ECONOMICS

JOSEPH E. STIGLITZ
STANFORD UNIVERSITY

JOHN DRIFFILL
BIRKBECK COLLEGE, UNIVERSITY OF LONDON

W · W · NORTON & COMPANY · NEW YORK · LONDON

Copyright © 2000, 1997, 1993 by W. W. Norton & Company, Inc.

The text of this book is composed in Zapf Book
with the display set in Kabel
Composition by TSI Graphics
Manufacturing by Courier Companies
Book design by Antonina Krass

Library of Congress Cataloging-in-Publication Data

Stiglitz, Joseph E.
    Economics/Joseph E. Stiglitz, John Driffill.
        p.   cm.
    Includes bibliographical references and index.
    ISBN 0-393-97584-3 (pbk.)
    1. Economics.   I. Driffill, John.   II. Title.

HB171.5   .S884   2000
330—dc21   99-086050

W. W. Norton & Company, Inc., 500 Fifth Avenue, New York, N.Y. 10110
    www.wwnorton.com

W. W. Norton & Company Ltd., 10 Coptic Street, London WCIA 1PU

1 2 3 4 5 6 7 8 9 0

CONTENTS IN BRIEF

CONTENTS

CHAPTER 5 USING DEMAND AND SUPPLY • 78

CHAPTER 6 TIME AND RISK • 99

CHAPTER 7 THE PUBLIC SECTOR • 115

PART TWO

PERFECT MARKETS

CHAPTER **8** THE CONSUMPTION DECISION • 137

CHAPTER **9** LABOUR SUPPLY AND SAVINGS • 161

CHAPTER 16 TECHNOLOGICAL CHANGE • 303

CHAPTER 17 IMPERFECT INFORMATION IN THE PRODUCT MARKET • 317

PART FOUR

POLICY ISSUES

CHAPTER 21 PUBLIC DECISION MAKING • 380

PART FIVE

FULL-EMPLOYMENT MACROECONOMICS

CHAPTER 22 MACROECONOMIC GOALS AND MEASURES • 391

CHAPTER **23** **THE FULL-EMPLOYMENT MODEL** • 416

CHAPTER **24** **USING THE FULL-EMPLOYMENT MODEL** • 439

PART SIX

UNEMPLOYMENT MACROECONOMICS

CHAPTER **30** FISCAL AND MONETARY POLICY • 563

PART SEVEN

DYNAMICS AND MACRO POLICY

CHAPTER **31** INFLATION: WAGE AND PRICE DYNAMICS • 579

CHAPTER **32** UNEMPLOYMENT: UNDERSTANDING WAGE RIGIDITIES • 606

CHAPTER **33** INFLATION VERSUS UNEMPLOYMENT: APPROACHES TO POLICY • 624

PART EIGHT

ISSUES IN MACROECONOMIC POLICY

CHAPTER **34** GROWTH AND PRODUCTIVITY • 647

CHAPTER **35** ECONOMIC INTEGRATION: THE EUROPEAN UNION • 672

CHAPTER **36** TRADE POLICY • 702

CHAPTER **37 ALTERNATIVE ECONOMIC SYSTEMS** • 716

CHAPTER **38 DEVELOPMENT** • 735

PREFACE

Introductory students should know the vitality of modern economics, and this book is intended to show it to them. It aims to provide an understanding of the principles of *modern* economics—both the principles that are necessary to understand how modern economists think about the world, and the principles that are required to understand current economic issues. But it is clear that the treatment of new topics, such as technological change, finance, incentives, and imperfect information, should be based upon the solid foundations of established fundamentals, such as the law of supply and demand, the theory of the firm, and traditional perspectives on unemployment, inflation, and growth.

The economic problems facing the world have changed dramatically in recent decades, and students should also know today's economic issues. Following the collapse of their Communist regimes, the countries of the former Soviet Union and eastern Europe are making slow and painful transitions to market economies. Several countries in East Asia, which had become known as the Tiger economies because of their unprecedented growth, found their progress abruptly interrupted in 1997 by waves of financial and subsequently real economic collapses, the Southeast Asian Crisis. The rapid development of these economies is cause for optimism that development is indeed possible. Their collapse into crisis in 1997 as a result of crony capitalism, weak regulation of financial markets, and the collapse of asset price bubbles exposes the fragility of financial markets and the importance of regulation and sound public policy. International trade, both in goods and in financial capital, was essential to their growth and has become increasingly important throughout the world. But the potentially huge flows of private finance unleashed by capital market liberalization have revealed their dangerous side. When investors in a country lose confidence and withdraw finance as they did in Mexico in 1995, financial flows can precipitate a crisis that the most-determined international cooperation may be able to stave off only with difficulty. The developed world is not immune to the consequences of international capital flows, as it found out in 1992 and 1993 when speculation substantially damaged the European Monetary System.

While the former Soviet Union disintegrated into several constituent states, members of the European Union continued to move towards greater integration, most conspicuously by launching Economic and Monetary Union in January 1999, the setbacks of 1992 and 1993 notwithstanding. Handing over monetary policy in Euroland to the European Central Bank and adopting the use of the Euro as its single currency in place of national monies—the mark, the franc, the lira, and so on—have raised fundamental questions about national sovereignty and government. While some have embraced greater integration with alacrity, apparently confident of the economic benefits it may bring and willing to pay the price of reduced independence, others have remained sceptical and hesitated to take what they conceived of as a leap into the unknown.

One of the intended benefits of integration is more rapid economic growth. The developed world's postwar Golden Age of high growth, low inflation, and low unemployment vanished in 1973, with the collapse of the Bretton Woods fixed exchange rate system and the arrival of a succession of oil price shocks. It was succeeded by a decade of rising unemployment, low growth, and rising inflation. The 1980s were a decade in which fighting inflation dominated macroeconomic policy, accompanied by microeconomic policies intended to increase productivity and growth: deregulation, privatization, and limitation of public spending and taxation. The 1990s witnessed a partial revival of growth and a return to low inflation. In Britain, and more spectacularly in the United States, unemployment fell to levels that had not been seen for twenty years and more.

As evidence of global warming mounted and other negative effects of human activity on the environment became more apparent, concern for the environment grew. While some improvements have been made in air and river quality, our expectations of environmental quality have grown too.

Medical advances have brought greater longevity but also much greater medical costs, particularly for the elderly. The aging populations of the developed world have brought problems of financing pensions to the top of the agenda in Britain and continental Europe, as well as in North America and Japan.

The role of government came to the fore in many of the economic developments of the last half-century. The welfare state established in Britain by the postwar Labour government and the apparent success of full-employment policies raised expectations of what the government could and should do on behalf of the population. The scale of government expenditure and taxation increased to the point where more than 40 percent of national income was taken in taxes. But in the 1980s the role of government came under scrutiny. Government was accused of having produced the "nanny state" and a dependency culture. Efforts were made to curtail the state's role. Nationalised industries were privatised across Europe. Defeated by the escalating burdens of providing generous benefits to growing numbers of unemployed and poor, even states like Sweden, strongly committed to vigorous public policy and comprehensive welfare provision, have scaled back state intervention. The growth in the role of the European Union and the rise in regionalism—in Britain through Scottish and Welsh devolution—have raised more questions about the economic (as well as the political) role of the state.

These are exciting issues, and they fill the pages of newspapers and the screens of television news programmes. An effective textbook on economic principles must prepare students to interpret and understand these important economic events. It also has to reflect the developments in economics that have accompanied them. Indeed, the changes in the discipline of economics over the past half-century have been as significant as the changes in world events.

The basic competitive model of the economy was perfected in the 1950s. Since then economists have gone beyond that model as they have come to understand its limitations better. Only in the last three decades has there been real progress in understanding incentives and imperfect information. The collapse of the Communist regimes of the Soviet Union and eastern Europe reflects their failure to provide good incentives. The banking crises that affected Southeast Asia and Japan highlight the importance of limited information and the need for sound regulation. The experience of the United Kingdom with privatised industries also shows the importance of effective regulation.

A thread running through the development of modern economics has been the integration of macroeconomics into economics as a whole and the end of the split between microeconomics and macroeconomics. Macroeconomic phenomena have to be related to underlying microeconomic principles; there is one set of economic principles, not two.

This book has been written with these points firmly in mind. Here are some of its most important features.

- Throughout the text, there are examples that relate economic theory to recent policy discussions. Policy perspective boxes are included, each of which provides a vignette on a particular issue. The policy discussions enliven the course and enrich the students' command of the basic material.

- Economists are famous for disagreeing with each other whenever possible. But in fact, on most issues differences among economists pale in comparison with differences among noneconomists. Fifteen points of consensus in economics which appear throughout the book draw attention to the remarkable extent of common ground occupied by economists.

- Instead of being stretched out to fill the entire microeconomics course, as is common, the competitive model is developed compactly in the first two parts of the book. This allows students to acquire a complete picture of the basic model before looking systematically at the role of imperfect markets.

- Economic incentives and the problems of incomplete information are given prominence. Chapter 19, for example, discusses the role that reputation plays in providing firms with incentives to maintain the quality of their products. Chapter 20 discusses how incentives can be used to motivate workers and managers.

- The presentation of macroeconomics has been organised to reflect its microeconomic foundations. The discussion in Part Five begins with an aggregate, full-employment model with perfectly flexible wages and prices. It moves on in Part Six to discuss the other extreme—and the focus of traditional macroeconomics—an unemployment model with rigid wages and prices. This leads in Part Seven to a discussion of the dynamics of adjustment in an economy in which wages and prices are neither perfectly flexible nor perfectly rigid and in which a principal concern is the rate of inflation. The aggregate supply and demand framework is used throughout the macroeconomic presentation. This organization allows the important topic of economic growth to be addressed early in the course in Chapter 24.

- International economics features prominently and is thoroughly integrated into the analysis. Trade is taken up at the outset in Chapter 3. On the macroeconomics side, the full-employment macroeconomic model set out in Chapter 25 is used to explain international capital flows and exchange rates in Chapter 26. International dimensions of unemployment (in Part Six) and dynamics of adjustment (in Part Seven) are addressed carefully, especially in relation to monetary theory and policy. International economic integration is the subject of Chapter 35 and trade policy is discussed in Chapter 36.

This book builds on all the experience and effort that went into the U.S. Edition of Joseph E. Stiglitz's *Economics* and benefits from the work of everyone who contributed to its success. A great debt of gratitude is owed to the publisher, W. W. Norton, with which it has been a great pleasure to work. Alan Cameron and Drake McFeely offered sustained encouragement with great patience, read and commented on the text with most helpful suggestions, and offered excellent ideas for close-up boxes and other examples. Sarah Stewart oversaw the editing and assembly of the final product with great care, efficiency, and speed.

The book has also benefited from the helpful comments of numerous reviewers. In particular, I would like to thank John Beath, University of St. Andrews; Angela Black, University of St. Andrews; Alan Carruth, University of Kent at Canterbury; John Fender, University of Birmingham; Andrew Hughes Hallett, University of Strathclyde; Anton Muscatelli, University of Glasgow; Paul Turner, University of Leeds; Alf Vanags, Queen Mary and Westfield College, University of London; David Vines, Oxford University; Christine Whitehead, London School of Economics; Rodney Wilson, University of Durham; Adrian Winnett, University of Bath; and Simon Wren-Lewis, University of Exeter.

Valuable adjuncts to the book are the *Study Guide* for students, the *Instructor's Manual* for teachers, and the *Test-Item File.* Christine Oughton of Birkbeck College carefully revised the *Study Guide* for the British Edition based on the U.S. Edition by Lawrence Martin of Michigan State University. Dorothy Manning of the University of Northumbria capably adapted the *Instructor's Manual* and the *Test-Item File,* originally created for the U.S. Edition by Alan Harrison of McMaster University and Dale Bails of Iowa Wesleyan University. I am grateful to each of these important contributors.

PART ONE

INTRODUCTION

I f we pick up a newspaper or turn on the television to watch the news, we are likely to be bombarded with statistics on unemployment rates, inflation rates, interest rates, exchange rates, and stock prices. How well are we doing in competition with other countries, such as the United States and Japan? Everyone seems to want to know. Political fortunes as well as the fortunes of countries, firms, and individuals depend on how well the economy does.

What is economics all about? That is the subject of Part One. Chapter 1 uses the story of the motor industry to illustrate many of the fundamental issues with which economics is concerned. The chapter describes the four basic questions at the heart of economics, and how it attempts to answer these questions.

Chapter 2 introduces the basic economic model and explains why property, profits, prices, and cost play such a central role in economic analysis.

A fact of life in the modern world is that individuals and countries are interdependent. All countries, and particularly wealthy countries like the United Kingdom or the United States, depend on foreign countries to provide vital imports as well as markets for their exports. Chapter 3 discusses the gains that result from trade: why trade, for instance, allows greater specialization and why greater specialization results in increased productivity. It also explains the patterns of trade: why each country imports and exports the particular goods it does.

Prices play a central role in enabling economies to function. Chapters 4 and 5 take up the question, what determines prices? Also, what causes prices to change over time? Why is water, without which we cannot live, normally so inexpensive, while diamonds, which we surely can do without, are very expensive? What happens to the prices of beer and cigarettes when the government imposes taxes on these goods? Sometimes the government passes laws requiring firms to pay wages of at least so much or forbidding landlords to charge rents that exceed a certain level. What are the consequences of these government interventions?

Chapter 6 introduces two important realities: economic life takes place not in a single moment of time but over long periods, and life is fraught with risk. Decisions today have effects on the future, and there is usually much uncertainty about what those effects will be. How does economics deal with problems posed by time and risk?

Finally, Chapter 7 turns to the pervasive role of the government in modern economies. Its focus is on why the government undertakes the economic roles it does and on the economic rationales for government actions. It also describes the various forms that government actions take and the changing roles of the government over time.

THE MOTOR INDUSTRY AND ECONOMICS

I magine the world 100 years ago: no cars, airplanes, computers (and computer games!), movies—to say nothing of atomic energy, lasers, and transistors. The list of inventions since then seems almost endless.

Of all the inventions that have shaped the world during the past century, perhaps none has had so profound an effect as the automobile. It has changed how and where people work, live, and play. But like any major innovation, it has been a mixed blessing: traffic jams on the one hand, access to wilderness areas on the other. And the new opportunities it created for some were accompanied by havoc for others. Some occupations—such as blacksmiths—virtually disappeared. Others—such as carriage makers—had to transform themselves (into car body manufacturers) or go out of business. But the gains of the many who benefited from the new industry far outweighed the losses of those who were hurt.

The story of the automobile is familiar. But looking at it from the perspective of economics can teach us a great deal about the economic way of thinking.

KEY QUESTIONS

1 What *is* economics? What are the basic questions it addresses?

2 In economies such as that of the United Kingdom, what are the respective roles of government and the private, or market, sector?

3 What are markets, and what are the principal markets that make up the economy?

4 Why is economics called a science?

5 Why, if economics is a science, do economists so often seem to disagree?

THE MOTOR INDUSTRY: A BRIEF HISTORY

The idea of a motorised carriage occurred to many, in Europe and the United States, at roughly the same time. But ideas by themselves are not enough. Translating ideas into marketable products requires solving technical problems and persuading investors to finance the venture.

If you visit a museum of early cars, you will see that the technical problems were resolved in a variety of ways, by many people working independently. The various automobile innovators could draw upon a stock of ideas "floating in the air." They also had the help of specialised firms that had developed a variety of new technologies and skills: for example, new alloys that enabled lighter motors to be constructed and new techniques for machining that allowed greater power, precision, and durability.

Henry Ford is generally given credit for having recognised the potential value of a vehicle that could be made and sold at a reasonable price. Before Ford, automobiles were luxuries, affordable only by the very rich. He saw the potential benefit from providing inexpensive transportation. After he introduced the Model T in the United States in 1909 at a bargain price of $900, he continued to cut the price—to $440 in 1914 and $360 in 1916. Sales skyrocketed from 58,000 in 1909 to 730,000 in 1916. Ford's prediction of a mass market for inexpensive cars had proved correct.

But success was neither sudden nor easy. To translate his idea into action Ford had to put to-gether a company to produce cars, figure out how to produce them cheaply, and raise the capital required to make all this possible.

Raising capital was particularly difficult, since the venture was extremely risky. Would Ford be successful in developing his automobile? Would someone else beat him to it? Would the price of a car be low enough for many people to buy it? If he was successful, would imitators copy his invention, robbing him of the mass market he needed to make money?

Ford formed a partnership to develop his first car. He was to supply the ideas and the work, while his partners supplied the funds. It took three partnerships before Ford produced a single car. The first two went bankrupt, with in each case, the financial partners' accusing Ford of spending all his time developing ideas instead of acting on them.

Were the first two sets of partners treated unfairly? After all, they knew the risks. Ford could have entered each partnership in good faith and simply been unable to deliver.

Even in the third case, his partners were unhappy: They claimed he managed to garner for himself the lion's share of the profits. Ford may have argued that his ideas were far more important than the mere dollars that the financiers provided to carry them out.

Whatever the truth in Ford's case, the general problem of who contributes more in a partnership and who should get what share of any profits occurs often.

Ford's success was due as much to his ability to come up with innovative ways of providing incentives and organising production as to his skill in solving technical problems. He demonstrated this ability with his original labour policies. He offered more than double the going wage and paid his workers the then princely sum of $5 a day. In exchange, Ford worked his employees hard; the moving assembly line he invented enabled him to set his workers a fast pace and push them to keep up. The amount produced per worker increased enormously. Still, it was clear that the high wages were ample compensation for the extra effort. Riots almost broke out as workers clamoured for the jobs he offered. Ford had rediscovered an old truth: in some cases, higher wages for employees can repay the employer in higher productivity, through greater loyalty, harder work, and less absenteeism.

Ford's success in increasing productivity meant that he could sell his cars far more cheaply than his rivals could. The lower prices and the high level of sales that accompanied them made it possible for him to take full advantage of the mass production techniques he had developed. At one point, however, Ford's plans were almost thwarted when a lawyer-inventor named George Baldwin Selden claimed that Ford had infringed on his patent.

Governments grant patents to enable inventors to reap the rewards of their innovative activity. These are generally for specific inventions, like a new type of braking system or transmission mechanism, not for general ideas. Ford's idea of an assembly line, for example, was not an invention that could be patented, and it was imitated by other car manufacturers. A patent gives the inventor the exclusive right to produce his invention for a limited time, thus helping to assure that inventors will be able to make some money from their successful inventions. Patents may lead to higher prices for these new products, since there is no competition from others making the same product. But the presumption is that the gains to society from the innovative activity more than compensate for the losses to consumers from the temporarily higher prices.

Selden had applied for, and been granted, a patent for a horseless, self-propelled carriage. He demanded that other car manufacturers pay him a royalty, which is a payment for the right to use a patented innovation. Ford challenged Selden's patent in court on the grounds that the concept of a "horseless, self-propelled carriage" was too vague to

be patentable. Ford won. Providing cars to the masses at low prices made Ford millions of dollars and many millions of people better off, by enabling them to go where they wanted to go more easily, cheaply, and speedily.

UPS AND DOWNS OF THE MOTOR INDUSTRY IN BRITAIN

While the early history of the motor industry in the United States is a great success story, the history of the industry in Britain has been a chequered one. Particularly since the Second World War, the fortunes of the motor industry in Britain have reflected many of the problems of British industry generally. Postwar optimism and expansion was followed by collapse in the face of international competition, which the British industry was poorly equipped to meet. There was a period in the 1960s and 1970s when it appeared that the best Britain could hope for was a period of elegant decline. Recently, there has been a revival in the car industry as foreign producers have established manufacturing plants in Britain and introduced new machinery, methods of production, and more cooperative relations between managers and workers.

Figures 1.1 and 1.2 show production, registrations of new cars, imports, and exports for Britain during the postwar period. Production rose strongly until 1964, after which it held roughly steady until 1972 when a period of decline set in, which continued until 1982. After that there was a modest recovery. Figure 1.1 also shows the continuing rise in registrations of new cars until 1990. From 1977 onwards, it is clear the number of new cars registered in Britain exceeded the numbers produced; this implies that, broadly speaking, there was a surplus of imports over exports in those years. Prior to 1977, the production of cars almost always exceeded registrations; this implies that Britain was a net exporter of cars. Figure 1.2 shows exports and imports of cars. Imports were very small until the late 1960s, and since then have risen substantially. They have fallen back in the recession since 1990. Exports are shown falling throughout the 1970s and the first half of the 1980s. A revival has occurred since 1986.

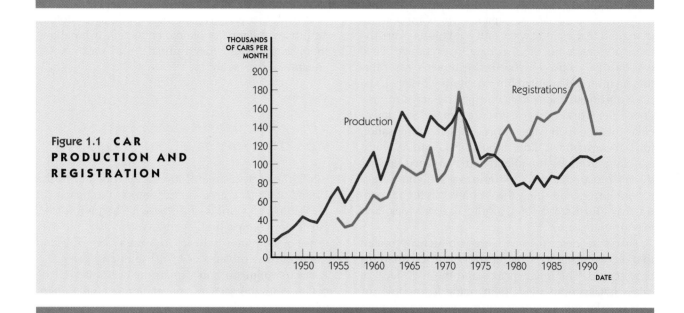

Figure 1.1 **CAR PRODUCTION AND REGISTRATION**

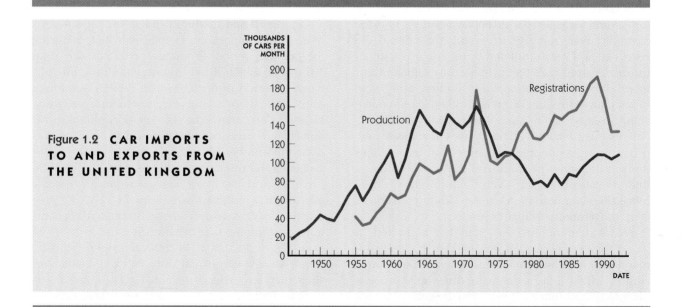

Figure 1.2 **CAR IMPORTS TO AND EXPORTS FROM THE UNITED KINGDOM**

INNOVATION AND PROTECTION

The development of the motor industry illustrates a number of economic issues. One of these is the relation between economies of scale, competition, and the extent of the market, a subject famously discussed by Adam Smith in *The Wealth of Nations*. Another is the many ways in which government influences the economy.

From its earliest days and into the years after the First World War, the motor industry was highly innovative. In those days, many small firms competed against each other, producing small numbers of each successive model of car until it was replaced by a new one incorporating the latest developments. The market for cars was small but growing fast. Cars were expensive but falling in price rapidly (like computers in the 1990s). In Britain, this development was able to take place sheltered from foreign competition, because in 1915 the British government had imposed a tariff of 33.3 percent on the import of cars. This tariff excluded virtually all foreign vehicles until the late 1950s when it was repealed. The presence of the tariff meant that foreign manufacturers who wanted to sell cars in Britain had to produce in Britain. Ford had set up a factory in 1911, and in fact became quite soon the largest producer in the country, producing around 6,000 Model T's a year by 1914; General Motors bought Vauxhall in 1929; and later on Chrysler bought another British manufacturer.

The many British firms were much smaller than Ford. During the interwar years (1918–1939), as car manufacture grew, Austin and Morris established themselves as the largest producers; others were the U.S. firms mentioned above, some familiar names—Jaguar, Rover—and some once famous but long since vanished—Standard, Rootes, Singer, Jowett, and many others.

As the motor industry matured, technical change in cars became less rapid, the demand for cars became larger and better established, and firms were able to produce larger numbers of each model. It became clear that there were advantages to very large manufacturers; they were able to produce at lower cost than smaller ones (i.e., they were able to take advantage of economies of scale). As a result, many smaller firms found themselves unable to compete, and either merged with others to form larger firms, were taken over, or closed down. Consequently, after the Second World War, the motor industry became more concentrated in the hands of a few producers.

INTERNATIONAL COMPETITION

Government intervention played a role in the industry in the interwar years via the tariff, and interventions by government of one form or another continued to influence it after 1945. The 33.3 percent tariff was cut substantially in the late 1950s, exposing the car industry to more foreign competition. In the early 1960s a succession of international negotiations which produced the General Agreement on Tariffs and Trade (GATT) began and further reduced tariff protection.

The background to the GATT process was the growing feeling around the world that tariffs were generally too high, and that there should be a general move towards free trade. Tariff barriers had been erected by many countries in the depression years of the 1930s, to keep out imports and protect employment. Although it had been a tempting policy for each country by itself to impose tariffs, this clearly had bad effects when all countries indulged in it. For an individual country, the idea that cutting imports increases demand for home-produced goods and causes more employment is superficially plausible. But the policy works by cutting the exports from other countries, where it therefore causes more unemployment. It was described by Keynes as a "beggar thy neighbour policy." When all countries follow this policy, they may all be able to reduce their imports, but at the same time they will all find that their exports have fallen as well. So none are better off; and in fact all are likely to be worse off.

By the 1950s and 1960s, which from today's vantage point look like a golden age of low inflation, low unemployment, and rapid economic growth, the underlying causes of the high tariffs had disappeared. Support grew for tariff cuts and a restoration of free trade, hence GATT. GATT was also stimulated by the technological changes that had taken place in many industries, including the motor industry. In a large part of manufacturing, economies of scale had grown in importance; the smallest firm that could fully exploit these economies and produce at the lowest cost had become very large relative to the domestic market. Without trade, these industries would be near monopolies if they were to be technically efficient. Opening markets to foreign trade enabled efficient production while maintaining some, though nevertheless imperfect, competition and allowed buyers of products to make a choice from more varieties.

The motor industry in Britain continued to grow after the Second World War until the early 1960s, and there were more mergers and takeovers intended to produce fewer, bigger firms that were thought to be capable of surviving in the now more competitive international market. Austin and Morris merged in 1952 to create the British Motor Corporation, which became the only large British-owned manufacturer. Nevertheless, the U.S. multinational firms (Ford, GM, and Chrysler which had taken over Rootes) increased their share of the British market. Car producers in Japan, Germany, and other European countries developed rapidly and gave British firms stiff competition in overseas export markets. The reduction of tariff barriers as part of the GATT process, from the mid-1960s onwards, enabled foreign producers to compete with local firms for the British market. The share of imports grew from 14 percent of the British market in 1970 to 27 percent in 1973. In 1995 the figure was roughly 50 percent.

NATIONALIZATION

The takeovers and mergers in the car industry in Britain nevertheless failed to produce a firm capable of survival in the increasingly competitive international market. The British Motor Corporation (BMC) fell into a prolonged decline, despite many attempts by governments to keep it alive. In 1968, it merged with a company called Leyland, emerged as the British Leyland Motor Corporation (BL), and con-

tained virtually all the British-owned car makers, including Rover and Jaguar. The state continued to intervene in the market during the 1960s and 1970s to keep this firm going. But it made losses throughout the 1970s and in 1975 it was nationalised and became a public corporation. The company was diagnosed as suffering from a variety of problems, including too little and too old capital equipment; poor relations between workers and management; many wildcat strikes, which frequently disrupted production; too little investment in design and development of new models; and a poor record for durability and reliability of its products. It was given large amounts of government loans and investments for restructuring.

Nationalization was a policy that had been followed consistently since 1945. It had been applied to coal, steel, railways, many ports, electricity, gas, and water supply. Many other industries either always had been publicly owned (like the post office) or were taken into public ownership. It was intended that they should be operated in the interests of the public as a whole and not just in the interests of their shareholders. In many cases, nationalised industries were public utilities (like water supply) whose production was regarded as being too important to be left to the vagaries of the market. In some cases (like railways and telephones, given the technology of the time), they were natural monopolies which could not be operated by private firms as competitive industries; nationalization protected the public from exploitation by a monopolist. In some cases (steel, coal, railways, and eventually the motor industry), they were declining industries that were either bankrupt or on the edge of bankruptcy. They were nationalised to protect jobs and in the hope that these ailing industries would eventually recover and could be returned to the private sector as profitable firms. Nationalization gave government greater control over the operation of these firms and industries, at the same time as it was providing funds for investment and also in many cases subsidies to help cover operating costs.

The policy of propping up declining industries by nationalization and subsidy was, by the mid-1970s, increasingly viewed as having failed. None of the lame ducks had ever managed to get off the ground. A gradual change in government policy occurred. Subsidies were cut and the objective of maintaining employment was given less emphasis. From 1977 and into the 1980s, under the leadership of Michael Edwardes, BL was "slimmed down." Employment and production capacity were reduced dramatically—employment by about half. In the 1980s BL began to collaborate with Honda: some of its new cars were largely Honda's with different badges.

In the 1980s, the postwar policy of nationalization was reversed. Many nationalised enterprises were privatised; that is, they were sold back to the private sector of the economy. As part of this policy, Jaguar, a profitable part of BL, was sold off to the private sector in 1984 and is now a part of Ford. Much of BL became the Rover Group and was sold off in 1988 to British Areospace, another recently privatised firm, for almost nothing, after the government had written off more than £1,500 million worth of its debts. (This deal was later investigated by the European Court of Justice because it was suspected of being against European laws on competition, which prevent firms from receiving government subsidies: Rover's debt write-off and other payments made to BAe as sweeteners in the sell-off could have qualified as illegal subsidies.) Since then, Rover has been bought by the German firm BMW.

INDUSTRIAL RELATIONS

Another aspect of government policy that affected the motor industry, as indeed it affected all industries, was the policy towards trade unions. Workers had over many difficult years, throughout the nineteenth century and in the early years of the twentieth century, fought for legal rights for their unions that would enable them to defend their interests. In the 1980s, a sequence of laws was passed that diminished union power. It became less easy for unions to call strikes, they were required to ballot members by post before strikes could be called, it was made easier for firms to dismiss strikers for breach of contract, pickets could only be mounted against employers with whom there was a dispute—secondary picketing was outlawed—and there were many other changes in

the law that reduced union power. Union membership fell from 14 million to 9 million during the 1980s. The frequency and length of strikes fell dramatically. On one hand, firms were able to introduce new, more efficient working practices; on the other hand, many workers came to feel that they were less secure in their jobs and wages and that their conditions of work were less good than they would otherwise have been. BL's management became much more aggressive towards the unions in the late 1970s and early 1980s. A leading shop steward, Derek Robinson, was symbolically sacked in 1979 for refusing to drop his opposition to a new recovery plan for the firm.

THE EXTENT OF THE MARKET

The thrust of many of the changes in technology and trading arrangements has been to create a move beyond national markets to much larger ones. Whereas at one time it may have made sense to talk about the British car market, it makes much less sense to do that today when the manufacture, sale, and purchase of cars in Britain is just a part of much wider activity. Until the late 1950s the production of cars in Britain was protected from foreign competition by a high tariff barrier. The British market was more or less independent of the rest of the world. British producers manufactured cars in Britain for British buyers. However, since tariff barriers fell and the scale of production grew, the boundaries at national borders have largely disappeared.

In the late 1980s and 1990s, there was a revival of motor manufacturing in Britain and exports grew. The structure of the industry is now different than it was in the 1950s and 1960s: of the six largest producers, three (Ford, Jaguar, and Vauxhall) are divisions of U.S. multinationals, one (Peugeot-Talbot) is part of a French firm, one (Nissan) part of a Japanese multinational, and one part of a German firm (BMW). Other new entrants are Japanese multinationals: Toyota and Honda. All of these firms build cars in several countries. Increasingly, they organise their operations at the level of Europe rather than a single country: engines made in Germany might be put into bodies made in Spain with electrics made in Britain. Ford is attempting to organise its business into a single global operation.

Continuing changes in technology have brought economies of scale to higher and higher levels of production, especially in the design and development of new models of cars; it might take sales throughout the world to recoup the costs of investing in a new model nowadays, as with the Ford Mondeo and other global models. This and the progressive cuts in tariff barriers that have taken place under GATT and in the European Union have led to an increasingly globalised motor industry. Most of the large producers sell cars throughout Europe. Any European country has a rather similar mixture of VW's, Renaults, Peugeots, Fiats, Fords, GM products, and so on—with a few BMW's, Mercedes, Volvos, Saabs, Jaguars, and other luxury makes thrown in. There is effectively a European market in cars.

Nevertheless, there are differences between the motor car markets in different European countries. They tend to display a bias in favour of domestic car makers. France is dominated by Renault and Peugeot; Italy by Fiat; and Germany by VW-Audi, BMW, and Mercedes. Competition from Japanese producers has been limited by a series of bilateral deals, each between an individual country and Japan, to limit Japanese imports. In Britain, the Japanese are limited to taking no more than 11 percent of the domestic market. In France, the limit is lower (3 percent); and in Italy, Spain, and Portugal, it is almost zero. Only in Germany are there few restrictions, and there Japanese producers had 16 percent of the market in 1990. These restrictions on imports from Japan have sheltered European manufacturers. The Japanese investments in Britain are partly a response to this: cars built in the United Kingdom by Japanese producers are not restricted, since they are European manufactures and are allowed free movement by the Single European Market (the SEM). The European Community agreed to drop all the restrictions on imported Japanese (and any other) cars by the end of 1999.

Under the SEM, it was intended that all tariff and nontariff barriers to the free movement of goods around Europe would have been dismantled by the end of 1992. In the motor trade, there are exceptions to this rule. It ought to be possible for a resident of Britain to buy a car from a dealer anywhere in Europe, shopping around for the best price. However, restrictive agreements imposed by manufacturers on dealers prevent this from happening. A dealer in some other European country will not sell to a buyer from the United Kingdom, who intends to bring the car to Britain and register it there. In some countries, the government authorities make it difficult to bring in a new car bought in another EU country and register it. Effectively, people who buy new cars have to buy them from a dealer in the country in which they plan to register them. These practices limit competition among dealers and car manufacturers, restrict buyers' ability to shop around for a good price, and help to keep car prices high in Europe. It was intended that these restrictions should have been phased out during the 1990s, but the car manufacturers and dealers who benefit from them were slow to respond.

In sum, it is clear that the concept of a national—British—market for cars has little meaning. It may be more useful to think of a European market, or even a global market. However, these large markets are imperfect. There are still costs and barriers to movement of these goods from place to place; the price of a car is not uniform throughout the world, or even throughout Europe. It is clear that it is not possible to define in an unambiguous way what the geographical extent of the market is.

WHAT IS ECONOMICS?

This narrative illustrates many facets of economics, but now a definition of our subject is in order. **Economics** studies how individuals, firms, governments, and other organizations within our society make **choices** and how those choices determine the way the resources of society are used. **Scarcity** figures prominently in economics: choices matter because resources are scarce. Imagine an enormously wealthy individual who can have everything he wants. We might think that scarcity is not in his vocabulary, until we consider that time is a resource and he must decide what expensive toy to devote his time to each day. Taking time into account, then, scarcity is a fact in everyone's life.

To produce a single product, like an automobile, thousands of decisions and choices have to be made. Since any economy is made up not only of automobiles but of millions of products, it is a marvel that the economy functions at all, let alone as well as it does most of the time. This marvel is particularly clear if you consider instances when things do not work so well: the Great Depression in the 1930s, when almost 25 percent of the work force could not find a job; the countries of the former Soviet Union today, where ordinary consumer goods like carrots or toilet paper are often simply unavailable; the developing economies of many countries in Africa, Asia, and Latin America, where standards of living have remained stubbornly low and in some places have even been declining.

The fact that choices must be made applies as well to the economy as a whole as it does to each individual. Somehow, decisions are made—by individuals, households, firms, and government—that together determine how the economy's limited resources, including its land, labour, machines, oil, and other natural resources, are used. Why is it that land used at one time for growing crops may at another time be used for an automobile plant? How was it that over the space of a couple of decades, resources were transferred from making horse-drawn carriages to making automobile bodies? That blacksmiths were replaced by car mechanics? How do the decisions of millions of consumers, workers, investors, managers, and government officials all interact to determine the use of the scarce resources available to society? Economists reduce such matters to four basic questions concerning how economies function:

1. What is produced, and in what quantities? There have been important changes in production over the past hundred years. In poorer countries today and in almost all countries a century ago, agriculture is or was the main form of economic activity. Now, in the richer developed countries, it makes up just 2 or 3 percent of national production. Although governments frequently extol the virtues of the man-ufacturing industry and exhort its regeneration, the proportion of manufacturing in national production continues to fall while the resources devoted to service industries, transport and communications, health, and education continue to grow.

What can account for changes like these? The economy seems to spew out new products like videocassette recorders and new services like automated bank tellers. What causes this process of innovation? The overall level of production has also shifted from year to year, often accompanied by large changes in the levels of employment and unemployment. How can economists explain these changes?

In most market economies, the questions of what is produced and in what quantities are answered largely by the private interaction of firms and consumers, but government also plays a role. Prices are critical in determining which goods are produced. When the price of some good rises, firms are induced to produce more of that good, to increase their profits. Thus, a central question for economists is, why are some goods more expensive than others? And why have the prices of some goods increased or decreased?

2. How are these goods produced? There are often many ways of making something. Textiles can be made with hand looms. Modern machines enable fewer workers to produce more cloth. Very modern machines may be highly computerised, allowing one worker to monitor many more machines than was possible earlier. The better machines generally cost more, but they require less labour. Which technique will be used, the advanced technology or the labour-intensive one? Henry Ford introduced the assembly line. More recently, car manufacturers have begun using robots. What determines how rapidly technology changes?

In the market economies, firms answer the question of how goods are produced, again with input from the government, which sets regulations and enacts laws that affect everything from the overall organization of firms to the ways they interact with their employees and customers.

3. For whom are these goods produced? Individuals who have higher incomes can consume more goods. But that answer only pushes the question back

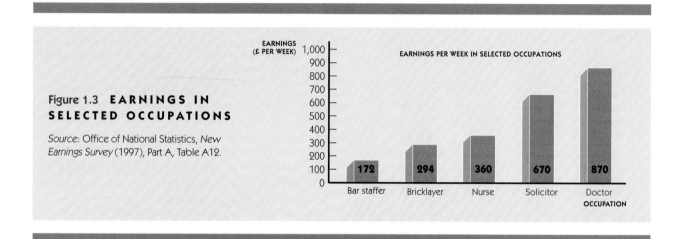

Figure 1.3 EARNINGS IN SELECTED OCCUPATIONS

Source: Office of National Statistics, *New Earnings Survey* (1997), Part A, Table A12.

one step: What determines the differences in income and wages? What is the role of luck, of education, of inheritance, of savings, of experience and hard work? These questions are difficult to answer. For now, suffice it to say that while incomes are primarily determined by the private interaction of firms and households, government also plays a strong role, with taxes, transfer payments, and various government spending programmes that redistribute income.

Figure 1.3 shows the relative pay in a variety of different occupations. It appears that the average doctor earns more than twice as much as the average nurse and four times as much as the average bar staffer.

4. Who makes economic decisions, and by what process? In a **centrally planned economy,** as the Soviet Union was, the government takes responsibility for virtually every aspect of economic activity. The government provides the answers to the first three questions. A central economic planning agency works through a bureaucracy to say what will be produced, by what method it will be produced, and who will consume it. At the other end of the spectrum are economies that rely primarily on the free interchange of producers and their customers to determine what, how, and for whom.

Most of the rich and broadly democratic countries of the developed world regard themselves as **mixed economies,** in which both the private and the public sectors play important roles. They vary greatly in the relative importance of these two parts; some are much more oriented towards the free market than others. The United States is often viewed as one of the world's most free-market oriented economies, while some of the Scandinavian countries, particularly Sweden and Norway, have very substantial public sectors. Most western European countries lie somewhere between these extremes. Within limits, producers make what they want to make, they use whatever method of production seems appropriate to them, and the output is distributed to consumers according to their income.

When economists examine an economy, they want to know to what extent economic decisions are made by the government and to what extent they are made by private individuals. In western Europe, while individuals for the most part make their own decisions about what kind of car to purchase, governments have inserted themselves in a number of ways: they have taken actions that affect the import of cars from outside the European Union, that restrict the amount of pollutants a car can produce, and that promote fuel efficiency and automobile safety.

A related question is whether economic decisions are made by individuals for their own interests or for the interest of an employer such as a business firm or government agency. This is an important distinction. We can expect people acting on their own behalf to make decisions that benefit themselves. When they act on behalf of organizations, however, a con-

BASIC QUESTIONS OF ECONOMICS

1 What is produced, and in what quantities?

2 How are these goods produced?

3 For whom are these goods produced?

4 Who makes economic decisions, and by what process?

flict of interest may arise. Observers often refer to corporations and governments as if they were a single individual. Economists point out that organizations consist, by definition, of a multitude of individuals and that the interests of these individuals do not necessarily coincide with one another or, for that matter, with the interests of the organization itself. Organizations bring a number of distinctive problems to the analysis of choice.

As you can see by their attention to decision making, economists are concerned not only with *how* the economy answers the four basic questions but also *how well.* They ask: Is the economy efficient? Could it produce more of some goods without producing fewer of others? Could it make some individuals better off without making some other individuals worse off?

MARKETS AND GOVERNMENT IN THE MIXED ECONOMY

The primary reliance on private decision making in western Europe and North America reflects widespread beliefs that this reliance is appropriate and necessary for economic efficiency; however, there are good reasons why certain interventions by government are desirable. Finding the appropriate balance between the public and the private sectors of the economy is a central issue of economic analysis.

MARKETS

The economic concept of markets is used to include any situation where exchange takes place, though this exchange may not necessarily resemble the traditional village markets. In department stores and shopping centres, customers rarely haggle over price. When manufacturers purchase the materials they need for production, they exchange money for them, not other goods. Most goods, from cameras to clothes, are not sold directly by producers to consumers. They are sold by producers to distributors, by distributors to retailers, and by retailers to consumers. All of these transactions are embraced by the concepts of **market** and **market economy.**

In market economies with competition, individuals make choices that reflect their own desires. And firms make choices that maximize their profits; to do so, they must produce the goods consumers want and they must produce them at lower cost than other firms. As firms compete in the quest for profits, consumers benefit, both from the kinds of goods produced and the prices at which they are supplied. The market economy thus provides answers to the four basic economic questions—what is produced, how it is produced, for whom it is produced, and how these decisions are made. And on the whole, the answers the market gives ensure the efficiency of the economy.

But the answer the market provides to the question of for whom goods are produced is one that not everyone finds acceptable. Like bidders at an auction, what market participants are willing and able to pay depends on their income. Some groups of individuals—including those without skills that are valued by the market—may receive such a low income that they could not feed and educate their children without outside assistance. Governments provide the assistance by taking steps to increase income equality. These steps, however, often blunt economic incentives. While social security and welfare payments provide an important safety net for the poor, the taxation required to finance them may discourage work and savings. If the government takes in income tax 50 pence out of every additional pound earned by a high-income worker, she may be inclined to work less hard. She may decide to work fewer hours each week and take longer holidays. If income taxes take 50 pence out of every pound of interest on savings, then she might decide to spend more now and save less. Like the appropriate balance between the public and private sectors, the appropriate balance between concerns about equality (often referred to as **equity concerns**) and efficiency is a central issue of modern economics.

THE ROLE OF GOVERNMENT

The answers that the market provides to the basic economic questions on the whole ensure efficiency. But in certain areas the solutions appear inadequate to many. There may be too much pollution, too much inequality, and too little concern about education, health, and safety. When the market is not perceived to be working well, people often turn to government.

The government plays a major role in modern economies. We need to understand both what that role is and why government undertakes the activities that it does. In the case of the car industry, governments intervene in many ways. The British government took over British Leyland—a forerunner of the current Rover Group—when it was foundering commercially. The European Union protects European producers against competition from outside Europe by the common external tariff it imposes on imports. Government regulations on safety and emissions, and the need to get a car through an annual mechanical test affect the cost of driving a car, as do the taxes on petrol. Laws that had protected trade unions and strengthened their bargaining position vis-à-vis employers in Britain were gradually amended in the 1980s in an attempt to increase the employers' grip on the industry.

Governments set the legal structure under which private firms and individuals operate. They regulate businesses to ensure that they do not discriminate by race or sex, do not mislead customers, are careful about the safety of their employees, and do not pollute air and water. In some industries, the government is the main producer of goods. Until recently all the public utilities in Britain—water, gas, and electricity—were publicly owned. Most countries' postal services are provided by publicly owned firms; most education is provided by government-owned schools. In other cases, the government supplies goods and services that the private sector does not, such as providing for the national defence, building roads, and printing money. Examples of this kind include the state retirement pensions paid almost to all old people, unemployment insurance payments (in Britain renamed the "job seekers' allowance"), and social security payments.

One can easily imagine a government controlling the economy more directly. In countries where decision-making authority is centralised and concentrated in the government, government bureaucrats might decide what and how much a factory should produce and set on the level of wages that should be paid. Various European governments run steel companies, coal mines, and the telephone system. At least until recently, governments in countries like the former Soviet Union and China attempted to control practically all major decisions regarding resource allocation.

THE THREE MAJOR MARKETS

The market economy revolves around exchange between individuals (or households), who buy goods and services from firms, and firms, which take **inputs,** the various materials of production, and produce **outputs,** the goods and services that they sell. In thinking about a market economy, economists focus their attention on three broad categories of markets in which individuals and firms interact. The markets in which firms sell their outputs to households are referred to collectively as the **product market.** Many firms also sell goods to other firms; the outputs of the first firm become the inputs of the second. These transactions too are said to occur in the product market.

CLOSE-UP: A FAILED ALTERNATIVE TO THE MIXED ECONOMY

Although the mixed economy now is the dominant form of economic organization, it is not the only possible way of answering the basic economic questions. Beginning in 1917, an experiment in almost complete government control was begun in what became the Soviet Union.

What was produced in such an economy, and in what quantities? Government planners set the targets, which workers and firms then struggled to fulfill.

How were these goods produced? Again, since government planners decided what supplies would be delivered to each factory, they effectively chose how production occurred.

For whom were these goods produced? The government made decisions about what each job was paid, which affected how much people could consume. In principle, individuals could choose what to buy at government-operated stores, at prices set by the government. But in practice, many goods were unavailable at these stores.

Who made economic decisions, and by what process? The government planners decided, basing the decisions on their view of national economic goals.

At one time, all this planning sounded very sensible, but as former Soviet premier Nikita Khrushchev once said, "Economics is a subject that does not greatly respect one's wishes." Many examples of Soviet economic woes could be cited, but two will suffice. In the shoe market, the Soviet Union was the largest national producer in the world. However, the average shoe was of such low quality that it fell apart in a few weeks, and inventories of unwanted shoes rotted in warehouses. In agriculture, the Soviet government had traditionally allowed small private plots. Although the government limited the time farmers could spend on these plots, publicly run farming was so unproductive that the 3 percent of Soviet land that was privately run produced about 25 percent of the total farm output.

Today the standard of living in the former Soviet Union is not only below that in industrialised nations like the United States and those of western Europe, but it is barely ahead of developing nations like Brazil and Mexico. Workers in the Soviet Union shared a grim one-liner: "We pretend to work and they pretend to pay us."

The collapse of the Soviet Union was, to a large extent, the result of the failure of its economic system. Much of this text is concerned with explaining why mixed economies work as well as they do.

On the input side, firms need (besides the materials that they buy in the product market) some combination of labour and machinery with which their goods can be produced. They purchase the services of workers in the **labour market.** They raise funds, with which to buy inputs, in the **capital market.**

Traditionally, economists have also highlighted the importance of a third input, land, but in modern industrial economies, land is of secondary importance. For most purposes, it suffices to focus attention on the three major markets listed here, and this text will follow this pattern.

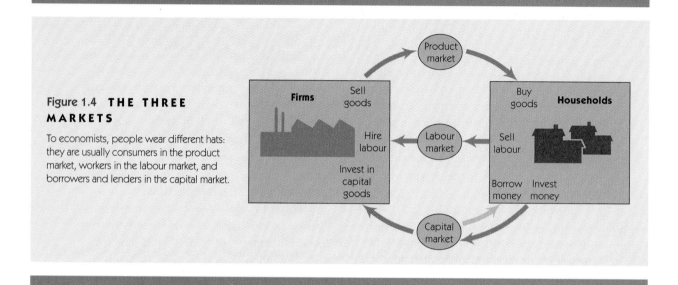

Figure 1.4 THE THREE MARKETS

To economists, people wear different hats: they are usually consumers in the product market, workers in the labour market, and borrowers and lenders in the capital market.

As Figure 1.4 shows, individuals participate in all three markets. When individuals buy goods or services, they act as **consumers** in the product market. When people act as **workers,** economists say they "sell their labour services" in the labour market. When individuals buy shares of stock in a firm or lend money to a business, economists note that they are participating in the capital market and refer to them as **investors.**

TWO CAVEATS

Terms in economics often are similar to terms in ordinary usage, but they can have special meanings. The terms **markets** and **capital** illustrate the problem.

Though the term *market* is used to conjure an image of a busy **marketplace,** there is no formal marketplace for most goods and services. There are buyers and sellers, and economists analyse the outcome as *if* there were a single marketplace in which all the transactions occurred.

Moreover, economists often talk about the "market for labour" as if all workers were identical. But workers obviously differ in countless ways. In some cases, these differences are important. We might then talk about the "market for skilled workers" or "the market for plumbers." But in other cases—such as when we are talking about the overall state of the economy and focusing on the unemployment rate

(the fraction of workers who would like jobs but cannot get them)—these differences can be ignored.

When newspapers refer to the capital market, they mean the bond traders and stockbrokers and the companies they work for in the City in London and other financial districts. When economists use the term *capital market,* they have in mind a broader concept. It includes all the institutions concerned with raising funds (and, as we will see later, sharing and insuring risks), including banks and insurance companies.

The term *capital* is used in still another way—to refer to the machines and buildings used in production. To distinguish this particular usage, in this book we refer to machines and buildings as **capital goods.** *Capital markets* thus refers to the markets in which funds are raised, borrowed, and lent. **Capital goods markets** refers to the markets in which capital goods are bought and sold.

MICROECONOMICS AND MACROECONOMICS: THE TWO BRANCHES OF ECONOMICS

The detailed study of product, labour, and capital markets is called **microeconomics.** Microeconomics (*micro* is derived from the Greek word meaning "small") focuses on the behaviour of the units—the firms, households, and individuals—that make up the economy. It is concerned with how the individual units make decisions and what affects those decisions. By contrast, **macroeconomics** (*macro* comes from the Greek word meaning "large") looks at the behaviour of the economy as a whole, in particular the behaviour of such aggregate measures as overall rates of unemployment, inflation, economic growth, and the balance of trade. The aggregate numbers do not tell us what any firm or household is doing. They tell us what is happening in toto or on average.

It is important to remember that these perspectives are simply two ways of looking at the same thing. Microeconomics is the bottom-up view of the economy; macroeconomics is the top-down view. The behaviour of the economy as a whole is dependent on the behaviour of the units that make it up.

The automobile industry is a story of both micro- and macroeconomics. It is a story of microeconomic interactions of individual companies, investors, and trade unions. It is also a story of global macroeconomic forces such as oil shortages and economic fluctuations. When car companies cut employment because demand has fallen, their problems boost the overall unemployment rate.

THE SCIENCE OF ECONOMICS

Economics is a **social science.** It studies the social problem of choice from a scientific viewpoint; this means that it is built on a systematic exploration of the problem of choice. This systematic exploration involves both the formulation of theories and the examination of data.

A **theory** consists of a set of assumptions (or hypotheses) and conclusions derived from those assumptions. Theories are logical exercises: *if* the assumptions are correct, *then* the results follow. If all college graduates have a better chance of getting jobs and Ellen is a college graduate, then Ellen has a better chance of getting a job than a nongraduate. Economists make predictions with their theories.

They may use a theory to predict what will happen if a tax is increased or if imports of foreign cars are limited. The predictions of a theory are of the form "If a tax is increased and if the market is competitive, then output will decrease and prices will increase."

In developing their theories, economists use models. To understand how economists use models, consider a modern car manufacturer trying to design a new automobile. It is extremely expensive to construct a new car. Rather than creating a separate, fully developed car for every engineer's or designer's conception of what she would like to see the new car be, the company uses models. The designers might use a plastic model to study the general shape of the vehicle and to assess reactions to the car's aesthetics. The engineers might use a computer model to study the air resistance, from which they can calculate fuel consumption, and a separate model for judging the car's comfort.

Just as engineers construct different models to study particular features of a car, so too economists construct models of the economy—in words or equations—to depict particular features of the economy. An economic model may describe a general relationship ("When incomes rise, the number of cars purchased increases"), describe a quantitative relationship ("When incomes rise by 10 percent, the number of cars purchased rises, on average, by 12 percent"), or make a general prediction ("An increase in the tax on petrol will decrease the demand for cars").

DISCOVERING AND INTERPRETING RELATIONSHIPS

A **variable** is any item that can be measured and that changes. Prices, wages, interest rates, and quantities bought and sold are all variables. What interests economists is the connection between variables. When economists see what appears to be a systematic relationship among variables, they ask, could it have arisen by chance or is there a relationship? This is the question of **correlation.**

Economists use statistical tests to measure and test correlations. Consider the problem of deciding whether a coin is biased. If you toss a coin 10 times and get 6 heads and 4 tails, is the coin a fair one? Or is it weighted to heads? Statistical tests say that the result of 6 heads and 4 tails could easily happen by chance, so the evidence does not prove that the coin is weighted. This does not prove that it is *not* weighted. The evidence is just not strong enough for either conclusion. But if you toss a coin 100 times and get 80 heads, statistical tests tell you that the possibility of this happening by chance with a fair coin is extremely small. The evidence supports the assertion that the coin is weighted.

A similar logic can be used on correlations in economic data. People with more education tend to earn higher wages. Does this connection occur merely by chance? Statistical tests show whether the evidence is too weak for a conclusion or it supports the existence of a systematic relationship between education and wages.

CAUSATION VERSUS CORRELATION

Economists would like to accomplish more than just asserting that different variables are indeed correlated. They would like to conclude that changes in one variable *cause* the changes in the other variable. The distinction between correlation and **causation** is important. If one variable causes the other, then changing one variable necessarily will change the other. If the relationship is just a correlation, this will not be true.

Earlier, we saw that imports of foreign cars into Britain rose and production in Britain fell during the 1970s. The two variables were negatively correlated. But does that prove that the fall in British production was caused by higher imports? This might have been the case if, for example, increased foreign productivity had enabled these producers to sell at lower prices in Britain. Conversely, is it possible that the increase in imports was caused by a fall in British production? This might have been caused by strikes and poor industrial relations cutting output from British producers. A third possibility is that both were caused by a third factor, such as a cut in tariffs when Britain joined the European Community in 1973. In

fact all these three factors were present during the 1970s. To be able to distinguish between these three explanations of the data and decide which explanation is valid, it would be necessary to have more information on changes in domestic car production and foreign imports, showing, for example, cases where they had moved in a variety of different directions, and the surrounding circumstances.

EXPERIMENTS IN ECONOMICS

Many sciences use laboratory experiments to test alternative explanations, since experiments allow the scientist to change one factor at a time and see what happens. But the economy is not a chemistry lab. Instead, economics is like astronomy in that both sciences must use the experiments that nature provides. Economists look for situations in which only one factor changes and study the consequences of changing that factor. A change in the income tax system is an example of a natural experiment. But nature is usually not kind to economists; the world does not stand still. As the tax system changes, so do other features of the economy, and economists often have a difficult time deciding whether changes are the result of the new tax system or of some other economic change. Sometimes they can use what is called **econometrics,** the branch of statistics developed to analyze the particular measurement problems that arise in economics.

In a few cases, mainly in the United States, economists have engaged in social experiments. For example, they have given a selected group of individuals a different income tax schedule or welfare program from that faced by another, otherwise similar, group. In recent years, a major new branch of economics, called **experimental economics,** has analysed certain aspects of economic behaviour in a controlled, laboratory setting. One way of seeing how individuals respond to risk, for example, is to construct a risky situation in such a setting and force individuals to make decisions and act on them. By varying the nature of the risk and the rewards, one can learn about how individuals will respond to different risks in real life situations. Similarly, different kinds of auctions can be simulated in a controlled laboratory setting to see how buyers respond. Both social and laboratory experiments have provided economists with valuable insights concerning economic behavior.

But even with all available tools, the problem of finding a variety of correlations between several different types of data and having to discern which connections are real and which are only apparent is a difficult one. Economists' interest in these questions is motivated by more than just curiosity. Often important policy questions depend on what one believes is going on. Whether a country thinks it worthwhile to pour more resources into higher education may depend upon whether it believes that the differences in wages observed between those with and without higher education are largely due to the skills and knowledge acquired during their studies or to differences in ability between those who complete their courses and those who do not.

The important lessons to remember here are (1) the fact of a correlation does not prove a causation; (2) the way to test different explanations of causation is to hold all of the factors constant except for one, and then allow that one to vary; and (3) data do not always speak clearly and sometimes do not allow any conclusions to be drawn.

WHY ECONOMISTS DISAGREE

Economists are frequently called upon to make judgments on matters of public policy. Should Britain join the European Monetary Union? Should the government reduce the deficit? Should inflation be reduced? If so, how? In these public policy discussions, economists often disagree. They differ in their views of how the world works, in their *description* of the economy, and in their predictions of the consequences of certain actions. And they differ in their values, in how they evaluate these consequences.

When they describe the economy and construct models that predict either how the economy will change or the effects of different policies, they are engaged in what is called **positive economics.** When they evaluate alternative policies, weighing up the various benefits and costs, they are engaged in what

is called **normative economics.** Positive economics is concerned with what is, with describing how the economy functions. Normative economics deals with what should be, with making judgments about the desirability of various courses of action. Normative economics makes use of positive economics. We cannot make judgments about whether a policy is desirable unless we have a clear picture of its consequences. Good normative economics also tries to be explicit about precisely which values or objectives it is incorporating. It tries to couch its statements in the form "If these are your objectives . . . , then this is the best possible policy."

Consider the normative and positive aspects of the proposal to restrict imports of Japanese cars. Positive economics would describe the consequences: the increased prices consumers have to pay, the increased sales of home-produced cars, the increased employment, and the increased profits. In the end, the question is *should there be restraints on imports of Japanese cars?* This is a normative question: Normative economics would weigh these various effects—the losses of the consumers, the gains to workers, and the increased profits—to reach an overall judgment. Normative economics develops systematic frameworks within which these complicated judgments can be made in a systematic way.

DISAGREEMENTS WITHIN POSITIVE ECONOMICS

Even when they describe how the economy works, economists may differ for two main reasons. First, economists may differ over what is the appropriate model of the economy. They may disagree about how well people and firms are able to perceive and calculate their self-interest and whether their interactions take place in a competitive or a noncompetitive market. Different models will produce different results. Often the data do not allow us to say which of two competing models provides a better description of some market.

Second, even when they agree about the appropriate theoretical model, economists may disagree about quantitative magnitudes; this will cause their predictions to differ. They may agree, for instance,

Despite the popular impression that in a room containing six economists you are bound to get at least seven opinions, when a number of professional economists in the United States were surveyed in 1990, their responses revealed substantial agreement on several controversial questions. And the views on which the economists agree are not always views that are generally held in the wider population.

The economists agreed that tariffs and quotas on international trade are bad things and that ceilings on rents reduce the availability of housing. They did not believe that the monopoly power of oil companies caused oil prices to rise. There was a fair degree of agreement that minimum wages increase unemployment, although on this question there was more diversity of opinion. Economists generally do not believe that the inability of firms to compete is a cause of trade deficits. They generally do believe that cash payments make people better off than equivalent payments in kind, such as food or shelter.

	Percentage of Economists Who Agree with		
	Disagree	Provisos	Agree
1. Tariffs and import quotas usually reduce general economic welfare.	6.5	21.3	71.3
2. A minimum wage increases unemployment among young and unskilled workers.	20.5	22.4	56.5
3. A ceiling on rents reduces the quantity and quality of housing available.	6.5	16.6	76.3
4. The cause of the rise in petrol prices that occurred in the wake of the Iraqi invasion of Kuwait was the monopoly power of large oil companies.	67.5	20.3	11.4
5. The trade deficit is primarily a consequence of the inability of firms to compete.	51.5	29.7	18.1

Source: Richard M. Alston, J. R. Kearl, and Michael B. Vaughan, "Is There a Consensus Among Economists in the 1990s?" American Economic Review, May 1992.

that reducing the tax on interest income will encourage individuals to save more, but they may produce different estimates about the amount of the savings increase. Again, many of these disagreements arise because of inadequate data. We may have many data concerning savings over the past century. But institutions and economic conditions today are markedly different from those of fifty or even ten years ago.

DISAGREEMENTS WITHIN NORMATIVE ECONOMICS

There are generally many consequences of any policy, some beneficial, some harmful. If you compare two policies, one may benefit some people more, another may benefit others. One policy is not unambiguously better than another. It depends upon what you care more about. A cut in the tax on the profits from the sale of stocks may encourage savings, but at the same time, most of the benefits accrue to the very wealthy; hence, it increases inequality. A reduction in taxes to stimulate the economy may reduce unemployment, but it may also increase inflation. Even though two economists agree about the model, they may make different recommendations. In assessing the effect of a tax cut on unemployment and inflation, for instance, an economist who is worried more about unemployment may recommend in favor of the tax cut, while the other, concerned about inflation, may recommend against it. In this case, the source of the disagreement is a difference in values.

But although economists may often seem to differ greatly among themselves, in fact they agree more than they disagree: their disagreements get more attention than their agreements. Most importantly, when they do disagree, they seek to be clear about the source of their disagreement: (1) to what extent does it arise out of differences in models, (2) to what extent does it arise out of differences in estimates of quantitative relations, and (3) to what extent does it arise out of differences in values? Clarifying the sources of and reasons for disagreement can be a very productive way of learning more.

CONSENSUS ON THE IMPORTANCE OF SCARCITY

Most of what we have discussed in this chapter fits within the areas on which there is broad consensus among economists. This includes the observation that the U.K. economy is a mixed economy and that there are certain basic questions that all economic systems must address. We highlight the most important points of consensus throughout the book. Our first consensus point concerns scarcity. It is the most important point of consensus in this chapter.

1 Scarcity

There is no free lunch. Having more of one thing requires giving up something else. Scarcity is a basic fact of life.

REVIEW AND PRACTICE

SUMMARY

1 Economics is the study of how individuals, firms, and governments within our society make choices. Choices are unavoidable because desired goods, services, and resources are inevitably scarce.

2 There are four basic questions that economists ask about any economy. (1) What is produced, and in what quantities? (2) How are these goods produced? (3) For whom are these goods produced? (4) Who makes economic decisions, and by what process?

3 Most developed countries have mixed economies; there is a mix between public and private decision making. The economy relies primarily on the private interaction of individuals and firms to answer the four basic questions, but government plays a large role as well. A central question for any mixed economy is the balance between the public and private sectors.

4 The term *market* is used to describe any situation where exchange takes place. In a market economy, individuals, firms, and government interact in product markets, labour markets, and capital markets.

5 Economists use models to study how the economy works and to make predictions about what will happen if something is changed. A model can be expressed in words or equations and is designed to mirror the essential characteristics of the particular phenomena under study.

6 A correlation exists when two variables tend to change together in a predictable way. However, the simple existence of a correlation does not prove that one factor causes the other to change. Additional outside factors may be influencing both.

7 Positive economics is the study of how the economy works. Disagreements within positive economics centre on the appropriate model of the economy or market and the quantitative magnitudes characterizing the models. Normative economics deals with the desirability of various actions. Disagreements within normative economics centre on differences in the values placed on the various costs and benefits of different actions.

KEY TERMS

centrally planned economy	product market	microeconomics	causation
mixed economy	labour market	macroeconomics	positive economics
market economy	capital market	theory	normative economics
	capital goods	correlation	

REVIEW QUESTIONS

1 Why are choices unavoidable?

2 How are the four basic economic questions answered in the economy?

3 What is a mixed economy? Describe some of the roles government might play or not play in a mixed economy.

4 Name the three main economic markets, and describe how an individual might participate in each one as a buyer and seller.

5 Give two examples of economic issues that are primarily microeconomic, and two examples that are primarily macroeconomic. What is the general difference between microeconomics and macroeconomics?

6 What is a model? Why do economists use models?

7 When causation exists, would you also expect a correlation to exist? When a correlation exists, would you also expect causation to exist? Explain.

8 "All disagreements between economists are purely subjective." Comment.

PROBLEMS

1 Characterise the following events as microeconomic, macroeconomic, or both.
  (a) Unemployment increases this month.
  (b) A drug company invents and begins to market a new medicine.
  (c) A bank loans money to a large company but turns down a small business.
  (d) Interest rates decline for all borrowers.
  (e) A union negotiates for higher pay and shorter hours of work.
  (f) The price of oil increases.

2 Characterise the following events as part of the labour market, the capital market, or the product market.
  (a) An investor tries to decide which company to invest in.
  (b) With practice, the workers on an assembly line become more efficient.
  (c) The opening up of the economies in eastern Europe offers new markets for European products.
  (d) A big company that is losing money decides

to offer its workers a special set of incentives to retire early, hoping to reduce its costs.

(e) A consumer roams around a shopping mall, looking for birthday gifts.

(f) The government needs to borrow more money to finance its level of spending.

3 Discuss the incentive issues that might arise in each of the following situations.

(a) You have some money to invest, and your financial adviser introduces you to a couple of software executives who want to start their own company. What should you worry about as you decide whether to invest?

(b) You are running a small company, and your workers promise that if you increase their pay, they will work harder.

(c) A large industry is going bankrupt and appeals for government assistance.

4 Name ways in which government intervention has helped the motor industry in the last two decades and ways in which it has injured the industry.

5 The back of a bag of cat litter claims, "Cats that use cat litter live three years longer than cats that don't." Do you think that cat litter causes an increased life expectancy of cats, or can you think of some other factors to explain this correlation? What evidence might you try to collect to test your explanation?

6 Life expectancy in Sweden is 78 years; life expectancy in India is 61 years. Does this prove that if an Indian moved to Sweden, he would live longer? That is, does this prove that living in Sweden causes an increase in life expectancy, or can you think of some other factors to explain these facts? What evidence might you try to collect to test your explanation?

2

BASIC PRINCIPLES

E veryone thinks about economics, at least some of the time. We think about money (we wish we had more of it) and about work (we wish we had less of it). But there is a distinctive way that economists approach economic issues, and one of the purposes of this course is to introduce you to that way of thinking. This chapter begins with a basic model of the economy. We follow this with a closer look at how the basic units that compose the economy—individuals, firms, and government—make choices in situations where they are faced with scarcity. In Chapters 3 through 5, we study ways in which these units interact with one another, and how those interactions add up to determine how society's resources are allocated.

KEY QUESTIONS

1 What is the basic competitive model of the economy?

2 What are incentives, property rights, prices, and the profit motive, and what roles do these essential ingredients of a market economy play?

3 What alternatives for allocating resources are there to the market system, and why do economists tend not to favour these alternatives?

4 What are some of the basic techniques economists use in their study of how people make choices? What are the various concepts of costs that economists use?

THE BASIC COMPETITIVE MODEL

Though different economists employ different models of the economy, they all use a basic set of assumptions as a point of departure. The economist's basic competitive model has three components: assumptions about how consumers behave, assumptions about how firms behave, and assumptions about the markets in which these consumers and firms interact. The model ignores government, because we need to see how an economy without a government might function before we can understand the role of government.

RATIONAL CONSUMERS AND PROFIT-MAXIMISING FIRMS

Scarcity, which we encountered in Chapter 1, implies that individuals and firms must make choices. Underlying much of economic analysis is the basic assumption of **rational choice,** that people weigh the costs and benefits of each possibility. This assumption is based on the expectation that individuals and firms will act in a consistent manner, with a reasonably well-defined notion of what they like and what their objectives are and with a reasonable understanding of how to attain those objectives.

In the case of an individual, the rationality assumption is taken to mean that he makes choices and decisions in pursuit of his own self-interest. Different people will, of course, have different goals and desires. Sally may want to drive a Porsche, own a yacht, and have a large house; to attain those objectives, she knows she needs to work long hours and sacrifice time with her family. Andrew is willing to accept a lower income to get longer holidays and more leisure throughout the year.

Economists make no judgments about whether Sally's preferences are better or worse than Andrew's. They do not even spend much time asking why different individuals have different views on these matters or why tastes change over time. These are important questions, but they are more the province of psychology and sociology. What economists are concerned about are the consequences of these different preferences. What decisions can they expect Sally and Andrew, rationally pursuing their respective interests, to make?

In the case of firms, the rationality assumption is taken to mean that firms operate to maximise their profits.

COMPETITIVE MARKETS

To complete the model, economists make assumptions about the places where self-interested consumers and profit-maximising firms meet: markets. Economists begin by focusing on the case where there are many buyers and sellers, all buying and selling the same thing. You might picture a crowded outdoor market to get a sense of the number of buyers and sellers, except that you have to picture everyone buying and selling just one good.

Suppose all the market stalls are full of oranges. Each of the farmers would like to raise his price. That way, if he can still sell his oranges, his profits go up. Yet with a large number of sellers, each is forced to charge close to the same price, since if any farmer charged much more, he would lose business to the farmer next door. Profit-maximising firms are in the same position. In an extreme case, if a firm charged any more than the going price, it would lose *all* its sales. Economists label this case **perfect competition.** In perfect competition, each firm is a **price taker;** this simply means that because the firm cannot influence the market price, it must accept that price. The firm takes the market price as given because it cannot raise its price without losing all sales and, at the market price, it can sell as much as it wishes. Even if it sold ten times as much, this would have a negligible effect on the total quantity marketed or the price prevailing in the market. Markets for agricultural goods would be, in the absence of government intervention, perfectly competitive. There are so many wheat farmers, for instance, that each farmer believes he can grow and sell as much wheat as he wishes and have no effect on the price of wheat. (Later in the book, we will encounter markets with limited or no competition, like monopolies, where firms can raise prices without losing all their sales.)

On the other side of our market are rational individuals, each of whom would like to pay as little as possible for her oranges. Why can't she pay less than the going price? Because the seller sees another buyer in the crowd who will pay the going price. Thus, the consumers also take the market price as given and focus their attention on other factors—their taste for oranges, primarily—in deciding how many to buy.

This model of consumers, firms, and markets—rational, self-interested consumers interacting with rational, profit-maximising firms, in competitive markets where firms and consumers are both price takers—is the **basic competitive model.** The model has one very strong implication: if actual markets are well described by the competitive market, then the economy is efficient: resources are not wasted, it is not possible to produce more of one good without producing less of another, and it is not even possible to make anyone better off without making someone else worse off. These results are obtained without government.

Virtually all economists recognise that actual economies are not *perfectly* described by the competitive model, but most still use it as a convenient benchmark, as we will throughout this book. We will also point out important differences between the predictions of the competitive model and observed outcomes, which will guide us to other models that provide better descriptions of particular markets and situations. Economists recognise too that, while the competitive market may not provide a *perfect* description of some markets, it may provide a good description—with its predictions matching actual outcomes well, though not perfectly. As we shall see, economists differ in their views about how many such markets there are, how good the match is, and how well alternative models do in rectifying the deficiencies of the competitive model in particular cases.

INGREDIENTS IN THE BASIC COMPETITIVE MODEL

1 Rational, self-interested consumers

2 Rational, profit-maximising firms

3 Competitive markets with price-taking behaviour

PRICES, PROPERTY RIGHTS, AND PROFITS: INCENTIVES AND INFORMATION

For market economies to work efficiently, firms and individuals must be informed and have incentives to act on available information. Indeed, incentives can be viewed as being at the heart of economics. Without incentives, why would individuals go to work in the morning? Who would undertake the risks of bringing out new products? Who would put aside savings for a rainy day? There is an old expression about the importance of having someone "mind the store." But without incentives, why would anyone bother?

Market economies provide information and incentives through *prices*, *profits*, and *property rights*. Prices provide information about the relative scarcity of different goods. The **price system** ensures that goods go to those individuals and firms who are most willing and able to pay for them. Prices convey information to firms about how individuals value different goods.

The desire for profits motivates firms to respond to the information provided by prices. By producing what consumers want in the most efficient way, in a way that uses the least scarce resources, they increase their profits. Similarly, rational individuals' pursuit of self-interest induces them to respond to prices: they buy goods that are more expensive—in a sense relatively more scarce—only if they provide commensurately greater benefits.

For the profit motive to be effective, firms need to be able to keep at least some of their profits. Households also need to be able to keep at least some of what they earn or receive as a return on their investments. (The return on their investments is simply what they receive back in excess of what they invested. If they receive back less than they invested, the return is negative.) There must, in short, be **private property,** with its attendant **property rights.** Property rights include both the right of the owner to use the property as she sees fit and the right to sell it.

These two attributes of property rights give individuals the incentive to use property under their control efficiently. The owner of a piece of land tries to work out the most profitable use of the land, for example, whether to build a store or a restaurant. If he makes a mistake and opens a restaurant when he should have opened a store, he bears the consequences: the loss in income. The profits he earns if he makes the right decision—and the losses he bears if he makes the wrong one—give him an incentive to think carefully about the decision and do the requisite research. The owner of a store tries to make sure that her customers get the kind of merchandise and the quality of service they want. She has an incentive to establish a good reputation, because if she does so, she will do more business and earn more profits.

The store owner will also want to maintain her property—which is not just the land anymore but includes the store as well—because she will get more for it when the time comes to sell her business to someone else. Similarly, the owner of a house has an incentive to maintain *his* property, so that he can sell it for more when he wishes to move. Again, the profit motive combines with private property to provide incentives.

INCENTIVES VERSUS EQUALITY

While incentives are at the heart of market economies, they come with a cost: inequality. Any system of incentives must tie compensation with performance. Whether through differences in luck or ability, the performances of different individuals will differ. In many cases, it will not be possible to identify why performance is high. The salesperson may claim that the reason his sales are high is superior skill and effort, while his colleague may argue that it is just luck.

If pay is tied to performance, there will inevitably be some inequality. And the more closely compensation is tied to performance, the greater the inequality. The fact that the greater the incentives, the greater the resulting inequality is called the **incentive-equality trade-off.** If society provides greater incentives, total output is likely to be higher but there will also probably be greater inequality.

HOW THE PROFIT MOTIVE DRIVES THE MARKET SYSTEM

In market economies, incentives are supplied to individuals and firms by prices, profits, and property rights.

One of the basic questions facing society in the choice of tax rates and welfare systems is how much would incentives be diminished by an increase in tax rates to finance a better welfare system and thus reduce inequality? What would be the results of those reduced incentives?

WHEN PROPERTY RIGHTS FAIL

Prices, profits, and property rights are the three essential ingredients of market economies. We can learn a lot about why they are so important by examining a few cases where property rights and prices are interfered with. Each example highlights a general point. Any time society fails to define the owner of its resources and does not allow the highest bidder to use them, inefficiencies result. Resources will be wasted or not used in the most productive way.

Ill-Defined Property Rights: Fishing Rights Fish are a valuable resource, but the sea in which they live is typically not owned by anyone who can control access to it and restrict fishing. This has led to recurrent problems all over the world. When most of the North Sea was regarded as international water, anyone was free to fish there without limit. The North Sea was overfished: the fish population was reduced to a point where fishing became unprofitable. This undermined the livelihoods of fishing people all around its coasts. But individual fishing people had no incentive to restrain their own fishing. If they did not take the fish, someone else would. No one had a right to any particular fish in the sea. More recently, the countries bordering the North Sea have extended their control to much more of it and have cooperated to place restrictions on fishing there. The

European Community has agreed on a limit on fishing by each member country. This policy has allowed the fish stocks to grow back to a healthier size and has raised the amount of fish that can be taken from the North Sea.

Entitlements as Property Rights Property rights do not always mean that you have full ownership or control. A **legal entitlement,** such as the right to occupy an apartment for life at a rent that is controlled, is viewed by economists as a property right. Individuals do not own the apartment and thus cannot sell it, but they cannot be thrown out, either.

These partial and restricted property rights result in many inefficiencies. Because the individual in a rent-controlled apartment cannot (legally) sell the right to live in her apartment, as she gets older she may have limited incentives to maintain its condition, let alone improve it.

CONSENSUS ON INCENTIVES

Incentives, prices, profits, and property rights are central features of any economy, and highlight an important area of consensus among economists. This brings us to our second point of consensus:

2 Incentives

Providing appropriate incentives is a fundamental economic problem. In modern market economies, profits provide incentives for firms to produce the goods individuals want and wages provide incentives for individuals to work. Property rights also provide people with important incentives not only to invest and to save but to put their assets to the best possible use.

RATIONING

The price system is only one way of allocating resources, and a comparison with other systems will help to clarify the advantages of markets. When individuals get less of a good than they would like at the terms being offered, the good is said to be **rationed.** Different **rationing systems** are different ways of deciding who gets society's scarce resources.

Rationing by Queues Rather than supplying goods to those willing and able to pay the most for them, a society could give them instead to those most willing to wait in a queue. Tickets are often allocated by queues, whether they are for movies, sporting events, or rock concerts. A price is set, and it will not change no matter how many people line up to buy at that price. (The high price that touts can get for tickets is a good indication of how much more than the ticket price people would have been willing to pay.)

Rationing by queues is thought by many to be a more desirable way of supplying medical services than the price system. Why, it is argued, should the rich—who are most able to pay for medical services—be the ones to get better or more medical care? Using this reasoning, the National Health Service (NHS) in Britain provides free medical care to everyone on its soil. To see a doctor in Britain, all you have to do is wait in a queue. Rationing medicine by queues turns the allocation problem around: since the value of time for low-wage workers is lower, they are more willing to wait, and therefore they get a larger share of medical services than they would if the price system was used to allocate NHS facilities.

In general, rationing by queues is an inefficient way of distributing resources, because the time spent in a queue is a wasted resource. There are usually ways of achieving the same goal within a price system that can make everyone better off.

Rationing by Lotteries Lotteries allocate goods by a random process, like picking a name from a hat.

They are often used when the scarce items cannot be divided up among all the persons who want them. Tickets to very popular concerts—the Last Night of the Proms, for example—are sometimes allocated by lottery or ballot. Like queue systems, lotteries are thought to be fair because everyone has an equal chance. However, they are also inefficient, because the scarce resources do not go to the individual or firm that is willing and able to pay (and therefore values them) the most.

Rationing by Coupons Most governments in wartime use **coupon rationing.** People are allowed so many litres of petrol, so many kilogrammes of sugar, and so much flour each month. To get the good, they have to pay the market price and produce a coupon. The reason for coupon rationing is that without coupons prices might soar, and so inflict a hardship on poorer members of society.

Coupon systems take two forms depending upon whether coupons are tradable or not. Coupons that are not tradable give rise to the same inefficiency that occurs with most of the other nonprice systems—goods do not in general go to the individuals who are willing and able to pay the most. There is generally room for a trade that will make all parties better off. For instance, I might be willing to trade some of my flour ration for some of your sugar ration. But in a nontradable coupon system, the law prohibits such transactions. When coupons cannot be legally traded, there are strong incentives for the establishment of a **black market,** an illegal market in which the goods or the coupons for the goods are traded.

OPPORTUNITY SETS

We have covered a lot of ground so far in this chapter. We have seen the economist's basic model, which relies on competitive markets. We have seen how prices, the profit motive, and private property supply the incentives that drive a market economy. And we have had our first glimpse at why economists believe that market systems, which supply goods to those who are willing and able to pay the most, provide the most efficient means of allocating what the economy produces. They are far better than the nonprice rationing schemes that have been employed. It is time now to return to the question of choice. Market systems leave to individuals and firms the question of what to consume. How are these decisions made?

For a rational individual or firm, the first step in the economic analysis of any choice is to identify what is possible—what economists call the **opportunity set,** which is simply the group of available options. If you want a sandwich and you have only roast beef and tuna in the refrigerator, then your opportunity set consists of a roast beef sandwich, a tuna sandwich, a strange sandwich combining roast beef and tuna, or no sandwich. A ham sandwich is out of the question. Defining the limitations facing an individual or firm is a critical step in economic analysis. One can spend time yearning after the ham sandwich, or anything else outside the opportunity set, but when it comes to making choices and facing decisions, only what is within the opportunity set is relevant.

BUDGET AND TIME CONSTRAINTS

Constraints limit choices and define the opportunity set. In most economic situations, the constraints that limit a person's choices—that is, the constraints that are relevant—are not sandwich fillings, but time and money. Opportunity sets whose constraints are imposed by money are referred to as **budget constraints;** opportunity sets whose constraints are prescribed by time are called **time constraints.** A billionaire may feel that his choices are limited not by money but by time, whereas for an unemployed worker, time hangs heavy. Lack of money rather than time limits his choices.

The budget constraint defines a typical opportunity set. Consider the budget constraint of Alfred, who has decided to spend £100 on either cassette recordings or compact discs. A CD costs £10, a cassette £5. So Alfred can buy 10 CDs or 20 cassettes, or 9 CDs and 2 cassettes, or 8 CDs and 4 cassettes. The

Table 2.1 ALFRED'S OPPORTUNITY SET

Cassettes	CDs
0	10
2	9
4	8
6	7
8	6
10	5
12	4
14	3
16	2
18	1
20	0

various possibilities are set forth in Table 2.1. And they are depicted graphically in Figure 2.1:[1] the number of cassettes purchased is measured along the vertical axis, and the number of CDs is measured along the horizontal axis. The line marked B_1B_2 is Alfred's budget constraint. The extreme cases, where Alfred buys only CDs or only cassettes, are represented by the points B_1 and B_2 in the figure. The dots between these two points, along the budget constraint, represent the other possible combinations. The cost of each combination of CDs and cassettes must add up to £100. The point chosen by Alfred is labeled E, where he purchases 4 CDs (for £40) and 12 cassettes (for £60).

Alfred's budget constraint is the line that defines the outer limits of his opportunity set. But the whole opportunity set is larger. It also includes all points below the budget constraint. This is the shaded area in Figure 2.1. The budget constraint shows the maximum number of cassettes Alfred can buy for each number of CDs purchased, and vice versa. Alfred is always happiest when he chooses a point on his budget constraint rather than below it. To see why,

---

[1] See the chapter appendix for help in reading graphs.

Figure 2.1 ALFRED'S BUD-GET CONSTRAINT

The budget constraint identifies the limits of an individual's opportunity set between CDs and cassettes. Points B_1 and B_2 are the extreme options, where he chooses all of one and none of the other. His actual choice is point E. Choices from the shaded area are possible but less attractive than choices on the budget constraint.

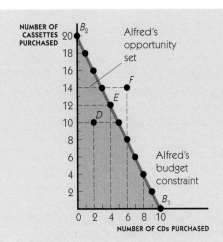

compare points E and D. At point E, he has more of both goods than at point D. He would be even happier at point F, at which he has still more cassettes and CDs, but that point, by definition, is unattainable.

Figure 2.2 depicts a time constraint. The most common time constraint simply says that the sum of what an individual spends her time on each day—including sleeping—must add up to 24 hours. Figure 2.2 plots the hours spent watching television on the horizontal axis and the hours spent on all other activities on the vertical axis. People—no matter how rich or how poor—have only 24 hours a day to spend on different activities. The time constraint is quite like the budget constraint. A person cannot spend more than 24 hours or fewer than 0 hours a day watching television. The more time she spends watching television, the less time she has available for all other activities. Point D (for dazed) has been added to the diagram at 5 hours a day.

Figure 2.2 AN OPPORTU-NITY SET FOR WATCHING TV AND OTHER ACTIVITIES

This opportunity set is limited by a time constraint, which shows the trade-off a person faces between spending time watching television and spending it on other activities. At 5 hours of TV time per day, point D represents a typical choice.

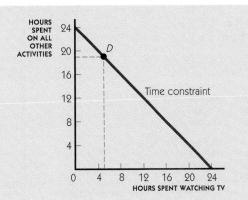

THE PRODUCTION POSSIBILITIES CURVE

Firms and societies also face constraints. They must make choices limited to opportunity sets. The amounts of goods a firm or society could produce, given a fixed amount of land, labour, and other inputs, are referred to as its **production possibilities.**

Take one much-discussed example: a simple description of a society in which all economic production is divided into two categories, military and civilian. Of course, each kind of spending has many different elements, but for the moment, let's discuss the choice as between the two broad categories. For simplicity, Figure 2.3 refers to military spending as guns and civilian spending as butter. The production of guns is given along the vertical axis, the production of butter along the horizontal. The possible combinations of military and civilian spending—of guns and butter—is the opportunity set. Table 2.2 sets out some possible combinations: 90 million guns and 40 million tonnes of butter, or 40 million guns and 90 million tonnes of butter. These possibilities are depicted in Figure 2.3. In a choice involving production decisions, the boundary of the opportunity set—giving the maximum amount of guns that can be produced for each amount of butter and vice versa—is called the **production possibilities curve.**

Table 2.2 PRODUCTION POSSIBILITIES FOR THE ECONOMY

Guns (millions)	Butter (millions of tonnes)
100	0
90	40
70	70
40	90
0	100

When we compare the individual's opportunity set with society's production possibilities curve, we notice one major difference. The individual's budget constraint is a straight line, whereas society's production possibilities curve bows outward. There is a good reason for this. An individual typically faces fixed **trade-offs:** if Alfred spends £10 more on CDs (that is, he buys one more CD), he has £10 less to spend on cassettes (he can buy two fewer cassettes).

On the other hand, the trade-offs faced by society are not fixed. If a society produces only a few guns, it will use those resources—the people and ma-

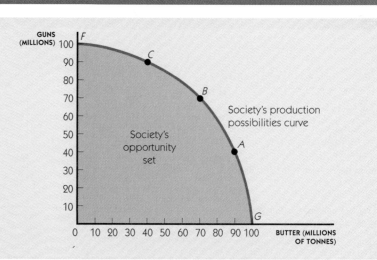

Figure 2.3 THE GUNS-AND-BUTTER TRADE-OFF

A production possibilities curve can show society's opportunity set. This one describes the trade-off between military spending (guns) and civilian spending (butter). Points F and G show the extreme choices, where the economy produces all guns or all butter. Notice that unlike the budget and time constraints, the production possibilities line curves, reflecting diminishing returns.

chines—that are best equipped for gun making. But as society tries to produce more and more guns, doing so becomes more difficult; it will increasingly have to rely on those who are less good at producing guns. It will be drawing these resources out of the production of other goods, in this case, butter. Thus, when the economy increases its production of guns from 40 million a year (point *A*) to 70 million (*B*), butter production falls by 20 million tonnes, from 90 million tonnes to 70 million tonnes. But if the production of guns is increased further, to 90 million (*C*), an increase of only 20 million, butter production has to decrease by 30 million tonnes, to only 40 million tonnes. For each increase in the number of guns, the reduction in the number of tonnes of butter produced gets larger. That is why the production possibilities curve is curved.

For another example, assume that a firm owns land that can grow wheat but not sweet corn, and land that can grow sweet corn but not wheat. In this case, the only way to increase wheat production is to move workers from the sweet corn fields to the wheat fields. As more and more workers are put into the wheat fields, production of wheat goes up, but each successive worker increases production less. The first workers might pick the largest and most destructive weeds. Additional workers lead to better weeding, and better weeding leads to higher output. But the additional weeds rooted up are smaller and less destructive, so output is increased by a corre-

Table 2.3 DIMINISHING RETURNS

Labour in Sweet Corn Field (no. of workers)	Sweet Corn Output (tonnes)	Labour in Wheat Field (no. of workers)	Wheat Output (tonnes)
1,000	60,000	5,000	200,000
2,000	110,000	4,000	180,000
3,000	150,000	3,000	150,000
4,000	180,000	2,000	110,000
5,000	200,000	1,000	60,000

spondingly smaller amount. This is an example of the general principle of **diminishing returns.** Adding successive units of any input such as fertilizer, labour, or machines to a fixed amount of other inputs—seeds or land—increases the output, or amount produced, but by less and less.

Table 2.3 shows the output of the sweet corn and wheat fields as labour is increased in each field. Assume the firm has 6,000 workers to divide between wheat production and sweet corn production. Thus, the second and fourth columns together give the firm's production possibilities, which are depicted in Figure 2.4.

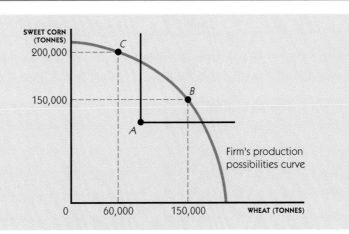

Figure 2.4 THE WHEAT-AND-CORN TRADE-OFF

This production possibilities curve shows that as wheat production increases, it becomes necessary to give up larger and larger amounts of sweet corn. Or to put the same point a different way, as sweet corn production falls, the resulting increase in wheat production gets smaller and smaller. Point *A* illustrates an inefficient outcome in this opportunity set.

INEFFICIENCIES: BEING OFF THE PRODUCTION POSSIBILITIES CURVE

There is no reason to assume that a firm or an economy will always be on its production possibilities curve. Any inefficiency in the economy will result in a point such as A in Figure 2.4, below the production possibilities curve. One of the major quests of economists is to look for instances in which the economy is inefficient in this way.

Whenever the economy is operating below the production possibilities curve, it is possible for us to have more of every good—more wheat and more sweet corn, more guns and more butter. No matter which goods we like, we can have more of them. That is why we can unambiguously say that points below the production possibilities curve are undesirable. But this does not mean that every point on the production possibilities curve is better than any point below it. Compare points A and C in Figure 2.4. Sweet corn production is higher at C, but wheat production is lower. If people do not like sweet corn very much, the increased sweet corn production may not adequately compensate them for the decreased wheat production.

There are many reasons why the economy may be below the production possibilities curve. If land better suited for the production of sweet corn is mistakenly devoted to the production of wheat, the economy will operate below its production possibilities curve. If some of society's resources—its land, labour, and capital goods—are simply left idle, as happens when there is a depression, the economy operates below the production possibilities curve. The kinds of inefficiencies discussed earlier in the chapter with inadequately or improperly defined property rights also result in operating below the production possibilities curve.

COST

The beauty of an opportunity set like the budget constraint, the time constraint, or the production possibilities curve is that it specifies the cost of one option in terms of another. If the individual, firm, or society is operating on the constraint or curve, then it is possible to get more of one thing only by sacrificing some of another. The cost of one more unit of one good is how much you have to give up of the other.

Economists thus think about cost in terms of trade-offs within opportunity sets. Let's go back to Alfred choosing between CDs and cassettes in Figure 2.1. The trade-off is given by the **relative price,** the ratio of the prices of CDs and cassettes. In our example, a CD cost £10, a cassette £5. The relative price is £10 ÷ £5 = 2; for every CD Alfred gives up, he can get two cassettes. Likewise, societies and firms face trade-offs along the production possibilities curve, like the one shown in Figure 2.3. There, point A is the choice where 40 million guns and 90 million tonnes of butter are produced. The trade-off can be calculated by comparing points A and B. Society can have 30 million more guns by giving up 20 million tonnes of butter.

Trade-offs are necessary because resources are scarce. If you want something, you have to pay for it; you have to give up something. If you want to go to the library tomorrow night, you have to give up going to the movies. If a sawmill wants to make more two-by-four beams from its stock of wood, it will not be able to make as many one-by-four boards.

OPPORTUNITY COSTS

If someone were to ask you right now what it costs to go to a movie, you would probably answer, "Seven pounds," or whatever you paid the last time you went. But with the concept of trade-offs, you can see that a *full* answer is not that simple. To begin with, the cost is not the £7 but what that £7 could otherwise buy. Furthermore, your time is a scarce resource that must be included in the calculation. Both the money and the time represent opportunities forgone in favor of going to the movie, or what economists refer to as the **opportunity cost** of the movie. To apply a resource to one use means that it cannot be put to any other use. Thus, we should consider the next-best use of any resource when we think about putting it to any particular use. This next-best use is the formal measurement of opportunity cost.

Some examples will help to clarify the idea of opportunity cost. Consider a student, Sarah, who enrolls in college. She thinks that the fee for tuition and room and board represents the costs of her education. But the economist's mind immediately turns to the job she might have had if she had not enrolled in college. If Sarah could have earned £15,000 from September to June, this is the opportunity cost of her time, and this forgone income must be added to the college bills in calculating the total economic cost of the academic year.

Now consider a business firm that has bought a building for its headquarters that is bigger than necessary. If the firm could receive £3 per month in rent for each square foot of space that is not needed, then this is the opportunity cost of leaving the space idle.

The analysis can be applied to the government as well. The government owns a vast amount of land. In deciding whether it is worthwhile to convert some of that land into a national park, the government needs to take into account the opportunity cost of the land. The land might be used for growing timber or for

CLOSE-UP: OPPORTUNITY COSTS OF MEETINGS

Businesses often neglect one of the most important opportunity costs of all: the time of their top employees. The personnel agency Accountemps tried to measure some of that wasted time by surveying 200 executives from the 1,000 largest U.S. companies. The executives estimated that they spent an average of 15 minutes a day on hold on the telephone, an average of 32 minutes a day reading or writing unnecessary memos, and an average of 72 minutes a day at unnecessary meetings. Now multiply those numbers by 48 weeks (assuming that the executives take 4 weeks of vacation each year). The average executive would be spending 60 hours per year on telephone hold, 128 hours per year on unnecessary memos, and 288 hours a year in unnecessary meetings!

Of course, estimates like these are more for illustration than precision. Moreover, it may be impossible to tell in advance whether a meeting will be useful; the only way to have a productive meeting, after all, may be to risk having an unproductive one. But even taking the particular numbers with a grain of salt, it seems likely that many businesses schedule meetings believing that since they do not have to pay extra for people to attend, the cost of the meetings is zero. They ignore the opportunity cost, the fact that their highly paid managers could be doing something else with their time.

One semiserious proposal is that businesses should measure and display the opportunity cost of their meetings with a scoreboard placed discreetly in the corner of their meeting rooms. As everyone entered the meeting room, she would enter her hourly salary, and the scoreboard would then start adding up the cost of everyone's time. For example, if there were 20 executives in a meeting who earned an average of $45 per hour, then the scoreboard would ring up $900 for every hour of meeting time. We could also include an opportunity cost of using the meeting room, of needing to call back people from other companies who called during the meeting, and so on. Surely, as the scoreboard showed the opportunity cost of the regular afternoon meeting climbing into four figures, there would be powerful incentive to finish quickly and let everyone return to her other tasks.

Source: "Executives on Hold 60 Hours a Year," *San Jose Mercury News*, 10 July, 1990, p. 7A.

grazing sheep. Whatever the value of the land in its next-best use, this is the economic cost of the national park. The fact that the government does not have to buy the land does not mean that the land should be treated as a free good.

Thus, in the economist's view, when rational firms and individuals make decisions—whether to undertake one investment project rather than another, whether to buy one product rather than another—they take into account *all* of the costs, the full opportunity costs, not just the direct expenditures.

SUNK COSTS

Economic cost includes costs, as we have just seen, that noneconomists often exclude, but it also ignores costs that noneconomists include. If an expenditure has already been made and cannot be recovered no matter what choice is made, a rational person would ignore it. Such expenditures are called **sunk costs.**

To understand sunk costs, let's go back to the movies, assuming now that you have spent £7 to buy a movie ticket. You were skeptical about whether the movie was worth £7. Half an hour into the movie, your worst suspicions are realized: the movie is a disaster. Should you leave the movie theater? In making that decision, the £7 should be ignored. It is a sunk cost; your money is gone whether you stay or leave. The only relevant choice now is how to spend the next 90 minutes of your time: watch a terrible movie or go and do something else.

Or assume you have just purchased a fancy laptop computer for £2,000. But the next week, the manufacturer announces a new computer with twice the power for £1,000; you can trade in your old computer for the new one by paying an additional £400. You are angry. You feel you have just paid £2,000 for a computer that is now almost worthless, and you have had hardly any use out of it. You decide not to buy the new computer for another year, until you have had at least some return for your investment. Again, an economist would say that you are not approaching the question rationally. The past decision is a sunk cost. The only question you should ask yourself is whether the extra power of the fancier computer is worth the additional £400. If it is, buy it. If not, don't.

MARGINAL COSTS

The third aspect of cost that economists emphasise is the extra costs of doing something, what economists call the **marginal costs.** These are weighed against the additional or **marginal benefits** of doing it. The most difficult decisions we make are not whether to do something. They are whether to do a little more or a little less of something. Few of us waste much time deciding whether to work. We have to work; the decision is whether to work a few more or a few less hours. A country does not consider whether to have any army; it decides whether to have a larger or smaller army.

Jim has just obtained a job for which he needs a car. He must decide how much to spend on the car. By spending more, he can get a bigger and more luxurious car. But he has to decide whether it is worth a few hundred (or thousand) marginal pounds for a larger car or for extra items like fancy hubcaps, power windows, and so on.

Polly is considering flying to Rome for the weekend. She has three days off work. The air fare is £200, and the hotel room costs £100 a night. Food costs the same as at home. She is trying to decide whether to go for two or three days. The *marginal* cost of the third day is £100, the hotel room cost. There are no additional transport costs involved in staying the third day. She needs to compare the marginal cost with the additional enjoyment she will have from the third day.

People, consciously or not, think about the trade-offs at the margin in most of their decisions. Economists, however, bring them into the foreground. Like opportunity costs and sunk costs, marginal costs are one of the critical concepts that enable economists to think systematically about the costs of alternative choices.

BASIC STEPS OF RATIONAL CHOICE

Identify the opportunity sets.

Define the trade-offs.

Calculate the costs correctly, taking into account opportunity costs, sunk costs, and marginal costs.

REVIEW AND PRACTICE

SUMMARY

1 The basic competitive model consists of rational, self-interested individuals and profit-maximising firms, interacting in competitive markets.

2 The profit motive and private property provide incentives for rational individuals and firms to work hard and efficiently. Ill-defined or restricted property rights can lead to inefficient or counterproductive behaviour.

3 Society often faces choices between efficiency, which requires incentives that enable people or firms to receive different benefits depending upon their performance, and equality, which requires people to receive more or less equal benefits.

4 The price system in a market economy is one way of allocating goods and services. Other methods include rationing by queue, by lottery, and by coupon.

5 An opportunity set illustrates what choices are possible. Budget constraints and time constraints define individuals' opportunity sets. Both show the trade-offs of how much of one thing a person must give up to get more of another.

6 A production possibilities curve defines a firm's or society's opportunity set, representing the possible combinations of goods that the firm or society can produce. If a firm or society is producing below its production possibilities curve, it is said to be inefficient, since it could produce more of either good (or both goods) without producing less of the other.

7 The opportunity cost is the cost of using any resource. It is measured by looking at the next-best use to which that resource could be put.

8 A sunk cost is a past expenditure that cannot be recovered, no matter what choice is made in the present. Thus, rational decision makers ignore them.

9 Most economic decisions concentrate on choices at the margin, where the marginal (or extra) cost of a course of action is compared with its extra benefits.

KEY TERMS

perfect competition	opportunity set	trade-offs	marginal costs
basic competitive model	budget constraints	diminishing returns	marginal benefits
price system	time constraints	opportunity cost	
rationing systems	production possibilities	sunk costs	

REVIEW QUESTIONS

1 What are the essential elements of the basic competitive model?

2 Consider a lake in a national park where everyone is allowed to fish as much as he wants. What outcome do you predict? Might this problem be averted if the lake were privately owned and fishing licences were sold?

3 Why might government policy to make the distribution of income more equitable lead to less efficiency?

4 List advantages and disadvantages of rationing by queue, by lottery, and by coupon. If the government permitted a black market to develop, might some of the disadvantages of these systems be reduced?

5 What are some of the opportunity costs of going to college? What are some of the opportunity costs the government should consider when deciding whether to widen a highway?

6 Give two examples of a sunk cost, and explain why they should be irrelevant to current decisions.

7 How is marginal analysis relevant in a decision about which car or which house to purchase? After deciding the kind of car to purchase, how is marginal analysis relevant?

PROBLEMS

1 Imagine that many businesses are located beside a river, into which they discharge industrial waste. There is a city downstream, which uses the river as a water supply and for recreation. If property rights to the river are ill defined, what problems may occur?

2 Suppose an underground reservoir of oil resides under properties owned by several different individuals. As each well is drilled, it reduces the amount of oil that others can take out. Compare how quickly the oil is likely to be extracted in this situation with how quickly it would be extracted if one person owned the property rights to drill for the entire pool of oil.

3 In some countries, hunting licences are allocated by lottery; if you want a licence, you send in your name to enter the lottery. If the purpose of the system is to ensure that those who want to hunt the most get a chance to do so, what are the flaws of this system? How would the situation improve if people who won licences were allowed to sell them to others?

4 Imagine that during time of war, the government imposes coupon rationing. What are the advantages of allowing people to buy and sell their coupons? What are the disadvantages?

5 Kathy, a student, has £20 a week to spend; she spends it either on junk food at £2.50 a snack or on petrol at 60 pence a litre. Draw Kathy's opportunity set. What is the trade-off between junk food and petrol? Now draw each new budget constraint she would face if:

    (a) A kind relative started sending her an additional £10 per week.
    (b) The price of a junk food snack fell to £2.
    (c) The price of petrol rose to 70 pence a litre.

In each case, how does the trade-off between junk food and petrol change?

6 Why is the opportunity cost of having a child greater for a woman with a university degree than it is for a woman who left school at 18?

7 Bob likes to divide his recreational time between going to movies and listening to compact discs. He has 20 hours a week available for recreation; a movie takes 2 hours to see, and a CD takes 1 hour to listen to. Draw his time budget constraint. Bob also has a limited amount of income to spend on recreation. He has £60 a week to spend on recreational activities; a movie costs £5 and a CD costs £12. (He never likes to listen to the same CD twice.) Draw his budget constraint. What is his opportunity set?

APPENDIX: READING GRAPHS

Whether the old saying that a picture is worth a thousand words under- or overestimates the value of a picture, economists find graphs extremely useful.

For instance, look at Figure 2.5; it is a redrawn version of Figure 2.1, showing the budget constraint—the various combinations of CDs and cassettes he can purchase—of an individual, Alfred. More generally, a graph shows the relationship between two variables, here, the number of CDs and the number of cassettes that can be purchased. The budget constraint gives the maximum number of cassettes that can be purchased, given the number of CDs that have been bought.

In a graph, one variable (here, CDs) is put on the horizontal axis, and the other variable on the vertical axis. We read a point such as E by looking down to the horizontal axis and seeing that it corresponds to 4 CDs and by looking across to the vertical axis and seeing that it corresponds to 12 cassettes. Similarly, we read point A by looking down to the horizontal axis and seeing that it corresponds to 5 CDs and by looking across to the vertical axis and seeing that it corresponds to 10 cassettes.

In Figure 2.5, each of the points from the table has been plotted, and then a curve has been drawn through those points. The curve turns out to be a straight line in this case, but we still use the more general term. The advantage of the curve over the individual points is that with it, we can read from the graph points on the budget constraint that are not in the table.

Sometimes, of course, not every point on the graph is economically meaningful. You cannot buy half a cassette or half a CD. For the most part, we ignore these considerations when drawing our graphs; we simply pretend that any point on the budget constraint is possible.

SLOPE

In any diagram, the amount by which the value along the vertical axis increases from a change in a unit along the horizontal axis is called the **slope,** just like the slope of a mountain. Slope is sometimes described as rise over run, meaning that the slope of a

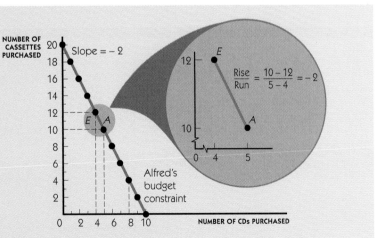

Figure 2.5 READING A GRAPH: THE BUDGET CONSTRAINT

Graphs can be used to show the relationship between two variables. This one shows the relationship between the variable on the vertical axis (the number of cassettes Alfred can buy) and the variable on the horizontal axis (the number of CDs).

The slope of a curve like the budget constraint gives the change in the number of cassettes that can be purchased as Alfred buys one more CD. The slope of the budget constraint is negative.

NUMBER OF CASSETTES PURCHASED

Slope = – 2

$\dfrac{\text{Rise}}{\text{Run}} = \dfrac{10 - 12}{5 - 4} = -2$

Alfred's budget constraint

NUMBER OF CDs PURCHASED

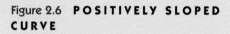

Figure 2.6 **POSITIVELY SLOPED CURVE**

Incomes increase with the number of years of schooling.

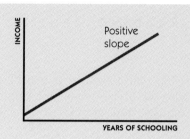

line can be calculated by dividing the change on the vertical axis (the rise) by the change on the horizontal axis (the run).

Look at Figure 2.5. As we move from E to A, increasing the number of CDs by 1, the number of cassettes purchased falls from 12 to 10. For each additional CD bought, the feasible number of cassettes that can be purchased falls by 2. So the slope of the line is

$$\frac{\text{Rise}}{\text{Run}} = \frac{10 - 12}{5 - 4} = \frac{-2}{1} = -2.$$

When, as in Figure 2.5, the variable on the vertical axis falls when the variable on the horizontal axis increases, the curve, or line, is said to be **negatively sloped.** A budget constraint is always negatively sloped. But when we describe the slope of a budget constraint, we frequently omit the term *negative.* We say the slope is 2, knowing that since we are describing the slope of a budget constraint, we should more formally say that the slope is negative 2. Alternatively, we sometimes say that the slope has an absolute value of 2.

Figure 2.6 shows the case of a curve that is **positively sloped.** The variable along the vertical axis, income, increases as schooling increases, giving the line its upward tilt from left to right.

In later discussions, we will encounter two special cases. A line that is very steep has a very large slope; that is, the increase in the vertical axis for every unit increase in the horizontal axis is very large. The extreme case is a perfectly vertical line, and we say then that the slope is infinite (Figure 2.7A). At the other extreme is a flat, horizontal line; since there is

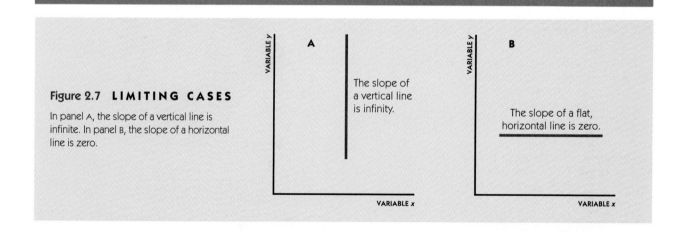

Figure 2.7 **LIMITING CASES**

In panel A, the slope of a vertical line is infinite. In panel B, the slope of a horizontal line is zero.

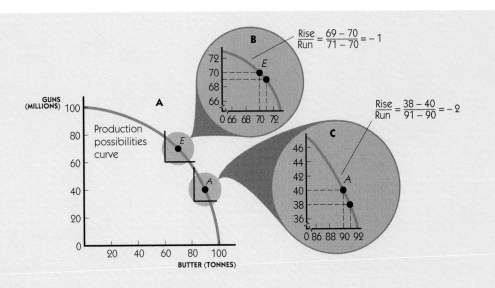

Figure 2.8 THE GUNS-AND-BUTTER TRADE-OFF

Panel A shows a trade-off between military spending (guns) and civilian spending (butter), where society chooses point E. Panel B is an enlargement of the area around E, which focuses on the slope there, which measures the marginal trade-offs

society faces near that point. Similarly, panel C is an enlargement of the area around A and shows the marginal trade-offs society faces near that point.

no increase in the vertical axis no matter how large the change along the horizontal, we say that the slope of such a curve is zero (Figure 2.7B).

Figures 2.5 and 2.6 both show straight lines. Everywhere along the straight line, the slope is the same. This is not true in Figure 2.8, which repeats the production possibilities curve shown originally in Figure 2.3. Look first at point E. Panel B of the figure blows up the area around E, so that we can see what happens to the output of guns when we increase the output of butter by 1. From the figure, you can see that the output of guns decreases by 1. Thus, the slope is

$$\frac{\text{Rise}}{\text{Run}} = \frac{69-70}{71-70} = -1.$$

Now look at point A, where the economy is producing more butter. The area around A has been blown up in panel C. Here, we see that when we increase

butter by 1 more unit, the reduction in guns is greater than before. The slope at A is

$$\frac{\text{Rise}}{\text{Run}} = \frac{38-40}{91-90} = -2.$$

With curves such as the production possibilities curve, the slope differs as we move along the curve.

INTERPRETING CURVES

Look at Figure 2.9. Which of the two curves has a larger slope? The one on the left appears to have a slope that has a larger absolute value. But look carefully at the axes. Notice that in panel A, the vertical axis is stretched relative to panel B. The same distance that represents 20 cassettes in panel B represents only 10 cassettes in panel A. In fact, both panels

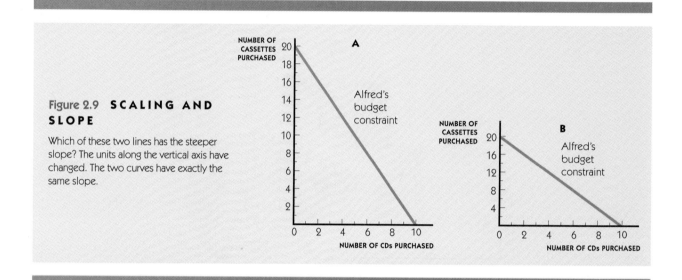

Figure 2.9 **SCALING AND SLOPE**

Which of these two lines has the steeper slope? The units along the vertical axis have changed. The two curves have exactly the same slope.

represent the same budget constraint. They have exactly the same slope.

This kind of cautionary tale is as important in looking at the graphs of data that were common in Chapter 1 as it is in looking at the relationships presented in this chapter that produce smooth curves. Compare, for instance, panels A and B of Figure 2.10.

Which of the two curves exhibits more variability? Which looks more stable? Panel B appears to show that inflation does not change much over time. But again, a closer look reveals that the vertical axis has been stretched inp panel A. The two curves are based on exactly the same data, and there is really no difference between them.

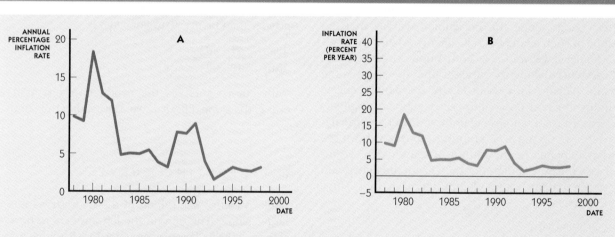

Figure 2.10 **INFLATION IN THE UNITED KINGDOM**

Which graph shows greater variability in the inflation rate? The two graphs display the same data. The vertical scale has been changed.

CHAPTER 3

TRADE

A creature on another planet looking down at a developed modern economy on Earth might compare human activity to an enormous ant colony. Each ant seemingly has an assigned task. Some stand guard. Some feed the young. Some harvest food and others distribute it. Some shuffle paper, scribble notes in books, and type on computer keyboards at computer consoles. Others work in factories, tightening screws, running machines, and so on. How is all of this activity coordinated? No dictator or superintelligent computer is giving instructions. Yet somehow an immense amount is accomplished in a reasonably coordinated way. Understanding how a complex economy operates—how it is that certain individuals do one task and others do another, how information is communicated and decisions made—is a central objective of economics.

This chapter discusses the problem of economic interdependence at two levels: individuals and firms within a country, and countries within the world economic community. Many of the same principles apply at both levels.

KEY QUESTIONS

1 Why is trade (exchange) mutually beneficial?

2 What are the similarities and differences between trade (exchange) between individuals within a country and trade between countries?

3 What determines what any particular country produces and sells on the international market? What is meant by comparative advantage, and why does it play such an important role?

4 What are the gains from specialization?

5 How valid is the argument, so often heard in political circles, that trade should be restricted?

THE BENEFITS OF ECONOMIC INTERDEPENDENCE

We begin by considering the benefits of trade, specifically the exchange of those goods which are already available in the economy.

THE GAINS FROM TRADE

When individuals own different goods, have different desires, or both, there is an opportunity for trades that benefit all parties to the trade. Scotland produces more Scotch whisky than can be consumed in Britain, but Britain cannot produce rice. The United States produces more rice than Americans want, but they want Scotch whisky. Trade can benefit both countries.

Voluntary trade involves only winners. If the trade would make a loser of any party, that party would choose not to trade. Thus, a fundamental consequence of voluntary exchange is that it benefits everyone involved.

"FEELING JILTED" IN TRADE

In spite of the seemingly persuasive argument that individuals only voluntarily engage in trade if they think they will be better off as a result, people often walk away from a deal believing they have been hurt. It is important to understand that when economists say that a voluntary trade makes the two traders better off, they do not mean that it makes them both happy.

Imagine, for example, that Frank brings an antique rocking chair to a flea market to sell. He is willing to sell it for £100 but hopes to sell it for £200. Helen comes to the flea market planning to buy such a chair, hoping to spend only £100 but willing to pay as much as £200. They argue and negotiate, eventually settle on a price of £125, and make the deal. But when they go home, they both complain. Frank complains the price was too low, and Helen that it was too high.

From an economist's point of view, such complaints are self-contradictory. If Frank *really* thought £125 was too low, he would not have sold at that price. If Helen *really* thought £125 was too high, she would not have paid the price. Economists argue that people reveal their preferences not by what they say but by what they do. If one voluntarily agrees to make a deal, one also agrees that the deal is, if not perfect, at least better than the alternative of not making it.

Two common objections are made to this line of reasoning. Both involve Frank's or Helen's taking advantage of the other. The implication is that if a buyer or a seller can take advantage, then the other party may be a loser rather than a winner.

The first objection is that either Frank or Helen may not really know what is being agreed to. Perhaps Helen recognises the chair is an antique but, by neglecting to tell Frank, manages to buy it for only £125. Perhaps Frank knows the rockers fall off but sells the chair without telling this to Helen, thus keeping the price high. In either case, lack of relevant information makes someone a loser after the trade.

The second objection concerns the equitable division of the **gains from trade.** Since Helen would have been willing to pay as much as £200, anything she pays less than that is **surplus,** the term economists use for a gain from trade. Similarly, since Frank would have been willing to sell the chair for as little as £100, anything he receives more than that is also surplus. The total pound value of the gain from trade is £100—the difference between the maximum price Helen was willing to pay and the minimum price at which Frank was willing to sell. At a price of £125, £25 of the gain went to Frank, £75 to Helen. The second objection is that such a split is not fair.

Economists do not have much patience with these objections. Like most people, they favour making as much information public as possible, and they think vendors and customers should be made to stand behind their promises. But economists also point out that second thoughts and "if only I had known" are not relevant. If Frank sells his antique at a flea market instead of having it valued by reputable antique dealers, he has made a voluntary decision to save his time and energy. If Helen buys an antique at a flea market instead of going to a reputable dealer, she knows she is taking a risk.

The logic of free exchange, however, does not say that everyone must express happiness with the result. It simply says that when people choose to make a deal, they prefer making it to not making it. And if they prefer the deal, they are by definition better off *in their own minds* at the time the transaction takes place.

The objections to trade nonetheless carry an important message: most exchanges that happen in the real world are considerably more complicated than the Frank-Helen chair trade. They involve problems of information, estimating risks, and expectations about the future. These complications will be discussed throughout the book. So without going into too much detail at the moment, let's just say that if you are worried that you do not have the proper information to make a trade, shop around, get a guarantee or expert opinion, or buy insurance. If you choose to plunge ahead without these precautions, don't pretend you don't have other choices. Like those who buy a ticket in a lottery, you know you are taking a chance.

ECONOMIC RELATIONS AS EXCHANGES

Individuals in our economy are involved in masses of voluntary trades. They trade their labour services (time and skills) to their employer for money. They then trade this money with a multitude of merchants for goods (like petrol and groceries) and services (like plumbing and hair styling). The employer trades the goods it produces for money and trades this money for labour services. Even your savings account can be viewed as a trade: you give the bank £100 today in exchange for the bank's promise to give you £105 at the end of the year (your original deposit plus 5 percent interest).

TRADE BETWEEN COUNTRIES

Why is it that people engage in this complex set of economic relations with others? The answer is that people are better off as a result of trading. Just as individuals *within* a country find it advantageous to trade with one another, so too do countries find trade advantageous. Just as it is impossible for any individual to be self-sufficient, it is impossible for a country to be self-reliant without sacrificing its standard of living. How has interdependence between countries affected the three main markets in the economy?

Interdependence in the Product Market A high proportion of goods sold in Britain are manufactured overseas. More than half the cars are **imports.** Many clothes are made in the Far East. Many consumer durables—refrigerators, washing machines, and so on—are made in other European countries. Indeed, it is something of a rarity to see a product that admits to being made in Britain.

As Figure 3.1 shows, imports have grown persistently as a fraction of the gross domestic product (GDP), and they amounted to 29 percent of it in 1995. Of all expenditure in the United Kingdom, 29 percent went, directly or indirectly, on imported goods. That may be no surprise. Indeed, that may be a

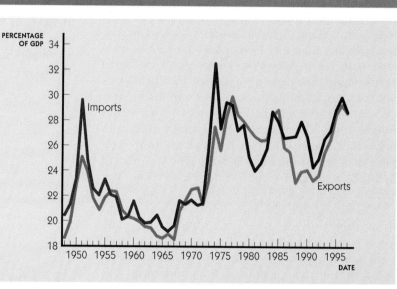

Figure 3.1 **U.K. IMPORTS AND EXPORTS**

Imports and exports are expressed as a percentage of GDP. Notice that trade has grown over time. After a long period of trade surpluses, the late 1980s and 1990s have seen a return of trade deficits. *Source:* Office of National Statistics, *Economic Trends,* Annual Supplement 1998 (1999), Table 1.3.

surprisingly low figure, given the media attention devoted to imports, and their prominence in the shops.

It may be more surprising that **exports** have almost kept pace with imports. Both have grown from around 20 percent of GDP in 1960 to almost 30 percent in 1995. From 1977 to 1983, exports were greater than imports. Despite frequent discussions about the poor quality of products, their unreliability, and the lack of competitiveness, the export performance of the United Kingdom should not be considered a failure.

Some European countries are more open than Britain, especially smaller countries such as Denmark, the Netherlands, and Belgium. There an even greater proportion of national production is exported, and a greater proportion of goods sold there are imported. By contrast, larger economies' exports and imports are smaller relative to their gross domestic products. In Japan and the United States, exports and imports each amount to around 10 percent of the GDP.

Interdependence in Capital Markets At the same time as countries have bought goods from each other, they have also borrowed large sums of money from each other and made large loans to each other. In the late nineteenth century, Britain invested quite

heavily in the developing countries of North and South America and accumulated a large stock of assets in the rest of the world. Even in the 1980s, as a relatively small economy, Britain had substantial stocks of assets held abroad. Britain's net wealth held abroad reached around £100 billion in 1986. This figure is the difference between two much larger figures. Gross assets held by British residents in the rest of the world amounted to approximately £1,000 billion. Assets in the United Kingdom owned by residents of other countries amounted to slightly less.

In recent years, restrictions on international trading in financial and real assets have been dismantled in many countries. Financial markets have been deregulated. Capital markets have become much more interdependent. A news item that affects the value of shares on the Tokyo stock exchange sends a shock wave around the world in a flash. Stock markets in London and New York are affected almost immediately.

Interdependence in Labour Markets In the 1990s we saw only small and limited flows of people between countries. But present populations are a legacy of great flows of people in the nineteenth century, when famine and poverty drove half the population of Ireland out of the country, a large fraction of the Swedish population emigrated to the United States, and substantial numbers of people emigrated from other European countries to North and South America. In this century migration has substantially enlarged the populations of Canada and Australia.

The European Union (EU) has removed barriers to the movement of labour. Citizens of EU are free to live and work anywhere in the community. This is intended to enable better use to be made of the skills available in the workforce of Europe by matching them to employment opportunities wherever they arise in the union.

MULTILATERAL TRADE

Many of the examples to this point have emphasised two-way trade. Trade between two individuals or countries is called **bilateral trade.** But exchanges between two parties is often less advantageous than trade between several parties, called **multilateral trade.** Japan has no domestic oil; it imports oil from Arabian countries. The Arabian countries want to

sell their oil, but they want wheat and food, not the cars and television sets that Japan can provide. The United States can provide the missing link by buying cars and television sets from Japan and selling food to the Arabian countries. This three-way trade, shown in Figure 3.2, offers gains that two-way trade cannot.

The scores of countries active in the world economy create patterns far more complex than these simplified examples. Figure 3.3 illustrates the construction of a Ford Escort in Europe and dramatises the importance of multilateral and interconnected trade relations. The parts that go into an Escort come from all over the world. Similar diagrams could be constructed for many of the components in the diagram; the aluminum alloys may contain bauxite from Jamaica, the chrome plate may use chromium from South America, and the copper for wiring may come from Chile.

Multilateral trade means that trade between any two participants may not balance. In Figure 3.2, the Arabian countries send oil to Japan but get no goods (only yen) in return. No one would say that the Arabian countries have an unfair trade policy with

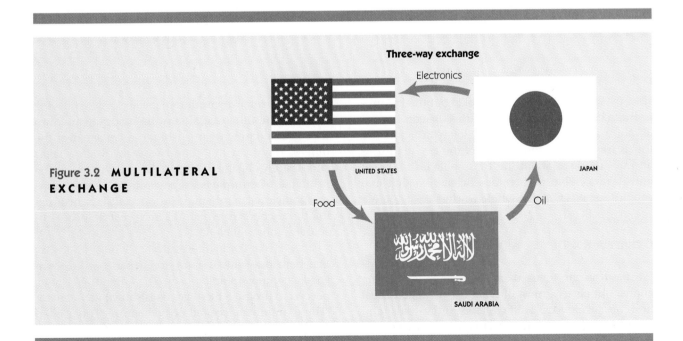

Figure 3.2 **MULTILATERAL EXCHANGE**

Three-way exchange

Electronics

UNITED STATES

JAPAN

Food

Oil

SAUDI ARABIA

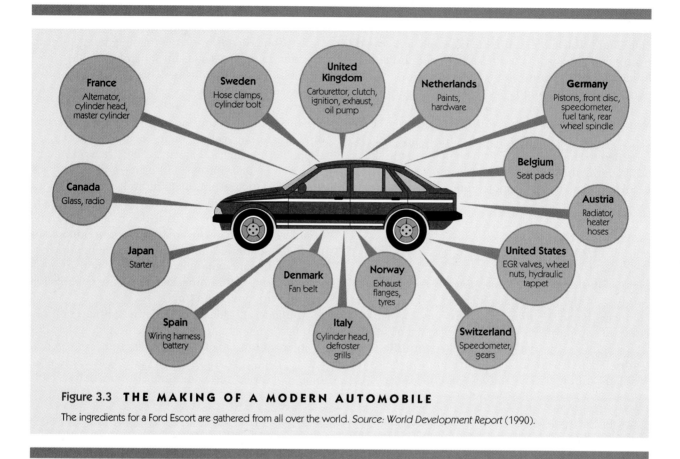

Figure 3.3 THE MAKING OF A MODERN AUTOMOBILE

The ingredients for a Ford Escort are gathered from all over the world. *Source: World Development Report* (1990).

Japan. There is little point in looking at the balance of trade between a pair of countries. Britain, for example, may have a large trade deficit with Japan. But this is irrelevant to the welfare of the two countries and to questions about the trade policies of Japan and Britain. What matters are Britain's deficit and Japan's surplus with the whole world.

COMPARATIVE ADVANTAGE

We have so far focused on exchanges of existing goods. But clearly, most of what is exchanged must first be produced. Trade allows individuals and countries to concentrate on what they produce best.

Some countries are more efficient at producing almost all goods than other countries are. The pos-session of superior production skills is called having an **absolute advantage,** and these advanced countries are said to have an absolute advantage over the others. How can the countries with disadvantages successfully engage in trade? The answer lies in the principle of **comparative advantage,** which states that individuals and countries specialise in producing those goods in which they are *relatively,* not absolutely, more efficient.

To see what comparative advantage means, let's say that both the United States and Japan produce two goods, computers and wheat. The amount of labour needed to produce these goods is shown in Table 3.1. (These numbers are all hypothetical.) The United States is more efficient (spends fewer worker hours) at making both products. It can rightfully claim to have the most efficient computer industry in the world, and

Table 3.1 LABOUR COST OF PRODUCING COMPUTERS AND WHEAT (WORKER HOURS)

	United States	Japan
Labour required to make a computer	100	120
Labour required to make a tonne of wheat	5	8

yet it imports computers from Japan. Why? The *relative* cost of making a computer (in terms of labour used) in Japan, relative to the cost of producing a tonne of wheat, is low, compared to in the United States. That is, in Japan, it takes 15 times as many hours (120/8) to produce a computer as a tonne of wheat; in the United States, it takes 20 times as many hours (100/5) to produce a computer as a tonne of wheat. While Japan has an absolute *dis*advantage in producing computers, it has a *comparative* advantage.

The principle of comparative advantage applies to individuals as well as countries. The president of a company might type faster than her secretary, but it still pays to have the secretary type her letters, because the president may have a comparative advantage at bringing in new clients, while the secretary has a comparative (though not absolute) advantage at typing.

PRODUCTION POSSIBILITIES CURVES AND COMPARATIVE ADVANTAGE

The easiest way to understand the comparative advantage of different countries is to use the production possibilities curve first introduced in Chapter 2. Figure 3.4 depicts hypothetical production possibilities

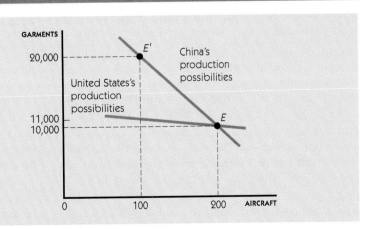

Figure 3.4 EXPLOITING COMPARATIVE ADVANTAGE

The production possibilities schedules for China and the United States, each manufacturing two commodities, textiles and airplanes, illustrate the trade-offs of different levels of production. Point E shows the current level of production for each country; point E' illustrates a production decision that better exploits each country's comparative advantage.

curves for two countries, China and the United States, producing two commodities, textiles (garments) and aircraft. On both curves, point E represents the current level of production. Let us look at what happens if each country changes its production by 100 aircraft.

China has a comparative advantage in producing textiles. If it reduces its aircraft production by 100, its textile production can be increased by 10,000 garments. This trade-off between aircrafts and garments is called the **marginal rate of transformation.** By contrast, if the United States reduces its plane production by 100 planes, its textile production can be increased by only 1,000 garments. We can now see why the world is better off if each country exploits its comparative advantage. If China moves from point E to point E' (decreasing its plane production by 100), it can produce 10,000 more garments. If the United States at the same time increases its plane production by 100, it will produce only 1,000 fewer garments. In the new situation, the world production of planes is unchanged, but the world production of garments has increased by 9,000. So long as the production trade-offs differ—that is, so long as the marginal rates of transformation differ—it pays for China to specialise increasingly in textiles and for the United States to specialise increasingly in planes. Notice that the analysis only requires knowledge about the production trade-offs. We do not need to know how much labour or capital is required in either country to produce either aircraft or garments.

Though it pays countries to increase the production and export of goods in which they have a comparative advantage and to import goods in which they have a comparative disadvantage, this may not lead to complete specialization. Thus the United States continues to be a major producer of textiles, in spite of heavy imports from the Far East. This does not violate the principle of comparative advantage: not all textiles require the same skill and expertise in manufacturing. Thus, while China may have a comparative advantage in inexpensive textiles, the United States may have a comparative advantage in higher-quality textiles. At the same time, the comparative advantage of other countries is so extreme in producing some goods that it does not pay for the United States to produce them at all: TVs, VCRs, and a host of other electronic gadgets, for example.

COMPARATIVE ADVANTAGE AND SPECIALIZATION

To see the benefits of specialization, consider the pencil. A tree, containing the right kind of wood, must be felled; it must be transported to a sawmill and there cut into pieces that can be further processed into pencil casings. Then the graphite that runs through the pencil's center, the eraser at its tip, and the metal that holds the two together must each be produced by specially trained people. The pencil is a simple tool. But to produce it by oneself would cost a fortune in money and an eternity in time.

Why Specialization Increases Productivity Specialization increases productivity, thus enhancing the benefits of trade, for three reasons. First, specialising avoids the time it takes a worker to switch from one production task to another. Second, by repeating the same task, the worker becomes more skilled at it. And third, specialization creates a fertile environment for invention.

Dividing jobs so that each worker can practice and perfect a particular skill (called the **division of labour**) may increase productivity hundreds or thousands of times. Almost anyone who practices a simple activity—like sewing on a button, shooting a basketball, or adding a column of numbers—will be quite a lot better at it than someone who has not practiced. Similarly, a country that specialises in producing sports cars may develop a comparative advantage. With its relatively large scale of production, it can divide tasks into separate assignments for different people; as each becomes better at his own tasks, productivity is increased.

At the same time, the division of labour often leads to invention. As someone learns a particular job extremely well, she might figure out ways of doing it better—including inventing a machine to do it. Specialization and invention reinforce each other. A slight initial advantage in some good leads to greater production of that good, thence to more invention, and thence to even greater production and further specialization.

Limits of Specialization The extent of division of labour, or specialization, is limited by the size of the market. There is greater scope for specialization in

Problem: Using the earlier example of Japan and the United States producing wheat and computers, calculate the trade-offs and show the gains from specialization. Assume that both countries have 240,000 worker hours, initially divided equally between producing wheat and computers.

Solution: First, draw the production possibilities curves, as in the following figures. Since the costs (in worker hours) of producing each unit of each commodity are fixed, the production possibilities schedule is a straight line. If the United States used all its labour to produce computers, it would produce 2,400 computers; if it used all its labour to produce wheat, it would produce 48,000 tonnes of wheat. If Japan used all its labour to produce computers,

it would produce 2,000 computers; if it used all its labour to produce wheat, it would produce 30,000 tonnes of wheat.

In both curves, use point A to mark the current point of production, at which labour is equally divided between computers and wheat.

Next, calculate the slope of the production possibilities curve, giving the trade-offs. In the United States, increasing wheat output by 1,000 tonnes leads to a reduction of computers produced by 50, while reducing wheat output by 1,000 tonnes in Japan leads to an increase in computers produced of 66⅔. Thus, each shift of wheat production by 1,000 tonnes from Japan to the United States increases world computer production by 16⅔.

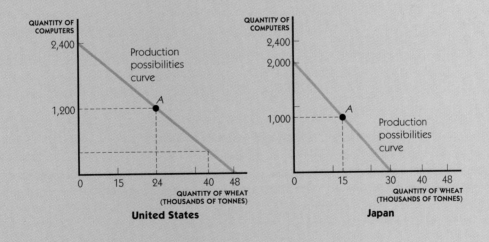

United States   **Japan**

---

mass-produced goods like picture frames than in custom-made items like the artwork that gets framed. That is one reason why the costs of production of mass-produced goods have declined so much. Similarly, there is greater scope for specialization in a

big city than in a small town. That is why small shops specialising in a particular food or type of clothing thrive in cities but are rare in smaller towns.

The very nature of specialization limits gains. Repetitive jobs can lead to bored and unproductive

CLOSE-UP: WHAT DOES BRITAIN EXPORT AND IMPORT?

This chapter has focused on comparative advantage to explain the pattern of imports and exports. Where does Britain's comparative advantage lie? Looking at the trade figures reveals the following information:

IMPORTS[a] INTO AND EXPORTS[b] FROM THE UNITED KINGDOM, BILLIONS OF POUNDS, 1997

Trade Sector	Exports	Imports
Food	6.55	13.81
Beverages and tobacco	4.56	2.98
Crude materials	2.50	6.15
Fuels	10.34	6.56
Animal and vegetable oils	0.27	0.65
Chemicals	21.97	17.87
Manufactured goods	22.62	28.64
Machinery	79.11	82.18
Miscellaneous manufactures	21.64	27.18
Other goods	1.95	1.63
Total	171.49	187.64

[a]Imports are measured CIF.

[b]Exports are measured FOB.

Source: Central Statistical Office, *Annual Abstract of Statistics* (1998), Tables 12.3 and 12.4.

The table shows that the pattern of comparative advantage is less easy to discern than might have been thought. For these broad categories of goods—food, fuels, chemicals, and so on—it turns out that Britain exports in most cases almost as much as it imports. Machinery is by far the largest category of goods for both imports and exports. Exports of chemicals exceed imports by over £3 billion, reflecting the strength of the chemical and pharmaceutical industries in Britain. Exports of food are less than half the level of imports, reflecting Britain's long-standing comparative disadvantage as an agricultural producer, despite the effects of subsidies to agriculture which have stimulated farm production. But notice that exports of beverages and tobacco exceed imports by roughly 1.5 billion, showing the contribution of whisky and gin production. The surplus in trade in fuels shows the continuing effect of North Sea oil production. The overall picture is less clear than the simple theory suggests, with a lot of trade apparently going in both directions.

However, within these broad figures, there are goods for which Britain's exports are dominant:

whisky (where the United Kingdom had 81.1 percent of world exports in 1990), jet engines (44.5 percent), small aircraft (21 percent), regenerated fibre yarn (28.3 percent), explosives and pyrotechnics (39.4 percent), retail insecticides (17.2 percent), nonchocolate sugar confectionary (12.5 percent), and developed cinema film (21.6 percent) (data from "Where Britain is Best," *Management Today*, February 1994).

A number of British firms account for a large fraction of total exports from the United Kingdom and export a large fraction of their output. The top exporters in 1996 were as shown in the table to the right.

Firm	Exports (£ million)	Percent Exports (of U.K. turnover)
British Aerospace	5,248	85
BP	4,483	20
Rover Group	4,005	62
Shell UK	3,357	48
IBM UK	3,069	60
British Steel	2,722	55
Ford Motor Co	2,611	37
Rolls Royce	2,512	59
Motorola	2,208	79
Zeneca	2,076	85

Source: "The FT Exporter," *Financial Times*, October 1997.

This list of firms contains a combination of high-tech, represented by IBM and Motorola in electronics, Zeneca in pharmaceuticals and agrichemicals, and Rolls Royce and British Aerospace in aircraft and defence equipment; medium-tech, in the form of British Steel, Ford, and Rover; and natural-resource-based industry represented by Shell and BP, reflecting Britain's position as an oil producer.

workers. And single-track specialization inhibits the new insights and ideas that can come from engaging in a variety of work activities.

WHAT DETERMINES COMPARATIVE ADVANTAGES?

Earlier we learned that comparative advantage determines the pattern of trade. But what determines comparative advantage? In the modern world, this turns out to be a complex matter.

Natural Endowments In first laying down the principle of comparative advantage in the early 1800s, the great British economist David Ricardo used the example of Portugal's trade with Britain. In Ricardo's example, Portugal had an absolute advantage in producing both wool and wine. But it had a comparative advantage in producing wine, and Britain had a comparative advantage in producing wool. In this and other early examples, economists tended to assume that a country's comparative advantage was determined largely by its **natural endowments.** Countries with soil and climate that are *relatively* better for grapes than for pasture will produce wine; countries with soil and climate that are relatively better for pasture than for grapes will produce sheep (and hence wool).

In the modern economy, natural endowments still count: countries that have an abundance of low-skilled labour relative to other resources, such as China, have a comparative advantage in producing goods like textiles, which require a lot of handwork. But in today's technological age, countries can also act to *acquire* a comparative advantage.

Acquired Endowments Japan has little in the way of natural resources, yet it is a major player in international trade, in part because it has **acquired endowments.** Japan's case underscores the principle that by saving and accumulating capital and building large factories, a country can acquire a comparative advantage in goods, like steel, that require large amounts of capital in their production. And by devot-

THE FOUR BASES OF COMPARATIVE ADVANTAGE

Natural endowments, which consist of geographical determinants such as land, natural resources, and climate

Acquired endowments, which are the physical capital and human skills a country has developed

Superior knowledge, including technological advantages, which may be acquired either as an accident of history or through deliberate policies

Specialization, which may create comparative advantages between countries that are similar in all other respects

---

ing resources to education, a country can develop a comparative advantage in those goods that require a skilled labour force. Thus, the resources—human and physical—that a country has managed to acquire for itself can also give rise to comparative advantage.

Superior Knowledge In the modern economy, comparative advantage may come simply from expertise in using resources productively. Switzerland has a comparative advantage in watches because, over the years, the people of the country have accumulated superior knowledge and expertise in watch making. Belgium has a comparative advantage in fine lace; its workers have developed the requisite skills. A quirk of fate might have led Belgium to acquire a comparative advantage in watches, and Switzerland in lace.

Although patterns of specialization sometimes occur as an accident of history, in modern economies they are more likely to be a consequence of deliberate decisions. The United States's semiconductor industry is a case in point. This industry manufactures the tiny silicon brains that control computers. Semiconductors were invented by an American, Robert Noyce, and in the 1970s, the United States had a powerful comparative advantage in manufacturing semiconductors; but Japan managed to become a close competitor in the 1980s. The rise of the U.S. semiconductor industry was built in part on decisions by its federal government to fund the necessary research (primarily so the semiconductors could be used in guided missiles and other weapons). The rise of the Japanese industry was similarly based on decisions by that government to support its semiconductor industry.

Stories like that of the semiconductor industry have led some economists to argue that government should

encourage certain industries, in order for them to gain a technological advantage, for instance, through the support of research relevant to that industry.

Specialization Earlier we saw how comparative advantage leads to specialization. Specialization may also lead to comparative advantage. The Swiss make fine watches and have a comparative advantage in that market based on years of unique experience. Such superior knowledge, however, does not explain why Britain, Germany, and the United States, which are at roughly the same level of technological expertise in building cars, all trade cars with one another. How can each country have a comparative advantage in making cars? The answer lies in specialization.

Both Britain and Germany may be better off if Britain specialises in producing sports cars and Germany in producing luxury cars, or conversely, because specialization increases productivity. Countries enhance or develop a comparative advantage by specialising just as individuals do. As a result, similar countries enjoy the advantages of specialization even when they specialise in different variations of basically similar products.

THE PERCEIVED COSTS OF INTERNATIONAL INTERDEPENDENCE

If the argument that voluntary trade must be mutually beneficial is so compelling, why has there been, from time to time, such strong antitrade sentiment in

Manchester is known as the home of free trade. Indeed, the city's main concert hall, which its excellent orchestra, the Hallé Orchestra, has used as its home base for many years, is called the Free Trade Hall.

The reason for all this is the growth of the cotton and other manufacturing industries in Manchester in the early nineteenth century, when the price of wheat in Britain was maintained at a minimum of 80 shillings a bushel by the operation of the Corn Laws, laws which imposed a variable levy on imports of wheat so as to keep the price in Britain from falling below this level. This import duty on wheat pleased the agricultural landowners and was stoutly defended by them. By raising the incomes produced by their farms, it maintained their traditional affluence. However, the manufacturers of the growing towns of the North and Midlands were fiercely opposed to the Corn Laws. The wages they had to pay their workers were heavily dependent on the price of bread, and thus on the price of wheat: the manufacturers had to pay the workers enough to feed themselves. Cheap bread meant low wages for the workers and more profits for the manufacturers. Free trade meant the end of the Corn Laws, relative impoverishment of the landowning classes, and greater wealth for the growing class of businesspeople and industrial entrepreneurs.

Initially the landowners—richer, more numerous, and politically more influential—had the upper hand. But in the early decades of the nineteenth century the power of the new class of industrialists rose and began to match that of the landowners. Their arguments in favour of free

trade were given intellectual force by the work of David Ricardo. Eventually, the free trade lobby won the day and the Corn Laws were repealed in 1846, paving the way for the growth in size and wealth of the city of Manchester and the other great industrial cities of northern England.

The workers did not immediately benefit from free trade. The industrial workers were at least no worse off in real terms: their wages (measured in terms of money) fell, but the amount of bread their wages could buy did not fall. But the agricultural workers, particularly those of southern England, were worse off, as falling farm incomes led to farm workers' being turned out of their jobs or kept on at starvation wages. The journalist and social critic of the period William Cobbett wrote about the misery of the agricultural poor in his book *Rural Rides* (1830). Rural poverty contributed to the flow of people out of the country and into the towns looking for work and provided the labour force for the growing industries of Manchester and Birmingham. Eventually, the rapid growth of industry did lead to rising real wages, though much later in the nineteenth century. Free trade was partly responsible for the more rapid industrialization and growth of Britain than of the continental European countries, and for Britain's economic supremacy at the end of the nineteenth century.

Free trade is in principle capable of bringing benefits to the entire economy; in practice there are usually big gainers and big losers from changes in trade policies; arguments about them are frequently very highly politicised, and settled by political and not economic considerations.

many countries? This antitrade feeling is often labeled **protectionism,** because it calls for "protecting" the economy from the effects of trade. Those who favour protectionism raise a number of concerns. Some of the objections to international trade parallel the objections to trade among individuals noted earlier. Did they get a fair deal? Was the seller in a stronger bargaining position? Such concerns, for individuals and countries, revolve around how the *surplus* associated with the gains from trade is divided. Weak countries may feel that they are being taken advantage of by stronger countries. Their weaker bargaining position may mean that the stronger countries get *more* of the gains from trade. But this does not contradict the basic premise: both parties gain from voluntary exchange. All countries—weak as well as strong—are better off as a result of voluntary exchange.

But an important difference exists between trade among individuals and trade among countries. Some individuals within a country benefit from trade and some lose. Since the trade as a whole is beneficial to the country, the gains to the winners exceed the losses to the losers. Thus, in principle, those who benefit within the country could more than compensate those who lose. In practice, however, those who lose remain losers and obviously oppose trade, using the argument that trade results in lost jobs and reduced wages. These concerns have become particularly acute as unskilled workers face competition with low-wage unskilled workers in Asia and Latin America: how can they compete, without lowering their wages?

These concerns played a prominent role in the debate in 1993 over ratification of the North American Free Trade Agreement (NAFTA), which allows Mexican goods into the United States with no duties at all. Advocates of NAFTA pointed out that (1) more jobs would be created by the new export opportunities than would be lost through competition from Mexican firms and (2) the jobs created would pay higher wages, reflecting the benefits from specialization in comparative advantage.

Opponents of NAFTA, in particular, and trade, in general, are not swayed by these arguments but instead stress the costs to workers and communities as particular industries shrink in response to foreign imports. Still the textile worker in North Carolina who loses his job a a result of imports of inexpensive clothing from China cannot instantly convert himself into a computer programmer in California or an aircraft engineer working for Boeing. But the fact is that jobs are being destroyed and created all the time, irrespective of trade. And over the long run, the economic incentive of the new jobs at Boeing may induce someone in the Midwest to leave his semiskilled job and get the training that makes him eligible for one of the skilled jobs at Boeing. The vacancy created may be filled by someone who moves in from Kentucky, leaving a vacancy there for the laid-off textile worker in North Carolina.

Because of the practical complications and the very real costs of retraining and relocation, there is increasing recognition that government may need to play a role in facilitating job movements. To the extent that such assistance increases the number of winners from trade, it should reduce opposition to trade.

While the perceived costs of economic interdependence cannot be ignored—especially when they become the subject of heated political debate—the fact that the country as a whole benefits from freer trade is one of the central tenets on which there is a consensus among the vast majority of economists. Trade is the subject of our third consensus point.

3 Trade

There are gains from voluntary exchanges. Whether between individuals or across national borders, all can gain from voluntary exchange. Trade allows parties to specialise in activities in which they have a comparative advantage.

REVIEW AND PRACTICE • 55

REVIEW AND PRACTICE

SUMMARY

1 The benefits and costs of economic interdependence apply to individuals and firms within a country as well as to countries within the world. No individual and no country is self-sufficient.

2 Both individuals and countries gain from voluntary trade. There may be cases in which there are only limited possibilities for bilateral trade (exchange between two parties), but the gains from multilateral trade (exchange between several parties) may be great.

3 The principle of comparative advantage asserts that countries should export the goods in which their production costs are *relatively* low.

4 Specialization tends to increase productivity for three reasons: specialising avoids the time it takes a worker to switch from one production task to an-

other, workers who repeat a task become more skilled at it, and specialization creates a fertile environment for invention.

5 A country's comparative advantage can arise from natural endowments, acquired endowments, superior knowledge, or specialization.

6 There is basic difference between trade among individuals and trade among countries: with trade among countries, some individuals within the country may be worse off. Though in principle, those who gain could more than compensate those who lose, such compensations are seldom provided. Though free trade enhances national income, fears about job loss and wage reductions among low-skilled workers have led to demands for protection. Government assistance to facilitate the required adjustments may be desirable.

KEY TERMS

gains from trade

surplus

imports

exports

bilateral trade

multilateral trade

absolute advantage

comparative advantage

marginal rate
of transformation

division of labour

natural endowments

acquired endowments

protectionism

REVIEW QUESTIONS

1 Why are all voluntary trades mutually beneficial?

2 Describe a situation (hypothetical if need be) where bilateral trade does not work but multilateral trade is possible.

3 What are some of the similarities of trade between individuals and trade between countries? What is a key way in which they differ?

4 Does a country with an absolute advantage in a product necessarily have a comparative advantage in that product? Can a country with an absolute disadvantage in a product have a comparative advantage in that product? Explain.

5 Why does specialization tend to increase productivity?

6 "A country's comparative advantage is dictated by its natural endowments." Discuss.

7 "If trade with a foreign country injures anyone in this country, the government should react by passing protectionist laws to limit or stop that particular trade." Comment.

PROBLEMS

1 Four players on a school baseball team discover that they have each been collecting baseball cards, and they agree to get together and trade. Is it possible for everyone to benefit from this agreement? Does the fact that one player starts off with many more cards than any of the others affect your answer?

2 Leaders in many developing countries of Latin America and Africa have often argued that because they are so much poorer than the wealthy countries of the world, trade with the more-developed economies of Europe and North America will injure them. They maintain that they must first become self-sufficient before they can benefit from trade. How might an economist respond to these claims?

3 If the United Kingdom changes its immigration quotas to allow many more unskilled workers into the country, who is likely to gain? Who is likely to lose? Consider the impact on consumers, on businesses that hire low-skilled labour, and on low-skilled labour in both the United Kingdom and the workers' countries of origin.

4 David Ricardo illustrated the principle of comparative advantage in terms of the trade between Britain and Portugal in wine (port) and wool. Suppose that in Britain it takes 120 labourers to produce a certain quantity of wine, while in Portugal it takes only 80 labourers to produce that same quantity. Similarly, in Britain it takes 100 labourers to produce a certain quantity of wool, while in Portugal it takes only 90. Draw the opportunity set for each country, assuming that each has 72,000 labourers. Assume that each country commits half its labour to each product in the absence of trade, and designate that point on your graph. Now describe a new production plan, with trade, that can benefit both countries.

5 In the 1980s, Britain and other western European countries negotiated with the Japanese a system of voluntary export restraints (VERs) whereby the Japanese agreed to limit the number of cars they would export to Europe. Similar arrangements were established between the United States and Japan. Who would have benefited from these VERs in Japan, and who in Europe? Who was injured by them? Consider the firms that make cars in Japan and in Europe, their workers, and the consumers who buy cars.

6 For many years, an international agreement called the Multifibre Agreement has limited the amount of textiles that the developed economies of Europe and North America can buy from poor countries in Latin America and Asia. Textiles can be produced by relatively unskilled labour with a reasonably small amount of capital. Who benefits from the protectionism of the Multifibre Agreement, and who suffers?

CHAPTER 4

DEMAND, SUPPLY, AND PRICE

C hoice in the face of scarcity, as we have seen, is the fundamental concern of economics. The **price** of a good or service is what must be given in exchange for the good. When the forces of supply and demand operate freely, price measures scarcity. As such, prices convey critical economic information. When the price of a resource used by a firm is high, the company has a greater incentive to economise on its use. When the price of a good that the firm produces is high, the company has a greater incentive to produce more of that good, and its customers have an incentive to economise on its use. In these ways and others, prices provide the economy with incentives to use scarce resources efficiently. This chapter describes how prices are determined in competitive market economies.

KEY QUESTIONS

1 What is meant by demand? Why do demand curves normally slope downwards? On what variables, other than price, does the quantity demanded depend?

2 What is meant by supply? What do supply curves normally slope upwards? On what variables, other than price, does the quantity supplied depend?

3 Why do economists say that the equilibrium price occurs at the intersection of the demand and supply curves?

4 How do shifts in the demand and supply curves affect the equilibrium price?

THE ROLE OF PRICES

Prices are the way participants in the economy communicate with one another. Assume a drought reduces drastically the supply of potatoes. Households will need to reduce their consumption of potatoes or there will not be enough to go around. But how will they know this? Suppose newspapers across the country ran an article informing people they would have to eat fewer potatoes because of a drought. What incentive would they have to pay attention to it? How would each family know how much it ought to reduce its consumption? As an alternative to the newspaper article, consider the effect of an increase in the price of potatoes. The higher price conveys all the relevant information. It tells families potatoes are scarce at the same time as it provides incentives for them to consume fewer of them. Consumers do not need to know anything about why potatoes are scarce, nor do they need to be told by how much they should reduce their consumption of them.

Price changes and differences present interesting problems and puzzles. In the late 1980s, house prices in many parts of Britain rose by around 50 percent, and then just as rapidly fell by 50 percent between 1990 and 1993. Why? During the same period, the price of bread rose persistently although slowly, while the price of computers fell dramatically. Why? The wage rate, or salary paid to workers, is just the price of labour. Why do women earn only 70 percent of what men earn on average? Why is the price of water, without which we cannot live, very low in most cases, but the price of diamonds, which we can surely live without, very high? The simple answer to all these questions is that in market economies, price is determined by supply and demand. Changes in prices are determined by changes in supply and demand.

Understanding the causes of changes in prices and being able to predict their occurrence is not just a matter of academic interest. One of the events that precipitated the French Revolution was the rise in the price of bread, for which the people blamed the government. Large price changes have also given rise to recent political turmoil in several countries, including Morocco, the Dominican Republic, Russia, and Poland.

Noneconomists see much more in prices than the impersonal forces of supply and demand. It was the landlord who raised the rent on the apartment; it was the oil company or the owner of the petrol station who raised the price of petrol. These people and companies *chose* to raise their prices, says the noneconomist, in moral indignation. True, replies the economist, but there must be some factor that made these people and companies believe that a higher price was not a good idea yesterday but is today. And economists point out that at a different time, these same impersonal factors can force the same landlords and oil companies to cut their prices. Economists see prices, then, as symptoms of underlying causes and focus on the forces of demand and supply behind price changes.

DEMAND

Economists use the concept of **demand** to describe the quantity of a good or service that a household or firm chooses to buy at a given price. It is important to understand that economists are concerned not just with what people desire but with what they choose to buy given the spending limits imposed by their budget constraint and given the prices of various goods. In analysing demand, the first question they ask is how the quantity of a good purchased by an individual changes as the price changes, keeping everything else constant.

THE INDIVIDUAL DEMAND CURVE

Think about what happens as the price of chocolate bars changes. At a price of £2.00, you might never buy one. At £1.20 you might buy one as a special treat. At 50

pence, you might buy a few, and if the price declined to 25 pence, you might buy a lot. Figure 4.1 summarises Roger's weekly demand for chocolate bars at different prices. We can see that the lower the price, the larger the quantity demanded. We can also draw a graph that shows the quantity Roger demands at each price. The quantity demanded is measured along the horizontal axis, and the price is measured along the vertical axis. The points are plotted in Figure 4.1.

A smooth curve can be drawn to connect the points. This curve is called the **demand curve.** The demand curve gives the quantity demanded at each price. Thus, if we want to know how many chocolate bars a week Roger will demand at a price of 40 pence, we simply look along the vertical axis at the price 40 pence, find the corresponding point *A* along the demand curve, and then read down to the horizontal axis. At a price of 40 pence, Roger buys 6 chocolate bars each week. Alternatively, if we want to know at what price he will buy just 3 chocolate bars, we look along the horizontal axis at the quantity 3, find the corresponding point *B* along the demand curve, and then read across to the vertical axis. Roger will buy 3 chocolate bars at a price of 60 pence.

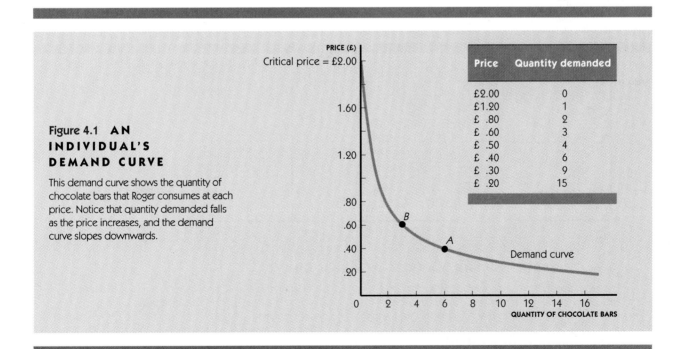

Figure 4.1 AN INDIVIDUAL'S DEMAND CURVE

This demand curve shows the quantity of chocolate bars that Roger consumes at each price. Notice that quantity demanded falls as the price increases, and the demand curve slopes downwards.

Price	Quantity demanded
£2.00	0
£1.20	1
£ .80	2
£ .60	3
£ .50	4
£ .40	6
£ .30	9
£ .20	15

As the price of chocolate bars increases, the quantity demanded decreases. This can be seen from the numbers in Figure 4.1 and in the shape of its demand curve, which slopes downwards from left to right. This relationship is typical of demand curves and makes common sense: the cheaper a good is (the lower down we look on the vertical axis), the more of it a person will buy (the farther right on the horizontal axis); the more expensive, the less a person will buy.

THE MARKET DEMAND CURVE

Suppose there was a simple economy made up of two people, Roger and Jane. Figure 4.2 illustrates how to add up the demand curves of these two individuals to obtain a demand curve for the market as a whole. We add the demand curves horizontally by taking, at each price, the quantities demanded by Roger and by Jane and adding the two together. Thus, in Figure 4.2, at the price of 30 pence, Roger demands 9 chocolate bars and Jane demands 11, so that the total market demand is 20 bars. The same principles apply no matter how many people there

are in the economy. The **market demand curve** gives the total quantity of the good that will be demanded at each price. Figure 4.3 summarises the information for our example of chocolate bars; it gives the total quantity demanded by everybody in the economy at various prices. If we had a figure like Figure 4.1 for each person in the economy, we would construct Figure 4.3 by adding up, at each price, the total quantity purchased. Figure 4.3 tells us, for instance, that at a price of £1.20 per chocolate bar, the total market demand is 1 million bars and that lowering the price to 80 pence increases market demand to 3 million.

Figure 4.3 also depicts the same information in a graph. As with Figure 4.1, price lies along the vertical axis, but now the horizontal axis measures the quantity demanded by everyone in the economy. Joining the points in Figure 4.3 together, we get the market demand curve. If we want to know what the total demand will be when the price is 60 pence per bar, we look on the vertical axis at the price 60 pence, find the corresponding point *A* along the demand curve, and read down to the horizontal axis; at that price, total demand is 4 million chocolate bars. If we want to know what the price will be when the demand

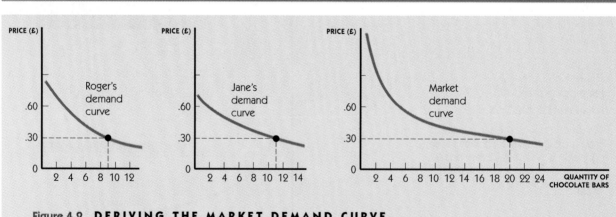

Figure 4.2 DERIVING THE MARKET DEMAND CURVE

The market demand curve is constructed by adding up, at each price, the total of the quantities consumed by each individual. The curve here shows what market demand would be if there were only two consumers. Actual market demand, as depicted in Figure 4.3, is much larger because there are many consumers.

Figure 4.3 THE MARKET DEMAND CURVE

The market demand curve shows the quantity of the good demanded by all consumers in the market at each price. The market demand curve is downward sloping, for two reasons: at a higher price, each consumer buys less, and at high enough prices, some consumers decide not to buy at all; they exit the market.

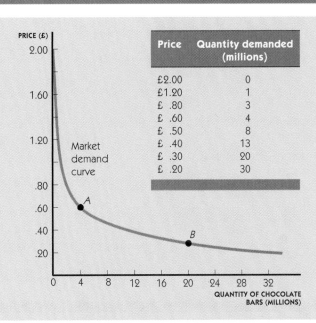

Price	Quantity demanded (millions)
£2.00	0
£1.20	1
£ .80	3
£ .60	4
£ .50	8
£ .40	13
£ .30	20
£ .20	30

equals 20 million, we find 20 million along the horizontal axis, look up to find the corresponding point B along the market demand curve, and read across to the vertical axis; the price at which 20 million chocolate bars are demanded is 30 pence.

Notice that just as when the price of chocolate bars increases, the individual's demand decreases, so too when the price increases, market demand decreases. Thus, the market demand curve also slopes downwards from left to right. This general rule holds both because each individual's demand curve is downward sloping and because as the price is increased, some individuals will decide to stop buying altogether. We have already examined the first of these reasons, but the second deserves a closer look.

In Figure 4.1, for example, Roger **exits the market**—consumes a quantity of zero—at the price of £2.00, at which his demand curve hits the vertical axis.

SHIFTS IN DEMAND CURVES

As the price of a good increases, the demand for that good decreases—when everything else is held constant. But in the real world, everything is not held constant. Any changes other than the price of the good in question shift the (whole) demand curve—that is, change the amount that will be demanded at each price. How the demand curve for chocolate has

DEMAND CURVE

The demand curve gives the quantity of the good demanded at each price.

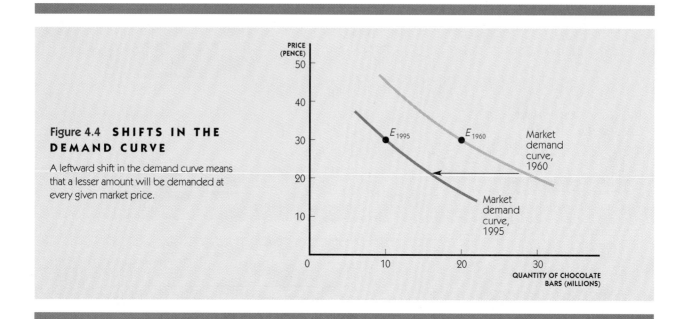

Figure 4.4 SHIFTS IN THE DEMAND CURVE

A leftward shift in the demand curve means that a lesser amount will be demanded at every given market price.

shifted as people have become more weight conscious provides a good example. Figure 4.4 shows hypothetical demand curves for chocolate bars in 1960 and in 1995. We can see from the figure, for instance, that the demand at a price of 30 pence has decreased from 20 million (point E_{1960}, the original equilibrium) to 10 million (point E_{1995}), as people have reduced their "taste" for chocolate.

SOURCES OF SHIFTS IN DEMAND CURVES

Two of the factors that shift the demand curve—changes in income and changes in the price of other goods—are specifically economic factors. (Look at Figure 4.5.) As an individual's income increases, she

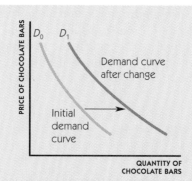

Figure 4.5 A RIGHTWARD SHIFT IN THE DEMAND CURVE

If, at each price, there is an increase in the quantity demanded, then the demand curve will have shifted to the right, as depicted. An increase in income, an increase in the price of a substitute, or a decrease in the price of a complement can cause a rightward shift in the demand curve.

normally purchases more of any good. Thus, rising incomes shift the demand curve to the right. At each price, she consumes more of the good.

Changes in the prices of other goods, particularly closely related goods, will also shift the demand curve for a good. For example, when the price of margarine increases, some individuals will substitute butter. Two goods are **substitutes** if an increase in the price of one *increases* the demand for the other. Butter and margarine are thus substitutes. When people choose between butter and margarine, one important factor is the relative price, that is, the ratio of the price of butter to the price of margarine. An increase in the price of butter and a decrease in the price of margarine both increase the relative price of butter. Thus, both induce individuals to substitute margarine for butter.

Chocolate and potato crisps can also be considered substitutes, as the two goods satisfy a similar need. Thus, an increase in the price of potato crisps makes chocolate relatively more attractive, and hence leads to a rightward shift in the demand curve for chocolate. (At each price, the demand for chocolate is greater.)

Sometimes, however, an increase in a price of other goods has just the opposite effect. Consider an individual who takes sugar in her coffee. In deciding on how much coffee to demand, she is concerned with the price of a cup of coffee *with* sugar. If sugar becomes more expensive, she will demand less coffee. For this person, sugar and coffee are **complements;** that is, an increase in the price of one *decreases* the demand for the other. A price increase of sugar shifts the demand curve of coffee to the left. (At each price, the demand for coffee is less.) Simi-larly, a *decrease* in the price of sugar shifts the demand curve for coffee to the right.

Noneconomic factors can also shift market demand curves. The major ones are changes in tastes and changes in the composition of the population. The earlier chocolate example was a change in taste.

Population changes that shift demand curves are often related to age. Young families with babies purchase disposable nappies. The demand for new houses and flats is closely related to the number of new households, which in turn depends upon the number of individuals of marriageable age. The population has been growing older, on average, both because life expectancies are increasing and because birthrates fell somewhat after the baby boom that followed the Second World War. So there has been a shift in demand away from nappies and new houses. Economists working for particular firms and industries spend considerable energy ascertaining population effects, called **demographic effects,** on the demand for the goods their firms sell.

Sometimes demand curves shift as the result of new information. The shifts in demand for alcohol and meat—and even more so for cigarettes—are related to improved consumer information about health risks.

Changes in the availability of credit also can shift demand curves—for goods like cars and houses that people typically buy with the help of loans. When banks, for example, reduce the money available for consumer loans, the demand curves for cars and houses shift.

Finally, what people think will happen in the future can shift demand curves. If people think they may become unemployed, they will reduce their

SOURCES OF SHIFTS IN MARKET DEMAND CURVES

A change in income	A change in tastes
A change in the price of a substitute	A change in information
A change in the price of a complement	A change in the availability of credit
A change in the composition of the population	A change in expectations

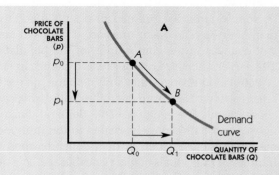

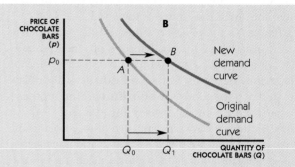

Figure 4.6 MOVEMENT ALONG A DEMAND CURVE VERSUS SHIFT IN A DEMAND CURVE

Panel A shows an increase in quantity demanded caused by a lower price—a movement along a given demand curve. Panel B illustrates an increase in quantity demanded caused by a shift in the entire demand curve, so that a greater quantity is demanded at every market price. Panel C shows a combination of a shift in a demand curve (the movement from point A to B) and a movement along a demand curve (the movement from B to C).

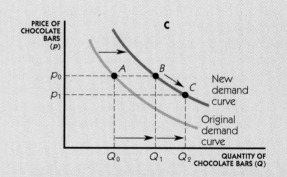

spending. In this case, economists say that their demand curve depends upon expectations.

SHIFTS IN A DEMAND CURVE VERSUS MOVEMENTS ALONG A DEMAND CURVE

The distinction between changes that result from a *shift* in a demand curve and changes that result from a *movement along* a demand curve is crucial to understanding economics. A movement along a demand curve is simply the change in the quantity demanded as the price changes. Figure 4.6A illustrates a movement along the demand curve from point A to point B; *given a demand curve,* at lower prices, more is consumed. Figure 4.6B illustrates a shift in the demand curve to the right; *at a given price,* more is consumed. Quantity again increases from Q_0 to Q_1, but now the price stays the same.

In practice, both effects are often present. Thus, in Figure 4.6C, the movement from point A to point C—where the quantity demanded has been increased from Q_0 to Q_2—consists of two parts: a change in quantity demanded resulting from a shift in the demand curve (the increase in quantity from Q_0 to Q_1), and a movement along the demand curve due to a change in the price (the increase in quantity from Q_1 to Q_2).

SUPPLY

Economists use the concept of **supply** to describe the quantity of a good or service that a household or firm would like to sell at a particular price. Supply in economics refers to such seemingly disparate choices as

One of the several risks of agriculture is the weather. Depending on how the season's frosts, rainfall, and sunshine turn out, the crops might be large or small. This has always been used as an argument for subsidising agriculture, or at least stabilising farm incomes in some way. In practice, many schemes have involved stabilising prices of agricultural goods, and these may have effects that are very different from stabilising farmers' incomes from year to year.

When the Brazilian coffee harvest is hit by some climatic disaster, the world supply of coffee is substantially reduced, as Brazil is one of the major producers. The world supply curve of coffee shifts to the left. The world market price of coffee then rises to meet the demand for it. The supply curve has shifted to the left, and the new market equilibrium is higher up the old demand curve, with a higher price and a smaller amount of coffee traded. How does this effect the incomes of coffee producers? Their incomes might have either fallen or risen; while production and sales have fallen, the price has increased. Total income—the product of sales and price—may have moved in either direction or remained unchanged. Consequently the movements of market prices for goods such as coffee, whose supply curve is prone to fluctuations due to weather and so on, seem likely to provide producers with some insurance against movements in their total income.

What would the consequences of a price stabilization scheme be? Suppose the government bought coffee (and stored it for the future) to prevent prices from falling below some minimal point and conversely brought coffee out of its stores and sold it on the market if price tended to rise above some upper limit. Such a scheme would make the demand curve for coffee much flatter. An increase in the supply of coffee (due to a remarkably good harvest, for example) relative to the normal supply would now be able to cause only a small fall in the price. And conversely, a reduction in the supply (brought about by a poor harvest) would produce only a small rise in the price. With a scheme that involved perfect price stabilization, there would be no variation in the price at all. The government's scheme would buy all the coffee that exceeded the market demand at the stabilised price or supply the market from its stocks when there was excess demand for coffee. How would variations in harvests affect coffee producers' incomes under these conditions? Good harvests would cause high incomes, and bad harvests low incomes. Producers would have a guaranteed price but not a guaranteed income. It is thus not clear that a price stabilization scheme of this kind would be of benefit to producers.

It is no accident that agricultural stabilization schemes that have had the support of producers have tended to stabilise prices at levels above the average market equilibrium price, and have therefore led to chronic excess production.

the number of chocolate bars a firm wants to sell and the number of hours a worker is willing to work. As with demand, the first question economists ask is how does the quantity supplied change when price changes, keeping everything else the same?

Figure 4.7 shows the number of chocolate bars that the Melt-in-the-Mouth Chocolate Company would like to sell, or supply to the market, at each price. As the price rises, so does the quantity supplied. Below 40 pence, the firm finds it unprofitable to produce. At 80 pence, it would like to sell 85,000 chocolate bars. At £2.00, it would like to sell 100,000.

Figure 4.7 also depicts these points in a graph. The curve drawn by connecting the points is called the **supply curve.** It shows the quantity that Melt-in-the-Mouth will supply at each price, holding all other factors constant. As with the demand curve, we put the price on the vertical axis and the quantity supplied on the horizontal axis. Thus, we can read point A on the curve as indicating that a price of 60 pence the firm would like to supply 70,000 chocolate bars.

In direct contrast to the demand curve, the typical supply curve slopes upwards from left to right; at higher prices, firms will supply more.[1] This is because higher prices yield suppliers higher profits—giving them an incentive to produce more.

---

[1] Chapter 9 will describe some unusual situations where supply curves may not be upward sloping.

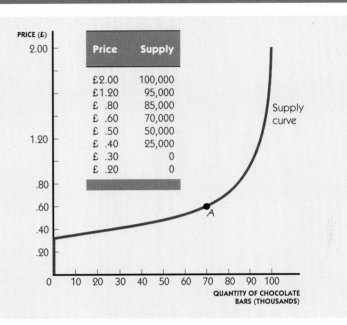

Figure 4.7 ONE FIRM'S SUPPLY CURVE

The supply curve shows the quantity of a good a firm is willing to produce at each price. Normally a firm is willing to produce more as the price increases; this is why the supply curve slopes upwards.

Price	Supply
£2.00	100,000
£1.20	95,000
£ .80	85,000
£ .60	70,000
£ .50	50,000
£ .40	25,000
£ .30	0
£ .20	0

MARKET SUPPLY

The **market supply** of a good is simply the total quantity that all the firms in the economy are willing to supply at a given price. Similarly, the market supply of labour is simply the total quantity of labour that all the households in the economy are willing to supply at a given wage. Figure 4.8 tells us, for instance, that at a price of 80 pence, firms will supply 70 million chocolate bars, whereas at a price of 20 pence, they will supply only 5 million.

Figure 4.8 also shows the same information graphically. The curve joining the points in the figure is the **market supply curve.** The market supply curve gives the total quantity of a good that firms are willing to produce at each price. Thus, we read point

A on the market supply curve as showing that at a price of 30 pence, the firms in the economy would like to sell 20 million chocolate bars.

As the price increases, the quantity supplied increases, other things equal. The market supply curve slopes upwards from left to right for two reasons: at higher prices, each firm in the market is willing to produce more; and at higher prices, more firms are willing to enter the market to produce the good.

The market supply curve is calculated from the supply curves of the different firms in the same way that the market demand curve is calculated from the demand curves of the different households: at each price, we add horizontally the quantities that each of the firms is willing to produce.

Figure 4.9 shows how this is done in a market

SUPPLY CURVE

The supply curve gives the quantity of the good supplied at each price.

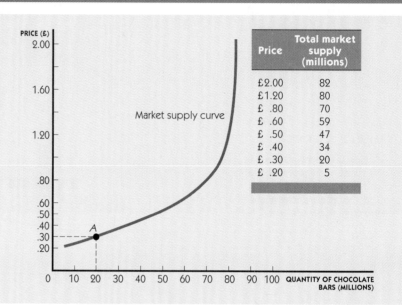

Figure 4.8 **THE MARKET SUPPLY CURVE**

The market supply curve shows the quantity of a good that all firms in the market are willing to supply at each price. The market supply curve is normally upward sloping, both because each firm is willing to supply more of the good at a higher price and because higher prices entice new firms to produce.

Price	Total market supply (millions)
£2.00	82
£1.20	80
£ .80	70
£ .60	59
£ .50	47
£ .40	34
£ .30	20
£ .20	5

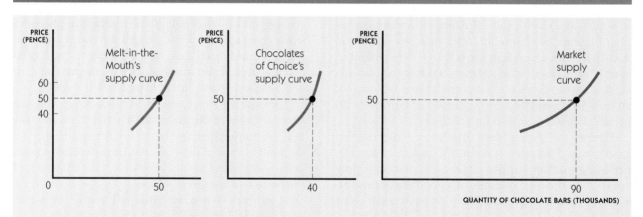

Figure 4.9 **DERIVING THE MARKET SUPPLY CURVE**

The market supply curve is constructed by adding up the quantity that each of the firms in the economy is willing to supply at each price. This figure shows what market supply would be if there were only two producers. Actual market supply, as depicted in Figure 4.8, is much larger because there are many producers.

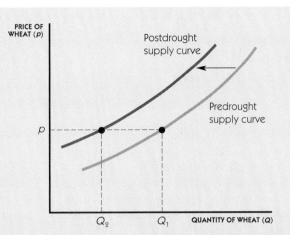

Figure 4.10 SHIFTING THE SUPPLY CURVE TO THE LEFT

A drought or other disaster (among other possible factors) will cause the supply curve to shift to the left, so that at each price, a smaller quantity is supplied.

with only two producers. At a price of 50 pence, Melt-in-the-Mouth Chocolate produces 50,000 bars, while the Chocolates of Choice Company produces 40,000. So the market supply is 90,000 bars.

SHIFTS IN SUPPLY CURVES

Just as demand curves can shift, supply curves too can shift, so that the quantity supplied at each price increases or decreases. Suppose a drought hits wheat production. Figure 4.10 illustrates the situa-

tion. The supply curve for wheat shifts to the left, which means that at each price of wheat, the quantity firms are willing to supply is smaller.

SOURCES OF SHIFTS IN SUPPLY CURVES

There are several sources of shifts in market supply curves, just as in the case of the market demand curves already discussed. One is changing prices of the inputs used to produce a good. Figure 4.11 shows

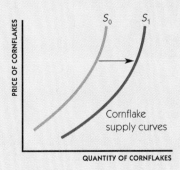

Figure 4.11 SHIFTING THE SUPPLY CURVE TO THE RIGHT

An improvement in technology or a reduction in input prices (among other possible factors) will cause the supply curve to shift to the right, so that at each price, a larger quantity is supplied.

S O U R C E S O F S H I F T S I N M A R K E T S U P P L Y C U R V E S

A change in the prices of inputs

A change in technology

A change in the natural environment

A change in the availability of credit

A change in expectations

that as corn becomes less expensive, the supply curve for cornflakes shifts to the right. Producing cornflakes costs less, so at every price, firms are willing to supply a greater quantity. That is why the quantity supplied along the curve S_1 is greater than the quantity supplied, at the same price, along the curve S_0.

Another source of shifts is changes in technology. The technological improvements in the computer industry over the past two decades have led to a rightward shift in the market supply curve. Yet another source of shifts is nature. The supply curve for agricultural goods may shift to the right or left depending upon weather conditions, insect infestations, or animal diseases.

Reduction in the availability of credit may curtail firms' ability to borrow to obtain inputs needed for production, and this too will induce a leftward shift in the supply curve. Finally, changed expectations can also lead to a shift in the supply curve. If firms

believe that a new technology for making cars will become available in two years' time, this belief will discourage investment today and will lead to a temporary leftward shift in the supply curve.

S H I F T S I N A S U P P L Y C U R V E V E R S U S M O V E M E N T S A L O N G A S U P P L Y C U R V E

Distinguishing between a movement *along* a curve and a *shift* in the curve itself is just as important for supply curves as it is for demand curves. In Figure 4.12A, the price of chocolate bars has gone up, with a corresponding increase in quantity supplied. Thus, there has been a movement along the supply curve.

By contrast, in Figure 4.12B, the supply curve has shifted to the right, perhaps because a new produc-

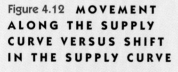

Figure 4.12 **MOVEMENT ALONG THE SUPPLY CURVE VERSUS SHIFT IN THE SUPPLY CURVE**

Panel A shows an increase in quantity supplied caused by a higher price—a movement along a given supply curve. Panel B illustrates an increase in quantity supplied caused by a shift in the entire supply curve, so that a greater quantity is supplied at every market price.

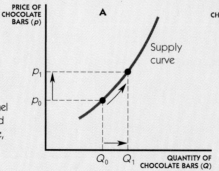

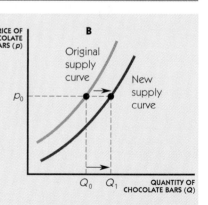

tion technique has made it cheaper to produce chocolate bars. Now, even though the price does not change, the quantity supplied increases. The quantity supplied in the market can increase either because the price of the good has increased, so that for a *given supply curve,* the quantity produced is higher, or because the supply curve has shifted, so that at a *given price,* the quantity supplied has increased.

LAW OF SUPPLY AND DEMAND

This chapter began with the assertion that supply and demand work together to determine the market price in competitive markets. Figure 4.13 puts a market supply curve and a market demand curve on the same graph to show how this happens. The price actually paid and received in the market will be determined by the intersection of the two curves. This point is labeled E_0, for equilibrium, and the corresponding price (30 pence) and quantity (20 million)

are called, respectively, the **equilibrium price** and the **equilibrium quantity.**

Since the term **equilibrium** will recur throughout the book, it is important to understand the concept clearly. Equilibrium describes a situation where there are no forces (reasons) for change. No one has an incentive to change the result—the price or quantity consumed or produced in the case of supply and demand.

Physicists also speak of equilibrium in describing a weight hanging from a spring. Two forces are working on the weight. Gravity is pulling it down; the spring is pulling it up. When the weight is at rest, it is in equilibrium, with the two forces' just offsetting each other. If one pulls the weight down a little bit, the force of the spring will be greater than the force of gravity and the weight will spring up. In the absence of any further intrusions, the weight will bob back and forth and eventually reach its equilibrium position.

An economic equilibrium is established in the same way. At the equilibrium price, consumers get precisely the quantity of the good they are willing to buy at that price, and producers sell precisely the quantity they are willing to sell at that price. Neither producers nor consumers have any incentive to change.

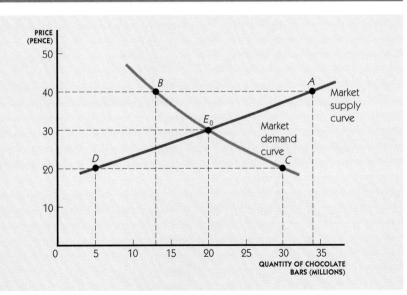

Figure 4.13 SUPPLY AND DEMAND EQUILIBRIUM

Equilibrium occurs at the intersection of the demand and supply curves, at point E_0. At any price above E_0, the quantity supplied will exceed the quantity demanded, the market will be out of equilibrium, and there will be excess supply. At any price below E_0, the quantity demanded will exceed the quantity supplied, the market will be out of equilibrium, and there will be excess demand.

CLOSE-UP: THE STRUCTURE OF ECONOMIC MODELS

Every economic model, including the model of how supply and demand determine the equilibrium price and quantity in a market, is constructed of three kinds of relationships: identities, behavioral relationships, and equilibrium relationships. Recognizing these component parts will help in understanding not only how economists think but also the source of their disagreements.

The market demand is equal to the sum of individual demands. This is an identity. An identity is a statement that is true simply because of the definition of the terms. In other words, market demand is *defined* to be the sum of the demands of all individuals. Similarly, it is an identity that market supply is equal to the sum of the supplies of all firms; the terms are defined that way.

The demand curve represents a relationship between the price and the quantity demanded. Normally, as prices rise, the quantity of a good demanded decreases. This is a description of how individuals behave and is called a behavioral relationship. The supply curve for each firm is also a behavioral relationship.

Economists may disagree over behavioral relationships. They may agree about the direction of

the relationship but disagree about the strength of the connection. For any given product, does a change in price lead to a large change in the quantity demanded or a small one? But they may even disagree over the direction of the effect. As later chapters will discuss, in some special cases a higher price may lead to a *lower* quantity supplied.

Finally, an equilibrium relationship exists when there are no forces for change. In the supply and demand model, the equilibrium occurs when the quantity demanded is equal to the quantity supplied. An equilibrium relationship is not the same as an identity. It is possible for the economy to be out of equilibrium, at least for a time. Of course, being out of equilibrium implies that there are forces for change pushing towards equilibrium. But an identity must always hold true at all times, as a matter of definition.

Economists usually agree about what an equilibrium would look like, but they often differ on whether the forces pushing the markets towards equilibrium are strong or weak, and thus on whether the economy is typically close to equilibrium or may stray rather far from it.

But consider the price of 40 pence in Figure 4.13. There is no equilibrium quantity here. First find 40 pence on the vertical axis. Now look across to find point *A* on the supply curve, and read down to the horizontal axis; point *A* tells you that at a price of 40 pence, firms want to supply 34 million chocolate bars. Now look at point *B* on the demand curve. Point *B* shows that at a price of 40 pence, consumers only want to buy 13 million bars. Like the weight bobbing on a spring, however, this market will work its way back to equilibrium in the following way. At a

price of 40 pence, there is **excess supply.** As producers discover that they cannot sell as much as they would like at this price, some of them will lower their price slightly, hoping to take business from other producers. When one producer lowers his price, his competitors will have to respond, for fear that they will end up unable to sell their goods. As price comes down, consumers will also buy more, and so on, until the market reaches the equilibrium price and quantity.

Similarly, assume that the price is lower than 30

pence, say 20 pence. At the lower price, there is **excess demand:** individuals want to buy 30 million bars (point *C*), while firms only want to produce 5 million (point *D*). Consumers unable to purchase all they want will offer to pay a bit more; other consumers, afraid of having to do without, will match these higher bids or raise them. As price starts to increase, suppliers will have an incentive to produce more. Again the market will tend towards the equilibrium point.

To repeat for emphasis: at equilibrium, no purchaser and no supplier has an incentive to change the price or quantity. In competitive market economies actual prices tend to be the equilibrium prices, at which demand equals supply. This is called the **law of supply and demand.** Note: this law does not mean that at every moment of time the price is precisely at the intersection of the demand and supply curves. As with the example of the weight and the spring, the market may bounce around a little bit when it is in the process of adjusting. What the law of supply and demand does say is that when a market is out of equilibrium, there are predictable forces for change.

USING DEMAND AND SUPPLY CURVES

The concepts of demand and supply curves—and market equilibrium as the intersection of demand and supply curves—constitute the economist's basic model of demand and supply. This model has proven to be extremely useful. It helps explain why the price of some commodity is high and that of some other commodity is low. It also helps *predict* the consequences of certain changes. Its predictions can then be tested against what actually happens. One of the reasons that the model is so useful is that it gives reasonably accurate predictions.

Figure 4.14 repeats the demand and supply curves for chocolate bars. Assume, now, however, that sugar becomes more expensive. As a result, at each price, the amount firms are willing to supply is reduced. The supply curve shifts to the left, as in panel A. There will be a new equilibrium, at a higher price and a lower quantity of chocolate bars consumed.

Alternatively, assume that people become more

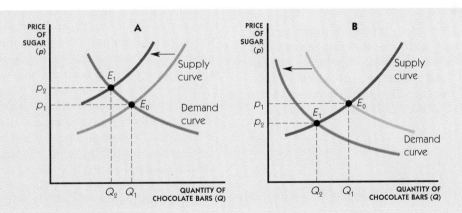

Figure 4.14 USING SUPPLY AND DEMAND CURVES TO PREDICT PRICE CHANGES

Initially the market for chocolate bars is in equilibrium at E_0. An increase in the cost of sugar shifts the supply curve to the left, as shown in panel A. At the new equilibrium E_1, the price is higher and the quantity consumed is lower. A shift in taste away from candy results in a leftward shift in the demand curve, as shown in panel B. At the new equilibrium E_1, both the price and the quantity consumed are lower.

health conscious, and as a result, at each price fewer chocolate bars are consumed: the demand curve shifts to the left, as shown in panel B. Again, there will be a new equilibrium, at a lower price and a lower quantity of chocolate bars consumed.

This illustrates how changes in observed prices can be related either to shifts in the demand curve or to shifts in the supply curve. When the war in Kuwait interrupted the supply of oil from the Middle East in 1990, that was a shift in the supply curve. The model predicted the result: an increase in the price of oil. This increase was the natural process of the law of supply and demand.

CONSENSUS ON THE DETERMINATION OF PRICES

The law of supply and demand plays such a prominent role in economics that there is a joke about teaching a parrot to be an economist simply by teaching it to say "supply and demand." That prices are determined by the law of supply and demand is one of the most long-standing and widely accepted ideas of economists. It forms our fourth point of consensus.

4 Prices

> *In competitive markets, prices are determined by the law of supply and demand. Shifts in the demand and supply curves lead to changes in the equilibrium price. Similar principles apply to the labour and capital markets. The price for labour is the wage, and the price for capital is the interest rate.*

PRICE, VALUE, AND COST

Price, to an economist, is what is given in exchange for a good or service. Price, in this sense, is determined by the forces of supply and demand. Adam Smith, often thought of as the founder of modern economics, called our notion of price "value in exchange" and contrasted it to the notion of "value in use":

The things which have the greatest value in use have frequently little or no value in exchange; and, on the contrary, those which have the greatest value in exchange have frequently little or no value in use. Nothing is more useful than water, but it will purchase scarce any thing; scarce any thing can be had in exchange for it. A diamond, on the contrary, has scarce any value in use; but a very great quantity of other goods may frequently be had in exchange for it.[2]

The law of supply and demand can help to explain the diamond-water paradox and many similar examples where "value in use" is very different from "value in exchange." Figure 4.15 presents a demand curve and a supply curve for water. Individuals are willing to pay a high price for the water they need to live, as illustrated by point *A* on the demand curve. But above some quantity, *B*, people will pay almost nothing more for additional water. In most of the inhabited parts of the world, water is readily available, so it gets supplied in plentiful quantities at low prices. Thus, the supply curve of water intersects the demand curve to the right of *B*, as in the figure; hence the low equilibrium price. Of course, in the desert, the water supply may be very limited and the price, as a result, very high.

To an economist, the statements that the price of diamonds is high and the price of water is low are statements about supply and demand conditions. They say nothing about whether diamonds are more important or better than water. In Adam Smith's terms, they are not statements about value in use.

Price is related to the *marginal* value of an object, that is, the value of an additional unit of the object. Water has a low price not because the *total* value of water is low—it is obviously high, since we could not live without it—but because the marginal value, what we would be willing to pay to be able to drink one more glass of water a year, is low.

Just as economists take care to distinguish the words *price* and *value*, they also distinguish the *price* of an object (what it sells for) from its *cost* (the expense of making the object). This is another crucial distinction in economics. The costs of producing a good affect the price at which firms are willing to supply that good. An increase in the costs of production

---

[2] *The Wealth of Nations* (1776), Book 1, Chapter IV.

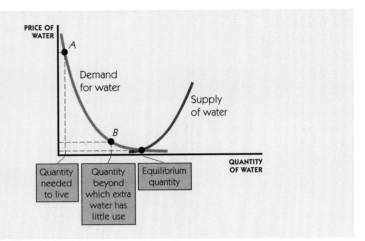

Figure 4.15 SUPPLY AND DEMAND FOR WATER

Point A shows that people are willing to pay a relatively high price for the first few units of water. But to the right of B, people have plenty of water already and are not willing to pay much for an additional amount. The price of water will be determined at the point where the supply curve crosses the demand curve. In most cases, the resulting price is extremely low.

will normally cause prices to rise. And in the competitive model, *in equilibrium*, the price of an object will normally equal its cost of production (including the amount needed to pay a firm's owner to stay in business rather than seek some other form of employment). But there are important cases—as we shall see in later chapters—where price does not equal cost.

In thinking about the relationship of price and cost, it is interesting to consider the case of a good in fixed supply, such as land. Normally, land is something that cannot be produced, so its cost of production can be considered infinite (though there are situations where land can be produced, as the Netherlands testifies). Yet there is still an equilibrium price of land, where the demand for land is equal to its (fixed) supply.

REVIEW AND PRACTICE

Summary

1 An individual's demand curve gives the quantity demanded of a good at each possible price. It normally slopes downwards; this means that the person demands a greater quantity of the good at lower prices and a lesser quantity at higher prices.

2 The market demand curve gives the total quantity of a good demanded by all individuals in an economy at each price. As the price rises, demand falls, both because each person demands less of the good and because some people exit the market.

3 A firm's supply curve gives the amount of a good the firm is willing to supply at each price. It is normally upward sloping; this means that firms supply a greater quantity of the good at higher prices and a lesser quantity at lower prices.

4 The market supply curve gives the total quantity of a good that all firms in the economy are willing to produce at each price. As the price rises, supply rises, both because each firm supplies more of the good and because some additional firms enter the market.

5 The law of supply and demand says that in competitive markets, the equilibrium price is that price at which quantity demanded equals quantity supplied. It is represented on a graph by the intersection of the demand and supply curves.

6 A demand curve *only* shows the relationship between quantity demanded and price. Changes in tastes, in demographic factors, in income, in the prices of other goods, in information, in the availability of credit, or in expectations are reflected in a shift of the entire demand curve.

7 A supply curve *only* shows the relationship between quantity supplied and price. Changes in factors such as technology, the prices of inputs, the natural environment, expectations, or the availability of credit are reflected in a shift of the entire supply curve.

8 It is important to distinguish movements along a demand curve from shifts in the demand curve, and movements along a supply curve from shifts in the supply curve.

KEY TERMS

demand curve	complements	supply curve	excess supply
substitutes	demographic effects	equilibrium price	excess demand

REVIEW QUESTIONS

1 Why does an individual's demand curve normally slope downwards? Why does a market demand curve normally slope downwards?

2 Why does a firm's supply curve normally slope upwards? Why does a market supply curve normally slope upwards?

3 What is the significance of the point where supply and demand curves intersect?

4 Explain why, if the price of a good is above the equilibrium price, the forces of supply and demand will tend to push the price towards equilibrium. Explain why, if the price of the good is below the equilibrium price, the market will tend to adjust towards equilibrium.

5 Name some factors that could shift the demand curve out to the right.

6 Name some factors that could shift the supply curve in to the left.

PROBLEMS

1 Imagine a company canteen that sells pizza by the slice. Using the following data, plot the points and graph the demand and supply curves. What is the equilibrium price and quantity? Find a price at which excess demand would exist and a price at which excess supply would exist, and plot them on your diagram.

Price per slice (£)	Demand (number of slices)	Supply (number of slices)
.50	420	0
1.00	210	100
1.50	140	140
2.00	105	160
2.50	84	170

2 Suppose a severe drought hit the sugarcane crop. Predict how this would affect the equilibrium price and quantity in the market for sugar and the market for honey. Draw supply and demand diagrams to illustrate your answers.

3 Imagine that a new invention allows each coal miner to mine twice as much coal. Predict how this would affect the equilibrium price and quantity in the market for coal and the market for heating oil. Draw supply and demand diagrams to illustrate your answer.

4 Tastes have shifted away from beef and towards chicken. Predict how this change affects the equilibrium price and quantity in the market for beef, the market for chicken, and the market for hamburger stands. Draw supply and demand diagrams to illustrate your answers.

5 In recent decades, it has become more acceptable for married women with children to work. Predict how this increase in the number of workers is likely to affect the equilibrium wage and quantity of employment. Draw supply and demand curves to illustrate your answer.

5

USING DEMAND
AND SUPPLY

T
he concepts of demand and supply are among the most useful in economics. The demand and supply framework explains why management consultants are paid more than lawyers or why the income of skilled workers has increased more than that of unskilled workers. It can also be used to predict what the demand for housing or disposable nappies will be 15 years from now or what will happen if the government increases the tax on cigarettes. Not only can we predict that prices will change, we can predict by how much they will change.

This chapter has two purposes. The first is to develop some of the concepts required to make these kinds of predictions and to illustrate how the demand-and-supply framework can be used in a variety of contexts.

The second is to look at what happens when people interfere with the workings of competitive markets. Rents may seem too high for poor people to afford adequate housing. Farmers may demand compensation for depressed beef prices and the slaughter of bovine spongiform encephalopathy–infected cattle. Political pressure constantly develops for government to intervene on behalf of the group that has been disadvantaged by the market—whether it be poor people or farmers. The second part of this chapter traces the consequences of political interventions into the workings of some markets.

KEY QUESTIONS

1 What is meant by the concept of elasticity? Why does it play such an important role in predicting market outcomes?

2 What happens when market outcomes are interfered with, as when the government imposes price floors and ceilings? Why do such interferences give rise to shortages and surpluses?

SENSITIVITY TO PRICE CHANGES: THE PRICE ELASTICITY OF DEMAND

If tomorrow supermarkets across the country were to cut the price of bread or milk by 5 percent, the quantity demanded of these items would not change much. If stores offered the same reduction on pre-

mium ice cream, however, demand would increase substantially. Why do price changes sometimes have small effects and other times large ones? The answer lies in the shape of the demand and supply curves.

The demand for ice cream is more sensitive to price changes than the demand for milk is, and this is reflected in the shape of the demand curves as illustrated in Figure 5.1. The demand curve for ice cream (panel A) is much flatter than the one for milk (panel B). When the demand curve is somewhat flat, a change in price, say from £2 a litre to £2.10, has a

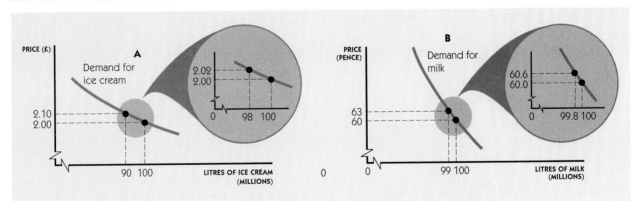

Figure 5.1 ELASTIC VERSUS INELASTIC DEMAND CURVES

Panel A shows a hypothetical demand curve for ice cream. Note that quantity demanded changes rapidly with fairly small price changes, indicating that demand for ice cream is elastic. The telescoped portion of the demand curve shows that a 1 percent rise in price leads to a 2 percent fall in quantity demanded. Panel B shows a hypothetical demand curve for

milk. Note that quantity demanded changes very little, regardless of changes in price; this means that demand for milk is inelastic. The telescoped portion of the demand curve shows that a 1 percent rise in price leads to a 0.2 percent fall in quantity demanded.

large effect on the quantity consumed. In panel A, the demand for ice cream decreases from 100 million litres at a price of £2.00 a litre to 90 million litres at a price of £2.10 per litre.

By contrast, when the demand curve is steep, it means that a change in price has little effect on quantity. In panel B, the demand for milk decreases from 100 million litres at 60 pence a litre to 99 million litres at 63 pence a litre. But saying that the demand curve is steep or flat just pushes the question back a step: why are some demand curves steeper than others?

The answer is that though substitutes exist for almost every good or service, substitution will be more difficult for some goods and services than for others. If substitution is difficult, when the price of a good increases, the quantity demanded will not decrease much and, when the price falls, the quantity demanded will not increase much. The typical consumer does not substitute milk for beer—or for anything else—even if milk becomes a good deal cheaper.

When substitution is easy, on the other hand, a fall in price may lead to a large increase in quantity demanded. For instance, there are many good substitutes for ice cream, including sorbets and frozen yogurts. The price decrease for ice cream means that these close substitutes have become relatively more expensive, and the demand for ice cream would thus increase significantly.

For many purposes, economists need to be precise about how steep or how flat the demand curve is. For precision they use the concept of the **price elasticity of demand** (in brief, the price elasticity or the elasticity of demand). The price elasticity of demand is defined as the percentage change in the quantity demanded divided by the percentage change in price. In mathematical terms,

$$\text{Elasticity of demand} = \frac{\text{percentage change in quantity demanded}}{\text{percentage change in price}}.$$

If the quantity demanded changes 8 percent in response to a 2 percent change in price, then the elasticity of demand is 4.

(Price elasticities of demand are *negative* numbers; that is, when the price increases, quantities demanded are reduced. But the convention is to simply refer to the elasticity as a number with the understanding that it is negative.)

It is easiest to calculate the elasticity of demand when there is just a 1 percent change in price. Then the elasticity of demand is simply the percent change in the quantity demanded. In the telescoped portion of Figure 5.1A, we see that increasing the price of ice cream from £2.00 a litre to £2.02—a 1 percent increase in price—reduces the demand from 100 million litres to 98 million, a 2 percent decline. So the price elasticity of demand for ice cream is 2.

By contrast, assume that the price of milk increases from 60 pence a litre to 60.6 pence (again a 1 percent increase in price), as shown in the telescoped portion of Figure 5.1B. This reduces demand from 100 million litres per year to 99.8 million. Demand has gone down by 0.2 percent; therefore the price elasticity of demand is 0.2. Larger values for price elasticity indicate that demand is more sensitive to price changes. Smaller values indicate that demand is less sensitive to price changes.

The revenue received by a firm in selling a good is price times quantity. We write this in a simple equation. Letting R denote revenue, p price, and Q quantity,

$$R = pQ.$$

This means that when price goes up by 1 percent, whether revenue goes up or down depends on the magnitude of the decrease in quantity. If quantity decreases by more than 1 percent, then total revenue decreases; by less than 1 percent, it increases.

We can express this result in terms of the concept of price elasticity. When the elasticity of demand is greater than unity—the change in quantity more than offsets the change in prices—we say that the demand for that good is **relatively elastic,** or *sensitive* to price changes, and revenue decreases as price increases and increases as price decreases.

In the case in which the price elasticity is **unity,** or 1, the decrease in the quantity demanded just offsets the increase in the price, so price increases have no effect on revenue. If the price elasticity is less than unity, then when the price of a good increases by 1 percent, the quantity demanded is reduced by less than 1 percent. Since there is not much reduction in demand, elasticities in this range, between 0 and 1, mean that price increases will increase revenue. And

PRICE ELASTICITY OF DEMAND

Elasticity	Description	Effect on Quantity Demanded of 1% Increase in Price	Effect on Revenues of 1% Increase in Price
0	Perfectly inelastic (vertical demand curve)	0	Increased by 1%
Between 0 and 1	Inelastic	Reduced by less than 1%	Increased by less than 1%
1	Unitary elasticity	Reduced by 1%	Unchanged
Greater than 1	Elastic	Reduced by more than 1%	Reduced (The greater the elasticity, the more revenue is reduced.)
Infinite	Perfectly elastic (horizontal demand curve)	Reduced to 0	Reduced to 0

price decreases will decrease revenue. We say the demand for that good is **relatively inelastic,** or *insensitive* to price changes.

Business firms must pay attention to the price elasticity of demand for their products. Suppose a cement producer, the only one in town, is considering a 1 percent increase in price. The firm hires an economist to estimate its price elasticity of demand, so that the firm will know what will happen to sales if it raises its price. The economist tells the firm that its elasticity of demand is 2. This means that if the price of cement rises by 1 percent, the quantity sold will decline by 2 percent.

The firm's executives will not be pleased by this finding. To see why, assume that initially the price of cement was £1,000 per tonne, and 100,000 tonnes were sold. To calculate revenue, you multiply the price times the quantity sold. So initially revenue is £1,000 × 100,000 = £100 million. With a 1 percent increase, the price will be £1,010. If the elasticity of demand is 2, then a 1 percent price increase results in a 2 percent decrease in the quantity sold. With a 2 percent quantity decrease, sales are now 98,000 tonnes. Revenue is down to £98.98 million (£1,010 × 98,000), a fall of just slightly over 1 percent. Because of the high price elasticity of demand, this cement firm's price *increase* leads to a *decrease* in revenue.

The price elasticity of demand works the same way for price decreases. Suppose the cement producer is considering decreasing the price of cement by 1 percent, to £990. With an elasticity of demand of 2, sales will increase by 2 percent, to 102,000 tonnes. Thus, revenue will *increase* to £100,980,000 ($990 × 102,000), that is, by a bit less than 1 percent.

EXTREME CASES

There are two extreme cases that deserve attention. One is that of a flat demand curve, a curve that is perfectly horizontal. We say that such a demand curve is perfectly elastic or has **infinite elasticity,** since even a slight increase in the price results in demand's dropping to zero. The other case is that of a steep demand curve, a curve that is perfectly vertical. We say that such a demand curve is perfectly inelastic or has **zero elasticity,** since no matter what the change in price, demand remains the same.

PRICE ELASTICITIES

The price elasticity of demand for some goods is much higher than for others. Food, for example, typically has a very low elasticity of demand: changes in price tend not to affect demand very much. But the

Table 5.1 SOME PRICE ELASTICITIES IN THE BRITISH ECONOMY

Good	Price Elasticity of Demand
Inelastic demands	
Bread	0.221
Meat	0.439
Vehicle operation	0.011
Rail travel	0.541
Clothing	0.720
Elastic Demands	
Expenditure abroad	1.626
Catering	2.605
Entertainment	1.399

Source: A. S. Deaton, "The Measurement of Income and Price Elasticities," European Economic Review 6 (1975): 261–273.

demand for luxury goods—expensive cars, skiing holidays, perfumes—tends to be more sensitive to price. Table 5.1 gives price elasticities of demand for some categories of goods. Bread and meat have low elasticities of demand. A 10 percent rise in the price of bread is estimated to cause the demand for bread to fall by 2.21 percent, for example. Surprisingly, or perhaps not, the demand for "vehicle operation" (effectively meaning car ownership) is extremely low, and the demand for rail travel is also low. By contrast with these, expenditure abroad is relatively price sensitive, as is the demand for "catering" (meals in restaurants and the like) and the demand for entertainment. A 10 percent rise in the price of restaurant meals is predicted to cut the demand for them by 26.05 percent. (Of course, it should be noted that these estimates are based on data on demand for goods over the period 1954 to 1972. Behaviour may have changed since then. Certainly the growth in the number of restaurants in London, their astronomical prices, and the difficulty of getting a table in recent years suggest that something has changed!)

ELASTICITY AND SLOPE

The elasticity of a curve is not the same as its slope. The best way to see the distinction is to look at the **linear** demand curve. The linear demand curve is a straight line, depicted in Figure 5.2. With a linear demand curve, the quantity demanded is related to the price by the equation

$$Q = a - bp.$$

If $a = 120$ and $b = 2$, at a price of 10, $Q = 100$; at a price of 11, $Q = 98$; at a price of 12, $Q = 96$; and so forth.

The demand curve also gives the price at which a particular quantity of the good will be demanded.

Figure 5.2 LINEAR DEMAND CURVE

The linear demand curve is a straight line; it is represented algebraicly by the equation $Q = a - bp$. The slope of the demand curve is a constant. However, the elasticity varies with output. At low outputs (high prices) it is very high. At high outputs (low prices) it is very low.

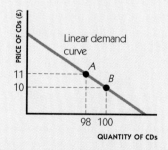

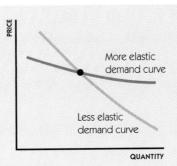

Figure 5.3 COMPARING ELASTICITIES

If two demand curves intersect, at the point of intersection, the flatter demand curve has the greater price elasticity.

Thus, we can rewrite the equation to read

$$p = \frac{a}{b} - \frac{Q}{b},$$

so that (with $a = 120$ and $b = 2$ as before) at $Q = 100$, $p = 10$; at $Q = 99$, $p = 10.5$; and at $Q = 98$, $p = 11$.

Slope gives the change along the vertical axis per unit change along the horizontal axis. Recall that when we draw the demand curve, we put price on the vertical axis and output on the horizontal axis.

$$\text{Slope} = \frac{\text{change in price}}{\text{change in quantity}} = \frac{\Delta p}{\Delta Q},$$

where the symbol Δ—the Greek letter delta—signifies a change. Thus, ΔQ means the change in quantity and Δp means the change in price. Equivalently, slope is the change in price for a unit change in quantity. In our example, as we change quantity by 1, price changes by 1/2. More generally, the slope of the linear demand equation above is $1/b$.[1]

[1]To see this, observe that at $Q + 1$, the price is

$$\frac{a}{b} - \frac{Q+1}{b}.$$

The change in price is

$$\frac{a}{b} - \frac{Q}{b} - \left(\frac{a}{b} - \frac{Q+1}{b} \right) = \frac{a}{b} - \frac{Q}{b} - \frac{a}{b} + \frac{Q+1}{b} = \frac{1}{b}.$$

The elasticity, as we know, is given by

$$\text{Elasticity} = \frac{\text{percentage change in quantity}}{\text{percentage change in price}}.$$

The percentage change in quantity is

Percentage change in quantity
$$= \frac{\text{change in quantity}}{\text{quantity}} = \frac{\Delta Q}{Q}.$$

Similarly,

Percentage change in price
$$= \frac{\text{change in price}}{\text{price}} = \frac{\Delta p}{p}.$$

We can now rewrite the expression for elasticity:

$$\text{Elasticity} = \frac{\Delta Q/Q}{\Delta p/p} = \frac{\Delta Q}{\Delta p} \frac{p}{Q}$$

$$= b \frac{p}{Q}$$

$$= \frac{1}{\text{slope}} \frac{p}{Q}.$$

Everywhere along a linear demand curve, the slope is the same; but the elasticity is very high at low levels of output and very low at high levels of output.

The formula for elasticity has one other important implication, illustrated in Figure 5.3. Of two demand curves going through the same point, the flatter demand curve has the higher elasticity at the point of intersection. At the point where they intersect, p and Q (and therefore p/Q) are the same. Only the slopes differ. The one with the smaller slope has the greater elasticity.

SMALL VERSUS LARGE PRICE CHANGES

Often, economists are interested in what will happen if there is a large price change. For instance, if an additional £1 in tax is imposed on a pack of 20 cigarettes, what will happen to demand?

When price changes are small or moderate, we can *extrapolate*. That is, often we have information about the effect of a small price change. We then extrapolate, assuming that a slightly larger price change will have proportionately larger effects. For example, if a 1 percent change in price results in a 2 percent change in quantity, then a 3 percent change in price will probably result in an approximately 6 percent change in quantity.

With large price changes, however, such extrapolation becomes riskier. The reason is that *price elasticity is typically different at different points along the demand curve.*

THE DETERMINANTS OF THE ELASTICITY OF DEMAND

In our earlier discussion, we noted one of the important determinants of the elasticity of demand: the availability of substitutes. There are two important determinants of the degree of substitutability: the relative price of the good consumed and the length of time it takes to make an adjustment.

When the price of a commodity is low and the consumption is high, a variety of substitutes exists. Figure 5.4 illustrates the case for aluminium. When the price of aluminium is low, it is used as a food wrap (aluminium foil), as containers for canned goods, and in aeroplane frames because it is lightweight. As the price increases, customers seek out substitutes. At first, substitutes are easy to find, and the demand for the product is greatly reduced. For example, plastic wrap can be used instead of aluminium foil. As the price rises still further, tin is used instead of aluminium for cans. At very high prices, say near point A, aluminium is used only where its lightweight properties are essential, such as in aeroplane frames. At this point, it may take a *huge* price increase before some other material becomes an economical substitute.

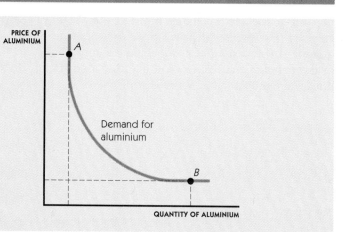

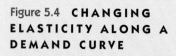

Figure 5.4 **CHANGING ELASTICITY ALONG A DEMAND CURVE**

Near point A, where the price is high, the demand curve is quite steep and inelastic. In the area of the demand curve near B, the demand curve is very flat and elastic.

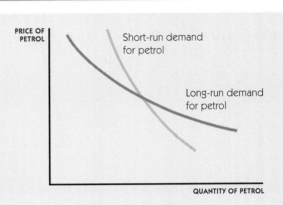

Figure 5.5 ELASTICITY OF DEMAND OVER TIME

Demand curves tend to be inelastic in the short run, when there is little time to adapt to price changes, but more elastic in the long run.

A second important determinant of the elasticity of demand is time. Because it is always easier to find substitutes and to make other adjustments when you have a longer time to make them, the elasticity of demand is normally larger in the *long run*—when all adjustments can be made—than it is in the *short run*—when at least some adjustments cannot be made. Figure 5.5 illustrates the difference in shape between short-run and long-run demand curves for petrol.

The sharp increase in oil prices in the 1970s provides an outstanding example. The short-run price elasticity of petrol was 0.2 (a 1 percent increase in price led to only a 0.2 percent decrease in quantity demanded), while the long-run elasticity was 0.7 or more; the short-run elasticity of fuel oil was 0.2, and the long-run elasticity was 1.2. In the short run, consumers were stuck with their old cars, their drafty houses, and their old fuel-wasting habits. In the long run, however, consumers bought smaller cars, became used to houses with slightly lower temperatures, installed better insulation in their homes, and turned to alternative energy sources. The long-run demand curve was therefore much more elastic (flat) than the short-run curve. Indeed, the long-run elasticity turned out to be much larger than anticipated.

How long is the long run? There is no simple answer. It will vary from product to product. In some cases, adjustments can occur rapidly; in other cases, they are very gradual. As old cars wore out, they were replaced with more fuel-efficient cars. As boilers wore out, they were replaced with more efficient ones. New homes are now constructed with more insulation, so that gradually, over time, the fraction of houses that are well insulated is increasing.

THE PRICE ELASTICITY OF SUPPLY

Supply curves normally slope upwards. As with demand curves, they are steep in some cases and flat in others. The degree of steepness reflects the sensitivity of supply to price changes. A steep supply curve, like the one for oil in Figure 5.6A, means that a large change in price generates only a small change in the quantity firms supply. A flatter curve, like the one for chicken in Figure 5.6B, means that a small change in price generates a large change in supply. Economists have developed a precise way of representing the sensitivity of supply to prices in a way that parallels the one already introduced for demand. The **price elasticity of supply** is defined as the percentage change in quantity supplied divided by the percentage change in price (or the percentage change in quantity supplied corresponding to a price change of 1 percent).

$$\text{Elasticity of supply} = \frac{\text{percentage change in quantity supplied}}{\text{percentage change in price}}.$$

Figure 5.6 **DIFFERING ELASTICITIES OF SUPPLY**

Panel A shows a supply curve for oil. It is inelastic: quantity supplied increases only a small amount with a rise in price. Panel B shows a supply curve for chicken. It is elastic: quantity supplied increases substantially with a rise in price.

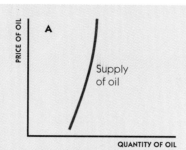
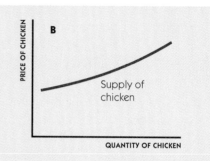

The elasticity of supply of oil is low; an increase in the price of oil will not have a significant effect on the total supply. The elasticity of supply of chicken is high; farmers can relatively easily cut their production of chickens when the price falls, putting their resources into the production of some other product. They can increase their production of chickens when a price rise makes it more profitable.

As is the case with demand, if a 1 percent increase in price results in more than a 1 percent increase in supply, we say the supply curve is elastic. If a 1 percent increase in price results in less than a 1 percent increase in supply, the supply curve is inelastic. In the extreme case of a vertical supply curve—where

the amount supplied does not depend at all on price—the curve is said to be perfectly inelastic or to have *zero* elasticity; and in the extreme case of a horizontal supply curve, the curve is said to be perfectly elastic or to have *infinite* elasticity.

Just as elasticity differs at different points of the demand curve, so too does it on the supply curve. Figure 5.7 shows a typical supply curve in manufacturing. An example might be ball bearings. At very low prices, plants are just covering their operating costs. Some plants shut down. In this situation, a small increase in price elicits a large increase in supply. The supply curve is relatively flat (elastic). But eventually, all machines are being worked, and fac-

Figure 5.7 **CHANGING ELASTICITY ALONG A SUPPLY CURVE**

When output is low and many machines are idle, a small change in price can lead to a large increase in quantity produced; the supply curve is flat and elastic. When output is high and all machines are working close to their limit, it takes a very large price change to induce even a small change in output; the supply curve is steep and inelastic.

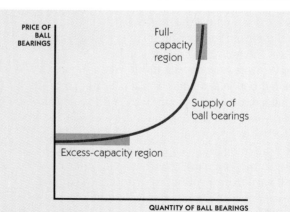

PRICE ELASTICITY OF SUPPLY

Elasticity	Description	Effect on Quantity Supplied of 1% Increase in Price
0	Perfectly inelastic (vertical supply curve)	0
Between 0 and 1	Inelastic	Increased by less than 1%
1	Unitary elasticity	Increased by 1%
Greater than 1	Elastic	Increased by more than 1%
Infinite	Perfectly elastic (horizontal supply curve)	Infinite increase

tories are working all three shifts. In this situation, it may be hard to increase supply further, so that the supply curve becomes close to vertical (inelastic). That is, however much the price increases, the supply will not change very much.

Economists distinguish between the responsiveness of supply to price in the short run and in the long run, just as they do with demand. The long-run supply elasticity is greater than the short-run. We define the short-run supply curve as the supply response *given the current stock of machines and buildings*. The long-run supply curve assumes that firms can adjust the stock of machines and buildings.

Farm crops are a typical example of a good whose supply in the short run is not very sensitive to changes in price; that is, the supply curve is steep (inelastic). After farmers have done their planting, they are committed to a certain level of production. If the price of their crop goes up, they cannot go back and plant more. If the price falls, they are stuck with the crop they have. In this case, the supply curve is relatively close to vertical, as illustrated by the steeper curve in Figure 5.8.

The long-run supply curve for many crops, in contrast, is very flat (elastic). A relatively small change in price can lead to a large change in the quantity supplied. A small increase in the price of beans relative to the price of sweet corn may induce many farmers to shift their planting from sweet corn and other crops to beans, generating a large increase in the quantity of beans. This is illustrated in Figure 5.8 by the flatter curve.

Earlier, we noted the response of consumers to the marked increase in the price of oil in the 1970s. The long-run demand elasticity was much higher than the short-run. So too for supply. The higher prices drove firms to explore for more oil in the North Sea off the coast of Great Britain, the United States, Canada, and Mexico. Though the alternative supplies could not be increased much in the short run (the short-run supply curve was inelastic, or steep), in the long run new supplies were found. Thus, the long-run supply elasticity was much higher (the supply curve was flatter) than the short-run supply elasticity.

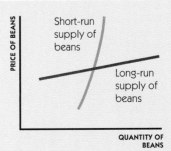

Figure 5.8 ELASTICITY OF SUPPLY OVER TIME

Supply curves may be inelastic in the short run and very elastic in the long run, as in the case of agricultural crops like soybeans.

USING DEMAND AND SUPPLY ELASTICITIES

When the demand curve for a good such as wine shifts to the right—when, for instance, wine becomes more popular, so that at each price the demand is greater—there is an increase in both the equilibrium price of wine and the quantity demanded, or consumed. Similarly, when the supply curve for a good such as corn shifts to the left—because, for instance, of a drought that hurt the year's crop, so that at each price farmers supply less—there is an increase in the equilibrium price of corn and a decrease in quantity. Knowing that a shift in the demand or supply curve will lead to an adjustment in both price *and* quantity is helpful, but it is even more useful to know whether most of the impact of a change will be on price or on quantity. For this, we have to consider the price elasticity of both the demand and supply curves.

Figure 5.9 illustrates the typical range of outcomes. If the supply curve is highly elastic (approaching the horizontal, as in panel A), a shift in the demand curve will be reflected more in a change in quantity than in price. If the supply curve is *relatively* inelastic (approaching the vertical, as in panel B), a shift in the demand curve will be reflected more in a change in price than in quantity. If the demand curve is highly elastic (approaching the horizontal as in panel C), a shift in the supply curve will be reflected more in a change in quantity than in price.

Figure 5.9 ELASTICITY OF DEMAND AND SUPPLY CURVES: THE NORMAL CASES

Normally, shifts in the demand curve will be reflected in changes in both price and quantity, as seen in panels A and B. When the supply curve is highly elastic, shifts in the demand curve will result mainly in changes in quantities; if it is relatively inelastic, shifts in the demand curve will result mainly in price changes. Likewise, shifts in the supply curve will be reflected in changes in both price and quantity, as seen in panels C and D. If the demand curve is highly elastic, shifts in the supply curve will result mainly in changes in quantities; if it is relatively inelastic, shifts in the supply curve will result mainly in price changes.

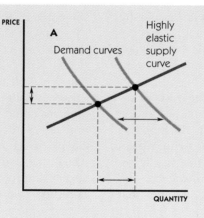

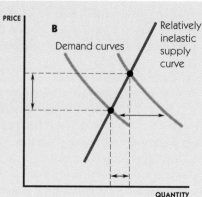

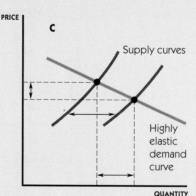

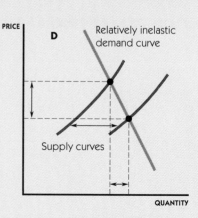

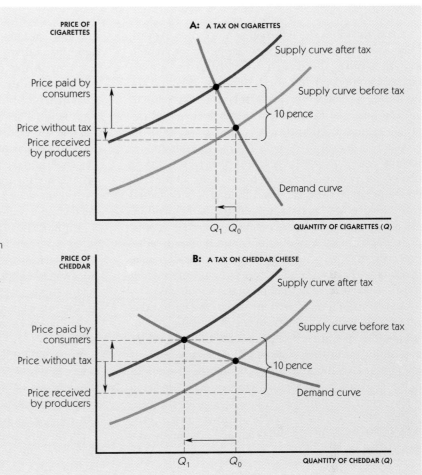

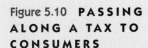

Figure 5.10 PASSING ALONG A TAX TO CONSUMERS

A tax on the output of an industry shifts the supply curve up by the amount of the tax. Panel A shows that if the demand curve is relatively inelastic, as it is for cigarettes, then most of the tax will be passed on to consumers in higher prices. Panel B shows that if the demand curve is relatively inelastic, as it is for cheddar cheese, then most of the tax cannot be passed along to consumers in higher prices and must instead be absorbed by producers.

Finally, if the demand curve is *relatively* inelastic (approaching the vertical as in panel D), a shift in the supply curve will be reflected more in a change in price than in quantity.

The extreme cases can be easily seen by extending the graphs in Figure 5.9. If one tilts the supply curve in panel A to be completely flat (perfectly elastic), a shift in the demand curve will have no effect on price. If one tilts the supply curve in panel B to be vertical (perfectly inelastic), a shift in the demand curve will have no effect on quantity.

Because demand and supply curves are likely to be less elastic (more vertical) in the short run than in the long run, shifts in the demand and supply curves are more likely to be reflected in price changes in the short run but quantity changes in the long run. In fact, short-run price increases signal firms to in-

crease their production. Therefore, short-run price increases can be thought of as responsible for the output increases that occur in the long run.

For many questions of public policy, understanding the law of supply and demand is vital. One of the important ways economists use this law is in projecting the effect of taxes. Assume that the tax on a pack of cigarettes is increased by 10 pence, that the tax is imposed on cigarette manufacturers, and that all the companies try to pass on the cost increase to consumers by raising the price of a pack 10 pence. At the higher price, fewer cigarettes will be consumed, with the decrease in demand's depending on the price elasticity of demand. With lower demand, firms may reduce their price; how much depends on the price elasticity of supply. The new equilibrium is depicted in Figure 5.10A.

For firms to produce the same amount as before, they must receive 10 pence more per pack (which they pass on to the government). Thus, the supply curve is shifted up 10 pence. Since the demand for cigarettes is relatively inelastic, this shift will result in a large increase in price and a relatively small decrease in quantity demanded.

When a tax on producers results in consumers' paying a higher price, economists say the tax is passed on or shifted to consumers. The fact that the consumer bears the tax (even though it is collected from the producers) does not mean that the producers are powerful or have conspired together. It simply reflects the system of supply and demand. Note, however, that the price did not rise the full 10 pence. Producers receive slightly lower after-tax prices and therefore bear a small fraction of the tax burden.

A tax imposed on a good for which the demand is very elastic leads to a different result. Assume, for instance, that the government decides to tax cheddar cheese (but no other cheeses). Since many cheeses are almost like cheddar, the demand curve for cheddar cheese is very elastic. In this case, as Figure 5.10B makes clear, most of the tax is absorbed by the producer, who receives (net of tax) a lower price. Production of cheddar cheese is reduced drastically as a consequence.

SHORTAGES AND SURPLUSES

The law of supply and demand works so well in a developed modern economy, most of the time, that everyone can take it for granted. If you are willing to pay the market price—the prevailing price of the good, determined by the intersection of demand and supply—you can obtain almost any good or service. Similarly, if a seller of a good or service is willing to charge no more than the market price, he can always sell what he wants to.

When the price is set so that demand equals supply—so that at that price, any individual can get as much as she wants and any supplier can sell the amount he wants—economists say that the **market clears.** But when the market does not clear, there

are shortages or surpluses. To an economist, a **shortage** means that people would like to buy something but they simply cannot find it for sale at the going price. A **surplus** means that sellers would like to sell their product but they cannot sell as much of it as they would like at the going price. These cases where the market does not seem to be working are often the most forceful reminders of the importance of the law of supply and demand. The problem is that the going price is not the market equilibrium price.

Shortages and surpluses can be seen in the standard supply-and-demand diagrams shown in Figure 5.11. In both panels A and B, the market equilibrium price is p^*. In panel A, the going price p_1 is below p^*. At this price, demand exceeds supply; you can see this by reading down to the horizontal axis. Demand is Q_d; supply is Q_s. The gap between the two points is the shortage. With the shortage, consumers scramble to get the limited supply available at the going price.

In panel B, the going price p_1 is above p^*. At this price, demand is less than supply. Again we denote the demand by Q_d and the supply by Q_s. There is a surplus in the market of $Q_s - Q_d$. Now sellers are scrambling to find buyers.

At various times and for various goods, markets have not cleared. There have been shortages of apartments in New York; farm surpluses have plagued both western Europe and the United States; in 1973, there was a shortage of petrol, with long lines of cars outside petrol stations. Unemployment is a type of surplus, in which people who want to work find that they cannot sell their labour services at the going wage.

In some markets, like the stock market, the adjustment of prices to shifts in the demand and supply curves tends to be very rapid. In other cases, such as in the housing market, the adjustments tend to be sluggish. When price adjustments are sluggish, shortages or surpluses may appear as prices adjust. Houses tend not to sell quickly, for instance, during periods of decreased demand, which translate only slowly into lower housing prices.

When the market is not adjusting quickly towards equilibrium, economists say that prices are **sticky.** Even in these cases, the analysis of market equilibrium is useful. It indicates the direction of the changes; if the equilibrium price exceeds the current price, prices will tend to rise. Moreover, the rate

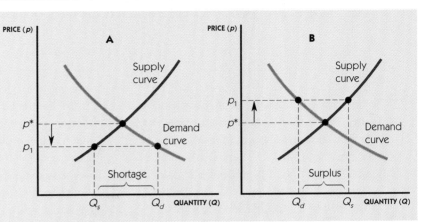

Figure 5.11 SHORTAGES AND SURPLUSES

In panel A, the actual price p_1 is below the market-clearing price p^*. At a price of p_1, quantity demanded exceeds quantity supplied, and a shortage exists. In panel B, the actual price p_1 is above the equilibrium price $p.^*$ In this case, quantity supplied exceeds quantity demanded, and there is a surplus, or glut, in the market.

at which prices fall or rise is often related to the gap, at the going price, between the quantity demanded and the quantity supplied.

INTERFERING WITH THE LAW OF SUPPLY AND DEMAND

The law of supply and demand, which governs how prices are set, can produce results that some individuals or groups do not like. For example, a reduced supply of oil may lead to a higher equilibrium price for oil. The higher price is not a malfunction of the law of supply and demand, but this is little comfort to those who use petrol to power their cars and oil to heat their homes. Low demand for unskilled labour may lead to very low wages for unskilled workers. An increase in the demand for apartments in New York City leads, in the short run (with an inelastic supply), to an increase in rents—to the delight of landlords but the dismay of renters.

In each of these cases, pressure from those who did not like the outcome of market processes has led government to act. The price of oil and natural gas was, at one time, regulated; minimum wage laws set a minimum limit on what employers can pay, even if the workers are willing to work for less; and rent

control laws at times have limited what landlords can charge. The concerns behind these inteferences with the market are understandable, but the agitation for government action is based on two errors.

First, someone (or some group) was assigned blame for the change: the oil price rises were blamed on the oil companies, low wages on the employer, and rent increases on the landlord. As already explained, economists emphasise the role of anonymous market forces in determining these prices. After all, if landlords or oil companies are basically the same people today as they were last week, there must be some reason that they started charging different prices this week. Sometimes the price increase is the result of producers' colluding to raise prices. This was the case in 1973, when the oil-exporting countries got together to raise the price of oil. The more common situation, however, is illustrated by the increase in the price of oil in August 1990, after Iraq's invasion of Kuwait. There was no collusion this time. The higher price simply reflected the anticipated reduction in the supply of oil. People rushed to buy, increasing short-term demand and pushing up the equilibrium price.

The second error was to forget that as powerful as governments may be, they can no more repeal the law of supply and demand than they can repeal the law of gravity. When they interfere with its working, the forces of supply and demand will not be balanced. There will be either excess supply or excess

Britain has always had higher taxes on beer, wine, and spirits than its nearby continental neighbours. The raising of the excise duties on beer, wines, spirits, and cigarettes has been a long-cherished ritual element of the chancellor of the Exchequer's annual Budget Speech—20 pence on a bottle of whisky, 10 pence on a bottle of wine, 3 pence on a pint of beer, and so on—a litany with which all Brits are familiar. These taxes used to be a sure source of revenue for the Exchequer. The demand for all these goods is relatively inelastic, so putting up the price causes only a small reduction in consumption. Back in the bad old days before Britain's membership in the European Union eliminated them, tight restrictions on the import of these goods into the United Kingdom kept the U.K. market for them separate from the market in the continental countries. It was possible to have higher prices in Britain than on the Continent because it was illegal to import these goods into Britain without paying the British taxes on them. The European Union has swept that all away. The EU's free movement of goods within the union requires that British residents buy unlimited quantities of alcoholic drinks and cigarettes anywhere in the union and bring them into Britain for their own use.

Calais is crowded with wine superstores, and the cross-channel ferries and the Channel Tunnel Shuttle heave with cars and vans stuffed to the gills with drinks and smokes. The pubs and off-licences of southeastern England complain bitterly that their trade has been decimated by legal and illegal cross-border shopping. Numbers of people have been caught illegally selling these imports through off-licences and other shops. The cost in lost tax revenue to the government is put at billions of pounds per year.

The possibility of cross-border shopping has dramatically changed the benefits to the government of imposing heavy taxes on these goods. As demand for them now leaks away when prices rise, there may be little or no increase in revenue from a tax increase. Indeed, it might be that tax cuts would bring more revenue, as the lower rate of tax on each item sold might be more than offset by the greater number of taxed items sold in Britain. In recent years, the British government has moderated the tax rises on these goods. The tax on spirits has fallen to historically low levels (as a percentage of the before-tax price of the goods); the tax on wine has fallen.

The cross-border shopping is not all one way. Some goods, such as clothing, have at times been cheaper in Britain than in France, partly because the rate of value-added tax has been lower in Britain than in France.

The cross-border shopping that takes place between Britain and France is only a small part of the picture. The possibilities for it on the Continent across the land borders between neighbouring EU states are much greater and a source of real concern to governments. There is an argument for EU countries to coordinate their taxes. Since it may be socially inefficient for countries to compete with one another on taxes, each trying to set lower taxes to attract business and expand their tax base, they could benefit from agreeing with their neighbours on tax rates. Such collaboration remains in its infancy. For a variety of historical reasons, tax rates differ from country to country. Wine producer interests in France have kept duties on wine low. The British puritanical attitude to alcohol and tobacco is not shared in the Mediterranean parts of the EU, although it strikes a chord in Scandinavia. So far the effects of the EU have been good for consumers of alcohol and tobacco in Britain and less good for off-licences in Kent.

demand. Shortages and surpluses create problems of their own, often worse than the original problem the government was supposed to resolve.

Two straightforward examples of government's overruling the law of supply and demand are **price ceilings,** which impose a maximum price that can be charged for a product, and **price floors,** which impose a minimum price. Rent control laws are price ceilings, and minimum wage laws and agricultural price supports are price floors. A closer look at each will help highlight the perils of interfering with the law of supply and demand.

PRICE CEILINGS: THE CASE OF RENT CONTROL

Price ceilings—setting a maximum charge—are always tempting to governments because they seem an easy way to assure that everyone will be able to afford a particular product. Typically the result has been to create shortages at the controlled price. Peo-

ple want to buy more of a good than producers want to sell, because producers have no incentive to produce more of the good. Those who can buy at the cheaper price benefit; producers and those unable to buy suffer.

The effect of **rent control laws**—setting the maximum rent that a landlord can charge for a one-bedroom flat, for example—is illustrated by Figure 5.12. In panel A, R^* is the market equilibrium rental rate, at which the demand for housing equals the supply. However, the local government is concerned that at R^*, many poor people cannot afford housing in the city, so it imposes a law that says that rents may be no higher than R_1. At R_1, there is an excess demand for flats. While the motives behind the government action may well have been praiseworthy, the government has created an artificial scarcity.

The problems caused by rent control are likely to be worse in the long run than in the short run, because long-run supply curves are more elastic than short-run supply curves. In the short run, the quantity of flats does not change much. But in the long

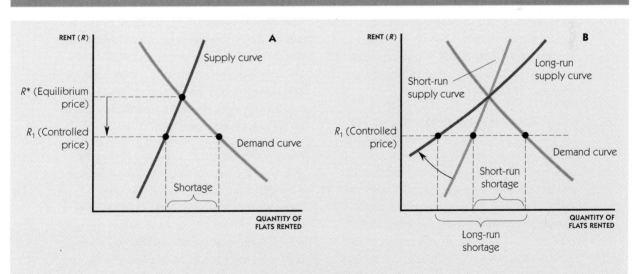

Figure 5.12 A PRICE CEILING: RENT CONTROL

Rent control laws limit the rents flat owners may charge. If rents are held down to R_1, below the market-clearing level R^*, as in panel A, there will be excess demand for flats. Panel B shows the long-run response. The supply of rental housing is more elastic in the long run, since landlords can refuse to build new flats for rent, or they can sell existing flats. The price ceiling eventually leads to the quantity supplied's being even further below the quantity demanded.

CLOSE-UP: INTERFERING WITH THE MARKET FOR HOUSING

Housing is an important aspect of life for everyone. Governments affirm their belief that everyone should have adequate and affordable housing. And so the housing market in most countries has been felt to be too important to be simply left alone. There is everywhere a variety of subsidies, price controls, rationing schemes, and public provision of housing.

In Britain the majority of households currently live in owner-occupied housing, which has been subsidised through tax relief on mortgage interest, the absence of capital gains tax on a principal residence, and the exclusion from tax of the value of the flow of services (effectively a form of income) derived from owning and occupying a house or flat. There is a substantial rented sector, in which most of the dwellings are publicly owned—council housing—and there remains a small privately rented sector. The rents on council housing have almost always been below the market rental, and council housing has been rationed and allocated to people according to various criteria—income, years of residence in the town in question, needs, and so on—and waiting lists used to be many years long in the 1950s and 1960s.

The privately rented sector was once very large. In the nineteenth century and early decades of the twentieth century, many people of all income levels routinely rented their homes and invested their wealth in other forms. Through the twentieth century, the privately rented sector has gradually dwindled away to almost nothing. In the 1950s notorious examples of flagrant exploitation and bullying of relatively poor tenants came to light—it became known as Rachmanism after a particularly egregious practitioner. Rent controls and other measures to protect tenants, such as protection against eviction, were

enacted in the 1960s. While these protected existing tenants, the laws reduced the returns available to landlords, both honest and dishonest, to a point below which it was not worthwhile building accommodation for rent (or converting existing accommodation). Much rental property was sold for owner occupancy; many converted flats were converted back into single-household owner-occupied houses, and the supply of privately rented housing fell until it accounted for a tiny fraction of the market.

The effect of the shrinkage of the privately rented housing sector and the growth of owner occupancy has been to reduce the mobility of labour, since buying and selling houses is a very costly and time-consuming business. It has also made housing more expensive for young people, who lack financial resources or sufficiently secure incomes to be able to buy into the owner-occupied market and who are not able to qualify for publicly provided housing (council houses), and less costly for people moving into the owner-occupied sector. This was seen as a problem by the Thatcher and Major governments (1979–1997), whose on-your-bike philosophy of encouraging the unemployed to move in search of work ran into the obstacle of a labour market immobilised by the lack of rental housing.

Andrew Oswald, of the University of Warwick, argues on the basis of evidence drawn from many countries that countries with more owner-occupied housing have higher equilibrium unemployment rates, other things being equal, giving some support to this view. In recent years there has been a revival of privately rented housing in Britain. An important factor was that landlords became more confident that they could recover a property at the end of a tenancy: tenants no longer had a (virtual) right to occupy a property in perpetuity whether they paid the rent or not. In the very depressed housing market in the early 1990s many people were not able to sell houses but were able to rent them instead, and this experience stimulated the provision of rented housing. There has been a growing recognition that, in an economy in which work increasingly requires people to be mobile, it makes sense for there to be forms of housing tenure that are consistent with mobility of labour.

Sources: A. J. Oswald, "The Missing Piece of the Unemployment Puzzle," Inaugural lecture, University of Warwick. Text available from http://www.warwick.ac.uk/fac/soc/Economics/papers/inaugura.pdf. B. McCormick, "Housing and Unemployment in Great Britain," *Oxford Economic Papers*, 1983, Vol. 35, pp. 283–305.

run, the quantity of flats can decline for several reasons, as landlords try to minimize the losses from rent control. Flats may be abandoned as they deteriorate; they can be sold instead of rented; and landlords may not wish to construct new ones if they cannot charge enough in rent to cover their costs.

Figure 5.12B illustrates how the housing shortages under rent control will increase over time. Rent control results in all *existing* renters' being better off, at least as long as the landlord stays in the business. But the quantity of available rental housing will decrease, so that many would-be residents will be unable to find rental housing in the market. Since renters tend to be poorer than those who can buy a home, a shortage of rental housing will tend to hurt the poor most.

PRICE FLOORS: THE CASE OF AGRICULTURAL SUPPORTS

Just as consumers try to get government to limit the prices they pay, sellers would like the government to put a floor on the prices they receive: a minimum wage for workers and a minimum price on agricultural products for farmers. Both groups appeal to fairness. The price they are receiving is inadequate to cover the effort (and other resources) they are contributing.

Farmers, because of their political influence, have in many countries, at various times succeeded in persuading government to impose a floor on the prices of many agricultural products—a price that is above the market equilibrium, as illustrated in Figure 5.13.

Figure 5.13 PRICE FLOORS

If the government imposes a price floor on, say, wheat—at a price in excess of the market equilibrium—there will be excess supply. Either the government will have to purchase the excess and put it into storage or discard it in some way, or it will have to limit production.

The consequences should be obvious: supply exceeds demand. To sustain the price, government has had to purchase and stockpile huge amounts of agricultural goods. The cost of supporting the price at these above-market levels has been in the billions. The Common Agricultural Policy in Europe has been scaled back in recent years but still takes up the majority of the budget of the European Commission.

As government interferes with the law of supply and demand, it is led into a labyrinth of problems. To reduce supplies, it has imposed production limitations. Imposing limitations is not only administratively cumbersome but impedes the adaptability of the market. This is because quotas are based on past production, but some areas should be expanding and others contracting in response to changed circumstances. The quota system does not allow this to happen easily. In order to sell surplus European farm production on world markets, exports have to be subsidised. But these subsidies have angered other countries, which view them as unfair competition. These subsidies have caused problems with most of Europe's trading partners, particularly the United States and Canada.

Governments are aware of these problems, but the political pressures to maintain high prices keep farm subsidies in place.

ALTERNATIVE SOLUTIONS

Large changes in prices cause distress. It is natural to try to find scapegoats and to look to the government for a solution. Such situations call for compassion, and the economists' caution can seem coldhearted. But the fact remains that in competitive markets, price changes are simply the impersonal workings of the law of supply and demand; without price changes, there will be shortages and surpluses. The examples of government attempts to interfere with the workings of supply and demand provide an important cautionary tale: one ignores the workings of the law of supply and demand only at one's peril. This does not mean, however, that the government should simply ignore the distress caused by large price and wage changes. It only means that government must take care in addressing the problems; price controls, including price ceilings and floors, are unlikely to be effective instruments.

Later chapters will discuss ways in which government can address dissatisfaction with the consequences of the law of supply and demand by making use of the power of the market rather than trying to fight against it. For example, if the government is concerned with low wages paid to unskilled workers, it can try to increase the demand for these workers. A shift to the right in the demand curve will increase the wages these workers receive. The government can do this either by subsidising firms that hire unskilled workers or by providing more training to these workers and thus increasing their productivity.

If the government wants to increase the supply of housing to the poor, it can provide housing subsidies for the poor, which will elicit a greater supply. If the government wants to conserve on the use of petrol, it can impose a tax on it. Noneconomists often object that these sorts of economic incentives have other distasteful consequences, and sometimes they do. But government policies that take account of the law of supply and demand will tend to be more effective, with fewer unfortunate side effects, than policies that ignore the predictable economic consequences that follow from disregarding the law of supply and demand.

REVIEW AND PRACTICE

SUMMARY

1 The price elasticity of demand describes how sensitive the quantity demanded of a good is to changes in the price of the good. When demand is inelastic, an increase in price has little effect on quantity demanded and the demand curve is steep; when demand is elastic, an increase in price has a large effect on quantity demanded and the curve is flat. Demand for necessities is usually quite inelastic; demand for luxuries is elastic.

2 The price elasticity of supply describes how sensitive the quantity supplied of a good is to changes in the price of the good. If price changes do not induce much change in supply, the supply curve is very steep and is said to be inelastic. If the supply curve is very flat, indicating that price changes cause large changes in supply, supply is said to be elastic.

3 The extent to which a shift in the supply curve is reflected in price or quantity depends on the shape of the demand curve. The more elastic the demand, the more a given shift in the supply curve will be reflected in changes in equilibrium quantities and the less it will be reflected in changes in equilibrium prices. The more inelastic the demand, the more a given shift in the supply curve will be reflected in changes in equilibrium prices and the less it will be reflected in changes in equilibrium quantities.

4 Likewise, the extent to which a shift in the demand curve is reflected in price or quantity depends on the shape of the supply curve.

5 Demand and supply curves are likely to be more elastic in the long run than in the short run. Therefore a shift in the demand or supply curve is likely to have a larger price effect in the short run and a larger quantity effect in the long run.

6 Elasticities can be used to predict to what extent consumer prices rise when a tax is imposed on a good. If the demand curve for a good is very inelastic, consumers in effect have to pay the tax. If the demand curve is very elastic, the quantities produced and the price received by producers are likely to decline considerably.

7 Government regulations may prevent a market from moving towards its equilibrium price, leading to shortages or surpluses. Price ceilings lead to excess demand. Price floors lead to excess supply.

KEY TERMS

price elasticity of demand

infinite elasticity

zero elasticity

price elasticity of supply

market clearing

sticky prices

price ceilings

price floors

REVIEW QUESTIONS

1 What is meant by the elasticity of demand and the elasticity of supply? Why do economists find these concepts useful?

2 Is a perfectly elastic demand or supply curve horizontal or vertical? Is of a perfectly inelastic demand or supply curve horizontal or vertical? Explain.

3 If the elasticity of demand is unity, what happens to total revenue as the price increases? What if the demand for a product is very inelastic? What if it is very elastic?

4 Under which condition will a shift in the demand curve result mainly in a change in quantity? In price?

5 Under which condition will a shift in the supply curve result mainly in a change in price? In quantity?

6 Why do the elasticities of demand and supply tend to change from the short run to the long run?

7 Under which circumstances will a tax on a product be passed along to consumers?

8 Why do price ceilings tend to lead to shortages? Why do price floors tend to lead to surpluses?

PROBLEMS

1 Suppose the price elasticity of demand for petrol is 0.2 in the short run and 0.7 in the long run. If the price of petrol rises 28 percent, what effect on quantity demanded will this have in the short run? In the long run?

2 Imagine that the short-run price elasticity of supply for a farmer's wheat is 0.3, while the long-run price elasticity is 2. If prices for wheat fall 30 percent, what are the short- and long-run changes in quantity supplied? What are the short- and long-run changes in quantity supplied if prices rise by 15 percent? What happens to the farmer's revenues in each of these situations?

3 Assume that the demand curve for spirits is highly inelastic and the supply curve for spirits is highly elastic. If the tastes of the drinking public shift away from spirits, will the effect be larger on price or on quantity? If the government decides to impose a higher tax on manufacturers of spirits, will the effects be larger on price or on quantity? What is the effect of an advertising program that succeeds in discouraging people from drinking? Draw a diagram to illustrate each of your answers.

4 Imagine that wages (the price of labour) are sticky in the labour market, that is, wages do not change in the short run, and that a supply of new workers enters that market. Will the market be in equilibrium in the short run? Why or why not? If not, explain the relationship you would expect to see between the quantity demanded and supplied, and draw a diagram to illustrate. Explain how sticky wages in the labour market affect unemployment.

5 For each of the following markets, explain whether you would expect prices in that market to be relatively sticky or not:

(a) The stock market
(b) The market for car workers
(c) The housing market
(d) The market for cut flowers
(e) The market for pizza-delivery people

6 Suppose a government wishes to ensure that its citizens can afford adequate housing. Consider three ways of pursuing that goal. One method is to pass a law requiring that all rents be cut by one-quarter. A second method offers a subsidy to all builders of homes. A third provides a subsidy directly to tenants equal to one-quarter of the rent they pay. Predict what effect each of these proposals would have on the price and quantity of rental housing in the short run and in the long run.

CHAPTER

TIME AND RISK

A recurring theme in political debate in Britain, the United States, and many other countries is the question of whether the country is investing enough in its future. The *choices* we make today affect living standards tomorrow. Much of economics is thus *future oriented*. The basic principles of making choices and markets—the law of supply and demand—apply here as well. But there are some distinctive aspects of future-oriented choices that contrast with the static nature of the conventional supply-and-demand equilibrium analysis. The first part of this chapter focuses on those aspects. We show how prices in the present, for instance, are linked to expectations of prices in the future.

Various governments in recent years have begun to enact policies to encourage entrepreneurship. A large percentage of new jobs are created in new and small businesses. But starting new businesses is risky—one of the many risks that permeate the economy. How do individuals and firms respond to risks? And how does uncertainty affect markets? The function of insurance is to protect against risk. Homeowners typically buy fire insurance, for instance. But many risks cannot be protected against so easily. A firm planning to bring out a new product, for example, cannot buy insurance to protect against the risk that it will fail in the marketplace. How well market economies handle the problems created by risk has much to do with their success. The second part of this chapter investigates insurance and other markets that protect against risk.

KEY QUESTIONS

1 How do we compare a pound received next year or in five years' time with a pound received today?

2 What determines the demand for an asset like gold, which is purchased mainly with the intent of selling it at some later date? What determines shifts in the demand curve for assets?

3 Why do people buy insurance?

4 Why are there many risks for which insurance is not available?

5 How do the different ways that firms raise funds in the capital market affect the risks borne by the investors who provide those funds? Why do some firms have to pay a higher interest rate on what they borrow than do others?

INTEREST

When you put money into a bank account you are involved in a future-oriented transaction. You have loaned your money to the bank, and the bank has promised to pay you back. But banks offer more than security; they offer you a *return* on your savings. This return is called **interest.** If you put £1,000 in the bank at the beginning of the year and the interest rate is 10 percent per year, you will receive £1,100 at the end of the year. The £100 is the payment of interest, while the £1,000 is the repayment of the **principal,** the original amount lent to the bank.

To an economist, the interest rate is a price. Normally, we express prices in terms of pounds and pence. If the price of an orange is 20 pence, that means we must give up 20 pence to get one orange. Economists talk about the relative price of two goods as the amount of one good you have to give up to get one more unit of the other. The relative price is the ratio of the two "pound-pence" prices.

For example, if the price of an apple is 10 pence and the price of an orange is 20 pence, then the relative price (that is, the ratio of the prices) is 2. If we wish to consume one more orange, we have to give up two apples. Thus, the relative price describes a trade-off. Similarly, if the interest rate is 10 percent, by giving up £1.00 worth of consumption today, a saver can have £1.10 worth of consumption next year. Thus, the rate of interest tells us how much fu-

ture consumption we can get by giving up £1.00 worth of current consumption. It tells us the relative price between the present and the future.

THE TIME VALUE OF MONEY

Interest rates are normally positive. If you have £1.00 today, you can put it into the bank and, if the interest rate is 5 percent, receive £1.05 at the end of next year. In short, £1.00 becomes, in this example, £1.05 next year.

A pound today is worth more than a pound in the future. Economists call this the **time value of money.** The concept of **present discounted value** tells us precisely how to measure the time value of money. The present discounted value of £100 a year from now is what you would pay today for £100 a year from now. Suppose the interest rate is 10 percent. If you put £90.91 in the bank today, at the end of the year you will receive £9.09 interest, which together with the original amount will total £100. Thus, £90.91 is the present discounted value of £100 a year from now if the interest rate is 10 percent.

There is a simple formula for calculating the present discounted value of any amount to be received a year from now: just divide the amount by 1 plus the annual rate of interest. The annual rate of interest is often denoted by r.

To check this formula, consider the present discounted value of £100. According to the formula, it is £100/$(1 + r)$. In other words, take the present discounted value, £100/$(1 + r)$, and put it in the bank.

USING ECONOMICS: THE EFFECTS OF COMPOUND INTEREST

We are all familiar with the small rates of interest offered by banks and building societies on savings accounts, often, in recent years, just a few percent per annum, and with the snail-like pace with which balances in these accounts grow as interest is added to them each year. However, over longer periods of time, compound interest turns out to have very powerful effects. How much will £1 be worth if it is invested at a rate of interest of 5 percent per annum, with all the interest reinvested each year, after 10 years? After 20 years? After 50 years? After 100 years? What if the rate of return is only 4 or 3 percent instead of 5 percent? If £1 is invested for one year at 5 percent, it becomes £1.05, and if all that is reinvested, it becomes $(1.05)^2$ after a second year, $(1.05)^3$ after a third year, $(1.05)^n$ after an nth year, and so on. The following table shows the value of £1, earning interest at various rates, after various periods of time.

After only 10 years, the returns are not much dif-

ferent from the returns that simple interest would produce, but after longer periods, the greater returns produced by higher rates of return become more marked. After 100 years, a rate of 5 percent per annum produces £131.50, whereas a return of 4 percent produces £50.50. A small difference in the rate of return becomes an enormous difference in the final value of the fund after longer periods.

While no individual is going to be very interested in returns to saving over a period as long as 100 years, these calculations have relevance to the growth of countries. For example, they show that a small difference in the rate of growth of two countries, sustained over a long period of time, will lead to a very great difference in their income levels. They also show that the value of £1 to be received at some time in the future might be very small. If the appropriate rate of interest to use is 5 percent, then £1 to be received in 20 years time is worth £1/2.65 = 38 pence today.

RATE OF RETURN

Years Invested	1 Percent	2 Percent	3 Percent	4 Percent	5 Percent
10	1.10	1.22	1.34	1.48	1.63
20	1.22	1.49	1.81	2.19	2.65
50	1.64	2.69	4.38	7.11	11.47
75	2.11	4.42	9.18	18.95	38.83
100	2.70	7.24	19.22	50.50	131.50

At the end of the year you will have

$$\frac{£100}{1 + r} (1 + r) = £100.$$

This confirms our conclusion that £100/(1 + r) today is the same as £100 one year from now.

If the interest rate increases, the present discounted value of £100 a year from now will decrease. If the interest rate should rise to 20 percent, for example, the present discounted value of £100 a year from now becomes £83.33 (100/1.2).

The concept of present discounted value is im-

PRESENT DISCOUNTED VALUE

$$\text{Present discounted value of £1,000 next year} = \frac{£1.00}{1 + \text{interest rate}}.$$

Denoting the interest rate by r, the right-hand side of the equation becomes

$$\frac{£1.00}{1 + r}.$$

portant because so many decisions in economics are oriented to the future. Whether the decision is made by a person buying a house or saving money for retirement or by a company building a factory or making an investment, the decision maker must be able to value money that will be received one, two, five, or ten years in the future.

THE MARKET FOR LOANABLE FUNDS

The previous section explained how the interest rate is a price, similar to the price of any other good, like apples and oranges. The price of borrowing a pound (which you have to pay back in a year) is the pound plus the annual rate of interest. In calculating the present discounted value, firms or individuals take the interest rate as given. But obviously the interest rate changes over time. How is the interest rate determined? Like other prices, the interest rate is determined by the law of supply and demand.

At any given time, there are some people and companies who would like to borrow, so they can spend more than they currently have. Rachel has her first job and knows she needs a car; George needs kitchen equipment, tables, and chairs to open his sandwich shop. Others would like to save, or spend less than they currently have been spending. John is putting aside money for his children's education and for his retirement; Bill is putting aside money to make a down payment on a house.

Exchanges that occur over time are called **intertemporal trades.** The gains from trade discussed in Chapter 3 apply equally well here. When one individual lends money to another, both gain. John and Bill can lend money to Rachel and George. John and Bill will get paid interest in the future, to compensate them for letting Rachel and George use their funds now. Rachel and George are willing to pay the interest because to them, having the funds today is worth more than waiting. The borrower may be a business firm like the one owned by George, who believes that with these funds he will be able to make an investment that will yield a return far higher than the interest rate he is charged today. Or the borrower may be an individual facing some emergency, such as a medical crisis, that requires funds today. The borrower may simply be a free spirit, wishing to consume as much as he can (as much as lenders are willing to give him) and letting the future take care of itself.

How is the supply of funds to be equated with the demand? As the interest rate rises, some borrowers will be discouraged from borrowing. Rachel may decide to ride her bicycle to work and postpone buying a new car until she can save up the money herself (or until interest rates come down). At the same time, as the interest rate rises, some savers may be induced to save more. Their incentives for saving have increased. John realizes that every extra pound he saves today will produce more money in the future, so he may put more aside.[1] Figure 6.1 shows

[1] In Chapter 9, we will see that there is some controversy about whether higher interest rates always induce people to save more.

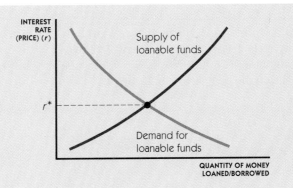

Figure 6.1 SUPPLY AND DEMAND FOR LOANABLE FUNDS

The amount of money loaned and borrowed is the quantity, and the interest rate is the price. At the equilibrium interest rate r^*, the supply of loanable funds equals the demand.

the supply and demand curves for loanable funds. Here the interest rate is the price, and the amount of money loaned and borrowed is the quantity. At r^*, the demand for funds equals the supply of funds.

We can now explain why the equilibrium interest rate is positive. If it were zero or negative, prospective borrowers would demand more funds than prospective savers would be willing to supply. Indeed, negative interest rates would mean that people could borrow to consume today and pay back less in the future and that savers would receive less in the future than the amount they saved. Only at a positive interest rate can the demand for loans be equated to the supply.

In our economy, borrowers and lenders do not usually meet face to face. Instead, banks and other financial institutions serve as intermediaries, collecting savings from those who want to save and disbursing money to those who want to borrow. These intermediaries help make the market for loans work smoothly. For their services, the intermediaries charge fees, which can be measured as the difference between the interest rate they pay savers and the interest rate they charge borrowers.

INFLATION AND THE REAL RATE OF INTEREST

The interest rate, we have seen, is a price. It tells how many pounds we can get next period if we give up one pound today. But except for misers like Scrooge who store money for its own sake, pounds are of value only because of the goods that can be bought with them. Because of inflation—the increase in prices over time—pounds in the future buy fewer goods than pounds today. In deciding both whether to borrow and whether to lend, individuals want to know how much *consumption* they get tomorrow if they give up a pound's worth of consumption today. The answer is given by the **real rate of interest.** This is distinguished from the **nominal rate of interest,** the rate one sees posted at one's bank and in the newspaper, which simply describes the number of pounds one gets next year in exchange for a pound today. There is a simple relationship between the real interest rate and the nominal interest rate: the real interest rate equals the nominal interest rate minus the rate of inflation (the annual rate of change of prices on average). If the nominal interest rate is 10 percent and the rate of inflation is 6 percent, then the real interest rate is 4 percent. By lending out (or saving) a pound today, you can increase the amount of goods that you get in one year's time by 4 percent.

Consider an individual who decides to deposit £1,000 in a savings account. At the end of the year, at a 10 percent interest rate, she will have £1,100. But prices meanwhile have risen by 6 percent. A good that cost £1,000 in the beginning of the year now costs £1,060. In terms of purchasing power, she has only £40 extra to spend (£1,100 − £1,060)—4 percent more than she had at the beginning of the year. This is her real return. In an inflationary economy, a borrower is in a similar situation. He knows that if he borrows money, the pounds he gives back to repay the loan will be worth less than the pounds he receives today. Thus, what is relevant for individuals to know when deciding either how much to lend (save) or how much to borrow is the *real* interest rate, which takes account of inflation. It is the real interest rate that should appear on the vertical axis of Figure 6.1.

THE MARKET FOR ASSETS

Gardeners today would have been shocked at the price of tulip bulbs in early seventeenth-century Holland, when one bulb sold for the equivalent of £11,000 in today's prices. The golden age of tulips did not last long, however, and in 1637, prices of bulbs fell by over 90 percent. Dramatic price swings are not only curiosities of history. Between 1973 and 1980, the price of gold rose from £98 to £613, or 525 percent; then from 1980 to 1985, it fell to £318. On October 19, 1987, prices in the U.S. stock market fell by one-half *trillion* dollars, almost 25 percent. Even a major war would be unlikely to destroy a quarter of the U.S. capital stock in a single day. But there was no war or other external event to explain the 1987 drop.

How can the demand-and-supply model of Chapters 4 and 5 explain these huge price swings? Supply curves for these goods certainly could not have shifted so dramatically. Nor could changes in tastes, incomes, or other goods have caused such fantastic shifts in demand. The solution to this puzzle does lie in shifts of the demand curve but not directly for the reasons we saw in Chapter 4.

The first step in the solution is to recognise that the goods in the examples above are unlike ice cream cones, newspapers, or any other goods that are valued by the consumer mainly for their present use. Gold, land, stock, and even tulips in seventeenth-century Holland are all examples of **assets.** Assets are long lived and thus can be bought at one date and sold at another. For this reason, the price individuals are willing to pay for them today depends not only on today's conditions—the immediate return or benefits—but also on some expectation of what tomorrow's conditions will be, in particular, on what the assets can be sold for in the future.

The concept of present discounted value tells us how to measure and compare returns anticipated in the future. Changes in present discounted value shift demand curves, as shown in Figure 6.2, because the amount that someone is willing to pay today depends on the present discounted value of what she believes she can get for it in the future.

Present discounted values can change for two reasons. First, they can change because the interest rate changes. An increase in the interest rate reduces the present discounted value of the pounds you expect to receive in the future. This is one reason why increases in the interest rate are often accompanied by drops in the price of shares on the stock market, and vice versa. Smart investors thus try to forecast interest rates accurately. Second, present discounted values can change because of a change in the expected price of an asset at the time one expects to sell it. Again, this will lead to a shift in the demand curve. Such expectations can be quite volatile; this explains a great deal of the volatility in asset prices.

To see how expectations concerning future events affect *current* prices, consider a hypothetical example. Suppose that, when plans to build the channel tunnel were finalised, people realised that, when the tunnel came into operation, say in ten years time, land in northern France would become more valuable, because of its improved train and road connections to London and Paris (say by £10,000 per hectare). But, they would have thought, in nine years time it would be recognised that in just one year more, the land would increase in value. And so, in nine years time, investors would be willing to pay almost £10,000 more

REAL INTEREST RATE

Real interest rate = nominal interest rate − rate of inflation.

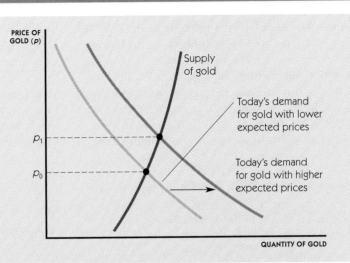

Figure 6.2 HOW EXPECTATIONS CAN SHIFT DEMAND

Expectations that the price of an asset will rise in the future can cause the demand curve to shift out to the right, thus raising the current price.

PRICE OF GOLD (p)

Supply of gold

Today's demand for gold with lower expected prices

p_1

p_0

Today's demand for gold with higher expected prices

QUANTITY OF GOLD

per hectare for the land, even though the tunnel would not be open at that time. But then, on the same principle, people would realise that in eight years time the increase in land values of almost £10,000 per hectare would be just one year away, and therefore people in eight years time would be willing to pay something just short of that amount more for the land. Working backwards like this makes it apparent that if people are confident land is going to be much more valuable in ten years, its price rises today.

Thus, while changes in tastes or technology or incomes or the prices of other goods *today* could not account for some of the sharp changes in asset values described at the start of this section, changes in expectations concerning any of these variables in the future will have an effect *today* on the demand. Markets for assets are linked together over time. An event that is expected to happen in 10 or 15 or even 50 years can have a direct bearing on today's market.

Changes in expectations about future returns or interest rates, then, can be reflected in large changes in asset prices today. How do individuals and firms form expectations? Partly by looking at past experience. If a company has steadily grown more valuable, investors may come to expect that pattern to continue. If every time inflation rates increase the banking authorities act to slow the economy by rais-

ing interest rates, people come to expect inflation to be followed by higher interest rates.

Psychologists and economists have studied how individuals form expectations. Sometimes people are **myopic,** or shortsighted. They expect what is true today to be true tomorrow. The price of gold today is what it will be tomorrow. Sometimes they are **adaptive,** extrapolating events of the recent past into the future. If the price of gold today is 5 percent higher than it was last year, they expect its price next year to be 5 percent higher than it is today.

When people make full use of all relevant available past data to form their expectations, economists say that their expectations are **rational.** While the price of gold rises during an inflationary period, the price of gold also goes down when inflation subsides. Thus, if a person knows that economic analysts are predicting lower inflation, he will not expect the gold price increases to continue. Even when individuals form their expectations rationally, they will not be right all the time. Sometimes they will be overly optimistic, sometimes overly pessimistic (although in making their decisions, they are aware of these possibilities). But the assumption of rational expectations is that on average they will be right.

The 1970s were a period when adaptive expectations reigned. Many investors came to expect prices of assets such as land and housing to continue to rise rapidly. The more you invested, the more money you made. The idea that the price of a house or of land might fall seemed beyond belief—even though history is full of episodes (most recently during the 1930s) when such prices fell dramatically. The collapse of the housing market in Britain in the late 1980s reminded investors of the importance of incorporating historical data in forming expectations.

But in this, as in all types of fortune-telling, history never repeats itself exactly. Since the situation today is never precisely like past experience, it is never completely clear which facts are the relevant ones. Even the best-informed experts are likely to disagree. When it comes to predicting the future, everyone's crystal ball is cloudy.

THE MARKET FOR RISK

Most of us do not like the risk that accompanies almost all future-oriented economic activity. We might spend a few pounds on some lottery tickets, but for the most part, we try to avoid or minimise serious risks. Psychologists who have studied this risk-avoidance behaviour focus on the anxiety to which uncertainty gives rise. Economists refer to individuals who demonstrate risk-avoidance behaviour as **risk averse.**

RESPONDING TO RISK

Even though most individuals are risk averse, our economy needs to encourage risk taking. New ventures are risky, but they are the engine of economic growth. Our economy has developed a number of ways by which risks are transferred, transformed, and shared. The institutions and arrangements by which this is done are known collectively as the **market for risk.**

AVOIDING AND MITIGATING RISK

The simplest way to respond to risk is to avoid it: don't gamble. But if everyone avoided all risks, economic activity would come to a standstill. No invest-

ments would be made. Firms wouldn't even hire workers: there is always the chance that an employee won't work out.

So risks cannot be avoided. But there is much individuals and firms can do to reduce the degree of risk and soften its impact. Firms invest in fire detection and suppression equipment to reduce the damage from a fire. Thorough research—obtaining as complete information as possible—before undertaking an investment project reduces the risk.

MAINTAINING OPTIONS

A second way to respond to risk is to keep one's options open. Many uncertainties get resolved over time. At the beginning of the week, Tim doesn't know whether it will rain on Saturday. By Friday, the weather forecasters will have provided him with much better information—a better estimate of the probability of rain. By Saturday morning, he will have a still better estimate. Tim would like to go to the football game on Saturday afternoon, provided it does not rain. If it rains, he would rather go to the movies. But by Friday all the football tickets will be sold out. He has to make his decision earlier. He may decide to buy the ticket on Monday, knowing that there is a chance that he will not use it (if it rains). Buying the ticket on Monday maintains his options. Failing to buy the ticket forecloses the option of going to the football game. On Saturday morning it does rain. Tim recognises that the expenditure on the football ticket is a sunk cost. Even though he spent the money, he prefers spending an extra £5 and going to the movies to getting cold and drenched at the football game. It was worth spending the money to keep his options open.

Businesses often spend considerable amounts to maintain options. They may enter a market, for example, knowing they will lose money for the next year or two. But they hope to learn a lot from the experience, and they know that if they fail to enter the market, it will be much harder (costlier) to enter it later. It is worth losing money for a while to keep their options open.

DIVERSIFYING

A third response to risk is: don't put all of your eggs in the same basket. Firms, for instance, may enter several lines of business to reduce risk. Farmers may grow several different crops. If things go badly in one area, there is a good chance they will go better in some other area.

TRANSFERRING AND SHARING RISK

A fourth response to risk is to transfer or share it. If I had no insurance and my house burnt down, it would be a financial calamity for me. But if some rich person agreed to pay me £100 if my house burnt down, his £100 loss would not have a major effect on his finances. He would be willing to accept the small risk, for a fee a bit above the payment he expected to make on average if my house did burn down. Thus, if there were a 1 percent chance that my house would burn down, the expected payment of someone who agreed to pay me £100 if my house burnt down would be

Expected payment
= probability of loss × payment in event of loss
= .01 × £100 = £1.

The *risk premium* is the *extra* payment an individual or firm must receive to be willing to bear risks. If he were willing to accept the risk in return for a payment of £1.10, then the £.10 would be the risk premium. I would be more than willing to pay him £1.10 to absorb the risk. Ideally, I would like to find 1,000 such people to insure my £100,000 house, for then, I would have completely transferred the risk of a fire to them.

Insurance firms are the institutions in our economy that specialise in absorbing risks. The earliest insurance firms—collectively known as Lloyd's of London—did nothing more than pull together a group of investors willing to absorb large risks, such as those associated with shipwrecks. Today, most insurance firms absorb risk directly.

LIMITS ON INSURANCE AS PROTECTION AGAINST RISK

Even though insurance companies specialise in absorbing risks, individuals and firms cannot buy insurance to protect themselves against all types of risk. A business, for example, cannot buy insurance that protects it against the risk that the demand for its product will fall or the risk that a competitor will develop a better product that will drive the company into bankruptcy. Economists have identified two inherent problems that limit the use of insurance as a mechanism for handling risk: adverse selection and moral hazard. Although the following discussion focuses on these problems in the context of insurance, they apply more generally to methods of sharing risk, including stocks and bonds.

Adverse Selection   The probability that an individual will have an accident depends on characteristics of that individual's life and behaviour that an insurance firm cannot perfectly observe. If the accident probabilities of different individuals could be accurately estimated, then in a competitive insurance market, premiums would accurately reflect those accident probabilities. For example, "hot dog" skiers would pay higher medical insurance rates, reflecting their higher average medical expenses, than people with safer pastimes.

But insurance firms do not know everything about each individual's risks. Insurance rates can only be based on observable factors; auto insurance rates, for example, depend on the record of past accidents, age of driver, and type of vehicle. The same rate is charged to all people with identical observable traits. When an insurance company perceives that the premium it is charging for a particular group of individuals is too low for the risks of the group, it raises the premium. This is when the problem of adverse selection can appear.

The **adverse selection** problem arises when insurance companies try to raise their premiums and the best risks stop buying insurance. The best risks may decide to either self-insure (not buy insurance from any company) or switch to another company. The worst risks—those who know that they really need insurance because they are unhealthy, for example, and so will not self-insure or those who cannot get insurance elsewhere—stick with the firm. As the best risks leave, the *average* riskiness of the insured risks worsens. It may deteriorate so much that average profits fall; the increased average riskiness more than offsets the increased premiums.

Though the term *adverse selection* was coined to capture this *adverse* effect on the mix of those buying insurance as premiums increase, it has come to refer to the whole array of actions that can affect the mix of those buying insurance.

CLOSE-UP: THE LLOYD'S INSURANCE MARKET

The Lloyd's insurance market was, until rocked by scandals a few years ago, one of the jewels in the City in London's crown. Since then, it has looked rather tarnished. Lloyd's had its origins in groups of men who would meet in a City coffeehouse in the eighteenth century and offer insurance on ships and their cargoes. The market developed into one of the most powerful forces in insurance. It is unusual in that it relies on individuals' using their personal wealth as the backing for the insurance offered, and these individuals have unlimited liability—not the usual limited liability—for the risks they take on: all their assets can be taken to meet claims arising from the risks they accept. People with enough personal wealth can put themselves forward as "names," and can then accept risks up to a limit, which depends on their wealth. Most names are not actively involved in underwriting, that is, accepting risks. Instead this job is delegated to specialists who have expert knowledge of particular fields of insurance. Names join with others to form syndicates, and these syndicates sell insurance, using specialist expertise to assess risks, set appropriate premiums, and so on.

In return for placing their personal wealth at risk (running the risk that all or part of it may be seized to meet insurance claims), names get an income, which is based on the insurance premiums their syndicates collect less the claims that have to be met. By pooling and spreading many risks, underwriting syndicates aim to have a relatively riskless stream of income from premiums. Of the large number of insurance policies each syndicate has issued, only a fraction typically will make claims in each year, while all pay premiums. If risks are properly assessed and premiums set appropriately, then the probability of claims' being larger than the year's premium income will be very small. Consequently, becoming a Lloyd's

name has for many years seemed to be a means for wealthy people to make their wealth work twice for them, once when it earns interest, rents, dividends, and profits in the usual way and a second time when it earns a stream of income from being the backing for the insurance policies sold by Lloyd's.

However, in the late 1980s all this began to go badly wrong. Lloyd's was famous for being willing to offer insurance (at a price) on any risk, and among the less-quantifiable risks the market had taken on were many for exposure to asbestos, for which firms were insuring themselves against claims that might come from their workers or customers. These insurance policies provided insurance for very long periods of time. Claims made on these policies began to outstrip all the expectations on which the premiums had been based, and claims came in decades after the insurance policies had been sold. It was evident that many policies had been sold at premiums that were much too low and that Lloyd's syndicates would make huge losses. In addition, it was argued that many syndicates had been very badly run and that the expert practitioners in the market had used the inactive names to take all the losses while ensuring that they themselves were not financially injured by the fiasco. The names, called upon to make enormous payments, in some cases to the point of personal ruin and bankruptcy, to meet claims, sued Lloyd's for having mismanaged their affairs and argued for various rescue packages to be put in place which would limit their losses and spread the losses more widely. Claims made on some Lloyd's policies were not met promptly while all these arguments raged. After several enquiries and court cases, a variety of rescue packages were put in place, and the market attempted to recover its position.

However, the events of recent years have undermined the confidence of potential names, many have withdrawn, and the underwriting capacity of the market has shrunk. The confidence of Lloyd's customers was also weakened. Lloyd's reputation for always meeting claims on its policies was damaged. At the same time, more insurance business was being done by large insurance companies, which, despite limited liability, had enormous capital assets with which to back underwriting activity, much greater than those of Lloyd's. Consequently the rationale for the long-established structure of the market—private individuals acting as names with unlimited liability—appears no longer valid, and Lloyd's is moving towards the use of corporate wealth and towards accepting limited liability.

For many kinds of insurance, such as fire insurance, adverse selection problems may not be too bad. The critical information (determining the likelihood of a fire) can easily be observed, for instance, by building inspectors. But for many of the kinds of risks against which individuals would like to buy insurance, adverse selection effects are important. With health or automobile insurance, for instance, an insurance firm is likely to find it difficult to determine any particular individual's risk. Even worse, consider the problem of measuring the risk that a firm's new product will fail to meet expectations. It would be nearly impossible for an insurance company to decide precisely what the prospects for the product are. The business firm itself is certainly more likely to be better informed than the insurance company about the markets in which it is trying to sell its product. Not surprisingly, then, because of their disadvantage in obtaining crucial information, insurance firms do not supply insurance against such business risks.

Moral Hazard   A second problem faced by insurance companies is an incentive problem: insurance affects people's incentives to avoid whatever contingencies they are insured against. A person who has no fire insurance on a house, for example, may choose to limit the risk of fire by buying smoke alarms and home fire extinguishers and being especially cautious. But if that same person had fire insurance, he might not be so careful. Indeed, if the insurance would pay more than the house's market value, he might even be tempted to burn his own house down to collect the insurance.

This general feature of insurance, that it reduces the individual's incentives to avoid the insured-against accident, is called **moral hazard.** Of course, from an economist's point of view, what is at issue is not a question of morality but only a question of incentives. If a person bears only a portion or none of the consequences of his actions—as he does when he has purchased insurance—his incentives are altered.

Moral hazard concerns may not be important for many kinds of insurance; an individual who buys a large life insurance policy and thus knows that her children will be well cared for in the event of her demise is hardly likely to take much bigger risks with her life. But for many kinds of risks against which a firm's managers would *like* to buy insurance, moral hazard concerns are important. For example, if a company could buy insurance to guarantee a minimum level of profit, managers would have less incentive to exert effort. When moral hazard problems are strong, insurance firms will offer limited—even no—insurance.

THE RISK-INCENTIVE TRADE-OFF

We have seen that insurance reduces incentives. The greater the insurance coverage, the more incentives are reduced. If my house is insured for only 50 percent of any loss, I have a strong incentive to make sure that there is no fire. If it is insured for 100 percent of any loss, I have little incentive to expend any resources to avoid a fire.

The resources of the National Health Service in Britain are always very tightly stretched. There are long queues for operations, and the care provided is not always to the standard that patients would like. Health service managers and doctors are obliged to make choices as to how to distribute the NHS's limited resources between treatment for different diseases and how to prioritise different kinds of patients for treatment. These choices are always controversial. Doctors and NHS managers would like to deny that there is any rationing, but it clearly exists. One issue that has come to the surface from time to time, always a source of controversy, is whether smokers should receive treatment with the same priority as nonsmokers or be given lower priority. The argument for giving smokers lower priority is based on the moral hazard effect of insurance.

If treatment is available for everyone, smoker or not, on the same basis, then there is no disincentive to smoking (arising from differential NHS treatment). The existence of free medical insurance through the NHS indeed then encourages smoking, because NHS treatment for smoking-induced illnesses, like cancers and heart and circulatory illnesses, reduces the cost of smoking to the smoker. The encouragement of smoking by the provision of national health insurance is an example of moral hazard. Private medical insurance would be very likely to charge higher premiums to smokers (to the extent that the amount of smoking could be identified by the insurers) because of the higher risk of illness among smokers. The NHS is not able to discriminate by differentiating the insurance premiums for different people. It is therefore sometimes argued that the NHS should compensate by giving less treatment—less speedy or perhaps simply refusing treatment—to smokers. There are two arguments, which tend to get mixed up. One is an incentive argument, which is that if the premiums cannot be adjusted for the different risks posed by different people, then the level of insurance should be adjusted. The other is a moral argument, that people who have to some extent inflicted illness on themselves by their choice of smoking have a weaker moral claim on the NHS than the deserving sick, who have fallen ill despite leading wholesome and virtuous lives.

The treatment of smokers is merely the tip of the iceberg. If smoking, then why not dangerous sports, lack of exercise, weight, substance abuse, and many other lifestyle choices that have implications for the individual's likely demands on the NHS? This clearly opens the most terrifying Pandora's box of moral tangles, suitable only for treatment by long discussions on off-peak quality radio programmes and clearly beyond the scope of this book. Nevertheless, the use of NHS resources and its implications for behaviour offer an interesting illustration of moral hazard.

There is thus a risk-incentive trade-off. The more the individual divests himself of risk, the weaker his incentives to avoid bad results and to foster good results. This principle applies in many contexts other than simple insurance markets. A store manager whose salary is guaranteed faces little risk but also has little incentive. If his pay depends on the store's sales, he has stronger incentives but faces greater risk. In spite of his best efforts, sales may be low, perhaps because of an economic downturn or perhaps because buyers have simply turned away from his products; in either case, his income will be low.

In many cases, the market reaches a compromise: partial insurance, providing the purchaser of insurance with some incentives but also making her bear some risk. With private medical insurance, for example, it is common for an insurance company to pay only some percentage (like 80 percent) of expenses (this is called coinsurance). In this case, an individual will have a financial motivation to be cautious in the use of medical care but still be largely protected.

Similarly, a firm that borrows money for a project is generally required to invest some of its own funds in the project or to supply the lender with collateral, that is, to provide the lender with an asset that the firm forfeits if it fails to repay the loan. Lenders know that with more of their own money at stake, borrowers will have better incentives to use the funds wisely.

ENTREPRENEURSHIP

Innovation gives life to a capitalist economy. It also demonstrates the vital roles played by time and risk. Consider for a moment the many new products and new processes of production that have so enriched (or at least altered) everyone's life in the last century: fast food, transistors, computers, aeroplanes, cars, televisions—the list is endless. Each of these innovations required more than just an idea. It needed people willing to follow the advice of David Lloyd George, a former prime minister of Great Britain, who said: "Don't be afraid to take a big step if one is indicated. You can't cross a chasm in two small jumps."

Innovations require people and businesses to take risks. Innovators need capital too, since those who have innovative ideas, like Henry Ford, often do not have the capital to carry them out. They must turn to others to supply them with resources, generally in exchange for part of any eventual return. After all, someone who lends to an innovator bears a risk, and he must receive compensation to be willing to undertake this risk.

In forming judgments about whether to pursue a possible innovation, innovators and investors form expectations about the future. But because they are dealing with new ideas, products, and processes, the expectations of reasonable men and women may differ. When the returns are in and the project has proved to be a success or a failure, it is often difficult to ascertain the reasons why, even with the wisdom of hindsight. Thus, those whose jobs require them to make decisions—the lending officers of banks, the managers of pension funds and other financial institutions, the leaders of corporations—face a difficult task. But lack of any simple formula does not mean that there are not better and worse ways of making these decisions. Forming expectations and evaluating risks are like playing football in a fog; you cannot always tell what is going on, but skilled players with good foresight still have an advantage.

Thus, **entrepreneurs**—the individuals responsible for creating new businesses, bringing new products to market, developing new processes of production—face all the problems we have discussed. All business decision making involves risk taking. But entrepreneurs who take responsibility for managing a new business generally face more risk than managers of established companies. Businesses often require additional financing for new projects, but new enterprises almost always require extensive outside financing. The problem of selection, of determining which of a set of potential investment projects and entrepreneurs ought to receive funds, is particularly acute, since because these projects are new, they have yet to establish a reputation. Lenders may be reluctant, for instance, to provide funds for fear of default.

Since entrepreneurs cannot buy insurance to cover most of the risks they face, they must be willing to bear the risks themselves. Entrepreneurs need a return to compensate them for their efforts and the risks they undertake. Similarly, those who provide these new enterprises with capital must receive a return greater than they might receive elsewhere, to compensate them for the additional risks they have to bear. There has been ongoing concern about the effect of a variety of public policies, especially tax policy, on these returns. Does the current tax system discourage entrepreneurship? Can policies be designed to encourage it? These questions will be addressed later in this book.

AN OVERVIEW OF FINANCIAL MARKETS

Our economic system is often referred to as capitalism, reflecting the importance that capital markets, or more generally, financial markets, play in our economy. The central role of these markets constitutes a fifth consensus point among economists.

5   Financial Markets

Financial markets are a central part of modern economies. They are essential for raising capital for new enterprises, expanding new businesses, and sharing risks.

REVIEW AND PRACTICE

SUMMARY

1 Much of economics is future oriented; this means that households and firms must form expectations about the future and cope with problems of risk and uncertainty.

2 The interest rate is a price. It equates the supply of funds by savers and the demand by borrowers. Savers receive interest for deferring consumption, and borrowers pay interest so that they can consume or invest now and pay later.

3 The fact that the market interest rate is positive means that a pound received today is worth more than a pound received in the future. This is the time value of money. The present discounted value of a pound in the future is the value in pounds today of receiving a pound in the future, given the prevailing rate of interest.

4 The real interest rate, which measures a person's actual increase in buying power when she saves money, is equal to the nominal interest rate (the amount paid in pounds) minus the inflation rate.

5 What investors are willing to pay today for an asset depends largely on what they believe they can sell it for in the future. Changes in expectations can thus shift the demand curve for an asset and change current prices.

6 Most people are risk averse. They respond to risks by trying to avoid them and mitigate their impacts, by keeping options open, by diversifying, and by transferring risks to and sharing risks with others.

7 Among the most important institutions for absorbing risks are insurance firms. Insurance firms face two problems. One is that people who buy insurance tend to be those most at risk, and charging higher prices for insurance will discourage those less at risk from buying insurance at all. This effect is called adverse selection. The second problem is that insurance reduces the incentives individuals have to avoid whatever they are insured against. This is called moral hazard.

8 Entrepreneurial innovation plays a cental role in modern economies.

KEY TERMS

interest	real rate of interest	adaptive	moral hazard
principal	nominal rate of interest	risk averse	entrepreneurs
present discounted value	assets	adverse selection	
intertemporal trades	myopic		

REVIEW QUESTIONS

1 Who is on the demand side and who is on the supply side in the market for loanable funds? What is the price in that market?

2 Which would you prefer to receive: £100 one year from now or £100 five years from now? Why? Would your answer change if the rate of inflation were zero?

3 What is the relationship between the nominal interest rate and the real interest rate?

4 True or false: "Demand curves depend on what people want now, not on their expectations about the future." Explain your answer.

5 What is mean by *risk averse?* What are some consequences of the fact that most people are risk averse?

6 Why do people pay insurance premiums if they hope and expect that nothing bad is going to happen to them?

7 Would you expect a borrower's rate of interest to be higher if the borrower were a large automobile company or a small restaurant owner? Why?

8 Why is there a trade-off between risk and incentives? Give an example of this trade-off.

PROBLEMS

1 Imagine that £1,000 is deposited in an account for five years; the account pays 10 percent interest per year, compounded annually. At the end of the first year, the account is credited with £100 interest, and then starts earning interest on the interest, and similarly at the end of each successive year. How much money will be in the account after five years? What if the rate of interest is 12 percent? What if the annual rate of interest is 12 percent but the interest is compounded monthly?

2 Suppose you want to buy a car three years from now and you know that the price of a car at that time will be £10,000. If the interest rate is 7 percent per year, how much will you have to set aside today to have the money ready when you need it? If the interest rate is 5 percent, how much will you have to set aside today?

3 Suppose a government has passed laws that put a ceiling on the rate of interest that can be charged; these laws are called usury laws. Using a supply-and-demand diagram, show the effect of interest rate ceilings on the quantity (supply) of lending. Who is better off as a result of such laws? Who is worse off?

4 Imagine that you win the lottery but find that your £10 million prize is paid out in five chunks: a £2 million payment right away, and then £2 million every five years until you have received the total. Calculate the present discounted value of your winnings if the annual interest rate is 10 percent. What would it be if the annual interest rate were 15 percent? How does a higher annual interest rate affect the present discounted value?

5 A motor insurance company offers policies some of which have a zero excess and some of which have a £100 excess. (The excess is the part of the claim that the insured person pays, not the insurance company.) Drivers who choose the policy with the zero excess turn out to make more frequent claims than the ones who choose policies with the £100 excess. Why might this happen? What is the name for it?

6 You hire someone to paint your house. Since it is a large job, you agree to pay him by the hour. What moral hazard problem must you consider? Explain the trade-off between risk and incentive in this situation.

APPENDIX: CALCULATING PRESENT DISCOUNTED VALUE

In the text, we described how to calculate the present discounted value (PDV) of a dollar received a year from now. The present discounted value of a dollar received two years from now can be calculated in a similar way. But how much *today* is equivalent to, say, £100 two years from now? If I were given £PDV today, and I put it in the bank, at the end of the year, I would have £PDV$(1 + r)$. If I left it in the bank for another year, in the second year I would earn interest on the total amount in the bank at the end of the first year, $r \times$ £PDV$(1 + r)$. Therefore, the total interest I would earn over the two-year period is

$$\begin{aligned} \text{PDV}(1 + r) + [r \times \text{PDV}(1 + r)] \\ = \text{PDV}(1 + r)(1 + r) \\ = \text{PDV}(1 + r)^2. \end{aligned}$$

In performing these calculations, we have taken account of the interest on the interest. This is called **compound interest.**

(By contrast, **simple interest** does not take into account the interest you earn on interest you have previously earned.) If the rate of interest is 10 percent and is compounded annually, £100 today is worth £110 a year from now and £121 (*not* £120) in two years' time. Thus, the present discounted value today of £121 two years from now is £100. Table 6.1 shows how to calculate the present discounted value of £100 received next year, two years from now, and three years from now.

We can now see how to calculate the value of an investment project that will yield a return over several years. We look at what the returns will be each year, adjust them to their present discounted values, and then add these values up. Table 6.2 shows how this is done for a project which yields £10,000 next year and £15,000 the year after and which you plan to sell in the third year for £50,000. The second column of the table shows the return in each year. The third column shows the discount factor—what we multiply the return by to obtain the present discounted value of that year's return. The calculations assume an annual interest rate of 10 percent. The fourth column multiplies the return by the discount factor to obtain the present discounted value of that year's return. In the bottom row of the table, the present discounted values of each year's return have been added up to obtain the total present discounted value of the project. Notice that it is much smaller than the number we obtain simply by adding up the returns, which is the undiscounted yield of the project.

Table 6.1 PRESENT DISCOUNTED VALUE OF £100

Year Received	Present Discounted Value
Next year	$\dfrac{1}{1 + r} \times 100 = \dfrac{100}{1 + r}$
Two years from now	$\dfrac{1}{1 + r} \times \dfrac{100}{1 + r} = \dfrac{100}{(1 + r)^2}$
Three years from now	$\dfrac{1}{1 + r} \times \dfrac{100}{(1+r)^2} = \dfrac{100}{(1 + r)^3}$

Table 6.2 CALCULATING PRESENT DISCOUNTED VALUE OF A THREE-YEAR PROJECT

Year	Return	Discount Factor ($r = 0.10$)	Present Discounted Value ($r = 0.10$)
1	£10,000	$\dfrac{1}{1.10}$	£ 9,091
2	£15,000	$\dfrac{1}{(1.10)^2} = \dfrac{1}{1.21}$	£12,397
3	£50,000	$\dfrac{1}{(1.10)^3} = \dfrac{1}{1.331}$	£37,566
Total	£75,000	—	£59,054

CHAPTER 7

THE PUBLIC SECTOR

In earlier chapters, we saw how the profit system provides firms with the incentive to produce the goods consumers want. Prices give firms the incentive to economize on scarce resources. Prices also coordinate economic activity and signal changes in economic conditions. Private property provides incentives for individuals to invest in and to maintain buildings, machines, land, cars, and other possessions. Chapter 3 examined the incentives individuals and countries have to engage in mutually advantageous trades and to specialise in areas of comparative advantage. Chapters 4 and 5 showed how, in free markets, prices are determined by the interaction of demand and supply.

We have thus seen how the private market answers the four basic questions set out in Chapter 1: *What is produced and in what quantities* is determined by the interaction of demand and supply, reflecting both the goods consumers want and what it costs firms to produce those goods. *How it is produced* is determined by competition among firms, which produce the goods in the least expensive way possible in order to stay in business. *For whom* it is produced is determined by the incomes of individuals in the economy. Those with high incomes get more of the economy's goods and services, and those with low incomes get less. These incomes, in turn, are established by the demand and supply for labour, which determine what workers are paid, and the demand and supply for capital, which determine the return people get on their savings. Who makes the decisions? Everyone. Which goods are produced depends on

KEY QUESTIONS

1 What distinguishes the private from the public sector?

2 What explains the economic roles the government has undertaken?

3 What are externalities and public goods, and why do they imply that markets may not work well?

4 What are the various ways the government can affect the economy and attempt to achieve its economic objectives?

5 How has the role of government changed in recent decades? And how does the role of government vary from one industrial country to another?

6 What are some of the current controversies concerning the roles of government? Why do failures of the market system not necessarily imply that government action is desirable?

millions of decisions made in households and firms throughout the economy. Moreover, firms, competing against one another, have incentives to choose as managers those most able to make the hard decisions—whether to enter some new market or to develop some new product—that every firm must face if it is to survive.

Economists recognise that the government must set and enforce the basic laws of society and provide a framework within which firms can compete fairly against one another. Beyond this, however, economists' understanding of the market's ability to answer the basic economic questions leads them to look hard at any additional function the government serves: why are private markets not serving that function? This chapter will explore the roles the government has undertaken, and how and why it carries out those roles.

THE CHANGING ROLE OF GOVERNMENT

The question of the appropriate balance between the public and private sectors is subject to constant debate, with different countries' giving different answers. In Switzerland, the public sector is small and government economic activities are severely limited. In the former Soviet Union and China, the govern-

ment tried to control, or **nationalise,** virtually all aspects of economic activity, though the difficulty of doing this created increasing pressures for change. Between these extremes lies a wide spectrum: free market economies like Hong Kong, where businesses do not face most of the regulations facing businesses in western Europe and the United States; welfare state economies like Sweden, where the government takes major responsibilities for health care, child care, and a host of other social services but where there is also a large private sector; and a number of European economies, like Great Britain, where the government has until recently dominated major industries like steel, coal, railroads, airlines, and public utilities. The United States is nearer the free market end of this spectrum than most countries with industrialised, developed economies.

Government has almost always been responsible for certain activities that the vast majority of citizens believe are fundamentally public functions—the justice system, police protection, and national defence, for example. But government's role in other areas has changed over time, usually in response to perceived failures of the market economy. The economic role of the state in Britain widened greatly after the end of the Second World War with the establishment of the welfare state and the wave of nationalizations which took large chunks of industry into public ownership. In the late 1940s National Insurance and National Assistance were greatly extended. The National Health Service was established. The railways, the coal industry, and the steel industry were among the important industries (referred to at the time as the "commanding heights" of the economy) that were nationalised. Since then the public provision of education—nursery schools, postcompulsory secondary education, and further and higher education—have all expanded enormously.

The postwar period saw British governments in common with many in Europe and North America assume a responsibility to maintain full employment, remembering the terrible years of depression in the 1920s and 1930s and following the publication of J. M. Keynes's *The General Theory of Employment, Interest and Money* (1936).

The tendency for the role of the state to grow was resisted firmly in the 1980s, in both Britain and the United States. It was argued that the state had grown too big, taxes had become too high, red tape had become too great a constraint on business, incentives to create wealth had become too weak, and the welfare state had created a "dependency culture." Attempts were made to **deregulate** many aspects of life. Notably, the City in London was deregulated in the Big Bang of September 1986. **Privatization** became all the rage. The British government attempted to sell off most of the industries it had acquired and to privatise such things as the prisons and the post office. Sustained attempts to cut tax rates eventually led to pressure on public funds for education, health services, defence, and the social security budget.

The British experience of government retreat has been shared elsewhere. Even in Sweden, tax rates have been cut and welfare benefits trimmed in the 1990s.

THE PICTURE IN STATISTICS

While there has been growth in government expenditure in Britain, as measured by the share of government expenditure in the GDP, over the last century, most of the growth took place in the first half of the century. In 1986, general government (central and local) expenditure was 43 percent of the GDP. (Central government expenditure, including the cost of payments from central to local government, was 38 percent of GDP, and local government spending was 11.8 percent.) In 1996, general government spending was 42 percent of GDP, of which 10.8 percent was local government spending. The Thatcher and Major governments made strenuous efforts to reduce the share of government expenditure in GDP but met with only limited success. Figure 7.1 shows the path of expenditure over recent years.

Figure 7.1 **THE SHARE OF GOVERNMENT EXPENDITURE IN U.K. GDP**

The total has remained fairly constant, falling from 43.2 percent in 1986 to 38.5 percent in 1989. Since then it rose back up to 43.9 percent in 1993 and then began falling slowly. *Source: U.K. National Income and Product Accounts.*

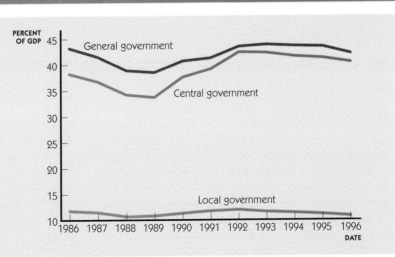

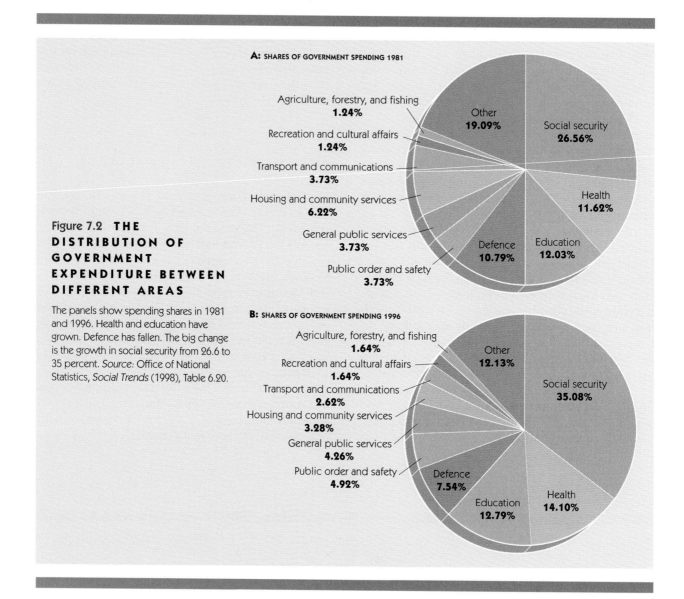

A: SHARES OF GOVERNMENT SPENDING 1981

Agriculture, forestry, and fishing
1.24%

Recreation and cultural affairs
1.24%

Transport and communications
3.73%

Housing and community services
6.22%

General public services
3.73%

Public order and safety
3.73%

Other
19.09%

Social security
26.56%

Health
11.62%

Defence
10.79%

Education
12.03%

B: SHARES OF GOVERNMENT SPENDING 1996

Agriculture, forestry, and fishing
1.64%

Recreation and cultural affairs
1.64%

Transport and communications
2.62%

Housing and community services
3.28%

General public services
4.26%

Public order and safety
4.92%

Other
12.13%

Social security
35.08%

Defence
7.54%

Education
12.79%

Health
14.10%

Figure 7.2 THE DISTRIBUTION OF GOVERNMENT EXPENDITURE BETWEEN DIFFERENT AREAS

The panels show spending shares in 1981 and 1996. Health and education have grown. Defence has fallen. The big change is the growth in social security from 26.6 to 35 percent. *Source:* Office of National Statistics, *Social Trends* (1998), Table 6.20.

While the total expenditure has changed relatively little as a percentage of GDP, the pattern of expenditure between government departments has changed, as Figure 7.2 shows. There has been a conspicuous rise in the share of expenditure devoted to social security, which was as low as 14.7 percent in 1960, from 26.6 percent in 1981 to 35.1 percent in 1996. The growth of social security spending (in Britain fueled by growing unemployment, families living in poverty, pensioners, and so on) has become a major problem for governments throughout the developed world. The share of expenditure devoted to defence has fallen from 17.1 percent in 1960 to 10.8 percent in 1981 to 7.5 percent in 1996, as Britain's military role in the world has shrunk. The share of spending on education has risen modestly from 9.8 percent in 1960 to

12 percent in 1981 to 12.7 percent in 1996, while health spending has also risen, from 9.2 percent in 1960 to 11.6 percent in 1981 to 14.1 percent in 1996.

CENTRAL AND LOCAL GOVERNMENT

Within government, in most countries, there are several different bodies responsible for making decisions on taxes, expenditure, and regulations. There are typically several different levels of government. In Britain, for example, there is a *central government* consisting of the parliament at Westminster, ministers and departments responsible for running the government, and various government agencies. There are also *local governments* which consist of either one layer, in the metropolitan districts or in the unitary authorities, or two layers in the rest of the country, where there is typically a county council and beneath it a district council. In principle, central government has responsibility for issues that affect the nation as a whole, such as setting taxes on incomes and expenditure, national defence, health care, and the system of justice. Local governments have responsibility for matters that affect the local community. City councils and district councils have been responsible for things like refuse collection, local public transport, and local roads. County councils have in principle had responsibility for issues that affect a whole region, not just a single town. They have taken over education, public libraries, and local roads and regional public transport.

Local governments are able to set some local taxes. In Britain these have until recently taken the form of property taxes—the "rates." But in the 1980s several changes were made to local government finance. First, the rates were abolished and replaced by the "community charge" (poll tax), which was more or less a lump-sum tax on persons, not a property tax; and this was replaced in 1991 by the Council Tax, which was in effect a property tax. The freedom of local governments to make independent decisions and their responsibilities have been changed frequently by central government in Britain. The Thatcher government in particular centralised government, taking functions away from local govern-

ments and reducing their freedom to set local taxes and spending.

The United States has a stable system of federal government, in which the national government—the federal government—state governments, and local governments have clearly defined responsibilities and powers to raise taxes. Germany is also a decentralised federal republic. The constituent states—the Länder—have considerable fiscal independence. France, by contrast, has a tightly centralised system of government.

WHAT DISTINGUISHES THE PRIVATE AND PUBLIC SECTORS?

In a democracy, two important features distinguish private from public institutions. First, the people responsible for running public institutions are elected or appointed by someone who is elected. The legitimacy of the person holding the position is derived directly or indirectly from the electoral process. Second, any government has certain rights of compulsion. For instance, the government has the right to force its citizens to pay taxes; if they fail to do so, it can confiscate their property and even imprison them. The government has the right to force its young people to serve in the armed forces at wages below those that would induce them to volunteer. The government also has the right to take private property for public use, provided it compensates the owner.

Its ability to use compulsion means that the government can do things private insitutions cannot do. Once a decision has been made to build a public road, for instance, the government can make sure that everyone helps to pay for it. Sometimes governments create rules to bind their own hands, so that they cannot do *anything* they wish. For instance, the government has established elaborate hiring procedures for government organizations that private firms generally do not find worthwhile. The owner of a private firm can decide whom she wants to hire; if she hires someone incompetent, she and her firm suffer. If the manager of a public enterprise hires someone incompetent, however, the public pays. The government's strict hiring procedures help avoid bad hiring, but they may also result in rigidities that make it difficult for government enterprises to compete against private firms for the most talented individuals.

These and other constraints imposed on the public sector—as well as the absence of the profit motive which provides the private sector with strong incentives to be efficient, reduce costs, and produce what consumers want—put the public sector at a general disadvantage relative to the private sector in markets that work well. It is the job of economists, concerned with the most efficient solutions to economic problems to ask: When do markets work well? When do they fail? And, when they fail, when might government improve matters?

ADAM SMITH'S "INVISIBLE HAND" AND THE CENTRAL ROLE OF MARKETS

Arguments in favour of private markets can be traced back to Adam Smith's 1776 masterpiece, *The Wealth of Nations*. Smith argued that workers and producers, interested only in helping themselves and their families, were the root of economic production. The public interest would best be promoted by individuals pursuing their own self-interest. As Smith put it:

Man has almost constant occasion for the help of his brethren, and it is in vain for him to expect it from their benevolence only. He will be more likely to prevail if he can interest their self-love in his favor, and show them that it is for their own advantage to do for him what he requires of them. . . . It is not from the benevolence of the butcher, the brewer, or the baker, that we expect our dinner, but from their regard to their own interest. We never talk to them of our own necessities but of their advantages.[1]

Smith's insight was that individuals work hardest to help the overall economic production of society when their efforts help themselves. He argued that an "obvious and simple system of liberty" provided

the greatest opportunities for people to help themselves and thus, by extension, to create the greatest wealth for a society.

Smith used the metaphor of the **invisible hand** to describe how self-interest led to social good: "He intends only his own gain, and he is in this as in many other cases led by an invisible hand to promote an end which was no part of his intention. . . . By pursuing his own interest he frequently promotes that of the society more effectually than when he really intends to promote it."

Economics has progressed since Adam Smith, but his fundamental argument still has great appeal. A greater liberty for individuals in country after country has indeed led to huge increases in production that have benefited if not everyone, almost everyone. Nevertheless, it is not difficult to find discontent with the market. There is concern that markets produce too much of some things, like air and water pollution, and too little of other things, such as support for the arts or child care facilities. Generally, concerns with market outcomes can be placed into three broad categories: those that are based on ignorance of the laws of economics, those having to do with the redistribution of income, and those having to do with genuine failures of private markets.

GOVERNMENT AND IGNORANCE OF ECONOMICS

"Wouldn't the world be a better place if we still lived in the Garden of Eden?" epitomises complaints about markets that ignore the laws of economics. Things have a price because they are scarce. If the price of oil is high, it is because oil is scarce and the high price reflects that scarcity. In Chapter 4, we saw that economists regard such situations not as market failures but as the hard facts of economic life. Much as everyone would like to live in a world where all individuals could have almost everything they wanted at a price they could afford, this is simply unrealistic. Those calling on government to "solve" the problem of scarcity by passing laws about prices simply shift the problem. They reduce prices for some and cause shortages for everyone else.

[1] Book 1, Chapter 2.

CLOSE-UP: ADAM SMITH—FOUNDER OF MODERN ECONOMICS

Adam Smith, the founder of modern economics, was a professor of moral philosophy at the University of Glasgow, in the latter part of the eighteenth century. His great masterpiece, *The Wealth of Nations,* was published in 1776, the year the United States signed the Declaration of Independence. The American Revolution coincided with two other revolutions. The industrial revolution marked the transformation of the economy both from agriculture to industry and from rural to urban life. A revolution in ideas and ideology began to question the earlier view that social institutions had been accepted as a matter of course, as part of a God-given order. Intellectuals began to inquire into the functions of social institutions (schools, churches, government) and to consider changes that could make society better off. This thinking is strongly reflected in the Federalist papers that form the background of the U.S. Constitution, and in the French Revolution at the turn of the nineteenth century.

No precise date or place marks the beginning of

either the industrial or the ideological revolution. Glasgow was at the center of both, and this was perhaps no accident: both revolutions fed upon each other. The key idea in Adam Smith's economics was that individuals, in pursuing their self-interest, could more assuredly attain the common interest than if it were pursued by government (at that time, a monarch). This view contrasted with the earlier *mercantilist* view, which held that government should actively pursue the commercial interests of the country, particularly by promoting exports. Because of his emphasis on markets, Adam Smith is often held up as a champion of very limited government. A closer look at his *The Wealth of Nations* shows a far more balanced view. Though he did not use the modern market failures vocabulary, he recognised many limitations of markets, and he saw government as performing an important role, such as supporting education. He also recognised the tendencies for firms to try to reduce or suppress competition, as well as the adverse consequences of lack of competition.

GOVERNMENT AND REDISTRIBUTION

A second category of complaints against the market represents a dissatisfaction with the distribution of income. Market economies may be productive and efficient at producing wealth, but they may also cause some people to get very rich and others to starve. Someone who has a rare and valuable skill will, by the laws of supply and demand, receive a high income. Someone else who has few skills, and common ones at that, will find his wage low—perhaps even too low for survival. This situation de-

scribes an economy with a very unequal distribution of income.

Most economists see an important role for the government in income redistribution, taking income from those who have more and giving it to those who have less. in their view, society need not accept whatever distribution of income results from the workings of private markets. Income and inheritance taxes on the rich and welfare programmes for the poor are part of the government's role in redistribution.

Concern for greater economic equality is a generally accepted role for government, but there is still much disagreement about the benefits and costs of programmes aimed at reducing inequality. And even if government reaches agreement on the degree to which income inequality should be reduced, economists will disagree as to what is the best method because income redistribution affects incentive.

Questions of redistribution are often posed as, How should the economy's pie be divided? What size slice should each person get? Often redistribution is viewed as simply cutting the pie differently, giving the poor somewhat larger slices and the rich somewhat smaller. But if the process of redistributing income weakens economic incentives and makes the economy less productive, the size of the whole pie may shrink. Then the poor get a larger share of a smaller pie. The rich are much worse off now; they get a smaller share of a smaller pie. If the size of the pie has shrunk enough, even the poor may be worse off. By designing government redistribution programmes appropriately, it may be possible to limit the size of these effects on productivity.

GOVERNMENT AND MARKET FAILURES

The final category of discontent with private markets consists of cases where the market does indeed fail in its role of producing economic efficiency. Economists refer to these problems as **market failures** and have studied them closely. When there is a market

failure, government may be able to correct the market failure and enhance the economy's efficiency.

STABILIZATION OF THE ECONOMY

The most dramatic examples of market failure are the periodic episodes of high unemployment that have plagued capitalist economies. It is hard to tout the virtues of an efficient market when a third of the industrial labour force and capital stock sits idle, as it did in the Great Depression of the 1930s. Although many economists believe there are forces that eventually restore the economy to full employment, the costs of waiting for the economy to correct itself—in terms of both forgone output and human misery—are enormous, and virtually all governments today take it as their responsibility to *try* to avoid extreme fluctuations in economic activity—both the downturns (when much of the economy's resources, its workers and machines, remain idle) and the booms (which may result in high inflation). The causes of these fluctuations, and how and whether the government can succeed in significantly reducing them are topics in macroeconomics, to which Parts Four to Six of this book are devoted.

When the economy's scarce resources are idle, the economy is operating below its production possibilities curve, as shown in Figure 7.3. As usual, the curve has been simplified to two goods, guns and

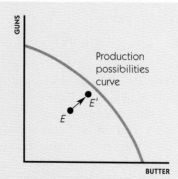

Figure 7.3 **AN ECONOMY OPERATING BELOW FULL POTENTIAL**

The economy is at point E, below the edge of its production possibilities curve. The government seeks to have it operate closer to the curve, at point E' for instance.

butter, which represent the general output levels in the public and private sectors. The government attempts to move the economy from point E to a point E' closer to the production possibilities curve.

Even when the economy is at full employment, resources will not be efficiently allocated if (1) competition is limited, (2) there are externalities, (3) public goods are involved, (4) markets are missing, or (5) information is limited.

LACK OF COMPETITION

Competition is essential for a market to function efficiently. Competition is what forces firms to look for more efficient ways of producing goods and to meet the desires of consumers more effectively. Without competition, prices will be higher and production lower than with competition. But life for the firms themselves is easier without competition, and profits are higher. Thus, firms try to reduce the extent of competition. Governments have passed numerous laws, called monopoly and merger and fair trading laws, attempting to enhance competition in the market economy.

EXTERNALITIES

But even when there is competition, the market may supply too much of some goods and too little of others. One of the reasons for this is the presence of **externalities.** Externalities are present whenever an individual or firm can take an action that directly affects others but for which it neither pays nor is paid compensation. It therefore does not bear all the consequences of its action. (The effect of the action is "external" to the individual or firm.) Externalities are pervasive. A hiker who leaves litter, a driver whose car emits pollution, a child who leaves a mess behind after he finishes playing, a person who smokes a cigarette in a crowded room—all create externalities. In each case, the actor is not the only one who must suffer the consequences of his action; others suffer them too. Externalities can be thought of as instances when the price system works imperfectly. The hiker is not charged for the litter she creates, nor does the car owner pay for the pollution it makes.

The examples so far are negative externalities. A common example of a negative externality is a factory that emits air pollution. The factory benefits from emitting the pollution, since by doing so, it can make its product more cheaply than if it put in pollution-control devices. Society as a whole bears the negative external costs of pollution. If the factory had to pay for its pollution, it would find ways to produce less of it. And indeed, government environmental regulations are often aimed at just that goal.

Externalities can also be positive. A common example of a positive externality is a new invention. When someone makes a new discovery that leads to greater economic productivity, other people (or companies) benefit. The inventor receives, through the prices he charges, only a fraction of the total gains to society from the invention. Other firms will copy it and learn from it. Inventions like the laser and the transistor have benefited consumers, both by providing new products and allowing other products to be made less expensively. While the individual researcher bears the costs of making a discovery, society receives positive external benefits. If everyone who benefited from an invention had to pay money to the inventor, there would be far higher incentives for research and development. And indeed, patents and other government laws enable the inventors to get a larger return than they otherwise would.

When externalities are present, the market's allocation of goods will be inefficient. When the production of a good such as steel entails a negative externality—like smoke and its effect on the air—the market level of production is too high. This is because the producer fails to take into account the social costs in deciding how much to produce. To put it another way, the price of steel determined in competitive markets by the law of supply and demand only reflects *private costs*, the costs actually faced by firms. If firms do not have to pay *all* of the costs (including the costs of pollution), equilibrium prices will be lower and output higher than they would be if firms took social costs into account.

The government can offset this effect in several ways. For instance, it might impose a tax. Panel A of Figure 7.4 shows the demand and supply curves for steel and depicts the market equilibrium Q_0 at the intersection of the two curves. If the government imposes a tax on the production of steel, the supply

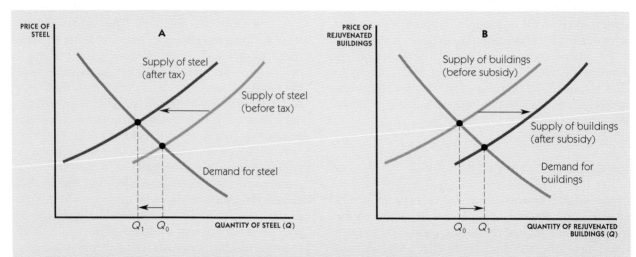

Figure 7.4 SUPPLY, DEMAND, AND EXTERNALITIES

The steel industry produces a negative externality of pollution. In panel A, a tax on steel production shifts the supply curve to the left, reducing both steel production and pollution. In panel B, a subsidy for rejuvenated buildings, which create the positive externality of neighbourhood beautification, shifts the supply curve to the right, causing more buildings and neighbourhoods to be renovated.

curve will shift to the left—the quantity produced at each price will be lower—and the equilibrium level of production Q_1 will be less.

When the production of a good involves positive externalities, the market level of production is too low, and the government can try to enlarge the supply. The rejuvenation of an apartment building in a decaying part of a city is an example of a positive externality; it will probably enhance the value of buildings around it. Panel B of Figure 7.4 shows the demand and supply curves for rejuvenated buildings. A government subsidy to rejuvenation shifts the supply curve to the right, increasing the number of rejuvenated buildings from Q_0 to Q_1.

PUBLIC GOODS

A particular category of goods, called **public goods,** is an extreme case of positive externalities. Public goods are goods which cost nothing extra for an additional individual to enjoy (their consumption is **nonrivalrous**) and which it costs a great deal to ex-clude any individual from enjoying (they are **nonexcludable**). The standard example of a public good is defence. Once the country is protected from attack, it costs nothing extra to protect each new baby from foreign invasion. Furthermore, it would be virtually impossible to exclude a newborn from the benefits of this protection.

Public parks along the sides of a road are another example. Anyone driving along the road enjoys the view. The fact that one person is enjoying the view does not exclude others from enjoying it; and it would in fact be expensive to stop anyone who is driving along the road from benefiting from the view. A lighthouse to guide ships around dangerous shoals or rocks is still another example of a public good. No additional costs are incurred as an additional ship navigates near the lighthouse, and it would be difficult to shut off the light in the lighthouse at just the right time to prevent a ship passing by from taking advantage of the lighthouse.

A **pure public good** is one for which the marginal cost of providing it to an additional person is strictly zero and which it is impossible to exclude

The externalities created by driving and smoking are becoming increasingly apparent, and governments use them as arguments for raising taxes, to discourage activities that create negative externalities. From the economic point of view, this makes good sense. When people drive around in cars, they ignore the costs they impose on others—the costs of causing accidents, creating congestion on the roads, and polluting the atmosphere. The taxes on cars (the road fund licence) and fuel compensate to some extent for these costs and reduce the overconsumption of car use. The British government has had the policy of increasing the duty on petrol each year by more than the rate of inflation. With petrol at 70 pence a litre, an extra 5 pence in duty on a litre of petrol would put up the price to 75 pence, a 7 percent increase. If the elasticity of demand for petrol were 0.5, this would reduce demand by 3.5 percent. If the policy is applied for a number of years, it might eventually induce a substantial fall in driving.

Leaded petrol is a worse polluter than unleaded, and the duty on leaded is higher, so that it cost roughly 6 pence a litre more than unleaded in 1998. Over a period of ten years or so, up to 1998, in which this tax and price difference opened up, the demand for leaded petrol

fell substantially. The elasticity of demand for leaded as opposed to unleaded petrol is much greater than the elasticity of demand for petrol in general, and a small price difference has created a big switch in demand. in this instance, incentives created by taxation have had a major effect.

It is often argued (usually by the motoring organizations) that motorists pay too much tax already, because the revenue from taxes on cars, car use, petrol, and so on, more than pays for the roads that are built and maintained. But paying for the costs is not the appropriate criterion for efficient taxes. The taxes should impose on the motorist an extra cost at the margin (that is, for the extra mile driven) that equals the cost of the extra externalities that it causes. If the marginal congestion cost is high, then the taxes should be high too.

It is also argued that the taxes generated by motoring should be earmarked for spending on public transport. A policy like this may buy political support for high taxes on cars and car use, but it makes no economic sense. Subsidies and spending on public transport should be determined by the size of the benefits they bring, which will only accidentally equal the revenue raised from taxes on cars.

people from receiving. Many public goods that government provides are not *pure* public goods in this sense. It is possible, though relatively expensive, to exclude people from (or charge people for) using an uncrowded motorway; the cost of an additional person using an uncrowded motorway is very, very small but not zero.

Figure 7.5 compares examples of publicly provided goods against the strict definition of a pure public good. It shows the ease of exclusion along the horizontal axis and the (marginal) cost of an additional individual using the good along the vertical axis. The lower left-hand corner represents a pure public good. Of the major public expenditures, only national defence is close to a pure public good. Completely uncongested motorways, to the extent they exist, are another example. The upper right-hand corner represents a pure private good (health ser-

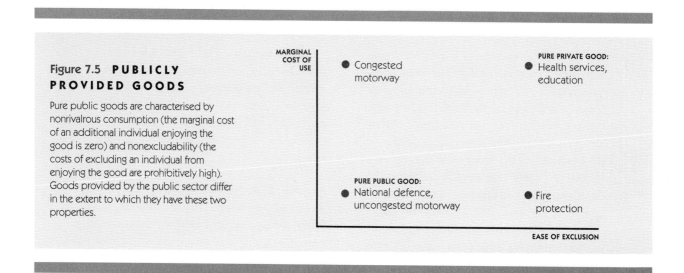

Figure 7.5 PUBLICLY PROVIDED GOODS

Pure public goods are characterised by nonrivalrous consumption (the marginal cost of an additional individual enjoying the good is zero) and nonexcludability (the costs of excluding an individual from enjoying the good are prohibitively high). Goods provided by the public sector differ in the extent to which they have these two properties.

vices or education), for which the cost of exclusion is low and the marginal cost of an additional individual using the good is high.

Many goods are not pure public goods but have one or the other property to some degree. Fire protection is like a private good in that exclusion is relatively easy; individuals who refuse to contribute to the fire brigade can simply not be helped in the event of a fire. But fire protection is like a public good in that the marginal cost of covering an additional person is low. Most of the time, firefighters are not engaged in fighting fires but are waiting for calls. Protecting an additional individual has little extra cost. Only in that rare event when two fires break out simultaneously will there be a significant cost to extending fire protection to an additional person.

Sometimes the marginal cost of using a good to which access is easy (a good that possesses the property of nonexcludability) will be high. When an uncongested motorway becomes congested, the costs of using it rise dramatically, not in terms of wear and tear on the road but in terms of the time lost by drivers using the road. In the past it has been costly to exclude by charging for road use; as a practical matter, this has only been done on toll roads, and, ironically, the toll booths often contributed to the congestion. (In future, electronic systems may enable cheap monitoring and charging for road use.)

Many of the goods that are publicly provided, such as education and health services, have high costs associated with providing the service to additional individuals. For most of these goods, exclusion is also relatively easy. In fact, many of these goods and services are provided privately or both publicly and privately in some countries. Though they are publicly provided in this country, they are not *pure* public goods, in the technical sense in which the term is defined.

Private markets undersupply public goods. If a single shipowner used the port near which a lighthouse is constructed, he could weigh the costs and benefits of the lighthouse. But if there were one large shipowner and many smaller owners, it would not pay any one of the small owners to build the lighthouse; and the large shipowner, in deciding whether to construct the lighthouse, would only take into account the benefits he would receive, not the benefits to the small shipowners. If the costs of construction exceeded the benefits that he alone would receive, he would not build the lighthouse. But if the benefits accruing to *all* the shipowners, large and small, were taken into account, those benefits would exceed the costs; it would then be desirable to build the lighthouse.

One can imagine a voluntary association of shipowners getting together to construct a lighthouse in this situation. But what happens if some small shipowner refuses to contribute, thinking that even if he does not contribute, the lighthouse will be built anyway? This is the **free-rider** aspect of public goods; because it is difficult to preclude anyone from using them, those who benefit from the goods have an incentive to avoid paying for them. Every shipowner has an incentive to "free ride" on the efforts of others. When too many decide to do this, the lighthouse will not be built.

Governments bring an important advantage to bear on the problem of public goods. They have the power to coerce citizens to pay for them. There might be *some* level of purchase of public goods—lighthouses, parks, even police or fire services—in the absence of government intervention. But society would be better off if the level of production were increased and citizens were forced to pay for the increased level of public services through taxes.

MISSING MARKETS

Market economies only work well when there are, in fact, markets or good substitutes for markets. Before government provided unemployment insurance, disability insurance, and social security, individuals could not purchase these forms of insurance in the market.[2] In many areas, flood insurance, crop insurance, or even theft insurance is not available. These

are all examples of important **missing markets.** In later chapters, we will consider the reasons for these missing markets. For now, we simply note that the absence of these markets has served as an impetus for government programs to fill the gaps.

INFORMATION AND KNOWLEDGE

The efficiency with which it handles information is one of the great strengths of the market economy. Producers do not have to know what each consumer likes; and consumers do not have to know the details of production of any of the products that they consume. Prices convey information about scarcity. Working through the law of supply and demand, prices convey information from consumers to producers about how consumers value different goods, and from producers to consumers about the resources required (at the margin) to produce different goods.

But some kinds of information, like information about the weather, are public goods: the marginal cost of an additional individual's benefiting from the information is negligible, and the cost of excluding individuals from the information may be considerable. This kind of information can also be important for efficient functioning of the economy, but markets do not produce efficient amounts of it. Thus, weather information has been supplied in Britain by a publicly funded body, the Meteorological Office. (Despite the public good character of the information it produces, the British government has been attempting to privatise it.)

---

[2] Even in those limited instances in which insurance was available, the price was much higher than could be simply justified by the risks.

Earlier, we saw how innovations typically give rise to externalities. Research can be thought of as the process of acquiring information, and innovation as the process of translating ideas, information, into new products. Later, we will discuss the array of government actions and programmes that are trying to ensure not only that the level of resources allocated to knowledge acquisition is appropriate but that it is directed in the right way.

BEYOND MARKET FAILURES

Markets, when they work well and do not suffer from one of the market failures just described, ensure that the economy is efficient—that resources are not wasted and that the economy operates on its production possibilities curve.

But efficiency is not everything. Even when a market is efficient, it may result in a distribution of income in which some individuals have hardly enough to live on, while others live in opulence.

Government actions are, of course, not limited to issues of economics. Governments try, for instance, to discourage robbery, rape, and murder. By and large, however, so long as an individual's action does not directly affect another, individuals are left to do what they please. I may think it strange that someone prefers vanilla to chocolate ice cream, or cherry to blueberry pie, but why should I impose my preferences? The principle that individuals are the best judges of what is in their own interests and that their preferences should be respected is called the **principle of consumer sovereignty.** There are, however, instances when government violates this principle: by smoking marijuana, an individual may cause no one else harm, yet governments in most states have made smoking marijuana illegal. Often, other rationales (such as externalities) for such actions are put forward; yet the underlying basis for government action remains inconsistent with the principle of consumer sovereignty. For instance, from 1920 to 1933, it was illegal to produce or sell alcoholic beverages in the United States. One of the reasons for this prohibition was the ill effects of drinking on others (such as alcohol-related accidents); but the view that drinking was *morally* wrong was what provided the fervor to the prohibition movement.

Government intervenes not only to discourage or prohibit certain actions but to encourage or force others. It requires parents to send their children to school, for instance. Goods the government encourages because it believes there is some public interest in their consumption that is not an externality (although it goes beyond the private interests of those consuming the goods) are called **merit goods.** There are also important instances where government discourages the consumption of certain goods, overriding consumer sovereignty even though there may be limited or no externalities.

GOVERNMENT'S OPTIONS

Once society has decided that government should do something, there is a second question: how can government accomplish society's ends most efficiently? Government has four choices. It can do something directly, it can provide incentives for the private sector to do something, it can instruct the private sector to do something, or it can do some combination of these.

TAKING DIRECT ACTION

One option is for government simply to take charge itself. If it believes there is a market failure in the provision of medical care, for instance, it can nationalise the medical sector, as Britain did after the Second World War. If government believes there is a market failure in the airline or railway industry, it can nationalise the industry or the part of the industry with which it is not content and run the industry or port itself. If government believes there is a market failure in the provision of housing for the poor, it can build housing.

Direct action does not require government to produce the good itself. It can also purchase the good from the private sector. Local governments in Britain currently often buy refuse collection services from private companies.

Many countries have publicly provided pensions. In Britain there is a state pension, the small weekly payment that is available to all over a certain age, providing that they have made enough National Insurance contributions over their working lives. Everyone who works in Britain is obliged to make National Insurance contributions, and everyone is entitled to this minimum pension, regardless of any other income. For many people, the state pension is much too small, and they save so that they have much larger incomes after their retirement. But for a considerable number of people, the state pension (plus any other state welfare benefits they are entitled to) is all they have to live on in old age. Effectively, people are forced to save more than they would choose to if left to themselves. The flat-rate state pension has fallen to a very low level, relative to most people's earnings, lower in fact for many than the level of welfare benefits they would be entitled to, and the relation between contributions and payments has been weakened. There are plans to introduce a compulsory-contribution-based second pension on top of the existing scheme. The ex-

isting level of forced saving is thought to be inadequate.

Why do governments legislate for compulsory saving? In this respect they are ignoring consumer sovereignty. Evidently there is a belief that many people would not save enough for retirement, left to themselves, by being too optimistic about their needs in retirement or the possibilities of making savings later, feeling that immediate needs are more pressing than saving, being myopic and ignoring the future, or believing that someone (the government, relatives perhaps) will help them out in the end. Governments obviously feel that it would not be credible to threaten to let old people fend for themselves, regardless how poor, that there would be intense political pressure to do something. Governments would end up bailing out old people one way or another, and so the forced saving.

Thus pensions are treated as a merit good. Public provision is an example of government's taking direct action to achieve a socially desirable outcome.

PROVIDING INCENTIVES
TO THE PRIVATE SECTOR

Government can also choose to operate at a distance, pricing incentives to alter the workings of private markets in desirable ways. It can provide such incentives directly through subsidies or indirectly through the tax system. Taxes on fuel can be used to encourage energy conservation. Accelerated depreciation allowances and other measures that give firms a tax break for investing in new machines have been used to encourage investment. And special provisions of the tax code encourage employers to provide pensions for their employees by reducing the costs of these benefits to the firm.

Subsidies and taxes put the government in the position of manipulating the price system to achieve its ends. If the government is worried about the supply of adequate housing for the poor, for example, it can provide builders with direct payments, or it can grant tax reductions for those who make investments in slum areas. Both lower the price to the builder of constructing housing. If the government wants to encourage oil conservation, it can impose a tax on oil or petrol, which will encourage conserva-

There are some wide disparities in government expenditures between countries. The following data show the total expenditure and its distribution among different departments for five countries—the United Kingdom, the United States, Japan, Australia, and the Netherlands. Britain, at 43.2 percent, is towards the high end; of the five shown, only the Netherlands has more, at 52.4 percent. Many European countries would be clustered around the Netherlands, with relatively generous welfare states and high tax burdens. The United States and Japan have the smallest public sectors—23.1 percent and 24.1 percent of their respective GDPs. (But note that the figure for the United States covers only federal spending, and omits state and local spending, which may increase its total.) The United States spends a lot on defence but very little on education (at the federal level; most educational spending is state and local) and has a small social security budget. Japan spends very little on defence, more than the United States on social security, practically nothing on health, which is largely privately financed, but rather a lot on "other" spending. The Netherlands is distinguished by its enormous social security bill, and it is also a big spender on education.

Which of these is the most desirable situation? Many European countries have chosen the combination of high taxes, generous social benefits, and public provision of health and education. The United States is at the low tax–low public spending end of the spectrum: low taxes, low benefits, private health insurance, and much private funding of higher education. The choices countries make reflect their preferences between a social, collectivist model and an individualistic, competitive model. Britain is somewhere in the middle and vacillates, drawn first to one model and then to the other.

Source: Government Finance Statistics Yearbook (1995).

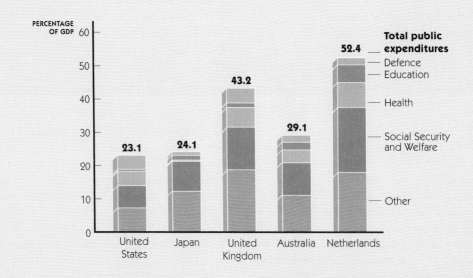

tion by raising the price. It can also tax cars that are not energy efficient, raising their price. The increase in the tax on leaded petrol relative to lead-free petrol caused a massive switch towards the nonpolluting lead-free petrol.

ENFORCING ACTION IN THE PRIVATE SECTOR

Concern about the effectiveness of incentives in achieving the desired result or about their costs (in tax forgiveness or outright payments) may lead government to require the desired action using legal sanctions to get people to comply. Government may require that automobile manufacturers produce fuel-efficient cars, specifying particular standards for miles per litre of fuel. Property developers who want to get planning permission for a large housing project may be required to provide a certain number of units for low-income individuals, to help improve a local road, or to build a local school. In all these cases, the government requirement does not show up as a cost on the government's budget. These requirements do have costs, however. These costs are borne indirectly by workers, firms, and consumers and can be very high.

COMBINING OPTIONS

The government often combines two or more courses of action in its attempts to achieve some objective. In the housing market, the British government provides some housing directly for low-income families through council housing. Other rented housing is privately provided but publicly subsidised through housing associations. Privately owned (owner-occupied) housing is subsidised by the tax treatment of interest on mortgage payments.

GOVERNMENT FAILURES

Whenever there is a market failure, there is a *potential* role for government. Government needs to consider each of the alternatives discussed in the previous section and assess the likelihood that one or the other alternative will succeed. Such an assessment may conclude that it is better not to intervene after all. Recent decades have provided numerous examples of government programmes that either have not succeeded to the extent their sponsors had hoped or have failed altogether. The slum clearance and rebuilding programmes of the 1950s and 1960s in Britain have in some cases created worse housing problems than the ones they were meant to solve. The social security system is said to have created a dependency culture which perpetuates poverty. Out of the failures and limited successes of government programmes has emerged a better understanding of the causes of government failure.

IMPERFECT INFORMATION

Imperfect information poses a problem in the public as well as the private sector. The government

GOVERNMENT'S OPTIONS

Taking direct action
   Producing a good or service
   Purchasing a good or service

Providing incentives to the private sector
   Subsidies
   Taxes
Enforcing private-sector action

would like to make sure, for instance, that public welfare assistance goes only to those who really need it. But it is costly to sort out the truly deserving from those who are not. Spending more on screening applicants lets fewer of the undeserving through the application process. But spending more on administration leaves less to spend on benefits. As always, there are trade-offs.

INCENTIVES AND THE EFFICIENCY OF GOVERNMENT

Problems of incentives can be worse in the public than in the private sector. Homeowners, for example, have an incentive to maintain their property, not only because an attractive house is more enjoyable to live in but also because when they sell, an attractive house will yield a higher price. Owners of a private apartment building, similarly, have incentives to maintain the building. And tenants in private apartments have an incentive not to abuse the property (they can be evicted or fail to have their lease renewed). Tenants in public housing have no such incentives. From their perspective, the quality of their apartment building or housing estate is like a public good; each individual has too little incentive to maintain public amenities. Managers of public housing have no incentives comparable to those of private landlords, since they typically have limited discretion in evicting tenants or even in refusing to renew leases. The problem of incentives is made worse in the public sector because public officials work under conditions of salary and job tenure that can make it difficult to hire first-rate workers or to reward workers for efficient performance. The rules make it difficult to pay good public officials a salary comparable to what similarly qualified and hardworking people receive in the private sector or to offer them opportunities for rapid promotion. It may even be more difficult to fire or demote incompetent and lazy workers.

Elected officials need funds to run their campaigns, and this makes them particularly attentive to those who can assist with campaign finances. The influence of the European farm lobby in obtaining support, far out of proportion to the number of voters whose livelihood depends on agriculture, is frequently attributed to this sort of special interest lobbying. Unions and many other groups provide funds to political parties that are sympathetic to their views. Naturally, lobbyists for these special interest groups claim they are not buying politicians but simply providing them with information needed to make an informed judgment—and then supporting those who have seen the truth. Some economists, including Nobel Prize winners James Buchanan and George Stigler, go so far as to see the problems of the public sector as perhaps the inevitable consequence of the political process.

WASTE IN GOVERNMENT

Some people view the public sector as being necessarily less efficient than the private sector. This is a view that has propelled many changes over the last twenty years. Privatization was to some extent driven by this view. The spectacular cuts in employment and unexpectedly high profits made by some of the privatised firms give support to it. It lay behind efforts to induce local governments to purchase many services from outside suppliers rather than supplying them themselves. It has also driven reforms in the National Health Service, where an internal market has been created in an attempt to create competition among providers of health services. Here the beneficial effects of introducing competition have been less clear. The new system has greatly increased the number and cost of managers and administrators in the NHS.

There are other counterexamples to the presumption of public-sector inefficiency. The administrative costs of many private insurance companies—amounting to up to 30 percent or more of the premiums—are considerably higher than the administrative expenses of public social insurance, such as social security. France's state-run electricity company is reputedly as efficient as any private firm.

There are also theoretical reasons to question the conclusion that public enterprises are doomed to be less efficient. This is because *some* of the problems generating inefficiencies in the public sector plague the private sector also. Just as public-sector employees typically do not receive any incentive pay (that is, pay is not linked to performance, so there are few *direct* returns to performing better), for instance, neither do most employees in the private sector. And large (with more than 500 employees) corporations—which still produce one-half of the economy's output—face bureaucratic problems no less than does government.

A consensus is thus emerging among economists that although the government is *often* less efficient than private firms performing similar tasks, it is not necessarily so.

UNFORESEEN RESPONSES TO A PROGRAMME

The success or failure of programmes in the public sector depends not only on public officials but also on how the private sector responds. Predicting those private responses is difficult, and many government programmes have faced problems because of this difficulty. A problem throughout Europe is the growth of welfare spending. The high rates of social security provision and generous pensions in many European countries were established in an age of low unemployment, with relatively few households living in poverty and relatively few pensioners. The rise in European unemployment, the growth in the

number of households in poverty, and the increasing proportion of elderly persons in the population have raised the cost of these programmes to a point where they have become unsupportable. Governments are attempting to cut welfare costs in the United Kingdom, Sweden, Germany, France, Italy, and many other countries.

Single mothers were accustomed at one time—in the 1950s and 1960s—to social stigma as well as poverty, receiving little help from the welfare state. But with more enlightened attitudes welfare provision has improved, and the social stigma largely disappeared. The problem for the state is that there has as the same time—whether the relationship is causal or coincidental is not entirely clear—been an unexpectedly large growth in the number of single parents, mostly mothers, on welfare benefits. In Britain the much-reviled Child Support Agency was set up to track down the feckless fathers and require them to pay for the support of their children, to relieve the state of the burden. In the United States there is a belief that the design of the welfare programmes encourages single parenthood. The unexpected consequences of welfare support to single parents has led to questioning the wisdom of making such generous welfare support available.

SOURCES OF PUBLIC FAILURES

Imperfect information

Problems of incentives, particularly for those charged with administering government programmes

Failure to assess the full consequences of government programmes, including responses of the private sector

Waste in government

REVIEW AND PRACTICE

SUMMARY

1 Government plays a pervasive role in the economy of almost every industrialised country. In Britain, government expenditures account for over 40 percent of national income. Elsewhere the share ranges

from just over 30 percent in Japan to around 60 percent in Sweden. In almost all countries, the share has grown dramatically since the 1950s. The major reason for this increase has been increased expenditures on social security and welfare, health programmes, and interest payments.

2 In a democracy, the public sector differs from the private in two main ways. Its legitimacy and authority are derived from the electoral process; it also has certain powers of compulsion, such as requiring households and firms to pay taxes and obey laws.

3 By and large, private markets allocate resources efficiently. But in a number of areas they do not, as is the case with externalities and public goods. Moreover, when the economy fails to use the available resources fully, there may be idle industrial capacity and unemployed workers. Even when the economy is efficient, there may be dissatisfaction with the distribution of income.

4 Individuals and firms produce too much of a good with a negative externality, such as air or water pollution, since they do not bear all the costs. They produce too little of a good with a positive externality, such as a new invention, since they cannot receive all the benefits.

5 Public goods are goods which cost little or nothing for an additional individual to enjoy but which it costs a great deal to exclude any individual from enjoying. National defence and lighthouses are two examples. Free markets underproduce public goods, since it is (by definition) difficult to prevent anyone from using them without paying for them.

6 Government has a variety of instruments it can use to change markets that are not functioning efficiently. It can take direct action, provide incentives to the private sector, or mandate action by the private sector.

7 While market failures provide a potential rationale for government action, government action may not provide an effective remedy. There are systematic reasons for government failure just as there are for market failure.

8 The proper balance between the public and private sectors is a major concern of economics.

KEY TERMS

nationalization	Smith's "Invisible hand"	externality	free-rider problem
deregulation	market failure	public good	principle of consumer sovereignty
privatization			

REVIEW QUESTIONS

1 Name some of the ways government touches the lives of all citizens, both in and out of the economic sphere.

2 "Since democratic governments are elected by the consent of a majority of the people, they have no need for compulsion." Comment.

3 How can individual selfishness end up promoting social welfare?

4 Name areas in which market failure can occur.

5 Why do goods with negative externalities tend to be overproduced? Why do goods with positive externalities tend to be underproduced? Give examples.

6 What two characteristics define a public good? Give an example.

7 What three broad types of instruments does government have to try to achieve its goals?

8 Does the presence of a market failure necessarily mean that government action is desirable? If not, why not?

9 Describe some of the major economic roles of government.

10 How has the size of government changed over time? How does the size of the British government compare with that of other industrialised countries?

PROBLEMS

1 In each of the following areas, specify how the government is involved, either as a direct producer, a regulator, a purchaser of final goods and services distributed directly to individuals or used within government, or in some other role:

(a) Education
(b) Mail delivery
(c) Housing
(d) Air travel
(e) National defence

In each of these cases, can you think of ways that part of the public role could be provided by the private sector?

2 Can you explain why even a benevolent and well-meaning government may sometimes have to use the power of compulsory purchase? (Hint: Consider the incentives of one person who knows that her property is the last obstacle to building a road.)

3 Explain why government redistribution programmes involve a trade-off between risk and incentives for *both* rich and poor.

4 Each of the following situations involves an externality. Say whether it is a positive or negative externality or both, and explain why free markets will overproduce or underproduce the good in question.

(a) A business performing research and development projects
(b) A business discharging waste into a nearby river
(c) A concert given in the middle of a large city park
(d) An individual smoking cigarettes in a meeting held in a small, unventilated room

5 When some activity causes a negative externality like pollution, would it be a good idea to ban the activity altogether? Why or why not? (Hint: Consider marginal costs and benefits.)

6 Roads are often referred to as public goods. That designation is basically fair but not perfect. What are the costs of exclusion? Can you describe a case where the marginal cost of an additional driver on a road might be relatively high? How might society deal with this problem?

PART TWO

PERFECT MARKETS

art Two explores in depth the basic microeconomic assumptions of rational, well-informed consumers interacting with profit-maximising firms in competitive markets. This set of assumptions, as we learned in Chapter 2, constitutes the basic economic model. Here, we study the implications of this model and examine the powerful insights it affords. It turns out that while this basic model is a good starting point, consumers are often not as well informed and markets are often not as competitive as the model assumes them to be. Part Three expands on and enriches the basic model in ways that make it more realistic.

The economy consists of three groups of participants—individuals or households, firms, and government—interacting in three markets—the labour, capital, and product markets. Part Two considers individuals and firms; the discussion of government is postponed to Part Three. The object in Part Two is to understand how a purely private market economy would operate. Chapters 8 and 9 discuss how individuals and households make their choices of which goods to consume, how much to save, and how much labour to supply. Chapters 10 and 11 analyse how firms make their decisions concerning how much to produce and how to produce it.

Finally, Chapter 12 brings households and firms together in the three markets. Households supply labour, and firms demand labour. The interaction of this supply and demand for labour determines wages. Similarly, households supply capital, and firms demand capital to build factories and buy new machines. Their interaction in the capital market determines the interest rate and the equilibrium level of savings and investment in the economy. Individuals take their income, both what they earn as workers and the return on their savings, and use it to buy goods. They demand goods. With the workers they have hired, machines they have purchased, and factories they have built, firms produce goods. Firms' supply of goods and households' demand for goods interact in the product market, and this interaction determines the prices of the myriad of goods we consume.

CHAPTER 8

THE CONSUMPTION DECISION

The millions of households in the economy taken together make an astounding number of spending choices every day. These decisions contribute to the overall demand for cars and bicycles, clothes and housing, and masses of other products available on the market. The members of each household also make decisions that affect how much income they will have to spend, like whether to work overtime or whether both partners in a marriage should work. They decide how much of their income to save. And they decide where to put the nest eggs they do save.

These four sets of decisions—about spending, working, saving, and investing—represent the basic economic choices facing the household. This chapter focuses on spending decisions and how these decisions are affected by taxes and other government policies. Chapter 9 discusses working and saving decisions. Chapter 10 deals with household decisions concerning how to invest savings.

These microeconomic decisions have macroeconomic consequences as well. Household decisions about whether to buy a car that is imported from abroad or one that is made domestically will affect the trade deficit. Choices about how much one should work will affect overall levels of unemployment and production. Household decisions about savings and investment will affect the future growth of the economy.

THE BASIC PROBLEM OF CONSUMER CHOICE

The first problem facing a consumer is easy to state, though hard to resolve: What should he do with whatever (after tax) income he has to spend? He must allocate (that is, divide) his available income among alternative goods. Should he buy CDs, go to the cinema, eat sweets, or purchase sweaters? In the absence of scarcity there would be an easy answer: have it all!

Chapter 2 provided the basic framework for economic decision making. The consumer defines his opportunity set, what is *possible* given the constraints he faces, and then chooses the most preferred point within this set. This chapter begins by reviewing how we define the opportunity set, and then asks how it changes—and how what the individual chooses changes—when incomes and prices change.

THE BUDGET CONSTRAINT

The individual's opportunity set is defined by the budget constraint. If, after taxes, a person's weekly pay comes to £300 and he has no other income, this is his budget constraint. Total expenditures on food, clothing, rent, entertainment, travel, and all other categories cannot exceed £300 per week. (For now we ignore the possibilities that individuals may borrow money, save money, or change their budget constraints by working longer or shorter hours.)

The line BC in Figure 8.1A shows a simplified individual budget constraint. A student, Fran, has a total of £300 each semester to spend on fun items. Figure 8.1 assumes that there are two goods, chocolate bars and compact discs. The simplified assumption of only two goods is an abstraction that highlights the main points of the analysis.

Let's say that a chocolate bar costs £1, while a compact disc costs £15. *If* Fran spent all her income on chocolate bars, she could purchase 300 bars (point B on the budget constraint). If she spent all her income on CDs, she could buy 20 CDs (point C on the budget constraint). Fran can also choose any of the intermediate choices on line BC. For example, she could buy 10 CDs (for £150) and 150 chocolate bars (for £150), or 15 CDs (£225) and 75 chocolate bars (£75). Each combination of purchases along the budget constraint totals £300.

As we learned in Chapter 2, a budget constraint diagram has two important features. First, although any point in the shaded area of Figure 8.1A is feasible, only the points on the line BC are relevant. This is because Fran is not consuming her entire budget if she is inside her budget constraint. Second, by looking along the budget constraint, we can see the trade-offs she faces—how many chocolate bars she has to give up to get 1 more CD, and vice versa. Look at points F and A. This part of the budget constraint is blown up in panel B. At point A, Fran has 10 CDs; at F, she has 11. At F, she has 135 chocolate bars; at A, 150. To get 1 more CD, she has to give up 15 chocolate bars.

These are her trade-offs, and they are determined by the relative prices of the two goods. If one good costs twice as much as another, to get 1 more unit of the costly good, we have to give up 2 units of the cheaper good. If, as here, one good costs 15 times as much as another, to get 1 more unit of the costly good, we have to give up 15 units of the less costly good.

The **slope** of the budget constraint also tells us what the trade-off is. The slope of a line measures how steep it is. As we move 1 unit along the horizon-

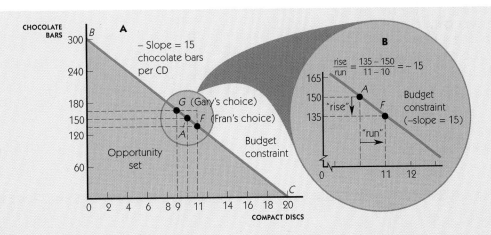

Figure 8.1 AN INDIVIDUAL'S BUDGET CONSTRAINT

Panel A is a budget constraint that shows the combinations of compact discs (at £15) and chocolate bars (at £1) that an individual could buy with £300. Fran chooses point F, with a relatively large number of CDs; Gary chooses point G, with a relatively large number of chocolate bars. Panel B shows that the trade-off of moving from 10 CDs to 11 (point A to F) is 15 chocolate bars.

tal axis (from 10 to 11 CDs), the slope measures the size of the change along the vertical axis. The slope is the rise (the movement up or down on the vertical axis) divided by the run (the corresponding horizontal movement). The slope of this budget constraint is thus 15.[1] It tells us how much of one good, at a given price, we need to give up if we want 1 more unit of the other good; it tells us, in other words, what the trade-off is.

Notice that the relative price of CDs to chocolate bars is 15; that is, a CD costs 15 times as much as a chocolate bar. But we have just seen that the slope of the budget constraint is 15 and that the trade-off (the number of chocolate bars Fran has to give up to get 1 more CD) is 15. It is no accident that these three numbers—relative price, slope, and trade-off—are the same.

[1] We ignore the negative sign. See the appendix to Chapter 2 for a more detailed explanation of the slope of a line.

This two-product example was chosen because it is easy to illustrate with a graph. But this logic can cover any number of products. Income can be spent on one item or a combination of items. The budget constraint defines what a certain amount of income can buy, which depends on the prices of the items. Giving up some of one item allows the purchase of more of another item or items.

Economists represent these choices by putting the purchases of the good upon which they are focusing attention, say CDs, on the horizontal axis and "all other goods" on the vertical axis. By definition, what is not spent on CDs is available to be spent on all other goods. Fran has £300 to spend altogether. A more realistic budget constraint for her is shown in Figure 8.2. The intersection of the budget constraint with the vertical axis, point B—where purchases of CDs are zero—is £300. If Fran spends nothing on CDs, she has £300 to spend on other goods. The budget constraint intersects the horizontal axis at 20 CDs (point C); if she spends all her income on CDs and

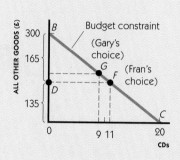

Figure 8.2 ALLOCATING A BUDGET BETWEEN A SINGLE GOOD AND ALL OTHERS

Some budget constraints show the choice between a particular good, in this case CDs, and all other goods. The other goods that may be purchased are collectively measured in money terms, as shown on the vertical axis.

CDs cost £15 each, she can buy 20. If she chooses a point such as *F*, she will buy 11 CDs, costing £165, and she will have £135 to spend on other goods (£300–£165). The distance 0*D* on the vertical axis measures what she spends on other goods; the distance *BD* measures what she spends on CDs.

CHOOSING A POINT ON THE BUDGET CONSTRAINT: INDIVIDUAL PREFERENCES

The budget constraint and a recognition of possible trade-offs is the starting point for the study of consumer behaviour. The process of identifying the budget constraints and the trade-offs is the same for *any* two people. If a person walks into a store (that only accepts cash) with £300, any economist can tell you his budget constraint and the trade-offs he faces by looking at the money in his pocket and the prices on the shelves. What choice will he make? Economists narrow their predictions to points on his budget constraint; any individual will choose *some* point along the budget constraint. But the point actually chosen depends on the individual's preferences: Fran, who likes to listen to music, might choose point *F* in Figure 8.1, while Gary, who loves chocolate might choose *G*.

Few people will choose either of the extreme points on the budget constraint, *B* or *C* in Figure 8.1, where only one of the goods is consumed. The rea-

son for this is that the more you have of a good—say, the more CDs you have relative to another good such as chocolate—the less valuable is an additional unit of that good relative to additional units of the other good. At points near *C*, it seems safe to assume that to most individuals, an extra CD does not look as attractive as some chocolate bars. Certainly, at *B*, most people would be so full of chocolate that an extra CD would look preferable.

Where the individual's choice lies depends on how she values the two goods. Chapter 2 emphasised the idea that in making decisions, people look at the *margin;* they look at the extra costs and benefits. In this case, the choice at each point along the budget constraint is between 1 more CD and 15 more chocolate bars. If Gary and Fran choose different points along the budget constraint, it is because they value the marginal benefits (how much better off they feel with an *extra* CD) and the marginal costs (how much it hurts to give up 15 chocolate bars) differently. Gary chooses point *G* in Figure 8.1 because that is the point where, for him, the marginal benefit of an extra CD is just offset by what he has to give up to get the extra CD, which is 15 chocolate bars. When Fran, who loves listening to music, considers point *G*, she realises that for her, at that point CDs are more important and chocolate bars less important than they are for Gary. So she trades along the line until she has enough CDs and few enough chocolate bars that, for her, the marginal benefits of an extra CD and the marginal costs of 15 fewer chocolate bars are equal. This point, as we have supposed, is *F*.

The same reasoning holds for a budget constraint like the one shown in Figure 8.2. Here, Gary and Fran are choosing between CDs and all other goods, measured in terms of pounds. Now in deciding to buy an extra CD, each compares the marginal benefit of an extra CD with the marginal cost, what has to be given up in other goods. With CDs priced at £15, choosing to buy a CD means giving up £15 of other goods. For Gary, the marginal benefit of an extra CD equals the cost, £15, when he has only 9 CDs and can therefore spend £165 on other goods. For Fran, who has more of a taste for CDs, the marginal benefit of an extra CD does not equal this marginal cost until she reaches 11 CDs, with £135 to spend elsewhere. Thus, the price is a quantitative measure of the marginal benefit.

WHAT HAPPENS TO CONSUMPTION WHEN INCOME CHANGES

When an individual's income increases, he has more to spend on consumption. Normally, he will buy a little more of many goods, although his consumption of some goods will increase more than that of others, and different individuals will spend their extra income in different ways. Jim may spend much of his extra income going out to eat in restaurants more often, while Bill may spend much of his extra income buying a more expensive car.

The **income elasticity of demand** (which parallels the *price* elasticity of demand presented in Chapter 5) measures how much the consumption of a particular good increases with income:

Income elasticity of demand

$$= \frac{\text{percentage change in consumption}}{\text{percentage change in income}}.$$

The income elasticity of demand, in other words, is the percentage change in consumption that would result from a 1 percent increase in income. If the income elasticity of demand of a certain good is greater than 1, a 1 percent increase in an individual's income results in a more than 1 percent increase in expenditures on that good. That is, the amount he spends on that good increases more than propor-

tionately with income. By definition, if the income elasticity of demand is less than 1, then a 1 percent increase in income results in a less than 1 percent increase in expenditures. In this case, the share of income a consumer spends on that good decreases with a rise in income.

As people's incomes increase, the types of goods they choose to buy also change. In particular, they have more money to spend on goods other than those required just to survive. For instance, while they may spend some of the extra income to buy better-quality food and other necessities, more money goes towards movies, more expensive cars, holidays, and other luxuries. Accordingly, poor individuals spend a larger percentage of their income on food and housing and a smaller percentage of their income on perfume. In other words, the income elasticity of necessities is less than 1, and the income elasticity of luxuries is greater than 1.

The consumption of some goods actually decreases as income increases and increases as income decreases. These goods are called **inferior goods.** They are in sharp contrast to **normal goods,** the consumption of which increases with income. In other words, goods for which the income elasticity is *negative* are, by definition, inferior, while all other goods are called normal. For instance, if Fran, who has been taking the bus to work, gets a large pay rise, she may find that she can afford a car. After buying the car, she will spend less on bus tickets. Thus, in this particular sense, bus trips represent an inferior good.

Figure 8.3 shows how typical families at different income levels spend their income. The fraction of spending on food steadily falls as income rises. The share spent on housing is roughly constant, and the share spent on motoring and fares and on leisure goods rises as total spending rises.

These figures are of practical importance. Because spending patterns differ by income level, rises in prices of certain goods do not affect all households equally. A rise in the price of fuel—electricity, gas, coal, and so on—will affect the poor more than the rich, since the poor spend more of their income on fuel than the rich do. This may partly explain the widespread opposition to the imposition of a value-added tax on domestic heating bills in Britain in 1994.

Table 8.1 gives some figures for the **income elasticity of demand** for a selection of goods. Bread ap-

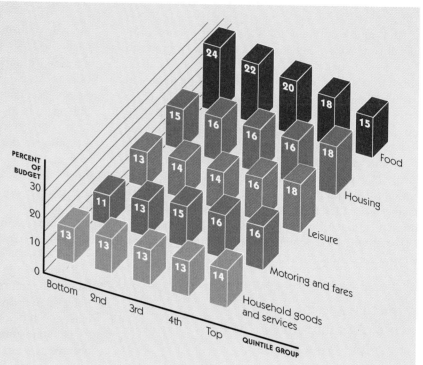

Figure 8.3 HOW HOUSEHOLDS OF DIFFERENT INCOMES SPEND THEIR MONEY

The figure shows the pattern of spending on different goods for households arranged in quintile groups—the poorest 20 percent of households, then the next 20 percent, and so on. Most striking is the fall in spending on food as a fraction of total spending. The share spent on housing is roughly constant. As might be expected, the share spent on motoring and fares and on leisure goods and services rises as total spending rises. *Source:* Office of National Statistics, *Social Trends* (1998), Table 6.5.

Table 8.1 SOME INCOME ELASTICITIES OF DEMAND

Elastic	
Beverages	1.369
Electricity	3.761
Wines and spirits	2.599
Expenditure abroad	1.143
Catering	1.638
Vehicle operation	5.393
Inelastic	
Bread	−0.499
Meat	0.289
Entertainment	0.893
Rail travel	−0.400

Source: A. S. Deaton, "The Measurement of Income and Price Elasticities," *European Economic Review* 6 (1975): 261–273. The elasticities are based on time-series data for the United Kingdom for the period 1954–1972, using a log-linear formulation of demand functions.

pears to have a negative elasticity: the demand for bread falls as income rises. Meat and entertainment have an elasticity that is positive but less than 1: as income rises, the demand for these things rises but not in proportion to income. Wines and spirits and "vehicle operation" have an elasticity greater than 1: demand for them rises more than in proportion to income. A 10 percent rise in income generates a 26 percent rise in the demand for wines and spirits.

A CLOSER LOOK AT THE DEMAND CURVE

In Chapter 4, we saw the principal characteristic of the demand curve: when prices rise, the quantity of a good demanded normally falls. Here, we take a closer look at why. This will help us understand why some goods respond more strongly to price changes, that is, have a greater price elasticity.

Calculations of the amount of revenue that a tax will raise have to take account of the effects of the tax on the consumption of the good in question. If the elasticity of demand for a good is high, then raising the tax on it will, if it raises the after-tax price of the good, reduce the amount consumed, and the revenue raised will be reduced. This is particularly true when the tax being considered is an increase in an already high tax. Take the case of cigarettes, for example. Suppose the price of a pack of 20 cigarettes is £2.50, of which £1.50 is tax and £1 is the before-tax price of cigarettes. Suppose the elasticity of demand for cigarettes is 0.3. What would be the effect on the demand for cigarettes of an additional 50 pence in tax? The price would rise by 50 pence, or 20 percent, to £3 a pack, and demand would fall by 6 percent (0.3 of 20 percent). What about tax revenue? Taxes are now higher by 50 pence at £2 per pack but demand is only 94 percent of original sales. Whereas previously for every 100 packs sold there would be £150 in tax revenue, there are now 94 packs sold with £188 in tax revenue, so revenue has increased by only 25 percent despite a 33 percent increase in the tax rate.

Let us return to our earlier example of Fran buying CDs in Figure 8.2. If the price of CDs rises from £15 to £20, Fran will face a new budget constraint. If she didn't buy any CDs, she would still have £300 to spend on other goods; but if she decided to spend all of her income on CDs, she could only buy 15 rather than 20. Her budget constraint is now the blue line in Figure 8.4.

The increase in the price of CDs has one obvious and important effect: Fran cannot continue to buy the same number of CDs and the same amount of other goods as she did before. Earlier, Fran bought

Figure 8.4 **EFFECT OF PRICE INCREASE**

An increase in the price of CDs moves the budget constraint down as shown. Fran must cut back on the consumption of some goods. Here, she is cutting back on the consumption of CDs and other goods.

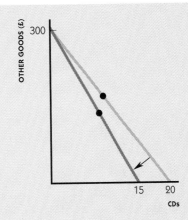

For many in the poorer countries, getting enough food to live on is a daily struggle. But for residents of wealthy countries, food is easy to come by. These differences in circumstances are reflected in differences in income and price elasticities. The left-hand column of the following table below lists selected countries from the poorest to richest, with their per capita income given as a percentage of per capita income in the United States in the second column. The third column gives an income elasticity for food in that country, while the fourth column lists a price elasticity for food.

Notice that the income elasticity of demand for food declines as income rises. This makes intuitive sense; as poor people receive more income, they will tend to spend a larger proportion of their additional money on food than wealthier people will. In India, a 10 percent increase in income will lead to a 7.6 percent increase in the quantity of food demanded. Looking at the fourth column, we see that for the richer countries such as the United States and Canada, a 10 percent increase in the price of food leads only to a 1 percent reduction in the quantity of food purchased.

Country	Per Capita Income (as % of U.S.)	Income Elasticity of Food	Price Elasticity of Food
India	5.9	0.76	−0.32
Nigeria	6.7	0.74	−0.33
Indonesia	7.2	0.72	−0.34
Bolivia	14.4	0.68	−0.35
Philippines	16.8	0.67	−0.35
Korea	20.4	0.64	−0.35
Poland	34.6	0.55	−0.33
Brazil	36.8	0.54	−0.33
Israel	45.6	0.49	−0.31
Spain	55.9	0.43	−0.36
Japan	61.6	0.39	−0.35
Italy	69.7	0.34	−0.30
United Kingdom	71.7	0.33	−0.22
France	81.1	0.27	−0.19
Germany	85.0	0.25	−0.17
Canada	99.2	0.15	−0.10
United States	100.0	0.14	−0.10

Source: Ching-Fun Cling and James Peale, Jr., "Income and Price Elasticities," in Henri Thell, ed., *Advances in Econometrics Supplement* (Greenwich, CT: JAI Press, 1989). Data are from 1980.

More of the expenditures on food in the richer countries are luxuries—restaurants, lobsters, steaks. One might have thought that this would imply that the price elasticity in richer countries would be larger than in poorer countries. But there is another effect that dominates. In poorer countries, people spend a much larger fraction of their income on food. When the price of food goes up, they almost have to reduce food consumption. This is not the case in the wealthier countries. Because expenditures on food represent a larger fraction of total expenditures in poor countries, the income effect of a rise in the price of food there is larger.

11 CDs. If she bought the same number of CDs, it would cost her £55 more, and she would have £55 less to spend on other goods. No matter what she does, Fran is worse off as a result of the price increase. It is *as if* she had less income to spend. When she has less income to spend, she reduces her expenditure on each good, including CDs. This part of the response to the higher price is called the **income effect.** An increase in income of about £55, or 18 percent (£55 out of £300), would offset the price increase.[2] Assume the income elasticity is approximately 1; that is, with income reduced by 18 percent, she would reduce purchases of CDs by 18 percent, which is about 2 CDs. This part of the reduction of the demand of CDs, from 11 to 9, is the income effect.

The magnitude of the income effect depends on two factors: how important the commodity is to the individual—that is, how large a fraction of the individual's income is spent on the good—and how large the income elasticity is. Since, in most cases, individuals spend a relatively small fraction of their income on any particular good, the income effect is relatively small. But in the case of housing, for example, on which individuals spend between a quarter and a third of their income on average, the income effect of an increase in the price of housing is significant.

Let us go back to Fran and the CDs. At the higher price, giving up 1 CD gets her more of other goods—more chocolate bars, more movies, more tapes, more sweaters. The relative price of CDs, or the trade-off between CDs and other goods, has changed. At the higher price, she *substitutes* goods that are

less expensive for the more expensive CDs. Not surprisingly, this effect is called the **substitution effect.** The magnitude of the substitution effect depends on how easily Fran can substitute other goods. If Fran still owns her tape player and if the price of tapes remains unchanged, then the substitution effect may be large. She may drop the number of CDs she purchases to 2. But if Fran has no tape player, if the only entertainment she likes is listening to music, and if she dislikes all the music played by the local radio stations, then the substitution effect may be small. She may drop the number of CDs she purchases only to 8.

DERIVING DEMAND CURVES

We can now see both how to derive the demand curve and why it has the shape it does. At each price, we draw the budget constraint and identify the point along the budget constraint that is chosen. As the price of CDs increases, Fran will choose points along the successive budget constraints with fewer CDs purchased: higher prices mean she is less well off, and therefore, through the income effect, decrease her purchases of all goods. The higher price *relative to other goods* means she will substitute other goods for CDs.

THE IMPORTANCE OF DISTINGUISHING BETWEEN INCOME AND SUBSTITUTION EFFECTS

Distinguishing between the income and substitution effects of a change in price is important for two reasons.

[2] Actually, it would slightly overcompensate. With the £55 increase, Fran could buy exactly the same bundle of goods as before, but as we shall shortly see, she will *choose* to reallocate her spending.

There have been proposals that governments could get a double benefit from environmental taxes. By raising taxes on environmentally damaging goods, like petrol and heating fuels, governments raise extra revenue. With their spending needs unchanged, they could then return some of this extra to taxpayers by cutting other taxes, such as income and value-added taxes. If cutting income taxes stimulates people to work more, the taxes both improve the environment and increase the potential output of the economy by encouraging more labour supply—a double benefit. Is it possible for a tax change that involves governments' taking with one hand and giving back with the other capable of working in this way? Would it really cut consumption of pollutants and reduce pollution?

The proposal relies on the substitution effect. Suppose Lucy has an income of £15,000 per year, of which £595 is spent on petrol—850 litres at 70 pence a litre. An additional tax of 14 pence a litre would raise the price to 84 pence a litre—a 20 percent rise in the price. If the elasticity of demand for petrol is 0.5, then Lucy's demand would go down by 10 percent to 765 litres, at a total cost of £643. The government's tax revenue would be £107. If this tax revenue is returned to consumers in a reduction in other taxes (such as the value-added tax and income tax), and supposing that Lucy is an average consumer, then she would get a tax cut exactly equal in value to the £107. If Lucy spends this income partly on petrol and partly on other goods in the same

proportions as her existing income—that is, 4 percent of her income on petrol—she would spend an additional £4 on petrol, taking the total to £647, buying a total of 770 litres, still 80 litres less than her original purchases of 850 litres.

So an increase in the tax on petrol combined with a refund of the extra tax revenue to consumers would reduce petrol consumption. There remains a possibility that if the fuel tax is returned through an income tax cut, there would be an increase in labour supply and potential national income.

This example may be reminiscent of the British government's controversial plan to impose a value-added tax at 17.5 percent on domestic heating fuel. The proposal was defeated eventually by the argument that it would impose suffering on old people, even though the government planned to increase pensions so that on average, old people would not lose by it. It was proposed that the state pension would be increased by the amount of additional tax that the average pensioner would pay on their heating fuel. Of course it is difficult to ensure that every single person over the age of 65 does not lose from the change. Those using a lot of heating fuel might have lost, but then many of these people were likely to have had higher incomes anyway. In this case a highly sensible tax proposal was defeated by emotive sloganising and lack of understanding of economics!

Understanding Responses to Price Changes
First, the distinction improves our understanding of
consumption responses to price changes. Thinking
about the substitution effect helps us understand
why some demand curves have a low price elasticity
and others a high price elasticity. It also helps us understand why the price elasticity may well differ at
different points along the demand curve. Recall
from Chapter 5 that when an individual is consuming lots of some good, substitutes for the good are
easy to find, and a small increase in price leads to a
large reduction in the quantity demanded; but as
consumption gets lower, it becomes increasingly difficult to find good substitutes.

Or consider the effect of an increase in the price
of one good on the demand for *other* goods. There is
always an income effect; the income effect, by itself,
would lead to a reduced consumption of all commodities. But the substitution effect leads to *increased* consumption of substitute commodities.
Thus, an increase in the price of Coke will lead to increased demand for Pepsi at each price; the demand
curve for Pepsi shifts to the right, because the substitution effect outweighs the slight income effect.

***Understanding Inefficiencies Associated with
Taxes*** A second reason to focus on income and
substitution effects is to identify some of the inefficiencies associated with taxation. The purpose of a
tax is to raise revenue so that the government can
purchase goods; it represents a transfer of purchasing power from the household to the government. If
the government is to obtain more resources, individuals have to consume less. Thus, any tax must have
an income effect.

But beyond that, taxes often *distort* economic activity. The distortion caused by taxation is associated
with the substitution effect. Take the window tax imposed in medieval England. It was intended to raise
revenue. It led, instead, to the construction of win-
dowless houses—a major distortion of the tax. Most
of the distortions associated with modern taxes are
somewhat more subtle. Take a tax on airline tickets
or on telephone calls. Reducing consumption of
things that are against society's interest can be a legitimate goal of taxation. But the government does
not think flying or making telephone calls is a bad

thing. The tax is levied to raise revenues. But it results in fewer air flights and telephone calls anyway—an unintentional consequence. Any tax leads
to *some* reduction in consumption, through the income effect. But most taxes also change relative
prices; so they have a substitution effect. It is the substitution effect that gives rise to the distortion. If the
substitution effect is small, the distortion is small; if
the substitution effect is large, the distortion is large.

UTILITY AND THE DESCRIPTION OF PREFERENCES

We have seen that people choose a point along their
budget constraint by weighing the benefits of consuming more of one good against the costs—what
they have to forgo of other goods. Economists refer
to the benefits of consumption as the **utility** that individuals get from the combination of goods they
consume. Presumably a person can tell you whether
he prefers a certain combination of goods to another. Economists say that the preferred bundle of
goods gives that individual a higher level of utility
than the other bundle of goods he could have chosen. Similarly, economists say that the individual will
choose the bundle of goods—within the budget constraint—that maximises his utility.

In the nineteenth century, social scientists, including the British philosopher Jeremy Bentham,
hoped that science would someday develop a machine that could measure utility. A scientist could
simply hook up some electrodes to an individual's
head and read off how happy she was. Most modern
economists believe that there is no *unique* way to
measure utility but that there are useful ways of
measuring changes in how well-off a person is.

For our purposes, a simple way to measure utility
will suffice: we ask how much an individual would
be willing to pay to be in one situation rather than in
another. For example, if Joe likes chocolate ice
cream more than vanilla, it stands to reason that he
would be willing to pay more for a scoop of choco-

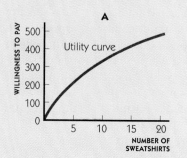

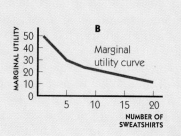

Figure 8.5 UTILITY AND MARGINAL UTILITY

Panel A shows that utility increases continually with consumption but tends to level off as consumption climbs higher. Panel B shows marginal utility; notice that it declines as consumption increases.

late ice cream than for a scoop of vanilla. Or if Diane would rather live in Cornwall than in London, it stands to reason that she would be willing to pay more for the West Country location.

Notice that how much a person is willing to pay is different from how much he *has* to pay. Just because Joe is willing to pay more for chocolate ice cream than for vanilla does not mean he will have to pay more. What he has to pay depends on market prices; what he is willing to pay reflects his preferences. Willingness to pay is an acceptable measure of utility, which is useful for purposes such as thinking about how an individual allocates his income along his budget constraint. But the hopes of nineteenth-century economists, that we could find some way of measuring utility that would allow us to compare how much utility Fran got from a bundle of goods with how much utility Gary obtained, are now viewed as pipe dreams.

Using willingness to pay as our measure of utility, we can construct a diagram like Figure 8.5A, which shows the level of utility Mary receives from sweatshirts as the number of sweatshirts she buys increases. This information is also given in Table 8.2. Here we assume that Mary is willing to pay £200 for 5 sweatshirts, £228 for 6 sweatshirts, £254 for 7 sweatshirts, and so on. Thus, 5 sweatshirts give her a utility of 200, 6 a utility of 228, and 7 sweatshirts a utility of 254. Mary's willingness to pay increases with the number of sweatshirts, reflecting the fact that additional sweatshirts give her additional utility. The extra utility of an additional sweatshirt, measured here by

the additional amount she is willing to pay, is the **marginal utility.** The numbers in the third column of Table 8.2 give the marginal (or extra) utility she received from her last sweatshirt. When Mary owns 5 sweatshirts, an additional sweatshirt yields her an additional or marginal utility of 28 (228 − 200); when she owns 6 sweatshirts, an additional one gives her a marginal utility of only 26 (254 − 228). Panel B traces the marginal utility of each of these increments.[3]

As an individual's bundle of goods includes more and more of a good, each successive increment increases her utility less. This is the law of **diminishing marginal utility.** The first sweatshirt is very desirable, and additional ones are attractive as well. But each sweatshirt does not increase utility by as much as the one before, and at some point, Mary may get almost no additional pleasure from adding to her sweatshirt wardrobe.

When Mary has a given budget and must choose between two goods that cost the same, say sweatshirts and pizza, each of which costs £15, she will make her choice so that the marginal utility of each good is the same. Table 8.2 shows Mary's willingness to pay (utility) for both sweatshirts and pizza. Look at what happens if Mary buys 20 sweatshirts with her £300 and no pizza. The marginal utility of the last sweatshirt is 12 and that of the first pizza is 18. If she switches £15 from sweatshirts to pizza, she loses a utility of 12 from

---

[3] Since marginal utility is the extra utility from an extra unit of consumption, it is measured by the slope of the utility curve in panel B.

the decreased sweatshirts but gains 18 from her first pizza. It obviously pays for her to switch.

Now look at the situation when she has decreased her purchases of sweatshirts to 17 and increased purchases of pizza to 3. The marginal utility of the last sweatshirt is 15 and that of the last pizza is also 15. At this point, she will not want to switch anymore. If she buys another sweatshirt, she gains 14, but the *last* pizza, her 3rd, which she will have to give up, has a marginal utility of 15; she loses more than she gains. If she buys another pizza, she gains 14, but the last sweatshirt (her 17th) gave her 15; again, she loses on balance. We can thus see that with her budget, she is best off when the marginal utilities of the two goods are the same.

The same general principle applies when the prices of two goods differ. Assume that a sweatshirt costs twice as much as a pizza. So long as the marginal utility of sweatshirts is more than twice that of pizzas, it still pays for Mary to switch to sweatshirts. To get one more sweatshirt, she has to give up two pizzas, and we reason, as before, that she will adjust her consumption until she gets to the point where the marginal utilities of the two goods, *per pound spent*, are equal. This is a general rule: in choosing between two goods, a consumer will adjust her choices to the point where the marginal utilities are proportional to the prices. Thus, the last unit purchased of a good that costs twice as much as another must generate twice the marginal utility as the last

Table 8.2 UTILITY AND MARGINAL UTILITY

Number of Sweatshirts	Mary's Willingness to Pay (Utility)	Marginal Utility	Number of Pizzas	Mary's Willingness to Pay (Utility)	Marginal Utility
0	0	50	0	0	18
1	50	45	1	18	16
2	95	40	2	34	15
3	135	35	3	49	14
4	170	30	4	63	13
5	200	28	5	76	12
6	228	26	6	88	11
7	254	24	7	99	10
8	278	23	8	109	9
9	301	22	9	118	8
10	323	21	10	126	7
11	344	20	11	133	6
12	364	19	12	139	5
13	383	18	13	144	4
14	401	17	14	148	
15	418	16			
16	434	15			
17	449	14			
18	463	13			
19	476	12			
20	488				

unit purchased of the other good; the last unit purchased of a good that costs three times as much must generate three times the marginal utility as the last unit purchased of the other good; and so on.

This general rule becomes even more powerful if we think about it in relation to a budget constraint diagram. We saw earlier that Fran chose the point along the budget constraint where the marginal *benefit* of an extra CD was equal to its price. The price measured what she had to give up in other goods to get one more CD. It was the marginal, or opportunity, cost of the extra CD. The reason Fran chose point *F* rather than *G* in Figure 8.1 is that *F* was the point where the marginal utilities of CDs and chocolate bars were proportional to their prices, or 15 to 1. For Fran, at *G* the marginal utility of an extra CD exceeded its price, while that of a chocolate bar was less than its price. As she moved down the budget constraint to *F*, the marginal utility of CDs decreased and that of chocolate bars increased, until the marginal utility of each equaled its price. We can express this in an equation,

$$MU_x = p_x,$$

which says that the marginal utility (*MU*) of any good (*x*) must equal its price (*p*).[4]

In the example we have just analysed, we assume Mary's willingness to pay for sweatshirts—her measure of utility—does not depend on how many pizzas, or other goods, she has. This is seldom the case. The utility, and hence marginal utility, of sweatshirts will depend on the number of pizzas, books, and other goods she has. Thus, even when the price of sweatshirts remains the same, if the price of other goods changes, she will change her consumption of those other goods *and* sweatshirts. The same thing will happen if Mary's income changes. The number of sweatshirts at which her marginal utility of an extra sweatshirt equals 15 will change. What matters for choices is *relative* price, so Mary will also change

her choices if the price of sweatshirts changes and other prices remain unchanged.

CONSUMER SURPLUS

Assume you go into a shop to buy a fizzy drink. The shop charges you 50 pence. You would have been willing to pay £1. The difference between what you paid and what you would have been willing to pay is called **consumer surplus.**

We can calculate the consumer surplus Mary gets from buying pizza from her demand curve. To see how we do this, use the marginal utility analysis of the previous section. We saw that at 11 pizzas, Mary is willing to pay £6 for one more; at 12, she is willing to pay £5.

Mary buys pizza up to the point where the price is equal to the marginal utility of the last pizza she chooses to buy. Of course, she pays the same price for each of the pizzas she purchases. Suppose pizzas cost £5 and Mary buys 13. The 13th pizza gives her a marginal utility of 5 and costs £5. Mary is getting a bargain: she would have been willing to pay more for the earlier pizzas. For her first pizza, she would have been willing to pay £18, for the second £16, and so forth. She would have been willing to pay a total of £144 (£18 + £16 + £15 + £14 + £13 + £12 + £11 + £10 + £9 + £8 + £7 + £6 + £5) for the 13 pizzas. The difference between what she *has* to pay for 13 pizzas £5 × 13, or £65—and what she would have been willing to pay, £144, is her **consumer surplus.** In this case, her consumer surplus is £79.

There is always some consumer surplus, so long as a consumer has to pay only a fixed price for all the items she purchases. The fact that demand curves are downward sloping means that the previous units the consumer purchases are more valuable than the marginal units. She would have been willing to pay more for these earlier units than for the last unit, but she does not have to.

In Figure 8.6, the total amount Mary would have been willing to pay for 13 pizzas is the total area under the demand curve between the vertical axis and 13, the combination of the purple and green shaded areas. This area is the sum of the willingness to pay for the 1st, 2nd, 3rd, and so on, up to the 13th pizza. The amount Mary actually has to pay is the green shaded area—the price, £5, times the quantity, 13 pizzas. Her consumer surplus is the *difference*,

---

[4] The result holds because we are measuring utility as willingness to pay. More generally, the result cited earlier, that the marginal utility per pound spent must be the same for all goods, can be written $MU_x/p_x = MU_y/p_y$ for any two goods *x* and *y*, or $MU_x/MU_y = p_x/p_y$; *the ratio of marginal utilities must equal the price ratio.*

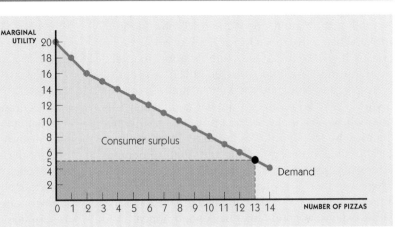

Figure 8.6 CONSUMER SURPLUS

The demand curve plots the amount Mary would be willing to pay for her 1st, 2nd, 3rd, and so on, pizza. The total amount she is willing to pay for 13 pizzas is the area under the demand curve up to the 13th pizza. The amount she actually has to pay is the green shaded area. The consumer surplus is the difference between the two, the purple shaded area above the line and below the demand curve, over the range of the quantity purchased.

the purple shaded area above the price line and below the demand curve, over the range of the quantity of purchases.

LOOKING BEYOND THE BASIC MODEL: HOW WELL DO THE UNDERLYING ASSUMPTIONS MATCH REALITY?

In the market economy, "For whom are goods produced?" has a simple answer: goods are produced for consumers. A theory of consumer choice is, therefore, critical to understanding market economies. The model of budget constraints and individual preferences sketched in this chapter is the economist's basic model of consumer choice. It is a powerful one whose insights carry well beyond this course. Still, the model has been criticised. Four criticisms are summarised here. The first has no economic merit. The other three are somewhat relevant. The first criticism is that the model does not reflect the thought processes consumers really go through. This line of criticism is like criticising the physicist's model of motion, which predicts with great precision how billiard balls will interact, simply because most billiard players do not go through the equations before taking a

shot. The appropriate question is whether the economic model of consumer choice can reliably be used to make predictions. By and large it can. Many businesses, for example, have found the model useful for predicting the demand for their products. And economists have used the model with remarkable success to predict consumer behaviour in a variety of circumstances.

The second criticism questions the model's assumption that individuals know what they like, which is to say that they have well-defined preferences. This criticism has merit. Having well-defined preferences means that if you gave someone a choice between two bundles of goods—one consisting of two apples, three oranges, and one pear and the other consisting of three apples, two oranges, and four pears—he could tell you quickly which he preferred. Furthermore, well-defined preferences imply that if you asked him tomorrow and the day after, he would give you the same answer. But in many cases, if you asked someone which of two things he preferred, he would say, "I don't know. Let me try them out." And what he likes may change from day to day. His preferences may, moreover, be affected by what others like. How else can we account for the frequent fads in foods and fashions as well as other aspects of our lives?

The third criticism has to do with the model's assumption that individuals know the price of each good in the market. People often do not know prices.

They know that there are bargains to be found, but they know it is costly to search for them. While we can talk meaningfully about the price of a tonne of wheat, what do we mean by the price of a couch or a house? If we are lucky and stumble onto a bargain, we might find a leather sofa for £1,000. If unlucky, even after searching all day, we may not find one for under £1,500. When we get the bargain leather sofa home, if we are lucky, we will find it is even better than we thought. If unlucky, the sofa will fall apart.

The final criticism points out that sometimes prices and preferences interact in a more complicated way than this chapter has depicted. People's attitudes toward a good can depend on its price. More expensive goods may have snob appeal. And when the quality of certain goods cannot easily be checked, individuals may judge quality by price. Because, on average, better (more durable) things are more costly, a cheap item is assumed to be of poor quality and an expensive item of good quality. In either case, demand curves will look quite different from those described in this chapter. Lowering the price for a good may actually lower the demand.

The fact that the basic economic model needs to be extended or modified for some goods in some instances does not deny its usefulness in the vast majority of situations where it provides just the information that businesses and governments need for making important decisions. Even in those instances where the model does not work so well, it provides a basic framework that allows us to enhance our understanding of the behaviour of households. By asking which of the assumptions underlying the model seems inappropriate in that particular situation, we are guided in our search for a better model of consumption.

REVIEW AND PRACTICE

SUMMARY

1 The amount of one good a person must give up to purchase another good is determined by the relative prices of the two goods and is illustrated by the slope of the budget constraint.

2 The demand curve for an individual is derived by tracing out the different quantities demanded of a good along a budget constraint as the price of the good changes and the budget constraint rotates.

3 Consumption of a normal good rises as income rises. Consumption of an inferior good falls as income rises.

4 As a good becomes more expensive relative to other goods, an individual will substitute other goods for the higher-priced good. This is the substitution effect. In addition, as the price of a good rises, a person's buying power is reduced. This is the in-

come effect. Normally, both the substitution effect and the income effect reduce the quantity demanded of a good as its price rises.

5 If two goods are complements, the demand for one decreases when the price of the other increases. If two goods are substitutes, the demand for one increases when the price of the other increases.

6 When substitution is easy, demand curves tend to be elastic, or flat. If substitution is difficult, demand curves tend to be inelastic, or steep.

7 Economists sometimes describe the benefits of consumption by referring to the utility that people get from a combination of goods. The extra utility of consuming one more unit of a good is referred to as the marginal utility of that good.

KEY TERMS

slope

income elasticity
of demand

inferior good

normal good

income effect

substitution effect

utility

marginal utility

diminishing marginal
utility

consumer surplus

REVIEW QUESTIONS

1 How is the slope of the budget constraint related
to the relative prices of the goods on the horizontal
and vertical axes?

2 How can the budget constraint appear the same
even for individuals whose tastes and preferences
differ dramatically?

3 Is the income elasticity of demand positive or negative for a normal good?

4 If the price of a normal good increases, how will
the income effect cause the quantity demanded of
that good to change?

5 If the price of a good increases, how will the income effect cause the quantity demanded of that
good to change?

6 Does a greater availability of substitutes make a
demand curve more or less elastic? Explain.

7 Why does marginal utility tend to diminish?

8 What is meant by consumer surplus?

PROBLEMS

1 Consider a student who has an entertainment budget of £120 per term and spends it on either concert
tickets at £10 apiece or cinema tickets at £6 apiece.
Imagine that cinema tickets start decreasing in price,
first falling to £4, then £3, then £2. Graph the four budget constraints, with visits to the cinema on the horizontal axis. If the student's demand curve for films is
represented by the function $D = 60 - 10p$, graph both
her demand curve for films and the point she will
choose at each price on the budget line.

2 Choose two normal goods and draw a budget constraint illustrating the trade-off between them. Show
how the budget line shifts if income increases. Arbi-
trarily choose a point on the first budget line as the
point a particular consumer will select. Now find
two points on the new budget line such that the new
preferred choice of the consumer must fall between
these points.

3 DINKs are households with "double income, no
kids," and such households are invading your neigh-

bourhood. You decide to take advantage of this influx
by starting a gourmet take-out food store. You know
that the price elasticity of demand for your food
from DINKs is 0.5 and the income elasticity of a demand is 1.5. From the standpoint of the quantity that
you sell, which of the following changes would concern you the most?

    (a) The number of DINKs in your neighbourhood
falls by 10 percent.
    (b) The average income of DINKs falls by 5 percent.

4 Compare one relatively poor person, with an income of £5,000 per year, with a relatively wealthy
person who has an income of £60,000 per year.
Imagine that the poor person drinks 15 bottles of
wine per year at an average price of £3 per bottle,
while the wealthy person drinks 50 bottles of wine
per year at an average price of £20 per bottle. If an
additional tax of £1 per bottle is imposed on wine,
who pays the greater amount? Who pays the greater
amount as a percentage of income? If a tax equal to

10 percent of the value of the wine is imposed, who pays the greater amount? Who pays the greater amount as a percentage of income?

Suppose there is an income elasticity of 0.62 for alcoholic beverages. Consider two people with incomes of £20,000 and £40,000. If all alcohol is taxed at the same rate, by what percentage of income will the tax paid by the £40,000 earner be greater than that paid by the £20,000 earner? Why might some people think this unfair?

5 Consider two ways of encouraging local governments to build or expand public parks. One proposal is for central government to provide grants for public parks. A second proposal is for the central government to agree to pay 25 percent of any expenditures for building or expansion. If the same amount of money would be spent on each program, which do you predict would be most effective in encouraging local parks? Explain your answer, using the ideas of income and substitution effects.

APPENDIX: INDIFFERENCE CURVES AND THE CONSUMPTION DECISION

This chapter explained the consumption decision in terms of the budget constraint facing the individual and the individual's choice of her most preferred point on the budget constraint. Effects of changes in prices on the quantity demanded were analysed in terms of income and substitution effects.

To facilitate a more rigorous analysis of choices and the consequences of changes in prices, economists have developed an extremely useful tool called **indifference curves.** Indifference curves give the combinations of goods among which an individual is indifferent or which yield the same level of utility. This appendix shows how indifference curves can be used to derive the demand curve and to separate more precisely changes in consumption into income and substitution effects.

USING INDIFFERENCE CURVES TO ILLUSTRATE CONSUMER CHOICES

In this chapter solutions to consumer choice problems were characterized as having two stages: first, identify the opportunity set, and second, find the most preferred point in the opportunity set. For consumers with a given income to spend on goods, the budget constraint defines her opportunity set. Figure 8.7 repeats the budget constraint for Fran, who must divide her income between chocolate bars and CDs. In the chapter, we simply said that Fran chose the most preferred point along the budget constraint. If she likes CDs a lot, she might choose point B; if she has a stronger preference for chocolate, she might choose point A.

The concept of the indifference curve can help us see which of these points she chooses.

The indifference curve shows the various combinations of goods that make a person equally happy. For example, in Figure 8.8, the indifference curve I_0 gives all those combinations of chocolate bars and compact discs that Fran finds just as attractive as 150 chocolate bars and 10 CDs (point A on the curve). At B, for instance, she has 12 CDs but only 130 chocolate bars—not so much chocolate, but in her mind the extra CDs make up for the loss. The fact that B and A are on the same indifference curve means that Fran is indifferent. That is, if you asked her whether she preferred A to B or B to A, she would answer that she couldn't care less.

Indifference curves simply reflect preferences between pairs of goods. Unlike demand curves, they have nothing to do with budget constraints or prices. The different combinations of goods along the indifference curve cost different amounts of money. The indifference curves are drawn by asking an individual which he prefers: 10 chocolate bars and 2 CDs or 15 chocolate bars and 1 CD? Or 11 chocolate bars and 2 CDs or 15 chocolate bars and 1 CD? Or 12 chocolate bars and 2 CDs or 15 chocolate bars and 1 CD? When he answers, "I am indifferent between the

Figure 8.7 BUDGET CONSTRAINT

The budget constraint defines the opportunity set. Fran can choose any point on or below the budget constraint. If she has strong preferences for CDs, she might choose B; if she has strong preferences for chocolate bars, she might choose point A.

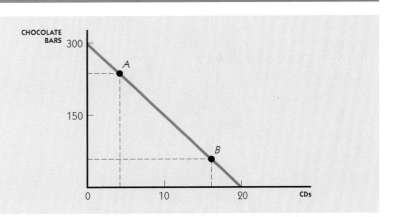

two," the two points that represent those choices are on the same indifference curve.

Moving along the curve in one direction, Fran is willing to accept more CDs in exchange for fewer chocolate bars; moving in the other direction, she is willing to accept more chocolate bars in exchange for fewer CDs. Any point on the same indifference curve, by definition, makes her just as happy as any other—whether it is point A or C or an extreme point like D, where she has many chocolate bars and very few CDs, or F, where she has relatively few chocolate bars but more CDs.

However, if Fran were to receive the same number of chocolate bars but more CDs than at A—say

150 chocolate bars and 15 CDs (point E)—she would be better off on the principle that more is better. The new indifference curve I_1 illustrates all those combinations of chocolate bars and CDs that make her just as well off as the combination of 150 chocolate bars and 15 CDs.

Figure 8.8 shows two indifference curves for Fran. Because more is better, Fran (or any individual) will prefer a choice on an indifference curve that is higher than another. On the higher indifference curve, she can have more of both items. By definition, we can draw an indifference curve for *any* point in the space of an indifference curve diagram. Also by definition, indifference curves cannot cross,

Figure 8.8 INDIFFERENCE CURVES

An indifference curve traces combinations of goods among which an individual is indifferent. Each reflects Fran's taste for CDs and for chocolate bars. She is just as well off (has an identical amount of utility) at all points on the indifference curve I_0: A, B, C, D, and F.

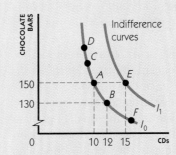

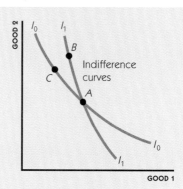

Figure 8.9 WHY INDIFFERENCE CURVES CANNOT CROSS

If two indifference curves crossed, a logical contradiction would occur. If curves crossed at point A, then Fran would be indifferent between A and B and between A and C, and therefore between B and C. But since B involves higher consumption of both goods than C, B is clearly preferred to C.

as Figure 8.9 makes clear. Assume that the indifference curves I_0 and I_1 cross at point A. That would mean that Fran is indifferent between A and all points on I_0 and between A and all points on I_1. In particular, she would be indifferent between A and B, between A and C, and accordingly between B and C. But B is clearly preferred to C; therefore, indifference curves cannot cross.

INDIFFERENCE CURVES AND MARGINAL RATES OF SUBSTITUTION

The slope of the indifference curve measures the number of compact discs that the individual is willing to give up to get another chocolate bar. The technical term for the slope of an indifference curve is the **marginal rate of substitution.** The marginal rate of substitution tells us how much of one good an individual is *willing* to give up in return for one more unit of another. This concept is quite distinct from the amount a consumer *must* give up, which is determined by the budget constraint and relative prices.

If Fran's marginal rate of substitution of chocolate bars for CDs is 15 to 1, this means that if she is given 1 more CD, she is willing to give up 15 chocolate bars. If she only had to give up 12 chocolate bars, she would be happier. If she had to give up 20, she would say, "That's too much. Having 1 more CD isn't worth

giving up 20 chocolate bars." Of course, Gary could have quite different attitudes towards CDs and chocolate bars. His marginal rate of substitution might be 25 to 1. He would be willing to give up 25 chocolate bars to get 1 more CD.

The marginal rate of substitution rises and falls according to how much of an item an individual already has. For example, consider point F back in Figure 8.8, where Fran has a lot of CDs and few chocolate bars. In this case, Fran already has bought all her favorite CDs; the marginal CD she buys now will be something she likes but not something she is wild about. In other words, because she already has a large number of CDs, having an additional one is less important. She would rather have some chocolate bars instead. Her marginal rate of substitution of chocolate bars for CDs at F is very low; for the sake of illustration, let's say that she would be willing to give up the marginal CD for only 10 chocolate bars. Her marginal rate of substitution is 10 to 1 (chocolate bars per CD).

The opposite situation prevails when Fran has lots of chocolate bars and few CDs. Since she is eating several chocolate bars almost every day, the chance to have more is just not worth much to her. But since she has few CDs, she does not yet own all of her favorites. The marginal value of another chocolate bar is relatively low, while the marginal value of another CD is relatively high. Accordingly, in this situation, Fran might insist on getting 30 extra chocolate bars before she gives up 1 CD. Her marginal rate of substitution is 30 to 1 (chocolate bars per CD).

As we move along an indifference curve, we increase the amount of one good (like CDs) that an individual has. In Fran's case, she requires less and less of the other good (chocolate bars) to compensate her for each one-unit decrease in the quantity of the first good (CDs). This principle is known as the **diminishing marginal rate of substitution.** As a result of the principle of diminishing marginal rate of substitution, the slope of the indifference curve becomes flatter as we move from left to right along the curve.

USING INDIFFERENCE CURVES TO ILLUSTRATE CHOICES

By definition, an individual does not care where he is on any *given* indifference curve. But he would prefer to be on the highest indifference curve possible. What pins him down is his budget constraint. As Figure 8.10 illustrates, the highest indifference curve that a person can attain is the one that just touches the budget constraint, that is, the indifference curve that is *tangent* to the budget constraint. The point of tangency (labeled E) is the point the individual will choose. Consider any other point on the budget constraint, say A. The indifference curve through A is below the curve through E; the individual is better off at E than at A. On the other hand, consider an indifference curve above I_0, for instance I_1. Since every point on I_1 lies above the budget constraint, there is no point on I_1 that the individual can purchase given his income.

When a curve is tangent to a line, the curve and line have the same slope at the point of tangency. Thus, the slope of the indifference curve equals the slope of the budget constraint at the point of tangency. The slope of the indifference curve is the marginal rate of substitution; the slope of the budget constraint is the relative price. This two-dimensional diagram therefore illustrates a basic principle of consumer choice: *individuals choose the point where the marginal rate of substitution equals the relative price.*

This principle makes sense. If the relative price of CDs and chocolate bars is 15 (CDs cost £15 and chocolate bars cost £1) and Fran's marginal rate of substitution is 20, Fran is willing to give up 20 chocolate bars to get 1 more CD but only *has* to give up 15; it clearly pays her to buy more CDs and fewer chocolate bars. If her marginal rate of substitution is 10, she is willing to give up 1 CD for just 10 chocolate bars; but if she gives up 1 CD, she can get 15 chocolate bars. She will be better off buying more chocolate bars and fewer CDs. Thus, if the marginal rate of substitution exceeds the relative price, Fran is better off if she buys more CDs; if it is less, she is better off if she buys fewer CDs. When the marginal rate of substitution *equals* the relative price, it does not pay for her to either increase or decrease her purchases.

INCOME ELASTICITY

Budget constraints and indifference curves show why, while goods normally have a positive income

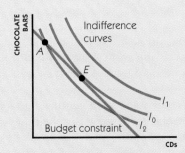

Figure 8.10 INDIFFERENCE CURVES AND THE BUDGET CONSTRAINT

The highest feasible indifference curve that can be reached is the one just tangent to the budget constraint, or indifference curve I_0 here. This individual's budget constraint does not permit her to reach I_1, nor would she want to choose point A, which would put her on I_2, since along I_2 she is worse off.

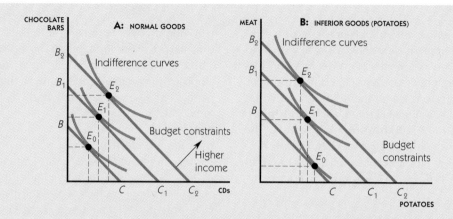

Figure 8.11 NORMAL AND INFERIOR GOODS WITH INDIFFERENCE CURVES

Panel A shows the case of two normal goods. An increase in income shifts the budget constraint out from BC to B_1C_1 to B_2C_2, and the consumption of both goods rises from E_0 to E_1 to E_2. Panel B shows the case of an inferior good. As the budget constraint shifts out, consumption of potatoes falls.

elasticity, some goods may have a negative income elasticity. As incomes increase, the budget constraint shifts out to the right in a parallel line, say from BC in Figure 8.11 to B_1C_1 to B_2C_2. The choices—the points of tangency with the indifference curves—are represented by the points E_0, E_1, and E_2. In panel A, we see the normal case, where as the budget constraint shifts out, more of both chocolate bars and CDs are consumed. But panel B illustrates the case of inferior goods. Potatoes are on the horizontal axis, and meat is on the vertical. As incomes rise, the points of tangency E_1 and E_2 move to the left; potato consumption falls.

USING INDIFFERENCE CURVES TO DERIVE DEMAND CURVES

Indifference curves and budget constraints can be used to derive the demand curve, to show what happens when prices increase. The analysis consists of two steps.

First, we identify what happens to the budget constraint as, say, the price of CDs increases. In the budget constraint drawn in Figure 8.12A, we find CDs on the horizontal axis and all other goods on the vertical axis. If Fran buys no CDs, she has £300 to spend on all other goods. At a CD price of £15, she can buy

up to 20 CDs. As the price of CDs increases, the budget constraint rotates. If she buys no CDs, the amount of other goods she can purchase is unchanged, at £300. But if she buys only CDs, the number of CDs she can purchase decreases in proportion to the increase in price. If the price rises to £30, she can buy half the number of CDs.

For each budget constraint, we find the point of tangency between the indifference curve and the budget constraint, the points labeled F_i, F, and F_d. This shows the point chosen along each budget constraint. Looking at the horizontal axis, we see, at each price, the quantity of CDs purchased. Panel B then plots these quantities for each price. At the price of £15, Fran chooses 11 CDs, at a price of £30, only 6.

SUBSTITUTION AND INCOME EFFECTS

Indifference curves also permit a precise definition of the substitution and income effects. Figure 8.13 plots Jeremy's indifference curve between CDs and chocolate. Jeremy's original budget constraint is line BC and his indifference curve is I_0; the point of tan-

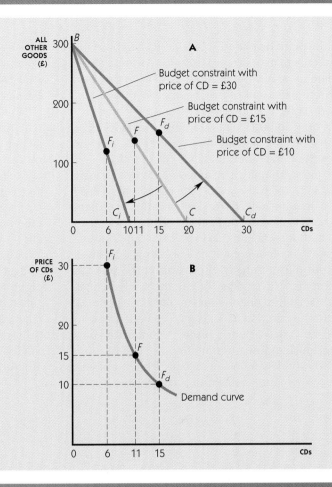

Figure 8.12 DERIVING DEMAND CURVES FROM SHIFTING BUDGET CONSTRAINTS

In panel A, the budget constraint rotates down to the left as the price of CDs increases, leading Fran to change consumption from F to F_i. The budget constraint rotates to the right when the price of CDs decreases, and Fran moves from F to F_d. Panel B shows the corresponding demand curve for CDs, illustrating how the rising prices lead to a declining quantity consumed.

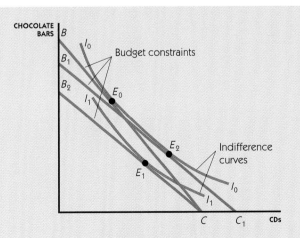

Figure 8.13 SUBSTITUTION AND INCOME EFFECTS WITH INDIFFERENCE CURVES

As the price of chocolate bars increases, the budget constraint rotates down. The change of Jeremy's choice from E_0 to E_1 can be broken down into an income and a substitution effect. The line B_1C_1 shows the substitution effect, the change that would occur if relative prices shifted but the level of utility remained the same. (Notice that Jeremy stays on the same indifference curve in this scenario.) The substitution effect alone causes a shift from E_0 to E_2. The shift in the budget constraint from B_1C_1 to B_2C shows the income effect, the change that results from changing the amount of income but leaving relative prices unchanged. The income effect alone causes a shift from E_2 to E_1.

gency, the point he chooses, is point E_0. Suppose the price of chocolate increases. Now he can buy fewer chocolate bars, but the number of CDs he can buy, were he to spend all of his income on CDs, is unchanged. Thus, his budget constraint becomes flatter; it is now line B_2C. While Jeremy originally chose point E_0 on the indifference curve I_0, now he chooses E_1 on the *lower* indifference curve I_1.

The price change has moved Jeremy's choice from E_0 to E_1 for two reasons: the substitution effect and the income effect. To see how this has happened, let's isolate the two effects. First, we focus on the substitution effect by asking what would happen to Jeremy's consumption if we changed relative prices but did not change how well off he was. To keep him just as well off as before the price change, we must keep him on the same indifference curve I_0. Thus, the substitution effect is a movement along an indifference curve. As the price of chocolate rises, Jeremy, moving down the indifference curve, buys more CDs and fewer chocolate bars. The movement from E_0 to E_2 is the substitution effect. The budget constraint B_1C_1 represents the *new* prices, but it does not account for the income effect, by definition, since Jeremy is on the same indifference curve that he was on before.

To keep Jeremy on the same indifference curve when we increase the price of chocolate requires giving Jeremy more income. The line B_1C_1 is the budget constraint with the new prices that would leave Jeremy on the same indifference curve. Because prices are the same, the budget constraint B_1C_1 is parallel to B_2C. We now need to take away the income that left Jeremy on the same indifference curve. We keep prices the same (at the new levels), and we take away income until we arrive at the new budget constraint B_2C and the corresponding new equilibrium E_1. The movement from E_2 to E_1 is called the income effect, since only income is changed. We have thus broken down the movement from the old equilibrium E_0 to the new one E_1 into the movement from E_0 to E_2, the substitution effect, and the movement from E_2 to E_1, the income effect.

LABOUR SUPPLY
AND SAVINGS

T he first of the four basic decisions of the household—how individuals choose to spend their money—was discussed in Chapter 8. How much money people have to spend depends, in turn, on two other basic decisions: how much they choose to work (and earn) and how much they save (or spend from savings). This chapter focuses on these two decisions. We will see that consumer theory can be supplied directly to analysing the work and saving decisions. We will also see how the supply curve for labour and the supply curve for savings can be derived, and why they have the shapes they do.

KEY QUESTIONS

1 How can the basic tools introduced in Chapter 8 to analyse consumers' expenditure decisions be applied to such important aspects of life as work, education, and savings?

2 What determines the number of hours an individual works or whether she chooses to work? How do

income and substitution effects help us to understand why labour suppy may not be very responsive to changes in wages, or savings to changes in interest rates?

3 Why do economists think of education as an investment and refer to the result as human capital?

THE LABOUR SUPPLY DECISION

Patterns of labour supply have changed greatly in the past three decades. The average work week for a manual worker in Britain has fallen from about 45 hours in 1947 to around 40 hours today. At the same time, the proportion of women in the labour force has increased enormously. As a result, the typical married household now devotes more hours to work outside the home than it did in 1900. The number of hours worked varies a lot from person to person. In Britain, in 1997, the distribution of hours of work was wide: 45 percent of women and 10 percent of men worked 30 hours a week or less, while 5 percent of women and 22 percent of men worked 51 hours a week or more—longer than the maximum normal working week of 48 hours proposed by the European Commission (see Figure 9.1). Many of the extra jobs in Britain in the 1980s provided part-time employment and jobs taken by women.

THE CHOICE BETWEEN LEISURE AND CONSUMPTION

Economists use the basic model of choice to help understand these patterns of labour supply. The decision about how much labour to supply is a choice between consumption, or income, and leisure. (Leisure to an economist means all the time an individual could po-

tentially work for pay that he actually spends not working. The time parents spend caring for their children, for example, is leisure in this special sense.) By giving up leisure, a person receives additional income, and therefore increases his consumption. By working less and giving up some consumption, a person obtains more leisure. An increase in income does not necessarily translate *immediately* into consumption; the individual has to decide whether to spend his extra income now or in the future. We tackle this later in the chapter. Here we assume that the person spends all his income.

Even though the typical job seems to represent a fixed time requirement, there are a variety of ways in which people can influence how much labour they will supply. Many workers may not have discretion as to whether they will work full time, but they have some choice in whether they will work overtime. In addition, many individuals moonlight; they take up second jobs that provide them with additional income. Most of these jobs—like driving a taxi—provide considerable discretion in the number of hours worked. Hence, even when people have no choice about how much they work at their primary job, they still have choices. Further, the fact that jobs differ in their normal work week means that a worker has some flexibility in choosing a job that allows her to work the amount of hours she wishes. Finally, economists believe that the social conventions concerning the standard work week—the 45-hour week that has become the 40-hour week—respond over time to the attitudes (preferences) of workers.

We now apply the analysis of Chapter 8, to an individual's choice between work and leisure. Figure 9.2 shows the budget constraint of Steve, who earns an

Figure 9.1 THE DISTRIBUTION OF HOURS OF WORK

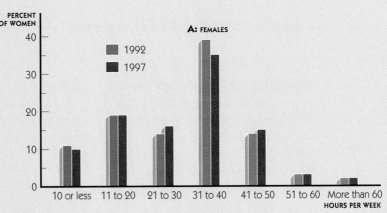

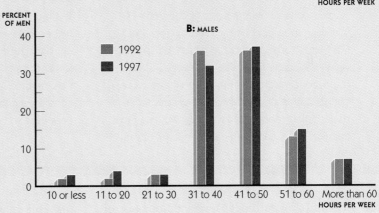

The figure shows the percentage of men and women who worked various numbers of hours per week during 1992 and 1997. Most men worked either 31 to 40 hours a week or 41 to 50 hours. There was a small increase in the percentage of men working longer hours. The distribution of women's working hours is much wider. A lot of women work less than 40 hours a week, with the biggest percentage's working between 31 and 40 hours. Interestingly, the percentage of women working more than 40 hours increased slightly between 1992 and 1997. *Source:* "Labour Force Survey," *Social Trends* (1998), Table 4.16.

Figure 9.2 A BUDGET CONSTRAINT BETWEEN LEISURE AND INCOME

Individuals are willing to trade leisure for an increase in income, and thus in consumption. The budget constraint shows Steve choosing E_0, with 10 hours of daily leisure, 6 hours of work, and £30 in daily wages.

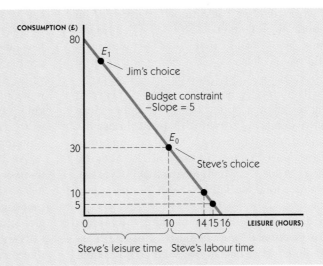

hourly wage of £5. Accordingly, for each hour less of leisure Steve enjoys—for each extra hour he works—he earns £5 more; that is, his consumption increases by £5. Underlying this budget constraint is his time constraint. He has only so many hours a day, say 16, to spend either working or at leisure. For each extra hour he works, he has 1 less hour of leisure. If he works 1 hour, his income is £5; if he works 2 hours, his income is £10; and so forth. If he works 16 hours—he has no leisure—his income is £5 × 16 = £80. The budget constraint trade-off is £5 per hour.

Steve will choose a point on the budget constraint according to his own preferences, just as he chose between two goods in Chapter 8. He must choose the appropriate trade-off between leisure and consumption. Let's suppose that he chooses point E_0. At E_0, he has 10 hours of leisure, which means that he works 6 hours out of a total available time of 16 hours and makes £30.

In deciding which of the points along the budget constraint to choose, Steve balances out the marginal benefits of what he can buy with an additional hour's wages with the marginal costs—the value of the hour's worth of leisure that he will have to forgo. Steve and his brother Jim assess the marginal bene-

fits and marginal costs differently: Steve chooses point E_0 and his brother chooses point E_1. Jim values the material things in life more and leisure less.

For Steve, at E_0, the marginal benefit of the extra concert tickets or other goods he can buy with the money he earns from working an extra hour just offsets the marginal cost of that hour, the extra leisure he has to give up. At points to the left of E_0, Steve has less leisure (so the marginal value of leisure is greater) and he has more goods (so the marginal value of the extra goods he can get is lower). The marginal benefit of working more exceeds the marginal costs, and so he works more—he moves towards E_0. Converse arguments apply to Steve's thinking about points to the right of E_0.

We can use the same kind of reasoning to see why the workaholic Jim chooses a point to the left of E_0. At E_0, Jim values goods more and leisure less; the marginal benefit of working more exceeds the marginal cost. At E_1, the marginal benefit of working an extra hour (the extra consumption) just offsets the marginal cost.

This framework can be used to analyse the effects of changes in income and wages on the work-leisure decision in the same way that we used it to analyse the

WAGE CHANGES AND LABOUR SUPPLY

As wages rise, individuals become better off. This income effect induces them to work less. Offsetting this is the substitution effect—the greater return to working provides an incentive to work longer hours. Either effect may dominate. Thus, the quantity of labour supplied may increase or decrease with wage increases.

effects of changes in income and prices on purchases of goods and services. For instance, an increase in income normally leads individuals to consume more of all "goods," including leisure: at fixed wages, as incomes rise, labour supply decreases.

Changes in wages have both an income effect and a substitution effect. An increase in wages makes individuals better off. When individuals are better off, they work less. This is the income effect. But an increase in wages also changes the trade-offs. By giving up one more hour of leisure, the individual can get more goods. Because of this, individuals are willing to work more. This is the substitution effect.

In the case of the typical good, we saw that the income and substitution effects reinforced each other. A higher price meant individuals were worse off, and this lead to reduced consumption of the good; and a higher price meant that individuals substituted away from the good whose price had increased. *With labour supply, income and substitution effects work in the opposite direction, so the net affect of an increase in wages is ambiguous.*

Figure 9.3A shows the normal case of an upward-sloping labour supply curve, where the substitution effect dominates. Panel B illustrates the case of a backward-bending labour supply curve. At high wages, the income effect of further increases in wages outweighs the substitution effect, so that labour supply decreases. The phenomenon of some high-income professionals' working only a four-day week may be evidence of a labour supply curve that is backward bending at high income levels.

If income and substitution effects just outweigh each other, then labour supply will be relatively unaffected by wage changes. The evidence is that, at least for men, the labour supply elasticity—the percentage increase in hours worked as a result of a 1 percent increase in real wages—is positive but small.

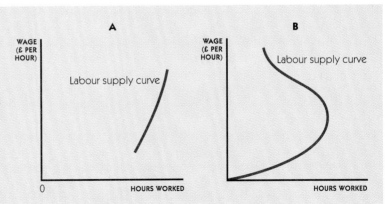

Figure 9.3 DERIVING THE LABOUR SUPPLY CURVE

Panel A shows the case in which the substitution effect exceeds the income effect by just a bit, so increases in wages lead to only a small change in labour supply, and the labour supply curve is almost vertical. In panel B, the substitution effect dominates the income effect at low wages, so that the labour supply curve is upward sloping; and the income effect dominates the substitution effect at high wages, so that the labour supply is downward sloping over that range. Thus, the labour supply curve bends backwards.

That is why in spite of the huge increase in wages over the past fifty years, average hours worked, for men, have not changed much.

LABOUR FORCE PARTICIPATION

The decision about how much labour to supply can be divided into two parts: whether to work and, if so, how much to work. The decision about *whether* to work is called the **labour force participation decision.** Figure 9.4 shows the labour supply curve for an individual, that is, how many hours he is willing to supply at each wage. The minimum wage at which the individual is willing to work, w_R, is called the **reservation wage.** Below the reservation wage, the individual does not participate in the labour force.

For men, the question of whether to work has traditionally had an obvious answer. Unless they were very wealthy, they have had to work to support themselves (and their families). The wage at which they would decide to work rather than not to was, accordingly, very low. For most men, a change in the wage still does not affect their decision of whether to work. It affects only their decision about how many hours to work, and even this effect is small.

Most women now work for pay too. For many years, most young unmarried women have worked. How-

ever, there has been an increase in the proportion of married women working. They have been returning to the labour force after the birth of children more quickly and in greater numbers than before. Nevertheless, the labour supply of women seems to be more sensitive to the wage rate than the labour supply of men does. Small changes in the wage rate thus have the potential of causing large changes in the fraction of women who work. The labour supply curve for women appears to be very elastic (flat). Some economists have estimated a female labour supply elasticity of the order of 1; that is, a 1 percent increase in wages leads to a 1 percent increase in labour supply.

During the postwar period in the United Kingdom, while the number of males employed has fallen form 15.8 million in 1949 to 14.3 million in 1997, the number of women workers has risen from 7.2 million in 1949 to 12.2 million in 1997 (see Figure 9.5). The change in women's labour supply can be viewed partly as a *shift* in the labour supply curve and partly as a *movement* along it. Figure 9.6 shows how the number of women participating in the labour force increases with the wage rate. Such a curve is called the labour force participation curve. If all women supplied a fixed number of hours (say, 35 hours per week), then the labour force participation curve and the female labour supply curve would look the same.

Job opportunities for women have improved greatly in the period since 1945. A lot of the growth of

Figure 9.4 **THE MARKET LABOUR PARTICIPATION DECISION**

The reservation wage W_R is the minimum wage at which an individual supplies labour.

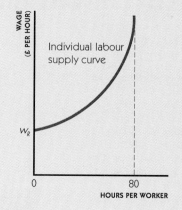

THE LABOUR SUPPLY DECISION • 167

Figure 9.5 MALE AND FEMALE EMPLOYMENT

Since 1949 the numbers of men employed in the United Kingdom has fallen slightly, from just under 16 million in 1949 to just over 14 million in 1997. The numbers of women have risen from just over 7 million to over 12 million during the same period. Women's labour force participation has grown strongly, as married women have reentered or remained in the labour force. The growth of the service industries since the 1980s has provided many more job opportunities for women, and many of them part time. As male unemployment has grown and as men have retired from work at progressively younger ages and stayed longer in education before entering the labour force, their numbers in jobs have slowly dwindled. *Source:* Central Statistical Office, *Annual Abstract of Statistics* (1998, 1987, 1968, 1960).

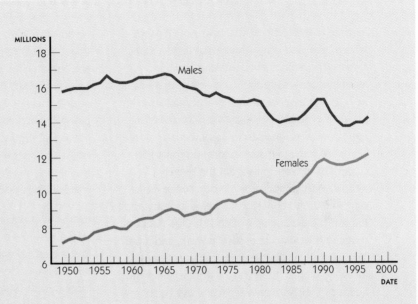

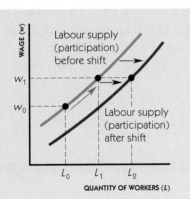

Figure 9.6 EXPLAINING CHANGES IN LABOUR FORCE PARTICIPATION

The increased labour force participation of women results in part from a movement along the supply curve resulting from higher wages (the movement from L_0 to L_1) and in part from a shift of the supply curve itself (the movement from L_1 to L_2).

employment in the 1980s was in the employment of women. Their earnings relative to men have also made modest gains. After the Equal Pay Acts of 1970, female wages in the United Kingdom rose from around 60 percent of comparable male wages in 1970 to around 70 percent in 1976.

TAX POLICY AND LABOUR SUPPLY

The effect of a change in wages on labour supply has important policy implications. For example, we often hear than an increase in taxes discourages people from working. An increase in tax rates is equivalent to a decrease in wages, since it decreases the after-tax wage received by the worker. But if the labour supply curve is backward bending, then a tax increase and its accompanying reduction in the after-tax wage can actually increase the labour supply.

Differences in views about the relative magnitudes of the income and substitution effects on labour supply have played an important role in re-

POLICY PERSPECTIVE: GROWTH OF FEMALE PARTICIPATION IN THE LABOUR FORCE

In some of the old industrial towns of England, where heavy industry—steel, shipbuilding, coal, railways—was once concentrated and the labour force was predominantly male, there is now a majority of women in the labour force. In towns like Middlesborough, the percentage of female workers has risen to 55 percent or more. There are some demand factors and some supply factors at work in this, but the two are deeply intertwined. Partly it is due to the decline in the traditional jobs in heavy industry and the rise in male unemployment. This has directly reduced the numbers of men in work, and it has also spurred many women to go out and look for work: women have sought work to meet the needs of their families when men have been unable to find it.

Allied to the rise in numbers of women looking for jobs has been a rise in the supply of suitable jobs. The shift from manufacturing to services has created a lot of jobs that do not require great physical strength or endurance but instead require good interpersonal skills. Call centres are a good example. Firms set up or use call centres to answer queries from customers, take bookings, sell products, and do many other transactions which once might have been done in a shop or office but which now are more often done over the telephone—again, a reflection of

technical advance and the falling costs of telecommunications. Many people think women are better suited to work of this kind than men are—more friendly and conciliatory over the phone, more willing to do things for other people. Also women are more likely to find this kind of work attractive whereas many men, particularly men who have had years of experience in traditional jobs in manufacturing, have not found it easy to adjust to service-sector jobs.

Many of the new jobs are dismissed as being "McJobs"—low pay, not very highly skilled, with low security of employment, and often part time. This may be too negative a view. More and more people want part-time work, for example, if they are balancing work and domestic commitments. Some people want to have a temporary job and do not want to make a career in whatever it happens to be. There is a growing workforce of young people, moving between education and work, financing their studies by working part time, American style. Providing there are plenty of these jobs and people can move into and out of them with ease, the fact that any particular one is not permanent does not matter.

Source: "The Future is Female," *The Guardian,* 8 August 1998.

cent debates over tax policy. When asked how they would respond to a tax increase, workers do not answer in terms of income and substitution effects. They say things like "I have to work longer hours to maintain my standard of living" or "I work less, because it doesn't pay to work so hard." But economists interpret these different responses in the analytical framework of income and substitution effects. In particular, economists are interested in

what happens *on average* and what happens to particular groups of people within the economy.

For men, the consensus is that the labour supply elasticity is relatively low, so that changing taxes has little effect on either labour force participation or hours worked. But some economists believe that men's labour supply elasticity is quite large and that the very high tax rate on high incomes that prevailed until the 1980s had a strong adverse effect on labour supply. Indeed, some "supply siders" (named for their emphasis on incentives that affect supply) predicted that high-income groups would supply so much more labour in response to a tax reduction that government revenue would increase (even with lower tax rates). The evidence by and large indicates that the labour supply response elasticity for men is actually low. Hours worked increased little if at all as a result of the tax cuts of the 1980s, and overall tax revenues dropped. But tax revenues from *upper* income groups did increase. It is not clear that the rich worked more as a result of the reduced tax rates, however. Two other explanations are at least as plausible. First, the lower tax rates meant that the value of avoiding taxes through tax shelters fell, and investors moved their money back into taxable activities. Second, and more important, wage inequality continued to increase over the period. The rich became richer not because they worked more hours but because they earned more per hour worked.

Changes in the income tax system have encouraged married women to participate in the labour market. In former times a married woman and her husband were taxed as if they were one person on the basis of their joint income. The important change has been to tax married couples as two separate people. This makes a big difference under a *progressive income tax regime*, one in which the marginal tax rate rises with the level of income. A married couple each earning £25,000 per annum would have been taxed as one person earning £50,000 under the old system, and they would have paid tax at the higher rate (currently 40 percent) on their marginal earnings. Currently they are taxed as two persons each earning £25,000 per annum and pay tax at the standard rate, currently 23 percent per annum on marginal earnings. Because each faces a lower tax rate, each has a greater incentive to work (on the basis of the substitution effect). This has induced a substantial increase in the labour supply of married women.

THE RETIREMENT DECISION

Retirement is another important aspect of the labour force participation decision. Life expectancy has been growing: a male aged 40 in the United Kingdom in 1901 had a life expectancy of 26.1 years,

whereas a male aged 40 in the United Kingdom in 1931 had a life expectancy of 29.5 years, in 1961 of 31.5 years, and in 1991 of 35.2 years. At the same time, retirement ages have been falling. In 1991, only 53.4 percent of males between the ages of 60 and 64 and 8.4 percent of those 65 or more were in the labour force; 23 percent of females aged between 60 and 64 and 3.1 percent of those aged 65 or more were in the labour force. Many people no longer work until the age of 65. Retirement before that age is more and more common. People are taking more years of retirement at the end of their lives.

These retirement decisions too can be understood in terms of a basic economic model. Increased lifetime wealth has led individuals to choose more leisure over their lifetime. The fact that when people are better off they wish to enjoy more leisure is, as we saw earlier, the income effect. The decision to retire earlier can be thought of as a decision to enjoy more leisure. Indeed, it makes sense for people to choose more leisure in their later years, when their productivity has reached its peak and their wages are not going to increase much further.

At the same time, wages today are much higher than they were fifty years ago. This means that it is more costly for people to retire early—the amount of consumption (income) they have to give up is larger. This is the substitution effect. Evidently, for many workers, the income effect dominates the substitution effect.

HUMAN CAPITAL AND EDUCATION

A nation's output depends not only on the number of hours people work but also on how productive those hours are. One of the important determinants of workers' productivity—and therefore wages—is education.

By taking more time for education, which usually means delaying entry into the labour force, people can increase their expected annual income. In addition, working *harder* at their studies and giving up leisure may result in better grades and skills, which in turn will result in higher wages in the future.

Thus, students face a trade-off between leisure today and consumption, or income, in the future.

For the student, taking a degree course has some costs, including living expenses and tuition fees. Some of the costs might be met by scholarships or other grants and subsidies. But there are other costs. In particular, there is the **opportunity cost** of the earnings that the student would have made if he or she had worked instead of studying. Economists say that the investment in education produces **human capital,** making an analogy to the **physical capital** investments that businesses make in plant and equipment. Human capital is developed by formal education, on-the-job learning, and many other investments of time and money that parents make in their children.

Expenditure on educational investments—human capital formation—is substantial. The British government spends just over 5 percent of the gross domestic product on it. This is only a part of the total, because it leaves out the additional expenditures made by individuals towards things like private school fees and it leaves out most of the forgone earnings of students of working age.

There has been a great increase in investment in education since 1945. In 1900 only 1.2 percent of each age group entered full-time higher education in Britain, in 1954 the figure was 5.8 percent, in 1962 it was 8.5 percent, in 1981 it was 13.5 percent, and by 1993 it had risen to over 25 percent. Enrollments in higher education rose from 1.18 million in 1990–91 to 1.90 million in 1995–96. Table 9.1 reports the growth in both male and female enrollment in both further and higher education.

EDUCATION AND ECONOMIC TRADE-OFFS

The production possibilities curve introduced in Chapter 2 can illustrate how decisions concerning investments in human capital are made. To accomplish this, we divide an individual's life into two periods: youth and later working years. Figure 9.7 depicts the relationship between consumption in youth and in later life. As the individual gives up consumption in his youth, staying in school longer in-

Table 9.1 ENROLLMENT IN FURTHER AND HIGHER EDUCATION IN THE UNITED KINGDOM, IN THOUSANDS

	1970–71	1980–81	1990–91	1995–96
Male				
Further ed.	1,007	851	987	1,110
Higher ed.	416	526	638	913
Female				
Further ed.	725	820	1,247	1,496
Higher ed.	205	301	537	987

Source: Office of National Statistics, *Social Trends* (1998), Table 3.8.

creases his expected future consumption because he can expect his income to go up. The curve has been drawn to show diminishing returns: spending more on education today (reducing consumption) raises future income, but each additional investment in education provides a smaller and smaller return.

Point *A* represents the case where Everett is a full-time student for the three years of a university degree course with little income until graduation (his youth) but with a high income in later life. Point *B* represents the consequences of leaving school at 18. When he does this, Everett has a higher income in his youth but a lower income in later life. Other possible points between *A* and *B* represent cases where Everett drops out of his university course after one or two years.

THE WIDENING WAGE GAP

Those who have a college or university education are paid more on average than those who leave school at 16 with few or no qualifications. Because unskilled workers generally cannot perform the same jobs as skilled workers, it is useful to think about the wages of the two groups as determined in separate labour markets, as illustrated in Figure 9.8.

Figure 9.7 EDUCATION AND THE TRADE-OFF BETWEEN CURRENT AND FUTURE CONSUMPTION

Point A represents a choice of a reduced income and better education in the present, with a higher income in the future. Point B represents the choice of higher income and less education now, with a lower level of income in the future.

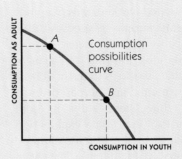

Panel A shows the demand and supply curves of unskilled workers, panel B those of skilled workers. The equilibrium wage for skilled workers is higher than that for unskilled workers.

What happens if a change in technology shifts the demand curve for skilled labour to the right, to DS_1, and the demand curve for unskilled labour to the left, to DU_1? The wages of unskilled workers will decrease from wu_0 to wu_1, and those of skilled workers will increase from ws_0 to ws_1. In the long run, this increased wage gap induces more people to acquire skills, so the supply of unskilled workers shifts to the

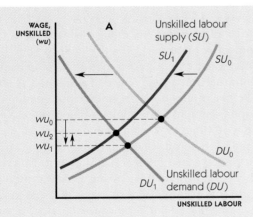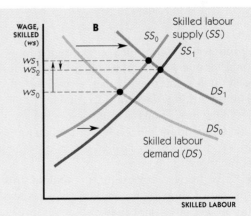

Figure 9.8 THE MARKET FOR SKILLED AND UNSKILLED LABOUR

In panel A, new advanced technology shifts the demand curve for unskilled labour to the left and reduces wages from wu_0 to wu_1. In panel B, the new technology shifts the demand curve for skilled labour out to the right and raises wages from ws_0 to ws_1. Over time, this increased difference in wages may lead more individuals to obtain skills, shifting the supply curve for unskilled labour back to the left, raising wages for unskilled labour somewhat from wu_1 to wu_2, and shifting the supply curve for skilled labour to the right, reducing wages for skilled labour from ws_1 to ws_2.

left, and that of skilled workers shifts to the right. As a result, the wage of unskilled workers rises from wu_1 to wu_2, and that of skilled workers falls from ws_1 to ws_2. These long-run supply responses thus dampen the short-run movements in wages.

Over the past two decades, the ratio of wages of graduates and other skilled workers to those of less-skilled and unskilled workers has increased enormously. Though there have been shifts in both demand and supply curves, the primary explanation of these shifts is a change in the relative demand for skilled labour, probably attributable largely to changes in technology.

Will the predicted shifts in long-run labour supply that result from unskilled workers' acquiring more skills—thus reducing the current wage gap—in fact occur? We cannot be certain. And if they do occur, how long will it take for the wage gap to be reduced to the levels that prevailed in the 1960s? In the meantime, many worry about the social consequences of steadily increasing wage (and income) inequality.

BUDGET CONSTRAINTS AND SAVINGS

The assumption that individuals spend their money in a rational manner, thinking through the alternatives clearly, holds for the savings as well as the spending-and-working decision. In making their saving decision, individuals are making a decision about *when* to spend, or consume. If they consume less today—if, that is, they save more today—they can consume more tomorrow.

We use the budget constraint to analyse this choice. Instead of showing the choice between two goods, the budget constraint now shows, as in Figure 9.9, the choice between spending in two time periods. This is similar to our discussion of human capital investment decisions. The only difference is that instead of youth and later working years, the two time periods here are working years and retirement years. Consider the case of Joan. She faces the lifetime budget constraint depicted in Figure 9.9. The first period is represented on the horizontal axis, the second on the vertical. Her wages during

her working life (the first period) are w. Thus, at one extreme, she could consume all of w in the first period (point C) and have nothing for her retirement. At the other extreme, she could consume nothing in the first period, save all of her income, and consume her savings with accumulated interest in the second (point B). If we use r to denote the rate of interest, her consumption in the second period is $w(1+r)$. Between these extremes lies a straight line that defines the rest of her choices. She can choose any combination of first- and second-period consumption on this line. This is Joan's two-period budget constraint.

By postponing consumption—that is, by saving—Joan can increase the total amount of goods that she can obtain because she is paid interest on her savings. The cost, however, is that she must wait to enjoy the goods. But what is the relative price, the amount of future consumption she has to trade for one more unit of current consumption? To put it another way, how much extra future consumption can she get if she gives up one unit of current consumption?

If Joan decides not to consume one more pound today, she can take that pound, put it in the bank, and get back at the end of the year that pound plus interest. If the interest rate is 10 percent, for every pound of consumption that Joan gives up today, she can get £1.10 of consumption next year. The relative price (of consumption today relative to consumption tomorrow) is thus 1 plus the interest rate. Because Joan must give up more than £1.00 of consumption in the second period to get an additional £1.00 worth of consumption today, current consumption is more expensive than future consumption. As was emphasised in Chapter 6, what Joan cares about in evaluating the trade-offs between consumption during her working years versus consumption in retirement is the *real* rate of interest, taking into account inflation.

In this example, where Joan's life is divided into a working period and a retirement period, what is relevant is the average length of time between the time that money is earned and saved, and the time that the savings are used in retirement. For an average person, this is perhaps 35 years. In making her calculations, Joan will take into account the fact that if she leaves her money in the bank, it will earn compound interest, meaning that interest will be paid on interest already earned, not just on the amount of principal saved.

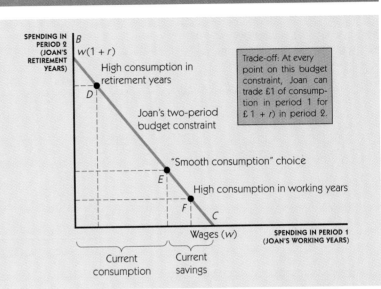

Figure 9.9 THE TWO-PERIOD BUDGET CONSTRAINT

The two-period budget constraint *BC* describes the possible combinations of current and future consumption available. Wages not spent in period 1 become savings, which earn interest. As a result, forgoing a pound of consumption today increases future consumption by more than a pound.

In recent years, the real rate of interest has been around 4 percent a year. If interest were not compounded, earning 4 percent a year for 35 years would simply provide an overall return of 35×4 percent = 140 percent. If Joan puts £1.00 in the bank today, in 35 years she will get back—in real terms—£2.40. However, if interest is compounded annually, for each dollar deposited the calculation is $(1 + .04)^{35}$. So the total interest paid will be 294.6 percent. If she puts £1.00 in the bank today, in 35 years she will get back—in real terms—£3.94 (that is, her original deposit *plus* the interest). Compound interest makes a big difference.

Thus, the slope of Joan's budget constraint is 3.94—for every pound of consumption she gives up during her working years, she gets £3.94 of additional consumption in retirement.

Joan chooses among the points on this budget constraint according to her personal preferences. Consider, for example, point *D*, where Joan is consuming very little during her working life. Since she is spending very little in the present, any additional consumption now will have a high marginal value. She will be relatively eager to substitute present consumption for future consumption. At the other extreme, if she is consuming a great deal in the present, say at point *F*, additional consumption today will have a relatively low marginal value, while future consumption will have a high marginal value. Hence, she will be relatively eager to save more for the future. She chooses point *E* in between where consumption in the two periods is not too different. She has **smoothed** her consumption; that is, consumption in each of the two different periods is about the same. This kind of saving, motivated to smooth consumption over one's lifetime and to provide for retirement, is called **life-cycle saving.**

SAVINGS AND THE INTEREST RATE

What happens to Joan's savings if the interest rate increases? Her new budget constraint is shown in Figure 9.10 as *B'C*. If she does no saving, the interest rate has no effect on her consumption. She simply consumes her income during her working years, with nothing left over for retirement. But for all other choices, she gets more consumption during her retirement years.

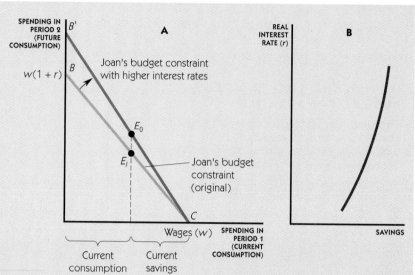

Figure 9.10 SAVINGS AND THE INTEREST RATE

An increase in the interest rate rotates the budget constraint out from *BC* to *B'C* (panel A). The fact that the individual is better off means that there is an income effect, leading to greater consumption in the present (and the future). Higher current consumption implies lower savings. However, the higher interest rate makes future consumption cheaper; the substitution effect, associated with the changed slope, leads to greater savings now (panel B). The savings function in panel B gives the level of savings at each level of real interest rate. The curve depicted has the typical shape: increases in the real interest rate lead to slight increases in savings; the substitution effect outweighs the income effect.

The increased interest rate has both an income and a substitution effect. Because Joan is a saver, higher interest rates make her better off. Because she is better of, she consumes more today; that is, she reduces savings. This is the income effect. But her return to savings—to postponing consumption—is increased. For each pound of consumption she postpones, she gets more consumption when she retires. This induces her to consume less—to save more. This is the substitution effect. Thus, the substitution and income effects work in opposite directions, and the *net* effect is ambiguous. Either may dominate. A higher interest rate may lead to more or less savings.

What happens on *average* is a difficult empirical question. Most estimates indicate that the substitution effect outweighs the income effect, so that an increase in the real interest rate has a slightly positive effect on the rate of savings.

The magnitude of the response of savings to interest rates is an important question. Government policies aimed at increasing the interest rate individuals receive, such as exempting certain forms of savings

THE SAVINGS DECISION

The savings decision is a decision of when to consume: today or tomorrow.

The slope of the budget constraint between consumption today and consumption tomorrow is determined by the rate of interest.

A principal motive of saving is to smooth consumption, so that consumption during working years and consumption during retirement years is about the same.

There has long been a concern that people in Britain do not save enough and a belief that higher savings would lead to faster growth of the economy. Some of the fast-growing countries of Asia—particularly Japan and Taiwan—have had very high rates of saving, which may well have contributed to their very rapid economic growth. Worry about low rates of saving is not confined to Britain: the United States also has very low rates of saving, and there too there is concern about it. Perhaps the British should take comfort from the spendthriftiness of the world's richest economy, drawing the inference that improvidence is no barrier to riches.

But what explains low savings in Britain? One explanation is that the relatively generous social security provision reduces the need for saving. The state pension, though small, may depress saving for retirement. The provision of free health care through the National Health Service reduces the need to save for medical expenses. Financial liberalization has made borrowing much easier. Many households have substantial wealth tied up in houses which is likely to depress saving. The rise in house prices over the course of the 1980s (notwithstanding the fall in prices between 1989 and 1993) made people feel much wealthier and caused saving to fall. Some people in fact used their housing wealth as an opportunity to take out more loans and increase their spending.

All these factors combine to cause people to save relatively little. They are present in other European countries as well as North America, to varying degrees, and affect saving there too. One perspective on different saving rates around the world is that the high rates of saving of Japan and Taiwan are the puzzles to be explained, rather than Britain's—or the United States's—low saving rate.

---

from taxation, are based on the belief that an increase in the interest rate on savings will significantly increase total (aggregate) savings in the economy. Since wealthy people save more, reducing taxes on interest—which increases the effective interest rate to the saver—obviously benefits them more.

OTHER FACTORS AFFECTING SAVINGS

We have now seen how individuals' decisons about savings can be looked at using the techniques of consumer choice analysis presented in Chapter 8. For savings, the two basic determinants are income and interest rates. As incomes rise, individuals want to consume more in their retirement, and hence must save more. As interest rates change, the income and substitution effect work in different directions, so the net effect is ambiguous.

The savings decision also involves an even more important determinant: social security. How much individuals need to save for their retirement depends on the size of the state pension they will receive when they retire. A generous social security system reduces the need to save for retirement. The National Insurance System in Britain was intended to ensure that retired people had at least a minimum income. In recent years, as the number of people over the retirement age has grown relative to total population, this commitment has become increasingly costly. The National Insurance Pension has been allowed to diminish relative to wages in order to cut the cost of providing it. As this has happened, the need for people to save for retirement, using company or private pension plans, or other savings, has grown. Increasingly many people in Britain have pension plans and other savings in addition to their right to state pensions.

AGGREGATE SAVINGS

The sum of the savings of all individuals in society is **aggregate** savings. At any time, some individuals are saving and others are spending their savings (or, as economists say, **dissaving**). Aggregate savings is the two activities taken together. The **aggregate savings rate** is aggregate savings divided by aggregate income. **Demographic** factors, in particular the rate of growth of the population, are important determinants of the aggregate savings rate. Retired people typically dissave. That is, they withdraw from savings accounts and sell stocks and bonds if they have any (to supplement their main income sources, social security and interest on investments). A more slowly growing population has a larger proportion of old people and, on that account, a lower aggregate savings rate than faster-growing populations with high birth rates.

The basic model provides great insight into the determinants of savings. But several motives for saving fall outside the basic model and have important implications for understanding the determinants of savings.

First, people typically want to leave something to their descendants. This is the **bequest** motive. The evidence suggests that the few wealthy people save more in toto over their lives than the much more numerous group that is the rest of society because of the bequest motive. If this is true, lower inheritance taxes might have much larger effects than more general efforts to increase the overall savings rate. Another motive for savings is the **precautionary** motive. This "saving for a rainy day" protects against emergencies for which one has no insurance coverage. Precautionary savings are particularly important for small businesses whose incomes can vary enormously from year to year. Still another (related) motive is to save for a particular purposes. **Target** savings are directed towards needs for which it may be hard to borrow sufficient funds, such as a deposit on a house.

REVIEW AND PRACTICE

Summary

1 The decision about how to allocate time between work and leisure can be analysed using the basic ideas of budget constraints and preferences. Individuals face a trade-off along a budget constraint between leisure and income. The amount of income a person can obtain by giving up leisure is determined by the wage rate.

2 In labour markets, the substitution and income effects of a change in wages work in opposite directions. An increase in wages makes people feel better off, and they wish to enjoy more leisure now as well as more consumption; this is the income effect. But the substitution effect of an increase in wages raises the opportunity cost of leisure and encourages more work. The overall effect of a rise in wages will depend on whether the substitution or income effect is larger.

3 An upward-sloping labour supply curve represents a case where the substitution effect of rising wages outweighs the income effect. A relatively vertical labour supply curve represents a case where the substitution and income effects of rising wages are nearly equal. A backward-bending labour supply curve represents a case where the substitution effect dominates at low wages (labour supply increases as the wage increases) but the income effect dominates at high wages (labour supply decreases as the wage increases).

4 The basic trade-off between leisure and income can also be used to analyse decisions such as when to enter the labour force (leave school) and when to retire (leave the labour force).

5 Human capital adds to economic productivity just as physical capital does. It is developed by education, on-the-job learning, and investments of time and money that parents make in their children.

6 In making a decision to save, people face a trade-off between current and future consumption. The amount of extra consumption an individual can obtain in the future by reducing present consumption is determined by the real rate of interest.

7 An increase in the real rate of interest makes individuals who save better off. The resulting income effect leads to an increase in current consumption (and future consumption) and a decrease in savings. An increase in the real rate of interest also makes it more attractive to save; this is the substitution effect, and it leads to a decrease in current consumption. The net effect is thus ambiguous, though in practice it appears that an increase in the real interest rate has a slightly positive effect on savings.

KEY TERMS

human capital

bequest savings motive

life-cycle savings

precautionary savings motive

target savings motive

REVIEW QUESTIONS

1 How do people make choices about the amount of time to work, given their personal tastes and relative wages in the market?

2 How will the income effect of a fall in wages affect hours worked? How will the substitution effect of a fall in wages affect hours worked? What does the labour supply curve look like if the income effect dominates the substitution effect? If the substitution effect dominates the income effect?

3 Describe how students invest time and money to acquire human capital.

4 How can a choice to consume in the present determine the amount of consumption in the future?

5 What is the price of future consumption in terms of present consumption?

6 For savers, how will the income effect of a higher interest rate affect current savings? How will the substitution effect of a higher interest rate affect current savings?

7 What are some of the other factors, besides incomes and interest rates, that affect savings?

8 What factors might account for the low U.K. savings rate?

PROBLEMS

1 Imagine that a wealthy relative dies and leaves you an inheritance in a trust fund that will provide you with £20,000 per year for the rest of your life. Draw a diagram to illustrate this shift in your budget constraint between leisure and consumption. After considering the ideas of income and substitution effects, decide whether this inheritance will cause you to work more or less.

2 Most individuals do not take a second job (moonlight), even if they could get one, for instance as a taxi driver. This is in spite of the fact that their basic job may require them to work only 37 hours a week. Most moonlighting jobs pay less per hour than the basic job. Draw a typical worker's budget constraint. Discuss the consequences of the kink in the budget constraint.

3 Under current economic conditions, let's say that an unskilled worker will be able to get a job at a wage of £5 per hour. Now assume the government decides to assure that all people with a weekly income of less than £150 will be given a cheque to bring them up to the £150 level. Draw one such worker's original budget constraint and the constraint with the welfare program. Will this welfare program be likely to cause a recipient who originally worked 30 hours to work less? How about a recipient who worked less than 30 hours? More than 30 hours? Explain how the government might reduce these negative effects by offering a wage subsidy that would increase the hourly wage to £6 per hour for each of the first 20 hours worked, and draw a revised budget constraint to illustrate.

4 This chapter analysed the savings decision of an individual who worked for one period, was retired the next, and received no social security payment in his retirement.

(a) Show how the budget constraint changes if the individual receives a fixed social security payment in retirement. Discuss what this does to savings.
(b) Show how the budget constraint changes if the individual is taxed in the first period of his life and receives a fixed social security payment in retirement. Discuss what this does to savings.

5 This chapter focused on how interest rates affect savers. If an individual is a net debtor (that is, he owes money), what is the income effect of an increase in interest rates. Will an increase in the interest rates that he has to pay induce him to borrow more or less?

6 In the context of the life-cycle model of savings, explain whether you would expect each of the following situations to increase or decrease household savings.

(a) More people retire before age 65.
(b) There is an increase in life expectancy.
(c) The government passes a law requiring private businesses to provide more lucrative pensions.

7 Explain how each of the following changes might affect people's motivation for saving.

(a) Inheritance taxes are increased.
(b) A government program allows students to obtain loans more easily.
(c) The government promises to assist anyone injured by natural disasters like floods and earthquakes.
(d) More couples decide against having children.
(e) The economy does far worse than anyone was expecting in a given year.

8 Economists are fairly certain that a rise in the price of most goods will cause people to consume less of those goods, but they are not sure whether a rise in interest rates will cause people to save more. Use the ideas of substitution and income effects to explain why economists are condident of the conclusion in the first case but not in the second.

APPENDIX: INDIFFERENCE CURVES AND THE LABOUR SUPPLY AND SAVINGS DECISIONS

This appendix investigates the labour supply and savings decisions using the indifference curve approach applied in this chapter to the consumption decision. Let's first look at the choice between leisure and consumption.

Figure 9.11 shows Tom's budget constraint between leisure and consumption. As we saw in this chapter, the trade-off along this budget constraint is between leisure and consumption: the less leisure, the more consumption, and vice versa. The slope of the budget constraint is the wage. The figure also shows two indifference curves; each gives the combinations of leisure and consumption among which Tom is indifferent. As usual, since people prefer more of both consumption and leisure if that is possible, Tom will move to the highest indifference curve he can attain. This will be the one that is just tangent to the budget constraint.

The slope of the indifference curve is the marginal rate of substitution between leisure and consumption. It measures the amount of extra consumption Tom requires to compensate him for forgoing one additional hour of leisure. At the point of tangency between the indifference curve and the budget

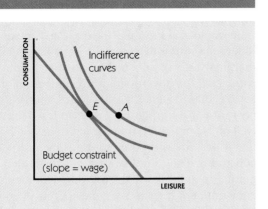

Figure 9.11 INDIFFERENCE CURVES AND LEISURE-INCOME CHOICES

An individual will choose the combination of leisure and income at point E. Point A would be more desirable, but it is not feasible. Other points on the budget line or inside it are feasible, but they lie on lower indifference curves and are therefore not as desirable.

constraint, point E, both have the same slope. That is, the marginal rate of substitution equals the wage at this point.

As in the earlier appendices, we can easily see why Tom chooses this point. Assume his marginal rate of substitution is £15 (pounds per hour), while his wage is £20 (pounds per hour). If he works an hour more—gives up an hour's worth of leisure—his consumption goes up by £20. But to compensate him for the forgone leisure, he only requires £15. Since he gets more than he requires by working, he clearly prefers to work more.

DECIDING WHETHER TO WORK

How to use indifference curves to analyse how people decide whether to work is shown in Figure 9.12. Consider a low-wage individual facing a welfare system in which there is a fixed level of benefits if one's income is below a threshold level. Benefits are cut off once income exceeds a certain level. The indifference curve I_0 is tangent to the budget constraint

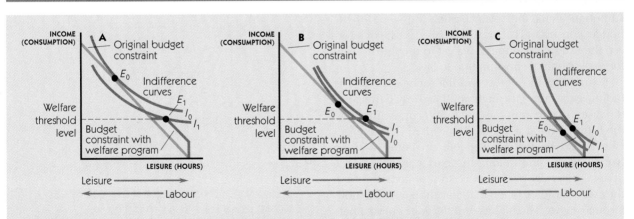

Figure 9.12 INDIFFERENCE CURVES AND WELFARE PROGRAMS

Panel A shows the case of an individual who chooses to work whether or not the welfare program exists. In panel B, before a welfare program is introduced, the individual is earning more than the welfare threshold. With the availability of welfare, she relies on welfare benefits to work less and move to a higher indifference curve. Panel C shows the case of someone who is earning less than the welfare threshold but would choose to work still less if the welfare program existed.

without welfare, and the point of tangency is E_0. The curve I_1 is the highest indifference curve consistent with the person receiving welfare.

The three possible cases are illustrated in panels A, B, and C. In panel A, the indifference curve I_0 through point E_0 is higher than the curve I_1. The individual chooses to work at E_0 and is unaffected by the welfare program. In panels B and C, the person works sufficiently little to be eligible for welfare; that is, I_1 is higher than I_0, and so he chooses point E_1. In panel B, the individual realises that if he works more, he will lose his welfare benefits. He earns just (little) enough to be eligible for welfare. In panel C, his marginal rate of substitution is equal to the wage rate; that is, the indifference curve I_1 is tangent to the budget constraint. The welfare system has only an income effect.

DECIDING HOW MUCH TO SAVE

The decision of how much to save is a decision about how much of lifetime income to consume now and how much to consume in the future. This trade-off is summarised in the two-period budget constraint introduced in this chapter, with present consumption measured along the horizontal axis and future consumption along the vertical axis. The slope of the budget constraint is $1 + r$, where r is the rate of interest, the extra consumption we get in the future from forgoing a unit of consumption today.

Figure 9.13 shows three indifference curves. The indifference curve through point A gives all the combinations of consumption today and consumption in the future among which the individual is indifferent (she would be just as well off, no better and no worse, at any point along the curve as at A). Since people generally prefer more to less consumption, they would rather be on a higher than a lower indifference curve. The highest indifference curve a person can attain is one that is tangent to the budget constraint. The point of tangency we denote by E. The individual would clearly prefer the indifference curve through A, but no point on that curve is attainable because the whole indifference curve is above the budget constraint. She could consume at F, but

the indifference curve through F lies below that through E.

As we learned in this chapter, the slope of the indifference curve at a certain point is equal to the marginal rate of substitution at that point. In this case, it tells us how much future consumption a person requires to compensate him for a decrease in current consumption by 1 unit, to leave him just as well off. At the point of tangency, the slope of the indifference curve is equal to the slope of the budget constraint. The marginal rate of substitution at that point, E, equals $1 + r$. If the individual forgoes a unit of consumption, he gets $1 + r$ more units of consumption in the future, and this is exactly the amount he requires to compensate him for giving up current consumption. On the other hand, if the marginal rate of substitution is less than $1 + r$, it pays the individual to save more. To see why, assume $1 + r = 1.5$, while the person's marginal rate of substitution is 1.2. Reducing his consumption by a unit, he gets 1.5 more units in the future, but he would have been content getting only 1.2 units. He is better off saving more.

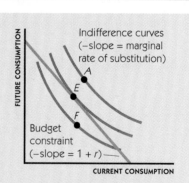

Figure 9.13 INDIFFERENCE CURVES AND SAVINGS BEHAVIOUR

An individual will choose the combination of present and future consumption at point E. Point A would be more desirable, but it is not feasible. Point F is feasible, but it lies on a lower indifference curve and is therefore less desirable.

CHANGING THE INTEREST RATE

With indifference curves and budget constraints, we can see the effect of an increase in the interest rate. Figure 9.14 shows the case of an individual, Maggie, who works while she is young and saves for her retirement. The vertical axis gives consumption during retirement years, the horizontal axis consumption during working years. An increase in the rate of interest rotates the budget constraint, moving it from BC to B_2C. It is useful to break the change down into two steps. In the first, we ask what would have happened if the interest rate had changed but Maggie remained on the same indifference curve. This is represented by the movement of the budget constraint form BC to B_1C_1. As a result of the increased interest rate, Maggie consumes less today; she saves more. This is the substitution effect, and it is seen in the movement from E_0 to E_2 in Figure 9.14.

In the second step, we note that, since Maggie is a saver, the increased interest rate makes her better off. To leave Maggie on the same indifference curve after the increase in the interest rate, we need to reduce her income. Her true budget constraint, after the interest rate increase, is B_2C, parallel to B_1C_1. The two budget constraints have the same slope because the after-tax interest rates are the same. The movement from B_1C_1 to B_2C is the second step. It induces Maggie to increase her consumption from E_2 to E_1. At higher incomes and the same relative prices (interest rates), people consume more every period; this implies that they save less. The movement from E_2 to E_1 is the income effect.

Thus, the substitution effect leads her to save more, the income effect to save less, and the net effect is ambiguous. In this case, there is a slight increase in savings.

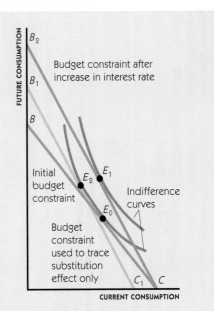

Figure 9.14 INCOME AND SUBSTITUTION EFFECTS OF A HIGHER INTEREST RATE

An increase in the interest rate rotates the budget constraint, moving it from BC to B_2C. The substitution effect describes what happens when relative prices are changed but Maggie remains on the same indifference curve; there is a shift in the budget line from BC to B_1C_1 and an increase in savings from E_0 to E_2. The income effect is the result of an outward shift of the budget line, keeping relative prices the same; the income effect is described by the shift from B_1C_1 to B_2C and the increase in present consumption from E_2 to E_1.

CHAPTER 10

THE FIRM'S COSTS

The previous four chapters focused on the decisions of households and individuals. In this chapter, the focus shifts to the decisions of firms. While households make decisions in pursuit of satisfaction, firms make decisions to maximise their profits. In their pursuit of profits, firms help to answer two of the four fundamental economic questions: What goods should be produced, and in what quantities? and How should these goods be produced? (The role firms play in answering the fourth question, Who makes the decisions? will be explored in detail in Chapter 12.)

The basic competitive model is, once again, our starting point. Many firms, all making the same product, compete with one another to sell that product to well-informed customers, who instantaneously recognise and act upon any price differences. Because customers are well informed about prices, all firms in a competitive market must accept the price set for their product by the forces of supply and demand in the market as a whole. Any firm trying to sell above that price will lose all its customers. Firms in competitive markets are, therefore, **price takers.** The classic example of competitive markets is agricultural markets—thousands of farmers, say, producing milk. A dairy farmer does not waste time wondering what price to set for the milk he has to sell. He knows he will get the going price.

A firm does have some control over its costs, however, because they are related to the firm's level of production. This chapter focuses on understanding the relationship between levels of production and costs. Chapter 11 shows how

KEY QUESTIONS

1 What do cost curves—curves relating costs to the level of production—look like in an economy where output depends on a single input to production?

2 What additional issues are raised when there are several inputs?

3 In the long run, firms can vary some inputs that they cannot vary in the short run. As a result, in the long run, cost curves may look different than they do in the short run. What is the relationship between long-run and short-run cost curves?

a firm uses this relationship to maximise its profits by minimising its costs.

Even though we talk in terms of production and goods, it is important to bear in mind that only one-third of the economy consists of industries that produce goods in the conventional sense—manufacturing, mining, construction, and agriculture. The other two-thirds of the economy produces primarily services—industries like transport, education, health care, wholesale and retail trade, and finance.

PROFITS, COSTS, AND FACTORS OF PRODUCTION

A business that fails to make a profit over time will cease to exist because it will not have enough money to pay its bills. If businesses are to continue, they are under pressure to make money. The motivation of making as much money as possible—maximising profits—provides a useful starting point for discussing the behaviour of firms in competitive markets.

The definition of **profits** is simple:

Profits = revenue − costs.

The **revenue** a business receives from selling its products is calculated as the quantity it sells of the product multiplied by the price of the product. A firm's **costs** are defined as the total expense of producing the good. What the firm uses to produce the goods are called inputs or **factors of production:** labour, materials, and capital goods. Labour costs

are what the company has to pay for the workers it hires and the managers it employs to supervise the workers. The costs of materials include raw materials and intermediate goods. Intermediate goods are whatever supplies the company purchases from other firms—as seeds, fertilizer, and fuel for a farm; iron ore, coal, coke, limestone, and electric power for a steel company.

All firms work to keep their costs as low as possible. Within limits, they can vary the mix of labour, materials, capital goods, and production processes they use; and they will do so until they find the lowest-cost method of producing a given quality of product. The simplest way of understanding how firms find the lowest cost point is to look at a firm with only two factors of production, one fixed and one variable.

PRODUCTION WITH ONLY TWO FACTORS

A wheat farmer with a fixed amount of land who uses only labour to produce his crop is our example. The more labour he applies to the farm (his own time, plus the time of workers that he hires), the greater the output. Labour is the single variable factor (input).

The relationship between the inputs used in production and the level of output is called the **production function.** Figure 10.1 shows the farmer's production function; the data supporting the figure are set forth in Table 10.1. The increase in the output corresponding to an increase in any factor of production, labour in this case, is the **marginal product** for that factor. For example, when the number of hours

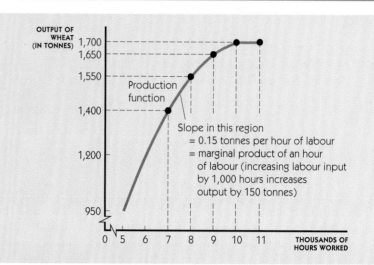

Figure 10.1 PRODUCTION FUNCTION WITH DIMINISHING RETURNS TO AN INPUT

As the amount of the input (labour) increases, so does the output (wheat). But there are diminishing returns to labour; each increase in labour results in successively smaller increases in wheat output. Since the slope of the curve is the marginal product of labour, on the graph, this means the slope flattens out as the amount of labour increases.

worked per year rises from 7,000 to 8,000, output increases by 150 tonnes, from 1,400 to 1,550. When the farmer is employing 8,000 hours, the marginal product of 1,000 more hours is 100 tonnes. The marginal product of an extra hour of labour will, accordingly, be 0.1 tonne. The marginal product is given in the last column of the table. Diagrammatically, it is given by the slope of the production function.

DIMINISHING RETURNS

In the case of the wheat farmer, as more and more labour is added to a fixed amount of land, the marginal product of labour diminishes. This is another application of the concept of **diminishing returns,** which we originally encountered in Chapter 2. In the case of a firm's production function, diminishing re-

Table 10.1 LEVEL OF OUTPUT WITH DIFFERENT AMOUNTS OF LABOUR

Number of Hours Worked	Amount of Wheat Produced (tonnes)	Marginal Product (additional tonnes produced by 1,000 additional hours of labour)
5,000	950	
		250
6,000	1,200	
		200
7,000	1,400	
		150
8,000	1,550	
		100
9,000	1,650	
		50
10,000	1,700	
		0
11,000	1,700	

DIMINISHING RETURNS

As more and more of one input is added, *while other inputs remain unchanged,* the marginal product of the added input diminishes.

turns implies that output increases less than proportionately with input. If labour is doubled, output is less than doubled. Increasing the number of hours worked from 7,000 to 8,000 raises output by 1,500 tonnes, but increasing the hours worked from 8,000 to 9,000 raises output by only 1,000 tonnes. Diminishing returns sets in with a vengeance at higher levels of input; moving from 10,000 to 11,000 hours worked adds nothing.

INCREASING RETURNS

Although a production function with diminishing returns is an important case, other cases do occur. Figure 10.2 shows a production function where increasing an input (here, labour) raises output more than proportionately. A firm with this kind of production function has **increasing returns.** In the single-input case depicted, it is clear that the marginal product of the input increases with the amount produced; that is, when the firm is producing a lot, adding one more worker increases output by more than it does when the firm is producing little.

Imagine a business that picks up refuse. If this business counts only one out of every five houses as customers, it will have a certain cost of production. But if the company can expand to picking up the refuse from two out of every five houses, while it will need more workers, the workers will be able to drive a shorter distance and pick up more refuse faster. Thus, a doubling of output can result from a less than doubling of labour. Many examples of increasing returns, like refuse collection, involve providing service to more people in a given area. Telephone companies and electricity companies are two other familiar instances.

CONSTANT RETURNS

In the case of increasing returns, output grows faster than input, while with diminishing returns, input grows faster than output. The intermediate case is one where if input changes, output changes at the same rate. This is the case of **constant returns.** Figure 10.3 shows constant returns, when the relationship between input and output is a straight line.

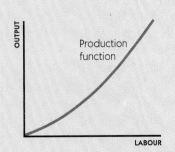

Figure 10.2 **PRODUCTION FUNCTION WITH INCREASING RETURNS TO AN INPUT**

As the amount of labour increases, so does output. But the returns to labour are increasing in this case; successive increases in labour result in successively larger increases in output. On the graph, this means the slope becomes steeper as the amount of labour increases.

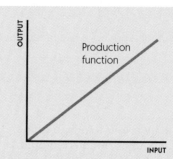

Figure 10.3 PRODUCTION FUNCTION WITH CONSTANT RETURNS TO AN INPUT

The marginal product of labour is constant, neither increasing nor diminishing as the firm expands production. On the graph, this means that the slope does not change.

FIXED VERSUS VARIABLE INPUTS

Firms typically require a certain level of input just to start production. Before it can open its doors, for instance, a firm may need land (or space) and some machines. It will have to hire someone to run the personnel office and someone to supervise the workers. These are called **fixed inputs,** because they do not depend on the level of output. The quantities of **variable inputs,** in contrast, rise and fall with the level of production. For instance, the firm can work its space and machines for one shift a day, or it can run them for all 24 hours. It simply hires more workers and uses more materials. These workers and materials are variable inputs.

Figure 10.4 shows a production function with fixed and variable inputs. At L_0, the fixed inputs are in place. At first, when the firm increases inputs beyond L_0, output increases more than proportionately. Output at L_2 is more than twice output at L_1, even though L_2 is twice L_1. This is due to the effect of the fixed input. As the variable input is increased, the

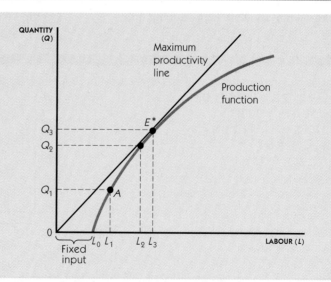

Figure 10.4 PRODUCTION FUNCTION WITH FIXED AND VARIABLE INPUTS

As the amount of labour increases, given the fixed inputs already in place, marginal returns to labour decrease, which is shown by the slope of the production function becoming flatter. Average productivity is given by the slope of a line from any point on the production function to the origin and will be highest at E^*.

increase in output generated by each successive unit of input decreases due to diminishing returns. Beyond L_3 the effect of diminishing returns outweighs that of the fixed input, and output rises *less* than proportionately with inputs.

The ratio of output to input at any point on the production function is called the **average productivity.** At point *A*, for example, the average productivity is the distance up the vertical axis from the origin (Q_1) divided by the distance along the horizontal axis (L_1). This is the slope of the line from the origin to *A*. The steepest line from the origin to the production function touches the production function at E^*. This is the level of production at which output per unit of input is maximised. Note that average productivity—the slope of the line from the origin to the production function—increases as output increases to point E^* and falls thereafter. Marginal productivity—the slope of the production function itself—continuously decreases as employment increases beyond L_0.

COST CURVES

The production function is important to the firm because the inputs it depicts determine the costs of production. The case of a production function with fixed inputs is the most common production function in the economy, and a look at the kinds of costs it generates will give us an overview of the major categories of costs upon which economists concentrate.

FIXED AND VARIABLE COSTS

The costs associated with fixed inputs are called **fixed costs** or **overhead costs.** Whether the firm produces nothing or produces at maximum capacity, it must meet the same fixed costs just to open for business. Figure 10.5 shows how costs depend on output. Panel A depicts fixed costs as a horizontal line; by definition, they do not depend on the level of output. As an example, consider a would-be wheat farmer who has the opportunity to buy a farm and its equipment for £25,000. His fixed costs are £25,000.

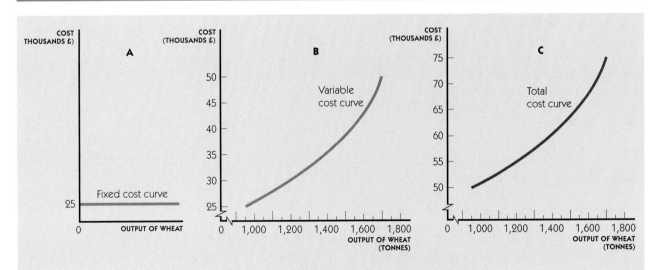

Figure 10.5 FIXED, VARIABLE, AND TOTAL COST CURVES

Panel A shows a firm's fixed costs; by definition, fixed costs do not depend on the level of output. Panel B shows a firm's variable costs, which rise with the level of production. The increasing slope of the curve indicates that it costs more and more to produce at the margin; this is a sign of diminishing returns. Panel C shows a total cost curve. It has the same slope as the variable cost curve but is higher by the amount of the fixed costs.

Table 10.2 THE COST OF PRODUCING WHEAT

Output (tonnes)	Labour Required (hours)	Total Variable Costs (at a wage of £5 per hour)	Total Costs (£)	Marginal Cost (£ per tonne)	Average Variable Costs (£ per tonne)	Average Total Costs (£ per tonne)
950	5,000	25,000	50,000	—	26.32	52.63
1,200	6,000	30,000	55,000	20.00	25.00	45.83
1,400	7,000	35,000	60,000	25.00	25.00	42.86
1,550	8,000	40,000	65,000	33.33	25.81	41.94
1,650	9,000	45,000	70,000	50.00	27.27	42.42
1,700	10,000	50,000	75,000	100.00	29.41	44.12

Variable costs correspond to variable inputs. These costs rise or fall with the level of production. Any cost that the firm can change during the time period under study is a variable cost. To the extent that such items as labour costs or material costs can go up or down as output does, these are variable costs. If we give our farmer only one variable input, labour, then his variable costs would be, say, £5 per hour for each worker. The variable costs corresponding to levels of output listed in Table 10.1 are shown in Table 10.2 and plotted in Figure 10.5B. As output increases, so do variable costs, so the curve slopes upwards.

TOTAL COSTS

Table 10.2 also includes a column labeled "Total costs." **Total costs** are defined as the sum of variable and fixed costs, so this column differs from the variable costs column by £25,000, the amount of the firm's fixed costs. The total cost curve, summarising these points, is shown in Figure 10.5C.

MARGINAL COST AND MARGINAL PRODUCT

As with the economic decisions we have discussed earlier in this book, the most important cost for the firm's decision makers is the **marginal cost.** This is the extra cost corresponding to each additional unit

produced.[1] In the case of the wheat farmer's costs (Table 10.2), as labour input is increased from 7,000 to 8,000 hours, output goes up from 1,400 to 1,550 tonnes, that is, 150 tonnes. To increase output by 1 tonne would require 1,000/150 hours, or 6.67 hours, of labour. At a cost of labour of £5 per hour, this comes to £5 × 6.67 = £33.33 per extra tonne of output. The marginal cost of a tonne of wheat is thus £33.33.

More generally, if MPL is the marginal product of labour (0.15 tonnes per hour) and w is the (hourly) wage (£5 per hour), the marginal cost of producing an extra unit of output if just w/MPL (£33.33 per tonne).

The marginal cost curve depicted in Figure 10.6 is upward sloping. This is the typical case. It reflects the fact that as more is produced, it becomes harder and harder to increase output further—an example of the familiar principle of diminishing marginal returns. (Marginal cost curves reflecting increasing or constant returns to scale have different shapes. These are discussed later in the chapter.)

---

[1] There is a simple relationship between the marginal cost curve and the total cost curve. Marginal cost is just the slope of total costs—the change in total costs (movement along the vertical axis, in Figure 10.5C) resulting from a unit change in output (movement along the horizontal axis).

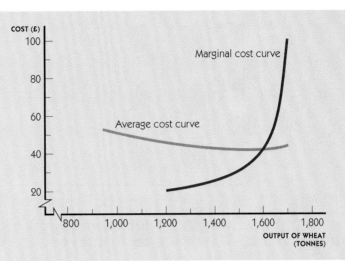

Figure 10.6 MARGINAL AND AVERAGE COST CURVES

The marginal costs are the extra costs of producing one more unit of output. With diminishing returns to an input, marginal costs increase with the level of output. Average costs, also shown here, are total costs divided by output.

AVERAGE COSTS

The final set of costs that concern the business firm are its **average costs.** These are simply total costs divided by output. The average cost curve gives average costs corresponding to different levels of output. Figure 10.6 also shows the average cost curve corresponding to the total cost curve depicted in Figure 10.5C. To find the average costs for any level of output, we draw a line from the origin to the point on the total cost curve for that level of output. The slope of that line is

$$\frac{\text{Total costs}}{\text{Output}} = \text{average costs.}$$

AVERAGE VARIABLE COSTS

The concept of **average variable costs** will be useful in the next chapter when we discuss the production decision. These are total variable costs divided by output.

THE U-SHAPED AVERAGE COST CURVE

The typical average cost curve is U-shaped. To see why, we examine the typical production function in more detail. Shown in Figure 10.7A, it is a slight vari-

ant of the production function with a fixed input we saw earlier (Figure 10.4). Three properties of this production function stand out.

1 Just to start production requires a significant input of labour, marked by L_0 in the diagram.

2 Because of diminishing returns, beyond some level of output it requires more and more labour to produce each additional unit of output. It may be almost impossible to increase output beyond some point. That is why the production function flattens out.

3 There is a level of output Q^* at which the output per unit input—average productivity—is maximised.

Panel B shows what these three properties imply for the total cost curve. First, there are fixed costs c_0. Second, diminishing returns mean that not only do total costs rise as output increases but the total cost curve becomes steeper and steeper.

That output per unit input is maximised at Q^* has one important implication. Average costs, total costs divided by output, are minimised at the output level Q^*. This is shown in Figure 10.8. With small outputs, average costs decline as output increases. If the *only* costs were fixed costs, then average costs (which

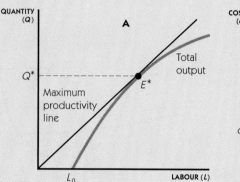
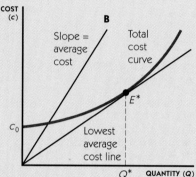

Figure 10.7 RELATING THE TYPICAL PRODUCTION FUNCTION TO THE TOTAL COST CURVE

Panel A shows a typical production function, with fixed costs and diminishing marginal returns. Average productivity is maximised at E^*. Panel B shows the total cost curve that corresponds to this typical production function. Diminishing returns cause the slope of the curve to become steeper; the point of lowest average costs—given by the slope of a line through the origin—corresponds to the point of highest average productivity.

would then equal the fixed costs divided by the output) would decrease in proportion to the increase in output. This same principle holds even if not all costs are fixed. Average costs still decline because there are more units of production by which to divide fixed costs. With large outputs, average costs increase, as the law of diminishing returns sets in with strength. Output increases less than proportionately with input; or equivalently, to get a 1 percent increase in output, one needs much more than a 1 percent increase in input.

Even if the average cost curve is U-shaped, the output at which average costs are minimised may be very great, so high that there is not enough demand to justify producing that much. Thus, when economists refer to declining average costs, they mean that those costs are declining over the level of output that is likely to prevail in the market.

Relationship between Average and Marginal Cost Curves The relationship between average costs and marginal costs is reflected in Figure 10.8. The marginal cost curve intersects the average cost curve at the bottom of the U—the *minimum* average cost. To understand why the marginal cost curve will *always* intersect the average cost curve at its lowest point, consider the relationship between average and marginal costs. As long as the marginal cost is below the average costs, producing an additional unit will pull down the average costs. Thus, everywhere that the marginal cost is below average costs, the average cost curve is declining. If marginal cost is above average costs, then producing an additional unit will raise the average costs. So everywhere that the marginal cost is above average costs, the average cost curve must be rising. The point between where the U-shaped average cost curve is falling and where it is rising is the minimum point.

ALTERNATIVE SHAPES OF COST CURVES

Earlier, we saw that production functions may exhibit increasing or constant returns. If there are in-

Figure 10.8 RELATING THE MARGINAL COST CURVE TO THE AVERAGE COST CURVE

The average cost curve is usually U-shaped. It initially declines as the fixed costs are spread over a larger amount of output, and then rises as diminishing returns to the variable input become increasingly important. With a U-shaped average cost curve, the marginal cost curve will cross the average cost curve at its minimum.

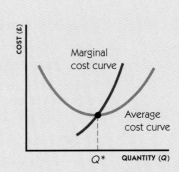

creasing returns, output increases more than proportionately with the input and total costs increase more slowly than output, as seen in panel A of Figure 10.9. In this case average and marginal costs decline, as illustrated in panel B.

If there are constant returns, doubling inputs doubles output, which will cost twice as much. In this case, total costs are simply proportional to output (panel C) and average and marginal costs are constant (panel D).

TOTAL CHANGING FACTOR PRICES AND COST CURVES

The cost curves shown thus far are based on the fixed price of each of the inputs firms purchase. An increase in the price of any factor, such as the wage,

Figure 10.9 COST CURVES WITH INCREASING OR CONSTANT RETURNS

Panels A and B show total, marginal, and average cost curves with increasing returns. Average costs decline as production increases. Panel C shows a total cost curve with constant returns; since returns to the variable factor are constant and fixed costs are zero, the total cost curve begins at the origin and its slope does not change. Panel D shows marginal and average costs with constant returns; marginal costs do not change, and so the average costs do not change either.

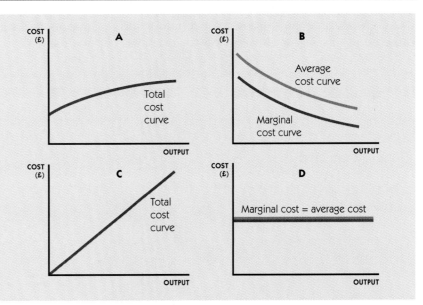

COST CONCEPTS

Total costs	Total costs of producing output = fixed costs + variable costs
Fixed, or overhead, costs	Costs that do not depend on output
Variable costs	Costs that do depend on output
Marginal cost	Extra cost of producing an extra unit = total costs of $(Q + 1)$ units minus total costs of Q units of output
Average costs	Total costs divided by output
Average variable costs	Total variable costs divided by output

the cost of machines, or the price of some raw material, shifts all of the cost curves—total, average, and marginal—upwards, as illustrated in Figure 10.10.

PRODUCTION WITH MANY FACTORS

The basic principles of the case with only two factors—one fixed, one variable—apply also to firms producing many products with many different inputs. The only fundamental difference is that with many factors it becomes possible to produce the same output in several different ways. Cost mini-

mization, therefore, involves weighing the costs of different mixes of inputs. (The analysis is somewhat more complicated, and is in the appendix to this chapter.)

COST MINIMIZATION

There are usually several ways a good can be produced, using different quantities of various inputs. Table 10.3 illustrates two ways of making car frames, one a highly automated process requiring little labour and the other a less-automated process that uses more assembly line workers. Table 10.3 shows the daily wage and capital costs for each process.

Figure 10.10 HOW CHANGING INPUT PRICES AFFECT COST CURVES

An increase in the price of a variable factor shifts the total, average, and marginal cost curves upward.

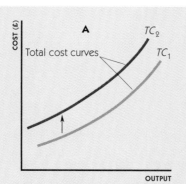

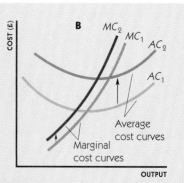

Table 10.3 COSTS OF PRODUCTION

Inputs	More-Automated Process	Less-Automated Process
Labour	50 worker hours @ £10 = £500	500 worker hours @ £10 = £5,000
Machines	5 machines @ £500 = £2,500	2 machines @ £500 = £1,000
Total	£3,000	£6,000

Each method produces the same quantity of output (say, 10,000 car frames per day). In this simple example, we assume all workers are identical (of equal skill) and hence get paid the same wage and that all machines cost the same. As we can see from Table 10.3, the less-automated process clearly costs more at the given costs of labour (£10 per worker per hour) and machines (rental costs equal £500 per day).

Although this table provides only two stark alternatives, it should be clear that in some cases the alternative possibilities for production will form a continuum, where the cost of one input increases a bit, the cost of another falls a bit, and output remains the same. In other words, the firm can smoothly substitute one input for another. For instance, in producing cars, different machines vary slightly in the degree of automation. Machines requiring less labour to run them cost more. When firms make their decisions about investment, they thus have a wide range of intermediate choices between the two described in Table 10.3.

THE PRINCIPLE OF SUBSTITUTION

One of the most important consequences of the principle of cost minimization in the case of multiple factors of production is that when the price of one input (say, oil) increases relative to that of other factors of production, the change in relative prices causes firms to substitute cheaper inputs for the more costly factor. This is an illustration of the general **principle of substitution** we encountered in Chapter 4.

In some cases, substitution is quick and easy; in other cases, it may take time and be difficult. When the price of oil increased fourfold in 1973 and doubled again in 1979, firms found many ways to economise on the use of oil. For instance, companies switched from oil to gas as a source of energy. More energy-efficient cars and trucks were constructed, often using lighter materials like ceramics and plastics. These substitutions took time, but they did eventually occur.

The principle of substitution should serve as a warning to those who think they can raise prices without bearing any consequences. Argentina has almost a world monopoly on linseed oil. At one time, linseed oil was universally used for making high-quality paints. Since there was no competition, Argentina decided that it would raise the price of linseed oil and assumed everyone would have to pay it. But as the price increased, paint manufacturers learned to substitute other natural oils that could do almost as well.

Raising the price of labour (wages) provides another example. British trade unions have in the past attempted to raise wages in a number of industries in which they have been strongly represented. In the short term they have been successful, but in the longer term high wages have encouraged firms to introduce labour-saving equipment and to use less labour. The dockworkers in the 1950s and 1960s used their key role in Britain's importing and exporting to improve their pay. But, over the years, trade moved away from the unionised ports (the ports in the Dock Labour Scheme) to nonunionised ports, like Felixstowe, where costs of handling the (then new) container ships were lower than elsewhere. Now employment at docks is a fraction of what it used to be, while the quantity of goods handled is

THE PRINCIPLE OF SUBSTITUTION

An increase in the price of an input will lead the firm to substitute other inputs for it.

vastly increased. The use of flexible working practices and more highly automated equipment (containers and so on) has greatly increased productivity.

Diagrammatic Analysis We can see the principle of substitution at work using our average cost diagrams. The car manufacturer described earlier has two ways of producing cars, each with its own average cost curve. Both are shown in Figure 10.11. The general principle of cost minimization requires that the firm use the method of production with the lowest average costs at the planned level of production. In the figure, at high levels of production, the more-mechanised process with average cost curve AC_2 dominates the less-mechanised process with average cost curve AC_1. A smaller-scale producer, however, uses the less-mechanised process. Assume now the cost of labour increases. This shifts up the cost curves for both ways of producing, but obviously,

the less-mechanised process—which is more dependent on labour—has its cost curve shifted up more. As a result, the critical output at which it pays to use the more-mechanised production process is lowered, from Q_1 to Q_2. Thus, as the price of labour is increased, more firms switch to a more-mechanised process—capital goods (machines) are substituted for labour.

An increase in the price of any input shifts the cost function up. The amount by which the cost function shifts up depends on several factors, including how much of the input was being used in the first place and how easy it is to substitute other inputs. If the production process uses a great deal of the input, then the cost will shift up a lot. If there is a large increase in the price of an input and the firm cannot easily substitute other inputs, then the cost curve will shift up more than it would if substitution of other inputs were easy.

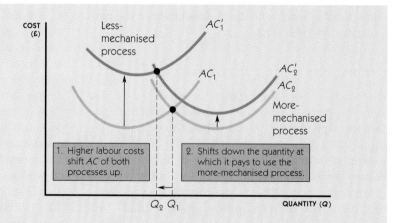

Figure 10.11 **MINIMISING COSTS AS INPUT PRICES CHANGE**

With two production processes, as the price of an input increases—in this case, labour—both average cost curves shift up. However, AC_1 relies more heavily on labour, so it shifts up more. This means that firms will switch to the more-mechanised technology of AC_2 at a lower level of output (Q_2 instead of Q_1), and there will tend to be a shift away from the more expensive input, labour, and toward the relatively cheaper input, capital.

COST (£)

Less-mechanised process

AC_1'

AC_1

AC_2'

AC_2

More-mechanised process

1. Higher labour costs shift AC of both processes up.

2. Shifts down the quantity at which it pays to use the more-mechanised process.

Q_2 Q_1

QUANTITY (Q)

Figure 10.12 **SHORT-RUN MARGINAL COST**

When there is excess capacity, the marginal cost of producing an extra unit may not increase much, and so the marginal cost curve is flat. But when capacity is approached, marginal costs may rise rapidly.

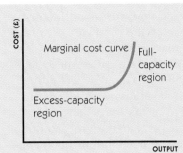

SHORT-RUN AND LONG-RUN COST CURVES

Up to this point, we have referred to the distinction between inputs that are fixed (their cost does not vary with quantity produced) and inputs that are variable (their cost does depend on quantity produced). We have side-stepped the fact that inputs and costs may be fixed for some period of time, but if the time period is long enough, they can vary with production. Take the inputs of labour and machines, for example. In the short run, the supply of machines may be fixed. Output is then increased only by increasing labour. In the longer run, both machines and workers can be adjusted. The short-run cost curve, then, is the cost of production with a *given* stock of machines. The long-run cost curve is the cost of production when all factors are adjusted.[2]

[2] The distinction between short-run and long-run costs corresponds to the distinction between short-run and long-run supply curves introduced in Chapter 5. Chapter 11 will make clear the relationship. It is an exaggeration to think that only capital goods are fixed in the short run while all labour is variable. In some cases, capital goods may easily be varied; a firm can, for instance, rent cars. And in some cases, as when a company has long-term contracts with its workers, it may be very difficult to vary labour in the short run.

SHORT-RUN COST CURVES

If we think of the number of machines as being fixed in the short run, and labour as the principal input that can be varied, our earlier analysis of production with a single variable factor provides a good description of short-run cost curves. Thus, short-run *average* cost curves are normally U-shaped.

The short-run *marginal* cost curve in Figure 10.12 presents a pattern often seen in manufacturing. Marginal costs are approximately constant over a wide range. As long as their newest machines are not being fully used, firms find that increasing production by 10 percent requires increasing the number of production workers by 10 percent and the inputs of other materials (raw materials, intermediate goods) by 10 percent. Idle machines are simply put to work. Eventually, however, the cost of producing extra units goes up. Workers have to work more hours (and often they get paid more—time and a half or double time—for these extra hours). Overworked machines break down more frequently. Older, poorer machines have to be put to use. At some level of output, it may be impossible, without extraordinary costs, to push a factory to a higher level of production in the short run.

We have thus identified two key properties of the short-run marginal cost curve. (1) When there is excess capacity, the marginal cost of producing each extra unit does not increase much; the marginal cost curve is relatively flat. (2) But eventually the marginal cost curve becomes steeply upward sloping. (Remember, we are focusing here on the short run, so we assume the number of machines is fixed; there is a particular capacity for which the plant was designed.)

Before we turn to the long run, it is useful to rethink the meaning of fixed versus overhead costs. So far, we have used these terms interchangeably, to mean costs that do not depend on the level of output. This in fact confuses two related, but distinct, concepts. Even if a firm could instantaneously adjust all factors of production, some overhead costs would still be required for the company to exist at all. From now on, **overhead costs** will be defined as costs that a firm must bear simply to operate, whether or not they can be varied in the short run. For a firm to be in business at all, for example, it probably needs telephone service. **Fixed costs** will be defined as costs that are fixed in the short run, whether or not they represent overhead costs. If a firm has a long-run labour contract, for example, its wage costs are fixed in the short run.

LONG-RUN COST CURVES

Even if the short-run average cost curves for a given manufacturing facility are U-shaped, the long-run average cost curve may not have the same shape. As production grows, it will pay at some point to build a second plant, and then a third, a fourth, and so on. Panel A of Figure 10.13 shows the total costs of producing different levels of output, assuming that the firm builds one plant. This curve is marked TC_1. It also shows the total costs of producing different levels of output assuming the firm builds two plants (TC_2) and three plants (TC_3). How many plants will the company build? Clearly, the firm wishes to minimise the (total) costs of producing at any level of output. Thus, the *relevant* total cost curve is the lower boundary of the three curves, which is heavily shaded. Between 0 and Q_1, the firm produces using one plant; between Q_1 and Q_2, it uses two plants; and for outputs larger than Q_2, it uses three plants.

We can see the same results in panel B, using average cost curves. Obviously, if the firm minimises

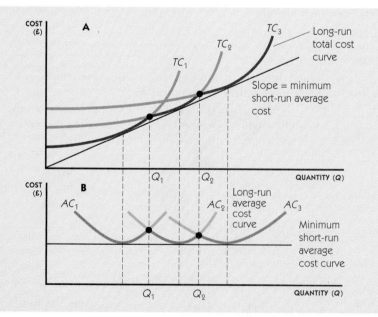

Figure 10.13 SHORT-RUN AND LONG-RUN COST CURVES

Panel A shows a series of long-run total cost curves, TC_1, TC_2, and TC_3, each representing a different level of fixed capital input. In the long run, a cost-minimising firm can choose any of these, so the long-run total cost curve will be the lowest cost of producing any level of output, as shown by the heavily shaded lower boundary of the curves. Panel B shows a series of short-run average cost curves, AC_1, AC_2, and AC_3, each representing a different level of fixed capital input. In the long run, a cost-minimising firm can choose any of these, so the long-run average cost curve will be the shaded lower boundary of the curves.

Some industries have lots of small firms; others have very few large firms. Farming is an industry in which there are many farms—thousands and thousands of them—despite the growth in the size of farms and the rise of "agribusiness" over recent decades. But in the sale of food in Britain, a handful of big supermarket chains have the bulk of the business. Sainsbury, Tesco, Asda, and a few others dominate the market. In the production of cars, a few big manufacturers dominate the world market: Ford, General Motors, Chrysler, VW-Audi, Renault, Fiat, Nissan, Honda, and a few more. In the production of (civil) aeroplanes, there are only a couple of firms at the world level—Boeing and Airbus Industrie—together with some smaller manufacturers.

What explains the dominance of some industries by just a few large firms, while others sustain a large number of smaller firms? There are a number of factors at work, but one of the more important is cost differences at different levels of production, that is, the shape of the cost curve. The world market for large passenger aircraft is not enormous—a few thousand new large jets a year on average—and each one costs millions of pounds. The long-run average costs of manufacturing an aeroplane appear to fall as the number built per year rises, up to a very large number—a number which is a large fraction of the world's

annual demand for planes. Economies of scale in aircraft manufacture are not exhausted until a manufacturer has a large fraction of the world market. The key element in this is the cost of developing a new plane—millions of pounds. This cost is a sunk cost (once it has been made): the firm has no way of recovering it, except by selling planes. It represents an enormous fixed element in the cost structure of a firm like Boeing.

The short-run variable costs of producing a plane—the costs of labour and capital and materials used in its production—are just a fraction of the long-run variable costs, which include also the development costs. For it to be worthwhile to develop a new plane, the manufacturer needs to believe that enough planes can be sold at a price that covers the direct inputs into each plane—labour, capital costs, materials—plus enough to cover the costs of development.

The same is true in car production. There are large fixed costs in developing a new model. The variable costs of each car produced may be quite small. Short-run variable costs of making a car may be constant, above a small scale of production. But when the costs of development are added, the long-run average costs diminish as the level of production grows.

---

the total costs of producing any particular output, it minimises the average cost of producing that output. The figure shows the average cost curves corresponding to the firm's producing with one, two, and three plants. The company chooses the number of plants that minimises its average costs, given the level of output it plans to produce. Thus, if the firm plans to produce less than Q_1, it builds only one plant; AC_1 is less than AC_2 for all outputs less than Q_1. If the firm plans to produce between Q_1 and Q_2,

it builds two plants, because AC_2 is, in this interval, less than either AC_1 or AC_3. Similarly, for outputs greater than Q_2, the firm builds three plants.

In this case, the long-run average cost curve is the heavily shaded bumpy curve in Figure 10.13B. For large outputs, the bumps look very small. In drawing long-run average cost curves, therefore, we typically ignore the bumps and draw smooth curves.

We now need to ask whether long-run average cost curves are normally flat or slope upwards or down-

Figure 10.14 **THE SHAPE OF THE LONG-RUN AVERAGE COST CURVE**

If there are many possibilities for varying the scale of the firm, such as by adding new machines and thus many short-run average cost curves, the long-run average cost curve defined by their joint boundary can be thought of as very flat, or smooth. In this case, the long-run average cost curve is drawn horizontal. The firm can increase output simply by replicating identical plants, and there are constant returns to scale.

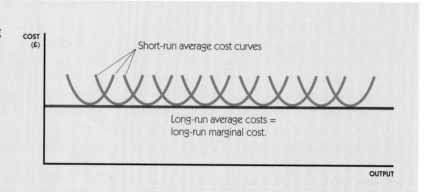

wards. To answer this question, remember how we analysed the shape of the short-run average cost curve, or the average cost curve with a single variable input. We first described the production function, relating the level of input to the level of output. If output increases less than proportionately with the input, there are diminishing returns, and the average cost curve is rising. If output increases more than proportionately with the input, there are increasing returns, and the average cost curve is falling.

Exactly the same kind of analysis applies when there are many inputs. We ask, what happens when all of the inputs increase together? When all of the inputs increase together in proportion, if output increases just in proportion, then there are **constant returns to scale;** if output increases less than proportionately, then there are **diminishing returns to scale;** and if output increases more than proportionately, then there are **increasing returns to scale,** or **economies of scale.**

Many economists argue that constant returns to scale are most prevalent in manufacturing; a firm can increase its production simply by replicating its plants. Then the long-run average and marginal costs equal minimum short-run average costs. The average and marginal cost curves for such a case are depicted in Figure 10.14, where there are many, many plants and the long-run average cost curve is flat. (The small bumps are caused by the fact that

output may not be a simple multiple of the output at which a plant attains its minimum average costs; but, as the figure shows, these bumps become relatively insignificant if output is very large.)

There are, however, also costs to establishing a firm—the overhead costs. The firm must bear these costs whether it operates 1, 2, or 100 plants. These overhead costs include not only the costs of the corporate headquarters but also the basic costs of designing the original plant. Thus, we more commonly think of the long-run average cost curve as slightly downward sloping, as in Figure 10.15A.

But sometimes small is beautiful, and big is bad. In these cases there are diminishing returns to scale. As the firm tries to grow, adding additional plants, it faces increasing managerial problems; it may have to add layer upon layer of management, and each of these layers increases its cost. When the firm is very small, the owner can watch all his workers. When the firm has grown to 10 employees, the owner can no longer supervise his workers effectively; a new supervisor maybe needed every time his firm hires 10 more workers. By the time the firm has grown to 100 workers, he has 10 supervisors. Now the owner spends most of his time looking after the supervisors, not the workers directly.

Eventually, the owner finds it difficult to keep tabs on the supervisors, so it becomes necessary to hire a manager for them. Notice that in this pattern, the number of supervisors and managers is a growing proportion of the workers in the firm. An organization with 10 workers requires only 1 supervisor; with 100 workers, it requires 10 supervisors and a manager; with 1,000 workers, 100 supervisors, 10 managers, and 1 supermanager. Besides the raw numbers of administrative people, decisions now must pass through a number of layers of bureaucracy, and communication will often be slower.

Eventually, average costs may start to increase, as illustrated in Figure 10.15B. Whether any particular industry is best described by Figure 10.14 or 10.15A or B depends on the importance of overhead costs and the extent to which managerial problems grow with size.

Increasing returns to scale are also possible in some industries, even for very large outputs. As the firm produces a higher output, it can take advantage of larger and more-efficient machines, which it would not pay a small firm to purchase. If there are increasing returns to scale, then the long-run average cost curve and the marginal cost curve will be downward sloping, as in Figure 10.15C.

LOOKING BEYOND THE BASIC MODEL: COST CURVES AND THE COMPETITIVENESS OF MARKETS

The degree of competition in an industry depends to a considerable degree on the structure of costs in that industry. This leads us to several insights that take us beyond the basic model. Consider the case of one company that is producing all the market wants in an industry with declining average costs. If any new company wishes to enter this market and produce less than the incumbent firm, its average costs will be higher than that of the incumbent company. So long as the original firm produces more than the entrant, its costs will be lower, so it can undercut the newcomer—and in fact charge a price so low that the new firm suffers a loss while the incumbent firm still makes a profit. Indeed, if the original merchant

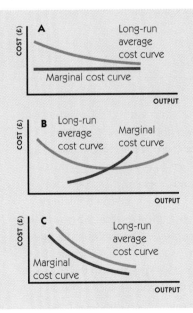

Figure 10.15 LONG-RUN AVERAGE COSTS

Panel A shows that with overhead costs, long-run average costs may be declining, but they flatten out as output increases. In panel B, with managerial costs increasing with the scale of the firm, eventually average and marginal costs may start to rise. Panel C shows that if there are increasing returns to scale, long-run costs may be continuously falling.

CLOSE-UP: HOW BIG IS BIG INDUSTRY?

While economic theory focuses on small competitive firms, in practice we see the economy dominated by very large firms, which are household names and have a global presence—firms like Microsoft, General Electric, Exxon, Coca-Cola, IBM, Shell, and many others. The *Financial Times* compiles a list of the world's 500 largest companies (measured by market capitalization). The largest (in September 1998) were:

Rank	Company	Country	Market Capitalization (U.S. $billions)
1	Microsoft	U.S.	272
2	General Electric	U.S.	259
3	Exxon	U.S.	172
4	Royal Dutch/Shell	Netherlands/U.K.	164
5	Merck	U.S.	155
6	Pfizer	U.S.	148
7	Intel	U.S.	144
8	Coca-Cola	U.S.	142
9	Wal-Mart	U.S.	123
10	IBM	U.S.	121
11	NTT	Japan	118
12	Philip Morris	U.S.	112
13	Novartis Ag	Switzerland	108
14	Johnson & Johnson	U.S.	105
15	Glaxo Wellcome	U.K.	105
16	Bristol Myers Squibb	U.S.	103
17	AT&T	U.S.	102
18	Roche	Switzerland	102

Source: Financial Times, 28 January 1999.

All these firms had market capitalizations over U.S. $100 billion (for comparison purposes, the gross output of the United Kingdom was roughly U.S. $1,250 billion in 1998). The biggest, Microsoft, approaches a market capitalization of U.S. $300 billion. How much competition do these very large enterprises face? Some of these firms have become very large through mergers with other firms, such as Glaxo Wellcome. Some have long-established positions in the super-league of global enterprises, such as Exxon, General Electric, and IBM. Others, such as Microsoft and Intel, have grown very rapidly through the development of new products.

The mere existence of very large firms does not imply an absence of competition. For example, IBM, once dominant in all aspects of the computer industry, has lost that position, although it remains a very large company. With the rise of the personal computer, it has been displaced by companies like Microsoft, Intel, Dell, and others; it retains a small market share. Microsoft has achieved a position of market power through its

Windows operating systems, but that dominance is being challenged by the development of new, competing operating systems, like Linux.

There are at least two views about the benefits of big firms. One is that globalization makes size an advantage, that size is now needed to compete in the global marketplace. The large firm is better able to develop, produce, distribute, and market products efficiently throughout the world. Another is that big established firms lose their innovative and competitive spirit and are not a recipe for growth. Younger, smaller firms are likely to be more dynamic. And indeed one sees firms moving up and down these rankings, joining them, and disappearing from them.

charges a price just equal to his average costs (or threatens to do so if an entrance tries to break into his market), there is now way that a rival can profitably enter.

If, in contrast, the incumbent firm is the only firm producing for the entire market but is on the upward-sloping portion of an average cost curve, a new company might aim at producing less with a lower average cost. Now, at least one new company will be able to undersell the original firm, and competitive forces will have some power.

The magnitude of the output at which average costs are minimised depends largely on the size of fixed costs, relative to the costs that vary with the level of output. In industries in which fixed costs are low, there will normally be many firms, since average costs will reach their minimum value at a relatively low level of output. Since the average cost curve may begin to rise quite rapidly beyond a relatively small output, small firms have the power to undersell larger firms, and there will be many firms in the market. Businesses with low fixed costs include real estate and travel agencies. In these industries, the typical firm is small, and there are thousands of them.

In industries in which fixed costs are high, however, the minimum average costs will be attained at a very high output, so there will be relatively few firms. Low-cost producers in these industries tend to be large firms, and relatively few fill the market demand. Makers of automobiles and household appliances are examples. Fixed costs loom large in the chemical industry too, so it is not surprising that many major chemicals are produced by only a few firms. In some industries, fixed costs are so large that average costs are declining throughout the output levels demanded in the market. In these cases, at least within any locality, there will be only one firm. Examples include electricity and other utility companies and cement plants. A main cost for most utilities is the cost of the wires (for electricity and telephone) or pipes (for water and sewage).

Expenditures to develop a new product are like high fixed costs in their effect on entry into a market. Firms can, of course, choose to spend more or less on research or on developing new products, but these costs do not increase with the firm's level of output. It is not surprising, then, that in many of the sectors of the economy in which research and development expenditures are important, there are relatively few firms. For example, the chemical industry is controlled by a small number of firms.

ECONOMIES OF SCOPE

Most firms produce more than one good. Deciding which goods to produce, and in what quantities, and how to produce them (the first and second basic economic questions) are central problems facing firm managers. The problems would be fairly straightforward were it not for some important interrelations among the products. The production of one product may affect the costs of producing another.

In some cases, products are produced naturally together; we say they are **joint products.** Thus, a sheep farm naturally produces wool, lamb meat, and mutton. If more lambs are slaughtered for meat, there will be less wool and less mutton.

If it is less expensive to produce a set of goods together than separately, economists say that there are **economies of scope.** The concept of economies of scope helps us understand why certain sets of activities are often undertaken by the same firms. Issues of economies of scope have also played an important role in discussions of regulation over the past two decades. In the United States at the time of the breakup of AT&T, which previously had dominated both local and long-distance telephone service as well as research in telecommunications, some economists argued against the breakup on the grounds that there were important economies of scope among these activities.

REVIEW AND PRACTICE

SUMMARY

1 A firm's production function specifies the level of output resulting from any combination of inputs. The increase in output corresponding to an increase in any input is the marginal product of that input.

2 Short-run marginal cost curves are generally upward sloping, because diminishing returns to a factor of production imply that it will take ever-increasing amounts of the input to produce a marginal unit of output.

3 The typical short-run average cost curve is U-shaped. With U-shaped average cost curves, the marginal and average cost curves will intersect at the minimum point of the average cost curve.

4 All profit-maximising firms choose the method of production that will minimise costs for the level of output they wish to produce, because the lowest costs will allow the highest amount of profits.

5 When a number of different inputs can be varied and the price of one input increases, the change in relative prices of inputs will encourage a firm to substitute relatively less expensive inputs; this is an application of the principle of substitution.

6 Economists often distinguish between short-run and long-run cost curves. In the short run, a firm is generally assumed not to be able to change its capital stock. In the long run, it can. Even if short-run average cost curves are U-shaped, long-run average cost curves can take on a variety of shapes. They can, for instance, be flat, continuously declining, or declining and then increasing.

7 Economies of scope exist when it is less expensive to produce two products together than it would be to produce each one separately.

KEY TERMS

profits	variable inputs	total costs	constant, diminishing, or **increasing returns to scale (economies of scale)**
revenue	average productivity	marginal cost	
production function	fixed or overhead costs	average costs	
marginal product	variable costs	average variable costs	economies of scope
fixed inputs			

REVIEW QUESTIONS

1 What is a production function? When there is a single (variable) input, why does output normally increase less than in proportion to input? What are the alternative shapes that the relationship between input and output takes? What is the relationship between these shapes and the shape of the cost function?

2 What is meant by these various concepts of cost: total, average, average variable, marginal, and fixed? What are the relationships between these costs? What are short-run and long-run costs? What is the relationship between them?

3 Why are short-run average cost curves frequently U-shaped? With U-shaped average cost curves, what is the relationship between average and marginal costs? If the average cost curve is U-shaped, what does the total cost curve look like?

4 What happens to average, marginal, and total costs when the price of an input rises?

5 If a firm has a number of variable inputs and the price of one of them rises, will the firm use more or less of this input? Why?

6 What are diminishing, constant, and increasing returns to scale? When might you expect each to occur? What is the relationship between these properties of the production function and the shape of the long-run average and total cost curves?

7 What are economies of scope, and how do they affect what a firm chooses to produce?

PROBLEMS

1 Tom and Dick, who own the Tom, Dick, and Hairy Barbershop, need to decide how many barbers to hire. The production function for their barbershop looks like this:

Number of barbers	Haircuts provided per day	Marginal product
0	0	
1	12	
2	36	
3	60	
4	72	
5	80	
6	84	

Calculate the marginal product of hiring additional barbers, and fill in the last column of the table. Over what range is the marginal product of labour increasing? Constant? Diminishing? Graph the production function. By looking at the graph, you should be able to tell at which point the average productivity of labour is highest. Calculate average productivity at each point to illustrate your answer.

2 The overhead costs of the Tom, Dick, and Hairy Barbershop are £80 per day, and the cost of paying a barber for a day is £40. With this information and the information in problem 1, make up a table with column headings in this order: Output, Labour required, Total variable costs, Total costs, Marginal cost, Average variable costs, and Average costs. If the price of a haircut is £5 and the shop sells 80 per day, what is the daily profit?

3 Using the information in problems 1 and 2, draw the total cost curve for the Tom, Dick, and Hairy Barbershop on one graph. On a second graph, draw the marginal cost curve, the average cost curve, and the average variable cost curve. Do these curves have the shape you would expect? Do the minimum and average cost curves intersect at the point you would expect?

4 Suppose a firm has the choice of two methods of producing: one method entails fixed costs of £10 and a marginal cost of £2; the other entails fixed costs of £20 and a marginal cost of £1. Draw the total and average cost curves for both methods. At which levels of output will the firm use the low-fixed-cost technology? At which levels of output will it use the high-fixed-cost technology?

5 A firm produces cars using labour and capital. Assume that average labour productivity—total output divided by the number of workers—has increased in the last few months. Does that mean that workers are working harder? Or that the firm has become more efficient? Explain.

APPENDIX: COST MINIMIZATION WITH MANY INPUTS

This appendix shows how the basic principles of cost minimization can be applied to a firm's choice of the mix of inputs to use in production. To do this, we make use of a set of concepts and tools similar to those presented in the appendix to Chapter 8, in the analysis of how households make decisions about what mix of goods to purchase.

ISOQUANTS

The alternative ways of producing a particular quantity of output can be graphically represented by **iso-** **quants.** The first part of the term comes form the Greek word *iso,* meaning "same," while "quant" is just shorthand for quantity. Thus, isoquants illustrate the different combinations of inputs that produce the same quantity.

Consider this simple extension of the example of Table 10.3 on page 193. A firm can buy three different kinds of machines, each of which produces car frames. One is a highly mechanised machine that requires very little labour. Another is much less automated and requires considerably more labour. In between is another technique. These represent three different ways of producing the same quantity.

Assume the firm wishes to produce 10,000 car frames a day. It could do this by using 5 highly mechanised machines or 2 of the moderately mechanised machines or 1 of the nonmechanised machines. The total capital and labour requirements for each of these possibilities are represented in Figure 10.16. The horizontal axis shows the capital requirements,

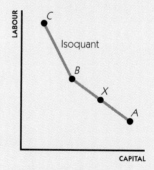

Figure 10.16 THREE ALTERNATIVE METHODS OF PRODUCING A CERTAIN AMOUNT

Point *A* represents the inputs for a highly mechanised way of producing a certain number of car frames; point *C* represents a technique of production that uses a much less expensive machine but more labour; point *B* represents a technique that is in between. By using different techniques in different proportions, the firm can use a combination of labour and capital on the line joining *A* and *B,* such as point *X.* The curve *ABC* is an isoquant.

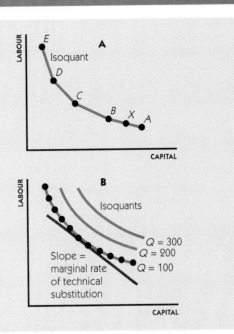

Figure 10.17 ISOQUANTS AND THE MARGINAL RATE OF SUBSTITUTION

Panel A shows an isoquant defined with many alternative techniques of production. Panel B shows that as the number of production techniques increases, isoquants appear as smooth curves. The slope of the isoquant tells how much of one input must be added to make up for the loss of a unit of the other input; this is the marginal rate of technical substitution.

while the vertical axis shows the labour requirements. The labour and capital associated with the highly mechanised production process is shown by point A, the moderately mechanised by point B, and the unmechanised by point C.

If the firm wishes, it can produce half its output on the highly mechanised machines and half on the moderately mechanised machines. If it chooses this option, its capital requirements will be halfway between the capital that would be required if it used only A or only B, and its labour requirements will also be halfway between. This halfway-between choice is illustrated by point X. By similar logic, the firm can achieve any combination of capital and labour requirements on the straight line joining A and B by changing the proportion of highly mechanised and moderately mechanised machines. And by changing the proportion of moderately mechanised and slightly mechanised machines, it can achieve any combination of capital and labour requirements on the straight line joining B and C. The curve ABC is the isoquant. It gives all those combinations of capital and labour requirements which can produce

10,000 automobile frames per day. All these input combinations give the same output.

Consider now what happens if many techniques are available instead of only three. The isoquant consists of points designating each of the techniques and the short line segments connecting these points which represent combinations of two techniques, as shown in Figure 10.17A. When many, many production techniques are available, the isoquant looks much like a smooth curve, and economists often draw it that way, as in panel B.

Many different isoquants can be drawn, each representing one particular level of output, as in panel B. Higher isoquants represent higher levels of production; lower isoquants represent lower levels.[3] There is also a simple relationship between the production

[3] People who have read the Chapter 8 appendix on indifference curves should recognise the similarities between isoquants and indifference curves: while indifference curves give those combinations of goods that yield the individual the same level of utility, the isoquant gives those combinations of goods (inputs) that yield the firm the same level of output.

functions discussed above and isoquants. The production function gives the output corresponding to each level of inputs. The isoquant tells which are the levels of inputs that can yield a given level of output.

MARGINAL RATE OF TECHNICAL SUBSTITUTION

The idea of the marginal rate of substitution was introduced in the appendix to Chapter 8 to describe how individuals are willing to trade off less of one good for more of another. The concept is also useful in analysing which technology firms will choose. In the case of firms, the marginal rate of substitution is defined not by individual preferences but by physical facts. If a firm reduces one input by a unit and then raises another input enough so that the final output remains the same, the amount of extra input required is called the **marginal rate of technical substitution.**

An example should help to clarify this idea. If a firm can reduce the amount of capital it uses by 1 machine, hire 2 more workers, and produce the same quantity, then it is possible for 2 workers to replace 1 machine. In this case, the marginal rate of technical substitution between workers and machines is 2/1. The marginal rate of technical substitution is just the slope of the isoquant, as Figure 10.17B shows diagrammatically: the slope simply tells how much of an increase in labour is needed to offset a one-unit decrease in capital to produce the same amount of output.[4]

Notice that the marginal rate of technical substitution and the slope of the isoquant change with the quantities of labour and capital involved. With fewer and fewer machines, it becomes increasingly difficult to substitute workers for machines. The marginal rate of technical substitution rises, and the slope of the isoquant becomes steeper and steeper. At the other end of the isoquant, with more and more machines, it becomes easier and easier to replace one of them. The marginal rate of technical substitution diminishes as the number of workers increases, and the slope of the isoquant becomes flatter. There is a **diminishing marginal rate of technical substitution** in production, just as there was a diminishing marginal rate of substitution in consumption.

The marginal rate of technical substitution can be calculated from the marginal products of labour and capital. If adding 1 more worker increases the output of automobile frames by 1, the marginal product of an extra worker in this industrial process is 1. Let us also imagine that adding 1 machine leads to an increase in car output of, say, 2 a day. So in this industrial process, the marginal product of a machine is 2. In this example, adding 2 workers and reducing machine input by 1 leaves output unchanged. Thus, the marginal rate of technical substitution is 2/1. In general, the marginal rate of technical substitution is equal to the ratio of the marginal products.

The principle of diminishing returns explains why the marginal rate of technical substitution diminishes as a firm adds more and more workers. As it adds more workers, the marginal product of an additional worker diminishes. As the number of machines is reduced, the marginal product of an additional machine is increased. When a firm considers the choices along an isoquant where machines are becoming more productive at the margin and workers are becoming less productive at the margin, it becomes increasingly costly to replace machines with additional workers.

Notice that calculating the marginal rate of substitution does not tell the firm whether it *should* substitute workers for machines, or machines for workers. The number by itself only provides factual information about what the trade-off would be, based on the technology available to the firm. To decide which combination of inputs should be chosen, the firm must also know the market prices of the various inputs.

COST MINIMIZATION

Minimising costs will require marginal decision making. Firms know the technology they are currently using and can consider changing it by trading

[4] Again, readers who earlier studied indifference curves will recall that the slope of the indifference curve is also called the marginal rate of substitution; it tells us how much more of one good is required when consumption of another good is reduced by one unit if we wish to leave the individual at the same level of welfare—on his indifference curve.

off some inputs against others. To decide whether such a trade-off will reduce costs, they can simply compare the market price of the input they are reducing with the price of the input they are increasing. If a firm can replace 1 machine with 2 workers and maintain the same output, and if a worker costs £12,000 a year and a machine costs £25,000 a year to rent, then by reducing machines by 1 and hiring 2 workers, the firm can reduce total costs. On the other hand, if a worker costs £13,000, it would pay to use 2 fewer workers (for a saving of £26,000) and rent 1 machine (for a cost of £25,000).

The only time that it would not pay the firm either to increase labour and reduce the number of machines or to decrease labour and increase the number of machines is when the marginal rate of technical substitution is equal to the relative price of the two factors. The reason for this is similar to the reason why individuals set their personal marginal rates of substitution equal to the ratio of market prices. The difference is that the individual's marginal rate of substitution is determined by individual preferences, while the firm's marginal rate of technical substitution is determined by technology.

ISOCOST CURVES

The **isocost** curve gives those combinations of inputs that cost the same amount. The isocost curve is analogous to an individual's budget constraint, which gives those combinations of goods that cost the same amount. If a firm faces fixed prices for its inputs, the isocost curve is a straight line, whose slope indicates the relative prices; that is, if each worker costs, say, £50 per day, then if the firm reduces the labour used by one, it could spend £50 per day on renting more machines. If renting a machine for a day costs £100, then the firm can rent one more machine with the amount it would save by reducing the input of labour by two. There are, of course, many isocost lines, one for each level of expenditure. Lower isocost lines represent lower expenditures on inputs. Costs along line C_1 in Figure 10.18 are lower than costs along C. The different isocost lines are parallel to one another, just as different household budget constraints representing different income levels are parallel.

Notice that all firms facing the same prices for inputs will have the same isocost lines. Similarly, different individuals with the same income face the same budget constraint, even when their preferences differ. However, the isoquant curves that describe each firm are based on the product the firm is making and the technology and knowledge available to the firm. Thus, isoquant curves will differ from firm to firm.

Isoquant curves and isocost lines can illuminate the behaviour of a cost-minimising firm. For example, any efficient profit-maximising firm will wish to maximise the output it obtains from any given expenditure. Or to rephrase the same point, the firm must reach the highest possible isoquant, given a particular level of expenditure on inputs, represented by a particular isocost line. The highest possi-

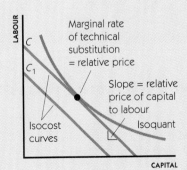

Figure 10.18 COST MINIMIZATION

Cost-minimising firms will wish to produce as much output as they can given a particular level of expenditure, so they will choose the highest isoquant they can reach with a given isocost curve, which will be the isoquant tangent to the isocost curve.

ble isoquant will touch the isocost line at a single point; the two curves will be tangent.

The problem of cost minimization can be described in a different way. Consider a firm that has a desired level of output and wishes to minimise its cost. The firm chooses an isoquant, and then tries to find the point on the isoquant that is on the lowest possible isocost line. Again, the cost-minimising firm will choose the point of tangency between the isocost line and the isoquant.

At the point of tangency, the slopes of the two curves are the same. The slope of the isoquant is the marginal rate of substitution. The slope of the isocost line is the relative price. Thus, *the marginal rate of technical substitution must equal the relative price.*

APPLYING THE DIAGRAMMATIC ANALYSIS

The isoquant/isocost diagram can be used to show how a change in relative prices affects the optimal mix of inputs. A change in relative prices changes the isocost line. In Figure 10.19, an increase in the wage makes the isocost curves flatter. The curve C is the original isocost curve that minimises the costs of producing output Q_0 (that is, C is tangent to the isoquant Q_0). The curve C_1 is the isocost line with the new higher wages that is tangent to the original isoquant. Obviously, to produce the same level of output will cost more if wages are increased. The figure also shows what this change in relative prices in the form of higher wages does to the cost-minimising combination of inputs: as one would expect, the firm substitutes away from labour towards capital (from point E_0 to E_1).

Of course, the magnitude of the substitution will differ from industry to industry, depending on an industry's isoquant. In addition, substitution is likely to be much greater in the long run than in the short run, as machines wear out, firms engage in research to find out how to conserve on the more expensive inputs, and so on. The figure represents these different possibilities for substitution. In panel A, the possibilities for substitution are very limited. The isoquant is very curved. This figure might illustrate a case where it is very difficult to substitute (at least in the short run) machines for labour—illustrated, perhaps, by the use of blast furnaces in producing steel. In panel B, substitution is very easy; the isoquant is very flat. This would illustrate an opposite case; for example, given the increased possibilities for automation afforded by modern technology, it is often relatively easy for a firm to substitute machines for labour.

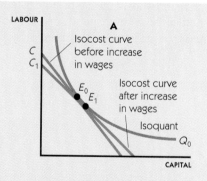
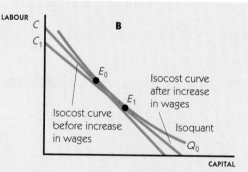

Figure 10.19 CHANGING FACTOR PRICES

This firm has chosen the level of production associated with the isoquant shown, and the cost-minimising combination of labour and capital for producing that amount is originally at E_0. But as wages rise, relative prices shift, and the cost-minimising method of producing the given amount becomes E_1. In panel A, an increase in wages leads to little substitution. But in panel B, an increase in wages leads to a much larger amount of substitution.

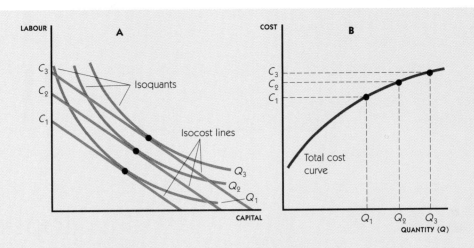

Figure 10.20 DERIVING THE TOTAL COST CURVE

The total cost curve describes how total cost changes at different levels of output. Panel A shows three isoquants representing different levels of output, and three isocost curves tangent to those isoquants, representing the least-cost way of producing each of these amounts. Panel B plots the actual level of costs for each of these levels of output, producing the familiar total cost curve.

DERIVING COST CURVES

The cost curves in this chapter represent the minimum cost of producing each level of output, at a particular level of input prices. Figure 10.20A shows the cost-minimising way of producing three different levels of output, Q_1, Q_2, and Q_3. Panel B then plots the actual level of costs associated with each of these levels of output. That is, the isocost curves tangent to the isoquants in panel A show the minimum level of costs associated with each output. Tracing out the costs associated with each level of output provides the total cost curve. And once we have the total cost curve, we know how to derive the marginal cost curve (the slope of the total cost curve) and the average cost curve (the slope of a line from the origin to the total cost curve).

PRODUCTION

C hapter 10 defined profits as the difference between revenue and costs. We learned that firms maximise their profits by balancing the extra benefits from producing one more unit, hiring one more worker, or buying one more machine with the extra costs. We also learned the basic tools for assessing the extra costs. In this chapter, we learn how to calculate the extra benefits and examine more closely how firms weigh extra costs against these extra benefits. This balancing process dictates the (rational) firm's production decision.

This chapter rounds out the discussion of markets because, in making their production decisions, firms provide the final ingredients for a complete model of the economy. With all the ingredients in hand—the basic economic decisions of individuals and households to maximise satisfaction and the basic economic decisions of firms seeking to maximise profits—we will be able to construct a complete model of the economy in Chapter 12.

KEY QUESTIONS

1 What determines the level of output a firm will supply at any given price? How do we derive, in other words, the firm's supply curve?

2 What determines whether or when a firm will enter or exit a market?

3 How do the answers to these questions enable us to analyse the market supply curve, why it is upward slopping and why it may be more elastic than the supply curve of any single firm?

4 How do we reconcile the economists' view that competition drives profits to zero with the accountants' reports showing that most of the time most firms earn positive profits?

5 What determines firms' demand for inputs, such as labour or capital? Why is the firms' demand curve for labour downward sloping?

REVENUE

Consider the hypothetical example of the High Strung Violin Company, manufacturer of world-class violins. The company hires labour; it buys wood, utilities, and other materials; and it rents a building and machines. Its violins sell for £40,000 each. Last year the company sold seven of them, for a gross revenue of £280,000. Table 11.1 gives a snapshot of the firm's financial health, its **profit-and-loss statement** for last year.

Table 11.1 PROFIT-AND-LOSS STATEMENT FOR THE HIGH STRUNG VIOLIN COMPANY

Gross revenue	£280,000
Costs	£180,000
Wages (including fringe benefits)	£150,000
Purchases of wood and other materials	£20,000
Utilities	£1,000
Rent of building	£5,000
Rent of machinery	£2,000
Miscellaneous expenses	£2,000
Profits	£100,000

We see that High Strung's revenues were £280,000 and its costs were £180,000, so its profits were £100,000. If its costs had been £400,000 instead of £180,000, its profits would have been −£120,000. The firm would have made a negative profit, in other words, a **loss.**

The relationship between revenue and output is shown by the **revenue curve** in Figure 11.1. The horizontal axis measures the firm's output, while the vertical axis measures the revenues. When the price of a violin is £40,000 and the firm sells nine violins, its revenue is £360,000; when it sells ten, revenue rises to £400,000.

The extra revenue that a firm receives from selling an extra unit is called its **marginal revenue.** Thus, £40,000 is the extra (or marginal) revenue from selling the tenth violin. It is no accident that the marginal revenue equals the price of the violin. A fundamental feature of competitive markets is that firms receive the same market price for each unit they sell. Thus, the extra revenue that firms in competitive markets receive from selling one more unit—the marginal revenue—is the same as the price of the unit.

COSTS

High Strung incurs costs corresponding to each level of output. Total costs are given in column 1 of Table 11.2 and depicted diagrammatically in Figure

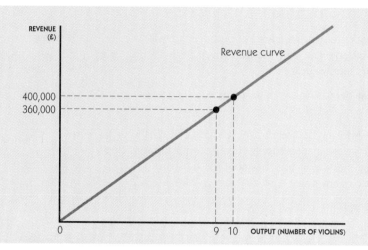

Figure 11.1 THE REVENUE CURVE

The revenue curve shows a firm's revenue at each level of output. For the firm in a competitive industry, price does not change as more is produced, so the revenue curve is a straight line with a constant slope. In this example, the revenue of each additional violin is always £40,000.

11.2A. Panel B shows the corresponding average and marginal costs. High Strung's average cost curve exhibits the typical U-shape that we associate with manufacturing firms.

Even before it builds its first violin, the company must spend £90,000. Space must be rented. Some employees have to be hired. Equipment must be purchased. No matter how many or how few violins High Strung produces, its fixed costs remain £90,000.

The *extra* cost of producing an additional violin, the marginal cost, is shown in column 3. Marginal cost is always associated with the additional cost of producing a *particular* unit of output. The marginal cost of increasing production from one to two violins, for example, is £10,000. Each additional violin costs £10,000 more until production reaches six violins. The extra (or marginal) cost of producing the seventh violin is £30,000. The marginal cost of producing the eighth violin is £40,000.

The High Strung Violin Company's average costs initially decline as its production increases, since the fixed costs can be divided among more units of production. But between six and seven violins, average costs begin to increase, as the effect of the increasing average variable costs dominates the effect of the fixed costs.

Table 11.2 HIGH STRUNG VIOLIN COMPANY'S COST OF PRODUCTION (THOUSANDS OF POUNDS)

Output	(1) Total Costs	(2) Average Costs	(3) Marginal Cost	(4) Total Variable Costs	(5) Average Variable Costs
0	90				
1	100	100	10	10	10
2	110	55	10	20	10
3	120	40	10	30	10
4	130	32.5	10	40	10
5	140	28	10	50	10
6	150	25	10	60	10
7	180	25.72	30	90	12.72
8	220	27.5	40	130	16.25
9	270	30	50	180	20
10	400	40	130	310	31

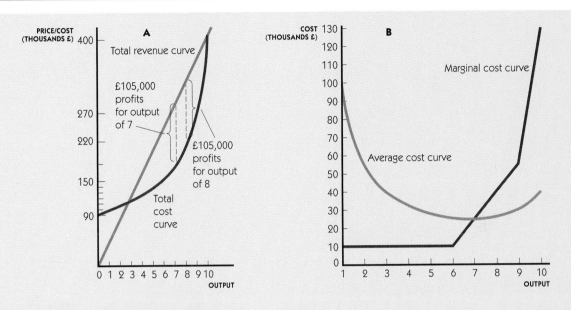

Figure 11.2 RELATING REVENUE AND COSTS

The firm's revenue and total cost curves can be diagrammed on the same graph, as in panel A. When total revenue exceeds total costs, the firm is making profits at that level of output. Profits, the difference between revenue and costs, are measured by the distance between the two curves; in this case, the highest level of profits is being made at a production level of 7 or 8. When total costs exceed total revenue, the firm is making losses at that level of output. When the two lines cross, the firm is making zero profits. The marginal and average cost curves for this company have their expected shape in panel B. Marginal cost is constant until a production level of 6, and then it begins to increase. The average cost curve is U-shaped.

BASIC CONDITIONS OF COMPETITIVE SUPPLY

In choosing how much to produce, a profit-maximising firm will focus its decision at the margin. Having incurred the fixed costs of getting into this market, the decision is generally not the stark one of whether to produce but whether to produce one more unit of a good or one less. For a firm in a competitive market, the answer to this problem is relatively simple: the company simply compares the marginal revenue it will receive by producing an extra unit—which is just the price of the good—with the extra cost of producing that unit, the marginal cost. As long as the marginal revenue exceeds the marginal cost, the firm will make additional profit by producing more. If marginal revenue is less than marginal cost, then producing an extra unit will cut profits, and the firm will reduce production. In short, the firm will produce to the point where the marginal cost equals the marginal revenue, which in a competitive market is equal to the price.

The marginal cost curve is upward sloping, just as the supply curves in Chapter 4 were upward sloping. This too is no accident: a firm's marginal cost curve is actually the same as its supply curve. The marginal cost curve shows the additional cost of producing

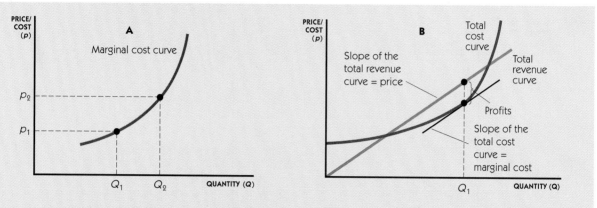

Figure 11.3 THE PROFIT-MAXIMISING LEVEL OF OUTPUT

A competitive firm maximises profits by setting output at the point where price equals marginal cost. In panel A, at the price of p_1, this quantity is Q_1. Panel B shows total revenue and total costs. Profits are maximised when the distance between the two curves is maximised, which is the point where the two lines are parallel (and thus have the same slope).

one more unit at different levels of output. A competitive firm chooses to produce at the level of output where the cost of producing an additional unit (that is, the marginal cost) is equal to the market price. We can thus read from the marginal cost curve what the firm's supply will be at any price: it will be the quantity of output at which marginal cost equals that price. Figure 11.2A shows the total revenue as well as total costs. We can see that profits—the gap between revenue and costs—are maximised at an output of either 7 or 8. If the price were just slightly lower than £40,000, profits would be maximised at 7, and if the price were just slightly higher than £40,000, profits would be maximised at 8.

The profit-maximising level of output, where price equals marginal cost, can be seen in panel A of Figure 11.3, which shows the marginal cost curve for a firm facing increasing marginal cost. The firm produces up to the point where price (which equals marginal revenue) equals marginal cost. If it produces more than that, the extra cost will be more than the extra revenue received. Figure 11.3 shows how much output the firm will produce at each price. At the price p_1, it will produce the output Q_1. At the price p_2, it will produce the output Q_2. With an upward-sloping marginal cost curve, it is clear that the firm will produce more as price increases.

The profit-maximising level of output can also be

EQUILIBRIUM OUTPUT FOR COMPETITIVE FIRMS

In competitive markets, firms produce at the level where price equals marginal cost.

seen in panel B of Figure 11.3, which shows the total revenue and total cost curves. Profits are the difference between revenue and costs. In panel B, profits are the distance between the revenue curve and the cost curve. The profit-maximising firm will choose the output where that distance is greatest. This occurs at Q_1. Below Q_1, price (the slope of the revenue curve) exceeds marginal cost (the slope of the total cost curve), so profits increase as output increases; above Q_1, price is less than marginal cost, so profits decrease as output increases.

ENTRY, EXIT, AND MARKET SUPPLY

We are now in a position to tackle the market supply curve. To do so, we need to know a little more about each firm's decision to produce. First let's consider a firm that is currently not producing. Under which circumstances should it incur the fixed costs of entering the industry? This is a relatively easy problem: the company simply looks at the average cost curve and the price. *If price exceeds minimum average costs, it pays the firm to enter.* This is because if it enters, it can sell the goods for more than the costs of producing them, thus making a profit.

Figure 11.4A shows the U-shaped average cost curve. Minimum average costs are c_{min}. If the price is less than c_{min}, then there is no level of output at which the firm could produce and make a profit. If the price is above c_{min}, then the firm will produce at the level of output at which price (p) equals marginal cost, Q^*. At Q^*, marginal cost exceeds average costs. (This is always true at output levels greater than that at which average costs are minimum.) Profit per unit is the difference between price and average costs. Total profits are the product of profit per unit and the level of output, the shaded area in Figure 11.4A.

Different companies may have different average cost curves. Some will have better management.

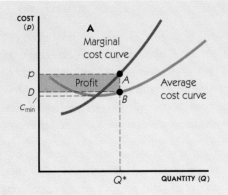
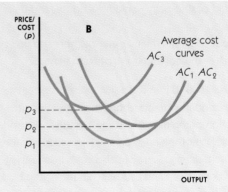

Figure 11.4 COST CURVES, PROFITS, AND ENTRY

Panel A shows that if price is above the minimum of the average cost curve, profits will exist. Profits are measured by the area formed by the shaded rectangle, the profit per unit (price minus average costs, corresponding to the distance AB) times the output Q^*. Panel B shows average cost curves for three different firms. At price p_1, only one firm will enter the market. As price rises to p_2 and then to p_3, first the firm whose cost curve is AC_2 and then the firm whose cost curve is AC_3 will enter the market.

House painting is a summer business, suitable for low-skilled labour on vacation from college. As a way of picking up some cash, Michael decided to start Presto Painters during the summer after taking introductory economics.

Just getting started involves some substantial fixed costs. Michael ran the business out of his parents' home, so he had no costs for office space. His fixed costs ended up looking like this:

Fixed Costs	
Used van	£500
Paint and supplies	£1,700
Flyers and signs	£400
Business cards and estimate sheets	£200
Phone line and answering machine	£200
Total	£3,000

Michael went to work drumming up business. He took calls from potential customers and knocked on doors, made estimates of what he thought it would cost to paint someone's house, and then offered him a price. Of course, he was in direct competition with many other painters and had to meet the competition's price to get a job.

Michael found that the going rate for labour was £3 per hour. (This adventure predated the introduction of the minimum wage.) In the real world, labour is not the only variable input required for house painting. There are also costs from buying additional paint and brushes, but for simplicity, assume he started off the summer with all the paint he needed. Thus, his variable costs were related to the labour he needed to hire.

Variable costs are also related to the amount of time it takes to paint a house, which varies de-

pending on the quality of the labour you can find. The variable costs for Presto Painters were:

Houses Painted	Hours of Labour Hired	Wage Bill
5	100	£300
10	300	£900
15	600	£1,800
20	1,000	£3,000
25	1,500	£4,500
30	2,100	£6,300

Given this information, Michael could calculate cost curves for Presto Painters (see next page).

On the basis of his marginal and average cost curves, Michael figured that if market conditions allowed him to charge £330 or more for a typical house, then he could make a profit by painting at least 25 houses. Roughly speaking, that is how his summer worked out; painting 25 houses for £330 apiece. Thus, he earned £150 in profits.

Or so he thought. Nowhere in this list of costs did Michael consider the opportunity cost of his time. He was getting paid £3 an hour for painting houses; he was out there stirring up business, hiring and organising workers, taking calls from customers, and dealing with complaints.

Imagine that Michael had an alternative job possibility as a waiter. He could earn £2.50 per hour (including tips) and work 40-hour weeks during a 12-week summer vacation. Thus, he could have earned £1,200 during the summer with little stress or risk. If this opportunity cost is added to the fixed costs of running the business, then his apparent profit turns into a loss. Since Presto

Painters did not cover Michael's opportunity cost *and* compensate him for the risk and aggravation of running his own business, he would have been financially better off sticking to the business of filling people's stomachs rather than painting their houses.

Number of Homes	Total Costs	Average Costs	Marginal Cost (per house)
0	£3,000		
5	£3,300	£660	£60
10	£3,900	£390	£120
15	£4,800	£320	£180
20	£6,000	£300	£240
25	£7,500	£300	£300
30	£9,300	£310	£360

Some will have a better location. Accordingly, firms will differ in their minimum average cost. As prices rise, additional firms will find it attractive to enter the market. Figure 11.4B shows the U-shaped average cost curves for three different firms. Firm 1's minimum average costs are AC_1, firm 2's minimum average costs are AC_2, and firm 3's minimum average costs are AC_3. Thus, firm 1 enters at the price p_1, firm 2 at the price p_2, and firm 3 at the price p_3.

SUNK COSTS AND EXIT

The converse of the decision of a firm to enter the market is the decision of a firm already producing to exit the market. Sunk costs are costs that are not recoverable, even if a firm goes out of business. The High Strung Violin Company, for example, may have had an extensive television advertising campaign. The costs of this campaign are sunk costs. There is no way this expenditure can be recouped if production ceases. If there were no sunk costs the decision to enter and the decision to exit would be mirror images of each other. Firms would exit the market when their average costs rose above the price. But if some costs remain even if a firm stops producing, the question facing that firm is whether it can recover some of these costs by continuing to produce.

Let us assume for simplicity that fixed costs are always sunk costs. A firm with no fixed costs has an average cost curve that is the same as its average variable cost curve. It will shut down as soon as the price falls below minimum average costs—the cost at the bottom of its U-shaped cost curve. But a firm *with* fixed costs has a different decision to make. Figure 11.5A depicts both the average variable cost curve and the average cost curve for such a case. As in the case with no sunk costs, the firm shuts down when price is below minimum average *variable* costs (costs that vary with the level of output) p_1. But if the price is *between* average variable costs and average costs, the firm will continue to produce, even though it will show a loss. It continues to produce because it would show an even bigger loss if it ceased operating. Since price exceeds average variable costs, the revenue it obtains exceeds the additional costs it incurs from producing. (Later in the chapter we will discuss the case in which fixed costs are not necessarily sunk costs.)

Different firms in an industry will have different average variable costs, and so will find it desirable to exit the market at different prices. Figure 11.5B shows the average variable cost curves for three different firms. Their cost curves differ; some may, for instance, have newer equipment than others. As the price falls, the firm with the highest minimum average variable costs finds it is no longer able to make

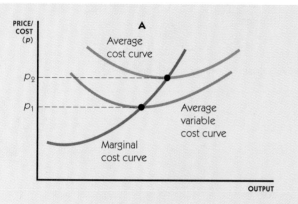
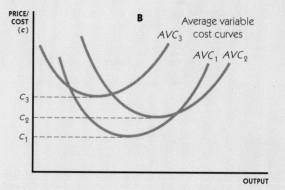

Figure 11.5 AVERAGE VARIABLE COSTS AND THE DECISION TO PRODUCE

Panel A shows a firm's average variable cost curves. In the short run, firms will produce as long as price exceeds average variable costs. Thus, for prices between p_1 and p_2, the firm will continue to produce, even though it is recording a loss (price is less than average costs). Panel B shows that firms with different average variable cost curves will decide to shut down at different price levels. As price falls below c_3, the minimum average variable costs for firm 3, firm 3 shuts down; as price falls still lower, below c_2, firm 2 shuts down. Finally, when price falls below c_1 firm 1 shuts down.

money at the going price and decides not to operate. Thus, firm 3 (represented by the curve AVC_3) shuts down as soon as the price falls below c_3, firm 2 shuts down as soon as the price falls below c_2, and firm 1 shuts down as soon as the price falls below c_1.

THE FIRM'S SUPPLY CURVE

We can now draw the firm's supply curve. As Figure 11.6A shows, for a firm contemplating entering the market, supply is zero up to a critical price, equal to the minimum average cost. Thus, for price below $p = c_{min}$, the firm produces zero output. For prices greater than c_{min}, the firm produces up to the point where price equals marginal cost, so the firm's supply curve coincides with the marginal cost curve. For a firm that has incurred sunk costs of entering the market (panel B), the supply curve coincides with the marginal cost curve so long as price exceeds the minimum value of average *variable* costs; when price is below the minimum value of average variable costs, the firm exists, so supply is again zero.

THE MARKET SUPPLY CURVE

With this information about the cost curves of individual firms, we can derive the overall market supply curve. Back in Chapter 4, the market supply curve was defined as the sum of the amounts that each firm was willing to supply at any given price. Figure 11.7 provides a graphical description of the supply curve for a market with two firms. If the price rises, the firms already in the market (firms 1 and 2) will find it profitable to increase their output and new firms (with higher average variable cost curves) will find it profitable to enter the market. Because higher prices induce more firms to enter a competitive market, the market supply response to an increase in price is greater than if the number of firms were fixed. In the same way, as price falls, there are two market responses. The firms that still find it profitable to produce at the lower price will produce less, and the higher-cost firms will exit the market. In this way, the competitive market ensures that whatever the product, it is produced at the lowest possible price by the most efficient firms.

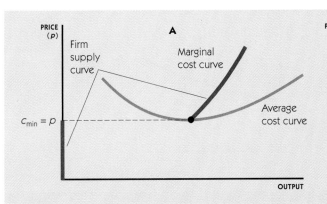
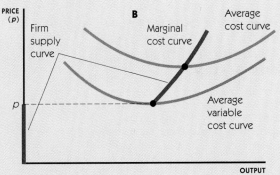

Figure 11.6 THE SUPPLY CURVE FOR A FIRM

Panel A shows that for a firm contemplating entering the market, supply is zero up to a critical price, equal to the firm's minimum average costs, after which the firm's supply curve coincides with the marginal cost curve. Panel B shows a firm that has already entered the market, incurring positive sunk costs; this firm will produce as long as price exceeds the minimum of the average variable cost curve.

Figure 11.7 THE MARKET SUPPLY CURVE

The market supply curve is derived by horizontally adding up the supply curves for each of the firms. More generally, as price rises, each firm produces more and new firms enter the market.

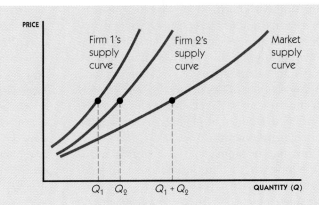

LONG-RUN VERSUS SHORT-RUN SUPPLY

As we saw in Chapter 10, in the short run the typical firm will have a U-shaped average cost curve, and a sharply rising marginal cost curve at output levels above the lowest point of the U. But its long-run average costs, and therefore marginal costs, are flatter. This is because adjustments to changes in market conditions take time, and some adjustments take longer than others. In the short run, you can add workers, work more shifts, run the machines harder (or reduce the rate at which these things are done), but you are probably stuck with your existing plant and equip-

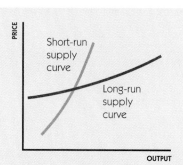

Figure 11.8 ELASTICITY OF SHORT-RUN AND LONG-RUN SUPPLY CURVES FOR A FIRM

Because there is a greater chance for a firm to adjust to changes in price in the long run, the price elasticity of the supply curve is greater in the long run than in the short run.

ment. In the long run, you can acquire more buildings and more machines (or sell them). Thus, the long-run supply curve for a firm is more elastic (flatter) than the short-run supply curve, as shown in Figure 11.8.

The same thing is true, only more so, for the industry—again because the number of firms is not fixed. Even if each firm can operate only one plant, the industry's output can be increased by 5 percent by increasing the number of firms by 5 percent. The extra costs of increasing output by 5 percent are approximately the same as the average costs. Accordingly, the long-run market supply curve is approximately horizontal. Under these conditions, even if the demand curve for the product shifts drastically, the market will supply much more of the product at pretty much the same price, as additional plants are constructed and additional firms enter the market.

Thus, the market supply curve is much more elastic in the long run than in the short run. Indeed, in the very short run, a firm may find it impossible to hire more skilled labour or to increase its capacity. Its

supply curve, and the market supply curve, would be nearly vertical. In what was called the short run in Chapter 10, machines and the number of firms are fixed, but labour and other inputs can be varied. Figure 11.9A shows the short-run supply curve. Contrast the short-run market supply curve with the long-run market supply curve. The short-run curve slopes up much more sharply. A shift in the demand curve has a larger effect on price and a smaller effect on quantity than it does in the long run. In the long run, the market supply curve may be horizontal. In this case, shifts in the demand curve have an effect *only* on quantity, as in panel B. Price remains at the level of minimum average costs; competition leads to entry to the point where there are zero profits.

It is worth asking, "How long is the long run?" That depends on the industry. For an electricity-generating company to change its capacity takes years. For most other firms, buildings and equipment can be added, if not within months, certainly within a year or two. Recent improvements in technology, like computer-

ADJUSTMENTS IN THE SHORT RUN AND IN THE LONG RUN

In the very short run, firms may be unable to adjust production at all; only the price changes.

In the short run, firms may be able to hire more labour and adjust other variable inputs.

In the long run, firms may be able to buy more machines, and firms may decide to enter or to exit.

The times required for these adjustments may vary from industry to industry.

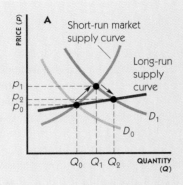
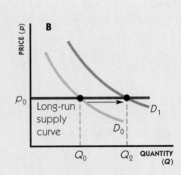

Figure 11.9 MARKET EQUILIBRIUM IN THE SHORT RUN AND IN THE LONG RUN

In panel A, the market equilibrium is originally at a price p_0 and an output Q_0. In the short run, a shift in the demand curve from D_0 to D_1 raises the price to p_1 and quantity to Q_1. In the long run, the supply elasticity is greater, so the increase in price is smaller—price is only p_2—and quantity Q_2 is greater. If supply is perfectly elastic in the long run, as shown in panel B, shifts in demand will only change the quantity produced in the long run, not the market price.

aided design and manufacturing, have made it possible for many companies to change what they are producing more rapidly, and thus have reduced the length of the long run and made supply curves more elastic than in the past.

LOOKING BEYOND THE BASIC MODEL: SUNK COSTS, ENTRY, AND COMPETITION

The degree of competition envisioned in the basic competitive model requires a large number of firms, vying with one another to sell a product. Competition among these firms drives the market price down to a level where there are no profits (as economists define them) in the market. (Recall that opportunity costs of the owners of the business and the cost of capital are included in the costs.)

Even without a large number of firms in the market, the predictions of the basic competitive model may still hold. Here is where the distinction between *fixed* and *sunk* costs becomes important. Fixed costs are costs that are incurred regardless of the scale of production of the firm. A building is a fixed cost in this sense. But if a company ceases to operate, it can resell the building and might well recover its cost. The cost of the building in this case, though fixed, is not sunk. Now take the case of a company that not only bought a building but spent a lot of money commissioning a logo, which it then mounted conspicuously on its building. If this firm went out of business it could recover the cost of its building but *not* its logo. Who wants the secondhand logo of a bankrupt company? Advertising expenditures are typically sunk costs. Expenditures on assets that can readily be put to other uses—buildings and cars—are, for the most part, not sunk.

The theory of **contestable markets** predicts that even in a market with only one firm, that firm will make zero profits, just as in a market with many firms *if* sunk costs are low. The threat that other firms will enter is sufficient to deter the single firm from raising its price beyond average costs. This result holds even in the presence of high fixed costs, so long as those fixed costs consist of buildings, cars, aeroplanes, and other assets that can easily be sold. A firm entering the industry has little to lose, since it can always reverse its decision and recover its investment.

But when the assets include major ones with no alternative use—such as a nuclear power plant—then the fixed costs become sunk costs, and the threat of competition diminishes. The firm that would otherwise have entered the market might now worry that if it entered, competition would get fierce. And the firm would be right to worry, as high sunk costs would make all firms reluctant to exit. If competition were fierce enough, the price might even drop below average costs, and still the firm's rivals might not leave. With prices below average costs, the new firm would not be able to get a return on its investment. Until it entered the market, the firm had an advantage: it had not taken on the sunk costs. Given the scenario just described, it might very well avert its gaze from the lure of the higher market prices, knowing they were like a mirage. The profits would disappear if the new firm tried to grab them by entering the market but would remain for the limited number of firms already in the market if they could keep the would-be newcomer out. Thus, markets with high sunk costs might be able to sustain high profits without much fear of entry—a clear departure from the basic competitive model.

ACCOUNTING PROFITS AND ECONOMIC PROFITS

We have learned in previous chapters that firms maximise profits, but now it appears that with competition, profits are driven to zero. To most individuals, this seems like a contradiction: if profits were truly zero, why would firms ever produce? How do we reconcile the conclusion that competition drives profits to zero with the fact that, throughout the economy, firms regularly report making profits?

The answer is that an accountant and an economist think about profits differently in two important respects. The first is that an economist takes opportunity costs into account. The second has to do with the economic concept of rent. Both deserve a closer look.

OPPORTUNITY COSTS

To begin to see how opportunity costs affect the economist's view of profits, consider a small firm in which the owner has invested £100,000. Assume the owner takes a small salary and devotes 60 hours a week to running the enterprise. An economist would argue that the owner ought to calculate his opportunity costs related to his investment of time and money into the business. The first is the best wage available to him if he worked 60 hours a week at an alternative job. His second opportunity cost is the return that the £100,000 invested in this enterprise would produce in another investment. These are the true costs of the owner's time and capital investment. To calculate profits of the firm as the economist sees them, these opportunity costs have to be subtracted out.

One can easily imagine a business whose accountant reports a profit equal to 3 percent of the capital investment. An economist would note that if the investment capital had been put in a bank account, it would have earned at least 5 percent. Thus, the economist would say the business is making a loss. Failure to take into account opportunity costs means that reported profits often overstate economic profits.

Taking opportunity costs into account is not always a simple matter because they include alternative uses of a firm's resources. Managerial time spent in expanding the firm in one direction, for example, might have been spent in controlling costs or expanding the firm in another direction. Land that is used for a golf course for the firm's employees might have been used for some other purpose, which could have saved more than enough money to buy golf club memberships for all who want them. In making decisions about resources like these, firms must constantly ask what price the resources might fetch in other uses.

Sometimes market data can provide appropriate prices for calculating opportunity costs. For example, the opportunity cost of giving huge offices to top executives can be gauged by the money those offices would bring if they were rented to some other company. But often the calculation is more difficult: how can, for example, a company measure the opportunity cost of the vice president who cannot be fired and will not retire for five years?

What about the costs associated with an expenditure already made, say on a building that is no longer really needed by the firm? The relevant opportunity cost of this building is not the original purchase or lease price but instead the value of the building in alternative uses, such as the rent that could be earned if the building were rented to other firms.

The fundamental point is that you cannot use past expenditures to calculate opportunity costs. Consider a car manufacturer that has purchased a parcel of land for £100,000 an acre. It turns out, however, that the company made a mistake and the land is worth only £10,000 an acre. The firm now must choose between two different plants for producing new cars, one of which uses much more land than the other. In figuring opportunity costs, should the land be valued at the purchase price of £100,000 an acre or what the land could be sold for—£10,000 an acre? The answer can make a difference between whether or not the firm chooses to conserve on land. From an economics viewpoint, the answer to this valuation problem should be obvious: the firm should evaluate costs according to the *current* opportunity costs. The fact that the company made a mistake in purchasing the land should be irrelevant for the current decision.

Individuals and firms frequently do compound their economic errors, however, by continuing to focus on past expenditures. Business executives who were originally responsible for making a bad decision may be particularly reluctant to let bygones be bygones. Publicly announcing that the correct market price of land is £10,000 an acre, for example, would be equivalent to announcing that a mistake had been made. Acknowledging such a mistake could jeopardise a business executive's future with the firm.

ECONOMIC RENT

A second difference between an economist's and an accountant's definition of profit concerns **economic rent.** Economic rent is the difference between the price that is actually paid and the price that would have to be paid in order for the good or service to be produced.

Although economic rent has far broader applications than its historic use to refer to payments made by farmers to their landlords for the use of their land, the example of rent for land use is still instructive. The critical characteristic of land in this regard is that its supply is inelastic. Higher payments for land (higher rents) will not elicit a greater supply. Even if landlords received virtually nothing for their land, the same land would be available. Many other factors of production have the same inelastic character. Even if you doubled his income Pete Sampras could not play more or better tennis. The extra payments for this kind of rare talent fall into the economist's definition of rent. Anyone who is in the position to receive economic rents is fortunate indeed, because these rents are unrelated to effort. They are payments determined entirely by demand.

Firms earn economic rent to the extent that they are more efficient than other firms. We saw earlier that a firm is willing to produce at a price equal to its minimum average costs. Some firms may be more efficient than others, so their average cost curves are lower. Consider a market in which all firms except one have the same average cost curve, and the market price corresponds to the minimum average costs of these firms. The remaining firm is super efficient, so its average costs are far below those of the other firms. The company would have been willing to produce at a lower price, at its minimum average costs. What it receives in excess of what is required to induce it to enter the market are rents—returns on the firm's superior capabilities.

Thus, when economists say that competition drives profits to zero, they are focusing on the fact that in competitive equilibrium, price equals marginal cost for every firm producing. A company will not in-

AN ACCOUNTANT'S VERSUS AN ECONOMIST'S PROFITS

Accounting profits: Revenues minus expenditures	Economic profits: Revenues minus rents minus economic costs (including opportunity costs of labour and capital)

CLOSE-UP: SUNK COSTS, CONTESTABILITY, AND THE CHANNEL TUNNEL

The completion of the channel tunnel was a great event—the culmination of nearly two centuries of schemes and plans—and it has transformed transport between Britain and the Continent. The shuttle, which carries vehicles and passengers through the tunnel, has provided fierce competition for the ferry companies, which previously had the market to themselves, and the ferry companies have undertaken a series of mergers in order to reduce competition amongst themselves on the Dover-Calais route (and the other nearby routes) and—they claim—to give the tunnel stiffer competition.

The cost structures of the ferries and the tunnel are very different, and this makes for an interesting competitive game between them. The tunnel was hugely expensive to construct, and the company that owns it is saddled with an enormous burden of debt—interest and capital—which has to be repaid from profits on the shuttle and the Eurostar rail services. The shareholders in Eurotunnel have not seen any dividends yet, and the banks who lent Eurotunnel money have had to lend more and have had their repayments rescheduled a number of times. There has been a string of last-minute financial rescue packages. Being able to pay the interest and capital depends on there being strong demand for Eurostar and shuttle services. The forecasts made by the company have always been very optimistic. At the prices needed to repay the debt, based on reasonable forecasts of demand, the ferry companies could easily undercut the tunnel.

But it does not matter whether the tunnel ever turns out to be profitable. The costs of building the tunnel are sunk costs. Whether they are repaid or not, the tunnel will exist, and the only thing the owners can do with it is to make as much from it as possible. The costs of running trains through it are very low, and providing the fares cover these variable costs, trains and shuttles will continue to be run. The tunnel will continue to operate even if the people who have provided the funds to build it never see any return.

The ferries have much higher variable costs of providing a service, and their fixed costs—the costs of the boats themselves—are much lower. Even the boats should be thought of as a variable cost, not a fixed cost, since they can be moved to and from other routes very quickly. The ferry companies need to charge fares that cover these higher variable costs in order to stay in the cross-channel business. Their minimum fares set a limit to the fares Eurotunnel can charge. Even if all the ferries left the cross-channel market, the market would be contestable. If Eurotunnel set fares too high, the ferries would come back to the business. Thus there would be potential competition to the tunnel, whether or not there were any actual competition. At present, Eurotunnel does not have enough capacity to take all the traffic; some goes by ferry. Consequently, Eurotunnel can set fares just enough below the ferries to ensure that all its capacity is used.

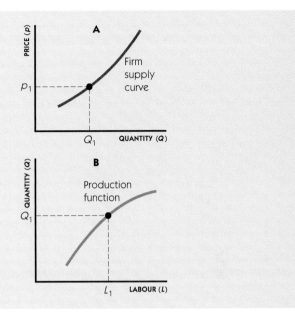

Figure 11.10 THE DEMAND FOR LABOUR

The demand for labour can be calculated from the firm's supply curve and the production function. Panel A shows how the firm, given a market price p_1, chooses a level of output Q_1 from its supply curve. Panel B shows that to produce the output Q_1 requires L_1 units of labour. The variable L_1 is the demand for labour.

crease profits by expanding production, and it will not pay for firms outside the industry to enter. We say that competition drives profits to zero at the margin.

In some cases, supplies of inputs are inelastic in the short run but elastic in the long run. An example is payment for the use of a building. In the short run, the supply of buildings does not depend on the return, and hence payments for the use of a building are rents, in the economist's sense. But in the long run, the supply of buildings does depend on the return; investors will not construct new buildings unless they receive a return equal to what they could obtain elsewhere. So the rent received by the building's owner is not a rent in the sense in which an economist uses the term.[1]

FACTOR DEMAND

In the process of deciding how much of each good to supply and what is the lowest-cost method of

[1] Economists sometimes use the term *quasi-rents* to describe payments for the use of buildings or other factors that are inelastically supplied in the short run but elastically supplied in the long run.

producing those goods, firms also decide how much of various inputs they will use. This is called **factor demand.** It is sometimes called a derived demand, because it flows from other decisions the profit-maximising firm makes. In Chapter 10, the analysis of costs was divided into two cases, one in which there was a single input, or factor of production, and one in which there were several factors. We proceed along similar lines here. Labour is used as our main example of an input. The same principles apply to any factor of production.

When there is only a single factor of production, say labour, then the decision about how much to produce is the same as the decision about how much labour to hire. As soon as we know the price of the good, we can calculate the supply (output) from the marginal cost curve; and as soon as we know the output the firm plans to produce, we know the labour required, simply by looking at the production function, which gives the output for any level of input of labour, or, equivalently, the labour required for any level of output. Thus, in Figure 11.10 at the price p_1, the output is Q_1 (panel A), and the labour required to produce that output (factor demand) is L_1 (panel B).

There is another way of deriving the demand for a factor. If a firm hires one more worker, for example,

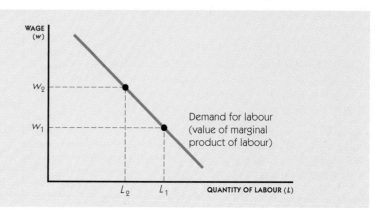

Figure 11.11 THE DEMAND CURVE FOR LABOUR

The value of the marginal product of labour declines with the level of employment. Since labour is hired up to the point where the wage equals the value of the marginal product, at wage w_1, employment is L_1, and at wage w_2, employment is L_2. The demand curve for labour thus traces out the values of the marginal product of labour at different levels of employment.

the extra cost is the wage w. The extra benefit of the worker is the price of the good times the extra output. The extra output corresponding to the extra worker is the marginal product of labour. (Marginal products can be calculated for any other factor of production as well.) The price of the good thus produced times the marginal product of labour is referred to as the **value of the marginal product of labour.** The firm hires labour up to the point where the value of its marginal product (the marginal benefit) equals its price, in this case, the wage.

Using p for the price of the good, MPL for the marginal product of labour, and w for the wage of the worker, we can write this equilibrium condition as

Value of marginal product of labor
$$= p \times MPL = w = \text{wage.}$$

From this equilibrium condition we can derive the demand curve for labour. Figure 11.11 plots the value of the marginal product of labour for each level of labour. Since the marginal product of labour decreases as labour increases, the value of the marginal product of labour decreases. When the wage is w_1, the value of the marginal product of labour equals the wage with a level of labour at L_1. This is the demand for labour at wage w_1. When the wage is w_2, the value of the marginal product of labour equals the wage with a level of labour at L_2. This is the demand for labour at a wage w_2. Thus, the curve giving the value of the marginal product of labour at each wage *is* the demand curve for labour.

It is easy to use this diagram to see the effect of an increase in the price of the good the firm produces. In Figure 11.12, the higher price increases the value of the marginal product of labour at each level of employment, and it immediately follows that at each wage, the demand for labour increases; the demand curve for labour shifts to the right.

Thus, the demand for labour depends on both the

FACTOR DEMAND

A factor of production will be demanded up to the point where the value of the marginal product of that factor equals the price. In the case of labour, this is the same as saying that the marginal product of labour equals the real product wage.

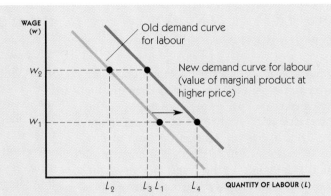

Figure 11.12 EFFECT OF A PRICE CHANGE ON THE DEMAND CURVE FOR LABOUR

An increase in the price received by a firm shifts the value of the marginal product of labour curve up, so that at each wage, the demand for labour is increased. At wage w_1, employment rises from L_1 to L_4; at wage w_2, employment rises from L_2 to L_3.

wage and the price the firm receives for the goods it sells. In fact, the demand for labour depends only on the ratio of the two, as we will now see.

If we divide both sides of the equation given the equilibrium condition by the price, we obtain the condition.

$$MPL = w/p.$$

The wage divided by the price of the good being produced is defined as the **real product wage.** It measures what firms pay workers in terms of the goods

the worker produces rather than in pound terms. Thus, the firm hires workers up to the point where the real product wage equals the marginal product of labour.

This principle is illustrated in Figure 11.13, which shows the marginal product of labour. Because of diminishing returns, the marginal product diminishes as labour (and output) increases. The demand for labour at the real product wage w_1/p is L_1, while the demand for labour at the real product wage w_2/p is L_2. As the real product wage increases, the demand for labour decreases.

Figure 11.13 THE FIRM'S DEMAND CURVE FOR LABOUR AND THE REAL PRODUCT WAGE

Firms hire labour up to the point where the real product wage equals the marginal product of labour. As the real product wage increases, the demand for labour decreases.

FROM THE FIRM'S FACTOR DEMAND TO THE MARKET'S FACTOR DEMAND

Once we have derived the firm's demand curve for labour, we can derive the total market demand for labour. At a given set of prices, we simply add up the demand for labour by each firm at any particular wage rate. The total is the market demand at that wage rate. Since each firm reduces the amount of labour that it demands as the wage increases, the market demand curve is downward sloping. Figure 11.14 shows how we add up diagrammatically the demand curves for labour for two firms, the High Strung Violin Company and Max's Fine Tunes Violin Company. At a wage of w_1, High Strung demands 30 workers and Max's Fine Tunes demands 30 workers, for a total demand of 60 workers. At a wage of w_2, High Strung demands 20 workers and Max's Fine Tunes demands 10 workers, for a total demand of 30 workers.

FACTOR DEMANDS WITH TWO OR MORE FACTORS

It is now time to relax our assumption that firms require only one factor of production. With more than one factor, when the price of any input falls, the demand for that input will increase for two reasons. First, the firm (and the industry as a whole) substitutes the cheaper input for other inputs, so that for each unit of output produced, more of the cheaper input is employed. Second, the lower price of the input lowers the marginal cost of production at each level of output, and this leads to an increase in the level of production. Since

Total demand for an input
= demand for the input per unit output × output,

and since both factor demand per unit of output and output have been increased, total demand for the input has increased.

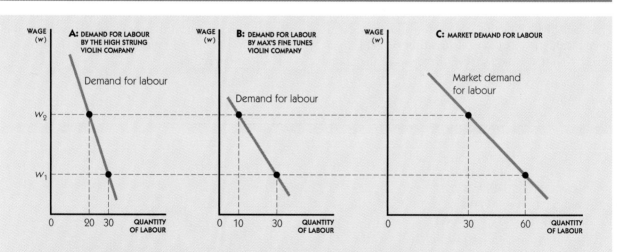

Figure 11.14 **THE MARKET DEMAND CURVE FOR LABOUR**

The market demand curve for labour at each wage is obtained by horizontally adding up the demand curves for labour of each individual firm. As the wage rises, at a fixed price of output, less labour is demanded.

When we draw the demand curve for labour, which shows the quantity of labour demanded at each wage, in the background we are keeping the price of output and the price of other inputs fixed. When any of these prices changes, the demand curve for labour shifts. For instance, as we have seen, if the price of output increases, the value of the marginal product of labour increases and the demand curve shifts to the right.

THE THEORY OF THE COMPETITIVE FIRM

We have now completed our description of the theory of the competitive firm. The firm takes the prices it receives for the goods it sells as given, and it takes the prices it pays for the inputs it uses, including the wages it pays workers and the costs of capital goods, as given. The firm chooses its outputs and inputs in order to maximise its profits.

We have seen where the supply curves for output and the demand curves for labour and capital that were used in Part 1 came from and why they have the shape they do. As prices increase, output increases; firms produce more, and more firms produce. Thus, supply curves are upward sloping.

As wages increase, with the price of other inputs fixed, firms' marginal cost curve shifts up. This causes them to produce less at each price of their output. The higher *relative* price of labour induces firms to substitute other inputs for labour; they use less labour to produce each unit of output. Therefore, the demand curve for labour (and other inputs) is downward sloping.

In the next chapter, we will use these results, together with the analysis of the household's behaviour in Chapters 8 and 9, to form a model of the entire economy.

REVIEW AND PRACTICE

SUMMARY

1 A revenue curve shows the relationship between a firm's total output and its revenue. For a competitive firm, the marginal revenue it receives from selling an additional unit of output is the price of that unit.

2 A firm in a competitive market will choose the output where the market price—the marginal revenue it receives from producing an extra unit—equals the marginal cost.

3 If the market price of a good exceeds minimum average costs, more firms will enter the market, since they can make a profit by selling the good for more that it costs to produce the good.

4 If the market price is below minimum average costs and a firm has no sunk costs, the firm will exit the market immediately. If the market price is below minimum average costs and a firm has sunk costs, it will continue to produce in the short run as long as it can at least cover its variable costs.

5 For a firm contemplating entering a market, its supply is zero up to the point where price equals minimum average costs. Above that price, the supply curve is the same as the marginal cost curve.

6 The market supply curve is constructed by adding the supply curves of all firms in an industry. As prices rise, more firms are willing to produce, and each firm is willing to produce more, so that the market supply curve is normally upward sloping.

7 The economist's and the accountant's concepts of profits differ in how they treat opportunity costs and rents.

8 A firm's demand for factors of production is derived from its decision about how much to produce. Inputs will be demanded up to the point where the value of the marginal product of the input equals its price.

9 The demand curve for factors of production is downward sloping for two reasons. Output is reduced as the price of the factor increases, and at each level of output, the firm substitutes away from the factor whose price has increased.

KEY TERMS

revenue curve

marginal revenue

economic rent

factor demand

real product wage

REVIEW QUESTIONS

1 In a competitive market, what rule determines the profit-maximising level of output? What is the relationship between a firm's supply curve and its marginal cost curve?

2 What determines firms' decisions to enter a market? To exit a market?

3 What is the relationship between the way an accountant uses the concept of profits and the way an economist does?

4 How do firms decide how much of an input to demand? Why is the demand curve for inputs (like labour) downward sloping?

5 Explain when and how the average variable cost curve determines whether firms will enter or exit the market.

PROBLEMS

1 The market price for painting a house in Centerville is £1,000. The Total Cover-up House-Painting Company has fixed costs of £4,000 for ladders, brushes, and so on, and the company's variable costs for house painting follow this pattern:

Output (houses painted)	2	3	4	5	6	7	8	9	10
Variable cost (in pounds)	2,600	3,200	3,600	4,200	5,000	6,000	7,200	8,600	10,200

Calculate the company's total costs, and graph the revenue curve and the total cost curve. Do the curves have the shape you expect? Over what range of production is the company making profits?

2 Calculate and graph the marginal costs, the average costs, and the average variable costs for the Total Cover-up House-Painting Company. Given the market price, at what level of output will this firm maximise profits? What profit (or loss) is it making at that level? At what price will the firm no longer make a profit? Assume its fixed costs are sunk; there is no market for used ladders, brushes, and so on. At what price will the company shut down?

3 Draw a U-shaped average cost curve. On your diagram, designate at what price levels you would expect entry and at what price levels you would expect exit if all the fixed costs are sunk. What if only half the fixed costs are sunk? Explain your reasoning.

4 Jose is a skilled electrician at a local company, a job that pays £15,000 per year, but he is considering quitting to start his own business. He talks it over

with an accountant, who helps him to draw up this chart with their best predictions about costs and revenues:

	Predicted annual costs	Predicted annual revenue
Basic wage	£5,000	£25,000
Rent of space	£3,000	
Rent of equipment	£4,500	
Utilities	£1,000	
Miscellaneous	£2,500	

The basic wage does seem a bit low, the accountant admits, but she tells Jose to remember that as owner of the business, he will get to keep any profits as well. From an economist's point of view, is the accountant's list of costs complete? From an economist's point of view, what are Jose's expected profits?

APPENDIX: ALTERNATIVE WAYS OF CALCULATING THE DEMAND FOR LABOUR

We have now seen three different ways for determining the demand for labour. One uses the condition for equilibrium output—price equals marginal cost—to determine the equilibrium level of output and then determine the required labour. The second is derived directly from the profit-maximising condition for the demand for labour: the value of the marginal product of labour is set equal to the wage. The third is to set the real product wage equal to the marginal product of labour. This appendix shows how these conditions are, in fact, alternative ways of writing the same condition.

With a single factor of production, labour, the extra cost of producing an extra unit of output is just the extra labour required times the wage. The extra labour required is $1/MPL$, 1 divided by the marginal product of labour. If 1 extra worker produces 2 violins a year, it takes 1/2 of a worker to produce an extra violin. Hence, the competitive equilibrium condition, price equals marginal cost, can be rewritten as

$$p = w/MPL.$$

If we multiply both sides of this equation by MPL, we obtain

$$p \times MPL = w,$$

the familiar condition, that the value of the marginal product ($p \times MPL$) equals the wage. And if we now divide both sides of the equation by p, we obtain

$$MPL = w/p,$$

the condition that the marginal product of labour equals the real wage. All of these conditions are in fact three ways of writing the same equation.

Two important consequences follow from these conditions. First, note that the demand for labour depends only on the real product wage, that is, the wage divided by the price of the good produced. If wages and prices both double, then the demand for labour and the supply of output are unaffected. Second, an increase in the wage, keeping prices fixed, reduces the demand for labour. This effect can be seen in several different ways. The real product wage has increased. Therefore, for the condition that the marginal product of labour equal the real wage to be satisfied, the marginal product of labour must increase. But the principle of diminishing returns says that to increase the marginal product of labour, the input of labour must be reduced.

Alternatively, an increase in the wage can be seen as increasing the marginal cost of hiring an additional unit of labour, while with a fixed price, the marginal benefit remains the same. Thus, at the old level of employment, the marginal benefit of the last worker hired is less than the marginal cost, and it pays firms to lower their level of production. At a high enough wage, the average variable costs of production may exceed the price, and the firm will shut down.

12

COMPETITIVE
EQUILIBRIUM

Now that we have considered each aspect of the basic competitive model separately—the consumption, work-and-savings, investment, and production decisions—it is time to put the pieces together. In doing so, we will come to understand how markets answer the basic questions posed in Chapter 1: what is to be produced and in what quantities, how these goods are to be produced and for whom, and, most fundamental, how these resource allocation decisions are to be made.

This chapter also provides a first glance at the interconnectedness of a modern economy. In the giant web of transactions that is the economy, pressure on any one part will affect all the rest. For example, in the late 1970s, the development of North Sea oil production gradually reduced the amount of oil imported into the United Kingdom. The oil production contributed directly to the prosperity of towns and regions that served the oil industry, like Aberdeen, in Scotland, where there was a boom in house prices as a result of the oil-induced prosperity. But the cut in oil imports contributed to an increase in the value of the pound relative to other currencies. This made it more difficult for manufacturing firms in the midlands to export their products abroad, depressing economic activity in the midlands and restraining the growth of house prices in that region. At the same time, the rise in the pound reduced the prices that consumers in the United Kingdom had to pay for imported goods, and on that account they were better off. Thus a disturbance in one part of the economy had effects that spread to many others.

Finally, this chapter explains why economists believe that, by and large, the market answers the fundamental economic questions efficiently.

KEY QUESTIONS

1 What is meant by the competitive equilibrium of the economy? Why is it that in competitive equilibrium, a disturbance to one part of the economy may have reverberations in others?

2 What implications does the interconnectedness of the economy have for policy issues such as the effects of a corporation tax?

3 What is the circular flow diagram, and how does it show the many links between the different parts of the economy?

4 Why do so many economists believe that, by and large, reliance on private markets is desirable? How do competitive markets result in economic efficiency?

5 If markets result in distributions of income that society views as unacceptable, should the market be abandoned or can the government intervene in a more limited way to combine efficient outcomes with acceptable distributions?

GENERAL EQUILIBRIUM ANALYSIS

In Chapter 4 where we introduced the idea of a market equilibrium, we focused on one market at a time. The price of a good was determined when the demand for that good equaled its supply. The wage rate was determined when the demand for labour equaled its supply. The interest rate was determined when the demand for savings equaled the supply. This kind of analysis is called **partial equilibrium analysis.** In analysing what is going on in one market, we ignore what is going on in other markets.

Interdependencies in the economy make partial equilibrium analysis overly simple because demand and supply in one market depend on prices determined in other markets. For instance, the demand for skis depends on the price of ski tickets, ski boots, and possibly even airline tickets. Thus, the equilibrium price of skis will depend on the price of ski tickets, ski boots, and airline tickets. But by the same token, the demand for ski tickets and ski boots will depend on the price of skis. Accordingly, the equilibrium price of ski tickets and ski boots will depend on the price of skis. **General equilibrium analysis** broadens the perspective, taking into account the interactions and interdependencies within the various parts of the economy.

EXAMPLE: CORPORATION TAX

Ascertaining the effect of a corporation tax—the tax the government imposes on the net income of companies—provides an example of why general equilibrium analysis is often essential. A partial equilibrium analysis of this tax is provided in Figure 12.1, where we have drawn the demand and supply curves for capital in the corporate sector. A corporation tax is shown as a tax on capital because much of a corporation's income is, in fact, a return on the capital invested in it. As can be seen, this tax drives a wedge between the price of capital paid by the firm and the return received by investors.

Who bears the burden of the tax? The partial equilibrium analysis shown in panel A of Figure 12.1 makes it clear that investors bear only a part of the burden. Their after-tax return is lowered but not by the full amount of the tax. Panel B, indeed, shows a case in which investors bear none of the burden, when the supply of capital is horizontal (infinitely elastic).

If investors do not bear the burden of the tax, who does? Because the interest rate that firms pay increases, firms' costs have gone up, and this will be reflected in higher equilibrium prices. Thus, consumers bear some of the costs. If sales decrease as a result, the demand for labour may decrease, and thus wages may fall, in which case workers will bear some of the burden. But other factors need to be taken into account as

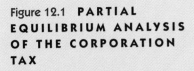

Figure 12.1 **PARTIAL EQUILIBRIUM ANALYSIS OF THE CORPORATION TAX**

In panel A, the tax, viewed as a tax on the return to capital in the corporate sector, leads to a lower return to investors and a higher cost of capital to firms. In panel B, the tax simply results in a higher cost of capital to firms.

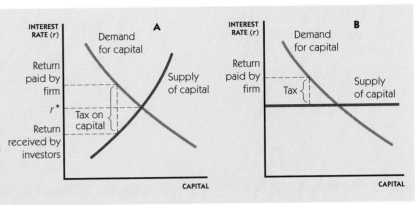

well. The higher cost of capital may induce firms to substitute labour for machines, in which case the demand for labour will increase. At higher prices to consumers, however, the return to working is reduced. In this case, workers may supply less labour.

Account must also be taken of the interactions between capital in the corporate and unincorporated sectors. Because over 80 percent of nonagricultural business takes place in the corporate sector, activities there have major ramifications on the rest of the economy. If investors find investing in the corporate sector less attractive, they will shift their savings to the unincorporated sector. As capital flows into the unincorporated sector, the return to the capital in that sector will be reduced until it equals the rate of return in the corporate sector. A full general equilibrium analysis needs to take all these factors into account.

General equilibrium analysis focuses on the fact that in equilibrium, the returns to all investments throughout the economy must provide the same rate of return per pound invested (adjusting for risk). An analysis of the corporate income tax that failed to take into account the responses in the unincorporated sector would be incomplete at best and could be seriously misleading. (Most economists agree that, in the long run, most of the burden of the corporation tax rests on workers and consumers, and relatively little on corporations, their shareholders, or others who have lent money—contrary to popular belief.)

WHEN PARTIAL EQUILIBRIUM ANALYSIS WILL DO

In the example of a corporation tax just given, general equilibrium analysis is clearly important. But can we ever focus on what goes on in a single market, without worrying about the reverberations in the rest of the economy? Are there circumstances in which partial equilibrium analysis will provide a fairly accurate answer to the effect of, say, a change in a tax? Fortunately, the answer is yes.

Partial equilibrium analysis is adequate, for example, when the reverberations from the initial imposition of a tax are so dispersed that they can be ignored without distorting the analysis. Such is the case when individuals shift their demand away from the taxed good towards many, many other goods. Each of the prices of those goods changes only a very little. And the total demand for factors of production (like capital and labour) changes only negligibly, so that the prices of different factors are virtually unchanged. Moreover, the slight changes in the prices of different goods and inputs have only a slight effect on the demand and supply curves of the industry upon which the analysis is focusing. In these circumstances, partial equilibrium analysis will provide a good approximation to what will actually happen.

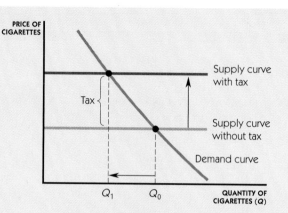

Figure 12.2 PARTIAL EQUILIBRIUM ANALYSIS OF THE EFFECT OF A TAX ON CIGARETTES

A tax on cigarettes raises the price of cigarettes and reduces consumption slightly. The second-round reverberations of this tax are sufficiently slight that they can be ignored.

EXAMPLE: A TAX ON CIGARETTES

The effect of a tax on cigarettes is an example where partial equilibrium analysis works well. What predictions can be made about the consequences of adding an additional 50 pence tax to a packet of cigarettes?

Figure 12.2 shows the tax as shifting the supply curve of cigarettes up by the amount of the tax. Demand is reduced from Q_0 to Q_1. Since expenditures on cigarettes are a small proportion of anyone's income, a 50 pence increase in their price will have only a small effect on overall consumption patterns. While the reduced quantity demanded of cigarettes (and the indirect changed demand for other goods) will have a slight effect on the total demand for labour, this effect is so small that it will have no noticeable change in the wage rate. Similarly, the tax will have virtually no effect on the return to capital.

Under these circumstances, where more distant general equilibrium effects are likely to be so faint as to be indiscernible, a partial equilibrium analysis of a tax on cigarettes is appropriate.

THE BASIC COMPETITIVE EQUILIBRIUM MODEL

General equilibrium analysis requires a model of the entire economy. To analyse the effects of imposing a tax or the immigration of labour or any other change, one "solves" for the full equilibrium before and after the change and looks at how each of the variables—wages, prices, interest rates, outputs, employment, and so forth—has changed.

To see how this is done, we focus on a simplified version of the full competitive equilibrium model.

In this simplified model, we assume all workers have identical skills. Ignoring differences in skill level enables us to talk about the labour market as if all workers received the same wage. Similarly, we ignore all aspects of risk in our analysis of the capital market. This allows us to use a single interest rate. Finally, we assume that all firms produce the same good; in other words, the product market consists of only one good. We now have an economy made up of three markets—the labour market, the capital market, and the product market—and can use general equilibrium analysis to trace through how they depend on one another.

In Chapter 9, we saw how households determine the amount of labour they wish to supply. Households supply labour because they want to buy goods. Hence, their labour supply depends on both wages and prices. It also depends on other sources of income. If we assume, for simplicity, that households' only other source of income is the return to their investments (their return to capital, or the interest on their investments), then we can see that the labour supply is connected to all three markets. It depends on the wage, the price of the single good, and the return to capital. In Chapter 10, we saw that the demand for labour depends on the wage, on the interest rate, and on the price at which the firm sells its product.

Equilibrium in the labour market requires that the

demand for labour equal the supply. Normally, when we draw the demand curve for labour, we simply assume that p, the price of the good(s) being produced, and r, the interest rate, are kept fixed. We focus our attention solely on the wage rate, the price of labour. Given p and r, we look for the wage at which the demand and supply for labour are equal. This is a partial equilibrium analysis of the labour market.

The labour market is only one of the three markets, even in our highly simplified economy. There is also the market for capital to consider. In Chapter 9, we saw how households determine their savings, which in turn determine the available supply of capital. The supply of capital is affected, in general, by the return it yields (the interest rate r) plus the income individuals have from other sources, in particular from wages. Since the amount individuals are willing to save may depend on how well off they feel, and how well off they feel depends on the wage rate relative to prices, we can think of the supply of capital too as depending on wages, interest rates, and prices. In Chapter 10, we learned how to derive the firms' demand for capital. This too will depend on the interest rate they must pay, the price at which goods can be sold, and the cost of other inputs.

Equilibrium in the capital market occurs at the point where the demand and supply for capital are equal. Again, partial equilibrium analysis of the capital market focuses on the return to capital, r, at which the demand and supply of capital are equal, but both the demand and the supply depend on the wage and the price of goods as well.

Finally, there is the market for goods. Chapters 8 and 9 showed how to derive the households' demand for goods. We can think of the household as first deciding on how much to spend (Chapter 9), and then deciding how to allocate what it spends over different goods (Chapter 8). Of course, with a single consumption good, the latter problem no longer exists. In our simplified model, then, we can think of the demand for goods as being determined by household income, which in turn depends on the wage, the interest rate, and the price of goods.

Similarly, in Chapter 11, we analysed how firms determine how much to produce: they set price equal to marginal cost, where marginal cost depends on wages and the interest rate. Equilibrium in the goods market requires that the demand for goods equal the supply of goods. Again, while in the simple partial equilibrium analysis we focus on how the demand and supply of goods depend on price p, we know that the demand and supply of goods also depend on both the wage rate and the return to capital.

The labour market is said to be in equilibrium when the demand for labour equals the supply. The product market is in equilibrium when the demand for goods equals the supply. The capital market is in equilibrium when the demand for capital equals the supply. The economy as a whole is in equilibrium only when all markets clear simultaneously (demand equals supply in all markets). The general equilibrium for our simple economy occurs at a common wage rate w, price p, and interest rate r, at which all three markets are also in equilibrium.

In the basic equilibrium model, there is only a single good, but it is easy to extend the analysis to the more realistic case where there are many goods. The same web of interconnections exists between different goods and between different goods and different inputs. Recall from Chapter 4 that the demand curve depicts the quantity of a good—for instance, beer—demanded at each price; the supply curve shows the quantity of a good that firms supply at each price. But the demand curve for beer depends on the prices of other goods and the income levels of different consumers; similarly, the supply curve for beer depends

EQUILIBRIUM IN THE BASIC COMPETITIVE MODEL

The labour market clearing condition: The demand for labour must equal the supply.

The capital market clearing condition: The demand for capital must equal the supply.

The goods market clearing condition: The demand for goods must equal the supply.

on the prices of inputs, including the wage rate, the interest rate, and the price of hops and other ingredients. Those prices, in turn, depend on supply and demand in their respective markets. The general equilibrium of the economy requires finding the prices for each good and for each input such that the demand for each good equals the supply, and the demand for each input equals the supply.

THE CIRCULAR FLOW OF FUNDS

General equilibrium analysis is not the only way to think about the interrelations of the various parts of the economy. Another way is to consider the flow of funds through the economy. Households buy goods and services from firms. Households supply labour and capital to firms. The income individuals receive, whether in the form of wages or the return on their savings, is spent to buy the goods that firms produce. All these transactions constitute what is called the **circular flow.**

The circular flow for a simplified economy—in which there are only households and firms, households do not save, and firms do not invest—is shown in Figure 12.3. This circular flow diagram serves two purposes. First, it keeps track of how funds flow

through the economy. We can see this by starting at A and following the circular flow round to the right. The top arrow shows that households pay money to firms to buy goods for their consumption. The lower arrow (B) shows that firms use the money to pay household members in the form of wages (for labour), rent (to the owners of land), and profit (to the owners of firms). The second purpose of the circular flow diagram is to focus on certain balance conditions in the economy that must always be satisfied. In the case of the simple flow in Figure 12.3, there is one balance condition. The income of households (the flow of funds from firms, lower arrow) must equal the expenditures of households (the flow of funds to firms, upper arrow).

Figure 12.4 expands the circular flow in three ways. First, savings and capital are included. Thus, the funds that flow from the firm to the household now include a return on capital (interest on loans, dividends on equities). The funds that flow from the household to the firm now include savings, which go to purchase machines and buildings. And firms now retain some of their earnings to finance investment.

Second, the circular flow now includes funds flowing into and out of the government. Thus, some households receive transfer payments from the government (benefits like social security payments and pensions). Some sell their labour services to the government rather than private firms. Some receive interest on loans to the government (as owners of government bonds). And there is now an important

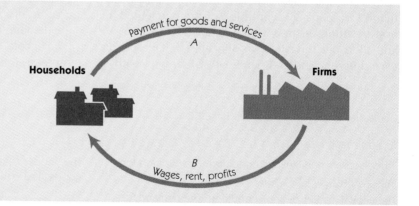

Figure 12.3 A SIMPLE CIRCULAR FLOW DIAGRAM

In this simple circular flow diagram, only labour and product markets and only the household and firm sectors are represented. It can be analysed from any starting point. For example, funds flow from households to firms in the form of purchases of goods and services. Funds flow from firms to households in the form of payments for the labour of workers and profits paid to owners.

Payment for goods and services
A

Households   Firms

B
Wages, rent, profits

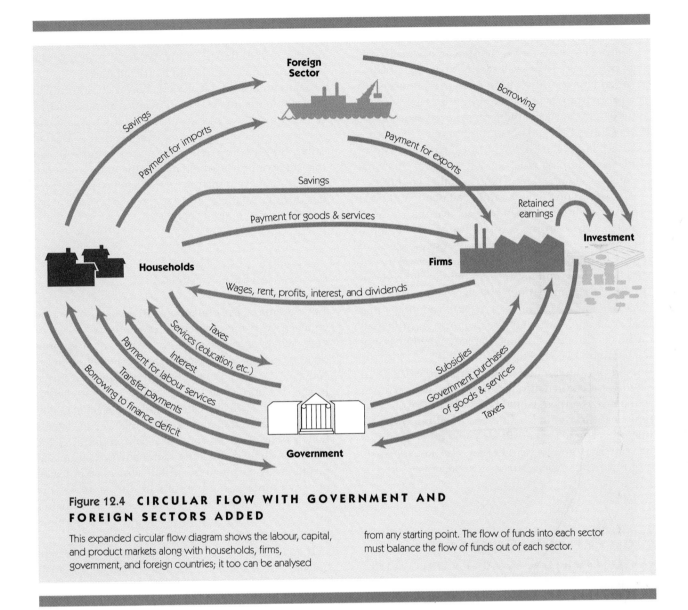

Figure 12.4 CIRCULAR FLOW WITH GOVERNMENT AND FOREIGN SECTORS ADDED

This expanded circular flow diagram shows the labour, capital, and product markets along with households, firms, government, and foreign countries; it too can be analysed from any starting point. The flow of funds into each sector must balance the flow of funds out of each sector.

additional outflow from households: income that goes to the government in the form of taxes. Similarly, firms have additional sources of inflow in the sales of goods and services they make to the government and in government subsidies to firms, and an additional outflow in the taxes they must pay to the government.

Just as the flow of funds into and out of households and firms must balance, the flow of funds into the government must balance the flow of funds out.[1] When there is a deficit—that is, when the government spends more than it collects in taxes—funds go into the government as borrowings. The govern-

[1] We ignore here the possibility that the government can simply pay for what it obtains by printing money.

ment finances the differences by borrowing (in our diagram, from households).

Third, Figure 12.4 adds the flow to and from foreign countries. Firms sell goods to foreigners (exports) and borrow funds from foreigners. Households buy goods from foreigners (imports) and invest funds in foreign firms. Again, there must be a balance in the flow of funds into and out of the country. A country's exports plus what it borrows from abroad (the flow of funds from abroad) must equal its imports plus what it lends abroad (the flow of funds to other countries).[2]

The interconnections and balance conditions making up circular flow analysis are the same as those that arise in the competitive general equilibrium model discussed earlier in the chapter. Even if the economy were not competitive, however, the interrelationships and balance conditions of the circular flow diagram would still be true. Thus, the circular flow diagram is a useful reminder that change in one element of the economy *must* be balanced by change in another element, whether or not the economy is competitive.

Let's put the circular flow diagram to work. Consider a reduction in the income tax. The flow of funds into the government would be reduced. The circular flow diagram reminds us flows in and out must remain balanced. That is, either some other tax must be increased, government borrowing must increase, or government expenditures must decrease.

COMPETITIVE GENERAL EQUILIBRIUM AND ECONOMIC EFFICIENCY

The first part of this chapter introduced the basic model of competitive general equilibrium. Competitive general equilibrium entails prices, wages, and returns to capital such that all markets—for goods, labour, capital (and other factors of production)—clear. A change in economic conditions, such as the

imposition of a tax, the migration of labour, or a sudden decline in supply of some good, results in a new equilibrium to the economy. We have seen how the effects of such changes can be traced out.

Economists are interested, however, not only in describing the market equilibrium, but in evaluating it. Do competitive markets do a good job in allocating resources? Chapter 7 introduced the idea of Adam Smith's "invisible hand," which implied that market economies are efficient. One of the most important achievements of modern economic theory has been to establish in what sense and under what conditions the market is efficient.

PARETO EFFICIENCY

To economists, the concept of efficiency is related to concern with the well-being of those in the economy. When no one can be made better off without making someone else worse off, the allocation of resources is called **Pareto efficient,** after the great Italian economist and sociologist Vilfredo Pareto (1848–1923). Typically when economists refer to efficiency, Pareto efficiency is what they mean. Saying that a market is efficient is a compliment. In the same way that an efficient machine uses its inputs as productively as possible, an efficient market leaves no way of increasing output with the same level of inputs. The only way one person can be made better off is by taking resources away from another, thereby making the second person worse off.

It is easy to see how a resource allocation might not be Pareto efficient. Assume the government is given the job of distributing chocolate and vanilla ice cream and pays no attention to people's preferences. Assume, moreover, that some individuals love chocolate and hate vanilla, while others love vanilla and hate chocolate. Some chocolate lovers will get vanilla ice cream, and some vanilla lovers will get chocolate ice cream. Clearly, this is Pareto inefficient. Allowing people to trade resources makes both groups better off.

To some, *all* economic changes represent nothing more than redistributions. Gains to one only subtract from another. Rent control is one example. In this view, the only effect of rent control is redistribution—landlords receive less and are worse off by the

---

[2] This condition can be put another way. The difference between imports and exports must equal the net flow of funds from abroad (the difference between what the country borrows from abroad and what it lends.)

same amount that their tenants' rents are reduced (and the tenants are better off). In some countries, unions have expressed similar views and see wage increases as having no further consequences than redistributing income to workers from those who own or who manage firms. This view is mistaken, because in each of these instances, there are consequences beyond the distribution. Rent control that keeps rents below the level that clears the rental housing market and minimum wages above those that clear the labour market both result in inefficiencies. For those concerned about renters who cannot afford the going rate or workers earning too little to support a family, there are better approaches that make the renters or workers as well as the landlords or employers better off than under rent control or minimum wage.

CONDITIONS FOR THE PARETO EFFICIENCY OF THE MARKET ECONOMY

For the economy to be Pareto efficient, it must meet the conditions of exchange efficiency, production efficiency, and product-mix efficiency. Considering each of these conditions separately shows us why the basic competitive model attains Pareto efficiency. (Recall the basic ingredients of that model: rational, perfectly informed households interacting with rational, profit-maximising firms in competitive markets, and in an environment in which the market failures discussed in Chapter 7 do not occur.)

EXCHANGE EFFICIENCY

Exchange efficiency requires that whatever the economy produces must be distributed among individuals in an efficient way. If I like chocolate ice cream and you like vanilla ice cream, exchange efficiency requires that I get the chocolate and you get the vanilla.

When there is exchange efficiency, there is no scope for further trade among individuals. Chapter 3 discussed the advantages of free exchange among individuals and nations. Any prohibition or restriction on trade results in exchange inefficiency. For instance, in war times, governments often ration scarce goods, like sugar. People are given coupons that allow them to buy, say, a pound of sugar a month. If sugar carries a price of 50 pence a pound, having 50 pence is not enough; you must also have the coupon. There is often considerable controversy about whether people should be allowed to sell their coupons or trade their coupons, say, a sugar coupon for a butter coupon. If the government prohibits the sale or trading of coupons, then the economy will not be exchange efficient; it will not be Pareto efficient.

The price system ensures that exchange efficiency is attained. In deciding how much of a good to buy, people balance the marginal benefit they receive by buying an extra unit with the cost of that extra unit, its price. Hence, price can be thought of as a rough measure of the *marginal* benefit an individual receives from a good, that is, the benefit a person receives from one more unit of the good. If all individuals face the same prices, their *marginal* benefits will be the same at the quantities they actually consume. For those who like chocolate ice cream a great deal and vanilla ice cream very little, this will entail consuming many more chocolate ice cream cones than vanilla. And conversely for the vanilla lover. Notice that no single individual or agency needs to know who is a chocolate and who is a vanilla lover for the goods to get to the right person. Not even the ice cream stores have to know individual preferences. Each consumer, by his own action, ensures that exchange efficiency is attained.

Notice too that if different individuals face *different* prices, then the economy will not, in general, be exchange efficient. This is because the marginal benefit of the good to the person who has to pay a high price will be far greater than to the person who pays a low price. If manufacturers charge some customers (say, those who buy in bulk) a lower price than others, then the economy will not be exchange efficient. If airlines charge different customers different prices, then the economy will also not be exchange efficient.

PRODUCTION EFFICIENCY

For an economy to be Pareto efficient, it must also have **production efficiency.** That is, it must not be possible to produce more of some goods without producing less of other goods. In other words, Pareto efficiency requires that the economy operate along the production possibilities curve first introduced in Chapter 2.

CLOSE-UP: PARETO IMPROVEMENT IN THE SKIES

Airlines want their planes to fly as full as possible. They also know that a certain percentage of people who purchased a ticket for any given flight are not going to show up. This gives the airlines an incentive to overbook flights. They sell more tickets than there are seats in the reasonable expectation that there will be room to take everyone who actually shows up. But sometimes everyone does show up, and a decision must be made about who will be bumped from the flight. Several methods of making this choice are possible.

In the 1960s, the airlines simply bumped whoever showed up last and gave those people tickets for a later flight. Bumped passengers had no recourse. This sort of policy causes high blood pressure.

To avoid imposing these costs on frustrated passengers, a second policy might be for the government to forbid airlines to overbook flights. But in that case, some planes would be forced to fly with empty seats that some people would have been willing to buy. Airlines would lose revenues, prices would have to rise to offset the lost revenue, and travelers who could have flown in the empty seats but could not get reservations under the no-overbooking rule would all be losers.

There is an alternative solution which is a Pareto improvement both over the practice of bumping and over rules forbidding no overbooking. Today airlines offer a free ticket on a future flight or other bonus as compensation to anyone willing to wait. People willing to accept such a deal are clearly better off in their own estimation. The airlines benefit because they are allowed to continue their practice of overbooking and thus keeping their flights as full as possible. In fact, since the person who receives a free ticket will often occupy a seat that would have been vacant anyway, the marginal cost of offering the free ticket for the airline is very close to zero. This is a real-world Pareto improvement. Everyone involved is at least no worse off and many are better off.

Source: Julian L. Simon, "An Almost Practical Solution to Airline Overbooking," *Journal of Transport Economics and Policy,* May 1968: 201–202.

Figure 12.5 shows the production possibilities curve for a simple economy that produces only two goods, apples and oranges. If the economy is at point *I*, inside the production possibilities curve, it cannot be Pareto efficient. Society could produce more of both apples and oranges, and by distributing them to different individuals, it could make people better off. Prices signal to firms the scarcity of each of the inputs they use. When all firms face the same prices of labour, capital goods, and other inputs, they will take the appropriate actions to economise on each of these inputs, ensuring that the economy operates along its production possibilities curve.

PRODUCT-MIX EFFICIENCY

The third condition for Pareto efficiency is **product-mix efficiency.** That is, the mix of goods produced by the economy must reflect the preferences of those in the economy. The economy must produce along the production possibilities curve at a point that reflects the preferences of consumers. The

THREE CONDITIONS FOR PARETO EFFICIENCY

1 Exchange efficiency: Goods must be distributed among individuals in a way that means there are no gains from further trade.

2 Production efficiency: The economy must be on its production possibilities curve.

3 Product-mix efficiency: The economy must produce a mix of goods reflecting the preferences of consumers.

price system again ensures that this condition will be satisfied. Assume that the economy is initially producing at a point along the production possibilities curve, E in Figure 12.5. Consumers decide that they like apples more and oranges less. The increased demand for apples will result in an increase in the price of apples, and this will lead to an increased output of apples; at the same time, the decrease demand for oranges will result in a decrease in the price of oranges, and this in turn will lead to a decreased output of oranges. The economy will move from E to a point such as E_1, where there are more apples and fewer oranges produced; the mix of goods produced in the economy will have changed to reflect the changed preferences of consumers.

LOOKING BEYOND THE BASIC MODEL: MARKET FAILURES AND THE ROLE OF GOVERNMENT

This chapter has brought together the pieces of the basic competitive model. It has shown how the competitive equilibrium in an ideal economy is achieved. To the extent that conditions in the real world match the approximations of the basic competitive model, there will be economic efficiency. Government will have little role in the economy beyond establishing a

Figure 12.5 **THE PRODUCTION POSSIBILITIES CURVE**

The production possibilities curve shows the maximum level of output of one good given the level of output of other goods. Production efficiency requires that the economy be on its production possibilities curve. Along the curve, the only way to increase production of one good (here, apples) is to decrease the production of other goods (oranges).

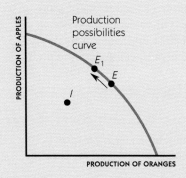

EFFICIENCY

An economy in competitive equilibrium is Pareto efficient.

Any Pareto-efficient resource allocation that society desires can be obtained through the market mechanism.

legal framework within which to enforce market transactions.

Views differ as to whether markets can be relied upon to deliver economic efficiency, prosperity, and acceptable distributions of resources. At one extreme there are people like the Austrian economist Friedrich von Hayek and the U.S. economist Milton Friedman, who believe in free markets and are suspicious of any government intervention. They tend to believe that markets are substantially competitive. Even where there are departures from the basic competitive model, they would still question whether government could bring about any improvement over the market's outcome. This leads to a view of economic policy and economic problems that has been described (by Willem Buiter, of the University of Cambridge) as Panglossian.

The predominant view among economists is that while the competitive model provides a useful benchmark, there are significant departures from it that create a presumption that government intervention in various ways might be able to improve the allocation of resources and the distribution of incomes. Some economists emphasise the role of imperfect competition. If the market for cigarettes is not competitive, the competitive model will probably yield incorrect predictions of the effects of a tax on cigarettes, for example. Other economists focus on the prevalence of imperfect information in the real world—firms do not have perfect information on the

qualities of their workers, investors do not have perfect information on the returns to different investment opportunities—which is likely, they argue, to cause labour and capital markets to function in ways quite different from those described by the basic competitive model. Others are concerned about externalities such as pollution of the environment, and the extent of unemployment, which appear to be departures from the basic competitive model.

However, these are differences of emphasis—differences of degree rather than of kind—and the common thread is the use of the competitive market model as a point of departure for a careful and reasoned study of its successes and failures and a willingness to consider the possibility of useful government intervention.

What are the consequences when the underlying assumptions are not valid? Which of the assumptions are most suspect? What evidence do we have with which we can assess either the validity of the model's underlying assumptions or its implications? The next part of this book is devoted to these questions and to the role of government that emerges from the answers.

A warning is in order before we embark on our study of market imperfections. That markets do not work perfectly—suggesting a possible role for government—does not necessarily mean that government intervention will improve matters.

TWO VIEWS OF THE BASIC COMPETITIVE MODEL

Free-market view: The competitive model provides a good description of the economy, and government intervention is not required.

Imperfect-market view: In many markets, the competitive model does not provide a good description, for instance, because competition is limited and information is imperfect. There are important market failures, evidence by unemployment and environmental pollution, which may require at least selective government intervention.

REVIEW AND PRACTICE

SUMMARY

1 When an economic change affects many markets at once, general equilibrium analysis is used to study the interactions among various parts of the economy. But when the secondary repercussions of a change are small, partial equilibrium analysis, focusing on only one or a few markets, is sufficient.

2 General equilibrium in the basic competitive model occurs when wages, interest rates, and prices are such that demand is equal to supply in all labour markets, in all capital markets, and in all product markets. All markets clear.

3 Circular flow of funds diagrams show capital, labour, and product market interrelationships between households, firms, government, and the foreign sector. The flow of funds in and out of each sector must balance.

4 Under the conditions of the basic competitive model, the economy's resource allocation is Pareto efficient; that is, no one can be made better off without making someone else worse off.

5 The distribution of income that emerges from competitive markets may possibly be very unequal. However, under the conditions of the basic competitive model, a redistribution of wealth can move the economy to a more equal allocation that is also Pareto efficient. No further government intervention is required.

6 Some economists hold that the basic competitive model provides an essentially accurate view of most of the economy; markets ensure economic efficiency, and there is only a limited role for government. Others maintain that many markets are quite imperfect, the basic competitive model provides no more than a starting point of analysis, and government intervention is required to deal with some of society's problems.

KEY TERMS

partial equilibrium analysis

general equilibrium analysis

circular flow

Pareto-efficient allocations

exchange efficiency

production efficiency

product-mix efficiency

REVIEW QUESTIONS

1 What is the difference between partial and general equilibrium analysis? When is each one especially appropriate?

2 List the principal flows into and out of firms, households, government, and the foreign sector.

3 How does the economy in general equilibrium answer the four basic economic questions: What is produced, and in what quantities? How are these goods produced? For whom are they produced? Who decides how resources are allocated?

4 What is meant by Pareto efficiency? What is required for the economy to be Pareto efficient? If the conditions of the basic competitive model are satisfied, is the economy Pareto efficient?

5 If the distribution of income in the economy is quite unequal, is it necessary to impose price controls or otherwise change prices in the competitive marketplace to make it more equal?

PROBLEMS

1 Decide whether partial equilibrium analysis would suffice in each of these cases or it would be wise to undertake a general equilibrium analysis:

(a) A tax on alcohol
(b) An increase in National Insurance contributions
(c) A drought that affects farm production
(d) A rise in the price of crude oil
(e) A major airline going out of business

Explain your answers.

2 Use the extended circular flow diagram, with the foreign sector included, to trace out the possible consequences of the following:

(a) A law requiring that businesses raise the wages of their employees
(b) A decision by consumers to import more and save less
(c) An increase in government expenditure financed by a rise in the corporation tax
(d) An increase in government expenditure without an accompanying increase in taxes

3 Explain how each of the following might interfere with exchange efficiency:

(a) Airlines that limit the number of seats they sell at a discount price

(b) A national health service that provides a *limited* amount of free health care to anyone who needs it after she has visited a general practitioner and waited in a long queue
(c) Firms that give volume discounts

In each case, what additional trades might be possible?

4 Assume that in the steel industry, given current production levels and technology, 1 machine costing £10,000 can replace 1 worker. Given current production levels and technology in the automobile industry, 1 machine costing £10,000 can replace 2 workers. Is this economy Pareto efficient; that is, on its production possibilities curve? If not, explain how total output of both goods can be increased by shifting machines and labour between industries.

5 Consider three ways of helping poor people to buy food, clothing, and shelter. The first way is to pass laws setting price ceilings to keep these basic goods affordable. The second is to have the government distribute coupons that give poor people a discount when they buy these necessities. The third is for the government to distribute income to poor people. Which programme is more likely to have a Pareto-efficient outcome? Describe why the other programmes are not likely to be Pareto efficient.

APPPENDIX: PARETO EFFICIENCY AND COMPETITIVE MARKETS

The concept of the marginal rate of substitution, introduced in the appendix to Chapter 8, can be used to see more clearly why competitive markets are Pareto efficient.

EXCHANGE EFFICIENCY

Exchange efficiency can be achieved only when all individuals have the same marginal rate of substitu-

tion, the amount of one good a person is willing to give up to get one unit of another. In competitive markets, individuals choose a mix of goods for which the marginal rate of substitution is equal to relative prices. Since all individuals face the same relative prices, they all have identical marginal rates of substitution; this ensures the exchange efficiency of the economy.

To see why exchange efficiency requires that all people have the same marginal rate of substitution, let's look at a simple example of Crusoe and Friday and their island economy. Assume that Crusoe's marginal rate of substitution between apples and oranges is 2; that is, he is willing to give up 2 apples for 1 extra orange. Friday's marginal rate of substitution between apples and oranges is 1; he willing to give up 1 apple for 1 orange. Since their marginal rates of substitution are not equal, we can make one of them better off without making the other worse off (or we can make both of them better off). The allocation is not Pareto efficient.

To see how this is done, suppose we take 1 orange away from Friday and give it to Crusoe. Crusoe would then be willing to give up 2 apples and would be just as well off as before. If he gave up only $1\frac{1}{2}$ apples to Friday, Friday would also be better off. Friday would have given up 1 orange in return for $1\frac{1}{2}$ apples; he would have been willing to make the trade if he had received just 1 apple in return.

It is easy to see that Crusoe and Friday will continue to trade until their marginal rates of substitution are equal. As Friday gives up oranges for apples, his marginal rate of substitution increases; he insists on getting more and more apples for each orange he gives up. Similarly, as Crusoe gives up apples and gets more oranges, his marginal rate of substitution decreases; he is willing to give up fewer apples for each extra orange he gets. Eventually, the two will have identical marginal rates of substitution, at which point trade will stop. Thus, the basic condition for exchange efficiency is that the marginal rates of substitution of all individuals must be the same.

PRODUCTION EFFICIENCY

The condition of production efficiency—when the economy is on its production possibilities curve—is very similar to the condition of exchange efficiency. An economy can only be productively efficient if the marginal rate of technical substitution between any two inputs in any two firms is the same. The marginal rate of technical substitution is the amount that one input can be reduced if another input is increased by one unit, while total output remains constant (see the appendix to Chapter 10).

Profit-maximising firms in a competitive economy choose a mix of inputs such that the marginal rate of technical substitution of different inputs is equal to the relative prices of those inputs. If all firms face the same relative prices of inputs, their marginal rates of technical substitution will all be the same, and production efficiency will result.

For example, consider a case involving the steel and auto industries. Assume that in steel, the marginal rate of substitution between capital expenditures and labour is £2,000; that is, if a company uses one more worker, it can save £2,000 on equipment (or equivalently, two £1,000 machines substitute for one worker). In the auto industry, the marginal rate of substitution is £1,000; one £1,000 machine substitutes for one worker. The marginal rates of substitution between inputs are not equal; this means that the economy is not productively efficient.

Consider a worker moving from the automobile to the steel industry. If the steel industry keeps its output at the same level, the additional worker in that industry frees up two machines. One of those machines can be transferred to the automobile industry, and production in that industry would stay at the same level. (We are assuming that in the automobile industry one £1,000 machine substitutes for one worker.) But one machine is left over. It can be used in the steel industry, the automobile industry, or both to increase production.

As we increase the number of workers in steel, the marginal productivity of labour in that industry will diminish, while as we reduce workers in the automobile industry, the marginal productivity of labour in that industry will increase; conversely for machines. As a result, the marginal rates of technical substitution will shift in the two industries, so that they are closer. Spurred on by the profit motive of the individual companies in competitive markets, labour and capital will tend to move between companies until marginal rates of technical substitution are equated, and production efficiency is reached. Thus, production efficiency, which means that the economy is on its production possibilities curve, requires that the marginal rate of technical substitution between any two inputs be the same in all uses.

PRODUCT-MIX EFFICIENCY

This third condition of Pareto efficiency requires that the economy operate at the point along the production possibilities curve that reflects consumers' preferences. Look at a particular point on the production possibilities curve in Figure 12.5, say point *E*. The **marginal rate of transformation** tells us how many extra units of one good the economy can get if it gives up one unit of another good—how many extra cases of beer the economy can produce if it reduces production of potato chips by a tonne or how many extra cars the economy can get if it gives up one tank. The slope of the production possibilities curve is equal to the marginal rate of transformation. The slope tells us how much of one good, measured along the vertical axis, can be increased if the economy gives up one unit of the good along the horizontal axis.

Product-mix efficiency requires that consumers' marginal rate of substitution equal the marginal rate of transformation. To see why this is so and how competitive economies ensure product-mix efficiency, consider an economy producing two fruits, apples and oranges. Assume that the marginal rate of substitution between apples and oranges is 2—individuals are willing to give up 2 apples for an additional orange—while the marginal rate of transformation is 1—they only have to give up 1 apple to get an additional orange. Clearly, it pays firms to increase orange production and reduce apple production.

The competitive price system ensures that the economy satisfies the condition for product-mix efficiency. We know that consumers set the marginal rate of substitution equal to the relative price. In a similar way, profit-maximising firms have an incentive to produce more of some goods and less of others according to the prices they can sell them for, until their marginal rate of transformation is equal to the relative price. If consumers and producers both face the same relative prices, the marginal rate of substitution will equal the marginal rate of transformation. Thus, product-mix efficiency comes about when both consumers and firms face the same prices.

To see more clearly why competitive firms will set the marginal rate of transformation equal to relative prices, consider a firm that produces both apples and oranges. If the company reallocates labour from apples to oranges, apple production is reduced and orange production is increased. Assume apple production goes down by 2 cases and orange production goes up by 1 case. The marginal rate of transformation is 2. If a case of apples sells for £4 and a case of oranges sells for £10, the firm loses £8 on apple sales but gains £10 on orange sales. It is clearly profitable for the firm to make the switch. The firm will continue to switch resources from apples to oranges until the marginal rate of transformation equals the relative price. The same result will occur even if oranges and apples are produced by different firms.[3]

Thus, the basic condition for product-mix efficiency, that the marginal rate of substitution must equal the marginal rate of transformation, will be satisfied in competitive economies because firms set the marginal rate of transformation equal to relative prices, and consumers set their marginal rate of substitution equal to relative prices.

---

[3] The concept of product-mix efficiency can be illustrated by superimposing a family of indifference curves (Chapter 8, appendix) in the same diagram with the production possibilities curve. Assume, for simplicity, that all individuals are the same. The highest level of welfare that one representative individual can attain is given by the tangency of her indifference curve with the production possibilities curve. The slopes of two curves that are tangent to each other are equal at the point of tangency. The slope of the indifference curve is the consumer's marginal rate of substitution; the slope of the production possibilities curve is the marginal rate of transformation. Thus, the tangency—and Pareto efficiency—requires that the marginal rate of substitution equal the marginal rate of transformation.

PART THREE

IMPERFECT MARKETS

n Part Two, the basic model of perfectly competitive markets was developed. If the real world matched up to its assumptions, then markets could be given free rein. They would supply efficient outcomes. If an outcome seemed inequitable, society would simply redistribute initial wealth and let markets take care of the rest.

In the two centuries since Adam Smith enunciated the view that markets ensure economic efficiency, the model has been investigated with great care. Most economists continue to believe that markets are, by and large, the most efficient way to coordinate an economy. However, they have found significant departures between modern economies and the competitive model. In Part Three, and later in Part Four, we will explore many of the ways in which the real world deviates from the competitive model. We can enumerate the basic differences here.

1 Most markets are not as competitive as those envisioned by the basic model. It is hard to think of a consumer product without attaching a brand name to it. The basic competitive model focuses on products like wheat or pig iron, for which the products produced by different firms are essentially identical, and are perfect substitutes for one another. In that model, there is no room for brand names. In the basic competitive model, if a firm raises its price slightly above that of its rivals, it loses all of its customers, as they switch; in the real world, a firm that raises its price slightly above that of its rivals, loses some, but far from all, of its customers. In the basic competitive model, when firms contemplate how much to produce, they take the market price as given, and do not need to consider how their rivals will react. In the real world, many firms spend enormous energies trying to anticipate the actions and reactions of rivals. In Chapters 13 to 15, we will take up failures of competition in product markets and government responses to them. In Chapter 18, we will also encounter restricted competition in the labour market.

2 The basic model simply ignores technological change. It assumes that all firms operate with a given technology. Competition in the basic model is over price, yet in the real world, a primary focus of competition is the development of new and better products and the improvements in production, transportation, and marketing that allow products to be brought to customers at lower costs and thus at a lower price. This competition takes place not between the multitude of small producers envisaged in the basic competitive model, but often between the industrial giants like Boeing and Airbus Industrie, and between the industrial giants and upstarts, like IBM and the many small computer firms that eventually took away a major share of the computer market.

Chapter 16 will enrich the model to help us understand better this more general view of competition, and to enable us to see how technological change can be encouraged.

3 The individuals and firms envisioned in the basic model have easy and inexpensive access to the information they need in order to operate in any market they enter. Buyers know what they are buying, whether it is stocks or bonds, a house, a car, or a refrigerator. Firms know perfectly the productivity of each worker they hire, and when a worker goes to work for a firm, he knows precisely what is expected of him in return for his promised pay.

Imperfections of information and competition arise in all markets—in product, labour, and capital markets—and in each they take on different forms. Consider, for instance, the product market (Chapter 17). Consumers cannot ascertain all the characteristics of a product before they buy it; they rely in part on the seller's reputation. They may worry that if the price is too low, the product is likely to be shoddy; they use price in part to *judge* quality—a quite different role from that upon which Part Two focused, with important consequences.

Or consider the labour market, discussed in Chapter 18: in the basic model, the employer knows precisely what he wants the worker to do, and he knows whether the worker has done what he is supposed to do. The employer pays the worker if and only if he does what he was contracted for. Issues of incentives, of motivating workers, simply never arise. In practice, designing compensation schemes—often based on performance—to motivate workers is a central concern of management.

Or consider the capital market: a central issue facing firms is how best to meet their capital requirements, whether by borrowing or issuing new equity. A somewhat surprising implication of the basic competitive model is that how the firm raises its capital makes no difference. Chapter 19 explains how factors not taken into account in that basic model help us understand why it does make a difference, and how firms actually make these crucial decisions.

While beyond the scope of Part Three, the following points are noted here to complete our comparison of the competitive model and the real world.

4 The competitive model assumes that the costs of bringing a good to market accrue fully and completely to the seller, and that the benefits of consuming a good go fully and completely to the buyer. In Chapter 7, however, we encountered the possibility of externalities, which are extra costs or benefits that do not figure in the market calculation. There may be positive externalities (such as national defence) and negative externalities (such as pollution). We will return to negative externalities in Part Four.

5 The basic model answers the question "What goods will be produced, and in what quantities?" by assuming that all desired goods that *can* be brought to market *will* be brought to market. Trees that bloom in gold coins and tablets that guarantee an eternal youth are out of the question. But if customers want to buy green hair colouring, cancer-causing tobacco products, or life insurance policies overladen with extras, then producers can be expected to supply such goods. However, there are many cases where markets have not provided goods or services that could be provided at a cost consumers would be willing to pay. Some of the most obvious examples are in insurance markets, where government has intervened with such programmes as unemployment insurance and Social Security. We first considered this problem of missing markets in Chapter 7, and will return to it in Part Four.

6 In the basic model, all markets clear—supply meets demand at the market price. Decades of evidence, however, suggest that labour markets often do not clear. The result is involuntary unemployment, sometimes on a massive scale. During the Great Depression, for instance, one out of four workers was out of a job. While beyond our scope in Part Three, the recurrence of involuntary unemployment in the economy is an important deviation from the competitive model of Part Two.

7 Even if markets are efficient, the way they allocate resources may appear to be socially unacceptable. We addressed this issue in Chapter 7, in the discussion of how government may redistribute income when the distribution produced by the market is deemed socially unacceptable. We will return to this subject in Part Four.

In the competitive model, there is little role for government, because markets ensure economic efficiency. The foregoing discussion highlights several reasons why there may be dissatisfaction with markets—why they may not in fact ensure efficiency or why, even if markets were efficient, the outcomes may not be acceptable. In each of these instances, government may be called upon. In each of the ensuing chapters, we will not only explore the limitations of the markets, but also describe and assess the roles government has undertaken to address those limitations

THE BASIC MODEL VERSUS THE REAL WORLD

The Basic Model	The Real World
1 All markets are competitive.	**1** Most markets are *not* characterised by the degree of competition envisioned in the basic model.
2 Technological know-how is fixed and cannot change.	**2** Technological change is a central part of competition in modern industrial economies.
3 Firms, consumers, and any other market participants have easy access to information that is relevant to the markets in which they participate.	**3** Good information may be impossible to come by, and in most cases is costly to obtain. In many markets, buyers of products know less than the sellers.
4 Sellers bear the full and complete costs of bringing goods to market, and buyers reap the full benefit.	**4** Externalities mean that market transactions may not accurately account for costs and benefits and the private market provides an inadequate supply of public goods.
5 All desired markets exist.	**5** Some markets may not exist, even though goods or services in that market might be provided at a cost consumers would be willing to pay.
6 There is no involuntary unemployment.	**6** There is involuntary unemployment.
7 Competitive markets provide an efficient allocation of resources.	**7** Efficiency is not enough. The income distribution generated by the market may be socially unacceptable.
8 There is little role for government.	**8** Government plays an important role in the economy. Among its roles are correcting market failure, providing social insurance, and redistributing income.

13

MONOPOLIES AND IMPERFECT COMPETITION

In the competitive model discussed in Part Two, markets have so many buyers and sellers that no individual household or firm believes its actions will affect the market equilibrium price. The buyer or seller takes the price as given, and then decides how much to buy or sell. At the market price, the seller can sell as much as she wants. But any effort to outfox the market has dramatic consequences. If, for instance, she raises her price above that of her competitors, her sales will be zero.

Not all markets are very competitive, however. For years, Kodak controlled the market for film. Some firms so dominated a product that their brand name became synonymous with the product, like Kleenex and Hoover.

In some industries, such as soft drinks (Coca-Cola, Pepsi, Schweppes), a handful of firms producing similar but not identical products dominate a market. When one such firm raises its price a little—say, by 2 or 3 percent—it loses some customers but far from all. If it lowers its price by 2 or 3 percent, it gains additional customers but not the entire market. As a result, these companies do not simply take the price as dictated to them by the market. They make the price. They are the **price makers.** Markets in which competition is limited are the subject of this chapter and the next.

KEY QUESTIONS

1 If there is only one firm in a market—a monopoly—how does it set its price and output? In what sense is the monopoly price too high?

2 Why do firms with no competition or imperfect competition face downward-sloping demand curves?

3 What are the barriers to entry that limit the number of firms in a market?

4 What does equilibrium look like in a market with imperfect competition, in which barriers to entry are small enough that profits are driven to zero, yet in which there are few enough firms that each faces a downward-sloping curve?

MARKET STRUCTURES

One way to simplify an economy is to break it up into its constituent markets. An example is the car market. The motor industry in Europe consists of firms like Ford and General Motors (both U.S. firms which have divisions in several European countries), Peugeot, Renault, Volkswagen, BMW, Mercedes, Fiat, Volvo, Saab, Rover (the only surviving British volume car producer, now owned by BMW), and a number of smaller producers like Alfa Romeo and Rolls-Royce. They compete for sales with firms from other countries, notably Japan and Korea.

When economists look at markets, they look first at the **market structure,** that is, at how that market is organised. The market structure that forms the basis of the competitive model of Part Two is called perfect competition. For example, there are so many wheat farmers (producers) that no individual wheat farmer can realistically hope to move the price of wheat from that produced by the law of supply and demand.

Frequently, however, competition is not perfect. Rather, it is limited. Economists group markets in which competition is limited into three broad structures. In the most extreme, there is no competition. A single firm supplies the entire market. This is called **monopoly.** Until recently local electricity companies had a monopoly in supplying electricity in their areas. Since one would expect the profits of a monopolist to attract entry into that market, for a firm to maintain its monopoly position, there must be some barrier to entry. Later, we learn what these barriers are.

In the second structure, several firms supply the market, so there is *some* competition. This is called **oligopoly.** The automobile industry is an example, with perhaps a dozen producers in Europe and three main producers in the United States. The defining characteristic of oligopolies is that the small number of firms forces each to be concerned with how its rivals will react to any action it undertakes. If General Motors offers low-interest-rate financing, for instance, the other companies may feel compelled to match the offer; and before making any such offer, GM will have to take this into account. By contrast, a monopolist has no rivals and thus considers only whether special offers help or hurt itself. And a firm facing perfect competition can sell as much as it wants at the market price without having recourse to any special offers.

In the third market structure, there are more firms than in an oligopoly but not enough for perfect competition. This is called **monopolistic competition.** An example is the market for clothing as represented by Marks and Spencer, Debenhams. Next, and other such chains of stores. Each chain has its own make of clothing, which no other chain sells. But the clothing in each chain is similar enough to that supplied by other chains that there is considerable competition. Even so, the clothing supplied by the different chains is different enough to make competition limited, so that the chain is not a price taker. The degree of competition under monopolistic competition is greater than that of oligopoly. This is because monopolistic competition involves a sufficiently large number of firms that each firm can ignore the reactions of any rival. If one company lowers its price, it may garner for itself a large num-

ALTERNATIVE MARKET STRUCTURES

Perfect competition: Many, many firms; each believes that nothing it does will have any effect on the market price.

Monopoly: One firm.

Imperfect competition: Several firms, each aware that its sales depend on the price it charges and possibly other actions it takes, such as advertising. There are two special cases:

Oligopoly: Sufficiently few firms that each worries about how rivals will respond to any action it undertakes.

Monopolistic competition: Sufficiently many firms that each believes that its rivals will not change the price they charge should it lower its own price.

ber of customers. But the number of customers it takes away from any single rival is so small that none of the rivals is motivated to retaliate.

With both oligopolies and monopolistic competition, there is some competition, but it is more limited than under perfect competition. These in-between market structures are referred to as **imperfect competition.**

This chapter focuses on monopoly and monopolistic competition. Oligopolies are left for Chapter 14. We begin with an analysis of how a monopolist sets its price and quantity, and how monopoly outcomes compare with competitive outcomes. We then switch to imperfect competition, a more common structure, and analyse the principal determinants of competition within any market. We follow this with an analysis of the barriers to entry that enable imperfectly competitive firms to sustain higher than normal profits for long periods of time. The final section looks at the case where barriers to entry are so weak enough that profits are driven to zero but competition is still sufficiently limited to enable each firm to change its prices without losing all its customers.

MONOPOLY OUTPUT

Economists' concerns about monopolies and other forms of restricted competition stem mainly from the observation that the output, or supply, of firms within these market structures is less than that of firms faced with perfect competition. To address these concerns, we consider a monopolist that charges the same price to all its customers and show how it determines its level of output.

A monopolist and a competitive firm are similar in some ways. Both try to maximise profits. In determining output, they compare the extra (or marginal) revenue they would receive from producing an extra unit of output with the extra (or marginal) cost of producing that extra unit. If marginal revenue exceeds marginal cost, it pays to expand output. Conversely if marginal revenue is less than marginal cost, it pays to reduce output. Thus, the basic principle for output determination for both a competitive firm and a monopolist is the same. Each produces at the output level at which marginal revenue equals marginal cost.

The essential difference between a monopolist and a competitive firm is that a competitive firm takes the price set by market forces. When such a firm increases production by one unit, its marginal revenue is just the price. For instance, the marginal revenue a wheat farmer receives from producing one more bushel of wheat is the price of a bushel of wheat. But the only way a monopolist can sell more is to lower the price it charges, so marginal revenue is *not* equal to the present market price.

The difference can be put another way. The demand curve facing a competitive firm is perfectly horizontal, as illustrated in Figure 13.1A. The price p^* is the market price. The firm can sell as much as it wants at that price and nothing at any higher price. In an industry such as wheat farming, if there are one million wheat farmers, each farmer on average accounts for one-millionth of the market. If a single average farmer even doubled his production, the total production would increase by one-millionth—

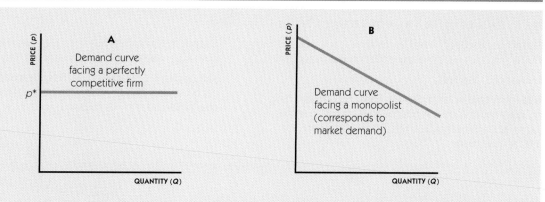

Figure 13.1 THE DEMAND CURVE FACING A PERFECTLY COMPETITIVE FIRM AND A MONOPOLIST

A price-taking, perfectly competitive firm can sell any quantity it wishes at the market price but cannot raise the price at all without losing all its business. It faces the horizontal demand curve shown in panel A. A monopolist provides all the output in a market, so an increased amount can only be sold at a reduced price. Panel B shows the downward-sloping demand curve—the market demand curve—faced by a monopolist.

a truly negligible amount that could be absorbed by the market with no perceptible change in price.

The demand curve facing a monopolist, in contrast, is downward sloping, as illustrated in Figure 13.1B. By definition, the monopolist controls the entire industry, so that a doubling of *its* output is a doubling of industry output, which will have a significant effect on price. If the monopoly supplier of aluminium had increased its production by 1 percent, the total supply of aluminium would have increased by 1 percent. Market prices would have fallen observably in response to a change in supply of even that magnitude.

The marginal revenue a monopolist receives from producing one more unit can be broken into two separate components. First, the firm receives revenue from selling the additional output. This additional revenue is just the market price. But to sell more, the firm must reduce its price. Unless it does so, it cannot sell the extra output. Marginal revenue is the price it receives from the sale of the one additional unit *minus* the loss in revenue from the price reduction on all other units. Thus, for a monopolist,

the marginal revenue for producing one extra unit is always less than the price received for that extra unit. (Only at the first unit produced are marginal revenue and price the same.)

This can be represented by a simple equation:

Marginal revenue
= (net increase in revenue from selling one more unit)
= price + $\Delta p \times Q$,

where Δp represents the change in price and Q represents the initial quantity sold. For a competitive firm, $\Delta p = 0$, so marginal revenue equals price. For a monopolist, Δp is negative, so marginal revenue is less than the price.

Figure 13.2A shows the output decision of a competitive firm. Marginal revenue is just equal to market price p^*. Panel B shows the output decision of a monopolist. Marginal revenue is always less than price. Note that with a monopoly, since marginal revenue is less than price and marginal revenue

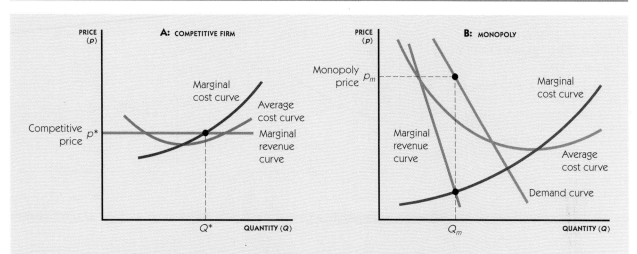

Figure 13.2 MARGINAL REVENUE EQUALS MARGINAL COST

A perfectly competitive firm gains or loses exactly the market price (p^*) when it changes the quantity produced by one unit. To maximise profits, the firm produces the quantity where marginal cost equals marginal revenue, which in the competitive case also equals price. Panel B shows the

downward-sloping marginal revenue curve for a monopolist. A monopolist also chooses the level of quantity where marginal cost equals marginal revenue. In the monopolistic case, however, marginal revenue is lower than price.

equals marginal cost, marginal cost is less than price. The price is what individuals are willing to pay for an extra unit of the product; it measures the marginal benefit to the consumer of an extra unit. Thus, the marginal benefit of an extra unit exceeds the marginal cost. This is the fundamental reason that monopolies reduce economic efficiency.[1]

The extent to which output is curtailed depends on the magnitude of the difference between marginal revenue and price. This in turn depends on the shape of the demand curve. When demand curves are very elastic (relatively flat), prices do not fall much when output increases. As shown in Figure 13.3A marginal revenue is not much less than price. The firm produces at Q_m, where marginal revenue equals marginal cost. The monopoly output Q_m is

slightly less than the competitive output Q_c, where price equals marginal cost. When demand curves are less elastic, as in panel B, prices may fall a considerable amount when output increases, and then the extra revenue the firm receives from producing an extra unit of output will be much less than the price received from selling that unit.

The larger the elasticity of demand, the smaller the discrepancy between marginal revenue and price. This can be seen simply by using the definitions of the elasticity of demand and marginal revenue:

Elasticity of demand

$$= \frac{\text{change in market quantity}}{\text{market quantity}} \bigg/ \frac{\text{change in price}}{\text{price}}$$

$$= \frac{\Delta Q}{Q} \bigg/ \frac{\Delta p}{p}.$$

If we consider a change in quantity of 1 (as we do

---

[1] Chapter 15 will describe more precisely how the magnitudes of the losses associated with monopoly can be quantified.

Figure 13.3 MONOPOLY AND THE ELASTICITY OF DEMAND

In panel A, a monopoly faces a very elastic market demand, so prices do not fall much as output increases, and monopoly price is not much more than the competitive price. In panel B, a monopoly faces a less elastic market demand, so prices fall quite a lot as output increases, and price is substantially above marginal cost.

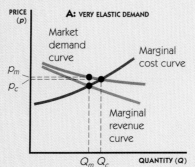

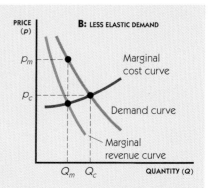

when we calculate marginal revenue), so that $\Delta Q = 1$,

$$\text{Elasticity of demand} = -\frac{1}{Q} \Big/ \frac{\Delta p}{p} = -\frac{p}{Q\,\Delta p}$$

and

Marginal revenue

$$= \text{price} + \text{change in price} \times \text{quantity sold}$$

$$= p + Q\,\Delta p$$

$$= p\left(1 + \frac{Q\,\Delta p}{p}\right)$$

$$= p(1 - 1/\text{elasticity of demand}).$$

Hence, if the elasticity of demand is 2, marginal revenue is 1/2 of price. If the elasticity of demand is 10, marginal revenue is 9/10 of price.

AN EXAMPLE: THE ABC-MENT COMPANY

Table 13.1 gives the demand curve facing the ABC-ment Company, which has a monopoly on the production of cement in its area. There is a particular price at which it can sell each level of output. As it lowers its price, it can sell more cement. Local builders will, for instance, use more cement and less wood and other materials in constructing a house.

For simplicity, we assume cement is sold in units of 1,000 cubic metres. At a price of £10,000 per unit (of 1,000 cubic metres), the firm sells 1 unit; at a price of £9,000, it sells 2 units; and at a price of £8,000, 3 units. The third column of the table shows the total revenue at each of these levels of produc-

THE FIRM'S SUPPLY DECISION

All firms maximise profits at the point where marginal revenue (the revenue from selling an extra unit of the product) equals marginal cost.

For a competitive firm, marginal revenue equals price.

For a monopoly, marginal revenue is less than price.

Table 13.1 DEMAND CURVE FACING ABC-MENT COMPANY

Cubic Metres (thousands)	Price	Total Revenues	Marginal Revenues	Total Costs	Marginal Cost
1	£10,000	£10,000		£15,000	
			£8,000		£2,000
2	£9,000	£18,000		£17,000	
			£6,000		£3,000
3	£8,000	£24,000		£20,000	
			£4,000		£4,000
4	£7,000	£28,000		£24,000	
			£2,000		£5,000
5	£6,000	£30,000		£29,000	
			0		£6,000
6	£5,000	£30,000		£35,000	

tion. The total revenue is just price times quantity. The marginal revenue from producing an extra unit (of 1,000 cubic metres) is just the difference between, say, the revenues received at 3 units and 2 units or 2 units and 1 unit. Notice that in each case, the marginal revenue is less than the price.

Figure 13.4 shows the demand and marginal revenue curves, using data from Table 13.1. At each level of output, the marginal revenue curve lies below the demand curve. As can be seen from Table 13.1, not only does price decrease as output increases, but so does marginal revenue.

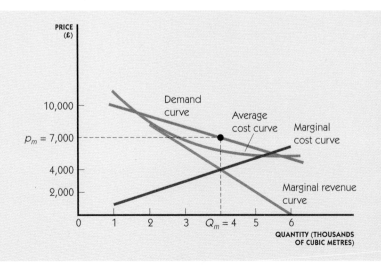

Figure 13.4 DEMAND AND MARGINAL REVENUE

At each level of output, the marginal revenue curve lies below the demand curve.

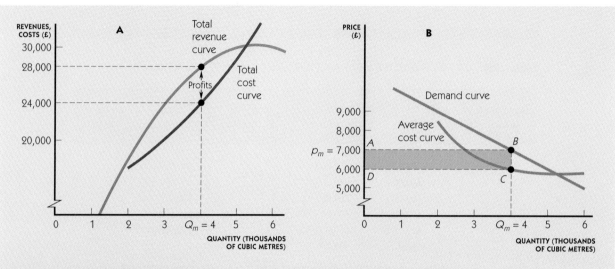

Figure 13.5 PRICE EXCEEDING AVERAGE COSTS MEANS PROFIT

Panel A shows profits to be the distance between the total revenue and total cost curves, maximised at the output Q_m = 4,000 cubic metres. Profits occur when the market price is above average costs, as in panel B, so that the company is (on average) making a profit on each unit it sells. Monopoly profits are the area *ABCD*, which is average profit per unit times the number of units sold.

The output at which marginal revenue equals marginal cost—the output chosen by the profit-maximising monopolist—is denoted by Q_m. In our example, Q_m = 4,000 cubic metres. When the number of cubic metres increases from 3,000 to 4,000, the marginal revenue is £4,000, and so is the marginal cost. At this level of output, the price p_m is £7,000 (per 1,000 cubic metres), which is considerably in excess of marginal cost, £4,000. Total revenue, £28,000, is also in excess of total costs, £24,000.[2]

MONOPOLY PROFITS

Monopolists maximise their profits by setting marginal revenue equal to marginal cost. The total level of monopoly profits can be seen in two ways as shown in Figure 13.5. Panel A shows total revenue and total

[2] In this example, the firm is indifferent between producing 3,000 or 4,000 cubic metres. If the marginal cost of producing the extra output exceeds £4,000 by a little, then it will produce 3,000 cubic metres; if the marginal cost is a little less than £4,000, then it will produce 4,000 cubic metres.

costs (from Table 13.1) for each level of output of the ABC-ment Company. The difference between revenue and costs is profits—the distance between the two curves. This distance is maximised at the output Q_m = 4,000 cubic metres. We can see that at this level of output, profits are £4,000 (£28,000 − £24,000). Panel B calculates profits using the average cost diagram. Total profits are equal to the profit per unit multiplied by the number of units produced. The profit per unit is the difference between the unit price and the average cost, and total monopoly profits is the shaded area *ABCD*. Again, the sum is £4,000: (£7,000 − £6,000) × 4. In Chapter 11, we saw that competition drives profits to zero. This means price is equal to the minimum average cost of the least efficient firm in the industry. The difference between what the least efficient firm gets in net revenue and what more efficient, lower-cost firms receive—as we also saw in Chapter 11—is not profit to an economist. It is, rather, rent (because, for instance, a firm has more knowledge than its competitors, and thus lower costs, yet faces the same market price as all other firms) and opportunity cost (the return the firm's owner would have received if she had invested her capital and time elsewhere).

Rent and opportunity cost are present in competitive markets as well as in monopolies. But for monopolists, there is a different kind of return that cannot be traced to opportunity cost or rents on technological capabilities. Even after taking these factors into account, a monopolist enjoys an extra return because it has been able to reduce its output and increase its price from the level that would have prevailed under competition. This return is called a **pure profit.** Because these payments are not required to elicit greater effort or production on the part of the monop-

olist (in fact, they derive from the monopolist's *reducing* the output from what it would be under competition), they are also called **monopoly rents.**

PRICE DISCRIMINATION

The basic objective of monopolists is to maximise profits, and they accomplish this by setting marginal revenue equal to marginal cost, so price exceeds marginal cost. Monopolists can also engage in a vari-

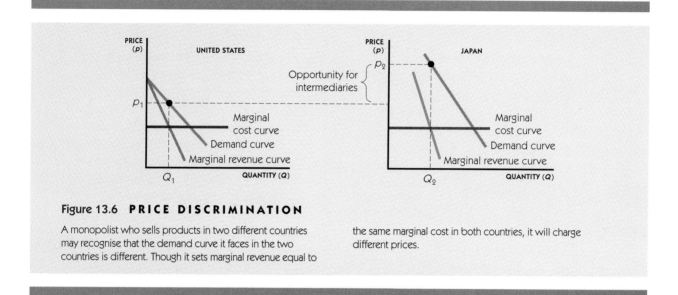

Figure 13.6 PRICE DISCRIMINATION

A monopolist who sells products in two different countries may recognise that the demand curve it faces in the two countries is different. Though it sets marginal revenue equal to the same marginal cost in both countries, it will charge different prices.

ety of other practices to increase their profits. Among the most important is **price discrimination,** which means charging different prices to different customers or in different markets.

Figure 13.6 shows a monopolist setting marginal revenue equal to marginal cost in the United States and in Japan. The demand curves the firm faces in the two countries are different. Therefore, though marginal costs are the same, the firm will charge different prices for the same good in the two countries. (By contrast, in competitive markets, price equals marginal cost, so that regardless of the shape of the demand curves, price will be the same in the two markets, except for the different costs of delivering the good to each market.) With prices in the two countries differing, intermediary firms will enter the market, buying the product in the country with the low price and selling it in the other country. A company may attempt to thwart the intermediaries—as many companies do—by, for instance, having distinct labels on the two products and refusing to provide service or honour any guarantees outside the country in which the good is originally delivered.

Within a country, a monopolist can also price discriminate *if* resale is difficult and *if* it can distinguish between buyers with high and low elasticities of demand. An electricity company can make its charge for each kilowatt-hour depend on how much elec-

tricity the customer uses, because of restrictions on the retransmission of electricity. If the company worries that large customers faced with the same high prices that it charges small customers might install their own electric generators or switch to some other energy source, it may charge them a lower price. An airline with a monopoly on a particular route might charge business customers a higher fare than vacationers. They do so knowing that business customers have no choice but to make the trip, while vacationers have many alternatives. They can travel elsewhere, on another day, or by car or train. Such business practices enable the monopolist to increase its profits relative to what they would be if it charged a single price in the market. Firms facing imperfect competition also engage in these practices as we will see. Airlines again provide a telling example.

IMPERFECT COMPETITION

In most markets, there is more than a single firm. In the perfectly competitive model of Part Two, firms compete against one another while believing they cannot affect the price—that if they raise their price, they will lose all their business. But outside agriculture, imperfect competition is more typical. Firms compete, often vigorously, against one another. But each believes that if it lowers its price, it can capture some but not all of the sales from other firms; and if it raises its price, it will lose some but not all of its customers. The first systematic analysis of imperfect competition was undertaken by Joan Robinson of the University of Cambridge whose seminal work *The Economics of Imperfect Competition* was published in 1933.

One way to assess the competitiveness of a particular market is to consider what will happen if a firm in that market raises its price. What percentage of its sales will it lose; in other words, what is its elasticity of demand? Firms in a perfectly competitive market face horizontal demand curves. The elasticity of demand for their output is infinite. By the same token, they are price takers. If they raise their price at all, they lose all their customers. They have no **market power,** a term meant to suggest the ability of a firm to throw its weight around, the way a monopoly can. As imperfect competition sets in, the demand curve facing a firm in the industry begins to slope downwards. The more downward sloping the demand curve, the more market power the firm has.

Two factors affect the elasticity of the demand curve facing a firm, and, therefore, its market power. The first is the number of firms in the industry, more generally, how concentrated production is within a few firms. The second is how different the goods produced by the various firms in the industry are.

NUMBER OF FIRMS IN THE INDUSTRY

Competition is likely to be greater when there are many firms in an industry than when a few companies dominate. Table 13.2 gives the percentage of output that is produced by the top five firms in a variety of industries ranging from hand tools to clothing, hats, and gloves. The fraction of output produced by the top five firms in an industry is called the **five-firm concentration ratio,** one of several measures used to study industry concentration. When the five-firm percentage is high, as in the tobacco industry, companies have considerable market power. This is true even when they produce similar or identical

Table 13.2 FIVE-FIRM CONCENTRATION RATIOS IN THE UNITED KINGDOM BASED ON NET OUTPUT IN 1992

Pharmaceutical products	51
Hand tools and finished metal goods	12
Telecommunications equipment	36
Motor vehicles and engines	84
Bread, biscuits, and flour confectionary	45
Tobacco	99
Clothing, hats, and gloves	20

Source: U.K. Department of Trade and Industry, "Census of Production," *Business Monitor* PA1002 (1995).

products. When it is low, as in the case of clothing, hats, and gloves, market power is low; each firm faces a practically horizontal demand curve.[3]

PRODUCT DIFFERENTIATION

In addition to the number of firms in a market—and how concentrated production is—the amount of competition depends on how similar the goods produced by different firms are. In some industries, the goods produced are essentially identical; iron produced by one firm is essentially the same as iron produced by any other. More typically, the firms in an industry with imperfect competition produce goods that are **imperfect substitutes**—goods sufficiently similar that they can be used for many of the same purposes but different enough that one may be somewhat better than another, at least for some purposes or in some people's minds. Kellogg's Corn Flakes and the supermarket's own brand may look alike. But many people purchase the Kellogg's version, even though it is more expensive.

The fact that similar products nonetheless differ from one another is referred to as **product differ-**

---

[3] In both theory and practice, a critical issue in evaluating the extent of competition is defining the relevant market, an issue taken up in Chapter 15.

entiation. Firms in imperfect markets spend considerable effort to produce goods that are slightly different from those of their competitors.

SOURCES OF PRODUCT DIFFERENTIATION

Many of the differences between products can be seen, heard, or tasted by consumers. But geography can also provide the basis for product differentiation. People are willing to pay more for milk at a nearby convenience store than at a supermarket farther away.

In cases where consumers find it difficult to assess the quality of a product before they purchase it, they rely heavily on firm reputations. They may buy a particular brand of aspirin even though it is more expensive than the supermarket's own brand, because they believe it is of a higher quality. In fact, aspirin itself is just acetylsalicylic acid, nothing more or less. Still, the binding agents that hold the pill together may differ, so the effects may differ. Consumers are often willing to pay more for goods with a trademark than for generic brands.

Ignorance and the costs of obtaining information often make the products of one firm an imperfect substitute for another. A consumer sees a dress for £45. She might know or suspect that some other store is selling the same dress for £35, but she does not know which other store, she is not sure it is in stock there, and it will take time to walk around looking for the store, and so she buys the dress at £45 anyway. If the store had raised its price to £55, she probably would have made the effort to search. If a store raises its prices, more customers decide to search out the bargains, and sales go down.

HOW PRODUCT DIFFERENTIATION IMPLIES IMPERFECT COMPETITION

When goods are perfect substitutes, individuals will choose whichever is cheapest. In an imaginary world where all brands of cornflakes are perfect substitutes for all consumers, they would all sell at the same price. If one brand lowered its price slightly, all consumers (assuming they knew this) would switch to it. If it raised its price slightly, all consumers would switch to a rival brand. That is why the demand curve facing the manufacturer of a perfectly substitutable good is horizontal, as illustrated in Figure 13.7A.

By contrast, if most consumers view the different brands as imperfect substitutes, the demand curve facing each firm will be downward sloping as in panel B. This, we have already learned, implies a departure from perfect competition. Some individuals may prefer sogginess and be willing to pay more for cornflakes that rapidly become soggy. Others may prefer crispness and be willing to pay more for cereal that does not become soggy. Assume that Kellogg's Corn Flakes become soggy more slowly than

Figure 13.7 DEMAND CURVES WITH PERFECT AND IMPERFECT COMPETITION

Panel A shows the demand curve for a perfectly competitive firm: if it raises its price, all its customers will find substitutes. The marginal revenue curve for the firm is the same as its demand curve. Panel B shows the demand curve and marginal revenue curve facing a firm with only imperfect substitutes for its products.

CLOSE-UP: IS *XEROX* THE SAME AS *PHOTOCOPY?*

You may have heard someone say, "I'm going to Xerox that document." What that person usually means is, "I'm going to photocopy that document on a machine that may or may not have been made by Xerox." Until the early 1970s, the Xerox company was almost synonymous with photocopying. The company had invented the photocopier, it held a group of more than 1,700 closely interrelated patents on the photocopying process, and it received about 95 percent of all copying machine sales in the United States.

In 1972, the Federal Trade Commission charged that Xerox was using its many patents as a way of monopolising the photocopy market. Instead of using the patents to protect a new invention for a limited amount of time, the FTC argued, Xerox was making them part of a strategy to monopolise the market indefinitely.

After several years of investigation and argument, a consent order was announced. Essentially, Xerox did not admit it had done anything wrong, but it agreed to change anyway. In July 1975, Xerox agreed to allow other competitors to use its patents and even to give its competitors access to some future patents. In addition, Xerox was required to drop all outstanding lawsuits against other companies for infringing on its patents. A spokesperson for the FTC maintained that these steps (and some others) would "eliminate the principal sources of Xerox's dominance of the office copier industry."

No longer fearing a lawsuit for infringing on a Xerox patent, entrants started pouring into the photocopy market, led by the Japanese firm Ricoh. The Ricoh DT1200 entered the market in 1975, and by 1976 Ricoh was the domestic market leader in copiers. Prices for photocopiers fell sharply. By 1980, Xerox was receiving only 46 percent of U.S. copier sales. Among the cheaper machines, the company held only 31 percent of the market. And the downward trend was continuing.

Through the 1980s, Xerox made several efforts to regain its growth path. It tried to move into the fields of computers and computer systems. It bought an insurance company and two investment banking firms. The move into computers was apparently more successful than the one into finance. As the 1990s began, the company was trying to sell off its financial subsidiaries and refocus its attention on laser printers and "smart" copying machines that could be linked with computers and fax machines. No longer collecting the profits of limited competition, Xerox had been transformed into another scrambling firm, worried about being surpassed by other firms and looking for an edge in the highly competitive market for office systems products.

Sources: Business Week, 16 December 1972, p. 24, 12 October 1981, p. 126, 13 February 1989, p. 90; *Wall Street Journal,* 17 April 1975, p. 8, 31 July 1975, p. 7; *Fortune,* 17 June 1991, p. 38.

---

the store brand. As the price for Kellogg's increases above that of the supermarket's own brand, individuals who care less about crispness will switch to the supermarket's brand. They are not willing to pay the price differential. But some are willing to pay a lot more for crisp flakes. Hence, Kellogg's does not lose all its customers, even if it charges considerably more than the supermarket brand. By the same token, when Kellogg's lowers its price below that of the supermarket brand, it does not steal all the customers. Those who love sogginess will pay more for the supermarket brand.

It matters little whether the differences between the brands are true or simply perceived differences.

BASES OF PRODUCT DIFFERENTIATION

1 Differences in characteristics of products produced by different firms

2 Differences in location of different firms

3 Perceived differences, often induced by advertising

The supermarket brand and Kellogg's Corn Flakes could be identical, but if Kellogg's advertisements have convinced some consumers that there is a difference, they will not switch even if the price of Kellogg's is higher. Numerous studies attest to the fact that consumers often see differences where none exist. One study put the same soap into two kinds of packages, one marked Brand A, the other marked Brand B. People were asked to judge which brand cleaned their clothes more effectively. Half saw no difference, but the other half claimed to see significant differences. Another study put the same beer into three kinds of bottles, one labeled premium, the second labeled standard, the third labeled discount. After drinking the differently bottled beers over an extended period of time, consumers were asked which they preferred. The "premium" beer was chosen consistently.

BARRIERS TO ENTRY: WHY IS COMPETITION LIMITED?

Normally, profits attract other firms to enter the market. For a monopoly to persist, some factors must prevent competition from springing up. Similarly, when there are profits with imperfect competition, some factors must prevent other firms' entering and eroding those profits. Such factors are called **barriers to entry.** They take a variety of forms, ranging from government rules that prohibit or limit competition (for reasons that may be good or bad), to technological reasons that naturally limit the number of firms in a market, to market strategies that keep potential competitors at bay.

When there are few barriers to entry, a monopoly can only be temporary; the profits of the monopolist will attract entry, and the firm's monopoly position will be lost. When there are many barriers, even if they only serve to delay entry, there *is* cause for concern, particularly when firms themselves take actions to create the barriers.

GOVERNMENT POLICIES

Many early monopolies were established by governments. In the seventeenth century, the British government gave the East India Company a monopoly on trade with India. The salt monopoly in eighteenth-century France had the exclusive right to sell salt. Even today, governments grant certain monopoly franchises. Most of the railways in Britain are operated by franchise holders that have local monopolies. Independent television services in the United Kingdom are franchised to companies who have local monopolies.

The most important monopolies granted by government today, however, are patents. As we learned in Chapter 1, a patent gives inventors the exclusive right to produce or to licence others to produce their discoveries for a limited period of time (20 years in the EU, 17 in the United States). The argument for patents is that without them, copycat firms would spring up with every new invention, inventors would make little money from their discoveries, and there would be no economic incentive to invent.

Occasionally governments set policies that restrict entry, allowing some but only limited competition. Licencing requirements in many of the professions (law, accounting, medicine), whose ostensible purpose is to protect consumers against incompetent practitioners, may at the same time limit the number of qualified practitioners, and thus limit competition.

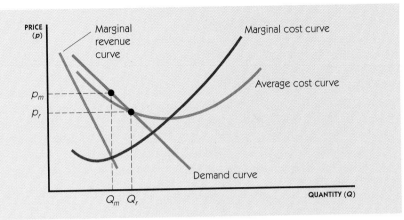

Figure 13.8 NATURAL MONOPOLY

In a natural monopoly, market demand intersects average costs in the downward-sloping portion of the average cost curve, at quantity Q_r and price p_r. Any firm that attempts to enter the market and produce less than Q_r will have higher average costs than the natural monopoly. Any firm that tries to enter the market and produce more than Q_r will find that it cannot sell all its output at a price that will cover its average costs.

SINGLE OWNERSHIP OF AN ESSENTIAL INPUT

Another barrier to entry and source of monopoly power is a firm's exclusive ownership of something that is not producible. For example, an aluminium company might attempt to become a monopolist in aluminium by buying all the sources of bauxite, the essential ingredient. A single South African company, De Beers, has come close to monopolising the world's supply of diamonds. There are in fact relatively few instances of such monopolies.

INFORMATION

Information does not pass through the economy in the full and complete way envisioned in the basic competitive model of Part Two. In considering barriers to entry, we encounter two of many ways that information—and the lack thereof—affects market outcomes. First, firms engage in research to give them a technological advantage over competitors. Even if they do not get a patent, it will take time before what they learn is disseminated to rivals. The fact that firms outside the industry do not know the trade secrets of the industry provides an important barrier to entry. Coca-Cola helps maintain its position in the soft-drink market by guarding its formula with the greatest care.

Second, consumers have imperfect information concerning the products being sold by different firms.

As a new firm, you must not only let potential buyers know about your product, you must convince them that your product is a better value than that of your rivals. When goods differ markedly in qualities that cannot easily be detected, it may not suffice simply to sell at a lower price. Customers may interpret the lower price as signaling lower quality. Thus, to get customers to try your product, you may have to advertise heavily and give away free samples. Entry costs like these constitute another significant barrier to entry.

ECONOMIES OF SCALE AND NATURAL MONOPOLIES

The technology needed to produce a good can sometimes result in a market with only one or very few firms. For example, until recently, if two electricity companies were to have competed in supplying electricity in a region, each would have needed to have had its own network of power supply cables. This would clearly have been inefficient. Similarly, in many regions there is only one supplier of cement. These situations are called **natural monopolies.**

A natural monopoly occurs whenever the average costs of production for a single firm are declining up to levels of output beyond those likely to emerge in the market. When the average costs of production fall as the scale of production increases, we say there are economies of scale, a concept first introduced in Chapter 10. In Figure 13.8, the demand curve facing a monopoly intersects the average cost curve at an output level at which average costs are still declining. At large enough outputs, average costs might start to increase, but that level of output is irrelevant to the actual market equilibrium. For instance, firms in the cement industry have U-shaped average cost curves, and the level of output at which costs are minimised is quite high. Accordingly, in smaller, isolated communities, there is a natural monopoly in cement.

A natural monopolist is protected by the knowledge that it can undercut its rivals should they enter. Since entrants typically are smaller and average costs decline with size, their average costs are higher. Therefore the monopolist feels relatively immune from the threat of entry. So long as it does not have to worry about entry, it acts like any other monopolist, setting marginal revenue equal to marginal cost, as in Figure 13.8, where it produces at the output Q_m and charges p_m.

Whether a particular industry is a natural monopoly depends on the size of the output at which average costs are minimised relative to the size of the market. With high enough demand, the monopolist will be operating along the rising part of the average cost curve. At this point, the monopolist can be undercut by an entrant, since a new firm that enters at the output at which average costs are minimised has costs that are lower. Thus, with high enough demand, the industry is no longer a natural monopoly. In populous regions, there may be several producers of cement, so that instead of a monopoly, there is an oligopoly.

Among the most important determinants of market size are transport costs. Among the most important determinants of the quantity of output at which average costs are minimised is the size of the fixed costs. The larger the expenditures of the firm just to begin production, the larger the scale of production at which average costs are minimised.

Fixed costs also help explain why only a limited number of firms produce each variety of a good and why the variety of goods is limited. Setting up dyes to make a slight variant of an existing car, for example, may be very expensive. Automobile companies tend to produce cars in only a limited range of colours. Some individuals might prefer a car that is bright orange but most car manufacturers do not offer this option. Presumably this is because they realise that additional costs to paint some cars bright orange would exceed the marginal revenue they would receive from providing this option.

Because both technology and transportation costs may change over time, the number of firms in a market may change. Long-distance telephone service used to be a natural monopoly. Telephone messages were transmitted over wires, and it would have been inefficient to duplicate wires. As the demand for telephone services increased, and as alternative technologies like satellites developed, long-distance service ceased to be a natural monopoly. Several major firms compete to provide long-distance services. Further technical advances have allowed the introduction of competition in local telephone services, even though they continue to use wires.

MARKET STRATEGIES

Some monopolies and oligopolies cannot be explained by any of the factors discussed so far. They are not the result of government policies and are not natural monopolies; nor can information problems explain the lack of entry. Many firms, whose original monopoly position may have been based on some technological innovation or patent, manage to maintain their dominant positions even after their patents expire, at least for a time. Kodak, Polaroid, and IBM are three examples. These firms maintained their dominant positions by the pursuit of market strategies that deterred other firms from entering their market.

When a company thinks about entering an industry dominated by a single firm, it must assess not only the current level of profits being earned by that firm but also what profits will be like after it has entered. If a potential entrant believes that the incumbent firm is likely to respond to entry by lowering its price and fighting a fierce competitive battle, then the potential newcomer may come to believe that while prices and profits look high now, they are likely to drop precipitously if it actually does enter the market.

Established firms would thus like to pursue a strategy to convince potential entrants that even though they are currently making high levels of profits, these profits will disappear should the new firm enter the market. There are three major ways to create this belief, collectively called **entry-deterring practices:** predatory pricing, excess capacity, and limit pricing.

Predatory Pricing If prices have fallen drastically in a certain market every time there has been entry in the past, then new firms may be reluctant to enter. This is because an incumbent firm may deliberately lower its price below the new entrant's cost of production, in order to drive the new arrival out and discourage future entry. The incumbent may lose money in the process, but it hopes to recoup the losses when the entrant leaves and it is free to raise prices to the monopoly level. This practice is called **predatory pricing** and is an illegal trade practice. However, shifting technologies and shifting demand often make it difficult to ascertain whether a firm has actually engaged in predatory pricing or simply lowered its price to meet the competition. Firms that lower their prices always claim that they were forced to do so by their competitors.

In the famous case in the British courts in 1992, British Airways (BA) was sued by Richard Branson over "dirty tricks" in its competition with his airline, Virgin Atlantic. While Branson did everything possible to avoid becoming involved in a price war with BA, the tactics used by BA were certainly viewed as predatory. The BA sales staff posed as Virgin staff and poached customers away from Virgin with offers of special deals on BA flights (like Concord). The BA staff hacked into Virgin's computers to get information on Virgin passengers. British Airways dismissed Branson's claims of dirty tricks as a publicity ploy, for which libel it eventually paid over half a million pounds in damages to Richard Branson (*The Economist*, 30 January 1993).

Excess Capacity Another action firms can take to convince potential rivals that prices are likely to fall if they enter the market is to build up production facilities in excess of those currently needed. By building extra plants and equipment, even if they are rarely used, a firm poses an extra threat to potential entrants. A newcomer will look at this **excess capacity** and realise that the incumbent firm can increase production a great deal with minimal effort. The excess capacity serves as a signal that the incumbent is willing and able to engage in fierce price competition.

Limit Pricing Other strategies for deterring entry involve clever patterns of pricing. A potential entrant may know what price is charged on the market and may have a good idea of its own costs of production. But it is not likely to know precisely the cost curve of the incumbent firm. The established firm can try to persuade potential entrants that its marginal cost is low and that it could easily reduce its price if threatened with a new entrant to the market.

Suppose a potential entrant knows that a monopolist firm's marginal revenue is 70 percent of price. If the monopolist charges a price of £10, then the marginal revenue (the extra revenue from selling one more unit) is £7. Reasoning that the monopolist is setting marginal revenue equal to marginal cost, the

BARRIERS TO ENTRY

Government policies: These include grants of monopoly (patents) and restrictions on entry (licencing).

Single ownership of an essential input: When a single firm owns the entire supply of a nonproducible input, entry is by definition precluded.

Information: Lack of technical information by potential competitors inhibits their entry; lack of information by consumers concerning the quality of a new entrant's product discourages consumers from switching to the new product, and thus inhibits entry.

Economies of scale: With a natural monopoly, economies of scale are so strong that it is efficient to have only one firm in an industry.

Market strategies: These include policies (such as predatory pricing, excess capacity, and limit pricing) aimed at convincing potential entrants that entry would be met with resistance, and thus would be unprofitable.

potential entrant might use a £7 marginal cost figure in deciding whether it pays to enter.

The monopolist is aware that such a calculation is probably going on. Thus, it has an incentive to make its costs look lower than they are, and hence to make entry look less attractive than it really is. It can do this by setting its price below its marginal cost. If it can persuade the potential entrant that marginal cost has to be below £6 (rather than £7) for entry to be profitable, it has protected its monopoly position that much better.

This is an example of a broader practice known as **limit pricing,** in which firms charge less than the ordinary monopoly price and produce at a level beyond that at which marginal revenue equals marginal cost because they are afraid that at higher prices, entry will be encouraged. This may happen simply because a firm realises that high profits attract attention. The greater attention focused on a market, the more likely it is that some entrepreneur will believe that entry is profitable.

Some entry-deterring devices, such as maintaining excess capacity, may be socially wasteful. Others, such as limit pricing, will benefit consumers, at least in the short run, though the long-run deleterious effects of monopoly or limited competition remain.

EQUILIBRIUM WITH MONOPOLISTIC COMPETITION

Barriers to entry are sufficiently weak in some markets that firms enter to the point where profits are driven to zero. But even then competition is imperfect if products are differentiated. With each firm producing a slightly different product, each faces a downward-sloping demand curve. In this section, we analyse the case where fixed costs are sufficiently large to ensure that each firm faces a downward-sloping demand curve but there are *enough* firms so that each firm can ignore the consequences of its actions on others. This is the case of monopolistic competition, first analysed by Edward Chamberlin of Harvard University in 1933.

Figure 13.9 illustrates a market in which there is monopolistic competition. Assume initially that all firms are charging the same price, say p_1. If one firm

were to charge a slightly lower price, it would steal some customers away from other firms. If there were 20 firms in the market, this price-cutting firm would attract more than one-twentieth of the total market demand. But if it should raise its price above that of its rivals, it would lose customers to them. Each firm assumes that the prices charged by other firms will remain unchanged as it changes its price or the quantity it produces. The demand curve facing each firm is thus the one shown in the figure.

In deciding how much to produce, the firm sets marginal revenue equal to marginal cost. The market equilibrium is (p_1, Q_1), with marginal revenue's equaling marginal cost. In the equilibrium depicted in Figure 13.9, price exceeds average costs. One can think of this situation as a sort of minimonopoly, where each firm has a monopoly on its own brand name or its own store location.

But if existing firms are earning monopoly profits, there is an incentive for new competitors to enter the market until profits are driven to zero, as in the perfectly competitive model. *This is the vital distinction between monopolies and monopolistic competition.* In both cases, firms face downward-sloping demand curves. In both cases, they set marginal revenue equal to marginal cost. But in monopolistic competition, there is entry. Entry continues so long as profits are positive. As firms enter, the share of the industry demand of each firm is reduced. The demand curve facing each firm thus shifts to the left, as depicted in panel B. This process continues until the demand curve just touches the average cost curve, at point (p_e, Q_e). At that point, profits are zero.

Figure 13.9 also shows the firm's marginal revenue and marginal cost curves. As we have said, the firm sets its marginal revenue equal to its marginal cost. This occurs at exactly the level of output at which the demand curve is tangent to the average cost curve. This is because at any other point, average costs exceed price, so profits are negative. Only at this point are profits zero. Accordingly, this is the profit-maximising output.

The monopolistic competition equilibrium has some interesting characteristics. Notice that in equilibrium, price and average costs exceed the minimum average costs at which the goods could be produced. *Less is produced at a higher price.* But there is a trade-off here. Whereas in the perfectly competitive market every product was a perfect substitute for every other

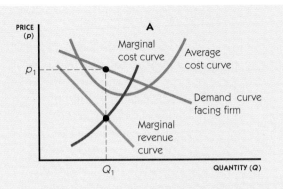
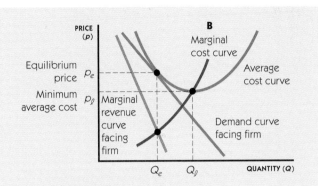

Figure 13.9 PROFIT MAXIMISING FOR A MONOPOLISTIC COMPETITOR

A monopolistic competitor chooses the quantity it will produce by setting marginal revenue equal to marginal cost, and then selling that quantity (Q_1) for the price given on its demand curve (p_1). In panel A, the price charged is above average costs, and the monopolistic competitor is making profits, enticing other firms to enter the market. As firms enter, the share of the market demand of each firm is reduced, and the demand curve facing each firm shifts to the left. Entry continues until the demand curve just touches the average cost curve (panel B). When the firm produces Q_e, it just breaks even; there is no incentive either for entry or exit.

one, in the world of monopolistic competition there is variety in the products available. People value variety and are willing to pay a higher price to obtain it. Thus, the fact that goods are sold at a price above the minimum average costs does not necessarily mean that the economy is inefficient.

Whether the market results in too little or too much product variety remains a contested subject. Either can occur. The important point to realise here is that there is a trade-off. Greater variety can only be obtained at greater cost.

SCHUMPETERIAN COMPETITION

The famous Harvard economist Joseph Schumpeter envisaged a rather different form of monopolistic competition from that which we have discussed above. He saw different markets dominated at different times by one or two firms, depending on which had technological superiority. But the dominant firms are also constantly subjected to competition for supremacy as new innovations supplant old. Even when the lead firm is not supplanted by a competing one, the threat of entry keeps the lead firm on its toes.

While each company dominates the market, it acts like a monopolist: it sets marginal revenue equal to marginal cost, producing less than would be produced under perfect competition. But if it wishes to maintain its position, the firm must reinvest profits in further expenditures to make new products and to develop new, cheaper ways of producing.

In Schumpeter's view, the disadvantage of the monopoly aspects of imperfect markets—the reduction in output—was more than offset by the advantages of the greater research the extra profits funded. Chapter 17 will take a closer look at these questions.

CLOSE-UP: IBM—FROM THE EDGE OF MONOPOLY TO THE EDGE OF COMPETITION

IBM committed itself to computers in the 1950s and rapidly asserted its dominance in the business of large mainframe computers. IBM machines were often the most technologically advanced, and in the few cases where they might not have been the best, they still had an extraordinary reputation for great service and support. Back in the days when computers were more than a little mysterious to most of their users, that reputation mattered a lot.

IBM was never a literal monopoly. Throughout the 1960s and 1970s, competition came from firms like Control Data, Honeywell, Sperry Univac, Burroughs, and NCR. But by 1980, IBM still had over 80 percent of the world market for mainframe computers. It was common for the company's sales to grow every year by double-digit percentages.

But by the early 1990s, its market share had slipped dramatically. In 1990, it had only 15 percent of the fastest-growing segment of the market, personal computers. Upstarts—Apple, Compaq, Dell, AST—as well as foreign producers—NEC and Toshiba—dominated the market. IBM was forced to make dramatic cutbacks. For the first time in its history, there were massive layoffs. It engaged in large-scale restructuring, trying to make itself nimble enough to compete in the fast-moving market. Less than two decades after the Justice Department had tried to break up IBM, charging that it was too close to a monopoly, it was scrambling for market share. It is a real-world example of Schumpeter's vision of markets with dominant firms only able to maintain their position temporarily in the face of intense technological competition from new entrants.

REVIEW AND PRACTICE

SUMMARY

1 Economists isolate four broad categories of market structure: perfect competition, monopoly, oligopoly, and monopolistic competition (the last two are collectively referred to as imperfect competition).

2 A perfectly competitive firm faces a horizontal demand curve; it is a price taker. In markets in which there is imperfect or no competition, each firm faces a downward-sloping demand curve and is a price maker.

3 Both monopolists and firms facing perfect competition maximise profit by producing at the quantity where marginal revenue is equal to marginal cost. However, marginal revenue for a perfect competitor is the same as the market price of an extra unit, while marginal revenue for a monopolist is less than the market price.

4 Since with a monopoly, price exceeds marginal revenue, buyers pay more for the product than the marginal cost to produce it; there is less production in a monopoly than there would be if price were set equal to marginal cost.

5 Imperfect competition occurs when a relatively small number of firms dominate the market and/or when firms produce goods that are differentiated by their characteristics, by the location of the firms, or in the perception of consumers.

6 Monopolies and imperfect competition may be sustained by either natural or human-made barriers to entry.

7 With monopolistic competition, barriers to entry are sufficiently weak that entry occurs until profits are driven to zero; there are few enough firms that each faces a downward-sloping demand curve, but a sufficiently large number of firms that each ignores its rivals' reactions to what it does.

KEY TERMS

monopoly

oligopoly

monopolistic competition

imperfect competition

pure profit or monopoly rents

price discrimination

product differentiation

barriers to entry

natural monopoly

predatory pricing

limit pricing

REVIEW QUESTIONS

1 What is the difference between perfect and imperfect competition? Between oligopoly and monopolistic competition?

2 Why is price equal to marginal revenue for a perfectly competitive firm but not for a monopolist with imperfect competition?

3 How should a monopoly choose its quantity of production to maximise profits? Explain why producing either less or more than the level of output at which marginal revenue equals marginal cost will reduce profits. Since a monopolist need not fear competition, what prevents it from raising its price as high as it wishes to make higher profits?

4 What are the primary sources of product differentiation?

5 What are barriers to entry? Describe the principal ones.

6 What is a natural monopoly?

7 Describe market equilibrium under monopolistic competition. Why does the price charged by the typical firm exceed the minimum average costs, even though there is entry?

PROBLEMS

1 Explain how it is possible that at a high enough level of output, if a monopoly produced and sold more, its revenue would actually decline.

2 Assume there is a single firm producing cigarettes and the marginal cost of producing cigarettes is a constant. Suppose the government imposes a 10-pence tax on each pack of cigarettes. If the demand curve for cigarettes is linear, will the price rise by more or less than the tax?

3 Describe possible strategies a furniture firm might use to differentiate its products.

4 Suppose a petrol station on a busy road is surrounded by many competitors, all of whom sell identical petrol. Draw the demand curve the petrol station faces, and draw its marginal and average cost curves. Explain the rule for maximising profit in this situation. Now imagine that the petrol station offers a new additive called zoomol and begins an advertising campaign that says: "Get zoomol in your petrol." No other station offers zoomol. Draw the demand curve faced by the station after this advertising campaign. Explain the rule for maximising profit in this situation, and illustrate it with an appropriate diagram.

5 Explain how consumers may benefit from predatory pricing and limit pricing in the short run but not in the long run.

6 Why might it make sense for a monopolist to choose a point on the demand curve where the price is somewhat lower than the price at which marginal revenue equals marginal cost?

APPENDIX A: MONOPSONY

In any market, imperfections of competition can arise on either the buyer or seller side. In this chapter, we have focused on imperfect competition among the sellers of goods. When there is a single buyer in a market, the buyer is called a **monopsonist.** Though monopsonies are relatively rare, they do exist. The government is a monopsonist in the market for a variety of high-technology defence systems.

In some labour markets, a single firm may be close to a monopsonist. In many markets, an employer may face an upward-sloping supply curve for labour, or at least labour with particular skills. Firms that dominate the town or region in which they are located, as the coal industry (run by the British Coal Board or British Coal) used to do in the valleys of South Wales, for example, are likely to face an upward-sloping supply curve for labour.

The consequences of monopsony are similar to those of monopoly. The basic rule remains: produce at the point where marginal revenue equals marginal cost. The buyer firm is aware, however, that if it buys more units, it will have to pay a higher price. Then if the firm cannot price discriminate, the marginal cost of buying one more unit is not only what the company has to pay for the last unit but also the higher price it must pay for all previously purchased units.

In the case of a labour market, Figure 13.10 illustrates the consequence. Chapter 11 showed that in competitive markets, firms hire labour up to the point where the value of the marginal product of labour (*MPL*) equals the wage, the marginal cost of hiring an additional worker. Figure 13.10 shows the curve that represents the value of the marginal product of labour; it declines as the number of workers hired increases. Figure 13.10 also shows the labour supply curve, which is upward sloping. From this, the firm can calculate the marginal cost of hiring an additional worker, the wage *plus* the increase in wage payments to all previously hired workers. Clearly, the marginal cost curve lies above the labour supply curve. The firm hires workers up to the point L^*, where the value of the marginal product of labour is equal to the marginal cost. Employment is lower than it would have been had the firm ignored the fact that as it hires more labour, the wage it pays increases.

APPENDIX B: DEMAND FOR INPUTS UNDER MONOPOLY AND IMPERFECT COMPETITION

In Chapter 11, we saw that competitive firms hire labour up to the point where the value of the marginal product (the value of what an extra hour of

Figure 13.10 MONOPSONY

As a monopsonist buys more of an input, it must pay not only a higher price for the marginal unit but a higher price for all the units it buys; thus, the marginal cost of buying an input exceeds the price. The monopsonist sets the marginal cost of the input equal to the value of its marginal product at employment level L^* and sets the wage at w_m. In a competitive labour market, a firm hires labour up to point L_c, at wage w_c. Thus, a monopsonist hires less labour at a lower wage than competitive firms would.

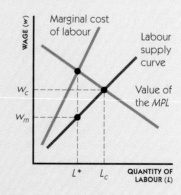

Figure 13.11 MARGINAL REVENUE PRODUCT CURVE

Firms hire labour up to the point where the marginal revenue product of an extra worker equals the marginal cost. In a competitive labour market, the marginal cost of labour is just the wage.

labour would produce) is equal to the wage. Similarly, any other factor of production is hired up to the point where the value of its marginal product is equal to its price. From this, we could derive the demand curve for labour (or any other input).

A quite similar analysis applies with imperfect competition. A monopolist hires labour up to the point where the extra revenue it produces—what economists call the marginal revenue product—is equal to the wage. In competitive markets, the value of the marginal product is just equal to the price of the output times the marginal physical product, the extra quantity that is produced. In a monopoly, the marginal revenue product (MRP) is equal to the marginal revenue yielded by producing one more unit

(MR) times the marginal physical product (MPP): $MRP = MR \times MPP$.

The quantity of labour that will be hired is illustrated in Figure 13.11, which shows the marginal revenue product curve. It is downward sloping, for two reasons: the more that is produced, the smaller the marginal physical product (this is just the law of diminishing returns), and the more that is produced, the smaller the marginal revenue. The firm hires labour up to the point where the marginal revenue product equals the wage, point L_0. If the wage increases from w_0 to w_1, the amount of labour hired will fall, from L_0 to L_1. Thus, the demand curve for labour is downward sloping with imperfect competition, just as it is with perfect competition.

CHAPTER 14

OLIGOPOLIES

In industries characterised by monopolistic competition, there are enough firms that each assumes its actions have no effect on the actions of its competitors. But in many industries, called oligopolies, there are so few firms that each worries about how its rivals will react to anything it does. This is true of the airline, cigarette, aluminium, automobile, and a host of other industries. Airlines that offer frequent flier bonuses, for instance, can expect their competitors to respond with similar offers.

If an oligopolist lowers its price, it worries that rivals will do the same and it will gain no competitive advantage. Worse still, a competitor may react to a price cut by engaging in a price war and cutting the price still further. Different oligopolies behave in quite different ways. The oligopolist is always torn between its desire to outwit competitors and the knowledge that by cooperating with other oligopolists to reduce output, it will earn a portion of the higher industry profits.

This chapter examines the key question facing an oligopolistic firm—whether it will earn higher profits colluding with rivals to restrict output or competing with rivals by charging lower prices. The analysis of oligopoly behaviour is divided into three sections. The first discusses collusion, or cooperation, and the problems firms confront in colluding. The second shows how firms may restrict competition, even when they do not formally collude. The third describes what happens if firms in an oligopoly compete.

1 Under what conditions will the firms in an industry collude in order to charge high prices? What are the incentives to collude?

2 What practices do firms in an oligopoly engage in to restrict the force of competition and hence increase their profits?

3 What are the main forms that competition among oligopolists takes? How do they compare in terms of the level of prices and output, and how the market responds to changes in economic conditions?

COLLUSION

In come cases, oligopolists try to **collude** to maximise their profits. In effect, they act jointly as if they were a monopoly and split up the resulting profits. The prevalence of collusion was long ago noted by Adam Smith, the founder of modern economics: "People of the same trade seldom meet together, even for merriment and diversion, but the conversation ends in a conspiracy against the public, or in some contrivance to raise prices."[1] A group of companies that formally operate in collusion is called a **cartel.** The Organization of Petroleum Exporting Countries (OPEC), for instance, acts collusively to restrict the output of oil, to raise oil prices and hence the profits of member countries.

In the late nineteenth century, in the United States two or more railroads ran between many major cities. When they competed vigorously, profits were low. So it did not take them long to discover that if they acted collusively, they could raise profits by raising prices.

In 1994 the European Commission found 32 European cement producers guilty of having used secret agreements to rig the market for over ten years. They were accused of colluding to reduce price differences between European Union member states, to remove temptations to undermine local monopolies. The commission obtained records of their secret

[1] *The Wealth of Nations*, Book 1, Chapter 10, Part II.

meetings. But while cartels increase industry profits, it is hard to maintain the cooperative behaviour required. We now look at three problems facing cartels.

THE PROBLEM OF SELF-ENFORCEMENT

Cartels seek to restrict output and thus to raise prices above marginal cost. The central difficulty facing cartels is that it pays any single member of the cartel to cheat. That is, if all other members of the cartel restrict output, so that price exceeds marginal cost, it pays the last member of the cartel to increase its output and take advantage of the higher price. This firm is said to be free riding on the cartel; the other firms pay the price of collusion by restricting their output, while the free rider gets the higher price without giving up any sales. But if too many members of a cartel cheat by increasing their output beyond the agreed-upon levels, the cartel breaks down. This happened to the OPEC oil cartel during the 1980s. Producers (other than Saudi Arabia) systematically increased production beyond their allotted quotas.

The incentives for any member of a cartel to cheat are illustrated in Figure 14.1, in which all members of a cartel face the same constant marginal cost. The figure shows the market demand curve and the output Q_c and price p_c at which the cartel's joint profits are maximised; that is, where marginal revenue for the cartel as a whole equals marginal cost. But the marginal revenue for the cartel as a whole is not the marginal revenue for any one firm. Any firm thinks it can cheat on the cartel and get away with it. If it shaves its price just lower than p_c and increases its

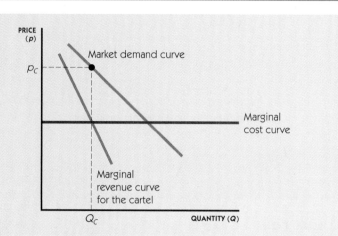

Figure 14.1 INCENTIVES TO CHEAT ON A CARTEL

The existence of a large gap between price and marginal cost provides a strong incentive for each member of a cartel to cheat; p_c is the cartel price.

production, it makes a profit of approximately p_c minus the marginal cost on that additional unit. With a large gap between price and marginal cost, the incentive to cheat is strong.

A factor that further encourages some members of a cartel to cheat on the collusive agreement is that members frequently believe they are not getting their fair share. This problem has plagued the OPEC oil cartel. Each country within the cartel faces different economic circumstances. Oil-rich skeikdoms have per capita incomes among the highest in the world. But for poor countries like Indonesia, oil revenues are a potential resource for development. No simple principles exist to help these countries decide how much each should produce or who should bear the burden of cutting back production in order to sustain a high market price. Those who feel they are being unfairly treated are most likely to try to cheat on the collusive agreement.

Thus, the first major problem facing cartels is how to enforce their collusive arrangement on their members. This self-enforcement is a particular problem in countries of the European Union, the United States, and elsewhere where laws have been passed that prohibit collusive behaviour. This makes it impossible for firms to get together and sign legally binding contracts that would require each firm to keep output low and prices high.

But the profits from collusion can be so great that firms have taken the risks involved in violating the

law. In 1994, 16 European steel companies were heavily fined by the EC for operating a cartel to raise steel prices.

THE PROBLEM OF COORDINATION

In countries where explicit collusion is illegal, members of an oligopoly who wish to take advantage of their market power must rely on **tacit collusion.** Tacit collusion is an implicit understanding that the oligopoly's interests are best served if its members do not compete too vigorously and particularly if they avoid price cutting. However, the interests of particular firms may not coincide exactly. And an implicit agreement by its very nature makes it difficult to specify what each firm should do in every situation. When cost or demand curves shift, perhaps because of changes in technology or changes in tastes, the members of a cartel need to get together to agree upon the appropriate changes in output and prices. A new technology or development may benefit one firm more than another, and that firm will wish to increase output more than the others. If the oligopolists could bargain together openly, they might be able to make a deal. But since the law prohibits them from such a straightforward solution, inventive oligopolists have developed a number of ways to circumvent this coordination problem.

One approach is for a particular firm to become the **price leader.** That firm, often the second- or third-largest member of the industry, sets the price, and others follow. According to some economists, American Airlines used to be the price leader in the U.S. airline industry. As costs (say, of fuel) or demand conditions changed in the airline industry, American would announce new fare structures, and the other airlines would simply match them. It is hard to prove that collusion has occurred in this type of sequence; the firms simply claim that they are responding to similar market forces.

Yet another approach is to develop **facilitating practices** that serve to make collusion easier. One example is the "meeting-the-competition clause," in which at least some members of the oligopoly commit themselves, often in advertisements, to charging no more than any competitor. The department stores in the John Lewis Partnership use the slogan "never knowingly undersold." To the consumer, this looks like a great deal. To see why this practice may actually lead to higher prices, think about it from the perspective of rival firms. Assume that the department store is selling for £100 an item that costs the store £90; its selling costs are £5, so it is making a £5 profit on the sale. Consider another store that would like to steal some customers away. It would be willing to sell the item for £95, undercutting the first store. But then it reasons that if it cuts its price, it will not gain any customers, since the first store has already guaranteed to match the lower price. Further, the second store knows that it will make less money on each sale to its current customers. Price cutting simply does not pay. It thus appears that a practice that seemingly is highly competitive in fact may facilitate collusion.

In many cases, oligopolists create a variety of cooperative arrangements that involve sharing inventories, research findings, or other information. In electronics and other high-technology industries, exchanging research information is particularly important. Any firm that cheated on the collusive price arrangement would find itself cut out from these cooperative arrangements.

THE PROBLEM OF ENTRY

The third major problem cartels face is similar to the problem faced by a monopolist. High profits enjoyed by the members of the cartel attract entry from other firms or cause nonmembers of the cartel to expand production. This was one of the fates that befell OPEC. When its members raised the price of oil, noncartel countries like the United Kingdom, Canada, and Mexico increased their production of oil.

Some economists, such as William Baumol of New York and Princeton Universities, have argued that in some markets just the threat of entry is strong enough to keep prices low, even if a firm controls over 90 percent of the market. If prices were ever so slightly above costs of production, there would be rapid entry, forcing prices down. In these cases, **potential competition,** the possibility of entry, is sufficient to keep prices low. The costs of entry and exit have to be relatively small, however, for potential competition to be effective. Otherwise, firms will not enter, even when they see high prices, unless they have reason to believe that prices will remain high after entry.

Markets such as these, in which potential competition suffices to ensure competitive prices, are called **contestable.** At one time, advocates of the theory of contestable markets used airlines in the United States as the basic example of a contestable entry. An airline could easily enter a market in which price exceeded costs (for example, the San Francisco–Los Angeles market), and thus potential competition would ensure low prices, even when there

LIMITS TO COLLUSION

Self-enforcement; incentives for each firm to cheat

Coordination problems in responding to changed economic circumstances

Entry

were only one or two airlines flying a particular route. But by the end of the 1980s, as airline prices skyrocketed on many routes on which competition was limited, potential competition did not seem strong enough to keep prices down. Potential entrants recognised that there were significant costs to entering a market—customers had to be informed, they had to be persuaded to switch from the usual carrier, airline offices had to be opened, and so forth—and experience had taught them that once they entered, prices would fall, making it impossible for them to recover these costs.

It is remarkable how many oligopolies persist with limited entry. There has been some entry into the film industry (Fuji), but it remains dominated by a few firms. Other oligopolies, such as the automobile, cigarette, and aluminium industries, have remained relatively intact over long periods of time. Even the number of attempts at entry has been limited. This suggests that if the barriers to entry discussed in Chapter 13 are strong enough, as appears to be the case in many situations, potential entry may provide an adequate threat to prevent firms from charging prices in excess of costs.

GAME THEORY: THE PRISONER'S DILEMMA

In recent years, economists have used a branch of mathematics called game theory to study collusion among oligopolists. The participants in a game are allowed to make certain moves, defined by the rules of the game. The outcomes of the game—what each participant receives—are referred to as its payoffs and depend on what each player does. Each participant in the game chooses a strategy; he decides what moves to make. In games in which each player has the chance to make more than one move (there is more than one round, or period), moves can depend on what has happened in previous periods. Game theory begins with the assumption that each player in the game is rational and knows that his rival is rational. Each is trying to maximise his own payoff. The theory then tries to predict what each player will

do. The answer depends on the rules of the game and the payoffs.

One example of such a game is called the **Prisoner's Dilemma.** Two prisoners, A and B, alleged to be conspirators in a crime, are put into separate rooms. A police officer goes into each room and makes a little speech: "Now here's the situation. If your partner confesses and you remain silent, you'll get five years in prison. But if your partner confesses and you confess also, you'll only get three years. On the other hand, perhaps your partner remains silent. If you're quiet also, we can only send you to prison for one year. But if your partner remains silent and you confess, we'll let you out in three months. So if your partner confesses, you are better off confessing, and if your partner doesn't confess, you are better off confessing. Why not confess?" This deal is offered to both prisoners.

The following diagram shows the results of this deal. The upper left-hand box, for example, shows the result if both A and B confess. The upper right-hand box shows the result if prisoner A remains silent but prisoner B confesses. And so on.

		Prisoner A	
		Confess	Remain silent
Prisoner B	Confess	A: 3 years B: 3 years	A: 5 years B: 3 months
	Remain silent	A: 3 months B: 5 years	A: 1 year B: 1 year

From the combined standpoint of the two prisoners, the best option is clearly that they both remain silent and each serve one year. But the self-interest of each individual prisoner says that confession is best, whether his partner confesses or not. However, if they both follow their self-interest and confess, they both end up worse off, each serving three years. The Prisoner's Dilemma is a simple game in which both parties are made worse off by independently following their own self-interest. Both would be better off if they could get together to agree on a story and to threaten the other if he deviated from the story.

The Prisoner's Dilemma comes up in a variety of contexts. For example, during the years of the Cold

War, the arms race between the United States and the former U.S.S.R. was described in these terms. Each party reasoned that if the other side built weapons, it needed to match the buildup. And if the other side did not build, it could acquire an advantage by building. Even though both sides might have been better off by agreeing not to build, their incentives pushed them towards a situation where both continued to do so.

The game can also be directly applied to collusion between two oligopolists. Assume that both firms agree to cut back their production, so they obtain higher prices and higher profits. But each oligopolist reasons the following way. Whether my rival cheats or not, it pays for me to expand production. If my rival cheats, then he gets all the advantages of my restricting output but pays none of the price. And if he does not cheat and keeps production low, it pays for me to cheat. As both firms reason that way, production expands and prices fall to a level below that at which their joint profits are maximised.

In the examples of the Prisoner's Dilemma presented so far, each party makes only one decision. But if firms (or countries) interact over time, then they have additional ways to try to enforce their agreement. For example, suppose each oligopolist announces that it will refrain from cutting prices as long as its rival does. But if the rival cheats on the collusive agreement, then the first oligopolist will respond by increasing production and lowering prices. Won't this threat ensure that the two firms cooperate?

Consider what happens if the two firms expect to compete in the same market over the next ten years, after which time a new product is expected to come along and shift the entire configuration of the industry. It will pay each firm to cheat in the tenth year, when there is no possibility of retaliation, because the industry will be completely altered in the next year. Now consider what happens in the ninth year. Both firms can figure out that it will not pay either one of them to cooperate in the tenth year. But if they are not going to cooperate in the tenth year anyway, then the *threat* of not cooperating in the future is completely ineffective. Hence in the ninth year, each firm will reason that it pays to cheat on the collusive agreement by producing more than the agreed-upon amount. Collusion breaks down in the ninth year. Reasoning backwards through time, this logic will lead collusion to break down almost immediately.

Economists have tried to set up laboratory experiments, much like those used by other sciences, to test how individuals actually behave in these different games. The advantage of this sort of **experimental economics** is that the researcher can change one aspect of what is going on at a time, to try to determine what are the crucial determinants of behaviour. One set of experiments has looked at how individuals cooperate with one another in situations like the Prisoner's Dilemma. These experiments have a tendency to show that participants often evolve simple strategies that, although they may appear irrational in the short run, can be effective in inducing cooperation (collusion) as the game is repeated a number of times. One common strategy is tit for tat. If you increase your output, I will do the same, even if doing so does not maximise my profits. If the rival firm believes this threat, especially after it has been carried out a few times, the rival may decide that it is more profitable to cooperate and keep production low rather than to cheat. In the real world, such simple strategies may play an important role in ensuring that firms do not compete too vigorously in those markets where there are only three or four dominant firms.

RESTRICTIVE PRACTICES

If members of an oligopoly could easily get together and collude, they would. Their joint profits would thereby be increased. They would have a problem of how to divide the profits, but each of the members of the oligopoly could be better off than it would be if they competed. We have seen, however, that there are significant impediments to collusion. If the members of an industry cannot collude to stop competition and cannot prevent entry, at least they can act to reduce competition and deter entry.

Chapter 13 described some of the ways firms act to deter entry. Here, we look at practices firms engage in that **may** serve to *restrict* competition, called **restrictive practices.** While these practices may not be quite as successful in increasing profits for the firms as the collusive arrangements already discussed, they do succeed in raising prices. In some cases, consumers may be even worse off than with outright collusion. Many restrictive practices are aimed at the wholesalers and retailers who sell a producer's goods. When one firm buys or sells another firm's products, the two companies are said to have a vertical relationship. Such restrictive practices are called **vertical restrictions,** as opposed to the price-fixing arrangements among producers or among wholesalers in a local market, which are referred to as **horizontal restrictions.**

An example of a vertical restriction is **dealership arrangements.** A car manufacturer, for instance, gives a particular garage in an area the right to act as a dealer for that make of car. The dealer is the only supplier of new cars of that make in that area, and it may also be the sole supplier of authorised servicing and repair of these cars. The dealer's mechanics may, for example, be provided with training by the manufacturer. The dealer will usually be the only supplier in the area of spare parts from the manufacturer. Manufacturers try to get dealers spread across the economy, spaced far enough apart for each to have a reasonably large market without competing for business with adjacent dealers but close enough together to ensure that there is a dealer reasonably close to any potential customer. This is a way of limiting competition between dealers for a particular make of car and preventing prices from being reduced by competition.

These arrangements reduce the amount of intrabrand competition—the competition between, say, Volkswagen dealers—but it might increase the amount of interbrand competition—the competition between, say, Volkswagen and Ford dealers.

Another example of a restrictive practice is **exclusive dealing,** in which a producer insists that any firm selling its products not sell those of its rivals.

When you go into a Shell petrol station, for instance, you can be sure you are buying petrol refined by Shell, not Texaco or Mobil. Like most refiners, Shell insists that stations that want to sell Shell sell only its brand of petrol.

A third example of a restrictive practice is **tie-ins,** in which a customer who buys one product must buy another. British banks usually insist that people who take out a mortgage with them also use the bank's insurance policies. Nintendo designs its console so that it can only be used with Nintendo games. In effect, it forces a tie-in sale between the console and the computer games. In the early days of computers, IBM designed its computers so that they could only be used with IBM peripherals, such as printers.

A final example of a restrictive practice is **resale price maintenance.** Under resale price maintenance, a producer insists that any retailer selling his product must sell it at the list price. This practice is also designed to reduce competitive pressures at the retail level. (Resale price maintenance was abolished in Britain in 1976.)

Firms engaging in the restrictive practice *claim* they are doing so not because they wish to restrict competition, but because they want to enhance economic efficiency. The motor dealership system, for example, is said to be necessary to allow dealers to obtain a return on the capital invested in their businesses and offer a better service by carrying a bigger stock of new models and spare parts. Exclusive dealing contracts, they say, provide incentives for firms to focus their attention on one producer's goods.

Regardless of these claims, restrictive practices often reduce economic efficiency. Also whether they enhance or hurt efficiency, restrictive practices may lead to higher prices by limiting competitive pressures.

Some restrictive practices work by increasing the costs of, or otherwise impeding, one's rivals (**raising**

FORMS OF RESTRICTIVE PRACTICES

Dealership arrangements	Tie-ins
Exclusive dealing	Resale price maintenance

rival's costs). In the 1980s, several major airlines developed computer reservation systems that they sold at very attractive prices to travel agents. If the primary goal of these systems had been to serve consumers, they would have been designed to display all the departures near the time the passengers desired. Instead, each airline's system displayed only its own flights—United's, for instance, focused on United flights—although with additional work, the travel agent could find out the flights of other airlines. Airlines benefited from these computer systems, not because they best met the needs of the consumer but because they put competitors at a disadvantage and thereby reduced the effectiveness of competition.

An exclusive dealing contract between a producer and a distributor is another example of how one firm may benefit from hurting its rivals. The contract may force a rival producer to set up its own distribution system, at great cost. The already-existing distributor might have been able to undertake the distribution of the second product at relatively low incremental cost. The exclusive dealing contract increases total resources spent on distribution.

THE MANY DIMENSIONS OF COMPETITION AMONG OLIGOPOLISTS

In the perfectly competitive markets of Part Two, competitive behaviour is clear and simple. Firms work to lower their costs of production. They can sell as much as they want at the going market price. They don't have to worry about clever marketing strategies, new products, advertising; but these, and a host of other decisions, are the battlefields on which competition among oligopolists occurs. This competition is fierce with firms' constantly trying to outwit rivals and anticipate their responses. It is like a game, but one in which not all the rules are clear, let alone written down. The first supermarket chain to cut prices may have anticipated being able to increase its market share and its profits at the expense of the other chains. But when all the other supermarkets had cut their prices to match the price cuts

of the first chain, it was probably the case that all were worse off than they had been before the price war, including the firm that started it.

PRICE AND OUTPUT COMPETITION

Even in the limited domain on which we have focused so far, determining prices and output, the life of an oligopolist is complicated. At one level of analysis, the oligopolist firm is just like a firm facing monopolistic competition. The oligopolist faces a demand curve specifying how much output it believes it can sell at each price it charges, or what the firm believes it will receive if it tries to sell a particular quantity. The oligopolist chooses the point along that demand curve at which its profits are maximised. It sets, in other words, marginal revenue equal to marginal cost. But while true, this statement hides all the real difficulties in an analysis of oligopoly. What an oligopolist will sell at any particular price, or what the market price will be if it produces a particular level of output, depends on what its rivals do.

Economists have investigated the behaviour of oligopolies under different assumptions concerning what each firm believes about what its rival will do.

COURNOT COMPETITION

An oligopolist firm may believe that its rivals are committed to producing a given quantity and selling it on the market and that they will keep this quantity fixed no matter what level of output the firm chooses to produce. If the firm considers producing more, it expects that its rivals will cut their prices until they sell the production level to which they are committed. Competition where an oligopolist firm assumes its rivals' output levels are fixed is called **Cournot competition,** after Augustin Cournot, a French economist and engineer, who first studied it in 1838. Industries such as aluminium or steel, where the major part of the cost of production is the cost of machinery and, once capital goods are in place, variable costs are relatively unimportant, are often thought of as industries where Cournot competition prevails. Adding new machinery would be expensive, and not using machinery to its capacity would save the firm relatively little money. Output is then determined, at least in the short run, by the production capacity of the firm's capital goods.

BERTRAND COMPETITION

In Cournot competition, each firm maximises profits by choosing what it will produce. In making its calculations, it assumes the level of output of its rivals is fixed. This assumption, we saw, is plausible for industries in which it takes time to change production capacity and in which capital goods represent the bulk of all production costs. But in many industries, it is easy to expand capacity. A taxicab company in a large city can easily buy a new car and hire new drivers. While increasing the total number of planes in service may take some time, an airline that wishes to increase the number of planes flying the London–Amsterdam route can do so quickly. Firms in these industries can be thought of as choosing a price to charge and adjusting their output to meet whatever demand arises at that price. They choose the price so as to maximise their profits, given their beliefs about the behaviour of their rivals. One commonly made assumption is that their rivals' prices are fixed. Oligopolies in which each firm chooses its price to maximise its profits on the assumption that its rivals' prices are fixed are said to have **Bertrand competition,** after the French economist Joseph Bertrand, who first studied this form of competition in 1883.

If rivals keep their prices unchanged, then the oligopolist may steal many of its rivals' customers when it lowers its price. But as long as the goods produced by two rivals are imperfect substitutes (for any of the reasons discussed in Chapter 13), when one firm lowers its price below that of its rivals, it does not capture *all* the customers.

KINKED DEMAND CURVES

A third hypothesis about how oligopolistic rivals may respond says that rivals match price cuts but do not respond to price increases. In this situation, an oligopolist believes that it will not gain much in sales if it lowers its price, because rivals will match the price cut, but it will lose considerably if it raises it price, since it will be undersold by rivals who do not change their prices. The demand curve facing such an oligopolist appears kinked, as in Figure 14.2. The curve is very steep below the current price p_1, reflecting the fact that few sales are gained as price is lowered. But it is relatively flat above p_1, indicating that the firm loses many customers to its rivals, who refuse to match the price increases.

Figure 14.2 also presents the marginal revenue curve, which has a sharp drop at the output level corresponding to the kink. Why does the marginal revenue curve have this shape, and what are the consequences? The drop in the marginal revenue curve follows from the fact that the increase in the price from a reduction in sales by a unit is much smaller than the fall in the price if the firm wants to increase sales by a unit. Increases in output beyond Q_1 raise relatively little additional revenue, since to sell the increased output, price must fall by a consid-

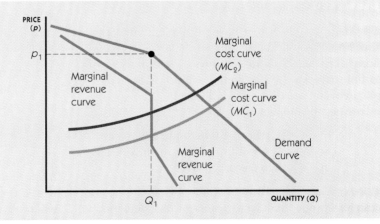

Figure 14.2 A KINKED DEMAND CURVE

The demand curve facing a firm is relatively flat at price levels above the current level (p_1), showing that an oligopolist will lose a large amount of sales if it increases its price and rivals do not. However, the demand curve is relatively steep at prices below the current level, showing that the oligopolist will not gain much in sales if it lowers its price, since rivals will follow. The sharp drop in marginal revenue means that a firm may not change its level of price or output, even if marginal cost shifts.

COMPETITION AMONG OLIGOPOLISTS

Cournot competition: Each firm believes its rivals will leave their output unchanged in response to changes in the firm's output.

Bertrand competition: Each firm sets its price believing its rivals will leave their own price unchanged in response to changes in the firm's price.

Kinked demand curves: Each firm believes its rivals will match price cuts but not price increases.

erable amount; any price cut by a firm is matched by its rivals, so relatively few customers are gained. But at levels of output less than those at the kink, marginal revenue is quite high, because as we have seen, the demand curve is relatively flat to the left of Q_1. With a flat demand curve, price and marginal revenue are close together.

The drop in the marginal revenue curve means that at the output Q_1 at which the drop occurs, the extra revenue lost from cutting back production is much greater than the extra revenue gained from increasing production. This has one important implication. Small changes in marginal cost, from MC_1 to MC_2, have no effect on output or price. Thus, firms that believe they face a kinked demand curve have good reason to hesitate before changing their prices.

REVIEW AND PRACTICE

SUMMARY

1 Oligopolists must choose whether to seek higher profits by colluding with rival firms or by competing. They must predict what their rivals will do in response to any action they take.

2 A group of firms that have an explicit and open agreement to collude is known as a cartel. Although cartels are illegal in most countries, firms have tried to find tacit ways of facilitating collusion, for example, by using price leaders and "meeting the competition" pricing policies.

3 If the threat of potential entry is sufficient to cause firms to set price and output at competitive levels, the industry is said to be contestable.

4 Even when they do not collude, firms attempt to restrict competition with practices like dealership arrangements, exclusive dealing, tie-ins, and resale price maintenance. In some cases, a firm's profits may be increased by raising its rival's costs and making the rival a less effective competitor.

5 In Cournot competition, an oligopolist chooses its output under the assumption that its rivals' output levels are fixed.

6 In Bertrand competition, each firm chooses the price of its product on the assumption that its rivals' prices are fixed.

7 If the rivals to an oligopolist match all price cuts but do not match any price increases, then the oligopolist faces a kinked demand curve. A kinked demand curve will lead to a marginal revenue curve with a vertical segment, which implies that the firm will often not change its level of output or its price in response to small changes in costs.

KEY TERMS

cartel   **Cournot competition**   **Bertrand competition**   **kinked demand curve**

Prisoner's Dilemma

REVIEW QUESTIONS

1 Why is the analysis of oligopoly more complicated than that of monopoly, perfect competition, or monopolistic competition?

2 Name some ways that firms might use tacit collusion if explicit collusion is ruled out by law.

3 What is a contestable market?

4 Name and define three restrictive practices.

5 Explain why Cournot competitors may produce more and charge a lower price than monopolists but produce less and charge a higher price than perfect competitors.

6 What expectations must an oligopolist have about the behaviour of its rivals if it believes that it faces a kinked demand curve?

7 Why might a firm that faces a kinked demand curve not change its price even when its costs change?

PROBLEMS

1 Explain why every member of a cartel has an incentive to cheat on its agreement. How does this fact strengthen the ability of laws that outlaw explicit collusion to do their job?

2 How might cooperative agreements between firms—to share research information, share the costs of cleaning up pollution, or help avoid shortfalls of supplies—end up helping firms to collude in reducing quantity and raising price?

3 Consider two oligopolists, with each choosing between a high and a low level of production. Given their choices of how much to produce, their profits will be:

Explain how firm B will reason that it makes sense to produce the high amount, regardless of what firm A chooses. Then explain how firm A will reason that it makes sense to produce the high amount, regardless of what firm B chooses. How might collusion assist the two firms in this case?

4 Explain how dealership arrangements, exclusive dealing, tie-ins, and resale price maintenance might help an oligopolist to make higher profits. How might a firm make the case that these practices add to efficiency?

		Firm A	
		High production	Low production
High production		A: £2 million B: £2 million	A: £1 million B: £5 million
Firm B			
Low production		A: £5 million B: £1 million	A: £4 million B: £4 million

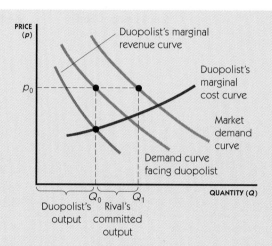

Figure 14.3 COURNOT COMPETITION IN A DUOPOLY

For a duopolist in a situation of Cournot competition, the firm's demand curve and the market demand curve are parallel, separated by the amount that the rival firm is committed to producing. Given the demand curve, the duopolist maximises profit in the usual way, by setting its marginal revenue equal to marginal cost.

APPENDIX: DESCRIBING THE MARKET EQUILIBRIUM FOR OLIGOPOLY

In this appendix, we take a closer look at how firms in an oligopoly behave and interact to determine the market equilibrium.

COURNOT COMPETITION

Under Cournot competition, each firm assumes its rival's output is constant. For simplicity, we focus on the case of a **duopoly,** a market in which there are only two firms, as illustrated in Figure 14.3.

The duopolist's demand curve in this case is simply the market demand curve shifted over to the left by the amount of output the rival is committed to producing.[2] Given this demand curve, we can draw the marginal revenue curve, and the firm produces at the point where marginal revenue equals marginal cost.

[2] This demand curve is sometimes referred to as the residual demand curve.

Normally, the equilibrium output with Cournot competition is less than with perfect competition but greater than with monopoly. With monopoly, the firm can be thought of as setting marginal revenue equal to marginal cost. With perfect competition, marginal revenue is just price. With monopoly, marginal revenue is lower than price. It is price minus what the firm loses on its earlier sales, that is, the reduction in price from producing one more unit. This is also the case with Cournot competition. Thus, output is lower than it is with perfect competition. But if there are two identical firms, each is producing only half the total output. Hence, what it loses in profits on earlier sales is smaller than under monopoly. Part of the lost revenue from lower prices is borne by the rival firm, which under the Cournot assumption is expected to maintain its output. Marginal revenue is closer to price. So, because at any level of output the marginal revenue is higher with Cournot competition than with monopoly, equilibrium output is also higher.

To describe the market equilibrium we need to see how the firms interact. The central tool in this analysis is the **reaction function,** which specifies the level of output of each firm given the level of output of the other firm. It shows, in other words, the reaction of one firm to the actions of the other. Consider the aluminium industry in the period after the Second World War; the two largest firms in the United States were Alcoa and Reynolds. The reaction

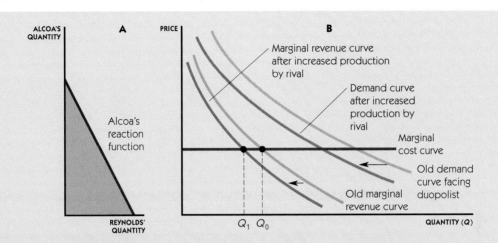

Figure 14.4 THE REACTION FUNCTION

The reaction function in panel A shows how much Alcoa will choose to produce for every level of output by Reynolds. Note that Alcoa's output declines as Reynolds's increases. Panel B shows why this is so. An increase in the rival's output shifts the demand curve facing the firm to the left. Similarly, the marginal revenue curve shifts to the left, and as a result, output is reduced.

function for Alcoa is plotted in Figure 14.4A. It is downward sloping.

To see why this is so, we need to recall how each Cournot oligopolist decides how much to produce. It sets marginal revenue equal to marginal cost as in panel B. If Reynolds increases production, the demand facing Alcoa at any given price is reduced. Equivalently, if Alcoa wants to sell the same amount as before, it must lower its price. Figure 14.4 shows the new demand and marginal revenue curves; they are to the left of the corresponding curves when Reynolds produced less. Accordingly, the optimal level of output is lower: as Reynolds increases production, Alcoa decreases production.

We apply the same analysis to Reynolds in Figure 14.5. The reaction curve shows Reynolds's level of output along the horizontal axis, given Alcoa's output along the vertical axis. The market equilibrium is the intersection of the reaction functions, point E. This point depicts the equilibrium output of Alcoa given the output of Reynolds, and it depicts the output of Reynolds given the output of Alcoa. The inter-

section of the reaction functions is an equilibrium because, given each firm's beliefs about the behaviour of its rival, neither firm wishes to change what it does. There are, in short, no pressures to change. Each firm is maximising its profits, given its belief that the rival is committed to producing its current level of output.

BERTRAND COMPETITION

Figure 14.6 uses reaction functions to describe the market equilibrium of a Bertrand duopoly. A Bertrand duopolist assumes that its rival's price is fixed. This duopoly consists of two mattress companies, Supersleeper and Heavenlyrest, which produce imperfect substitutes. The reaction function in this case gives the price charged by one firm, given the price charged by its rival. As Supersleeper increases its price, Heavenlyrest finds it optimal to increase its own price. That is why the reaction function is positively sloped. The equilibrium is at E.

Figure 14.5 MARKET EQUILIBRIUM WITH COURNOT COMPETITION

Equilibrium will be at the intersection of the two reaction functions, where each firm is maximising its profits given its belief that the output of the other firm is fixed. At that point, there is no pressure for either firm to change output.

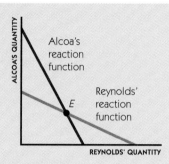

Figure 14.6 EXCLUSIVE DEALING TO RAISE RIVALS' COSTS

Equilibrium will be at the intersection of the two reaction functions, where each firm is maximising its profits given its belief that the price of the other firm is fixed. As one firm increases its price, the profit-maximising price of its rival increases, so the reaction functions are positively sloped.

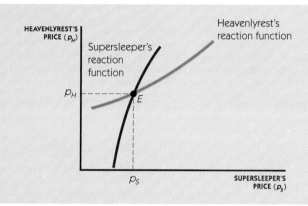

With price-setting (Bertrand) competition, firms believe that they face more elastic demand curves than they do with quantity-setting (Cournot) competition. This can easily be seen when we consider the extreme case where the two goods produced by two different firms are perfect substitutes. Then if one firm charges slightly less than its rival, it garners for itself the entire market; if it charges slightly more, it loses all of its sales. Each firm faces a horizontal demand curve. Thus, even when there are only two firms, if each believes the other has fixed its price and will not change the price in response to changes in prices it charges and if the two firms produce *perfect* substitutes, the market outcome is competitive.

We can see this process of competition as follows. Assume both firms have constant marginal and average costs of production. Since each company believes its rival will not budge its price so long as price exceeds marginal cost, each one will find that it pays it to shave its price by a small amount. By doing so, it steals the whole market. But the rival firm, thinking the same way, then undercuts still further. The process continues until the price is bid down to the point where there are zero profits. It does not pay to cut prices any further.

In general, the products produced by two duopolists are not perfect substitutes but differ somewhat, so that each firm faces a downward-sloping demand curve. In equilibrium, price exceeds marginal cost. Output is less than it would be with perfect competition but more than it would be with Cournot competition.

15

GOVERNMENT POLICIES TOWARDS COMPETITION

I n the minds of most people, monopolies are not a good thing. They smell of income inequities and undemocratic concentrations of political power. To economists, however, the concern is economic efficiency. Motivated by both political and economic concerns, government has taken an active role in promoting competition and in limiting the abuses of market power. In this chapter, we review the economic effects of limited competition and look at government policies to reduce its negative effects.

KEY QUESTIONS

1 Why is government concerned with monopolies and imperfect competition? In what sense do markets with monopolies and imperfect competition result in inefficiency?

2 How have different governments attempted to address the problem posed by a natural monopoly?

3 How have governments used public policies to break up monopolies, to impede the ability of any single firm to attain a dominant position in a market, and to outlaw practices designed to restrict competition?

THE DRAWBACKS OF MONOPOLIES AND LIMITED COMPETITION

Four major sources of economic inefficiency result from monopolies and other imperfectly competitive industries: restricted output, managerial slack, insufficient attention to research and development, and dissipation of profits through rent-seeking behaviour. The problems can be seen most simply in the context of monopolies (the focus here), but they also arise in imperfectly competitive markets.

RESTRICTED OUTPUT

Monopolists, like competitive firms, are in business to make profits by producing the kinds of goods and services customers want. But monopolists can make profits in ways not available to competitive firms. One way is to drive up the price of a good by restricting output, as discussed in Chapter 14. Consumers, by *choosing* to buy the monopolist's good, are revealing that they are better off than they would be without the product. But they are paying more than they would if the industry were competitive.

A monopolist who sets marginal revenue equal to marginal cost produces at a lower level of output than a corresponding competitive industry—an industry which has the same demand curve and costs but in which there are many producers rather than one—where price equals marginal cost. Figure 15.1 shows that the monopoly output Q_m is much smaller than the competitive output Q_c, where p_c equals marginal cost. The price under monopoly p_m is thus much higher.

The price of a good, by definition, measures how much an individual is willing to pay for an extra unit of a good. It measures, in other words, the marginal benefit of the good to the purchaser. With perfect competition, price equals marginal cost, so that in equilibrium the marginal benefit of an extra unit of a good to the individual (the price) is just equal to the marginal cost to the firm of producing it. At the monopolist's lower level of output, the marginal benefit of producing an extra unit—the price individuals are willing to pay for an extra unit—exceeds marginal cost.

By comparing the monopolist's production decision to the collective output decisions of firms in a competitive market, we can estimate the value of the loss to society when there is a monopoly. To simplify the analysis, in Figure 15.2 marginal cost is assumed to be constant, the horizontal line at the competitive price p_c. The monopolist produces an output of Q_m, at the point where marginal revenue equals marginal cost, and finds that it can charge p_m, the price on the demand curve corresponding to the output Q_m.

Two kinds of losses result, both related to the concept of consumer surplus introduced in Chapter 8. There we learned that the downward-sloping demand curve implies a bounty to most consumers. At points left of the intersection of the price line and demand curve, people are willing to pay more for the good than they have to. With competition, the consumer surplus in Figure 15.2 is the entire shaded area between the demand curve and the line at p_c.

Figure 15.1 WHY MONOPOLY OUTPUT IS INEFFICIENT

With perfect competition price is set equal to marginal cost, with output at quantity Q_c and price p_c. A monopolist will set marginal revenue equal to marginal cost and produce at quantity Q_m and price p_m, where the market price exceeds marginal cost.

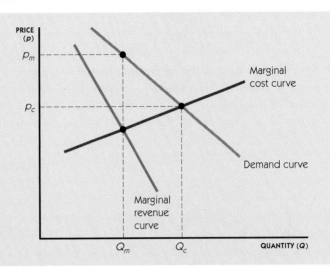

The monopolist cuts into this surplus. First, it charges a higher price p_m than would be obtained in the competitive situation. This loss is measured by the rectangle *ABCD*, the extra price times the quantity actually produced and consumed. This loss to consumers is not a loss to society as a whole. It is a transfer of income as the higher price ends up as revenue for the monopoly. But second, it reduces the quantity produced. While production in a competitive market would be Q_c, with a monopoly it is the

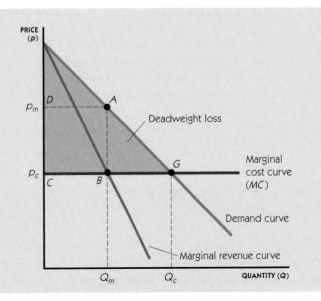

Figure 15.2 MEASURING THE SOCIAL COSTS OF MONOPOLY

The higher, monopoly price removes some of the consumer surplus. Part of this loss (the rectangle *ABCD*) is simply a transfer of income from consumers to the monopolist; the remainder (the triangle *ABG*) is known as the deadweight loss of monopoly.

lower amount Q_m. This second kind of loss is a complete loss to society and is called the **deadweight loss** of a monopoly. Consumers lose the surplus to the right of Q_m, denoted *ABG*, with no resulting gain to the monopolist.

Some economists, such as Arnold Harberger of the University of California, Los Angeles, have argued that these costs of monopoly are relatively small, amounting to perhaps 3 percent of the monopolist's output value. Others believe the losses from restricting output are higher. Whichever argument is right, output restriction is only one source of the inefficiencies monopolies introduce into the economy.

MANAGERIAL SLACK

Chapter 10 argued that any company wants to minimise its costs of production, and any profit-maximising firm will make the highest possible level of profits when it keeps its costs as low as possible. But in practice, companies already making a lot of money without much competition lack the incentive to hold costs as low as possible. The lack of efficiency when firms are insulated from the pressures of competition is referred to as **managerial slack.**

In the absence of competition, it can be difficult to tell whether managers are being efficient. How much should it cost to make a telephone call from London to Tokyo or New York, for example? When British Telecom had a monopoly of long-distance telephone services, it might have claimed that its costs were as low as possible. However, such claims are very difficult to verify. Since it has had to compete with firms such as Mercury, Cable and Wireless, Swiftcall, and all the other suppliers of long-distance telephone calls, British Telecom has cut the prices of such calls.

REDUCED RESEARCH AND DEVELOPMENT

Competition motivates firms to develop new products and less expensive ways of producing goods. A monopoly, by contrast, may be willing to let the profits roll in, without aggressively encouraging technological progress.

Not all monopolists stand idly by, of course. Bell Labs, now succeeded by Lucent Technologies, the research division of the U.S. telephone company AT&T, was a fountain of important innovations throughout the period during which AT&T was a virtual monopolist in telephone service. The laser and the transistor are but two of its innovations. But AT&T was also in a unique position. The prices it charged were set by government regulators, and those prices were set to encourage the expenditure of money on research. From this perspective, AT&T's research contribution was as much a consequence of government regulatory policy as of anything else.

RENT SEEKING

The final source of economic inefficiency under monopoly is the temptation for monopolists to spend their extra profits in economically unproductive ways. A major example is devoting resources to obtaining or maintaining their monopoly position by deterring entry. Since the profits a monopolist receives are called monopoly rents, the attempt to acquire or maintain already existing rents by acquiring or maintaining a monopoly position in some industry is referred to as **rent seeking.**

Sometimes a firm's monopoly position is at least partly the result of government protection. Many developing countries grant a company within their country a monopoly to produce a good, and they bar imports of that good from abroad. In these circumstances, firms will give money to lobbyists and politicians to maintain regulations that restrict competition so that they can keep their profits high. Such activities are socially wasteful. Real resources (including labour time) are used to win favourable rules, not to produce goods and services. There is thus legitimate concern that the willingness of governments to restrict competition will encourage firms to spend money on rent-seeking activities rather than on making a better product.

How much would a firm be willing to spend to gain a monopoly position? The firm would be willing to spend up to the amount it would obtain as monopoly profits. The waste from this rent-seeking activity can be much larger than the loss from the reduced output.

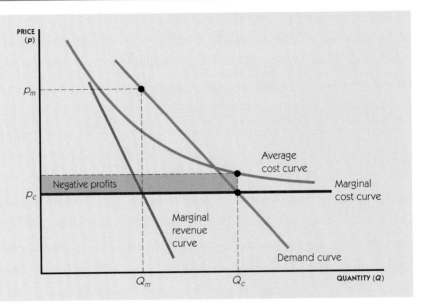

Figure 15.3 A PROBLEM WITH REGULATING NATURAL MONOPOLY

A natural monopoly will set marginal revenue equal to marginal cost and produce at quantity Q_m and price p_m. In perfect competition, price would be equal to marginal cost, at Q_c and p_c. However, the perfectly competitive outcome is not possible in this case, since it would force the natural monopoly to produce at below its average costs, and thus to be making losses.

PRICE
(p)

p_m

p_c

Negative profits

Average cost curve

Marginal cost curve

Marginal revenue curve

Demand curve

Q_m Q_c QUANTITY (Q)

FURTHER DRAWBACKS OF LIMITED COMPETITION

We saw in Chapters 13 and 14 that markets in which a few firms dominated were more prevalent than monopolies. Relative to monopolies, some of the inefficiencies just discussed are smaller under limited competition. Output is lower than under perfect competition but higher than under monopoly, for example. And competition to produce new products (research and development) is often intense, as we shall see in the next chapter. But other inefficiencies are worse in markets with limited competition than in monopoly markets. Firms under imperfect competition, for example, expend major resources on practices designed to deter entry, to reduce the force of competition, and to raise prices. Such expenditures may increase profits, but they waste resources and make consumers worse off. Under imperfect competition, firms may also maintain excess capacity, again to deter entry. Firms may gain a competitive advantage over a rival, not by lowering their own costs but by raising his, for instance, by depriving him of the use of existing distribution facilities. They may also spend money on uninformative advertising.

POLICIES TOWARDS NATURAL MONOPOLIES

If imperfect competition is as disadvantageous as the previous analysis has suggested, why not simply require that competition be perfect? To answer this question, we need to recall the reasons, discussed in Chapter 13, why competition is imperfect.

One reason is government-granted patents. Monopoly profits provide the return to inventors and innovators that is necessary to stimulate activities vital to a capitalist economy. We will discuss these issues more extensively in Chapter 16.

A second reason is that the cost of production may be lower if there is a single firm in the industry. This is the case with natural monopoly. Natural monopolies present a difficult policy problem. Like any other firm, a natural monopolist will produce at the level where marginal revenue equals marginal cost, at Q_m in Figure 15.3. At this level, it will charge a price of p_m, which is higher than the marginal cost at that point. Thus, it will produce less and charge more than it would if price were equal to marginal cost, as would be the case with perfect competition (the output level Q_c and the price p_c in Figure 15.3).

But in the case of natural monopoly, the very nature of the decreasing cost of technology precludes perfect competition. Indeed, consider what would happen if price were set equal to marginal cost. With a natural monopoly, average costs are declining and marginal cost is below average costs. Hence, if price were equal to marginal cost, it would be less than average costs, and the firm would be losing money. Profits would be negative, as shown by the shaded area in Figure 15.3. If the government wanted a natural monopoly to produce at the point where marginal cost equaled price, it would have to subsidise the company to offset these losses. Taxes would have to be raised to generate the money for the subsidies; this would impose other economic costs. Moreover, the government would probably have a difficult time ascertaining the magnitude of the subsidy required. Managers and workers in such a firm have a way of exaggerating their estimates of the wages they need to produce the required output.

Following are three different solutions government has found to the problem of natural monopolies.

NATIONALIZATION AND PRIVATIZATION

Many countries have responded to the issues raised by natural monopolies by taking them into public ownership, or **nationalising** them. In Britain this has been true of the railways, telephones, and supply of electricity, gas, and water. Most of the nationalization in Britain was carried out by the Labour government of 1945 to 1951. It was intended that a nationalised industry would not abuse its monopoly position and act against the public interest; it would not restrict output and charge monopoly prices.

However, there have been problems with nationalised industries. Managers working in them may have lacked adequate incentives to cut costs and innovate rapidly. Their ability to obtain subsidies to cover losses, as in the case of the railways, may have weakened their incentives to cut costs. Governments have yielded to the temptation to interfere with nationalised industries to achieve other objectives than their efficient operation. They have, for example, encouraged them from time to time not to cut employment when it conflicted with the government's desire

to reduce unemployment. In some European countries, such as Sweden, the provision of public sector jobs has been used systematically to keep down unemployment. In Britain, nationalised industries have had their investment plans constrained by the Treasury. Their borrowing has been a part of the Public Sector Borrowing Requirement—the overall borrowing of the government—and has been limited as part of efforts to limit overall public sector borrowing and to keep down the size of the national debt.

Firms may have been under pressure to provide some services at below their marginal cost, with the losses made up out of profits on other parts of the business, a practice known as **cross-subsidization.** An example is that British Rail was required to maintain some loss-making services financed out of revenue from more profitable routes. (In recent years, such practices have been abandoned, in favour of a system that makes profits and losses on different parts of the business more transparent, and any subsidies given to support the loss-making services explicit.) Another example of cross-subsidization is the post office's practice of charging the same price for delivering a piece of mail between any two points in the United Kingdom regardless of whether these are two points in the same large city, or somewhere in the Outer Hebrides and a remote farm in Cornwall.

Growing dissatisfaction with the working of nationalised industries has led to a policy of selling them back to the private sector of the economy, or **privatization,** in the 1980s, not only in Britain but also in other European countries. British Telecom, British Gas, and the water and electricity companies are among the nationalised natural monopolies that were privatised in the 1980s. Since they were sold back to the private sector, there have been some dramatic cuts in employment, especially in British Telecom, indicating that there were cost savings to be made. Many of these companies have also made enormous profits since privatization, and the prices of their shares have risen dramatically; this has led to widespread suspicion that the state sold them at prices that were much too low.

REGULATION

Privatization alone does not solve all the problems created by these industries. Although privatization has typically been associated with efforts to construct or reestablish competitive environments, in which the privatised firms will have to operate and which will enforce behaviour in the public interest, it has not always been possible to do this, particularly where the privatised firms have a natural monopoly. In such cases it is necessary to add further restraints on their behaviour, to prevent them from abusing their monopoly position. This is the process of **regulation.** There is considerable expertise in regulation in the United States where many utilities—water, electricity, and gas companies—and telephones have traditionally been private companies subject to regulation by the state or federal governments.

In Britain a number of new regulatory agencies have been established—the Office of Electricity Regulation (OFER), the Office of Gas Regulation (OFGAS), the Office of Telephone Regulation (OFTEL) to look after electricity, gas, and telephones respectively—and many of them have applied a formula called "**RPI minus** x" to regulate firms: the price these firms charge must not rise by more than the retail price index (RPI) less x percent per annum, where x is the estimated rate of productivity growth in excess of the average economywide productivity growth of which these firms are believed to be capable.

The aim of regulation is to keep the price as low as possible, commensurate with the monopolist's need to obtain an adequate return on its investment. In other words, the regulators try to keep price equal to average costs, where average costs include a normal return on what the firm's owners have invested in the firm. If the regulators are successful, the natural monopoly will earn no monopoly profits. Such a regulated output and price are shown in Figure 15.4 and Q_r and p_r.

Two criticisms have been leveled against regulation as a solution to the natural monopoly problem. The first is that regulations often take an inefficient form. The sources of inefficiency are several. The intent is to set prices so that firms obtain a fair return on their capital. But to make the highest level of profits, firms respond by increasing their amount of capital as much as possible, which can lead to too much investment. In addition, the structure of prices may be set so that some groups, often businesses, may be charged extra-high prices to make it possible to subsidise other groups. This problem of cross-subsidies

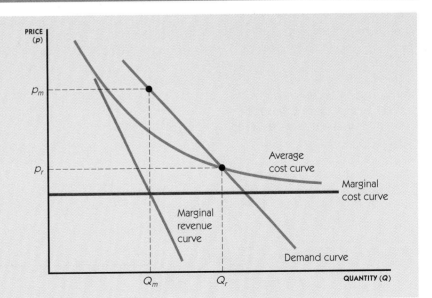

Figure 15.4 REGULATING NATURAL MONOPOLY

Government regulators will often seek to choose the point on the market demand curve where the firm provides the greatest quantity at the lowest price consistent with the firm's covering its costs. The point is the quantity Q_r and price p_r, where the demand curve intersects the average cost curve.

is no less a problem for natural monopolies if they are privately owned and regulated than it is if they are owned and operated by the government. Further, firms' incentives to innovate are weakened every time they lower costs. Recently regulators have recognised that unless they reward innovation, it will not happen. They have agreed to allow the utilities to retain much of the increased profits they obtain from improved efficiency, at least for a few years.

The second criticism is that the regulators lose track of the public interest. The theory of **regulatory capture** argues that regulators are pulled frequently into the camps of those they regulate. This could happen through bribery and corruption, but the much likelier way is just that over time, employees of a regulated industry develop personal friendships with the regulators, who in turn come to rely on their expertise and judgment. Worse, regulatory agencies (of necessity) tend to hire from firms in the regulated industry. By the same token, regulators who demonstrate an "understanding" of the industry may be rewarded with good jobs in that industry after they leave government service.

ENCOURAGING COMPETITION

The final way government deals with the hard choices posed by natural monopolies is to encourage competition, even if imperfect. To understand this strategy, let us first review why competition may not be viable when average costs are declining over the relevant range of output.

If two firms divide the market between them, each faces higher average costs than if any one firm grabbed the whole market. As illustrated in Figure 15.5, Q_d denotes the output of each firm in the initial duopoly and AC_d its average costs. By undercutting its rival, a firm would be able to capture the entire market *and* have its average costs reduced. By the same token, a natural monopolist knows that it can charge a price above its average costs AC_m without worrying about entry. Rivals that might enter, trying to capture some of the profits, know that the natural monopolist has lower costs because of its larger scale of production and so can always undercut them.

Even under these conditions, some economists

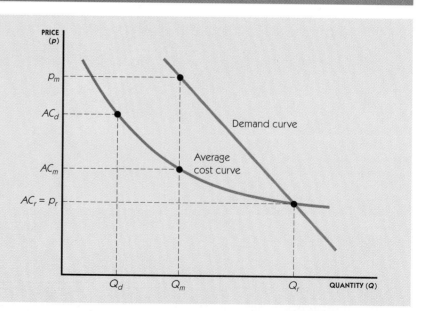

Figure 15.5 WHY COMPETITION MAY NOT BE VIABLE WITH DECREASING AVERAGE COSTS

If two firms share a market, each producing Q_d, one firm could double its output to Q_m, lower its costs, and undercut its rival. The larger firm has a cost advantage over a smaller competitor.

APPROACHES TO NATURAL MONOPOLY

Public ownership

Regulation

Competition

have argued (as noted in Chapter 14) that a monopolist would not in fact charge higher than average costs, because a rival could enter at any time and grab the whole market. In this argument, all that is required to keep prices low is potential competition.

Most economists are not so sanguine about the effectiveness of potential, as opposed to actual, competition. Airline behaviour provides the most convincing demonstration of the importance of having more than one firm in the market. Routes between many cities are natural monopolies. These markets have experienced wild price fluctuations. The cycle starts with the natural monopolist charging higher than average costs. Another carrier (or carriers) enters the market. Prices fall dramatically as they try to force each other out. One carrier leaves. Prices rise again. And so on.

In the late 1970s and the 1980s, many governments became convinced that more competition should be introduced into markets. The British government has attempted to deregulate bus services and to introduce competition in telephones. Electricity generation and distribution were separated when the industry was privatised, and there are now competing generators of electricity. The Big Bang in the City in London in 1987 was aimed at removing restrictions on the business done by financial companies and increasing competition on the stock market. The ownership of railway track (and other fixed infrastructure) has been separated from the operation of railway services, with the aim of introducing competition into the provision of railway services. The European Commission has been attempting to deregulate air travel in Europe to allow more competition. Airlines in the United States have been substantially deregulated.

How effective these changes have been is not clear. European air fares were very high compared with fares elsewhere in the world. Increased competition has improved services and lowered fares on busier routes such as London–Paris and London–Amsterdam where now more than two airlines provide service. Bus deregulation in Britain has been controversial. Services are thought to have improved on heavily used routes but to have deteriorated elsewhere. However, this is what might have been expected to happen when cross-subsidization between routes ended. In the initial period after deregulation, many new bus operators put on services. There followed a period of settling down, in which many of the new operators left the market. In some cases the old bus companies remained as the sole survivors, and bus services were eventually largely unaffected by deregulation. In many industries in which privatization was associated with breaking up the industry either vertically (as for example in the separation of electricity generation and distribution) or horizontally (as in the separation of railway operations into many different firms each operating on different sets of routes) to create competition, there has been subsequent re-integration, as some regional electricity companies have bought others or moved into generation, and as some rail operators have bought up others. Consequently there is concern that intended competition is being whittled away.

GOVERNMENT POLICIES

Only some of the failures of competition arise from natural monopolies. Other imperfections, as we have seen, are the result of sharp business practices to develop market power by deterring entry or promoting collusion. When encouraging competition doesn't work, government sometimes resorts to enforcing competition through legislation.

In a number of industries, privatization has been accompanied by attempts to create a competitive market structure. When the railways in Britain were privatised, the track, signaling, and other infrastructure were kept together in one company, Railtrack, while the job of operating rail services was sold off to a number of operating companies. These were allowed to bid for franchises to operate services on particular routes. The ownership of rolling stock was sold off to yet more firms, which lease it to operating companies. The franchises give the operating companies rights to operate rail services for a fixed period of time, typically periods between 7 and 15 years. Companies like Richard Branson's Virgin won the franchise for the West Coast Main Line and for Inter-City Cross-Country. The bus company Stagecoach won the franchise for South-West Trains. While in most cases it is not possible to have two operators providing services on the same routes and competing directly, it is possible for a number of firms to build up expertise in running railways and be in a position to compete for franchises when they expire, and the experiences of operators on other franchises provides a point of comparison against which the performance of each operator can be judged.

However, the initial ownership structure has not proved durable. There has been some consolidation, as some of the original owners following privatization have sold out, while others have extended their ownership and control of rail firms. Stagecoach has bought out one of the rolling stock leasing companies, introducing some vertical integration, which may act against competition. Stagecoach has also acquired more bus companies and in some areas controls both bus and rail services, giving it a local monopoly on public transport. This has some advantages, in that it allows for better coordination of bus and rail services—it brings the possibility of an integrated transport network—but it also may make it easier for anticompetitive practices to develop.

There have been similar developments in other industries. In electricity supply, two generators of electricity, National Power and Powergen, were separated from the Regional Electricity Companies (the RECs). The idea was that the RECs should buy electricity from the cheapest generator, and then pass it on to their customers—ordinary households and firms. This structure is intended to produce competition between the different electricity generating companies. There have been a number of takeovers of RECs. In 1996, controversially, the Monopolies and Mergers Commission (as the current Competition Commission was then named) allowed proposed mergers between generators and RECs, Powergen and Midland Electric, and National Power and Southern Electricity ("Short Circuit," *The Economist*, 13 April 1996, pp. 27–28). These mergers will weaken the incentive of those RECs to seek out the cheapest source of electricity that they can. It will make it easier for the generators to fix prices, by giving them a captive market for their electricity. The electricity industry has been changing continuously since 1996. There has been an influx of new gas-powered generating capacity, as some of the RECs have extended their operations to include generation as well as distribution of electricity. From 1998, the RECs do not have a local monopoly within their own regions of supply of electricity to households and firms. Other firms, such as the gas companies, are able to sell electricity to households. The growth in the number of firms generating electricity increases competition in that part of the industry, but the vertical integration, whereby generation and distribution are done by the same company, is likely to reduce competition.

Maintaining effective competition in these privatised industries will depend on the policies of the competition authorities in Britain, and many people believe that they are unlikely to take a tough enough stand against the producers and distributors to protect the interests of their customers.

As we will see, these policies have often been controversial. Consumer groups and injured businesses tend to support them, arguing that, without them, firms would focus more on competition-reducing strategies than on producing in a less expensive way products that customers like. Many businesses, however, claim that such policies interfere with economic efficiency. For instance, even if the most efficient way to distribute its products is through dealership arrangements, the firm might worry that such a contract might be illegal.

MONOPOLIES AND MERGERS POLICY

We have seen that market power is a bad thing since it enables firms to put up prices and restrict supply, and it causes economic inefficiency. There are good reasons for governments to prevent firms from obtaining market power and those who have market power from using it. In Britain, a number of laws exist to promote competition and prevent the acquisition and abuse of market power, and a number of government agencies exist to enforce these laws. Monopolies policy in Britain is complicated by the existence of European Union laws which apply in Britain as well as British laws, and the two are not in every way mutually compatible. There are inconsistencies between them.

Under British law, the Fair Trading Act of 1973 set up the Office of Fair Trading to monitor competition and monopoly in Britain. The director-general of fair trading (DGFT) and the secretary of state for trade and industry have the power to refer a case to the Competition Commission (another government agency) if it appears that a monopoly exists. A monopoly is defined as a situation in which a company has at least 25 percent of the relevant market. A complex monopoly occurs if two or more companies have between them a market share of at least 25 percent and are acting as if they were a monopolist.

The Competition Commission investigates cases referred to it and reports back to the secretary of state on whether a monopoly exists and whether it acts against the public interest. If it does, the secretary of state may attempt to do something about it. He or she may attempt to remedy its effects or prevent the monopolistic activities from recurring or may accept an undertaking from the firm(s) in question to stop acting against the public interest.

When two or more firms propose to merge with each other, the secretary of state can refer the case to the Competition Commission if their merger would create or enhance a monopoly or if the merger involves the takeover of firms with sufficiently large assets. A merger that the Competition Commission judges to be likely to operate against the public interest can be prohibited by the secretary of state or allowed to go ahead only under specified conditions.

Another act of Parliament, the 1980 Competition Act, deals with **anticompetitive practices** (as distinct from restrictive trade practices, of which more subsequently). An anticompetitive practice is defined quite broadly, as a course of conduct that is likely to restrict or distort competition. The DGFT is empowered to investigate suspected anticompetitive practices, and either refer the firm involved to the Competition Commission for further investigation or get an undertaking from the firm that it will stop doing whatever it is that is anticompetitive.

DEFINING MARKETS

The definition of monopoly used in British law depends on the size of the firm relative to the relevant market: 25 percent is the critical size for a monopoly. The debate thus centers on what is the relevant market. We have learned that the extent to which a firm's demand curve is downward sloping, so it can raise prices without losing all its customers—its market power—is related to both the number of firms in the industry and the extent of product differentiation. The problem of defining markets for the purposes of enforcing competition policy is related to both factors.

Geographical Bounds   International trade has become increasingly important, and Britain's exports make up over a quarter of national production. In many industries, imports and exports are so important that for many products it would make no sense to define the industry as the British producers of these products. In some industries the bounds may be the European Union, in others the world, and in yet others something between the two.

In the motor industry, for example, the firms that manufacture in Britain (Rover, Jaguar, the U.K. divisions of Ford, General Motors, Nissan, Peugeot, and so on) face competition from other European producers like Fiat, BMW, Renault, Mercedes, Volkswagen, and Volvo, as well as from Japanese and Korean producers. There has been, in a very small way, competition from some producers from eastern Europe, like Lada and Yugo, and this area may offer more competition in the future. It could be argued that this industry is effectively a global one. Certainly, inside the European Union, where there is free trade between countries, there is a European market, not meaningfully a British market. Indeed, the manufacture of cars is spread out around Europe so that a car assembled in Britain is likely to be made up of parts made all over Europe and beyond. The firms operating in Britain include parts of companies that have their head offices in the United States, France, and Japan as well as Britain and have manufacturing plants in several countries. The same is true of more and more manufacturing industries.

Product Differentiation   The other issue is: what products should be included in the relevant market? If the industry consisted of several firms in the same location, all producing identical goods, the issue would not arise. But where each firm is located in a different place and each produces something slightly different, the extent of the market is blurred at the edges. In defining the market for motor cars, should off-road 4 × 4 vehicles like Land Rovers, or commercial vehicles like small vans be included? Should the market for family saloon cars be separated from a market for luxury cars (Jaguar, Rolls-Royce, Mercedes)? Some consumers make substitutions between these different goods depending on their prices, and so the producers of them are to some extent competing with each other.

CURBING RESTRICTIVE TRADE PRACTICES

Restrictive agreements—which include agreements made by two or more firms that affect conditions of supply or distribution, such as create a cartel—are dealt with separately from monopolies and mergers. They are covered under British law by the 1976 Restrictive Trade Practices Act. All restrictive trade agreements have to be registered with the DGFT who must take them before the Restrictive Trade Practices Court. Here it is presumed that these practices are against the public interest unless the firms involved can prove otherwise.

It is worth noting that British policy does not outlaw the mere existence of a monopoly or a restrictive trade practice (RTP): the monopoly or restrictive trade practice has to operate against the public interest in order for it to be outlawed. The public interest is defined as taking account of many different things: effective competition, the interests of consumers, innovation and the entry of new firms, a balanced distribution of employment and industry, and the competitive position of U.K. producers. This gives a lot of discretion to the government and the public bodies that implement the law.

A consequence of the law in Britain is that, the **structure** of an industry (that is, the number of firms in it and their size) is not enough to justify intervention against a monopoly or RTP. The **conduct** of the firm(s) involved (that is, the way in which it sets price and acts towards competitors, and so on), the **performance** of the industry (in other words, its profitability, investment, exports, amount of innovation, and other factors which might indicate whether it is acting in the public interest) matter as well.

EUROPEAN UNION LAW

The EU has laws on monopolies and competition under Articles 85 and 86 of the Treaty of Rome, which prohibit anticompetitive agreements between firms and the use of a dominant market position if these features affect trade between member states of the EU. The European Commission (EC) can fine firms found guilty of breaking its competition laws, as it did in the case of a number of European steel producers in 1994. The commission's decisions can be reviewed by the European Court of Justice.

The EU's laws only apply when trade between member countries of the EU is involved, and so they do not cover all firms and industries. They differ from much of British law because they are concerned with the **economic effects** of monopoly or restrictive agreements rather than their **form.** The European definition of monopoly does not depend on the fraction of the market taken by a firm; instead it depends on the abuse of market power by the firm. Similarly, a restrictive trade agreement only violates Articles 85 and 86 if it operates against competition. As trade within Europe grows, and the single European market acquires more force, there is growing pressure on countries in the EU to make their competition laws consistent with those of the EC.

A criticism that is often leveled against the laws in Britain is that they provide very weak penalties for firms that violate them and thus little incentive for firms to comply. Typically, firms that are found to be violating the laws have been required to stop the practices involved and may be required to give undertakings that they will not resume anticompetitive practices. They have not been required, for example, to pay back monopoly profits that they have earned through their abuse of market power or through anticompetitive practices or restrictive trade agreements.

There have only been a few cases where stronger punishments have been imposed on monopolists in Britain. In a recent case a number of the largest brewing companies in Britain were ordered to reduce the number of pubs they owned and ran as tied houses after the Monopolies and Mergers Commission (as the Competition Commission was named at that time) ruled that a complex monopoly operated against the public interest in the supply of beer. The brewers sold off a number of pubs to other companies. The intention was that this should increase the number of free houses in which the products of more than one brewer should be on sale, so drinkers would have more choice of beer.

In another recent spectacular case, Richard Branson obtained damages from British Airways, which had been using a variety of sharp practices to take customers away from his airline, Virgin Atlantic, and reinforce its dominant market position. In this case Branson himself sued BA for damages in the civil courts in Britain. He threatened to use the U.S. courts as well, because he had much greater power to extract damages from BA under U.S. law.

Both the European Union laws and the U.S. laws impose much bigger penalties on violators than do the British ones. Under Articles 85 and 86 of the Treaty of Rome, firms can be fined up to 10 percent of their annual turnover. A number of European steelmakers were fined for operating a cartel in early 1994 under these laws. In the United States, firms can be required to pay punitive damages of up to three times the value of the losses they have imposed on competing firms as a result of their breaches of the U.S. antitrust laws.

Another feature of the U.S. laws is that aggrieved firms can bring antitrust actions against their competitors. Thus enforcement is partly in private hands and does not depend on the government administration, as is the norm in Britain. Cases in the United States are decided, and penalties imposed, by the law courts. Again this takes the enforcement of the law outside the hands of administrative officials and politicians. This procedure has some bad effects: firms can use an antitrust suit (or the threat of one) to influence a competitor's behaviour, for example, by preventing a merger from taking place while a case is being heard. But it also has good effects, in

POLICY PERSPECTIVE:
THE EUROPEAN COMMISSION FIGHTS CARTELS

1994 was a big year for the Competition Commissioner of the European Commission, Karel van Miert.

In February 1994 the European Commission fined 16 leading European steelmakers £79 million for running a cartel in the supply of steel beams to the construction industry. The largest single fine, £24 million, was imposed on British Steel. It was alleged that prices had been fixed, that confidential information had been exchanged between firms, and that the firms had reached an agreement to divide up the market between them.

In July 1994, the commission fined 19 cartonboard producers a total of £104 million, describing them as having formed Europe's "most pernicious" cartel. The participants had met in luxury Swiss hotels to agree to price rises and concealed their activities by drawing up bogus minutes of their meetings. The cartel operated between 1987 and 1990 and was uncovered in 1991, through a series of unannounced inspections carried out in April 1991 following complaints by the customers of these companies. Eventually, one of the participants came clean with the commission.

And finally in November 1994, the commission fined 33 European cement producers 248 million ecus (or £193 million, using the exchange rate prevailing at the time) for having run a cartel over a ten-year period. Although the members of the cartel kept no minutes of their collusive meetings, the commission found enough evidence of collusion, having conducted a series of raids on the headquarters of all the leading EU cement companies. The members of the cartel agreed not to ship cement across internal EU borders and exchanged information on prices so as to align prices and remove the incentive to export cement. A number of notes exchanged by members of the cartel exposed their sharing of markets. The cartel kept Greek cement out of the European Union after 1986.

Cement is an industry particularly prone to cartelization and anticompetitive practices. Cement has a long history of cartels, both legal and illegal. In 1989, the German Cartel Office fined German producers £100 million for price fixing; in 1992 the Italian antitrust authority imposed fines of £2 million on a cartel in southern Italy. In 1987 a 50-year-old legal pricing arrangement was ended in Britain; a legal cartel in Switzerland established in 1911 was dismantled only in 1994.

National markets are dominated by a few large companies, because the cost of setting up a modern cement works (put at £100 million for a medium-sized plant) is so high and its output is very large in relation to national demand. The demand for cement, by the construction industry, is highly cyclical, giving a great temptation to price stabilization through clandestine agreements. The cement market in Britain is dominated by three firms—Blue Circle, Rugby, and Castle—which have over 90 percent of the market; in France four firms have over 90 percent of the market. The European Commission argued that cement can be traded profitably over long distances and that the appropriate definition of the market is Europe and not individual member states.

Sources: Geoff Stewart, "Cartels," *Economic Review,* September 1994, pp. 25–26; "Brussels Fines Carton Board Price Fixers Record £104.27m," *Financial Times,* 14 July 1994; "How the Cement Cartel Came Unstuck," *Financial Times,* 2 December 1994.

that it might prevent someone like the secretary of state for trade and industry from using his discretion for other purposes than to promote competition. For example, it has often been claimed in Britain that potential mergers have been referred to the Competition Commission and effectively prevented from happening simply to prevent non-British firms from taking over British ones.

While the United States has pursued a consistent line in its competition policy ever since the time of the great robber barons of the late nineteenth century like John D. Rockefeller or Andrew Carnegie, the government of the United Kingdom has had a more ambivalent attitude to it. Indeed, during the 1950s and 1960s, when Britain's falling share of world trade and persistent deficits on the balance of payments were a continuous source of political concern, mergers between large companies within Britain were encouraged, even when they produced

firms that had a dominant position in the markets within the United Kingdom. The argument used was that the larger merged firms were needed to compete effectively with large firms outside the United Kingdom. So, for example, in the motor industry a number of smaller firms—Austin, Morris, Wolseley, Riley, and MG—were absorbed into the British Motor Corporation, which eventually merged with others to become British Leyland and finally Rover. A similar process of mergers established British Aerospace. The government of the United Kingdom has at times leaned more towards promoting competition (a tendency exhibited by Margaret Thatcher as prime minister and Norman Tebbit as secretary of state for trade and industry in the 1980s), and at other times leaned more towards promoting British industry, with less regard for competition (a tendency exhibited by Michael Heseltine as president of the Board of Trade in the early 1990s).

REVIEW AND PRACTICE

SUMMARY

1 Economists have identified four major problems resulting from monopolies and imperfect competition: restricted output and excessive profits, managerial slack, lack of incentives for technological progress, and a tendency towards wasteful rent-seeking expenditures.

2 Since for a natural monopoly average costs are declining over the range of market demand, a large firm can undercut its rivals. And since marginal cost for a natural monopoly lies below average costs, an attempt by regulators to require it to set price equal to marginal cost (as in the case of perfect competition) will force the firm to make losses.

3 Taking ownership of a natural monopoly allows the government to set price and quantity directly. But it also subjects an industry to political pressures and the potential inefficiencies of government operation.

4 When natural monopolies are in the hands of private companies, they are regulated. Government reg-

ulators seek to keep prices as low and quantity as high as is consistent with the natural monopolist's covering its costs. However, regulators must also face problems of cross-subsidies and the possibility of being captured by the industry they are regulating.

5 In some cases, competition may be as effective as public ownership or government regulation at keeping prices low.

6 A large part of government policy towards industry is concerned with promoting competition, both by prohibiting any firm from dominating a market and by restricting practices that interfere with competition.

7 Monopolies may be allowed to exist and mergers between large companies may be allowed to go ahead if it is ruled that they do not operate against the public interest. A loss of competition may be balanced against lower costs for the merged or monopolistic producer than there would be otherwise.

KEY TERMS

managerial slack   cross-subsidization   regulatory capture   "RPI minus x"

rent seeking

REVIEW QUESTIONS

1 What does it mean when an economist says that monopoly output is "too little" or a monopoly price is "too high"? By what standard? Compared with what?

2 Why might a monopoly lack incentives to hold costs as low as possible?

3 Why might a monopoly lack incentives to pursue research and development opportunities aggressively?

4 What might an economist regard as a socially wasteful way of spending monopoly profits?

5 Explain why the marginal cost curve of a natural monopoly lies below its average cost curve. What are the consequences of this?

6 If government regulators of a natural monopoly set price equal to marginal cost, what problem will inevitably arise? How might nationalization or regulation address this problem?

7 What is the regulatory capture hypothesis?

PROBLEMS

1 The post office charges the same price to deliver a first-class letter between any two points in the United Kingdom. Other carriers may argue that they could provide a postal service between big cities for a much lower price. What does this imply about cross-subsidization in the post office? What might be the consequences of allowing competitors to offer a postal service between places of their own choosing, while continuing to require the post office to deliver mail from any point in the country to any other point?

2 Do the large reductions in employment which have taken place at British Telecom since it was privatised demonstrate that the private sector is more efficient than the public sector?

3 Explain the incentive problem involved if regulators assure that a natural monopoly will be able to cover its average costs.

4 Explain how some competition, even if not perfect, may be an improvement for consumers over an unregulated natural monopoly. Explain why such competition will not be as good for consumers as an extremely sophisticated regulator and why it may be better than many real-world regulators.

5 Should a monopoly be allowed to exist on the grounds that it would lead to greater efficiency in the use of resources?

CHAPTER 16

TECHNOLOGICAL CHANGE

T he great strength of the market economy has been its ability to increase productivity, raise living standards, and innovate. Yet, the basic competitive model upon which we focused in Part Two simply *assumed* the state of technology as given.

If we are to understand what determines the pace of innovation, we must go beyond the standard competitive model.

First, industries in which technological change is important are almost necessarily imperfectly competitive. Second, the basic competitive model of Part Two assumes that individuals and firms receive all the benefits and pay all the costs of their actions. This assumption takes no account of the externalities produced by technological change. There is little doubt that we have all benefited from the multitude of inventions that have occurred in the last century. Just imagine what life would be like without the radio, television, cars, aeroplanes, washing machines, dishwashers, antibiotics—the list is endless. Alexander Graham Bell, Henry Ford, the Wright brothers, Alexander Fleming were all rewarded for their inventions, some richly so. But the creation of these new products confers benefits beyond what consumers have to pay for them. Inventions possess certain characteristics of public goods.

This chapter shows why technological change is inevitably linked to imperfect competition. It then discusses the public good aspects of technological change and alternative ways to promote it.

KEY QUESTIONS

1 In what ways is the production of knowledge—including the knowledge of how to make new products and how to produce things more cheaply—different from the production of ordinary goods, like shoes and wheat?

2 Why is the patent system important in providing incentives to engage in research and development?

3 How may patents, as essential as they are for encouraging competition in research, at the same time reduce some aspects of competition?

4 How can government encourage technological progress?

LINKS BETWEEN TECHNOLOGICAL CHANGE AND IMPERFECT COMPETITION

In modern industrialised economies, much competition takes the form of trying to develop both new products and new ways of making old products. Firms devote a considerable amount of their resources to R & D—research (discovering new ideas, products, and processes) and development (perfecting, for instance, a new product to the point where it is brought to the market). In industries in which technological change (and therefore R & D) is important, such as computers and drugs, firms strive to earn profits by introducing new and better (at least in the eyes of consumers) goods or less costly methods of production. Only through such profits can the investment in R & D pay.

Technological change and imperfect competition are inevitably linked for three major reasons. First, in order to make R & D expenditure pay, and therefore stimulate innovation, inventions are protected from competition by patents. Patents are specifically designed to limit competition. Second, industries where technological change is important typically have high fixed costs—costs that do not change as output increases. This characteristic implies decreasing average costs over a wide range of output, another characteristic of imperfect competition. Finally, industries characterised by rapid technological change are also industries where the benefits of increasing experience in a new production technique can lead to rapidly decreasing costs. All these make entry difficult and reduce competition in the sense defined by the basic competitive model.

PATENTS

A **patent** grants for a limited time to authors and inventors the exclusive right to their respective writing and discoveries. The limited time for inventors is currently 20 years in Europe and 17 years in the United States. During this period, other producers are precluded from producing the same good, or even making use of the invention in a product of their own, without the permission of the patent holder. Patent holders can sell to others the right to use their product in exchange for a payment called a royalty.

THE TRADE-OFF BETWEEN SHORT-RUN EFFICIENCY AND INNOVATION

The patent system grants the inventor a temporary monopoly, allowing her to appropriate some part of the returns on her inventive activity. In Chapter 13, we learned that relative to competitive markets, monopolies result in lower output and higher prices. In spite of this and in spite of the competition policies discussed in Chapter 13, why does government sanction these monopolies?

In Chapter 12, where we explained why competitive markets, with price equal to marginal cost, ensure economic efficiency, we assumed that the technology was given. We refer to the kind of economic efficiency that ignores concerns about innovation and invention as **short-run efficiency.**

But the overall efficiency of the economy requires balancing these short-run concerns with the long-run objectives of stimulating research and innovation. Innovation requires firms to reap a return on their investment, and that in turn requires some degree of monopoly power. An economy in which the balancing of short- and long-run concerns is appropriately done is said to be **dynamically efficient.**

A key provision of the patent law for the trade-off between short-run efficiency and the innovation necessary for dynamic efficiency is the **life of the patent.** If the life of a patent is short, then firms can appropriate the returns from their innovation for only a short time. There is less incentive to innovate than if the patent protection (and monopoly) lasted longer, but the economy has greater short-run efficiency. If the life of a patent is long, then there are large incentives to innovate, but the benefits of the innovation are limited. Consumers, in particular, must wait a long time before prices fall. The 20-year patent period is intended to strike a balance between the benefits to consumers and the return to investments in R & D.

AN EXAMPLE: THE SWEET MELON COMPANY

Figure 16.1 illustrates the effect of a patent owned by the Sweet Melon Company on a new, cheaper process for producing frozen watermelon juice. To make it simple, the marginal cost of production is constant in this example. Before the innovation, all producers face the same marginal cost c_0. Sweet Melon's innovation reduces the marginal cost of production to c_1. Imagine that this industry is perfectly competitive before the innovation, so that price equals marginal cost c_0. But now Sweet Melon is able to undercut its rivals. With patent protection, the firm sells the good for slightly less than p_0. Its rivals drop out of the market because at the new, lower price, they cannot break even. Sweet Melon now has the whole market. The company sells the quantity Q_1 at the price p_1, making a profit of AB on each sale. Total profits are the shaded area $ABCD$ in the figure. The innovation pays off if the profits received exceed the cost of the research.

What happens when the patent expires? Other firms enter the industry, using the less expensive technology. Competition forces the price down to the now lower marginal cost c_1 and output expands to Q_2. The new equilibrium is at E. Consumers are clearly better off. Short-run economic efficiency is enhanced, because price is now equal to marginal cost. But Sweet Melon reaps no further return from its expenditures on research and development.

If no patent were available, competitors would immediately copy the new juice-making process, and the price would drop to c_1 as soon as the innovation became available. Sweet Melon would receive absolutely no returns. (In practice, of course, imitation takes time, during which the company would be able to obtain *some* returns from the innovation.) If the patent were made permanent, consumers would benefit only a small amount from the innovation, since other companies could not compete. Output would remain at Q_1, slightly greater than the original output, and the price would remain high.

BREADTH OF PATENT PROTECTION

How broad a patent's coverage should be is as important as its duration. If an inventor comes up with a product quite similar to one that has already been

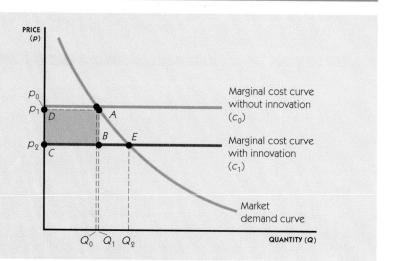

Figure 16.1 ECONOMIC EFFECT OF PATENTS

Here, an innovation has reduced the marginal cost of production from c_0 to c_1. Before the innovation, the equilibrium price is p_0, which equals c_0. However, an innovator with a patent will drop the price to p_1, just below p_0, and sell the quantity Q_1. Total profits are the shaded area $ABCD$. When the patent expires, competitors reenter the market, price falls to p_2, which equals c_1, and profits drop to zero.

CLOSE-UP: JOSEPH SCHUMPETER AND SCHUMPETERIAN COMPETITION

The economist most known for emphasising the role of innovation in market economies is the economist Joseph Schumpeter. Schumpeter began his career in Austria (serving from spring to October 1919 as minister of finance to the emperor of the Austrian-Hungarian Empire) and ended his career as a distinguished professor of economics at Harvard University. His vision of the economy was markedly different from that of the competition equilibrium model. That model focuses on equilibrium, a state of the world in which there is no change. He questioned the very concept of equilibrium. To him the economy was always in flux and the economist's role was to understand the forces driving those changes.

Schumpeter argued that the economy was characterised by a process of creative destruction. An innovator could, through his new product or lower costs of production, establish a dominant position in a market. But eventually, that dominant position would be destroyed, as a new innovator took his place.[1]

He worried that the giant corporations he saw being formed during his life would stifle innovation and end this process of creative destruc-tion. His fears, so far, have been unfounded; indeed, many of the largest firms, like IBM, have not been able to manage the innovative process in a way that keeps up with upstart rivals.

Modern day Schumpeterians often turn to biology to help them understand the process of change. They describe changes as *evolutionary*. They see a slow process of change, with many random elements. Firms that are the fittest—by luck or skill manage to discover new products or new ways of doing business that are better, in the particular environment, than their rivals'—manage to survive, and their practices spread to other firms.

As respect for and understanding of the importance of innovation has grown, so too have the number of economists who think of themselves as Schumpeterians. And the Schumpeter Society of Austria provides an award every year to honour someone in the Schumpeterian tradition. In 1994, the award went to an American, Ted Turner, founder of CNN.

---

[1] We discussed this kind of competition—a succession of monopolies—in "Schumpeterian Competition," Chapter 13.

---

patented yet slightly different, can this inventor also get a patent for his variant? Or does the original patent cover minor variants? Chapter 1 discussed the patent claim of George Baldwin Selden, who argued that his patent covered all self-propelled, petrol-powered vehicles. He tried to force Henry Ford and the other pioneers of the automobile industry to pay royalties to him, but Ford successfully challenged the patent claim. Recently controversies over patents have hit genetic engineering and super-conductivity. Does a firm that decodes a fraction of a gene and establishes a use for that information, for example, get a patent? If so, does the patent cover the fraction in question or the whole gene?

The original innovators have every incentive to claim broad patent coverage affecting their own product and those which are in any way related. Later entrants argue for narrow coverage, so that they will be allowed to produce variants and applications without paying royalties. As usual in economics, there is a trade-off. Broad coverage ensures that the inventor reaps more of the returns of her innovation. But excessively broad coverage inhibits innovation, as others see their returns to further developing the idea squeezed by the royalties they must pay to the original inventor.

TRADE SECRETS

If patents protect the profits of innovation, why do many firms not bother to seek patent protection for their new products and processes? A major reason is that a firm cannot get a patent without disclosing the details of the new product or process—information that may be extremely helpful to its rivals in furthering their own R & D programmes.

To prevent such disclosure, companies sometimes prefer to keep their own innovations a **trade secret.** A trade secret is simply an innovation or knowledge of a production process that a firm does not disclose to others. The formula for Coca-Cola, for example, is not protected by a patent. It is a trade secret. Trade secrets play an important role in metallurgy, where new alloys are usually not patented. Trade secrets have one major disadvantage over patents. If a rival firm *independently* discovers the same new process, say for making an alloy, it can use the process without paying royalties, even though it was second on the scene.

Some of the returns to an invention come simply from being first in the market. Typically, the firm that first introduces a new product has a decided advantage over rivals, as it builds up customer loyalty and a reputation. Latecomers often have a hard time breaking in, even if there is no patent or trade secret protection.

R & D AS A FIXED COST

Patents and trade secrets are not the only reason that industries in which technological change is important are generally not perfectly competitive. A second explanation is that R & D expenditures are fixed costs. That is, the costs of inventing something do not change according to how many times the idea

is used in production.[1] The amount of fixed costs helps determine how competitive an industry is. The greater the fixed costs, the more likely that there will be few firms and limited competition.

Because expenditures on research and development are fixed costs, industries with large R & D expenditures face declining average cost curves up to relatively high levels of output. We saw in Chapter 10 that firms typically have U-shaped average cost curves. The presence of fixed costs means that average costs initially decline as firms produce more, but for all the reasons discussed in Chapter 10, beyond some level of output average costs increase. When there are large fixed costs, large firms will have lower average costs than small firms and enjoy a competitive advantage (see Figure 16.2). Industries with large fixed costs thus tend to have relatively few firms and limited competition. It is not surprising, therefore, that the chemical industry—where R & D is tremendously important—is highly concentrated.

Increased size also provides firms with greater incentives to undertake research. Suppose a small firm produces one million pens a year. If it discovers a better production technology that reduces its costs by £1 per pen, it saves £1 million a year. A large firm that makes the same discovery and produces ten million pens a year will save £10 million a year. Thus, large firms have more incentive to engage in research and development, and as they do, they grow more than their smaller rivals do.

But while a large firm's research-and-development department may help the firm win a competitive advantage, it may also create managerial problems. Bright innovators can feel stifled in the bureaucratic environment of a large corporation, and they may also feel that they are inadequately compensated for their research efforts. In the computer industry, for example, many capable people have left the larger firms to start up new companies of their own.

Thus, size has both its advantages and disadvantages when it comes to innovation. Important inven-

---

[1] R & D expenditures can themselves be varied. Differences in the expenditure level will affect when new products will be brought to market and whether a firm will beat its rivals in the competition for new products.

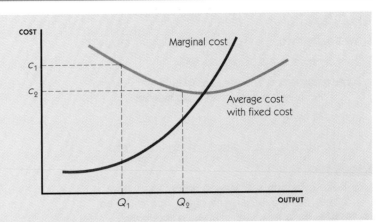

Figure 16.2 COSTS OF RESEARCH AND DEVELOPMENT

R & D costs are fixed costs; they do not vary with the scale of production. In industries that are R & D intensive, average costs will be declining over a wide range of outputs. Firms with low levels of output (Q_1) have higher average costs than those with higher output (Q_2).

tions and innovations, such as nylon, transistors, and the laser have been produced by major corporations; on the other hand, small enterprises and individual inventors have produced Apple computers, Polaroid cameras, and Kodak film, all of which became major corporations as a result of their success. One objective of monopolies and merger policies is to maintain an economic environment in which small, innovative firms can compete effectively against established giants.

LEARNING BY DOING

Some increases in productivity occur not as a result of explicit expenditures on R & D but as a by-product of production. As firms gain experience from production, their costs fall. This kind of technological change is called **learning by doing.** This systematic relationship between cumulative production experience and costs—often called the **learning curve**—was first discovered in the aeroplane industry, where as more planes of a given type were produced, the costs of production fell dramatically.

This is the third reason why technological change and imperfect competition go together—because the marginal cost falls as the scale of production (and the experience accumulated) increases. The first firm to enter an industry has a particular advantage over other firms. Even if some of what the first company has learned spills over to other firms, not all of it does. Because of the knowledge the first firm has gained, its costs will be below those of potential rivals, and thus it can always undercut them. Since potential entrants know this, they are reluctant to enter industries where learning by doing has a significant impact on costs. By the same token, companies realise that if they can find a product that provides significant benefits from learning by doing, the profits they earn will be relatively secure. Hence, just as firms race to be the first to obtain a patent, so too they race to be the first to enter a product market in which there is a steep learning curve. This behaviour is commonly displayed in the computer chip industry.

When learning by doing is important, firms will produce beyond the point where marginal revenue equals *current* marginal cost, because producing more today has an extra benefit. It reduces future costs of production. How much extra a firm produces depends on the steepness of the learning curve.

ACCESS TO CAPITAL MARKETS

Banks are generally unwilling to lend funds to finance R & D expenditure, because the results are

COMPETITION AND TECHNOLOGICAL CHANGE

HOW COMPETITION AFFECTS TECHNOLOGICAL CHANGE

Competition spurs R & D:

> A new innovation enables firms to enjoy profits (profits are driven to zero in standard markets).

> Unless firms innovate, they will not survive.

Competition impedes R & D:

> Competitors may imitate, thus eroding returns from innovation.

> Competition erodes the profits required to finance R & D.

HOW TECHNOLOGICAL CHANGE AFFECTS COMPETITION

R & D spurs competition:

> R & D provides an alternative to prices as a way for firms to compete; it is one of the most important areas for competition in modern economies.

R & D impedes competition:

> Patents give a single firm a protected position for a number of years.

> The fixed costs of R & D give large firms an advantage and mean that industries in which R & D is important may have few firms.

> Learning by doing gives a decided advantage to the first entrant into a market.

> Limited access to capital markets for financing R & D is a disadvantage to new and small firms.

often very risky and these risks cannot be insured. When a bank makes a loan for a building, if the borrower defaults, the bank ends up with the building. If the bank lends for R & D and the research project fails or a rival beats the firm to the patent office, the bank may end up with nothing. Inventors also often have a hard time judging the prospects of an R & D endeavour; inventors are always optimistic about their ideas. This difficulty is compounded because an inventor may be reluctant to disclose all the information about his idea, either to banks or potential investors, lest some among them steal his idea and beat him to either the market or the patent office.

For established firms in industries with limited competition and growing demand, financing their research expenditure presents no serious problem. They can pay for R & D out of their profits. That is why, for the economy as a whole, most research and development occurs in such firms. But raising capital is a problem for new and small firms, and also for firms in industries where intense competition limits the profits that any one company can earn. Thus, a firm's dominant position in an industry may be self-perpetuating. Its greater output means that it has more to gain from innovations that reduce the cost

of production. Its greater profits give it more resources to expend on R & D.

Today much of the research and development in new and small companies is financed by venture capital firms. These firms raise capital, mainly from pension funds, insurance companies, and wealthy individuals, which they then invest in the most promising R & D ventures. Venture capital firms often demand, as compensation for their risk taking, a significant share of the new enterprise, and they usually keep close tabs on how their money is spent. They also sometimes specialise in particular areas, such as computer technology or biotechnology. In less glamorous industries, it is often difficult to find financing for research and development.

BASIC RESEARCH AS A PUBLIC GOOD

R & D expenditures on inventions or innovations almost always give rise to externalities. Externalities arise, as we learned in Chapter 7, whenever one individual's or firm's action produces costs or benefits to others. The total benefits produced by an R & D expenditure are referred to as its **social benefit.** Even with patents, inventors appropriate only a fraction of the social benefit of an invention. A firm that discovers a cheaper way of producing is likely to lower its price during the life of the patent to steal customers away from its rivals. This benefits consumers. After the patent expires, consumers benefit even more as rivals beat the price down further. And the benefits of an invention in one area spill over to other areas. The transistor, which revolutionised electronics, was invented at the research laboratories of the U.S. telephone company AT&T. Then AT&T reaped the benefits from its direct application to telephone equipment. But the benefits in better radios, television sets, and other products accrued to others.

From society's viewpoint, a particularly valuable kind of R & D is **basic research.** Basic research is the kind of fundamental inquiry that produces a wide range of applications. Basic research in physics, for example, led to the ideas behind so many of the things we take for granted today—the laser, the transistor, atomic energy. The returns to firms from any basic research they might undertake—which would dictate the amount of R & D spent on basic research in the absence of government intervention—are negligible in comparison to its social benefits. Indeed, the externalities flowing from basic research are so extreme that it can be considered a public good.

Public goods are defined by two properties. First, it is difficult to exclude anyone from the benefits of a public good. Basic research involves the discovery of underlying scientific principles or facts of nature. Such facts—like superconductivity, or even the fact that there exist certain materials that exhibit superconductivity at temperatures considerably above absolute zero—cannot be patented.

Second, the marginal cost of an additional individual enjoying a public good is zero. We say that consumption is nonrivalrous. An additional person's being informed of a basic discovery does not detract from the knowledge that the original discoverer has, though it may, of course, reduce the profits the original discoverer can make out of the discovery. Indeed, sharing the fruits of basic research as soon as they are available can yield enormous benefits, as other researchers use this knowledge in their quest for innovations.

Table 16.1 EXPENDITURE ON RESEARCH AND DEVELOPMENT IN VARIOUS COUNTRIES IN 1996 AS A PERCENTAGE OF GDP

United Kingdom	1.9
Germany	2.3
France	2.3
Italy	1.1
Japan	2.8 (1995)
Canada	1.7
United States	2.5

Source: Economic Trends, August 1998.

As with all public goods, private markets yield an undersupply of basic research. Accordingly, governments in most countries provide money to support basic research. In Britain it is done by the Department of Education and Science which gives funds to the research councils (the names of which seem to change continuously) and supports basic research in the universities. In France the equivalent body is the Centre Nationale pour la Recherche Scientifique, in the United States there is the National Science Foundation, and in other countries there are analogous organizations.

There is ongoing concern in most countries about whether enough R & D is taking place and whether the government is giving it enough support. Table 16.1 shows R & D expenditure as a proportion of GDP in 1996 in a number of countries. Japan tops the list. The United Kingdom is near the bottom of the list; only Canada and Italy have less R & D.

Most R & D is performed by private businesses, as Table 16.2 shows, and this largely consists of applied research and developmental work. The next-biggest contributor is higher education, and here more of the research is basic, long-term, so-called blue sky research, undertaken in the spirit of scientific inquiry, with less focus on short- or medium-term applicability (although, as we know very well, this kind of research often has enormous and profound long-term benefits). Industrial R & D is concentrated in a

Table 16.2 RESEARCH AND DEVELOPMENT EXPENDITURE IN THE UNITED KINGDOM IN 1996 (IN MILLION POUNDS)

Total R & D expenditure	14,340
Civilian	12,254
Defence	2,085
Performed by:	
Government	1,495
Research councils	575
Businesses	9,301
Higher education	2,792
Private nonprofit organizations	177
Total as a percentage of GDP	1.94
Distribution of R & D performed by businesses, by industry:	
Manufacturing	6,943
Chemicals	626
Pharmaceuticals	1,852
Mechanical engineering	605
Electrical engineering	1,265
Transport equipment	997
Aerospace	812
Other manufacturing	786
Services	2,358
Total	9,301

Source: Economic Trends, August 1998.

small number of recognisably high-tech industries—pharmaceuticals, aerospace, electrical machinery, and so on.

Britain's relatively low total expenditure on R & D may be due to a number of causes. It may be that Britain's high-tech industries do less R & D (relative to their size) than the same industries in other countries do. There is in fact little evidence for this. Or it could be that Britain has relatively little high-tech industry. Neither of these views is based on a clear idea of the costs and benefits of more R & D expenditure or of what constitutes the optimal amount of R & D. These concerns, which are beyond the scope of this book, are the subject of much contemporary research in economics.

GOVERNMENT PROMOTION OF TECHNOLOGICAL PROGRESS

While there is widespread agreement that government should encourage innovative activity through the protection of intellectual property rights and through support of basic R & D, other ways by which the government promotes R & D have been far more controversial.

SUBSIDIES

Government support for applied research has been attacked by critics. Among the reasons given is that the government has a bad record in picking what to subsidise. As evidence, they note that the Concorde, the supersonic aeroplane developed with the support of the British and French governments, has never been able to pay for itself. Many advocates of this view still support broad-based subsidies, such as R & D tax credits, which do not depend on government selection of particular projects.

But there are still supporters of more active involvement of government in R & D, who claim there are large positive externalities associated with applied research, implying that the private sector underinvests in applied research. Policies aimed to support particular sectors of the economy are called **industrial policies.**

Advocates of public support for applied R & D admit that government has not always picked winners. But they claim R & D is by its very nature risky and a record of complete success cannot be expected.

A rationale for government R & D expenditures in competitive industries is that an industry made up of many firms will fall further below the socially efficient level of R & D expenditure than industries in which a few firms dominate (and can, therefore, reap for themselves most of the benefits of their R & D investment).

Advocates of government technology programmes argue, further, that government should work in partnership with industry to increase the effectiveness of its R & D investment. They advocate requiring industry to put up money of its own and making the competition for funds very broad.

Subsidies have, however, raised the spectre of unfair competition in the international arena. Countries facing competition from foreign firms with government subsidies impose countervailing duties, that is, taxes on imports that are intended to offset the benefits of these subsidies. The concern is if, for instance, Europe and the Untied States become engaged in a contest to support some industry, the industry will benefit but at the expense of the taxpayers in all the countries. Thus, international agreements have tried to reduce the extent of subsidization. Broad-based R & D subsidies (such as through the tax system) are still permitted, but more narrowly focused subsidies are either prohibited or put into the category of questionable practices.

PROTECTION

Firms in developing countries often argue that they need to be insulated from competition from abroad in order to develop the knowledge base required to compete effectively in world markets. This is the **infant industry argument for protection.** Most economists are skeptical. They see this argument mainly as an attempt at rent seeking by firms that will use any excuse to insulate themselves from competition so they can raise prices and increase profits. The best way to learn to compete is to compete, not to be isolated from competition. If some help is needed to enable firms to catch up, it should be provided in the form of subsidies, the costs of which are explicit and obvious, unlike the hidden costs of higher prices that result from protection.

RELAXING COMPETITION POLICIES

The competition policies explored in Chapter 15 were founded on the belief that government should push markets towards the model of perfect competition. But an increasing awareness of the importance of R & D in modern industrial economies has led some to argue for change.

TECHNOLOGICAL CHANGE AND THE BASIC COMPETITIVE MODEL

Basic Competitive Model	Industries in Which Technological Change Is Important
Fixed technology	The central question is what determines the pace of technological change. Related issues include what determines expenditure on R & D and how learning by doing affects the level of production.
Perfect competition, with many firms in industry	Competition is not perfect; industries where technological change is important tend to have relatively few firms.
Perfect capital markets	Firms find it difficult to borrow to finance R & D expenditures.
No externalities	R & D confers benefits to those besides the inventor; even with patents, the inventor appropriates only a fraction of the social benefits of an invention.
No public goods	Basic research is a public good: the marginal cost of an additional person's making use of a new idea is zero (nonrivalrous consumption), and it is often difficult to exclude others from enjoying the benefits of basic research.

A major argument for change is that cooperation aimed at sharing knowledge and coordinating research among firms in an industry has the effect of internalising the externalities of R & D. But governments worry that cooperation in R & D could easily grow into cooperation in other areas, such as price setting, which would not serve the public interest. There is a danger that a joint research venture might involve agreements between firms that fall foul of the Restrictive Trade Practices Act in Britain. It might be that their project would lead to the firms' colluding (or at least appearing to collude) on prices or output levels and being punished under the European Commission's powers. However, governments attempt to limit the conflict between the policies of promoting innovation and promoting competition. The European Union gives exemptions from the competition laws (which are based on Articles 85 and 86 of the Treaty of Rome) for collaborative R & D projects. The United States introduced a National Collaborative Research Act in 1984 to protect this kind of R & D. Competition policy in Britain makes no special provision for collaborative R & D; however, it can be claimed that it acts in the public interest, which is an accepted defence of practices that might be considered anticompetitive.

REVIEW AND PRACTICE

SUMMARY

1 Industries in which technological change is important are almost necessarily imperfectly competitive. Patents are one way the government makes it difficult and costly for firms to copy the technological innovations of others. A firm with a patent will have a government-enforced monopoly. The expenditures on R & D are fixed costs; when they are large, there are likely to be few firms in the industry, and price competition is more likely to be limited.

2 Long-lived and broad patents discourage competition (at least in the short run) but provide greater incentives to innovate. Short-lived and narrow patents reduce the incentive to innovate but encourage competition.

3 Learning by doing, in which companies (or countries) that begin making a product first enjoy an advantage over all later entrants, may be a source of technological advantage.

4 Research and development generally provides positive externalities to consumers and other firms. But since the innovating firm cannot capture all the social benefits from its invention, it will tend to invest less than a socially optimal amount.

5 Basic research has both the central properties of a public good: it is difficult to exclude others from the benefits of the research, and the marginal cost of an additional person's making use of the new idea is zero.

6 A number of government policies encourage technological advance: patents, direct spending on research, tax incentives to encourage corporate R & D, temporary protection from technologically advanced foreign competitors, and relaxing competition laws to allow potential competitors to work together on research projects.

KEY TERMS

patent	learning by doing	industrial policy	infant industry argument for protection
trade secret	learning curve		

REVIEW QUESTIONS

1 In what ways do industries in which technological change is important not satisfy the assumptions of the standard competitive model?

2 Why are industries in which technological change is important not likely to be competitive?

3 Why do governments grant patents, thereby conferring temporary monopoly rights? Explain the trade-off society faces in choosing whether to offer long-lived or short-lived patents and whether to offer broad or narrow patents.

4 How does the existence of learning by doing provide an advantage to incumbent firms over prospective entrants?

5 Why might it be harder to raise capital for R & D than for other projects? How can established firms deal with this problem? What about start-up firms?

6 How do positive externalities arise from research and development? Why do externalities imply that there may be too little expenditure on research by private firms?

7 Explain how basic research can be thought of as a public good. Why is society likely to underinvest in basic research? What is the economist's reason for supporting government subsidies in areas that help produce new technology?

8 What are industrial policies? What are the arguments for and against government support of research in particular industries?

9 What possible trade-off does society face when it considers loosening its competition laws to encourage joint research and development ventures?

PROBLEMS

1 Imagine that the European Commission is considering a bill to reduce the current 20-year life of patents to 8 years. What negative effects might this change have on the rate of innovation? What positive effect might it have for the economy?

2 Suppose that many years ago, one inventor received a patent for orange juice, and then another inventor came forward and requested a patent for lemonade. The first inventor maintained that the or-

ange juice patent should be interpreted to cover all fruit juices, while the second inventor argued that the original patent included only one particular method of making one kind of juice. What trade-offs does society face in setting rules for deciding cases like this?

3 Although a patent assures a monopoly on that particular invention for some time, it also requires that the inventor disclose the details of the invention.

Given this requirement, under what conditions might a company (like Coca-Cola) prefer to use a trade secret rather than a patent to protect its formula?

4 Why might a company invest in research and development even if it does not believe it will be able to patent its discovery?

5 Learning by doing seems to be important in the semiconductor industry, where the United States and Japan are the main producers. Explain why U.S. and Japanese firms may race to try to bring out new generations of semiconductors. Draw a learning curve to illustrate your answers. If learning by doing is important in the semiconductor industry, why might other countries try to use an infant industry strategy to develop their own semiconductor industry?

CHAPTER 17

IMPERFECT INFORMATION IN THE PRODUCT MARKET

I t was never any secret to economists that the real world did not match the model of perfect competition. Theories of monopoly and imperfect competition such as those covered in Chapters 13 to 16 have been propounded from Adam Smith's time to the present.

Another limitation of the model of perfect competition has recently come to the fore: its assumption of **perfect information**—that market participants have full information about the goods being bought and sold. By incorporating **imperfect information** into their models, economists have come a long way in closing the gap between the real world and the world depicted by the perfect competition, perfect information model of Part Two.

This chapter provides a broad overview of the major information problems of the product market, the ways in which market economies deal with them, and how the basic model of Part Two has to be modified as a result. In the following chapter, we will see how information problems affect labour markets (Chapter 18). In Parts Four and Five, we will see how many of the most important macro-economic problems can be traced, at least in part, to information problems.

KEY QUESTIONS

1 Why is information different from other goods, such as hats and cameras? Why, in particular, do markets for information often not work well?

2 When does the market price affect the quality of what is being sold? How does the fact that consumers believe price affects quality influence how firms behave?

3 When customers have trouble differentiating good from shoddy merchandise, what are the incentives firms have to produce good merchandise? What role does reputation play?

4 Why is it that, in the same market, identical or very similar goods will sell at different prices? How does the fact that search is costly affect the nature of competition?

5 How does advertising affect firm demand curves and profits? Why may the firms in an industry be better off if they collectively agree not to advertise?

6 What has government done to address the problem of imperfect information? Why do these efforts have only limited success?

THE INFORMATION PROBLEM

The basic competitive model assumes that households and firms are well informed. This means that they know their opportunity set, or what is available. More striking, they know every characteristic of every good, including how long it will last. Were these assumptions true, shopping would hardly be a chore.

The model also assumes that consumers know their preferences, what they like. They know not only how many oranges they can trade for an apple but also how many oranges they are willing to trade. In the case of apples and oranges this may make sense. But how do students know how much they are going to enjoy, or even benefit from, their education before they have experienced it? How does an individual know whether she would like to be a doctor or a lawyer? She gets some idea about what different professions are like by observing those who practice them, but her information is at best imperfect.

According to the basic model, firms too are perfectly well informed. They all know the best available technology. They know the productivity of each applicant for a job. They know the prices at which inputs can be purchased from every possible supplier (and all of the inputs' characteristics). And they know the prices at which they can sell the goods, not only today but in every possible circumstance in the future.

HOW BIG A PROBLEM?

That individuals and firms are not perfectly well informed is, by itself, not necessarily a telling criticism of the competitive model, just as the criticism that markets are not perfectly competitive does not cause us to discard the model. The relevant questions have to do with the danger that the competitive model will mislead us. Are there important economic phenomena that can be explained only by taking into account imperfect information? Are there important predictions of the model that are incorrect as a result of the assumptions concerning well-informed consumers and firms?

Increasingly, over the past two decades, economists have come to believe that the answer to these questions is yes. We have already seen evidence of this. Graduates may receive a higher income than nongraduates, not only because they have learned things that make them more productive but because their degree helps them through a sorting process. Employers cannot glean from an interview which applicants for a job will be productive workers. They therefore use a degree to help them identify those who are better at learning. Graduates *are*, on average, more productive workers. But it is wrong to conclude from this that graduation has necessarily *increased* their productivity. It may simply have enabled firms to sort out more easily the more productive from the less productive.

The same problems arise when people invest in the stock market. The basic maxim for success in investing is simple. Buy when the price is low, and sell when the price is high. The problem is how to know when the price of a stock is low or high.

HOW PRICES CONVEY INFORMATION

The price system provides brilliant solutions for some information problems. We have seen how prices play an important role in coordinating production and communicating information about economic scarcity. Firms do not have to know what John or Julia likes, what their trade-offs are. The price tells the producer the marginal benefit of producing an extra unit of the good, and that is all he needs to know. Similarly, a firm does not need to know how much iron ore is left in the world, the cost of refining iron ore, or a thousand other details. All it needs to know is the price of iron ore. This tells the company how scarce the resource is, how much effort it should expend in conserving it. Prices and markets provide the basis of the economy's incentive system. But there are some information problems that markets do not handle or do not handle well. And imperfect information sometimes inhibits the ability of markets to perform the tasks it performs so well when information is good.

MARKETS FOR INFORMATION

Information has value; people are willing to pay for it. In this sense, we can consider information just as we do any other good. There is a market for information with its price, just as there is a market for labour and a market for capital. Indeed, our economy is sometimes referred to as an information economy. Every year, investors spend millions on newsletters that give them information. Magazines sell specialised information about hundreds of goods.

However, the markets for information are far from perfect, and for good reasons. The most conspicuous one is that information is *not* just like any other good. When you buy a chair, the furniture dealer is happy to let you look at it, feel it, sit on it, and decide whether you like it. When you buy information, you cannot do the same. The seller can either say, "Trust me. I'll tell you what you need to know," or show you the information and say, "Here's what I know. If this is what you wanted to know, please pay me." You would rightfully be skeptical in the first scenario, and might be unwilling to pay in the second. After you were given the information, what incentive would you have to pay?

In some cases, there is a basic credibility problem. You might think, if a stock tipster *really* knows that a stock is going to go up in price, why should he tell me, even if I pay him for the information? Why doesn't he go out and make his fortune with the information? Or is it that he really is not sure and would just as soon have me risk my money rather than risk his?

Most important, even after the firm or consumer buys all the information he thinks is worth paying for, his information is still far from perfect. Let's look now at some of the consequences of imperfect information.

THE MARKET FOR LEMONS AND ADVERSE SELECTION

Have you ever wondered why a three-month-old used car sells for so much less—often 20 percent less—than a new car? Surely cars do not deteriorate that fast. The pleasure of owning a new car may be worth something, but in three months, even the car you can buy new will be "used." But a thousand pounds or more is a steep price to pay for this short-lived pleasure.

George Akerlof has provided a simple explanation, based on imperfect information. Some cars are worse than others. They have hidden defects which become apparent to the owner only after she has owned the car for a while. In the United States such defective cars are called lemons. One thing after another goes wrong with them. While warranties may

CLOSE-UP: INSURANCE BROKERS AND INDEPENDENT FINANCIAL ADVISERS

People go to insurance brokers when buying insurance policies such as life insurance or car insurance. The broker's job is to collect information on policies that might be available and find one suited to the customer's needs at the best price—to find the best policy for the customer. Insurance is a very complicated area, there are many different policies available with different features, and gathering all the information takes a long time. For an inexperienced person, it would certainly involve a lot of hard work to understand the detail of all the available policies and decide on the best one. Indeed, notoriously, most people do not even look at the fine print on the insurance policies they take out. It makes much sense for someone to specialise in gathering all the information, become an expert on insurance policies, and give advice to people wanting to take out policies.

But who pays the broker for his advice? The customer does not pay directly for advice. The practice in Britain for many years was for the insurance companies themselves to pay the brokers, by paying a commission to the broker on each policy sold. This clearly creates a problem, because it need not necessarily be in the broker's interests to give a consumer impartial advice. Depending on the size of the commissions available, the broker may have a financial incentive to recommend the policy that gives the higher commission even if it is not in the consumer's interests. The fact that the broker's payment is a commission from the company may open up a conflict of interest between the broker and the customer. Brokers argue that they nevertheless act in the customer's interest, because they have an interest in securing business in the long term and they want to protect their

reputations for giving sound, impartial advice. Some steps have been made in recent years to reduce the incentive problem in this relationship. Insurance companies and brokers are required to disclose the size of the commissions paid—information that used to be kept secret in the past. Some brokers return part of the commission to the customer as a discount on the premiums. Nevertheless, the incentive and information structure in insurance broking appears to be less than satisfactory.

Under the new regulatory regime introduced in Britain since the Big Bang in the City in London in 1986, banks and other financial advisers have been required to give much more information to customers in order to make clear what financial interest the adviser may have in the advice being given. For example, some banks offer financial advice, but as they sell their own financial products—insurance policies, savings schemes, and so on—they are permitted to advise only on their own products, not on their merits relative to products of other financial institutions, while other institutions, such as some Building Societies, do not sell their own range of financial products and can offer themselves as independent financial advisers.

This mis-selling of private pensions, which has cause a considerable furore, may be an example of what can go wrong when the regulatory structure is too lax. Several insurance companies began selling private pensions in the late 1980s, and they advised numbers of people to switch from company pension schemes into their private schemes. Highly reputable insurance companies such as Prudential were involved in this.

However, it has since come to light that many people were given bad advice, and the move to a private pension has cost them dear, either by providing them with lower pensions for given contributions or by requiring higher contributions to maintain the same pension. Several insurance companies have been taken to court and have been required to pay large sums in compensation to people who were badly advised.

Despite the greater amount of information given in recent years under the new regulatory arrangements to people taking financial advice, a situation in which advisers have a financial stake in the sale of the products on which they are advising does not look like one in which consumers are likely to get impartial advice. There is a new view that the regulatory system for financial markets in Britain needs to be strengthened further.

reduce the financial cost of having a lemon, they do not eliminate the bother—the time it takes to bring the car to a garage, the anxiety of knowing there is a good chance of a breakdown. The owners, of course, know they have a lemon and would like to pass it along to someone else. Those with the worst lemons are going to be the most willing to sell their car. But at a high used car price, they will be joined by owners of better quality cars. As the price drops, more of the good cars will be withdrawn from the market as the owners decide to keep them. And the average quality of the used cars for sale will *drop*. We say there is an adverse selection effect. The mix of those who elect to sell changes adversely as price falls. We encountered adverse selection in the insurance market in Chapter 6. We will encounter adverse se-

lection again in our discussion of labour market imperfections (Chapter 18).

Figure 17.1 shows the consequences of imperfect information for market equilibrium in the used car market. Panel A depicts, for each price (measured along the horizontal axis), the average quality of used cars being sold in the market. As price increases, quality increases. Panel B shows the supply curve of used cars. As price increases, the number of cars being sold in the market increases, for all the usual reasons. The demand curve is also shown. This curve has a peculiar shape: upward as well as downward sloping. The reason is that as price increases, the average quality increases. But demand depends not just on price but on quality—on the value being offered on the market. If, as price falls, quality deteri-

Figure 17.1 A MARKET WITH LEMONS

Panel A shows the average quality of a used car increasing as the price increases. Panel B shows a typical upward-sloping supply curve but a backward-bending demand curve. Demand bends back because buyers know that quality is lower at lower prices, and they thus choose to buy less as the price falls. Panel B shows the market equilibrium is at point *E*.

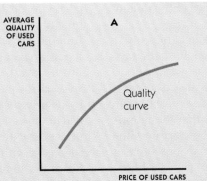

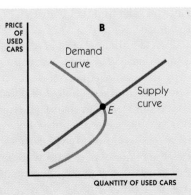

orates rapidly, then quantity demanded will *fall* as price falls; consumers are getting less for their pounds. The equilibrium is depicted in panel B.

This particular example is often referred to as one with **asymmetric information.** That is, the seller of the used car has more information about the product than the buyer. Many markets are characterised by asymmetric information. One of the consequences of asymmetric information is that there may be relatively few buyers and sellers, far fewer than there would be with perfect information. Economists use the term **thin** to describe markets in which there are relatively few buyers and sellers. In some situations, a market may be so thin as to be essentially nonexistent. Economists say the economy has an **incomplete** set of markets. The used car market, for example, is a thin one. Buyers may know that there are some legitimate sellers, those who for one reason or another always want to drive a new car. But mixed in with these are people who are trying to dump their lemons. The buyers cannot tell the lemons apart from the good cars. Rather than risk it, they simply do not buy. (Of course, the fact that demand is low drives down the price, increasing the proportion of lemons. It is a vicious cycle.)

SIGNALING

If you have a good car and you want to sell it, you would like to persuade potential buyers that it is good. You could tell them that it is not a lemon, but why should they believe you? There is a simple principle: *actions speak louder than words.* What actions can you take that will convince buyers of the quality of your car?

The fact that a manufacturer is willing to provide a five-year, 50,000-mile warranty on its cars says something about the confidence it has in its product. The warranty is valuable, not only because it reduces the risk of having to spend a fortune to repair the car but also because the buyer believes that the manufacturer would not have provided the warranty unless the chances of defects were low. Actions such as this are said to signal higher quality. A signal is effective if it differentiates—here between high-quality cars and low-quality cars. The cost to the producer of a five-year guarantee is much higher for a car that

is likely to fall apart within five years than for a car that is unlikely to break down. Customers know this, and thus can infer that a firm willing to provide this warranty is selling high-quality cars.

When you go to a car dealer, you want to know that it will still be around if you have trouble. Some firms signal that they are not fly-by-nights by spending a great deal of money on their showroom. This indicates that it would be costly for them to just pack up and leave. (There are, of course, other reasons why they may spend money on a fancy showroom.)

Actions such as providing a better guarantee or a larger showroom are taken not just for the direct benefit that the consumer receives from them but because those actions make consumers believe that the product is a better product or the firm is a better firm to deal with. In a sense, the desire to convey information distorts the decisions made relative to what they would have been in a perfect-information world.

JUDGING QUALITY BY PRICE

There is still another clue that buyers use to judge the quality of what they are about to purchase. This is price. Consumers make inferences about the quality of goods on the basis of the price charged. For example, they know that on average, if the price of a used car is low, the chance of getting a lemon is higher. Firms know that consumers know this.

In markets with imperfect information, firms *set* their prices. And in setting their prices, they take into account what customers will think about the quality of the good being sold. Concerns about consumers correctly or incorrectly making inferences about quality impede the effectiveness of price competition. In the used car example, we saw that, as price rose, the average quality of cars on the market increased. But if firms think customers believe that cars being sold at a lower price are lower quality—that the quality deteriorates more than the price declines—they will not lower the price because they will think lower prices *lose* their customers. Under such circumstances, even if the firms cannot sell all they would like at the going price, they will still not cut prices.

A situation can be sustained in which there is a seeming excess supply of goods. Imperfect information means that equilibrium will be achieved away from the intersection of the supply and demand curves. This is a profound result, one we will trace through many of the chapters that follow.

Information problems fascinate economists because they turn the basic competitive model upside down. Prices convey critical information in a market economy. Sellers will manipulate prices when they can to control the information conveyed. Buyers, for their part, see through these manipulations. And their concern that the seller is trying to pass off a lemon discourages trade. When information problems like these are severe, markets are thin or even nonexistent. Alternatively price competition may be limited. Even when there is an excess supply of goods, firms may not cut their prices and the market may not clear.

THE INCENTIVE PROBLEM

We have seen throughout this book that providing incentives that motivate individuals to do the right thing, to make the right choices, is one of the central economic problems. The central problem of incentives, in turn, is that individuals do not bear the full consequences of their actions.

In the basic competitive model of Part Two, private property and prices provide incentives. Individuals are rewarded for performing particular tasks. The problem arises when an individual is not rewarded for what he does or when he does not have to pay the full costs of what he does. In our economy, incentive problems are pervasive.

In product markets, firms must be given the incentive to produce quality products. Again, the incentive problem is an information problem. If customers could always tell the quality of the product they were getting, firms that produced higher-quality products would always be able to charge a higher price and no company could get away with producing shoddy goods. Most of us have had the experience of going to a newly established restaurant, having a good meal, and then returning to find that the quality had deteriorated. Evidently something went wrong with incentives.

MARKET SOLUTIONS

In simple transactions, incentive problems can be solved with schemes of penalties and rewards. You would like a document typed. You sign a contract with someone to pay him £25 to deliver the typed document by tomorrow at 5:00 P.M. The contract stipulates that fifty pence will be deducted for each typographical error, and £1 for every hour the paper is late. The contract has built-in incentives for the paper to be delivered without errors and on time.

But most transactions, even simple ones, are more complicated than this one. The more complicated the transaction, the more difficult it is to solve the incentive problem. You want your grass mowed, and your neighbour's 12-year-old son wants to mow it. You want him to take care of your power mower. When he sees a rock in the mower's path, he should stop and pick it up. But what incentive does he have to take care of the mower? If you plan to charge him for repairs if the mower does hit a rock, how can you tell whether the rock was hidden by the grass? If he owned his own mower, he would have the appropriate incentive. That is why private property combined with the price system provides such an effective solution to the incentive problem. But your neighbour's son probably does not have the money to buy his own power

CLOSE-UP: THE MEDICAL PROFESSION AND THE MEDICAL CARE INDUSTRY

Medicine abounds with information problems—fascinating from an intellectual perspective but maybe rather worrying if you happen to need a doctor. The key feature of medical advice and treatment is that the customer—the patient—has typically very little information on which to judge the quality of the advice being offered or the competence of the person offering it. The establishment of a professional organization solves the second problem, the quality of the practitioner. By setting up a professional body, such as the British Medical Association, allowing membership only to people who have passed exams and established their competence, and allowing only persons who are members to practice medicine in Britain, the BMA is able to offer a sort of guarantee, so that the customer at least knows that the practitioner is competent.

However, that does not solve all the problems. The professional body may have an incentive to restrict entry into the profession, limit the supply of qualified practitioners, and thereby increase the price. It is not clear that such bodies have an incentive to act in the public interest. In Britain that problem is partly solved by the existence of the National Health Service, which has had for many years a monopoly on the employment of doctors and been able to regulate their salaries. (The question of doctors' pay was one of the most difficult sticking points in the establishment of the NHS in 1948. Whether it was solved satisfactorily from the public viewpoint is a moot question. Aneurin Bevan, the government minister who saw it through, remarked that he had silenced the consultants' opposition by having "stuffed their mouths with gold.") The government has also regulated the supply of doctors by controlling the public provision of places in

medical schools, thus taking a grip on both the supply of and demand for doctors.

Nevertheless, given a fixed amount to spend in the NHS, there is a question of whether resources within it are allocated appropriately. Do doctors offer treatment as cheaply and effectively as possible? Is there a temptation for them to treat too few patients too well, using too many innovative techniques and treating interesting cases rather than dull but needful ones? Again, given that the doctors have a monopoly on the expert knowledge needed to answer the question, the wider community is not well informed. The attempts to set up internal markets in the NHS can be seen as a response to this kind of issue. By separating the providers of health care (the hospitals) from the buyers (general practitioners acting on behalf of their patients) and giving the general practitioners funds, allowing them to seek care from any hospital, pressure is put on providers to provide the kind of treatment patients want at lowest cost. This has shaken up the NHS considerably but has not been a complete success, since it has imposed a greatly increased administrative burden, which has consumed some or all of the efficiency gains.

A number of different incentive and informational problems arise when health care is left to the private market, as in the United States. Widespread private health insurance has created a problem of escalating medical costs, since doctors have had (until recently, with changes in insurance practices) little incentive to contain costs. The litigiousness of the United States has burdened doctors with very costly professional indemnity insurance, and further led to doctors'

mower. Then an incentive problem is inevitable. Either you let him use your lawn mower and bear the risk of his mistreating it, or you lend him money to buy his own and bear the risk of his not paying you back.

Many private companies must hire people to run machinery worth hundreds or thousands of times more than a lawn mower. Every company would like its workers to exert effort and care, to communicate clearly with one another and take responsibility. Beyond private property and prices, the market economy has other partial solutions to these incentive problems, loosely categorised as contract solutions and reputation solutions.

CONTRACT SOLUTIONS

When one party (firm) agrees to do something for another, it typically signs a contract, which specifies the conditions of the transaction. For example, a firm will agree to deliver a product of a particular quality at a certain time and place. There will normally be escape clauses. If there is a strike, if the weather is bad, and so on, the delivery can be postponed. These **contingency clauses** may also make the payment depend on the circumstances and manner in which the service is performed.

Contracts attempt to deal with incentive problems by specifying what each of the parties is to do in each situation. But no one can think of every contingency. And even if one could, it would take a prohibitively long time to write down all the possibilities.

There are times when it would be extremely expensive for the supplier to comply with all the terms of the contract. He could make the promised delivery on time, but only at a very great cost; if the buyer would only accept a one-day delay, there would be great savings. To provide suppliers with the incentive to violate the terms only when it is economically worthwhile, most contracts allow delivery delays, but with a penalty attached. The penalty is what gives the supplier the incentive to deliver in a timely way.

Sometimes the supplier may think it simply is not worth complying with the contract. If he violates the agreement, he is said to be in **breach** of the contract. When a contract has been breached, the parties sometimes end up in court, and the legal system stipulates what damages the party breaking the contract must pay to the other side. Contracts, by stipulating what parties are supposed to do in a variety of circumstances, help resolve incentive problems. But no matter how complicated the contract, there will still be ambiguities and disputes. Contracts are incomplete and enforcement is costly, and thus they provide only a partial resolution of the incentive problem.

REPUTATION SOLUTIONS

Reputations play an extremely important role in providing incentives in market economies. A reputation is a form of guarantee. Even though you may know that you cannot collect from this guarantee yourself—it is not a money-back guarantee—you know that the reputation of the person or company will suffer if it does not perform well. The incentive to maintain a reputation is what provides firms with an incentive to produce high-quality goods. It provides the contractor with an incentive to complete a house on or near the promised date.

SOLUTIONS TO INCENTIVE PROBLEMS IN MARKET ECONOMIES
Private property and prices   Reputations
Contracts

For reputation to be an effective incentive mechanism, firms must lose something if their reputation suffers. The something is, of course, profits. For reputations to provide incentives, there must be profits to lose.

Thus, we see another way that markets with imperfect information differ from markets with perfect information. In competitive markets with perfect information, competition drives price down to marginal cost. In markets in which quality is maintained as the result of a reputation mechanism, whether competitive or not, price must remain above marginal cost.

Why, in markets where reputation is important, doesn't competition lead to price cutting? If price is too low, firms do not have an incentive to maintain their reputation. Consumers, knowing this, come to expect low-quality goods. This is another reason that cutting prices will not necessarily bring firms more customers. Most consumers, at one time or another, have encountered companies that tried to live off their reputation. For example, in the 1950s and 1960s, Rover cars enjoyed a deserved reputation for quality, solidity, and dependability. But, in more recent years, the name Rover has been attached to less expensive cars, some of them formerly made by British Leyland. Rather than improving the image of these vehicles, as was intended, the Rover name has itself been besmirched, despite all efforts to restore it.

Competition is frequently very imperfect in markets where reputation is important. The necessity of establishing a reputation acts as an important barrier to entry and limits the degree of competition in these industries. Given a choice between purchasing the product of an established firm with a good reputation and the product of a newcomer with no reputation at the same price, consumers will normally choose the established firm's good. Why try a new cola drink when you know that you like the tastes of Pepsi and Coca-Cola? The newcomer must offer a sufficiently low price, often accompanied with strong guarantees. In some cases, newcomers have almost to give away their product in order to establish themselves. Entering a market thus becomes extremely expensive.

THE SEARCH PROBLEM

A basic information problem, as noted at the beginning of this chapter, is that consumers must find out what goods are available on the market, at what price, and where. Households must learn about job opportunities as well as opportunities for investing their funds. Firms, by the same token, have to figure out the demand curve they face, and where and at what price they can obtain inputs. Both sides of the market need, in other words, to find out about their opportunity sets.

In the basic competitive model of Part Two, a particular good sells for the same price everywhere. If we see what look like identical shoes selling for two different prices at two neighbouring stores—£25 at one and £35 at the other—it must mean (in that model) that the stores are really selling different products. If the shoes are in fact identical, then what the customer must be getting is a combination package, the shoes plus the service of having the shoes fitted. And the more expensive store is providing a higher quality of service.

In fact, however, essentially the same good may be sold at different stores for different prices. And you may not be able to account for the observed differences in prices by differences in other attributes, like the location of the store or the quality of the service provided. In these cases, we say there is **price dispersion.** If search were costless (or information perfect, as in the standard competitive model), consumers would search until they found the cheapest price. And no store charging more than the lowest price on the market would ever have any customers.

Price dispersion, combined with variations in quality, means that households and firms must spend considerable energies in searching. Workers search for a good job. Firms look for good workers. Consumers search for the lowest prices and best values. The process by which this kind of information is gathered is called **search.**

Search is an important, and costly, economic activity. Because it is costly, a search stops before you have *all* the relevant information. You know there are bargains out there to be found, but it is just too expensive to find them. You might worry that you will be disappointed the day or week after buying a new computer if you find it for sale at 10 percent less. But in truth, there should be no regrets. There was a chance that you would not find a better buy or that next week you would not even be able to buy it at the price offered today. You looked at these risks, the costs of further search, the benefits of being able to get the computer today and use it now (compared with the benefits of waiting and the chance of find-

ing it at a still lower price). After a careful balancing of the benefits and costs of further waiting, you decided to purchase now.

In Figure 17.2 the horizontal axis plots the time spent in searching, while the vertical axis measures the expected marginal benefit of searching. On the one hand, the expected marginal benefit of searching declines with the amount of search. In general, people search the best prospects first. As they search more and more, they look at less and less likely prospects. On the other hand, the marginal cost of additional search rises with increased search. This reflects the fact that the more time people spend in search, the less time they have to do other things. The opportunity cost of spending an extra hour searching thus increases. The amount of search chosen will be at the point where the expected marginal benefit just equals the marginal cost.

An increase in price (or quality) dispersion will normally increase the return to searching; there is a chance of picking up a really good bargain, and the difference between a good buy and a bad buy is larger. Thus, the expected benefit curve shifts up, and the amount of search will increase from T_1 to T_2.

Search is costly, and this has important implications for how *markets* work. The fact that in equilibrium there can exist price dispersion is only one example.

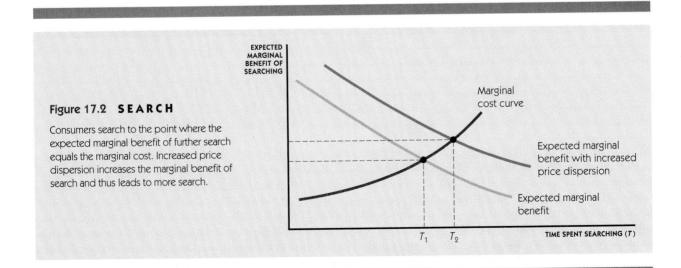

Figure 17.2 SEARCH

Consumers search to the point where the expected marginal benefit of further search equals the marginal cost. Increased price dispersion increases the marginal benefit of search and thus leads to more search.

Modern manufactured goods and many services—washing machines, computers, cars, insurance policies, package holidays, mobile phone contracts—are very complicated, and evaluating the relative merits of all the alternatives would be a time-consuming business. Many of these goods are hard to evaluate without trying them out, and a key feature of many of them, their durability, is difficult to know in advance. Some of these goods (mobile phones and computers, for example) may meet needs that many people were never aware that they had. Consequently the world differs very much from the paradigm offered by the competitive equilibrium model. People are not choosing among goods which have properties that are perfectly understood and over which they have well-defined preferences. The lack of information that most consumers face has been dealt with in a variety of different ways.

One of the most conspicuous and enduring of these is the Consumers' Association, and the magazine *Which?* which it publishes. *Which?* carries out comparative studies of consumer goods and provides summaries and evaluations of alternatives, makes recommendations, and identifies best buys.

The fact that people are willing to pay for *Which?* indicates the value set on information about consumer goods.

Of course, *Which?* is just a part of the picture. Magazines and newspapers are full of information about goods and services, from the wine column of the Sunday paper to the book review and the *Times Literary Supplement* to the interior decorating magazines. There is a whole spectrum of information sources available. The quality of the information varies. While *Which?* is paid for by the people who buy it and has every incentive to give sound advice, some magazines—the computer magazines, for example—are 90 percent advertising and clearly depend for their revenue on it. Their recommendations to buy the latest piece of equipment, lavishly advertised in the magazine, clearly deserve to be read with a critical eye.

SEARCH AND IMPERFECT COMPETITION

Firms know search is costly and take advantage of that fact. They know they will not lose all their customers if they raise their prices. And if a store lowers its price slightly, it will not immediately attract *all* the customers from the other stores. Customers have to learn about the competitive price advantage, and this takes time. Moreover, even when people do hear of the lower price, they may worry about the quality of the goods being sold, the nature of the service, whether the goods will be in stock, and so on.

The fact that search is costly means that the demand curve facing a firm will be downward sloping. Competition is necessarily imperfect.

Consider, for instance, the demand for a Walkman. When you walk into a store, you have some idea what it should sell for. The store asks £40 for it. You may know that somewhere you might be able to purchase it for £5 less. But is it worth the additional time, trouble, and expense to drive to the other stores that might have it, looking for a bargain? Some individuals are willing to pay the extra £5 simply to stop having to search. As the store raises its price to, say, £45 or £50, some people who would have bought the Walkman at £40 decide that it is worth continuing to shop around. The store, as it raises its price, loses some but not all of its customers. Thus, it faces a downward-sloping demand curve. If search were costless, everyone would go to the store selling the Walkman at the lowest price, and any store charging more than that would have no sales. Markets in which search is costly are, accordingly, better described by the models of imperfect competition introduced in Chapters 13 and 14.

SEARCH AND INFORMATION INTERMEDIARIES

Some firms play an important role by gathering information and serving as intermediaries between producers and customers. These firms are part of the market for information discussed in the beginning of the chapter. One of the functions of good department stores, for example, is to economise on customers' search costs. The stores' buyers seek out literally hundreds of producers, looking for the best buys and the kinds of goods that their customers will like. Good department stores earn a reputation for the quality of their buyers. Customers still have a search problem—they may have to visit several department stores—but the problem is far smaller than if they had to search directly among producers.

ADVERTISING

Customers have an incentive to find out where the best buys are. Firms have a corresponding incentive to tell customers about the great deals they are providing. Companies may spend great sums on advertising to bring information about their products, prices, and locations to potential customers.

In the classic joke about advertising, an executive says, "We know half the money we spend on advertising is wasted, but we don't know which half." That joke says a lot about the economics of advertising. Many firms spend 2 percent, 3 percent, or more of their total revenues on advertising.

Advertising can serve the important economic function of providing information about what choices are available. When a new airline enters a market, it must convey that information to potential customers. When a new product is developed, that fact has to be made known. When a business is having a sale, it must let people know. A firm cannot just lower its price, sit on its haunches, and wait if it wants to be successful. Companies need to recruit new customers and convey information in an active way.

Take the typical beer or car advertisement. It conveys no information about the product but seeks to convey an image, one with which potential buyers will identify. That these advertisements succeed in persuading individuals either to try a product or to stick with that product and not try another is a reminder that consumer behaviour is much more complicated than the simple theories of competitive markets suggest. Few people decide to go out and buy a car or a new suit solely because they saw a TV advertisement. But decisions about what kinds of clothes to wear, what beer to drink, or what car to drive are affected by a variety of considerations, including how peers view them or how they see themselves. These views, in turn, can be affected by advertising.

To emphasise the different roles played by advertising, economists distinguish between **informative advertising** and **persuasive advertising.** The intent of the former is to provide consumers with information about the price of a good, where it can be acquired, or what its characteristics are. The intent of persuasive advertising is to make consumers feel good about the product. This can even take the form of providing disinformation, to confuse consumers into thinking there is a difference among goods when there really is not.

ADVERTISING AND COMPETITION

Advertising is both a cause and a consequence of imperfect competition. In a perfectly competitive industry, where many producers make identical goods, it would not pay any single producer to advertise the merits of a good. You do not see advertisements for

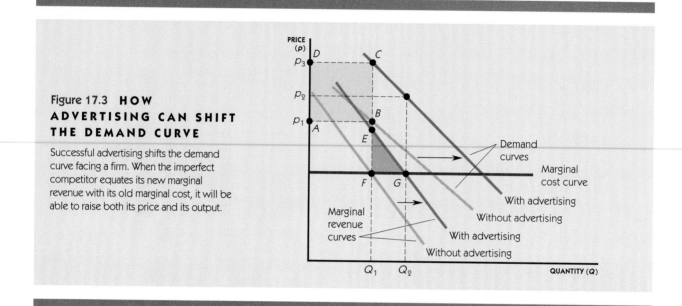

Figure 17.3 HOW ADVERTISING CAN SHIFT THE DEMAND CURVE

Successful advertising shifts the demand curve facing a firm. When the imperfect competitor equates its new marginal revenue with its old marginal cost, it will be able to raise both its price and its output.

wheat or corn. If such advertising were successful, it would simply shift the demand curve for the product out. The total demand for wheat might increase, but this would have a negligible effect on the wheat grower who paid for the advertisement. If all wheat farmers could get together, it might pay them to advertise as a group. In past years, associations of producers of eggs (with the slogan "Go to work on an egg!"), milk, and lamb have done just that.

ADVERTISING AND PROFITS

The objective of advertising is to shift the demand curve. The increase in advertising by one firm may divert customers away from rivals or it may divert customers away from other products. Advertising a particular brand of cigarettes may be successful in inducing some smokers to switch brands and in inducing some nonsmokers to smoke.

When a firm is already in an imperfectly competitive situation, advertising shifts the demand curve for its product out, as in Figure 17.3. The increase in profits consists of two parts. First, the firm can sell the same quantity it sold before but at a higher price—p_3, rather than p_1. Profits then increase by

the original quantity (Q_1) times the change in price $(p_3 - p_1)$, the rectangle $ABCD$ in the figure. Second, by adjusting the quantity it sells, it can increase profits still further. This is because the advertising has shifted the firm's marginal revenue curve up. As usual, the imperfectly competitive firm sets marginal revenue equal to marginal cost, so it increases output from Q_1 to Q_2. The additional profits thus generated are measured by the area between the marginal revenue and marginal cost curves between Q_1 and Q_2. Marginal cost remains the same, so the second source of extra profits is the shaded area EFG. The net increase in profits is the area $ABCD$ plus the area EFG minus the cost of advertising.

So far, in studying the effect of an increase in advertising on one firm's profits, we have assumed that other firms keep their level of advertising constant. The effect of advertising on both industry and firm profits is more problematical once the reactions of other firms in the industry are taken into account. To the extent that advertising diverts sales from one firm in an industry to another, advertising may, in equilibrium, have little effect on demand. For example, assume that Nike shoe advertisements divert customers from Reeboks to Nikes and vice versa for Reebok advertisements. Figure 17.4 shows the de-

CONSEQUENCES OF IMPERFECT INFORMATION

Adverse selection problems

    Thin or nonexistent markets

    Signaling

    Possibility that markets may not clear

Incentive problems

    Desirability of designing incentive schemes

    Increased importance of contracts and reputations

Search problems

    Price dispersion

    Imperfect competition

mand curve facing Reebok (1) before advertising, (2) when only Reebok advertises, and (3) when both companies advertise. The final demand curve is the same as the initial demand curve. Price and output are the same; profits are lower by the amount spent on advertising. We have here another example of a Prisoner's Dilemma. If the firms could cooperate and agree not to advertise, they would both be better off. But without such cooperation, it pays each to advertise, regardless of what the rival does. The government-mandated ban on cigarette advertising on radio and TV may have partially solved this Prisoner's Dilemma for the tobacco industry—in the name of health policy.

In practice, when all cigarette firms advertise, the advertisements do more than just cancel each other out. Some people who might not otherwise have smoked are persuaded to do so, and some smokers are induced to smoke more than they otherwise would have. But the shift in the demand curve facing a particular firm when all companies advertise is still much smaller than it is when only that firm advertises.

GOVERNMENT AND INFORMATION

Information problems may result not only in inefficient markets but even in market failures. Govern-

---

Figure 17.4 HOW ADVERTISING CAN CANCEL OTHER ADVERTISING

If only one company advertises, the demand curve for its product may shift out. But if both companies advertise, the resulting demand curve may be the same as it would be if neither advertised.

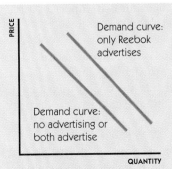

ment concern for market failure resulting from ill-informed consumers has motivated a number of pieces of **consumer protection legislation.** In most countries advertising and product descriptions are regulated so as to avoid misleading consumers. Food manufacturers are required to list the ingredients of their products on the package. In Britain, the Trade Descriptions Act makes it illegal for firms to sell products under false or misleading descriptions, and the Advertising Standards Council regulates advertisements on the television and other media. Manufactured goods that meet a set of criteria for being well made, reliable, and having other desirable properties can display a sign saying that they meet the appropriate "British standards." The stock exchange requires firms whose shares are listed on it to disclose financial information to the public.

Yet much of this legislation is of only limited effectiveness. One problem comes when consumers try to absorb and process the information. A cereal manu-facturer may disclose not only what is required but a host of other information, which may or may not be of importance. How is the consumer to know what to pay attention to? He cannot absorb everything. Occasionally, as in the case of warnings about the dangers from smoking, government regulators, aware of these problems of information absorption, have required the disclosures to be of a specific form and size lettering to make them stand out. But that kind of intervention on a more massive scale would probably be, at the very least, extremely costly.

Another problem with outlawing deceptive advertising is the difficulty of drawing a clear line between persuasion and deception. Advertisers are good at walking along the edge of any line; a suggestive hint may do where an explicit claim might be called deceptive. Having Parliament or the courts draw a line between informative and noninformative advertising seems an impossible task.

REVIEW AND PRACTICE

SUMMARY

1 The model of perfect competition assumes that participants in the market have perfect information about the goods being bought and sold and their prices. But this is not the case in the real world, and economists have thus incorporated imperfect information into their models of the economy.

2 A problem of adverse selection may arise when consumers cannot judge the true quality of a product. As the price of the good falls, the quality mix changes adversely, and the quantity demanded at a lower price may actually be lower than at a higher price.

3 Producers of high-quality products may attempt to signal that their product is better than those of competitors, for instance by providing better guarantees.

4 When consumers judge quality by price, there may be some price that offers the best value. Firms will have no incentive to cut price below this best-value price, even when, at this price, the amount they would be willing to supply exceeds demand. As a result, the market can settle in an equilibrium with an excess supply of goods.

5 When there is perfect information, private property and prices can provide correct incentives to all market participants. When information is imperfect, two methods of helping to provide correct incentives are contracts with contingency clauses, and reputations.

6 Advertising attempts to change consumers' buying behaviour, either by providing relevant information about prices or characteristics, by persuasion, or both.

KEY TERMS

imperfect information

asymmetric information

thin or incomplete markets

contingency clauses

price dispersion

consumer protection legislation

REVIEW QUESTIONS

1 Why are markets for information not likely to work well?

2 Why would "lemons" not be a problem for consumers in a world of perfect information? Why do they lead to a backward-bending demand curve in a world of imperfect information?

3 Why is signaling unnecessary in a world of perfect information? What does it accomplish in a world of imperfect information?

4 Explain why, if consumers think that quality increases with price, there will be cases where firms will have no incentive to cut prices in an attempt to attract more business.

5 How do contingency clauses in contracts help provide appropriate incentives? What are some of the problems in writing contracts that provide for all the relevant contingencies?

6 What role does reputation have in maintaining incentives? What is required if firms are to have an incentive to maintain their reputations? How might the good reputation of existing firms serve as a barrier to the entry of new firms?

7 What are the benefits of searching for market information? What are the costs? How does the existence of price dispersion affect the benefits? Could price dispersion exist in a world of perfect information? How does the fact that search is costly affect the nature of competition in a market?

8 Describe how advertising might affect the demand curve facing a firm. How do these changes affect prices? Profits?

9 "For most practical purposes, information problems can be solved by government requirements that information be disclosed to potential buyers and investors." Discuss.

PROBLEMS

1 The We Pick 'Em Company collects information about horse races and sells a newsletter predicting the winners. Why might you possibly be predisposed to distrust the accuracy of the We Pick 'Em newsletter?

2 When you apply for a job, possible employers have imperfect information about your abilities. How might you try to signal that you would be a good employee?

3 Explain how the incentives of someone to look after a car she is renting may not suit the company that is renting the car. How might a contingency contract help to solve this problem? Is it likely to solve the problem completely?

4 A certain mail order company has a long-standing policy that it will take back anything it has sold, at any time, for any reason. Why might it be worthwhile for a profit-maximising firm to enact such a policy?

5 Would you expect to see greater price dispersion within a larger conurbation or between several small towns that are 50 miles apart? Why?

6 How do the costs of search help to explain the existence of department stores?

18

IMPERFECTIONS IN THE LABOUR MARKET

Part Two emphasised the similarity between the labour market and markets for goods. Households demand goods and firms supply them, with the price system as intermediary. Likewise, firms demand labour and workers supply it, with the wage as intermediary. Firms hire labour up to the point where the value of the marginal product of labour is equal to the wage, just as they would buy coal up to the point where the value of the marginal product of coal was equal to the price of coal.

This chapter takes another look at the labour market. Just as we saw in the preceding five chapters some of the ways in which product markets differ from the way they are depicted in the basic competitive model, here we will also see important ways in which labour markets, like product markets, are characterised by imperfect competition. Unions are the most obvious manifestation, and we will take a look at their history as well as their impact on wages and employment—the prices and quantities of the labour market.

Information problems have an even more significant impact on the labour market than on product markets. This is partly because workers are not like lumps of coal. They have to be motivated to work hard. And they are concerned with their conditions of work and how their pay compares with others'. Firms are aware of the importance of these considerations in attracting and keeping workers and design employment and compensation policies that take them into account.

KEY QUESTIONS

1 How do unions affect the wages of their workers? Of workers in general? What limits the power of the unions? Why have unions been declining in strength?

2 How do we explain the large differences in wages paid to different workers, even to workers who appear to have similar abilities? What role does discrimination play?

3 How do firms seek to motivate workers, to ensure that they put out effort commensurate with their pay, and to select good workers? In what sense can the problem of providing workers' incentives be viewed as a consequence of imperfect or limited information?

TRADE UNIONS

Trade unions are organizations of workers, formed to obtain better working conditions and higher wages for their members. The main weapon they have is the threat of a collective withdrawal of labour, known as a **strike.**

A BRIEF HISTORY

Trade unions in Britain developed over a long period of time. Associations of workers began to form in the seventeenth and eighteenth centuries, but they developed most rapidly in the nineteenth century, during the industrial revolution, when large numbers of people were brought together to work in factories, mills, and coal mines and on the railways. During this period, unions fought for and gradually achieved acceptance as part of the economic and social structure. In 1900, there were more than 1,300 unions in Britain, with around two million members among them.

During the twentieth century, the number of unions has steadily fallen, as smaller unions have merged with or joined larger ones. There were 453 unions in 1979 and 268 in 1992. Membership in unions grew until 1920, and then it fell sharply in the severe recession of the 1920s as Figure 18.1 shows. Membership then recovered and continued to grow until 1979, when it reached a peak of over 13 million.

Since then, membership has fallen to 9 million in 1992 and to 8 million at the end of 1995.

What has accounted for the changes in union membership over the century? A great increase in membership occurred between 1966 and 1979. In this period of time, unions appeared to be particularly powerful and were successful in obtaining wage increases for their members. Their power arose partly from the commitment to full employment recognised by the governments of the period, which meant that unions did not have to worry that wage demands would lead to unemployment.

This was a period of time in which inflation was a large and growing political and economic problem. As part of the response to it, governments in Britain introduced **prices and incomes policies** by which they tried to intervene directly in markets for goods and labour and limit the growth of wages and prices. Unions were asked (or required) to limit their wage demands. These policies brought unions into negotiations with the government and the representatives of employers (like the Confederation of British Industry [CBI]). These three-sided discussions ("beer and sandwiches at number 10") put the unions in the position of influencing national economic policy and helped to create the illusion if not the substance of trade union power. In a number of strikes, the government rather than the unions conceded defeat. A notorious example is the strike in the coal industry in 1973–74 which led to the collapse of the Conservative government of Edward Heath. A change in the law regulating trade unions, the Industrial Relations Act of 1971, strongly disliked by the trade union movement, was repealed in 1974 by the succeeding Labour government. The

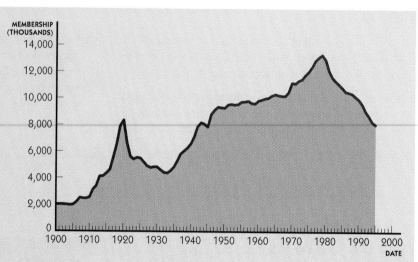

Figure 18.1 TRADE UNION MEMBERSHIP IN THE UNITED KINGDOM, 1900–1995

Trade union membership grew strongly until 1920, fell back in a slump until 1933, and then recovered. After peaking in 1979 it has fallen back to eight million in 1995. *Sources:* Office of National Statistics, *Annual Abstract* (1998); *Employment Gazette*, U.K. Department of Employment June 1994; A. H. Halsey, ed., *Social Trends in Britain since 1900* (Basingstoke: MacMillan, 1988).

Labour governments of 1974 to 1979 attempted to retain the cooperation of the unions in restraining the growth of wages, through a series of voluntary incomes policies; unions were asked rather than required to restrain their wage demands. However, cooperation broke down in the winter of 1979 when there was a series of strikes by workers employed by local councils—the so-called winter of discontent. In this period unions appeared to be a powerful force in the economy. Attempts by governments to pass laws restricting union power failed. Their power, real or apparent, is often cited as a cause of the rapid growth of membership that took place at the time.

Since 1979 there has been a remarkable fall in membership. This is partly attributed to the fall in employment in heavily unionised industries in the deep recession of the early 1980s, and partly to the subsequent rise in the employment of women, part-time workers, and workers in service industries, all of which are groups in which unions have not been prominent.

There have been several changes in the law relating to trade unions, which have reduced their power. Acts of Parliament limiting trade union power were passed in 1980, 1982, 1984, 1988, and 1993. They prevent unions from using secondary picketing to support a strike; that is, unions are not allowed to picket at places of work other than the ones directly involved in the dispute. The rights of workers not to belong to a union have been strengthened. Strikes have to be preceded by secret postal ballots. Unions and their officials can be sued for the consequences of illegal industrial action. It has been made easier for employers to sack workers during a strike.

The Conservative governments since 1979 have not attempted to use prices and incomes policies and have attempted not to become involved in disputes with unions. Three-way discussion between government, employers, and unions on economic policy has been deliberately avoided. Privatization of nationalised industries has had the effect that workers in those industries are no longer employed by the government; this has kept the government further from being involved in industrial disputes in those industries.

The Thatcher government had the intention of reducing union power and enabling "management to manage." A tougher management style in firms in Britain has been encouraged. Whether because of these exhortations or because of changes in the law or because of the high rate of unemployment that has existed for much of the period, firms have been less willing to accommodate union demands and have responded more toughly to strikes or threats of

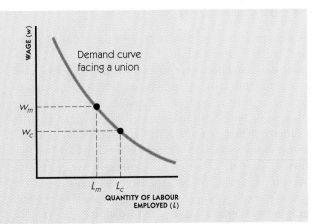

Figure 18.2 THE UNION AS A MONOPOLY SELLER OF LABOUR

Unions can be viewed as sellers of labour, with market power. When they increase their wage demands, they reduce the demand for their members' labour services.

strikes. The collapse of the miners' strike in 1984 signaled the determination of the government not to yield to union demands. In a number of recent cases, including a Timex watch factory in Dundee and a printing company, Arrowsmiths, in Bristol, a firm has sacked the striking workers and hired a new workforce to replace them.

Another factor that may have influenced union power is competition: unions my be unable to raise wages for their workers in competitive markets. When firms' costs are raised, their profits are reduced. In a competitive market, firms do not have the opportunity of raising their prices, as they would lose demand to other firms. The prospect of the loss of profits may have stiffened the firms' resistance to union wage demands. Markets may have become more competitive in the 1980s because of freer trade (the Single European Market in Europe) and the deregulation of various industries.

These developments in the 1980s have made unions seem a lot less powerful, and the advantages of joining unions may appear to many workers to have fallen. Hence membership has fallen also.

ECONOMIC EFFECTS

The source of union power is collective action. When workers join together in a union, they no longer negotiate as isolated individuals. The threat of

a strike (or a go-slow) poses many more difficulties for an employer than does the threat of any single employee's quitting.

In the perfectly competitive model of labour markets, workers are price takers, facing a given market wage. But unions have some power to be price setters. Figure 18.2 shows the demand curve for labour facing a union.[1] It is downward sloping, reflecting the union's monopoly power. As a result of this power, a worker at a given level of skill who works in a unionised establishment will be paid more than a comparable worker in a competitive industry. The firm would like to hire that lower-priced, nonunion worker, and the nonunionised worker could easily be induced to move, but the firm's agreement with the union prevents this from happening. However, as the union raises the price of labour (the wage), firms will employ fewer workers. Higher wages are obtained at the expense of lower employment. In Figure 18.2, when wages rise from the competitive level w_c to w_m, employment is reduced from L_c to L_m.

[1] Chapter 11 showed how the demand curve for labour is derived in competitive markets. Firms hire labour up to the point where the wage equals the value of the marginal product of labour. The derivation of the demand curve for labour in monopolies and imperfectly competitive markets follows along similar lines. Firms hire labour up to the point where the marginal revenue, the extra revenue they obtain from selling the extra output they produce from hiring an extra unit of labour, is equal to the wage.

SHORT-RUN GAINS AT THE EXPENSE OF LONG-RUN LOSSES

Sometimes unions can increase both employment and wages. They present the employer with, in effect, two alternatives: either pay high wages *and* maintain the same employment level, or go out of business. If the employer already has sunk costs in machines and buildings, he may concede to the union demands. In effect, the union thus takes away some of the employer's monopoly profits and/or return to capital. In competitive markets, where there are no monopoly profits, the higher wages can only come out of employers' return to capital. But these employers will lose interest in investing in more capital. As capital wears out, the employer has less and less to lose from the union threat. As he refuses to invest more, jobs decrease. Even if the union makes short-run gains, they come at the expense of a long-run loss in jobs.

EFFECTS ON NONUNION WORKERS

The gains of today's union members may not only cost future jobs, they may also be at the expense of those in other sectors of the economy, for two reasons. First, the higher wages may well be passed on to consumers in the form of higher prices, particularly if product markets are not perfectly competitive. Second, the increased wages (and reduced employment) in the union sector drive down wages in the nonunionised sector, as the supply of nonunion labour increases. Some argue the opposite—that high union wages "pull up" wages in nonunion firms. The nonunion firms may, for instance, pay higher wages to reduce the likelihood of unionization. In particular sectors this effect is important, but most economists believe that the overall effect on nonunion workers is negative.

JOB SECURITY AND INNOVATION

As explained in Chapter 16, the economy as a whole benefits from innovation, but particular groups are likely to suffer. In an innovative economy, those workers who are dislocated by new inventions are expected to learn new skills and seek out new jobs. Without labour's shifting in response to changes in demand (resulting either from new technologies or changes in tastes), the economy will be inefficient.

Technological changes may threaten the job security unions seek for their members. As a result, unions have attempted to retard innovations that might decrease the demand for their members' labour services. There has been a long battle to get unions to abandon so-called restrictive practices and to accept the changes in working practices and manning levels made possible by technical change. For example, the restrictive practices used by the printing unions prevented the Fleet Street newspapers for many years from using computer typesetting. Eventually several papers moved from Fleet Street to Wapping where they had new offices set up, employed new staff, and introduced the new technology against the vigorous opposition of print unions like the Society of Graphical and Allied Trades (SOGAT). Job transitions are necessary for economic efficiency, but they are costly and the costs are borne largely by the workers. Before the advent of unions and laws providing unemployment compensation, the human toll was considerable. Individuals could not buy insurance against these employment risks but they could form unions, and union attempts to enhance job security were a response to this important problem.

UNIONS AND POLITICS

Unions in Britain and in most European countries have developed close links with political parties to advance the interest of workers through the democratic process. In Britain, the Labour Party was largely a creation of the trade union movement, which has had until recently a major influence on the policies that the party has pursued. During the recent periods of Labour government, 1945 to 1951, 1964 to 1970, and 1974 to 1979, the unions have been able to advance their cause in a number of ways. They have been able to influence government policy and have had access to government ministers in times of industrial disputes. In exchange, Labour governments have been able to obtain some cooperation from the unions, expressed in the form of wage restraint and support for voluntary incomes policies. The amount of this kind of cooperation between governments and unions in the United Kingdom has been fairly small. But in other European countries, like Sweden, the Netherlands, and Germany, there have been more successful experiences of cooperation between the "social partners"—meaning unions, employers, and government.

Unions frequently support economic policies that appear, at least in the short term, to benefit their members and strengthen their bargaining position, like the European Commission's proposals that place an upper limit on weekly hours of work, and proposals for minimum wage legislation. Unions have been strong supporters of subsidies for loss-making firms, especially among the industries that used to be in public ownership, like the railways, steel, coal mining, and shipbuilding.

LIMITS ON UNION POWER

In almost all countries, no union has a monopoly on *all* workers. At most, a union has a monopoly on the workers currently working for a particular firm or industry. Thus, the power of unions is partly attributable to the fact that a firm cannot easily replace its employees. When a union goes on strike, the firm may be able to hire some workers, but it is costly to bring in and train a whole new labour force. Indeed, most of the knowledge needed to train the new workers is in the hands of the union members. While one sack of wheat may be very much like another, one worker is not very much like another. Workers outside the firm are not perfect substitutes for workers, particularly skilled ones, inside.

THE THREAT OF REPLACEMENT

In those industries in which skills are easily transferable across firms, or a union has not been successful in enlisting the support of most of the skilled workers, a firm can replace striking workers, and union power will be limited. In the United Kingdom, it was very rare before the 1980s for a firm to sack its workforce and hire a new one. Since then, however, it has happened on a number of occasions, partly because the law has been changed so that it has become easier for firms to do this. Since 1982, firms have no longer been required to give workers on strike the same protection from dismissal as those who are working normally.

In many cases, however, workers' skills are firm-specific. Just as, from the employers' perspective, workers outside the firm are not perfect substitutes for workers within, from the workers' perspective, one job is not a perfect substitute for another. Thus, there is often value both to workers and firms in preserving established employment relationships. The two parties are tied to each other in what is referred to as a bargaining relationship. The bargaining strengths of the two sides are affected by the fact that a firm, at a cost, can obtain other employees, and employees, at a cost, can get other jobs. The total amount by which the two sides together are better off continuing their relationship than ending it is referred to as the "bargaining surplus." A large part of the negotiations between unions and management are about how to split this surplus.

THE THREAT OF UNEMPLOYMENT

Higher wages—other things being equal—mean lower levels of employment. When job opportunities in general are weak, concern about the employment consequences of wage demands increases.

In the early 1980s, there was a deep recession in which unemployment rose rapidly to three million in the United Kingdom. Exports from British manufacturers were made less competitive by a greatly increased value of the pound in the foreign exchange markets. Many manufacturing firms faced greatly reduced demand for their products and were on the edge of bankruptcy. Employed union members were in such a position that if they lost their jobs, the alternative was unemployment rather than, as had been the case in the 1960s and 1970s, a job in another firm or industry. While the threat of unemployment appeared to weaken the bargaining position of the union and to some extent unions were willing to make smaller wage demands in return for reduced threats of redundancies, a remarkable feature of the 1980s was that wage inflation did not fall by much. Unions continued to press for and obtain wage increases despite the high unemployment. A consequence of this was a fall in employment in unionised firms which may have contributed to the fall in union membership.

By contrast with the United Kingdom, when unions in the United States found their bargaining position undermined by a deep recession in the early 1980s, wage inflation fell very quickly. Unemployment fell back quite rapidly to normal U.S. levels, unlike in the United Kingdom (and much of Europe) where unemployment has remained persistently high. This illustrates one aspect of the greater flexibility of labour markets in the United States as compared with those in the United Kingdom.

INSIDERS AND OUTSIDERS—EMPLOYEE POWER WITH OR WITHOUT UNIONS

Whether or not workers are represented by a trade union, they may nevertheless have a considerable bargaining advantage in their dealings with the firm relative to people who are not employees.

If the competitive model were fully applicable to the labour market, existing workers would be identical with other potential workers outside the firm—unemployed people (with the same qualifications and experience) looking for jobs or people employed in other firms. There would be no costs or benefits to a firm from replacing its existing workforce with a new one composed of outsiders. If existing workers were paid more than replacement workers, the employer would have an incentive to replace them. Wages would then be affected very much by conditions in the labour market.

However, almost all jobs are very different from the picture of them painted by the competitive model. In almost all cases workers have detailed knowledge of the working of the firm that employs them, knowledge not shared by outsiders. The process of hiring suitable new workers is expensive and time consuming for employers. To become useful workers, new employees need to learn the peculiarities of their new firm and establish good working relationships with existing workers. Firms rely on existing workers to train new recruits in the ways of the firm and to cooperate with them. Even if a firm wanted to replace its existing workforce with a new one, the existing workers are legally protected from dismissal except under specified conditions, such as redundancy or inability to work satisfactorily. Being able to hire someone else to do the job more cheaply is not among the reasons that firms can give for dismissing staff (although firms have some freedom to vary the terms of the contract under which people are employed).

For all these reasons, incumbent employees (insiders) are in a strong bargaining position with the employer, relative to outsiders. If the firm attempts to replace them with less expensive recruits, they are able to withdraw their cooperation from the training of new recruits and working with them, and thus render them ineffective. They may use or abuse their knowledge of the firm's operations to make the firm work less effectively, without actually failing to do their work (as defined in their contracts of employment) satisfactorily.

This idea has been developed by Assar Lindbeck (of the University of Stockholm) and Dennis Snower (of London University) into a theory, called the **insider-outsider theory.** It explains why wages and conditions of work for existing workers do not respond immediately—if ever—to conditions in the labour market outside the firm. There may be high unemployment, with many looking for work, but that need not lead to the insiders'—the currently employed by the firm—facing lower wages or poorer conditions. The bargaining power of the insiders protects them from competition from the outsiders—the currently unemployed and people working in other firms. It can be used to explain why pay responds to the financial condition of the firm, as reflected in its profits or amount of business, rather than outside labour market conditions. It can explain why unemployment is persistent because after a fall in employment, unions continue to look after the workers who are still employed and do not concern themselves too much with the welfare of the unemployed. This phenomenon, also called **hysteresis** in labour markets, has been analysed by a number of economists, including the U.S. economists Olivier Blanchard of the Massachusetts Institute of Technology and Lawrence Summers of Harvard University.

The implication of these theories is that the presence or absence of a formal union need not make so much difference. Some of the factors that give existing workers bargaining power are independent of explicit unionization and will have similar consequences. Part of the problem of labour markets in Europe—Eurosclerosis, high wages, high unemployment, lack of flexibility—may be due to high insider power. A contrast is drawn with the United States where insider power is allegedly lower. The compe-

UNIONS AND IMPERFECT COMPETITION IN THE LABOUR MARKET

Economic effects:

Higher wages for union members, with fewer union jobs and lower wages for nonunion members

Improved job security, sometimes at the expense of innovation and economic efficiency

Minimum wages, improved working conditions, other gains achieved through the political process

Determinants of union power:

Political and legal environment

Economic environment: threat of replacement and unemployment

tition from the unemployed poses a much greater threat to the insiders there than it does in Europe. As a result, labour markets in the United States adjust faster when there is unemployment. Wages fall, or at least their rate of increase slows down, and the unemployed get reabsorbed into jobs more quickly than in Europe.

WAGE DIFFERENTIALS

The basic competitive model suggests that if the goods being sold are the same, prices will also be the same. Wages are the price in the labour market; but even in the absence of unions, similar types of workers performing similar types of jobs are sometimes paid quite different wages. For example, some secretaries are paid twice as much as others. How can economists explain differences like these?

They begin by pointing to **compensating wage differentials.** Understanding compensating wage differentials begins with the observation that although different jobs may have the same title, they can be quite different. Some jobs are less pleasant, require more overtime, and are in a less convenient location. These are **nonpecuniary** attributes of a job. Others include the degree of autonomy provided the worker (that is, the closeness with which her actions are supervised) and the risk she must bear, whether in a physical sense or from the variability in income. Economists

expect wages to adjust to reflect the attractiveness or unattractiveness of these nonpecuniary characteristics. Compensating wage differentials arise because firms have to compensate their workers for the negative aspects of a job.

Other differences are accounted for by differences in the productivity of workers: These are **productivity wage differentials.** Some workers are much more productive than others, even with the same experience and education.

Compensating and productivity wage differentials fall within the realm of basic competitive market analysis. But other wage differentials are due to imperfect information. It takes time to search out different job opportunities. Just as one store may sell the same object for a higher price than another store, one firm may hire labour for a lower wage than another firm. The worker who accepts a lower-paying job simply because he did not know about the higher-paying one down the street faces an information-based differential.

Limited information has important implications for firms. First, in the standard competitive model, firms face a horizontal supply curve for labour. If they raise wages ever so little above the market wage, they can obtain as much labour as they want. In practice, mobility is more limited. Even if workers at other firms knew about the higher wage offer, they might be reluctant to switch. They may not be well matched for the job, or the employer may be offering high wages because the work is in one way or another unattractive.

Second, firms worry about the quality of their workforce. If an employer offers a higher wage to

The Labour government elected in May 1997 made a preelection commitment to introduce a minimum wage, and there has been much discussion and analysis of its likely effects and the level at which it should be set. The simple analysis of a minimum wage says that, to the extent that it has any effect at all, it raises the wage for groups of workers whose free market equilibrium wage would have been below the minimum wage, and it also causes some of these people to become unemployed. Thus it makes some people better off but others worse off. This analysis assumes that there is a competitive market for labour. Opponents point to the unemployment effect of a minimum wage and argue that there are better ways of raising the incomes of low-paid workers that do not create so much economic inefficiency at the same time. Supporters of the idea disclaim the likelihood of a minimum's causing job losses and instead argue that it protects workers from exploitation by low-wage employers, who, it is claimed, also increase the social security bill, as their low-paid employees become eligible for social security benefits.

Many other countries have experience of a minimum wage, which can be used to give some insight into what might result in Britain from its introduction. There is a minimum wage in the United States, for example, which affects only very low paid workers. France has a rather high minimum wage which affects a great many workers. Studies in the United States have found that the minimum wage has not reduced employment.

The argument is that employers do not lose all their workers if they cut the wage they offer, and conversely, in order to hire more workers, they have to offer higher wages. In other words, employers have some monopsony power in the labour market. When the market is left alone, employers have an incentive to hold wages down in order to save on labour costs. The marginal cost of an employee exceeds the wage paid to that person, because the wage rate offered to all employees has to be raised in order to attract an additional worker; the excess of the marginal cost over the wage rate is the cost to the employer of raising the wages of all the other workers by enough to attract the additional worker. The profit-maximising employer hires workers until the marginal cost of hiring the extra worker equals the marginal revenue produced by hiring. At this point the monopsonistic employer is paying a wage that is less than the marginal revenue produced by the worker, and thus the wage is less than it would be in a competitive market (and less than it should be if resources are to be allocated efficiently in the economy) and employment is lower.

By imposing a minimum wage, these employers might have to pay a higher wage than in the unfettered marketplace. However, the marginal cost of hiring an additional worker is just the minimum wage; there is no element of increasing the wage bill for the existing workers. Thus the imposition of a minimum wage might actually lower the marginal cost to the firm of hiring a new worker, and so cause more employment rather than less. The U.S. results were derived from the analysis of employment in fast-food outlets in New Jersey and Pennsylvania. Some people find it hard to believe that employers such as McDonald's and Burger King have any monopsony power, and the analysis has been controversial. Nevertheless it is supported by evidence on the abolition of the wages councils in Britain in 1983, which had set a minimum wage in several industries: there has been no evidence that they ever destroyed any jobs. In any event this is the economically respectable argument for the view that a minimum wage need not cost jobs. This argument only applies to a low minimum, set only slightly above the free market wage, of course. Set high enough, a minimum wage is bound to cost jobs, as everyone agrees.

The discussion of the appropriate level of the minimum wage created suggestions from as high as £4.26 (from the Trades Union Congress) to as low as £3 from various employers' organizations. Figures based on the wages set by the old wages councils uprated for average earnings growth would emerge at roughly £3.40. A minimum wage set at half of average male earnings (notwithstanding that this poses major problems of definition) might have produced £3.75 an hour. In the event, a figure of £3.60 has been seized upon, with a rate of £3 for workers under the age of 21.

Variations in the minimum wage will be very important, in order to prevent its having a negative effect on employment. Teenagers have much lower earnings (less than half) than older workers on average. People on recognised training courses also get lower wages and should have a lower minimum wage. Regional differences in wages are smaller and could not easily form the basis of a differentiated minimum wage.

In the end, there is widespread agreement, uniting supporters and opponents, that a minimum wage will not have a major impact on the economy, for good or ill. It may have a positive effect for some low-paid workers. It looks like a policy whose totemic political significance far exceeds its economic importance.

Sources: Martin Wolf, "A Policy with No Point," *Financial Times*, 22 April 1997; Alan Manning, "If It's Good Enough for Everyone Else, It's Good Enough for Us," *The Independent*, 11 May 1997.

---

someone working for another firm, and the worker accepts, the employer might worry. Did the worker's current employer—who presumably knows a lot about the worker's productivity—fail to match the job offer because the worker's productivity does not warrant the higher wage? Does the worker's willingness to leave demonstrate lack of loyalty or an unsettled nature? If so, will he stick with the new firm long enough to make his training worthwhile? These concerns again impede labour mobility, as employers prefer to keep their existing labour force even when there are lower-paid workers with similar credentials whom they might be able to recruit at a lower wage.

There are a variety of other impediments to labour mobility, including the costs of moving from one city to another.

Different groups of individuals may differ in their mobility. For instance, older workers may be much more reluctant to move than younger workers. Sometimes, firms take advantage of these differences to pay lower wages. Knowing that older workers will not leave even if wages fail to keep pace with infla-

tion, employers may hold back raises from them, discriminating against their age and lower mobility.

DISCRIMINATION

Discrimination is said to occur if two workers of seemingly similar *work-related* characteristics are treated differently. Paying higher wages to more-educated workers is not discrimination, as long as the higher level of education is related to higher productivity. If older workers are less productive, then paying them lower wages is not discrimination. But if older workers are just as productive as younger workers, then taking advantage of their lower mobility *is* discrimination.

Forty years ago, there was open and outright discrimination in the labour market. Some employers simply refused to hire members of various racial and other minority groups. Today much of the discrimination that occurs is more subtle. Firms seek to hire the best workers they can for each job at the lowest cost possible, operating with imperfect information. We have seen how, in making predictions about future performance, employers use whatever information they have available. On average, employers may have found that recruits with a degree from one of the United Kingdom's ancient universities were more successful in the firm than recruits with a degree from one of the newer universities. If it turned out that many of the nonwhites who had been successful in getting to universities had gone to the newer universities, then the procedure of picking recruits from the graduates of the ancient universities would effectively screen out many nonwhite workers. This more subtle form of discrimination is called **statistical discrimination.**

Some discrimination is neither old-fashioned prejudice nor statistical discrimination. Employers may just feel more comfortable dealing with people with whom they have dealt in the past. In a world in which there is so much uncertainty about who is a good worker and in which a bad worker can do enormous damage, top management may rely on certain trusted employees for recommendations. And such judgments are inevitably affected by friendships and other ties. Many claim that if discrimination is to be eliminated, this form of discrimination, based on "old boy networks," has to be broken.

When firms pay lower wages to, say, women or minorities, it is called **wage discrimination.** Today, wage discrimination is perhaps less common than **job discrimination,** where disadvantaged groups have less access to better-paying jobs. Women are often said to face a "glass ceiling": they can climb up to middle management jobs but can't get beyond them to top management.

Some market forces tend to limit the extent of discrimination. If a woman is paid less than a man of comparable productivity, it pays a firm to hire the woman. Not to hire her costs the firm profits. To put it another way, the firm pays a price for discriminating. If there are enough firms that put profits above prejudice, then the wages of women will be bid up towards the level of men of comparable productivity.

The British government responded to racial discrimination by passing a Race Relations Act in 1968 and another in 1976, which made it illegal to act in such a way as to create racial tension or hatred and established the Commission for Racial Equality to promote equality and help to eradicate cases of racial discrimination. Sexual discrimination has been met by the passing of the Equal Pay Act of 1970 and the Sex Discrimination Act of 1975. The laws in Britain are weak in that, while discrimination is illegal, the discriminators are required to do little more than stop doing it. There are no direct penalties for discrimination. Laws imposed in Britain by the European Commission have more teeth. In a recent case, a number of women in the armed services who were dismissed by the Ministry of Defence when they became pregnant have been given large awards as compensation for lost earnings and careers by the courts.

Despite the weakness of the British laws, the earn-

EXPLANATIONS OF WAGE DIFFERENTIALS

Unions: Unions may succeed in obtaining higher wages for their workers.

Compensating differentials: Wage differences may correspond to differences in the nature of the job.

Productivity differentials: Wage differences may correspond to differences in productivity among workers.

Information-based differentials: Wage differences may reflect the fact that workers do not have perfect information about the opportunities available in the market and employers do not view workers as perfect substitutes.

Imperfect labour mobility: Differentials will not be eliminated by individuals moving between jobs.

Discrimination: Wage differentials and hiring and promotion decisions can sometimes be traced to nothing more than racial or gender differences.

ings of women relative to men rose from around 60 percent—where they had been for decades—to around 70 percent in the five years following the passage of the 1970 Equal Pay Act. Since then, however, there has been little further improvement in women's pay relative to men's.

The laws in the United States have gone a lot further to promote nondiscrimination. A programme of **affirmative action** has required many firms acting as contractors for the U.S. government to keep quotas of jobs for women and members of minority racial groups. Quotas have been controversial. People in favour argue that they are needed to overcome subtle forms of discrimination which are widespread. People against argue that quotas are themselves discriminatory and may, for example, lead to the employment of a minority person instead of a better-qualified white male. They argue also that whereas the laws were intended to stop people from thinking in terms of gender or racial categories, quotas have exactly the opposite effect and perpetuate racial and gender distinctions.

MOTIVATING WORKERS

The discussion to this point has treated workers as if they were machines. Workers have a price—the wage—analogous to the price of machines. But even to the most profit-hungry and coldhearted employer, people are different from machines. They bring adaptability and a multitude of skills and experiences to a job. Most machines can only do one task, and even robots can only do what they are programmed to do. However, machines have one advantage over humans. Except when they break down, they do what they are told. But workers have to be motivated if they are to work hard and to exercise good judgment.

This can be viewed as an information problem. In the basic competitive model of Part Two, workers were paid to perform particular tasks. The employer knew perfectly whether the worker performed the agreed-upon task in the agreed-upon manner. If the worker failed to do so, he did not get paid. The pay was the only form of motivation required. But in reality, workers frequently have considerable discretion. Employers have limited information about what a worker is doing at each moment. So they have to motivate their workforce to exercise their abilities to the fullest.

To motivate workers, employers use both the carrot and the stick. They may reward workers for performing well by making pay and promotion depend on performance, and they may punish workers for shirking by firing them. Sometimes a worker is given considerable discretion and autonomy; sometimes he is monitored closely. The mix of carrots and sticks, autonomy and direct supervision, varies from job to job and industry to industry. It depends partly on how easy it is to supervise workers directly and partly on how easy it is to compensate workers on the basis of performance.

PIECE RATES AND INCENTIVES

When workers can be paid for exactly what they produce, with their pay increasing for higher productivity and falling for lower productivity, they will have appropriate incentives to work hard. The system of payment in which a worker is paid for each item produced or each task performed is called a **piece-rate system.** But relatively few workers are paid largely, let alone exclusively, on a piece-rate system. Typically, even workers within a piece-rate system get a base pay *plus* additional pay, which increases the more they produce.

Why don't more employers enact a piece-rate system if it would improve incentives? One major reason is that piece rates leave workers bearing considerable risk. A worker may have a bad week because of bad luck. For example, salespeople, who are often paid commissions on the basis of productivity—a form of piece rate—may simply find the demand for their products lacking.

A firm, by providing a certain amount of guaranteed pay, gives the worker a steady income and reduces the risk she must bear. But with lower piece-rate compensation, the worker has less incentive to work hard. There is thus a trade-off between risk and incentives. Thus, compensation schemes must find some balance between offering security and offering incentives linked to worker performance. In many jobs, employers or managers achieve this balance by offering both a guaranteed minimum compensation (including fringe benefits) and bonuses that depend on performance.

A second reason more employers do not use piece-rate systems is a concern for quality. For workers on an assembly line, for example, the quantity produced may be easily measured but quality cannot. If the workers' pay just depends on the number of items produced, the worker has an incentive to emphasise quantity over quality. The result may be less profitable for the firm than a lower quantity of higher-quality output.

In any case, most workers are engaged in a variety of tasks, only some of which can easily be defined and rewarded by means of a piece-rate system. For example, although employers would like experienced workers to train new workers, employees who are paid on a piece-rate system have little incentive to do this or to help their co-workers in other ways. Similarly, when salespeople are paid on the basis of commissions, they have little incentive to provide information and service to potential customers whom they perceive as not likely to be immediate buyers. Even if providing information enhances the likelihood that a customer will return to the store to buy the good, there is a fair chance that some other salesperson will get the commission.

EFFICIENCY WAGES

When output is easily measured, then the carrot of basing pay at least partially on performance makes sense. And when effort is easily monitored, then using the stick of being fired for failure to exert adequate effort makes sense. But monitoring effort continuously is often expensive. An alternative is to monitor less frequently, and impose a big penalty if the worker is caught shirking. One way of imposing a big penalty is to pay above-market wages. Then, if a worker is fired, he suffers a big income loss. The higher the wage, the greater the penalty from being fired. Similarly, rewarding with higher pay workers who are observed to be working hard whenever they

are monitored provides incentives for workers to continue to work hard.

These are examples where higher wages help motivate workers and lead to increased productivity. There are additional reasons why it may pay a firm to pay high wages. High wages reduce labour turnover, lead to more loyalty and higher quality work by employees, and enable the firm to attract more productive workers. This two-way link is captured by **efficiency wage theory.** This theory says that not only do higher productivities result in higher wages but also higher wages result in higher productivity. While wages increase with productivity, you cannot tell what is causing what.

Efficiency wage theory provides an explanation for some wage differentials. In jobs where it is very costly to monitor workers on a day-to-day basis or where the damage a worker can do is very great (for instance, by punching one wrong button, the worker can destroy a machine), employers are more likely to rely on high wages to ensure workers perform well.

These "wages of trust" may explain why wages in more capital-intensive industries (that require massive investments) are higher for workers with otherwise comparable skills than wages in industries using less capital are. They may also explain why workers entrusted with the care of much cash (which they could abscond with) are paid higher wages than other workers of comparable skills are. It is not so much that they receive high wages because they are trustworthy but that they become more trustworthy because they receive high wages, and the threat of losing those high wages encourages moral behaviour.

OTHER INCENTIVES

After paying piece rates, bonuses, and higher-than-market wages, among the most important incentives to increase job performance are enhanced promotion possibilities for those who perform well, with pay rising with promotions, and contests among workers. Contests are particularly useful when it is hard to determine the difficulty of the task a worker is performing. Consider a firm trying to work out how much to pay its sales force when it is promoting a new product. If a salesperson is successful, does that represent good selling technique or is the new product able to sell itself? All sales representatives are in roughly the same position. The representative who sells the most wins the contest and gets a bonus.

At the top end of the corporate hierarchy, the top executives of the largest firms are paid high salaries often running to hundreds of thousands of pounds. Why is this? Economists continue to debate the issue. Some interpret these salaries as the payoffs of contests, others as reflecting the large contributions of these managers or wages of trust. But some suspect that top managers have enough control to divert a considerable amount (though but a small fraction) of a firm's resources to their own betterment in the form of higher compensation.

In recent years, firms have explored the consequences of alternative ways of encouraging worker motivation and hence worker productivity. Some use teams. When pay depends on team performance, members of a team have an incentive to monitor and help one another. The car manufacturer Volvo believes that such team arrangements have increased the productivity of its own workforce. Some firms have encouraged worker participation in decision making. Such participation may help both sides see that there is more to be gained by cooperation than by conflict. For instance, new ways of producing

CLOSE-UP: FRINGE BENEFITS

Fringe benefits form a part of the total compensation for almost all employees, and they are a large fraction of the total for some. They include things like pension contributions and National Insurance contributions made by the employer, private health insurance (which is becoming increasingly widespread), and the provision of a car. Firms may have or pay for membership in sports or health clubs or, in years gone by, brass bands. Depending on how wages are measured, holiday entitlements and paid leave for sickness may be included as fringe benefits. Firms may offer bonuses, which may also be viewed as fringe benefits. Many firms speak of the total compensation package that they offer, emphasising that the wage or salary is just a part of the deal.

Why do employers like to offer compensation in these different ways, rather than just offering a straightforward wage or salary? And why do employees like to get paid in this way? One reason is tax efficiency. The tax paid by the firm and the

worker on the benefits provided by the firm may be less than the worker would pay on the equivalent wage. This explains the prevalence of company cars in Britain, where half of all new cars are bought by firms. In recent years taxation of company cars has been increased, and their importance may be expected to diminish. Another factor is to encourage workers to stay with the firm. Company pension schemes often reward workers who stay with the firm for long periods rather than moving frequently from job to job. Firms are likely to do this when long-standing workers are likely to have experience of great value to the firm or when hiring and training new workers is expensive. A third factor is that firms may be able to buy benefits or services more cheaply than their employees could buy them individually. For example, a group membership in a private health insurance scheme or a health or sports club may be cheaper than many individual memberships.

Piece rates, or pay based on measured output

Efficiency wages, or higher wages to workers who work harder, which introduce an extra cost to those dismissed for unsatisfactory performance

Relative performance: promotions, contests

Team rewards, or pay based on team performance

goods can make both the firm and the workers better off; if the company sells more goods, all share in the benefits.

At least in the long run, wages and labour costs respond to reflect the attitudes of workers. If workers find that a certain firm provides an attractive workplace, the wages it must pay to recruit people may be lower than other firms' wages, and the people that it recruits will work harder and stay longer. If workers as a whole become concerned about having more autonomy, more say in decision making, or any other attribute of the workplace, it will pay firms to respond to their concerns.

REVIEW AND PRACTICE

SUMMARY

1 The proportion of workers in unions has declined since 1979. Possible reasons include the decline of manufacturing industries, in which unions have traditionally been strong, relative to service industries; foreign competition; a more antiunion legal structure.

2 Overall, there is little evidence that workers today receive higher pay than they would have in the absence of unions, though union workers may gain some at the expense of nonunion workers.

3 Union power is limited by the ability of companies to bring in new, nonunion workers and by the threat of unemployment to union workers.

4 Explanations for wage differentials include compensating differentials (differences in the nature of jobs), productivity differentials (differences in productivity between workers), imperfect information (workers do not know all the job opportunities that are available), and discrimination.

5 Employers try to motivate workers and induce high levels of effort through a combination of direct supervision, incentives for doing well, and penalties for doing badly. They pay wages higher than workers could get elsewhere (efficiency wages), give promotions and bonuses, base pay on relative performance (contests), and grant team rewards.

KEY TERMS

compensating wage differentials

statistical discrimination

piece-rate system

efficiency wage theory

REVIEW QUESTIONS

1 Has the power of unions in the economy been shrinking or growing in the last few decades? Why?

2 What effect will successful unions have on the level of wages paid by unionised companies? On the capital investment in those companies? What effect will they have on wages paid by nonunionised companies?

3 How might greater job security for union workers possibly lead to their becoming less efficient?

4 Does it make sense for a union to resist the intro-duction of an innovation in the short run? In the long run?

5 What are alternative explanations for wage differentials?

6 How do piece rates provide incentives to work hard? Why is there not a greater reliance on piece-rate systems?

7 What is efficiency wage theory?

PROBLEMS

1 In what ways are labour markets similar to prod-uct markets? In what ways are they different?

2 Explain how both these points can be true simultaneously:
 (a) Unions manage to raise the wage paid to their members.
 (b) Unions do not affect the average level of wages paid in the economy.

3 How might each of the following factors affect the power of unions?
 (a) Foreign imports increase.
 (b) The national unemployment rate falls.
 (c) Company profits increase.

4 Suppose a worker holding a job that pays £7 per hour applies for a job with another company that pays £10 per hour. Why might the second company be suspicious about whether the worker is really worth £10 per hour? How might the worker attempt to overcome those fears?

5 Imagine that a company knows that if it cuts wages 10 percent, then 10 percent of its employees will leave. How might adverse selection cause the amount of work done by the remaining workers in the company to fall by more than 10 percent?

6 Advances in computer technology have allowed some firms to monitor their typists by a system that counts the number of keystrokes they make in a given workday. Telephone operators are sometimes monitored to determine how many calls they take and how long they spend on an average call. Would you expect such monitoring to increase productiv-ity? Why or why not?

7 When someone is promoted from middle man-agement to top executive, his salary often doubles or more. Why does this seem puzzling, from the per-spective of the theory of competitive markets? Why might a profit-maximising firm do this?

PART FOUR

Policy Issues

T he basic competitive model presented in Part Two focused on the private sector—on firms and households. Yet government plays a central role in our modern economy. In developed countries, between 30 and 60 percent of the economy's output passes through the hands of the government (at the local or central level). Chapter 7 presented a brief overview of the economic role of government, and Part Three showed how government seeks to encourage competition and promote technological change. But we have yet to discuss some of the most important activities of the government—what the government does and why.

In Chapter 19 we return to the subject of externalities, introduced in Chapter 7, and consider the impact of negative externalities upon the environment. We explore the market failures that give rise to pollution and review the ways governments have attempted to remedy those failures. We also examine whether markets provide adequate incentives to conserve natural resources such as oil and minerals. Finally, we discuss circumstances in which the consumption of products is mandated (as in compulsory education) or prohibited (as in illegal drugs) by government. Here, government intervention is based not only on economic efficiency but also on other grounds.

Even when markets are efficient, how they allocate resources may be socially unacceptable. Such concerns are raised by poverty and homelessness. The distribution of income is a major concern of modern societies and their governments. Chapter 20 discusses recent changes in income distribution, and describes and evaluates the tax system.

Government social insurance programmes are discussed in Chapter 20 too. Markets often fail to provide insurance against some of the most important risks that individuals face, including the loss of a job and being disabled and unable to work. Chapter 20 looks at these social insurance programmes and the problems they face today, as well as the broader role of government in redistribution.

Government differs from households and firms in many ways, not the least of which is the form of decision making. In a democratic society, some individuals would like the government to spend more money on education, others on parks, others on bombers. How *collective* decisions are made and the influences upon those decisions have significant effects on the allocation of resources. Chapter 21 discusses these factors and some of the problems facing collective decision making.

In Part Four we complete our discussion of the many ways in which the real world is different from the basic model—except for one. The basic model assumes that all markets clear, including the labour market. But at times involuntary unemployment becomes a fact of life. At times, such as during the Great Depression when one out of four workers was without a job, there is massive unemployment. Later parts of the book address the causes of this unemployment and what government can do about it.

CHAPTER 19

EXTERNALITIES
AND THE
ENVIRONMENT

In this and the next two chapters, we probe the economic role of government, a topic first treated in broad terms in Chapter 7. Beyond providing a legal framework within which economic relations take place, government may have an economic role to play when markets fail to produce efficient outcomes. This justification is known as the **market failures approach** to the role of government.

We already know several ways in which markets can fail to produce efficient outcomes. For example, competition may be less than envisaged by the basic model, and less-than-perfect competition produces inefficient economic outcomes. Competitive markets may, for all the reasons set forth in Chapter 16, fail to produce the technological innovation needed by a thriving economy. Government has responded with patent laws and other legislative efforts to spur innovation.

Markets may also fail in the face of information problems (Chapter 17). For instance, producers tend to know more about their products than they reveal to customers. Government has responded with truth-in-advertising laws.

One market failure has not yet been adequately discussed. This failure arises when there are externalities—costs and benefits of a transaction that are not fully reflected in the market price. When we first encountered externalities in Chapter 7, our focus was on positive externalities, such as those associated with goods that are publicly provided. Here we shift the focus to negative externalities and the issues of environmental protection and natural resource depletion.

1 Why do externalities such as pollution result in a market failure? What alternative policies can government employ to remedy this market failure?

2 What are the market forces that lead to an efficient use of society's natural resources? What may impede markets from using scarce natural resources efficiently?

NEGATIVE EXTERNALITIES AND OVERSUPPLY

Perfect competition assumes that the costs of producing a good and the benefits of selling it all accrue to the seller and that the benefits of receiving the good and the costs of buying it all accrue to the buyer. This is often not the case. As was explained in Chapter 7, the extra costs and benefits not captured by the market transaction are called externalities.

Externalities can be either positive or negative, depending on whether individuals enjoy extra benefits they did not pay for or suffer extra costs they did not incur. Goods for which there are positive externalities—such as research and development—will be undersupplied in the market. In deciding how much of the good to purchase, each individual or firm thinks only about the benefits it receives, not the benefits conferred upon others. By the same token, goods for which there are negative externalities, such as air and water pollution, will be oversupplied in the market. The fact that the market might not fully capture the costs and benefits of a trade provides a classic example of a market failure and a possible role for the public sector.

Figure 19.1A shows the demand and supply curves for a good, say steel. Market equilibrium is the intersection of the curves, the point labeled E, with output Q_p and price p_p. Chapter 12 explained why, in the absence of externalities, the equilibrium E is efficient. The price reflects the marginal benefit individuals receive from an extra unit of steel (it measures their marginal willingness to pay for an extra unit). The price also reflects the marginal cost to the firm of producing an extra unit. At E, marginal benefit equals marginal cost.

Consider what happens if, in the production of steel, there is an externality: producers are polluting the air and water without penalty. The **social marginal cost**—the marginal cost borne by all individuals in the economy—will now exceed the **private marginal cost**—the marginal cost borne by the producer alone. Note that in a competitive industry, the supply curve corresponds to the horizontal sum of all producers' *private* marginal cost curves. Panel B contrasts the two situations. It shows the social marginal cost curve for producing steel lying above the private marginal cost curve. Thus, with social marginal cost equated to social marginal benefit, the economically efficient level of production of steel will be lower, at Q_s, than it would be, at Q_p, if private costs were the only ones.

Thus, the level of production of steel, which generates negative externalities, will be too high in a free market. We can also ask, what about the level of expenditure on pollution abatement? Such expenditures confer a positive externality on others; the benefits of the equipment, the cleaner air, accrue mainly to others. Figure 19.2 shows a firm's demand curve for pollution-abatement equipment in the absence of government regulation. It is quite low, reflecting the fact that the firm itself derives little benefit. That is, the firm's marginal private benefit from expenditures on pollution-abatement equipment is small. The firm sets its marginal private benefit equal to the marginal cost of pollution abatement; this results in a level of expenditure on pollution abatement at E. The figure also depicts the marginal social benefit of pollution abatement, which is far greater than the marginal private benefit. Efficiency requires that the marginal social benefit equal the marginal cost, point E'. Thus, economic efficiency requires greater expenditures on pollution abatement than there would be in the free market.

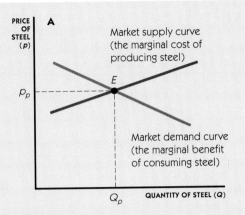 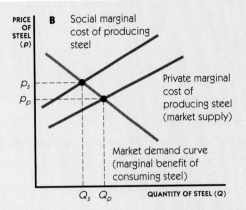

Figure 19.1 HOW NEGATIVE EXTERNALITIES CAUSE OVERSUPPLY

In a perfectly competitive market, the market supply curve is the (horizontal) sum of the marginal cost curves of all firms, while market demand reflects how much the marginal consumer is willing to pay. In panel A, the intersection or equilibrium, at quantity Q_p and price p_p, will be where marginal cost is equal to the marginal benefit for society as a whole.

The private marginal cost includes just the costs actually paid by the producing firm. If there are broader costs to society as a whole, like pollution, then the social costs will exceed the private costs. If the supplier is not required to take these additional costs into account (as in panel B), production will be at Q_p, greater than Q_s, where price equals social marginal cost, and the quantity produced will exceed the amount where marginal cost is equal to marginal benefit for society as a whole.

Figure 19.2 HOW POSITIVE EXTERNALITIES CAUSE UNDERSUPPLY

The private marginal benefit includes just the benefits received by the firm, but since pollution-abatement equipment provides a positive externality, it will have a social marginal benefit that is higher. If the firm takes only its private benefit into account, it will operate at point E, using less equipment than at the point where marginal benefits are equal to marginal costs for society as a whole (E').

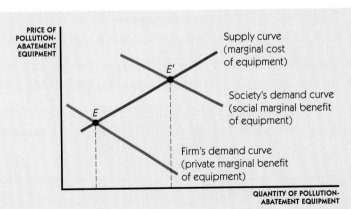

One of the government's major economic roles is to correct the inefficiencies resulting from externalities. Among the many types of negative externalities, perhaps the most conspicuous are those that harm the environment.

ENVIRONMENTAL PROTECTION AND CONSERVATION: EXAMPLES

Chloro-fluoro-carbons (CFCs), gases which once were used as propellants in aerosol cans and as coolants in air conditioners and refrigerators, appear to have destroyed some of the ozone layer of the atmosphere—risking major climatic changes and possibly exposing individuals to radiation that may cause cancer. This is a worldwide externality. A major treaty among the nations of the world was signed in early 1990 that would eventually ban the use of these and related gases. The nature of the externality in this case was clear: the use of these gases anywhere could have disastrous effects on everyone.

Another major international treaty was signed in Rio de Janeiro in 1992. Since the beginning of the industrial revolution, enormous quantities of fossil fuels—coal, oil, and gas—have been burned. When they burn, they produce carbon dioxide (CO_2). Carbon dioxide is absorbed into the oceans and used by plants in photosynthesis. But the rate of emissions in recent decades has been far greater than the rate of absorption, so much so that the concentration of CO_2 in the atmosphere is 25 percent higher than it was at the beginning of the industrial revolution. Worse, in the next few decades, it is projected to double, or more, unless strong actions are taken. The United Nations convened an international panel of scientists to assess both the extent of these dramatic changes in the earth's atmosphere and their consequences. Their findings were alarming. These and other gases create a "greenhouse gas" effect, trapping radiation arriving at the earth and leading to global warming. While the magnitude of the warming effect is likely to be small—only a few degrees—the potential harm is great: a partial melting of the earth's ice caps, a rise in sea levels, a flooding of low-lying countries such as Bangladesh, and an increase in the spread of deserts.

At Rio, the developed countries agreed to restrain their level of emissions, returning them to their 1990 level by the year 2000. Since emissions increase with energy use, and energy use normally increases with economic growth, achieving this goal will require both substantial increases in energy efficiency and switching from energy sources (such as coal) that produce high levels of emissions to those that produce little or none (such as hydroelectric power.)

These are examples of global externalities. Most externalities are more local. Many of the world's cities are choking with smog, for example, caused largely by automobile exhausts. Many rivers, streams, and lakes are so polluted that they are unsafe to drink or to swim in.

POLICY RESPONSES TO PROBLEMS IN THE ENVIRONMENT

As the negative externalities associated with pollution and other environmental issues are increasingly recognised, the alternative ways government can curtail their bad effects have received considerable attention from economists and others. This section evaluates several of the major options.

PROPERTY RIGHTS RESPONSES

Large-scale environmental degradation is a conspicuous form of negative externalities. Having identified them as market failures, what can the government do to improve matters? Some economists, led by Nobel laureate Ronald Coase, argue that government should simply rearrange property rights. **Coase's theorem** says that, with appropriately designed property rights, markets could take care of externalities without direct government intervention. Consider, for example, the case of a small lake in which anyone can fish without charge. Each person fishing ignores the fact that the more fish he takes out of the lake, the fewer fish there are for others to take out. If the government were to rearrange property rights

The average American eats 63 pounds of beef, 50 pounds of pork, and 46 pounds of chicken in a year, and one never hears concerns that this consumption will drive cows or pigs or chickens into extinction. Relatively few Americans eat whale meat, yet in certain countries like Japan, whale meat is considered a delicacy. In 1986, fearing that whales were being hunted into extinction, an international convention passed a moratorium on all commercial whaling. Why does the market system work to assure plenty of cows and pigs and chickens but threaten to exterminate certain breeds of whales?

Economists approach this question by analysing the property rights in each case. The farmers who raise cows and pigs and chickens own them, and thus have an incentive to build up the supply of animals. But no country or individual owns the ocean or the whales in it. Thus, although there is an economic incentive to hunt whales and sell their meat, there is no individual or company with a direct economic incentive to help nurture and increase the overall number of whales.

This pattern has been called the "tragedy of the commons." When an area is owned in common, like the ocean, everyone has an economic incentive to exploit it, but no one has an economic incentive to care for it. The result can be the disappearance of the whales in the ocean.

Of course, the problem of the commons is not limited to whales. The decimation of the bison on the commonly owned U.S. prairie is another example, as is the pollution in the commonly owned air and water.

Soon after the moratorium on whaling for commercial purposes was passed in 1986, several countries felt a sudden need to hunt whales for scientific purposes. Japan, for example, announced in 1987 an urgent need to kill for research purposes nearly half the number of whales they had been catching for commercial purposes. Iceland announced that it would be shipping much of the whale meat from its "research whales" to Japan, where the meat would sell at premium prices. More recently, international agreements have placed tight limits on the number of whales that can be caught. As a result, the number of Minky whales quickly made a recovery, to the point where limited commercial whaling has begun once again.

Sources: Figures on meat consumption come from *Statistical Abstract of the United States* (1990), Table 202; information about whaling in 1986 and 1987 comes from Timothy Appel, "Japan Finds Loophole in Whaling Ban," *Christian Science Monitor*, 15 April 1987, p. 1.

and grant to a single individual the right to fish, then he would have every incentive to fish efficiently. There would be no externalities. He would take into account the long-run interests as well as the short-run. He would realise that if he fished too much this year, he would have fewer fish next year. If it were a large lake, he might let others do the fishing and charge them for each fish caught or regulate the amount of fish they could catch. But the prices he charged and the regulations he imposed would be designed to ensure that the lake was not overfished.

The point of this example is that the problem of overfishing is solved with only limited government intervention. All the government has to do is assign the property rights correctly.

The appeal of Coase's theorem is that it assigns a minimal role to government. Government simply makes the property rights clear and leaves the efficient outcome to private markets. Opportunities to apply the theorem are limited, however, because the costs of reaching an agreement may be high, particularly when large numbers of individuals are involved. Imagine the difficulties of assigning property rights to the atmosphere and having all the individuals adversely affected by air pollution negotiating with all those contributing to it!

Today there is general agreement that while assigning property rights clearly may take care of some externality problems, most externalities, particularly those concerning the environment, require more active government intervention. Some forms this intervention might take include regulatory measures, financial penalties, subsidization of corrective measures, and creating a market for the externality.

REGULATION

An obvious government response to the need for intervention to address environmental externalities is to regulate. Electric utilities that burned high-sulphur coal might not be allowed to emit sulphur dioxide into the atmosphere. They might be required to install scrubbers, devices that remove the sulphur from the fumes. And cars could be required to have catalytic converters. This approach is sometimes called the **command and control approach.**

The approach has disadvantages. The same environmental benefits often can be achieved at much lower costs than the specificity of the regulations demand. This is partly because the regulations do not (and can not) allow for the myriad of variations in circumstances facing different firms, and partly because the regulatory process is always slow (at best) in incorporating newly developing technologies. Worse still, the command and control approach fails to provide incentives for the development of new technologies to reduce environmental damage, since it often does not allow the technologies, even if they do a better job.[1] Moreover, politics inevitably intrudes into the setting of regulations, typically resulting in higher than necessary costs.

---

[1] On the other side, advocates argue that in some cases the tight regulations have forced the development of new technologies to meet environmental standards that could not be met with existing technologies.

TAXES AND SUBSIDIES

Most economists believe that taxes and subsidies provide a better way than regulation to encourage the behaviour society wants. Taxes are the stick, while subsidies are the carrot. Both share the aim of adjusting private costs to account for social costs.

Taxes on pollution are similar to fines for violating regulations in one respect; they both increase the cost of and thereby discourage pollution. But taxes differ from regulation in a fundamental way. Regulations are a clumsy weapon. They penalise firms for polluting over a specified level, but polluters who stay just below that level escape any penalty. Pollution taxes can be set so that they reduce aggregate pollution by the same amount as a regulator would under a command and control system. But the economic effects are very different. Taxes add the cost of pollution to the costs a company has to cover to remain in business. As a result, companies will have the incentive to reduce their pollution as far as possible and to find new, low-cost ways of reducing pollution, rather than keeping it just below the legal standard. This is efficient pollution abatement, in which the producers who pollute less have their reward in lower costs.

Subsidies are an alternative way of providing incentives to reduce pollution, perhaps in the form of tax credits for pollution-abatement devices. Subsidies are economically inefficient. Take the case of a steel firm. With subsidies, firms are not paying the full costs. Part of the costs are being picked up by the government. This allows producers to sell (and users to buy) steel at lower than its full cost of production and keeps pollution above the socially efficient level. This, of course, is why firms prefer subsidies to taxes.

THE MARKETABLE PERMIT RESPONSE

Still another approach to curbing pollution is **marketable permits.** Companies purchase (or are granted) a permit from the government that allows them to emit a certain amount of pollution. Again, the government can issue the amount of permits so that the company produces the same level of pollution that there would be under the command and control approach. However, companies are allowed to sell their permits. Thus, if a company cuts its pollution in half, it could sell some of its permits to another company that wants to expand production (and hence its emissions of pollutants).

The incentive effects of marketable permits are very much like those of taxes. A market for pollution permits encourages development of the best possible antipollution devices, rather than keeping the pollution just under some government-set limit. If the government wishes to reduce pollution over time, the permits can be designed to reduce the amount of pollution they allow by a set amount each year. In the United States, this sort of shrinking marketable permit was used to reduce the amount of lead in petrol during the early 1980s. Variants of this idea have recently been adopted to help control other forms of air pollution, such as sulphur dioxide.

WEIGHING THE ALTERNATIVE APPROACHES

Incentive programs, such as taxes or marketable permits, have an important advantage over direct controls, like regulations. The issue of pollution is not whether it should be allowed. After all, it is virtually impossible to eliminate all pollution in an industrial economy. Nor would it be efficient to do so; the costs would far exceed the benefits. The real issue is how sharply pollution should be limited. The *marginal* benefit has to be weighed against the marginal cost. This is not done under regulation. If government ascertains the marginal social cost of pollution and sets charges and permits accordingly, private firms will engage in pollution control up to the point at which the marginal cost of pollution control equals the marginal social return of pollution abatement (which is, of course, just the marginal cost of pollution). Each firm will have the correct marginal incentives.

Governments often prefer direct regulations because they believe that they can control the outcomes better. But such control can be illusory. If an unreachable standard is set, it is likely to be repealed. For example, as vehicle manufacturers have found the costs of various regulations to be prohibitive, they have repeatedly appealed for a delay in the enforcement of the regulations, often with considerable success.

It must also be kept in mind that choosing the socially efficient method of pollution abatement is the easy part of the policy problem. Figuring out the right level of pollution to aim for is much harder. Uncertainty about the consequences of pollution abounds and how to value certain options is an issue of hot debate. To what extent can environmental degradation be reversed? How much value should be placed on the extinction of a species like the spotted owl or the preservation of the Arctic wilderness? No matter what approach is chosen to externalities and the environment, such questions will remain controversial.

NATURAL RESOURCES

A recurrent theme among environmentalists is that our society is exhausting its natural resources too rapidly. We are using up oil and energy resources at

---

SOLVING THE PROBLEM OF EXTERNALITIES

Externalities, which occur when the extra costs and benefits of a transaction are not fully summed up in the market price, give rise to market failure. Four main solutions have been proposed and used:

1 The reassignment of property rights

2 Regulations that outlaw the negative externality

3 Tax and subsidy measures to encourage the behaviour society wants

4 Marketable permits

an alarming rate, hardwood timber forests that took hundreds of years to grow are being cut down, and supplies of vital resources like phosphorus are dwindling. There are repeated calls for government intervention to enhance the conservation of our scarce natural resources. Those who believe in the infallibility of markets reply, nonsense! Prices give the same guidance to the use of natural resources that they give to any other resource, these people say. Prices measure scarcity and send consumers and firms the right signals about how much effort to expend to conserve resources, so long as consumers and firms are well informed and so long as there is not some other source of market failure.

There is, in fact, some truth in both positions. Prices, in general, do provide signals concerning the scarcity of resources, and *in the absence of market failures*, those signals lead to economic efficiency. We have seen some cases where a private economy without government intervention will not be efficient—when there are negative externalities (pollution) or when a resource (like fish in the ocean) is not priced.

But what about a privately owned resource, like bauxite (from which aluminium is made) or copper? The owner of a bauxite mine has a clearly defined property right. Let's assume that he pays a tax appropriate to any pollution his mining operation causes. Thus, the price he charges will reflect both social and private costs. The question of resource depletion now boils down to the question of whether his bauxite is worth more to him in the market or in the ground. The answer depends on what bauxite will be worth in the future, say thirty years from now. If it is worth more thirty years from now, he will keep the bauxite in the ground even though he may not be alive. That way he maximises the value of his property, and he can enjoy his wise decision by selling the mine when he retires. The price at which he sells it should reflect the present discounted value of the bauxite.

If this miner and all other bauxite producers choose to bring the bauxite to market today, depleting the world's supply of bauxite, there are two possible reasons. Either this is the socially efficient outcome—society values bauxite more highly today than it will tomorrow—or the miners have miscalculated the value of bauxite thirty years from now and underestimated future prices, though they have every incentive to get as accurate a forecast as they can. If they have indeed miscalculated, we might view the result as a market failure; but there would be no reason to expect a government bureaucracy to do any better than the firms at guessing future prices.

However, from society's viewpoint there are two plausible reasons why private owners may undervalue future benefits of a natural resource. First, in countries where property rights are not secure, owners of a resource may feel that if they do not sell it soon, there is a reasonable chance that the resources will be taken away from them. There may be a revolution, for example, in which the government will take over the resource with no or only partial compensation to the owners. Even in countries where owners are not worried about government confiscating their property, increased regulations might make it more expensive to extract the resource in the future. Second, individuals and firms often face limited borrowing opportunities and very high interest rates. In these circumstances, capital markets discount future returns at a high rate, far higher than society or the government would discount them.

Higher interest rates induce a more rapid depletion of resources. Suppose an oil company is deciding whether to extract some oil today or to wait until next year. For simplicity, assume there are no extraction costs, so the net return to selling the oil is just its price. If the price of a barrel of oil is the same today as a year from now, the firm's decision is simple. The firm will sell the oil today. But what if the price of oil is expected to go up 10 percent? Now the firm must compare the present discounted value of the oil sold a year from now with what it could receive today. To calculate the present discounted value, we simply divide next year's price by 1 plus the interest rate. If the interest rate is 10 percent, then a dollar a year from now is worth 10 percent less than a dollar today. So if the interest rate is less than 10 percent, it pays the firm to wait; if the interest rate is more than 10 percent, it pays the firm to extract the oil today. At higher interest rates, firms have a greater incentive to extract oil earlier.

REVIEW AND PRACTICE

SUMMARY

1 Government may have a role in the economy when markets fail to produce an efficient outcome. When positive or negative externalities exist, markets will not provide an efficient outcome.

2 One way to deal with externalities is to assign clear-cut property rights.

3 Governments may deal with environmental externalities by imposing regulatory measures (the command and control approach), levying taxes and granting subsidies, or issuing marketable permits.

4 In a perfect market, natural resources are used up at an efficient rate. However, privately owned resources may be sold too soon, for two reasons. First, owners may fear that if they do not sell the resources soon, new government rules may prevent them from selling at all or, in any case, lower the return from selling them in the future. Second, interest rates facing owners may be higher, so they may value future income less than society in general does. High interest rates lead to a faster exploitation of natural resources.

KEY TERMS

market failures approach

social marginal cost

private marginal cost

Coase's theorem

command and control approach

REVIEW QUESTIONS

1 Name several market failures. Why do economists see the existence of these market failures as a justification for government action?

2 Why will a free market produce too much of goods that have negative externalities, like pollution? Why will a free market produce too little of goods that have positive externalities, like pollution control?

3 What are the advantages and limitations of dealing with externalities by assigning property rights?

4 What are the advantages of marketable permits over command and control regulation? What are the advantages of using taxes for polluting rather than subsidies for pollution-abatement equipment?

5 How do markets work to allocate natural resources efficiently? In which cases will markets fail to give the correct signals for how quickly a resource like oil should be depleted?

PROBLEMS

1 Foggy Bottom and Great Trilling-on-the-Wold are two neighbouring villages. Great Trilling is considering holding a grand and loud firework display to celebrate the millennium, which will create a negative externality (noise pollution) for Foggy Bottom. Suppose the local magistrates decide that any village has the right to prevent any other village from creating noise pollution. If the firework display creates a negative externality, how might the Great Trilling Village Council apply the lessons of Coase's theorem to get the firework display they want?

Suppose instead that the magistrates decide that no village has the right to prevent any other village from holding celebrations, no matter how loud and bright. How may the Foggy Bottom Village Council apply the lessons of Coase's theorem to reduce the disturbance the village suffers from the fireworks in Great Trilling?

2 The manufacturer of trucks produces pollution of various kinds. Producing a truck creates a pollution cost to society of £3,000. Imagine that the supply of trucks is competitive, and market supply and demand are given by the following data:

Price (thousand £)	19	20	21	22	23	24	25
Quantity supplied	480	540	600	660	720	780	840
Quantity demanded	660	630	600	570	540	510	480

Graph the supply curve for the industry and the demand curve. What are equilibrium price and output? Now graph the social marginal cost curve. If the social costs of pollution were taken into account, what would be the new equilibrium price and output?

If the government is concerned about the pollution emitted by truck plants, explain how it might deal with the externality through fines or taxes and through subsidies. Illustrate the effects of taxes and subsidies by drawing the appropriate supply and demand graphs. (Don't bother worrying about the exact units.) Why are economists likely to prefer fines to subsidies?

3 Consider a small lake (such as the North Sea) with a certain number of fish. The more fish that one person fishing takes out, the fewer fish are available for others to take out. Use graphs depicting private and social costs and benefits to fishing to describe the equilibrium and the socially efficient level of fishing. Explain how a tax on fishing could achieve the efficient outcome. Explain how giving a single individual the property right to the fish in the lake might also be used to obtain an efficient outcome.

The more fish taken out this year, the fewer fish will be available next year. Explain why if there is a single owner of the lake, the fish will be efficiently extracted from it. Assume that anyone who wants to fish can do so. Would you expect that too many fish would be taken out this year?

4 Consider a crowded room with an equal number of smokers and nonsmokers. Each smoker would be willing to pay £1.00 to have the right to smoke. Each nonsmoker would be willing to pay £.50 to have the room free from smoke. Assume there is a rule that says that no smoking is allowed. Could everyone be made better off if smoking is allowed? How? If property rights to clean air are assigned to the nonsmokers, how might the efficient outcome be obtained? What difference does it make to the outcome whether there is initially a rule that smoking is allowed or smoking is not allowed? What problems might you envision occurring if no smoking is allowed, unless all the nonsmokers agree to allow smoking?

CHAPTER 20

TAXES, TRANSFERS, AND REDISTRIBUTION

During this century, governments have become increasingly involved in reducing inequality in the distribution of income provided by the market. Without help, some families have too little income to do more than barely survive. Children who have the bad fortune to be born into impoverished families face bleak life prospects. Most developed countries have therefore sought to provide a safety net for the poor. Some have taken the more active stance of promoting equality of opportunity. Many have also developed benefit programs that help people, regardless of income, in times of need (such as illness, unemployment, or old age).

Income redistribution is inextricably linked to taxation, because virtually every tax system in the world today changes the proportion of income enjoyed by different groups in society. After a look at the case for income redistribution, this chapter takes up the two major ways government alters the distribution of income: taxes and public benefit programmes (transfers).

THE CASE FOR INCOME REDISTRIBUTION

Income redistribution policies are justified in ways different from other governmental economic policies. The roles of government developed in earlier chapters are based on the premise that public sector intervention may be appropriate to ensure efficient outcomes when there are market failures—whether from lack of competition, imperfect information, or the presence of externalities. In such situations, markets fail to provide completely satisfactory answers to two of the basic economic questions: "What goods are produced, and in what quantities?" and "How are the goods produced?"

When it comes to the question "For whom are the goods produced?" to which this chapter is devoted, the rationale for public sector intervention is different. Individuals' incomes determine who consumes the goods produced in a market economy. People with higher skills or more capital, for instance, earn higher incomes and therefore get to consume more of the goods produced. Labour and capital markets may be efficient, in the sense that wages and returns to capital get the incentive structure right for the economy. But the market distribution may result in some individuals' having enormous incomes and others' being homeless, with inadequate food and medical care. Thus, the case for income redistribution is not based on the pursuit of economic efficiency. It is based on overriding social value. There is a general consensus that when the market results in incomes so low that people cannot sustain a minimally decent standard of living, government should help out. *How* it helps out is crucial, however, because redistribution programmes often interfere with economic efficiency.

TAXES

Tax revenue is raised from a wide variety of sources. An important group of taxes, those on incomes of different kinds, are referred to as **direct taxes.** They include **income tax** and **corporation tax,** and also the **National Insurance contributions** (sometimes referred to as **payroll taxes**), that individuals and their employers have to pay from the individuals' earnings.

Another important group of taxes, levied on expenditures, is referred to as **indirect taxes.** These include **Value-Added Tax** (VAT), which is levied at the same rate on all goods and services with a few exceptions, and **excise duties,** which are levied most conspicuously on diesel and petrol; beer, wines, and spirits; and tobacco. The same agency of the British government that collects VAT and excise duties, H.M. Customs and Excise, also collects **customs duties** on imports from outside the European Union, but these are getting progressively less important as trade barriers are taken down.

Local governments in the United Kingdom have raised their own revenue from taxes on property. Historically these have been called the **rates**—a tax based on an ancient theoretical calculation of the rental value of a property. The rates were abolished in the late 1980s by the Thatcher government and replaced (for private households, not businesses) by the **community charge** (as the government called it), otherwise known as the **poll tax** (by everybody else). The poll tax was a fixed charge payable by each adult, with some allowances for persons with low incomes, intended to meet a part of the cost of services provided by local governments. It proved monumentally unpopular, contributed to the downfall of Mrs. (as she then was) Thatcher, and had a brief life. It was replaced in 1993 by the **council tax,** which is a tax based

on the capital value of property. Businesses now pay a separate property tax, the uniform business rate.

As a result of these taxes, few transactions escape some form of taxation. Figure 20.1 shows the relative importance of these taxes as sources of revenue. The income tax raises just over a quarter of central government revenue. The VAT is next in size, at just under one-fifth, followed by social security contributions (almost all of this is National Insurance contributions paid by employees, employers, and the self-employed). Excise duties yield about a tenth of revenue, corporation tax about the same, and business rates somewhat less. The vast bulk—over three-quarters—of local government revenue comes from grants made to it by central government. The community charge (and its successor the council tax)

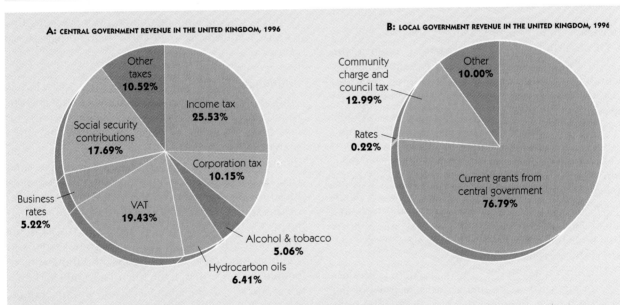

A: CENTRAL GOVERNMENT REVENUE IN THE UNITED KINGDOM, 1996

- Other taxes **10.52%**
- Income tax **25.53%**
- Social security contributions **17.69%**
- Corporation tax **10.15%**
- Business rates **5.22%**
- VAT **19.43%**
- Alcohol & tobacco **5.06%**
- Hydrocarbon oils **6.41%**

B: LOCAL GOVERNMENT REVENUE IN THE UNITED KINGDOM, 1996

- Community charge and council tax **12.99%**
- Other **10.00%**
- Rates **0.22%**
- Current grants from central government **76.79%**

Figure 20.1 **SOURCES OF TAX REVENUE FOR CENTRAL AND LOCAL GOVERNMENT**

Panel A shows central government tax revenue. The income tax raises just over a quarter of the total, followed in importance by the value-added tax, which raises just under 20 percent. Social security contributions were also very large. Altogether, the main direct taxes (income taxes, social security contributions, and corporation tax) raise over half of total revenue. Taxes on alcohol, tobacco, and petrol and other fuels are also significant. Panel B shows how heavily dependent on central government are local governments in Britain. They have little power to affect their revenue by changing the rate of the council tax. *Source:* U.K. National Income and Product Accounts ("The Blue Book") (Office of National Statistics, 1998).

raises only a small fraction of local government revenue, reflecting the extent to which local governments have little freedom of choice to decide their revenue and expenditures.

CHARACTERISTICS OF A GOOD TAX SYSTEM

Government tax revenues amount to more than 40 percent of the National Income in the United Kingdom. Not surprisingly, there is great concern about how the government raises its revenue. At one time, the art of taxation was likened to the problem of how to pluck a goose without making it squawk. The basic fact of life is that everyone enjoys government services but few enjoy paying taxes. Even so, there is substantial agreement about what constitutes a good tax system. It has five characteristics.

Fairness   In most people's minds, the first criterion is fairness. But fairness, like beauty, is often in the eye of the beholder. In trying to define fairness, economists focus on two principles: **horizontal equity,** which says that individuals who are in identical or similar situations should pay identical or similar taxes, and **vertical equity,** which says that people who are better off should pay more taxes.

Tax systems in which the rich pay a larger fraction of their income than the poor are said to be **progressive,** while those in which the poor pay a larger fraction of their income than the rich are called **regressive.** If rich people pay more taxes than poor but not proportionately more, the tax system is still considered regressive.

The income tax in the United Kingdom is moderately progressive, since higher average rates of tax apply to higher incomes. However, National Insurance contributions are only progressive at some of the lower ranges of the income scale, where the average rate of contribution rises with earnings. Because there is an upper ceiling on contributions, this tax becomes regressive at higher earnings. Taken together, National Insurance contributions and the income tax produce a tax that is not very progressive.

Efficiency   The second criterion for a good tax system is efficiency. The tax system should interfere as little as possible with the way the economy allocates resources, and it should raise revenue with the least costs to taxpayers. Very high taxes may discourage work and savings, and therefore interfere with the efficiency of the economy. Taxes that select out particular goods to be taxed—such as excise taxes on perfume, boats, and airline tickets—discourage individuals from purchasing those goods, and therefore also interfere with efficiency.

The income tax system has several provisions that have the effect of encouraging some types of economic activity and discouraging others. A famous example is the subsidy given to interest on mortgages via the tax system. Mortgage interest up to a limit—currently the interest on a mortgage of up to £30,000—used not to be liable to tax: taxpayers could deduct it from their income when computing taxable income. This has been a powerful force behind people's buying their own houses rather than renting them in Britain: the growth of the property-owning democracy. More recently, this subsidy has been reduced and is being progressively phased out.

Administrative Simplicity   The third criterion is administrative simplicity. It is costly—to the government and therefore to those who pay taxes—to collect taxes and administer a tax system. Although many income taxpayers never need to complete an income tax return, millions of hours are spent each year by the taxpayers who are required to complete these forms. Millions more are spent by the businesses that have to fill in much more complicated forms for VAT, PAYE (the pay-as-you-earn system for withholding income tax from employees' pay), and National Insurance contributions. And thousands of people are employed in the Inland Revenue and Customs and Excise checking forms and working out tax liabilities. In addition, with a good tax system, it should be difficult to evade the taxes imposed.

Flexibility   The fourth criterion is flexibility. As economic circumstances change, it may be desirable to change tax rates. With a good tax system, it should be relatively easy to do this.

Transparency   The fifth criterion is transparency. A good tax system is one in which it can be ascertained what each person is paying in taxes. The principle of transparency is analogous to the principle of "truth in advertising." Taxpayers are consumers of public services. They should know what they (and others) are paying for the services they are getting.

GRADING THE U.K. TAX SYSTEM

How well does the U.K. tax system fare, on the basis of these five criteria? Equally important, have the major changes in the tax laws over the past years improved the tax system?

Fairness The combination of income tax and employees' National Insurance (NI) contributions in the United Kingdom is broadly progressive. Individuals with very low incomes pay no tax or NI. All persons are entitled to a personal allowance of £4,195 (in the 1998–99 tax year). Income tax is then paid on the next £4,300 of income at a rate of 20 percent, on the next £22,800 at 23 percent (the standard rate), and then on any income above this at 40 percent. National Insurance contributions start when weekly income

reaches £64. At that level of income, the contribution to be paid jumps from zero to £1.28. The **marginal tax rate**—the ratio of additional tax to additional income—is very large at that point, since, in principle, the extra income that takes weekly income from £64 to £65 attracts additional NI contributions of £1.28. The marginal tax rate is thus (approximately) 100 × 1.28/1.00 percent = 128 percent. There is a spike in the graph of the marginal tax rate at this point. Contributions are £1.28 plus 10 percent of the income that lies between £64 and £485 per week. There are no extra contributions paid on incomes above £485 per week.

Combining employees' NI contributions and income tax for the 1998–99 tax year gives the average and marginal tax rates shown in Figure 20.2. The marginal tax rate rises from zero at £3,328 per annum, and there is a spike at this point. It then rises with income in steps but falls from 33 percent to 23 percent at earnings of £25,220 a year—the effective ceiling for NI contributions—and then jumps back up to 40 percent at an income of £31,235 a year when the higher (40 percent) rate of income tax cuts in. The **average tax rate,** which is the total tax paid divided

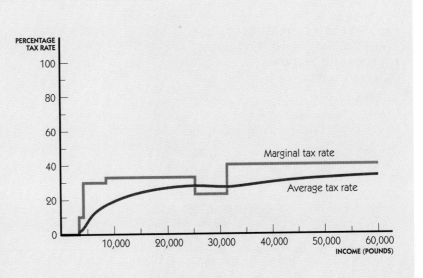

Figure 20.2 AVERAGE AND MARGINAL RATES OF DIRECT PERSONAL TAXES

The figure shows the combined effects of income tax and employees' National Insurance contributions. There is a spike in the marginal rate at the income level where £1.28 in NI contributions suddenly become payable; the average rate of tax jumps up at that point. The marginal rate rises in a few steps to 33 percent, then falls back to 23 percent when the ceiling on NI contributions is reached, then goes up to 40 percent when the higher rate of income tax kicks in. The combined effect is to make the tax system nearly proportional above moderate levels of income. The average rate of tax rises to approximately 27 percent at an income of £15,000 per year and to about 33 percent at an income of £60,000 per year.

by the total income, rises gradually with income, but it falls for incomes between £25,220 and £31,235 for which the marginal tax rate (23 percent) is less than the average tax rate. The average tax rate rises again at higher income levels.

The U.K. tax system is fairly progressive at moderate income levels—between £5,000 and £15,000 a year—and much less progressive at higher income levels. It becomes, in fact, roughly **proportional** (that is, the average tax rate is more or less constant) at higher income levels. The amount of progressivity is further reduced by the tax allowance given for interest payments on mortgages and the exemption from capital gains tax of capital gains less than a threshold amount in each year. Both of these features of the system are of more benefit to people with middle and high incomes than to people with low incomes.

However, to assess the progressivity of the tax system, it is necessary to look at the effects of all taxes on incomes, including the indirect taxes like excise duties on beer and cigarettes and VAT as well as direct taxes other than the income tax (principally the corporation tax). In fact it is necessary to look be-

yond taxes and consider also the effects of government expenditure on goods and services and on direct payments made to people to raise low incomes, in order to determine how much redistribution of income takes place.

Even if such a thorough calculation is carried out, appearances can be deceptive. The burden of a tax does not necessarily fall on the person or firm that is directly responsible for the payment. For example, the division between the employer's and the employee's National Insurance contribution does not matter, at least in the long run. The employer is concerned only with the cost of labour including all taxes, and the employee is concerned with wages less all taxes. As Figure 20.3 shows, it would make no difference whether the employer had to pay all of the National Insurance contributions or the employee had to pay them. In the second case, with a gross wage higher than in the first case, the net wage (after paying the employee's NI) received by the employee and the total labour cost (including any employer's NI contributions) paid by the employer would be exactly the same as in the first case. Similarly, firms are often said to pass on higher taxes (such as excise

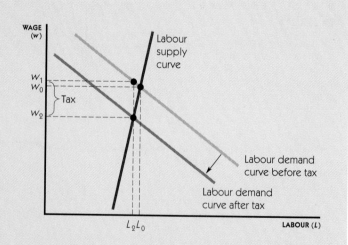

Figure 20.3 THE INCIDENCE OF EMPLOYERS' AND EMPLOYEES' NATIONAL INSURANCE CONTRIBUTIONS

The diagram shows that it does not matter whether National Insurance contributions are levied on employers or employees. The employer is concerned only with the total cost of employing the worker, and the worker only with the wage net of National Insurance contributions. Shifting the contributions from the firm to the worker would merely raise the before-tax wage by the amount of the shift but leave unchanged both the total cost to the employer and the worker's wage after NI contributions. It would also leave unchanged the amount of employment in equilibrium. Imposing a National Insurance contribution reduces employment form L_0 to L_2. The gross cost to the employer is raised from w_0 to w_1, while the net wage received by the worker goes down from w_0 to w_2, regardless of how the NI contribution is split between them.

taxes) to consumers in the form of higher prices. Whether they in fact do this depends on the slopes of the market demand and supply curves.

The effects of the corporation tax are particularly difficult to assess. It is sometimes argued that companies do not pay their fair share of taxes. However, the costs of these taxes do not ultimately fall on companies; they fall on persons: the workers in the company may get lower wages, the consumers who buy its products may pay higher prices, and the owners of the company may get lower returns on their investment in it.

Efficiency During the 1980s, various changes were made to the tax system in Britain by the Conservative government of the time. There was shift from direct taxation to indirect taxation. The rates of income tax were reduced, and there was a substantial increase in the rate of value-added tax.

The rate of income tax in the 1994–95 tax year was 20 percent on the first £3,000 of a person's taxable income, 25 percent (the standard rate) on the next £20,700, and 40 percent on any higher income. In 1978–79, the standard rate was 33 percent, and tax rates on higher incomes went up to 83 percent on the highest incomes. On top of that, investment income—interest on savings and dividends on shares, for example—could be charged an additional 15 percent tax, so that the top rate of tax payable was in theory as high as 98 percent. It was argued that very high marginal tax rates had a strong disincentive effect on work effort; it discouraged hard work and entrepreneurial behaviour from highly qualified and able workers. Objective evidence for these claims remains scarce.

High rates of taxation encourage people to avoid taxation legally. They might rearrange their portfolios of financial assets to take advantage of any tax concessions available on certain assets, for example. High tax rates encourage people to spend time and money trying to discover clever ways of avoiding taxes (legally), and paying accountants and others to help them do this: they encourage people to devote resources to tax avoidance.

High tax rates also encourage do-it-yourself (DIY) work. The reason is that the work you do for yourself, as a plumber or an interior decorator, for example, is not taxed, whereas the work you do for your employer as a chartered accountant, again for example, is taxed. If the tax rate is high enough, your before-tax rate of pay as a plumber or decorator might be bigger than your after-tax rate of pay as an accountant, even if it were less than your before-tax rate of pay as an accountant. If the tax rate were high enough, it might cause the accountant to do less accounting and more DIY plumbing and decorating. This is economically inefficient: resources have been diverted away from their best use.

High rates of income tax encourage the growth of the "black economy" in which people work for cash and do not declare their earnings to the Inland Revenue.

For these reasons high rates of tax appear to lead to inefficient uses of resources in the economy. The reduction in the rates of the income tax, combined with the increase in the value-added tax, have reduced taxes more for people with high incomes than for people with average or low incomes. This causes the distribution of incomes (after tax) to widen, and not everyone has been happy with this effect of the tax changes.

The United Kingdom was not alone in cutting high marginal rates of income taxes. In the 1980s under President Ronald Reagan, income tax rates in the United States were reduced, to a maximum of 33 percent. Sweden, traditionally a country with very high marginal tax rates as well as generous social benefits, has cut income tax rates. (Professor Assar Lindbeck, of the University of Stockholm and for many years the chairperson of the committee which selects Nobel prizewinners in economics, has argued long and hard for such changes to be made, on grounds of economic efficiency.) The Netherlands and Denmark have made changes in the same direction.

A conspicuous feature of the income tax system in Britain has been tax relief for interest paid on mortgages. This provision has encouraged owner occupation. In the early 1990s, about 70 percent of households in Britain owned the house they lived in. At the same time the market for privately rented accommodation has shrunk, partly because landlords renting out property do not get the same subsidy that owner occupation gets as mortgage interest tax relief and partly because controls on rents have also reduced the rate of return that landlords can get by investing in property for rental.

While owner occupancy is thought to have some beneficial effects on society, because owner occupiers take better care of their houses than tenants and because perhaps they express more concern about the quality of life in the communities in which they live since they have a bigger stake in them than tenants have, it has also proved to have some bad effects. Buying and selling a house is an expensive and time-consuming activity, and owner occupiers tend to be less able to move to new areas when employment opportunities move. The shrinkage of the privately rented market has made it harder for younger, more mobile workers to find housing. It has also reduced opportunities for people who do not have established jobs with regular and predictable incomes and who therefore cannot get mortgages with which to buy a flat or house.

Tax relief on mortgage interest is finally being phased out of the tax system, even though it was until recently an article of faith of the Conservative government under the then Mrs. Thatcher. Tax relief was available at a rate of 10 percent in the 1997–98 tax year and on a maximum loan of £30,000. It is likely to be reduced further. The cost of tax relief to the Treasury is estimated at £3 billion to £4 billion, which is a substantial fraction of the total income tax revenue of £67 billion in 1996.

Administrative Simplicity   The costs of collecting taxes varies from tax to tax. The system of property taxes in Britain—the rates—was cheap to collect and administratively simple. Properties and their owners are easily identifiable, and the taxpayers—property owners—were not able to avoid paying the tax. The replacement community charge, or poll tax, proved very expensive to administer. Estimates of the costs of collection as a fraction of revenue were much higher than for the old rating system. A register of adult residents liable to pay the tax in each community had to be compiled. There were many more poll taxpayers than there had been ratepayers. Keeping track of people who moved from one locality to another was difficult. Some people did not put their names on the register of electors in order to make it more difficult for local authorities to find them and present them with poll tax bills. The costs of identifying people who refused to register, prosecuting them in the courts, and collecting taxes proved to be very expensive.

The advantage of keeping the tax laws simple and widely accepted, limiting the number of taxpayers, and not changing the tax laws frequently is that administrative costs can be kept down. The disadvantage may be that simple tax laws do not meet the goals of horizontal and vertical equity as effectively as complicated ones, and the government cannot use the tax laws to subsidise some activities and penalise others as much it would like to.

Flexibility   It is useful for governments to be able to change tax rates from time to time as the need for revenue changes. Simpler tax systems with fewer complicated exemptions and special provisions tend to be more flexible: there are fewer tax rates and thresholds to change. The British government is able to change taxes at will, with little effective debate or opposition. The budget is announced by the chancellor of the exchequer in the November budget statement and is usually passed into law with little amendment.

By contrast with Britain, the separation of powers between the president and Congress in the United States and the complexity of the U.S. tax codes has made changing taxes in the United States a much slower and more cumbersome business. In the early 1980s the unwillingness of the Congress and the president to agree to raise taxes and take the blame for tax increases from the media and the voters led to an enormous federal budget deficit and high interest rates and contributed to economic problems in the United States and around the world.

Transparency   While personal income taxes are very transparent—individuals can see clearly how much they pay—indirect taxes and corporation taxes are less so. It is less clear to people how much they pay in various ways for government services through corporation tax. It is sometimes argued that particular taxes should be related to particular government expenditures: that taxes on petrol and cars should be spent on roads, for example. However, there are many good reasons why there should be no connection between the two. Even National Insurance contributions, which originally were intended to be a kind of insurance premium and calculated in a similar way, with benefits related to the level of contributions and the risks that were insured, are now set merely as a part of the general tax system, unrelated to benefits. There is pressure to amalgamate National Insurance contributions into the income tax.

TRANSFERS

In addition to tax policy, government affects the income distributions through **transfer programmes.** Transfers are payments that households receive without having to engage in any current productive activity in return. Transfer payments can be private, such as company pensions or grants for higher education. Government engages in a wide range of transfer programmes. Two major groups of government transfer programmes concern us here: **means-tested transfers,** the direct purpose of which is to redistribute income from upper-income to lower-income people, and **social insurance,** which protects individuals, irrespective of income, in times of need.

SOCIAL SECURITY AND THE WELFARE STATE

The welfare state in Britain was established immediately after the Second World War in the late 1940s, under the Labour government of Clement Attlee. It was intended that education and health care should be freely available to everyone regardless of income and that people should be protected from poverty whether caused by the absence of work or low pay. The National Health Service was set up to provide universal free medical care, and the system of National Insurance and social security was established to make sure that no one was subjected to the worst extremes of poverty. The safety net for incomes was established.

The principle that there should be a social safety net has never been challenged, but there has been continuous argument as to how generous the benefits should be. The Thatcher government criticised the welfare state for inducing a "dependency culture" among the people who receive benefits from it. It is said, with some justification, that state benefits for unemployment or low income reduce people's incentives to find work and fend for themselves. Changes in state welfare benefits have been made and more are proposed, aimed at increasing incentives and cutting the cost of the welfare state. Recently the idea has been revived that voluntary charities should bear some of the burden of providing for the needs of poor people.

Even in Sweden, a particularly egalitarian and socially cohesive country, where the social safety net was particularly well developed, the growth of unemployment and the growth of the costs of generous state benefits has caused a reevaluation of how much the state can (or is willing to) provide. Reducing costs and increasing incentives almost always makes the people receiving benefits worse off, makes the poor poorer, and widens the distribution of incomes. The extent of the welfare state is always a controversial issue because it involves making a value judgment between equality on the one hand and economic efficiency on the other.

WHO ARE THE POOR?

The poor include people living in households in which no one is working and people on low wages. People not working include old people who have retired from the labour force and disabled persons. They also include people who are looking for work but cannot find it and people who are neither old nor disabled but who are not looking for work. This may possibly be because they have become discouraged after a long period of unemployment and unsuccessful job hunting or because they are receiving benefits that are big enough relative to the earnings they could command in a job to make job hunting not a worthwhile activity.

Low pay arises for a number of reasons. One is low education and training, as was discussed in Chapter 9. Another factor may be discrimination. Despite the equal pay acts and the race relations acts, women and members of ethnic minorities in Britain get paid less than white males in the labour force, even after allowing for all the other factors—such as age, experience, education and training, and the industry or occupation in which they work—that might affect a person's wage. Part-time workers also get paid less than equivalent full-time workers; part-time work has often been available in relatively low-paid jobs. Workers who can only work part time have thus found themselves restricted to low-paid jobs. This is a problem that is faced by, among others, single parents, who find themselves only able to work part time.

SOCIAL SECURITY AND NATIONAL INSURANCE PROVISION IN BRITAIN

A whole range of welfare benefits have come into being to assist—at least in a modest way—people who have become poor or unemployed.

The **National Insurance** scheme was intended to provide a number of benefits to protect workers from becoming unemployed through market conditions, ill health, or old age. It provides an unemployment benefit (the dole) to people who become unemployed through market conditions, an invalidity benefit and sick pay for persons unable to work through ill health, and a basic pension automatically to people who reach the required age, currently 65 for men and 60 for women. There are a number of other benefits as well. The unemployment benefit and the basic pension are paid out at a flat rate—the same amount for everyone independently of things like previous wages or the number of years (above a minimum) that contributions have been made.

The scheme was originally based on an insurance principle: benefits were available to workers who had previously made contributions to it (employees' and employers' National Insurance contributions). The contributions are effectively an insurance premium. The benefits are then available independently of other income or wealth; they are not **means tested.** While the insurance principle is maintained, the link between the amount of contributions and the amount of benefits has become rather weak. The benefits are said to be **contributory benefits.**

The sizes of the state pension and unemployment benefits have dwindled over the years relative to earnings. Whereas the state pension was intended to provide a basic income on which retired people could live, it is now so low that it is very often topped up with additional means-tested benefits. The unemployment

benefit is so low that many unemployed people receive additional benefits as well, and it is these additional benefits which determine their total income while unemployed, not the unemployment benefit. The unemployment benefit was intended to tide people over a temporary period of unemployment while they looked for another job, and the benefit is paid out for a maximum period of a year. People who remain unemployed for longer than a year—the **long-term unemployed**—continue to be supported by social security but through different benefits.

REFINEMENTS OF THE BENEFITS SYSTEM

In the late 1960s, a brief experiment was made with earnings-related unemployment benefits. But this was eventually abandoned, and benefits went back to being paid at a flat rate.

In 1994, the government renamed the unemployment benefit the "jobseekers allowance," making it payable for only six months rather than a year and putting much greater pressure on recipients of it to search actively for jobs. In the 1950s and 1960s, unemployment benefits were paid out at the same office as the one where vacant jobs were advertised—the Labour Exchange—and the officers who administered claims for benefits also directed unemployed people to suitable vacant jobs. It was a condition of getting benefits that unemployed people had to chase up these vacancies and try to get jobs. In the 1970s, the two functions were separated: claims for unemployment benefits were dealt with at Social Security Benefits Offices, and vacancies were advertised at Jobcentres. As a result, less pressure was put on the unemployed to search actively for vacancies. It has been argued that this change has been partly responsible for the growth of long-term unemployment in Britain. The last decade has seen an attempt to reverse this in order to get the unemployed to search more vigorously for jobs and reduce unemployment.

PENSIONS

To raise the size of the state pension and to tie it more closely to an individual's contributions, the government introduced some years ago a State

Earnings Related Pension Scheme (SERPS), which provides higher pensions for people who make higher contributions in addition to the basic NI contributions. This scheme is intended for people who do not have other pension plans, for example, with their own employer or with an insurance company.

As life expectancy has grown, the costs of providing the basic flat-rate state pension have grown. Almost half of all social security expenditure goes on support for the elderly. The future of the basic state pension is being questioned by the British government. It is being suggested that it might not be necessary to have a non-means-tested benefit for the elderly any longer. If the pension were means tested, the government would save the cost of providing it to old people who have other substantial sources of income. Increasingly many people have pensions provided to them through schemes with their employer—occupational pensions—or private pensions they have obtained through insurance companies. The government has been encouraging the growth of private pensions, so that fewer old people will need to rely on the state pension.

OTHER SOCIAL SECURITY BENEFITS

In addition to the benefits provided by the National Insurance scheme, there are a host of others. These are described as **noncontributory benefits,** because eligibility for them does not depend on having made any contributions. Most of these benefits are, however, means tested: they are only available to people who have sufficiently low incomes and sufficiently few assets. Most of them are also nontaxable. They include the child benefit, one-parent benefit, industrial disablement benefit, industrial death benefit, war pension, benefits for invalidity and disablement, income support, family credit, housing benefit, community charge/council tax benefit, and the social fund. The most important of these, in terms of cost, are the child benefit, income support, and housing benefit.

The child benefit is a fixed sum per child payable to all households with children regardless of income (it is not a *means-tested* benefit). At the end of 1996, 7.3 million families received it on account of approximately 12.8 million children, and it cost £6.6 billion in 1996–97.

Income support is payable to all persons who are not working more than 16 hours per week and whose income and wealth fall below a certain level; it takes their income up to that level. There were 5.8 million recipients in 1996–97, and it cost £14.5 billion. Most of the unemployed receive support from it, because they have used up their rights to unemployment benefits by having been unemployed for more than six months or because they were ineligible for unemployment benefits. Many unemployed people receive income support as a supplement to unemployment benefits, and many pensioners receive it as a supplement to their pensions. In addition to income support, many people with low incomes can claim housing benefits and council tax benefits which cover the cost of their housing. More than five million people received this in 1996–97. Expenditure on it was £10.8 billion.

THE POVERTY TRAP

One of the most notorious problems created by the benefit system is the **poverty trap.** If the main earner in a household with no income were to find a job, the benefits received by the household would be reduced, once her income passed beyond a certain (rather low) point. Income support, the housing benefit, and other benefits—such as entitlement to free dental care, medical prescriptions, and school meals for children—would gradually be lost. Over some ranges of income, as earnings grow, the loss of benefits may be as great as or greater than the increase in income. The household faces an effective tax rate of over 100 percent. Naturally this creates a very strong disincentive to work. Unless a person can find a job with a good rate of pay, there may be little point in finding any work, because it will not increase the household's income after taxes and benefits. There may be other reasons for which someone may want to work, reasons concerned with morale and employment prospects for the more distant future. But in terms of the immediate effect on net income, the poverty trap provides a strong barrier.

Efforts to provide poor and unemployed people with greater incentives to find work have been largely unsuccessful. It has been suggested that the benefits system should be simplified, so that there are fewer benefits, and the interaction between them is better understood. They should be coordinated so as to avoid creating a poverty trap. The problem is that to provide stronger incentives without making the poor poorer is expensive, because it means letting people keep some of their benefits as their incomes rise. This leads to a large increase in expenditure. Alternatively, reducing benefits for the poorest people seems harsh and widens the inequality of incomes. Attempts are being made to improve the targeting of benefits to cut the costs of the system. *Targeting* means ensuring that the benefits go to the people in the greatest need. However, it does not help to reduce the problem of the poverty trap; it makes it worse.

The pressure to reduce expenditure on the social security system would be less intense if the total expenditure on it had not grown so much over the last decades. As Table 20.1 shows, expenditure on social security had risen to 13.4 percent of the gross domestic product in 1993–94, up from 7.3 percent in 1966. Even under more favourable macroeconomic conditions, with lower unemployment, in 1996–97 it was still 12.2 percent of the GDP. Part of the rise is associated with the rise in unemployment that has occurred since the 1960s; part of it is associated with the increase in life expectancy and the number of retired persons in the population.

A NEGATIVE INCOME TAX

A scheme for simplifying taxes and social security and avoiding the danger of creating a poverty trap is a **negative income tax.** This is an idea which has a lot of appeal for economists but which has so far not been adopted in practice. The idea is that if an individual's income were to fall below a certain level (the break-even level), the income tax would go into reverse, and instead of the taxpayer's paying income tax to the Inland Revenue, he would get a payment from the Inland Revenue in proportion to the shortfall of his income below the break-even level.

If, for example, the break-even income were £3,445 per annum and the tax rate on incomes below this level were 50 percent, then a person with a before-tax income of £2,000 would get back from the Inland Revenue 50 percent of £3,445 – £2,000, that is, £722.50, making his after-tax income £2,722.50. The

Table 20.1 THE COST OF SOCIAL SECURITY IN BRITAIN

Social Security Benefits as a Fraction of GDP	
Year[a]	Expenditure/GDP (%)
1966	7.3
1971	6.7
1976	8.4
1979–80	10.8
1984–85	13.7
1989–90	10.1
1991–92	11.9
1992–93	13.0
1993–94	13.4
1994–95	13.0
1995–96	12.7
1996–97	12.2

Composition of Social Security Benefits in 1996–97	
	£ million
Contributory Benefits	
Retirement pension	39,990
Jobseekers allowance	904
Incapacity benefit	7,605
Noncontributory benefits	
Child benefit	6,603
Family credit	2,047
Income support	14,854
Housing benefit and council tax benefit	10,764
Total	91,604

[a] Years referred to are years ending 31 March.

Source: Annual Abstract of Statistics (Office for National Statistics 1998), Table 3.5.

person with a before-tax income of zero would get a payment of 50 percent of £3,445, or £1,722.50, which forms the **guaranteed minimum income.** An alternative way of looking at the negative income tax is to say that everyone gets a payment of £1,722.50, and everyone pays income tax of 50 percent of income between £0 and £3,445 a year. (And of course everyone pays whatever tax is determined by the income tax code on income above £3,445.) This scheme would replace the many existing benefits that have developed piecemeal: the unemployment benefit, state pension, income support, child benefit, free prescriptions, housing benefit, and so on.

The attraction of such a scheme is that it would be simple to administer. It would also make it clearer to people what the benefits were when they took a job, and it would prevent a poverty trap from occurring: it ensures that a person who finds work gets to keep 50 percent of the additional pay he is able to earn. This has much better incentive effects than the current set of social security benefits and taxes. The difficulty of a scheme like this is that if it had a reasonably high minimum income without imposing too high a marginal tax rate, it would be expensive. Alternatively, if the costs of the scheme were to be limited, the problem would be either that it would not guarantee people a sufficiently high minimum income or that the marginal tax rate would be too high.

THE COSTS AND BENEFITS OF REDISTRIBUTION

Tax, welfare, and social insurance programs all play an important role in answering one of the fundamental questions posed in Chapter 1: For whom are goods produced (who gets to enjoy the goods that are available)? Each group in society would like to pay as little in taxes as possible and receive as many benefits as possible, and complaints about fairness abound. But issues of what is fair may never be resolved. And economists worry that at least some attempts to make sure everyone has a fair slice may so reduce the size of the economic pie to be divided that almost everyone is worse off.

EQUITY-EFFICIENCY TRADE-OFFS

Economists enter the discussion of redistribution to clarify the costs and consequences of various pro-

grammes, including different tax systems. Systems that tax the rich more heavily or provide support for the poor regardless of their employability are likely to have adverse effects on incentives. Economists try to calculate precisely how important these effects are.

All economists agree that as government redistributes more income to the poor, it has to raise taxes on the rich and middle-income individuals; this weakens their incentives to work. But economists disagree about the magnitudes of the trade-offs. Most economists agree that at high enough tax rates, incentives are greatly reduced. The high marginal tax rates of 60 percent or more that used to prevail in Europe probably had large negative effects on efficiency. But whether at current marginal tax rates an increase in taxation would have a *large* effect on incentives is much more debatable.

We have seen how economists focus on the trade-offs—between equity (how the pie is divided) and efficiency (the size of the pie) and between reductions in the risks of life (through the provision of social insurance) and economic incentives. Beyond these trade-offs lie basic issues of social values, of what kind of society we want to have, *recognising the economic constraints on the choices that we can make.* These values touch not only on issues of efficiency, equality, and risk protection but also on individual rights and social responsibilities.

INCOME INEQUALITY

Economists often represent the degree of inequality in an economy by a diagram called the **Lorenz curve.** The Lorenz curve shows the cumulative fraction of the country's total income earned by the poorest 5 percent, the poorest 10 percent, the poorest 15 percent, and so on. If there were complete equality, then 20 percent of the income would accrue to the lowest 20 percent of the population, 40 percent to the lowest 40 percent, and so on. The Lorenz curve would be a straight 45-degree line. If incomes were very concentrated, then the lowest 80 percent might receive almost nothing and the top 5 percent might receive 80 percent of total income; in this case, the Lorenz curve would be very bowed. Twice the area between the 45-degree line and the Lorenz curve is a commonly employed measure of inequality, called the **Gini coefficient.**

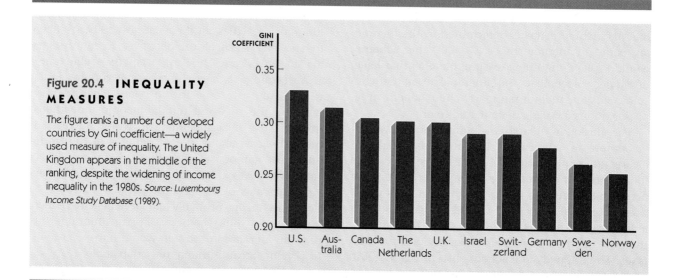

Figure 20.4 **INEQUALITY MEASURES**

The figure ranks a number of developed countries by Gini coefficient—a widely used measure of inequality. The United Kingdom appears in the middle of the ranking, despite the widening of income inequality in the 1980s. *Source: Luxembourg Income Study Database* (1989).

Figure 20.4 shows the Gini coefficient for a number of countries. The United Kingdom comes fifth in the ranking, after the United States, Canada, Australia, and the Netherlands. The United States has the most unequal distribution of income. At the other end of the scale, Sweden and Norway have the least inequality of incomes.

It has often been claimed that inequality of incomes has grown in the United Kingdom over the last 15 years or so. The facts seem to confirm this belief. In terms of the disposable income of households, the share of income received by the poorest fifth of the population has fallen from 10 percent in 1979 to 7 percent in 1990 and 1991 taken together, while the income of the top fifth of the population has risen from 35 to 41 percent (see Table 20.2). The table shows the percentage of total disposable income received by individuals, ranked by the disposable income of the household, adjusted for the size and composition of the household. So, for example, the poorest fifth of individuals in 1979 received 10 percent of the total income, while the richest fifth received 35 percent. Disposable income is earnings, pensions, annuities, investment income, and other income, plus social security benefits in cash less income tax, National Insurance contributions, and the community charge in the relevant years. The in-

crease in inequality between 1979 and 1990–91 is illustrated in Figure 20.5 in the form of the Lorenz curve. In terms of real disposable incomes, the median individual in the bottom fifth of the population became only 3 percent better off between 1979 and

Table 20.2 **SHARE OF DISPOSABLE INCOME RECEIVED BY QUINTILE GROUPS OF INDIVIDUALS IN THE UNITED KINGDOM**

Year	Bottom Fifth	2nd Fifth	3rd Fifth	4th Fifth	Top Fifth
1979	10	14	18	23	35
1981	10	14	18	23	36
1987	9	13	17	23	39
1988–89	8	12	17	23	40
1990–91	7	12	17	23	41

Source: Social Trends (Central Statistical Office, 1994).

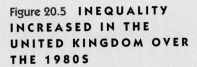

Figure 20.5 INEQUALITY INCREASED IN THE UNITED KINGDOM OVER THE 1980S

The figure shows the Lorenz Curve for income distribution in the United Kingdom for 1979 and 1990–91 using the data from Table 20.2. Both Lorenz curves lie below the straight line which would denote complete equality, and the curve for 1990–91 lies below that for 1979, showing that incomes became more unequally distributed in the intervening period.

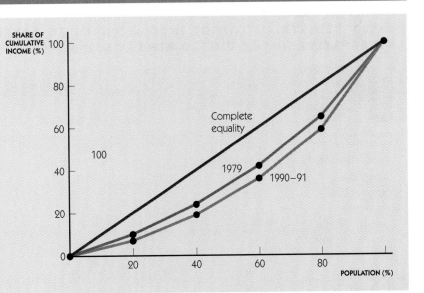

THE MARKET FAILURE ROLES OF GOVERNMENT

MARKET FAILURES	EXAMPLES OF GOVERNMENT RESPONSES
Market not competitive	Monopolies and mergers policies
Product markets (Chapters 13–16)	Regulation of pollution; provision of national defence
Labour markets (Chapter 18)	Public support of basic research; patents
Public goods and externalities (Chapters 7, 19)	Consumer protection legislation (including securities regulations)
Basic research as a public good; externalities associated with R & D (Chapter 16)	Macroeconomic policies to be discussed
Imperfect information and thin (incomplete) markets (Chapter 17)	Compulsory education; prohibition against drugs
Unemployment (to be discussed in Chapters 25–34)	Social security and tax programs
Merit goods and bads; distrust of consumer sovereignty (Chapter 19)	
Redistribution (Chapter 20)	

Table 20.3 REDISTRIBUTION OF INCOME THROUGH TAXES AND BENEFITS IN THE UNITED KINGDOM 1995-96

| | Quintile Groups of Households Ranked by Equivalised Disposable Income | | | | | |
	Bottom	2nd	3rd	4th	Top	All
Total original income	2,430	6,090	13,790	22,450	41,260	17,200
Plus cash benefits:						
Contributory	1,860	2,280	1,710	1,180	770	1,560
Noncontributory	3,050	2,380	1,650	950	430	1,690
Gross income	7,340	10,750	17,150	24,580	42,450	20,450
Less:						
National insurance contributions and income tax	540	930	2,480	4,470	9,660	3,610
Local taxes	590	590	650	710	820	670
Disposable income	6,210	9,230	14,020	19,400	31,980	16,170
Less indirect taxes	1,930	2,340	3,290	4,090	5,090	3,350
After-tax income	4,280	6,890	10,730	15,310	26,890	12,820
Plus benefits in kind:						
Education	1,810	1,300	1,420	1,070	830	1,290
NHS	1,890	1,830	1,730	1,520	1,330	1,660
Housing subsidy	90	80	40	20	10	50
Travel subsidies	50	70	60	60	140	70
School meals and welfare milk	100	30	10			30
Final income	8,230	10,200	13,990	17,980	29,980	15,920

Source: Social Trends (Central Statistical Office, 1998), Table 5.20.

1990–91, while the median individual in the top fifth became more than 48 percent better off.

Although inequality of incomes has grown, taxes, social security benefits, and other government expenditures redistribute income towards poorer households. Table 20.3 shows incomes before and after taxes and benefits for households at five different income levels in the United Kingdom. Final income, which allows for the effects of taxes, social security benefits, and the value of goods and services directly provided by the state (or benefits in kind)—education, the National Health Service, housing sub-

sidy, travel subsidies, school meals, and welfare milk—is much more equally distributed than total original income—earnings, occupational pensions (not the state pension), annuities, investment income, and other sources of income.

The value of benefits in cash (unemployment benefit, income support, state retirement pension, and so on) decreases as household income rises. Direct taxation is slightly progressive: higher-income households pay higher fractions of their gross incomes in direct taxes. Indirect taxes are regressive, however: the amount of tax paid rises with income, but it does

CLOSE-UP: WELFARE REFORM—THE NEW DEAL AND THE WFTC

There have been a number of major changes in welfare provision in Britain recently. One is the New Deal for the unemployed. Another is the introduction of the Working Families' Tax Credit (WFTC). Both are part of continuing efforts to improve incentives while maintaining social protection for the poor, in other words, to combine equity with efficiency.

The New Deal, introduced in April 1998, covers people between 18 and 24 years old who have been unemployed for more than six months. As a condition of continuing to receive the unemployed person's jobseekers allowance, the person has to accept (1) a programme of training or education for up to a year, (2) six months' work experience with the Environmental Task Force, (3) six months' work experience in the voluntary sector, or (4) six months' work experience in a job. Employers get a subsidy of £60 per week for six months.

The scheme is intended to encourage unemployed persons into work or more training, in the belief that this enhances their future employability, and that it has immediate benefits for society as well. There is no guarantee of course that these six-month subsidised jobs will prove more lasting or that the training will win a job for the trainees. There are other potential problems. The subsidised jobs may just displace other nonsubsidised jobs which might have existed instead of these; firms may design job openings to attract the subsidy.

The effects of the scheme in practice are not yet clear. The scheme is a kind of "welfare-to-work" scheme and has similarities with some that have been tried in the United States recently, like Restart and Workfare. The scheme is the latest in a long line of schemes designed to tackle high youth unemployment and private sector employers' underinvestment in the training of young workers.

The Working Families' Tax Credit, introduced in October 1999, is a move towards a negative income tax. It will be handled by the Inland Revenue, not the Department of Social Security. It is intended to address the problem of the poverty trap by reducing to 55 percent the effective tax rate faced by families receiving it: an extra 1 pound earned will lose 55 pence of WFTC payments. This compares with a rate of 70 percent with the current family credit, which it replaces.

The basic amount of tax credit in the WFTC is planned to be £48.80 a week for each family (in 1998–99 prices). There will also be tax credits for each child, £14.85 a week up to 11 years old, £20.45 for 11 to 16 year olds, and £25.40 for 16 to 18 year olds. There will be an extra tax credit of £10.80 for people working 30 hours or more a week, and a childcare tax credit worth 70 percent of eligible childcare with up to maximum costs of £100 a week for families with one child and £150 for families with two or more children. The maximum amount of WFTC is payable below the threshold income of £90 a week. The government expects that the WFTC will provide around £5 billion a year of support and affect about 1½ million working families by 2001.

The effects of this scheme will also take some years to become clear. The WFTC remains one of many social security schemes, and its effects depend partly on how it interacts with other aspects of welfare provision. But the introduction of these new schemes, which make attempts to combine welfare support with improvements to incentives to work, shows that governments take account of the economic principles set out in this book.

Sources: Peter Dolton, "Old Problem, New Deal," *Economic Review*, September 1998, pp. 24–25; *Financial Statement and Budget Report*, H.M. Treasury, March 1998.

not rise in proportion to income; the fraction of income paid in indirect tax falls as income rises. The value of benefits in kind is clearly progressive. All in all, the total original income of the average of the poorest fifth of households, £2,430, is raised to a final income of £8,230. The total original income of the average of the richest fifth of households, £41,260, falls to a final income of £29,980.

Finally, it is important to remember that these comparisons assume that if all the taxes and benefits and government expenditures were removed, the before-tax incomes and prices would remain unchanged. That is unlikely to happen. There would probably be many changes in wages, profits, and prices and employment levels if all that government activity were abolished. Therefore the comparisons made might be either an understatement or an overstatement of the redistributive effects of taxes and benefits, depending on how the economy responded.

REVIEW AND PRACTICE

SUMMARY

1 Even if markets are efficient, there may be dissatisfaction with the resulting distribution of income.

2 Inequality—both in terms of wages and income—in the United Kingdom increased during the 1980s and early 1990s.

3 In Britain, the important sources of central government revenue are incomes taxes, National Insurance contributions, excise duties, and the value-added tax. Local government gets about three-quarters of its revenue as a grant from the central government, and the rest from the council tax.

4 A tax system can be judged by five criteria: horizontal and vertical equity, efficiency, administrative simplicity, flexibility, and transparency.

5 There exists a variety of social security benefits in Britain intended to relieve poverty: the unemployment benefit (now the jobseekers allowance), state pension, housing benefit, child benefit, income support, and many others.

6 All public assistance programmes force society to balance the concerns of equity, which involve helping those in need, with the concerns of efficiency, which involve making sure that both people and taxpayers have good incentives to work.

7 Although the income tax in Britain may be mildly progressive (the average rate of tax that is paid rises with income), the effects of other taxes and benefits are to produce a much more complicated system. At higher income levels, it is roughly proportional. At some low income levels, the marginal tax rate exceeds 100 percent, giving rise to the poverty trap.

KEY TERMS

individual income tax	excise tax	progressive tax	poverty trap
corporation tax	horizontal equity	regressive tax	Lorenz curve
payroll tax	vertical equity	transfer programmes	Gini coefficient
value-added tax			

Review Questions

1 Will an efficient market necessarily produce a fairly equal distribution of income? Discuss.

2 What is the main source of central government revenue? Of local government revenues?

3 What are the five characteristics of a good tax system? How well does the U.K. tax system fare in terms of their criteria? What is the difference between horizontal equity and vertical equity? What is the difference between a progressive and a regressive tax?

4 How can redistribution take place through the National Insurance system, where all workers contribute and all retired people receive benefits?

5 What is a Lorenz curve? What does it reveal?

Problems

1 Explain how a tax subsidy for a good with positive externalities (like research and development) can help economic efficiency. Then explain how a tax subsidy for other goods without such externalities could injure efficiency.

2 Assume that a country has a simple tax structure, in which all income over £10,000 is taxed at 20 percent. Evaluate a proposal to increase the progressivity of the tax structure by requiring all those with incomes over £100,000 to pay a tax of 80 percent on income in excess of £100,000. Draw a high-wage earner's budget constraint. How does the higher tax rate affect his budget constraint? What happens to his incentives to work? Is it possible that imposing the tax actually will reduce the tax revenues the government receives from the rich?

3 Imagine that it was decided to fund an increase in social security benefits by increasing the payroll tax on employers. Would this prevent employees from being affected by the higher tax? Draw a diagram to illustrate your answer.

4 Draw Lorenz curves for the following countries. Which country has the greatest and least inequality?

	Lowest fifth	Second fifth	Third fifth	Fourth fifth	Top fifth
			Percentage of total income received by		
United States	4.7	11.0	17.4	25.0	41.9
Japan	8.7	13.2	17.5	23.1	37.5
Germany	6.8	12.7	17.8	24.1	38.7

CHAPTER 21

PUBLIC DECISION
MAKING

Except in a dictatorship, government actions do not reflect the preference of any single individual. Rather, they are the result of public choices. The importance of **public choice** theory was recognised when James Buchanan of George Mason University was awarded the Nobel prize for his pioneering work on this topic. In this chapter we look at how public choices are made.

KEY QUESTIONS

1 Does majority voting in a democracy provide a unique answer to policy issues? If so, what can we say about it?

2 What is the role of bureaucrats and interest groups in decision making in a democracy?

3 Why does government frequently fail to achieve its stated objectives? What are the sources of government failure?

4 What should be the relationship between central and local governments? What activities should be undertaken at each level?

DECISION MAKING IN A DEMOCRACY

In a democracy, the wishes of the majority are supposedly reflected in the actions government takes. But the United Kingdom is not a direct democracy, where citizens vote for or against each law. Rather citizens vote for members of Parliament, along with local elected officials, who, in turn, make our laws. Laws have to be introduced and passed by both houses of Parliament. Political scientists focus on the whole range of issues and actors that define the political process, including coalition formation, interest groups, and the media. Economists have a narrower focus, analysing how rational individuals express their preferences through the political process of voting and how, in models of the political process, their votes are reflected in the public choices that mark collective decision making.

THE VOTING PARADOX

Governments are not always consistent in their actions. This may not be surprising, given that government choices do not reflect the preferences of a single individual. This is referred to as the **voting paradox.** More fundamentally, majority voting may not yield a determinate outcome even when only three people choose among only three alternatives, as was noted more than two hundred years ago by the Frenchman the Marquis de Condorcet. Consider the simple example of three people who want to go to a movie together. They have narrowed their choices down to three movies, which they rank in this way.

	Jessica's Preferences	Ralph's Preferences	Brutus's Preferences
First choice	Young and Romantic	Third and Goal to Go	Automatic Avengers
Second choice	Third and Goal to Go	Automatic Avengers	Young and Romantic
Third choice	Automatic Avengers	Young and Romantic	Third and Goal to Go

When they compare each of the movies, they find that *Young and Romantic* is preferred over *Third and Goal to Go* by a 2–1 margin and *Third and Goal to Go* is preferred to *Automatic Avengers*, also by a 2–1 margin. Taking this information alone, they might reason that since *Young and Romantic* is preferred over *Third and Goal to Go* and *Third and Goal to Go* is preferred over *Automatic Avengers*, *Young and Romantic* is also preferred to *Automatic Avengers*. But when they put it to a vote, they find that *Automatic Avengers* is preferred to *Young and Romantic* by a 2–1 margin. There is no majority winner. Majority voting can compare any two of these choices but is incapable of ranking all three of them.

Nobel laureate Kenneth Arrow proved an even more remarkable result. All voting systems (two-thirds majority, weighted majority, or any other), under some circumstances, yield the same kind of indecision. Inconsistencies are simply inherent in the decision-making process of any democratic government. The only way around this problem, to ensure that consistent choices are made, is to entrust a single individual with all decisions. Such a system yields consistent choices but is hardly democratic!

THE MEDIAN VOTER

Fortunately, inconsistencies in democratic decision making are not inevitable. What would happen if there were a vote over a single issue, such as how much to spend per pupil in state-run schools? Some individuals want more to be spent, some less. Whose preferences dominate? The answer depends, of course, on the rules by which decisions are made. The **median voter theory** provides a remarkably simple prediction of the outcome in the case of majority voting. It is the median voter—half of the population want more to be spent than this voter, and half want less—whose preferences dominate. For instance, suppose the median voter wants £2,000 per pupil to be spent and there are 40,001 voters. Then 20,000 voters want more than £2,000 to be spent, and 20,000 want less than £2,000 to be spent. What would happen if there were a vote between spending £2,000 and spending £1,000? Clearly £2,000 would win, because the median voter would vote for £2,000 and all the 20,000 people who wanted a larger amount to be

spent would vote for £2,000; so £2,000 would get at least 20,001 votes, and the proposal to spend £1,000 would get a maximum of 20,000 votes. In any vote between the median voter's first choice, £2,000, and any other amount to be spent on the schools, the median voter's first choice will win.

Voters, of course, do not decide most issues directly, but elect politicians who vote on issues. Politicians, however, want to get elected. To increase the likelihood that they get elected, they take positions that will increase their members' votes. If both parties take positions to maximise their votes, both will take positions reflecting the views of the median voter.

To understand this point, consider an imaginary world in which the only issue that matters is how much the government is going to spend. Suppose that the amounts that people would like the government to spend can be arranged from smallest to largest. Suppose there are two parties, and one party takes the position reflecting the individual at the 40th percentile. That is, 40 percent would like the government to spend less, 60 percent would like it to spend more. The other party will win simply by taking a position close to that of the voter representing the 41st percentile. That party would get 59 percent of the vote—a landslide. Of course, the first party knows this and tries to find a position such that the opposition cannot undercut it and win a majority. There are thus strong incentives for both parties to take positions closely reflecting the views of the median voter.

This theory explains why voters often feel that they do not have a choice: the two parties are both trying to find the middle position, so that they will not be defeated. It also gives us a way of forecasting government behaviour: government will approximate the interests of the median voter.[1]

It is important that the median voter theory does not resolve the voting paradox. As long as there is a single variable being voted upon—say the level of expenditure on education—and different individuals have a "most-preferred" level and vote for outcomes closer to that level, then the median voter will determine the outcome. But when alternatives cannot be simply ranked in terms of more or less (as in the

---

[1] The principle that both parties will gravitate towards the center (reflecting the views of the median voter) was first analysed by the economist-statistician Harold Hotelling.

three-movie example given earlier), the voting paradox will arise and there is no clear theoretical prediction of the outcome of the electoral process.

In some countries political parties have converged, and there are few differences between them
on policy issues. In such places the median voter
theory seems to be borne out in practice. But this is
not universal. In Britain, there have been periods of
convergence, like the 1950s and early 1960s, when a
middle-of-the-road consensual approach to government policy prevailed. There was a common belief
in the value of a mixed economy and the welfare
state, shared by the Conservative Party and the
Labour Party. It was known as "Butskellism," after
R. A. Butler, a prominent Conservative, and Hugh
Gaitskell, the leader of the Labour Party, of the time.
Margaret Thatcher repudiated the centrist tendency
when she became leader of the Conservative Party in
1975 and led a polarization of policy positions. The
Conservatives under her leadership took up a more
radical free market position, while Labour moved to
the left. Evidently British politics do not conform to
the median voter model.

INTEREST GROUPS AND RENT SEEKING

The median voter theory is neat, but frequently government action does not even remotely reflect the
interests of the median voter. Rather, it more nearly
represents the interests of particular groups.

One economic explanation for this has to do with
the increasing needs of candidates for funds to run
successfully for election and the willingness of
special-interest groups to provide those funds as
long as their interests are served. There has been a
growth in single-issue politics and lobbying. People
with particular interests have found it possible to increase their political influence by forming a lobbying
organization and offering their electoral support to
candidates who support the special interests of the
group. This tendency has developed furthest in the
United States, but there are signs of it in Britain also,
where politicians shade their policies to attract the
Green vote or the animal rights vote or whatever.

Economists refer to these activities as **rent seeking.** Rents, as we learned in Chapter 11, are returns
enjoyed by a factor of production that go beyond
those required to elicit its supply. The term *rent
seeking* is used when individuals or firms devote
their energies to the procurement of rents or other
special favours from the government. Government,
through its power to tax, to set tariffs, to provide subsidies, and to intervene in other ways with private
markets, can affect the profitability of various enterprises enormously. An attempt by European car producers to restrict competition from outside the
European Union would be referred to as rent seeking. As a result of protection, they find they can get
higher prices and make bigger profits.

As long as the government has the discretion to
grant rents and other special favours, firms and individuals will find it pays to engage in rent-seeking
behaviour—that is, to persuade government to grant
them tariffs or other benefits—and the decisions of
government will accordingly get distorted. It makes
little difference whether this behaviour comes in the
form of direct bribes, as is frequently the case in developing countries, or contributions to the funds of
political parties, which may influence the formulation
of government policy. Either way, a second aspect of
government behaviour has emerged: governments
respond to the rent-seeking behaviour of special-
interest groups.

BUREAUCRACIES

The final aspect of government behaviour that we
will take up is the **theory of bureaucracy,** which involves a principal-agent problem. The government
consists not only of elected officials but also of those
appointed by elected officials and civil service,
whose job it is to administer government programmes. Just as in the private sector managers' interests may not perfectly coincide with those of
shareholders, in the government sector also public
managers may not do what the electorate or their
elected representatives would ideally like—or what
is, in some broader sense, in the public interest.

It is a notorious fact that British government ministers—elected politicians—sometimes find that
their civil servants prevent them from pursuing the
policies they would like to pursue. The character Sir

Ensuring that politicians act in the interests of the voters and not in their personal interests or for some interest group is a tricky business. It is impossible to prevent the decisions made by governments from affecting the wealth and well-being of the politicians themselves. Indeed, many people go into politics to try to improve society, and if they are successful, they will benefit from it, along with everyone else. But everyone accepts that there must be limits on politicians' promoting policies where they have a direct interest in the outcome. Getting the balance right became a big issue in the mid-1990s in the final years of the Major government (1990 to 1997) and the early years of the Blair government. Accusations of sleaze dogged the last years of the Major government, which was never able to shake them off. The new Labour dawn which broke in May 1997 promised to be unclouded by accusations of sleaze. But in the event it has been the subject of similar accusations.

The cash-for-questions affair involved consulting firms' effectively paying members of Parliament for asking questions on various issues of importance to the industrial groups employing the consultants, attempting to influence the legislation under discussion. This was held to be completely improper. The MPs involved either resigned or were voted out of office at the 1997 general election. Geoffrey Robinson, paymaster general in the Blair government, having been involved in formulating legislation on the taxation of income from trusts held overseas, was found to be the beneficiary of trusts in the Channel Islands that escaped the taxes, and this caused an enormous outcry. However, it was determined that he had given up control of his wealth, that it was controlled on his behalf by persons who did not have access to privileged information, and that he had properly reported his financial affairs to Parliament. The Major government established a commission—the Nolan Commission—on standards in public life, to determine what information politicians and other public officials should report on their personal financial affairs and what steps they should take to ensure that conflicts of interest were, if not eliminated, then at least limited in scale.

The problems of separating politics and public affairs from private life seems so great that there will be no end to accusations of sleaze and corruption's being traded among politicians and in the press—some of them reflecting genuine improprieties, others attempts by politicians of one party to get an advantage over politicians of another party, and others the media whipping up a storm to promote sales of their own products.

Humphrey in the television programme *Yes Minister* has made famous the image of the wily civil servant outwitting the politician and ensuring that the policies pursued (which even the minister himself, at least eventually, wishes to pursue) are precisely the ones the civil servants want to pursue. Harold Wilson's Labour government which came to power in 1964 encountered strong suspicion on the part of civil servants. Several now well-known tactics were used by civil servants to ensure that some policies were not followed. Lady Thatcher complains loudly in her memoirs about the obstructiveness of civil servants on some issues.

Whether this is a good or a bad thing is open to question. The British civil service has a long history of attracting intellectuals of the highest calibre, classical scholars from Oxford and Cambridge, communicating with each other in brilliant memoranda. It has also a long tradition of impartiality and public service, and independence from the government of the day. It may be that the policies promoted by the civil service would be better than the ones desired by the politicians. The complaint made by the politicians is that the civil servants are too conservative (with the well-known small *c*); arguably, this may be no bad thing.

The European Union suffers a worse case of the same disease. Its civil servants, the European Commission, are able to take a leading role in the formulation of policy, which may differ markedly from that of the politicians, who come together in the Council of Ministers. Under the highly active M. Jacques Delors, who was president of the commission from 1984 to 1994, the European Community (as it was until 1993) became much more federalist in its stance, and the bureaucracy in Brussels became much more interventionist in the affairs of member states. While this was supported by some politicians, some member countries, particularly Britain, expressed strong opposition.

The point of these examples is that the principal-agent problem in government, with the politicians as the principals and the civil servants as the agents, leads to a state of affairs where policies that are put into effect reflect not only the desires of the politicians but also those of the civil servants.

Even if they are partly concerned with doing a good job, bureaucrats are also concerned with their own careers. For instance, concern about making mistakes may lead them to act in a risk-averse manner. Because it is so difficult to assess the "output" of administrators, performance may be judged more on the extent to which an individual has conformed to certain "bureaucratic" procedures, which partially accounts for the proliferation of red tape. Bureaucrats may have an interest in expanding their spheres of influence, just as any businessperson has an interest in the growth of her business. But while a businessperson expands her business by providing a good at a cheaper price, bureaucrats expand their influence by persuading the legislature either that they need more funds or personnel to do what has to be done, or that there should be more of whatever it is they do. This leads to competition among bureaucrats that may have deleterious effects.

INCENTIVES AND THE EFFICIENCY OF GOVERNMENT

There are problems of efficiency in the public sector just as there are in the private sector. Government departments and government agencies—the office that issues driving licences and vehicle licences, the Department of Social Security, and local government offices—have monopoly positions and do not face the same kind of pressures on them to cut costs and lower prices that firms in competitive markets face. Conservative governments in Britain since 1979 have made a big issue of public sector waste and inefficiency. Their concern with it has driven a number of their policies: privatization of nationalised industries was prompted in part by it, local councils have been forced to contract out local services like rubbish collection and building maintenance to private companies, and internal markets have been established in the National Health Service. Some recent attempts to improve the quality of government services in Britain have been promoted under the banner of the Citizen's Charter.

The incentives that public sector workers face do not always lead them to pursue the interests of the public. Doctors in the National Health Service may have been able to pursue their clinical interests—treating patients with new and interesting methods and to a standard which the doctors felt appropriate, but with too little regard for the patients who were waiting for treatment or not getting treated at all. Recent controversial changes have encouraged hospitals to become independent self-governing organizations (NHS trusts), able to compete with each other to provide (sell) operations to general practitioners, who buy them on behalf of their patients. Managers seem to have gained power in deciding how to allocate resources in hospitals, and the doctors have lost influence.

Local authorities may not have had sufficient incentive to collect rubbish at the lowest cost. They may have operated too much to suit the interests of the local government workers and too little to suit the interests of local residents.

CLOSE-UP: SOFT BUDGET CONSTRAINTS AND COST OVERRUNS

The new British Library building was opened in 1998 after twenty or thirty years of planning, construction delays, budget changes, and cost overruns. The building was originally intended to cost 116 million pounds and eventually cost a total of 515 million. Happily the final product has been greeted with approval. It is architecturally distinguished, it will provide a very pleasant environment for study and research, it greatly increases the storage space of the library and the accessibility of its vast collections, and it provides a worthy successor to the famous round reading room in the British Museum where the library had previously been housed.

The problem of containing the costs of public investment projects and of cost overruns is very widespread. For small projects, the problem is not severe. The government agency can invite private sector contractors to tender for the project and accept the most attractive tender. Contracts can be written to put the burden of risk onto the shoulders of the contractor. If the project turns out to be costlier or to take longer than planned, the contractor suffers the loss, not the government agency. The problem arises for large-scale projects, where the risks are too great to be shouldered by one or more private sector firms and, indeed, governments cannot find firms willing to bear the risk. For these projects, the contracts specify sharing risks or, sometimes, having the government or public body bear all the risk. Examples include the European fighter aircraft project, development of computing systems for government departments and health authorities, building of the Channel Tunnel, and projects like the building of the British Library.

When government bears some risk, there is an incentive problem. The contractor can argue that costs have increased and that the government should pay more to cover the increase. The contractor probably has much better information than the government agency, which may not be able to argue against the contractor's claims. The contractors have an incentive to submit optimistic bids in the first place in order to win contracts, which makes it more likely that more detailed work will reveal cost increases which can be justified. Contractors know that government agencies can increase the budget for projects if necessary, particularly when some funds have already been spent and the alternative to accepting a cost increase is to have an incomplete building (say) and much higher costs of getting it completed with other builders. This is the problem of **soft budget constraints.** For big public projects, the contractor may have the final credible threat that if the cost increases are not met, then the contractor will just be forced into bankruptcy. In this case, whatever the contract says, the government is left carrying the risk.

So cost overruns arise from a classic combination of informational imperfections, misaligned incentives, and soft budget constraints. These interactions between government and contractors are examples of principal-agent problems.

In the case of the British Library and other large public investments, there is often also the problem that delays and changes in budgets, which further conspire to increase costs, are imposed by the principal (the government).

Source: "Watchdog Shows Library Cost Over-runs," *Financial Times*, 15 May 1996, p. 11.

387 RESPONSES TO GOVERNMENT POLICIES • 387

Schools may not have had a strong enough incentive to promote the welfare of pupils, and have had too strong an incentive to serve the interests of teachers. A recent government response has been to enforce a national curriculum on schools in Britain, following the example of France and some other continental European countries, which have managed to maintain higher standards of achievement in schools. The government has also published league tables of schools' performance; allowed parents greater choice of the school to which their children are sent; and allowed schools to opt out of local authority control, make more of their own decisions on how to spend money within the school, and receive grants direct from the central government.

While many of these changes have been attempts to introduce more competition into the provision of public services and move them further away from day-to-day political control, attempts which have been controversial in most cases and clearly successful in only a few, they have very clearly led to setting up a lot of so-called Quangos: quasi-autonomous nongovernmental organizations. Whereas schools and hospitals once were clearly controlled by elected politicians, the new bodies—the NHS trusts, and so on—have no clear responsibility to politicians although they continue to receive and spend public funds to deliver services. The incentives facing a lot of these new bodies are obscure. Many people argue that the introduction of private sector attitudes into organizations that have to provide public services has undermined a tradition of service and high standards in the public sector. Others applaud real or imagined cost savings. The effects of many of these changes in the organization of government services is still unclear.

While elected politicians—or at least some of them—have argued that government agencies and public sector organizations do not always act in the public interest, it is also clear that elected politicians themselves have incentives to act in ways that serve their own interests and not those of the general public. The desire to stay in power and get reelected makes politicians particularly sensitive to the interests of small groups of voters who might be able to tip the scales in an election. Farmers throughout Europe, in the United Sates, and in Japan seem to enjoy political influence that is disproportionate to their small numbers and their contribution to the national income. Governments in France and Germany rely heavily on the agricultural vote to hold on to power. As a consequence, Europe has been saddled with the enormously wasteful Common Agricultural Policy. Japan has tariffs that keep the price of rice in Japan at several times the world price. The United States also has expensive subsidies for farmers.

British members of Parliament can and do supplement their parliamentary salaries by acting as consultants to various business organizations, and their services are often in demand as nonexecutive directors on the boards of companies. While they officially declare their interests in these firms and do not allow them to influence their support or opposition to issues debated and voted on in Parliament, the existence of these directorships and consultancies keeps alive the suspicion that firms are able to pay politicians for supporting measures that are in the firms' interests. The people or groups who give political parties financial support, which they need to fight elections, may find their support rewarded by legislation that promotes their interests. To some extent this is perfectly natural and legitimate. Nevertheless, the danger of large firms' or other groups' buying politicians is such that in the United States gifts to political parties and candidates are limited in size, and the sums that candidates are allowed to spend on campaigns are also limited. In Britain, the Labour Party complains that big business is able to make large gifts to the Conservative Party while the Conservatives attempt to check the ability of the trades unions to pass on their members' contributions to the Labour Party. It is clear that elected politicians may be pursuing their own interests in getting reelected by promoting the sectional interests of their financial backers rather than promoting a wider public interest.

UNFORESEEN RESPONSES TO GOVERNMENT POLICIES

Government policies may fail to solve social and economic problems in the way they are supposed to for another reason: the private sector does not respond

CLOSE-UP: DEVOLUTION

After years of argument and fierce opposition from the Conservative governments of Thatcher and Major, the Labour government under Blair has taken steps towards devolution in Scotland and Wales. Scotland is to have a parliament and Wales an assembly. This reverses a centuries-long trend towards the centralization of government in Britain, since England annexed Wales in the Middle Ages and the Act of Union of 1707 united England and Scotland (or perhaps one should go back to Alfred the Great who unified southern England in the ninth century). At a more local level, centralization has removed powers from local governments (from the county, district, and borough councils and from the metropolitan county and district councils), both powers to determine local taxes and powers to set the form and level of local spending. Local responsibility for schools, for example, has been diminished by the ability of some schools to get their funding direct from central government and by control of the national curriculum, which lies outside local government's hands. Local taxation, the council tax, raises only a small fraction of local expenditure, the bulk of which is met by grants from central to local government, and the rates of council tax are limited by central government.

The establishment of a parliament in Scotland with powers to set laws and to raise taxes is a major step, one of several towards stronger regional and local government. Others include the plans to increase the powers of mayors in London and other big cities.

A properly federal structure in Britain looks some way off, because there would need to be a parliament for England, in parallel with the Scottish parliament and the Welsh assembly (with the same powers as the others), and a similar body in Northern Ireland, each of which would decide matters of interest within its respective area. The government of the United Kingdom would then deal with matters of interest to all four areas, particularly defence and foreign policy. Such a fully federal structure would parallel that in the United States, where states have many legislative and tax-raising powers. The dominance of England militates against this happening in Britain. Politicians do not like to give up power. For the government in Westminster to give up some of its powers over Scotland and Wales may be just tolerable, but to lose control of England is still unthinkable.

The celebrated West Lothian Question is raised by the fact that, with a Scottish parliament but no English one, Scotland would be represented in its own parliament and at Westminster, while England wold be represented only at Westminster. Scottish MPs would get to vote on English issues, whereas English MPs would not get to vote on Scottish issues. While this has traditionally been used as an argument against Scottish devolution, it looks increasingly like an argument for carrying devolution further and setting up an English parliament as well.

to the policies in the way that was predicted. Predictions about how people will respond to policies are inevitably surrounded by error. In Britain the growth of the social security budget has exceeded all expectations. Standing at roughly £107 billion per year for 1996, it consumes roughly one-third of all government expenditure, which was approximately £300 billion per year at that time, and a substantial fraction of national income (£740 billion in 1996). Social security may have contributed to the rise in long-term unemployment in Britain. A more extreme view is that it has created a cycle of depen-

SOURCES OF PUBLIC FAILURES

Imperfect information

Incentives

    Constrained ability to make long-term commitments

    Political pressures—power of lobbyists

Budgeting and spending constraints

Unintended consequences

Unforeseen changes in behaviour resulting from government action

dency, which people, once in, find hard to get out of. The availability-for-work test, which is applied to recipients of social security benefits, sometimes has perverse effects, by preventing the unemployed from taking training courses which would increase their job prospects. Benefit recipients cannot take part-time or low-paying jobs without losing benefits; this discourages attempts to find such work.

Such things are not confined to Britain. In the Netherlands, a generous programme of benefits for people who were unable to work because they were invalids, which could be obtained provided a doctor would certify invalidity, has led to an enormous growth in the numbers of invalids in the Netherlands, to the point where the scheme has had to be cut back. In the United States, the programme of almost free medical care for the aged, Medicare, has become much more costly than expected. These programmes may have created a group of people who have come to depend on them, so that terminating them or cutting them back looks like harsh treatment of numbers of relatively poor people and may be politically difficult, especially when these groups of dependents become numerous enough to affect election results materially.

It is possible to give numerous examples of policies that have had unforeseen effects. The programme of federally guaranteed student loans in the United States became very expensive (for the U.S. government) when many ex-students found that it was advantageous to declare bankruptcy and avoid having to repay the loan. The recently introduced student loan programme in Britain may be more costly to the Treasury than has been planned if loans prove difficult to recover.

REVIEW AND PRACTICE

SUMMARY

1 Different voters have different views about what the government should do. In some cases, majority voting may not yield a determinate outcome. In other cases, the choices made in majority voting reflect the preferences of the median voter.

2 Government actions sometimes reflect the interests of particular groups, who seek special favours. The activities they engage in to get these special favours are called rent-seeking activities.

3 Sources of systemic public failure include weak or distorted incentives, budgeting and spending rigidities, and inability to foresee fully the consequences of government programmes, particularly changes in behaviour.

4 Centralised provision of public goods and services is preferred when externalities and national public goods, or income distribution issues are involved. Decentralised provision is preferred for local public goods, is more responsive to community preferences and needs, and facilitates experimentation in different ways to solve common problems.

KEY TERMS

public choice   median voter theory   rent seeking   theory of bureaucracy

voting paradox

REVIEW QUESTIONS

1 What is the voting paradox?

2 Who is the median voter? Why does the median voter matter so much in a system of majority rule?

3 What role do special-interest groups and bureaucrats play in determining what government does?

4 In what ways does government face different constraints from those facing firms in the private sector? What effects do the differences have on incentives?

5 Describe the advantages and disadvantages of providing public goods and services at the local or state level versus at the national level.

PROBLEMS

1 A prime minister is trying to decide which of three goals he should put at the top of his agenda—deficit reduction (d), a tax cut (m), or preserving the safety net for the poor (p). He puts the matter before his advisers in three separate meetings. Assume he has three advisers, and he takes a vote in each meeting. His political adviser's ranking is {m–d–p}, his economic adviser's ranking is {d–p–m}, and his health care adviser's ranking is {p–m–d}. What is the outcome?

2 Suppose you are considering building a food stand along a mile-long strip of beach but you know that one other vendor is planning to build a stand too. If visitors are evenly distributed along the beach, and people will buy from whichever food stand is closest to them, where should you decide to build your stand? If the goal is to have the shortest possible average distance for people to get to food, where should the two stands be located? (Hint: Think about the situation of two political parties competing for the median voter.)

3 While the median voter predicts that the two political parties will converge towards the center, in practice the two parties often seem far apart. Use median voter theory to predict the outcome of a two-stage election. In the first stage, voters within each party choose their candidate. If, in the first stage, voters do not vote strategically—that is, they vote for their preferred candidate, not for the candidate that they think will win—describe the outcome of the political process. How might the fact that voters at the extremes of the political spectrum are more likely to vote affect the outcome?

4 Suppose that for a programme of government spending, the central government paid half of the total amount spent but left it to the local government to decide how much to spend on the programme within its jurisdiction. How might such a cost-sharing arrangement affect the level of expenditure? How might the wealth of the local area affect the extent to which it might take advantage of such a programme?

PART FIVE

FULL-EMPLOYMENT MACROECONOMICS

T here is widespread belief among the public that government is responsible for maintaining the economy at full employment, with stable prices, and for creating an economic environment in which growth can occur.

Although most economists still agree with these sentiments, there are dissenting views. Some claim that the government has relatively little power to control most of the fluctuations in output and employment; some argue that, apart from isolated instances such as the Great Depression of the 1930s, neither inflation nor unemployment is a major economic problem (though they obviously remain political problems); and some believe the government has been as much a cause of the problems of unemployment, inflation, and slow growth as a part of their solution. We will explore these various interpretations in greater depth in the chapters that follow.

The problems of unemployment, inflation, and growth relate to the performance of the entire economy. Earlier in the book, we learned how the law of supply and demand operates in the market for oranges, apples, or other goods. At any one time, one industry may be doing well, another poorly. Yet to understand the forces that determine how well the economy as a whole is doing, we want to see beyond the vagaries that affect any particular industry. This is the domain of macroeconomics. Macroeconomics focuses not on the output of single products like orange juice or peanut butter nor on the demand for masons or bricklayers or computer programmers. Rather, it is concerned with the characteristics of an entire economy, such as the overall level of output, the total level of employment, and the stability of the overall level of prices. What accounts for the "diseases" that sometimes affect the economy—the episodes of massive unemployment, rising prices, or economic stagnation—and what can the government do, both to prevent the onset of these diseases and to cure them once they have occurred?

Macroeconomic *theory* is concerned with what determines the level of employment and output as well as the rate of inflation and the overall growth rate of the economy, while macroeconomic *policy* focuses on what government can do to stimulate employment, prevent inflation, and increase the economy's growth rate.

We begin our study of macroeconomics in Chapter 22 by learning the major statistics used to assess the state of the economy—the rates of unemployment, inflation, and growth. Chapter 23 then builds on the microeconomic analysis of Part Two to construct an *aggregate* model of the economy. Paralleling our earlier discussions, we focus on labour, product, and capital markets. We see how the demand and supply for labour determines the real wage and how the real wage changes in response to shifts in either of these curves. We then see how the price level and the interest rate are determined in the product and capital markets. In this basic aggregate model, we assume there is full employment. The rate of growth is determined, in part, by the level of investment that emerges from the market equilibrium. And changes in the price level (and the rate of inflation) are determined by changes in the money supply.

International trade plays an increasingly important role in all the developed economies. Exports have been expanding far faster than the world economy as a whole has been growing. Many countries finance trade surpluses and deficits by extensively borrowing from abroad. Thus, international economic relations affect both the product and capital markets, as Chapter 23 also discusses.

The National Income Accounts show that there is an unbreakable connection between the government deficit, the balance of payments current account deficit, and the net saving of the private sector of the economy. Chapter 24 explores some important consequences of this accounting identity.

MACROECONOMIC GOALS AND MEASURES

J
ust as doctors find it useful to take a patient's temperature to help them judge the patient's condition, economists use statistics to get a measure of the state of the economy. Statistics on unemployment, inflation, and growth are three of the most commonly used, though they give only a rough and incomplete picture. These three areas have also been the main concerns of governments in the choice of macroeconomic policy.

The importance of unemployment, inflation, and growth for policy has varied from time to time and place to place. In the 1950s and 1960s, great emphasis was placed on low unemployment. By the 1980s, in most of the developed countries of the world, attention had shifted to inflation. Inflation was viewed as a more-pressing problem, and also it seemed more capable of treatment: many governments had come to believe that it was more responsive to their policies than unemployment. Governments have always wanted to promote economic growth. Rapid growth has occurred at some times in some places, like Japan, Germany, and Hong Kong. But how to achieve it has remained a mystery. The recipes for success used in the fast-growing economies have proved impossible to copy successfully elsewhere.

This chapter introduces these major goals of macroeconomic policy, and the statistics that are used to measure them. Although statistics generally get a bad press ("lies, damn lies, and statistics," Disreali said), they are essential, never accurate, and must be used with caution. A change in the inflation rate or the unemployment rate by a few tenths of a percentage point between one month and

KEY QUESTIONS

1 What are the main objects of macroeconomic policy?

2 How are unemployment, output, growth, and inflation measured?

3 What are some of the central problems in measuring these variables?

the next conveys little useful information, just as there is rarely cause for concern when a patient's temperature fluctuates by a tenth of a degree. But large or persistent changes in the figures—an increase in the measured unemployment rate from 5 to 10 percent, for example—generally indicate that something significant has occurred.

The sections in this chapter discuss unemployment, inflation, and growth and explain how each is measured.

THE THREE MACROECONOMIC ILLS

Chapter 1 characterised the economy in terms of a set of interconnected labour, product, and capital markets. The diagram often referred to as the circular flow diagram in Figure 1.4 shows firms' obtaining labour and capital from households and using it to produce goods, which are then sold to households, which buy the goods with the income they earn providing labour and capital to firms. Given these interconnections, it is not surprising that problems in one part of the economy may be manifested in other parts. The symptoms in one part may indicate disease elsewhere in the system.

Later chapters will enable us to understand the entire system. Here we focus on the symptoms, each of which is most closely associated with a particular part of the system.

Unemployment has been high on the agenda since the 1930s, when it affected almost a quarter of the workforce. The whole of the developed world, not only the United Kingdom and the United States

but also the continental European countries, particularly Germany, were wracked by the Great Depression. While the 1950s and 1960s were a golden age of low unemployment, it returned to high levels throughout Europe in the 1980s and 1990s. In Spain it exceeds 20 percent, in France it stands at more than 12 percent, and in Germany it is roughly 10 percent. It is difficult to believe in such conditions that the demand for labour equals its supply: there appears to be a significant departure from the basic competitive model.

In recent years **inflation** has been represented as a terrible economic dragon to be slain. Macroeconomic policy since around 1980 in North America, the United Kingdom, and continental Europe has been dedicated to its eradication. The European Union has made low inflation a key objective of the Economic and Monetary Union. In developing countries, inflation has been much worse: 10,000 percent per annum in the Ukraine in the early 1990s. Latin American countries have suffered regular bouts of **hyperinflation,** the treatment for which, administered by the International Monetary Fund, has sometimes been almost as unpleasant as the disease.

While unemployment usually reflects short-run fluctuations in income, and inflation concerns movements in prices, the great long-term concern is with real standards of living, that is to say with economic growth. Real living standards are compared among countries. The United Kingdom has fallen back compared with many countries because it has grown less quickly. The Asian Tigers—Singapore, Hong Kong, Taiwan, and South Korea—grew rapidly until summer 1997 when the Asian financial crisis broke out in Thailand. The Chinese economy has also grown rapidly in recent years, and if it continues to grow as it is expected to do, it will soon challenge the hegemony of the West in economic affairs.

GROWTH

In the middle of the nineteenth century, the average standard of living in Britain was the highest in the world. Since then, the standard of living has risen but by less than in many countries, and now Britain has only a relatively moderate standard of living. Many European countries, Canada, the United States, and Japan have higher standards of living today than the United Kingdom does. Britain's slow rate of economic growth has been a puzzle and a source of anxiety for policymakers for decades. The British economy has resisted a succession of economic policies aimed at making it grow faster.

However, concern about growth rates and productivity is not confined to Britain. The United States may still have the highest standard of living in the world, but nevertheless the rate of growth of the U.S. economy in the 1970s and 1980s has been slow and the gap in living standards between the United States and other countries has been narrowing. This has been a growing cause of concern to policymakers in the United States.

MEASURING OUTPUT

The output of the economy consists of millions of different goods. We could report how much of each good the economy produced: 1,362,478 hammers, 473,562,382 potatoes, 7,875,342 watches, and so forth. Such data may be useful for some purposes, but they do not provide us with the information we want. If next year the output of hammers goes up by 5 per-

cent, the output of potatoes goes down by 2 percent, and the output of watches rises by 7 percent, has total output gone up or down? And by how much?

We need a single number that summarises the output of the economy. But how do we add up the hammers, potatoes, watches, and billions of other products produced in the economy? We do this by adding the money value of all the final goods (goods that are not used to make other goods) produced and arriving at a single number that encapsulates the production of the economy. This number is called the **gross domestic product,** or **GDP.** It is the standard measure of the output of an economy and sums up the total money value of the goods and services produced by the residents of a country during a specified period. The GDP includes everything from buttons to air travel and from haircuts to barrels of oil. It makes no difference whether the production takes place in the public or private sector or whether the goods and services are purchased by households or government.[1]

There is one problem with using money as a measure of output. The value of a pound changes over time. Chocolate bars, books, cinema tickets, and hammers, all cost more today than they did ten years ago. Another way of saying this is that a pound does not buy as much now as it did ten years ago. We do not want to be misled into believing that the output is higher when in fact only prices have risen.

To purge the measurement of GDP of the effects of inflation, a figure called **real GDP** is computed. The goods produced in the economy in successive

---

[1] We use prices not only because they are a convenient way of making comparisons but also because prices reflect how consumers value different goods. If the price of an orange is twice that of an apple, it means an orange is worth twice as much (at the margin) as an apple.

years are evaluated at a common set of prices, the prices prevailing in a given base year. Table 22.1 gives a numerical example. The GDP measured in current prices, **nominal GDP,** rises from £423.40 million in 1985 to £481.10 million in 1986 and to £518.60 million in 1987. The GDP measured in 1985 prices, or real GDP, rises from £423.40 million in 1985 to £456.5 million in 1986 and to £471.25 million in 1987. Some of the growth in nominal GDP is caused by the growth in prices, not the growth in output.

A measure of the growth in the price level is the ratio of the GDP at current prices to the GDP at base year prices. This is called the implicit GDP deflator. It is a price index, similar to the retail price index. There is an important difference, however. The retail price index measures the cost of the same basket of goods (the basket of goods consumed in the base year) at the prices in successive years relative to its cost in the base year. By contrast, the implicit GDP deflator measures the cost of a different basket of

Table 22.1 CALCULATING AN INDEX OF GDP

Year 1985	Potatoes	Watches	Hammers
Output (in millions)	473 lb	7.8	1.3
Prices (in £s)	0.05	50	7.5
Nominal GDP	$= (473 \times 0.05) + (7.8 \times 50) + (1.3 \times 7.5) = 423.40.$		
Real GDP at 1985 prices	$= (473 \times 0.05) + (7.8 \times 50) + (1.3 \times 7.5) = 423.40.$		
Index of real GDP	$= 100.$		
Implicit GDP deflator	$= 100 \times 423.40/423.40 = 100.$		

Year 1986	Potatoes	Watches	Hammers
Output (in millions)	480 lb	8.5	1.0
Prices (in £s)	0.06	52	9.3
Nominal GDP	$= (480 \times 0.06) + (8.5 \times 52) + (1.0 \times 9.3) = 481.10.$		
Real GDP at 1985 prices	$= (480 \times 0.05) + (8.5 \times 50) + (1.0 \times 7.5) = 456.5.$		
Index of nominal GDP	$= 100 \times 481.10/423.40 = 113.39.$		
Index of real GDP	$= 100 \times 456.5/423.40 = 107.82.$		
Implicit GDP deflator	$= 100 \times 481.10/456.5 = 105.17.$		

Year 1987	Potatoes	Watches	Hammers
Output (in millions)	500 lb	8.7	1.5
Prices (in £s)	0.07	53	15.0
Nominal GDP	$= (500 \times 0.07) + (8.7 \times 53) + (1.5 \times 15.0) = 518.60.$		
Real GDP at 1985 prices	$= (500 \times 0.05) + (8.7 \times 50) + (1.5 \times 7.5) = 471.25.$		
Implicit GDP deflator	$= 100 \times 518.60/471.25 = 110.05.$		

goods (the basket of goods produced in the current year) at the prices in successive years relative to its cost in the base year.

In the example, the implicit GDP deflator is 100.00 in 1985 and 105.17 in 1986. While nominal GDP grew by 13.39 percent between 1985 and 1986 (the index of nominal GDP is 113.39 in 1986), real GDP grew by only 7.82 percent. The remainder is accounted for by higher prices: the GDP deflator grew by 5.17 percent. Note that the index of nominal GDP is the product of the index of real GDP and the GDP deflator, divided by 100 (113.39 = 107.82 × 105.17/100). The growth in nominal GDP is approximately equal to the sum of the growth in real GDP and the growth in the GDP deflator (13.39 approximately equals 7.82 + 5.17). Conversely, the growth in real GDP is approximately equal to the growth in nominal GDP less the growth in the GDP deflator.

REAL GDP IN THE UNITED KINGDOM SINCE 1945

Figure 22.1 shows real GDP (at 1985 prices) in the United Kingdom from 1945 to 1996. Figure 22.2 shows the percentage rate of growth in real GDP from one year to the next. The GDP has generally grown but not smoothly. There have been several occasions when it has fallen: between 1945 and 1946, between 1956 and 1957 (just), between 1973 and 1975, more deeply between 1980 and 1982, and between 1991 and 1992. Figure 22.2 shows that there has been a clear pattern of cycles in the growth of GDP: some years of more rapid growth followed by a year or more of slow growth. For example, after a fall from 1945 to 1946, GDP grew in 1947, 1948, 1949, and 1950, and then stagnated between 1950 and 1951. A cyclical pattern of this kind is repeated in the following years. The cycles differ in their length and amplitude.

Periods of rapid growth are called **booms,** and periods of weak growth are called **recessions.** The succession of booms and recessions is referred to as **business cycles.** Businesspeople are particularly interested in predictions of when a recession will end (when the economy "bottoms out"), or when a boom will end and the economy will slow down and go into a recession (when the economy "peaks"), because business profits are particularly sensitive to the timing of these turning points. However, despite the large macroeconomic models that have been built precisely in order to make forecasts of such things, turning points in the business cycle have proved difficult to predict with any accuracy.

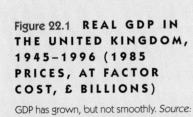

Figure 22.1 **REAL GDP IN THE UNITED KINGDOM, 1945–1996 (1985 PRICES, AT FACTOR COST, £ BILLIONS)**

GDP has grown, but not smoothly. *Source: Office of National Statistics, Economic Trends,* Annual Supplement (1998).

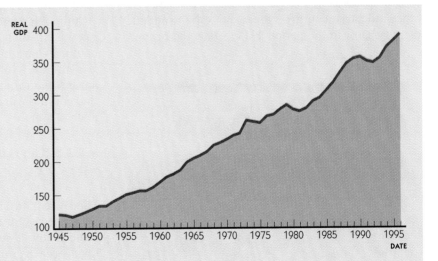

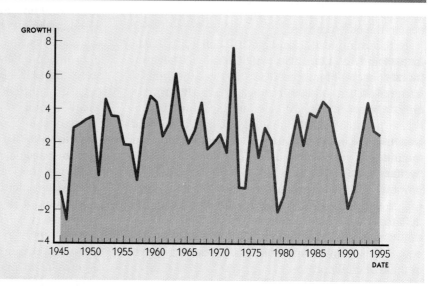

Figure 22.2 **REAL GDP GROWTH RATE IN THE UNITED KINGDOM, 1945–1995 (PERCENT PER ANNUM)**

By focusing on real GDP, we can see the cyclical patterns more clearly. *Source:* Office of National Statistics, *Economic Trends*, Annual Supplement (1998).

There are some variables that frequently signal a change in the direction of the economy, such as surveys of business or consumer confidence, and firms' orders for new machines. These variables which anticipate a downturn or an upswing are called **leading indicators.**

As Table 22.2 shows, the growth rate of the United Kingdom has compared unfavourably with that of other industrial countries throughout the twentieth century. Only in the period 1913 to 1950 did France

and Germany grow marginally more slowly, and both suffered great devastation of their stocks of capital equipment in the two world wars of that period. During the golden age of rapid growth among the industrialised economies, 1950 to 1973, Japan's growth stands out as being remarkably high. Since 1973, there has been a marked slowdown in growth among the industrialised economies.

Although some of the differences in growth rates may seem small, they accumulate over time. If two countries start off with the same GDP but one has a growth rate which is greater by 0.7 percent per annum than that of the other, then the GDP of the first country will double relative to that of the second after 100 years.

MEASURING GDP: THE VALUE OF OUTPUT

There are three approaches to measuring GDP (whether real or nominal), each of which yields the same result. Two concentrate on output data. The third—relying on the fact that the value of output all becomes income to someone—uses income figures to obtain a measure of output.

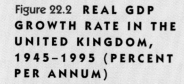

Table 22.2 GROWTH RATES OF REAL GDP, PERCENT PER ANNUM

Period	U.K.	France	Germany	U.S.	Japan
1913–1950	1.29	1.15	1.28	2.79	2.24
1950–1973	3.03	5.04	5.92	3.63	9.27
1973–1987	1.75	2.16	1.82	2.51	3.73

THE FINAL GOODS APPROACH

On the face of it, measuring GDP is a straightforward task, albeit massive. One gathers together the money values of all goods and services sold in a country, and then adds them up. Unfortunately, matters are not this simple, because it is first necessary to distinguish between final goods and intermediate goods. Final goods—like automobiles, books, bread, and shoes—are sold to consumers. Final goods also include goods sold to firms as *investments* in fixed capital and inventories. These investments are an addition to a firm's *stock* of buildings, machinery, and vehicles or to its *stock* of raw materials, work-in-progress, or finished goods. It is important to distinguish between goods sold to firms which are final goods and those which are *intermediate* goods. Intermediate goods are used up in the production process, like flour in baking bread or steel in making cars. Capital equipment is of course eventually used up but only very gradually. Factories and machinery last many years before they are worn out. Intermediate goods are used to produce outputs—such as coal when used to make steel, or apples when used to make applesauce. A good such as an apple can be either a final or an intermediate good, depending on how it is used. The **final goods approach** to GDP adds up the total money value of goods and services produced, categorised by their ultimate users.

The reason it is so important to distinguish between final and intermediate goods is that the value of final goods *includes* the value of the intermediate goods that went into making them. When Ford sells a car for £12,000, that figure may include £100 worth of Dunlop tyres. It would be double counting to list in GDP the revenues of both the car maker and the tyre producer. Likewise for the steel, plastic, and other components that go into the car. In fact, cases where some intermediate goods are used to produce other intermediate goods could even lead to triple or quadruple counting.

One way of calculating the value of the final goods of the economy is to consider where those goods go. There are four possibilities. Some final goods are consumed by individuals; we call this **aggregate consumption** (and we include all consumption goods, regardless of where they are produced). Some are used by firms to build buildings and make machines; this is called **aggregate investment** (again, we include all investment goods, regardless of where they are produced). Some are purchased by government and are called **government spending.** And, some of the goods, called **exports,** go abroad. If we didn't import (that is, buy from abroad) any goods, then GDP would simply consist of goods that went for private consumption, for private investment, to the government, or for export. But not all consumption, investment, or government purchases are produced at home. We, therefore, need a final step to get GDP by this method. We have to subtract the amount imported. Thus,

$$GDP = C + I + G + X - M,$$

where C = consumption, I = investment, G = government purchases, X = exports, and M = imports. The difference between exports and imports is referred to as **net exports.** This equation is an **identity;** that is, it is always true (by definition) that GDP equals consumption plus investment plus government expenditures plus net exports.

THE VALUE-ADDED APPROACH

A second way to calculate the value of GDP is to study the intermediate goods directly. The production of most items occurs in several stages. Consider the car. At one stage in its production, iron ore, coal, and limestone are mined. At a second stage, these raw materials are delivered to a steel mill. A third stage finds a steel company combining these ingredients to make steel. Finally, the steel and other inputs,

GDP equals consumption plus investment plus government expenditures plus exports minus imports.

CLOSE-UP: MEASURING PRODUCTIVITY AND GROWTH

The figures for gross domestic product are often taken at face value, as an authoritative measure of the economy's production. But a recent change in the way the figures are computed and presented was a reminder that even such a widely trusted and widely used statistic is based on many assumptions which are open to scrutiny and argument. In September 1998, the Office of National Statistics (ONS) started to present National Income statistics according to new international standards, the United Nations Systems of National Accounts 1993 (SNA 93) and the European System of Accounts 1995 (ESA 95). These are intended to make international comparisons easier. When the new figures were released, they showed that GDP growth had been greater than had previously been believed and gave an indication of the degree of uncertainty surrounding the figures.

The new system of accounts involves many detailed changes. But one of the most important is in the way that productivity in the public sector is measured. Until 1998, the quantity of output from public sector services was measured by the quantity of inputs—the output of the NHS by the numbers of nurses and doctors, and so on, and the output of education by the numbers of teachers. A result of this is that productivity growth in these activities was by definition impossible, as far as the national income accounts were concerned. The output of one teacher or one nurse was constant, regardless of how many students were taught, how effectively they were taught, how many patients were treated, and so on.

It is highly ironic that at the same time, during the 1980s and 1990s, the public sector was required by the government to make productivity gains, and the amount of money allocated to public services assumed that these would be made, and that a given number of students would be taught with fewer teachers or that a given number of patients would be treated with progressively fewer doctors and nurses.

A consequence of measuring the outputs of these activities by the inputs into them is that the growth in the gross domestic product was underestimated previously. With the new accounts, revised figures show faster economic growth than the previous figures did. The new accounts make a start at measuring productivity in public services, using a range of performance indicators, such as student numbers to measure education output, an index of activity in hospitals to measure health service output, and the numbers of benefit claims for social security to measure output of the Department of Social Security.

The same kind of problems that arises in the measurement of public services—measuring their outputs—arises in connection with services in the private sector. Changes in quantity and quality of services are hard to measure accurately. While productivity in manufacturing has been studied extensively and there is a well-developed methodology for measuring it, productivity in services is less well studied and less well understood. As services account for an increasing proportion of the GDP (currently between 60 and 70 percent in most developed countries), it is increasingly important to measure their output and productivity accurately if the estimates of economic growth are to be useful.

Sources: Office of National Statistics, *Economic Trends,* August 1998 and October 1998; DeAnne Julius and John Butler, "Inflation and Growth in a Service Economy," *Bank of England Quarterly Bulletin,* November 1998, pp. 338–346; Anna Brueton, "Recent Changes to the National Accounts, Balance of Payments, and Monetary Statistics," *Bank of England Quarterly Bulletin,* November 1998, pp. 361–367.

such as rubber and plastics, are combined by the car manufacturer to make a car. The difference in value between what the car maker pays for intermediate goods and what it receives for the finished cars is called the firm's **value added.**

Value added = firm's revenue − costs of intermediate goods. The GDP can be measured by calculating the value added at each stage of production.

GDP = sum of value added of all firms.

THE INCOME APPROACH

The third method used to calculate GDP involves measuring the income generated by selling products, rather than the value of the products themselves. This is known as the **income approach.** Firms do five things with their revenue. They pay for labour, they pay interest, they buy intermediate goods, they pay indirect taxes such as value-added taxes and excise taxes, and they enjoy what is left over as profits.

Revenue = wages + interest payments + costs
of intermediate inputs + indirect taxes + profits.

But we already know that the firm's value added is its revenue minus the costs of intermediate goods. Therefore,

Value added = wages + interest payments
+ indirect taxes + profits.

And since the value of GDP is equal to the sum of the value added of all firms, GDP must also equal the sum of the value of all wage payments, interest payments, taxes, and profits for all firms:

GDP = wages + interest payments
+ indirect taxes + profits.

People receive income from wages, capital, and profits of the firms they own (or own shares in). Thus, the right-hand side of this identity is just the total income of all individuals plus government revenue from indirect taxes. This is an extremely important result, one economists use frequently, so it is worth high-

lighting: *aggregate output equals aggregate income.*

The notion of income just used to calculate GDP differs slightly from the way individuals commonly perceive income, and it is important to be aware of the distinction.

First, people are likely to include in their view of income any capital gains they earn. **Capital gains** are increases in the value of assets and accordingly do not represent production (output) in any way. The national income accounts used to calculate GDP, which are designed to focus on the production of goods and services, do not include capital gains.

Second, profits that are retained by a firm are included in national income, but individuals may not perceive these retained profits as part of their own income. Again, this is because the GDP accounts measure the value of production, and profits are part of the value of production, whether those profits are distributed to shareholders or retained by firms.

COMPARISON OF THE FINAL GOODS AND INCOME APPROACHES

Earlier we learned how to break down the output of the economy into four categories—consumption, investment, government expenditures, and net exports. We break down the income of the economy into three categories—payments to workers, consisting mainly of wages; payments to owners of capital, including profits, interest, and rents; and taxes. As Table 22.3 shows, the value of GDP is the same whether calculated in output or income terms.

That the value of output is equal to the value of income—that GDP measured either way is identical—is no accident. It is a consequence of the circular flow of the economy. What each firm receives from selling its goods must go back somewhere else into the economy—as wages, profits, interest, or taxes. The income to households flows back in turn either to firms—in consumption goods households purchase or in savings, which eventually are used to purchase plant and equipment by firms—or to government—in taxes or in newly issued government bonds. Similarly, the money spent by the government must have come from somewhere else in the economy—either from households or corporations as taxes or through borrowing.

Table 22.3 TWO APPROACHES TO U.K. GDP, 1996

Expenditure (£ millions)		Incomes (£ millions)	
Consumers' expenditure	473,509	Income from employment	400,354
Government expenditure	155,732	Self-employment income	69,898
Investment in fixed capital	114,623	Gross profits of companies	101,409
Investment in inventories	2,917	Gross profits of public corporations	3,959
Exports	217,147	Gross profits of general government enterprises	681
(−) Imports	(−) 222,603	Rent	63,850
Statistical discrepancy	975	Imputed charge for consumption of nontrading capital	4,333
GDP at market prices	742,300	(−) Stock appreciation	(−) 973
(−) Taxes on expenditure − subsidies	(−) 99,384	Statistical discrepancy	(−) 595
GDP at factor cost	642,916	GDP at factor cost	642,916

Source: Office of National Statistics, *Annual Abstract of Statistics* (1998), Table 14.1.

ALTERNATIVE MEASURES OF OUTPUT

Gross national product is a measure of the incomes of residents of a country, including income they receive from abroad (wages, returns on investment, interest payments) but not including similar payments made to those abroad. By contrast, GDP ignores income received from or paid overseas. It is thus a measure of the goods and services produced *within* the country.

The treatment of machines and other capital goods (buildings) is a problem in measuring national output. As machines are used to produce output, they wear out. Worn-out machines are a cost of production that should be balanced against total output.

As an example, consider a firm that has a machine worth £1,000 and uses that machine, with £600 of labour, to produce £2,000 worth of output. Furthermore, assume that at the end of the year the machine is completely worn out. The firm then has a *net* output of £400: £2,000 minus the labour costs *and* minus the value of the machine that has worn out.

ALTERNATIVE APPROACHES TO MEASURING NATIONAL OUTPUT

Measuring output of final goods

Value of final output:

Consumption + investment + government expenditures + net exports

Sum of value added in each stage of production

Measuring income

Employee compensation + profits, rents, interest + indirect taxes

Output = income

Table 22.3 gives data on U.K. GDP for 1996, using both the expenditure and income approaches. They are taken from the "Blue Book"—the U.K. *National Income and Expenditure Accounts*. At first sight the table looks slightly more complicated than the explanation of GDP in this chapter might suggest. On closer inspection the differences can easily be reconciled. The small differences illustrate the frequent observation that reality is slightly more complicated and messy than our theories would like it to be.

How does the table differ from the explanation of GDP in the text? On the expenditure side, we have seen that

GDP = consumption + investment + government expenditure + exports – imports.

In the table, investment is subdivided into two categories: fixed investment (new factory and office buildings, machinery, vehicles, and so on) and inventories (additional stocks of materials and work in progress acquired by firms). The separation is maintained because the two kinds of investment have different properties. Inventory investment is much more volatile than fixed investment. In addition, taxes net of subsidies have been subtracted from the measure of GDP at market prices to obtain a measure of GDP "at factor cost." As the name implies, GDP at market prices measures output using market prices that include VAT and excise duties and other indirect taxes (less any subsidies). GDP at factor cost measures output at prices that exclude these items.

Finally, on the expenditure side, there is an item "statistical discrepancy." This reflects the fact that the values for expenditure—consumers' expenditure, investment, government expenditure, and so on—are estimates. They are derived from surveys and are not accurate down to the last pound. While the value of GDP derived from measures of expenditure should in theory equal the value of GDP derived from measures of income, in practice the two figures generally differ. The statistical discrepancy allocates the differences to expenditure and income measures of GDP.

On the income side, we have seen that in principle

GDP = labour income + profits + interest payments + indirect taxes.

In the table, income from work (labour income) has been divided into income from employment and self-employment income. Profits have been subdivided according to the type of firm: companies, public corporations, and general government enterprises.

The item "imputed charge for consumption of nontrading capital" refers to the value of the services provided by houses, vehicles, and other goods that households own and, effectively, rent to themselves. This item is also included in the estimate of consumers' expenditure on the expenditure side of the accounts. Interest payments are included in rents.

"Stock appreciation" is deducted from the total because it forms a component of the profits reported by firms but it does not correspond to the production of goods or services. It merely reflects a rise in the prices of goods held in their inventories.

The reduction in the value of the machine is called the machine's **depreciation.** Since machines wear out at all sorts of different rates, accounting for how much the machines in the economy have depreciated is an extremely difficult problem. The GDP figures take the easy road and make no allowance for depreciation. The term *gross* in "gross domestic product" should serve as a reminder that the statistic covers all production. Economists sometimes use a separate measure that includes the effects of depreciation, called **net domestic product (NDP),** which subtracts an estimate of the value of depreciation from GDP:

NDP = GDP − depreciation.

The problem is that economists have little confidence in the estimates of depreciation. For this reason they usually use the GDP figure as the measure of the economy's output. Since GDP, GNP, and NDP go up and down together, for most purposes, it does not much matter which one you use as long as you are consistent.

MEASURING THE STANDARD OF LIVING

The GDP tells something about the overall level of a country's economic activity, the goods and services produced in market transactions. But it is only part of the measure of a society's overall well-being. Other social indicators are often employed for this, such as literacy rates (the percentage of the population that can read or write), infant mortality rates (the fraction of infants that die), and life expectancy.

GDP does not reflect environmental degradation which may accompany economic growth. And GDP statistics may be misleading: consider a poor country that decides to harvest its hardwood forests to increase its income. These forests take centuries to grow. Harvesting the forest increases the measured output of the economy but decreases the country's assets. The output is not sustainable. The United Nations is creating a new set of national accounts, called **Green GDP,** which attempts to incorporate some of the effects on the environment and natural resources. In the hardwood forest example, Green GDP would subtract from conventional GDP the decrease in the natural resource base. Policymakers would then know that the conventionally measured increase in GDP from cutting down the hardwood forest is short lived. It is based not on an addition to society's wealth but rather a subtraction from it.

UNEMPLOYMENT

Since the end of the Second World War, most governments have made full employment one of their main economic objectives. It is often asserted that everybody who wants to work and is capable of working should be able to get a job. In recent years, there has been a retreat from the objective of full employment to a more modest objective of a low level of unemployment. Full employment has turned out to be difficult to define and impossible to achieve.

There are several reasons why unemployment has been viewed as a social and economic problem. One reason is that, on almost anyone's definition, unemployment represents a waste of resources for the economy as a whole. If the unemployed were employed, the production of goods and services in the economy would be higher. Government spending on unemployment benefits would be lower, and the tax rates needed to finance government spending might be lower. The people who would have been unemployed would be better off. Everybody could be made better off.

Another reason is that unemployed people suffer economic hardship. Unemployed persons often feel rejected by and alienated from the mainstream of society. Having a job is important to most people's self-esteem. Family relationships may be put under strain by unemployment. There is evidence that unemployment and poverty are associated with poor health. Young workers who are unemployed appear to be more likely to end up involved in crime and do not develop basic work habits and skills; this leads to more economic and social problems in the future. Older workers who become unemployed have often found it difficult to get back into work, and have remained unemployed for long periods of time or have effectively been forced into early retirement. For a variety of reasons, which trade under the name "ageism," employers have been reluctant to take them on.

The problem of unemployment has been magnified because of its concentration in particular regions or among particular groups of people. Unemployment has often been concentrated in particular regions or towns, when a major industry or firm has shut down: coal and steel in South Wales, the textile industries in Lancashire and Yorkshire, and shipbuilding on the Tyne and the Clyde, to take some examples from Britain. The local concentration of unemployment caused by a large firm's closing down affects the whole local economy. Other local firms tend to contract or go bankrupt, because they lose business. Branches of national companies—the banks and high-street shops—might also close down. These knock-on effects cause more local unemployment. Residents of regions affected this way have found their wealth further diminished by falling values of local property. The concentration of unem-

ployment among young, unskilled male workers, particularly near the centres of large cities and among various racial minority groups, accentuates the social and economic problems that unemployment creates. All these factors have contributed to the regional problem in Britain and other industrial countries. They all add to the pressure on governments to do something about unemployment.

Before developing policies, however, it is wise to try to understand how the economy works at the macro level. Otherwise, to pursue the medical analogy, the cure may be worse than the disease.

MEASUREMENTS AND DEFINITIONS OF UNEMPLOYMENT

Generally speaking *unemployment* occurs when people who want to and are able to work cannot find a job. This definition is not absolutely clear-cut. It does not lead to an unambiguous and universally agreed measurement of the number of people unemployed. The extent of the disagreement, as we shall see, shows up in arguments about what the true rate of unemployment is.

In Britain until 1998 the most widely publicised and used figures for unemployment were those produced by the Department of Employment based on the number of people claiming unemployment-related benefits, as a percentage of the total workforce. This is the so-called claimant count measure of unemployment. The workforce consists of employees ("employees in employment"), the self-employed, persons on work-related government job-training schemes (mainly Youth Training [YT] and the Job Training Scheme [JTS]), the armed services, and the unemployed. Table 22.4 shows the numbers of men and women in these categories of the workforce in the United Kingdom in 1997. Since in 1997 there were 1,600,000 unemployed persons and 28,107,000 in the workforce, the unemployment rate was 1,600/28,107, or 5.69 percent. (This was roughly the lowest unemployment rate since 1980.)

Table 22.4 THE LABOUR FORCE IN THE UNITED KINGDOM, MID-JUNE 1997

	Total	Male	Female
Workforce	28,107,000	15,515,000	12,592,000
Unemployed	1,600,000	1,222,000	377,000
H.M. Forces	210,000	195,000	15,000
Self-employed	3,338,000	2,487,000	851,000
Employees in employment	22,792,000	11,507,000	11,285,000
Work-related government training programmes	167,000	104,000	64,000

Source: Office of National Statistics, *Annual Abstract of Statistics* (1998), Table 6.1.

The definitions used in calculating the official unemployment figures (based on the claimant count) in Britain were changed frequently in the 1980s, generally with the effect of reducing the official unemployment rate. As a result this became a somewhat discredited and politicised statistic. Many people claimed that it underrepresents "true" unemployment, by excluding some people who are unemployed in terms of the preceding definition. That is, they want to work at existing wages and are looking for work. For example, men over the age of 60 who have been unemployed for over a year are excluded from the figures. They are treated as having left the labour force. People who are not eligible for unemployment benefits cannot be included in the official figures even if they are available for and looking for work. This excludes those persons whose spouses work and who have been unemployed for over a year when the family income is high enough to exclude them from social security benefits. These exclusions reduce the official figure below the true figure.

However, other factors cause the official figure to be too high. It includes people who are receiving benefits, even if they do not want to work at the available wage rates, and merely give the appearance of looking for work to satisfy the (increasingly strict) criteria laid down by the benefit offices. On the basis of the definition, these people should not be counted as unemployed.

An alternative method of measuring unemployment is to carry out a survey, as is done in the United States. A representative sample of households is asked whether any members of it are currently seeking work. This method avoids some of the shortcomings of the method based on the number of people claiming benefits but introduces some new ones of its own. It includes people who claim to be looking for work, even if they are in fact not doing so. It excludes discouraged workers, people who have given up looking for work because the prospects of finding it seem so poor. These are often people who have been unemployed a long time.

In the United Kingdom, surveys have been carried out since the early 1980s, and they give a different measure of unemployment than the figures based on the claimant count. During the 1980s, the unemployment figure based on surveys of the labour force (and published by the Organization for Economic Cooperation and Development [OECD]) were generally between 1 and 2 percent higher. This discrepancy illustrates that there is no unambiguously correct measurement of the rate of unemployment.

In 1998 the Office of National Statistics began to publish a quarterly unemployment rate based on the labour force survey, using concepts and definitions that meet internationally agreed standards. The figures obtained using the International Labour Office (ILO) definition of unemployment have now replaced the old claimant count figures. Figure 22.3 shows the two series from the first quarter of 1995 to the third quarter of 1998. It confirms that the claimant count tends to be between 1 and 1.5 percent lower than the ILO-survey-based measure of unemployment.

HOW MUCH UNEMPLOYMENT IS THERE?

Figure 22.4 shows the unemployment rate in the United Kingdom between 1915 and 1990. (There is an observation missing in 1919, and there are two breaks in the series—one in 1939 and the other in 1980—because definitions were changed.) The

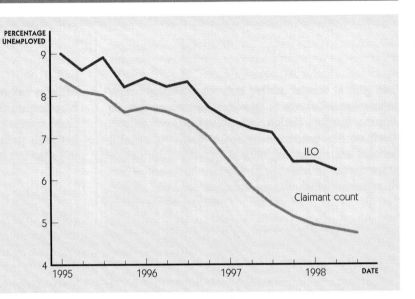

Figure 22.3 ILO VERSUS CLAIMANT UNEMPLOYMENT IN THE UNITED KINGDOM, QUARTERLY

The new ILO measures of unemployment tend to be about 1 to 1.5 percent higher than the claimant count.

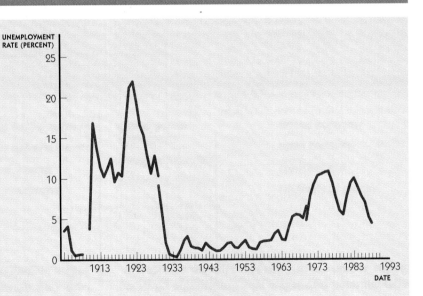

**Figure 22.4
UNEMPLOYMENT IN THE UNITED KINGDOM, 1913–1998**

Unemployment was generally above 10 percent between 1920 and 1939. It was then very low during the 1950s and 1960s. But it was drifting slowly upwards and has been much higher in the 1980s and 1990s. *Sources:* Mitchell, *British Historical Statistics;* Office of National Statistics, *Annual Abstract of Statistics* (1998).

slump in the 1920s and 1930s stands out very clearly. Unemployment rarely fell below 10 percent between the wars and was above 20 percent in 1931 and 1932. From the Second World War until 1975 unemployment never rose above 5 percent. In retrospect, this period now looks like a golden age of low unemployment. (This was also a period of low inflation and rapid economic growth.) It is worth noting, however, that even in this period, when the numbers unemployed fell as low as 264,500 in 1955, unemployment never fell to zero: there have always been some people unemployed. A third period, starting in 1980, shows an upward jump in unemployment relative to the preceding period. Since 1980, unemployment has sometimes exceeded 10 percent and has never fallen below 5 percent. Unemployment in 1990 was 1,618,000, its lowest for a decade, and had risen above 3 million by 1993.

Figure 22.5 compares unemployment in several countries over the 1980s. Some European countries, including the United Kingdom and France, had high unemployment throughout the period. For these countries, unemployment in the 1980s was much higher than at any time since the Second World War. This increase in unemployment pre-

sented a great problem: how to explain it and how to get back to the sustained low unemployment rates of the 1950s and 1960s. The United States has had on average slightly lower unemployment rates than these countries. Also, the 1980s do not look as bad in the United States, compared with its own history, as they do in Britain and France. Meanwhile, some countries, including Japan and Sweden, maintained very low unemployment rates, between 1 and 4 percent throughout the 1980s. How have they done it? The question this raises is whether other countries could, or would wish to, achieve such low rates of unemployment. Why, in 1999, was 4.5 percent unemployment seen as a crisis in Japan while 6 percent in Britain was a cause for rejoicing?

These figures show the great variety that exists in the experience of unemployment over time and across countries.

FORMS OF UNEMPLOYMENT

It is useful to distinguish between different kinds of unemployment. Before Christmas, there is a de-

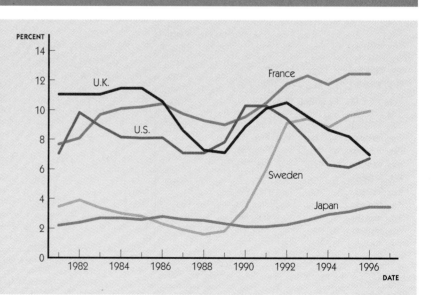

Figure 22.5 STANDARDISED UNEMPLOYMENT RATES

Much of Europe, including the United Kingdom and France, has suffered high unemployment. The United States has had slightly less. Japan has maintained much lower rates. Sweden's enviable record of low unemployment came to an end in the 1990s, and Sweden now shares Europe's high rates. *Source:* OECD, *Labour Force Statistics*, 1998.

FORMS OF UNEMPLOYMENT

Seasonal	Structural
Frictional	Cyclical

mand for sales staff to work in department stores. Building work slows down in the winter because of the weather. Tourism increases in the summer, and so does the number of jobs that cater to tourists. Unemployment that varies with the seasons is called **seasonal unemployment.** Since these movements in employment and unemployment reflect normal seasonal patterns, the unemployment rate you see reported on the news is adjusted according to the average amount of seasonal unemployment. These adjustments are called seasonal adjustments. Thus, if, on average, the unadjusted unemployment rate is normally 0.4 percent lower in the summer than at other times, the seasonally adjusted unemployment rate for July will be the measured unemployment rate plus 0.4 percent.

While workers in building, agriculture, and tourism regularly face seasonal unemployment, other workers become unemployed only as part of a normal transition from one job to another. This kind of unemployment is referred to as **frictional unemployment.** If people could move from job to job instantaneously, there would be no frictional unemployment. In a dynamic economy, with some industries growing and others declining, there will always be movements from one job to another, and hence there will always be frictional unemployment.

Some unemployment occurs because the location of the unemployed does not match the location of available jobs or because the skills of the unemployed do not match the skills needed for vacant jobs. This kind of unemployment is often called **structural unemployment.** Substantial structural unemployment is found quite often side by side with job vacancies, because the unemployed lack the skills required for the newly created jobs. For example, there may be vacancies for computer programmers, while building workers are unemployed. By

the same token, there may be labour shortages in those parts of the economy that are expanding (as in the southeast) and unemployment in areas that are suffering decline (as in the old industrial areas of South Wales, the midlands, and the North).

Unemployment that increases when the economy goes into a recession and decreases when the economy goes into a boom is called **cyclical unemployment** and is the fundamental concern of this part of the book. Government policy has tended to be aimed at reducing both the frequency and magnitude of this kind of unemployment, by reducing the frequency and magnitude of the recessions that give rise to it. Government also seeks to reduce its impact, by providing unemployment compensation for those temporarily thrown out of work.

As the economy goes into a recession, the demand for labour—the number of hours to be worked—decreases; if the decreased demand were spread uniformly among all workers, the social disruption would be limited; but in fact, most workers have a slight reduction in work, while a few workers simply lose their jobs. And unskilled workers and minorities are especially likely to become unemployed. Unemployment rates among these groups often soar in a downturn.

INFLATION

In the 1920s, the price of a pint of beer was a few pence. In 1968 it was around 2 shillings (10p). Now it is roughly £2. This steady price rise is no anomaly. Most other goods have undergone similar increases over time. This increase in the general level of prices is called **inflation.** While unemployment tends to be concentrated in certain groups within the population, everyone is affected by inflation. Thus, it is not surprising that when inflation becomes high, it almost always rises to the top of the political agenda.

It is not inflation if the price of only one good goes up. It *is* inflation if the prices of *most* goods go up. The **inflation rate** is the rate at which the *general level* of prices increases.

MEASURING INFLATION

If the prices of all goods rose by the same proportion, say by 5 percent, over a period of a year, measuring inflation would be easy: the rate of inflation for that year would be 5 percent. The difficulties arise from the fact that the prices of different goods rise at different rates, and some goods even decline in price. To determine the change in the overall price level, economists calculate the *average* percentage increase in prices. But since some goods loom much larger in the typical consumer's budget than others, this calculation must reflect the relative purchases of different goods. A change in the price of housing, for example, is much more important than a change in the price of pencils. If the price of pencils goes down by 5 percent but the price of housing goes up by 5 percent, the overall measure of the price level should go up.

Economists have a straightforward way of reflecting the differing importance of different goods. They ask, what would it cost consumers to purchase the same bundle of goods this year that they bought last year? If, for example, it cost £5,500 in 1996 to buy what it cost consumers only £5,000 to purchase in 1995, we say that prices, *on average,* have risen by 10 percent. Such results are frequently expressed in the form of a **price index,** which, for ease of comparison, measures the price level in any given year relative to a common base year.

The price index for the base year is, by definition, 100. The price index for any other year is calculated by taking the ratio of the price level in that year to the price level in the base year and multiplying it by 100. For example, if 2000 is our base year and we want to know the price index for 2001, we first calculate the ratio of the cost of a certain bundle of goods in 2001 (£5,500) to the cost of the same bundle of goods in 2000 (£5,000), which is 1.1. The price index in 2001 is therefore 1.1 × 100 = 110. The index of 110, using 2000 as a base, means that prices are 10 percent higher, on average, in 2001 than in 2000.

There are several different price indices, each using a different bundle of goods. To track the movement of prices that are important to households, the government collects price data on the bundle of goods that represents how the average household spends its income. This index is called the **retail price index,** or **RPI.** To determine this bundle, the results of the family expenditure survey are used.

EXPERIENCE WITH INFLATION IN THE UNITED KINGDOM

Figure 22.6 shows the inflation rate between 1915 and 1995. There is a clear upward drift in inflation from 1921 to 1995, which is evident despite the many short-term fluctuations in the inflation rate. As with unemployment rates, there are again a number of periods that can be identified. In the first, inflation was volatile after the end of the First World War. High inflation between 1915 and 1919 was followed by rapidly falling prices in 1920 to 1921. In the second period, running from 1924 until 1937, when unemployment was very high, the price level was actually falling for much of the time. In the third period, which ran from 1940 until 1972, inflation was always under 10 percent and mostly under 5 percent—the golden age again. In the fourth period, from 1973 until the present, things went bad from the inflation perspective. Inflation was never higher than in 1974–75 when it reached almost 25 percent. It has fallen since then to lower levels.

The rise in inflation in the 1970s was common to many countries. Something very similar happened in the rest of Europe and in the United States. Nevertheless, these inflation rates appear very small beside Germany's 1923 experience with inflation, that of some Latin American countries at various times, and that of Israel. Between 1980 and 1990, inflation averaged nearly 400 percent a year in Bolivia and over 100 percent a year in Israel. In Japan, on the other hand, it was only 1.3 percent.

Figure 22.6 **INFLATION RATE IN THE UNITED KINGDOM, 1915–1995**

The inflation rate has drifted upwards but there are many short-term fluctuations.
Source: Retail price index, Office of National Statistics, *Economic Trends,* Annual Supplement (1998).

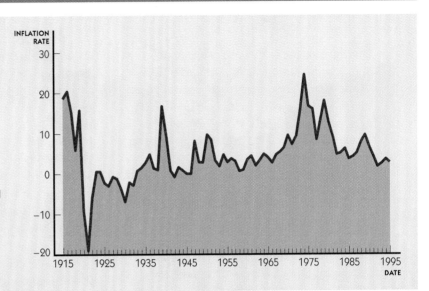

THE IMPORTANCE OF INFLATION

Why does inflation matter? There can be no doubt that it matters to politicians, who have made a fetish of zero inflation. At times since 1979 policy seems to have been driven by nothing else. Policies with the stated aim of "squeezing inflation out of the system" or "continuing to bear down on the rate of inflation" have been pursued almost to the complete exclusion of other objectives. Politicians express concern about inflation because doing so wins them votes, and so some voters presumably dislike inflation.

Nevertheless, for some people, inflation has brought benefits rather than costs. People with mortgages on their houses have gained from inflation. The values of houses have risen relative to the value of the debts owed to the banks and building societies, leaving owners better off. (The higher interest rates and repayments on mortgages, which have often accompanied higher inflation, have not wiped out this gain.) Workers generally have not lost from inflation, because wages have, as a rule, risen by more than prices. Persons receiving state benefits and pensions have been protected against inflation

by the *indexation* of benefits to the price level, a process of building in an automatic increase in benefits to preserve their purchasing power when prices rise.

There are several arguments to the effect that inflation imposes costs on society. One is that unexpected inflation causes transfers of wealth from lenders to borrowers when the value of loans or credits is fixed in money terms, because the real value of the loan is reduced by the rise in prices. The number of hours that the borrower has to work or the quantity of produce he must sell to pay back the loan falls when prices (and wages) rise. When inflation is both more variable and more unpredictable, then borrowing and lending become more risky activities. This may affect saving and the accumulation of wealth in the economy.

In Britain, the argument is often made that inflation has made housing attractive relative to other forms of investment, because of the way that the tax subsidies to housing are increased by inflation. This has resulted in there being too large a stock of houses and too little industrial capital, and thereby contributed to Britain's low productivity.

A second argument is that inflation may make the

USING ECONOMICS:
CALCULATING THE RETAIL PRICE INDEX

Encapsulating the movements of many prices into a single figure, an index, provides an easy way to look at price trends over time. Suppose that in 1995 an average household spent £500 per month to buy a basket of goods. Assume that in 2000 it cost £600 to buy the same basket of goods. Then the price index for 2000 is just the ratio of the cost in 2000 to the cost in 1995, multiplied by 100. That is,

RPI for 2000 = (600/500) × 100 = 120.

This says that 120 is the price index for 2000, taking 1995 as the base year. (The index for 1995 itself, using 1995 as the base year is obviously 100.) Alternatively, prices have risen by 20 percent.

The advantage of a price index is that once there is an index number for each year, then the price level in that year can be compared with the price level in any other year. The retail price index for 1947 was 7.50, while in 1994 it was 144.1 (taking 1987 as the base year). Prices in 1994 were therefore 100 × (144.1/7.50) = 1,921 percent of the 1947 level; they had risen by 1,921 percent in the intervening period. The following figure shows the retail price Index from 1915 to 1995 using 1987 as the base year. It shows that there has been a roughly thirtyfold increase in prices over the whole period, most of which has occurred since 1945.

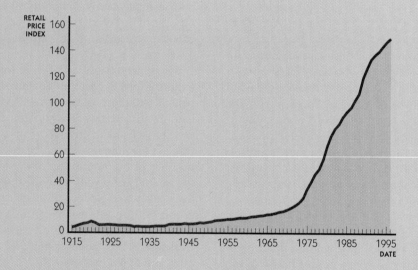

price system less efficient in guiding resources to the best uses, by increasing the variability of relative prices. When there is no inflation, the prices of individual goods are likely not to change frequently or by very much when they do change. People can keep in mind a fairly clear idea as to how much things cost. If a loaf of bread has cost 80 pence for the last ten years, then a 70 pence loaf is clearly a bargain and may be expected to attract a lot of demand.

When prices are increasing quickly, relative prices of goods tend to change all the time, because not all shops put up all their prices by the same proportion at the same time. When average prices are rising at 5 percent a month (to take a fairly extreme example), some months the price of bread in some shops may go up by 20 percent, and some months not change at all. With the prices of all goods doing the same thing—sometimes rising by a large amount, then staying unchanged for a while—relative prices tend to fluctuate a lot.

It is then much harder for people to keep in mind a clear idea of what things normally cost relative to each other. They will tend to respond less to price incentives, because they will be less able to spot them. The efficacy of relative prices in guiding the allocation of resources will be reduced. In addition, greater variability of relative prices may cause people to spend more time trying to find out what normal prices are and looking for bargains, causing more resources to be wasted.

ALTERNATIVE MEASURES OF INFLATION

The retail price index is one measure of inflation, based on what the average consumer pays. Other price indices can be calculated using different market baskets. A different measure of prices is the **producer price index** (or **wholesale price index**), which measures the average level of prices of goods sold by producers. This index is useful because it gives us an idea of what will happen to consumer prices in the near future. Usually, if producers are receiving higher prices from their sales to wholesalers, eventually retailers will have to charge higher prices. This will be reflected in a higher retail price index.

Earlier in the chapter we observed that real GDP is nominal GDP adjusted for the price level. The price index we use for calculating real GDP is called the **GDP deflator.** It represents a comparison between what it would cost to buy the total mix of goods and services in the economy today and in a base year. In other words, the GDP deflator is a weighted average of the prices of different goods and services, where the weights represent the importance of each of the goods and services in GDP.

CONNECTING THE THREE MAJOR VARIABLES

Often the major macroeconomic variables move together in systematic ways. For example, when the economy is in a recession, as it was in 1992, unemployment tends to be higher, inflation tends to be lower, and growth comes to a standstill. These connections make sense. After all, when the economy is suffering hard times, businesses reduce their output, lay off workers, and do not hire new workers. In addition, businesses that are having a hard time selling products in a competitive market are less likely to raise prices.

FLOWS AND STOCKS

The GDP, GNP, and NDP are all measures of output *per year*. Rate measurements such as these are called **flows.** When a news report says, "The quarterly GDP figures, just released, show that GDP was £700 billion per year," it does not mean that £700 billion of goods and services was produced during the quarter. Rather, it means that £175 billion was produced during the quarter, so that if that rate of production were maintained for a whole year, the total value of goods and services would be £700 billion.

Price indices have come to play an increasingly important role in economic life, in spite of the dry, technical flavour that seems to pervade most discussion of them. Various social security benefits, such as the National Insurance Retirement Pension, are uprated annually in line with the rise in the retail price index. Income tax brackets and allowances are also revised in the light of the increase in the RPI. Perhaps most spectacularly, the Bank of England's Monetary Policy Committee (MPC) sets interest rates so as to achieve a target 2.5 percent per year rate of increase in the RPI (to be precise, in the RPI excluding mortgage interest payments, the RPIX, as it is known). Therefore if the RPI overstates the rate of inflation, the real incomes of old age pensioners rise (which might, of course, be a very good thing, since the pension is set at a level that most people think is unreasonably low) and real inflation-adjusted income tax payments fall. Both these things tend to increase the government's borrowing. Also, if the RPI overstates inflation, it may cause the MPC to raise interest rates too much, in the belief that inflation is above the target when in fact it is not.

There are three reasons why the RPI may overstate inflation. The first is the "fixed basket" problem. The RPI is calculated by comparing how much it costs to purchase a particular basket of goods that represents an average consumer's expenditure pattern. But expenditure patterns change steadily over time, while the market basket is revised relatively infrequently. As people buy more of the goods which have become relatively less expensive and fewer of those which have become relatively more expensive, the

index increasingly overweights goods whose relative prices are rising.

The second problem is with quality adjustments. New products that can do new better things than older products constantly enter the market. To compare the prices of the new products with the old, some quality adjustment has to be made. If the price goes up by 10 percent but the product lives longer and does better than the old one, in a real sense the price increase is less than 10 percent and may even be a price reduction. The quality adjustments may sometimes be easy: one machine can do what two machines did before. But usually the comparisons are difficult. If we measure the quality of computers by calculations per minute, memory, and disk storage, the rate of decrease in computer prices is phenomenal. But even this does not fully reflect the quality improvement. We can do things with the computer now that were unimaginable 25 years ago at any price. And how do we treat a new drug that cures a previously incurable disease?

Statisticians attempt to measure quality changes and make appropriate adjustments. Nevertheless, there is a suspicion that the RPI overstates the true rate of inflation. The same concerns have arisen in the United States where it is believed that the Consumer Price Index (the CPI, the U.S. equivalent of the RPI used in the United Kingdom) overstates inflation by 1/2 to 1 percent per year. The U.K. Office of National Statistics is refining methods for measuring quality changes, especially for services where the problems are particularly acute.

Flow statistics need to be contrasted with **stock** statistics, which measure an item at a single point in time. Among the most important stocks is the capital stock—the total value of all the buildings and machines that underlie the productive potential of the economy.

The relationships between stocks and flows are simple. The stock of capital at the end of 1996, for example, consists of the stock of capital at the end of 1995 plus or minus the flows into or out of this stock during 1996. Investment is the flow into the capital stock. Depreciation is the flow out of the capital stock.

Similarly, we can look at the *number* of unemployed individuals as a stock. This number at the end of 1996 consists of the number at the end of 1995 plus or minus the flows into or out of the unemployment pool during 1996. Layoffs, dismissals, resignations, and new entry into the labour force can be thought of as flows into the unemployment pool; new hires represent flows out of the unemployment pool.

REVIEW AND PRACTICE

SUMMARY

1 The three central macroeconomic policy objectives of the government are low unemployment, low inflation, and high growth. Macroeconomics studies how these aggregate variables change as a result of household and business behaviour and how government policy may affect them.

2 The period between 1950 and 1973 appears in retrospect to have been a golden age of low unemployment, low inflation, and rapid economic growth. For the United Kingdom, and also for continental Europe, North America, and Japan, it stands out clearly from both the preceding and following periods.

3 Gross domestic product is the typical way of measuring national output. Real GDP adjusts GDP for changes in the price level.

4 The GDP can be calculated in three ways: the final goods approach, which adds the value of all final goods produced in the economy; the value-added approach, which adds the difference between firms' revenues and costs of intermediate goods; and the income approach, which adds together all income received by those in the economy. All three methods give the same answer.

5 Unemployment imposes costs both on individuals and on society as a whole, which loses what the unemployed workers could have contributed and ends up supporting them in other ways.

6 Seasonal unemployment, such as building in areas with harsh winters, occurs regularly depending on the season. Frictional unemployment results from people's being in transition between one job and another. Structural unemployment refers to the unemployment generated as the structure of the economy changes, so that the new jobs being created have requirements different from the old jobs being lost. Cyclical unemployment increases or decreases with the level of economic activity.

7 The inflation rate is the percentage increase of the price level from one year to the next. In different countries at different times, inflation has sometimes been very high, with prices' increasing by factors of tens or hundreds in a given year.

8 The amount of inflation between two years is measured by the percentage change in the amount it would cost to buy a given basket of goods in those years. Different baskets define different price indexes, such as the retail price index and the producer price index.

9 Many macroeconomic variables seem to move together in systematic ways. For example, in a boom, unemployment tends to fall, inflation tends to rise, and productivity tends to rise. In a recession, the reverse happens.

10 Economists distinguish between flows—such as output per year—and stocks—such as the stock of capital.

KEY TERMS

unemployment rate	recession	net domestic product (NDP)	cyclical unemployment
inflation	business cycles	Green GDP	retail price index
gross domestic product (GDP)	value added	labour force participation rate	deflation
real GDP	capital gains		producer price index or wholesale price index
nominal GDP	gross national product (GNP)	seasonal unemployment	GDP deflator
boom	depreciation	frictional unemployment	flows
		structural unemployment	stocks

REVIEW QUESTIONS

1 What are the three main goals of macroeconomic policy?

2 What is the difference between nominal GDP and real GDP?

3 What is the difference between the final outputs approach to measuring GDP, the value-added approach, and the income approach?

4 What is the difference between GDP, GNP, and NDP?

5 What has happened in the last two decades to the rate of change of productivity?

6 What is the difference between frictional unemployment, seasonal unemployment, structural unemployment, and cyclical unemployment?

7 When there is a reduction in the number of hours worked in the economy, is this normally shared equally by all workers? Are workers in some groups more affected by increased unemployment than those in other groups?

8 When the prices of different goods change at different rates, how do we measure the rate of inflation?

9 Are all groups of people affected equally by inflation? Why or why not?

PROBLEMS

1 Geoffrey spends his pocket money on three things: hamburgers, magazines, and video rentals. He has £30 per month to spend on them, and he rents 4 videos at £2 each, buys 5 hamburgers at £2 each, and buys 4 magazines at £3 each. Setting the current value of the price index to 100, calculate a Geoffrey Price Index (GPI) for this basket of goods for the three following cases:

(a) The price of videos goes up to £3.
(b) The price of videos goes up to £3 and the price of hamburgers falls by 40 pence.

(c) The price of videos goes up to £3, the price of hamburgers falls by 40 pence, and the price of a magazine rises to £4.

2 An increase in the retail price index will often affect different groups in different ways. Think about how different groups will purchase items like housing, travel, or food in the RPI basket, and explain why they will be affected differently by increases in the overall RPI. How would you calculate an urban RPI or a rural RPI?

3 Given the following information about the U.K. economy, how much did the U.K. implicit GDP deflator rise between 1965 and 1975? Between 1975 and 1985?

	1965	1970	1975	1980	1985	1990
Nominal GDP (£ billions)	31.5	44.0	95.7	201.0	306.7	477.7
Real GDP at 1985 prices	205.3	232.8	257.6	278.2	306.7	356.3

4 Much of this chapter has discussed how economists adjust the data to find what they want to know, for example, adjusting for inflation or dividing by the population level. What adjustments might you suggest for analysing education expenditures? Social security expenditures?

5 Firms typically do not fire workers quickly as the economy goes into a recession, at least not in proportion to the reduction in their output. How might you expect output per worker and output per hour to move over the business cycle?

23

THE FULL-EMPLOYMENT MODEL

I f we look at history in decades, the market economy creates jobs for almost all who seek them. The economic theories in the next part of the book explain why there are important episodes in which markets fail to create enough jobs and what the government can do about them. In this part of the book, we will see how the economy works in the long run, when it creates jobs at the rate of new entry into the labour force. We focus on the aggregate behaviour of the economy—on movements of such macroeconomic variables as output and wages—when resources are fully employed. We show how competitive markets, when they work well, help explain the vitality of the economy.

KEY QUESTIONS

1 In an economy operating at full employment, what determines the real wage, level of output, and investment?

2 How is the economy affected by government expenditures and international trade? When government increases its expenditures but raises taxes to pay for the increased expenditures, what happens to investment? How might the answer differ between a small country like Switzerland, a medium sized country like the United Kingdom, and a large country like the United States?

3 How are markets in the economy interlinked?

MACROECONOMIC EQUILIBRIUM

The model we employ here is the basic competitive model of Part Two. In it, large numbers of households and firms interact in the labour, product, and capital markets. Households supply labour to firms that use the labour to produce goods and compensate workers by paying them wages. Households also save, and those savings finance firms' investments such as the plant and equipment that firms need to produce. For the use of their funds, households receive interest and dividends from firms. With the income they earn from working and the return they earn from their savings, households buy the products that firms produce.

Two key lessons emerge from the basic competitive model. First, all markets are interrelated. What goes on in one market has an impact on others. The demand for labour, for instance, depends on the level of output (the product market). Second, wages, interest rates, and prices adjust to equate demand and supply. In this part of the book, we continue to focus on labour, product, and capital markets and to assume that the adjustments in wages, interest rates, and prices are sufficiently rapid that, for practical purposes, all markets are always in equilibrium. That is, they all clear, with demand equal to supply. This assumption is not only a convenient starting point, but it gives us powerful insights into some of the basic macroeconomic questions. We began the chapter with the observation that *somehow* the economy creates jobs for the millions of new entrants into the labour force each year. It has done this without any government official or private individual managing the whole process. The magic of the market—the adjustment of wages and prices equilibrating the labour market—guides this process, and the model we present here explains how this happens.

The analysis here differs in one important way from the kind of microeconomic analysis we have seen previously. In macroeconomics, we focus on aggregates, on total output, rather than the output of individual products. We focus on total employment and on average prices, which we refer to as the price level. We also proceed as if there is a single good being produced or a single kind of labour. That is, we can picture the economy as if all firms produce the same commodity and all workers are identical. In looking at these aggregates, we ignore the richness of the microeconomic detail we dealt with earlier. Hidden behind an increase in the price level are a myriad of changes in relative prices. Some prices have gone up faster than this average, some have gone up more slowly, and some may have even decreased. The basic premise of macroeconomics is that we can say a great deal about the aggregates without inquiring into the smaller details.

THE LABOUR MARKET

By assumption, in the basic competitive model, all markets clear. In the labour market, the fact that the demand for labour equals the supply implies that there is full employment. No worker who wishes to get a job (for which she is qualified) at the going market wage will fail to get one. Adjustments in wages ensure that this will occur. Of course, when economists say that there is full employment of the labour force—that the demand for labour is equal to the supply—there may still be a large amount of unemployment as conventionally measured. As we learned in Chapter 22, there is always some frictional unemployment in modern economies, as workers in transition between jobs or just entering the labour force search for new positions. Some people may be able to get more social security benefits than they could get wages. Thus, full employment should not be equated with an unemployment rate of zero.

The assumption of zero unemployment, while it is clearly unrealistic, is a useful simplification, particularly for studying changes in the economy in periods in which unemployment is relatively low or for comparing the economy at different periods in which unemployment was low, such as 1989 and 1999.

In the aggregate labour market, the relationship between wages (w) and the price level (P) is very important. Economists distinguish between real and nominal wages. The real wage is the nominal wage adjusted for increases in the price level. Dividing the nominal wage by the price level gives us the real wage, or w/P. This means that if wages and the price level change together, the real wage will remain the same. For example, suppose that nominal wages and the price level both increase by 2 percent during the

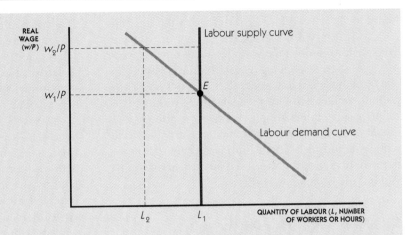

Figure 23.1 EQUILIBRIUM IN THE LABOUR MARKET

Equilibrium in the labour market is at the intersection of the aggregate demand and supply curves for labour. If the real wage is above w_1/P, where demand equals supply, there will be unemployment, putting pressure on wages to fall as workers compete to offer their services. Below w_1/P, there will be excess demand for labour, which will put pressure on wages to rise.

course of a year. The real wage would be exactly the same as it was at the beginning of the year, because the increase in the nominal wage would be offset by a proportional increase in prices. Alternatively, if the price level is held constant, changes in the nominal wage represent changes in the real wage, and if the nominal wage is held constant while the price level increases (or decreases), the real wage will fall (or rise).

Figure 23.1 shows the aggregate labour market, with the real wage (w/P) on the vertical axis, the quantity of labour (L) on the horizontal axis, and the aggregate demand and supply curves for labour. With a given set of machines and technology, the aggregate demand for labour depends on the wages firms must pay, the prices firms receive for the goods they produce, and the prices they have to pay for other inputs, including raw materials and machines. Holding the prices of goods and inputs constant, the aggregate demand curve traces out the quantity of labour demanded by firms at different wages. At lower wages, the quantity of labour demanded is greater. There are two reasons for this. First, as wages fall relative to the cost of machines, it pays firms to substitute workers for machines. Second, as the wage falls, labour becomes relatively less expensive compared with the price of the goods it produces (so at the old level of employment, the value of the marginal product of the last unit of labour hired would exceed the wage), and

again employers will hire more workers. Thus, the demand curve for labour slopes down, as shown in the diagram.

Figure 23.1 also shows an aggregate labour supply curve. To simplify matters, we assume that labour supply is inelastic.[1] That is, individuals are either in the labour force, working a full (40-hour) work week, or they are not. They do not enter and exit the market as wages go up and down, nor do they reduce or increase the hours they work in response to such changes. One advantage of making the assumption that the hours worked per week is fixed is that we can put *either* the number of hours worked (per week) or the number of workers hired on the horizontal axis of Figure 23.1. The demand and supply of labour hours (per week) is simply 40 times the demand and supply of workers.

Basic supply and demand analysis implies that market equilibrium should occur at the intersection of the demand and supply curves, point E. The rea-

---

[1] Recall the definition of elasticity from Chapter 5: the percentage change in quantity divided by the percentage change in price. Thus, an inelastic labour supply means that a 1 percent increase in price results in a small percentage increase in supply. A perfectly inelastic labour supply curve is vertical: that means the labour supply does not change at all when wages increase.

son for this is simple: if the wage happens to be above the equilibrium wage w_1/P, say at w_2/P, the demand for labour will be L_2, much less than the supply L_1. There will be an excess supply of workers. Those without jobs who want jobs will offer to work for less than the going wage, bidding down the wages of those already working. The process of competition will lead to lower wages, until eventually demand again equals supply. Likewise, if the wage is lower than w_1/P, say at w_3/P, firms in the economy will demand more labour than is supplied. Competing with one another for scarce labour services, they will bid the wage up to w_1/P.

SHIFTS IN THE DEMAND AND SUPPLY OF LABOUR

The basic competitive model makes clear predictions of the consequences of shifts in the demand and supply of labour. Consider first shifts in the supply curve of labour. This can occur because there are more young people reaching working age than there are old people retiring, because of new immigrants, or because of social changes that lead more women to join the labour force. The consequences of such a shift in the labour supply curve are de-

picted in Figure 23.2. The supply curve (here depicted as vertical) shifts to the right. The equilibrium real wage falls. The economy responds to the lower wages by creating more jobs. The wages (the price of labour) indicate to firms that labour is less scarce, in a sense, than it was before, and so firms should economise less in the use of labour.

Consider now the effects of a shift in the demand curve for labour. First consider the case of a decrease in investment leading to a reduction in the quantity of machines available for use by workers. This reduces the productivity of workers, thereby shifting the demand curve for labour to the left, as depicted in panel A of Figure 23.3. For a given real wage, firms want to hire fewer workers than before.

Panel B depicts the effects of technological progress on the demand for labour. Workers are more productive and the labour demand curve shifts to the right.

These examples suggest that increases in investment and technology imply an increase in the demand for labour represented by a rightward shift in the labour demand curve. Although this is generally true, it may be the case that the demand for some types of labour, especially unskilled labour, declines with investment in new machines and technology, while the demand for skilled workers increases. In

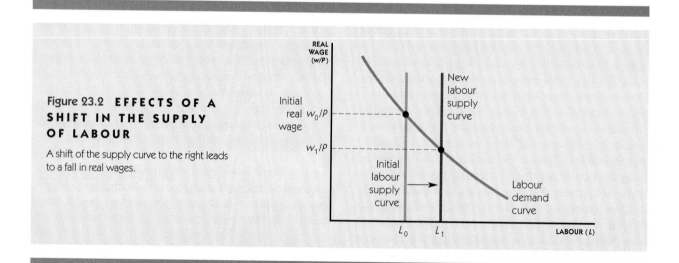

Figure 23.2 EFFECTS OF A SHIFT IN THE SUPPLY OF LABOUR

A shift of the supply curve to the right leads to a fall in real wages.

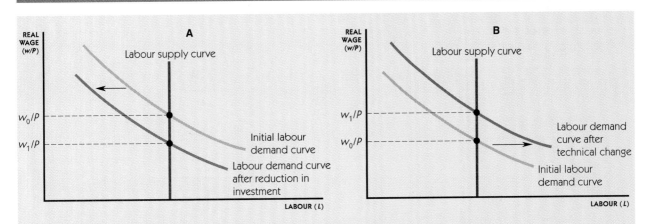

Figure 23.3 EFFECTS OF CHANGES IN INVESTMENT AND TECHNOLOGY

New investment or technological change shifts the demand curve for labour. Panel A shows a reduction in investment. Workers have fewer machines to work with, and the demand curve for labour shifts to the left, lowering real wages. Panel B shows an increase in technology. The demand curve shifts to the right, as workers' marginal productivity increases, leading to higher real wages.

this case, the labour market is really made up of two markets: that of skilled and that of unskilled workers. An increase in investment or technology may increase the demand for skilled workers as in panel B but decrease the demand for unskilled workers as in panel A. This represents one of the cases where merely studying the market for all labour is not sufficient to understand an interesting macroeconomic phenomenon—the increase in wage inequality based on skill levels.

THE PRODUCT MARKET

Just as the real wage adjusts to ensure that the demand for labour equals the supply, so too—in our basic competitive model—prices adjust to ensure that the demand for goods equals the supply.

LABOUR MARKET EQUILIBRIUM

Real wages adjust to equate labour demand with labour supply.

A rightward shift in labour supply lowers the real wage, inducing firms to create additional jobs equal to the increased labour supply.

Technological change or new investment induces changes in the real wage, so that all workers remain fully employed. The real wage adjusts to equate supply and demand.

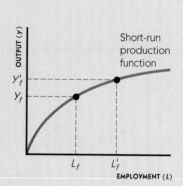

Figure 23.4 SHORT-RUN PRODUCTION FUNCTION

In the short run, with given technology and a given set of plant and equipment, as more labour is employed, output increases but with diminishing returns. (Each successive increase in input results in smaller increases in output.) The full-employment level of employment is L_f, so the full-employment level of output is Y_f. An increase in the labour supply generates a movement along the short-run production function; the full-employment level of output will increase to Y_f'.

AGGREGATE SUPPLY

At any point in time, the economy has a certain capital stock, a set of machines and buildings that, together with labour and materials, produces output. If more workers are hired, output increases. The relationship between employment and output is called the **short-run production function,** depicted in Figure 23.4. There are diminishing returns. As more workers are hired, output goes up but at a diminishing rate. The most productive machines are used first; if more labour is put to work, it is assigned to older and less productive machines.

We have been assuming that there is a fixed supply of labour. With this fixed supply of labour, the economy has a certain productive capacity, also referred to as the potential GDP or the **full-employment level of output.** This level of output is also referred to as the **aggregate supply.** It represents the amount of goods that firms would be willing to supply, given their plant and equipment, assuming wages and prices are flexible, and adjust so that everyone is fully employed.

Output can occasionally exceed capacity: for short spurts, such as during wars, output can be increased further, by deferring maintenance, running machines three shifts, and so forth.

If the labour supply increases, even with a fixed stock of machines, the capacity of the economy increases. This is a movement along the short-run production function. Figure 23.4 shows that if employment increases from L_f to L_f' then output increases from Y_f to Y_f'.

The **aggregate supply curve** gives the level of aggregate supply at each price level. Note that if real wages adjust to clear the labour market, then the level of aggregate supply does not depend at all on price. Thus, Figure 23.5 depicts the aggregate supply curve (sometimes referred to as the **long-run aggregate supply curve,** since it is based on the long-run assumption that labour markets clear) as vertical. We have seen that an increase in the labour force leads to a shift in the aggregate supply curve to the right, as depicted.[2]

AGGREGATE DEMAND AND EQUILIBRIUM OUTPUT

Aggregate demand is the sum total of the goods and services demanded by all the households, firms, and government in the economy, plus foreigners wishing to buy the country's goods and services. In Chapter

[2] Later, we will see how technological change and investment shift the short-run production function out, and even with a fixed labour supply, also shift the aggregate supply curve to the right.

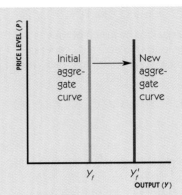

Figure 23.5 AGGREGATE SUPPLY CURVE

If real wages adjust to clear the market, the aggregate supply curve is vertical. If the labour force grows, the aggregate supply curve shifts to the right.

22, we divided aggregate output into four components: consumption, investment, government expenditures, and (net) exports. Analyses of aggregate demand thus focus on identifying the demand for each of these components.

The **aggregate demand curve** gives the quantity of goods and services demanded at each price level, and has the shape of the demand curves encountered earlier in this book. In particular, it is downward sloping, as depicted in Figure 23.6. The reason for this can be seen by focusing on consumption, which accounts for 70 percent of aggregate demand.

Households' demand for real consumption (that is, consumption taking into account changes in the price level) depends on their real wealth. When individuals are wealthier, they purchase more goods. An important part of individuals' wealth is their money and other financial assets denominated in pounds, for instance, savings bonds promising to pay a fixed sum of money after one or two years. When the price level increases, the real value of these assets decreases. Households' real wealth thus decreases and hence their consumption decreases. Higher price levels will be associated with lower levels of con-

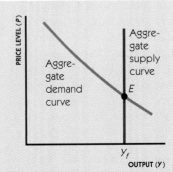

Figure 23.6 AGGREGATE DEMAND CURVE

The aggregate demand curve is downward sloping. Equilibrium in the product market occurs at the intersection of the aggregate demand and supply curves.

PRODUCT MARKET EQUILIBRIUM

In equilibrium, output is equal to the full-employment level of output, that is, the output that can be generated by the available labour force working with the given plant and equipment.

Increases in the labour supply (rightward shifts in the labour supply curve), increases in the stock of plant and equipment as a result of net investment, and technological change all increase the full-employment level of output.

sumption and lower levels of aggregate demand, as depicted in Figure 23.6.[3]

The equilibrium, the intersection of the aggregate demand and supply curves, determines the price level and output. Since we know that, in equilibrium, demand equals supply, and supply is fixed at Y_f, equilibrium output equals Y_f.

THE CAPITAL MARKET

We turn now to the capital market. Equilibrium in the capital market requires that savings (the supply of funds) equal investment (the demand for funds).

SAVINGS

The most important determinants of savings are income and interest rates. Each year, families have to decide how much of their income they spend on current consumption and how much they save for future consumption, for retirement, for emergencies, to pay for their children's college education, or to buy a new car or a new home. On average, families with higher incomes spend more and save more. Of course, what is relevant is how much income households have to spend; this is called their **disposable income**—their income after taxes. Thus,

when the government increases taxes, it reduces disposable income, and when disposable income is reduced, household savings are reduced.

In this chapter, we assume that the stock of plant and equipment as well as the labour supply are given. With wages and prices adjusting to ensure that the labour market clears, aggregate output is fixed. We now make use of an important result from Chapter 22: we saw there that national income equals aggregate output. The money that is used to purchase goods has to go into somebody's pockets, and thus becomes income. If aggregate output is given, so is aggregate income. Here, we also assume that taxes are fixed, so that with aggregate income given, aggregate disposable income is fixed.

With taxes fixed, our focus is on the interest rate, which is the return on savings. Figure 23.7 shows two different possibilities. In panel A, savings increase with the interest rate, while in panel B, savings respond only slightly to changes in the interest rate. Empirical studies suggest that savings are slightly sensitive to interest rates; that is, the savings curve is almost vertical. It looks more like panel B than panel A.

But doesn't a higher interest rate provide greater incentives to save? The answer is yes, but there is another effect: at higher interest rates, individuals do not need to put aside today as much as they otherwise would to retire or to buy a home. At higher interest rates, savers are better off. Individuals who are better off consume more and save less. We refer to this as the income effect, in contrast to the incentive or substitution effect. The two effects pull in opposite directions and essentially offset each other. That is why savings are not very sensitive to the interest rate.

Of course, when individuals look at the return to savings, they take into account inflation—the fact that a pound in the future may buy less than a pound

[3] Later in this chapter, we will see that there are other reasons why the aggregate demand curve may have the shape depicted.

Figure 23.7 SAVINGS AND THE REAL INTEREST RATE

Different savings curves are shown in panels A and B. In panel A, savings increase with the interest rate. In panel B, savings are only slightly sensitive to the interest rate—a relationship which is supported by empirical evidence.

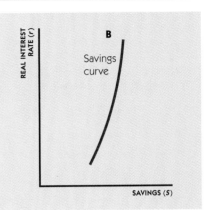

today. Thus the relevant interest rate for savings is the *real* interest rate, which is just the nominal interest rate minus the rate of inflation. If the nominal interest rate is 10 percent, and the rate of inflation is 4 percent, then the real interest rate is 6 percent. As in the macroeconomic analysis of the labour and product markets, where we ignore differences between the variety of wages and prices, here we ignore the differences between the various interest rates at play in the economy. We simply refer to the interest rate in general.

INVESTMENT

Economists use the word *investment* in two different ways. Households think of the stocks and bonds they buy as investments—**financial investments.** These financial investments provide the funds for firms to buy capital goods—machines and buildings. The purchases of new machines and buildings represent firms' investments, referred to as **capital goods investments.** In macroeconomics, when we refer to investments, it is to capital, not financial, investments.

Firms invest in order to increase their capacity to produce, to be able to produce more goods. They expect returns from the sale of these extra goods to cover the cost of additional workers and raw materials required to increase production, as well as the cost of the funds to finance the investment, and so to leave them with a profit.

There are thus two key determinants of investment: firms' expectations concerning the future, which we will assume for now to be fixed, and the interest rate. Many firms borrow to finance their investment. The cost of these funds—what they have to pay the bank for using its funds—is the interest rate. Since a firm pays back a debt with pounds that have less purchasing power due to inflation, the relevant cost of funds is the real interest rate.

The higher the interest rate, the fewer investment projects are profitable, that is, the fewer the projects which, after paying the bank its interest, will yield a return to the investor sufficient to compensate him for the risks he undertakes. Even if the firm is flush with cash, the interest rate matters. The interest rate becomes the opportunity cost of the firm's money, what it could have obtained if, instead of making the investment, it had simply decided to lend the money to some other firm or the government.

The **investment function** gives the level of (real) investment at each value of the real interest rate. The investment function slopes downwards to the right: investment increases as the real interest rate decreases. This is depicted in Figure 23.8, which shows the real interest rate on the vertical axis and the real investment level on the horizontal axis.

There is another way of seeing why the interest rate matters: while the firm puts out money today to buy machines, the returns it receives, in increased profits, do not occur until the future. A pound re-

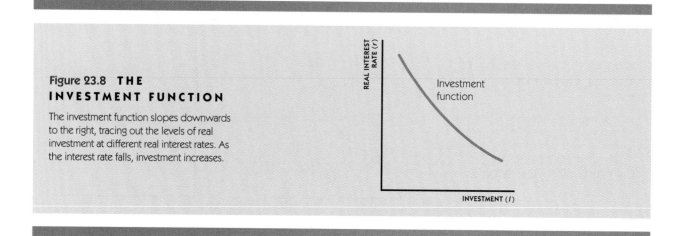

Figure 23.8 THE INVESTMENT FUNCTION

The investment function slopes downwards to the right, tracing out the levels of real investment at different real interest rates. As the interest rate falls, investment increases.

ceived in the future is not worth as much as a pound today, because of the time value of money: a pound today could have been put in the bank and earned interest; if the interest rate is 7 percent, in ten years, the pound will have doubled to £2. We thus say that the **present discounted value** of £2 ten years from now is £1. (The present discounted value of £1 in the future is what someone would be willing to pay today for it.) An increase in the interest rate reduces the present discounted value of future money. At a 14 percent interest rate, £1 put in the bank today has doubled to £2 in five years and quadrupled to £4 in ten years. Thus, £1 in ten years is worth only 25p, while at 7 percent it is worth 50p. An investment is undertaken if the present discounted value of (expected) profits is more than the cost; with an increase in the interest rate, fewer investments meet this criterion. The aggregate level of investment thus decreases.

EQUILIBRIUM IN THE CAPITAL MARKET

In a **closed economy,** that is, an economy that does not trade with the rest of the world, or borrow from or lend to it, equilibrium in the capital market requires that savings equal investment, as depicted in Figure 23.9. Panels A and B show the effect of an increased demand for investment at each interest rate. In panel A, both the equilibrium real interest rate

and equilibrium savings and investment are increased, while in panel B only the equilibrium real interest rate is changed. Because savings are not sensitive to the real interest rate, and savings must equal investment, investment remains unchanged. By contrast, a rightward shift in the savings curve, so that at every real interest rate savings increases, results in a reduction in the real interest rate and an increase in investment. This is shown in panel C. Because the savings curve is almost vertical, the major impact of a shift in the savings curve is a change in investment.

However, no developed countries are closed economies. Most are **open economies:** they engage in substantial trade with each other, and lend and borrow on world financial markets.

The United Kingdom may best be viewed as a **small open economy;** that is to say, it takes as given the world prices of the goods it trades and the world real interest rate at which it can lend and borrow internationally. The United Kingdom is small in the sense that the amount of borrowing or lending done by U.K. residents on world markets is too small to affect world interest rates. The United States, by contrast, is not a small economy. When the United States, either its firms or its government, increases borrowing on world markets, interest rates may rise throughout the world. The United States should be classified as a **large open economy.**

For a small open economy, equilibrium occurs at the world real interest rate as shown in Figure 23.10.

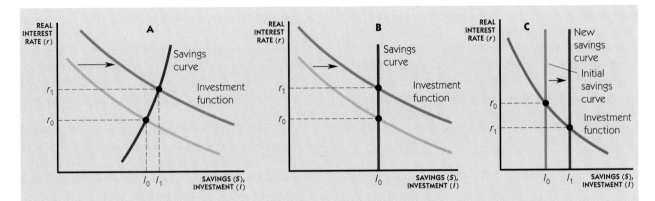

Figure 23.9 EQUILIBRIUM IN THE CAPITAL MARKET

Equilibrium requires the demand for funds (investment) equal the supply (savings). The level of desired investment decreases as the real interest rate increases.

We assume the economy is at full employment. In panel A, savings increase slightly with increases in the real interest rate. In panels B and C, savings are not interest sensitive, so the savings curve is a vertical straight line. The equilibrium level of investment is simply equal to the full-employment level of savings.

A shift in the investment function—so that at every real interest rate the demand for investment is increased—is depicted in panels A and B. In panel A, investment is increased from I_0 to I_1, while in panel B, with inelastic savings, the only effect is to increase the real interest rate from r_0 to r_1 and leave investment (and savings) unchanged. Panel C shows a rightward shift in the savings curve. The level of savings increases at each real interest rate, resulting in a decrease of the real interest rate from r_0 to r_1 and an increase in investment from I_0 to I_1.

Figure 23.10 SUPPLY OF SAVINGS IN A SMALL OPEN ECONOMY

In a small open economy, the real interest rate r^* is determined by the international capital market. That in turn determines the level of investment I^*. In the figure, savings are assumed to be fixed, unaffected by the interest rate. If domestic savings equal S_0, the shortfall B_0 is made up by borrowing from abroad. A reduction in savings to S_1 leads to increased borrowing B_1 but leaves investment unchanged.

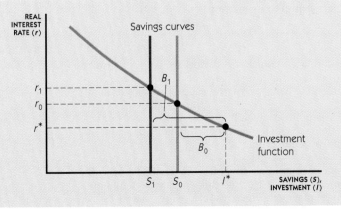

At the interest rate r^*, the country invests an amount I^*, while it saves S_0. The difference $(B_0 = I^* - S_0)$ is borrowed from abroad. If savings were to fall to S_1, then foreign borrowing would rise to B_1 $(I^* - S_1)$. The real interest rate would be unchanged at r^*.

By contrast, if this had been a closed economy, the equilibrium level of savings *and* investment would have been at S_0 with the equilibrium at r_0. The fall in savings from S_0 to S_1 would have caused investment to fall to S_1 also and the real interest rate to rise to r_1.

THE GENERAL EQUILIBRIUM

We can now describe the general equilibrium of the economy, the real wages, price level, and interest rate at which the labour, product, and capital markets all clear.

The real wage adjusts to ensure the demand for labour equals the supply. This determines the equilibrium real wage. The price level adjusts to ensure that aggregate demand equals aggregate supply, which in turn is equal to the full-employment level of output. Thus, equilibrium output is equal to potential GDP, the output which the labour supply, working with the available capital stock, can produce. Finally, borrowing from abroad adjusts to ensure that, at this full-employment level of output and at the world real interest rate, savings plus foreign borrowing are equal to investment.[4]

---

[4] We can, in fact, show that if savings are equal to investment at the full-employment level of output, then aggregate demand equals aggregate supply at that level of output.

In our simplified model there are four sources of aggregate demand, investment, consumption, government expenditure, and net exports:
$$Y^d = C + I + G + (X - Z).$$
Since national output always equals national income, full-employment output Yf equals full-employment income, and full-employment incomes are either saved, consumed, or paid in taxes:
$$Y_f = C + S + T \quad \text{or} \quad S = Y_f - C - T.$$

USING THE GENERAL EQUILIBRIUM MODEL

The general equilibrium model is useful because it allows us to understand the effects of various changes in the economy—from the market in which these changes originate to all the other markets in the economy.

Consider the effect of the introduction of personal computers to the economy. The marginal product of workers increases, causing a shift in the demand curve for labour to the right. The equilibrium real wage increases as shown in Figure 23.11A.

Given the greater productivity of workers and the fixed labour supply, full-employment output increases, as shown by a rightward shift in the aggregate supply curve (panel B). Aggregate demand may rise due to an increase in investment (at every value of the real interest rate) as firms take advantage of the available profit opportunities opened up by the new computer technology. At the same time, the increase in income leads to an increase in consumption and savings at each interest rate. If aggregate demand rises by the same amount as aggregate supply, the price level is unchanged. Of course, the shift in the aggregate demand curve at P_0 may be greater or less than the increase in aggregate supply, so the price level may either increase or decrease.

The increased investment and savings at each interest rate are represented by a rightward shift in both the investment and savings functions (panel C). In equilibrium the amount of borrowing from abroad may either rise or fall at the world real interest rate. As the diagram has been drawn, there is no change in net borrowing from abroad.

While we have focused here on the current effects

Since the total demand for goods $C + I + G + (X - Z)$ equals incomes generated by production $C + S + T$, it must be true that
$$C + S + T = C + I + G + (X - Z),$$
or rearranging,
$$S + (T - G) + (Z - X) = I.$$
Thus it is identically true that investment (I) is financed by private savings (S), government savings $(T - G)$, and borrowing from abroad $(Z - X)$, which is equal to the current account deficit.

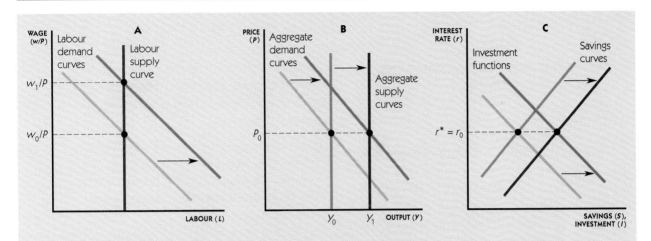

Figure 23.11 EFFECTS OF INTRODUCING PERSONAL COMPUTERS INTO THE ECONOMY

Panel A depicts the labour market. Personal computers increase the marginal product of workers, resulting in a rightward shift of the labour demand curve and an increase in the equilibrium real wage from w_0 to w_1. Panel B depicts the product market. With the increased productivity of workers, the aggregate supply curve shifts to the right. Output increases from Y_0 to Y_1. If aggregate demand increases (due to an increase in investment and an increase in consumption from higher incomes), the aggregate demand curve will shift to the right. If at P_0 the increase in aggregate demand is the same as the increase in aggregate supply, the price level will remain at P_0. Panel C depicts the capital market. Investment increases as firms purchase computers, and savings increase as a result of increased income. Both the investment and savings curves shift to the right. There may be no net effect on the interest rate (r_0), as shown here.

of these changes, there are important future effects. In the future, there will be more plant and equipment. The economy's future capacity will increase. Thus, not only are all markets linked today, but markets today are also linked with markets in the future.

EXTENDING THE BASIC FULL-EMPLOYMENT MODEL

Macroeconomics is concerned with policy: what are the impacts, for instance, of increasing government expenditure or increasing the money supply? The basic full-employment aggregate model can incorporate government expenditures and money, and thus be used to address these policy questions.

GOVERNMENT

Introducing government into the analysis affects both the product market and the capital market. In the product market, government expenditures add to aggregate demand, but taxes reduce disposable income and thus subtract from aggregate demand.

Focusing on the capital market makes the effects of government on the general equilibrium clear. In an open economy, the reduction in savings caused by taxation shifts the savings curve to the left. In equilibrium, the amount of foreign borrowing rises. This is illustrated in Figure 23.12. The situation in a closed economy is illustrated in Figure 23.13, the reduction in disposable income from taxes shifts the savings rate to the left, reducing equilibrium savings from S_0 to S_1. With an unchanged investment sched-

Increased government expenditures, even when matched by increased taxes, crowd out private investment in a closed economy. It is easy to quantify the effect. Assume the government increases its expenditure by £100 billion and increases taxes on individuals by £100 billion. With higher taxes, individuals have a disposable lower income, and so—at any interest rate—they save less. For simplicity, assume that for each extra hundred pounds of after-tax income, individuals save ten pounds. Thus, the increased £100 billion of taxes reduces savings by £10 billion. For simplicity, assume that savings are completely insensitive to the interest rate; that is, the savings curve is a vertical straight line. Then, if savings equal investment, and savings are reduced by £10 billion, so is investment. In the new equilibrium, aggregate output is unchanged (at the full-

employment level), government expenditures are increased by £100 billion, offset by a reduction of consumption of £90 billion and of investment by £10 billion.

If savings have a slight positive elasticity, then as interest rates rise, there will be increased savings. Thus, investment will be less and consumption more than if savings are totally insensitive to the interest rate.

In an open economy, where borrowing can be obtained from abroad, the rise in the interest rate will be smaller than in the closed economy, and it will be zero in a small open economy that borrows at the world real interest rate. In the small open economy, investment does not fall. Instead borrowing from abroad rises by £10 billion and net exports fall by £10 billion.

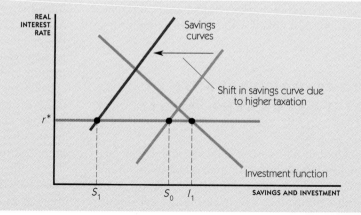

Figure 23.12 GOVERNMENT EFFECTS ON THE CAPITAL MARKET IN AN OPEN ECONOMY

In an open economy, an increase in government expenditures and taxation causes no increase in the rate of interest and consequently there is a fall in investment. However, the fall in savings, from S_0 to S_1 at the world real interest rate r^*, causes an increase in borrowing from abroad from $(I - S_0)$ to $(I - S_1)$.

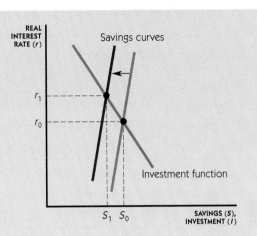

Figure 23.13 GOVERNMENT EFFECTS ON THE CAPITAL MARKET IN A CLOSED ECONOMY

Government taxes reduce disposable income and savings, resulting in a leftward shift of the savings curve from S_0 to S_1. The equilibrium interest rate rises from r_0 to r_1, and the investment level falls.

ule, the equilibrium interest rate rises and the equilibrium investment level falls.

Government also affects the composition of output. Figure 23.14 shows how an increase in government expenditure matched with an increase in taxes changes the composition of output in a small open economy. The total size of the pie is unchanged; we assume that the economy remains at full employment. Thus, the effect of government is simply to change how the pie is divided. Net exports and consumption are both lowered—or **crowded out**—to make room for increased government expenditures. Even if government increases taxes by an amount to fully pay for the increased expenditure—in our

Figure 23.14 EFFECT OF AN EQUAL INCREASE IN GOVERNMENT EXPENDITURES AND TAXES ON THE COMPOSITION OF OUTPUT

In a small open economy an increase in government expenditures financed by an increase in taxes leads to a decrease in consumption and net exports. Government expenditures are said to crowd out private expenditure.

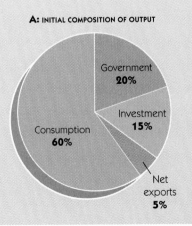

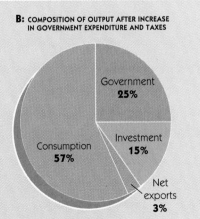

A: INITIAL COMPOSITION OF OUTPUT

Government 20%
Investment 15%
Consumption 60%
Net exports 5%

B: COMPOSITION OF OUTPUT AFTER INCREASE IN GOVERNMENT EXPENDITURE AND TAXES

Government 25%
Investment 15%
Consumption 57%
Net exports 3%

The real interest rate reflects the balance between the supply of savings and the demand for investment. In the late 1980s and early 1990s nominal interest rates rose around the world, and it looked for a time as if real interest rates had also risen substantially. Was this a sign of a world capital shortage? There were several factors at work at the time to suggest that the demand for capital and investment had risen substantially while the supply might, if anything, have shrunk. There was strong demand for capital from the newly opened-up economies of Russia and eastern Europe, particularly eastern Germany, into which the German government began to pour huge amounts of investment. At the time the Asian Tigers (Thailand, South Korea, Malaysia, Indonesia, and Taiwan) were growing very rapidly, so much that their demand for capital might outstrip even their very high savings rates. Many developing countries that had previously discouraged foreign investment were actively seeking it. At the same time the supply of savings, particularly in the large developed economies of Europe and North America, was diminished: savings rates had fallen relative to the levels of a decade before.

Since the early 1990s, real interest rates have fallen back as demand for investment has fallen. World growth has slowed. The crisis in Southeast Asia from 1997 onwards has reduced investment demand there and has diminished the prospects for growth and profits in the rest of the world as well. The rise in real rates of the early 1990s looks with the benefit of hindsight to have been a temporary blip.

Taking a longer perspective and looking back, the following diagram shows the real interest rate from the end of 1957 to 1993. It is an average for five large economies (the United Kingdom, Germany, France, the United States, and Japan). The outstanding feature is the dramatic fall in real rates in the 1970s and their strong bounce back in the 1980s and 1990s.

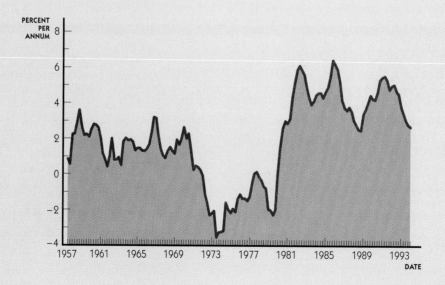

example, by 3 percent of GDP—consumption is reduced by less, as individuals adjust in part by reducing savings.

THE MONEY SUPPLY

Government may also play a role in the economy by changing the amount of money in circulation. This is done through monetary policy, a subject we will consider later in this book. For now, it is important to understand the consequences of changes in the money supply for the full-employment model.

By and large, economists agree that in a full-employment economy, money affects the price level but little else. In particular, it does not affect the quantity of goods produced or the number of workers employed. We can use an imaginative example to understand the point. Suppose that instantaneously, the entire supply of money in the economy was increased by a multiple of 10. In effect, we have tacked a zero onto the money supply. So £5 notes are now worth £50, £10 notes are now worth £100, £20 notes are now worth £200, your bank account of £250 is now worth £2,500, and so on. Shops, acting perfectly efficiently and knowing that the money supply has multiplied by 10, would increase their prices tenfold. Thus, the amount of goods and services produced and consumed would be the same; there would be

no real effect. The only difference would be the numbers on the bills, bank statements, and price tags.

The lesson is more general: an increase in the supply of money accompanied by a proportionate increase in the price level has no real effect on the economy. When changing the money supply has no real effect, we say that money is *neutral*. If the economy is at full employment and prices are perfectly flexible, prices will increase proportionally with the money supply. Thus, the **neutrality of money** is a basic property of the full-employment model. We can see this by tracing through the effects of an increase in the money supply in the product, labour, and capital markets, as shown in Figure 23.15.

Panel A of Figure 23.15 shows the aggregate supply and aggregate demand curves. An increase in the money supply represents an increase in money balances held by the public, so private wealth increases. This results in a rightward shift of the aggregate demand curve. The price level increases from P_0 to P_1, but the equilibrium level of output remains at Y_0.

In panel B we see the aggregate supply and aggregate demand curves for labour. In the labour market, the increase in the price level will be matched by an increase in the nominal wage from w_0 to w_1, so that the real wage remains at its original level: $w_0/P_0 = w_1/P_1$. At this real wage, the demand for labour continues to equal its supply. Thus the effect on the labour market of an increase in the price level is simply a proportionate increase in the nominal

There is much talk of globalization. Some of it makes sense and some of it doesn't—globaloney, in a term popularised by Professor Paul Krugman of the Massachusetts Institute of Technology (although originally coined by Claire Booth Luce). There is a fear in the West (meaning western Europe and North America) that jobs, particularly low-skill jobs, are being moved from the West to developing countries in Asia and Latin America where labour is cheaper and profits are higher. Western Europeans worry about jobs moving to eastern Europe. Germany in particular is concerned about the prospect of firms' moving factories to Poland, the Czech Republic, Hungary, and other nearby countries. In Canada and the United States there was concern that NAFTA would cause jobs to shift to Mexico.

These aspects of globalization are driven partly by the cuts in tariffs and other forms of protection, which enable goods to be traded without impediment: they can be made in one place and sold in another without incurring additional taxes or being subject to quotas. But also they are driven by open capital markets: firms are able to invest their funds in whichever country they wish in search of profits. Free trade in goods and open capital markets go hand in hand. Free trade in goods raises the profitability of setting up plants in developing countries; open capital markets enable firms to realise those profits by taking the funds there and setting up the plants.

From the global point of view, it makes sense for capital to be mobile in this way. Global efficiency is promoted by firms' investing where the rate of return is the greatest. If the return to investment in one country is 8 percent while it is 24 percent in another, £1 billion invested in the second country rather than the first yields an extra £160 million a year. In the short term it may produce problems in some areas, from whose perspective it looks as if "their" jobs are being taken away by cheap labour elsewhere. But at the same time it brings benefits in the countries which receive the investment, by creating new employment, which is very often better paid than the existing jobs in those countries and making use of otherwise underused skills in the labour force.

Nevertheless, when capital is mobile in this way, countries often become very sensitive to the possibility that their exports are not given the same degree of access to foreign markets as foreign goods are given to their markets. The United States, and to a lesser degree Europe, has been engaged in a long-running argument with Japan and some other Asian countries (such as Taiwan) about access to their markets. It is claimed for example that a number of very tight regulations on goods sold in Japan, while apparently quite evenhanded in their treatment of Japanese and foreign-made goods, are actually devised so as to give a big advantage to Japanese-made goods. A frequently cited example is car parts. Japan imposes strict tests on parts not made by the original manufacturer of the vehicle. This effectively excludes U.S. manufacturers from supply vehicle parts in Japan. Achieving free trade in goods and reciprocally free access of goods and capital remains fraught with problems.

Part of the complaint of the United States and Europe against Japan, Taiwan, and others, is based on Japan and others' large trade surpluses and the United State's large deficit. From one perspective this seems to be an entirely rea-

wage. There is no real effect; the equilibrium real wage and the equilibrium level of employment L_0 are not affected.

In the capital market, real savings and investment both depend on the real interest rate, which is not affected by the increase in the price level. Accordingly, in panel C, neither the savings curve nor the investment function shifts. At each real interest rate, *nominal* savings and investment would increase by an amount exactly proportional to the increase in the money supply. Why? Because households and firms must increase the money amount of savings and investment in order to maintain the value of savings and investment relative to the higher price level. But panel C shows the levels of *real* savings and investment at each real interest rate. The equilibrium real interest rate r_0 remains the same. The overall result once again displays the neutrality of money because

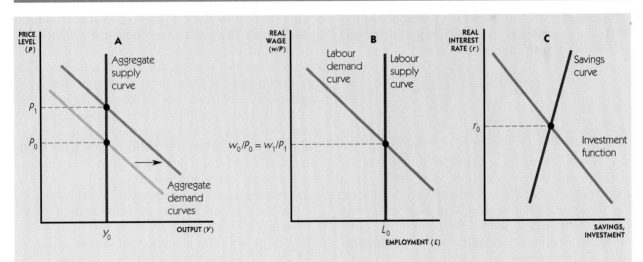

Figure 23.15 EFFECTS OF AN INCREASE IN THE MONEY SUPPLY

Panel A shows the product market. The increase in the money supply results in a rightward shift of the aggregate demand curve. The price level rises from P_0 to P_1, and the equilibrium level of output remains at Y_0. Panel B shows the labour market. The nominal wage (w) increases in proportion to the increase in the price level, so that the real wage is unaffected. Panel C shows the capital market. The savings and investment curves giving the real levels of those variables both shift to the right, in proportion to the increase in the price level. The real interest rate r_0 is unaffected.

there are no real effects in the capital market. Only the *nominal* levels of savings and investment change in proportion to the change in the price level.

The neutrality of money highlights the important distinction economists make between real and nominal phenomena. As we have seen here and in earlier chapters, in referring to nominal variables, such as nominal GDP and nominal wages, we mean the current money value of those variables, that is, the value *without* adjustments for changes in the price level. As this example shows, our full-employment model with flexible prices makes a perfect distinction between real and nominal phenomena. Relationships between real variables—which are the focus of the model—are completely independent of changes in nominal variables.

While the neutrality of money is a basic property of our full-employment model with flexible prices, it is important to keep in mind the limitations of the model. If price increases themselves had literally no consequences, inflation would not be a matter of much concern. But as we learned in Chapter 22, it is a concern. Later chapters will explore the more complicated effects of increases in the money supply when the economy is not at full employment and prices are not perfectly flexible.

CONSENSUS IN MACROECONOMICS

Macroeconomic issues are often on the front pages of the newspapers and nightly on television. There is good reason for this. As we learned in Chapter 22, the macroeconomic problems of unemployment, slow growth, and inflation have substantial, widespread consequences. With modest productivity gains, the concern is with slow economic growth; when the unemployment rate increases, the focus is on impending recession; when the consumer price index goes up faster, attention shifts to inflation. These problems and the ways to address them are often hotly debated, giving rise to controversy. In this context, the views of economists often appear to be contradictory, and the old saw about how any two economists will give you three opinions may seem true. But in fact, there is remarkable consensus among economists about basic macroeconomic principles. In this chapter we have encountered our sixth and seventh points of consensus:

6 Effects of government expenditures at full employment

When the economy is at full employment, and the economy is closed, increases in government expenditures must come at the expense of private consumption and/or investment. Even when matched with increases in taxes, such increases crowd out private investment, since the increased taxes will normally lead to a reduction in savings. If the economy is open, government expenditures lead to increased foreign borrowing.

7 Neutrality of money

At full employment, an increase in the money supply only leads to a proportionate increase in prices and wages, with no real consequences.

LOOKING FORWARDS

This chapter has used the basic competitive model to analyse the full-employment macroeconomic equilibrium of the economy. We have seen how real wages adjust to ensure that the demand for labour always equals the supply, even in the face of changes in technology and new investments which might replace workers. We have seen how prices and borrowing from abroad or interest rates adjust in the face of shifts in the demand for investment so that the economy continues to produce at its productive capacity and so that savings and borrowing continue to equal investment at the full-employment level of output.

In the long run, wages, prices, and interest rates do adjust in much the manner described here. In the short run, however, they may not. If they did adjust to shifts instantaneously, then the full-employment model would not only be a good description of how the economy in the long run is able to create enough new jobs to match the increase in labour supply, but it would also be a good description of the economy in the short run. But wages and prices in particular may be sticky, that is, fail to adjust to the market clearing levels. This has profound implications for how the economy behaves in the short run, as we shall see in the following two parts. First, however, we take a closer look at our full-employment model.

REVIEW AND PRACTICE

SUMMARY

1 Macroeconomic equilibrium focuses on equilibrium levels of aggregates: employment, output, and investment. In a full-employment competitive equilibrium, each is determined by equating demand and supply. Full employment is attained as a result of flexible wages and prices.

2 The real wage equates the demand for labour with the supply of labour. Increases in the labour supply are reflected in lower real wages, which induce firms to create additional jobs to match the increased supply.

3 The full-employment level of output is that level of output which the economy can produce with its given stock of plant and equipment when labour is fully employed. It will increase with increases in the labour supply.

4 The price level adjusts to equate aggregate demand to aggregate supply.

5 In a closed economy, the real interest rate (which takes account of inflation) equates investment and savings. The desired level of investment decreases with increases in the real interest rate. Savings depend on disposable income and the real interest rate.

With flexible wages and prices, labour is fully employed, so output is always at the full-employment level. Since aggregate output equals national income, if taxes are fixed, disposable income will be fixed. Hence, in a full-employment economy, the interest rate is the main variable of concern in determining savings. Savings increase slightly with increases in the real interest rate.

6 In a closed economy, government expenditures, when paid for by increases in taxes, crowd out consumption and investment. In a small open economy, investment is unchanged and foreign borrowing increases.

7 Shifts to the left in the savings curve lead to reduced investment in a closed economy and to increased foreign borrowing in a small open economy.

8 All the markets in the economy are interlinked. Changes in one market have effects on all other markets.

9 In a full-employment economy with perfectly flexible wages and prices, money is neutral; increases in the money supply are simply reflected in increases in prices.

KEY TERMS

short-run production function

full-employment level of output

aggregate supply

aggregate supply curve

aggregate demand curve

disposable income

financial investments

capital goods investments

investment function

present discounted value

closed economy

open economy

crowding out

neutrality of money

REVIEW QUESTIONS

1 How do competitive markets with flexible wages and prices ensure that labour is always fully employed? What induces firms to create just the right number of additional jobs to match an increase in the number of workers?

2 Describe the effects of shifts in the labour supply curve on equilibrium real wages and potential GDP (full-employment level of output).

3 What determines the economy's productive capacity or aggregate supply or potential GDP? How does aggregate supply increase when labour supply increases?

4 What is the aggregate demand curve? Why is it downward sloping? Why is the aggregate supply curve vertical? What determines the price level?

5 What is the investment schedule? Why does investment decrease when the real interest rate increases? What role do expectations play in investment?

6 What determines the level of savings? Explain why, if taxes are fixed, disposable income in a full-

employment economy is fixed. Explain why savings may not be very sensitive to the real rate of interest.

7 How is the equilibrium rate of interest determined?

8 How do government expenditures matched by taxes affect the market equilibrium?

9 What difference does it make whether the economy is closed or open? Illustrate by examining the effects of an increase in government expenditure.

10 How does the U.K. economy differ from a closed economy?

PROBLEMS

1 In the text, we assumed that the labour supply did not depend on the real wage. Assume that at higher real wages, more individuals wish to work. Trace through how each of the steps in the analysis has to be changed. (Show the equilibrium in the labour market. What happens to real wages, employment, GDP, and savings if the labour supply curve shifts to the right?)

2 An increase in capital resulting from an increase in investment allows a given number of workers to produce more. Show the effect on the short-run production function and the full-employment level of output. It may be the case that while the short-run production function shifts upwards, its slope becomes flatter at some levels of employment (output). What does this imply for the aggregate demand curve for labour? Is it possible that the equilibrium real wage could fall?

3 Firms hire workers up to the point where the real wage equals the marginal product of labour, the extra output that an extra worker produces. Explain why the slope of the short-run production function is the marginal product of labour. Explain why, with diminishing returns, an increase in the real wage leads

to a lower level of demand for labour. Draw an example of a shift outwards in the short-run production function, caused by technological change, which causes (at any real wage) the demand for labour to decrease. To increase.

4 Explain how income and substitution effects offset each other in the supply curve of labour. In the supply curve for savings.

5 Trace through how the effects of a change in one market—such as an increase in the supply of labour—has effects on other markets. How is it possible for there to be a large increase in the labour supply while real wages change relatively little.

6 Trace through the effects of an increase in taxes without a corresponding increase in government expenditures or an increase in government expenditures without a corresponding increase in taxes.

7 What are some of the reasons that, even in an open economy, investment and savings may be highly correlated.

8 "Even if, in an open economy, a decrease in savings does not decrease investment, future generations are worse off." Discuss.

USING THE FULL-
EMPLOYMENT
MODEL

T he Maastricht Treaty and Economic and Monetary Union in Europe brought the question of government deficits and debt levels to the forefront of everyone's attention. The treaty set a maximum deficit of 3 percent of the GDP and a maximum debt of 60 percent of the GDP as conditions for entry into the Monetary Union. The Stability and Growth Pact, which has been taken up within the Monetary Union, further enshrines a policy of strictly limiting debts and deficits. The British government in 1997 and 1998 also set out its own principles for guiding fiscal policy, which set limits to deficits and debt. In this chapter we use the model developed in Chapter 23 to elucidate the consequences of debts and deficits. The size of the government's fiscal deficit is connected to the size of the country's trade deficit. In the past, trade deficits have been seen as important limits on the government's ability to use policies aimed at economic growth. The full-employment model can also be used to help us understand the trade deficit and how it might be affected by various policies.

In Chapter 22 we described the three fundamental economic problems of growth, unemployment, and inflation. By assumption, the full-employment

1 What are the consequences of large fiscal deficits and high levels of national debt?

2 Why do some countries have persistent trade deficits, while others appear to run persistent surpluses? What are the consequences?

3 How do deficits affect economic growth? What other policies can be used to promote economic growth?

model of Chapter 23 cannot directly shed light on the problem of unemployment, though in the next chapter we will explain how simply by changing one of the critical assumptions of that model, there can be unemployment. In the last chapter we saw how the full-employment model provides us with useful insights into inflation, with the price level's increasing in proportion to the money supply. In this chapter, we also show how the full-employment model provides us with useful insights into the problem of growth.

THE DEFICIT

When the government spends more than it receives in taxes and other revenues in any given year, it has a deficit, often referred to as the **fiscal deficit,** to distinguish it from the gap between imports and exports, which is called the trade deficit. It must borrow to finance the deficit. In Britain the government's deficit became negative for a short period in the late 1980s. However, the deficit subsequently rose, and for some years in the 1990s it exceeded the Maastricht Treaty's critical 3 percent limit. By the late 1990s borrowing had been reined back to within the 3 percent limit.

The *national debt* is the cumulative amount the government owes. There has been considerable concern over the rise in national debt as a percentage of GDP since 1990. Figure 24.1 shows the ratio of debt to GDP for recent years, the fall to just over 34 percent

in 1990 and the subsequent rise. However, seen in a wider perspective, Britain's national debt is currently small. Figure 24.2 shows the national debt for selected years of the twentieth century. Both world wars caused the debt to shoot up. It reached over 200 percent of the GDP in 1945; since then it has fallen steadily. As Figure 24.3 shows, while Britain had a high ratio of government *borrowing* to GDP in 1995, relative to a number of other countries, the ratio of its accumulated national debt to GDP was relatively low.

In this chapter we use the model of Chapter 23 to give a qualitative picture of the consequences of government borrowing. Whereas in Chapter 23 we discussed the effects of an increase in government expenditure matched by higher taxes, here we consider an increase in government expenditure unmatched by an increase in taxes. As before, the openness of the economy to international trade and capital flows is an important determinant of the effects. Two extremes are examined, an open economy and a closed economy.

AN OPEN ECONOMY

If the government increases its spending without increasing taxes, it must borrow the difference. The government's deficit D can be thought of as the negative of *public savings* S_g. Thus,[1]

$$D \equiv -S_g.$$

---

[1] The symbol $\equiv$ means "is defined as" or "is identical to."

Figure 24.1 **PUBLIC SECTOR DEBT HELD OUTSIDE THE PUBLIC SECTOR AS A PERCENTAGE OF GDP**

Debt as a percentage of GDP has fallen and then risen again in recent years, but these levels are small relative to the broader historical trends shown in Figure 24.2. *Source:* Office of National Statistics, *Annual Abstract of Statistics* (1998), Table 16.3.

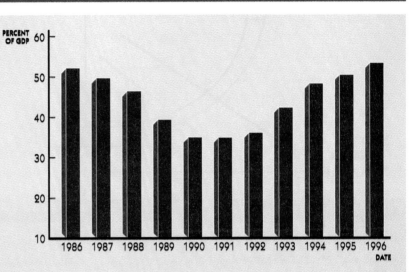

Figure 24.2 **U.K. NATIONAL DEBT-TO-GDP RATIO, SELECTED YEARS, 1900–1980**

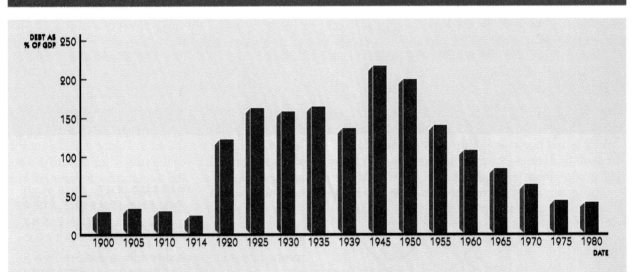

The main increases in the debt-to-GDP ratio occurred in the two world wars. The period of active Keynesian policy coincided with an enormous fall in the debt-to-GDP ratio in the United Kingdom. *Source:* Mitchell, *British Historical Statistics.*

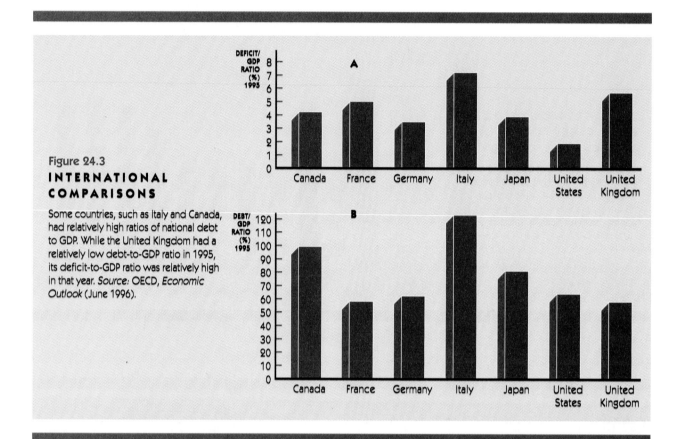

Figure 24.3

INTERNATIONAL COMPARISONS

Some countries, such as Italy and Canada, had relatively high ratios of national debt to GDP. While the United Kingdom had a relatively low debt-to-GDP ratio in 1995, its deficit-to-GDP ratio was relatively high in that year. *Source:* OECD, *Economic Outlook* (June 1996).

The sources of funds to meet government borrowing are two: (1) the private sector of the economy (households and firms), which has available for lending to the government an amount equal to the excess of its savings (S_p) over its investment in new capital equipment and other goods (I), and (2) the foreign sector, since the rest of the world may lend to finance the government's deficit. Foreign financing could be thought of as foreign savings (S_f).

Putting all this together, we can write

$$D \equiv -S_p - I + S_f.$$

Rearranging this expression, we have

$$I \equiv S_g + S_p + S_f,$$

which says that private sector investment is financed by savings by government, the private sector, and the rest of the world.

A *small open economy* can borrow any amount from the rest of the world at the going world real interest rate (r^*) and thus the supply curve of foreign lending S_f is horizontal, as in Figure 24.4. Domestic savings S are defined as the sum of public and private savings: $S \equiv S_g + S_p$. The demand for investment is a downward-sloping function of the real interest rate.

An increase in government spending and the deficit cuts domestic savings from S_0 to S_1 in Figure 24.4, and therefore foreign borrowing rises while domestic investment remains unchanged.

A CLOSED ECONOMY

In a closed economy, there is no recourse to foreign borrowing to meet a government deficit. A higher deficit has to be met by either higher private savings

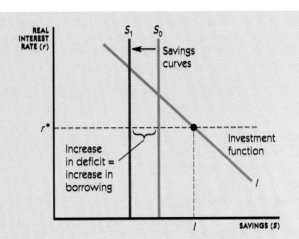

Figure 24.4 EFFECTS OF INCREASED DEFICITS IN AN OPEN ECONOMY

Increased deficits shift the national savings curve to the left. Investment is unaffected, but foreign borrowing increases.

or lower investment. Given fixed private savings, investment must fall (see Figure 24.5). When savings fall from S_0 to S_1, investment falls by the same amount and the real interest rate rises. Lower domestic investment will reduce the future capital stock and income of the economy.

A LARGE OPEN ECONOMY

The United States is a large open economy—with features that represent a cross between a closed economy and a small open economy. When the

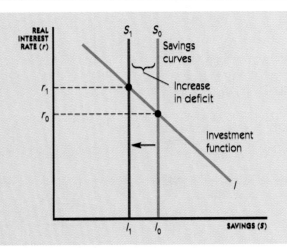

Figure 24.5 EFFECTS OF INCREASED DEFICITS IN A CLOSED ECONOMY

Increased deficits reduce national savings. With a leftward shift in the savings curve, the equilibrium level of interest rates is higher and the equilibrium level of investment is lower.

In a closed economy, an increase in government expenditure not accompanied by an increase in taxes (or a decrease in taxes, not accompanied by a corresponding decrease in government expenditures) results in higher interest rates and decreased investment, while in a small, open economy, interest rates and investment remain unchanged but foreign borrowing increases.

United States has a deficit, it borrows more from abroad, but interest rates rise and some investment is crowded out. A rough rule of thumb is that between one-third and one-half of the deficit is offset by increased foreign borrowing.

If we look at who has bought the additional bonds the U.S. government has been issuing in recent years, we note that some but not all of the higher deficit has been financed by foreigners. But the consequences are equally or even more disturbing if foreigners do not *directly* finance the deficit. A high deficit can lead to increased foreign indebtedness directly as the government borrows directly from abroad, or it can increase foreign debt indirectly by sopping up available domestic savings so that Americans no longer have the money to invest in U.S. businesses and foreigners come in to fill the gap. Some economists have described the latter situation by saying that government borrowing can *crowd in* foreign investment.

THE TRADE DEFICIT

The **trade deficit** is the difference between imports and exports in any given year. Britain has had a chronic trade deficit throughout much of the postwar period. However, North Sea oil improved the trade balance in the late 1970s and early 1980s. The shift from fixed to floating exchange rates in 1972 also relaxed the constraint on the economy imposed by the trade deficit. Figure 24.6 shows Britain's imports and exports for the period 1960 to 1996 and the trade deficit

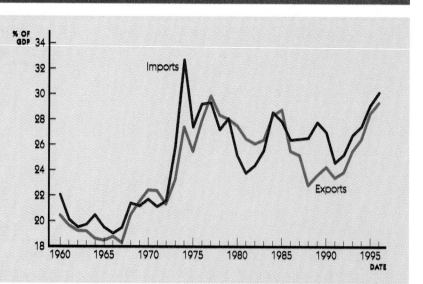

Figure 24.6 **IMPORTS AND EXPORTS IN THE U.K. ECONOMY, 1960–1996**

Both imports and exports have grown as a fraction of GDP in Britain, though most of the growth occurred between the mid-1960s and the mid-1970s. Imports and exports constitute about 30 percent of the GDP. *Source: Annual Abstract* (1998 and 1992); Mitchell, *British Historical Statistics*.

appears as the difference between them. Britain's persistent deficits are clearly revealed in Figure 24.6.

Trade deficits have been to some extent associated with fiscal deficits. In the United States in the mid-1980s, there was much discussion of the "twin deficits," a concurrence of a high government fiscal deficit and a high trade deficit. This is no accident: the two are in fact closely related. The reason for this we already noted: for an open economy, an increase in government expenditure not matched by an increase in taxes (or a decrease in taxes not matched by a reduction in government expenditures) results in an increased deficit and increased foreign borrowing. We will now see why increased foreign borrowing implies an increase in the trade deficit.

CAPITAL FLOWS

To see the relationship between foreign borrowing and the trade deficit, we first need to see the links between trade flows and capital flows. Let's trace what happens when someone in Britain buys a German car. It seems like a simple matter: he pays in sterling to his dealer. His dealer buys the car in sterling from an importer. The importer buys the car from the German manufacturer, who wants to be paid in German marks. For the importer, this is no problem: he goes to a bank, say in Germany, and exchanges his pounds for marks. But the bank won't just hold those pounds. It will sell them, either to someone wanting to purchase British goods or to someone wanting to invest in a sterling-denominated asset.

We call the money coming into the United Kingdom to buy investments, to be deposited in U.K. banks, to buy U.K. government bonds, or to lend to British residents for any reason—including buying a German car—**capital inflows.** Pounds going to other countries for similar purposes are called **capital outflows.** For most purposes, we are interested in **net capital inflows,** the inflows minus the outflows.

As we have seen, every pound a U.K. resident spends to buy a foreign import eventually comes back, either to buy British exports or to buy an investment in the United Kingdom. We can express this relation by a simple equation:

Imports into the United Kingdom
    = exports + capital inflows.

Subtracting exports from both sides of this equation, we obtain the basic trade identity:

Trade deficit ≡ imports − exports ≡ capital inflows.

Thus, a trade deficit and an inflow of foreign capital are two ways of saying the same thing. This can be put another way: the only way that domestic consumers and businesses can import more from abroad than they export abroad is if foreigners are willing to make up the difference by lending to or investing in the domestic economy.

In a world of multilateral trade, the accounts between any particular country and the domestic economy do not have to balance. Assume Japan and Europe are in trade balance and the United States and Europe are in trade balance, but Japanese investors like to put their money into Europe and Europeans like to invest in the United States. Europe has zero net capital inflows with a positive capital inflow from Japan offset by a capital outflow to the United States. In this situation, the U.S. trade deficit with Japan is offset by a capital inflow from Europe. But what must be true for any country is that total imports minus total exports (the trade deficit) equal total capital inflows.

The basic trade identity can describe a capital outflow as well as a capital inflow. In the 1950s, the United States had a substantial trade surplus, as the country exported more than it imported. Europe and Japan did not receive enough dollars from selling exports to the United States to buy the imports that they desired, and they borrowed the difference from the United States. There was a net capital outflow from the United States, which gradually accumulated. Japan now exports more than it imports, with the difference equal to its capital outflows.

EXCHANGE RATES

If a country borrows more (or less) from abroad, the **exchange rate** ensures that net imports adjust. The exchange rate tells how much of one currency exchanges for a given amount of another. For instance, in August 1998, one pound could be exchanged for approximately 235 yen. Exchange rates may change rapidly. By the beginning of 1999, a pound was worth only 195 yen—a fall in value of 20 percent in three

POLICY PERSPECTIVE:
CONTAINING FISCAL DEFICITS

The new government which took office in Britain in May 1997 introduced a set of principles by which, it argued, fiscal policy should be guided. They are aimed at limiting the size of deficits and the national debt while at the same time avoiding the problem that limiting government expenditures in order to limit borrowing has in the past caused a reduction in public sector investment. A key element of the plan is that government expenditure should be considered in two parts: current spending and capital spending. Capital spending includes that on new roads and hospitals. The current fiscal deficit is defined as the excess of current spending over revenues.

The first rule for fiscal policy is the so-called golden rule that, on average, the current deficit should be zero. This rule permits borrowing to finance current spending when GDP and tax revenues are temporarily low, and repayment of debt when tax revenues are temporarily high; but on average it implies no borrowing. Borrowing is reserved for the finance of public investments. The second rule for fiscal policy is that the level of the national debt should be held to a "stable and prudent level."

It is hoped that these rules will limit the size of the national debt without discouraging public investment. Earlier attempts in the 1980s to limit the total amount of government borrowing, using a target for the public sector borrowing requirement, which includes both current and capital expenditure, may have had the effect of causing cuts in public sector investment. Public sector net investment was between 1 and 2 percent of the GDP in the period 1980 to 1996,

having been between 5 and 8 percent in the period 1963 to 1975. Compared with other countries, there is little public investment in Britain. General government gross investment in Britain in 1995 was less than 2 percent of GDP, compared with over 6 percent in Japan, 3 percent in France, between 2.5 and 3 percent in Germany and the United States, and more than 2 percent in Italy and Canada: Britain's figure was the lowest among the G7 countries. Certainly this corresponds to the widespread view that public investment has been tightly squeezed.

Under the new rules, borrowing for public investments will not be counted in the attempts to balance the government's current budget on average. This should make it easier for a government to invest in things like the London Underground or the High-Speed Rail Link to the Channel Tunnel.

However, these new rules may not be consistent with the borrowing limits in Euroland, as the countries that have joined EMU (Economic and Monetary Union) in Europe are called. In Euroland, the Stability and Growth Pact (SGP) limits overall borrowing to a maximum of 3 percent of GDP, regardless of whether it is for investment or current spending. In principle, if there were to be more public investment than 3 percent of GDP, all financed by borrowing, it would violate the SGP and the country would incur penalties.

Sources: H.M. Treasury, "A Code for Fiscal Stability" and "Fiscal Policy: Current and Capital Spending" (1997–98). (Available on the internet at http://www.hm-treasury.gov.uk along with related papers.)

Figure 24.7 **EQUILIBRIUM IN THE MARKET FOR POUNDS**

The exchange rate is the relative price of two currencies. The equilibrium exchange rate e_e occurs at the intersection of the supply and demand curves for pounds.

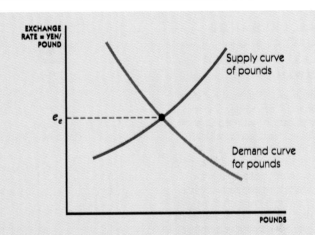

months. When the pound has become less valuable relative to the yen, we say it has **depreciated.** The yen has become more valuable; it has **appreciated.**

The exchange rate is thus a price—the relative price of two currencies. Like any price, the exchange rate is determined by the laws of supply and demand. For simplicity, let us continue to focus on the exchange rate between the pound and the yen (ignoring the fact that, in the world trading system, all exchange markets are interlinked). Figure 24.7 depicts the market for pounds in terms of the exchange rate with the yen. The exchange rate in yen per pound is on the vertical axis, and the quantity of pounds is on the horizontal axis. The supply curve for pounds represents the quantity of pounds supplied by people in Britain to purchase Japanese goods and to make investments in Japan. At higher exchange rates—when the pound buys more yen—people will supply higher quantities of pounds. The supply curve for pounds thus slopes upwards to the right. The demand curve for pounds represents the pounds demanded by the Japanese to purchase U.K. products and to make investments in the United Kingdom. At higher exchange rates—when it takes more yen to buy one pound—the Japanese demand lower quantities of pounds; this results in a demand curve which slopes downwards to the right. The

equilibrium exchange rate e_e lies at the intersection of the supply and demand curves for pounds.

Now we can see how the exchange rate connects the flow of capital and goods between countries. We continue with the case of the United Kingdom and Japan. Suppose the United Kingdom wants to borrow more from Japan. Higher U.K. interest rates will attract more Japanese investment to the United Kingdom. Japanese demand for pounds increases at each exchange rate, shifting the demand curve for pounds to the right, as depicted in Figure 24.8. The higher interest rates will also make Japanese investments relatively less attractive to investors in Britain, who will therefore increase their investments at home. People in Britain will be willing to supply fewer pounds at each exchange rate, shifting the supply curve for pounds to the left. These shifts in the supply and demand curves for pounds cause the exchange rate to rise from e_0 to e_1—the pound appreciates and the yen depreciates.[2] Since the pound can now buy more Japanese products, U.K. imports increase (Japanese exports increase). Changes in the

[2] Later, in Chapter 31, we shall see that matters are somewhat more complicated. Investors have to take into account expectations concerning changes in the exchange rates as well.

Figure 24.8 EXCHANGE RATE EFFECTS OF INCREASED FOREIGN BORROWING

The equilibrium exchange rate is e_0 before the increase in U.K. borrowing from Japan. Higher interest rates in the United Kingdom attract Japanese investment to the United Kingdom, shifting the demand curve for pounds to the right. At the same time, more people in Britain decide to invest in the United Kingdom rather than abroad; this is represented by a shift to the left of the supply curve for pounds. The exchange rate rises from e_0 to e_1. At the higher exchange rate, the pound buys more yen, so U.K. imports of Japanese products increase. Conversely, U.K. exports decrease.

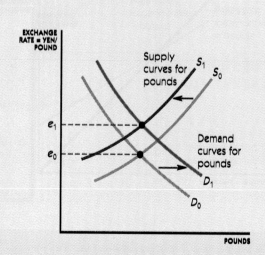

exchange rate thus ensure that the trade deficit moves in tandem with foreign borrowing.

THE SAVINGS-INVESTMENT IDENTITY

We can now return to the issue discussed at the beginning of this section, the link between fiscal deficits and trade deficits. When the fiscal deficit increases, the government's demand for borrowing increases. To the extent that this is not financed by a change in domestic investment or saving, it has to be financed by borrowing from abroad. As foreign residents attempt to buy the domestic currency, in order to buy government bonds, the demand for domestic currency on the foreign exchange market rises. This causes its price to rise. In the pound-yen example pursued so far, if the U.K. government increases its borrowing, the additional demand for pounds on the foreign exchange market will cause the price of pounds to rise in terms of yen.

This has the effect of making goods exported from the United Kingdom more expensive in foreign countries and reducing demand for them, which has the effect of reducing the demand for pounds on the foreign exchange market. At the same time, foreign goods imported into the United Kingdom become cheaper in terms of pounds, increasing British demand for them. This produces an increase in the supply of pounds to the foreign exchange market. At some level, the appreciated pound causes an increase in the net supply of pounds arising out of imports and exports, large enough to meet the additional demand for pounds arising out of the government's additional borrowing. The effect of additional government borrowing therefore is to cause an appreciation of the currency and a trade deficit.

In terms of the national income and product accounts, we can write:

GDP ≡ government expenditures on goods and
    services
    + consumers' expenditures
    + investment
    + exports − imports.

Rearranging this accounting identity,

Trade deficit ≡ government expenditures on goods
and services
+ consumers' expenditures
+ investment
– GDP.

The right-hand side of this expression denotes the excess of the total consumption of and investment in goods over the domestic production of them. Since GDP is equal to the total of consumers' expenditures, savings, and tax payments by domestic residents, we can write:

$$\text{Trade deficit} \equiv (G + C + I) - (C + S + T)$$
$$\equiv (G - T) + (I - S),$$

where $(G - T)$ denotes the government deficit, and $(I - S)$ the deficit of the private sector (the extent to which private investment cannot be financed by private savings). The sum of these deficits—the public sector deficit and the private sector deficit—has to be met by borrowing from abroad, or capital inflows. The trade deficit identity makes it clear that an increase in government expenditure (G) with no corresponding increase in tax revenue (T) or a reduction in private savings (S) or an increase in investment (I) will lead to an increase in the trade deficit. The mechanism by which this is brought about is an appreciation of the currency, as we explained. The larger trade deficit, and the larger rate of borrowing from abroad that goes with it, may involve foreign residents' increasing the quantity of domestic government bonds that they own or buying property or shares in companies in the domestic economy.

ARE TRADE DEFICITS A PROBLEM?

Trade deficits have very often been regarded as a problem. In the United Kingdom in the 1950s and 1960s, the tendency for trade to go into deficit as a result of weak export performance was seen as a brake on economic growth. By contrast the rapidly growing economies of Japan and Germany enjoyed strong trade surpluses. In the 1990s, the rapidly growing Asian economies—Taiwan, Singapore, and Hong Kong—had large surpluses. The United States had a very large trade deficit in the 1980s which preoccupied its policymakers. It was seen as a serious problem, along with the associated federal fiscal deficit.

However, from the perspective of the full-employment macroeconomic model, there appears to be no presumption that a trade deficit is either a good or a bad thing. A deficit occurs when the domestic economy's total *absorption* (that is, consumption plus investment plus government expenditures) exceeds its production of goods and services and the shortfall is met by imports from abroad. (An equivalent statement of the same position is that expenditures on goods and services exceeds income, and the difference is met by borrowing from abroad.) The consequence of a deficit is that residents of the rest of the world build up more claims on the domestic economy.

If a country persistently runs a trade deficit, then its debts to the rest of the world rise and the interest payments on these debts rise also. For some heavily indebted countries, such as some in Africa and Latin America, interest on foreign debt has amounted to a substantial fraction of the value of their annual bud-

BASIC TRADE IDENTITIES

Capital inflow = trade deficit.

Investment = private savings + government savings + capital inflows.

LONG-RUN CONSEQUENCES OF PERSISTENT TRADE DEFICITS

Increased foreign indebtedness, leading eventually to

Increased interest and dividend payments abroad, and if foreign borrowing is not used to finance additional in-

vestments that yield returns sufficient to pay the increased interest and dividend payments,

Lower living standards

gets. Consequently Argentina has had to run a large trade surplus to pay the interest on its accumulated debts abroad. The United States ran large deficits during the 1980s as a consequence of which it went from having positive net foreign assets of over $100 billion in 1986 to having net foreign debts of over $100 billion in 1992, making it the largest net debtor in the world.

However, countries' ability to run trade deficits and surpluses contributes to the efficient allocation of resources around the world. During the late nineteenth century, when there were profitable investment opportunities in then-developing economies like Argentina, Britain invested heavily abroad. British financial surpluses were invested in railways and industries abroad, enabling rapid growth. Britain became the world's biggest net creditor and enjoyed a large flow of income from its foreign wealth. The returns earned by foreign investments exceeded the returns that might have been earned on investments in Britain.

Trade surpluses and deficits can result from countries' effectively smoothing the path of income over time. A temporary increase in national income might cause the residents of a country to want to invest most of it and spread out an increase in consumption over time. This would entail running a trade surplus while income was high, building up net foreign assets, and consuming the income generated

by them in the future. Thus there would be a trade surplus when income was high followed by a deficit when income returned to its normal level; the trade deficit would be paid for by interest on assets held abroad. This is one explanation for the large trade surpluses run by Britain in the years of peak North Sea oil production in the early 1980s as a result of which Britain's net overseas assets grew dramatically.

USING THE BASIC MODEL TO ANALYSE A TRADE DEFICIT

The full-employment model can be used both to provide insights into the origins of a trade deficit and to think about policies that might reduce it. As we have seen, an increase in the government's deficit—a decrease in national savings—in an open economy leads to more foreign borrowing; and increased foreign borrowing leads to an increased trade deficit. Exchange rates adjust to accommodate the trade deficit.

To reduce the trade deficit, we can either shift the investment function to the left as in Figure 24.9A or shift the aggregate savings curve to the right as in Figure 24.9B. The former obviously is not very desirable; it means that the economy will be less productive in the future. That is why attention has focused

REDUCING THE TRADE DEFICIT

Increase private savings.

Reduce the fiscal deficit.

Reduce investment.

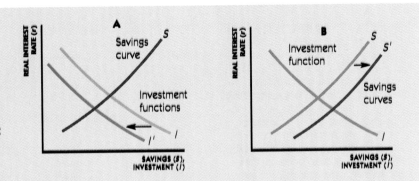

Figure 24.9 POLICIES TO REDUCE THE TRADE DEFICIT

The trade deficit can be reduced either by shifting the investment function to the left (panel A) or the savings function to the right (panel B).

on shifting the aggregate savings curve. There are two ways to do this: either increase government savings (reduce the deficit) or increase private savings.

GROWTH

The full-employment model can also be used to analyse policies that might promote economic growth. There are three keys to increased growth: (1) a more productive labour force—the result of improved edu-

cation and training; (2) more and better capital—the result of increased investment in plant and equipment and investment in **infrastructure**, such as roads and airports; and (3) technological progress—partially the result of public and private expenditures on research and development. Expenditures in all three categories are referred to as **investments**, which are expenditures made today that reap benefits in the future. Investments in people are often called **human capital.** All three of these investments shift future short-run production functions out, as depicted in Figure 24.10, so that the level of output that can be obtained at any level of employment is increased.

In a closed economy, it is possible to increase in-

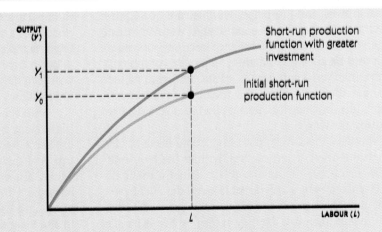

Figure 24.10 INCREASING THE ECONOMY'S PRODUCTIVE POTENTIAL

Improved education and training, the result of investments in people; more and better capital, the result of investments in plant and equipment; and improved technology, the result of investments in research and development and technology—all shift the short-run production function out, so that the level of output produced by any level of employment is increased.

Figure 24.11 EFFECT OF AN INCENTIVE TO INVESTMENT

An incentive to investment shifts the investment function to the right, from curve I to curve I'. In an open economy, with the world real interest rate at r^*, the level of investment will increase from I_0 to I_2 with no increase in interest rates and with the extra investment financed by borrowing from abroad. In a closed economy, with no recourse to foreign borrowing, the level of investment goes up from I_0 to I_1 and the rate of interest goes up from r^* to r' to stimulate additional saving.

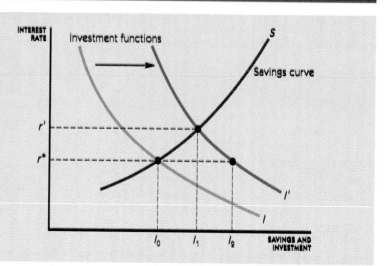

vestment by shifting the savings function to the right. In an open economy, investment can also be increased by shifting the investment function to the right. In an open economy, operating with a given world real interest rate, shifting the savings function to the right will increase the trade surplus or reduce the trade deficit, and eventually lead to bigger net foreign wealth, but it will not raise domestic production.

STIMULATING INVESTMENT

Governments have used tax policy as a way of shifting the investment function, as illustrated in Figure 24.11. One such policy is **accelerated depreciation.** When a firm buys a machine that lasts, say, ten years, it should be allowed to deduct 10 percent of the cost of the machine each year from its profits, to reflect the fact that over time, the machine is becoming worth less and less. The deduction is called a **depreciation allowance.**

However, the government may allow firms to depreciate equipment more rapidly than the true rate. Thus, firms may be able to pretend that a machine that lasted ten years only lasted five and deduct 20 percent of its value in each of the first five years of its life. This means that taxes they pay in the first five years are lower. Obviously, a pound today is worth far more than a pound five years from now: with accelerated

depreciation, the present discounted value of the tax reductions associated with depreciation allowances is greatly increased. This makes investments more attractive, shifting the investment function to the right.

STIMULATING SAVINGS

Governments frequently try to shift the savings function by providing tax incentives to saving. Saving for pensions in most countries has tax benefits. In Britain, contributions to approved pension schemes are tax-free. In the 1980s a British government introduced Personal Equity Plans (PEPs) which allowed dividends and capital gains to be taken tax-free. Similarly tax exempt special savings accounts (TESSAs) allowed tax-free interest on savings accounts. A successor to these schemes, the personal savings account (PSA), allows tax-free returns on a range of assets.

These schemes may have had the effect of diverting savings from one form to another, rather than increasing the total amount of savings. To some degree this was their intention. The PEPs were intended to widen share ownership across the population. In large part these schemes merely increased the income and wealth of people who already held assets in shares and bank and building society accounts.

In open economies like Britain policies to shift the overall savings curve are less likely to increase

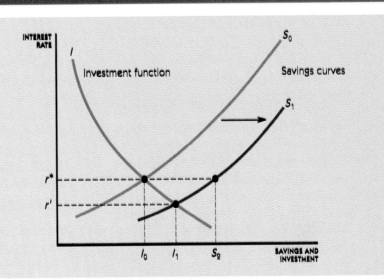

Figure 24.12 EFFECTS OF POLICIES TO STIMULATE SAVINGS

In an open economy, a tax incentive that shifted the savings curve to the right from S_0 to S_1 would not affect investment but would lead to a trade surplus and a capital outflow (equal in size to the length S_2I_0). In a closed economy, the shift in the savings function S_0 to S_1 would push the real interest rate down from r^* to r' and lead to a rise in investment from I_0 to I_1.

domestic investment, as illustrated in Figure 24.12. The shift simply sends the savings abroad, in the form of a reduction in net imports and a corresponding increase in investment abroad. The situation would be different in a closed economy, where higher levels of savings would lower the interest rate and thereby stimulate domestic investment.

REDUCING THE DEFICIT

We saw earlier that reducing the deficit is equivalent to shifting the aggregate savings curve to the right. But we need to emphasise that the net effect on growth depends on how the deficit is cut. In Figure 24.13 we

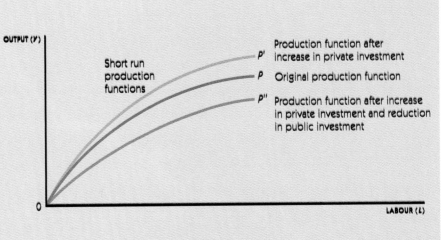

Figure 24.13 EFFECT OF DEFICIT REDUCTION ON ECONOMIC GROWTH

The lower deficit shifts the aggregate savings curve to the right, leading to lower interest rates and higher investment. This shifts the future short-run production function out from OP to OP'. But if the deficit reduction is accomplished by cutting back productive public investments, the effect of these lower investments is to shift the short-run production function in. It is possible that the net effect may actually be to lower future output, as illustrated by the curve OP''.

CLOSE-UP: INTERNATIONAL ASSET POSITIONS

The accumulated debts of some of the third world debtor countries are notoriously large. But the developed countries themselves have also run up large debts and deficits.

The trade deficit of a country is identically equal to the sum of the government's deficit ($G - T$) and the private sector's deficit ($I - S$). And when the country runs a trade deficit, it has to be financed by the rest of the world's buying financial assets from the country in question. This adds to the stock of assets owned by the rest of the world and correspondingly diminishes the net overseas wealth of the country.

The picture is more complicated because the residents of a country can buy more assets in the rest of the world, providing the residents of the rest of the world buy assets in the country, without there being a trade deficit or surplus. For example, British residents might buy stocks in U.S. companies while Americans buy stocks in U.K. companies, without there being a trade imbalance. There can be a complicated pattern of ownership of assets whose relative values can change because of stock markets and exchange rates going up or down. When this is the case, the value of the net overseas assets of a country (the difference between the value of the assets that the country owns in the rest of the world and the value of the assets that the rest of the world owns in that country) can change quickly and in a way that seems only loosely related to the trade balance.

Nevertheless, some fairly clear patterns emerge. The first figure that follows shows the overseas assets and liabilities of the United Kingdom from 1980 to 1997. Both assets and liabilities have grown strongly, from around 500 billion U.S. dollars in 1980 to around 3,000 billion in 1997. The net asset position is a small difference between two very large numbers. Since all these figures are estimated with substantial error, the net asset figure has to be treated with great caution: the margins of error are enormous. The gross asset and liability figures are greatly affected by the revaluation of existing assets.

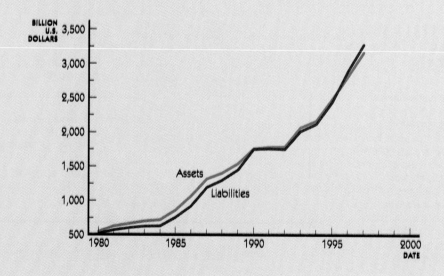

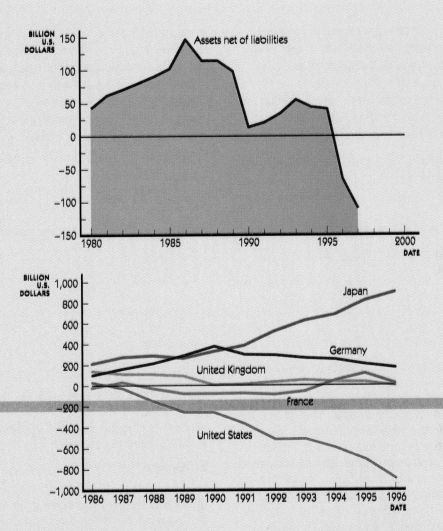

BILLION U.S. DOLLARS

Assets net of liabilities

(Top figure: net assets 1980–2000, ranging from 150 to −150)

BILLION U.S. DOLLARS

Japan

Germany

United Kingdom

France

United States

(Bottom figure: net wealth 1986–1996, five countries, ranging from 1,000 to −1,000)

The net assets of the United Kingdom (second following figure) show growth from 1980 until 1986, followed by decline until 1990, growth until 1993, and decline since. The growth in the late 1970s was fueled by the United Kingdom's earnings from North Sea oil and the associated trade surpluses. To these were added in the early 1980s the effects of tight monetary and fiscal policy, which further increased the trade surpluses. From 1986 the economy was growing, policy was much looser, and the trade balance went into deficit. The period of net asset growth from 1990 to 1993 corresponds to a tight monetary policy (and to an allegedly overvalued pound), and the period from 1993 onwards to a period of sustained growth and modest trade deficits.

The third figure that follows shows comparative figures for five countries for selected years between 1986 and 1996. The outstanding feature is the persistent decline in U.S. net overseas wealth to −870 billion dollars in 1996 and the rise in that of the Japanese to 890 billion dollars. This has been a consequence of persistent U.S. trade deficits and Japanese surpluses. By comparison, the French, German, and British net asset positions look very small. Germany's net assets fell substantially after 1990, following the deficits induced by unification, while France's position was bolstered in 1990 by the surpluses associated with tight money under the "Franc fort" policy.

While the United States rages against persistent Japanese trade surpluses, it nevertheless makes sense for the Japanese to invest overseas (which is the corollary of their trade surplus) at a time when the returns to investment in Japan are particularly low relative to returns in other countries, such as the United States. Trade imbalances and international capital flows are part of the mechanism that brings about an efficient allocation of resources around the world by steering funds to places where the return on investment is greatest.

Sources: IMF, *International Financial Statistics Yearbook* (1998); *Bank of England Quarterly Bulletin*, November 1997.

illustrate a case where deficit reduction leads to lower growth. As we saw earlier, the shift in the aggregate savings curve to the right leads to lower interest rates and increased private investment. This shifts the economy's future short-run production function out to OP'. But if the government reduces the deficit by cutting back on productive public investments, such as research, investments in education, or infrastructure, the future short-run production function shifts in to OP''—below where it was before the deficit reduction. A pound of deficit reduction does not, in general, result in an increase of private investment by a pound because the investment function is upward sloping, so that even if public investment is *less* productive than private investment, deficit reduction attained through investment reduction can lower economic growth.[3] And there is evidence that public investments in education, research, and infrastructure may yield higher marginal returns than private investment.

[3] Only if the investment function were a horizontal straight line would a shift in the savings curve to the right by a pound result in an increase in investment by a pound.

CONSENSUS IN MACROECONOMICS

From this chapter emerges an eighth point of consensus in macroeconomics:

8 Growth

Increases in standards of living require increases in productivity; increases in productivity require expenditures on research and development, investments in new technology, plant, equipment, and infrastructure and increases in the skills of the labour force.

In a closed economy, investment can be increased either by shifting the investment curve to the right (such as by accelerated depreciation) or by shifting the savings curve to the right (such as by preferential tax treatment). Some preferential tax treatments may actually lower national savings, since the induced private savings are less than the increased deficit. Similarly, deficit reduction, in a closed economy, will result in increased private investment, but if the deficit reduction is attained through reducing public investment, future output and living standards may actually be reduced.

REVIEW AND PRACTICE

Summary

1 National debt levels have changed markedly over the years. In 1945 Britain's debt was more than two year's GDP. In 1989, it had fallen to less than 40 percent of one year's GDP.

2 In a closed economy, increases in the deficit lead to lower private investment and increased interest rates. The net effect of reductions in the deficit depend on how it is reduced. If generated by reductions in public investment, growth is likely to be reduced, as the increased private investment is unlikely to be sufficient to offset the reduced public investment.

3 In a small open economy, increases in the deficit have no effect on investment but lead to larger trade deficits and increased foreign indebtedness. Cumulative increases in foreign indebtedness will make future citizens worse off, as they have to pay interest on the foreign indebtedness.

4 The trade deficit must equal capital inflows. Policy options for reducing a trade deficit and foreign borrowing include decreasing investment (a bad idea for long-term growth), increasing household and business savings (a good idea if the government could do it), or reducing the government's fiscal deficit.

5 The savings-investment identity for an open economy says that the sum of private savings, capital flows from abroad, and government savings is equal to investment. This identity implies that a change in any one factor must also involve offsetting changes in other factors.

6 Increases in investments in human capital, plant and equipment, infrastructure, and improved technology all shift out the short-run production curve, increasing the full-employment output of the economy and the economy's rate of growth. Investment can be stimulated through incentives such as accelerated depreciation or, in a closed economy, by increasing the rate of savings through tax concessions. Because of a low interest elasticity of savings, tax concessions may not be very effective.

Key Terms

fiscal deficit	exchange rates	infrastructure	depreciation allowance
trade deficit	depreciate	human capital	interest elasticity of savings
capital flows (capital outflow, inflow)	appreciate	accelerated depreciation	

Review Questions

1 What is the relationship between the deficit and the level of the debt?

2 What are the consequences of an increased deficit for private investment in an open economy and in a closed economy?

3 Why do the consequences for growth of deficit reduction depend on whether the deficit reduction is accomplished by cutting government investment, by cutting government consumption expenditures, or by raising taxes?

4 How have Britain's net assets held abroad changed during the twentieth century? What sectors have influenced it?

5 What is the relationship between the trade deficit and an inflow of foreign capital?

6 What is the relationship between the trade deficit and the fiscal deficit?

7 What is the exchange rate? How is it determined? What role do adjustments in the exchange rate play in ensuring that capital inflows equal the trade deficit?

8 What are the consequences of persistent trade deficits?

9 What is the savings-investment identity for an open economy?

10 How may government stimulate investment and savings?

11 How do efforts to increase economic growth differ in a small open economy compared to those in a closed economy?

PROBLEMS

1 Suppose a certain country has private savings of 6 percent of GDP, foreign borrowing of 1 percent of GDP, and a balanced budget. What is its level of investment? If the budget deficit is 1.5 percent of GDP, how does your answer change?

2 Why does it matter if a country borrows abroad to finance the expansion of its railways or the increase in social security benefits for the elderly?

3 Assume investments in human capital yield a return of 15 percent, private investments yield a total return of 10 percent, and public investments in research yield a return of 25 percent. Assume the deficit is £100 billion per year and the government wishes to eliminate it. What will be the impact on economic growth of a deficit reduction package that consists of reducing defence expenditures by £50 billion, education expenditures by £40 billion, and research expenditures by £10 billion?

4 The primary deficit is defined as the difference between government expenditures *excluding interest payments* and tax revenues; it represents what the deficit would have been, had the government not inherited any debt. The following table shows the U.S. primary deficit measured in billions of U.S. dollars over time. Discuss why the concept of a primary deficit may or may not be useful or relevant.

5 If the economy is growing at 5 percent per year and the debt-to-GDP ratio is 50 percent, what is the critical value of the deficit-to-GDP ratio, such that if the deficit-to-GDP ratio exceeds that number, the debt-to-GDP ratio will increase and, if the deficit-to-GDP ratio falls short of that number, the debt-to-GDP ratio will decrease.

6 The foreign indebtedness of the United States is greater than that of Mexico, Brazil, and Argentina combined. But does this necessarily mean that the United States has a larger debt problem than those countries? Why or why not? Can you think of a situation in which an individual with debts of larger value may actually have less of a debt problem?

7 If Parliament were to pass a law prohibiting foreigners from buying British government securities, would this prevent government borrowing from leading to capital inflows? Discuss.

8 Japan had large trade surpluses during the 1980s. Would this cause Japan to be a borrower or a lender in international capital markets?

9 If a country borrowed $50 billion from abroad one year and its imports were worth $800 billion, what would be the value of its exports? How does the answer change if, instead of borrowing, the country loaned $100 billion abroad?

10 Since other countries benefit from exporting their products to the United States, why shouldn't the U.S. government charge them for the privilege of selling in the United States?

Year	Primary deficit	Actual deficit
1980	21.3	73.8
1985	82.8	212.3
1990	37.2	221.4
1995	−68.4	163.8

PART SIX

UNEMPLOYMENT MACROECONOMICS

P art Five explored full-employment macroeconomics. The basic assumption was that the economy operates as envisioned in the basic competitive model: prices, wages, and interest rates adjust quickly and fully to ensure that all markets clear. Most importantly, the demand for labour equals the supply of labour. The assumption may be unrealistic, but the model is instructive. We saw how deficits crowd out investment and increase foreign borrowing, and we got to look more closely at economic growth.

The full-employment model needs to be modified to take up two further fundamental macroeconomic questions: unemployment and inflation. In this part, we take up unemployment, reserving inflation for Part Seven. Over the long run, most economies manage to create jobs to keep pace with the increasing number of workers. But in the short run, mismatches between demand and supply occur.

Here, in Part Six, we examine the problem of maintaining the economy at full employment. The most fundamental difference in our analysis in this part of the book is that we drop the assumption that wages and prices instantaneously adjust to clear all markets. For simplicity, we assume that they do not adjust at all, that they are fixed. In Part Seven, we will take up the in-between case, exploring how wages and prices adjust and why they often change so slowly.

Chapter 25 provides an overview of the macroeconomics of unemployment and introduces some of the basic concepts. The next two chapters focus on the product market. Chapter 26 looks at aggregate demand, which, as we will see, in situations of unemployment determines the level of aggregate output. Chapter 27 looks more closely at two of the most important components of aggregate demand, consumption and investment.

Chapters 28 to 30 focus on the capital market and the links between that market and the product market. We begin with a discussion, in Chapter 28, of money. Chapter 29 then discusses monetary theory—how changes in the supply of money, interest rates, and the availability of credit affect the level of economic activity and how government changes the supply of money and credit availability. Chapter 30 puts the entire unemployment model with fixed prices and wages together, focusing on how fiscal and monetary policy can be used to restore the economy to full employment. To reach a better understanding of the roles these two alternative policy instruments play, it contrasts both their consequences and the difficulties that are faced in using them effectively.

CHAPTER 25

OVERVIEW OF UNEMPLOYMENT MACROECONOMICS

P eople worry about jobs. They worry about layoffs. If they are laid off, they worry about how long it will take to get another job. In all market economies, there is some unemployment. In a dynamic economy, some firms and industries are shrinking—jobs are being lost—at the same time that new jobs are being created. It takes time for individuals to switch from one job to another. But at times, as we saw in Chapter 22, the unemployment rate becomes very high. Labour markets do not clear: the demand for labour is much less than the supply. In such situations, governments take on the responsibility of reducing the unemployment rate, not necessarily to zero but at least to a low level.

We have seen how all markets of the economy are interlinked. The labour market is linked to the product market and the product market to the capital market. The labour market is particularly sensitive to changes in the product market: if output goes down, so too will the demand for labour. If real wages adjust too slowly, there will be unemployment. In this chapter, we do not ask why they adjust slowly; that is a question postponed until Part Seven. We focus instead on the consequences. After a few words about macroeconomic models, we discuss the labour market, then the product market, and finally the capital market. The chapter closes by applying the framework to discuss some recent macroeconomic events.

KEY QUESTIONS

1 How do economists analyse what determines levels of aggregate output and employment in the short run, when wages and prices are fixed?

2 What causes shifts in the aggregate demand and supply for labour? Why may unemployment result if wages fail to adjust in response to these shifts?

3 What is the aggregate demand curve? What happens when the price level is fixed at a level at which aggregate demand is less than aggregate supply? What are the consequences of a shift in the aggregate demand curve in these circumstances?

4 How can we use aggregate demand curves to interpret some of the major macroeconomic episodes of the past fifty years?

MORE ABOUT MACROECONOMIC MODELS

Part Five developed the full-employment macroeconomic model. The critical assumption of Part Five was that wages and prices adjust so that all markets—including the labour market—clear: there is no unemployment. The basic way in which this part differs from Part Five is that here, we are concerned about the problem of unemployment. The basic explanation for unemployment is that wages do not adjust quickly enough to shifts in either the demand or supply curve for labour, so that *at least for a while and sometimes for extended periods of time,* the demand for labour at market wages and prices may be less than the supply. In this part of the book, to simplify matters, we assume wages and prices are fixed; that is, they do not adjust at all. Economists say that such wages and prices are **rigid.** The results are much the same as they would be if they adjusted slowly, that is, adjusted in the direction required by market clearing, but too slowly to ensure that the demand and supply for, say, labour were equated. While some prices—such as those on the stock market—adjust quickly, others—wages in particular—adjust slowly. When firms and workers bargain over wage increases, they frequently consider the rate of price inflation, the wage increases granted in other

firms, the profitability of the firm, and the firm's ability to employ its existing workforce. It is generally expected that wages in a firm or industry will rise in line with wages elsewhere in the economy and that they should keep pace with inflation and reward productivity growth. Rarely is the level of unemployment an important direct influence in wage bargaining. Even in nonunionised firms, circumstances internal to the firm and its workers—profitability, wages relative to wages paid elsewhere, employment projections—matter more than aggregate labour market conditions. Consequently wages tend to adjust only slowly when there is an excess supply of labour in the economy as a whole.

The fact that slow adjustments can lead to persistent unemployment is one of the reasons that macroeconomists focus so much on dynamics—how and in particular, *how fast* things change. In Part Seven of the book, we will describe the dynamics of the economy, focusing in particular on price and wage adjustments. We will analyse how and how fast the economy adjusts.

This part of the book focuses on the short run, a time span that might range from a week or a month up to a few years. Although investment is occurring in the economy, we assume the net change in the capital stock is so small in the short term that it can be ignored. Except when we focus explicitly upon *changes* in government actions, we will also assume that tax rates, levels of expenditures, and the money supply are all fixed.

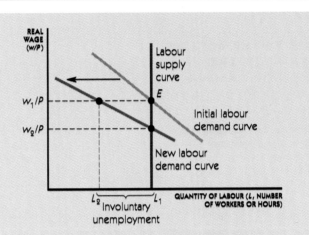

Figure 25.1 **EFFECTS OF A SHIFT IN THE DEMAND FOR LABOUR WITH FIXED WAGES**

Equilibrium in the labour market is at the intersection of the aggregate demand and supply curves for labour. If the demand for labour decreases and the wage is fixed, employed labour decreases from L_1 to L_2.

THE LABOUR MARKET

Since unemployment is our key concern in this part of the book, our discussion naturally begins with the labour market. In Chapter 23, we described equilibrium in the labour market as the intersection of the aggregate demand and supply curves for labour. Both depended on real wages. We are assuming now that prices are fixed, so we do not have to distinguish between nominal and real wages.

In the earlier discussion of the labour market, we simplified the analysis in two ways. We assumed that each worker supplied exactly 40 hours of labour—no more and no less—per week and that real wages did not affect aggregate supply.[1] Thus, the aggregate supply curve was vertical. Wages were flexible, so that they adjusted to equate demand and supply, to w_1/P in Figure 25.1.

But what happens if wages do not adjust quickly?

[1] The fact that each worker works 40 hours means that we can put on the horizontal axis either the number of workers or the number of hours worked.

Assume, for some reason, that the demand curve for labour suddenly shifts to the left, so that at each wage, fewer workers are demanded. At the old equilibrium wage w_1/P, the supply for labour exceeds the demand. However, if the wage is stuck at the original level w_1/P—above the wage at which the demand for labour equals the supply—firms will still only hire the amount demanded. More workers will be willing to work than can get jobs at that wage. Those without jobs will be involuntarily unemployed. In Figure 25.1 the demand for labour will only be L_2, while the supply is L_1. The distance between these two points measures the amount of involuntary unemployment. At this high wage, the supply of labour exceeds the demand.

Involuntary unemployment arising from reductions in the demand for labour (combined with wage rigidity) would be much less of a social problem if the impact could be spread over the entire population. Even if the demand for labour were reduced by 10 percent and wages did not fall, the consequences would be limited if each worker worked 10 percent fewer hours. The problem in that case would be *underemployment*. Each person in the economy might work only 36 hours per week, when she wished to work 40 hours.

In the modern industrial economy, the problem is different. Most workers continue to work the same or only a slightly reduced number of hours when the

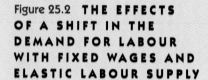

Figure 25.2 **THE EFFECTS OF A SHIFT IN THE DEMAND FOR LABOUR WITH FIXED WAGES AND ELASTIC LABOUR SUPPLY**

If wages do not fall when the demand for labour shifts to the left, involuntary unemployment results. If wages adjust, employment decreases, but this is a voluntary change.

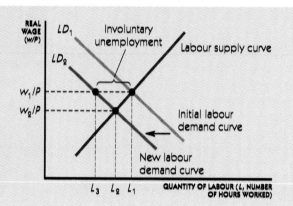

labour market goes out of equilibrium, but an unfortunate few will find no full-time job at all at the going wage. This is the problem of unemployment. Whenever the supply of labour exceeds the demand at the going wage, there will be "rationing": some individuals will not be able to sell all the labour they would like. But the impact of this rationing is not evenly spread in the economy; some workers will manage to sell little if any of their labour services, while others will be fully employed. Many of the social problems associated with a reduced demand for labour result from the fact that the economic burden is so concentrated.

The analysis is little different if we assume an upward-sloping rather than vertical labour supply curve. This would mean that workers change the number of hours they work in response to wage changes, supplying less labour at lower wages and more labour at higher wages. And at low wages, some individuals may decide not to work at all. Consider Figure 25.2, which shows an upward-sloping labour supply curve and a labour demand curve, LD_1. The initial equilibrium entails a wage of w_1/P and employment of L_1 (hours worked). Now suppose there is a reduction in labour demanded at each wage, represented by the leftward shift of the labour demand curve from LD_1 to LD_2. If wages adjusted quickly, there would be a new equilibrium with

wages at w_2/P and a lower level of employment at L_2. In this case, the reduction in employment is referred to as **voluntary unemployment.** At the lower wage w_2/P fewer people wish to work—those who wish to work have jobs, and those who are unemployed have chosen not to work.

By contrast, if wages remain at w_1/P after the shift of the labour demand curve, then employed labour falls to L_3. At this wage, the number willing to work is much higher: it remains at L_1. The workers who cannot get jobs represent **involuntary unemployment.** They are willing and able to work at the going wage w_1/P but simply cannot find jobs.

Most economists believe that the individual's labour supply curve, while not perfectly inelastic (or vertical), is relatively inelastic and that much of the responsiveness of the aggregate labour supply to wages comes from decisions to participate in the labour force (rather than in the desired number of hours worked per week). Moreover, as we have noted, when demand for labour is less than the supply, the shortfall usually takes the form mostly of reduction in employed workers, rather than hours worked per worker. For simplicity, in the following analysis, we shall assume that the hours worked per worker are fixed and that reductions in the demand for labour hours are translated directly into reductions in employment.

UNEMPLOYMENT
AND WAGE RIGIDITIES

If we look at data on real wages—wages adjusted for changes in the price level—we see that wages vary little with economic conditions. Given the relatively small changes in real wages, the magnitude of the changes in employment cannot be explained by movements along a fixed, steep labour supply curve. Then how can we account for such large changes in employment?

There are but two possibilities. One is that the labour supply curve is not only not fixed but shifts dramatically—in a way just offsetting shifts in the labour demand curve—so that in spite of large variations in employment, real wages remained unchanged. Few economists accept this account. Even if there are sudden, dramatic shifts in the labour supply curve, it is hard to believe that these would occur in just the right amount to offset shifts in the labour demand curve.

Economists have focused their attention on the other possible explanation: at least at times, demand for labour is less than supply; the labour market is not in equilibrium. How does such a situation arise? First, there is a shift in the demand curve for labour, as we illustrated in Figures 25.1 and 25.2.

Such shifts can occur fairly rapidly, mainly because of changes in output. Second, wages fail to fall enough to restore equilibrium (where demand for labour equals supply), resulting in involuntary unemployment. Because there is widespread agreement over this explanation, we may present it as our ninth point of consensus:

9 Unemployment

Unemployment is typically generated by shifts in the aggregate demand curve for labour when wages fail to adjust. The shifts in the aggregate demand curve for labour typically arise from changes in aggregate output.

UNEMPLOYMENT AND THE
AGGREGATE SUPPLY OF LABOUR

While most unemployment arises from sudden leftward shifts in the demand curve for labour, occasionally large rightward shifts in the supply curve for labour can also give rise to unemployment, as illustrated in Figure 25.3. Normally, aggregate labour supply changes only slowly, such as through demographic changes or changes in labour force participation rates. But there are circumstances in which aggregate supply can shift dramatically in a short

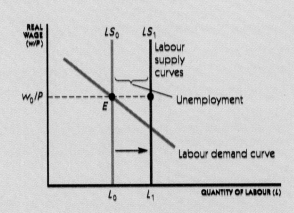

Figure 25.3

UNEMPLOYMENT AND THE AGGREGATE SUPPLY OF LABOUR

Unemployment may arise from rightward shifts of the aggregate supply curve for labour, when wages fail to adjust. The initial equilibrium wage is w_0/P, at the intersection of the aggregate demand curve for labour and the initial aggregate supply curve for labour (LS_0). The aggregate supply curve for labour then shifts from LS_0 to LS_1. The real wage remains at w_0/P, where the quantity of labour demanded L_0 is less than the quantity of labour supplied, resulting in unemployment.

BASIC ISSUES IN THE ANALYSIS OF UNEMPLOYMENT

1 What causes shifts in the demand curve for labour?

2 Why do wages fail to adjust?

span of time. For instance, in the early 1990s, Israel was faced with a flood of Jewish immigrants from Russia, increasing its labour force by more than 10 percent. In the short run, real wages did not adjust quickly enough, and unemployment rose. Remarkably, within five years, the unemployment rate was back down, though the adjustment seems to have been more through a compensating shift in the aggregate demand curve for labour than a lowering of the real wage. Another instance of *potentially* rapid shifts in the labour supply curve is associated with changes in tax laws, which might induce a smaller or larger fraction of the population to join the labour force, though in practice such changes appear to take place more gradually.

THE PRODUCT MARKET IN THE SHORT RUN

To understand unemployment we must understand what causes changes in output. Thus, we now turn to the product market. Later, in Part Seven, we will return to another basic issue of unemployment: what causes real wages to adjust slowly?

Just as the demand and supply curves for labour were the basic tools for analysing the labour market, the aggregate supply and demand curves for goods provide the framework for analysing the product market. Recall the graph of the product market from Chapter 23. Redrawn here as Figure 25.4, it shows the vertical aggregate supply curve and the downward-sloping aggregate demand curve intersecting at point E. As we know from Chapter 23, the aggregate supply curve defines the economy's full-employment level of output, denoted as Y_s. At point E the economy is at full employment at the price level P_0.

Like the assumption of fixed wages in our short-run analysis of the labour market, we assume that prices are fixed in the short-run analysis of the product market. In the short run, prices change little in response to movements of the aggregate demand and supply curves. Car manufacturers, for instance, typically change their prices only when new models come out. There are costs to changing prices—such as those of printing new catalogues and price lists—

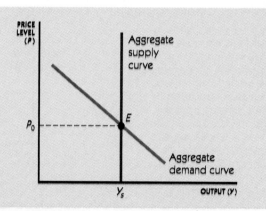

Figure 25.4 **THE PRODUCT MARKET**

The full-employment level of output Y_s is given by the vertical aggregate supply curve. The aggregate demand curve intersects the aggregate supply curve at the price level P_0. Full-employment equilibrium is at point E, the intersection of the aggregate demand and supply curves.

CLOSE-UP: G-7 AND THE WORLDWIDE JOBS PROBLEM

In March 1994, the leaders of the seven major industrialised countries (called the G-7) convened in Detroit. Their agenda: the first ever jobs summit to discuss the worldwide jobs problem and what might be done about it. Through the 1980s and into the 1990s, Europe had been plagued with a high level of unemployment. In Ireland and Spain, almost one in five remained unemployed. In the Netherlands, though the official unemployment statistics were better, the disability rolls—again, one in five—disguised what was really going on; more generous disability benefits and an absence of tight screening led many who were thrown out of jobs to apply for disability rather than unemployment benefits. The United States was beginning to bring unemployment under control, but in many other countries, unemployment continued to be a problem as the following graph indicates.

All countries agreed that the major source of the problem was with low-skilled and unskilled workers. The demand curve for these workers had not shifted to the right enough to offset the increased supply of such workers, and in some countries, the demand curve for these workers may have even shifted to the left. Though a variety of explanations have been put forward, the most widely accepted is changes in technology, which have increased the demand for those with skills (such as the ability to use computers) relative to those without skills. The responses to

these shifts in labour supply and demand curves have varied from country to country. In the United States, real wages of unskilled labour fell. In Europe, higher minimum wages helped prevent such a drop in real wages at the bottom of the skill distribution. Real wages of those employed in Europe increased over the 1970s through the 1990s by about 2 percent per year, in contrast to the virtual stagnation in the United States.

While the focus of attention was on unskilled workers, in Europe the problem seemed to be more widespread. Total job creation in the private sector in the first half of the 1990s was virtually nil, in contrast to the United States where more than seven million jobs were created in the private sector from 1993 to 1995. While there is no universally accepted explanation of Europe's poor job performance, one widely held view focuses on more rigid labour markets, in which it is harder for firms to fire workers. But the flip side of greater job security is that firms become more nervous about taking on more workers.

Thus, in Europe fewer people had jobs, but those who did did better. The European solution involved greater inequality among the unskilled workers (higher wages versus no wages) and a loss of economic efficiency, as human resources were vastly underutilised.

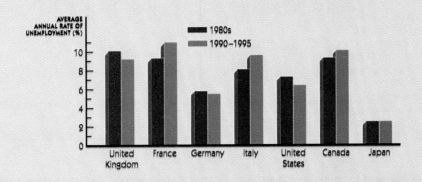

and risks; if a firm raises its price and its rivals do not, it might price itself out of the market and lose customers. While there are a few markets, such as the stock market or the market for gold, in which prices adjust to shifts in the demand and supply curves on a daily or faster basis, for most goods and services, whether sold by producers, wholesalers, or retailers, there is considerable price rigidity.

Consider what happens in the short run if aggregate demand shifts to the left, as depicted in Figure 25.5. At price level P_0, firms will produce only the quantity that they can sell, Y_1, which is below the full-employment level of output. One result of the reduced output will be a decrease in the demand for labour. Because of fixed wages in the labour market, this results in involuntary unemployment. Eventually, prices and wages may adjust, and if the aggregate demand curve remains in its new position (AD_1), the economy may move down the aggregate demand curve towards the future full-employment equilibrium E_f. But this process of adjustment is beyond the scope of our concern here. In the short run—a period that may span a year or more—the economy will be stuck at P_0, with output below capacity and involuntary unemployment.

Another scenario is also possible and is illustrated in Figure 25.6. At price level P_0, demand exceeds supply, output is limited by aggregate supply (Y_s), and there is upward pressure on prices, anticipating the economy's eventual movement up the aggregate supply curve towards the future full-employment equilibrium E_f. Under such circumstances the problem is not unemployment but inflation, a subject we will consider in detail in later chapters. For now, the point to remember is that inflation becomes a concern when demand exceeds supply at a given price level; unemployment is the opposite problem, when demand at a given price level is less than the full-employment supply Y_s.

THE ECONOMY BELOW CAPACITY

The economy may fall below the full-employment level of output for any number of reasons. Anything that decreases the demand (at a given price level) for consumption, investment, government expenditures, or net exports can give rise to a leftward shift in the aggregate demand curve, bringing the economy to a level of output below the full-employment level. For instance, an economic downturn in Mexico, Japan, or the United States will decrease its demand for European goods, decreasing our exports to it at any price level. Or, if businesses lose confidence in the future, they will be less willing to invest. Such unexpected shifts in the aggregate demand curve are referred to as **demand shocks.**

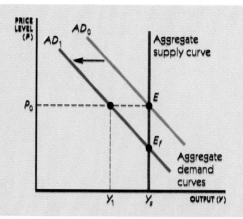

Figure 25.5 **OUTPUT BELOW CAPACITY**

With the price level fixed at P_0, if the aggregate demand curve shifts to the left, the economy will fall below the full-employment level of output Y_s. Output will be given by the aggregate demand curve at P_0, the level of output Y_1. Eventually, if the aggregate demand curve remains at AD_1, the economy will move down the aggregate demand curve towards the future full-employment equilibrium E_f.

Figure 25.6 EXCESS DEMAND

If the aggregate demand curve shifts to the right (from AD_0 to AD_1), aggregate demand will exceed the economy's capacity to produce at P_0. There will be excess demand and upward pressure on prices. Eventually, the economy will move up the aggregate supply curve towards the future full-employment equilibrium at E_f.

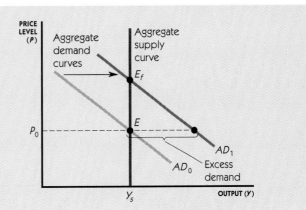

Occasionally, shifts in the supply schedule can also give rise to excess capacity—a wave of immigration faster than the economy can absorb or improvements in technology that increase the economy's productive capacity, even with an unchanged labour supply. When such shifts are sudden and unanticipated, they are referred to as **supply shocks.**

However it gets there, when the economy falls below the full-employment level of output, the options for policymakers are clear: either wait for the economy to adjust to a new full-employment equilibrium, or take action to shift the aggregate demand curve to the right and reestablish the full-employment level of output at the existing price level. Policymakers have tended to take action. As the economist John Maynard Keynes once said: "In the long run, we are all dead." That the economy will resume full employment in the long run offers little solace to the unemployed. Figure 25.7 depicts the economy beginning at a level of output below capacity at Y_0. By shifting the aggregate demand curve to the right, the economy can be brought to the full-employment level of output, or at least closer to it, and faster than if markets were allowed to adjust on their own.

Figure 25.7 ATTAINING FULL EMPLOYMENT

At price level P_0, if the government can shift the aggregate demand curve enough to the right, the economy can be moved to operate at full capacity. When the aggregate demand curve shifts from AD_0 to AD_1, output increases from Y_0 to Y_1. With the aggregate demand curve at AD_2, the economy attains the full-employment equilibrium at P_0.

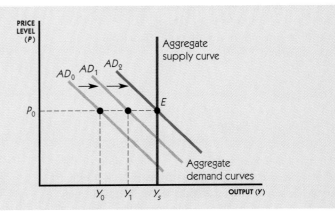

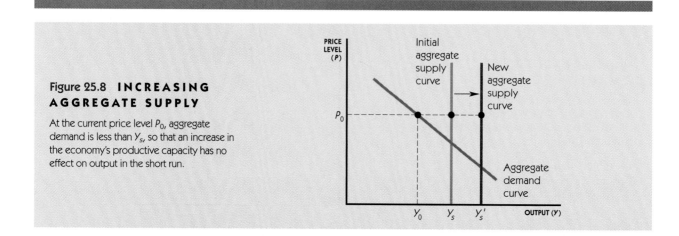

Figure 25.8 INCREASING AGGREGATE SUPPLY

At the current price level P_0, aggregate demand is less than Y_s, so that an increase in the economy's productive capacity has no effect on output in the short run.

Anything that increases the demand (at a given price level) for consumption, investment, government expenditures, and net exports may lead to a rightward shift in the aggregate demand curve. One option for government is to increase its expenditures. For instance, by increasing defence expenditures, aggregate demand at each price level would increase, shifting the aggregate demand curve to the right. With excess capacity in the economy, this would result in increased output.

Raising government expenditures in response to involuntary unemployment is an act of **fiscal policy**. By fiscal policy, economists refer to changes in government expenditures and taxes directed at improving macroeconomic performance, including increasing output when there is excess capacity. Economists sometimes refer to a government effort to stimulate the economy through fiscal policy as a **fiscal stimulus**.

THE SUPPLY SIDE OF THE MARKET

So far we have focused on the demand side of the market, and shifts in aggregate demand. What effect do increases in aggregate supply have on involuntary unemployment when the economy is below capacity?

Increased capacity of the economy may result from new investment or new technology. This shifts

Y_s to the right. Figure 25.8 shows a rightward shift of the aggregate supply curve when the economy is initially below capacity at the price level P_0. The result is only an increase in the amount by which aggregate supply exceeds aggregate demand at P_0. There is no effect on output.

On the other hand, when there is excess demand for goods (see Figure 25.6), an increase in aggregate supply will reduce the magnitude of the excess demand for goods, and thus the magnitude of the inflationary pressures. This was part of the rationale for the supply-side policies of the 1980s, which were supposed to lead to increased labour supply and increased investment. As it turned out, the supply-side effects were small and were overwhelmed by demand effects arising out of monetary policy.

THREE MORE POINTS OF CONSENSUS

The important results of this analysis of aggregate demand and supply can be summarised in our tenth, eleventh, and twelfth points of consensus.

10 Stimulating the Economy When It Is below Capacity

When the economy has excess capacity, an increase in aggregate demand at each price level results in an increase in aggregate output, with relatively little effect on prices.

The increase in aggregate demand can, of course, come from any source: an increase in consumption by households, expenditures by government, investment by firms, or net exports.

11 The Effect of Overstimulating the Economy

When the economy is close to capacity, with most machines and workers fully employed, then a further increase in the demand for goods and services at each price level results in upward pressure on prices and has little effect on output.

12 Supply-Side Effects When There Is Excess Capacity

When the economy has excess capacity, increases in capacity have little effect on output.

LINKS WITH THE CAPITAL MARKET

We have now discussed the labour and product markets, two of the three central markets of the economy. These are both linked to the capital market in important ways.

In the capital market, interest rates are influenced by **monetary policy**—the actions of the **central bank,** which is responsible for controlling the money supply and interest rates. The central bank can lower and raise interest rates, with important consequences for the product and labour markets. Consider first the product market. Low interest rates may encourage the construction industry and other investment activities, leading to a higher demand for goods and a higher level of output. If the central bank detects a lull in economic activity, it may choose to lower the interest rate. Figure 25.9 shows the effect of lower interest rates on the product market. There is a rightward shift of the aggregate demand curve. If the economy is initially operating with excess capacity, the shift in the aggregate demand curve leads to an increase in aggregate output. We could then trace through the effects on the labour market: higher aggregate output leads to a higher level of employment.

On the other hand, if the central bank is worried that the inflation rate is about to increase, it typically raises the interest rate. A situation with inflationary pressure is usually one where, at the current price level, aggregate demand exceeds the economy's full-employment level of output, as depicted in Figure 25.6. A higher interest rate dampens the level of aggregate demand; at each price, the quantity of investment that firms wish to make is reduced, so that the aggregate demand curve shifts to the left. If the central bank's assessment of the economic situation is correct, then the leftward movement of the aggregate demand curve simply decreases the upward pressure on prices, without having much effect on output. But if it increases interest rates too far, it will

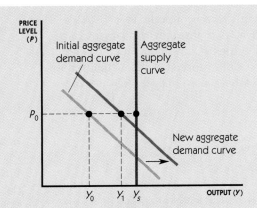

Figure 25.9 THE LINK BETWEEN THE CAPITAL MARKET AND THE PRODUCT MARKET

Lower interest rates lead to increased investment. This in turn leads to a rightward shift in the aggregate demand curve. If the economy is initially operating with excess capacity, aggregate output increases.

INTERDEPENDENCIES AMONG MARKETS

Changes in the capital market—such as lower interest rates—have immediate and direct impacts on the product market, shifting the aggregate demand curve.

Changes in the product market—such as increased aggregate demand—have impacts on the labour market, shifting the demand curve for labour.

---

shift the aggregate demand curve too much to the left, so that aggregate demand at the current price level P_0 will be less than Y_s: output will fall and unemployment will increase.

We have thus come full circle: all the markets of the economy are interconnected. So too are all the major policy concerns. The central bank may stimulate the economy by cutting the interest rate. On the other hand, aggressive action to contain inflation by restraining the economy—by raising the interest rate—discourages investment and may lead to lower growth. If the central bank acts excessively aggressively, it may overshoot, lowering output and inducing unemployment. Rather than just curtailing inflation, it may push the economy into a recession. Later chapters will pursue these links, as well as the trade-offs for policymakers.

MACROECONOMIC LESSONS FROM THE POSTWAR PERIOD

The wide areas of macroeconomic consensus have been developed in part through a series of hard-learned lessons in the decades following the Second World War. The brief historical sketches that follow highlight some of the major policy discussions of the period.

MR. BARBER'S DASH FOR GROWTH

In the early 1970s in Britain, unemployment grew rapidly, from 2.6 percent in 1970 to 3.4 percent in 1971 to 3.8 percent in 1972. The chancellor of the exchequer, Anthony (later Lord) Barber, in his budget in March 1972, introduced a very expansionary fiscal policy. Taxes were cut and government expenditures increased. The changes had the effect of shifting the aggregate demand curve out to the right. As the economy was believed to have a lot of spare capacity at the time, it was predicted that output would rise without a large increase in the price level. In terms of Figure 25.10, the economy was on the flat part of the AS curve. The shift in the aggregate demand curve should have moved the equilibrium from Y_0 to Y_1.

However, as luck would have it, in 1973, as the effect of the budget was working its way through the economy (in practice tax cuts do not affect consumers' expenditures instantaneously), there was an enormous rise in oil prices, when OPEC used its monopoly power for the first time. The value of the pound in terms of foreign currencies also fell sharply. Both of these things had the effect of raising the position of the AS curve.

The level of unemployment fell rapidly in response to the dash for growth but quickly rose again, and inflation shot upwards. Unemployment fell to 2.7 percent in 1973 and to 2.6 percent in 1974 but was back up to 4.0 percent in 1975 and 5.5 percent in 1976. Inflation rose from 7.1 percent in 1972 to 9.2 percent in 1973 to 16.1 percent in 1974, and to 24.3 percent in 1975.

Although the boost to aggregate demand given by the Barber budget of 1972 succeeded temporarily in reducing unemployment, the disastrous rise in inflation that followed in its wake undermined support for the use of fiscal expansion (following in a simple-minded way Keynes's prescriptions) to reduce unemployment. This was the last occasion when a deliberate policy of vigorous aggregate demand management was used in Britain. The Labour minister James (later

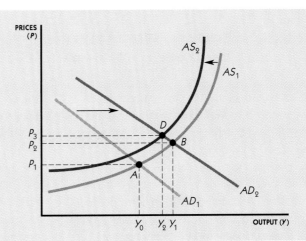

Figure 25.10 MR. BARBER'S DASH FOR GROWTH

The fiscal expansion of 1972 was intended to move the British economy from A to B on AS_1 with a large increase in output and only a small rise in prices. In fact the AS curve shifted up to AS_2 partly because of the rise in oil prices in 1973 and partly because the value of the pound in terms of foreign currencies fell. The result was a move back from B to D, where prices were higher and real output lower.

Lord) Callaghan, who succeeded Barber as chancellor in 1974 and became prime minister in 1976, famously remarked after this debacle that "we can no longer spend our way out of a recession."

MRS. THATCHER AND THE SUPPLY SIDE

When Mrs. Thatcher took office as prime minister in 1979, inflation was 13.4 percent in Britain and unemployment around 5 percent. The new Conservative government was determined to use a tight monetary and fiscal policy to reduce inflation and at the same time to make the economy more productive by using various supply-side measures, such as reducing trade union power, increasing competition, privatising public enterprises, and reducing tax rates.

In terms of aggregate demand and supply analysis, we can suppose that in 1973 the economy was operating on the steep part of the AS curve as at A in Figure 25.11. The cuts in aggregate demand were intended to reduce prices, without creating much

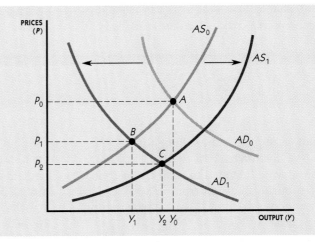

Figure 25.11 THE SUPPLY-SIDE INTENTIONS OF THE THATCHER GOVERNMENT

A large cut in demand was to lower prices without greatly cutting output, as the economy moved from A to B. A shift in the aggregate supply curve was intended to increase output from B to C.

lower output, as at point *B*, by shifting the aggregate demand curve down from AD_0 to AD_1. The supply-side measures were intended to push the aggregate supply curve out to the right from AS_0 to AS_1 and bring the economy to point *C*, with higher output and lower prices.

Things did not work out this way. Unemployment rose steadily and peaked at 11.1 percent of the workforce in 1986, before falling again to 5.8 percent in 1990. Inflation fell more rapidly, to roughly 4.5 percent in 1983, and stayed at around that rate until 1988. There is little evidence that the policies shifted the aggregate supply curve out far to the right. The reduction in inflation was mainly the result of a severe reduction in aggregate demand, with only a small outward shift in aggregate supply (Figure 25.12).

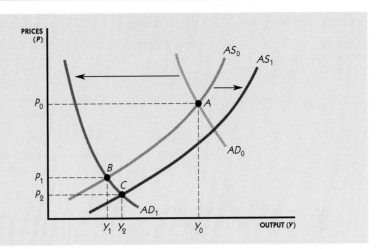

Figure 25.12 THE RESULTS OF THE THATCHER YEARS

The demand cut of the early 1980s caused a bigger than intended fall in output. The shift in the aggregate supply curve from AS_0 to AS_1 proved modest, and output fell substantially, from Y_0 to Y_2, overall.

REVIEW AND PRACTICE

SUMMARY

1 Unemployment macroeconomics assumes that wages and prices are fixed in the short run.

2 To explain unemployment, we need to explain why the aggregate labour market does not clear. If real wages do not adjust to shifts in the aggregate supply and demand curves for labour and either the demand curve for labour shifts to the left or the supply curve for labour shifts to the right, then the quantity of labour supplied will exceed the quantity demanded at the prevailing wage, and there will be involuntary unemployment.

3 The demand curve for labour shifts because of a fall in the production of goods by firms, as a result of a decrease in the demand for their products at each price level.

4 In the product market, if aggregate demand at a given price level is less than the economy's full-employment output (capacity), output will be limited by aggregate demand. Shifting the aggregate demand curve to the right will increase output and employment and may restore the economy to full employment.

5 If, at a given price level, aggregate demand exceeds aggregate supply, output will be limited by aggregate supply and there will be upward pressure on prices.

6 All markets in the economy are interrelated. Thus disturbances in the product market have consequences for the labour market, and disturbances in the capital market have consequences for the product market. For instance, when there is involuntary unemployment, lower interest rates may result in increased investment, which increases output and employment.

KEY TERMS

voluntary unemployment

involuntary unemployment

demand shocks

supply shocks

fiscal policy

fiscal stimulus

monetary policy

central bank

REVIEW QUESTIONS

1 If the labour market always cleared, would there be any unemployment? What does it mean for the labour market not to clear? What gives rise to unemployment?

2 If the labour market always clears, can there be variations in the level of employment?

3 What inferences do you draw from the following two facts?
(a) The labour supply curve is relatively inelastic.
(b) Large variations in employment coexist with relatively small variations in real wages.

4 What might shift the aggregate demand curve for labour?

5 If prices are rigid and at a level *above* that at which aggregate demand equals supply, what will be the level of output? What will happen if the aggregate demand curve shifts to the left? To the right? If the aggregate supply curve shifts to the left? To the right?

6 If prices are rigid and at a level *below* that at which aggregate demand equals supply, what will be the level of output? What will happen if the aggregate demand curve shifts to the left? To the right? If the aggregate supply curve shifts to the left? To the right?

7 What are some of the ways in which the various markets of the economy are interlinked?

8 Use the aggregate demand and supply curve framework to describe some of the major macroeconomic episodes of the postwar period.

PROBLEMS

1 Suppose that there is a rapid growth in labour supply because, say, the baby-boom generation reaches working age. If wages adjust, what effect will this have on the equilibrium level of wages and quantity of labour? If wages do not adjust, how does your answer change? In which case will unemployment exist? Draw a diagram to explain your answer. What is the effect of the increased labour supply on the product market? Illustrate your answer diagrammatically.

2 How would a cut in the rates of income tax that caused workers to want to work harder affect the level of prices and output in the economy? How does the answer differ in the case where the economy is working at full capacity from the answer in the case where the economy has considerable spare capacity and unemployment?

3 In the aftermath of unification in 1991, demand for investment goods in Germany grew dramatically and led to a boom in Germany. How would you expect this to have affected the aggregate demand curve in other European countries?

4 In the early 1990s, there was a massive wave of Russian immigrants into Israel. Yet, within a few years, unemployment returned to normal levels and real wages had not fallen. Using aggregate demand and supply curves for goods and labour, explain how this could have occurred. (Hint: new immigrants generate additional demand for goods as well as additional supplies of labour.)

5 When Bill Clinton became president of the United States in 1993, the U.S. unemployment rate was in excess of 7 percent. There was worry about the speed of economic recovery. He proposed—but Congress rejected—a small stimulus package, consisting mainly of increased investment. Show diagrammatically what this might have done to the aggregate demand curve and the level of output at a given price level. Critics worried that the government would have had to borrow more money to pay for the additional expenditures and that this would have driven up interest rates, discouraging private investment. If this had happened, show what would have happened to the aggregate demand curve and the level of output at a given price level in the United States.

6 While for the most part, macroeconomics focuses on aggregate employment, ignoring distinctions among different categories of workers, it sometimes focuses on broad categories, such as skilled and unskilled workers. Assume, for simplicity, that there are just these two categories, and that for the most part, they cannot be substituted for each other.

(a) Draw demand and supply curves for skilled and unskilled workers, marking the initial equilibrium in each market.

(b) Assume now that there is a technological change that increases the demand for skilled labour at each wage, while it shifts the demand curve for unskilled labour to the left. If wages do not adjust, can there be vacancies of one type of labour at the same time there is unemployment of another type?

7 How might a fall in the price of oil affect the aggregate supply curve, and so the level of prices and output?

8 An outward shift in the aggregate supply curve, with a given aggregate demand curve, is predicted to lower prices and raise output. In practice, the price level rarely falls: prices have risen in the United Kingdom in every year since 1945. How do you explain this?

26

AGGREGATE DEMAND

n Chapter 25 we learned that the major cause of unemployment was a shift in the demand curve for labour, without a commensurate fall in the real wage. We also learned that the major cause of a shift in the demand curve for labour was a reduction in aggregate output. Thus, to understand events in the labour market, we must understand the product market: what determines the level of output and its changes?

The objective of this and the following chapters is to answer this question, focusing on situations where supply imposes no constraints, that is, where there is excess capacity of machines and unemployment of labour. In this simple scenario, output is determined entirely by aggregate demand.

The task of this chapter is to explain what determines the level of aggregate demand at any particular set of wages and prices, what causes changes in aggregate demand, and why output can be so volatile.

1 When the economy has excess capacity, what determines the aggregate level of output?

2 What are the components of aggregate expenditures?

3 How do consumption and imports increase with income?

4 Why, if investment or government expenditures or exports increase by a pound, does aggregate output increase by more than a pound? What determines the amount by which it increases?

INCOME-EXPENDITURE ANALYSIS

Let us return for a moment to the aggregate demand and supply framework that we introduced in Chapter 25, focusing on a situation where the economy has a large excess capacity. Figure 26.1 shows the aggregate demand and supply curves and a price level P_0 such that there is a large excess supply: at P_0, aggregate demand is much less than the economy's capacity to produce. In this situation, a shift in the aggregate demand curve from AD_0 to, say, AD_1 leads to an increase in aggregate output from Y_0 to Y_1.

But what determines the level of aggregate demand at each price level? And what determines changes in

this level of demand? Recall the four components of aggregate output and demand: consumption, investment, government expenditures, and net exports. Aggregate demand at any price level is just the sum of consumption, investment, government expenditures, and net exports demanded at that price level. We can think of this demand as the expenditures in four parts of the economy: households on consumer goods, firms on investment goods, government on public goods and services, and foreigners on net exports.

The trick to solving for the equilibrium level of output and the equilibrium level of aggregate demand is the **aggregate expenditures schedule.** The term *aggregate expenditures* refers to the total of expenditures on consumption, investment, government goods and services, and net exports. The aggregate expenditures schedule traces out the

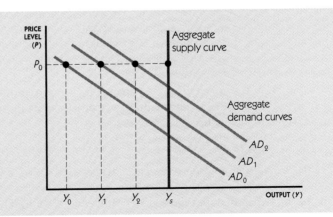

Figure 26.1 SHIFTS IN THE AGGREGATE DEMAND CURVE WHEN THERE IS EXCESS SUPPLY

When the economy has excess capacity, shifts in the aggregate demand curve result in different levels of output at the fixed price level P_0.

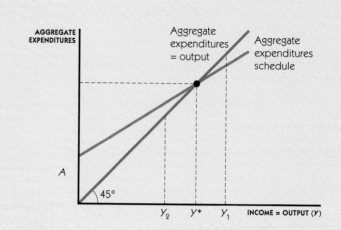
relationship, at a fixed price level, between aggregate expenditures and national income—the aggregate income of everyone in the economy. It is depicted in Figure 26.2, where the vertical axis measures aggregate expenditures and the horizontal axis measures national income.

The aggregate expenditures schedule has three critical properties. First, it is upward sloping; as national income goes up, so do aggregate expenditures. Changes in other variables (like interest rates, tax rates, and exchange rates) cause the aggregate expenditures schedule to shift up or down, and they may even change the slope.

Second, as income increases by a pound, aggregate expenditures increase by less than a pound. The reason for this is that consumers save some of their increased income. Figure 26.2 also shows a line through the origin at a 45-degree angle. The slope of this line is unity. All along this line, a £1 change in the vertical axis (aggregate expenditures) is matched by a £1 change in the horizontal axis (income). By contrast, the aggregate expenditures schedule is flatter than the 45-degree line since aggregate expenditures increase less than pound for pound with increased income.

Third, even if national income were zero, aggregate expenditures would remain positive. This is reflected in the fact that the aggregate expenditures schedule intercepts the vertical axis at a positive

level, point A. (We will discuss the reasons for this later in the chapter.)

The facts that (1) the aggregate expenditures schedule is flatter than the 45-degree line through the origin and (2) aggregate expenditures are positive, even when income is zero, imply that the aggregate expenditures schedule intersects the 45-degree line, as seen in Figure 26.2.

What is the relationship between the aggregate expenditures schedule and the aggregate demand schedule discussed in Chapter 25? The aggregate expenditures schedule shows expenditures, at each level of price and income; the aggregate demand curve shows aggregate demand (or expenditures) at each level of price—when the level of income has been adjusted to its (short-run) equilibrium level. This brings us to our central question: What determines the (short-run) equilibrium level of output, when there is excess capacity? Besides the aggregate expenditures schedule, we need two more concepts for our analysis.

THE NATIONAL INCOME-OUTPUT IDENTITY

National income is equal to national output (as shown in Chapter 22). This reflects the fact that

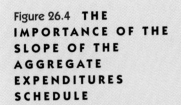

Figure 26.4 **THE IMPORTANCE OF THE SLOPE OF THE AGGREGATE EXPENDITURES SCHEDULE**

The flatter the aggregate expenditures schedule, the smaller the magnitude of the increase in output resulting from a given upward shift in the schedule.

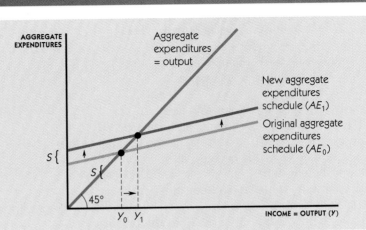

penditures schedule (the value of AE when $Y = 0$) and c is the slope of the aggregate expenditures schedule (an increase in Y of £1 increases AE by £c). The fact that the slope is less than 45 degrees implies that c is between 0 and 1. Equilibrium requires aggregate expenditures to equal income, which under our simplifying assumptions, equals Y:

$$AE = Y.$$

Substituting the second equation into the first equation yields

$$Y = b + cY,$$

which can be solved for Y:

$$Y = b/(1 - c).$$

An upward shift in the aggregate expenditures schedule corresponds to an increase in b, say to $b + 1$. Then Y increases by an amount $1/(1 - c)$. Since c is less than 1, $1/(1 - c)$ is greater than 1. If $c = 0.9$, then $1 - c = 0.1$ and $1/(1 - c) = 10$, so that an upward shift in the aggregate expenditures schedule by £1 increases GDP by £10. This basic property is called the multiplier. Later in the chapter we will take a closer look at it.

A LOOK FORWARDS

We have just learned two of the central principles of macroeconomics: (1) shifts in the aggregate expenditures schedule determine changes in the equilibrium output of the economy, and (2) the magnitude of those changes is greater than the magnitude of the shift up or down in the aggregate expenditures schedule and increases with the slope of the aggregate expenditures schedule. The remainder of this chapter explores the implications of these principles. Two questions are addressed.

The first question is: What determines the slope of the aggregate expenditures schedule, that is, the extent to which aggregate expenditures increase as income increases? As we have seen, the greater that slope, the larger the increase in output from any upward shift in the schedule. The second question is: What causes shifts in the aggregate expenditures schedule? And what, if anything, can the government do to shift the schedule? The possibilities for government are an important issue. In Chapter 25, we saw that unemployment is created when there is a shift in the demand curve for labour without a corresponding downward adjustment of wages. The primary reason for a shift in the demand curve for labour is a change in the equilibrium level of output. When output is low, the demand for labour is low. If government can increase the equilibrium level of output by somehow shifting the aggregate expenditures schedule, then it can increase the level of employment.

To answer these questions, we need to take a closer look at each of the four components of aggregate expenditures: (1) consumption goods, such as food, television sets, or clothes, all of which are purchased by consumers; (2) investment in capital goods, machines or buildings that are bought by firms to help them produce goods; (3) government purchases, both goods and services bought for current use (public consumption) and goods and services like buildings and roads bought for the future benefits they generate (public investment); and (4) net exports. We say net exports, because we have to subtract from the value of goods sold abroad the value of those goods and services bought by domestic households, businesses, and government that are produced abroad, that is, imports.

Using *AE* for aggregate expenditures, *C* for consumption spending, *I* for investment spending, *G* for government spending, and *E* for net exports, we can set out the components of aggregate expenditures in equation form:

$$AE = C + I + G + E.$$

This equation is nothing more than a definition. It says that consumption spending, investment spending, government spending, and net exports add up to aggregate expenditures. Net exports is sometimes written as $X - M$, where X stands for exports and M for imports. We now take a brief look at each of these categories.

CONSUMPTION

The most important determinant of consumption is income. On average, families with higher incomes

Table 26.1 RELATIONSHIP BETWEEN INCOME AND CONSUMPTION

Income	Consumption
£ 5,000	£ 6,000
10,000	10,500
20,000	19,500
30,000	28,500

spend more. Table 26.1 shows the relationship between consumption and income for a hypothetical family. The same information is depicted graphically in Figure 26.5A, with the amount of consumption given along the vertical axis and income along the horizontal axis. The upward slope of the line indicates that consumption for this family increases as income does. The relationship between a household's consumption and its income is called its **consumption function.** Every family has different consumption patterns because the tastes and circumstances of families differ, but the pattern shown in Table 26.1 is typical.

Aggregate consumption is the sum of the consumption of all the households in the economy. Just as when a typical family's income rises its consumption increases, when the total income of the economy rises, aggregate consumption increases. For purposes of macroeconomics, it is the **aggregate consumption function,** the relationship between aggregate consumption and aggregate income, that is of importance. And the measure of income that is important is disposable income, or what people have after paying taxes. But because we are assuming no government for the moment, disposal income equals national income. The relationship between aggregate consumption and national income is given in Table 26.2 (on p. 484), and the aggregate consumption function is depicted graphically in Figure 26.5B.

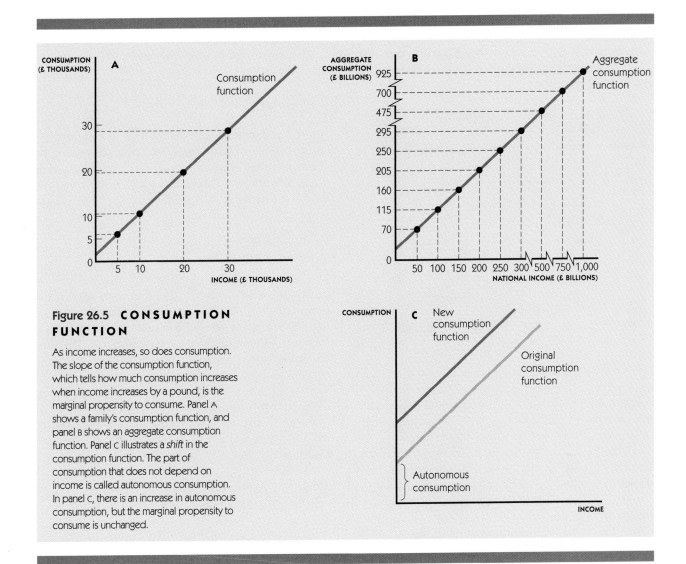

Figure 26.5 **CONSUMPTION FUNCTION**

As income increases, so does consumption. The slope of the consumption function, which tells how much consumption increases when income increases by a pound, is the marginal propensity to consume. Panel A shows a family's consumption function, and panel B shows an aggregate consumption function. Panel C illustrates a *shift* in the consumption function. The part of consumption that does not depend on income is called autonomous consumption. In panel C, there is an increase in autonomous consumption, but the marginal propensity to consume is unchanged.

THE MARGINAL PROPENSITY TO CONSUME

The amount by which consumption increases when disposable income increases by £1 is called the **marginal propensity to consume** (*MPC*). In the hypothetical consumption function illustrated in Figure 26.5B, the marginal propensity to consume is 0.9:

when disposable income goes up by £1 billion, aggregate consumption goes up by £900 million.

The slope of the aggregate consumption function conveys important information. It tells us by how much aggregate consumption (measured along the vertical axis) rises with a unit increase of aggregate disposable income (horizontal axis). In other words, the slope of the aggregate consumption function is the marginal propensity to consume. In panels A and

Table 26.2 AGGREGATE CONSUMPTION AND NATIONAL INCOME (BILLIONS OF POUNDS)

National Income	Consumption (C)
£ 50	£ 70
100	115
150	160
200	205
250	250
300	295
500	415
750	700
1,000	925

B of Figure 26.5, the fact that consumption increases as income rises is reflected in the upward slope of the consumption function, and the marginal propensity to consume is equal to this slope. Flatter slopes would illustrate lower marginal propensities to consume.

Figure 26.5C shows a shift in the consumption function. The intercept with the vertical axis—the level of consumption that would prevail even if disposable income were zero—is increased. This part of consumption, which does not depend on the level of income, is sometimes called **autonomous consumption.**[1] With the shift depicted in Figure 26.5C, the marginal propensity to consume remains unchanged; that is, the slope of the consumption function is the same. Sometimes both autonomous consumption and the marginal propensity to consume change.

As usual, we have to be careful to distinguish between changes in consumption that result from *movements along a consumption function*—the increase in consumption that results from higher incomes—and changes in consumption that result from a *shift in the consumption function*. Chapter 27

---

[1] People can consume even when their income is zero by using up savings.

will discuss some of the factors that lead to shifts in the consumption function.

The consumption function can be written mathematically as

$$C = a + mY_d,$$

where C is consumption, a is the level of autonomous consumption, m is the marginal propensity to consume (the extra amount spent on consumption when disposable income increases by one unit), and Y_d is disposable income, income after paying taxes.

THE MARGINAL PROPENSITY TO SAVE

Individuals have to either spend or save each extra unit of disposable income, so savings and consumption are mirror images of each other. The definition income = consumption plus savings tells us that when disposable income rises by one unit, if aggregate consumption increases by 0.9, aggregate savings increase by 0.1. The higher level of savings stemming from an extra unit of income is called the **marginal propensity to save** (*MPS*). This is the counterpart of the marginal propensity to consume, and the two must always sum to 1:

Marginal propensity to save
+ marginal propensity to consume = 1.

A high marginal propensity to consume means that there is a low marginal propensity to save.

INVESTMENT

We now turn to the second major component of GDP—investment. Investment varies greatly from year to year, and, as we learned in Chapter 23, depends on the level of interest rates. Now, however, our focus is on the relationship between aggregate expenditures and national income as described by the aggregate expenditures schedule. We assume the level of investment is unrelated to the level of income this year. This assumption is made largely to simplify the analysis, but it also reflects the view that investment is primarily determined by firms' estimates of the economic prospects over the future. Accordingly, investment levels are not greatly affected by what happens this year and, in particular, not greatly affected by the level of national income (see Table 26.3). We can now analyse equilibrium output in a simplified economy with no government and no foreign trade. Aggregate expenditures thus consist only of consumption and investment.

Table 26.3 combines the information from Table 26.2 with a fixed level of investment, £25 billion. Because we have assumed away government—both taxes and expenditures—disposable income is the same as national income. Table 26.3 shows the level of aggregate expenditures for various levels of national income. Aggregate expenditures consist of the sum of consumption and investment, shown in the fourth column of the table and plotted in Figure 26.6. Because

Table 26.3 SOME COMPONENTS OF AGGREGATE EXPENDITURES (BILLIONS OF POUNDS)

Y_d	C^a	I	Total
£ 50	£ 70	£25	£ 95
100	115	25	140
150	160	25	180
200	205	25	230
250	250	25	275
350	340	25	365
500	475	25	500
750	700	25	725
1,000	925	25	950

^{a}This table uses the consumption function $C = 0.9Y_d + 25$.

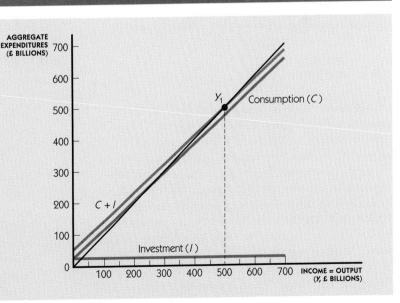

Figure 26.6 A SECOND VIEW OF OUTPUT DETERMINATION: CONSUMPTION PLUS INVESTMENT

Investment is fixed, so the aggregate expenditures schedule is a fixed amount above the consumption function alone. The slope of $C + I$ is the same as that of the consumption function; it is just the marginal propensity to consume.

USING ECONOMICS: CALCULATING EQUILIBRIUM OUTPUT

Equilibrium output can be calculated as follows. Since

$$C = a + mY,$$

$$AE = C + I = a + mY + I,$$

and, in equilibrium, aggregate expenditures equal income,

$$AE = Y,$$

we have

$$Y = a + mY + I,$$

or

$$Y = \frac{a + I}{1 - m}.$$

As a numerical example, let a = £200 billion, I = £100 billion, and m = 1/2. When we substitute all these, we get Y = £600 billion.

we assume investment does not depend on current income, the slope of the upper line in Figure 26.6 is exactly the same as the slope of the consumption function: as income increases, aggregate expenditures increase by the same amount that consumption does, that is, by the marginal propensity to consume. The slope of the aggregate expenditures schedule is still the marginal propensity to consume. The equilibrium—the intersection of the aggregate expenditures schedule and the 45-degree line—is at Y_1 (£500 billion).

THE MULTIPLIER

One of the fundamental insights of income-expenditure analysis is that factors shifting the aggregate expenditures schedule will have a compound effect on output. Consider, for instance, an upward shift in the aggregate expenditures schedule induced by an increase in investment of £1 billion. We continue to assume that the marginal propensity to consume (MPC) is 0.9. The first-round effect of the extra investment spending, shown in Table 26.4, is straightforward: output increases by £1 billion as firms purchase capital goods. This is only the beginning, however. The value of this increased output is distributed to the members of the economy as income, in the form of either higher wages, higher interest

payments, or higher profits that become income to the firms' owners. Given that the marginal propensity to consume is 0.9, this will lead consumption demand to increase by 0.9 × £1 billion = £900 million. This second-round effect creates a £900 million increase in output and thus income, which in turn

Table 26.4 EFFECTS OF AN INCREASE IN INVESTMENT OF £1 BILLION (MILLIONS OF POUNDS)

First round	£1,000
Second round	900
Third round	810
Fourth round	729
Fifth round	656
Sixth round	590
Seventh round	531
Eighth round	478
Ninth round	430
Tenth round	387
Eleventh round	349
Sum of twelfth and successive rounds	£3,140
Total increase	£10,000

THE MULTIPLIER

An increase in investment leads to an increase in output that is a multiple of the original increase.

The multiplier equals $1/(1 - MPC)$, or $1/MPS$.

brings on a third-round increase of consumption of $0.9 \times £900$ million = £810 million. In the next round, output is increased by $0.9 \times £810,000$, then by 0.9 times that amount, then by 0.9 times that amount, and so on. In this example, when all the increases are totaled, a £1 billion increase in investment will lead to a £10 billion rise in equilibrium output.

Unfortunately, the multiplier process also works in reverse. Just as an increase in investment leads to a multiple increase in national output, a decrease in investment leads to a multiple decrease in national output. In our example, with an MPC of 0.9, if investment decreases by £1 billion, national output will decrease by £10 billion. The relationship between any change in investment expenditures and the resulting eventual change in national output is called the investment multiplier, or just **multiplier** for short. An increase in government expenditures or net exports has a similar multiplier effect.

In our simple model, with no trade and no government, the multiplier has a simple mathematical form: $1/(1 - MPC)$. As we learned earlier, any income an individual does not consume is saved, and an increase of income by one unit must be spent either on consumption or on savings. Therefore, $1 - MPC = MPS$, the marginal propensity to save. This result allows us to rewrite the basic formula for the multiplier:

$$\text{Multiplier} = \frac{1}{1 - MPC} = \frac{1}{MPS}.$$

In other words, the multiplier is the reciprocal of the marginal propensity to save. If the marginal propensity to consume is 0.9, the marginal propensity to save is $1 - 0.9 = 0.1$, and the multiplier is 10.

GOVERNMENT AND TRADE

The basic operation of the multiplier is unchanged when government and foreign trade are included in the analysis. Changes in government expenditure

USING ECONOMICS: CALCULATING THE MULTIPLIER

Earlier, we showed that

$$y = \frac{a + I}{1 - m}.$$

To see the multiplier, assume that I increases by a unit. Now

$$y_1 = \frac{a + I + 1}{1 - m}.$$

The change in Y, $Y_1 - Y$, is found by subtraction:

$$Y_1 - Y = \frac{1}{1 - m}.$$

The smaller m, the marginal propensity to consume, is, the flatter the aggregate expenditures schedule is and the smaller the multiplier is. If $m = 0.9$, the multiplier is 10. If $m = 0.8$, the multiplier is 5.

and net exports lead, through a multiplier, to larger changes in equilibrium output. But, as we will see, the effects of government and trade change the size of the multiplier.

THE EFFECTS OF GOVERNMENT

Government serves as a double-edged sword in the macroeconomy: its spending increases aggregate expenditures at the same time that its taxes reduce the amount of people's income. Let us take taxes first. Since consumption depends on individuals' disposable income—the amount of income they have available to spend after paying taxes—government taxes also reduce consumption.

Total income equals total output, denoted Y. Disposable income is simply total income minus taxes T:

Disposable income = $Y - T$.

Taxes do two things. First, since at each level of national income disposable income is lower with taxes, consumption is lower. Taxes shift the aggregate expenditures schedule down. Second, when taxes increase with income, the multiplier is lower (the slope of the aggregate expenditures schedule is smaller). This is because taxes typically go up with income. When total income increases by one unit, therefore, consumption increases by less than it otherwise would, since a fraction of the increased income goes to government.

Without taxes, when investment goes up by one unit, income rises by one unit, which leads to an increase in consumption determined by the marginal propensity to consume. This increase in consumption then sets off the next round of increases in national income. If, when income goes up by one unit, government tax collections increase by 0.25, then disposable income increases by only 0.75. So the increase in consumption with taxes is one-quarter smaller than it is without. In other words, the consumption function is flatter, as shown in Figure 26.7A. Because the slope of the aggregate consumption function is flatter, the slope of the aggregate expenditures schedule is flatter, as illustrated in panel B. And because the slope of the aggregate expenditures schedule is flatter, the multiplier is smaller.

How about government spending? The answer to this question would be simpler if the government's expenditures were always equal to its revenues. However, the government can spend more than it raises in taxes, by borrowing. When annual government expenditures exceed tax revenues, there is a **deficit.** There is some debate about the effects of deficits. Here we make the simplifying assumption that the deficit itself (as opposed to the spending imbalance that created the deficit) has no *direct* effect on either consumption or investment.

We also assume that government expenditures do not increase automatically with the level of income; they are assumed to be fixed, say at £135 billion. Thus, while taxes shift in the aggregate expenditures schedule down and flatten it, government expenditures shift the aggregate expenditures schedule up by the amount of those expenditures, as shown in Figure 26.7C. In this panel, the upward shifts in the aggregate expenditures schedule from government expenditures have been superimposed on the downward shifts in the aggregate expenditures schedule from taxes depicted in panel B. Note that the contributions of investment I (which, in the example of Figure 26.7, are still assumed to be £25 billion) and government expenditures G raise the schedule but do not change its slope. The slope in panel C is the same as in panel B. Equilibrium again occurs at the intersection of the aggregate expenditures schedule and the 45-degree line. Increased government expenditures can have a powerful effect in stimulating the economy. But if the economy is in a serious recession, the government may have to increase expenditures a great deal to raise output to the full-employment level.

THE EFFECTS OF INTERNATIONAL TRADE

The analysis so far has ignored the important role of international trade. This is appropriate for a closed economy, an economy that neither exports nor imports, but not for an open economy, one actively engaged in international trade. The United Kingdom and other industrialised economies are very much open economies.

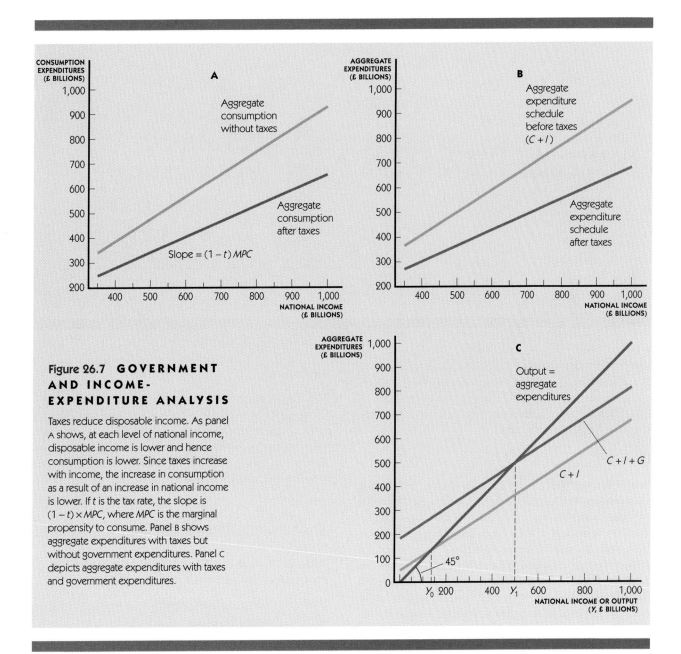

Figure 26.7 GOVERNMENT AND INCOME-EXPENDITURE ANALYSIS

Taxes reduce disposable income. As panel A shows, at each level of national income, disposable income is lower and hence consumption is lower. Since taxes increase with income, the increase in consumption as a result of an increase in national income is lower. If t is the tax rate, the slope is $(1 - t) \times MPC$, where MPC is the marginal propensity to consume. Panel B shows aggregate expenditures with taxes but without government expenditures. Panel C depicts aggregate expenditures with taxes and government expenditures.

International trade can have powerful effects on national output. To begin with, exports expand the market for domestic goods. But just as exports expand the market for domestic goods, imports decrease it. Therefore, imports and exports affect the aggregate expenditures schedule in different ways.

Net exports have fluctuated considerably, as shown in Figure 26.8. They improved after the famous devaluation of November 1967 but subsequently slid into deficit following the Barber boom of 1972, the floating of sterling, and the oil shock of 1973. North Sea oil rescued the United Kingdom's

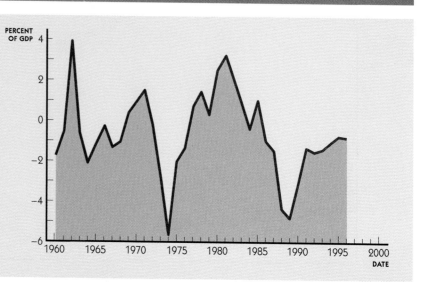

Figure 26.8 NET EXPORTS FROM THE UNITED KINGDOM, 1960–1996

Net exports have fluctuated widely in the period since 1960, ending up roughly in balance by the mid-1990s.
Source: Office of National Statistics, *Economic Trends* (1997), various tables.

net export position after 1975. The Lawson boom of the mid- and late 1980s is associated with another slide in net exports, until the restrictive policies of the 1990s restrained demand and brought the export position back towards balance.

IMPORTS

When households' incomes rise, they not only buy more domestically made consumer goods, they also buy more goods from abroad. We can illustrate an **import function** in much the same way that we illustrated a consumption function. (We have assumed investment and government expenditures to be fixed here, so for now there is no schedule relating either of these to income.) The import function shows the levels of imports corresponding to different levels of income. Table 26.5 shows hypothetical levels of imports for different levels of national income. The import function is depicted in Figure 26.9.

Imports increase with income. The **marginal propensity to import** gives the amount of each extra unit of income spent on imports. If the marginal propensity to import is .3, then if income goes up by £1,000, imports go up by .3 × £1,000 = £300. In Figure 26.9, the marginal propensity to import is given by the slope of the import function.

EXPORTS

What foreigners buy from the United Kingdom depends on the income of foreigners and not directly on income in the United Kingdom. Exports may also depend on other factors, such as the marketing effort of British firms and the prices of British goods relative to those of foreign goods. Our focus here is

Table 26.5 IMPORTS AND NATIONAL INCOME (BILLIONS OF POUNDS)

National income	Imports
£ 100	£ 30
200	60
300	90
400	120
500	150
1,000	300

When we add government, the equation for aggregate expenditures becomes

$$AE = C + I + G = a + mY_d + I + G,$$

where Y_d is disposable income. For simplicity, we assume a given fraction t of income is paid in taxes, so

$$Y_d = Y(1 - t).$$

Hence, in equilibrium, with aggregate expenditures' equaling income,

$$AE = Y = a + mY(1 - t) + I + G$$

or

$$Y = \frac{a + I + G}{1 - m(1 - t)}$$

Hence,

$$Multiplier = \frac{1}{1 - m(1 - t)}$$

If $m = 0.8$ and $t = 0.25$, the multiplier = 2.5. By contrast, the multiplier without taxes is 5, twice as large. The reason that the multiplier is larger without taxes than with is simple. Without taxes every unit of extra income translates into 0.8 units of extra expenditure. With taxes, when income goes up by a unit, consumption increases by only $0.8 \times (1 - 0.25) = 0.6$ units.

to determine output in the United Kingdom. For simplicity, we assume that these other factors are fixed and do not depend on what happens in the United Kingdom. In particular, we assume that foreigners' incomes do not depend significantly on incomes in the United Kingdom. Hence, the level of exports is taken as fixed at £150 billion.

Exports minus imports (net exports) is sometimes referred to as the **balance of trade.** Net exports at each level of national income are given in Table 26.6. At very low levels of income, net exports are positive. That is to say, exports exceed imports. As income increases, imports increase, with exports remaining unchanged. Eventually imports exceed exports; the balance of trade becomes negative.

Trade, like taxes, has the effect of flattening the aggregate expenditures schedule. This is because as income increases, some of it goes to buy foreign

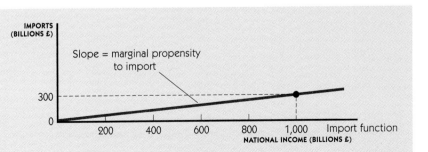

Figure 26.9 **THE IMPORT FUNCTION**

Imports (M) increase steadily as disposable income (Y) rises. The slope of the import function is determined by the marginal propensity to import.

Table 26.6 NET EXPORTS (BILLIONS OF POUNDS)

National income	Exports	Imports	E (Exports – imports)
£100	£150	£ 30	£120
200	150	60	90
300	150	90	60
400	150	120	30
500	150	150	0
600	150	180	–30
700	150	210	–60

economy, when income increases by a unit, aggregate expenditures increase by the marginal propensity to consume *minus* the marginal propensity to import. The difference between the two can be thought of as the marginal propensity to consume domestically produced goods.

This can be seen in Table 26.7, which calculates, for different levels of national income, the level of consumption, investment, government expenditures, and net exports. Every time aggregate income increases by £1,000 billion, disposable income increases by only £700 billion; and while consumption increases by £630 billion, net exports *fall* (because imports increase) by £300 billion, so the net increase in aggregate expenditures is only £330 billion. In a closed economy with no government, aggregate expenditures would have increased by £900 billion.

At an income of £500 billion (a disposable income of £350 billion), net exports are zero. At higher levels of income, net exports are negative. At lower levels, they are positive. Thus, trade increases aggregate expenditures at lower levels of national income, and decreases aggregate expenditures at higher levels of national income. At low levels of income, the stimulation provided by exports more than offsets the

goods rather than domestically produced goods. Hence, aggregate expenditures—spending for goods produced within the country—increase by a smaller amount. In a closed economy, when income increases by a unit, aggregate expenditures increase by the marginal propensity to consume. In an open

Table 26.7 AGGREGATE EXPENDITURES SCHEDULE (BILLIONS OF POUNDS[a])

National income	Consumption	Investment	Government expenditures	Exports	Imports	Aggregate expenditure
£ 0	£ 25	£25	£135	£150	£ 0	£335
100	88	25	135	150	30	368
200	151	25	135	150	60	401
300	214	25	135	150	90	434
400	277	25	135	150	120	467
500	340	25	135	150	150	500
600	403	25	135	150	180	533
700	466	25	135	150	210	566
800	529	25	135	150	240	599
900	592	25	135	150	270	632
1,000	655	25	135	150	300	665

[a]The figures in the table assume that disposable income is 70 percent of national income and the consumption function is

$C = 25 + 0.9Y_{di}$

that is, the marginal propensity to consume is 0.9, and the marginal propensity to import is 0.3.

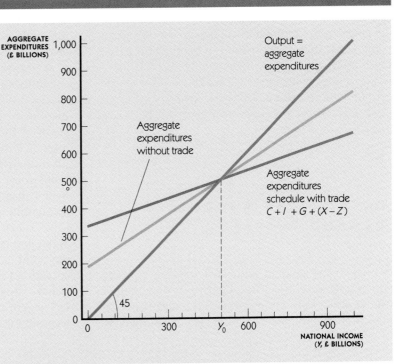

Figure 26.10 INCOME-EXPENDITURE ANALYSIS WITH A FOREIGN TRADE SECTOR

Adding a fixed level of exports raises the aggregate demand function. But adding imports makes the slope of the function flatter, since some of national income is now going to buy products produced outside the country. The multiplier is reduced.

losses from imports; at higher levels of income just the opposite happens.

In Figure 26.10, the income-expenditure analysis diagram is again used to show how the level of output is determined. As before, the equilibrium condition that output equals aggregate expenditures, $Y = AE$, is represented by the 45-degree line. The aggregate expenditures schedule now adds all of its components: $C + I + G + (X - Z)$. The slope of this line is even flatter than in Figure 26.7C. This is because, as income increases, net exports—one of the components of aggregate expenditures—decrease. Equilibrium again occurs at the intersection of the aggregate expenditures schedule and the 45-degree line, the output level Y_0 in Figure 26.10.

We know that whenever the aggregate expenditures schedule is flattened, the multiplier is lowered. To see precisely how this works in the case of trade, think again about how the multiplier works through various rounds in the economy. The first-round effect of the increase in investment is augmented by the second-round effect of the rise in consumption induced by the higher income of those producing the investment goods. This is augmented by the third-round effect of the increase in consumption induced by the higher income of those involved in producing the second round. And so on. But now, when investment rises by £1 billion, the second-round effect is only the increase in consumption of domestically produced goods. If the marginal propensity to consume is 0.9, the tax rate is 0.3, and the marginal propensity to import is 0.3, the increase in *domestically produced* consumption goods is £330 million (not £630 million, as it would be without trade, or £900 million, as it would be without taxes or government).[2] Not only is the second-round effect smaller, the third-round effect is also smaller.

[2] Of the £1 billion, the government takes 30 percent, leaving households with £700 million. Households consume 90 percent of this amount, but 30 percent of the increase in national income is spent on imports, so only £330 million of the £630 million increase in consumers' expenditures represents an increase in demand for domestically produced goods.

If more of the income generated on each successive round is not spent on goods produced within the country, the multiplier will be smaller. When income generated in one round of production is not used to buy more goods produced within the country, economists say there are **leakages.** In a closed economy there are two leakages: savings and taxes. In an open economy there are three leakages: savings, taxes, and imports.

BACK TO THE AGGREGATE DEMAND CURVES

We began the chapter with an aggregate demand and supply schedule. The objective of this chapter was to show how at any price level, aggregate demand—and equilibrium output—is determined. We can use the analysis to *derive* the aggregate demand curve simply by asking, what happens to aggregate demand—and equilibrium output—when the price level changes? To answer that question, all we have to ascertain is, how does the aggregate expenditures schedule shift when the price level increases or decreases? When the price level rises, at each level of income, consumers will consume less, since the real value of their bank balances will have decreased. Also, if *current* price levels are higher relative to (fixed beliefs about) *future* price levels, then households may *substitute* against current consumption (which has become relatively expensive) for future consumption. In either case, the aggregate expenditures schedule shifts down, as depicted in Figure 26.11, and equilibrium output falls. Thus, while Y_0 is the point on the aggregate demand schedule corresponding to P_0, Y_1 is the point on the aggregate demand schedule corresponding to P_1. Later chapters will explore more fully how changes in the price level shift the aggregate expenditures schedule.

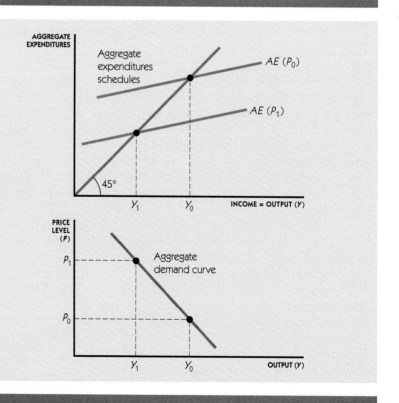

Figure 26.11 DERIVING THE AGGREGATE DEMAND CURVE

Panel A shows the effect of an increase in the price level from P_0 to P_1 on the aggregate expenditures schedule. It decreases equilibrium output from Y_0 to Y_1. Panel B traces out the equilibrium values of aggregate demand (and output) corresponding to different price levels.

LIMITATIONS OF THE INCOME-EXPENDITURE APPROACH

This chapter has analysed the determination of national output by focusing exclusively on the aggregate expenditures schedule, which underlies the aggregate demand curve. But what happened to aggregate supply? Isn't that important too?

Recall that aggregate demand rules the roost when there is excess capacity. That is, changes in aggregate demand alone determine what happens to national output when there are idle machines and workers that could be put to work if only there were sufficient demand to purchase the goods they produce.

There are many times when there is excess capacity in the economy and when the approach taken here, ignoring capacity constraints, makes perfect sense. There are other times, however, when the economy is working close to capacity. In such situations, aggregate supply has to be brought into the picture.

REVIEW AND PRACTICE

SUMMARY

1 Income-expenditure analysis shows how the equilibrium level of output in the economy is determined when there is excess capacity, so that aggregate demand determines the level of output. Throughout the analysis, the price level is taken as fixed.

2 Equilibrium output is determined by the intersection of the 45-degree line and the aggregate expenditures schedule. The aggregate expenditures schedule shows the level of aggregate expenditures at each level of national income, while the 45-degree line represents the points where aggregate expenditures equal output (income).

3 Shifts in the aggregate expenditures schedule give rise to changes in the equilibrium level of output. The magnitude of the increase in output resulting from an upward shift in the aggregate expenditures schedule depends on the slope of the schedule. Much of macroeconomic analysis focuses on what determines the slope of the aggregate expenditures schedule, what causes shifts in the schedule, and how government can shift the schedule.

4 Aggregate expenditures are the sum of consumption, investment, government expenditures, and net exports. Net exports are the difference between exports and imports.

5 Consumption increases as disposable income increases, and the relationship between income and consumption is called the consumption function. The amount by which consumption increases when disposable income increases by a unit is called the marginal propensity to consume (*MPC*). The amount by which savings increase when disposable income increases by a unit is called the marginal propensity to save (*MPS*). Since all income must be saved or consumed, the sum of the *MPC* and *MPS* must be 1.

6 The multiplier is the factor by which a change in one of the components of aggregate expenditures must be multiplied to get the resulting change in national output. In a simple model without government spending, taxes, or net exports, the multiplier for changes in investment is $1/(1 - MPC)$, or $1/MPS$.

7 Government spending increases aggregate expenditures, and taxes reduce disposable income and therefore consumption. When taxes increase with income, consumption increases by less than it otherwise would, since a fraction of the increased income goes to government. The aggregate expenditures schedule is flatter, and the multiplier is smaller.

8 Exports increase aggregate demand, and imports reduce aggregate demand. Imports increase with income, but exports are determined by factors in other countries. Trade flattens the aggregate expenditures schedule, because as income increases, some of it goes to buy foreign rather than domestic goods. As a result, the multiplier is smaller.

9 The aggregate expenditures schedule is used to derive the equilibrium level of output at each price level (assuming that there is excess capacity in the economy). As the price level increases, the aggregate expenditures schedule shifts down and equilibrium output decreases. The aggregate demand curve then traces out the equilibrium level of output at each price level.

KEY TERMS

aggregate expenditures schedule	consumption function	marginal propensity to save	marginal propensity to import
income-expenditure analysis	marginal propensity to consume	multiplier	balance of trade
planned and unplanned inventories	autonomous consumption	import function	

REVIEW QUESTIONS

1 What is the aggregate expenditures schedule? What are the components of aggregate expenditures?

2 How is the equilibrium level of output determined? Why are points on the aggregate expenditures schedule above the 45-degree line not sustainable? Why are points on the aggregate expenditures schedule below the 45-degree line not sustainable?

3 What is a consumption function? What determines its slope? What is an import function? What determines its slope?

4 What is the consequence of a shift in the aggregate expenditures schedule? Give examples of what might give rise to such a shift.

5 Illustrate the difference between a change in consumption resulting from an increase in income with a given consumption function and a change in consumption resulting from a shift in the consumption function.

6 Why is the sum of the marginal propensity to save and the marginal propensity to consume always 1?

7 Show that the magnitude of the effect of a given shift in the aggregate expenditures schedule on equilibrium output depends on the slope of the aggregate expenditures schedule. What determines the slope of the aggregate expenditures schedule? How is it affected by taxes? By imports?

8 How can changes of a certain amount in the level of investment or government spending have a larger effect on national output? What is the multiplier?

9 What is the relationship between the aggregate expenditures schedule and the aggregate demand curve? How does the aggregate expenditures schedule shift when the price level increases? How can the aggregate demand curve be derived?

PROBLEMS

1 In the economy of Consumerland, national income and consumption are related in this way:

| National income | £1,500 | £1,600 | £1,700 | £1,800 | £1,900 |
| Consumption | £1,325 | £1,420 | £1,515 | £1,610 | £1,705 |

Calculate national savings at each level of national income. What is the marginal propensity to consume in Consumerland? What is the marginal propensity to save? If national income rose to £2,000, what do you predict consumption and savings would be?

2 To the economy of Consumerland add the fact that investment will be £180 at every level of output. Graph the consumption function and the aggregate expenditures schedule for this simple economy. What determines the slope of the aggregate expenditures schedule? What is the equilibrium output?

3 Calculate the first four rounds of the multiplier effect for an increase of £10 billion in investment spending in each of the following cases:

    (a) A simple consumption and investment economy where the *MPC* is 0.8

    (b) An economy with government but no foreign trade, where the *MPC* is 0.8 and the tax rate is 0.4

    (c) An economy with an *MPC* of 0.8, a tax rate of 0.4, and a marginal propensity to import of 0.4

4 If, at each level of disposable income, savings increase, what does this imply about what has happened to the consumption function? What will be the consequences for the equilibrium level of output?

5 Use the income-expenditure analysis diagram to explain why a lower level of investment, government spending, and net exports all have similar effects on the equilibrium level of output.

6 In a more stable economy (where national output is less vulnerable to small changes in, say, exports), government policy is less effective (changes in government expenditures do not do much to stimulate the economy); in a less stable economy, government policy is more effective. Explain why there is a trade-off between the stability of the economy and the power of government policy.

CHAPTER 27

CONSUMPTION
AND INVESTMENT*

Now that we have developed the overall framework of income-expenditure analysis, we take a closer look at two of the components of aggregate expenditures, consumption and investment. Examining them will help us understand both why the level of economic activity fluctuates and what policies the government might pursue to reduce those fluctuations or to stimulate the economy.

* This chapter may be skipped or taken up after subsequent chapters without loss of continuity.

KEY QUESTIONS

1 Why may current consumption not be very dependent on current income, and what implications does this have for the use of tax policy to stimulate the economy?

2 What other factors determine the level of aggregate consumption?

3 What are consumer durables, and why are expenditures on them so volatile?

4 What are the major determinants of the level of investment? What role do variations in real interest rates and the availability of credit play? What role is played by changing perceptions of risk and the ability and willingness to bear risk?

5 Why is the variability in investment and expenditures on consumer durables so important?

CONSUMPTION

The consumption function presented in Chapter 26 said that the demand for goods and services by households is determined by the level of disposable income. As disposable income goes up, so does con-

sumption. If disposable income is known, the consumption function can be used to predict this year's consumption spending.

This simple consumption function, often referred to as the Keynesian consumption function, is a good starting point, as Figure 27.1 illustrates. Income varies from year to year, and so does consumption. If they moved as the simple consumption function predicts, a straight line could be drawn through all the points in Figure 27.1. The relationship is close to the

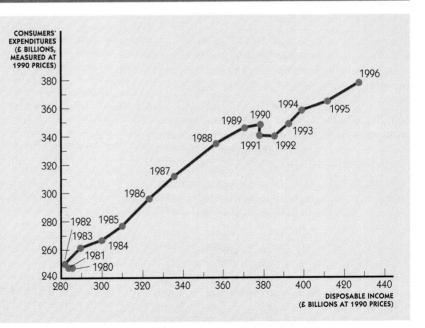

Figure 27.1 CONSUMPTION AND DISPOSABLE INCOME IN THE UNITED KINGDOM, 1980–1996

There is an approximately linear relationship between consumer's expenditures and their disposable income, although there was a clear drop in spending relative to income in the early 1990s which may reflect the fall in wealth associated with the collapse of the housing market. *Source:* Office of National Statistics, *Economic Trends,* Annual Supplement (1997).

CONSUMERS' EXPENDITURES (£ BILLIONS, MEASURED AT 1990 PRICES)

DISPOSABLE INCOME (£ BILLIONS AT 1990 PRICES)

linear relationship predicted by the theories. Still, economists have sought to develop even better predictors of consumption.

FUTURE-ORIENTED CONSUMPTION FUNCTIONS

In the decades after Keynes's time, many economists questioned his idea that current consumption depends primarily on current income. They argued that individuals, in making consumption decisions, look at total income over their lifetime, averaging good years with bad and recognising that income typically increases with experience.

Nobel laureate Franco Modigliani, for instance, emphasised that people save for retirement. He called this motive **life-cycle savings,** to convey the notion that individuals will save during their working years so they will not have to curtail their consumption after they retire. Milton Friedman, also a Nobel laureate, emphasised how the future affects consumption today by pointing out that people save in good years to carry them through bad years. His view is called the **permanent income hypothesis.** Permanent income is a person's average income over her lifetime. Friedman stressed that consumption depends not so much on current income as on total lifetime income, averaging good years with bad. While Modigliani emphasised the role of savings in smoothing consumption between working and retirement years, Friedman emphasised its role in smoothing consumption between good and bad years. Underlying both views is the notion that people like their consumption patterns to be stable.

These future-oriented theories of savings and consumption yield different consequences from the basic Keynesian or traditional theory that consumption simply depends on this year's income. Consider an individual who happens to get a windfall gain in income one year—perhaps he wins £1 million in the national lottery. If the marginal propensity to consume is 0.9, the Keynesian consumption function predicts that he will consume £900,000 of his winnings that year. The future-oriented consumption theories suggest that the lucky winner will spread the extra income over a lifetime of consumption.

Similarly, if the government temporarily lowers income taxes for one year, the future-oriented consumption theories predict that a taxpayer will not dramatically increase consumption in that year but will spread over his lifetime the extra consumption that the one-year income tax reduction allows. Thus, they suggest that *temporary* tax changes will be much less effective in stimulating consumption than the Keynesian model predicts.

Figure 27.2 compares the future-oriented consumption function and the Keynesian consumption function for the household. Suppose a household were to have a onetime increase in its disposable income. If consumption responds according to the Keynesian consumption function, it will increase from C_0 to C_1 as shown in panel A.

The future-oriented theories predict that consumption will not change very much. We can see this in two different ways. Panel B shows consumption depending on average disposable income over a person's lifetime. Now the change in this year's income from Y_0 to Y_1 has little effect on average disposable income, and hence little effect on consumption. Panel C puts this year's disposable income on the horizontal axis, as does panel A. The difference in the slope between the consumption functions in panels A and C reflects the difference between Keynes's views and those of the future-oriented theorists. Consumption, in the latter view, is not very sensitive to current disposable income; this is why the line is so flat.

The principle that consumption depends not just on income this year but also on longer-run considerations holds at the aggregate level as well. Figure 27.3 shows the implications of future-oriented theories for aggregate expenditures and the determination of equilibrium output. Since the relationship between changes in today's income and changes in consumption is weaker than in the Keynesian model, the aggregate expenditures schedule is now much flatter; that is, increases in current income lead to relatively small changes in consumption and aggregate expenditures. This in turn has strong implications for the multiplier. An increase in, say, investment, which shifts the aggregate expenditures schedule up, increases equilibrium output by an amount only slightly greater than the original increase in investment. The multiplier is very small.

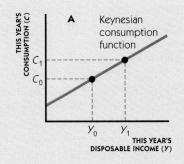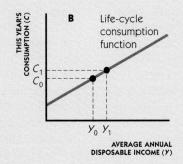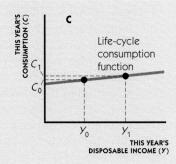

Figure 27.2 EFFECT OF A TEMPORARY INCOME CHANGE IN THE LIFE-CYCLE MODEL

With the Keynesian consumption function, panel A, a temporary change in income results in a large change in consumption. In the life-cycle model, panel B, a temporary change in income has only a small effect on average annual income over a lifetime, and thus leads to only a small change in consumption. Panel C shows how the life-cycle model predicts that consumption will react in response to *this year's income*. Since consumption does not change by much, the life-cycle consumption function is very flat.

WEALTH AND CAPITAL GAINS

The future-oriented consumption theories suggest not only that current income is relatively unimportant in determining consumption but also that variables Keynes ignored may be important. For instance, wealthier people consume more (at each level of current income). Since consumption is related to wealth, changes in consumption will be affected by changes in wealth.

The distinction between income and wealth as a determinant of consumption is important. It corresponds to the distinction between flows and stocks. Flows are measured as rates. Both income and con-

Figure 27.3 THE LIFE-CYCLE MODEL AND DETERMINING NATIONAL OUTPUT

Since changes in today's income have much weaker effects on current consumption in the life-cycle model, the aggregate expenditures schedule is much flatter; this implies that the multiplier is lower.

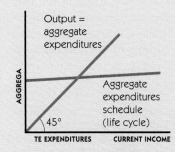

sumption are flow variables. They are measured as pounds *per year*. Wealth is a stock variable.[1] It is measured simply by the total value of one's assets. Future-oriented theories emphasise that there is no reason that an individual's current consumption should be related to his current income. What he consumes should be related to how well off he is, and that is better measured by his wealth.[2] Capital gains, or changes in the value of assets, change an individual's wealth. Thus, these theories predict that when stock market or property prices rise in value and people expect this change to last for a long time, individuals who own these assets will increase their level of consumption. They will do so because their overall wealth has grown, even if they do not immediately receive any income from the increase in value.

There is some evidence to support this view. Many economists believe that in the United States the stock market crash of 1929, which preceded the Great Depression, contributed to that Depression by generating a downward shift in the consumption function. On the other hand, when the stock market fell by over 22 percent on a single day in October 1987, consumption did not decline sharply in the way one might have expected. People responded only slightly to this capital loss. One reason for this is that individuals respond to changes in wealth only slowly, and in 1987 their consumption had not yet fully responded to the increases in stock market prices that had occurred during the preceding few years. A prolonged and persistent decline in the stock market might, however, have an extremely depressing effect on consumption.

In the United Kingdom, a large increase in house prices in 1987 and 1988 was associated with rapidly growing consumers' expenditures. It appeared that consumers were borrowing against the increased value of the houses and spending some of the proceeds on consumption. The process was aided by the recent liberalization of financial markets and greater availability of funds for lending to the housing market. In 1989 and the following years, a sharp rise in interest rates and a long recession brought house prices down very sharply. It was one of the few occasions in the United Kingdom when nominal house prices fell. The rapid and unexpected fall in people's net wealth (the value of their assets less their loans and debts) appeared to have caused a considerable fall in consumption. Figure 27.4A and B illustrates the association of the rising ratio of wealth held in the form of houses to other forms of wealth, due to the rise in house prices, with the low fraction of personal disposable income saved, which took place during the boom of the late 1980s in the United Kingdom.

RECONCILING CONSUMPTION THEORY WITH FACTS

The permanent income and life-cycle hypotheses contain large elements of truth. Families do save for their retirement, so life-cycle considerations are important. And households do smooth their consumption between good years and bad, so permanent income considerations are relevant. Even so, household consumption appears to be more dependent on current income than either theory would suggest. There are two reasons for this, durable goods and credit rationing. Each plays an important role in consumption.

DURABLE GOODS

Goods such as cars, refrigerators, and furniture are called **durable goods.** Purchasing a durable good is like an investment decision, because such goods are bought for the services they render over a number of years. Decisions to postpone purchasing a durable good have quite different consequences from decisions not to buy food or some other nondurable. If you do not buy strawberries today, you will have to do without them. But not buying a durable does not mean you will do without. It simply means you may have to make do with the services provided by an older durable. The costs of postponing the purchase of a new car are often relatively low; you can make do with an old car a little bit longer.

When a household's income is temporarily low, rather than borrowing to purchase durables, the household simply postpones the purchase. Similarly,

---

[1] Other stock variables in macroeconomics include capital stock; other flow variables include the interest rate.
[2] Future-oriented theories take an expansive view of what should be included in wealth: they include *human capital,* the present discounted value of future wage income. (See Chapter 6 or a definition of present discounted value.)

RATIO

A

Ratio of housing to non-housing wealth (personal sector)

1980 1981 1982 1983 1984 1985 1986 1987 1988 1989 1990 1991 1992

DATE

Figure 27.4 A COMPARISON OF HOUSING PRICE INCREASES AND CONSUMPTION

Panel A depicts the ratio of housing prices to other forms of wealth, highlighting the dramatic increases in housing prices in 1987 and 1988. Panel B traces savings rates. The decrease in household saving (increase in consumption) in 1987 and 1988 is probably related to the increase in housing prices shown in panel A. *Sources:* Central Statistical Office, *Economic Trends;* Bank of England; OECD.

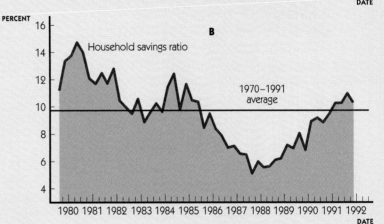

PERCENT

B

Household savings ratio

1970–1991 average

1980 1981 1982 1983 1984 1985 1986 1987 1988 1989 1990 1991 1992

DATE

if a worker worries about losing his job, he may cut back durable purchases. These fluctuations in purchases of durables, together with the variations in investment, seem to account for much of the variation in economic activity over the business cycle. Variations in the services provided by durable goods—and hence in true consumption—are much smaller.

CREDIT RATIONING

Empirical studies show that even nondurable consumption expenditures seem more dependent on current income than the future-oriented theories suggest. These theories, in particular the permanent income hypothesis, assume that when an individual has a bad year, he can maintain his consumption at a steady level. They assume, in other words, either that the household has a large stock of savings to draw on while its income is temporarily low or that the household can easily borrow.

For many people, neither of these conditions is true. Most individuals have few liquid assets upon which to draw. They may have considerable savings tied up in a pension scheme, but they cannot draw upon these until they retire. They may have some equity in their house, but the last thing they want to do is sell their home. Moreover, it is precisely in times of need, when a person is unemployed or a business is

Close-up: An Empirical Puzzle and an Ingenious Theory—Friedman's Permanent Income Hypothesis

The genesis of Milton Friedman's permanent income hypothesis was an empirical puzzle. The story of how he solved it illustrates insightful economic analysis at work.

When economists plotted aggregate disposable personal income in various years with the corresponding level of aggregate consumption, they obtained something like panel A of the following figure. These data suggested a consumption function in which consumption increases proportionately with income. But, when economists plotted the consumption of different income groups against their current income for any particular year, they obtained something more like panel B. This suggests a consumption function in which consumption increases less than proportionately with income. The problem Friedman set himself was how to reconcile the data.

His ingenious solution was to say that consumption is related to people's long-term, or "normal," income, what he called their permanent income. Friedman observed that people with low incomes included a disproportionate number who were having unusually bad years. And correspondingly, those with very high incomes included a disproportionate number having unusually good years. Those having a bad year did not reduce their consumption proportionately; those having a particularly good year did not increase their consumption proportionately. Friedman was thus able to explain how, over time, aggregate consumption could rise in proportion to income for the population as a whole, even though the consumption of any particular household increased less than proportionately with current income.

Stanford University economist Robert Hall has pointed out an unsettling consequence of the permanent income hypothesis. If the level of consumption a person chooses depends on perma-

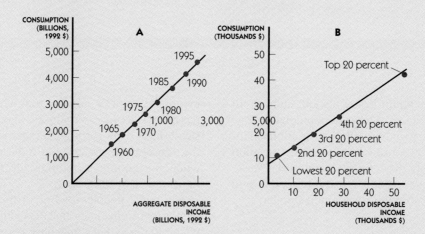

Panel A shows that as income has increased over time, consumption has increased almost in proportion. Panel B illustrates the fact that individuals with higher income increase their consumption somewhat less than proportionately, especially at the highest income levels. *Sources: ERP* (1995), Table B-28; *Consumer Expenditure Survey* (1988).

doing badly, that banks are least forthcoming with funds. (As the saying goes, banks only lend to those who don't need the money!)

Credit rationing occurs when people are unable to obtain funds at the market rate of interest, because of the risks associated with lending to them. Many people are credit rationed. For those who have no assets and are credit rationed, cutting back on consumption when income declines is not a matter of choice. For these individuals, consumption depends heavily on current income.

If people were not credit rationed, short-term unemployment would not be as important a problem as it appears to be. The suffering caused by temporary layoffs would be much less. To see why, we need to look again at the concept of total wealth. Assume, for instance, that Evan will work for 40 years, that his initial salary is £25,000 per year, that his salary increases in real terms at 5 percent per year, and that 5 percent is the real rate of interest. Then the present discounted value of his lifetime earnings is £1 million. This is his wealth, assuming that he has no unexpected windfall, no inheritance from his great-aunt, and no other assets. Imagine that Evan loses his job and is unemployed for half a year. At first glance, that looks like a personal calamity. But upon closer inspection, we see that it represents a loss of only a bit more than 1 percent of his lifetime wealth.

If Evan could borrow six months' pay, he would have no trouble paying it back, and the period without work would be no tragedy; his lifestyle would be constrained but insignificantly. Since he would have to cut expenditures by only a bit more than 1 percent, cutting out a few visits to the cinema, a fancy restaurant meal or two, and a few other activities would do the trick. However, for most people, losing a job for half a year would be a major disaster, not because of the reduction in total lifetime wealth but because most individuals face important constraints on the amount they can borrow. Without a job, they cannot obtain loans, except possibly at very high interest rates. Because of these credit constraints, for most lower- and many middle-income individuals, the traditional Keynesian consumption function is all too relevant. When their current income is reduced, their consumption is necessarily reduced.

MACROECONOMIC IMPLICATIONS OF CONSUMPTION THEORIES

The alternative theories of consumption we have explored so far have two sets of macroeconomic implications. First, the future-oriented theories of consumption, in arguing that consumption does not depend heavily on current income, maintain that the aggregate expenditures schedule is flat and therefore the multiplier is low. This is both good news and bad news for the economy. It is good news because a small multiplier means that decreases in the level of investment lead to much smaller decreases in the level of national income than they would if the multiplier were large. It is bad news because it means that government efforts to stimulate the economy through temporary reductions in taxes—or to dampen an overheated economy through temporary increases in taxes—will be less effective than if the multiplier were larger.

Second, by identifying other determinants of consumption, future-oriented theories help explain why the ratio of consumption to disposable income may shift from year to year. Expectations concerning future economic conditions, changes in the availability of credit, or variations in the price of houses or shares of stock are among the factors that can give rise to such shifts in the consumption function. These shifts in turn give rise to larger variations in the equilibrium level of national output. Indeed, they help explain how a slight downturn in economic activity can become magnified. With a downturn, consumers may lose confidence in the future. They worry about layoffs and cut back on purchases of durables. At the same time, banks, nervous about the ability of borrowers to repay loans should the downturn worsen, become more restrictive. Even those adventurous souls willing to buy a new car in the face of the uncertain future may find it difficult to find a bank willing to lend to them. The net effect is a downward shift in the consumption function, exacerbating the initial decline in national income.

INVESTMENT

Variations in the level of investment are probably the principal cause of variations in aggregate expenditures, and hence in national output. Just how volatile investment is can be seen in Figure 27.5. In recent years, investment has varied from 16 to 20 percent of GDP.

The investment spending relevant for aggregate expenditures includes three broad categories. The first is firms' purchases of new capital goods, which include, besides buildings and machines, the vehicles, cash registers, and desks that firms use. These make up the **plant and equipment** portion of overall investment. Firms also invest in **inventories** as they store their output in anticipation of sales or store the raw materials they will need to produce more goods. The third investment category consists of households' purchases of new homes. The purchases of previously owned capital goods or houses do not count, because they do not increase output. Households' financial investments such as stocks and bonds are a related but different concept. Usually when an individual buys, say, a share of stock, she buys it from someone else. She makes an investment, but someone else makes a "disinvestment." There is simply a change in who owns the economy's assets. There is, however, a close relationship between investment in new capital goods and the capital market in general: when firms issue new shares or borrow funds by issuing bonds, they procure the resources with which to purchase new capital goods. (In this way, financial investments and capital investments—with which we are concerned here—are closely linked.)

We restrict our focus in this discussion to business investment, which includes two of our three major investment categories: plant and equipment, and inventories. The third major investment category—consumers' demand for new housing—is best

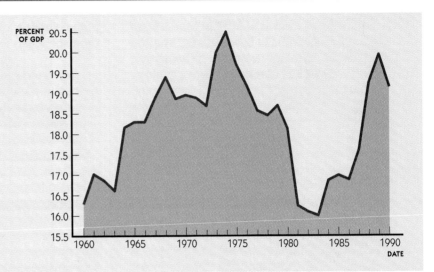

Figure 27.5 **THE VARIABILITY OF INVESTMENT IN THE UNITED KINGDOM**

The share of investment ("gross domestic fixed capital formation") in GDP in recent years has fluctuated somewhat. *Sources: Central Statistical Office, Annual Abstract (1992); Mitchell, British Historical Statistics.*

analysed as a very long lived durable good, using the principles governing the demand for durable goods developed earlier in this chapter.

Three questions concern us here. What determines the level of business investment? Why is it so variable? And how does government influence it? We direct these questions first to plant and equipment investment and then to inventory investment.

INVESTMENT IN PLANT AND EQUIPMENT

To undertake an investment, firms must believe that the expected future returns will be large enough to compensate them for the risks of the investment. Moreover, firms are aware that money in the future is worth less than money today; if they have £1 this year, they can put it in the bank and get it back *with interest* next year. As the interest rate rises, future pounds are worth less relative to today's pound. That means there will be fewer projects with future returns large enough to offset forgone interest. To put it another way, think of the firm as having to borrow the money for the investment project. Higher interest rates increase the cost of undertaking the project. Fewer projects will have a sufficiently high return to pay these higher interest costs. Thus, higher interest rates lead to lower levels of investment. The relationship between interest rates and investment is the investment schedule introduced in Chapter 23 and is depicted as the downward-sloping curve in Figure 27.6. Of course, what matters for investment is the real interest rate, the cost of funds taking into account the effect of inflation. If the *nominal* interest rate increases but future prices increase in an offsetting way, firms' investment will be unaffected. (The real interest rate is the nominal interest rate minus the rate of inflation.) And, of course, what matters for long-term investment is the long-term real interest rate—over the period of the investment.

EXPECTATIONS AND RISK

Perhaps the hardest part of the firm's investment decision is predicting future returns. In some cases, there are **technological risks:** the firm may be using a new technology which could prove unreliable. In most cases, there are **market risks.** Will there be a market for the product? At what price will it sell? What wage will workers demand in the future? What will be the price of electricity and other inputs? The firm has no crystal ball: it has to make an educated guess, recognising that there is uncertainty.

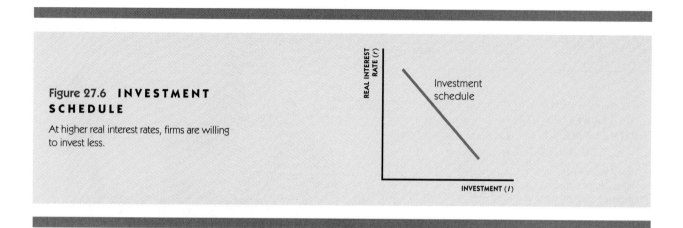

Figure 27.6 INVESTMENT SCHEDULE

At higher real interest rates, firms are willing to invest less.

Typically, firms insist on being compensated for bearing risks. There are three major determinants of the amount that firms require to compensate them for bearing risks: the magnitude of the risks, their ability to share the risks, and their willingness to bear the risks. When the economy goes into a recession, typically firms perceive that the risks of investing are greater. The primary way that firms share risks is through the stock market. In companies whose shares are widely held, large numbers of individuals share risks. When the stock market is booming, firms find it easy to issue new shares and thus to spread risks more widely. Finally, the ability and willingness of firms to bear risks depends on their own financial strength. If their net worth has been eroded by a series of losses and they have had to borrow to remain afloat, their ability and willingness to bear risks will be reduced.

THE ACCELERATOR

One of the most important determinants of expectations of returns to investment is future sales. When sales are up today, firms may expect future sales to be high, and perhaps even increasing. With high and increasing sales, firms will want to have more capital; that is, they want to invest more. Thus, an increase in government expenditures today not only gives rise to an even larger increase in output through the multiplier but to a still larger increase, as the higher output generates more investment, which further stimulates the economy. The fact that

increases in output beget further increases in output as a result of increased investment is referred to as the **accelerator.**

AVAILABILITY OF FUNDS

There is one more important determinant of investment. The analysis so far has assumed that firms can borrow funds at the market rate of interest. Particularly in economic downturns, many firms *claim* they cannot borrow as much as they would like. When they cannot borrow, they must resort to **retained earnings**—their profits, less what they pay out to shareholders in dividends—to finance their investment.

In the recession of the early 1990s, many firms found that banks would not lend to them to keep their businesses going during the period of low sales. The banks which had been lending freely to small businesses in the boom of the late 1980s, thereby contributing to the rise in demand and inflation, tightened up the criteria they used for lending to small firms. Additionally, they charged high rates of interest on those loans that they were willing to make. This was in part because banks had changed their assessment of the riskiness of loans to small firms and demanded a high risk premium built into the interest rate. The banks argued that they were not the cause of the problem, which was in fact that there were too few "good" borrowers and too few borrowers prepared to pay realistic interest rates.

In fact, most firms—even those that can easily borrow—finance most of their investments out of retained earnings. But even if they cannot borrow from banks, large firms have two other sources of funds: they can issue new shares on the stock market, or they can issue new bonds on the bond market. But typically, in an economic downturn, the stock market does not fare well, so that firms would have a hard time issuing new shares; current owners would have to give up a large share of their firm—more than they think it is worth—to raise a limited amount of funds. And the bond market is likely to be no more friendly, requiring what the borrower may feel is an exorbitant interest rate to compensate for what is perceived as the high risk of lending in the midst of a recession. Thus, as a practical matter, particularly in an economic downturn, many firms view the availability of funds as a major constraint on their investment.

RECESSIONS

As the economy goes into a recession, typically the investment schedule shifts to the left, as depicted in Fig-

Figure 27.7 THE EFFECT OF A RECESSION ON INVESTMENT

As the economy enters a recession, expectations of profits decrease, the ability to share risks decreases, and the availability of financing decreases. This leads to a shift in the investment schedule to the left.

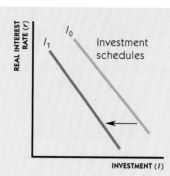

ure 27.7. Expectations of profits decrease, risks appear larger, the ability to share risks is decreased, and the ability and willingness to bear risks is reduced. Moreover, firms that are not able to borrow and have to use retained earnings to finance investment have fewer funds available for investment. And banks—with their capital base eroded from higher defaults and with a perception of a greater risk of default for new loans—may be less willing to make loans. Under these circumstances, even large changes in real interest rates may be unable to generate much additional investment.

A LOOK AT THE DATA

There is considerable evidence that lowering interest rates does stimulate investment. Some kinds of investments—such as investment in housing—are viewed to be more interest sensitive than others—such as inventories, which we will discuss shortly. The increases in interest rates in Britain in 1989 and 1990 caused an enormous collapse in house prices. Only in 1996 did the housing market in Britain begin to recover.

While interest rates are an important determinant of investment, they are not the only determinant: as we have seen, changes in expectations, perceptions of risk, and willingness to bear risk may all shift the investment schedule. Indeed, in certain periods of time, most of the variations in investment appear related to these other variables. Figure 27.8 shows investment as a percentage of the GDP in the United Kingdom for the period 1930 to 1990 and estimates of the real interest rate for selected years. The real interest rates are constructed by taking the nominal yield on long-term government bonds and subtracting an estimate of the future inflation rate that was forecast at the time. This estimate is surrounded by a wide margin of uncertainty, and so, therefore, are any estimates of real interest rates. There is no evidence of a negative relation between investment and real interest rates. Real interest rates have in fact varied little over the period, from 2.5 to 5 percent. Real interest rates were low in the 1930s, when investment was also low. During the 1980s, when real interest rates were relatively high, investment was not particularly low.

WHY INVESTMENT MAY BE LOW IN RECESSIONS

There are low expectations of future profits.

Banks' being unwilling to lend and low firm profits make it impossible for firms to finance investment projects.

Perceptions of greater risk and lower ability to bear risk make banks less willing to lend and firms less willing to invest.

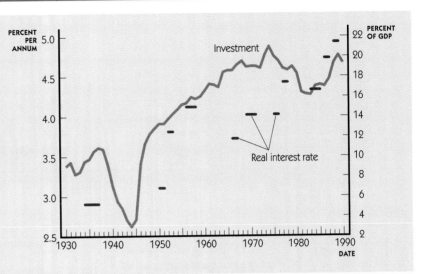

Figure 27.8 REAL INTEREST RATES AND INVESTMENT IN THE UNITED KINGDOM

Historical data for the United Kingdom do not suggest a negative relationship between investment and real interest rates. *Sources:* Central Statistical Office, *Annual Abstract of Statistics* (1992); Mitchell, *British Historical Statistics;* M. Scott, "Real Interest Rates: Past and Future," *National Institute Economic Review* (1993).

We now know why investment in plant and equipment can be volatile: changes in expectations, availability of funds, and a firm's net worth, as well as interest rates can affect investment. Indeed, Keynes thought firms' investment decisions were so unpredictable as to be based on "animal spirits."

INVENTORY INVESTMENT

One of the most volatile components of investment is inventories—the materials that are held in storage either awaiting use in production or for sale to customers.

Although inventory investment is not large, on average, as a fraction of GDP, it is highly variable. Inventories can be both accumulated and reduced quickly, and inventory investment can fluctuate from +1 percent of GDP one year to −1 percent of GDP the next. These changes in this component of aggregate demand can have substantial effects on the economy as it moves between booms and recessions. Figure 27.9 shows inventory investment in the United Kingdom for the period 1930 to 1990.

There is a cost to holding inventories. If firms borrow funds to finance their inventories, planning to pay back the loans after selling the inventoried products,

they must pay interest on these funds while the products remain unsold. If a company finances the inventories itself, it faces an opportunity cost. The funds that pay for the inventory could be used for other purposes. Beyond the cost of the inventory itself, storage space costs money, as does spoilage or deterioration in the process of storage.

Given the costs, why do firms hold inventories? One reason is that inventories on the input side facilitate production. This is called the **production-facilitating function** of inventories. It is very costly, for instance, for a printing plant to run out of paper and have workers and machines standing idle until more arrives. On the output side, customers often rely upon the producer to supply the good to them when they need it. To do that, the producer must maintain inventories sufficient to meet anticipated sales. If there are delays in fulfilling an order, the customer may turn elsewhere.

Inventories also enable firms to save money by producing at a steady rate. It is expensive to let sales dictate the level of production. There would be too much variation from day to day or even month to month. Workers and machines might be left idle or forced to work overtime. Thus, firms prefer to set a steady level of production, which, when combined with the unsteady demand for their products, pro-

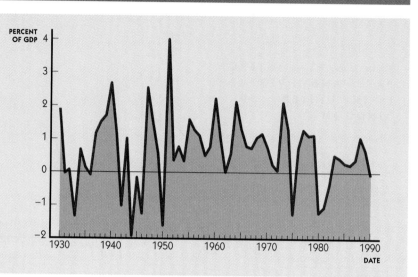

Figure 27.9 INVENTORY INVESTMENT

The diagram shows the "value of the physical increase of goods and works in progress" for the United Kingdom, 1930 to 1990. Inventory investment, although on average a small fraction of GDP—around 1 percent—is a highly volatile one.

duces inventory. To smooth production, firms put goods into inventories in slack periods and take them out of inventories in peak times. This is called the **production-smoothing function** of inventories.

In the production-facilitating explanation, inventories are positively correlated with the level of output and aggregate expenditures: inventories increase when the level of output is high. In the production-smoothing explanation, inventories are negatively correlated with aggregate expenditures: they go up when expenditures go down. This pattern would seem to suggest that inventories reduce fluctuations in national output, by allowing firms to keep an even level of production.

In fact, however, rather than serving to dampen business fluctuations, inventories seem to exacerbate them. Inventories vary far more than output, and as was mentioned earlier, they seem to be a major contributing factor to fluctuations in aggregate expenditures. This is true even for inventories of consumer goods, which should serve a particularly smoothing role.

One reason for the variability of investment in inventories may again be the risk-averse behaviour of firms and the availability of credit. When the economy enters a recession, firms often find that their net worth is decreased. They are less willing to make

any kind of investment, including inventory investment. Where possible, they would like to "disinvest," or convert their assets back into cash. By far, the easiest kind of disinvestment is to sell off inventories. When a business faces credit rationing, it may be forced to sell its inventories to raise the requisite capital. And even if it is not yet forced to sell off its inventories, it may fear future credit rationing and, in anticipation, seek to reduce its inventories.

UNINTENDED INVENTORY ACCUMULATIONS

Often, as the economy goes into a recession, inventories build up involuntarily. Retailers, for instance, make orders based on expected sales; if the sales fail to materialise, the shop holds the unsold merchandise as "inventory." This unintended inventory accumulation can feed back quickly into production, as shops reduce their factory orders in response to their larger than desired inventories. Lower orders lead quickly to a cutback in production. The cutbacks in production as firms try to restore inventories to normal size relative to sales are referred to as "inventory corrections." Cyclical variabilities induced by inventories are called inventory cycles.

CLOSE-UP: JUST-IN-TIME INVENTORY MANAGEMENT

A recent change in the way that companies manage their inventories may have an effect on the stability of the economy. In the 1970s Toyota pioneered a new system of inventory management called "just-in-time." Instead of holding large stocks of parts and materials at its factories, Toyota reduced inventories to a bare minimum and relied on developments in information technology and efficient delivery services to keep the factories supplied with the materials needed. This system spread through Japanese industry in the 1970s and to the United States and other western economies in 1980s.

Besides saving on the costs of holding stocks, just-in-time systems may have helped firms to modernise in other ways. *The Economist* described it the following way. "A favorite analogy is with water in a river. When the level of water falls, rocks start to appear. The rocks can be removed rather than hit." In other words, carrying big inventories can allow a company to cover up various organizational problems. Cutting inventories can be a powerful tool for overall efficiency.

The widespread adoption of just-in-time systems may have significant effects on macroeconomic stability. For instance, a strike at General Motors (GM) brake manufacturing plants in the United States in March 1995 brought production throughout GM to a halt within two weeks because inventories of brakes ran out, no cars could be made, and 200,000 workers had to be laid off.

At the same time, the stability of the economy may be enhanced, because just-in-time may reduce the violent swings in inventory investment that have been a common feature of previous business cycles. If firms hold few inventories, they will match closely production to demand, rather than continuing to produce, allowing inventories to grow when demand begins to fall, and subsequently cutting back production sharply to clear the surplus stocks.

Source: Richard J. Schonberger, "The Transfer of Japanese Management Approaches to U.S. Industry," *The Economist*, 25 April 1987, p. 68.

POLICIES TO STIMULATE INVESTMENT

While the government cannot control all of the determinants of investment, it has a variety of instruments that may affect it. If the business community is convinced of the government's commitment to economic stability, businesses may perceive less risk and be more willing to invest. But predicting, let alone controlling, the psychology of business executives is at best a tricky business.

The British government has used the rules for corporation tax to influence investment decisions. Depreciation allowances in particular have been used for this purpose. By allowing firms to depreciate capital equipment rapidly (for tax purposes), the effective cost of investment is reduced. **Accelerated depreciation** means that the firm can set the cost of an investment against its profits in the year in which the investment is made, rather than over the true economic life of the capital equipment. This cuts the cost of investment.

For example, take an investment of £1 million in capital equipment, which depreciates at 10 percent a year. That is to say that it is worth £900,000 after 1 year, £810,000 after 2 years, £729,000 after 3 years, and so on. If the firm were restricted to charging only the true economic depreciation against its gross profits, it would be able to charge depreciation of

WAYS OF STIMULATING INVESTMENT

1 Increasing business confidence: government's demonstrating a commitment to maintaining high levels of employment and output

2 Lowering the cost of investment: subsidies to investment through the tax system

3 Increasing the availability of credit or making it available on more attractive terms (monetary policy; direct government lending programmes)

only £100,000 in the first year, £90,000 in the second, £81,000 in the third, £72,900 in the fourth, and so on. With a corporation tax rate of 40 percent, the tax savings would be 40 percent of those amounts in each year. The capitalised value of these tax savings (or their **present discounted value**) at an interest rate of 5 percent per annum would be (in £ thousands)

$$0.4 \times [100 + 90/(1.05) + 81/(1.05)^2 + 72.9/(1.05)^3 + \ldots]$$
$$= 280.$$

If the firm is allowed to deduct the full cost of its capital investment in the first year, then it charges the full £1 million against its gross profits and reduces its net profits by £1 million. The tax saved in the first year is £400,000. This compares with the comparable capitalised tax savings of £280,000 when accelerated depreciation is not allowed. Accelerated depreciation saves the firm 12 percent of the cost of the investment, in this particular case.

But temporary tax changes are a cumbersome tool, requiring action by government. Temporary tax changes may also distort how resources are allocated, though the macroeconomic gains—in higher levels of output—may well be worth the microeconomic losses from these distortions.

For the most part, however, the government relies on monetary policy, which affects both the availability of credit and the terms on which firms can borrow. Firms raise funds through the capital market. How and when the government, through monetary authorities, affects the capital market (interest rates and availability of credit) are important, complex questions that we will explore in the next three chapters. For now, it is worth noting once again the interrelationships among all the pieces of the macroeconomic puzzle. What goes on in the product market (the determination of the equilibrium level of output) affects the labour market (the level of unemployment in the economy), and what goes on in the capital market (interest rates and the availability of credit) affects investment and thus the product market.

REVIEW AND PRACTICE

SUMMARY

1 The Keynesian consumption function stresses the importance of current disposable income in determining consumption. In contrast, future-oriented consumption theories focus on an individual's total wealth, including what he will receive as income over his entire life; savings serves to smooth consumption. Thus, the life-cycle hypothesis says that people save during their life so they can spend after retirement. The permanent income hypothesis argues that people save in good years to offset the bad years.

2 In the traditional (Keynesian) consumption function, the government could manipulate this year's consumption by changing this year's income tax rate. In the future-oriented theories, temporary income tax reductions would have a limited effect in stimulating consumption, since people are considering a longer horizon than this year for their consumption decisions.

3 Both the life-cycle and permanent income models predict that consumption will depend on lifetime wealth and that capital gains will therefore affect consumption.

4 Household consumption appears to be more dependent on current income than either the life-cycle or permanent income theory suggests. Consumers can easily postpone the purchase of durables when current income falls. Also, limitations on their ability to borrow (credit rationing) may keep the consumption of many people with little savings close to their current income.

5 Future-oriented theories of consumption suggest that the aggregate expenditures schedule is flat and the multiplier is low.

6 Variations in the level of investment are probably the principal reason for variations in total aggregate expenditures. The three main categories of investment are firms' purchases of plant and equipment, firms' increase or decrease of inventories, and households' purchases of new homes.

7 While investment depends on the real rate of interest, historically, much if not most of the variation in investment is attributed to other factors, such as changes in expectations, perceptions of risk, and willingness and ability to bear risk, all of which shift the investment schedule.

8 As income increases, investment tends to increase, partly because expectations of future sales increases, partly because as GDP increases, profits increase, increasing the availability of funds for investment. The relationship between income and investment is called the accelerator.

9 Most firms finance most of their investment out of retained earnings. When firms cannot borrow or raise money in the stock market—or can do so only at very unattractive terms—firms may perceive the lack of availability of funds as limiting their investment.

10 Investment is low in a recession because of low expectations of future profits; an unwillingness of banks to lend; a lack of profits, which makes it impossible for firms to finance investment projects on their own; and perceptions of greater risk and a lower ability to bear risk, which make banks less willing to lend and firms less willing to invest.

11 Inventories serve to both facilitate production and smooth production. Variations in inventory accumulation contribute to the economy's fluctuations; a slight unanticipated downturn in the economy leads to unintended inventory accumulation, and as firms cut back orders to reverse this unintended inventory accumulation, output falls.

12 Government can stimulate investment by increasing business confidence, especially through a demonstrated commitment to maintain the economy at high levels of employment and output, by subsidising investment through the tax system and by lowering interest rates and increasing the availability of credit.

KEY TERMS

life-cycle savings

permanent income hypothesis

durable goods

accelerator

retained earnings

production-facilitating function

production-smoothing function

accelerated depreciation

REVIEW QUESTIONS

1 What is the difference between the Keynesian model of consumption, the life-cycle model, and the permanent income model?

2 Why do the life-cycle and permanent income hypotheses predict that temporary tax changes will have little effect on current consumption?

3 What factors affect consumer expenditures on durables? Why are these expenditures so volatile?

4 How will the existence of credit rationing make consumption more dependent on current income than the future-oriented consumption theories would suggest?

5 What are the principal forms of investment? Why does the level of investment depend on the real interest rate? What are other important determinants of the level of investment in plant and equipment?

Historically, what role have these various determinants played in variations in the level of investment?

6 What is the accelerator, what gives rise to it, and what are its consequences?

7 What are the possible sources of funds for firms that wish to invest? Why might availability of funds play an important role in investment?

8 Why does investment tend to fall in a recession?

9 Why do firms hold inventories? What are the costs and benefits of holding inventories? What are unintended inventory accumulations, and what role do they play? Why might inventory investment be as volatile as it is?

10 How can government stimulate investment?

PROBLEMS

1 Under which theory of consumption would a temporary tax cut have the largest effect on consumption? Under which theory would a permanent rise in social security benefits have the largest effect on consumption? Under which theory would permanently higher unemployment insurance benefits have the largest effect on consumption? Explain.

2 Which theory of consumption predicts that aggregate savings will depend on the proportion of retired and young people in the population? What is the relationship? Which theories predict that consumption will not vary a great deal according to whether the economy is in a boom or recession? Why?

3 If the government made it easier for people to borrow money, perhaps by enacting programmes to help them get loans, would you expect consumption behaviour to become more or less sensitive to current income? Why?

4 How would you predict that a crash in the stock market would affect the relationship between con-

sumption and income? How would you predict that rapidly rising prices for houses would affect the relationship between consumption and income? Draw shifts in the consumption function to illustrate. How do your predictions differ depending on whether the consumer is a Keynesian, life-cycle, or permanent income consumer?

5 A company that expects the long-term real interest rate to be 3 percent is considering a list of projects. Each project costs £10,000, but they vary in the amount of time they will take to pay off and in how much they will pay off. The first will pay £12,000 in two years; the second, £12,500 in three years; the third, £13,000 in four years. Which projects are worth doing? If the expected interest rate was 5 percent, does your answer change? You may assume that prices are stable.

6 Take the projects in problem 5 and reevaluate them, this time assuming that inflation is at 4 percent per year and the nominal values of the payoffs are unchanged. Are the projects still worth doing?

7 Draw a diagram to show how investment is affected in each of the following situations.

(a) The government introduces accelerated depreciation allowances.

(b) Businesses believe the economic future looks healthier than they had previously thought.

(c) The government reduces the real interest rate.

8 Imagine that the government raises personal income taxes but also gives a subsidy to investment which is worth the same amount. Describe under which circumstances this combination of policies would be most effective in stimulating aggregate demand. Consider differing theories of consumption, and the choice between permanent and temporary changes in the tax rates.

9 Explain how purchasing a durable good is like an investment. How might an increase in the interest rate or a change in credit availability affect the demand for durables?

10 Explain why if most inventories were held for reasons of production smoothing, inventory accumulation would actually serve to stabilise the economy. Why do economists focus on movements in inventories of consumption goods to argue that there are important factors other than production smoothing that determine patterns of inventory holding? What is one possible explanation of the observed pattern?

Why would you expect the desired level of inventory holdings to increase with the level of output? Explain why this accelerator relationship might contribute to economic instability. How would you expect changes in the rate of interest, changes in the costs of storage, and innovations in inventory management techniques to affect the desired inventory-sales ratio?

APPENDIX: THE INVESTMENT-SAVINGS IDENTITY

We typically think of savings and investment together. Both are virtues: "A penny saved is a penny earned." Increased investment enhances the future productivity of the economy. It is sometimes argued—especially in the United Kingdom where the rate of economic growth has been slow, and the fraction of income saved low—that, to raise economic growth, countries should save more. The implicit assumption is that higher savings would automatically lead to higher investment.

When a *closed* economy is operating along its production possibilities curve, with all resources fully utilized, increased savings—reduced consumption—mean that more capital goods can be produced. Then savings and investment will move together. But when the economy is operating below its production possibilities curve, increased savings—reduced consumption—may simply push the economy further below that curve.

In *open* economies, savings and investment do not have to change together even when the economy is on its production possibilities curve. This is because the economy can undertake investment, even when there is little domestic saving, by borrowing from abroad.

The income-expenditure analysis of Chapter 26 focused on the relationship between aggregate expenditures and income. Equilibrium occurs when aggregate expenditures equal national income. An alternative way of describing how national output is determined focuses on savings and investment. We look at a simple model first, in which disposable income equals national income. For this to be the case, we assume that taxes are zero and all of a firm's profits are paid out as dividends. To simplify further, we assume there are no government savings or dissavings, or any flow of funds from abroad. Later we will loosen up these assumptions to get a fuller picture.

By definition individuals can either spend their income today or save:

$$\text{Income} = \text{consumption} + \text{savings}. \qquad (27.1)$$

With no government purchases or net exports, we know from the components of aggregate expenditures that firms can produce only two kinds of goods: consumer goods and investment goods. Thus, output Y can be broken into its two components:

$$Y = \text{consumption} + \text{investment}. \qquad (27.2)$$

These two identities can be combined to form a new one. Since the value of national output equals national income,

$$Y = \text{income}, \qquad (27.3)$$

we can use the right-hand sides of equations 27.1 and 27.2 to get

$$\begin{aligned} &\text{Consumption} + \text{savings} \\ &\quad = \text{consumption} + \text{investment}. \end{aligned} \qquad (27.4)$$

Subtracting consumption from both sides of the equation yields

$$\text{Savings} = \text{investment}. \qquad (27.5)$$

One way to understand this identity is to think of firms as producing a certain amount of goods, the value of which is just equal to the income of the individuals in the economy (because everything firms take in they pay out as income to someone). The income that is not consumed is, by definition, saved. On the output side, firms either sell the goods they produce or put them into inventory for sale in future years. Some of the inventory buildup is planned, be-

cause businesses need inventories to survive. Some of it is unplanned; businesses may be surprised by an economic downturn that spoils their sales projections. Both intended and unintended inventory buildups are considered investment. Thus, the goods that are not consumed are, by definition, invested.

Equality 27.5 can be transformed into an equation determining national output, once it is recognised that in equilibrium firms will cut back production if there is unintended inventory accumulation. Because firms will cut back, in equilibrium the amount companies invest is the amount they wish to invest (including inventories), given current market conditions. The equilibrium condition, then, is that

$$\text{Investment} = \text{desired investment}. \qquad (27.6)$$

Now switch over to the savings side of equality 27.5. The consumption function presented earlier tells how much people wish to consume at each level of income. But since what is not consumed is saved, the consumption function can be transformed into a savings function, giving the level of savings at each level of income. Savings is income minus consumption:

$$\text{Savings} = \text{income } (Y) - \text{consumption}. \qquad (27.7)$$

Figure 27.10 shows the savings function. The slope of this curve, the amount by which savings increase with income, is the marginal propensity to save, which is 1 minus the marginal propensity to consume.

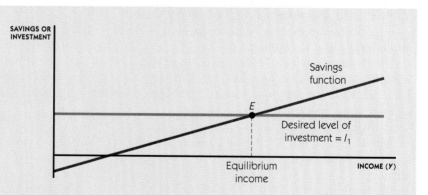

Figure 27.10 THE SAVINGS FUNCTION AND NATIONAL INCOME

As income increases, the amount individuals desire to save increases. The amount by which saving increase as the result of an increase in income—the slope of the savings function—is called the marginal propensity to save. In equilibrium, savings equal investment. Thus, equilibrium occurs at the intersection of the savings function and the level of investment.

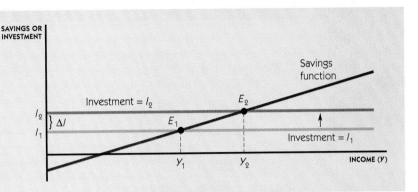

Figure 27.11 USING THE SAVINGS-INVESTMENT DIAGRAM

A shift in investment from I_1 to I_2 leads to an increase in output from Y_1 to Y_2; the increase in output is a multiple of the original increase in investment.

Since savings must equal investment and in equilibrium investment must equal desired investment, then in equilibrium,

$$\text{Savings} = \text{desired investment}. \qquad (27.8)$$

Figure 27.10 shows a fixed level of desired investment I_1, which is horizontal because investment is assumed to be unaffected by the level of income. Equilibrium occurs at the intersection of the desired investment curve and the savings curve, point E.

As with income-expenditure analysis, savings-investment analysis shows how an increase in investment leads to an increase in output that is a multiple of itself. Figure 27.11 shows that as investment shifts up from I_1 to I_2, the equilibrium shifts from E_1 to E_2, and output increases from Y_1 to Y_2. The change in output is again larger than the change in investment

ΔI. This should not surprise us, since income-expenditure analysis and savings-investment analysis are two ways of looking at the same thing.

The Paradox of Thrift   We can use a similar diagram to illustrate what may seem a paradoxical result. When the economy's resources are not fully employed, and increase in thrift—the level of savings at each level of income—may have no effect at all on the equilibrium level of savings or investment. The only effect of greater thrift is to lower national income and output. Figure 27.12 shows the effect of an upward shift in the savings function; at each level of income, savings are higher. But in equilibrium, savings equal investment. With investment fixed, savings, in equilibrium, must also be fixed. To attain that level of savings (equal to the level of investment), income must be lowered from Y_1 to Y_2.

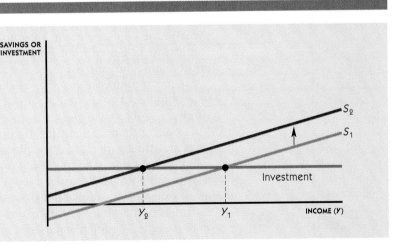

Figure 27.12 THE SAVINGS FUNCTION AND THE PARADOX OF THRIFT

Given a level of investment fixed by other factors, increased thriftiness, reflected in an upward shift in the savings function, lowers output from Y_1 to Y_2 but leaves savings unchanged.

MONEY, BANKING, AND CREDIT

S ome say money is the root of all evil. Some say money makes the world go 'round. Actually, money does not *do* anything in and of itself. Part of the economy is made up of real people working with real machines to make goods that satisfy needs directly. Money for the most part is just paper or a record in a bank's computer. It satisfies needs only indirectly, when it is spent.

In Chapter 23 we encountered the principle of money neutrality. At full employment, an increase in the money supply only leads to a proportionate increase in prices and wages, with no real consequences. Yet controlling the supply of money is considered such an important function of government that failure to exercise that control properly has been blamed not only for inflations but also for depressions. In the short run, the economy may deviate significantly from full employment, and under such conditions monetary policy may affect output and employment substantially.

We have emphasised that all markets are interlinked. Fluctuations in aggregate output cause fluctuations in employment. Changes in aggregate output can be traced to changes in the level of aggregate demand, which in turn can be related to changes in the level of investment. Investment depends on interest rates and other aspects of the capital market.

So it is to the capital market that we now turn. We will see in this and the next two chapters how government can—through monetary policy—affect interest rates and the availability of credit, and thus the level of investment in the short term. This chapter will explain what money is, what it does, and why it is so important. The following two chapters will show how, why, and when monetary policy affects the level of economic activity.

1 What *is* money? What economic functions does it serve?

2 What is meant by the money supply, and how is it measured?

3 What institutions in our economy are responsible for controlling the money supply and determining monetary policy?

4 How do modern economies create money through the banking system? How do monetary authorities affect the creation of money and the availability of credit? How do they, in other words, affect the supply of money and credit?

MONEY IS WHAT MONEY DOES

We use the term *money* to mean much more than just bank notes and coins. When someone asks how much money you make, he means what is your income. When someone says, "He has a lot of money," she means he is wealthy, not that he has stashed away lots of cash. When someone accuses corporations of being "interested only in making money," she means they are interested only in making profits.

Economists define money by the functions it serves, and we must look at these functions before we can develop a formal definition of money.

MONEY AS A MEDIUM OF EXCHANGE

Money's first function is to facilitate trade—the exchange of goods or services for mutual benefit. This is called the **medium of exchange** function of money. Trade that occurs without money is called **barter.** Barter involves a direct exchange of one good or service for another. Two families agree to take turns baby-sitting for each other, or a doctor and a lawyer agree to trade consultations. Nations sometimes sign treaties phrased in barter terms. A certain amount of oil, for example, might be traded for a certain amount of machinery or weapons.

Barter works best in simple economies. One can imagine an old-style farmer bartering with the blacksmith, the tailor, the grocer, and the doctor in his small town. For simple barter to work, however, there must be a **double coincidence of wants.** That is, one individual must have what the other wants, and vice versa. Henry has potatoes and wants shoes, Joshua has an extra pair of shoes and wants potatoes. Bartering can make them both happier. But if Henry has firewood and Joshua does not need any of that, then bartering for Joshua's shoes requires one or both of them to go searching for more people in the hope of making a multilateral exchange. Money provides a way to make multilateral exchange much simpler. Henry sells his firewood to someone else for money and uses the money to buy Joshua's shoes. The convenience of money becomes even clearer when one considers the billions of exchanges that take place in a modern economy.

Any easily transportable and storable good can, in principle, be used as a medium of exchange. And a wide variety of items have served that function. Indeed, the item chosen as money can be thought of as a social convention. The reason you accept money in payment for what you sell is that others will accept it for things you want to buy. Different cultures in different times have used all sorts of items as money. American Indians used wampum; South Sea Islanders used cowrie shells. In the Second World War prisoner-of-war camps and in many prisons of today, cigarettes serve as a medium of exchange.

For a long time, gold was the major medium of exchange. However, the value of a gold coin depends on its weight and purity, as well as on the supply and demand for gold in the gold market. It would be expensive to weigh and verify the quality of gold every time you engaged in a transaction. So one of the functions of governments, right up into the twentieth century, was to mint gold coins, certifying their weight and quality. But because gold is soft, it wears thin with use. Criminals have also profited by shaving the edges off gold coins. The ridges on some modern coins are a carryover from coins developed to deter this practice.

Today all the developed countries of the world use paper as well as metal coins for currency, printed by the government specially for this purpose. However, most business transactions use not currency but cheques drawn on banks, credit cards whose balances are paid with cheques, or funds wired from one bank to another. Economists consider chequing account balances to be money, just as cash is, because they are accepted as payment at most places and thus serve the medium of exchange function. Since most people have much more money in their chequing accounts than they do in their wallets, it should be evident that the economists' measure of the money supply is much larger than the amount of notes and coins in circulation.

MONEY AS A STORE OF VALUE

People will only be willing to exchange what they have for money if they believe they can later exchange the money for the goods or services they want. Thus, for money to serve its role as a medium of exchange, it must hold its value, at least for a short while. This function is known as the **store of value** function of money. There was a time when governments feared that paper money by itself would not be accepted in the future, and so paper money was not as good a store of value as gold. People had confidence in paper money only because it was backed by gold (if you wished, you used to be able to exchange your paper money for gold).

Today, however, all major economies have **fiat money**—money that has value only because the government says it has value and because people are willing to accept it in exchange for goods. The bank-

notes issued by the Bank of England attempt to make their owners feel secure with the words, "I promise to pay the bearer on demand the sum of five pounds," in the case of the five pound note. (This is in fact a meaningless statement. Once upon a time, when the pound sterling was backed by gold, the Bank of England had an obligation to exchange notes for gold. But nowadays, the only thing the Bank of England will offer in exchange for one five pound note is another five pound note.) The fact that it is legal tender means that if you owe someone £50, you have fully discharged that debt if you give her a £50 note.

There are many other stores of value. Gold, which is no longer money because it no longer serves as a medium of exchange, nevertheless continues to serve as a store of value. In India, for instance, people hold much of their savings in the form of gold. Land, corporate stocks and bonds, oil and minerals—all are stores of value. None of them is perfectly safe, in the sense that you cannot be precisely sure what they can be exchanged for in the future. But cash, chequing account balances, and other forms of money are not a perfectly safe store of value either. If prices change, then what you can buy with the cash in your pocket or bank account will change.

MONEY AS A UNIT OF ACCOUNT

In performing its roles as a medium of exchange and a store of value, money serves a third purpose. It is a way of measuring the relative values of different goods. This is the **unit of account** function of money. If a banana costs 25 pence and a peach 50 pence, then a peach is worth twice as much as a banana. A person who wishes to trade bananas for peaches can do so at the rate of two bananas for one peach. Money thus provides a simple and convenient yardstick for measuring relative market values.

Imagine how difficult it would be for firms to keep track of how well they were doing without such a yardstick. The ledgers might describe how many of each item the firm bought or sold. But the fact that the firm sold more items than it purchased would tell you nothing about how well that firm was doing. You need to know the value of what the firm sells relative to the value of what it purchases. Money pro-

CLOSE-UP: ALTERNATIVE MONIES

The normal and almost universally accepted situation is that the central bank of the country is the sole supplier of currency. However things have not at all times and in all places been this way.

The Scottish banks still issue their own bank notes, in a faint echo of the practice in the nineteenth century and earlier when many banks in England and Scotland (and, indeed, in other countries also) issued their own notes. In Scotland today the notes are issued one for one against deposits held against them by the banks at the Bank of England. In effect they are merely replacing Bank of England notes one for one with Scottish notes. It is merely relabeling. In the nineteenth century individual banks in many British towns were issuing their own notes to their customers without such controls in place. The banks were not regulated so as to prevent them from issuing too many notes given the size of their reserves of gold or their capital. There were only weak controls on the quality of their portfolio of loans. There were consequently frequent banking crises and collapses until effective bank regulation and controls were established. The English banks lost their right to issue their own notes, but the Scots retained theirs, though tightly circumscribed.

The use of cigarettes as a medium of exchange in prisoner-of-war camps in the Second World War is well known. Cigarettes were usable as a currency in an economy where there was no central bank issuing notes because they have a number of desirable properties as money. They are small, light, reasonably durable, and divisible, so suitable for small transactions. They also have intrinsic value: many people wanted to smoke them. This put a floor under their value as money. If their money value fell below this, people would simply smoke the cigarettes, reducing the money supply until the price of cigarettes rose (or the price of other goods in terms of cigarettes fell) sufficiently. They were universally acceptable in exchange because everyone correctly believed that everyone else would accept cigarettes in payment, even if not everyone wanted to smoke them.

In other places more varied goods have been used, with mixed success, as money. And in some places, barter survived until recently. Stanley Jevons, the great British economist and one of the towering figures in the development of economics, tells of a singer, Mademoiselle Zélie of the *Théâtre Lyrique*, who was paid for a performance in the Society Islands with "three pigs, twenty-three turkeys, forty-four chickens, five thousand cocoanuts, besides considerable quantities of bananas, oranges and lemons." Back in Paris this would have been worth a good deal at the market. "In the Society Islands, however, pieces of currency were very scarce; and as Mademoiselle could not consume any considerable portion of the receipts herself, it became necessary in the meantime to feed the pigs and the poultry with the fruit." Perishable goods such as these are clearly less suited to use as an international medium of exchange.

Source: W. S. Jevons, "Barter," *Money and the Medium of Exchange* (23d ed.; London: Kegan Paul, 1910), pp. 1–7. Reprinted in *Monetary Theory*, R. W. Clower, ed., (New York: Penguin, 1969).

Despite the presence of regulations intended to limit banks' investment activity and lessen the chances of bank failure, there has been a string of failures. In some cases the failing banks have been rescued by the central bank, and in others they have been allowed to fail.

In the United Kingdom, the biggest set of failures of recent times occurred in 1973–74, when many so-called near-banks collapsed. They had been set up specifically to evade restrictions on the lending activities of the normal banks and leant money heavily to property speculators: there was an enormous boom in property prices at that time. When the property market collapsed, many of these loans went bad: the borrowers became unable to repay, and the collateral was insufficient, because of the property price collapse. The scale of potential failures was sufficient to threaten the stability of the entire banking system in Britain. The Bank of England organised an enormous financial rescue attempt—the lifeboat operation—which succeeded in maintaining the stability of the system, though at considerable cost to the public.

In other cases, banks have been allowed to collapse. The Bank of Credit and Commerce International collapsed spectacularly in 1991 as a result of fraud with the loss of £13 billion, but as it posed no general threat to the stability of the banking system, it was allowed to collapse. When Baring's Bank, a small but distinguished and long-established investment bank, collapsed in 1996, as a result of the failed speculative activities of its Singapore trader Nick Leeson, the Bank of England did not attempt to prevent failure or effect a rescue. In this case also it was judged that there was no threat to the banking system as a whole, and the bank was allowed to fail.

While people who hold small deposits in failing banks are protected against losing the bulk of their money, large depositors are not so protected, and in Baring's case would have made substantial losses. Arguably people who make large deposits in banks should share some of the risk of loss, in order to encourage them to be watchful of the financial stability of the institution in which they deposit money. Many politicians take the naive view that banking regulations should be sufficiently strict and regulators sufficiently vigilant that such failures should never ever occur. The governor of the Bank of England, called before a parliamentary committee to explain why the Bank's regulatory procedures had not prevented the Baring's collapse, robustly defended the Bank's record and wisely remarked that such rigorous regulation would be so costly as to be counterproductive.

There were massive bank failures in the Far East, in Thailand, South Korea, Malaysia, Indonesia, and Japan in 1997 and 1998, associated with the Southeast Asian Crisis. One of the biggest was the failure of Long Term Credit Bank in Japan in 1998. In the United States a so-called hedge fund, Long Term Capital Management, collapsed in 1998 with the loss of $4.8 billions of capital. This case raised ironic smiles because it had been set up in part by Professors Myron Scholes and Robert Merton (University of Chicago), joint winners of the 1997 Nobel Prize for Economics, and had based its investments on the most-advanced economic principles.

Worldwide, the biggest and most extensive systemic collapse of recent years was that of the Savings and Loan Associations (S & Ls) in the United States. The S & Ls are equivalent to building societies in the United Kingdom. They had a reputation for being very cautious lenders and very safe institutions. But they got caught out in the 1980s when they found themselves holding long-term fixed-interest-rate mortgages (which they had issued in days when interest rates were low) but had to pay high interest rates in order to maintain their deposits. Regulations were relaxed to allow S & Ls to make riskier loans, with higher returns than mortgages. But many, realising that they were probably heading for bankruptcy anyway, made highly speculative investments, knowing that if they failed, their depositors would be insured (by the Federal Deposit Insur-ance Corporation) and that if the investments paid off, the S & Ls would make good profits: a no-lose situation for the S & Ls. In the event, there were failures on an unprecedented scale, and the bailout cost U.S. taxpayers $100 billion.

The moral of these (true) stories is that effective banking regulations can at best limit the frequency of failure and protect the system from the effects of collapses of some banks within it and that inappropriate regulations can bring about spectacular disasters.

vides the unit of account, the means by which the firm and others take these measurements.

We are now ready for the economic definition of **money.** Money is anything that is generally accepted as a medium of exchange, a store of value, and a unit of account. Money is, in other words, what money does.

MEASURING THE MONEY SUPPLY

The quantity of money is called the **money supply,** a stock variable like the capital stock. Most of the other variables discussed in this chapter are stock variables as well, but they have important effects on the flow variables (like the level of economic activity, measured as dollars *per year*).

What exactly should be included in the money supply? A variety of items serve some of the functions of money but not all of them. For example, the chips issued in casinos for gambling serve as a medium of exchange inside the casino and perhaps even in some nearby shops and restaurants. But no place outside the casino is obliged to take them; they are neither a generally accepted medium of exchange nor a unit of account.

The economists' measure of money begins with the currency and coins that we carry around. Economists then expand the measure of money to include other items that serve the three functions of money. Current accounts, or **sight deposits** (so called because you can get your money back on sight), are included in the money supply, as are some other forms of bank accounts. But what are the limits? There is a continuum here, running from items that everyone would agree should be called money to items that can work as money in many circumstances, to items that can occasionally work as money, to items that would never be considered money.

The Bank of England publishes figures for a number of monetary aggregates. The narrowest definition is **M0**—"the wide monetary base"—which consists of notes and coin in circulation outside the Bank of England, plus bankers' operational deposits in the Banking Department of the Bank of England.

A wider definition is **M2:** This consists of the notes and coin, and sterling retail deposits held with the U.K. banks and building societies by residents of the United Kingdom (*residents* here means everyone excluding banks or building societies). Bank retail deposits are defined as being all non-interest-bearing deposits plus "chequable" sight or time deposits regardless of maturity, plus other deposits up to £100,000 with less than one month to maturity. Building society retail deposits are transaction accounts and other deposits up to £100,000 with no more than one month to maturity.

A yet wider definition is **M4:** This includes the notes and coin and all sterling deposits at U.K. banks and building societies held, once again, by the U.K. nonbank nonbuilding society sector. This includes all sight and time deposits of any size.

The Bank of England also publishes a number called **M3H** which is comparable to the broad money aggregates published in other European Community countries (*H* is for harmonised). The M3H includes M4 and also the foreign currency deposits of U.K. residents with banks and building societies in the United Kingdom and the sterling and foreign currency deposits of public corporations held with banks and building societies in the United Kingdom. The M3H is slightly larger than M4—by about 5 percent.

Over the years a number of different definitions of the money supply have been offered. The M1, M3, and £M3 (sterling M3) definitions have been used in the recent past. The control of £M3 was a key element in the medium-term financial strategy of the Thatcher government in Britain from 1980 onwards. The definitions have changed as time has passed because the regulations governing banks and building societies have changed, the banks and building societies have introduced new financial products, and there have been changes in the usage and importance of different kinds of financial instruments. The conversion of the Abbey National from a building society to a bank in 1989 led to the discontinuation of M3 as a measure of the money supply.

The older definitions of the money stock (such as M3) excluded deposits held in building societies, because building society deposits were believed not to be used much for transactions. It used to be relatively more difficult to put money into and get it out of a building society account; a transaction using a building society account had to involve cash or a bank cheque as well. However, since financial markets were deregulated in the mid-1980s in Britain, building societies have been able to offer cheques on their accounts. Many building society accounts are now usable just like bank accounts, and there is no argument for including only bank deposits and no building society deposits in the definition of the money stock.

In a similar way, the usefulness of M1, which excluded interest-bearing current accounts from its definition of the money stock, was undermined by the growing use of interest-bearing current accounts (sight deposits).

One of the difficulties of the use of measures of the money stock is that they do not all grow at the same rate. This has lead to confusion over the state of monetary policy, and difficulty in making inferences about what is happening in the economy. Figure 28.1 shows the growth rates of M0 and M4 from 1970 to 1996. Note M4 grew quite rapidly until 1990, whereas M0 grew much more slowly.

MONEY AND CREDIT

One of the key properties of money, as noted, is that it is a medium of exchange. However, many transactions today do not entail the use of any of the measures presented so far: M0, M2, or M4. They involve credit, not money. In selling a suit of clothes or a piece of furniture or a car, shops often do not receive money. They receive, rather, a promise from you to pay money in the future. Credit is clearly tied to money: what you owe the shop is measured in pounds. You want something today, and you will have the money for it tomorrow. The shop wants you to buy today and is willing to wait until tomorrow or next week for the money. There is a mutually advantageous trade. But because the exchange is not *simultaneous,* the shop must rely on your promise.

Promises, the saying goes, are made to be broken. But if they are broken too often, shops will not be able to trust buyers, and credit exchanges will not occur. There is therefore an incentive for the development of institutions, such as banks, to ascertain who is most likely to keep economic promises and to help ensure that once such a promise has been made, it is kept.

When banks are involved, the shop does not need to believe the word of the shopper. Rather, the shopper must convince the bank that he will in fact pay. Consider a car purchase. Suppose a bank agrees to give Luke a loan, and he then buys the car. If he later breaks his promise and does not pay back the loan, the car dealer is protected. It is the bank that tries to force Luke to keep his commitment.

Modern economies have relied increasingly on credit as a basis of transactions. Banks in Britain have a long tradition of granting overdrafts to firms and in-

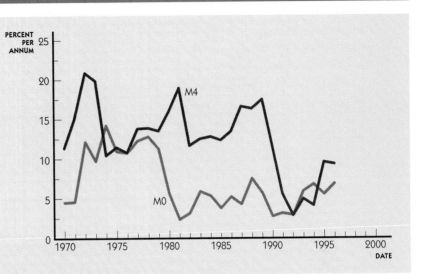

Figure 28.1 MONEY STOCK GROWTH IN THE UNITED KINGDOM, 1970–1996

Stocks of monetary aggregates outstanding: M0 end 1996, £24,800 million; M4 end 1996, £569,431 million. These figures are seasonally adjusted. *Source:* Bank of England, reported in *Economic Trends*, Annual Supplement, Office of National Statistics (1997), Table 5.2.

dividuals. Credit is made available to them up to an agreed limit as it is needed. With Visa and Master-Card and the variety of other credit cards that came into widespread use in the 1970s and 1980s, credit has also been extended to millions of consumers, who now can purchase goods even when they have no cash or current account balances on hand. There are a variety of ways that people who own houses can get credit using their ownership of the property either as collateral for the loan or at least to indicate to the lender that they are likely to repay the loan.

These innovations make it easier for people to obtain credit. But they have also altered the way economists think about the role of money in the economy—blurring definitions that once seemed quite clear.

THE FINANCIAL SYSTEM IN MODERN ECONOMIES

Broadly speaking, a country's **financial system** includes all institutions involved in moving savings from households and firms whose income exceeds their

expenditures and transferring it to other households and firms who would like to spend more than their income and liquid assets allow. Here we take a closer look at the most important of these institutions.

The financial system not only allows consumers to buy cars, televisions, and VCRs even when they do not have the cash to do so. It also enables firms to invest in factories and new machines. Sometimes money goes directly from, say, a household doing some saving to a firm that needs some additional cash. In the United States, corporations sometimes sell bonds to raise cash. These are like loans for fixed periods of time—90 days, 180 days, 5 years, 15 years, for example—at predetermined interest rates. When Ben buys a newly issued bond from General Motors, he is lending money directly to GM. In Britain, the corporate bond market is less commonly used. But individuals often lend money directly to small firms, like family businesses.

But most of the funds flow through **financial intermediaries.** These are firms that stand in between the savers, who have the extra funds, and the borrowers, who need them. The most important group of financial intermediaries is the banks, but there are many other groups of financial intermediaries as well, including life insurance companies

CLOSE-UP: A GLOSSARY OF FINANCIAL TERMS

One of the problems of defining money is that there are many financial assets differing in the ease or convenience or effectiveness with which they can be used as a means of payment or store of value. Each tends to be very similar to the next, so that it is not clear where to draw the line in deciding what is and what is not money. Indeed, much of the financial services industry is devoted to devising new financial instruments which plug the gaps in the spectrum currently on offer in an attempt to tease customers away from rival institutions. Some assets that serve, progressively less satisfactorily, the functions of money are:

Notes and coin

Universally acceptable as means of exchange but insecure—too easily stolen or lost—and only suitable for small transactions.

Travelers cheques

Cheques issued by firms such as American Express. Used less and less as credit cards make cash available in increasingly many places around the globe. Still used in the United States, where there are more local banks and fewer national networks.

Sight deposits, or current accounts

Bank deposits from which money can be drawn on sight, or demand. Sometimes pay low interest rates, reflecting the cost of providing transfer services (as well as the monopoly power of the large banks).

High interest cheque accounts

Attempt to combine the liquidity of cheques with the returns of a less liquid savings account. They usually offer a limited number of free withdrawals by cheque per year or limit the minimum size of cheque withdrawal or combine both of these.

Savings deposits, or deposit accounts

Sometimes referred to as "time deposits" to denote the period of notice needed for a withdrawal. Tend to offer higher interest rates to compensate for the loss of liquidity.

Certificates of deposit

Referred to as "CDs." Usually available only in very large denominations and held by large companies. Often have a fixed term before they can be cashed in and may be transferable between holders.

Eurodollars, Eurosterling, and other Euro-currencies

Not to be confused with the Euro. Bank deposits in dollars held in banks outside the United States, or sterling accounts held outside the United Kingdom, and so on. A market that developed as a result of "petrodollars," the surpluses earned by the oil producers after the 1973 oil shock, combined with restrictions on interest rates in the United States at the time. An initially largely unregulated market, often credited with increasing the volatility of the international financial system.

and building societies. All are engaged in looking over potential borrowers, ascertaining who are good risks, and monitoring their investments and loans. The intermediaries take "deposits" from consumers and invest them. By putting the funds into many different investments, they diversify and thus reduce the risk. One investment might turn sour, but it is unlikely that many will. This provides the intermediary with a kind of safety it could not obtain if it put all its eggs in one basket. Financial institutions differ in who the depositors are, where the funds are invested, and who owns the institutions.

THE BANKING SYSTEM

In most developed economies, the basis of the financial system is **fiat money**—paper money, printed at virtually no cost and deriving value from being kept in limited supply. It has no intrinsic value (unlike gold, for example). The key player in the financial system in such economies is accordingly the supplier of the paper money, the **central bank.** In Britain, the central bank is the Bank of England, in Germany the Bundesbank, in France the Banque de France, in the United States the Federal Reserve System, and in Japan the Bank of Japan.

Central banks serve a number of functions in the financial system. One is to act as a banker to the other banks in the economy and to act as the "lender of last resort." In this capacity the central bank holds deposits made with it by the other banks in the economy. These the other banks use as **reserve assets** which they can (in principle) draw upon if they need to pay out cash to their depositors and which are used to settle transactions between banks. As lender of last resort, the central bank lends to other banks, if necessary, to ensure that depositors at these banks can be confident of always being able to obtain their deposits in cash and to reduce the danger of a **run on the banks.**

A related function, often but not necessarily carried out by central banks, is to act as the **regulator** of the banking system. In this capacity it imposes conditions on persons or firms who want to act as banks and monitors the activities of banks, to reduce the danger of banks' becoming insolvent and to limit the chance that it (the central bank) will have to act as lender of last resort.

A third role performed by many but not all central banks is to act as the banker for the government. In this capacity they either lend directly to the government or arrange loans for the government through the financial markets, and manage the financing of the national debt. In some countries the central bank has been required to lend directly to the government to supply its needs for cash. In some instances, this has led to the central bank's simply printing money for the government to spend, and so to inflation and hyperinflation. In other countries, partly to avoid the dangers of hyperinflation, the central bank has been prohibited from lending directly to the government.

In Britain, the role of the Bank of England in **debt management**—advising the government on how to finance its deficit and on the management of the national debt—has always been viewed as one of its key roles. Providing funds to the British government was the main reason that the Bank of England was established.

A natural consequence of the key position in the financial system occupied by the central bank is that it is in a position to influence most if not all of the financial markets in the economy. It can use the rate of interest at which it is willing to lend to other financial institutions to manipulate interest rates. It can use its ability to buy and sell government and other securities in the financial markets to influence interest rates—the rates of return on those securities—and it may be able to regulate the quantity of money circulating in the economy.

CREATING MONEY IN MODERN ECONOMIES

In order to see how a central bank can influence the money stock and interest rates, we need to examine the way banks run their businesses, making loans and investments. Most money in the economy does not consist of notes and coins but of bank deposits; and bank deposits come into existence largely as a

CLOSE-UP: A GLOSSARY OF FINANCIAL INTERMEDIARIES IN BRITAIN

A variety of financial intermediaries take funds from the public and lend them to borrowers or invest the funds. There are legal and regulatory differences between these institutions, but the main differences relate to the kinds of loans or investments they make.

Banks

A wide category of institutions in the United Kingdom are classed as banks by the Bank of England and were regulated by it until the establishment of the Financial Services Agency in 1998. They take deposits and make loans and investments. While there was once a clear distinction between banks and building societies, that distinction has all but disappeared. Building societies have become much more like banks, in that they provide accounts with cheque books, and debit and credit cards. Meanwhile, banks lend on mortgages for housing purchases, once almost exclusively the preserve of the building societies. Some building societies have in fact become banks.

Life insurance companies

They collect premiums from policyholders, out of which they pay claims. They have become more closely connected with banks and building societies, which increasingly try to sell their customers services other than banking. Life insurance policies have become used very much in mortgage contracts—so-called endowment mortgages, which at one time had small tax advantages for borrowers and still have large advantages (in the shape of commissions) for insurance salespeople and financial advisers.

Building societies

They were originally restricted to taking deposits and using them to make loans for house purchases. More recently they have become like banks and offer a wider range of services, like cash machines, chequebooks, and credit cards. They are also allowed to raise funds by borrowing on wholesale money markets and not just by taking deposits from persons (the so-called retail market). Many have abandoned their old mutual status (they were owned by their depositors) and have floated themselves on the stock market as public limited companies. The distinction between building societies and banks has become very blurred.

Unit trusts

Individuals can buy units in these trusts. The proceeds are invested in different types of stocks and bonds. Different funds invest in different kinds of assets. Some buy stocks that pay few dividends but have a lot of capital growth; others attempt to find stocks that pay high dividends but offer little capital growth. Some try to find a safe if relatively low return; others go for a high average return accompanied by more risk.

Investment trusts

They are rather like unit trusts, except that you buy shares in the investment trust, which is a company whose purpose is to invest in other companies. The price of the shares depends on the value of the assets owned by the trust but curiously is generally much less than the value of the assets. The discrepancy, known as the investment trust discount, has been as high as 40 or 50 percent at times but is currently on the order of 10 percent. Investment trusts have much smaller assets in the aggregate than unit trusts in the United Kingdom.

Pension funds · They collect pension contributions from members and invest them in a variety of stocks and bonds, land, property, or works of art (in the famous case of the National Coal Board Pension Fund). They are intended to provide pensions for their members after they retire from work. Sometimes they are embezzled (illegally) by the persons or companies who have set up the fund (as in the case of Robert Maxwell and the Mirror Group newspapers) or raided (legally) by the firms that set them up to provide the firm with additional funds, when it can be claimed that the pension fund has more resources than it needs to meet its future claims.

---

result of banks' making loans to their customers. Banks, it is said, "create" money by their lending activities. The money supply of today is created not by a mint or printing press but largely by the banking system. When you put money into the bank, the bank does not simply take the currency down to its vault, put it into a little slot marked with your name, and keep it there until you are ready to take it out. Instead, banks realise that not all their thousands of depositors will withdraw their money on any given day. Some will come by next week, some in two weeks, and some not for a year or more. In the meantime, the bank can lend out the money deposited in its vault and charge interest. The more money the bank can persuade people to deposit, the more it can lend out, and thus the more money the bank will earn. To attract depositors, the band pays interest on its deposits, effectively passing on (after taking its cut) the interest earned on its loans.

How much can safely be lent out? Money retained by a bank in case those who have deposited money want it back is called its **reserves.** How much needs to be kept as reserves? Should the bank keep reserves of 5 percent of deposits? Of 20 percent of deposits? The less it keeps as reserves, the more money it can earn, but the greater the possibility that it will not have enough funds on hand if a large number of depositors want their deposits back at the same time. To understand how these reserves work and how they affect the supply of money and credit avail-

able in the economy, we need to take a close look at the typical bank's balance sheet.

THE BANK'S BALANCE SHEET

Bankers see the world backwards. Where else would loans be called "assets" and deposits be called "liabilities"? This is the perspective shown on a bank's **balance sheet.** Like any firm's balance sheet, it describes the bank's **assets** and **liabilities.** Assets are what the firm owns, including what is owed to it by others. That is why the bank's loans appear as assets on its balance sheet. Liabilities are what it owes to others. We can think of the bank's depositors as having loaned money to the bank. They can get their money back when they wish. That is why deposits are treated by the bank as liabilities.

Table 28.1 shows the balance sheet of Mid-Lloyd Bank. Its assets are divided into four categories: loans, government bonds, liquid assets, and cash reserves at the Bank of England. Reserves of cash and liquid assets are held to meet the probable needs of customers withdrawing their deposits.[1] Cash reserves at the Bank of England are required to be at

---

[1] Note that the required reserve ratios are changed from time to time. They have typically ranged between 0.25 and 1.00 percent in recent years.

Table 28.1 THE BALANCE SHEET OF MID-LLOYD BANK

Assets		Liabilities	
Loans	£50 billion	Deposits	£55 billion
Government bonds	£ 5 billion	Net worth	£11.3 billion
Liquid assets	£ 6 billion		
Cash reserves at the Bank of England	£ 0.3 billion		
Total	£61.3 billion	Total	£61.3 billion

least 0.5 percent of a bank's deposits. In addition to these legally required reserves at the Bank of England, banks hold more reserves (also at the Bank of England), so-called bankers' operational deposits, to meet their day-to-day needs for settling transactions between banks and for meeting their own customers' demands for cash. The 0.5 percent required cash reserve acts as a tax on banks for the services provided by the Bank of England.

Liquid assets include Treasury bills with only a short time to maturity and other government bills, local government bills, and private sector bills ("commercial bills"). These assets are not cash, but they can be readily sold for cash at an almost certain price, and then used to meet the demands from customers withdrawing deposits. The Bank of England is typically willing to buy (or borrow) these assets from the banks when they need extra cash. The advantage to the banks of holding these assets is that they yield a higher return to the banks than do reserves at the Bank of England; the banks sacrifice a small degree of liquidity in exchange for a greater yield.

The ratio of liquid assets to deposits held by the banks is the subject of "prudential regulation" by the Bank of England. While liquid assets do not have to amount to some minimal fixed percentage of deposits, banks are required to keep an amount that can be judged "prudent" given the kinds of deposits it holds. For example, deposits held in current accounts in which turnover is rapid, with many payments of money into the accounts and many payments out of them, and a relatively small average balance, suggest a need for large liquid assets, because any balances could quickly disappear. By contrast, deposits held in high-interest accounts, in which three months' notice is required before a withdrawal can be made (or there is a penalty of three months' loss of interest) and cheques have to be for at least £500, suggest the need for relatively small reserves of liquid assets. The bank is not likely to be caught short of cash by sudden large withdrawals from such accounts.

The government bonds owned by the banks are usually of longer periods to maturity than are the Treasury bills included in the liquid assets. They are an investment of the banks, yielding a low but secure return: the British government is thought to be unlikely to default on its debts. They are not liquid assets. While these investments can be sold at any time for cash in the market for government bonds—the "gilt-edged" market—their capital value is somewhat uncertain. The least liquid category of asset held by banks is loans to customers. These also make up the bulk of banks' assets. Most loans are made for at least some stated minimal duration, and the bank cannot get its money back before the loan is due to be repaid.

The liabilities of Mid-Lloyd Bank are divided into two categories. The larger is deposits of customers, and this may include current accounts and deposit or savings accounts of various kinds. The other item is the net worth, or **capital,** of the bank. This is the difference between the bank's assets and its other liabilities (in practice, mainly deposits; in this illustration, entirely deposits). The bank's capital can act as a kind of buffer to protect the depositors against fluctuations in the value of the bank's assets. For example, if the bank's assets include £1 billion of loans to a developing country, on which the borrower defaults, the bank has to remove the value of that asset from its balance sheet. If the bank writes down the value of its assets by £1 billion on the left-hand side of the balance sheet, it also has to reduce an item on the right-hand side by the same amount. It owes its depositors the same amount as before. The liability that is reduced is the bank's capital. When banks make provision for bad debts, they are adding to their capital and investments, in order to increase the size of this buffer and reduce the risk that when these debts go bad and have to be written off, the remaining assets of the banks are not big enough to cover their deposits.

In recent years, bank regulators have paid more and more attention to the need to ensure that banks have enough capital to protect their depositors. It is not enough to ensure that banks have sufficient cash and liquid assets to meet the need for withdrawals. In 1988, regulators from around the world meeting in Basle agreed to impose a uniform minimal **capital adequacy requirement** on banks: from 1992, banks are required by this agreement to maintain capital of at least 8 percent of their assets.

HOW BANKS CREATE MONEY

To see how banks create money, consider all the banks in the country as if they were one big bank. Now suppose that a wealthy individual deposited £1 million in cash (previously hidden under the mattress) into a bank account. The bank knows it has to keep 0.5 percent of deposits as cash reserves at the Bank of England, and it may wish to keep a further 0.5 percent of its deposits in the form of cash reserves in its own vaults to meet possible withdrawals by customers. But the remainder (99 percent) of its deposits it can use to make loans, to buy liquid assets, and to make other investments. The bank may wish to keep a further 9 percent of the deposits in other liquid assets, to protect it in case of sudden needs for cash. If the bank at first deposits half of the £1 million with the Bank of England and keeps the other half in its vaults, then the initial effect of the deposit of £1 million on the bank's balance sheet is to increase liabilities (deposits) by £1 million and to increase assets by £1 million (cash reserves at Bank of England by £.5 million and cash reserves in vaults, part of the liquid assets of the bank, by £.5 million).

When the bank makes a loan to a customer, it credits the amount of the loan to her bank account. When that customer uses the loan to pay people, she writes cheques which transfer the money from her bank account to the bank accounts of other people. So the money (bank deposits) created by the loan remain in the banking system. The bank's balance sheet is therefore increased on the assets side by the amount of the loan it makes and on the liabilities side by the amount of the extra bank deposits created by the loan. If the bank makes a loan of £1 million to the customer, its loans and its deposits both rise by £1 million. For the banking system as a whole, making loans does not cause it to lose cash, unless the people who take out the loans keep them in cash rather than as bank deposits which are then passed on to the accounts of other persons when payments are made.

The same is true if the bank buys liquid assets, such as Treasury bills or commercial bills from other members of the public or from companies. When it buys a Treasury bill, it pays for it by increasing the bank deposit of the person or company from whom it buys the Treasury bill. If the bank buys a £1 million commercial bill from Imperial Chemical Industries, it adds the commercial bill to its assets and adds a deposit of £1 million owned by ICI to its liabilities.

As a result the bank knows that, having received a deposit of £1 million in cash, which adds to its reserves at the Bank of England and to its vault cash, it can make additional loans, of say £90 million, and purchase liquid assets, of say £9 million. (This assumes that the bank has customers who want to take out additional loans of at least this amount.) These two actions will add £99 million to the bank's assets and liabilities. Taking this together with the initial effects of the £1 million deposit, we find that the bank's deposits have risen by a total of £100 million, and so have its assets. The increase in the assets is made up of £.5 million in reserves at the Bank of England, £0.5 million in cash in the bank's own vaults, £9 million in additional liquid assets, and £90 million in loans. Table 28.2 illustrates the effects of these transactions on the bank's balance sheet.

In this example the final effect of someone's depositing £1 million of cash in the banking system is to allow the banking system to increase deposits by £100 million. The ratio 1:100 between cash and deposits is there because the bank only wants to keep £1 in reserves of cash (half in the vault, half at the Bank of England) for every £100 of deposits. The

Table 28.2 CHANGES IN THE BANK'S BALANCE SHEET

A. Initial Effect of a Deposit of £1 Million, Half Deposited with the Bank of England and Half Kept as Cash in the Bank's Vaults

Assets		Liabilities	
Cash reserves at Bank of England	£.5 m	Deposits	£1 m
Cash in vault	£.5 m		

B. Effect of the Bank's Making a Loan of £1 Million and Buying a Commercial Bill from ICI for £1 Million

Assets		Liabilities	
Loans	£1 m	Deposits	£2 m
Liquid assets	£1 m		

C. Combined Effects of a Deposit of £1 Million, of Which £.5 Million Is Deposited with the Bank of England and £.5 Million Is Retained as Cash in the Vaults, a Purchase of Further Liquid Assets of £9 Million, and Making Loans of £90 Million

Assets		Liabilities	
Reserves of cash at Bank of England	£ .5 m	Deposits	£100 million
Cash in vaults	£ .5 m		
Liquid assets	£ 9 m		
Loans	£90 m		

ratio is called the **money multiplier.** The banking system is able, by making loans and investments, to convert £1 of cash into £100 of bank deposits. This is the sense in which the banking system is able to create money.

The example could be taken to suggest that changes in the supply of money are caused by people's depositing money with the banking system or withdrawing it. A small deposit of cash is capable of producing a large increase in the money supply, and a small withdrawal appears capable of causing a large contraction in it, when the process just described is put into reverse. This suggests that the stock of money may be very volatile. In practice, changes in the money supply occur for other reasons. The pattern of cause and effect in practice is not as simple as the example suggests. The example suggests that the availability of cash reserves to the banks fixes or limits the money stock. In principle, it is possible for banks' reserves to be limited or controlled by the central bank to limit the money supply.

In the United Kingdom, the money supply has not been controlled in this way. The Bank of England has normally made it possible for the banks to obtain cash reserves when they need them. So in practice, in Britain, the demand for bank deposits and bank loans has determined the amount of cash reserves, not the other way round.

Suppose, for example, that the bank just described wanted to make additional loans of £90 million but lacked any spare cash reserves. The bank could make the loans of £90 million, and it could also purchase, from firms or ordinary people, Treasury bills and commercial bills worth £10 million. These actions would increase the bank's assets and liabilities by £100 million, but they would leave it short of cash reserves. The bank needs to keep an additional £.5 million at the Bank of England, and it may wish to keep an additional £.5 million in its vaults. How is it to get hold of these reserves? The bank can offer to sell, to the Bank of England, Treasury and commercial bills worth £1 million, and take half the proceeds in cash to keep in its vault and leave half on deposit at the Bank of England. If it were to do this, it would convert some of its liquid assets into cash reserves and meet its legal and prudential requirements for reserves and liquidity.

The Bank of England typically is willing to accommodate the needs of banks for cash reserves and buy up bills. However, it can exert some influence on the banks, by fixing the price at which it will buy bills. This affects the interest rate that the banks pay for their reserves. The lower the price the Bank of England pays for bills, the higher the interest rate.

The effects on the balance sheet of the banking system of selling Treasury bills to the Bank of England and the effects on the balance sheet of the Bank of England are illustrated in Table 28.3. The banking system—the commercial banks—reduce their holdings of bills (liquid assets) and increase their holdings of cash reserves. Both of these are their assets. There is no change in their liabilities. The Bank of England increases its assets (its holdings of bills) and its liabilities (deposits held at the bank by the commercial bankers). The Bank of England's liabilities consist of notes and coin held outside the Bank and bankers' deposits. This quantity (with the exclusion of bankers cash ratio deposits) is the **wide monetary base, M0,** sometimes described as the stock of **high-powered money,** since it forms the basis of the multiple expansion of deposits through the banking system.

Table 28.3 makes an important point: that the stock of high-powered money consists of the liabilities of the Bank of England. In principle, the Bank can control its liabilities and its assets. It only incurs greater liabilities when it acquires more assets, by buying securities—bills and bonds—from banks or individuals outside the Bank of England, and paying them with cash (notes and coins) or giving them bank deposits at the Bank of England. In principle, the Bank can engage in **monetary base control** as a means of controlling the money supply. However, this has not been used significantly in the United Kingdom. Other countries, such as Germany and the United States, have relied more on the control of the monetary base to control the money supply.

Table 28.3 EFFECTS ON BALANCE SHEETS OF A COMMERCIAL BANK'S SELLING TREASURY BILLS TO THE BANK OF ENGLAND

Mid-Lloyd Bank

Assets		Liabilities	
Cash reserves at Bank of England	+£1 million	Deposits	No change
Liquid Assets	–£1 million	Net worth	No change
Loans	No change		

Bank of England

Assets		Liabilities	
Treasury and commercial bills	+£1 million	Notes and coin held outside the Bank of England	No change
Other government securities	No change	Deposits of commercial banks	+£1 million

THE INSTRUMENTS OF MONETARY POLICY

SHORT-TERM INTEREST RATES

The principal instrument used by the Bank of England to control the money supply and generally credit conditions in the United Kingdom is the control of short-term interest rates. It does this by influencing rates of interest paid in the money markets on Treasury and other bills and on government bonds with short times left before they mature. The Bank of England, acting on behalf of the government, sells each week a quantity of new Treasury bills to the banks and other financial institutions. The banks hold these as part of their reserves of liquid assets, and there is active trade in new and second-hand Treasury bills. It is the existence of continuous trading in these bills that makes them liquid, of course. At any time, someone owning Treasury bills can sell them in the financial markets at a price that reflects the prevailing rate of interest. The price varies therefore, but there is no problem about finding a buyer.

The Bank of England enters the market for Treasury bills and short-dated government bonds every day (not quite according to the timetable of the one-time president of the Board of Trade Michael Hesel-

CLOSE-UP: THE BALANCE SHEET OF BANKS IN THE UNITED KINGDOM, END OF DECEMBER 1992

Sterling liabilities (£ millions)		Sterling Assets (£ millions)	
Notes outstanding	2,084	Notes and coin	4,317
Sight deposits	179,947	Deposits at the Bank of England	
Time deposits	298,722	Cash ratio deposits	1,420
Certificates of deposit	50,812	Other	−42
Total deposits	529,481		
		Loans to financial markets	155,253
Items in suspension and transmission	10,324	Bills	11,022
Capital	68,920	Advances	380,911
		Investments	33,925
		Other	29,311
Total sterling liabilities	610,809	Total sterling assets	617,378

Other Currency Liabilities (£ millions)		Other Currency Assets (£ millions)	
Deposits	756,055	Market loans and advances	675,233
Items in suspense and transmission	11,702	Bills	11,675
Capital	20,800	Investments	82,980
		Other assets	12,100
Total other currency liabilities	788,557	Total other currency assets	781,988
Total liabilities, £ millions	1,399,366	Total assets, £ millions	1,399,366
(Eligible liabilities	406,697)		

Source: Bank of England Quarterly Bulletin, 1993.

The balance sheet figures reveal some important features of the banking system. First, notice that of the banks' total assets and liabilities, over half are not in sterling at all; they are in foreign currencies. This underlines the importance of London as an international financial centre and shows how important the rest of the world is to the U.K. banks. The banks' sterling assets and liabilities are roughly the same. Overall, the banks do not take large positions in the foreign exchange markets; they are not net sellers or buyers of sterling.

Of the banks' sterling assets, the largest category is "advances," which are mainly loans to customers in the private sector of the United Kingdom. The other big item is loans to financial markets, mainly deposits held at other banks. Only a small amount of assets—less than 2 percent—are held in Treasury and other bills, and a very small fraction is held at the Bank of England—£1.4 billion out of sterling assets of £617 billion, relative to "eligible liabilities" of £406 billion and just over 3 percent of eligible liabilities. The banks hold much more in cash in their vaults—£4.3 billion—than on deposit at the Bank of England. These figures underline the point that the banks mainly make loans and advances to customers. Buying government stocks and Treasury bills is a relatively small part of their business.

The capital funds of the banks—£69 billion in sterling and £20 billion in other currencies—are the assets of the banks which are not matched by other liabilities and which provide a cushion against, for example, bad debts or some of the banks' investments yielding a low rate of return.

On the liabilities side of the balance sheet, it appears that time deposits—those which cannot be withdrawn without notice—are bigger than sight deposits. The Scottish banks still have £2 billion of their own banknotes outstanding. Certificates of deposit are tradable bank deposits that carry interest and have a fixed date on which the money in the deposit can be obtained. Large firms can buy and sell these bank deposits without needing to transfer deposits directly.

---

tine, before breakfast, before lunch, and before dinner but nevertheless frequently and regularly). It invites banks to offer to sell to it bills that are nearing the date of maturity, and it takes up some of these offers, naturally the best ones and as many as it believes appropriate. By doing this, the Bank gives the banks cash (in the form of deposits held at the Bank of England) which they can use to meet their needs for reserves and operational reserves and which they can also use to obtain notes and coin to meet the demands made by their customers.

In 1997 the Bank of England began to use the Repo market in its open market operations. Repo contracts involve the Bank in buying an asset (a government bond, for example) for a period of time at the end of which it is sold back to the seller. It effectively involves the Bank in lending reserves to the financial market using the asset as collateral. It enables a wider range of assets to be used in the Bank's dealings with the money markets. The Bank of England uses its announced Repo rate (the rate of interest that is used in its repo contracts) as the principal method of influencing interest rates in the economy. However, the institutions and practices in financial markets evolve continuously, and none of these procedures are set in stone. They are very likely to change with the passage of time. The use of Repo markets has brought the Bank of England's procedures for intervening in money markets much closer to the procedures used in other European countries, such as Germany.

The Bank of England has in the past used a number of means to influence rates of interest. It has used indirect means, such as dropping loud hints as to which interest rates it thinks are appropriate. Another method has been to buy lots of bills, providing the banks with a lot of cash relative to their needs when it wanted interest rates to fall. Conversely, it has bought only small amounts of bills, leaving the banks relatively short of cash and having to offer high rates of interest in order to sell bills and meet their needs. These traditional operations—buying and selling Treasury bills—affect the cash and liquidity of the banks and influence the rates of interest at which these financial institutions lend to and borrow from each other for short periods of time—overnight, one day, seven days, one month, and so on. These money market rates of interest affect the rates of interest that the banks offer to their ordinary customers—individuals and firms—on deposits and loans. Banks have adopted the practice of setting a base rate and setting other interest rates relative to it.

RESERVE REQUIREMENTS

In principle, the Bank of England could use changes in reserve requirements to control the supply of money. We have seen that the money multiplier, which relates the amount of reserves banks hold to the size of their deposits, depends on the reserve ratio: the fraction of deposits that banks hold as cash reserves, either in their vaults or at the Bank of England. If banks keep 1 percent of their deposits in the form of cash reserves, then deposits can be no more than 100 times the size of their reserves. By raising the fraction of deposits that banks have to keep in the form of reserves, the Bank of England can reduce the maximum size of deposits for any given amount of reserves. If the Bank insisted on banks' keeping reserves at the Bank equal to 10 percent of their deposits, deposits could be no more than 10 times the size of the banks' reserves at the Bank of England. If the Bank of England then limited the availability of reserves, by limiting its purchases of Treasury and other bills, it could control the maximum size of the money supply. If the Bank wanted to reduce the money supply, it could raise the required reserve ratio.

Since 1980, changes in reserve requirements have not been used in Britain as a means of controlling the money supply. This is partly because the availability of reserves has not been used to control the money stock. Banks have been able to obtain reserves when needed. The interest rate at which reserves have been available has been used to influence the conditions in financial markets. When the availability of reserves is not used to limit the money supply, there is little point in changing reserve ratios. Prior to 1980, changes in reserve ratios were used. Banks were required to make additional deposits with the Bank of England, called special deposits, which effectively raised the reserve ratio, at times during the 1960s and 1970s when there was an attempt to tighten monetary conditions. A scheme called supplementary special deposits (the "corset") was used in the late 1970s to restrain the growth of the money supply. It required the banks to make extra deposits with the Bank of England when their deposits grew above some target level. It acted as a penalty paid by the banks if they allowed the money supply to grow too fast. It effectively limited the apparent growth of the money supply but created a number of other unintended and undesirable results. (It created difficulties in interpreting money supply figures, and it distorted the efficient allocation of financial resources.)

In general, the use of variable reserve requirements to manipulate the money supply has been reduced, because they act as a tax on banks and, like almost all taxes, distort the allocation of resources and create inefficiencies. An example of this is that, in the 1970s, the application of reserve requirements in the United Kingdom led to the growth of a number of fringe banks which did not have to satisfy the reserve requirements, and so avoided paying the implicit tax. They were able to compete for business against the existing banks. They made extensive loans for property development. Many became insolvent in a crash in property prices in 1974 and had to be rescued in a "lifeboat" operation launched by the Bank of England.

Nevertheless, required reserve ratios are used as part of the process of controlling the money supply in the United States and Germany. In both countries, the banks are required to keep a large fraction of deposits on reserve at the central bank—the Federal Reserve Banks and the Bundesbank, respectively—and more use is made of the availability of reserves than in the United Kingdom in the control of the money supply. In Europe, with the introduction of the single market in financial services, there is growing pressure for harmonization of banking regulations. The German banks believe that they are subject to unfair competition from others, such as the British banks, which do not need to keep such a large fraction of deposits on reserve, and thus pay a smaller implicit tax.

The European Central Bank (ECB) has inherited many practices from the German Bundesbank, and one is the use of reserve requirements, to which it attaches much greater weight than the Bank of England does. The ECB imposes a minimum reserve ratio of 2 percent on banks within its control, which is applied to most bank deposits (overnight deposits, deposits with agreed maturity of up to two years, deposits redeemable at notice up to two years, debt securities issued with agreed maturity up to two years, and money market paper). The relatively low rate of 2 percent reflects the growing international pressure of competition in banking. Since the reserve requirement acts as a tax on banks, there is pressure not to impose a higher tax than banks would face in other jurisdictions; the danger is that banking activity would simply relocate to those low-tax jurisdictions.

THE STABILITY OF THE BANKING SYSTEM

The fractional reserve banking system explains how banks create money, and it also explains how they can get into trouble. Well-managed banks, even before the advent of present-day reserve requirements and other controls, kept reserves equal to their expected day-to-day needs for cash. A bank could quickly get into trouble if one day's needs for cash exceeded its reserves.

If, for good reasons or bad, depositors were to lose confidence in a bank all at the same time, they would attempt to withdraw all their funds at once. The bank would simply not have the money available, since most of it would have been lent out in loans that could not be recalled instantaneously. This situation is called a **bank run.** Bank runs were common in Britain in the early nineteenth century, when regulation and supervision of banks was weak, many banks were able to issue their own bank notes, and banks did not have recourse to the resources of institutions like the Bank of England to bail them out of difficulties. A bank run could drive a healthy and soundly run bank out of business very quickly. If a rumour spread that a bank was in trouble and a few depositors ran to the bank to clean out their accounts, then other investors would feel they were foolish not to run down to the bank themselves and withdraw their deposits. One vicious rumour could result in a healthy bank's shutting down and the panic's setting off a run on other banks, thus destabilising the banking system and the whole local economy.

REDUCING THE THREAT OF BANK RUNS

Over the course of the nineteenth and early twentieth centuries the banking system gradually developed in such a way as to reduce the risk of panics and bank runs. Most countries evolved towards a system in which a central bank acted as a lender of last resort and required banks to hold reserves, and either the central bank or another institution regulated the banks and supervised their activities. In Britain the Bank of England until 1998 acted as both the lender of last resort and as the regulatory and supervisory body. In 1998 the role of banking supervision and regulation was taken over by the newly established Financial Services Agency.

There are three levels of protection for British banks against bank runs. The first is that the Bank of England acts as the lender of last resort. When a bank faces a run, it can borrow funds from the Bank

of England to tide it over the crisis. The Bank of England here is providing liquidity. Knowing that the bank is sure to be able to meet its obligations, its depositors have no need to run to the bank. There is a distinction to be drawn between a bank's having a liquidity problem, when it has too few liquid assets but enough assets overall to cover its liabilities, that is to say, it is solvent, and a bank's not having enough assets overall, and being therefore both illiquid and insolvent.

The second line of defence is the setting of reserve requirements for which the Bank of England has been responsible. These ensure that reckless bank executives who might be willing to get by on minuscule reserves are unable to do so.

The third line of defence is provided by the assets in the bank of the owners of the bank. Most banks were begun by investors who put up some money in exchange for a share of the bank's ownership. The net worth of the firm, the difference between the bank's assets and liabilities, is this initial investment, augmented or decreased over time by the bank's profits and losses. If the bank makes bad investments, then the shareholders can be forced to bear the cost (up to the limits imposed by limited liability, in most cases; the exceptions are where banks are partnerships). The cushion provided by the shareholders not only protects depositors, it also encourages the bank to be more prudent in making loans. If the bank makes bad loans, the owners risk their entire investment. But if the owners' net worth in the bank is too small, the owners may see themselves in a "Heads I win, tails you lose" situation. If risky investments turn out well, the extra profits accrue to the bank; if they turn out badly, the bank goes bankrupt, but since the owners have little at stake, they have little to lose. To protect against this danger, the government requires banks to maintain certain ratios of net worth to deposits. These are called **capital requirements.** Capital requirements protect against insolvency; they mean that if the bank invests badly and many of its loans default, the bank will still be able to pay back depositors. (By contrast, reserves and the ability to borrow from the Bank of England protect against illiquidity; they ensure that if depositors want cash, they can get it.) On occasion—more frequently in recent years—a bank will make so many bad loans that its net worth shrinks to the point where it can no longer satisfy the capital requirements.

A final measure that is used to stabilise banking systems in many countries is deposit insurance. In the United States, for example, the Federal Deposit Insurance Corporation (FDIC) was established in 1933. Federal banks and savings and loan associations have to buy insurance from it, with which deposits of up to $100,000 are insured against loss. This further reassures depositors that there is no need to rush to the bank to withdraw money in fear of a bank failure. Even if the bank fails, the FDIC will pay. The existence of the FDIC not only insures depositors, but it also increases the stability of the banking system. Its mere existence makes the risk against which it insures much less likely to occur. It is as if life insurance somehow prolonged life. Depositor insurance of this transparent and unconditional kind does not exist in the United Kingdom. Protection of depositors has depended heavily on whether and how failing banks have been rescued. The depositors in the Bank of Credit and Commerce International which failed in 1991 because of fraud only got back a proportion of their deposits. The depositors in banks that have been rescued have typically been protected.

Deposit insurance has an offsetting disadvantage, however. Depositors no longer have any incentive to monitor banks, to make sure that banks are investing their funds safely. Regardless of what the bank does with their funds, the funds are protected. Thus—to the extent that capital requirements fail to provide banks with appropriate incentives to make good loans—bank regulators must assume the full responsibility of ensuring the safety and soundness of banks.

Chapter 29 takes a closer look at the relations between monetary policy, the financial position of banks, money and credit, and the level of economic activity.

REVIEW AND PRACTICE

SUMMARY

1 Money is anything that is generally accepted in a given society as a medium of exchange, store of value, and unit of account.

2 There are many ways of measuring the money supply, with names like M0, M2, and M4. All include both currency and chequing accounts. They differ in what they include as assets that are close substitutes to currency and chequing accounts.

3 A buyer does not need money to purchase a good, at least not right away, if the seller or a financial institution is willing to extend credit.

4 Financial intermediaries, which include banks, savings and loans, mutual funds, insurance companies, and others, all have in common that they form the link between savers who have extra funds and borrowers who desire extra funds.

5 Government is involved with the banking industry for two reasons. First, by regulating the activities banks can undertake, government seeks to protect depositors and ensure the stability of the financial system. Second, by influencing the willingness of banks to make loans, government attempts to influence the level of investment and overall economic activity.

6 By making loans, banks can create an increase in the supply of money that is a multiple of an initial increase in the banks' deposits. If every bank loans all the money it can and every pound lent is spent to buy goods, purchased from other firms which deposit the cheques in their accounts, the money multiplier is 1 divided by the reserve requirement imposed by the central bank. In practice, the money multiplier is considerably smaller.

7 The central bank can affect the money supply by changing the reserve requirement, by changing the discount rate, or by open market operations.

8 Reserve requirements, capital requirements, and the central bank's acting as a lender of last resort have made bank runs rare.

KEY TERMS

medium of exchange	money	financial intermediaries	money multiplier
store of value	demand deposits	central bank	reserve requirements
unit of account	M0, M2, M4	reserves	

REVIEW QUESTIONS

1 What are the three characteristics that define money?

2 What are the differences between M0, M2, and M4?

3 When consumers or businesses desire to make a large purchase, are they limited to spending only as much money as they have on hand? Explain.

4 What are the two main reasons for government involvement in the banking system?

5 What are three ways for the central bank to reduce the money supply?

6 What has the government done to make bank runs less likely?

PROBLEMS

1 Identify which of money's three traits each of the following assets shares and which traits it does not share:
  (a) A house
  (b) A day pass for an amusement park
  (c) German marks held by a resident of Dallas, Texas
  (d) A painting
  (e) Gold

2 How might bank depositors be protected by legal prohibitions on banks' entering businesses like insurance or selling and investing in stocks or venture capital? What are the possible costs and benefits of such prohibitions for depositors and for the government?

3 Down Home Savings has the following assets and liabilities: £6 million in government bonds and reserves, £40 million in deposits, and £36 million in outstanding loans. Draw up a balance sheet for the bank. What is its net worth (or capital)?

4 What factors might affect the value of a bank's loan portfolio? If these factors are changing, explain

how this would complicate the job of a bank examiner trying to ascertain the magnitude of the bank's net worth. Why would the bank examiner be concerned about the value of the net worth?

5 While gardening in his backyard, lucky Bob finds a jar containing £100,000 in bank notes. After he deposits the money in his lucky bank, where the reserve requirement is 5 percent, how much will the money supply eventually increase?

6 Why is it that if the Bank of England sells Treasury bills, the money supply changes, but if a big company sells Treasury bills (to anyone other than the Bank of England), the money supply does not change?

7 "So long as the central bank stands ready to lend to any bank with a positive net worth, reserve requirements are unnecessary. What underlies the stability of the banking system is the central bank's role as a lender of last resort, combined with policies aimed at ensuring the financial viability of the banks—for instance, the net worth (or capital adequacy) requirements." Comment.

29

MONETARY
THEORY

n Chapter 28 we saw the close link between the creation of money and credit (loans). This chapter explains why the money supply and the availability of credit are important to the economy. Knowing this, we can understand how monetary policy—the collection of policies aimed at affecting the money supply and the availability of credit—works.

Changes in the money supply and in the availability of credit are really two sides of the same coin. We begin by looking at the central bank's direct effects on the money supply, then turn to its effects on credit availability.

KEY QUESTIONS

1 What determines the demand for money? How and why does it depend on the interest rate and the level of income?

2 How is the demand for money equilibrated to the supply of money?

3 What are the consequences of changes in the supply of money when prices are fixed? When will it lead to a change in real output? When will it largely lead to a change in the amount of money that individuals are willing to hold?

4 What are the channels through which monetary policy affects the economy? What role is played by changes in the real interest rate? In the availability of credit?

MONEY SUPPLY AND ECONOMIC ACTIVITY

In this chapter, we continue with our assumption that the price level is fixed. (Recall that if prices are completely flexible, changes in the money supply elicit proportionate changes in the price level, leaving the real stock of money unchanged.) In the case of fixed prices, if the central bank increases the money supply, there are only two possible results. First, people who get the additional money could just hold on to it. Their bank balances would grow but nothing would happen to the rest of the economy. In this case, monetary policy would be relatively ineffective—an outcome that is most likely when the economy is in a deep recession. Second, those who get the additional money could spend it. If the economy had excess capacity and prices were fixed, this increased spending (aggregate expenditures) would increase incomes and output.

What actually happens when the money supply is increased (assuming prices are fixed) is a combination of changed holdings of money and changed output. One of the purposes of this chapter is to understand the circumstances under which each of these effects predominates.

In Chapter 28, we considered several different ways of measuring the money supply—M0, M2, and M4. For much of our discussion, we do not have to be precise about which definition we have in mind. Much of the theory assumes that money is cash plus non-interest-bearing sight deposits, an old definition which used to be called M1. However, because there is now a continuous transition from accounts that pay no interest to ones that do and from accounts on which there is no penalty for immediate withdrawal to ones in which there is, this definition is of little practical use. Most of the arguments that follow are applicable to the broad money definition, such as the M4 figure currently used in the United Kingdom, which includes all bank and building society accounts held by residents of the United Kingdom in sterling, as well as notes and coin.

THE VELOCITY OF MONEY

The speed with which money circulates in the economy, its **velocity,** is as important to monetary policy as the money supply itself. If people keep money under the mattress for weeks after being paid, money circulates very slowly. In a bustling city, where money changes hands quickly, a given money supply supports many more transactions. The velocity of money is formally defined as the ratio of GDP to the money supply. If Y represents the real output of the economy, the quantity of goods produced in the economy, and P is a weighted average of their prices (the price level), PY is equal to nominal GDP (which, as we know, equals nominal aggregate income).

Using the symbol V to denote velocity and M as the money supply, we get

$$V \equiv PY/M.$$

This equation is sometimes referred to as the **equation of exchange.**

Let's use this **equation of exchange** to look at what happens when the money supply increases. If M increases, with the price level fixed, either V must decrease or Y must increase. This matches the possible consequences of an increase in the money supply with which we began the chapter. Individuals could simply hold the extra money, which would decrease velocity, or the amount bought Y may increase.

The essential problem of monetary theory is to know when each of these outcomes will result. When the *only* effect is on money holdings, monetary policy is completely ineffective in stimulating aggregate output and employment. But if there is *some* effect on output as well, then monetary policy can be a useful instrument in stimulating the economy. It may take a large dose of the medicine—a large increase in the money supply—to achieve any desired goal, but it can be done. To answer the question of when individuals will simply be willing to hold any additional supply of money, we have to understand the determinants of the demand for money.

THE DEMAND FOR MONEY

The velocity of money depends on how willing people are to hold, or keep, money. Because currency is an asset that bears no interest, it is like a hot potato; there are strong incentives to pass it along. Preferring to earn interest, people have an incentive to exchange currency for either goods or an interest-bearing asset like a Treasury bill. The only reason to hold currency is its convenience. You can buy groceries with currency but not with a Treasury bill, unless you convert your Treasury bill back to currency. To do that incurs costs (transaction costs).

THE EFFECT OF INTEREST RATES

People's willingness to hold money is a result of their balancing the benefits of holding money—the convenience—against the **opportunity cost** or the forgone interest—the interest that they could have earned if they had invested the money in their bank account (or in their pocket) in some other asset. If bank deposits pay interest of 0 percent and very short term government bonds (Treasury bills) pay 4 percent per year, then the cost of holding money is 4 percent per year. Today bank accounts pay interest, so the opportunity of cost of holding funds in them is lower than it used to be. Nevertheless, the difference between the interest paid on bank accounts and the return to other assets of similar risk deters people from holding money. We focus on the interest rate paid on Treasury bills for a simple reason: they are just as safe as money. The only difference is that Treasury bills yield a higher interest rate, but money is better as a medium of exchange.

The demand for money is much like the demand for any other good; it depends on the price. The inter-

---

USING ECONOMICS: CALCULATING VELOCITY

To see how velocity is calculated, use the identity velocity (V) = income (Y) divided by the money supply (M), and assume that $Y = £1,000$ billion per year and that $M = £800$ billion. In this case the velocity of circulation $V = 1,000/800 = 1.25$. If producing £1 of output required only one transaction, the average pound would have to circulate 1.25 times every year to produce output (or income) of £1,000 billion. If the money supply M were only £500 million, every pound would have to circulate twice per year for a national income of £1,000 billion.

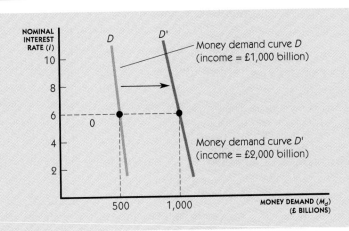

Figure 29.1 DEMAND CURVE FOR MONEY

The quantity demanded of money slopes down as the opportunity cost of holding funds—that is, the interest rate—increases. An increase in income causes a shift in the money demand function from *D* to *D'*.

est rate (*r*) the individual could have earned on a government bond can be thought of as the price of money, since it measures the opportunity cost of holding money. As the interest rate rises, the amount of money demanded declines, as shown in Figure 29.1.

THE EFFECT OF INCOME

The benefits of holding money are related to money's use as a medium of exchange. The more transactions people engage in, the more money they will want to hold. The demand for money arising from its use in facilitating transactions is called the **transactions demand for money.** This demand for money rises with *nominal* income: higher incomes mean that the value of goods bought will be greater, which implies that the value of transactions will be greater. In fact, the demand for money increases proportionately with the nominal value of income, which equals the value *PQ* of output: if prices double, then other things being equal, people will need to have twice the amount of money to engage in the same transactions. This is illustrated in Table 29.1, which shows a hypothetical example. Figure 29.1 shows that an increase in income shifts the demand curve to the right. With an income level of £1,000 billion, the demand for money is given by the curve on the left. Table 29.1 and Figure 29.1 illustrate the two basic properties of the demand for money. It de-

creases as the interest rate rises. And it increases, at a fixed interest rate, in proportion to income. Doubling the income level to £2,000 billion at any fixed interest rate shifts the demand curve for money out.

In equilibrium, the interest rate adjusts to make the demand for money equal the supply. Figure 29.2 shows supply curves for money as well as a demand curve. The supply of money is controlled by the central bank, through the instruments described in Chapter 28. The amount of money the government makes available does not depend at all on the interest rate. That is why the supply curves are vertical. The equilibrium interest rate with money supply MS_0 is i_0.

Table 29.1 DEMAND FOR MONEY

Nominal Interest Rate	Money Demand Income £1,000 Billion	Money Demand Income £2,000 Billion
2%	550	1,100
4%	525	1,050
6%	500	1,000
8%	475	950
10%	450	900

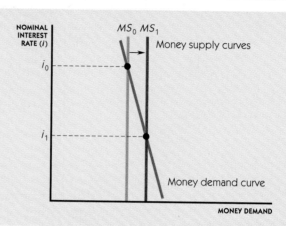

Figure 29.2 EQUILIBRIUM INTEREST RATES

The interest rate adjusts to make the demand for money equal the supply. In this diagram, a government-induced shift in the supply of money from MS_0 to MS_1 has a large effect on the interest rate, since the demand for money is relatively inelastic with respect to the interest rate.

The principles described in this section—that the nominal interest rate is the opportunity cost of holding money, that the demand for money decreases as the interest rate rises, and that the interest rate is determined to equate the demand and supply of money—are together sometimes called **Keynesian monetary theory,** or **traditional monetary theory.** Keynes used this theory to explain how monetary policy works when it works and why it sometimes does not work. To do this, he traced out the effects of a change in the supply of money on the interest rate, the effects of a change in the interest rate on investment, and the effects of a change in investment on the level of national income. We now take a closer look at each of the steps in this analysis.

HOW MONETARY POLICY MAY AFFECT THE ECONOMY THROUGH CHANGING INTEREST RATES

Figure 29.2 can also be used to show how changes in the money supply can lead to changes in the interest rates. Initially, the money supply is at MS_0 and the equilibrium interest rate is i_0. When the government increases the money supply to MS_1, the interest rate falls to i_1. In Figure 29.1, the demand for money is relatively inelastic, so that an increase in the supply of money at a given level of income causes a large decrease in the interest rate. As the interest rate falls, investment rises. As investment spending increases, income (which is the same as output) rises via the multiplier.

The increase in investment shifts the aggregate expenditures schedule up, as depicted in Figure 29.3, and results in a higher equilibrium level of output. Output increases from Y_0 to Y_1.

When income increases, the money demand curve shifts to the right, as shown in Figure 29.4. Thus, the eventual equilibrium attained will involve a smaller decrease in the rate of interest than i_1. The new equilibrium interest rate will lie somewhere between i_0 and i_1. In Figure 29.4, it is i_2.

We can trace out the equilibrium in the product market at i_2: panel A of Figure 29.5 shows the level of investment I_2 when the real interest is r_2, while panel B shows the aggregate expenditures schedule when investment is equal to I_2, and the equilibrium level of output Y_2. Notice that while money demand depends on *nominal* interest rates, denoted by i, investment depends on *real* interest rates, denoted by r. Since it is assumed here that inflation is zero, nominal and real interest rates are equal. That is, $i = r$. It is important to keep in mind that this is not always the case.

The aggregate expenditures schedule assumes a particular price level. A similar effect of an increase

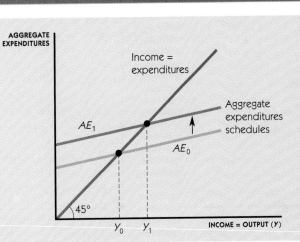

Figure 29.3 A MONETARY POLICY STIMULUS

An increase in the money supply may shift the aggregate expenditures schedule up, because of increased investment by firms, leading to an increased equilibrium output. A similar effect occurs at each price level.

in the money supply occurs at each price. In Chapter 26 we showed how to derive the aggregate demand curve by tracing out the intersection of the aggregate expenditures schedule with the 45-degree line at each price level. Since at each price level, the equilibrium level of output is higher, the aggregate demand curve has shifted to the right, as depicted in panel C. In this chapter, we are focusing on situations where price is fixed and there is excess capacity. We see clearly in panel C how the shift in the aggregate demand curve translates into an increase in aggregate output from Y_0 to Y_2.

The results of this section lead us to our thirteenth point of consensus in economics:

13 Using Monetary Policy to Stimulate the Economy

When there is excess capacity and prices are rigid, increasing the money supply normally stimulates the economy, leading to higher levels of output.

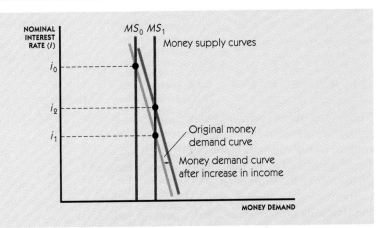

Figure 29.4 SECOND-ROUND EFFECTS OF INCREASED MONEY SUPPLY

In the first round, the increased money supply led to lower interest rates (Figure 29.2), which led in turn to higher levels of national income (Figure 29.3). This higher level of income now shifts the money demand curve up (since the demand for money at each interest rate is higher). The equilibrium interest rate is i_2.

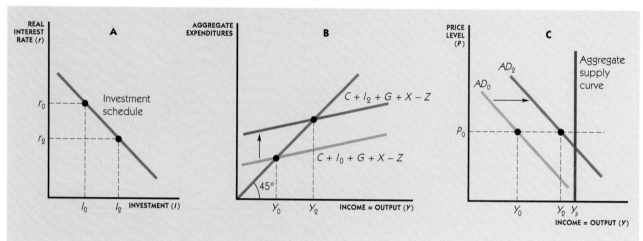

Figure 29.5 TRACING OUT THE FULL EFFECTS OF AN INCREASE IN MONEY SUPPLY

An increase in the money supply leads to a lower interest rate. Panel A shows that the lower interest rate leads to increased investment. Panel B shows that the increased investment shifts the aggregate expenditures schedule up, leading to a higher equilibrium output *at each price level*. Panel C shows that as a result, the aggregate demand curve shifts to the right.

While there is consensus on the conclusion that monetary policy can stimulate the economy, there is far less agreement about two other issues: the *quantitative effects*—the amount by which any given change in the money supply increases output—and the *channels*—the mechanisms through which monetary policy affects the economy.

WHAT DETERMINES THE EFFECTIVENESS OF MONETARY POLICY?

There are three principal determinants of how much an increase in the money supply increases output: (1) the elasticity of the demand for money, (2) the sensitivity of investment to the interest rate, and (3) the size of the multiplier.

Increasing the money supply will be less effective in increasing output when the demand for money is relatively elastic (when the money demand curve is relatively flat). When the demand for money is relatively elastic, an increase in the money supply has little effect on interest rates; interest rates decrease only slightly (see Figure 29.6A). *Other things being equal*, when the interest rate decreases a little, there is only a small increase in investment, resulting in a small increase in GDP (see Figure 29.6B).

Increasing the money supply will be less effective in increasing output when investment is not very sensitive to the interest rate (investment is inelastic). In this case a decrease in the interest rate resulting from an increase in the money supply will have little effect on investment, and therefore GDP.

An increase in investment has less of an effect on output when the multiplier is small. For any given increase in investment, the smaller the multiplier, the smaller the increase in GDP. Thus, an increase in the money supply will result in a smaller increase in output when the multiplier is smaller. And, as we saw in Chapter 26, the multiplier is smaller if (1) the marginal propensity to save is large, (2) tax rates are large, or (3) the marginal propensity to import is large.

Many economists—Keynes included—argue that when the economy is in a deep recession, monetary

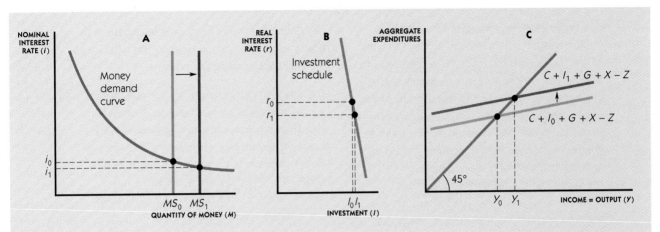

Figure 29.6 EFFECTS OF MONETARY POLICY IN A SEVERE RECESSION

Panel A shows that if the demand curve for money is flat, an increase in the money supply has little effect on interest rates. Panel B shows that if the investment schedule is steep, a decrease in interest rates has little effect on investment. Panel C shows that if investment is increased a little, the aggregate expenditure schedule shifts up very little, so that aggregate output increases very little.

policy is relatively ineffective. They believe that the demand curve for money appears as in Figure 29.6A: at least at low interest rates it is relatively flat. As a result, monetary authorities have a hard time driving the interest rate down further. Exacerbating the problem facing monetary authorities is a fact which takes us beyond the model of this chapter but is nonetheless real: in recessions, prices fall. In the Great Depression, prices fell by 25 percent. In the economic downturn in Japan between 1994 and 1999, prices fell slightly. What investors care about is *real interest rates*—the difference between the nominal interest rates and the rate of inflation. If the nominal interest rate falls but the rate of inflation falls more, real interest rates rise. With falling prices, real interest rates exceed the nominal interest rates. If prices are falling at 10 percent a year, then even a zero nominal interest rate corresponds to a 10 percent real interest rate—by historical standards, an extremely high real interest rate.

Moreover, given investors' pessimism about economic prospects, it takes a large fall in interest rates to induce firms to invest much more. Since by defin-

ition, in a recession, there is considerable excess capacity, the marginal return from extra investment is close to zero. New machines simply add to excess capacity, not to profits. Only if the new machines are much better than the old (using so much less labour that the savings offsets the additional capital costs) or if they are designed to make a new product, will it pay firms to make additional investments. Moreover, a lengthy period of losses will deplete a firm's cash reserves and increase its indebtedness. Facing the threat of bankruptcy, the firm will be reluctant to undertake additional new investments, even if it could persuade banks to lend it money. As a result of these negative factors, as the economy goes into a recession, not only will the investment schedule shift down but it also becomes relatively inelastic; that is, lower interest rates have only a small effect in inducing additional investment (see Figure 29.6B).

Since increasing the money supply has a small effect on interest rates, and the decrease in interest rates has only a small effect on investment, increasing the money supply has a small effect on output, as illustrated in Figure 29.6C.

CLOSE-UP: TARGETING THE MONEY SUPPLY

During the 1950s and 1960s in Britain, little attention was paid to the money supply. The Bank of England used its influence on interest rates to affect credit conditions in the economy and to influence aggregate demand. But the size of the money stock was not treated as a subject of interest. During the 1970s, as inflation became a greater concern, attention gradually shifted to controlling the stock of money itself. In 1980, the Conservative government of Margaret Thatcher organised its monetary policy around the medium term financial strategy, setting targets for the rate of growth of the money supply (sterling M3) for each year of the 1980s. The target growth rates were set to fall gradually, causing a reduction in the inflation rate without causing unemployment to rise. The Bank of England attempted to achieve these targets for the money growth rate by manipulating interest rates, raising them when the money supply was over the target and reducing them when it was under the target. This was the first time that an attempt had been made to control the money supply over a sustained period in Britain.

The policy did not have the intended effects. When interest rates were raised to reduce the money supply, the exchange rate shot up, and sterling reached a value of $2.40 to the pound late in 1980. Meanwhile the demand for money did not fall as expected. The picture was clouded by the effects of the removal of foreign exchange controls in 1979 and of the removal of other restrictions ("the corset") on the banking sector around the same time. The effect was to swell the stock of money. As a result, the signals coming from different variables were at odds. The large money supply suggested that policy was very loose, the high interest rates suggested that policy was moderately tight, and the very high exchange rate suggested a very tight monetary policy. There was considerable debate as to how these signals should be read and what was the true state of monetary policy.

The very high exchange rate hit the manufacturing industry hard. Demand and production fell rapidly, and unemployment began to rise very rapidly. It quickly became clear that the government's attempts to adhere to its monetary targets had plunged the economy into a very severe recession. The demand for money was much above predicted levels.

The government responded by revising its money supply targets upwards. And these targets were systematically breached in the following years. But unemployment continued to rise and inflation to fall. The cut in aggregate demand brought about by the high exchange rate was reinforced by a tight fiscal policy. The government was able to meet roughly its targets for public sector borrowing. When tax revenue fell and a wider deficit loomed, government spending was cut back and taxes were increased.

This episode, though crucial in establishing the government's noninflationary credentials and doing much to remove the inflationary psychology that had taken hold, revealed the dangers of targeting the money supply. Money demand functions appeared to have become very unstable. The historical relationship between money growth and inflation, which appeared to be well established in the 1970s, broke down decisively.

This prompted the enunciation of Goodhart's law, to the effect that no historically observed empirical regularity can survive the strain of being used as the basis of economic policy. (This law was set out by Professor Charles Goodhart of the London School of Economics, who is also a member of the Bank of England's Monetary Policy Committee.)

TRADITIONAL MONETARY THEORY

The nominal interest rate is the opportunity cost of holding money.

The demand for money decreases as the interest rate rises.

The interest rate equates the demand and supply for money.

TRADITIONAL THEORY OF MONETARY POLICY

When monetary policy is effective in generating increased output, it is because the policy induces a lower interest rate.

Monetary policy is ineffective in deep recessions, because:

1 The money demand curve is elastic, so changes in the money supply induce only small changes in interest rates.

2 Even large changes in the interest rate induce little change in investment and hence in aggregate demand.

Some economists have described the ineffectiveness of monetary policy in deep recessions by saying that it is like pushing on a string. While economists differ in their judgments about how deep a recession it takes before monetary policy becomes relatively ineffective, they agree on the basic principle. This brings us to our fourteenth point of consensus in economics:

14 Monetary Policy in a Deep Recession

> When the economy is in a deep recession, monetary policy is relatively ineffective in stimulating the economy to recover.

Some advocates of monetary policy claim, however, that all that matters is that there be some effect of monetary policy. A weak effect for a given percentage change in the money supply simply means that monetary authorities have to take more aggressive actions—increase the money supply by a larger percentage.

MONETARISM

While there is broad agreement on the two conclusions stated so far—that monetary policy can be used effectively to stimulate the economy, except when there is a deep recession, some economists—called **monetarists**—argue that the *only* effect of monetary policy is on the price level. They believe that the basic assumption underlying this chapter—that prices are

fixed—is simply wrong. They argue that prices are flexible, even in the short run. Thus, *all* that happens when the money supply increases is that the price level changes with no change in output or employment. In fact they believe that prices move approximately in proportion to the change in the money supply. They believe that the full-employment model discussed in Chapter 23 applies at all times. Some monetarists believe that even if there is unemployment and output is below the economy's capacity, increases in the money supply are still mostly reflected in changes in the price level.

To see how monetarists arrive at this conclusion, we need to return to the equation of exchange. The equation of exchange, as presented, was a *definition* of velocity. But the monetarists make one additional assumption—velocity is constant. Thus

$$M\bar{V} = PY,$$

where the bar over the V reminds us that it is fixed. If Y is assumed fixed (say at its full-employment level), then increases in M get translated into proportionate increases in P.

This equation also gives us a simple rule for the expansion of the money supply. If we want prices to be stable and real income is increasing at, say, 2 percent a year, then the money supply should increase at 2 percent a year. Monetarists believe that monetary policy should focus on the monetary aggregates (the measures of the money supply) and that money supply should increase in proportion to increases in real output. Doing this will lead to stable prices.

These are the *conclusions* of the monetarists. They can, however, be simply related to traditional monetary theory. Monetarists believe that the demand for money is just proportional to nominal output (income). It does not depend on the interest rate. Note the contrast with traditional Keynesian theory: while Keynes assumed that in deep recessions the demand curve for money was almost horizontal (the elasticity was very large), monetarists assume that the demand curve is vertical: Demand does not depend on the interest rate.

$$M^d = kY^m,$$

where Y^m is nominal national income (output). Since money demand equals money supply,

$$M^d = M^s,$$

increasing money supply increases nominal aggregate output (income) proportionately. Furthermore,

since nominal income is the price level P times the real output Y,

$$Y^m = PY,$$

if Y is *fixed*, then increasing nominal output (income) Y^m leads to an equiproportionate increase in the price level. In other words, if money supply doubles, in equilibrium, money demand must double. Money demand can only double if nominal aggregate output (income) doubles, and nominal aggregate output (income) can double only if the price level doubles.

Thus, the assumption that the demand for money does not depend on the interest rate is equivalent to the assumption that velocity (M/Y) is constant; and the theory that holds that because velocity is constant, increases in the money supply are reflected simply in proportionate increases in income is called the **quantity theory of money.** While there have been long periods for which velocity has been nearly constant, in recent years it has changed, and often in ways that are hard to predict, as Figures 29.7 and 29.8 illustrate.

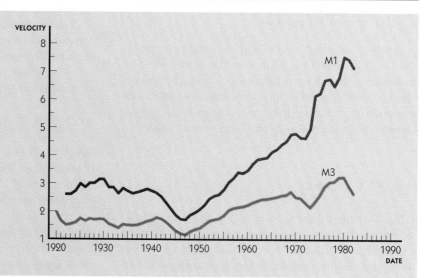

Figure 29.7 VELOCITY OF CIRCULATION OF WIDE AND NARROW MONEY

The velocity of circulation for both wide (M3) and narrow (M1) money have fluctuated somewhat. There has been a clear rise since 1945, with more erratic behaviour since 1970. This last has been a period of financial innovation, there have been a variety of different exchange rate regimes, and policy has been conducted in several very different ways.

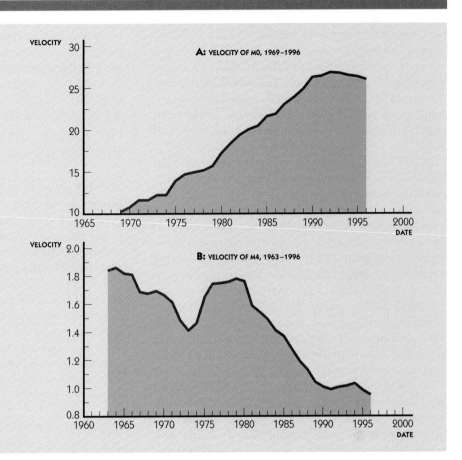

Figure 29.8 VELOCITY SINCE 1963

This figure shows velocity for the new monetary aggregates, in panel A for M0, the wide monetary base, and in panel B for M4, the new wider wide money measure. The velocity of M0 drifted steadily upwards until 1992 and then began to drift slowly down. The velocity of M4 was more erratic in the 1970s and 1980s. The rise in its velocity in the 1970s, due to restrictions on bank lending, and its reversal in the 1980s caught the government of the time unawares.

CRITICISMS OF THE TRADITIONAL THEORY OF THE DEMAND FOR MONEY

In traditional monetary theory, the mechanism by which monetary policy affects the economy is simple. When the government increases the supply of money, interest rates must fall in order for the demand for money to equal the supply; and lower interest rates induce more investment and consumer purchases of durables, stimulating aggregate demand. In recent years, changes in the financial system have led to a reexamination of this theory. In particular economists have raised several questions concerning the demand function for money underlying the theory. Some questions focus on the relationship between the demand for money and income, others on the effect of interest rates on the demand for money.

RELATIONSHIP BETWEEN MONEY AND INCOME

Earlier we saw that what particularly distinguishes money from other assets such as government Treasury bills is its role as a medium of exchange in facilitating transactions. Traditional monetary theory implies that the higher their income, the more money people will want to hold. In other words, there is a simple relationship between the volume of transactions and the level of income. This would be the case if most transactions were directly related to output—employers' paying wages and buying goods from suppliers, customers' buying goods from firms, and so on.

But in fact, in terms of their monetary value, most transactions are for exchanges of financial assets, not the purchase of goods and services. One individual thinks ICI stock is going to go down, and so he sells his shares. Another person thinks it is going to go up, and so she buys shares. The volume of these financial transactions has virtually no direct bearing on national output and income. Moreover, the *ratio* of these transactions to national income may change markedly with economic conditions. When there is greater uncertainty and change, there may be more such exchanges, as people take differing views of what the future holds and as individual circumstances change rapidly.

In the longer run, a number of other factors affect the relationship between money and income. For instance, not all transactions require payment by cash or cheque; today most transactions are made with credit. You need neither have money in a bank account nor cash in your pocket to buy a car or a holiday in Hawaii, so long as you can get credit. You can pay with a credit card or use a bank loan. Of course, some kinds of transactions are still not easily done with credit. In most places, for example, you still

have to pay for taxis with cash. But in Australia, taxis accept Visa, MasterCard, and American Express. The transactions that require money at the point of sale represent a relatively small and shrinking proportion of all transactions in the modern economy.

RELATIONSHIP BETWEEN INTEREST RATES AND THE DEMAND FOR MONEY

This brings us to the second set of criticisms: most money, as we have seen, is in the form of sight deposits, and today—unlike fifty years ago when traditional monetary theory was first formulated—sight deposits generally bear interest. Thus, the opportunity cost of holding money is not the interest rate but the *difference* between the return to holding a government bond, for example, and the interest paid on bank deposits. That difference relates to the bank's cost of running the chequing account. The existence of interest-bearing chequing accounts calls into question the extent to which the demand for money will rise or fall in response to changes in interest rates.

OTHER CRITICISMS OF TRADITIONAL MONETARY THEORY

Traditional monetary theory assumed that changing the money supply affected the economy through changes in *real* interest rates. Yet there have been

CRITICISMS OF TRADITIONAL MONETARY THEORY

There is no simple relationship between the demand for money and income.
> Most transactions involve not goods and services (output) but the exchange of assets. The connection between transactions related to output and those related to exchange may not be stable.
> Transactions do not necessarily need money; credit will do.

Today, more extensive use is made of credit (credit cards).

There is no simple relationship between real interest rates and the money supply.
> Today most money takes the form of sight (or demand) deposits and is interest bearing.
>> Thus, the opportunity cost of holding money is low and is not directly related to the interest rate.
> Changes in the rate of inflation may offset changes in the nominal interest rate.

CLOSE-UP: JAPAN IN A LIQUIDITY TRAP

The Japanese economy fell into a deep depression in the late 1990s, a situation worsened by the crises in neighbouring countries in Asia. By late in 1998, unemployment had risen to a record 4.3 percent, GDP had fallen by 1.8 percent over the previous year and industrial production by a massive 8.5 percent, consumer prices were falling slowly—down 0.3 percent over the previous year—and earnings were falling by 2.4 percent a year. The situation was dire. Despite many exhortations from international bodies like the IMF and the OECD, the policy response in Japan seemed weak and ineffectual. A succession of plans to cut taxes and raise government spending were announced but seemed inadequate in the face of Japan's own problems and the regional crisis that surrounded it. Part of the problem was no matter how much extra spending the Japanese government announced, there was a suspicion that the cautious Japanese civil service would frustrate the plans, so there would be no actual spending increase.

Monetary policy had been eased in Japan. Interest rates in late 1998 were practically zero. Short-term rates (overnight rates) were 0.19 percent per annum. Japan appeared to be in a Keynesian liquidity trap: the classic situation set out by Keynes in *The General Theory* in which no amount of expansionary monetary policy can stimulate demand and raise output and employment. The Japanese problem was worsened by two things. One was the response of cautious Japanese people to economic uncertainty, which was to save more. The other was that following a huge property boom, there was a massive surplus of commercial property in Japan and the return on investment was zero or negative. Both these factors served to limit the demand for goods.

The U.S. economist Paul Krugman suggested that the Bank of Japan should nevertheless print lots of money. He argued that even though it could not lower interest rates further, it might stimulate spending by making the banks more willing to lend, by simply "burning holes in peoples' pockets," by buying up the national debt, reducing the government's interest payments on it, and making way for more tax cuts or spending rises. To claims that such a policy might be inflationary, he responded that that would be a good thing. Arguably what Japan needs is the prospect of inflation in the future, because that would reduce the real interest rate below zero, make cash holding expensive, and may stimulate spending. The problem, on this analysis, is that the Bank of Japan has *too much* anti-inflationary credibility. It needs to commit itself to inflationary policy for the coming years. So far it has not found a way of doing it or been willing to do it.

This is not a diagnosis that is shared by the Japanese government, which focuses on the need to recapitalise the banking system. This has suffered from bad debts on a massive scale, partly as a consequence of its own lending practices.

The irony of the Japanese situation is to find the Keynesian liquidity trap coming back from the 1930s to haunt the world economy and still a difference of view as to how to respond, almost as wide as the divide between Keynes and the holders of orthodox views at the British Treasury in the 1930s.

Sources: Paul Krugman, "What Is Wrong with Japan?" *The Accidental Theorist,* (New York: Norton, 1998); Eisuke Sakakibara, "Academic Economists Reveal Vacuum of Thinking on Japan's Problems," letter in *Financial Times,* 30 October 1998.

long periods in which real interest rates have varied very little. Nominal interest rates tend to move up or down with inflation, so variations in real interest rates are far smaller than variations in nominal interest rates. Monetary policy seems to have effects that are far larger than would be indicated by the relatively small variations in real interest rates.

ALTERNATIVE MECHANISMS

Traditional monetary theory has thus been questioned on several fronts—both the theory of demand for money, which underlies it, and the role of interest rates. But monetary policy does seem to matter nevertheless. There are several alternative mechanisms through which monetary policy exercises its influence.

CREDIT AVAILABILITY

One channel is through credit availability. In Chapter 28, we looked at the two sides of the bank's balance sheet—its deposits (the money supply) and its assets, which include loans. Various actions of the central bank reduce both deposits (the money supply) and the supply of available loans. Figure 29.9 shows the demand and supply of credit. Restrictive monetary policy has the effect of reducing banks' supply of loans—shifting the loan supply to the left and increasing the equilibrium interest rate at which credit is made available, while decreasing the equilibrium level of lending.

At times, banks may ration the amount of credit they make available. They typically do not simply lend to anyone willing to borrow at the interest rates they charge. At times, they may not extend loans to all those deemed creditworthy who would like loans. They could, of course, raise the interest rate charged; but they may worry that by doing so, the best risks—those most likely to repay the loan—will go elsewhere or decide it is not worth borrowing at such interest rates. If interest rates—like other prices—remain fixed, then a shift in the loan supply curve has an even larger effect than when interest rates adjust, as Figure 29.9 illustrates.

Even when credit is not being rationed, banks respond to a situation of tighter credit by adjusting terms of the loan contract other than the interest rate: they may, for instance, require more collateral.

In any case, the shift in the availability of credit

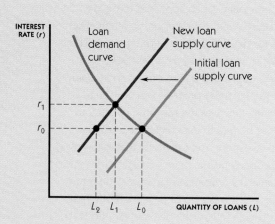

Figure 29.9 EFFECT OF MONETARY POLICY VIEWED THROUGH IMPACT ON CREDIT AVAILABILITY

Restrictive monetary policy reduces the supply of loans available at any interest rate. Thus, the equilibrium interest rate increases (from r_0 to r_1) and the quantity of loans made is reduced from L_0 to L_1. In some circumstances, interest rates appear to be rigid and do not adjust. There will then be credit rationing, with the demand for loans' exceeding the supply. In that case, the decrease in loans may even be greater, to L_2.

(the shift of the loan supply curve to the left) results in lower investment, because interest rates are higher (making it less attractive to undertake investments), because other terms of the loan contract are adjusted to make borrowing less attractive, or because funds required to undertake investments simply are not available.

PORTFOLIO THEORIES

An alternative channel by which monetary policy may affect the economy is through the price of shares and long-term bonds. At lower *nominal* interest rates, the value of long-term bonds increases. People feel wealthier, and because they feel wealthier, they consume more. Moreover, because bonds yield lower returns, investors turn to stocks. As the demand for stocks increases, their prices rise. Higher stock prices not only lead to increased consumption but also to increased investment: at the higher stock prices, more firms believe that it is a good time to issue new shares, to raise additional capital, and to finance new investments.

Portfolio theories argue that monetary policy affects the level of economic activity not only or so much through its *direct* impact on interest rates (as a result of the interaction of the demand for and supply of money) but through a variety of indirect mechanisms, as individuals adjust their **portfolios,** the bundle of assets—including stocks and bonds— that they hold. These adjustments in the demands for other assets result in changes in their prices, and it is through these changes that monetary policy ultimately has its most important effects.

INTEREST RATES AND THE HOUSING MARKET

In Britain, the connection between interest rates, house prices, and consumption has proved to be very strong in recent years. Lower interest rates reduce the cost of buying a house or flat. Put differently, the implicit rental cost of a stream of housing services is reduced. The rental cost of a piece of property is equal to the interest payable on the capital value of the property, plus the cost of maintenance and depreciation, and less the expected capital gain on the property. At lower interest rates, with other things unchanged, the rental cost is lower. This increases the demand for housing and, with a fixed supply of it, causes a rise in price (the capital value) of real property. Conversely, a higher interest rate raises the implicit rental cost of housing, reduces the demand for the stock of property, and lowers its price.

Fluctuations in the value of real property appear to have a large impact on consumption. A rise in property prices raises the wealth of people who own houses and may induce them to increase their rate of consumption. This factor appears to have been at work in Britain from 1989 to 1992, when a sharp increase in short-term interest rates caused a fall in property prices of 20 to 30 percent. This sharply reduced the net wealth of the personal sector of the United Kingdom and caused a sharp fall in consumers' expenditures and a rise in the personal savings ratio, as was discussed in Chapter 27.

This conclusion needs some qualifications. The change in consumption may have been caused in part by other things' going on at the same time. The British economy went into a recession in 1989, and consumption may have fallen relative to income because people feared becoming unemployed or had just revised their expected future incomes downwards. The effect of interest rates and house prices on consumption may operate not only because of the effect of the relative price of housing on the demand for it and on the effect of wealth on consumption but also because of credit rationing and liquidity constraints, which we have discussed. Higher interest rates may reduce the demand for housing because people cannot obtain as much credit when interest rates rise. Lenders may refuse to let people spend more than some fraction—say one-third—of their income on interest payments. When the interest rate rises, the maximum capital sum people can borrow falls. This reduces the demand for houses. Another effect is that when the interest rate rises, people who have mortgages find that their interest payments have risen, and their income net of interest payments falls.

MONETARY POLICY IN AN OPEN ECONOMY

In today's open, international economy, one of the most important ways by which monetary policy affects the level of economic activity is by affecting the exchange rate: lowering interest rates leads to a lower exchange rate—the number of yen that can be traded for a pound. A lower exchange rate makes domestic goods more attractive abroad and foreign goods less attractive here, and thus increases exports and decreases imports. For instance, between August 1998 and January 1999 the exchange rate between the pound and the yen fell approximately 20 percent. Thus, to a Japanese consumer, a £50 British shirt fell in price by 20 percent, from 11,750 yen to 9,750 yen. And to a British consumer, the price of Japanese goods increased by 25 percent. A computer that sold in Japan for 100,000 yen—and thus cost £425 in the United Kingdom—would now cost British residents £513. (In practice, the changes were somewhat less dramatic, since in the short run, exporters and importers absorb some of the variation in exchange rates.)

As exports increase and imports decrease, *net* ex- ports increase. As Figure 29.10 illustrates, an increase in net exports leads to an increase in aggregate output. In this section, we explain in more detail how monetary policy affects the exchange rate. We begin with a review of what determines the exchange rate.

HOW MONETARY POLICY AFFECTS EXCHANGE RATES

In Chapter 24, we saw that the yen-dollar exchange rate (for example) is determined by the intersection of the demand and supply curves for pounds in exchange for yen. The demand for pounds is determined in turn by Japan's demand for U.K. goods and Japan's desire to invest in the United Kingdom. Similarly, the supply of pounds is determined by U.K. demand for Japanese goods and U.K. residents' desire to invest in Japan. When the Bank of England lowers the interest rate, foreigners find it less attractive to invest in the United Kingdom, and U.K. residents find it more attractive to invest abroad. This shifts the demand for pounds to the left and the supply of pounds to the right, as in Figure 29.11. The net result is a decrease in the exchange rate, an increase in exports, and a decrease in imports.

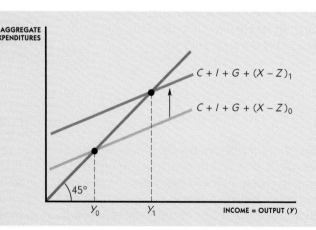

Figure 29.10 **IMPACT OF AN INCREASE IN NET EXPORTS ON AGGREGATE OUTPUT**

A depreciation of the exchange rate reduces the price of domestic goods relative to foreign goods, increasing exports and reducing imports. An increase in net exports shifts the aggregate expenditures schedule up and results in an increased equilibrium level of output.

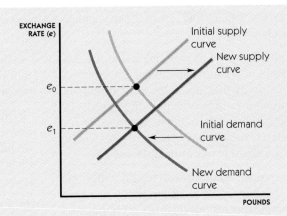

Figure 29.11 IMPACT OF MONETARY POLICY ON EXCHANGE RATES

A lowering of interest rates in the United Kingdom induces more U.K. residents to invest abroad, increasing the supply of pounds (at any exchange rate), and reduces the demand by foreigners to invest in the United Kingdom, reducing the demand for pounds (at any exchange rate). As a result, the new equilibrium exchange rate is lowered, falling from e_0 to e_1.

WHY TRADITIONAL CHANNELS OF MONETARY POLICY MAY BE LESS EFFECTIVE IN AN OPEN ECONOMY

While there is thus a new channel through which monetary policy exercises its influence, some of the other channels may in fact be much weaker in an open economy. One of the ways that we saw that monetary policy exercises its influence is reducing the availability of credit. But if firms can borrow abroad, then restricting credit from domestic banks simply induces borrowers to seek funds elsewhere. To be sure, not everyone has access to foreign banks. But the thousands of multinational firms do. And if enough of these firms switch their borrowing abroad, it frees up funds so domestic banks can continue their lending to those who do not have access to foreign banks.

REVIEW AND PRACTICE

SUMMARY

1 Theories concerning the effect of monetary policy on the economy focus on two sides of the banks' balance sheet, money and credit.

2 When prices are fixed, changes in the supply of money can cause changes in holdings of money or changes in output. When the economy has considerable excess capacity, normally output will increase; in deep recessions, the effect on output may be minimal.

3 Traditional theories of the demand for money focus on its dependence on the (nominal) rate of interest and on the level of income. Equilibrium requires the demand for money to be equal to the supply. Changes in the supply of money result in changes in the interest rate and, through changes in the interest rate, in the level of aggregate expenditures and equilibrium output.

4 In severe recessions, the interest elasticity of the demand for money may be high and the interest elasticity of investment is low, so monetary policy may be relatively ineffective.

5 The quantity theory of money holds that the demand for money does not depend on the interest rate and accordingly that the velocity of money is constant. Increases in money supply then result in proportionate increases in national income. In recent years, velocity has not only not been constant; it has changed in relatively unpredictable ways.

6 There are many difficulties with traditional monetary theory. Money is not used for many transactions, and many transactions involve exchanges of assets, which have little to do with income generation. Changes in technology and the structure of the economy may alter the money-income relationship. Most money bears interest, and the opportunity cost is only the difference between the interest rate money pays and the interest rate on Treasury bills.

7 Portfolio theories stress the effect of changes in monetary policy on the demand and supply of various assets (including money) and the resulting effect on prices of assets.

8 Credit availability theories stress the effects of monetary policy on the availability of credit (the supply of loans) by banks.

9 In an open economy, monetary policy is likely to have a smaller effect on interest rates and credit availability than it otherwise would. If the central bank attempts to restrict credit or raise interest rates, firms can borrow from abroad.

10 In an open economy, monetary policy has effects on exchange rates: a reduction in the money supply leading to higher interest rates leads to an appreciation of the domestic currency, a decrease in exports, and an increase in imports.

KEY TERMS

velocity

equation of exchange

transactions demand for money

monetarists

quantity theory of money

portfolio theories

REVIEW QUESTIONS

1 What might happen in response to a change in the money supply?

2 Why does demand for money fall as the interest rate rises? What is the opportunity cost of holding money that pays interest (such as sight deposits)?

3 What might cause changes in the relationship between the demand for money and income besides changes in the interest rate?

4 Why might changes in the money supply not lead to increases in the level of investment in a severe recession?

5 What assumptions are involved in the quantity theory of money? What conclusion can be drawn on the basis of those assumptions? What is the evidence concerning the constancy of the velocity of circulation?

6 What are alternative mechanisms by which portfolio theories suggest that monetary policy affects the economy?

7 Describe how monetary policy might affect investment or consumption *even if monetary policy has little effect at all on interest rates.*

8 How does the fact that an economy is open affect monetary policy? How do exchange rate changes affect equilibrium levels of output? How does monetary policy affect equilibrium exchange rates?

Problems

1 If GDP is £1,000 billion and the money supply is £250 billion, what is velocity? How does your answer change if GDP rises to £1,500 billion while the money supply remains the same? If GDP remains at £1,000 billion while the money supply increases to £500 billion, how does velocity change?

2 Graph the money demand curve from the following data, with quantity of money demanded given in billions of pounds.

Interest rate	7%	8%	9%	10%	11%	12%
Money demand	340	320	300	280	260	250

How do changes in national income affect the demand curve?

3 Using money supply and demand diagrams, explain how the elasticity of the money demand curve determines whether monetary policy can have a substantial effect on the interest rate.

4 Explain how the elasticity of investment with respect to interest rates determines if monetary policy can have a substantial effect on aggregate demand.

5 Explain how each of the following might affect the demand for money:
   (a) Interest is paid on chequing accounts.
   (b) Credit cards become more readily available.
   (c) Electronic fund transfers become common.

Would the changes in the demand for money necessarily reduce the ability of the central bank to use monetary policy to affect the economy?

6 How might an increase in national income affect the exchange rate? Before 1973 exchange rates were *fixed* by the government (with the government's buying and selling pounds in order to maintain the set exchange rate). Contrast the effects of an increase in investment on equilibrium output assuming the exchange rate is fixed with the effects if exchange rates are *flexible,* that is, are allowed to vary freely to equilibrate demand and supply.

7 Describe the impact of an appreciation of the yen relative to the U.S. dollar on the Japanese economy, using the aggregate expenditures schedule.

8 In the text, we saw that if output was growing at 2 percent per year, and velocity was constant, if the government wanted stable prices, it should expand the money supply at 2 percent. In fact, velocity has been falling gradually over time. Assume that velocity in any year does not depend on the interest rate, but year after year, it falls at the rate of 1 percent per year. What does this imply about the rate at which the monetary authorities should expand the money supply if they wish to maintain stable prices?

9 Assume that banks are worried that if they raise the interest rate, they will attract borrowers who are riskier, that is, less likely to repay their loans. Borrowers who realise that there is a good chance that they will not repay their loan may be less sensitive to increases in interest rates, while borrowers who invest in conservative, safe projects will decide that at high interest rates, it simply does not pay to borrow and invest. Why might this mean that as the bank raises its interest rates, its expected return (taking into account the probability of default) might decrease? Assume there was an interest rate at which the expected return was maximised; that is, further increases lead to a lowering of the expected return. What would happen if at that interest rate, the demand for funds exceeded the supply? Would banks raise the interest rate they charged anyway?

10 Use the equation of exchange to explain the alternative possible effects of changing the money supply.
   (a) What happens if velocity and output are constant?
   (b) What happens if price and velocity are constant?
   (c) What does traditional monetary policy say about the normal effect of monetary policy on velocity? What does this do to the magnitude of the effect on output compared to what it would have been had velocity been constant (assuming price is constant)?
   (d) What does traditional monetary policy say about what happens when the economy is in a deep recession?

11 Assume that for one reason or another, the interest rate on loans is fixed, and there is credit rationing. Show on a diagram what this implies.

Assume that there are firms that rely on borrowing to finance their investment projects. They invest all of their cash flow, plus what they can borrow. What happens to investment if they have a bad year—say their sales drop because of a temporary recession in the countries to which they export goods? Show what happens to investment and GDP if as a result of monetary policy, the supply of funds at each interest rate increases. Use the diagram to explain why monetary policy may be even more effective in such situations than if the interest rate adjusts.

If the multiplier is 2 and the government increases credit availability by £100 billion, what happens to GDP if the interest rate does not adjust? Assume that the interest rate always adjusts to equate the demand for and supply of funds (a closed economy) and that the interest rate elasticity of savings is 1, so that a lowering of the interest rate from 10 to 9 percent lowers savings by 10 percent. Assume that initially investment (equals savings) is £900 billion and that as a result of monetary policy, at each interest rate, £100 billion more funds are available for lending but that the interest rate falls from 10 to 9 percent. Calculate what happens to GDP now.

APPENDIX: AN ALGEBRAIC DERIVATION OF EQUILIBRIUM IN THE MONEY MARKET

The money demand equation can be written

$$M_d = M_d(r, Y),$$

where M_d is the demand for money and $Y = pQ$ is the value of national income. If M_s is the money supply, then the equilibrium condition that the demand for money equals the supply can be written

$$M_s = M_d(r, Y). \tag{29.1}$$

From Chapter 26, we know that in a closed economy

$$Y = C + I + G,$$

where I (investment) depends on the interest rate r and G (government expenditures) is assumed to be fixed. If consumption is just $(1 - s)$ times income Y, then

$$Y = (1 - s)Y + I(r) + G,$$

or

$$Y = [I(r) + G]/s. \tag{29.2}$$

Equations 29.1 and 29.2 provide us with two equations in two unknowns. The solution gives us the equilibrium income and interest rate. An increase in the money supply results in a new solution, with a lower interest rate and a higher level of national income.

CHAPTER 30

FISCAL AND MONETARY POLICY

There are three principal objectives of monetary and fiscal policy: maintaining full employment, promoting economic growth, and maintaining price stability. In Chapters 23 and 24, we saw that when the economy is at full employment, government policy can have significant effects on the growth rate, by affecting the level of investment. At full employment, there is a fixed-sized pie, and government actions affect how that pie is divided. But when there is unemployment and resources are not fully utilised, government actions can affect both the size of the pie and how it is divided. Even if a smaller share of national output goes to investment, if national output is increased enough, the level of investment will increase and long-run growth will be promoted.

This chapter pulls together the insights of earlier chapters of this part to see how fiscal and monetary policy may be used to stimulate the economy and promote economic growth. We will compare the effects of monetary and fiscal policy, and analyse several issues that arise in the application of policy today. Later chapters will explore how fiscal and monetary policy relate to the problem of maintaining price stability.

1 What difference does it make whether we use monetary or fiscal policy to help the economy out of a recession?

2 What are the economic effects of an increase in government expenditure accompanied by an increase in taxes of the same amount?

3 What might be the consequences of a balanced budget policy on economic stability?

FISCAL POLICY

In Chapter 25 we defined fiscal policy as efforts to improve macroeconomic performance through changes in government expenditures and taxes. Faced with output below the full-employment level, policymakers may help restore the economy to full employment through an increase in government expenditures or a reduction in taxes. Recall our aggregate expenditures diagram from Chapter 26. An increase in government expenditures shifts the aggregate expenditures schedule up, as shown in Figure 30.1A. Equilibrium output at each price level increases, and the aggregate demand schedule shifts to the right, as illustrated in Figure 30.1B. A tax cut puts more money in the pockets of consumers, leading to an increase in consumption. This also shifts the aggregate expenditures schedule up and results in a rightward shift of the aggregate demand curve. Either way, the economy is brought closer to the full-employment level of output.

IS IT WORTH INCURRING A DEFICIT TO GET OUT OF A RECESSION?

The problem with an increase in government expenditures or a tax cut is that it increases the deficit. There are two concerns. First, even if the fiscal stimulus makes us better off now, future generations are saddled with debt; this makes them worse off. However, if government expands its investment—in infrastructure, human capital, or research—future generations may be better off, provided the return on those investments exceeds the interest rate. Estimated returns in many of these areas are very high. Most estimates put the return on investment in research in excess of 20 percent, and estimates of the return on investment in education greatly exceed the interest rate.

But even if increased expenditures are spent on consumption, the outcome appears favourable. Assume the government spends £1 billion on public consumption goods. As a result of the multiplier, the net increase in current income (consumption) is much higher. If the multiplier is 2, national income increases by £2 billion. At some future date—say in the next boom—the increased indebtedness has to be paid off, with interest. But there is only £1 billion in increased indebtedness. The trade-off between an increase in national income today of £2 billion, with a reduction in consumption in the future to repay £1 billion in indebtedness, seems a favourable one. Indeed, the trade-off may be more favourable still if the government has borrowed money from its own citizens. In this case, the government will simply impose a tax on some individuals, in order to repay those who purchased bonds to finance the original expenditure. Then there would be a transfer of resources from taxpayers to bondholders but no reduction in aggregate consumption.

This trade-off in financing a fiscal stimulus is slightly less favourable than this calculation since the government's dissaving (deficit) soaks up some savings that would have been available for invest-

Figure 30.1 **EFFECT OF INCREASED GOVERNMENT EXPENDITURES**

Increased government expenditures shift the aggregate expenditures schedule up, and hence increase the equilibrium level of output at each price level. Hence the aggregate demand schedule shifts to the right—by an amount equal to the multiplier times the increase in government expenditures. At the initial fixed price level, P_0, equilibrium output increases by the amount of the shift—the multiplier times the increase in government expenditures.

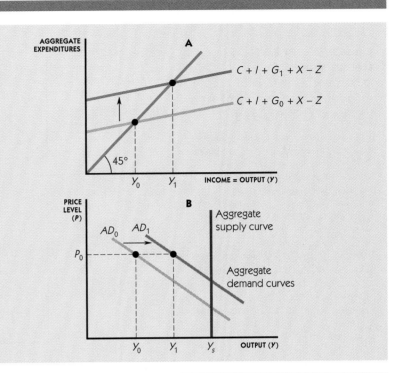

ment. The capital stock of the economy is thus smaller, and as a result, so is future national income; this too makes future generations worse off.

FISCAL POLICY UNDER FISCAL CONSTRAINTS

In recent years, with governments' in many countries running huge deficits, increasing government expenditures in a recession to stimulate the economy has often seemed politically impossible. The Maastricht Treaty, under which the countries of the European Union have formed a common currency, calls for them to reduce their deficits to 3 percent of GDP. Achieving this goal requires cutting back on expenditures or raising taxes, and so little room for increasing expenditures or lowering taxes to stimulate the economy. Similarly, in the United States, Congress now abides by a self-imposed constraint that it

will not increase expenditures (over agreed-upon levels) unless there is an agreement to increase taxes by a corresponding amount. Such action is unlikely, given that raising new taxes is so politically unpopular, especially in an economic downturn. In such situations, the government has no choice but to rely on monetary policy.

BALANCED BUDGET MULTIPLIERS

What happens if government matches increased expenditures with increased taxes? The **balanced budget multiplier** is the increase in GDP from a unit increase in government expenditures matched by a unit increase in taxes. The increased taxes reduce disposable income, and thus private consumption. This largely, but not completely, offsets the expansionary effect of the increased government expenditures. To see why it only partially offsets the ex-

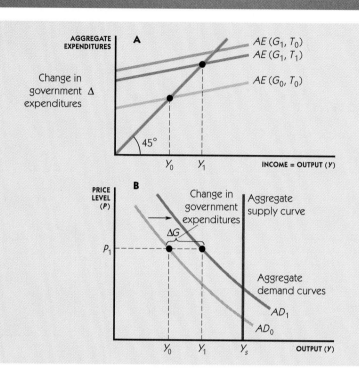

Figure 30.2 EFFECT OF INCREASED GOVERNMENT EXPENDITURES MATCHED BY TAX INCREASES

Three aggregate expenditures schedules appear in panel A. $AE(G_0, T_0)$ corresponds to aggregate expenditures before the increase in government spending and the matching tax increase. $AE(G_1, T_0)$ represents the effect of the increased government expenditures had there been no tax increase. $AE(G_1, T_1)$ shows the effect of the balanced budget increase in government spending; the balanced budget multiplier is unity, so the increase in output is equal to the increase in government spending. Panel B shows the aggregate demand curve shifting to the right by the amount of the increase in government spending.

pansionary effect, recall that a one unit reduction in disposable income only reduces consumption by the marginal propensity to consume. The net effect of the increased expenditure accompanied by increased taxes—after the multiplier has had a chance to run itself out—is that national income rises by the amount of the increased government expenditure (rather than a multiple of that amount, as would be the case if taxes were not raised). The balanced budget multiplier is unity.

Suppose that an increase in government expenditures of £1 billion is matched by an equal increase in taxes (ignoring, for simplicity, the dependence of taxes on income and ignoring exports and imports). The first round net effect is just

$$\text{£1 billion} - MPC \times \text{£1 billion} = (1 - MPC) \times \text{£1 billion},$$

where MPC is the marginal propensity to consume. The multiplier, as we know from Chapter 26, is

$$1/(1 - MPC),$$

so the net effect is

$$\frac{1}{1 - MPC}(1 - MPC) \times \text{£1 billion} = \text{£1 billion}.$$

The net effect is £1 billion. Figure 30.2 shows the result of this balanced budget increase in government expenditures. The aggregate demand curve shifts to the right, increasing output.

MONETARY POLICY

In earlier chapters we have seen how monetary policy can stimulate the economy. An increase in the money supply leads to lower interest rates and increased credit availability, stimulating investment. This shifts the aggregate expenditures schedule up and the aggregate demand schedule out, so that at

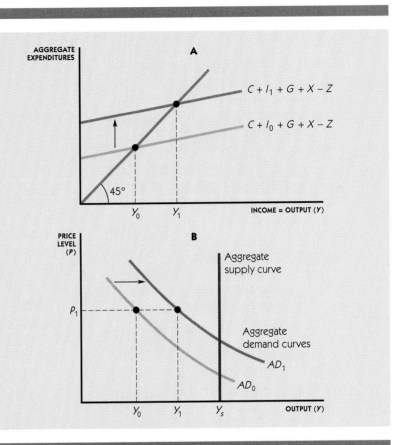

Figure 30.3 EFFECT OF MONETARY POLICY

An increase in the money supply leads to lower interest rates and increased credit availability, stimulating investment. This shifts the aggregate expenditures schedule up (panel A). The aggregate demand schedule shifts out, so that at any price level, aggregate output increases (panel B).

any price level, aggregate output increases (see Figure 30.3). As we saw in Chapter 29, an additional mechanism is at play in an open economy: as interest rates fall, exchange rates decrease, and exports increase while imports decrease. Thus, net exports increase, and again, the aggregate expenditures schedule shifts up.

INTERACTIONS BETWEEN MONETARY AND FISCAL POLICIES

So far, we have treated monetary and fiscal policies as if they were two distinct policies. In fact, there are important interactions between them. Consider the earlier discussion of a fiscal stimulus. If the monetary authorities simultaneously raise interest rates, monetary policy may partially or totally offset the expansionary effects of fiscal policy. The two are pulling in opposite directions. In the period following unification, Germany's fiscal policy was expansionary. High spending on the eastern part of the country was not matched by high taxes. Meanwhile, monetary policy, in the hands of the independent Bundesbank, was aimed at maintaining price stability, and therefore imposed high interest rates in order to restrain aggregate demand.

Sometimes the two policies work hand in hand. In Britain, in the early 1980s, a tight monetary policy aimed at reducing aggregate demand was reinforced by a tight fiscal policy. Indeed, as GDP and tax revenue fell, factors which by themselves would have led to a bigger fiscal deficit, the British government tight-

If the government reduces income taxes this year but keeps expenditures unchanged, the budget deficit will increase. This deficit is a liability for taxpayers. In the future, taxes will have to be increased (from what they otherwise would have been) to pay interest on the debt and to repay the debt. If taxpayers know that they will have to pay for a tax cut this year with higher taxes in the future and that their total lifetime income will remain unchanged, a tax cut (keeping government expenditures fixed) may have no effect on consumption. Clearly, this view goes beyond the permanent income and life-cycle models introduced earlier, which said a temporary tax cut would have an effect (if small) on total lifetime wealth, and therefore have a small effect on today's aggregate consumption.

The view that whether the government finances a given level of expenditures by taxes or by borrowing makes *no* difference to current consumption—that the two are perfectly equivalent—is called the Ricardian equivalence view, in honor of David Ricardo, the nineteenth-century English economist who also discovered the principle of comparative advantage. Ricardo described the equivalence theory, then dismissed it as irrelevant. In recent years, it has been resurrected and promoted by Robert Barro of Harvard University.

The theory of Ricardian equivalence suggests that the huge increases in government borrowing which have occurred in many developed countries in the 1980s should have led to huge increases in private savings. After all, when rational individuals see deficits, they should expect that taxes will increase some time in the future and begin setting aside funds to pay the bills. There has been no such increase in savings, however.

There are numerous reasons why Ricardian equivalence does not hold. Many individuals do not think and act in the way envisaged in the model. Many taxpayers have little idea about the true size of the deficit and do not take into account the consequences of higher future taxes. When individuals do not fully see and respond to these consequences in ways that fully offset them, we say there is a "public veil"—just as when they do not fully take into account what is going on inside corporations, we say there is a "corporate veil."

If the burden of repaying the public debt can be passed on to future generations—and if parents do not fully adjust bequests to their heirs to reflect this—then the tax reduction does represent an increase in the current generation's lifetime wealth, and accordingly aggregate consumption should rise for this generation.

ened fiscal policy further to prevent the deficit from increasing. Unemployment rose from 1.5 million to an all-time high in excess of 3 million people.

In a situation of excess supply and unemployment, a government might use the opposite combination of policies, that is, a loose, or expansionary, fiscal policy and a monetary policy that allowed the money stock to grow, so that interest rates did not rise. Economists sometimes refer to such monetary policies as **accommodative,** because the policies accommodate the changes in fiscal policy (or other

changes in the economic environment) that maintain the economy's macroeconomic performance.

Note that if the monetary authorities did nothing in the presence of a fiscal expansion, an increase in government expenditures—that is, kept the money supply constant—interest rates would rise. The increase in national income would lead to an increase in the demand for money, and for the demand for money to equal the fixed supply, interest rates would have to rise. The rise in the interest rates would discourage investment. The increased government expenditures would have partially crowded out private investment. The net expansion in the economy would be smaller—possibly far smaller—than if the monetary authorities had been more accommodative.

DIFFERENCES BETWEEN MONETARY AND FISCAL POLICIES

There are major differences between monetary and fiscal policies, in their effects on the composition of output, their efficacy, and the lags with which their effects are felt.

EFFECTS ON THE COMPOSITION OF OUTPUT

Assume, first, that we could use either monetary or fiscal policy to stimulate the economy to the same extent. If we use monetary policy, we lower interest rates, stimulating investment. Thus, future levels of income will be higher. Using monetary policy, governments can pursue both a high-growth and a full-employment strategy. If we use fiscal policy, with a fixed money supply, as incomes increase, interest rates rise so that the demand for money remains equal to the supply. Figure 30.4 contrasts the composition of GDP under alternative policies. While either fiscal or monetary policy may be able to restore the economy to full employment, they have different effects on future economic growth.

But these differences become less clear if government expenditures are for investments. A portion of government expenditures goes for physical investments, such as the construction of roads and buildings. Additionally, a portion is devoted to investment in people (investment in human capital) and investment in technology, both of which serve to increase economic growth. If the government stimulates the economy by increasing public investment rather than lowering interest rates and stimulating private investment, the impact on growth will depend on the relative rates of return of these two forms of investment.

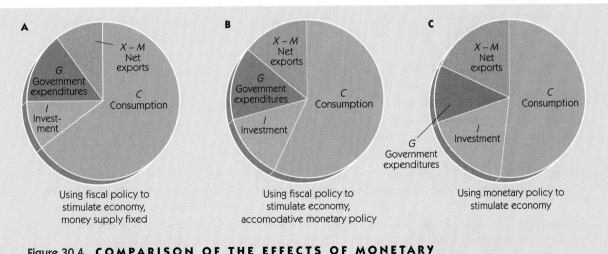

Figure 30.4 COMPARISON OF THE EFFECTS OF MONETARY AND FISCAL POLICIES

The share of investment is highest when monetary policy alone is used to restore full employment, and lowest when monetary authorities keep money supply constant, and increased government expenditures alone are used.

The 1990s saw the emergence of new institutional arrangements for monetary policy in many countries, with growing emphasis on independent central banks responsible for monetary policy. The Federal Reserve in the United States has a long-established independence from the rest of the U.S. government to conduct monetary policy; the Bundesbank established itself also as an independent central bank, responsible only for the stability of prices in Germany. Canada and Australia adopted new arrangements in the 1990s to make their central banks independent of the elected government and responsible for price stability. The Bank of England was made more independent in 1997 and given responsibility for achieving price stability. The European Central Bank is responsible for price stability, and also has independence from other parts of government both at the European and at the member state level.

The question that arises is how is coordination between the fiscal and the monetary authorities intended to emerge? Whereas in previous years when the elected government was responsible for both monetary and fiscal policy (through the chancellor of the exchequer or the finance minister), it was natural to coordinate monetary and fiscal policies, the establishment of independent central banks has removed the natural mechanism for achieving coordination. In the face of an impending recession, should the finance minister take fiscal action to stimulate demand or wait for the central bank to lower interest rates? If the finance minister and the central bank disagree about the appropriate speed or scale of tax cuts or interest rate cuts that are needed, how is the disagreement resolved? If the finance minister believes that urgent and large tax cuts are needed while the central bank disagrees,

the result will be tax cuts offset by rising interest rates. This will encourage consumption and discourage investment. If the central bank believes that interest rates should be cut while the finance minister does not, the result will be falling interest rates offset by rising taxes or falling government expenditures. This will stimulate investment and discourage consumption.

Lack of coordination leads to imbalance between fiscal and monetary policies, either to monetary policy that is too tight while fiscal policy is too loose, or to fiscal policy that is too tight while monetary policy is too loose.

During the 1950s and 1960s this issue, getting the right balance between monetary and fiscal policies, was widely discussed. It was believed to be desirable to stimulate investment in order to boost productivity and growth, and there was continual concern in Britain that the stimulation of aggregate demand relied too heavily on consumption. During the 1970s and 1980s, as concern shifted towards the control of inflation and away from the management of aggregate demand and as belief in the self-regulating properties of the economy grew, interest in the "policy mix" faded. The establishment of independent central banks, combined with the restoration of low inflation, has revived this old question in economic policy.

Since the European Central Bank has begun its operations with the intention of maintaining a hard noninflationary line and of refusing to enter into discussions that might compromise its independence of elected government officials, it is unclear how this question will be resolved.

Source: N. Rankin, "Is Delegating Half of Demand Management Sensible?" *International Review of Applied Economics* 12, no. 3 (1998), pp. 415–422.

DIFFERENCES IN THE EFFICACY OF MONETARY AND FISCAL POLICIES

Recall consensus point 14 from Chapter 29: when the economy is in a deep recession, monetary policy may be ineffective. Increases in the money supply may have little effect on interest rates, and decreases in the interest rate may have little effect on investment.

Questions have also been raised about the efficacy of some fiscal policies. In some circumstances, a tax reduction may not stimulate much consumption. Consumers—worried about the future and thinking that the tax reduction may not be permanent—save the additional funds.[1] But if the economy has been in an extended downturn, leaving many individuals credit constrained, even temporary tax cuts are likely to be effective in increasing consumption.

Many economists worry that increased deficits— tax cuts not matched by expenditure cuts, or expenditure increases not matched by tax increases— themselves dampen the economy. Since the government will have to turn to capital markets to finance the deficit, some private investment will be crowded out. The net impact of fiscal policy must take this into account: if increased deficit-financed government expenditures crowd out an equivalent amount of private investment, there will be no stimulative effect. In the open economy of the United Kingdom, this crowding out effect is not likely to be so dramatic. Still, there may be some offsetting effects through changes in the exchange rate, but because imports and exports adjust so slowly—sometimes taking up to two years to adjust fully—the offsetting effects may not reduce by much the efficacy of fiscal policy in the very short run.

[1] Chapter 27 analysed in more detail these future-oriented consumption decisions. Individuals base consumption not on their current income but on their lifetime or permanent incomes, and a one-time, once-and-for-all tax reduction has little effect on individuals' lifetime or permanent income.

DIFFERENCES IN THE LAGS OF MONETARY AND FISCAL POLICIES

Monetary and fiscal policies also differ in the speed with which they can take effect. Monetary policy stimulates the economy by lowering interest rates and increasing investment in equipment and housing. Even after firms see a decrease in interest rates, it may take some time before they place new orders for investment and before the capital goods industry starts producing the newly ordered items. Similarly, though in the long run lower interest rates lead to an increased demand for housing, it takes a while before plans are drawn up, planning permissions are obtained, and construction starts. Typically, it takes six months or longer before the effects of monetary policy are realised. By contrast increased government expenditures have a direct and immediate effect in increasing incomes.

There is another important source of delay: governments must decide to take action. They must see that the economy is in a downturn and that some kind of stimulus is needed. These lags in taking action are often significant. They are avoided through the use of **automatic stabilisers,** expenditures that automatically increase or taxes that automatically decrease when economic conditions worsen.

The economy has a number of these automatic stabilisers. Expenditures on unemployment compensation automatically go up in an economic downturn. So do other social insurance payments, as more individuals claim disability and other benefits. Similarly, income tax functions as an automatic stabiliser because of its progressive structure. A progressive tax system is one in which individuals with higher incomes pay a larger fraction of their income in taxes. As an individual's income increases, he moves into a higher tax bracket, and his average tax rate increases. Thus, when the total income (output) of the economy increases, average tax rates increase, and taxes as a fraction of GDP increase. Conversely, when the economy goes into a downturn, tax revenue will decline even if the tax rate is constant. But with a progressive tax system, they decline even more since the average tax rate declines. The fact that the tax system is progressive thus enhances its role as an automatic stabiliser.

In the 1980s and 1990s a number of countries found that their national debt levels were rising alarmingly and undertook fiscal restructuring. This involved rises in tax revenue or cuts in government expenditures or both, in order to improve the government's budget balance, and thus stem the growth in the national debt. Whereas the conventional wisdom was that these policies would cause a severe contraction in the economy, in fact, in a number of countries, the contractionary effect was short lived and was succeeded by a period of vigorous growth.

In Denmark, for example, the national debt grew from 29 percent of GDP at the beginning of 1980 to 65 percent at the end of 1982. The government was running a large fiscal deficit of 3.1 percent of GDP even before allowing for the cost of interest payments on the existing debt. The rapid growth in the debt threw into doubt the sustainability of the government's policies. Such was the alarm in financial markets that Danish long-term interest rates rose to 22 percent, while inflation was only 10 percent per year. Without policy changes, the national debt was likely to get out of control. A new conservative government elected in 1982 adopted a tight fiscal policy, cutting government expenditure and raising taxes. In addition the Danish crown was pegged to the German mark. As a result, interest rates fell dramatically. Far from causing a deep recession, Danish real GDP grew 3.6 percent per year from 1983 to 1986. There was strong growth in consumers' expenditure and a spectacular investment boom.

This is just one example. There were similar occurrences in Ireland from 1987 onwards and Italy from 1993 onwards. Further afield, Australia, in the period from 1987, provides an example of an expansionary "fiscal contraction." The Clinton administration adopted contractionary fiscal policies from 1993 onwards in the United States which, by cutting the national debt, may have strengthened the growth in the U.S. economy that followed.

Why is it that, in many cases, policies that have had the direct effect of cutting aggregate demand have been followed by periods of strong economic growth? It is clear that expectations of future government spending and taxation, and forecasts of the national debt have been important. Consumers may have taken cuts in government spending and borrowing as an indication that tax rates would be lower in the future, raising their expected future disposable income and leading them to increase their consumption immediately. Business confidence seems to have been boosted by these measures, perhaps because of forecasts of lower future taxes, perhaps because of expectations of a more stable economy, leading to increases in investment. It appears that a cut in government expenditure often "crowded in" a rise in private investment.

Since these episodes of fiscal retrenchment were usually accompanied by other measures, such as devaluation of exchange rates or monetary policy changes, it is difficult to disentangle precisely the role of the fiscal policy change from the whole. Nevertheless, they show that expectations of future government policy can have a powerful effect on people's immediate behaviour and on the development of the economy, sufficient to overwhelm the direct impact of the policy.

Sources: F. Giavazzi and M. Pagano, "Can Severe Fiscal Contractions Be Expansionary?" in *Macroeconomic Annual,* National Bureau of Economic Research (Boston: MIT Press, 1990), pp. 75–110; A. Alesina and S. Ardagna, "Fiscal Adjustments," *Economic Policy* 27 (October 1998), pp. 489–517.

CONSEQUENCES OF A BALANCED BUDGET POLICY

Many people have thought that it is irresponsible for government to have a deficit, reasoning that, like a business, government cannot permanently run at a loss. The huge deficits in the United States in the 1980s brought the issue to a head: there was a strong political movement to adopt a constitutional amendment requiring a balanced budget, known as the **balanced budget amendment.** The proposal for such an amendment passed the House of Representatives in 1995 and failed by one vote to achieve the required two-thirds majority in the Senate.

Most economists opposed the balanced budget amendment, largely because they believed that it would eliminate the ability of automatic stabilisers to work. As we have seen, automatic stabilisers typically result in expenditures' increasing and revenue's falling in economic downturns, leading to deficits in recessions. But under a balanced budget amendment, the government would be forced to *destabilise* the economy—either raising taxes or cutting expenditures as the economy went into a recession—when just the opposite medicine was required.

This destabilization of the economy in Britain was a consequence of the Medium Term Financial Strategy (MTFS) of the government of the 1980s. The MTFS set out targets for money growth and the fiscal deficit for each year from 1981 to 1986. When GDP fell more than expected, causing a larger than planned deficit, government expenditures were cut and taxes were raised to get the deficit back on target, even though the recession was deepening.

With fiscal policy's no longer being used to stabilise the economy—or worse, contributing to its instability—the burden of stabilization would be put squarely on the shoulders of the monetary authorities. This means that interest rates would have to fluctuate more than they otherwise would, causing greater expansions and contractions in the interest-sensitive sectors (housing, durable goods, and plant and equipment). Since the lags in monetary policy—the time between when an action is undertaken and when its effects are fully felt—would be long and variable (typically six months or more), the economy itself would exhibit greater variability. And there are times when monetary policy is relatively ineffective in stimulating the economy (when the response of the economy to lowering interest rates is small or smaller than anticipated), such as during the Great Depression. In such situations, the economic downturn would last longer and might be deeper than it would be if stronger automatic stabilisers were in place.

One proposal for reducing these destabilising effects is to balance not the actual budget but to set to zero the **full-employment deficit**—what the deficit would have been had the economy been operating at full employment. The full-employment deficit takes into account the changes in expenditures and revenue due to the current economic conditions. In a recession the full-employment deficit is smaller than the actual deficit. Most economists believe that the government is fiscally responsible so long as there is no full-employment deficit. Arguably, a policy of maintaining a balanced budget would be better pursued in terms of the full-employment budget deficit.

BALANCED BUDGETS AND STABILIZATION POLICY

1 An increase in government expenditure matched by an increase in tax revenue is expansionary.

2 Automatic stabilisers increase expenditures and reduce taxes automatically as the economy goes into a recession. Simple balanced budget rules would preclude the use of automatic stabilisers as well as eliminate the possibility of discretionary fiscal policy to stabilise the economy.

3 In practice, a policy balancing the budget would be likely to destabilise the economy and force the entire burden of stabilization onto monetary policy.

The text describes the important concept of the full-employment deficit (sometimes called the structural deficit). Suppose the economy has 5 percent unemployment, when it is generally believed that only 6 percent is possible without inflationary pressures developing. From Chapter 22 we know that there are always some people without jobs in the economy, because of such factors as frictional, seasonal, and structural unemployment. Thus we can assume that 6 percent unemployment corresponds to the full-employment level of output. Assume also that government's budget deficit is already £5 billion, GDP is £850 billion, and a 1 percentage point increase in the unemployment rate will be associated with a 2 percent decrease in output. What is the full-employment deficit?

Step 1.   Calculate the full-employment level of output. Increasing unemployment from 5 to 6 percent will cause a reduction in output of £17 billion.

Step 2.   Calculate the extent to which tax revenue decreases and expenditures increase as output falls. Suppose that tax revenue falls by £35 for every £100 fall in GDP and that government expenditures rise by £15. In toto the deficit rises by £50 for every £100 fall in GDP. A fall in GDP of £17 billion will cause an increase in the deficit of £8.5 billion.

Step 3.   Add these figures to the original deficit. The full-employment, or structural, deficit is then £5 billion + £8.5 billion = £13.5 billion. (As a percentage of GDP this is $100 \times 13.5/850$, or approximately 1.6 percent).

There are three conspicuous sources of uncertainty surrounding this calculation. One is the level of the unemployment rate at full employment (the NAIRU). This has always been surrounded with considerable uncertainty, partly because it has fluctuated so much over the past fifty years and partly because inflation responds slowly and with a lag to unemployment and also responds to other factors, so that pinning down a precise estimate of the NAIRU has been impossible. A second source of uncertainty lies in the effect of a fall in GDP on government spending and tax revenue; and a third is the effect of a rise in unemployment on GDP. Taken together, these elements of uncertainty leave the estimated structural deficit surrounded by considerable margins of error.

REVIEW AND PRACTICE

SUMMARY

1 Increasing government expenditure (without increasing taxes) stimulates the economy but generates a deficit. If the government spends the additional funds on investments that yield returns in excess of the interest rate, then increased government expenditure can make the economy stronger both today and in the future.

2 Increases in government expenditure matched by increases in taxes can still stimulate the economy, but there will be no multiplier effects.

3 Monetary policy stimulates the economy by increasing investment and net exports. Thus, stimulating the economy through monetary policy has a more positive effect on economic growth than doing so through fiscal policy unless the increased government expenditures are spent on investments. In deep recessions, however, monetary policy may not be very effective.

4 The lags associated with monetary policy may be longer than those associated with fiscal policy.

5 Automatic stabilisers help to stabilise the economy, without any policymaker making an active decision.

6 Most balanced budget policies would circumscribe the operation of automatic stabilisers and thus serve to destabilise the economy. All the burden of stabilization would be placed on monetary policy.

KEY TERMS

balanced budget
multiplier

accommodative
monetary policy

automatic stabilisers

balanced budget policy

full-employment deficit

REVIEW QUESTIONS

1 How does an increase in government expenditure shift the aggregate expenditures schedule and the aggregate demand curve? How does monetary policy shift the aggregate expenditures schedule and the aggregate demand curve?

2 If the economy is in a recession, describe the trade-off between today and the future associated with an increase in government expenditures. How does what the government spends its increased expenditures on affect the trade-off? If the government spends the funds on investments that yield high returns, is there still a trade-off? Even if the government spends the funds on public consumption, why might the trade-off still appear attractive?

3 What is the effect of an increase in government expenditure matched by an increase in taxes?

4 Compare the effects of monetary and fiscal policies on the level of investment and the composition of output.

5 What other factor(s) are important in the choice between monetary and fiscal policies?

6 What effect might a policy of balancing the budget have on the stability of the economy?

7 What are automatic stabilisers, and why are they important?

PROBLEMS

1 Show how a decrease in the price level leads to a shift in the aggregate demand curve if money supply remains unchanged.
   (a) First, use the demand and supply curves for money to show the effect on interest rates.
   (b) Then use the investment function to show the effect on investments.
   (c) Then use the aggregate expenditures schedule to show the effect on equilibrium output.

2 Show the differences in the effect of an increase in government expenditure when monetary authorities:
   (a) Keep the money supply constant.
   (b) Expand the money supply to keep the interest rate constant.
Trace out the effects on:
   (i) The demand and supply curves for money and the equilibrium interest rate
   (ii) The level of investment

(iii) The aggregate expenditures schedule and the equilibrium level of output at any fixed price

(iv) The aggregate demand schedule

3 Assume you are in charge of monetary policy. The economy is £10 billion below capacity, or 1 percent of its £1,000 billion capacity.

(a) You are told the government does not plan to increase government expenditures or change tax rates at all. How much must you increase the money supply? Assume:

(i) Money demand has an interest elasticity of 0.8 and an income elasticity of 1.

(ii) Investment elasticity is 0.8 and investment amounts to 10 percent of GDP (£99 billion).

(iii) The multiplier is 2.

(b) The government plans to increase expenditures to restore full employment, but it wants the monetary authorities to keep interest rates constant. By how much must they increase the money supply? (Use the same assumptions as in part a.) Assuming the multiplier is 2, by how much must government expenditure be increased?

(c) Now assume the monetary authorities are independent and have announced that they will not change the money supply. By how much will interest rates rise if the government is successful in restoring the economy to full employment? How will that affect investment? What does this imply for the required magnitude of increase in government expenditures?

4 When individuals become wealthier, they consume more. If prices fall, the *real value* of wealth which is denominated in monetary terms—like money and government bonds—increases. Would you expect this effect to be large or small?

Assume that government bonds and money represent 10 percent of national wealth and that an increase in real wealth of 10 percent leads to a 0.6 percent increase in consumption. Assume consumption represents 90 percent of GDP and the multiplier is 2. Assume prices fall by 5 percent. By approximately what percentage will GDP increase? Assume the economy is 10 percent below capacity. How long would it take the economy to be restored to full employment if prices continued to fall at the rate of 5 percent per year?

5 The economy is £10 billion below capacity, or 1 percent of its £1,000 billion capacity. The government contemplates stimulating the economy by alternative policies. Assume that the multiplier is 2 and that investment is completely interest inelastic. Calculate the required increase in government expenditures. Calculate the required increase in government expenditures if the government increases taxes in tandem. Can monetary policy be used to stimulate the economy?

6 Consider the extreme case where the individuals and firms within a country can borrow (or lend) as much as desired at a fixed real interest rate. Can monetary authorities affect the level of real investment? Assume that as the monetary authorities try to raise interest rates, funds flow in from abroad; as they flow in, they bid up the exchange rate. Trace through the effects of:

(a) The increased demand for the domestic currency by foreign investors wishing to invest in the country on the exchange rate

(b) The exchange rate on the aggregate expenditures schedule and on GDP

7 Eleven European countries formed the European Monetary Union in January 1999, in which there is a single currency. Exchange rates between the countries are fixed and there is a single interest rate for all the countries set by the European Central Bank. The governments have agreed that certain criteria must be met by members of EMU, under the terms of the Stability and Growth Pact (SGP). These include reducing the fiscal deficit as a share of GDP to below 3 percent. What might be the macroeconomic effects of this deficit reduction if:

(a) The European Central Bank does not adjust interest rates?

(b) Interest rates are reduced?

Why might the simultaneous reduction of deficits by all the countries lead to a larger reduction in output than if only one country reduced its deficit if the interest rates do not fall? Use diagrams to illustrate your answers.

8 Assume that the European Monetary Union produces the same interest rates in all countries within the Union. Assume that unemployment in one country within the Union, say France, increases. What can the government do to restore full employment?

Contrast what might be done about unemployment in France within the European Monetary Union with what might be done about unemployment in one of the states in the United States, say California. In what ways will the situation be similar? How will they differ?

9 Compare the effects on longer-term economic growth of using monetary rather than fiscal policy to stimulate an economy when capital flows freely internationally with the effects within a closed economy.

PART SEVEN

Dynamics and Macro Policy

S o far, we have discussed two of the three key macroeconomic problems: growth and unemployment. We now turn to the third, *inflation*. What causes it? Why is it a problem? What can government do about it?

This part of the book does more, however, than just round out our discussion of the three key macroeconomic problems. It also describes and explains the *dynamics of wage and price adjustments*. Part Five focused on full-employment economies, Part Six on economies with unemployment. We emphasised that the key distinction between the two was assumptions about adjustments. In Part Five, wages and prices adjusted quickly so that the labour market was always in equilibrium. In Part Six, wages and prices were fixed. We were taking a snapshot of the economy, before the dynamic process unfolded. We recognised that when the demand for labour was less than the supply at the current wages or when the demand for goods was less than the supply at the current price level, there were pressures for wages and prices to fall. But the adjustments do not occur instantaneously. Similarly, if initially the economy's resources were fully employed and there was a rightward shift in the aggregate demand curve, there would be excess demand for goods at the going price level. This creates upward price pressure, but again, prices do not adjust instantaneously.

The fact that wages and prices do not adjust instantaneously—that they are sticky—means that after any disturbance, there will be at least a period in which demand does not equal supply. If at current prices and wages demand is less than supply, output is limited by aggregate demand, so that an increase in aggregate demand—say as a result of increased government expenditure—increases output and employment.

Understanding why unemployment persists and why prices may rise, not just once but year after year, entails understanding the dynamics of adjustment. In this part, we will *describe* observed regularities in wage and price adjustments and *explain* both the consequences of these observed patterns and the sources of wage and price stickiness. Part Seven consists of three chapters. Chapter 31 describes wage and price dynamics and explains the major determinants of the rate of inflation. Chapter 32 takes a closer look at the labour market, to see why wages in particular often exhibit rigidities. Finally Chapter 33 brings together the insights of Parts One, Five, and Six to discuss some of the central policy issues in macroeconomics and the controversies surrounding them. Should the government intervene? And if so, what is the most effective form of intervention?

INFLATION: WAGE AND PRICE DYNAMICS

t is an axiom of political rhetoric that inflation is bad. Popular sentiment runs so strongly against inflation that it is usually taken for granted that the government should do something about it. But if the government needs to do something about inflation, we need to know what causes it. How do we explain why some countries have higher inflation rates than others? Or why does the United Kingdom have a lower inflation rate today than it did fifteen years ago?

If inflation is so disliked, why don't governments simply get rid of it? The answer is that, normally, inflation can only be reduced at a cost—only if the unemployment rate is allowed to increase. This chapter looks at the trade-off between inflation and unemployment, and how this trade-off can be changed. Many economists believe that in the long run, there is no trade-off: attempting to reduce unemployment to too low a level is a chimera. Not only does inflation increase, but it increases at a faster and faster rate, until inflation, not unemployment, becomes viewed as the central economic problem. This chapter explains these critical debates which underlie so much of current policy discussions.

KEY QUESTIONS

1 What are the costs of inflation? Why does it make a difference whether inflation is anticipated? How can the costs be ameliorated?

2 What is the trade-off between inflation and unemployment? How do expectations about inflation affect the level of inflation associated with any level of unemployment?

3 Why might inflation accelerate if the unemployment rate is kept at too low a level? How do these considerations affect government policies?

4 How do labour market factors and government policies affect this critical unemployment rate?

5 Why is it that once inflation starts, it tends to persist?

6 What role does monetary policy play in initiating or perpetuating inflation?

7 What are some of the reasons for wage and price rigidities?

THE COSTS OF INFLATION

We identified growth, unemployment, and inflation as the three key macroeconomic problems. Part Five discussed issues of growth, and Part Six of unemployment. Here we focus on inflation and the relationship between inflation and unemployment. While the costs of unemployment are apparent—not only is there a loss in output, but the misery of those who cannot secure gainful employment is palpable—the costs of inflation are more subtle and over the years have been greatly ameliorated.

People sense there is something wrong with the economy when there is high inflation. Workers worry that their pay will not keep pace with increases in the price level, and thus their living standards will be eroded. Investors worry that the returns they receive in the future will be worth less than the money they invested, leaving them with less than enough to live comfortably in their old age.

When inflation is anticipated, many of its economic costs disappear. Workers who know that prices will be rising by 10 percent this year, for example, may negotiate wages that rise fast enough to offset the inflation. Lenders know that the money they will be repaid will be worth less than the money

they lent, and they take this into account when setting the interest rate they charge or when deciding whether to make the loan.

But even when inflation is not perfectly anticipated, workers and investors can immunise themselves against the effects of inflation by having wages and returns **indexed** to inflation. For instance, when wages are perfectly indexed, a 1 percent increase in the price level results in a 1 percent increase in wages.

In recent years, social security payments and tax rates have both been indexed. Many countries, including the United Kingdom, Canada, and New Zealand, sell indexed government bonds so that savers can put aside money knowing that the returns will not be affected by inflation. In May 1996, the U.S. government announced its intention to begin selling indexed bonds.

WHO SUFFERS FROM INFLATION?

While indexing softens the effects of inflation, it is far from complete. So who suffers today from inflation? Many people may suffer a little, since indexing does not fully protect them, but some are more likely to suffer than others. Among the groups most imperfectly protected are lenders, taxpayers, and holders of currency.

Lenders Since most loans are not fully indexed, an unexpected increase in inflation means that the lender gets back from the borrower money that is of less real value than was expected. During the 1970s, when inflation was at its highest, the nominal rates of return that people earned on their investments in building society accounts, government bonds, and shares were often less than the rate of inflation; the real return was negative. If the inflation had been anticipated, nominal (and real) interest rates might have been higher.

The banks are often thought of as the biggest lenders in the economy, and it might be thought they had lost from the high inflation of the 1970s. However, that is not the case. The banks actually did rather well in the periods of high inflation. While real interest rates may have been negative, the gap between the rate of interest that banks paid on their deposits and the rate of interest they collected on loans widened in the 1970s: the banks were generally paying no interest on current account deposits at that time, and yet the interest charged on loans went up. Banks did well in the 1970s.

Taxpayers The tax system is only partially indexed, and inflation frequently hurts investors badly through the tax system. All returns to investment are taxed, including those that do nothing more than offset inflation. Consequently, real after-tax returns are often negative. Consider a rate of inflation of 10 percent and an asset that yields a return of 12 percent before tax. If the individual has to pay a 33 percent tax on the return, his after-tax yield is 8 percent—not enough to compensate him for inflation. His after-tax real return is −1 percent.

Holders of Currency Inflation also makes it expensive for people to hold currency because as they hold it, the currency loses its value. Since currency facilitates a variety of transactions, inflation interferes with the efficiency of the economy by discouraging the holding of currency. The fact that inflation takes away the value of money means that inflation acts as a tax on holding money. Economists refer to this distortionary effect as an **inflation tax.**

This distortion is not as important in modern economies, where bank accounts are frequently used instead of cash and typically pay interest. As the rate of inflation increases, the interest rate paid on bank accounts normally increases as well. Even in Argentina in the 1970s, when prices were rising by 800 percent a month, bank accounts yielded more than 800 percent a month. Still, poorer individuals who do not have bank accounts—and therefore must hold much of what little wealth they have in the form of currency—are adversely affected.

The Economy There are two costs of inflation to the economy as a whole. The first has to do with relative prices. Because price increases are never perfectly coordinated, increases in the rate of inflation lead to a greater variability of relative prices. If the shoe industry makes price adjustments only every three months, then in the third month, right before its price increase, shoes may be relatively cheap, while right after the price increase, shoes may be relatively expensive. On the other hand, the prices of groceries might change continually throughout the three-month period. Therefore, the ratio of the price of groceries to the price of shoes will continually be changing. When the average rate of inflation is only 2 or 3 percent per year, this does not cause much of a problem. But when the average rate of inflation is 10 percent per month, inflation causes real distortions in how society allocates its resources. When inflation gets very high, economies tend to allocate considerable resources to avoid the costs of inflation and to take advantage of the discrepancies in prices charged by different sellers. Rather than carrying money, which quickly erodes in value, people rush to deposit their money in interest-bearing bank accounts.

The second economywide cost of inflation arises from the risk and uncertainty that inflation generates. If there were perfect indexing, the uncertainty about the rate of inflation would be unimportant. But as indexing is not perfect, the resulting uncertainty makes it difficult to plan. People saving for their retirement cannot know what to put aside. Business firms borrowing money are uncertain about the price they will receive for the goods they produce. Firms are also hurt when they build wage increases into multiyear contracts to reflect *anticipated* inflation. If for any reason a firm finds that the prices it can charge increase less rapidly than anticipated in the contract, the employer suffers.

CLOSE-UP: HYPERINFLATION IN GERMANY IN THE 1920S

Following the First World War, Germany was required by the victorious Allied nations to make substantial reparation payments. But the sheer size of the reparations, combined with the wartime devastation of German industry, made payment nearly impossible. John Maynard Keynes, then an economic adviser to the British government, was among those who warned that the reparations were too large. To finance some of Germany's financial obligations, the German government started simply printing money.

The resulting increases in both the amount of circulating currency and the price level can be seen in the following figure. From January 1922 to November 1923, the average price level increased by a factor of almost 10 billion.* People made desperate attempts to spend their currency as soon as they received it, since the value of currency was declining so rapidly. One story often told by Keynes was how Germans would buy two beers at once, even though one was likely to get warm, for fear that otherwise, when it came time to buy the second beer, the price would have risen.

At an annual inflation rate of 100 percent, money loses half its value every year. If you save £100 today, in five years it will have buying power equal to only £3 at today's prices. It is possible for nominal interest rates to adjust even to very high inflation rates. But when those high inflation rates fluctuate in unanticipated ways, the effects can be disastrous.

Periods of hyperinflation create a massive redistribution of wealth. If an individual is smart or lucky enough to hold assets in a form such as foreign funds or land, then the hyperinflation will do little to reduce that person's actual wealth. Those who cannot avail themselves of these inflation-proof assets will see their wealth fall.

*Thomas Sargent, "The Ends of Four Big Inflations," in *Inflation*, Robert Hall, ed. (Chicago: University of Chicago Press, 1982), pp. 74–75.

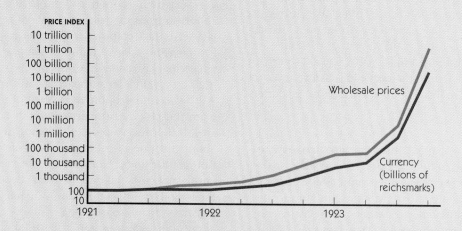

WHO GAINS FROM INFLATION?

While many people may lose from inflation, some groups perceive a gain from inflation. One conspicuous group in Britain is people who borrowed to buy property since the end of the Second World War. (Only people who have bought property since 1989 have lost money on their investments.) These people bought real property, the value of which rose as the general level of prices and wages rose with inflation. They financed the purchases by taking out loans (mortgages), mainly from building societies. The interest rate paid has moved up and down with inflation, but the tax system subsidised these loans greatly in times of inflation, until tax relief on mortgage interest was limited.

Suppose mortgage interest is tax deductible. Then, with 10 percent inflation, a 15 percent interest rate on mortgages (so that the real rate of interest before tax is 5 percent), and a tax rate of 33 percent on income, the net interest rate paid (after tax) is 10 percent (= 67 percent of 15 percent) and the real after-tax interest rate is 0 percent. Compare the situation when there is no inflation and the mortgage interest rate is 5 percent (so that again the real before-tax rate of interest is 5 percent). The after-tax interest rate is 67 percent of 5 percent, or 3.33 percent, and that is the real after-tax interest rate as well as the nominal after-tax interest rate. Inflation of 10 percent takes the real after-tax rate of interest from 3.33 percent to 0 percent, making borrowing for house purchase effectively free.

The subsidy to house purchase which is given by tax relief on mortgage interest is increased by inflation. It has encouraged people in Britain to invest heavily in housing rather than other assets and made the economy excessively sensitive to the state of the housing market. It may have reduced the flow of lending available to finance investment in industry in Britain.

MISPERCEIVED COSTS OF INFLATION

We have discussed two significant costs of inflation, but much of the aversion to inflation comes from a variety of forms of misperceptions. If a poll were conducted asking people whether they were hurt or helped by inflation, most would say they were hurt. Much of this is simply *perception*. People "feel" price increases much more vividly than they do the corresponding income increases. They "feel" the higher interest rates they have to pay on loans more than they do the decrease in the value of the money with which they repay lenders. A closer look at who benefits and who loses from unanticipated inflation suggests that there are probably more gainers than there are losers. This is simply because there are probably more debtors than lenders, and debtors benefit from unanticipated inflation.

In many inflationary episodes, many individuals not only *feel* worse off, they *are* worse off, but inflation itself is not the culprit. The oil price increases of 1973 set off a widespread inflation in the United States. The higher price of oil also made the United States poorer than it had previously been, because it was an oil importer. Someone's standard of living had to be cut, and inflation did the cutting. Frequently those whose incomes were cut—unskilled

---

COSTS OF INFLATION, ACTUAL AND PERCEIVED

Real costs

Variability in relative prices

Resources devoted to mitigating the costs of inflation and taking advantage of price discrepancies

Increased uncertainty

Misperceptions

Failing to recognise offsetting increases in income

Blaming inflation for losses in real income that occur during inflationary episodes but are caused by other factors

workers, whose wages did not keep pace with prices—cited as the *cause* of their lower incomes the inflation that accompanied the oil price increases. However, generalised price inflation was only a symptom. The underlying cause of that particular inflation, and of the reduced real incomes, was a sharp rise in the price of oil.

It is clear that the costs of inflation are different from, and undoubtedly lower than, what they were before indexing was so extensive. Today economists do not agree on the *magnitude* of the adverse effects of inflation. There is considerable evidence that high rates of inflation have strongly adverse effects on economic performance. But there is little evidence that at the moderate rates of inflation that the developed world has experienced in recent years, there are any significant adverse effects.

INFLATION AND UNEMPLOYMENT

While there is some debate about the *magnitude* of the costs of inflation, if it were costless to reduce inflation, clearly governments would do so. But lower inflation can typically be obtained only through higher unemployment. In this section, we analyse the relationship between inflation and unemployment.

In Parts Five and Six, we examined two different models of the economy: the full-employment and un-employment models. These models are based on opposite assumptions about prices and wages. In the full-employment model, we assumed that prices and wages are perfectly flexible. In the unemployment model, we assumed that prices and wages are fixed. The full-employment model gives us a useful picture of the economy in the long run. Eventually, prices and wages do adjust so that the economy returns to the full-employment level of output. The unemployment model is a closer picture of the economy in the very short run, in which prices and wages adjust very little, if at all. Our objective now is to understand the middle ground between the very short run of the unemployment model (with fixed wages and prices) and the long run of the full-employment model.

In Part Six the case when at the current price level P_0, aggregate demand fell short of aggregate supply is illustrated in Figure 31.1 by the aggregate demand curve AD_1. As we know, in this situation, output is limited by aggregate demand (Y_1). When the economy is below the full-employment level of output, policymakers may attempt to shift the aggregate demand curve to the right, increasing output and reducing unemployment. But if the aggregate demand curve is shifted too far to the right, say to AD_2 at the current price level P_0, where aggregate demand exceeds aggregate supply, upward price pressure is injected into the economy, and inflation rears its ugly head. On the other hand, if the initial situation is represented by AD_2, upward price pressure may be diminished by leftward shifts of the aggregate demand curve. If this is taken to extremes, the level of output may fall below the full-employment level.

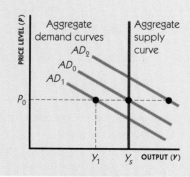

Figure 31.1 SHORT-RUN EQUILIBRIUM

When aggregate demand is less than aggregate supply at the current price level, output (Y_1) will be limited by aggregate demand and there will be involuntary unemployment. When aggregate supply is less than aggregate demand at the current price level, output will be limited by aggregate supply and there will be upward price pressure.

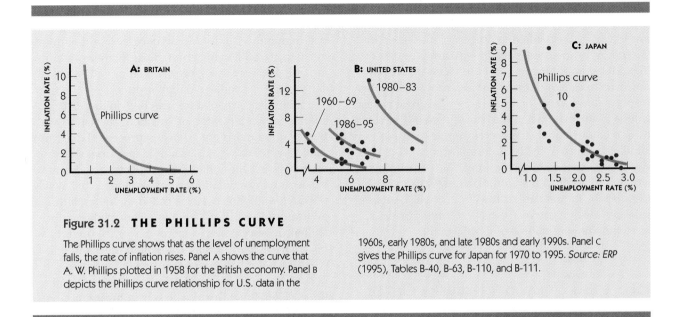

Figure 31.2 THE PHILLIPS CURVE

The Phillips curve shows that as the level of unemployment falls, the rate of inflation rises. Panel A shows the curve that A. W. Phillips plotted in 1958 for the British economy. Panel B depicts the Phillips curve relationship for U.S. data in the 1960s, early 1980s, and late 1980s and early 1990s. Panel C gives the Phillips curve for Japan for 1970 to 1995. *Source: ERP* (1995), Tables B-40, B-63, B-110, and B-111.

The problems of inflation and unemployment lie on opposite sides of the aggregate supply curve. This suggests that the unemployment rate and inflation, the rate of change in prices, are connected, which is indeed the case. The economy's adjustment to shifts in the aggregate demand and supply curves is represented in changes in rates of inflation and levels of unemployment. When aggregate demand exceeds aggregate supply, the economy will experience higher inflation as it moves to the future equilibrium level. On the other hand, when aggregate demand is less than aggregate supply, inflation will be down, but the unemployment rate will be high. In both cases, the size of the effects on the rates of inflation and unemployment will depend on the size of the gap between aggregate supply and aggregate demand; the larger the gap, the larger the effect. This interconnection between inflation and unemployment is the key to understanding the dynamics of adjustment—the middle ground between the full-employment and unemployment models we have studied thus far.

The challenge for economists and policymakers is threefold: (1) to determine the state of the economy at any given time, (2) to determine how policy can change the state of the economy favourably, and (3) to determine how inflation and unemployment are likely to change in the future. Two of the key factors they look at in assessing the state of the economy are the unemployment rate—a measure of the "tightness" of the labour market—and the rate of change of wages. In addition to looking at the labour market, economists and policymakers examine conditions in the product and capital markets, but for various reasons, unemployment and wages are an especially good gauge of where the economy is and where inflation is heading.

THE PHILLIPS CURVE

The framework for thinking about the rate of change of wages is the same as that used for thinking about the rate of change of prices. Just as the greater the gap between demand and supply, the more pressure there is for prices to increase, and so the *faster* will be the rate of price increases. So too in the labour market: the "tighter" the labour market, the faster we expect the price of labour—wages—to rise. This kind of relationship has been verified in a number of markets in a number of instances, as illustrated in Figure 31.2. The relationship is called the **Phillips curve** after A. W. Phillips, a New Zealander who taught economics in England in the 1950s.

In the curve that Phillips drew, the unemployment rate at which inflation is zero is positive. There are several reasons for this. In the economy, not every worker is qualified to do every job. There may be unemployment of carworkers and excess demand for computer programmers. If wages respond upwards to excess demand more strongly than they respond downwards to excess supply, average wages will be rising even when the excess demand for one type of labour equals the excess supply of the other. Similarly, there may be unemployment in South Wales and vacancies in London. But unemployed workers in South Wales cannot simply walk into jobs in London. By the same token, there will be some workers moving between jobs; in Chapter 22 we referred to this as frictional unemployment.

THE EXPECTATIONS-AUGMENTED PHILLIPS CURVE

In the 1970s, the stable relationship between unemployment and inflation seemed to disappear. The economy experienced high unemployment with high inflation. There was a simple explanation for this: the rate at which wages increase at any level of

unemployment depends on expectations concerning inflation. If workers expect prices to be rising, they will demand offsetting wage increases; and employers will be willing to grant those higher wage increases, because they believe that they will be able to sell what they produce at higher prices.

Inflationary expectations ran high in the 1970s, resulting in higher rates of inflation coexisting with higher unemployment. This is represented diagrammatically in Figure 31.3. The Phillips curve shifts up, incorporating the inflationary expectations. Because it accounts for inflationary expectations, the newly positioned Phillips curve is called the **expectations-augmented Phillips curve.** The Phillips curve shifted up successively during the 1970s, until it stabilised in the early 1980s. The Phillips curve stabilises when actual inflation equals expected inflation. This occurs at a special level of unemployment, sometimes called the **natural rate of unemployment,** indicated by U^* in Figure 31.3.

To better understand the role of the natural rate of unemployment, consider that expectations about inflation are affected both by recent experience and anticipated changes in policy and economic conditions. Take the simple case where expectations are simply adaptive; that is, they respond or adapt to re-

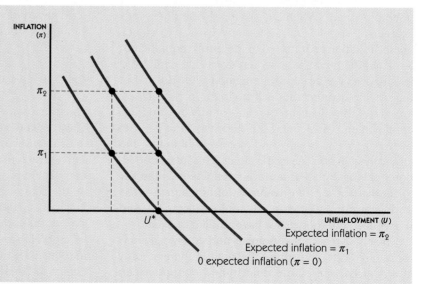

Figure 31.3 THE EXPECTATIONS-AUGMENTED PHILLIPS CURVE

The position of the Phillips curve depends on inflationary expectations. Increased expectations concerning inflation shift the Phillips curve up. The variable U^* is the natural, or nonaccelerating, inflation rate of unemployment (NAIRU). At U^*, if expected inflation is π_1, actual inflation is π_1; when expected inflation is π_2, actual inflation is π_2. At lower unemployment rates, inflation exceeds inflationary expectations, and eventually the Phillips curve shifts up still more. At higher unemployment rates, inflation is less than the expectations concerning inflation, and the Phillips curve shifts down.

cent experience. Assume the economy was initially in a situation where prices had been stable for an extended period of time. Given this historical experience, workers expect zero inflation. In Figure 31.3 the Phillips curve is the curve labeled $\pi = 0$. Suppose the government reduces unemployment below the rate U^* (where inflation equals expected inflation) and keeps it at the lower rate. This induces an increase in the inflation rate. As the inflation rate increases, the expectations-augmented Phillips curve shifts up, so there will be higher rates of inflation at each level of unemployment. If the government continues to maintain the unemployment rate below U^*, this will fuel higher expected inflation, resulting in another upward shift of the expectations-augmented Phillips curve. Thus, if the government attempts to maintain the unemployment rate below the natural rate, the inflation rate will continue to increase. As expectations adapt to each successive increase in the inflation rate, inflation increases still more. Accordingly, today, the natural rate is generally known as the **nonaccelerating inflation rate of unemployment,** or NAIRU for short. An economy cannot *permanently* lower its unemployment rate below the NAIRU without facing faster and faster rates of inflation. This has emerged as one of the central points of consensus among macroeconomists, bringing us to our fifteenth consensus point.

15 The Trade-off between Inflation and Unemployment

When the unemployment rate remains below the NAIRU, the rate of inflation increases; when it remains above the NAIRU, the rate of inflation decreases. An economy cannot permanently lower its unemployment rate below the NAIRU without facing ever-increasing rates of inflation.

An important result of this consensus is an emerging belief about policy: the government should not push the unemployment rate below the NAIRU.

A key issue is how fast does the expectations-augmented Phillips curve shift up when the unemployment rate is below the NAIRU? The answer depends in part on the economy's recent inflationary experience: if inflation has been high and volatile, everyone will be sensitised to inflation, inflationary expectations may respond quickly, and the expectations-augmented Phillips curve shifts

quickly. The amount by which the unemployment rate must be kept above the NAIRU for one year to bring down inflation by 1 percentage point is called the **sacrifice ratio.** In 1995, the sacrifice ratio for the United States was believed to be about 2. Recent data for the United Kingdom suggests a figure of roughly 2.25.

SHIFTS IN THE NAIRU

But while the *concept* of the NAIRU is now well accepted, economists do differ in their estimates of what the critical level of unemployment is below which inflation begins. This is because the NAIRU itself may vary over time. In Britain, inflation was steady at around 3 percent per annum in the period 1992 to 1996 as unemployment fell from around 3 million to less than 2 million. It is estimated that unemployment might be able to fall as low as 1.5 million before inflation rises significantly. These estimates put the NAIRU in the range of 5.5 to 7 percent of the labour force.

Many factors affect the NAIRU. The flow of new workers into the labour force affects the amount of frictional unemployment, as young workers are more prone to changing jobs. The degree of generosity of social security provision affects the vigour with which unemployed people search for jobs. Social security has been made less generous in Britain over the last twenty years. Changes in unemployment protection laws affecting unions are likely to have reduced the ability of unemployed workers to push up wages when there is unemployment in the economy. Union membership has declined. All these factors are likely to have reduced the NAIRU.

But it is difficult to estimate with any precision the strength, durability, and impact of these trends, so considerable uncertainty remains about the value of the NAIRU.

THE LONG-RUN PHILLIPS CURVE

The relationship between unemployment and the inflation rate *in the long run* is called the long-run Phillips curve, shown in Figure 31.4. The long-run Phillips curve is vertical at the level of unemployment that we have identified as the NAIRU. An economy can-

Figure 31.4 A VERTICAL LONG-RUN PHILLIPS CURVE

Assume initially that there is no inflation and that the government decides to "buy" less unemployment by allowing increased inflation. For a short time, unemployment is reduced to U_0, but then the inflationary expectations shift the expectations-augmented Phillips curve up, so that at π_1, unemployment increases back to U^*. If the government again attempts to lower the unemployment rate below U^*, it can only do so by allowing inflation to increase further to π_2. But this raises the Phillips curve yet again. If it kept inflation fixed at π_2, unemployment would rise again to U^*. Only by allowing the inflation rate to continue to increase can an unemployment rate below U^* be sustained. The only unemployment rate that can be sustained with a fixed rate of inflation is U^*: the long-run Phillips curve is vertical.

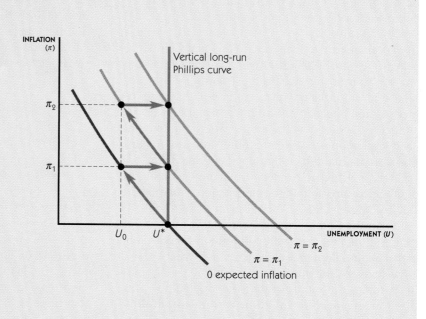

not *permanently* lower its unemployment rate below the NAIRU without facing faster and faster inflation. In cannot "buy" a lower unemployment rate by accepting just a slightly higher inflation rate. But there is still a short-term trade-off. In the short term, the economy may be able to obtain lower unemployment at the price of higher inflation.

RATIONAL EXPECTATIONS

In the previous example, the expectations-augmented Phillips curve shifts up gradually over time, as market participants experience higher inflation rates and build those expectations into their wage bargains.

INFLATION AND UNEMPLOYMENT: BASIC CONCEPTS

Phillips curve: Shows the relationship between inflation and unemployment; the lower the unemployment rate, the higher the inflation rate.

Inflation expectations-augmented Phillips curve: The level of inflation associated with any level of unemployment depends on expectations concerning inflation; the higher inflationary expectations, the higher the level of inflation associated with any level of unemployment. As inflationary expectations increase, the inflation expectations-augmented Phillips curve shifts up.

NAIRU: The NAIRU (the nonaccelerating inflation rate of unemployment) is the unemployment rate at which actual inflation equals expected inflation and both remain constant. It is positive. If the unemployment rate remains below the NAIRU, the rate of inflation will continue to accelerate. To reduce the rate of inflation requires keeping the unemployment rate below the NAIRU.

Long-run Phillips curve: The relationship between the inflation rate and unemployment in the long run, with full adjustment of inflationary expectations. It is generally believed to be vertical.

The sacrifice ratio counts the number of percentage point–years of unemployment that have to be endured in order to reduce the inflation rate by 1 percentage point. The unemployment rate and inflation rate in the United Kingdom for recent years are given here:

Year	Inflation[a]	Unemployment[b]
1988	3.3	8.7
1989	7.5	7.3
1990	7.7	7.1
1991	9.0	8.8
1992	4.1	10.1
1993	1.7	10.5
1994	2.0	9.6
1995	3.3	8.7
1996	2.9	8.2
1997	2.8	7.0
1998	2.7	6.2[c]

[a]Inflation = percentage change in RPI in January over January of preceding year.

[b]ILO standardised unemployment rates.

[c]1998 figures are authors' estimates.

Sources: Annual Abstract (1998), Table 14.8; OECD Quarterly Labour Force Statistics no. 2 (1998).

The fall in the inflation rate from 9.0 percent in 1991 to roughly 2.5 percent in January 1999 was accompanied by a period of relatively high unemployment. The NAIRU is difficult to estimate precisely, but notice that unemployment reached a minimum of 7.1 percent in 1990, and the unemployment rate in 1998 of 6.2 percent is believed to be below the sustainable rate. This suggests a NAIRU of roughly 7 percent. The cumulative excess of unemployment over 7 percent in the period 1991 to 1997 was 1.8 + 3.1 + 3.5 + 2.6 + 1.7 + 1.2 = 13.9 percentage point–years. The reduction in inflation was from 9.0 to 2.8 percent, a fall of 6.2 percentage points. The sacrifice ratio, taken as the ratio of 13.9 to 6.2 was therefore 2.25. That is to say, it took 2.25 percentage point–years of unemployment to reduce the long-run inflation rate by 1 percentage point.

This estimate has to be treated with caution, for several reasons. Firstly, it is not clear that the inflation rate in 1991 of 9.0 percent was a long-run inflation rate. Part of it may have been a temporary blip. Secondly, the estimate uses an assumed 7 percentage point NAIRU, which itself is subject to error. If either of these assumptions are varied, the estimated sacrifice ratio varies also. Finally, this estimate is based on one single deflationary episode, and it is possible that the sacrifice ratio has been different at other times. Nevertheless, this figure is of the same order of magnitude as has been found for other countries. For example, in the United States, the sacrifice ratio has been put roughly around 2.

Their expectations are assumed to *adapt* to what they actually experience.

In path-breaking work done in the 1970s that earned him the Nobel Prize in 1995, Robert Lucas suggested that the upward shift in the expectations-augmented Phillips curve could occur much more rapidly. Market participants did not have to wait until inflation actually occurred to build it into their expectations. They could *rationally anticipate* it. If, for instance, the government tried to stimulate the economy by expanding the money supply, firms and workers would rationally expect that prices would increase, and they would build that expectation into their behaviour. These expectations, based on an understanding of the structure of the economy, are referred to as **rational expectations.**

There is one very strong implication of rational expectations. Assume the government announced it was going to keep the unemployment rate below the NAIRU by expanding the money supply. Workers and firms would anticipate the increased inflation, and this would instantaneously shift up the expectations-augmented Phillips curve. Indeed, if the impact of the faster expansion of the money supply was fully anticipated, prices would rise proportionately; there would be no increase in the real money supply, and hence no effect on the level of economic activity. In this case the vertical long-run Phillips curve applies even in a relatively short time span, possibly even less than a year.

How quickly expectations adjust depends on economic circumstances. When inflation has been stable for an extended period of time, households and firms are likely to take the inflation rate as given. They will change expectations only gradually. But in economies that have experienced high and variable inflation, households and firms realise the importance of forming accurate predictions of inflation, and in that case, expectations are more likely to be highly responsive to changes in government policy.

There is one curious aspect of highly responsive expectations. While the government cannot reduce unemployment below the NAIRU without inflation's increasing very rapidly, there may also be little cost to the government's reducing the inflation rate. If firms and households believe that the government will reduce the inflation rate, inflationary expectations can be brought down almost overnight, with the consequent downward shift in the expectations-augmented Phillips curve. The trick, of course, is for the government to convince others that it will succeed in getting the inflation rate down.

It may not be easy to establish credibility, and the price may be high—running the economy at a high unemployment rate over an extended period of time. Some policymakers believe that establishing credibility requires a single-minded focus on inflation, so that everyone knows that at the first signs of incipient inflation, monetary policy will be contractionary. For some countries, the international financial institutions (the International Monetary Fund [IMF], in particular) have played a key role for countries that find themselves in financial difficulties. They often impose strong conditions for access to funds, including a firm commitment to control inflation. Investors and others, recognising how crucial such funds are for the government to continue to function, believe that such commitments have considerable credibility.

The issue of index-linked government bonds is held to increase the anti-inflationary stance of the government. The capital value of index-linked bonds goes up and down with the price level, and therefore reduces the government's incentive to create inflation. If the national debt is index linked, the government cannot reduce the real cost of refinancing it by using inflation. The British government has been issuing index-linked debt since the early 1980s, though not in large quantities. Only a small fraction of the national debt is index linked. Recently other countries have taken to issuing index-linked debt also.

INFLATION AGGREGATE DEMAND AND SUPPLY ANALYSIS

The previous section focused on the labour market—on unemployment—and described how the level of unemployment combines with inflationary expectations to determine the rate of inflation. Because wages and prices move in tandem, by studying the determinants of wage inflation, we are in fact studying the determinants of overall inflation. In this section, we take a closer look at the linkage between labour and product markets. This will enable us to see more closely the relationship between the dynamic analysis that we have just described, focusing on the rate of change of wages and price, and the static analysis of Parts Five and Six, which used the tools of the aggregate supply and demand curves.

AGGREGATE SUPPLY

We begin by focusing on the product market, on aggregate demand and supply. In earlier chapters, we described the economy's potential GDP, Y_s, the amount of output it could produce using the avail-

In recent years a number of countries, including the United Kingdom, Australia, Canada, Israel, and most recently the United States in 1996, have begun to issue index-linked bonds. In the United Kingdom they were initially issued in the early 1980s with the intention (at least in part) of providing an inflation-proof vehicle for the savings of the elderly, and they were known as "granny bonds." However, they have gained much wider acceptance, and a much bigger and more liquid market in them has developed.

Although economists believe the real long-term interest rate is the most relevant for investment decisions, calculating the real rate is somewhat difficult. The *nominal* long-term interest rate is clear. But how can we be sure about investors' inflation expectations? If the nominal interest rate rises only because of increased inflationary expectations, then the real long-term interest rate will not rise and investment will not be discouraged, at least not for that reason.

One way that the real long-term interest rate can be ascertained is for the government to issue bonds whose return is linked to the consumer price index, called indexed bonds. As the government auctioned off these bonds, the real interest rate it had to pay would provide valuable information to policymakers. Thus, a one-year indexed bond might promise to pay 3 percent real. Then, if the inflation rate turned out to be 2 percent, it would pay a total of 5 percent.

With indexed bonds, governments can figure out inflationary expectations. Assume the government can sell a £100 bond promising a real interest rate of 3 percent. That is, the buyer knows that he will get back, at the end of the year, £103 *plus* the inflation rate times £100. And assume that an ordinary one-year bond yields 5 percent. That implies that if there were no risk premium (that is, if bondholders did not have to be compensated for the uncertainty associated with the variability in real returns), investors expected inflation to be 2 percent. If the interest rate on unindexed bonds increases by 1 percent and the interest rate on indexed bonds remains unchanged, it implies that investors' expectations concerning inflation have increased by 1 percent.

Indexed bonds have a number of other important virtues. One is saving for retirement. Without indexing, a bondholder would face significant risk from increases in the inflation rate. If a bond pays 7 percent and inflation turns out to be 10 percent, the retiring individual will find himself much less well off than he thought.

Yet another advantage of indexed bonds is a likely reduction in the government's cost of borrowing. Since individuals and pension funds dislike bearing the inflation risk, they should be willing to pay extra for inflation insurance, and the government is in a better position to bear this risk than anyone else.

Figure 31.5 SHORT-RUN AGGREGATE SUPPLY CURVE

The short-run aggregate supply curve gives the level of output that will be produced at each price level, given a particular level of wages. By contrast, the long-run aggregate supply curve gives the level of output that will be produced when wages are flexible, and so labour and capital are working at what might be viewed a normal level of full capacity. Because for short periods of time, capital and labour can work more beyond this level, at high prices, short-run aggregate supply can exceed long-run aggregate supply.

The short-run aggregate supply curve has three portions: a flat portion where there is a large amount of excess capacity, a vertical portion when there is no spare capacity, and an upward-sloping portion in between.

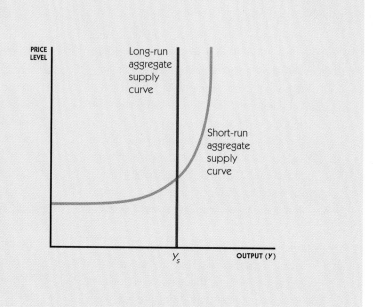

able labour supply and stock of plant and equipment. For simplicity, we assumed that labour supply was inelastic. As a result, changes in the price level did not draw more people into the labour force, and thus the economy's potential output was not sensitive to the price level.

Another way of thinking of the economy's aggregate supply is that it is the level of output that would be produced if wages and prices were perfectly flexible, so that labour was always fully employed. Because of this assumption that wages and prices can adjust fully to ensure full employment, economists sometimes call the vertical aggregate supply curve the **long-run aggregate supply curve.**[1]

Firms may not be willing to hire all the available workers if the price they receive for the goods is low *relative* to the wages they pay workers. The **short-run aggregate supply curve** assumes that wages are fixed; they do not fall to ensure that there is full employment. It asks how much are firms willing to supply at each price level? Typically, it has the shape depicted in Figure 31.5. The curve has three parts. If there is excess capacity, then there can be large increases in output with little or no increase in the price level—the horizontal portion. If the economy is using all of its resources fully, then no increase in the price level can elicit an increase in output—the vertical portion. And in between, there is an upward-sloping portion, where higher prices can coax producers to work their machines harder.

[1] Some economists think of the long-run aggregate supply curve as depicting the level that firms are willing to supply when the price level changes and wages change commensurately. Firms' demands for labour depend on the *real wage*, the wage divided by the price level. Thus, if when the price level falls, wages fall in tandem, leaving the real wage unchanged, the demand for labour will remain unchanged. The long-run aggregate supply curve is thus vertical. The position of the aggregate supply curve then depends on the *level* at which the real wage is fixed. Here, we assume that the real wage is at the level at which labour is fully employed, so the vertical long-run aggregate supply curve corresponds to the economy's potential output.

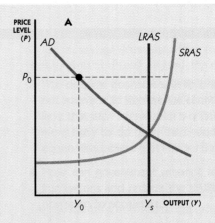

Figure 31.6 SHORT-RUN OUTPUT DETERMINATION

The graphs in panels A and B show aggregate demand (AD), long-run aggregate supply (LRAS), and short-run aggregate supply (SRAS) curves. In panel A, at P_0, aggregate demand is less than aggregate supply. Output equals Y_0. In panel B, at the current price P_1, the short-run aggregate supply exceeds the long-run aggregate supply, but aggregate demand is larger still. Output is determined by the short-run aggregate supply curve.

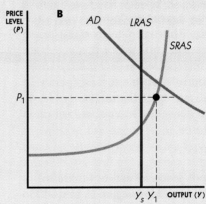

The relationship between the vertical portion of the short-run aggregate supply curve, the long-run (vertical) aggregate supply curve, and the NAIRU requires some discussion. In the short run, such as during a war, as we saw in Chapter 22, the economy can operate at more than 100 percent of capacity, as maintenance on machines is deferred. Moreover, for short periods of time workers may be induced to work overtime, and additional workers may be brought into the labour force temporarily. But it is not possible in the long run to defer maintenance or to induce workers to work, say, additional shifts. To the extent that one can work workers and machines overtime, the vertical portion of the short-run aggregate supply curve lies to the right of the long-run aggregate supply curve, as depicted in Figure 31.5. The position of the long-run aggregate supply curve represents the normal capacity of the economy. When the economy is operating beyond normal full capacity, there will be upward pressure on prices, and when it is operating below normal full capacity, there will be downward pressure on prices. Thus, the output of the long-run aggregate supply curve is that corresponding to the NAIRU; at that unemployment rate, the inflation rate is neither increasing nor decreasing.

SHORT-RUN EQUILIBRIUM

We can now see how equilibrium output *(in the short run)* depends on the price level. When the price level is very high, as in Figure 31.6A, aggregate demand is less than aggregate supply—the familiar case of Part Six. Firms only produce what they can sell. Output is equal to aggregate demand.

Figure 31.6B illustrates a case where at the current price, the short-run aggregate supply exceeds the long-run aggregate supply, but aggregate demand is larger still. Output is determined by the short-run aggregate supply curve.

The general principle here is: the short side of the market always dominates.

SHIFTS IN AGGREGATE DEMAND CURVES

We can use this framework to show the consequences of shifts in the aggregate demand curves on inflationary pressures. There are three situations. Figure 31.7A shows the aggregate demand curve initially intersecting the short-run aggregate supply curve along the horizontal portion of the aggregate supply curve. The initial price level is P_0 and the initial output is Y_0. There is large excess capacity. A rightward shift in the aggregate demand curve leads to a new equilibrium output Y_1. At Y_1, there is no ex-

cess demand for goods. There is no upward price pressure. Because there is so much excess capacity, the increase in aggregate demand has not resulted in any inflationary pressure.

Figure 31.7B shows the aggregate demand curve initially intersecting the short-run aggregate supply curve along the vertical portion of the aggregate supply curve. We assume initially the price is P_0, so again, in the initial situation, aggregate demand just equals aggregate supply. Now, however, a rightward shift in the aggregate demand curve leads to no change in aggregate output; after all, the economy is already operating at full capacity. But there is large upward pressure on prices. Inflation that starts with a rightward shift in the aggregate demand curve is referred to as **demand-pull inflation.**

Figure 31.7C shows the aggregate demand curve initially intersecting the short-run aggregate supply curve along the upward sloping portion of the aggregate supply curve. Again, we assume initially the

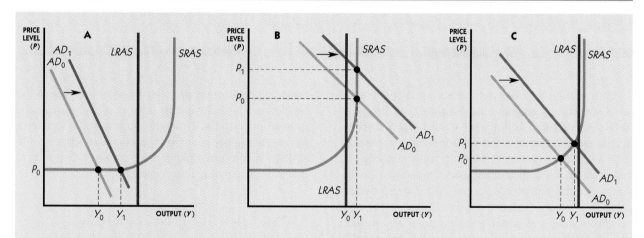

Figure 31.7 SHIFTS IN THE AGGREGATE DEMAND CURVE

The graphs in panels A, B, and C show aggregate demand (AD), long-run aggregate supply (LRAS), and short-run aggregate supply (SRAS) curves. In panel A, the initial equilibrium is along the horizontal portion of the short-run aggregate supply curve, so that rightward shifts in the aggregate demand curve lead to increased output but no upward price pressure. In panel B, the initial equilibrium is along the vertical portion of the aggregate supply curve, so

that rightward shifts in the aggregate demand curve lead to no increased output but considerable upward price pressure. In panel C, the initial equilibrium is along the upward-sloping portion of the aggregate supply curve. Rightward shifts in the aggregate demand curve lead to upward pressure on prices. If nothing else changed, eventually equilibrium would be restored with aggregate demand equaling aggregate supply at P_1 and with output higher than before.

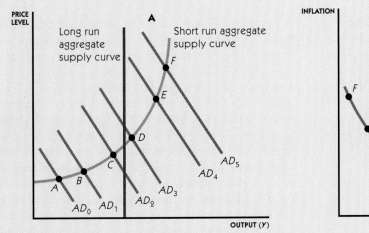

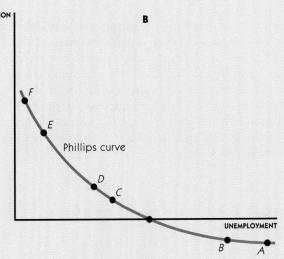

Figure 31.8 THE SHAPE OF THE PHILLIPS CURVE: TRANSLATING STATIC SHIFTS IN THE AGGREGATE DEMAND CURVE INTO MOVEMENTS ALONG THE PHILLIPS CURVE

When there is large excess capacity—when the unemployment rate is high—shifts in the aggregate demand curve result in large reductions in the unemployment rate and small increases in the inflation rate—the movement from A to B. When unemployment is very low, shifts in the aggregate demand curve result in small reductions in the unemployment rate and large increases in the inflation rate—the movement from E to F. In between, shifts in the aggregate demand curve result in moderate reductions in the unemployment rate and increases in the inflation rate—the movement from C to D.

price is P_0, where the aggregate demand equals aggregate supply. Again, a rightward shift in the aggregate demand curve gives rise to upward price pressure; but now, as the price level increases, output increases, since the aggregate supply curve (in this region) is upward sloping.

Thus, the extent to which the shift in the aggregate demand curve gets reflected in increased prices or increased output depends on the slope of the short-run aggregate supply curve: when it is hori-zontal, output increases and there is no price pressure; when it is vertical, output cannot increase but there are large upward pressures on price; and when it is upward sloping, output increases *and* there is upward price pressure. This static picture translates into the shape of the typical Phillips curve shown in Figure 31.8. When the unemployment rate is high, a given rightward shift in the aggregate demand curve (say, increasing aggregate demand at a given price level by 1 percent) results in a large re-

SHORT-RUN OUTPUT DETERMINATION

When the price level fails to adjust to equate aggregate demand and aggregate supply, the short side of the market dominates:

1 If at the given price level, aggregate demand is less than aggregate supply, the actual output will be given by aggregate demand.

2 If at the given price level, the short-run aggregate supply is less than aggregate demand, the actual output will be given by the short-run aggregate supply.

duction in the unemployment rate and very little increase in the rate of inflation (the movement from A to B); when the unemployment rate is low, a rightward shift in the aggregate demand curve by the same amount results in a small reduction in the unemployment rate and a large increase in the rate of inflation (the movement from E to F); in between, the changes in the unemployment and inflation rates are moderate (the movement from C to D).

SHIFTS IN THE AGGREGATE SUPPLY CURVE

Figure 31.9A and B shows two ways in which the short-run aggregate supply curve may shift. The curve may shift downward and to the right because of an increase in capacity (say, because of additional investment) or a decrease in costs (say, a fall in the

price of oil). This is shown in panel A. The result is that at the initial price level, there is downward price pressure. Panel B shows the short-run aggregate supply curve's shifting in the opposite manner, upwards and to the left. This may be caused by an increase in costs, such as occurred in the 1970s when oil prices rose dramatically. The result is upward price pressure at the initial price level, leading to inflation. Inflation that arises from this type of shift in the aggregate supply curve is called **cost-push inflation.**

A good example is provided by the experience of the United States in the early 1970s. In 1973, OPEC, consisting mainly of nations in the Middle East, decided to impose an embargo on the shipment of oil to certain Western nations, including the United States. Even after the embargo was lifted, OPEC restricted oil production, so that the price of oil rose dramatically. For the U.S. economy as a whole, the higher oil prices raised costs of production. The short-run aggregate supply curve shifted upwards

Figure 31.9 SHIFTS IN THE SHORT-RUN AGGREGATE SUPPLY CURVE

The short-run aggregate supply curve may shift downwards and to the right, due to increases in capacity or decreases in costs, or upwards and to the left, due to decreases in capacity or increases in costs. Panel A shows the shift downwards and to the right from AS_0 to AS_1, resulting in downward pressure at the original price level. As prices fall, output will increase. Panel B shows the shift upwards and to the left from AS_0 to AS_1, resulting in upward price pressure at the original price level.

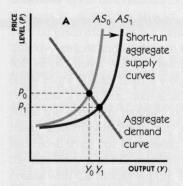

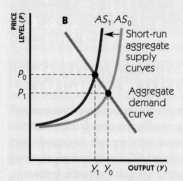

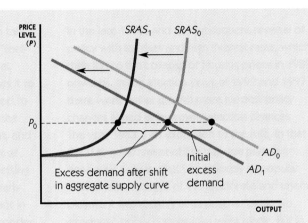

Figure 31.10 THE OIL PRICE SHOCK AND THE END OF THE VIETNAM WAR

The end of the Vietnam War shifted the aggregate demand curve to the left, from AD_0 to AD_1. If nothing else had happened, this would have put downward pressure on prices. But at the same time, the oil price shock shifted the short-run aggregate supply curve up, from $SRAS_0$ to $SRAS_1$. At the old price P_0, output was reduced, while upward price pressure persisted.

and to the left, resulting in inflationary pressures.

The timing could not have been worse. The increased government expenditure to finance the Vietnam War ignited inflation. As the Vietnam War wound down, reduced government expenditures would have led to a leftward shift in the aggregate demand curve, resulting in downward price pressure. But the upward shift in the short-run aggregate supply curve more than offset this effect, and the economy had **stagflation:** inflation went up as unemployment went up. This is illustrated in Figure 31.10. The inflationary episode that had begun with a rightward shift in the aggregate demand curve as a result of the Vietnam War was carried forwards with an upward shift in the aggregate supply curve as a result of the oil embargo.

This analysis could equally well be applied to Britain at the same time. The Barber boom, the result of a very expansionary fiscal policy in 1972,

caused demand to increase dramatically in 1972 and 1973. This was met by a leftward shift of the aggregate supply curve as the OPEC oil price hit, and there was also a rapid increase in wages.

INFLATION INERTIA

Earlier in the chapter, we described how if the unemployment rate remains at the NAIRU level, inflation will simply continue at a given rate. This tendency of inflation to persist is referred to as **inflation inertia.** Inflation inertia occurs because higher wages lead to higher prices (and expectations of higher prices), which in turn lead to higher wages. At the higher prices, firms are willing to pay and workers demand

SHORT-RUN AGGREGATE SUPPLY

The short-run aggregate supply curve has three portions: a vertical segment, where the economy is operating at full capacity; a horizontal segment, along which output can be increased with little or no increase in the price level; and an upward-sloping portion joining the two.

Shifts in the aggregate supply curve can either increase capacity, shifting the curve to the right, or decrease the price at which firms are willing to supply any level of output, shifting the curve downwards.

higher wages. And at higher wages, customers are willing to pay and firms demand higher prices.

It makes little difference how inflation is started, whether through a shift in the aggregate demand curve that gives rise to demand-pull inflation or through a shift in the aggregate supply curve that gives rise to cost-push inflation. Once started, wage increases give rise to price increases which give rise to further wage increases, in a seemingly never-ending cycle.

Expectations help to maintain inflation inertia. Workers base their demands for wage increases on their *expectations* of price increases; and firms may set their prices based on *expectations* of increases in wages and other costs.

When inflation inertia is strong, it can take long periods of unemployment to bring inflation down. With high unemployment, workers' moderate wage demands; lower wage demands translate into slower rates of increase in prices; as workers gradually realise that inflation is slowing down, this reinforces the moderation of their wage demands.

Sometimes, however, inflation can be stopped quickly, by reversing expectations. If the government puts into place policies that are thought to be effective in reducing inflation, then, for instance, workers may moderate their wage demands and firms will not be willing to grant increased wages since they do not anticipate that they will be able to get higher prices for the products they sell.

MONETARY POLICY

Inflation is the continual increase in money prices, year after year: it takes more money to buy a Coke or rent a house as time goes by. Thus, inflation is often viewed as essentially a monetary phenomenon. And in Part Five, where prices were perfectly flexible, we saw that this was the case. Increases in the money supply translated into increases in the price level, with no real effect on the economy. On the other hand, in Part Six, where prices were perfectly rigid, by assumption monetary policy did not have an *immediate* effect on inflation, but it did have an effect on output. In this part, which bridges the discussion

between perfectly flexible and perfectly rigid prices, we will see that in general monetary policy has an effect both on output and inflation.

Figure 31.11A shows that an increase in the money supply shifts the aggregate demand curve to the right. Assume that initially aggregate demand equaled (both short-run and long-run) aggregate supply and that initially there was no inflation. The shift in the aggregate demand curve leads at the current price level to upward price pressure, and as we have seen, this upward price pressure gradually translates into higher prices. With higher prices, output increases along the short-run aggregate supply curve. As output increases, so does employment. Panel B shows that the unemployment rate falls below the NAIRU, and as a result, inflation sets in. Thus, an increase in the money supply can begin an inflationary episode.

Excessively expansionary monetary policy, like a large increase in government expenditures or a large decrease in taxes, can generate demand-pull inflation. As we saw in the last section, once initiated—from any source—inflation inertia, with price increases' leading to wage increases and expectations of further price increases' leading to still further price increases, can keep inflation going.

MONETARY POLICY AND SUSTAINING INFLATION INERTIA

Monetary policy may also play a role in sustaining inflation inertia. If the money supply is allowed to increase in tandem with prices, inflation can persist. However, with restrictive policies, inflation can be reduced.

Whether monetary policy is being restrictive depends to a large extent on the rate of increase in the money supply. In Chapter 29, we saw that normally the demand for money (at any interest rate) increases with *nominal* income. If the economy's real growth is, say, 2 percent, and prices are increasing at 3 percent, then if the money supply is increased at the rate of 5 percent per year, the increased supply of money will just equal the increased demand at an

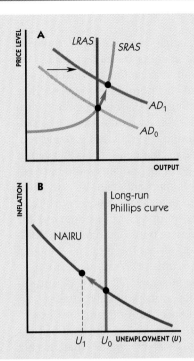

Figure 33.11 EXCESSIVELY EXPANSIONARY MONETARY POLICY SETS OFF INFLATION

Increasing the money supply shifts the aggregate demand curve to the right (panel A). There is upward price pressure. As prices rise, output increases along the short-run aggregate supply curve. As output increases, so does employment. In panel B the unemployment rate falls below the NAIRU, and as a result inflation accelerates.

unchanged interest rate. If the money supply increases less rapidly, interest rates must rise for demand to equal supply, reducing investment. The aggregate demand curve shifts to the left and inflationary pressures are reduced.

EXPECTATIONS AND FOREIGN EXCHANGE RATES

In Chapter 29, we saw that there were two channels through which monetary policy affected the economy: it affected interest rates, and thus investment, and in an open economy, it affected exchange rates, and thus net exports. In our earlier analysis, we noted that a decrease in the interest rate makes financial investment in the country less attractive, decreasing the demand for its currency and thereby decreasing the exchange rate. The lower exchange rate makes the country's goods more attractive abroad—increasing exports—and makes other countries' goods more expensive—decreasing imports. The result is an increase in net exports, shifting the aggregate demand curve to the right. The same logic applies to a restrictive monetary policy. Higher interest rates lead to a higher exchange rate and a decrease in net exports, shifting the aggregate demand curve to the left.

This analysis ignores one critical ingredient in the

INFLATION INERTIA

Inflation once started perpetuates itself:
   Increases in prices lead to increases in wages, which in turn lead to further increases in prices.
   Expectations of inflation get built into wage formation.

Monetary policy can dampen or accelerate inflation.

determination of exchange rates, a wild card which makes predicting the effect of monetary policy on exchange rates difficult: expectations. If investors in Britain hold yen, and the pound *depreciates,* they make a capital gain. Consider Jack who spent £1,000 to buy yen in August 1998, when the exchange rate was 230 yen to the pound. He received 230,000 yen. Four months later, the exchange rate was 200 yen to the pound. If he cashed in his yen, he would have received £1,150 for a 15 percent gain in only four months. If investors expect the pound to depreciate, they buy yen and sell pounds, so the demand for pounds decreases. Hence, the exchange rate falls—confirming their expectations. It is easy to see how a spiral of decreasing exchange rates can emerge, as—at least up to a point—each fall of the pound reinforces beliefs that the pound will fall further.

How investors and speculators form their expectations—and how monetary policy affects those expectations—is a complicated matter that is not completely understood. But inflationary expectations are an important determinant. If the United Kingdom's price level is expected to rise faster than Japan's price level, investors will believe that *in the long run* the pound must decline in value relative to the yen.

Expectations reinforce the dampening effect of tighter monetary policy when tighter monetary policy leads to an appreciation of the pound because of its effects on inflationary expectations: if investors believe that the monetary authorities are taking actions to dampen the economy—and hence reduce inflation—they will expect the pound to increase in value relative to the yen (compared to what it otherwise would have been), and this expectation of an increased value leads to higher demand for pounds today—and a higher exchange rate. The higher exchange rate makes imports more attractive to residents of Britain, while Japanese consumers find British goods more expensive, and so the United Kingdom will export less.

CAUSES OF WAGE AND PRICE RIGIDITIES

In this chapter and the chapters of Part Six, we have moved well beyond the picture of the economy offered by the full-employment model with perfectly flexible prices and wages. In that model, there is no involuntary unemployment, and while inflation may occur (whenever the money supply increases), it has no consequences. But in the real world there *is* unemployment, and inflation *is* a concern. And wages and prices are clearly not perfectly flexible. But neither, of course, are they perfectly fixed, as assumed in Part Six. They adjust, but only slowly. We have *described* in this chapter how wages and prices adjust—how, for instance, wages increase faster the lower the unemployment rate. These empirical regularities make sense; after all, the tighter the labour market, the more likely employers will be scrambling to hire workers and the more wages will rise.

But to economic theorists, these explanations are not fully satisfactory. Why don't wages and prices adjust faster than they do? If they did, unemployment might not be able to persist as long. Economists have identified three key reasons why wages and prices adjust slowly—adjustment costs, risk and imperfect information, and imperfect competition that gives rise to kinked demand and labour supply curves.[2]

ADJUSTMENT COSTS

The first explanation for price rigidities emphasises the costs of changing prices. When firms change their prices, they must print new menus and price lists or otherwise convey the change in prices to their customers. Changing prices costs money, and these costs are referred to as **menu costs.** Menu costs may be large, but advocates of the menu cost explanation of price rigidities, who include Gregory Mankiw of Harvard University and George Akerlof and Janet Yellen of the University of California at Berkeley, point out that even small costs can have big effects.

Let's use an analogy from physics. A ball rolling on a frictionless plane will roll on forever. Just as a

---

[2] In some cases, these explanations seem to explain too much; they suggest that under some circumstances, prices and wages will not adjust at all to, say, small changes in demand or costs. But the economy consists of many firms in different circumstances. Some may be in a situation where they do not respond at all, while others may respond fully. The *average* for the economy will reflect a *slow* response.

In the next chapter, we consider a set of explanations that pertain particularly to the labour market.

Figure 31.12 ADJUSTMENT COSTS

Shifts in the demand curve facing a firm necessitate adjustments in either the price charged or the quantity produced. How the firm adjusts depends in part on the costs of adjusting each and the risks associated with each. If the costs or risks of adjusting prices are high and of adjusting quantities are low, then the firm will leave price unchanged and lower quantity: there will be price rigidity.

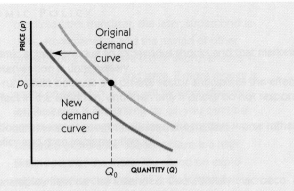

small amount of friction has a big effect on how the ball behaves—it eventually will stop—so too if each firm in the economy is slow to adjust its prices because of menu costs, even if these costs are small, the cumulative effects could still be significant. There could be powerful aggregate price rigidities.

When firms face a shift in the demand curves for their products, as in Figure 31.12, they must choose whether to adjust quantities or prices. While there are costs of adjusting either quantities or prices, the costs of adjusting quantities are almost always much greater. Facing such choices, firms will adjust prices rather than quantities. Accordingly, *in most instances the direct costs of making adjustments do not provide a convincing explanation of price rigidities.*

RISK AND IMPERFECT INFORMATION

Risk and imperfect information provide important reasons for price and wage rigidities. There is a great deal of uncertainty about the consequences of these changes. When a firm lowers its price, whether sales increase depends on how other firms in the industry respond and how its customers respond. If rivals respond by lowering their prices, the firm may fail to gain market share, and its profits simply plummet with the decline in prices. If rivals fail to respond, the

firm may gain a competitive advantage. Customers may think that this is just the first of several price decreases and decide to postpone purchases until prices get still lower; thus a decrease in price may even result in reduced sales. Similarly, the consequences of a firm's lowering its wages depend on how its workers and rival firms respond. Other firms might leave wages unchanged and use the opportunity to try to recruit the firm's best employees. Alternatively, they might respond by lowering wages in a corresponding manner. In one case profits would rise; in the other, they would fall.

The uncertainty associated with wage and price changes is often much greater than that associated with changing output and employment. When a firm cuts back on its production, provided it does not cut back too drastically, its only risk is that its inventories will be depleted below normal levels, in which case it simply increases production next period to replace the lost inventories. If production costs do not change much over time, there is accordingly little extra risk to cutting back production. Similarly, there is little risk to a firm's decreasing its employment simply by not hiring new workers as older workers leave or retire— much less risk than associated with lowering wages.

Since firms like to avoid risks, they try to avoid making large changes to prices and wages; they would rather accept somewhat larger changes in quantities—in the amount produced or in the hours worked. As a result wages and prices are sticky.

KINKED DEMAND CURVES

A third group of explanations attribute price rigidities to the shape of demand curves facing firms under imperfect competition. Recall that with perfect competition, a firm faces a horizontal demand curve. With imperfect competition, a firm faces a downward-sloping demand curve; in particular, the demand curve may have a kink, as illustrated in Figure 31.13. The kink means that firms lose many more sales when they raise prices above p_0 than they gain when they lower prices below p_0.

There are two reasons why the demand curve may be kinked, that is, why there are very different responses to price increases and price decreases. First, companies believe that if they raise their prices, their own customers will immediately know it and will start searching for stores selling the good at a lower price. But if they lower their prices without heavy expenditures on advertising, customers at other stores may not find out about their lower prices, so they gain few new customers.

Second, firms worry that if they raise their prices, their rivals will not match the increase, and hence they will lose customers from their relatively uncompetitive prices. But if they lower their prices, rivals will view this as a threat and will match the decrease, and the firm will gain little from its attempt to beat the market.

Kinked demand curves have one dramatic impli-cation: small changes in marginal costs may have no effect on the price firms charge. Even if the company's costs go down, it will continue to charge the price at the kink, p_0 in Figure 31.13. Firms worry, for instance, that if they cut their price in response to the lower marginal cost, other firms will simply match them and they will be no better off. Thus, kinked demand curves give rise to price rigidities: small changes, such as those resulting from a fall in wages, have no effect on either the output or pricing decisions of the firm.

A similar analysis applies to labour, in markets where firms have to pay higher wages to obtain more workers with the skills they require. There may be *different* responses to a firm's lowering its wages and increasing its wages. If a firm raises wages, rival firms may match its wages, because they worry that unless they do so, they will lose their best workers; if a firm lowers wages, the rival firms may fail to respond, taking advantage of their more competitive wages to attract the best workers. Thus, even if the value of the marginal product of a worker increases—either because the price of the goods that a firm sells has increased or because a change in technology has increased workers' productivity—firms may not raise the wage to attract additional workers, since, given the response of rivals, they would obtain few additional workers in spite of raising the wage significantly. Because the benefits of raising wages are less than the costs, the firm leaves its wage unchanged. There is a form of wage rigidity.

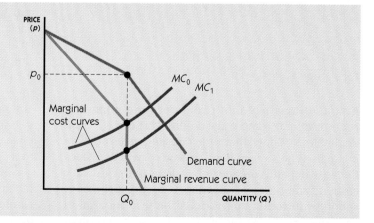

Figure 31.13 KINKED DEMAND CURVES AND PRICE INFLEXIBILITY

If firms lose many more sales from price increases than they gain from price decreases, their demand curve will be kinked. When the demand curve is kinked, the marginal revenue curve has a vertical section, since the extra revenue from price decreases is less than the lost revenue from price increases, and small changes in marginal cost will not lead to any change in price or output.

SOURCES OF WAGE AND PRICE STICKINESS

Adjustment costs

Risks associated with wage and price adjustments

Imperfect competition with kinked demand or labour supply curves

REVIEW AND PRACTICE

SUMMARY

1 *Other things equal*, lower levels of inflation are associated with higher levels of unemployment. This relationship is called the Phillips curve.

2 The level of inflation associated with any particular level of unemployment will increase as expectations of inflation increase. As a result, if the government tries to maintain the unemployment rate at a very low rate, the inflation rate will continually increase, as each increase in inflation is built into individuals' expectations. The Phillips curve which reflects the effects of inflationary expectations is called the expectations-augmented Phillips curve.

3 The unemployment rate at which the inflation rate is stable—at which actual inflation is equal to expected inflation—is called the NAIRU, the nonaccelerating inflation rate of unemployment.

4 The NAIRU can change because of changes in the structure of the labour force, increasing competition in labour and product markets which puts downward pressures on wages and prices, and government policies aimed at facilitating worker mobility.

5 With rational expectations, changes in policy can be reflected directly into inflationary expectations; the expectations-augmented Phillips curve can shift up immediately, without waiting for inflation actually to occur. By contrast, with adaptive expectations, the expectations-augmented Phillips curve only shifts up in response to recently realised inflationary experiences. With rational expectations, the trade-off between inflation and unemployment may be particularly unfavourable. There may be large increases in

inflation with little or no reductions in unemployment, in response to government *attempts* to lower the unemployment rate, for instance, through more expansionary monetary policy.

6 The short-run aggregate supply curve gives the amount that firms are willing to supply at each price level (given current wages). It has three portions: a horizontal portion (reflecting a price below which it is unprofitable to produce), a vertical portion (representing the full capacity of the economy), and an upward-sloping portion. When the economy operates along the horizontal portion, there is excess capacity.

7 When at the current price level, aggregate demand is greater than aggregate supply, there is upward pressure on prices. But wages and prices do not adjust instantaneously to clear labour and product markets. The rate of change in prices or wages is related to the magnitude of the gap.

8 There is considerable inflation inertia. Once started, inflation can persist as increases in wages lead to increased prices, and increases in prices lead to increased wages.

9 Monetary policy may allow the money supply to increase in tandem with prices, and thus help perpetuate inflation; or, by restricting the rate of increase of the money supply, it may dampen inflation.

10 Prices and wages may be slow to adjust for three reasons. Firms may face large costs of adjustments. Firms may adjust output and employment rather than prices because the uncertainties associated with changing prices may be greater. And firms may face kinked demand and labour supply curves, and with these kinks, they may not change prices even when marginal cost changes, or they may not change wages even when the demand for their goods (the price they receive) changes.

KEY TERMS

indexing

inflation tax

Phillips curve

expectations-augmented
Phillips curve

natural rate of
unemployment

nonaccelerating inflation
rate of unemployment

rational expectations

long-run aggregate
supply curve

short-run aggregate
supply curve

demand-pull inflation

cost-push inflation

menu costs

REVIEW QUESTIONS

1 Why is there a trade-off between inflation and unemployment in the short run?

2 What role do changes in expectations play in shifting the Phillips curve? What difference does it make whether expectations are adaptive or rational?

3 What is the NAIRU? Why, if unemployment is kept below the NAIRU, will the rate of inflation accelerate? Why might the long-run Phillips curve be vertical?

4 What factors affect the NAIRU?

5 What is the shape of the typical short-run aggregate supply curve?

6 What is the relationship between the dynamic analysis of the Phillips curve, and the static analysis of aggregate demand and supply curves?

7 What is inflation inertia? What factors contribute to its existence?

8 How does monetary policy affect inflation? What difference does it make whether there are rational expectations? Whether the economy is open?

9 What are some explanations for wage and price rigidities?

PROBLEMS

1 Why might the inflation effect of a one-time increase in a tax rate on final goods be different from other events that might start an inflationary spiral?

2 The sacrifice ratio measures the number of unemployment years required to bring down inflation by 1 percent. Thus, if the sacrifice ratio is 0.5, then one can bring down the unemployment rate by 1 percent either by increasing the unemployment rate by 0.25 percent for two years or by increasing the unemployment rate by 0.5 for one year or by 1 percent for a half year. If the sacrifice ratio is 1, then how long will it take to bring down the inflation rate by 2 percent?

3 Assume the government maintained the unemployment rate above the NAIRU by 1 percent for 2 years and the inflation rate increased by 1 percentage point, from 3 to 4 percent. Assume the costs of bringing down inflation are identical to the benefits (lower unemployment) associated with the increase in inflation. What must the government do to decrease the inflation rate to its original level? What is the sacrifice ratio?

4 If you were in the position of the governor of the Bank of England, with unemployment's falling towards 1.3 million and other indicators' suggesting the economy had relatively little excess capacity but no strong signs of incipient inflation, would you have argued that interest rates should be raised? Why or why not?

5 "If expectations adjust quickly to changes in economic circumstances, including changes in economic policy, then it is easy to start an inflationary episode. But under the same conditions, it is also easy to stop inflation." Discuss. If true, what implications might this finding have for economic policy?

6 Use aggregate supply and demand curves to explain whether (and when) the following events might trigger inflation:
   (a) An increase in business confidence
   (b) An increase in the Central Bank's base rate
   (c) The development of important new technologies
   (d) An increase in the price of imports
   (e) An increase in government spending

7 What would be the effect on the Phillips curve of an announcement that OPEC—the cartel of oil-producing countries—had fallen apart, and thus the price of oil was expected to fall dramatically?

8 While playing around with old economic data in your spare time, you find that on a number of occasions during the 1960s and 1970s, inflation and unemployment increased simultaneously. Does this evidence necessarily imply anything about the shape of the short-run or long-run Phillips curve? How might you interpret these data?

32

UNEMPLOYMENT: UNDERSTANDING WAGE RIGIDITIES

High and rising unemployment figures, announcements that firms are making people redundant, and large numbers of applicants for the few vacancies that exist are symptoms of recession. The economy loses output because productive resources are not fully utilised, firms' profits are reduced, and unemployed workers suffer economic hardships. But before recommending policies to reduce unemployment, it is necessary to understand its causes.

Although unemployment represents a situation where the supply of labour exceeds its demand, the macroeconomics of unemployment in Part Six looked at the product rather than the labour market. The reason is simple. Variations in output underlie most variations in employment. And variations in aggregate demand underlie most variations in output. Still, one important fact remains, which we emphasised in Chapter 23. No matter what the source of variation in the aggregate demand for labour, if real wages adjusted, full employment could be sustained. Unemployment is fundamentally a labour market phenomenon. It reflects a failure of real wages to adjust to changes in economic circumstances. The last chapter gave several reasons why wages and prices maybe sticky. This chapter focuses on special features of the labour market that may contribute to rigidities in wages, particularly in *real wages*.

KEY QUESTIONS

1 Why may wages not fall even when there is excess supply of labour?

2 Which policies may reduce either the extent of unemployment or the costs borne by those who are thrown out of work?

3 What are some of the problems facing the unemployment insurance system?

THE WAGE-EMPLOYMENT PUZZLE

It is difficult to reconcile observed changes in employment (or unemployment) and wages with the basic competitive model. If we applied the basic model to the labour market, we would predict that when the demand for labour goes down, as in a recession, the real wage also falls, as illustrated in Figure 32.1. A leftward shift in the demand for labour results in lower wages. If the supply of labour is unresponsive to wage changes (that is, the labour supply curve is inelastic), as depicted by the steepness of the line in Figure 32.1, the reduction in the real wage is large.

In the real world it doesn't seem to happen this way. In the 1920s and 1930s, despite very high unemployment and falling prices, real wage rates continued to rise. The cost of living index was 175 in 1924 and fell to 157 in 1930 and to 140 in 1933. (The index takes 1914 as a base year and so is 100 in that year.) The index of money wages (again taking 1914 as the base year) stood at 194 in 1924 and 191 in 1930 and fell to 183 by 1933. As a result, the index of real wages rose from 111 in 1924 to 122 in 1930 and to 131 in 1933, a rise of just under 20 percent over the 13-year period (Mitchell, *British Historical Statistics*, "Labour Force 21 Part C").

Figure 32.2 shows the real wage and unemployment rates during the 1980s. Real wages have not been much affected by changes in unemployment. In

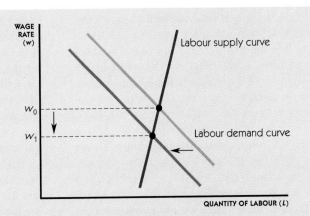

Figure 32.1 CHANGES IN THE DEMAND FOR LABOUR AND REAL WAGES

Traditional theory predicts that when the demand curve for labour shifts to the left, real wages fall.

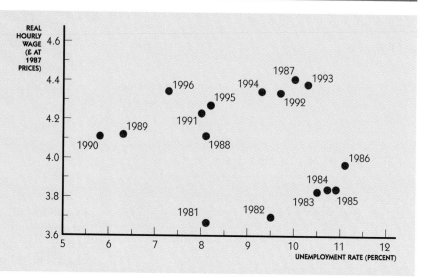

Figure 32.2 REAL WAGES AND UNEMPLOYMENT IN THE UNITED KINGDOM, 1981–1996

The figure plots the average hourly wage rates of full-time male manual workers in all industries in the United Kingdom. The unemployment rate is the overall unemployment rate for the United Kingdom. There has been no tendency for real wages to fall when unemployment was high. If anything the reverse appears to have been true. Real wages rose more strongly when unemployment was at its height. *Source:* Central Statistical Office, *Annual Abstract of Statistics* (1988, 1992, 1994, 1998).

fact, real wages rose strongly in the mid-1980s despite high unemployment. There are three possible explanations. The first is that the supply curve for labour is horizontal and the demand curve for labour has shifted, as shown in Figure 32.3A. In this case, the labour market has moved along the labour supply curve to a new point of equilibrium. Almost all economists reject this interpretation, because of the huge amount of evidence suggesting that the labour supply curve is relatively inelastic (steep), not flat.

The second possible interpretation is that there are shifts in the labour supply curve that just offset the shifts in the labour demand curve, as depicted in Figure 32.3B. The shifting demand and supply curves trace out a pattern of changing employment with little change in the real wage. Again, the labour market winds up at an equilibrium point. The reduced employment in the Great Depression was, in this view, due to a decreased willingness to supply labour—in other words, an increased desire for leisure. As we learned in Chapter 25, there have been marked changes in the supply of labour. But most economists do not see any persuasive evidence that the supply curve for labour shifts much as the economy goes into or comes out of a recession, let alone to the ex-

tent required in Figure 32.3B. And they see no reason why shifts in the demand curve for labour would normally be offset by shifts in the supply curve.

The third interpretation is that there has been a shift in the demand curve for labour, with no matching shift in the supply curve *and no corresponding change in the real wage*, as depicted in Figure 32.3C. The labour market is stuck in disequilibrium. At the wage w_0/P, the amount of labour that workers would like to supply remains at L_0. But as the demand for labour shifts, the number of workers hired at w_0/P falls from L_0 to L_1. The difference, $L_0 - L_1$, is the level of unemployment. If the wage does not fall, most economists—and virtually all of the general public— would say the unemployment is involuntary. People are willing to work *at the going wage,* but the work is not there. The same argument holds even if there is a slight shift in the labour supply curve and a slight change in the wage. The adjustment in the wage is too small to align demand with supply.

The question posed by panel c is fundamental to macroeconomics. How do we explain the apparent fact that wages do not fall in the face of a shift in the demand curve for labour? Reasons abound, as we will see in the following sections.

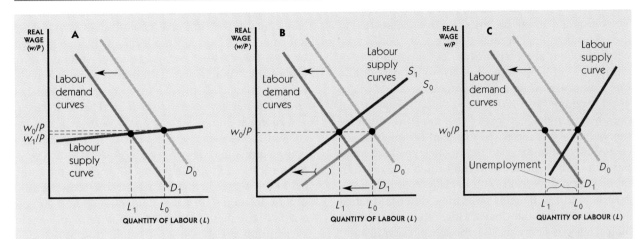

Figure 32.3 WHY WAGES DO NOT FALL WHEN DEMAND SHIFTS

Panel A shows a very elastic labour supply curve. A leftward shift in demand for labour from D_0 to D_1 will decrease employment without affecting wages. Panel B shows a shift in both supply and demand curves. Although the shift in demand for labour from D_0 to D_1 would reduce wages by itself, it is offset by a shift in the supply of labour from S_0 to S_1, leaving the wage level unchanged. In panel C, the demand for labour shifts from D_0 to D_1, but wages do not fall for some reason. Involuntary unemployment results.

EXPLANATIONS OF WAGE RIGIDITIES

Why don't wages fall enough to eliminate unemployment quickly? We looked at several explanations in the previous chapter. Two possibilities are important for the current discussion. First, firms may not be allowed to lower wages, because of union pressure or government legislation. Second, the efficient wage for the firm (i.e., the wage at which profits are maximised) may be at the current wage level. It may not pay the firm to reduce wage levels, even if the supply curve for labour changes. The reasons for wage stickiness may vary from industry to industry and may overlap.

UNIONS, CONTRACTS, AND GOVERNMENT REGULATIONS

One reason real wages may not decline as employment declines is that contracts and regulations are in place that keep them from doing so. In effect, there are wage floors, like the price floors we encountered in Chapter 5. The most conspicuous examples are trade union wage agreements.

TRADE UNIONS

The labour market in Britain has been dominated by trade unions. At their peak in the late 1970s, about 14 million people, over half the labour force, were members. Although membership fell substantially in the 1980s, it still stood at just below 9 million in 1998. The influence of unions spreads more widely than to the membership, because, in many workplaces where unions are responsible for bargaining with employers, not all employees are members, only a majority of them. As a result, many people's wages are determined by unions, even though they are not members. Union "coverage," as it is called, the fraction of the labour force whose pay and conditions are covered by union bargaining, has been as high as 80 percent of the workforce in the United Kingdom. In other European countries, especially in Scandinavia, Austria, and the Benelux countries, union influence is greater than in the United Kingdom. In the United States, it is considerably less, though still significant.

In Britain, unions have been particularly powerful in the public sector and in heavy industry. Coal, steel, and the railways were always bastions of trade unions. Unions have also been important in the electric power industry, shipbuilding, engineering, work at the docks, teaching, the post office, and the health service.

Unions bargain with employers over wages, principally, but also over other aspects of work, and in Britain agreements have generally been expected to last for a year. There is a well-defined "wage round" starting in the autumn of each year in which successive industries bargain over wages for the coming year.

Unions help to cause wage rigidities in a number of ways. One is that the existence of a union wage bargain prevents wages from adjusting to shifts in the supply of or demand for labour during the 12 months after the agreement is reached. A fall in labour demand in that period will lead to firstly, a cut in hiring new staff and the nonreplacement of workers who leave the firm, which allows employment to fall by "natural wastage," or attrition; secondly, a reduction in overtime hours and possibly the introduction of short-time working; and thirdly, redundancies, when some workers are dismissed (on grounds of being no longer needed, or redundant). Very often firms offer a payment to workers who are willing to accept voluntary redundancy. In the last resort, firms simply dismiss workers; that is to say, they make them compulsorily redundant.

Secondly, unions may be able to bargain for a wage that is above the level that would match labour demand with supply. Employers may find it less

costly to pay a higher wage than to fight through a long negotiation or sit out a strike, and have to work subsequently with difficult relations between workers and managers. British management has often been blamed for its weak response to the unions. Mrs. (now Lady) Thatcher made it one of her missions to restore management to the managers. (And, of course, to a large extent, she achieved her objective.)

Union bargaining, at least in the short run, has insulated the existing workers of the firm against the competition offered by the unemployed who are looking for jobs and may be willing to work for the same or lower wages. Unemployment has only caused unions to moderate wage demands when it threatened to engulf the currently employed workers in large numbers, as it did in 1981 and 1982. Otherwise, those covered by union contracts remained more or less immune to the dole queues, as Figure 32.3 shows.

In the long run, unions that maintain high wages may find that employment in the firm or industry falls and may eventually disappear. The demise of the British shipbuilding industry was hastened by high wages imposed by unions. The coal mining industry is another casualty of several unfavourable circumstances, among them high wages. Cheaper imported coal and other fuels for electricity generation have reduced the demand for deep-mined coal from Britain. The National Union of Mineworkers has virtually disappeared.

It may be a rational response to a declining industry for the workers in it to bargain for a wage that is high enough to make employment fall, so long as it falls slowly enough for natural wastage to take care of the necessary job losses.

A third reason why union bargaining slows down wage adjustment to unemployment is that unions seem to be very concerned about relative wages. No union likes to accept a lower wage increase than has been accepted in recent past settlements because that means a fall in the relative pay of its members. If the Ford workers get 5 percent, then the workers in the other car firms will want at least 5 percent. And if they get 5 percent, workers in other engineering industries and in the public sector unions will strengthen their resistance to settlements less than 5 percent. A so-called going rate of pay increase is quickly established. This behaviour by unions reduces the responsiveness of wage rates to variations

UNIONS

May reduce employment in unionised sectors.	Do not cover enough of the labour force to explain fully unemployment trends.
May slow down real wage adjustment, thus contributing to cyclical unemployment.	

in labour market conditions across geographical regions and across industries, and it slows down the response over time to a fall in labour demand relative to the supply. By doing this, it tends to worsen the problem of unemployment following a fall in the demand for labour.

Unions are not a complete explanation for rigid wages and unemployment. Their high visibility may attract more attention to them than they are due. They have played a role, however, which may be diminishing in the face of the recently introduced laws to restrict their powers, and falling membership and coverage.

IMPLICIT CONTRACT THEORY

Wage rigidities may come about even in the absence of a union or an explicit labour contract. This is because the relations between an employer and her employees are governed by a host of implicit understandings developed over time between the firm and its workers. These implicit understandings are referred to as an **implicit contract.**

Workers are generally risk averse. Many have fixed financial commitments like monthly rent, mortgage, or car payments. They do not want their wages to fluctuate with every change in the demand and supply of labour. Firms can bear these market fluctuations more easily. First, the owners of firms tend to be wealthier, with a larger cushion for adjusting to variations in income. Second, in the event of a temporary shortfall of funds, companies can borrow more easily than can most workers.

Given that firms are less vulnerable to economic fluctuations than individual workers, it pays companies to provide at least some indirect insurance to their workers. Workers will be willing to work for a dependable firm that pays a steady wage, even if that wage is lower on average than the highly varying wages they could get elsewhere. Such a firm provides a form of insurance to its workers through an implicit contract—an understanding that the wages will not vary with the month-to-month, or even year-to-year, variations in the labour market. That is, the firm behaves as *if* it had a contract with its workers guaranteeing the wage. It is called an implicit contract because it is an understanding, not a formal or explicit contract. In these circumstances, the wage workers receive can be thought of as consisting of two parts: the market wage (the wage the worker could receive elsewhere) plus an adjustment for the implicit insurance component. When the market wage is relatively low, the wage received by the worker may be higher than the market wage. The worker is receiving a benefit on the implicit insurance policy. When the market wage is high, the wage received by the worker may be lower than the market wage. The difference is the premium the worker pays for wage stability.

For many industries in which long-term employment relations are common, implicit contract theory provides a convincing explanation of why wages do not vary much. But it does not explain layoffs. The risk of most concern to workers is the complete cessation of their income. Thus, implicit contract theory seems to predict that rather than laying people off, firms will engage in **work sharing;** they will reduce the hours each person works. In Britain this is called "short-time working." It is used to a small extent. Most adjustments occur through layoffs and redundancies.

Proponents of the implicit contract theory try to explain layoffs in two ways. Both explanations are ultimately unsatisfactory. The first focuses on the fixed costs of employment and the idea that productivity shrinks more than proportionately with changes in the length of the workday. If a worker needs the first half-hour to settle into work, the last half-hour to get ready to leave, and a one-hour lunch break, then a six-hour day will lose the same two hours as an eight-hour day. So a firm seeking to cut its labour bill by 25 percent, by cutting its workday from 8 to 6 hours, would find its productivity reduced by 33 percent. This does not, in fact, explain layoffs, however, because the work sharing could simply take the form of fewer days a week rather than fewer hours a day.

The second explanation for layoffs given by implicit contract theorists is that unemployment insurance encourages layoffs. In most places, individuals are not eligible for unemployment benefits in the event of a layoff unless they work full time. (Some European countries now allow unemployment benefits for those who face reductions in their work week.) If a company trims the work week, it and its workers share the cost. If the company lays off workers instead, the government shares the cost. This is an unsatisfactory explanation because it once again only suggests a different form of work sharing—one in which there are short-term layoffs that take the form of job rotations. One group might be laid off for two months, the next group for the next two months, and so on. Job rotations such as these, in fact, are very rare in the real world. (They were used, though not extensively, in the interwar years.)

But the most telling criticism of implicit contract theory is that it does not really explain why wages of job seekers should fail to decline when there is unemployment. Even in the deepest recession, the labour market is like a revolving door, with people quitting jobs and some firms hiring new workers. Even if implicit contract theory could explain why some workers are laid off, it does not explain why employers do not pay new employees lower wages than they pay their existing workforce. If the wages paid to new employees fell sufficiently, presumably there would be no unemployment.

INSIDER-OUTSIDER THEORY

An explanation for why firms faced with recessionary conditions do not pay lower wages to new employees is provided by what is known as **insider-outsider theory.** Insiders in this case are those with jobs at a particular firm. Outsiders are people who want jobs at that firm.

Insider-outsider theory focuses on the importance of training costs. Each firm needs a labour force trained in the special ways that it operates. Most of the training is done by current employees, the insiders. The insiders recognise that by training new employees, outsiders, they are reducing their bargaining position with the firm. The company can promise to continue to pay them higher wages than the newcomers, but the insiders know this promise could be broken. In future bargaining situations, the employer can use the availability of the lower-wage workers to exert downward pressure on the wages of the other employees. Knowing this, the insiders refuse to cooperate with training the outsiders, unless the new employees' interests are made to coincide with their own. The firm can accomplish this only by offering similar pay. This results in wage stickiness and unemployment persists.

Insider-outsider theory holds, further, that even if the current employees were to train new, lower-paid workers, the firm should not take the new workers' willingness to work at a low wage seriously. For once an outsider has been trained, she becomes a trained insider able to extract from the firm higher wages.

Wage systems in which new workers are paid less than established workers doing the same job are called **two-tier wage systems.** Firms do not seem to like two-tier wage systems. Most such experiments—such as a contract between Ford and its workers in the United States signed in 1982, which provided that new workers be paid 85 percent of what previously hired workers received—are relatively short lived. The Ford experiment was abandoned in 1984.

MINIMUM WAGES

A minimum wage set by the government may result in unemployment. The minimum wage is a price floor. To the extent that workers would accept and firms would offer wages below the minimum if they were allowed to, the minimum wage would keep the demand for labour from equaling the supply. In Britain, until recently, only a small number of workers in catering and some other industries were affected by minimum rates of pay set by wages councils. They had little effect on employment in practice. They have been much more prevalent and have had more effect in the United States. However, minimum wages have recently become a subject of political debate in the United Kingdom. A universal minimum wage of £3.60 an hour was introduced in 1998 for virtually all adult workers. Of course it remains true that most workers are not directly affected by the minimum wage.

EFFICIENCY WAGE THEORY

Even in a world without contracts, explicit or implicit, wages may not fall enough to eliminate unemployment because firms may find they make more profits by paying a wage higher than the one at which the labour market would clear. If paying higher wages leads to higher productivity, then higher wages may improve a firm's profits.

When Henry Ford opened his automobile plant in the United States in 1914, he paid his workers more than double the going wage. He wanted his workers to work hard. He knew that his new technique of production—the assembly line—when combined with motivated workers, would increase his profits. Many modern companies apply the same philosophy.

WHY DOES PRODUCTIVITY DEPEND ON WAGES?

Three main reasons have been offered to explain why firms may benefit if they pay high wages: wages affect the quality of the workforce, the level of effort, and the rate of labour turnover. Each of these reasons has been extensively studied. For each, productivity may depend not just on the wage paid but also on the wage paid relative to that paid by other firms and on the unemployment rate.

Quality of the Labour Force   It is all too common for companies to discover after a wage cut that they have lost the best of their workers. Indeed, this is the reason frequently given by firms for not cutting wages. This is an example of adverse selection: the average quality of those offering to work for a firm is affected adversely by a lowering of the wage.[1] If a firm lowers wages, its best workers will most likely find a new job at the old (higher) wage and therefore will most likely leave.

Level of Effort   We can easily see that it would not pay any worker to make any effort on the job if all firms paid the market-clearing wage. A worker could reason as follows: "If I shirk—put out a minimal level of effort—I will either be caught or not. If I don't get caught, I get my pay and have saved the trouble of making an effort. True, if I am unlucky enough to be caught shirking, I risk being fired. But by the terms of the basic competitive model, I can immediately obtain a new job at the same wage. There is, in effect, no penalty for having been caught shirking."

Firms that raise their wages above the market-clearing level will find that they have introduced a penalty for shirking, for two reasons. First, if their workers are caught shirking and are fired, they will have to take the lower wage being offered by other firms. Second, if many firms offer higher-than-market-clearing wages, unemployment will result, since at the higher wages firms as a whole will hire fewer workers. Now a worker who is fired may have to remain unemployed for a time.

Consider a wage just high enough to induce the workers not to shirk. We know this wage must exceed the wage at which the demand for labour equals the supply. If one of the unemployed workers offers to work for a lower wage at a particular firm, he will not be hired. His promise to work is not credible. The firm knows that at the lower wage, it simply does not pay the worker to exert effort.

The no-shirking view of wages also provides a gloomy forecast for the consequences of unemployment benefits. Assume that the government increases unemployment benefits. Now the cost of being unemployed is lower; hence the wage a firm must pay to induce workers to work—that is, not to shirk—is higher. As a result, wages are increased, leading to a lower level of employment. The higher unemployment benefits have increased the unemployment rate.

Higher wages may lead to higher levels of effort

---

[1] It should be clear that we have now moved away from the assumption that all workers are identical.

CLOSE-UP: EFFICIENCY WAGES IN TANZANIA

One of the implications of efficiency wage theory—that employers may be able to get work done more cheaply by *increasing* wages—can lead to some topsy-turvy implications. Or as Alfred Marshall, a famous economist of the late nineteenth and early twentieth centuries put it: "Highly paid labour is generally efficient and therefore not dear labour; a fact which though it is more full of hope for the future of the human race than any other that is known us, will be found to exercise a very complicating influence." The first chapter of this book gave the example of Henry Ford taking advantage of efficiency wage theory by paying higher wages in the automobile industry. But the theory can have striking implications in developing countries too.

Consider the experience of the East African nation of Tanzania, formed by the union of Tanganyika and Zanzibar in 1964. When the area now known as Tanzania achieved independence in 1961, most wage earners worked on large plantations. Most of the workers were migrants, as is commonly the case in Africa, returning from the plantations to their home villages several times each year. The workers had low productivity and were not paid much. After independence, the government decreed that wage rates

for the plantation workers would triple. Plantation owners predicted disaster; such a massive increase in the price they paid for labour, they thought, could only drive them out of business. But the government responded with predictions based on efficiency wage theory, that higher wages would lead to a more productive and stable work force.

The government predictions turned out to be correct. Sisal, for example, is a plant cultivated because it produces a strong white fiber that can be used for cord or fibre. Overall production of sisal quadrupled under the efficiency wage policy. This occurred not because of a change in the overall physical capital available but because more motivated and highly skilled workers were better employed by the plantation owners. Over several years following the wage increase, however, employment in Tanzania's sisal industry fell from 129,000 to 42,000, thus illustrating how efficiency wages can increase unemployment.

Sources: Mrinal Datta-Chaudhuri, *Journal of Economic Perspectives,* Summer 1990, pp. 25–39; Richard Sabot, "Labor Standards in a Small Low-Income Country: Tanzania" (Overseas Development Council, 1988).

for another reason. They may lead to improved morale among the workers. If workers think the firm is taking advantage of them, they may reciprocate by taking advantage of the firm. If workers think their boss is treating them well—including paying them good wages—they will reciprocate by going the extra mile.

Rate of Labour Turnover Lowering wages increases the rate at which workers quit, the **labour turnover rate.** It is costly to hire new workers, to find the jobs that best match their talents and interests, and to train them. So firms seek to reduce their labour turnover rate by paying high wages. The lower the wages, the more likely it is that workers will find another job more to their liking, either because it pays a higher wage or for some other reason. Thus, while firms may save a little on their direct labour costs in the short run by cutting wages in a recession, these savings will be more than offset by the increased training and hiring costs incurred as demand rises again and they have to replace lost workers. We can think of what workers produce net of the costs of hiring and training them as their *net productivity*. Higher wages, by lowering these turn-over costs, lead to higher net productivity.

DETERMINING THE EFFICIENCY WAGE

If, as we have just seen, net productivity increases when a firm pays higher wages, then it may be profitable for an employer not to cut wages even if there is an excess supply of workers. This is because the productivity of the employer's workforce may decline so much in response to a wage cut that the overall labour costs per unit of production will increase.

The employer wants to pay the wage at which total labour costs are minimised, called the **efficiency wage.** The wage at which the labour market clears—the wage at which the supply of labour equals the demand for labour—is called the market-clearing wage. There is no reason to expect the efficiency wage and the market-clearing wage to be the same. **Efficiency wage theory** suggests that labour costs may be minimised by paying a wage higher than the market-clearing wage.

If the efficiency wage is greater than the market-clearing wage, it will still pay any profit-maximising firm to pay the efficiency wage. There will be unemployed workers who are willing to work at a lower wage, but it will not pay firms to hire them. At the lower wage, productivity will decline enough to more than offset the lower wage.

If productivity depends on wages because effort increases with the wage—the shirking view of wages—the efficiency wage *must* exceed the market-clearing level. But if productivity depends on wages for some other reason, the efficiency wage can be less than the market-clearing wage. In that case, competition for workers will bid up the wage to the competitive, market-clearing level. Firms would like to pay the lower, efficiency wage, but at that wage they simply cannot hire workers. In efficiency wage theory, the market-clearing wage thus forms a floor for wages.

In general, the efficiency wage for any firm will depend on two factors: the wage paid by other firms and the unemployment rate. The wage paid by other firms matters because if other companies pay a lower wage, a firm will find that it does not have to pay quite as high a wage to elicit a high level of effort. Workers know that if they are fired, the jobs they are likely to find will pay less. Thus, the cost of being fired is increased, and this spurs employees to work harder. The wages paid by other firms matter for other reasons as well. If wages paid by other firms are low, then the firm will lose fewer workers to other firms if it lowers its wages, and thus the cost of lowering wages—increased turnover rate—will be lower. Also, firms will find it easier to hire high-quality workers at any wage if the wages paid by competitors are lower.

The unemployment rate comes into play because as it increases, firms will again find that they do not have to pay quite as high wages to elicit a high level of effort. The workers know that if they are fired, they will have a harder time getting a new job.

Efficiency wage theory also suggests a slow adjustment process for wages. Each firm is reluctant to lower its wages until others do, for several reasons. The company worries that its best workers will be attracted by other firms. It worries that the morale of its workers, and thus their productivity, will be impaired if they see their wages are below that of similar firms. No company wants to be the leader in wage reductions. Each therefore contents itself with reducing its wages slowly and never much below those of other firms. Gradually, as wages in all firms are lowered, employment is increased and unemployment reduced.

These patterns are in contrast to the basic competitive model, which predicts that with a relatively inelastic supply curve for labour, there will be large and quick changes in wages in response to changes in the demand for labour. It is these wage changes that prevent unemployment.

WHY ARE THERE LAYOFFS?

Efficiency wage theory also helps explain why, if the economy needs a 25 percent reduction in labour supplied, workers do not simply work 30 hours rather than 40 and save jobs for the 25 percent of their colleagues who otherwise would be laid off.

According to efficiency wage theory, the reason workers do not just work 30 hours rather than 40 is that by reducing work proportionately among its workers, a firm will in effect be reducing overall pay proportionately. The company will fall back into the traps outlined above. If it lowers overall pay, it may

The introduction of a minimum wage in the United Kingdom in 1999 was surrounded by considerable controversy. Naturally, those ranged against it made the argument that a minimum wage would, to the extent that it raised the wages of some low-paid workers, also cause a reduction in their employment, and therefore be a mixed blessing for the poor. It has been claimed that a minimum wage is an ineffective method of relieving poverty. However, a considerable amount of analysis suggests that its effects, both positive and negative, will be modest and that there is little reason to expect a noticeable increase in unemployment.

The minimum wage was set at £3.60 per hour for adults and £3 per hour for persons between 18 and 21 for its introduction in 1999. This level is low relative to the minimum wage set by the wages councils, which had previously existed in some sectors of the U.K. economy, such as in hotels and catering, and which were phased out in 1993. Relatively few people will be directly affected by the minimum wage, and its impact on the wage bill of firms is likely to be small. Research by Professor Steve Machin of the Centre for Economic Performance at the London School of Economics and his colleagues suggests that 12 percent of those workers between 18 and 21 and 7.3 percent of workers aged 22 and above will be affected and that the overall wage bill will rise by only 0.7 percent. However, those workers who will be affected will be affected substantially, with a 27.7 percent increase in their wages on average. Workers who benefit particularly from the minimum wage are likely to be female and to work part time, in the private sector, in small firms, and without trade union recognition.

The negative effects on employment are likely to be small. Evidence on the effects of the minimum wages set by the wages councils suggests that they did not have negative effects on employment in the industries the councils used to cover. Evidence from the United States, where there has been a minimum wage for many years, supports this view. Professors David Card and Alan Kreuger from Princeton University in the United States examined the effects of New Jersey's raising its minimum wage in 1992, compared with the neighbouring state of Pennsylvania's keeping its unchanged. They found no significant adverse effects on employment.

Why does it appear that minimum wages set at moderate levels do not reduce employment, as standard economic theory would suggest? Two arguments are put forward. One is that labour markets are imperfect: many employers have to increase wages in order to attract more workers. Therefore such employers find it advantageous to limit their employment levels in order not to drive up wages. In other words, they have some monopsony power in labour markets. When a minimum wage is set, above the wage they currently pay, they may be willing to increase rather than decrease employment. The reason is that at the higher minimum wage level, there is a ready supply of labour, and employers no longer need to raise wages further in order to recruit more staff. As a result the marginal cost of labour may fall rather than rise when a minimum wage is introduced.

Another argument is based on efficiency wage theory. Higher wages lead to greater productivity, largely offsetting the additional costs of the higher wages. The minimum wage may also affect the wages of workers who would already earn an above-minimum wage, indicating that labour markets do not work like ordinary markets for goods. Employers seem to care about the effects of wages on productivity. Raising the minimum wage raises norms for the treatment of workers and creates a ripple effect. These factors all suggest that the beneficial wage effects are greater and the negative employment effects are smaller than a simple analysis would suggest.

Sources: David Card and Alan Kreuger, *Myth and Measurement* (Princeton, N.J.: Princeton University Press, 1995); Richard Dickens and Steve Machin, "Minimum Wage: Maximum Impact?" *CentrePiece* 3, no. 2 (Autumn 1998), pp. 10–13.

lose a disproportionate fraction of its better workers. These workers can obtain offers of full-time work and full-time pay, and they will find this more attractive than a job with 80 percent of full-time work and 80 percent of the pay. (They may enjoy the extra leisure, but it will not help meet the mortgage payments.) Furthermore, workers now working part time will find that their incentives to exert high levels of effort decline. If they get fired, losing a part-time job is not as serious as losing a full-time job. This ability to explain concentrated layoffs is one feature that sets efficiency wage theory apart from some of the alternative views of wage rigidity.

THE IMPACT OF UNEMPLOYMENT ON DIFFERENT GROUPS

One striking aspect of unemployment is that it affects different groups in the population very differently. In competitive markets, wages will adjust to reflect productivity. Groups with higher productivity will have commensurately higher wage rates, while groups with lower productivity will have lower wage rates. But people in both groups will have jobs. There would be no reason for different groups to have different unemployment rates.

Efficiency wage theory argues that there may be some kinds of labourers—such as part-time workers or those with limited skills—who, at any wage, have sufficiently low productivity that it barely pays a firm to hire them. To put it another way, while they may receive a low wage, the wage is only just low enough to offset their low productivity. Paying higher wages would not increase productivity enough to offset the wage increase. And paying lower wages would reduce productivity, making that option unworkable as well.

It is these groups, which lie right at the margin of the hiring decision, which will bear the brunt of the fluctuations in the demand for labour. Teenagers and young workers not only have higher average unemployment rates, they bear more than their proportionate share of the burden of variations in employment.

LIMITS OF EFFICIENCY WAGE THEORY

Efficiency wage theory may provide a significant part of the explanation for wage rigidities in a number of different situations: where training and turnover costs are high, where monitoring productivity is difficult, and where differences in individuals' productivity are large and important but it is difficult to ascertain them before hiring and training them. But efficiency wage considerations are likely to be less important in situations where workers are paid piece rates on the basis of how much they produce, or in situations where training costs are low and monitoring is easy. These situations may indeed exhibit greater wage flexibility, at least if there are no union pressures, implicit contracts, or insider-outsider considerations.

LABOUR HOARDING AND DISGUISED UNEMPLOYMENT

However high the unemployment statistics climb, they still may not fully reflect the underutilization of labour. Firms find it costly to hire and train workers. When they have a temporary lull in demand, they may not even lay workers off, for fear that once laid off, the workers will seek employment elsewhere. Thus, firms keep the workers on the job but may not fully utilise them. This is **labour hoarding** and can be thought of as a form of disguised unemployment. Employees are not really working, though they are showing up for work. Like open unemployment, it represents a waste of human resources.

The importance of disguised unemployment in the United States was brought home by an economist and U.S. presidential adviser, Arthur Okun. He showed that as the economy pulls out of a recession, output increases more than proportionately with employment; and as the economy goes into a recession, output decreases more than proportionately with the reduction in employment. This result is known as **Okun's law.** In Okun's study, for every 1 percentage point decrease in the unemployment rate, output increased by 3 percent. Today, most economists still think output increases more than proportionately with employment, though not as much as Okun suggested. Okun's finding seemed to run contrary to one of the basic principles of economics—the law of diminishing returns—which would have predicted that a 1 percentage point decrease in the unemployment rate would have less than a proportionate effect on output. The explanation for Okun's law, however, was simple. Many of those who were working in a recession were partially idle. As the economy heated up, they worked more fully, and this yielded the unexpected increase in output.

POLICY ISSUES

This chapter has examined a number of reasons why wages do not always adjust to the market-clearing level, where labour demand equals labour supply. All of them play a role in causing wage rigidity in practice. Money wage rates sometimes fall, as they did in the 1920s and 1930s, but the important thing for the hiring decisions of firms is the real wage—the money wage rate relative to prices. The real wage rate has shown great resilience in the face of apparently very large excess supplies of labour, both in the interwar period and in the 1980s.

When the labour market fails to clear continuously and involuntary unemployment results, there may be a role for the government to intervene to make wages more sensitive to disequilibrium. In Britain, since 1979, the problems of the labour market have been interpreted partly as a problem of rigidity, which we have just considered, but also partly a problem with the equilibrium itself: there are too many people unemployed when the market is in equilibrium. The diagnosis of this problem is that there is too much structural and frictional unemployment, even when there is no cyclical unemployment. The policies that have been adopted in Britain are aimed at reducing the equilibrium unemployment rate at the same time as increasing the flexibility of wages so that they deviate less from their equilibrium values when the economy is disturbed by shifts in the labour supply and demand curves. These policies include an attack on the unions, reductions in the levels of unemployment benefits and a harsher administration of the social security system, attempts to increase training, and attempts to increase labour mobility.

THE UNIONS

Unions have been viewed as a source of both wage rigidity and a high unemployment rate in equilibrium. Their role in the economy has appeared increasingly negative since the mid-1960s, as their ability to achieve increases in money wages despite higher and higher unemployment became apparent. During the 1980s a series of changes in the law reduced the power of unions in wage bargaining. They are now legally required to ballot members by post before calling a strike. Secondary picketing—at places other than the workplace directly involved in the dispute—is illegal. Unions and their officials are no longer immune from penalties when their members hold strikes or picket outside the legally permitted limits. All these changes have had the effect of reducing the incidence of strikes and the ability of unions to immunise their members from external labour market conditions. Their membership and influence has been further reduced by the fall in employment in the industries in which they were concentrated. The privatization and splitting-up of some

ALTERNATIVE EXPLANATIONS OF WAGE RIGIDITIES

1 Unions with explicit and implicit contracts prevent wages from falling. Insider-outsider theory explains why firms do not pay newly hired workers a lower wage.

2 Efficiency wage theory suggests that it is profitable for firms to pay above-market wages. This is because wages affect the quality of the labour force, labour turnover rates, and the level of effort exerted by workers.

nationalised industries has, to some degree, divided the interests of the workers in these industries and weakened their bargaining position.

UNEMPLOYMENT BENEFITS

Unemployment benefits are necessary to relieve, at least to a small extent, the economic hardships that fall on people who become unemployed. However, they also have the unfortunate effect of reducing the incentive of unemployed workers to look for jobs and increasing the length of time they remain unemployed. Because benefits effectively subsidise the unemployed in their search for new jobs, they make them too fussy about what sort of job to accept. So higher benefits increase wage rigidity and increase the equilibrium level of unemployment. The question is where should the balance be struck between insuring people against the loss of income involved in becoming unemployed, and inducing them to search efficiently for jobs and not be excessively choosy about which one they accept.

A disturbing aspect of high unemployment in Britain in the 1980s was the high incidence of long-term unemployment: people being unemployed for more than a year. At its peak in 1986, more than 48 percent of the unemployed had been unemployed for more than a year. Similar rates of long-term unemployment were found in some other European countries, such as Germany, but not in the United States and not in Sweden, where the unemployment benefit systems are very different. It has been argued that the administration of the benefit system was responsible for this. In the United Kingdom, after unemployment benefits expire after six months of unemployment, the unemployed are entitled to family income support, as is anyone on a low income. In the early 1980s, there was little or no attempt made by the job centres or benefit offices to ensure that the long-term unemployed were looking for work and pursuing vacancies. In fact it turned out that many long-term unemployed persons did not look for jobs with any vigour and not all were available for work. The long-term unemployed were not banging on the factory gates clamouring for work, and therefore contributing to the downward pressure on wages, in the same way as newly unemployed persons. This also contributes to a persistently high level of unemployment.

The policy response to these issues was to toughen the administration of benefits and to limit their growth. Benefits fell as a fraction of average wages during the 1980s, and a programme called Restart was introduced to check that long-term unemployed people were available for and looking for work. They were interviewed by benefit officers and helped to find vacancies for which to apply. Benefits were denied to people who did not meet tougher criteria for them. This was part of a series of measures unappetisingly (but reasonably) called "harrassment of the work-shy."

TRAINING

The unskilled always suffer higher rates of unemployment than the more-skilled workers. Firms report shortages of skilled labour even when unemployment is high. There rarely if ever appears to be a shortage of unskilled labour. Despite this, there is little sign of relative wages of unskilled workers decreasing enough to take up the surplus.

The concentration of unemployment among the

unskilled indicates a structural imbalance in the British labour market, a chronic excess supply of unskilled labour and an excess demand for skilled labour, which raises the measured rate of unemployment when the labour market overall is in equilibrium. This is one element of the mismatch between job vacancies and the unemployed which may contribute to persistently high unemployment.

A response to the skill shortage and to large numbers of unemployed workers with few potentially marketable skills has been an attempt to increase training. The youth training scheme, the job training scheme (JTS), and other training schemes currently take about 500,000 people, mainly between the ages of 16 and 18 (many of whom would have otherwise been unemployed), with the intention of providing training for them and having them enter the labour market with more job skills than they would otherwise have done. No 16 to 18 year olds who refuse a place in JTS (if one is offered) are eligible for unemployment benefits, and consequently can no longer be "unemployed." These schemes have been criticised for being window dressing, to reduce the unemployment figures without providing any real training. They certainly reduced unemployment figures, but it is likely that they also raised the job skills of this group.

Training schemes associated with the Restart programme have also been provided for people unemployed more than one year. These schemes reduce long-term unemployment automatically: even if people who come out the schemes go straight back into unemployment, they do so as newly unemployed people. The schemes then work as a recycling process for the unemployed. It is argued that they also improve the skills of long-term unemployed people, improve their morale, and increase their attachment to the labour market.

LABOUR MOBILITY

A factor allegedly contributing to persistently high unemployment in Britain has been the lack of labour mobility between regions. There have always been wide differences between unemployment rates between regions, which decades of half-hearted re-gional policies have (not surprisingly) failed to reduce. The old declining industrial regions have always had higher unemployment: South Wales, the North East, the Midlands, and Northern Ireland. There has been little net migration of workers from high to low unemployment regions. Regional mobility would reduce unemployment in the depressed regions, while at the same reducing the excess demand for labour in the booming ones, and allow a lower level of unemployment overall to be maintained when the labour market is in equilibrium.

The housing market may contribute to lack of mobility. The bulk of people live either in owner-occupied housing or in housing rented from local authorities. Both forms of housing make moving expensive or difficult. Owner occupiers in depressed regions (where house prices are low) find that their accumulated wealth in housing buys relatively little in the booming areas (where house prices tend to be high). A £30,000 terraced house in Hull cannot be traded for much in London.

Occupants of rented council property find that when they move, they are unable to rent from the local council in the place to which they are moving, because there are typically long waiting lists for council housing and the allocation criteria favour certain classes of existing local residents, not newcomers from outside. The alternative of moving to private sector rented housing or buying property is relatively more expensive. These costs of moving wipe out the benefits of higher pay or better employment prospects of a move to a different region unless these are substantially better than found locally.

There have been moves to encourage the market in privately rented housing. The rent controls, introduced in the early 1970s, limited landlords' ability to set rents according to the state of demand for (and supply of) property and gave protection for tenants ("sitting tenants" obtained an almost unlimited hold on a rented property). They led to the virtual extinction of the private rented sector in Britain, as landlords, whose returns on the rental of property were lower than the market rate of return on other assets, withdrew property from the rental market and sold it for owner occupation whenever they could. The market has not been completely deregulated, but new forms of tenancy have been created, which give landlords greater freedom, and weaken but do not eliminate the protections given to tenants. This is aimed at increasing the supply of rented housing available in an open market, where there are no queues or rationing and where workers who want to move will find it easier to leave one region and relocate to another.

REVIEW AND PRACTICE

SUMMARY

1 Involuntary unemployment exists when the supply of labour exceeds the demand for labour at the prevailing market wage. This happens when demand for labour at each wage level falls but real wages do not decline.

2 Explanations for why firms may be unable to reduce wages and thus unemployment include union contracts or implicit contracts, insider-outsider theory (which explains why firms do not pay lower wages to new hires), and minimum wage laws.

3 Reducing wages may lead to an increase in labour costs, because it may result in a lower average quality of workers as the best workers leave, lower effort, or higher turnover costs.

4 Firms often do not fully utilise their labour force in economic downturns. This labour hoarding means that as the economy expands, output increases more than in porportion to increases in employment.

5 Unemployment benefits reduce the costs to workers of being laid off, but they also reduce workers' incentives to work hard or to search for a new job. Firms' responses may lead to higher rather than lower unemployment.

KEY TERMS

implicit contract	insider-outsider theory	efficiency wage	Okun's law
work sharing	labour turnover rate		

REVIEW QUESTIONS

1 What gives rise to involuntary unemployment?

2 List reasons why firms may be unable or unwilling to reduce wages.

3 True or false: "The prevalence of unions is the primary reason for wage stickiness, and therefore for unemployment, in the British economy." Discuss your answer.

4 If an implicit contract is not written down, why would a firm abide by it? Why would a worker?

5 Why does implicit contract theory predict that work sharing is more likely than layoffs?

6 Give three reasons why productivity may depend on the level of wages paid.

7 How does an efficiency wage differ from a market-clearing wage?

8 How does efficiency wage theory help explain why different groups may have very different levels of unemployment?

9 What trade-off does society face when it attempts to expand economic security for workers with higher unemployment benefits or greater job security?

PROBLEMS

1 Suppose that a minimum wage of, say, £4.50 an hour were to be introduced. Explain why efficiency wage theory suggests that the effect on employment may be relatively small.

2 Would you be more or less likely to observe implicit contracts in industries where most workers hold their jobs for only a short time? What about industries where most workers hold jobs for a long time? Explain.

3 A number of businesses have proposed a two-tier wage scale, in which the wage scale for new employees is lower than the wage scale for current employees. Using the insights of insider-outsider theory, would you be more or less likely to observe two-tier wage scales in industries where a lot of on-the-job training is needed than in those where not much is needed?

4 The following figures represent the relationship between productivity and wages for the Doorware Company, which makes hinges.

Wage per hour	£2	£3	£4	£5	£6	£7	£8
Hinges produced per hour	20	24	33	42	52	58	60

Graph the productivity-wage relationship. From the graph, how do you determine the efficiency wage? Calculate output per pound spent on labour for the Doorware Company. What is the efficiency wage?

5 Would you be more or less likely to see efficiency wages in the following types of industries?
  (a) Industries where training and turnover costs are relatively low
  (b) Industries where it is difficult to monitor individual productivity
  (c) Industries that have many jobs where individual differences in productivity are relatively large

APPENDIX: DERIVATION OF THE EFFICIENCY WAGE

Figure 32.4 depicts a curve that represents one possible relationship between productivity and wages. We refer to this curve as the **wage-productivity curve.** Productivity here can be thought of as "the number of pins produced in an hour" or any similar measure of output. There is a minimum wage w_m, below which the firm will find it difficult if not impossible to obtain labour. At a very low wage, w_1, the company can only hire the dregs of the labour market—those who cannot get jobs elsewhere. Worker morale is low, and effort is low. Workers quit as soon as they can get another job, so labour turnover is high.

As the firm raises its wage, productivity increases. The company earns a reputation as a high-wage firm, attracting the best workers. Morale is high, turnover is low, and employees work hard. But eventually, as in so many areas, diminishing returns set in. Successive increases in wages have incrementally smaller effects on productivity. The firm is concerned with wage costs per unit of output, not wage costs per employee. Thus, it wishes to minimise not the wage but the wage divided by productivity.

This can be put another way. The company wishes to maximise the output per pound spent on labour (we are assuming that all other costs are fixed). Since productivity is defined as output per unit of time (pins per hour) and the wage is labour cost per unit of time (pounds per hour), dividing productivity by the wage produces the equation

$$\frac{\text{Productivity}}{\text{Wage}} = \frac{\text{output/unit of time}}{\text{pounds/unit of time}}$$

$$= \frac{\text{output}}{\text{pounds spent on labour}}.$$

Thus, a decision to make the ratio of output to pounds spent on labour as high as possible is mathematically equivalent to a decision to make the ratio of productivity to wages as high as possible. To tell which level of wages will accomplish this goal, Figure 32.4 shows the productivity-wage ratio as a line

Figure 32.4 **THE RELATIONSHIP BETWEEN PRODUCTIVITY AND WAGES**

As wages rise, productivity increases, at first quickly and then more slowly. The efficiency wage is the wage at which the ratio of productivity to wage is highest. It is found by drawing a line through the origin tangent to the wage-productivity curve.

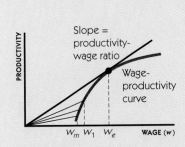

from the origin to a point on the wage-productivity curve. The slope of this line is the ratio of productivity (the vertical axis) to the wage (the horizontal axis).

As we draw successive lines from the origin to points on the wage-productivity curve with higher wages, the slope first increases and then decreases. The slope is largest for the line through the origin that is just tangent to the wage-productivity curve. The wage at this point of tangency is the wage at which labour costs are minimised: the efficiency wage w_e.

Changes in unemployment rates may shift the wage-productivity curve, as shown in Figure 32.5. At each wage, the productivity of the labour force is higher at the higher unemployment rate. Also, the efficiency wage—the wage at which the ratio of productivity to the wage is maximised—is lowered slightly. It falls from w_0 to w_1. The change in the efficiency wage may be relatively small, even if the shift in the curve relating productivity to wages is relatively large.

Figure 32.5 **SHIFTING THE PRODUCTIVITY-WAGE RELATIONSHIP**

If unemployment is low, workers have many alternative job possibilities. With the threat of being fired reduced, at each wage workers work less hard, so productivity is lower. In the case shown here, the efficiency wage will be lower when there is high unemployment than when there is low unemployment.

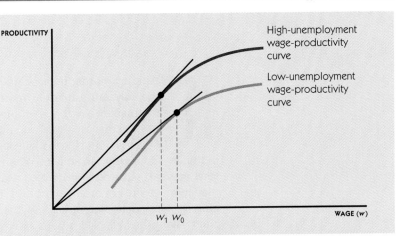

33

INFLATION VERSUS UNEMPLOYMENT: APPROACHES TO POLICY

Making economic policy can be like walking a tightrope. Lean too far one way, and unemployment increases. Lean too far the other way, and prices rise. It is even possible to have the worst of all worlds: simultaneous inflation, unemployment, and slow growth.

Many of the basic macroeconomic problems stem from variability in the level of economic activity. When the economy is dragging along, a jump start may be required to reignite it. But when the economy is racing, inflation may loom. Both unemployment and inflation cause economic hardship. Unemployment particularly affects the young, who have no cushion of accumulated savings to fall back upon, as well as minorities and unskilled workers. Inflation takes its toll among those retired people whose incomes do not rise commensurately with prices.

After briefly reviewing these costs, this chapter focuses on the major policy issues: Should the government intervene to stabilise the economy? If so, how? With monetary or fiscal policy? It then illustrates some of the basic issues by a historical review of the major policy debates over the past three decades.

THE IMPACT OF INFLATION AND UNEMPLOYMENT

When should policymakers act to stimulate or dampen the economy? Each decision involves a trade-off. Consider the problem facing policymakers as an economy begins to grow rapidly, unemployment falls, and house prices begin to rise. Everyone agrees that at some point inflation will set in. The question is, when? If, for instance, the policymakers act too early and raise interest rates too much, the recovery can stall, throwing the economy back into recession. If they wait too long, inflation will increase. What would be the costs of a higher level of inflation? How much would it cost to bring inflation down?

THE BASIC TRADE-OFFS

The discussions of earlier chapters have set the scene for how policymakers approach these decisions: the costs of high unemployment—including the loss in output—are apparent.

Inflation too has its costs, though the discussion of Chapter 31 suggested that at the low levels of inflation that have prevailed in most developed countries during the past 15 years, some of those costs are more perceived than real.

Chapter 31 also clarified the trade-offs. Today, the focus is not so much on trading a little more inflation for a temporary lowering of the unemployment rate. Governments recognise that they cannot permanently run the economy at a rate lower than the NAIRU without inflation accelerating, and most do not seem even willing to take advantage of the short-run gains from reduced unemployment, which typically occur earlier than the inflation costs, which are felt only with a lag. Today, the debate focuses more on risk: if there is uncertainty about the NAIRU, how aggressive or conservative should government be? How willing should it be to risk an increase in inflation, at the cost of failing to use the economy's resources as fully as they might be used? But in assessing these risks, economists continue to evaluate the costs of inflation and of unemployment. Not surprisingly, those who worry more about unemployment argue for more aggressive policies, while those who worry about inflation argue for more conservative policies.

DIFFERENT VIEWS OF TRADE-OFFS

Key to understanding these different positions is the recognition that unemployment and inflation impact different groups. Low-wage workers and other disadvantaged groups are the most likely to benefit from low unemployment policies. Since they have little savings, they bear little of the costs of inflation. The costs of *unanticipated* increases in inflation are typically borne most by those who hold long-term financial assets whose value is fixed in terms of money—who see the value of those assets decrease as nominal interest rates increase, as typically happens when inflation increases.

It is thus not surprising that unions typically push for more aggressive macroeconomic policies and that participants in financial markets push for more conservative policies. Since more aggressive policies typically entail lowering interest rates—a major cost for firms which typically borrow to finance inventories and purchases of plant and equipment—and lead to higher levels of output, both of which are good for business, it is also not surprising that businesses often support more aggressive policies.

PERSPECTIVES ON FLUCTUATIONS AND MACROECONOMIC POLICY

There is widespread agreement on the desirability of high growth, low unemployment, and low and stable inflation. But economists disagree about the role and means of government in pursuing these objectives. Some economists believe that government attempts at intervention have little effect, or worse, only destabilise the economy. Others argue that government interventions are generally successful.

For simplicity, we can split economists into two broad groups on these issues—interventionists and noninterventionists. Noninterventionists tend to have great faith in markets and little faith in government. Believing the economy adjusts quickly and efficiently to disturbances, noninterventionists see little role for government action. Interventionists argue that because markets adjust slowly, there may be extended periods of unemployment, and government policies can restore the economy to full employment faster than the market would do on its own.

The central challenge in managing the economy is its variability. It is not as if there is an isolated episode in which the aggregate demand curve shifts to the left, resulting in unemployment. The prescription then would be simple: use monetary or fiscal policy to shift the aggregate demand curve back to the right. The problem is that the economy is always changing, always fluctuating. Some noninterventionists accept that markets may adjust slowly but argue that government efforts do more harm than good. There is a real fear that because of the length of time it takes for policies to be put into effect, the government will be stimulating the economy just when it should be dampening it, and vice versa. There are some economists who think that government policies have contributed to the economy's fluctuations. Views concerning whether government should or should not intervene depend strongly on views concerning the origins and nature of the economy's fluctuations.

ECONOMIC FLUCTUATIONS

Figure 33.1A shows the movement of U.K. economic output over the past 40 years. A smooth line has been drawn through the data, tracing out the path the economy would have taken had it grown at a steady rate. This line represents the economy's **long-term trend.** The economy is sometimes above the trend line and sometimes below. Figure 33.1B shows the percentage by which the economy has been below or above the trend for the past 30 years. It also shows the unemployment rate, to illustrate the negative correlation between these deviations of output from trend and unemployment. The term *recession* is reserved for periods in which output declines, but even growth at a substantially lower rate represents an economic slowdown, with significant consequences.

Although there is clearly a cyclical pattern in economic activity and unemployment, as Figure 33.1B makes clear, the length of the cycles is quite variable,

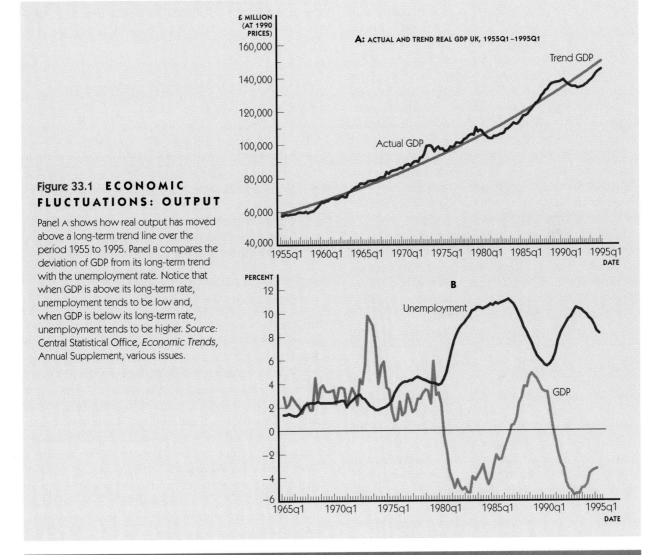

Figure 33.1 ECONOMIC FLUCTUATIONS: OUTPUT

Panel A shows how real output has moved above a long-term trend line over the period 1955 to 1995. Panel B compares the deviation of GDP from its long-term trend with the unemployment rate. Notice that when GDP is above its long-term rate, unemployment tends to be low and, when GDP is below its long-term rate, unemployment tends to be higher. *Source:* Central Statistical Office, *Economic Trends,* Annual Supplement, various issues.

and the amplitude varies from one cycle to the next. Again, this is evident from the diagram. The swings in unemployment and output have been much longer and of greater amplitude during the 1980s and 1990s than they were during the 1960s and 1970s.

While the length of downturns and upturns has been highly variable, there are still distinct patterns associated with the economy's fluctuations. In downturns, not only does output growth slow down (and sometimes even become negative), but unemployment increases. Hours worked per worker tend to decline, inflation tends to slow, and in some cases, prices even start to fall.

While economists agree that the economy has been marked by fluctuations exhibiting these distinctive patterns, they disagree about the *causes* and what government should do. Some believe that the underlying sources of the fluctuations are **exogenous** shocks, that is, disturbances originating outside the economy, such as wars that start a boom. Others focus on **endogenous** factors, that is, properties of the economy itself, such as a tendency of the economy to become overconfident in expansions, leading to overinvestment (including overinvestment in inventories), leading in turn to a downturn as investment slows down once the overinvestment is recognised. Today, most economists think economic fluctuations involve a mixture of exogenous and endogenous factors: an external shock (such as an increase in the price of oil) may hit an economy, but endogenous factors may sometimes amplify the initial effects and make them more persistent.

Some of the variation in economic activity is an inevitable consequence of people's inability to predict the future perfectly. There will be times in which firms overestimate demand and produce too much. When production exceeds sales, inventories build up. As inventories build up, firms are induced to cut back on their production. And by the same token, government interventions designed to stabilise the economy may not do so and may even exacerbate the fluctuations, because government cannot predict perfectly where the economy is going. Indeed, in many cases, it may not even know with much precision where the economy is today. Data gauging the health of the economy become available only with a lag.

Many economic downturns in the United Kingdom have followed a tightening of monetary policy, generally in the form of a sharp rise in interest rates. These policy changes have often been prompted by the emergence of inflation. During the 1950s and 1960s, when Britain was a member of a fixed exchange rate regime, the Bretton Woods system, the immediate reason for a package of tight fiscal and monetary policies was generally a deterioration in the balance of payments and the danger of a run on the pound.

There has always been a question as to whether, by better timing of policy actions, the economy could have been more finely tuned. By a more timely increase in interest rates, could aggregate demand have been kept moving precisely in step with aggregate supply, so that there was no tendency for inflation to pick up, and thus no need for the government to slam on the brakes?

Interventionists believe that appropriate policies can both reduce the endogenous forces that either give rise to or help sustain fluctuations—for instance by using the automatic stabilisers discussed in Chapter 30—and increase the likelihood that interventions stabilise the economy.

THE NONINTERVENTIONIST PERSPECTIVE

Those who share the view that government should not intervene to stabilise the economy differ in their reasons. Some believe that the economy is efficient, so that there is little that government can add; others believe that government action is ineffective, while still others believe that governments do have significant effects, but more often make matters worse. We now take a closer look at each of these perspectives.

REAL BUSINESS CYCLE THEORY: INTERVENTION IS UNNECESSARY

Intervention is clearly unnecessary if the economy always operates efficiently, at full employment. **Real business cycle** theorists attribute the economy's fluctuations to exogenous shocks, such as the 1973 and 1979 oil price increases but believe that markets adjust quickly—prices and wages are sufficiently flexible that full employment will be restored quickly—and certainly more quickly than it would take government to recognise a problem, take actions, and have an effect. Since the economy typically operates at full employment, government need only worry about inflation. But recall from our discussion in Part Five that when the economy is at full employment, prices tend to increase with the money supply. Price stability—and full employment—can be attained if the monetary authorities let the money supply expand at the rate of increase in real GDP.

NEW CLASSICAL MACROECONOMICS: INTERVENTION IS INEFFECTIVE

Some noninterventionists claim that the government cannot even have an effect on output in the short run, because the private sector largely blocks any government action. Thus, if the government increases the money supply, with rational expectations, all market participants recognise that this will simply have an effect on the price level. Price levels adjust in-

CLOSE-UP: THE POLITICAL BUSINESS CYCLE

In Britain in the mid-1990s there was much talk in political circles and in the media of the "feel-good factor," the elusive *je ne sais quoi* that makes the electorate feel happy and causes it to reelect the existing government. It appeared to have flown out of the window along with the house price boom and low unemployment, and despite the best efforts of the government of the time, there seemed to be no way of getting it back again. Politicians and the media clearly believe that the feelgood factor is important in getting the government reelected. Little wonder that politicians make a great effort to generate a feelgood factor when a general election looms.

It is, however, not entirely a matter of *je ne sais quoi*. There is a fairly well-established view of what it involves. Low or falling unemployment is an important factor. Rising house prices are helpful. A general sense of prosperity is important. Careful statistical analysis has shown that the probability of a government's getting re-elected is increased by these factors.

The consequence is that governments are prone to cut taxes and boost spending and to take other populist actions, in the run-up to an election. (In Britain, which is unusual in allowing governments great freedom of choice over the timing of elections, governments also choose to go to the country when conditions are ripe for it.) Preelection tax cuts and spending often cause excessive government borrowing and inflation in the years following an election, and the policies have to be reversed. This creates the political business cycle—fluctuations in the economy driven by election-induced policy changes.

In the United Kingdom, there was a spectacular example of this in 1987 when tax cuts continued despite growing signs of the development of a runaway boom in the economy. It led to inflation in the late 1980s and the subsequent reversal of policy with tax rises and high interest rates, which then led to the collapse of housing prices in 1989 onwards. In the election years of 1992 and 1997 there were similar though more modest policy changes aimed at improving election chances. The year 1983 is an exception to the rule, in that the U.K. government of the day was pursuing economic policies that were deeply unpopular with at least sections of the electorate and unemployment was roughly at its postwar peak. No economic policy concessions were made. But in that case the government was staking its reputation on its commitment to its long-term policy strategy of low inflation, and its election success was in the event rescued by the "Falklands factor"; the military success there greatly boosted the government's popularity. Evidence from many democratic developed economies supports the view that there is a political business cycle.

The mystery (at least for economists) is why the electorate is taken in by this manipulation, particularly as its effects are damaging in the longer term. Why do voters not see through these ploys? It may be that voters are not as farsighted or as rational as economic analysis generally supposes. Or it may be that poor economic performance may result either from the government's abstention from pre-election gimmicks or from genuine incompetence and that voters quite reasonably simply cannot determine which is the real cause. In any case rational voters will punish what they see as poor performance in the elections, and rational governments will try to ensure that they are not seen to deliver poor performance at election time.

Sources: Alberto Alesina, "Macroeconomics and Politics," *NBER Macroeconomics Annual* (1988); Torsten Persson and Guido Tabellini, "Political Economics and Macroeconomic Policy," in *Handbook of Macroeconomics*, J. Taylor and M. Woodford, eds. (Amsterdam: North-Holland, 1999).

stantaneously, so that the *real* money supply is unchanged. The expansionary effects of the increase in money supply are thus completely counteracted, and monetary policy has no *real* effects. Similarly, an increase in the government deficit is perfectly offset by an increase in private savings as households foresee the need for higher taxes in the future.

The view that policies are largely ineffective and that to the extent they are effective, it is only in the very short run—with no permanent gains—was strongly advanced by the **new classical economists,** led by Robert Lucas of the University of Chicago.

INTERVENTION IS COUNTERPRODUCTIVE

Faith in markets is one thing; faith in the ability of government to improve on markets is another. Some noninterventionists see more shortcomings in markets than real business cycle theorists and new classical economists do, but nonetheless have little confidence in the ability of government to improve macroeconomic performance. Indeed, some hold the view that intervention is counterproductive, for two reasons.

First, they recognise that there are important **lags**—between the time the government recognises a problem and takes action and between the time the action occurs and its macroeconomic effects are fully realised. By the time the effects are fully realised, the action may no longer be appropriate. Lags by themselves would not be a problem if the government could accurately forecast where the economy is going and the exact effects of policy on the economy. But everyone—including the government—sees the future with a cloudy crystal ball, and as a result, governments risk taking the wrong action.

Second, critics of strong interventionist policies argue that there are systematic political reasons that interventions are often misguided. Politicians want the economy to be strong before an election. They thus tend to overheat the economy, with gains in employment showing up before the election but costs, in terms of inflation, showing up (hopefully) only after the election.

RULES VERSUS DISCRETION: THE NONINTERVENTIONIST PERSPECTIVE

Critics of intervention claim that historically, whether because of political motivations or simply because of

the lags described earlier, the government has exacerbated the economy's fluctuations. When the government attempts to dampen a boom, its policies reducing demand take effect just as the economy is weakening, reinforcing the downward movement. Conversely, when the government attempts to stimulate the economy, the increase in demand kicks in as the economy is strengthening on its own, thereby igniting inflation. Thus, critics of government action, such as Milton Friedman, conclude that economic policy should be based on simple *rules* rather than the *discretion* of government policymakers. For example, **monetarists** like Friedman believe the government should expand the money supply at a constant rate, rather than adjusting the money supply in response to specific economic events or conditions. According to Friedman and others, by sticking to such rules, the government would eliminate a major source of uncertainty and instability in the economy: uncertainty about future government policy.

Furthermore, they believe not only that government should pursue certain rules but that it should have its hands tied, so that it has no choice. The reason for this is that even if the government today promised to follow certain rules—such as not trying to stimulate the economy should there be a downturn—it will not (or politically, cannot) follow those rules. The problem of whether the government will carry out a promised course of action is called the problem of **dynamic consistency.** The government may announce that a particular tax change is permanent, and it may even deceive itself into believing that the tax change is permanent. But with the passage of time, policies will change. And the fact that policies are likely to change—and that individuals and firms expect them to change—has enormous consequences for the behaviour of individuals and firms.

In 1979 the government of Margaret Thatcher came to power determined to reduce inflation. In its Medium Term Financial Strategy, announced in 1980, the government set out its plans to limit government expenditure and borrowing, and the growth of the money supply. As unemployment rose from 1.5 to over 3 million (11 percent of the workforce) in the early 1980s and the pound appreciated dramatically on the foreign exchange markets, there were loud cries for a relaxation of the policy. Indeed, many people believed that the policy *would* be relaxed. Despite rising unemployment, wages continued to increase by 7 to 8 percent per year. On this occasion, the policy was not changed. "The lady's not for turning" was Margaret Thatcher's famous battle cry. The budget of 1983 which tightened fiscal policy in the middle of Britain's deepest postwar recession underlined the commitment to the low inflation policy. In this instance, the policymakers substantially carried out their policies through much changed circumstances. But the fact that they were not believed at the outset contributed to the continuation of high wage increases throughout the 1980s, and this in turn contributed to the high cost of the policy, in terms of the high rate of unemployment that it produced.

THE INTERVENTIONIST PERSPECTIVE

The most compelling case for intervention is based on the belief that without intervention, recovery may take an unconscionably long time and that there are interventions which on balance can reduce the economy's fluctuations. As a practical matter, governments *must* intervene. Even to keep the money supply constant or to increase it at a fixed rate requires decisions: forecasts about what the money supply would be in the absence of action by the central bank and judgments about the consequences of particular actions.

The underlying assumption of the noninterventionists is that markets adjust quickly and so unemployment is, at most, a short-term affair. There have been periods in which this assumption seems unpersuasive: in the Great Depression, unemployment persisted for many years. Unemployment rates in some European countries have exceeded 10 percent for more than a decade. Earlier chapters have explained both the reasons for, and consequences of, wage and price stickiness. As a practical matter, when unemployment rates are high, governments are under enormous pressures to reduce them.

Today, the leading school of thought of economists who believe that government can and should intervene to stabilise the economy is called **New Keynesianism.** They share Lord Keynes's view that unemployment may be persistent and that though there may be market forces that restore the economy to full employment, those forces work so slowly that government action is required. The New Keynesian

theories differ from older Keynesian analyses in their emphasis on microeconomics; they share, for instance, with many real business cycle and new classical economists, a view that the economy consists largely of profit-maximising firms, though they typically believe that markets often deviate significantly from the *perfectly competitive* ideal assumed by real business cycle and new classical theories. But they have identified a variety of reasons—such as costs of adjustment and imperfections of information—why markets do not adjust quickly to disturbances.

Moreover, they agree that while there are forces that enable the economy to dampen and absorb exogenous shocks, there are also endogenous forces that sometimes amplify shocks and make them more persistent. Noninterventionists emphasise the former forces: when prices and wages adjust quickly, as firms cut back production in response to an inventory buildup, wages and prices fall. At these low prices and wages, firms decide it is a good time to buy new machines; households may decide it is a good time to buy durables and new houses. These decisions help raise aggregate demand, offsetting the dampening effect of the excess inventories.

By contrast, New Keynesian economists emphasise the forces within the economy that amplify fluctuations and help make those fluctuations persist. Thus the recession in Britain in the early 1990s was made worse by high interest rates, dramatic falls in house prices, and the banks' applying tougher criteria to borrowers before they would make loans. The falling house prices led to a number of people's being unable to sell houses, meanwhile spending a large fraction of their disposable income on interest payments on loans taken out for house purchases, and so cutting consumption of other goods. Many small businesses were unable to borrow from banks, which were now much more risk averse than they had been in the boom years of the late 1980s, and went into bankruptcy. All these effects contributed to a sharp and self-reinforcing fall in aggregate demand.

THE MULTIPLIER-ACCELERATOR

The most widely discussed of the systematic endogenous forces that amplify fluctuations is called the multiplier-accelerator. We already encountered the multiplier: an upturn in exports is amplified by the multiplier, so that the increase in GDP may be two or more times the increase in exports. But matters do not stop there: the increase in GDP leads firms to want to invest more to meet the increased demand for goods. Typically, it takes around £2 to £3 of capital to produce £1 of GDP. Thus, if firms expect output to increase by, say, £100 billion, they will want to increase their capital stock by £200 to £300 billion. This is called the **accelerator.** As firms increase their investment, GDP grows even more. Increased investment of £200 billion results in a further increase of GDP by £400 billion if the multiplier is 2. But this increase in GDP may give rise to a further increase in the demand for investment. Thus, the multiplier and accelerator help to amplify and propagate what was initially an exogenous shock—an increase in exports.

Not only does the structure of the economy serve to amplify and propagate external shocks, it may also, on its own, convert an expansion into a downturn. To see how this occurs, consider what happens as the economy continues to expand. Eventually, it hits constraints. For example, shortages of labour may impose a limit on the expansion of the economy. Once these constraints are hit, the economy stops expanding or at least stops expanding as fast. But when the economy expands at a slower rate, the demand for investment decreases. And because of the multiplier effects, this reduces aggregate demand. A downturn in the economy thus begins. As output declines, investment drops lower, further accentuating the decline. Investment comes to a standstill. But eventually the old machines wear out or become obsolete. Even to produce the low level of output associated with the recession, new investment is required. This new investment stimulates demand, which in turn stimulates investment; the economy turns up.

OTHER SOURCES OF AMPLIFICATION

There are other reasons that the internal structure of the economy may amplify fluctuations. For instance, firms rely heavily on profits as a source of investment. They may face constraints on the amounts they can borrow, and they may find it impossible to raise funds by issuing new shares or feel that the cost of doing so is so unattractive, that they would prefer to rely on internally generated funds. As the economy goes into a downturn, profits fall; decreased profits lead to decreased investment, exacerbating the economic downturn.

While New Keynesians agree that adjustments in interest rates and prices may *partially* offset these destabilising influences—lower prices providing greater impetus for firms to invest, for instance, in a recession—these adjustments are simply to weak to offset them fully.

POLICIES TO IMPROVE ECONOMIC PERFORMANCE

Interventionists claim not only that markets, by themselves, do not ensure full employment but that government interventions can *and have* contributed to the stability of the economy. While there *are* instances in the past in which government actions may have exacerbated an economic downturn, they believe that by and large the government's record is a positive one.

While academic economists often debate *whether* government should intervene, most policy debates center around *when* and *how.* There are three sets of policies designed to improve the economy's economic performance.

First, government should attempt to change the structure of the economy to make it more stable. Automatic stabilisers (discussed in Chapter 30), which automatically lead to increased government expenditures when the economy goes into a downturn, are the most important example.

Second, government should use *discretionary* policy to stimulate the economy when output is low and unemployment high and to dampen the economy when inflation is strong.

Third, government should attempt to lower the NAIRU, so that price stability (stable inflation) can be attained at a lower level of unemployment.

RULES VERSUS DISCRETION: AN INTERVENTIONIST PERSPECTIVE

Interventionists argue that discretionary macroeconomic policy can and has helped stabilise the econ-

SCHOOLS OF THOUGHT IN MACROECONOMIC POLICY

NONINTERVENTIONISTS

Real business cycle theorists believe that fluctuations in economic activity are due to exogenous shocks and that markets respond quickly to economic disturbances. Government intervention is unnecessary.

New classical economists think that policies can have no long-run effect because the private sector anticipates the effects of policy and undoes them. Policies can only have a real effect in the short run, and then only if prices do not respond quickly.

Others believe that even though markets adjust slowly, discretionary macroeconomic policies make matters worse rather than better because of lags in determining the need for policy and then implementing it.

INTERVENTIONISTS

New Keynesians think markets respond slowly, so periods of unemployment can be extended. Discretionary macroeconomic policy can be effective.

Business cycles are endogenous phenomena and forces exist that amplify fluctuations.

Governments should both engage in discretionary macroeconomic policies and design built-in stabilisers that make the economy more stable.

omy. They also argue that the historical record shows why it is not possible to follow simple rules. Consider, for instance, the simple rule discussed earlier—that the money supply should simply increase at a constant rate, the rate of increase of *real* GDP. Since the monetary authorities do not directly control the money supply, this still entails some discretion: they must forecast what will be happening to the economy and, on the basis of that, make judgments concerning which policies to undertake so that the money supply will expand at the desired rate. Policies based on control of the money supply were used in Britain and the United States in the 1970s and early 1980s. They continued to be used successfully in Germany until 1999. In Britain and the United States, however, their effects were unpredictable and led to unexpectedly severe recessions. Furthermore, as we saw in Chapter 29, the marked changes in the relationship between the monetary aggregates (money supply) and output which have occurred during the past two decades removed the theoretical underpinnings of this approach. Inevitably, central banks must use discretion, if only to judge whether there has been a change in the structure of the economy.

INFLATION-UNEMPLOYMENT TRADE-OFFS

What should the government do when it intervenes actively? The analysis of Chapter 31 provides the analytic basis for these decisions. Clearly, we would like to have both low rates of inflation and low rates of unemployment. But is there a trade-off? Can we get, say, lower rates of unemployment only by allowing the inflation rate to increase?

In the years immediately following the discovery of the Phillips curve, most economists thought that there was a trade-off. Those economists who thought the costs of inflation were high argued for a high unemployment rate, while those who thought the benefits of low inflation paled in comparison with the costs of unemployment argued for somewhat lower unemployment rates. Thus disagreements about policy largely hinged upon disagreements about the *costs* of inflation and unemployment. Economists who focused on the hardship that unemployment imposed on workers advocated low unemployment policies; those who focused on the impact of inflation on investors (including retired individuals who de-

In 1997 new arrangements for monetary policy were introduced in the United Kingdom. The Bank of England was given greater independence in carrying out monetary policy. It was given the freedom to set interest rates as it saw fit, independently of the views of the chancellor of the exchequer but with the responsibility for setting rates so as to achieve a target rate of inflation of 2.5 percent per annum. The Bank was required to set up a nine-person Monetary Policy Committee (MPC), consisting of officials from the Bank itself and outside experts, which would meet monthly and make the decision about interest rates. The government and the Bank of England made great play of these new arrangements.

They are intended to depoliticise monetary policy, putting it into the hands of officials and experts who have no interest in doing anything other than achieving the set inflation target. In particular, these officials have no interest in going soft on inflation and cutting interest rates in order to win elections. While the chancellor could take back the power to set interest rates himself, to do that would be a very public act which would be difficult to do, in practice, it is claimed. It would probably be interpreted as a signal that politicians were about to resort to inflationary monetary policies. The new arrangements are highly open and *transparent:* the Bank publishes the minutes of the MPC meetings and the evidence on which decisions were based in its quarterly *Inflation Report.* It includes information on the voting of individual committee members.

The new arrangements were controversial, and criticism was made of the MPC for keeping interest rates too high and not bringing them down quickly enough in the face of evidence that demand was falling and unemployment was likely to rise. This was, of course, precisely the politicians' intention: that the Bank should get the blame for pursuing unpopular policies which the government itself would have pursued had it retained the operational control of policy.

The minutes of the MPC meetings throw an interesting sidelight on the policy views of members of the MPC. When interest rates were rising in 1997 and early in 1998, the academic economists on the committee wanted to raise interest rates quickly and were on the whole much more hawkish than the Bank officials. The newspapers began to report the "aviary index" of the committee members on a scale that ran from hawk to dove. Interestingly, when interest rates began to fall in late 1998, the academics again were keen to act quicker and further in cutting rates than the Bank officials. Then the newspapers began to report the "activisim index." Professor Willem Buiter of the University of Cambridge, a prominent member of the committee, was identified first as a particularly hawkish and then as a strongly activist member of the committee. The cautious position adopted by the governor of the Bank of England, Mr. Eddie George, who was more likely to vote for less rapid changes in rates, was entirely consistent with his role in dealings with a previous chancellor of the exchequer, Kenneth Clarke, when he was dubbed "steady Eddie" by the press.

The argument often made for a cautious approach is that a rapid change would run the risk of having to be reversed soon afterwards, which would give the impression that the Bank was not particularly competent in forecasting the state of the economy or judging the effects of its policies. However, Professor Charles Goodhart of the London School of Economics, also a prominent member of the MPC, argued in the Keynes Lecture to the British Academy that reversals of interest rates would in fact be quite common—and should be quite common—if the MPC set interest rates at a level which, if sustained for the medium term and in the absence of unexpected developments, would drive the economy towards the inflation target. The unexpected developments in the economy that might cause a revision of interest rates would then clearly be equally likely to require an increase or a decrease.

Sources: J. Vickers, "Inflation Targetting in Practice: The U.K. Experience," *Quarterly Bulletin*, Bank of England, November 1998, pp. 368–375); Bank of England, *Quarterly Bulletin* and *Inflation Report*, various issues.

pend on interest payments to live) advocated low inflation policies.

But in the 1970s, as the unemployment rate and inflation rate increased together and as economists became more aware of the importance of inflationary expectations and inflation inertia, there developed an increasing consensus that the economy could not enjoy a sustained level of unemployment below the NAIRU, without ever-increasing inflation.

There still remained two elements of disagreement about the nature of the trade-off. First, while there was agreement that the long-run Phillips curve was (at least close to) vertical, some economists thought that in the short run—for a period of perhaps several years—the economy could experience lower unemployment while inflation increased only moderately. Others worried that with rational expectations, even short periods of low unemployment—unemployment below the NAIRU—could give rise to high levels of inflation. They saw the economy as standing on a precipice: leaning towards too low a level of unemployment quickly leads to soaring inflation.

The experiences of Britain, many other European countries, and the United States over the last 15 years suggests that these dangers are not so great. While inflation rates have been brought down to lower levels, on average, and have been held down for some years, there have been substantial fluctuations in unemployment rates. It appears that while inflation remains at a roughly constant low level, unemployment can vary widely. The economy does not stand on a precipice.

The second disagreement concerned the costs of "disinflation"—the name given to reducing the inflation rate. Assume policymakers made a mistake and pushed the unemployment rate below the NAIRU. Inflation increased slightly. What would it take to reduce inflation? Clearly, the economy would have to operate for a while at a higher level of unemployment—at a level above the NAIRU. Those who advocated a cautious policy—making sure that the unemployment rate never fell below the NAIRU—worried that the costs of reducing inflation were very high. In particular, they looked to the experience of the 1970s and 1980s: to wring the inflationary expectations of the 1970s (when inflation hit double-digit levels) out of the economy, the United Kingdom and the United States had to go through a deep recession.

But the evidence from attempts to reduce more moderate inflation suggests that the costs are low. Indeed, the loss in output and employment from "killing" inflation are matched by the gains in output and employment during the period in which unemployment remained below the NAIRU.

IMPLEMENTING POLICIES: TARGETS

So far, we have focused our discussion on *what are the trade-offs* and *what should be the objectives of macroeconomic policy.* But even when there is agreement about the objectives of macroeconomic policy, there may be disagreements about how best to achieve those objectives. For instance, the government might believe that the NAIRU is 5.6 percent and might wish to keep the unemployment rate at that level, but it does not directly control the unemployment rate. There may be an inflation target of 2.5 per-

CONTROVERSIES IN MACROECONOMIC POLICY

Evaluating the Costs of Inflation and Unemployment

How large are the costs of moderate inflation?

How large are the costs of unemployment?

Since the costs of inflation and the costs of unemployment are borne by different individuals, how do we value these different costs?

Trade-offs

How quickly will attempts to lower unemployment below the NAIRU lead to increases in prices and price expectations? How quickly will runaway inflation set in? Does the economy sit on a precipice?

Are there large costs associated with disinflation? What is the relationship between these costs and the benefits that the economy achieved in the period during which unemployment was lower than the NAIRU?

---

cent, but the government and the central bank do not control inflation directly. Over the years, economists have come up with a variety of targets—intermediate variables, not necessarily of interest for their own sake, but easier to control than the variables of real interest and (or thought at the time to be) closely related to the variables of real concern. Thus, in the late 1970s and early 1980s, many central banks focused on the **monetary aggregates,** the statistics describing the money supply (M0, M1, M3, and so on). Controlling these would, it was believed, stabilise the inflation rate. It was believed that there was a stable relationship between the money supply and nominal income. If the money supply increased by 3 percent, nominal income would increase by only 3 percent. And since most of the advocates of this theory believed that the economy normally operated at full employment, if the economy's full-employment output was growing at 3 percent, that would imply that there would be no inflation. (The rate of increase of nominal income is the rate of increase of real income plus the rate of increase of prices.) But just as the theory came to be widely believed, the empirical relationship fell apart, as we saw in Chapter 29. The ratio of the money supply (say M3) to nominal income appeared to vary in ways that were hard to predict. Thus, controlling the money supply was not a good target. At other times, central banks have focused on variables such as the real interest rate, the rate of inflation, or the unemployment rate. Today, in Britain as in many countries, the government and the cen-

tral bank take an eclectic approach, incorporating data about all of these variables (including the monetary aggregates) into their analyses.

STRUCTURAL POLICIES: REDUCING THE NAIRU

Discretionary monetary and fiscal policies, no matter how aggressively and well pursued, will never completely eliminate the economy's fluctuations. Governments therefore try to improve the structure of the economy, to dampen the fluctuations and to reduce the NAIRU, so that the economy can have lower unemployment rates without the threat of increasing inflation. The major set of policies aimed at dampening fluctuations are the automatic stabilisers, discussed in Chapter 30, which automatically reduce taxes and increase expenditures as the economy slows down. Here, we focus on policies aimed at lowering the NAIRU.

Government has tried to lower the NAIRU in several ways: by increasing labour mobility, increasing the competitiveness of the economy, controlling directly the increase in wages and prices, and moral suasion.

INCREASING LABOUR MOBILITY

By reducing the time that it takes for people to move from job to job the government can reduce frictional unemployment and thus lower the NAIRU. Policies to facilitate labour mobility include limiting the time for which unemployment benefits are available and making the criteria for eligibility stricter. A central part of Sweden's active labour policies is training programmes that provide those who have lost their jobs the skills required for the new jobs being created. Making rented housing more readily available may also enhance mobility.

Some government policies, particularly in Europe, have probably reduced labour mobility, and thus increased the NAIRU. There is concern that legislation intended to increase workers' job security (by making it more difficult for employers to fire them) has had the side effect of making employers more reluctant to hire new workers, and thus has impeded the process of job transition. Changing these laws, as has happened in Britain, may lower the NAIRU.

MAKING THE ECONOMY MORE COMPETITIVE

A second approach, which received considerable attention in the late 1970s and early 1980s, entails shifting the aggregate supply curve down and to the right, as illustrated in Figure 33.2. This increases output, and thus reduces inflationary pressure. One way of shifting the aggregate supply curve down and to the right is by reducing regulations that inhibit competition.

These and other measures making the economy more competitive may lower the NAIRU: a more competitive economy—particularly one that is more open to international competition—will have less pressure to increase prices and wages, even when the unemployment rate is low. Workers worry, for instance, that if they demand significant wage increases, the products they produce will not be able to compete with foreign imports, demand for what they produce will decrease, and they will face a risk of losing their jobs.

WAGE AND PRICE CONTROLS AND MORAL SUASION

In the 1950s and 1960s, many believed that competition—market forces—were insufficient to control price and wage increases. Large unions could demand—and get—large wage increases, regardless of the unemployment rate; and industries that were dominated by a few large producers could—and would—raise their prices, even when there was large excess capacity. In a number of instances, governments tried to reduce the inflationary pressures—at any level of unemployment—by imposing direct controls on wages and prices. Such controls, by interfering with how the price system serves to allocate resources, impose high costs on the economy and tend to be effective only for short periods of time. When the price controls are removed, prices increase rapidly, largely undoing any benefits from

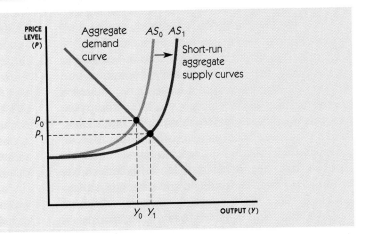

Figure 33.2 EFFECTS OF REDUCED INDUSTRIAL REGULATION

Reduced regulation that restricts competition is represented as a shift down and to the right of the short-run aggregate supply curve, from AS_0 to AS_1. Output increases and inflationary pressures are reduced.

the lower rates of price increases while the controls were in place. Today, few economists advocate price and wage controls as a way of lowering the NAIRU.

A less intrusive way that some governments have tried is moral suasion, or jawboning, in which they try to *persuade* firms and workers not to raise prices and wages. The government sets wage and price guidelines, with which it hopes workers and firms will voluntarily comply. The government often has considerable leverage beyond its appeal to moral rectitude, because it can threaten not to buy from firms that violate its suggestions. There is little evidence to suggest that these policies have had much effect. Today most economists are skeptical about the power of moral suasion to have any effect on price setting.

A BRIEF HISTORY OF MACROECONOMIC POLICY

The historical record, illustrated in Figure 33.1, shows clearly that fiscal and monetary policies have not been able to eliminate the economy's fluctuations. But fluctuations were smaller after than before the Second World War, and government policy may have played a role. In the following sections, we review briefly the major policy debates of the past fifty years.

THE HEYDAY OF DISCRETIONARY FISCAL POLICY: THE 1950s AND 1960s

The heyday of discretionary fiscal and monetary policies was the 1950s and 1960s. In that period the annual budget in Britain, then presented in March each year, in which the government set out its tax proposals for the coming financial year, was used to regulate aggregate demand in the British economy. With the benefit of hindsight, that period appears as a golden age of low unemployment, low inflation, and rapid growth. At the time, however, concern was frequently expressed about the level of unemployment and in-

flation, and Britain's poor performance relative to her trading partners. The main constraint on policy was seen as the balance of payments. Too rapid growth in Britain led to a deficit in the balance of payments and fears of a capital outflow and a run on the pound. The usual response was a package of fiscal and monetary policies aimed at cutting demand, with increases in interest rates to attract foreign financial capital back into Britain. In this period, there was a consensus that Keynes's model of the economy was the right one. Elaborate econometric models were constructed and used to guide policy. The small and frequent adjustments to aggregate demand were referred to as "fine tuning" the economy.

THE ERA OF INFLATION AND ANTI-INFLATIONARY POLICY

As inflation increased markedly in the 1970s, macroeconomics increasingly became focused on reducing inflation. The fact that inflation and unemployment both increased—an effect that became known as stagflation—cast doubt on the traditional concept of the Phillips curve, with a stable trade-off between inflation and unemployment. As we have seen, new classical economists focused attention on the role of expectations, which could change quickly. This meant that bad economic policy could quickly give rise to inflation, but it also meant that good economic policy could quickly bring inflation under control.

The failure of government policy to provide a stable macroeconomic environment provided renewed interest in rules-based policy. Adopting rules-based policies would bring an immediate reward: the *expectation* that inflation would thereby be controlled would immediately bring down the inflation rate. In particular, monetarism, which sought to bring inflation under control by fixing the rate of growth of the money supply, enjoyed a period of popularity in many industrialised economies, before becoming discredited as the relationship between money supply and national income became unstable.

The decade of the 1970s was one of economic uncertainty and instability. The collapse of the Bretton Woods system of fixed exchange rates changed the environment within which macroeconomic policy was carried out. It removed the balance of payments constraint on expansionary fiscal and monetary policies. However, the British government quickly discovered that this constraint had been replaced by another. While the balance of payments was no longer a constraint, the inflationary consequences of a depreciating currency did indeed provide such a constraint, following a policy experiment in 1972 (Mr Barber's "Dash for Growth") which had unexpected consequences.

The 1970s was also a decade of supply shocks, which arrived in the shape of dramatic rises in oil prices in 1973 and 1979 and worsening industrial relations. The combination of low inflation and unemployment of the 1950s had slipped out of reach. Inflation was 25 percent per year in 1975, and unemployment almost 1 million people.

Incomes policies were tried repeatedly during the 1970s in efforts to improve the unemployment-inflation trade-off—to get less unemployment without creating more inflation. In the end, they were judged to have failed. They were abandoned after the famous "winter of discontent" of late 1978 and early 1979 when cooperation between trade unions and a Labour government conspicuously disintegrated.

The effectiveness of Keynesian-style demand management policies appeared to be less and less over the decade. Control of the money supply took on increasing importance. James Callaghan, then chancellor of the exchequer, remarked in 1976, "We can no longer spend our way out of recession," in many ways sounding a death-knell for Keynesian demand management.

By 1979, when Margaret Thatcher's government came to office, the objectives of macroeconomic policy had changed. Inflation was now given much greater prominence. The instruments of policy had also changed. Controlling the money supply was the principal instrument of policy. Fiscal policy was stood on its head. Instead of being used to stabilise demand, it was used effectively to destabilise demand: government borrowing was to follow a preset course. Unemployment was no longer a target of policy. The rate of unemployment was allowed to settle where it might, since this was believed to be close to the NAIRU. The NAIRU was itself regarded as an unknown and shifting quantity, and thus there could not be a target unemployment rate, for fear of aiming above or below the NAIRU and thereby creating either inflation or deflation.

The Thatcher government pursued structural policies aimed at cutting the NAIRU: reform of trade union laws, changes in unemployment benefits and social security, amendments to job protection legislation, changes to the housing market, deregulation, privatization of public enterprises, all aimed (at least in part) at enhancing competition and flexibility of markets.

POLICY IN THE 1990S

Macroeconomic policy in Britain in the 1990s has continued to be dominated by the objective of achieving price stability, intertwined with issues arising out of Economic and Monetary Union in Europe.

While low inflation has remained the main target, the instruments of policy used to achieve it have continued to change. Between 1990 and September 1992, Britain was a member of the Exchange Rate Mechanism (ERM) of the European Monetary System and was required to keep the pound fixed within a band of DM 2.95 plus or minus 6 percent. Britain entered the system to make a commitment to a low inflation policy, tying the pound to the deutsche mark with its history of low inflation (at least in the post-1945 period). Many European countries have pursued the same policy with success during the 1980s and 1990s. However, in Britain's case, it proved impossible to remain in the ERM in 1992 when Germany's domestic economic situation caused her to maintain high interest rates, while Britain had a deepening recession. There was a speculative attack on the pound and the Italian lira in September 1992, as a result of which the pound left the ERM and reverted to being a floating currency.

Membership of the ERM had been intended to provide a framework for monetary policy and a nominal anchor for the price level in Britain. Since control of the money supply according to a preset target growth plan had proved an unreliable guide, the idea had been to fix the exchange rate instead, use interest rates to manage the exchange rate, leaving the money supply to be determined by the demand for money, and let inflation be determined, effectively, by German inflation.

When Britain left the ERM in September 1992, monetary policy in Britain was left, it was said, with-

The United Kingdom has been portrayed as a place where flexible labour markets have enabled unemployment to diminish as foreign investment has come into the country and new jobs have emerged to absorb the high unemployment of the 1980s. But at the same time it is often claimed that too many of the new jobs have been low pay, low security, part-time, low skill jobs in the growing service sector of the economy—McJobs, so-called in a reference to the near-casual employment provided by the big fast food chains. The United Kingdom has been likened to the United States, as a dynamic economy with a flexible labour market. It has been contrasted with the continental economies, Germany, France, Italy, and others, where workers enjoy extensive protection against losing their jobs and wages are protected by strong minimum wage provisions and strong unions but where, as a result, unemployment remains very high and job creation has been low.

The data shown in the following figure give the lie to this popular image. Job creation has been vastly greater in the United States, Japan, and Canada than in any European country in the period 1980 to 1993. The United Kingdom falls in between Germany and France in terms of job creation. The drift towards employment in services rather than in manufacturing and other production industries is, however, common to all developed economies. The McJobs issue in the United Kingdom is an echo of a similar concern about the growth of low quality employment in the United States.

Analysis of employment growth in the United States shows that in fact more than 60 percent of the new jobs have been in relatively highly paid occupations, such as finance and computer services. While part-time employment has been growing, the number of persons working part time because they were unable to find a full-time job has been falling. It seems that more and more people want to take up part-time work. These new kinds of jobs may be responding to people's preferences and providing high quality employment.

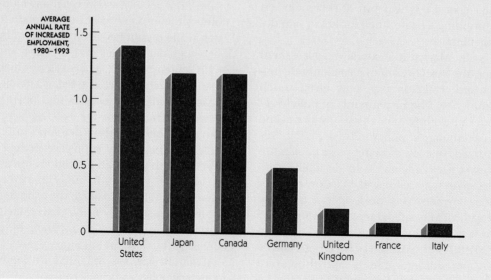

In the United Kingdom many new jobs have been created in the burgeoning new call centres, which in 1998 employed 1.1 percent of the U.K. workforce and are forecast to double that by 2001. They employ more than coal, steel, and vehicle production put together. These jobs are often part time and may involve work outside the normal working day, so-called unsocial hours. They receive typically no union recognition, and they offer employers unparalleled opportunities for monitoring their workers' performance. Might these be a disguised revival of the sweatshops of the past? In any event they provide employment in a number of high unemployment regions.

The call centres also offer an excellent opportunity for studying how workers respond to different systems of payment and supervision. Researchers at the Centre for Economic Performance at the London School of Economics are engaged in an extensive project on the topic.

Sources: Sue Fernlie, "Hanging on the Telephone," *CentrePiece* 3, no. 1 (Spring 1998), pp. 6–11; U.S. Bureau of Labour Statistics, U.S. Department of Labour.

out a clear guiding framework. Since then, the idea of an inflation target has been enunciated. Initially the government announced a target range for inflation of 1 to 4 percent and stated an intention of being in the lower half of the range by mid-1997. More recently the target has been set at 2.5 percent inflation per annum. The monetary instrument for achieving this objective is the short-term interest rate, which the Bank of England effectively sets. It uses all the information that can be obtained from the money supply, exchange rates, interest rates, wages and prices, GDP, and so on, to guide its policy.

Thus the change in monetary policy is that instead of having an *intermediate* target (the money supply in the 1980s, the exchange rate in the early 1990s), there is now only the *final target,* namely inflation itself, for monetary policy. This policy has been followed in other countries, such as Canada and New Zealand. Other countries have continued to use the money supply as an intermediate target, Germany being the prime example.

While maintaining or achieving price stability remained the prime economic objective of the 1990s, throughout the developed world, the secondary objective of policy became the limitation of government deficits and national debts. In Europe, the Maastricht Treaty and the criteria for membership in the EMU brought debts and deficits to the forefront of attention and caused deficit reduction to dominate the formulation of fiscal policy. European countries, including Britain, strove to reduce the fiscal deficit to below 3 percent of GDP. Besides this criterion on the deficit, the Maastricht Treaty also set an upper limit on the debt-to-GDP ratio of 60 percent. Many EMU members had debt levels far in excess of 60 percent.

The effects of the Maastricht criteria were to make fiscal policy contractionary. In a period of widespread recession in the early 1990s, European countries were cutting their fiscal deficits. Once again, this focus on deficit limitation undermines the ability of government expenditures and taxation to act as an automatic stabiliser and contributes to greater cyclical variability.

While the overall macroeconomic performance of the economy in the mid- to late 1990s was strong (the sum of the unemployment and inflation rates, known as the misery index, was the lowest it had been in three decades), there were many individuals whose enthusiasm over the economy did not match the economic statistics. Many workers felt insecure. There was reportedly an absence of the so-called feelgood factor. Economists traced this sense of insecurity to two trends.

One is the onward march of technical advance combined with competitive pressure which has led many large companies to downsize and delayer their workforces. Many white-collar jobs in the financial services industries are being lost in this way. More and more firms are employing staff on fixed-term and part-time contracts with less good compensation for redundancy. Many skilled salaried workers feel that their jobs are less secure than they once were.

A second factor is growing inequality of incomes. In Britain this is partly a result of tax changes, which have led to a less redistributive tax system, and partly a result of a widening gap between the wages of unskilled and skilled workers. Throughout Europe, a growing issue is the existence of a large number of relatively unskilled unemployed adult male workers whose employment prospects have worsened as a result of changes in technology, shifts in the pattern of trade, and economic development in the rest of the world.

Joseph Schumpeter, a famous economist of the early twentieth century who emphasised the role of innovation, described the market economy as a process of creative destruction: jobs were always being destroyed at the same time that new jobs were being created. For example, British Telecom has reduced its employment substantially since privatization. Nevertheless, overall employment in the telecommunications sector has increased as a result of the vast array of new products that have come about from enhanced competition in the sector. While the economy as a whole may benefit, particular individuals—those who lose their jobs—are worse off.

Those economists referred to earlier as interventionists believe not only that government should actively try to reduce the magnitude of economic fluctuations but also that it should reduce the costs of unemployment and transitions. While noninterven-

tionists argue that unemployment is at most a temporary phenomenon and that individuals should cope with it on their own (for instance, by putting aside savings), interventionists believe that the government-run unemployment insurance programme has made an important contribution in enhancing economic security. (This is true even if it may have, at the same time, led to higher unemployment rates because it reduced individuals' incentives to search for a new job.)

ECONOMIC CHALLENGES OF THE TWENTY-FIRST CENTURY

As we have seen, every period has its own economic problems. Just as it is difficult to predict the performance of the economy a year or two from now, it is hard to predict the central problems and controversies that will be facing the economy in five or ten years. It is probable that the challenges we have discussed in this chapter—maintaining full employment with stable prices and addressing the concerns of dislocated and low-wage unskilled workers—will still be there. It is also probable that the issue to which we turn in the next chapter—enhancing the rate of growth—will also be at the forefront. But whatever the problems, the kinds of analytic tools and ways of thinking that we have considered in this and the preceding two parts of the book will be a central part of the framework that policymakers use as they address those problems.

REVIEW AND PRACTICE

SUMMARY

1 Those who bear the cost of inflation tend to be different from those who bear the cost of unemployment. The latter costs tend to be concentrated especially among the unskilled.

2 The economy is constantly subjected to fluctuations. The fluctuations are partially generated exogenously, by disturbances from the outside, and partially endogenously, by the structure of the economy. The structure of the economy may also amplify exogenous

shocks, resulting in effects which persist long after the initial disturbance. Economic expansions have varied greatly in their duration, and contractions in their depth. Still, there are marked similarities among fluctuations in the manner in which different variables (like output, employment, and hours) move together.

3 Those who criticise active intervention argue that markets adjust quickly, so that unemployment is only short lived. Attempts by government to intervene are not only unnecessary but are largely ineffective, since they are offset by actions of the private sector. And to the extent that they do have effects, such policies often exacerbate fluctuations, because of the long lags and the limited information of the government and because political pressures result in the government's overheating the economy before elections.

4 Most governments believe that they should intervene to help stabilise the economy. Without government intervention, there may be long periods of high and persistent unemployment. While policymakers recognise that there are often long lags and that policy is made with imperfect information, so that at times, policy may be ill timed or counterproductive, on average, policy can be and has been stabilising.

5 Critics of discretionary policy believe governments should tie their hands, using fixed rules. But critics of fixed rules argue not only that this represents giving up on an important set of instruments but that fixed rules never work well, because they fail to respond to the ever-changing structure of the economy.

6 Current policy discussions recognise that the economy cannot be kept at unemployment rates below the NAIRU for long. The debate is over two questions. What is the level of the NAIRU and have changes in the structure of the economy raised or lowered it? What are the risks and rewards of aggressive policies trying to keep the unemployment rate at the NAIRU versus those of more cautious policies, which lower the unemployment rate only after evidence that the NAIRU is lower has mounted?

7 Those who argue for aggressive policies believe that the costs in lost output and economic insecurity from the failure to keep unemployment as low as possible without giving rise to large inflationary risks are significant, while the real costs of low inflation are small, especially when there is indexing. They also believe that it is not too costly to correct a mistake, that is, pushing the unemployment rate below the NAIRU for a short period of time. Those who argue for more cautious policies worry that once started, inflationary episodes are hard to bring under control, typically requiring extended periods of high unemployment. They think not only that the costs of inflation are high but also that the short-run benefits of reduced unemployment are more than offset by the risks of higher unemployment, should inflation be ignited and the government and central bank be forced to disinflate.

8 Governments can pursue policies that will serve both to stabilise the economy (automatic stabilisers) and to lower the NAIRU (by improving labour mobility, increasing competitiveness of markets, and moral suasion).

9 Each period in our economy's history has had its own economic problems, such as avoiding overheating the economy in the 1950s and 1960s, controlling inflation and avoiding stagflation in the 1970s, recovering from the recessions of 1981 to 1983 and 1991 to 1993. In the mid-1990s, with inflation under control, concerns focused on stimulating economic growth, enhancing economic security, and reducing the deficit.

KEY TERMS

exogenous	real business cycle
endogenous	monetarists

dynamic consistency	monetary aggregates
New Keynesianism	

REVIEW QUESTIONS

1 What are the alternative explanations of the sources of the economy's fluctuations? What is the relationship between views about the nature of these fluctuations and views about the role of government?

2 What are some of the controversies today in macroeconomic policy? What are some of the disagreements concerning the risks associated with pursuing an aggressive policy, maintaining the economy at a rate of unemployment as close to the NAIRU as possible?

3 How do inflation and unemployment affect different groups differently, and how do these differences affect views concerning macroeconomic policy?

4 Why do some economists believe that active government intervention in an attempt to stabilise the economy is either unnecessary or undesirable? What are the counterarguments?

5 Describe the rules versus discretion debate.

6 What steps may the government take to lower the NAIRU?

7 What is an intermediate target for the guidance of monetary policy?

8 Describe the principal macroeconomic problems of the past five decades.

9 What are some of the major macroeconomic challenges currently facing the country?

PROBLEMS

1 Describe the actions of the private sector that might offset the following actions of government. In which cases do you think the actions will *fully* offset the government actions?

(a) The government increases the money supply.

(b) The government attempts to increase aggregate demand by increasing government expenditures without increasing taxes.

(c) The government increases social security payments to the elderly in an attempt to make them better off. (Assume that the elderly currently receive some financial support from their children or that the individuals save for their retirement needs, with the level of savings determined in order to attain a certain standard of living in retirement.)

(d) The government attempts to reduce inequality by taxing inheritances.

2 In the United States, tax changes require the approval of both houses of Congress as well as of the president before they are put into effect. This is at best a very slow process, which may take years, or indeed, it may never happen at all. How might this feature have affected the balance between the use of fiscal and monetary policies for stabilising the economy in the United States?

3 Some critics of indexed bonds have argued that indexation will reduce government's resolve to fight inflation. Compare the *real* costs to government of an increase in inflation when the government has used, say, long-term indexed bonds and when it has used conventional long-term bonds to finance its borrowing. Compare the real costs to bondholders of an increase in inflation in the two circumstances. Do you think that indexation will increase or decrease the resolve to fight inflation?

Other critics of indexed bonds have argued that indexation imposes a huge risk on the government, because if inflation increases, the government will have to pay more interest. Proponents suggest that indexation reduces the risk faced by the government, because there is less variability in the *real* payments made by government. Assume the rate of inflation in the future may be either 5 percent or 15 percent (with equal probability). Compare the risks associated with an indexed bond paying 2 percent real interest and a nominal bond paying 12 percent. Which form of bond do you think is less risky from the government's perspective?

4 If the economy is in a boom, why might a multiplier-accelerator model predict that it will eventually slow down? If the economy is in a recession, why might the multiplier-accelerator model predict that it will eventually speed up?

5 In the traditional multiplier-accelerator model, an increase in GDP of £10 billion gives rise to an increased demand for additional capital. If the desired ratio of capital to output is 2 and if the £10 billion increase in output is believed to be permanent, what is the increase in the desired level of capital? Assume firms try to fill this gap in one year. What then is the increase in desired investment? If prices of capital goods rise in booms and fall in economic downturns, why might increases in output give rise to smaller increases in the demand for investment in booms and larger increases in economic downturns? What happens to the demand for investment if firms believe that the economic expansion will not be sustained?

6 A decision tree outlines the consequences of each decision depending on how some uncertainty is resolved. A decision tree follows for the government's decision to pursue an aggressive or a cautious unemployment-inflation policy. The NAIRU is either 5 or 6 percent, but the government is uncertain about the real value of the NAIRU. Under the aggressive strategy, it will set the unemployment rate at 5 percent; under the cautious strategy, it will set it at 6 percent. Each strategy has different consequences, depending on the real value of the NAIRU. These are outlined in the decision tree.

Aggressive Strategy: set unemployment at 5 percent

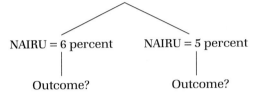

NAIRU = 6 percent NAIRU = 5 percent

Outcome? Outcome?

Cautious Strategy: set unemployment at 6 percent

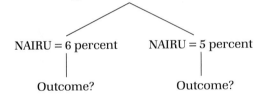

NAIRU = 6 percent NAIRU = 5 percent

Outcome? Outcome?

Fill in the outcomes for each branch of the decision tree under the following assumptions:

(a) It takes two years to discover the true NAIRU (if the government chooses the aggressive strategy when the NAIRU is actually 6 percent, higher inflation will occur in two years, indicating the real value of the NAIRU).

(b) Keeping the unemployment rate 1 percentage point below (above) the NAIRU for one year increases (decreases) the inflation rate by 1 percentage point.

(c) Decreasing (increasing) the unemployment rate by 1 percentage point increases (decreases) output by 2 percent.

(d) The GDP is initially at £1,000 billion.

(e) After the real NAIRU is discovered, the government changes the unemployment rate so as to return the inflation rate to its original level over a two-year period.

(f) Ignore any indirect effect of inflation on output.

What happens to output and inflation during the four-year period for each policy option? Evaluate the trade-offs between the aggressive and cautious policies.

PART EIGHT

ISSUES IN MACROECONOMIC POLICY

Unemployment and inflation, the subjects of Parts Six and Seven, are not the only economic concerns that make the news. The joys and horrors of European integration, starvation in Ethiopia, and economic crises in the formerly Communist countries of the Soviet Union and Eastern Europe are among other events that have grabbed headlines in the past decade. In this part of the book, we use the principles and insights developed in the preceding chapters to take a look at these and other current public policy issues.

In many countries, the United Kingdom and the United States prominent among them, there is concern about slow economic growth. Chapter 34 explores what causes economic growth and what policy measures can be used to stimulate it.

We hear much about regionalization and globalization in the media. Chapter 35 examines the issue that has loomed over Britain for decades—European integration. Chapter 36 takes a global rather than a regional perspective and examines international trade policy, including barriers to trade, fair trade laws, and international trade agreements.

The collapse of communism is undoubtedly one of the biggest events of the twentieth century, just as its rise was. In the aftermath of the First World War, the Soviet Union established an alternative economic system that, it was believed, would eventually dominate capitalism. In Chapter 37, we look at what the system's basic tenets were, why it failed, and the problems the countries that embraced it face today in making the transition to capitalism.

Most of the world lives in countries where incomes are but a fraction of those in western Europe, Japan, the United States, and the other developed countries. By the standards in these developing countries, referred to as the Third World, most people who consider themselves poor in the developed countries are indeed well off. In Chapter 38 we learn some of the major differences between the developed and developing countries. We also ask, what are some of the major issues facing these poorer countries as they struggle to grow and raise themselves out of the mire of poverty in which they have remained for centuries?

34

GROWTH AND PRODUCTIVITY

The period between 1950 and 1973 now appears as a golden age of rapid economic growth and stability in the developed world. This is particularly true for continental Europe, but also for the United Kingdom and North America. The performance of the United Kingdom, the United States, and Canada in the golden age was less impressive than that of the continental European countries, but it was nevertheless much better than their performance in the years that followed. Britain has spent the whole of the postwar period (1945 onwards) coming to terms with its declining role in the world, and there has been continued agonising over its poor record of economic growth. The United States has also grown relatively slowly in the postwar period. It has lost its position as the richest country in the world (in terms of real GDP per head of population) and worries about its relative decline.

Nevertheless, the rise in standards of living continues. Sustained economic growth, which took off in Britain in the late eighteenth century, is now regarded as a permanent and natural feature of the developed world. The real gross national product per head in Britain rose by a factor of four during the nineteenth century and has risen by roughly a factor of three and a half in the twentieth century (between 1900 and 1992). In toto, the real income of the United Kingdom per person has increased roughly by a factor of fourteen between 1800 and 1992. As growth has progressed, all aspects of life have changed dramatically. Life expectancy has risen, hours of work have fallen, and schooling and higher education have been massively expanded.

A major goal of this chapter is to understand what causes economic growth. A second is to understand why growth rates differ from country to country and from one time period to the next.

KEY QUESTIONS

1 What are the principal determinants of growth in the economy?

2 What factors might account for the variation in growth rates from time to time and from country to country?

3 Are there policies available to the government that might stimulate economic growth?

The rate of growth of the economy depends on two factors: the rate of increase in the number of hours worked, and the rate of increase in the output per hour worked, the *productivity* of the labour force.

In the 1950s and 1960s, Britain fell behind much of Europe in economic growth. In the 1980s, it had something of a revival. To see why growth rates change, we need to understand better the underlying forces giving rise to increases in the labour force and productivity.

EXPLAINING PRODUCTIVITY

Sustained growth in productivity (output per hour of work) took off in Britain in the late eighteenth century with a rash of new inventions that transformed the cotton industry. Arkwright's water frame (1769), Hargreaves's spinning jenny (1770), and Compton's mule (1779) transformed it in forty years from a tiny industry into the principal engine of the industrial

revolution, contributing 8 percent of Britain's GDP. The subsequent arrival of steam power, the development of the canals and then the railways, and the growth of the woolen industry, coal, iron, steel, and engineering contributed to the Industrial Revolution which made Britain in the middle of the nineteenth century the first industrial nation and the richest country in the world. Later in the nineteenth century, other countries—the United States and some continental European countries—began to catch up with Britain. By 1900, the United States was a richer country, and Britain's relative decline was already under way. As Figure 34.1 shows, in 1994, per capita real GDP in Britain was less than that of Canada, France, Germany, Italy, Japan, and the United States. Britain was, in other words, the poorest of the G7 (Group of 7) countries, the seven largest developed economies in the world. Figure 34.2 shows that the rate of growth of per capita real GDP over the period 1965 to 1990 was slower in Britain than in any other G7 country except the United States. Japan enjoyed particularly rapid growth over the period.

While countries have differed in their productivity growth rates, Figure 34.2 makes it clear that apart

Rate of growth of economy = rate of increase in the number of hours worked plus the rate of increase in the output per hour worked.

$$g_Q = g_H + g_P,$$

where g_Q = rate of growth of output
  g_H = rate of increase in number of hours worked
  g_P = rate of increase in productivity
    (output per hour).

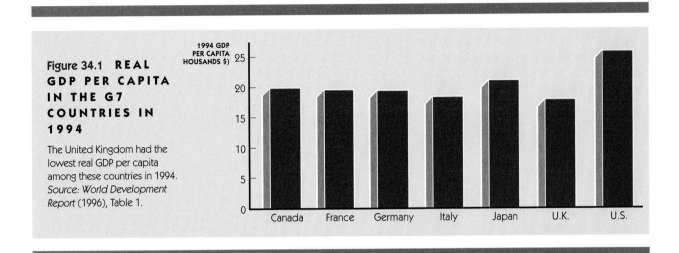

Figure 34.1 REAL GDP PER CAPITA IN THE G7 COUNTRIES IN 1994

The United Kingdom had the lowest real GDP per capita among these countries in 1994. *Source: World Development Report* (1996), Table 1.

from Japan the differences have been small. The other countries' growth rates lay roughly between 2 and 3.5 percent per annum. The importance of the differences is that they have cumulative effects. Suppose two countries start out with real incomes of £10,000 per head, but one country grows at 2.5 percent while the other grows at 3.5 percent. After thirty years, the country growing at 3.5 percent has a real income of £28,100 while the country growing at 2.5 percent has a real income of only £21,000.

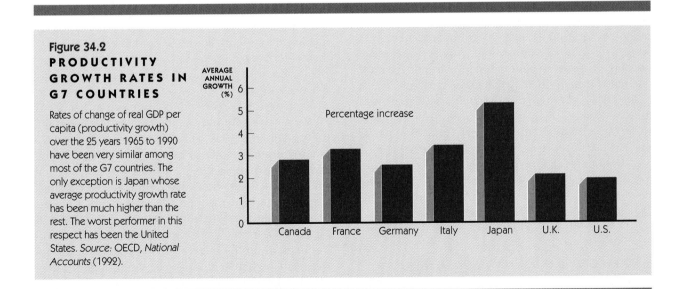

Figure 34.2 PRODUCTIVITY GROWTH RATES IN G7 COUNTRIES

Rates of change of real GDP per capita (productivity growth) over the 25 years 1965 to 1990 have been very similar among most of the G7 countries. The only exception is Japan whose average productivity growth rate has been much higher than the rest. The worst performer in this respect has been the United States. *Source:* OECD, *National Accounts* (1992).

Table 34.1 GROWTH OF REAL GDP PER HEAD IN THE UNITED KINGDOM COMPARED WITH OTHER COUNTRIES, 1950–1989

	United Kingdom	12-Country Median
1950–1973	2.4	3.4
1973–1979	1.5	2.0
1979–1989	2.1	1.9

Source: C. Bean and N. F. R. Crafts, "British Economic Growth since 1945: Relative Decline . . . and Renaissance?" in *Economic Growth in Europe since 1945*, N. F. R. Crafts and G. Toniolo, eds. (London: Cambridge University Press/Centre for Economic Policy Research, 1996).

Table 34.1 shows that during the golden age, 1950 to 1973, Britain's growth fell behind the median of 12 other industrial countries. (However, by Britain's own historical record, 2.4 percent per annum was good.) The 1970s were a period of slow growth everywhere. Britain's growth rate fell, though less than elsewhere, and the gap narrowed. In the 1980s, Britain's growth bounced back and slightly exceeded the 12-country median. Thus there may be grounds for optimism about its long-term position relative to other countries. The 1980s rebound has been the subject of a lot of controversy. It is still not clear whether it was a temporary blip or a more lasting change in Britain's productivity growth rate.

To see why productivity growth has varied over time and across countries, we need to understand what causes increased output per hour of work in the first place. There are four key factors: savings and investment, education and the quality of the labour force, reallocating resources from low to high productivity sectors, and research and development. The next four sections discuss each of these in turn.

SAVINGS AND INVESTMENT

Workers today are more productive than they were twenty or one hundred years ago because they have more and better machines. A European or American textile worker can produce far more than a textile worker in India, partly because of differences in the equipment they use. Many textile workers in India still use handlooms, similar to those used in Europe and America two hundred years ago.

Modern machines are expensive. Someone has to put aside money to buy them; someone has to save. If the savings rate is higher, there will be more investment; the quality and quantity of machines people have to work with will increase, and so will productivity. One of the distinguishing features of Japan and the other rapidly growing countries of East Asia is their remarkably high savings and investment rates, which greatly exceed those of Europe and North America.

Economists have attempted to estimate the contribution of investment to economic growth and to what extent lower rates of investment have contributed to lower rates of growth of productivity. Though there is some disagreement, perhaps the most widely accepted estimate is that of Robert Solow, who received a Nobel Prize for his contributions to growth theory. He estimated that over the past century, approximately one eighth of the increase in productivity resulted from investment.

Higher levels of investment relative to GDP result in more capital per worker. Economists call this **capital deepening.** As capital per worker increases, output per worker increases. Suppose an economy has an investment rate of 10 percent of GDP and a low level of capital per worker. Increasing its investment rate to 15 percent will raise the level of capital per worker, and thus productivity. This is illustrated in Figure 34.3. Increasing capital per worker from k_0 to k_1 raises output per worker. As the economy moves from the initial situation E_0 to the new one E_1, where output per worker (productivity) is higher, the growth rate increases.

In Chapters 23 and 24 we discussed the relationship between savings and investment. In a closed economy, savings equals investment, as illustrated in Figure 34.4. In the figure, we assume that savings do not depend on the interest rate. A reduction in savings leads to higher interest rates, and higher interest rates lead to lower investment.

In an open economy, matters are somewhat more complicated. Domestic savings need not equal in-

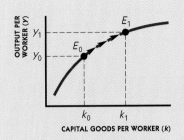

Figure 34.3 INVESTMENT AND PRODUCTIVITY

An increase in the investment rate (the ratio of investment to GDP) results in capital deepening. As capital per worker increases, output per worker increases.

vestment, because the country can finance investment from abroad. (If this is done, gross national product [GNP]—the measure of output that nets out payments of interest and dividends to foreigners—will increase less than GDP, which is simply the amount produced within a country; citizens of the country will have to share the benefits of higher productivity with foreigners.) Conversely, an open economy might save more than it invests and lend the excess abroad. In this case, the GNP will eventually exceed GDP, by the amount of the returns from net investments held abroad. During the nineteenth century and parts of the twentieth, Britain has been a major overseas investor. By 1913, in fact, 25 percent of Britain's total capital excluding land was held overseas. Britain's net wealth held abroad was substantially reduced by the borrowing needed to fi-

nance its activities in the Second World War and during a long period of trade deficits in the 1960s. But in the late 1970s, revenue from North Sea oil brought a temporary increase in GDP, and much of this was invested abroad.

Figure 34.5 compares the savings rates in developed countries. Savings in both the United Kingdom and the United States were considerably lower than in any other G7 country.

Figure 34.6 shows the sources of domestic savings in the United Kingdom. Note that these are gross savings and therefore exceed the net savings reported in Figure 34.5. Until recently, the government has on balance contributed to savings. The largest component of savings has been savings of firms (through undistributed profits), and personal savings have been only a moderate contributor. The total figure

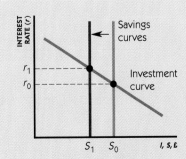

Figure 34.4 SAVINGS AND INVESTMENT

Lower savings rates lead to lower investment in a closed economy.

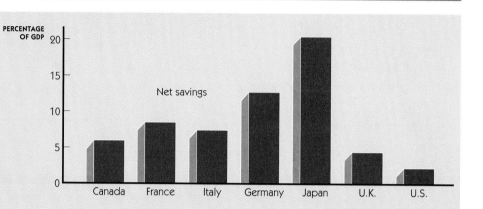

Figure 34.5 SAVINGS RATES IN DEVELOPED ECONOMIES

During the 1980s and 1990s, net savings rates in the United Kingdom and United States were low compared with the other G7 countries. Japan's savings rate was the highest by far. *Source:* OECD, *Economic Outlook* (1990).

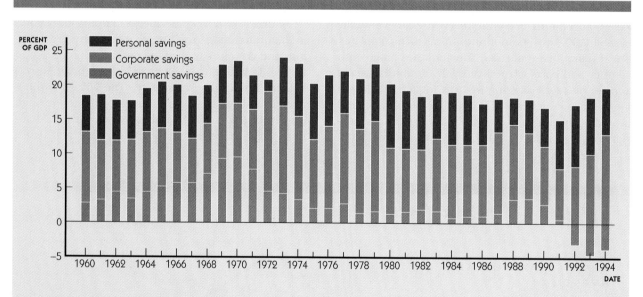

Figure 34.6 SAVINGS IN THE UNITED KINGDOM, 1960–1994

The bulk of gross savings in the United Kingdom has been provided by firms (corporate savings), through retained profits. The government has been a net saver for most of this period, but it became a net borrower in the 1990s. Personal savings have been small. *Source:* Office of National Statistics, *Economic Trends,* Annual Supplement (1996).

has amounted to between 15 and 25 percent of GDP. The rate of saving was noticeably high during the 1970s when inflation was at its height. This was probably because the definition of savings used here includes the appreciation in the value of assets.

Figure 34.7 shows the uses of savings for investment. To domestic savings has to be added the contribution from the rest of the world (foreign savings), which corresponds to the net inflow of financial capital into the United Kingdom. The total of domestic and foreign savings is then used on investment. The bulk of this is domestic fixed capital formation. A small amount is classified as the increase in the value of stocks of goods and other assets. This element includes both the increase in the quality of stocks held and also the increase in the value of existing stocks. Consequently Figure 34.7 shows a clear increase during the inflationary 1970s.

FACTORS THAT INFLUENCE SAVINGS

Throughout the postwar period, there has been concern in Britain that savings have been too low. A number of factors might have influenced savings rates. These include: the real rate of return to savings, the effect of the welfare safety net, the effects of financial market regulations, the housing market, and demographic changes.

During the 1970s, the real return to savings was negative. The nominal rate of interest was frequently below the rate of inflation. After paying income tax on the interest on savings, the real value of the returns—the quantity of goods that could be bought with the initial amount saved plus the interest on it after the period for which it had been saved—was often less than the real value of the initial amount saved. In the 1980s, the real returns became positive. Nominal interest rates exceeded inflation, and the rates of income tax were lowered. This may have stimulated saving to some extent, but all the evidence suggests that savings are not very sensitive to the real rate of return on them.

The social security safety net may have depressed savings. The protection it offers against unemployment and poverty, although limited, is thought to depress savings, by reducing the need to save for a rainy day sometime in the future. The small (and shrinking) state retirement pension reduces people's need to save to provide for their own retirement. State pension provision in Britain does not substitute public savings for private savings, because the state does not save national insurance contributions in

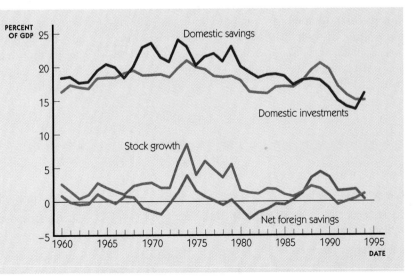

Figure 34.7 SAVINGS AND INVESTMENT, 1960–1994

Domestic savings plus foreign savings (the capital inflow in the balance of payments) are used to finance domestic investment (in fixed capital) plus the increase in the value of stocks of goods (inventories) held by firms and households. *Source:* Office of National Statistics, *Economic Trends*, Annual Supplement (1996).

order to pay out pensions in the future to the people who made the contributions. It pays out the contributions it gets in as pensions to current pensioners: it is a pay-as-you-go scheme. Although people correctly believe that they have wealth in the form of rights to a pension in the future, there is no fund, or stock of real or financial assets, to back that wealth.

Financial market regulation affects savings. Financial markets were deregulated during the 1980s. Building societies and banks began to compete more vigorously to attract deposits and were at the same time freer to make loans to people. The building societies' cartel which set interest rates was abolished. The queues for mortgages, which had existed, vanished. The greater ability to borrow probably caused a greater reduction in savings than the improved return to savings increased it. Overall, financial market deregulation probably contributed to lower savings.

The effects of financial markets in the late 1980s were coupled with the effects of a boom in house prices. Higher property values and easy access to loans enabled people to mortgage property in order to buy other goods, not property. This is called "equity withdrawal." Rising property values made people wealthier, so that rather than needing to save to increase their wealth, they were able to spend some of their higher wealth. This depressed savings in the late 1980s.

Demographic changes may also have affected savings. According to the **life-cycle model of consumption and savings,** people save most during the middle of their lives (25 to 60) while the young (less than 25) and old (more than 60) tend to save less and perhaps dis-save: they spend more than their income, and their wealth falls.

FACTORS AFFECTING INVESTMENT

Britain's slow growth has often been attributed to a low rate of investment and to a misallocation of investment. It is argued that the system by which firms get finance in Britain (and in the United States) makes it more costly and difficult to obtain finance than the system in countries like Germany and Japan does. A second argument is that the tax system has created distortions that have caused too much investment to go into housing rather than into manufacturing and other production industries. It was also believed that by the end of the 1970s the burden of restrictions on businesses and the power of organised labour had reduced managers' freedom to run firms effectively. Employment protection legislation and labour law had contributed to a reduction in the fraction of value added going to capital and reduced the rate of return on investment in industry.

Financial Markets and Investment   In Britain, as in the United States, Canada, and other Anglo-Saxon countries, firms get short-term finance from banks and long-term finance from their owners either directly (in the case of small firms) or indirectly through the stock market (in the case of large firms). British banks have avoided providing long-term loans and equity finance (buying firms' shares and thus taking a fraction of the profits in return for their stake). They have usually provided loans to finance working capital, such as for the cost of raw materials, or the value of the finished or partly finished goods that firms keep in their inventories. This has left firms exposed to the effects of short-term fluctuations in interest rates or of fluctuations in bankers'

FACTORS AFFECTING SAVINGS

Real returns to saving

Social security—unemployment benefits, state pensions, welfare benefits

Demographic changes

Financial market deregulation

Fluctuations in asset prices, particularly house prices

willingness to lend to them. Banks have cut off the supply of loans to firms at precisely the times they most needed them, during periods of recession, and have caused bankruptcies of viable firms.

Raising long-term finance is limited, in the case of a small firm, by the resources of its owners, or, in the case of large firm, by the costs of raising funds on the stock market. The direct costs of raising funds through a share issue are substantial. Indirectly, the stock market imposes costs through its alleged short-termism. Stock prices are very sensitive to current dividends and profits, not long-term future profits. Firms are induced to invest in projects that will pay off very quickly, rather than ones that will have beneficial long-term effects.

By contrast, banks in Germany and Japan have a different relationship with firms. They provide long-term loans which can be used for fixed capital investment. They become actively involved in production and investment decisions, give advice, and help to shape policies in the firms they finance. They provide relatively inexpensive, secure, long-term funding. They do not suffer from the British and U.S. stock markets' short-termism, it is alleged. The relationships between banks and firms in Japan and Germany are credited with a part of their success in the postwar era.

The Allocation of Investment   It is often claimed that too great a fraction of total investment in Britain has gone not into industry but into housing, as a result of subsidies to owner occupation and restrictions on the rented housing markets. Tax relief on the interest on mortgages and exemption of the principal residence of a family from capital gains tax encouraged investment in housing. Around 70 percent of households live in owner-occupied houses. The value of the tax relief is greater in times of high inflation and when the limit on the amount of relief was higher relative to the size of the typical mortgage as it was in the 1970s. Both inflation and the amount of tax relief have fallen substantially in the 1980s and 1990s.

POLICIES TO STIMULATE SAVING AND INVESTMENT

British governments have made modest attempts to stimulate saving and investment over the years.

There have been a number of policies aimed specifically at saving, including the introduction of Personal Equity Plans (PEPs) in the 1980s and the introduction of Tax Exempt Special Savings Accounts (TESSAs) in 1991. The PEPs allow people to invest in stocks and unit trusts up to a limited amount without any liability to capital gains tax or income tax. The TESSAs allow people to invest a limited amount tax-free in a bank or building society account. The PEPs may have been intended to influence the form in which people save, as much as the amount. They were intended to spread share ownership more widely. They have also generated business for the financial industries. For some holders of PEPs, the payment of taxes has merely been replaced by the payment of fees and commissions to the finance houses who administer the PEPs.

Many government policies not specifically aimed at saving and investment may have had effects on them nevertheless. Changes in labour law, intended to reduce the security of employed workers and weaken union power, may have enabled firms to lower costs and get a better return on their investments. Deregulation, cutting the burden of bureaucracy, and policies aimed at lowering inflation may have increased the return to investment.

An absence from the list of policies employed in Britain in the 1980s and 1990s, although much discussed in previous decades, was an industrial policy. This has often been aimed at promoting particular industries or firms. Such policies have been tried in the past and are judged to have failed. Governments, it is argued, are no better at picking winners than the financial markets are. British governments in the 1980s and 1990s reversed the policies of earlier governments and abandoned attempts to prop up declining industries like steel and coal, and have not attempted to stimulate the manufacturing industry. Meanwhile the European Commission has continued to support industry through its regional and structural funds.

WHY LOWER SAVINGS AND INVESTMENT IS NOT THE WHOLE STORY

As important as low savings and investment rates are in explaining low rates of growth of productivity, they are not the whole story. As we have seen, capital accumulation leads to increases in output per worker—in productivity. However, this effect is limited to the short run. When capital deepening is generated from an increase in savings and investment, the economy eventually reaches a new ratio of capital to worker. At the new level of capital to worker, the economy is indeed operating at a higher level of productivity, but the productivity *increase* has run its course. This is illustrated in Figure 34.8, which uses a hypothetical time series for real output to display the economy's growth path. Three segments of the growth path are evident. The first segment (*AB*) represents the economy's growth before the increase in savings and investment. The steep segment that follows (*BC*) represents the period of capital accumulation arising from the increase in savings and investment; as capital per worker increases, so does productivity and the growth rate of the economy. But once the new, higher level of capital per worker is reached, the economy resumes its original growth rate, represented by the third segment (*CD*).

This analysis may suggest that repeated increases in the level of savings and investment, generating continuous capital deepening, will result in long-run acceleration in the rate of productivity increase and therefore a long-run increase in the rate of economic growth. This is not the case. The flaw in the reasoning is overlooking the law of diminishing returns, which says that as the amount of capital goods

per worker continues to increase, successive increments of capital increase output per worker by less and less. Eventually, further increases in capital per worker will yield almost no increase in output per worker. Figure 34.9 shows that as the economy increases capital per worker from k_2 to k_3, the increase in output per worker is much smaller than when the economy increases capital per worker by a similar amount from k_1 to k_2.

Yet in fact, productivity growth did not diminish even in periods of rapid capital accumulation. Japan, for example, has had steadily increasing productivity growth along with large increases in capital goods per worker for the past quarter century.

The reason that productivity growth can continue over long periods is that capital deepening is not the only, or even primary, source of productivity increases. If we are to understand why the rate of productivity growth has not decreased, we need to look at these other sources, to which we now turn.

HIGHER QUALITY OF THE LABOUR FORCE

A second major source of productivity growth, after increased capital per worker, is a higher quality labour force.

Figure 34.8 SHORT-RUN AND LONG-RUN EFFECTS OF CAPITAL DEEPENING

Capital deepening increases output per worker (productivity), and therefore economic growth, but the effects on the rate of growth of productivity (as opposed to the level of productivity) are limited to the short run. The graph shows three segments of a hypothetical growth path. The segment *AB* represents the economy's growth before an increase in savings and investment. The steep segment *BC* represents the period of capital accumulation arising from an increase in savings and investment. Once the new, higher level of capital per worker is reached, the economy resumes its original growth rate, represented by the third segment, *CD*.

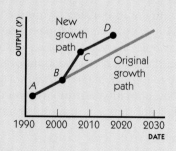

Figure 34.9 DIMINISHING RETURNS TO CAPITAL

With a given production function, the increase in capital goods per worker from k_2 to k_3 would result in a smaller increase in productivity than the corresponding increase from k_1 to k_2.

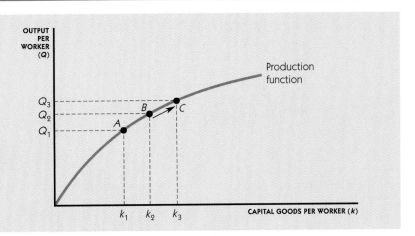

Recent discussions of the quality of the labour force have focused on workers' skills and the possibility that the United Kingdom is falling behind other countries. The more skilled the labour force, the higher the economy's productivity will be. The general consensus is that running a modern industrial economy requires a well-educated labour force. In addition, an economy on the cutting edge of technological change needs trained engineers and scientists to discover and shape those innovations.

Spending money on education and training improves workers' skills and productivity. These expenditures are investments, just like investments in machines and buildings. And just as expenditures on plant and equipment result in physical capital, we say that expenditures on education results in **human capital.** Thus, increases in human capital are one of the major sources of economic growth.

As economies have grown richer, the educational standards of their populations have grown. In the United Kingdom in 1820, the average person aged 15 to 65 had 2 years of education. In 1870, this had grown to 4.4 years. It was 8.8 years in 1913, 10.6 in 1950, 11.7 in 1973, and 14.1 in 1992 (Angus Maddison's estimates). Figure 34.10 gives figures for other major countries. While this may reflect just the effect

of higher incomes on the demand for education, it is universally believed that higher educational standards raise income levels, and therefore that the increases shown in Figure 34.10 have contributed to economic growth.

EXPANSION OF HIGHER EDUCATION IN BRITAIN

Since 1944 when the Butler Education Act made higher education affordable to more people, there has been steady growth in the fraction of people in Britain staying on at school to the age of 18 and then going on to higher education. Many new universities were created during the 1960s to meet a commitment to make university places available to all qualified 18 year olds. Nevertheless, the number of 18 to 22 year olds in higher education in Britain has consistently fallen a long way short of the numbers in many other European and North American countries. Changes in university funding and changes in the incentives and directives given to the universities have resulted in a large increase in participation in higher education in Britain in the 1990s. In 1996, over one-third of all the 18 to 22 year olds participated. This still falls short of the participation rates

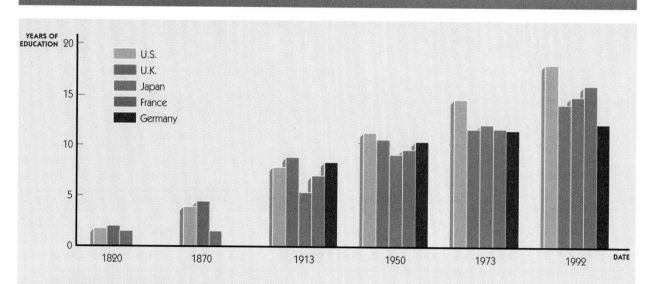

Figure 34.10 YEARS OF EDUCATION

The average amount of schooling, as measured by the years of schooling of the average member of the population, has risen gradually over the last two centuries. In the nineteenth century, Britain had the most highly educated workforce, on this measure. Since then, the United States has moved into the lead with around 18 years of education per person, while there are less than 15 in the United Kingdom. *Source:* Angus Maddison, *Dynamic Forces in Capitalist Development* (London: Oxford University Press, 1995), Table 2-3.

in the United States, Canada, Germany, France, and many other countries, where the rate is in many cases over 50 percent.

It is sometimes claimed that higher education in Britain is highly efficient, since students typically get degrees after three or four years' study, rather than four to six which has been common in continental Europe. However, it is also criticised for having been too specialised, producing too few scientists and engineers and producing too many with degrees in the arts and social sciences. Such concerns point to two issues. One is that the type of educational investment, not merely the total amount, is thought to matter. A second is that the belief persists that choices made by students about the area in which to study do not lead to an efficient allocation of economic resources.

SCIENTISTS AND ENGINEERS

It is often claimed by industrialists and government ministers that there is a shortage of scientists and engineers. But economists should ask how such a shortage would manifest itself and what evidence there is that it exists. A shortage might exist if wages and salaries did not respond to supply and demand but were fixed somehow, by historical precedent maybe, and employers of scientists found that at these wages there were not enough to be had. However, in practice, wages and salaries do respond to supply and demand, although perhaps not instantly, and relative wages and salaries reflect the balance of supply and demand for different groups of workers. In fact it turns out that the incomes and employment prospects of graduate scientists are not high relative to those of graduates in other subjects. On this measure, there appears to be not a shortage but rather an excess supply of scientists.

Through government control of the number of university places in different subjects, large numbers of places have been provided in science and engineering despite the fact that these subjects are unpopular student choices and graduates' earnings are low. The engineering professions appear to have generated an excess supply of engineers rather than an excess demand. By contrast the accounting profession has maintained high salaries by restricting entry—the professional examinations are notoriously difficult to pass and are used to limit the number of accountants—and attracting able people to work in it. Accountants seem to understand economics better than engineers.

CRAFT AND VOCATIONAL SKILLS

Another criticism of British education is that it has an academic bias which has left craft skills—such as skilled fitters, welders, lathe operators, and bricklayers—undersupplied. A long-standing system of apprenticeships, in which young workers, usually teenagers, worked alongside a skilled crafts worker and were trained in the craft over a period (often quite long, as long as five years) has been replaced by formal training in colleges of further education and other institutions. However, these have been treated as the Cinderella end of the postsecondary educational spectrum and not well funded. In addition, the basic academic component of the training offered to skilled manual workers has been poor relative to that offered in continental Europe. In a long series of studies, Professor S. G. Prais of the National Institute of Economic and Social Research has documented the weaknesses of British training, as compared with German and French training, which has provided a labour force better able to work in modern factories. Prais attributed much of the greater efficiency of German car factories in the 1960s and 1970s to the better-trained labour force, itself the product of effective craft training.

IS THERE A SHORTAGE OF MATHEMATICS AND SCIENCE TEACHERS?

The lack of mathematical ability and interest among students in postsecondary education may be partly due to a lack of good mathematics and science teachers. This itself is caused by the low pay of teachers relative to what mathematics and science graduates can earn in other careers. There is an economic argument for paying different amounts to teachers in different subjects, in order to balance supply and demand. However, there has always been resistance from the teachers' unions to paying different wages subject by subject.

COMPREHENSIVES AND GRAMMAR SCHOOLS

There is continuing debate over the merits of educating all children together in comprehensive schools, as opposed to separating them by ability or achievement and educating different streams separately. In the 1960s, comprehensive schools were introduced, and the selection of children at the age of 11 for academic grammar schools or vocational secondary modern schools was ended in most of Britain. The previous system was said to be socially divisive and to lower the aspirations and achievements of those allocated to secondary modern schools. On the other hand comprehensive schools are criticised for holding back the best students. This debate has continued unabated. There are signs that the balance of opinion is turning back in favour of streaming and perhaps to the reintroduction of academically selective schools. The continuation of debate shows how little is understood of the economic and social consequences of different educational systems. It also reflects continuing disagreement over where to strike the balance between equity and efficiency.

Concern about standards in education has led to the introduction of a national curriculum and testing of school children at intervals throughout their schooling. There has been in recent years a return to an emphasis on basic skills—reading, writing, and arithmetic—away from the individualistic approach developed in the 1960s and 1970s which gave more weight to creativity and interpretation.

REALLOCATING RESOURCES FROM LOW TO HIGH PRODUCTIVITY SECTORS

In 1801, 35.9 percent of the British labour force was employed in agriculture. The percentage fell to 21.7 in 1851, 8.7 in 1901, and 5.0 in 1951. Currently it is just a couple of percent. Meanwhile the fraction in manufacturing rose from 29.7 percent in 1801 to 42.9 percent in 1851, 46.3 percent in 1901, and 49.1 percent in 1951. Since then it has fallen back to about 25 percent, while the service sector has burgeoned. Figure 34.11 illustrates the change in the distribution of

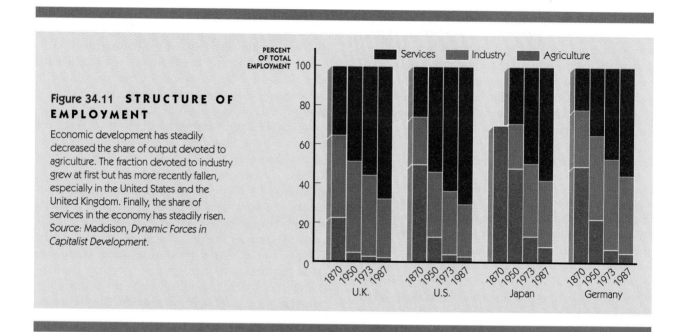

Figure 34.11 STRUCTURE OF EMPLOYMENT

Economic development has steadily decreased the share of output devoted to agriculture. The fraction devoted to industry grew at first but has more recently fallen, especially in the United States and the United Kingdom. Finally, the share of services in the economy has steadily risen. *Source:* Maddison, *Dynamic Forces in Capitalist Development.*

the labour force across industries for a number of countries.

The movement out of agriculture and into industry explains much of the productivity increase in the nineteenth century. While the level of productivity in agriculture was increasing rapidly, it remained lower than in industry. Thus, as workers shifted out of low-productivity jobs in agriculture into high-productivity jobs in manufacturing, average productivity in the economy increased. With almost all labour now out of agriculture—and with agricultural productivity increased to the point where incomes in that sector are comparable to those in the rest of the economy—this kind of shift can no longer be a source of overall productivity growth. But there remain other opportunities. The recent growth of services has been associated with new technology and products in services. Whereas services were once regarded as a sector relatively incapable of productivity growth, it has become clear that in the financial industries, telecommunications, and other services, advances in electronics and computing have permitted great productivity growth and development of new products.

TECHNOLOGICAL CHANGE

This final source of productivity growth may be the most important. Indeed, it has been estimated that as much as seven-eighths of all increases in productivity are due to technological progress. One of the major differences between the economy today and in 1900 is the routine nature of change in the modern economy. The prototype of the nineteenth- and early twentieth-century inventors was men like Thomas Edison and Alexander Graham Bell—lone individuals, working by themselves or with a small number of collaborators. Small entrepreneurs and innovators continue to play a role in developing new products, particularly in the computer industry. But the prototype of a modern research effort, like the U.S. programme to put a man on the moon, has thousands of scientists working together to accomplish in a few short years what would have been almost unimaginable earlier. Technological change in the modern economy is a large-scale, systematic effort. Modern research is centered in huge laboratories, employing thousands of people. While some of these laboratories are publicly run, like the European particle physics research establishment CERN in Geneva, many are private, like the research labs of Glaxo-Wellcome or the electronics giant Intel. Indeed, most major firms spend about 3 percent of their gross revenue on research and development.

The current level of technological progress has become so expected that it is hard to believe how different the view of reputable economists was in the early 1800s. Real wages of workers were little higher than they had been five hundred years earlier, when the bubonic plague destroyed a large part of the population of Europe and thereby created a great scarcity of labour. After half a millennium of at best slow progress, Thomas Malthus, one of the greatest economists of that time, saw population expanding more rapidly than the capacity of the economy to support it. What was missing from his dismal forecast was technological change.

EXPENDITURES ON R & D

A major determinant of the pace of technological expenditures is the level of expenditures on R & D. These expenditures are a form of investment; expenditures today yield returns in the future. There are two major sources of research funds—corporations and government. Government has primary responsibility for *basic* research—the development of new ideas—from developments in mathematics that eventually led to the computer to developments in our understanding of physics that eventually led to nuclear power, with a wide range of applicability. Industry has primary responsibility for *applied* research, the kind of research that leads to a new software programme, a newly designed telephone, or a better laser. In between, there is a vast gray area, with shared responsibility, and today, research moves from the university to the corporation with great speed. Basic advances in understanding genes quickly spawned firms using genetic engineering to make new drugs.

The amount spent on R & D varies from country to country, as Figure 34.12 shows. Across the G7 countries, it varies from just under 1.5 percent of GDP in Canada to almost 3 percent in Japan. The United Kingdom is towards the lower end of the spectrum with around 2 percent, more than Canada and Italy, but less than Germany, France, Japan, and the United States. Another measure of the amount of

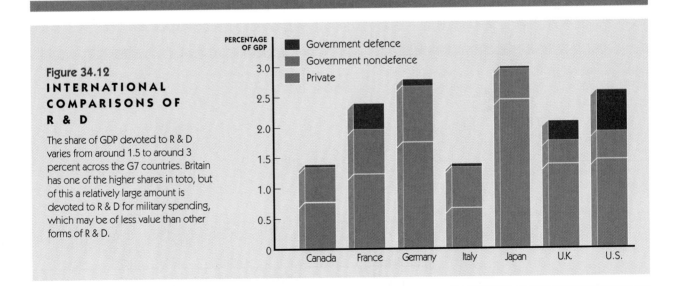

Figure 34.12
INTERNATIONAL COMPARISONS OF R & D

The share of GDP devoted to R & D varies from around 1.5 to around 3 percent across the G7 countries. Britain has one of the higher shares in toto, but of this a relatively large amount is devoted to R & D for military spending, which may be of less value than other forms of R & D.

innovative activity in a country is the number of patent applications it produces relative to its population size (see Figure 34.13). Germany and Japan lead the field by a long way. The United Kingdom, the United States, and France have lower rates of patent applications, and Canada and Italy have much lower ones. An interesting question is why Germany's and Japan's modestly higher R & D expenditures are associated with markedly higher patent applications. The number of patent applications may be associated with their lower fraction of total R & D spending devoted to defence-related R & D and a bigger fraction devoted to non-defence-related R & D.

The relation between R & D, patents, and growth is clearly not a simple one. Japan and Germany stand out as having had high growth at the same time as having high R & D expenditures and patent activity. Italy, however, has had rapid economic growth despite low R & D and patenting. It is not to be expected that R & D and patents translate into immediate effects on growth. New products and processes take time to spread through the economy. Some R & D spending and patents may have more effects on growth than others. Technology spills over from one country to another, so growth in any particular country may benefit from ideas generated in many countries. It used to be argued that while Britain had been an important source of fundamental scientific advances, it had often failed to turn them into commer-

cial successes, and the economic benefits of British science had been enjoyed elsewhere.

Nevertheless, there is a strongly held view that R & D expenditures contribute to growth, and indeed have a high rate of return for firms that make them. Some estimates put the rate of return as high as 25 percent. This, together with the fact that some of the returns to R & D may accrue to firms other than the ones carrying out the research, suggests that there is underinvestment in R & D. This is explained partly by the highly risky nature of R & D and the limitations on the ability to borrow to finance it.

OTHER FACTORS AFFECTING PRODUCTIVITY GROWTH

There are several other factors that may have affected productivity growth in recent years. One is concern about the growth of the service sector, and another is the possible effects of rising energy prices.

The Growth of the Service Industries   Some people have expressed concern that since the share of manufacturing in most economies is declining and services are becoming more prominent, the scope for future productivity growth will diminish. Service industries have in the past appeared to have had less productivity growth than manufacturing industries. However, many of the new services appear to break

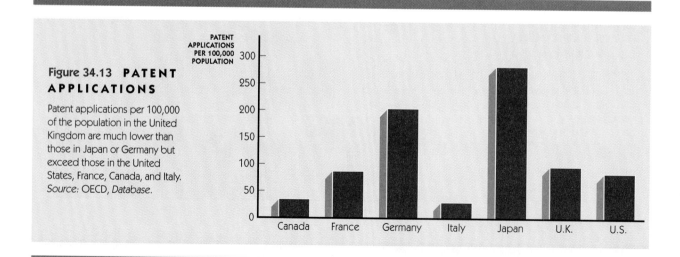

Figure 34.13 PATENT APPLICATIONS

Patent applications per 100,000 of the population in the United Kingdom are much lower than those in Japan or Germany but exceed those in the United States, France, Canada, and Italy. *Source:* OECD, *Database.*

that mold. The use of electronics and new technology in telecommunications and in banking and finance has permitted great productivity growth. Many new service industries, like software development, aid the growing microelectronics industries. Part of the record of low productivity growth in services may have resulted from the failure to measure changes in the quality of products and services. In service industries such as education and health care, where these are provided by the public sector, change in productivity may have been set at zero by assumption. The United Kingdom's national accounts, for example, make the *assumption* that the volume of output of public sector activities which are not sold on the market is equal to the volume of inputs. Thus the quantity of output produced by public spending on education is proportional to the number of teachers and other staff employed, and the volume of other inputs into the process of educational production (with these different inputs suitably weighted to allow for their relative importance). By construction therefore, the GDP figures do not allow for productivity growth in these areas. The effects of technological advances, new equipment and new drugs to enable doctors to treat more patients and to treat them more effectively for example, are not captured in the measured GDP figures.

Energy Prices In 1973 and again in 1979, there was a sharp rise in energy prices. In 1973, OPEC doubled the price of oil overnight. Following this, there was a worldwide slowdown in productivity growth. One possible reason for this was that the world contained a lot of capital equipment designed to operate with relatively inexpensive energy. Following the rise in oil prices, a lot of investment was carried out in order to replace old equipment with new more energy-efficient equipment. Much of R & D expenditures was devoted to developing new more energy-efficient machines and buildings. This may have diverted spending away from attempts to increase productivity. However, this analysis of the effects of the oil shocks is not universally accepted. Critics argue that energy represents only a small fraction of the GDP and note that the real price of energy had declined to its pre-1973 levels by the mid-1980s, questioning the long-run importance of the oil price rises of the 1970s.

TOTAL FACTOR PRODUCTIVITY

The preceding sections have discussed the ways in which various factors affect the growth rate of the economy. However, we have not so far tried to quan-

FACTORS CONTRIBUTING TO PRODUCTIVITY GROWTH

Capital accumulation
    Increasing national savings
        Low sensitivity to interest rates
    Increasing investment
        Tax concessions

Improved quality of labour force
    Education and training
    Educational reforms

Reallocation of labour from low productivity sectors
to high productivity sectors
    Movement from agriculture to industry

Technological progress
    Increased expenditures on R & D

tify the contributions to growth of the different factors. A method called **total factor productivity (TFP) analysis** is used to do this. It works by asking how much growth there would have been, based on the growth of capital and labour inputs in the economy and returns to capital and labour, in the absence of any technological progress.

Suppose the share of capital in output—the amount of output attributable to capital (the total returns to capital divided by GDP)—is 20 percent, and the growth of capital is 10 percent. The share of capital in output (20 percent), multiplied by capital growth (10 percent) gives us the amount that capital growth contributes to the growth of output (2 percent). The same logic applies to labour. But capital and labour do not account for all of growth. The part of growth that cannot be explained by increases in capital and labour is called the increase in total factor productivity. The rate of total factor productivity increase is calculated as follows:

$$\text{TFP} = g_Q - (S_K \times g_K) - (S_L \times g_L),$$

where S_K = share of capital in GDP
          S_L = share of labour in GDP
          g_Q = rate of growth of output
          g_K = rate of growth of capital
          g_L = rate of growth of labour.

The increase in total factory productivity reflects increasing efficiency with which an economy's resources are used. Some of this is the result of research and development, but at least prior to 1973,

much of the increase in total factor productivity could not be easily explained. The part that could not be explained was referred to as the **residual**—the part of growth that was left over after all the systematic sources of growth were taken into account.

Figure 34.14 uses the method just described to analyse the sources of productivity growth in Britain, Germany, and France, for three periods, 1913 to 1950, 1950 to 1973, and 1973 to 1987. The diagram shows how much higher was growth in the golden age (1950 to 1973) than either before or afterwards. During the golden age, total factor productivity growth was the major source of growth in France and Germany, though not in Britain. The gap between Britain and the continental countries opened in that period. The slowdown of growth in the 1970s and 1980s was common to all three countries and was associated with a very large fall in the contribution of TFP, but there was also lower capital accumulation and falling labour inputs. The falling labour inputs reflect falling normal hours of work, earlier retirement, and people withdrawing from the labour market because of unemployment (the discouraged worker effect), set against rising female participation. Grouping together the years 1973 to 1979 with the years 1979 to 1987 obscures the "Thatcher productivity miracle," which emerges only in Britain's not-so-bad productivity (TFP) performance compared with its neighbours for the period.

The difficulty of explaining the unusually high growth in the 1950s and 1960s presents major problems for long-term forecasting. It is not clear whether the rapid growth of productivity in the

USING ECONOMICS: CALCULATING TOTAL FACTOR PRODUCTIVITY

Between 1990 and 1994, it is estimated that GDP went up by 7.3 percent, the capital stock increased by 6.6 percent, the labour force—adjusted for improvements in education—by 6.5 percent. If the share of capital in output is 30 percent and of labour is 70 percent, what is the percent increase in total factor productivity over this period?

Start with the formula for total factor productivity (see p. 664):

$$TFP = g_Q - S_K \times g_K - S_L \times g_L.$$

The percent increase in total factor productivity equals the growth in national output (g_Q) minus the growth in output attributable to capital ($S_K \times g_K$) minus the growth in output attributable to labour ($S_t \times g_L$). Substituting the data for the period from 1990 to 1994,

$$TFP = 7.3 - (0.3 \times 6.6) - (0.7 \times 5.4)$$
$$= 1.54.$$

Figure 34.14 SOURCES OF ECONOMIC GROWTH

Growth of real GDP can be attributed to growth of inputs of labour and capital and to growth of productivity. Productivity growth is simply the part of total growth that cannot be explained. The gap between Britain and the continent was widest during the golden age, 1950 to 1973. In the more recent period, 1973 to 1987, the gap has narrowed considerably. France and Germany have slowed down a lot more than Britain. In the recent period, labour inputs have been falling rather than rising, as very slow population growth, falling hours of work, earlier retirement, and growing unemployment have more than offset the effects of rising participation of women and rising educational standards. *Source:* N. F. R. Crafts and G. Toniolo, "Postwar Growth: An Overview," in *Economic Growth in Europe since 1945*, Crafts and Toniolo, eds. (London: Cambridge University Press, 1996), Table 1.6, p. 9.

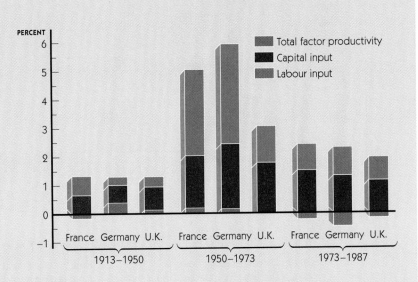

1950s and 1960s was due just to postwar reconstruction and the introduction into the economy of innovations held back by two decades of depression and war. Likewise it is not yet possible to say whether the 1970s and 1980s were an aberration caused by the introduction of new technology like computers whose full benefits have yet to be felt. Since then more substantial changes have occurred—further moves towards the creation of a Single European Market and towards Economic and Monetary Union, the unification of Germany, and the transition of central and eastern European countries to market economies, for example—and these are likely to affect growth. It is difficult to predict the future growth rate of economy.

GROWTH OF THE LABOUR FORCE

Earlier in the chapter, we noted that the total growth rate of the economy equaled the growth in hours worked plus the growth in output per hour worked (productivity).

The slowing of growth after 1973 in Britain, France, and Germany was partly due to a slowdown in the growth of labour inputs. As Figure 34.15 shows, total hours of work grew much more slowly in the period 1973 to 1992 than they had in previous periods. This was due to a combination of four factors: slow population growth, falling rates of partici-

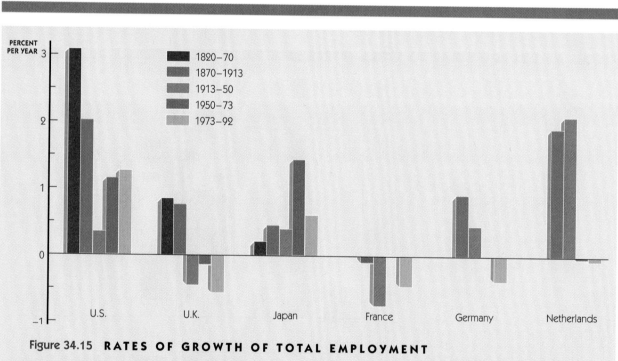

Figure 34.15 RATES OF GROWTH OF TOTAL EMPLOYMENT

Total hours of work—the number of people working multiplied by the average number of hours worked by each of them during the year—grew rapidly in the nineteenth century, and typically, they have grown more slowly in recent decades.

There is a big contrast between Europe on the one hand and Japan and the United States on the other. *Source:* Maddison, *Dynamic Forces in Capitalist Development.*

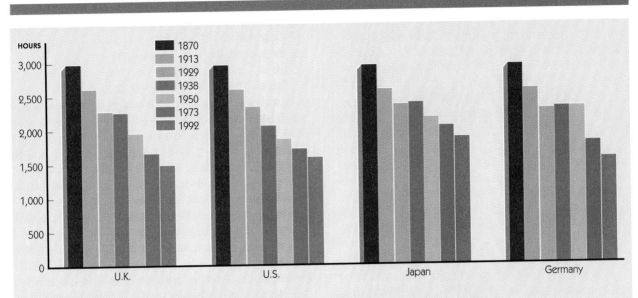

Figure 34.16 AVERAGE HOURS OF WORK PER PERSON PER YEAR

As wage rates have grown, the average number of hours worked per year by a typical worker has fallen, from around 3,000 in 1870 to between 1,500 and 2,000 in 1992. Of the four countries shown here, hours worked were the shortest in the United Kingdom and longest in Japan. *Source:* Maddison, *Dynamic Forces in Capitalist Development.*

pation (the fraction of the population that is members of the labour force), rising unemployment (among participants in the labour force), and falling hours of work. Falling hours of work is a continuation of a long-standing trend and has occurred in all economies, as Figure 34.16 shows. Hours of work per employed person have fallen steadily from just under 3,000 hours a year in 1870 to just under 1,500 in 1992 in the United Kingdom. There is concern that European economies have not been creating jobs on anything like the scale of the United States and Japan. By contrast with Europe, total labour inputs have continued to grow in these economies.

Growth in the labour force is driven by two factors: demographics and participation rates. The demographic factor includes the size and age distribution of the population. In Europe, population growth rates have been low throughout the postwar era, and changes in population growth have contributed relatively little to changes in GDP growth rates.

The decision whether to work—labour force participation—is affected by a variety of economic and noneconomic factors. There has been a marked increase in female labour force participation over the past quarter century, partially offset by a decrease in male labour force participation. Changes in attitudes towards women working, especially when they have children, as well as changes in desired family sizes, reduced discrimination, and increased educational opportunities for women have all contributed to increased female participation.

Participation rates for women (aged 15 to 64) have grown from 40 percent in 1950 to 63 percent in 1987 in the United Kingdom, while those for men have

Table 34.2 LABOUR PARTICIPATION RATES

Females as a Proportion of the Labour Force				
	1910	1950	1973	1987
United Kingdom	29	30.8	36.6	41.1
Average of 16 countries	29.6	30.4	36.3	41.9

Labour Force Participation Rates			
	Persons Aged 65+	Males Aged 15–64	Females Aged 15–64
United Kingdom, around 1950	16	93.9	40.1
Average of 16 countries, around 1950	22.3	91.3	38.1
United Kingdom, 1987	4.8	88.3	62.6
Average of 16 countries, 1987	8.4	83.4	60.6

Source: Angus Maddison, *Dynamic Forces in Capitalist Development* (London: Oxford University Press, 1991), p. 245, Table C2, and p. 247, Table C4.

fallen from 94 to 88 percent over the same period. Consequently, women accounted for 41 percent of the labour force in 1987, as opposed to 29 percent in 1910, 31 percent in 1950, and 37 percent in 1973 (see Table 34.2).

Slower growth of the labour force caused by slower growth of the population has a markedly different effect than slower growth caused by lower productivity. The latter is associated with slower increases in standards of living. By contrast, faster population growth may give rise to congestion and place higher demands on the environment. On the other hand, some economists believe that the rapid expansion of the economy as it seeks to adapt to the increased labour force gives rise to a dynamism which generates increased productivity: increased labour force growth (at least to a point) helps cause increased productivity growth. But the causation also works in reverse: economic slowdowns, such as the Great Depression, lead to low birth rates.

THE COSTS OF ECONOMIC GROWTH

Faith in the virtues of economic progress is widespread. Few openly embrace the alternative of economic stagnation and lower standards of living. Yet not everyone benefits from changes in technology. In the early 1800s, English workers destroyed labour-saving machinery rather than see it take over their jobs. They were referred to as **Luddites,** after their leader Ned Ludd, whose role may have been largely mythical. Concerns about workers thrown out of their jobs as a result of some innovation are no less real today.

What needs to be kept in mind, and has already been stressed earlier in the book, is that technological progress creates jobs as it destroys them. Of course, it can be hard to teach an old dog new tricks, so a middle-aged or older worker who loses her job may have difficulty in getting another that is even nearly as good. How much sympathy this displaced worker should receive is a matter on which reasonable people can disagree. Does a worker who is used to a certain wage have an inalienable right to this wage? Should we pay more attention to the plight of the worker who loses a job and is forced into another one at lower pay than to the benefits to the worker in the new industry who gets a better job? Should one worry more about the plight of the worker who loses a good job than about the plight of one who lacks the skills to get any good job in the first place?

Not surprisingly, technical progress frequently meets with resistance. While there is acceptance that such resistance is futile—change will eventually come—and that the benefits of progress exceed the costs, there is also recognition of the role of government in assisting individuals who are displaced by technological change in their transition to alternative employment. Such assistance can be thought of as a form of insurance. Most workers face the possibility that their jobs will be made technologically obsolete. Knowing that if they are thrown out of work for this reason, they will be at least partially protected adds to a sense of security, something most workers value highly. In the long run, such programmes can help increase the rate at which technological changes are adopted by making the prospect of losing a job less fearful.

More generally, we saw in Part Five that in the long run, with flexible wages, the economy will create enough jobs to match the supply. In Part Six, we saw that in the short run, wage and price rigidity may lead to significant unemployment but that there are government policies that can help ensure that the economy remains close to full employment. To the extent that government employs such policies, there will be fewer worries about jobs. There will be less resistance to new technologies that lead to job loss, as workers become more confident that the economy will at the same time generate new job opportunities.

Are There Limits to Economic Growth?

In the early 1800s, the famous British economist Thomas Malthus envisioned the future as one in which the ever-increasing labour force would push wages down to the subsistence level, or even lower. Any technological progress that occurred would, in his view, raise wages only temporarily. As the labour supply increased, wages would eventually fall back to the subsistence level.

Over the past century, there has been a decrease in the rate of population growth, a phenomenon perhaps as remarkable as the increase in the rate of technological progress. One might have expected improved medicine and health conditions to cause a population explosion, but the spread of birth control and family planning has had the opposite effect, at least in the developed countries. Today family size has decreased to the point where in many countries population growth (apart from migration) has almost halted. Those who worry about the limits to growth today believe that *exhaustible* natural resources—like oil, natural gas, phosphorus, or potassium—may pose a limit to economic growth as they are used up in the ordinary course of production.

Most economists do not share this fear, believing that markets do provide incentives for the wise use of most resources—that as any good becomes more scarce and its price rises, the search for substitutes will be stimulated. Thus, the rise in the price of oil led to smaller, more efficient cars, cooler but better insulated houses, and a search for alternative sources of energy like geothermal and synthetic fuels, all of which resulted in a decline in the consumption of oil.

Still, there is one area in which the price system does not work well—the area of externalities. Without government intervention, for example, producers have no incentive to worry about air and water pollution. And in our globally connected world, what one country does results in externalities for others. Cutting down the rain forest in Brazil, for example, may have worldwide climactic consequences. The developing countries feel that they can ill afford the costs of pollution control, when they can barely pay the price of any industrialization. Most economists do not believe we face an either-or choice. We do not have to abandon growth to preserve our environment. Nevertheless, a sensitivity to the quality of our environment may affect how we go about growing. This sensitivity is building a new consensus in favour of **sustainable development,** that is growth not based simply on the exploitation of natural resources and the environment in a way that cannot be sustained. In many cases, policies can be devised that improve economic efficiency, and thus promote economic growth, at the same time that they decrease adverse environmental effects. These include the elimination of energy subsidies and certain agricultural subsidies which induce farmers to use excessive amounts of fertilisers and pesticides.

The Prognosis

Though this century has been marked by large increases in productivity, the rate of productivity growth has not been steady. There have been periods of relative stagnation as well as periods in which the economy has burst forth with energy and growth. Was the decline in productivity growth of the 1970s and 1980s just a passing phase? Or were the high rates of productivity growth during the 1950s and 1960s the aberration?

The analysis of this chapter suggests grounds for both pessimism and optimism. There is no quick or easy reversal of many of the factors hampering productivity growth, but some of them are more easily altered. These include the failure of government to improve the economy's infrastructure, and the low level of expenditures on research and development, at least expenditures directed at improving the economy's productivity rather than increasing military prowess.

REVIEW AND PRACTICE

SUMMARY

1 The rates of growth of the world's major economies were much greater in the period between 1950 and 1973 than at any time before or since. Britain's growth was slow in that period, relative to other countries, and GDP per head in Britain fell below theirs. However, since 1973, Britain's growth has not slowed down so much as has growth elsewhere. Indeed, there was a revival of growth in Britain in the 1980s. It is not yet clear whether this will prove to be only a temporary improvement or a permanent one.

2 Some of the differences in growth rates between countries may look small, but even small differences, if sustained for a long period, have substantial effects on relative incomes.

3 There are four major sources of productivity growth: increases in the accumulation of capital goods (investment), a higher quality of the labour force, greater efficiency in allocating resources, and technological change.

4 There is considerable concern in many countries, including Britain and the United States, about the contribution made by education to growth. There is concern about standards in schools, and the quality of mathematical skills and scientific knowledge among school leavers. The number of students investing in higher education in Britain has recently been dramatically increased, but it is still a smaller fraction of the relevant age group than in the United States and many European countries.

5 As countries grow richer, the fraction of their resources devoted to agriculture falls. Over the last two centuries, the share of employment in agriculture has fallen in Britain to just over 2 percent. Industry first grows in importance as agriculture diminishes, but more recently services have taken over and industry in its turn has fallen back in importance. The world's developed countries are increasingly service economies. In Britain, services account for over 70 percent of employment.

6 Some economists have argued that the potential for technological progress is less in services than in industry and that for this reason rapid growth will be more difficult to sustain in the future.

7 There has long been concern that the world's supply of certain natural resources (like oil) will someday run out, causing economic growth to halt. However, most economists would argue that the price of resources will increase as they become more scarce, and this will encourage both greater conservation and a search for substitutes.

KEY TERMS

capital deepening

life-cycle model
of consumption and
savings

total factor productivity
analysis

sustainable development

REVIEW QUESTIONS

1 True or false: "Since growth-oriented policies might have an effect of only a percent or two per year, they are not worth worrying much about." Explain.

2 What are the four possible sources of productivity growth?

3 Why might growth rates among developed economies have fallen since the end of the golden age in the early 1970s?

4 What are the components of total savings in the economy? How have they varied over the last forty years or so?

5 Are policies to raise the rate of return on savings (such as the British government's PEPs and TESSAs) likely to lead to increased aggregate savings?

6 What is the link between changes in savings and changes in investment? What is the link between changes in the capital stock (investment) and the rate of growth of productivity in the short run? What is meant by capital deepening?

7 What are some costs of economic growth? Short of seeking to restrain growth, how might government deal with these costs?

8 What are some of the concerns about limits to economic growth? How have they been overcome in the past?

PROBLEMS

1 Will the following changes increase or decrease the rate of household savings?
  (a) The proportion of people in the 45 to 64 age bracket increases.
  (b) Government programmes provide secure retirement benefits.
  (c) Credit cards become much more prevalent.
  (d) The proportion of people in the 21 to 45 age bracket increases.
  (e) Government programmes to guarantee student loans are enacted.

2 Explain how the following factors would increase or decrease the average productivity of labour:
  (a) Successful reforms of the educational system
  (b) The entry of new workers into the economy
  (c) Earlier retirement
  (d) High unemployment rates during a recession

3 Suppose a firm is considering spending £1 million on R & D projects, which it believes will translate into patents that it will be able to sell for £2.5 million in ten years. Assume that the firm ignores risk. If the interest rate is 10 percent, is the firm likely to at-

tempt these R & D projects? If the government offers a 20 percent subsidy on R & D investment, how does the firm's calculation change?

4 Explain why a rapid influx of workers might result in a lower output per worker (a reduction in productivity). Would the effect on productivity depend on the skill level of the new workers?

5 Explain, using supply and demand diagrams, how a technological change such as computerization could lead to lower wages of unskilled workers and higher wages of skilled workers.

6 Using the model of Chapter 23, discuss the effect of:
  (a) An increased government deficit
  (b) An increased government expenditure, financed by taxes on households that reduce their disposable income
  (c) An investment subsidy on the level of investment for an open economy

How will such policies affect future living standards of those living in the country?

CHAPTER 35

ECONOMIC INTEGRATION: THE EUROPEAN UNION

Since the end of the Second World War in 1945 there has been a trend towards economic integration among nations. This has been driven partly by changes in technology and partly by political considerations. The General Agreement on Tariffs and Trade (GATT), under which there has been a series of rounds of multilateral trade negotiations, and its successor organization, the World Trade Organization (WTO), have led to a general reduction in tariffs, quotas, and other barriers, around the world, thereby increasing trade. Production processes have economies of scale up to higher and higher production levels. Transport and communications have been getting progressively cheaper. People in Europe eat fruit from South Africa, lamb from New Zealand, and beef from Argentina; they drive cars made in Japan, Korea, and many European countries other than the one they live in; their clothes are likely to have been produced in Singapore or China. Many large firms have their production processes scattered around several different countries. Every weekday morning at unsocial hours the airports of Europe are crowded with businesspeople waiting to be flown around the Continent for their daily business meetings. Travel has been getting cheaper, and telecommunications

KEY QUESTIONS

1 What are the costs and benefits of forming a customs union?

2 How does the concept of the European Single Market go beyond what is embodied in a customs union?

3 How does the Common Agricultural Policy operate? Is its reputation for inefficiency and waste justified?

4 What are the costs and benefits of a single currency in Europe?

5 Does the introduction of a single currency imply a need for more coordination of fiscal policies among European countries than would otherwise be needed?

6 Why has the European Central Bank been given complete independence from elected politicians? Why has it been given the single objective of stabilising prices?

7 Does European integration imply a loss of sovereignty for nation-states that are members of the European Union?

have been getting much cheaper, relative to the price of the average consumption bundle. Huge amounts of money are traded between currencies each day on the foreign exchange markets. For many countries, a very large proportion of their national production is sold abroad. For small European countries like Belgium and the Netherlands, the proportion is more than half.

These changes mean that the old standard assumption that *the economy* refers to the nation is becoming a poorer and poorer approximation to reality, as more and more transactions take place across national boundaries rather than within them.

These changes in technology and patterns of production, consumption, and trade have led to pressure for changes to governments' policies and institutions. But also, political changes have been made in order to propel economic integration more rapidly. The European Union, for example, is partly a response to changes in technology and partly an attempt to make the integration process go further and faster than it otherwise might.

The European Union is the largest, most highly developed, and widest ranging exercise in economic integration in the world. There are, however, many other examples of groups of countries getting together to try to organise mutually beneficial changes to their trading arrangements—typically cutting tariff barriers within their group—and developing other cooperative activities. The North American Free Trade Agreement (NAFTA) established free trade among the United States, Canada, and Mexico. The Association of South East Asian Nations (ASEAN) aims to develop free trade

in Southeast Asia, reinforced by the Asia-Pacific Economic Cooperation (APEC), an organization which aims at trade liberalization over a wider area. There are also similar organizations promoting local cooperation in South America and Africa. At the same time a spectacular example of economic and political disintegration has occurred: the collapse of the Soviet Union. However, that might be viewed as the collapse of an empire brought together by the military coercion of Russia rather than free association. There is now some sign of formerly Communist countries reestablishing cooperation and coordination. Belarus, for example, has recently formed an association with Russia.

Some writers have speculated that the economies of the developed world are forming up into three large regional economic blocs: Europe, North America, and Asia. It is suggested that the development of regional trading blocs will be detrimental to the world's economic well-being. However, there are other forces at work that counteract the trend to regionalization. The GATT process is leading to lower tariffs all around the world, and it is often said that there is a process of globalization going on. Manufacturing industries in developed countries are increasingly exposed to growing competition from the countries of Southeast Asia (Hong Kong, Singapore, Taiwan, and South Korea), which, though in the throes of a dreadful economic crisis, have been growing very rapidly until recently and were known as the Asian tigers, and also from developing countries. The kinds of concerns expressed in Europe, about jobs being lost in the high-income northern countries and shifting to low-income countries, are mirrored both in other regional trading blocs (NAFTA, for example) and at the level of the world as a whole.

"Europe" has been a controversial issue for a long time, and not only in Britain but also on the Continent. The ratification of the Maastricht Treaty was the subject of two referenda in Denmark in 1992 and 1993; Sweden and Norway held referenda on the question of whether to join the European Union. Spain has been involved in arguments within the European Union about fishing in waters off Ireland and Britain and in 1995 drew the EU into a dispute with Canada. France fiercely opposed some of the deals on agricultural products that the EC had negotiated as part of the Uruguay Round of GATT. Brussels's bureaucracy has been the butt of many jokes, for its rules on straight bananas and its threats to French cheeses and genetically impure British oak trees. The Common Agricultural Policy (CAP), the policy through which European farming is subsidised and protected from external competition, is thought by many to be a source of inefficiency, waste, and corruption. It is said to have led to high food prices, the beef mountain, the wine lake, milk quotas, and set-aside. A critical view of the CAP is not confined to Britain. French farmers are annoyed to find that it enables foreign produce to enter France.

The European Monetary System has been associated with some spectacular crises in the foreign exchange markets in recent years: in September 1992, speculation against the pound and the lira led Britain and Italy to leave the system; in August 1993, speculation against the franc and other currencies caused the system to be more or less abandoned. Nevertheless, the plans to set up a single European currency proceeded on track, and it was established on 1 January 1999, with 11 member countries, and managed by the European Central Bank. Opponents claim that it will lead to a loss of sovereignty of national governments and to the determination of important aspects of national economic policy by foreign bankers. These concerns are not felt in Britain alone. Many people in Germany, for example, are unhappy at the prospect of the replacement of the deutsche mark—which has become a symbol of the postwar stability and prosperity of the German economy—by a European currency which may be governed by less reliable forces.

The social chapter of the Maastricht Treaty, which sets out concerns about employment protection, industrial relations, and other social measures relating to labour markets, is another source of controversy. It is viewed in France and Germany as a way of ensuring that there is a level playing field in the European Union, preventing countries from using weak employment protection laws and poor social provisions (such as unemployment insurance, health care, and so on) to allow firms to undercut costs and attract employment from other EU countries, a policy which is disparaged as "social dumping." But there is a contrasting view that the social chapter imposes costs on firms and on economies as a whole, which will maintain inefficiencies in Europe and reduce its level of real income.

"Europe" brings together under a single heading a great many economic issues, as well as political and social ones. On many of these issues, as the previous examples illustrate, "Europe" is a focus of controversy and disagreement. This is arguably a natural feature of the process of integration. Economic integration involves several countries' cooperating with each other on a wide range of economic and social policies. They have to agree on things like the height of the common external tariff, the standards for labeling food products, weights and measures, and the support prices set for agriculture. They have to coordinate their monetary policies and, to some degree, their fiscal policies. Industrial policies, such as the extent to which the countries are willing to subsidise loss-making firms and the way they deal with monopolies, have to be coordinated—harmonised, in Eurospeak.

The motivation for cooperation is that it makes all the participating countries better off. It also involves each country in acting not in its own individual best interests, ignoring the others, but in the interests of the group. There is inevitably the question of how to distribute the benefits of cooperation: alternative arrangements benefit some countries more than others. This naturally leads to arguments and disagreements in the process of negotiating a common policy. On some issues, some countries may feel they gain little or lose, while on others, they gain a lot. There is a temptation for a country to withdraw from the common policy in order to get a better outcome by acting directly in its own interests. Withdrawal is a threat that a country may use in the bargaining process to influence the outcome in its favour. Countries may want to cooperate only on the matters on which they feel that the common policy is favourable to them. If they did this, it would lead to the Europe à la carte greatly despised by the European Commission, and it would undermine the basis on which countries agreed on other issues.

The other aspect of international cooperation that leads to controversy is its effects on democratic institutions, decision making, and sovereignty. In the European case it has involved setting up European institutions, in particular the European Commission, which can make some decisions, of the more routine kind, on behalf of the member states. On other issues, typically the most important and controversial ones, the unanimous agreement of all member countries (in the Council of Ministers) is needed. Yet other issues are decided by a qualified majority of countries. Decision making in an integrated Europe involves individual member states in transferring their sovereignty on some issues to European institutions, on certain other issues their sovereignty is pooled, and on many other issues they retain complete sovereignty. Naturally this affects the ability of national governments to govern independently. In some European countries this has been accepted as a natural and appropriate part of the process of integration; in others it has excited greater opposition. Clearly, individual countries want to retain as much autonomy and independence as possible, while enjoying the benefits of cooperation. This desire is enshrined in the concept of "subsidiarity," which is the idea that decisions should be taken at as local and decentralised a level as possible.

In this chapter we outline the economic arguments involved in three prominent aspects of "Europe": the Single Market, the Common Agricultural Policy, and the process leading towards Economic and Monetary Union (EMU). The aim is to draw attention to economic issues and to apply principles developed in earlier chapters of this book to understanding the effects of various policies and institutions.

THE GROWTH OF EUROPEAN INSTITUTIONS: A LITTLE BIT OF HISTORY

The European Union is a recent institution. It began life on 1 November 1993, with the ratification of the Maastricht Treaty. But the process that led to its formation began soon after the end of the Second World War and sprang from a deeply held view that cooperative economic and political arrangements between European countries were needed, partly to speed the reconstruction of the war-torn continental countries and partly to ensure that they were so closely bound together by economic and political ties that another European war would be impossible. Initially it involved France, West Germany, the Benelux countries (Belgium, the Netherlands, and Luxemburg), and Italy. The Treaty of Paris, signed in 1951, established the European Coal and Steel Community (ECSC), which was to coordinate developments of those industries, then still regarded as being among the commanding heights of the economy. The ECSC was joined in 1958 by the European Economic Community and the European Atomic Energy Community. In 1965, these three organizations were joined, as the European Community.

The number of countries in the EC grew in the 1970s. Britain, Denmark, and Ireland joined in 1973. (Earlier attempts by Britain to join in 1961 and 1967 had been vetoed by General Charles de Gaulle.) Greece joined the EC in 1981, and Spain and Portugal in 1986. The two main treaties that have changed the EC since then are the Single European Act, in 1986, and the Treaty on European Union (the Maastricht Treaty), in 1992. Sweden, Finland, and Austria joined the EU in 1995. While Norway and Switzerland have decided not to join the EU, there are several other countries, at the southeastern corner of Europe, Turkey and Cyprus, and to the east, former-Communist countries such as Poland, Hungary, and the Czech and Slovakian Republics, which would like to join.

There are two views about European integration.

One is that it should come about through ongoing efforts at cooperation and collaboration between nation-states. This was de Gaulle's view of a *Europe des patries,* and it is a view widely held in Britain. The other is the view that supranational institutions should be set up to take over some functions from the nation-states. This is a more federalist approach. These two different views of how to bring about integration among European countries exist side by side, with some tension and disagreement. The Gaullist view retains the independence of the member states, but it arguably would lead to less coordination and a slower process of integration, as each issue would have to be negotiated and agreed on by all members. National governments would retain all of their sovereignty. The federalist view involves much more ceding of the sovereignty of national governments to European bodies. It would encourage faster and more thorough going integration. The structure of the European Union and its institutions reflects and in a sense tries to balance these two contrasting approaches.

Bodies that reflect the cooperation among nation-states include the European Council (the heads of government of the EU states plus the president and a vice president of the European Commission) and the Council of Ministers. Together, they make the main policy decisions in the EU, and their agreement is needed on questions that affect European Community law. They decide whether to accept proposals made by the European Commission, on issues like the single currency. One of the heated issues in the Council of Ministers is the use of qualified majority voting rather than unanimity to reach decisions. The need for unanimity enables individual countries to protect their own interests, but it can paralyse the council if countries can veto measures unless they can obtain a benefit from each measure.

The supranational bodies are the European Commission and the European Parliament. The commission is like a civil service for the EU, in that a major function is to administer the policies determined by the European Council and the Council of Ministers. However, the commission is more powerful than a national civil service, because it can also make proposals and suggest policies to the European Council. By doing this, it can influence the way the EU develops. Jacques Delors, the commission president for

ten years from 1985 to 1995, was very active in this way and gave the commission a high profile. He vigorously pushed the EU towards economic and monetary union and was highly influential in the negotiations on the Maastricht Treaty. He fought for the inclusion of the social chapter of the treaty, for example. He was responsible for the social democratic and federalist leaning of the commission under his presidency.

The European Parliament is often dismissed as a talking shop. It can discuss policy and give its views, but has few powers to decide anything. It now approves the new European Commission, every five years when new commissioners are put forward. It can, if it wishes, vote against an entire commission, forcing a new one to be put forward. But it is unable to vote against individual commissioners, unlike the U.S. Congress which must approve presidential nominees for positions in the U.S. government and is able to reject individuals of whom it does not approve.

While the European Commission is a kind of executive branch of European government, and the European Parliament is an attenuated legislature, the role of the judiciary is filled by the European Court of Justice (ECJ). The ECJ makes judgments on the application of European law. For example, in 1994 it imposed large fines on steel manufacturers who were operating a cartel.

THE EUROPEAN UNION AS A CUSTOMS UNION

From the beginning, the European Economic Community was intended to be a **customs union:** an area within which there are no taxes or tariffs or quotas on goods crossing national boundaries within the customs union. Goods entering from outside the union may face a **common external tariff** imposed by all members of the union at the same rate. Although tariff barriers within the EC had been removed by the end of 1968, other restrictions on trade (so-called nontariff barriers) had still not been entirely removed by the end of 1992 when the Single European Market was supposed to have come into effect.

The reason for having a customs union in Europe

was to encourage trade between countries. Manufacturers in any one country would have access to all the markets of all countries in the union without having to pay tariffs. Each manufacturer would get free access to a larger market, but at the same time, it would face more competition from other European manufacturers in its home market. Renault would be able to sell in Italy and Germany and compete there with Fiat and VW/Audi without facing tariff barriers, but Fiat and VW/Audi would be free to sell in France at the same time. Consumers in all countries would effectively get greater choice of products. Greater competition among European firms was expected to lead to reductions in firms' profit margins and bring consumers the benefits of cheaper goods.

It was hoped that the larger markets that would be opened to each producer in Europe would enable each one to produce more efficiently—at a lower average cost of production—and to compete more effectively in markets outside the EC against producers from the other industrial giants, the United States and Japan. It was also hoped that the larger home market in Europe and the greater competition among European producers would stimulate more rapid innovation and growth of productivity in Europe.

THE EFFECTS OF A CUSTOMS UNION ON TRADE AND WELFARE

The classic economic analysis of the effects of forming a customs union was made by a U.S. economist, Jacob Viner, in 1950. He considered the effect of a small country's forming a customs union with another country and looked at the effects on a single industry. He distinguished two effects—**trade creation** and **trade diversion.** Trade creation occurs when the formation of the customs union causes one country to import a good from its partner in the union rather than to produce it itself. This involves production switching from a high cost producer to a low cost producer, and consequently is likely to raise economic welfare. It is likely to represent a move towards free trade. Trade diversion occurs when the

formation of the customs union causes a country to change the source of its imports, away from third countries outside the customs union, towards partner countries in the union. The reason this might happen is that the formation of the union allows imports from other countries in the customs union without a tariff, whereas imports from third countries, outside the customs union, continue to face a tariff. Even though the supplier inside the union has higher costs than the supplier outside the union, the different tariff treatment makes the supplier inside the union cheaper, once tariffs are taken into account. Trade diversion is likely to reduce economic welfare; it is likely to be a move away from free trade.

The creation of a customs union is likely to cause both trade creation and trade diversion. Trade is expanded between the members of the union, where there are no tariff barriers. This may be partly trade diversion, associated with a fall in trade between members of the union and countries outside it, and partly trade creation, when total imports and exports have risen. Whether the allocation of resources is more efficient than before depends on the balance of trade creation and trade diversion. Customs unions are more likely to be beneficial when they cause a lot of trade creation and little trade diversion. Thus a customs union between countries that are relatively similar to each other in terms of their industrial structures and dissimilar from the other countries with which they trade is more likely to improve welfare than a union between relatively dissimilar countries.

A numerical example might make clearer the ideas of trade creation and trade diversion. The numbers shown in Figure 35.1 are meant to illustrate the general point and are purely hypothetical. Suppose that in the refrigerator industry, there are three producers. Malaysia produces refrigerators at a cost of £250 each, however many are demanded; Italy produces them in any quantity for £300 each. The supply of refrigerators from British producers depends on the price. Suppose that at a price of £325, the British industry will produce 400,000 refrigerators per year but that this falls short of demand, which is 500,000 per year at this price. Initially, Britain has a tariff of 30 percent on imported refrigerators. Consequently, the tariff-inclusive price of a Malaysian refrigerator in Britain is £325, and of an Italian refrigerator is £390. The market price for a refrigerator in Britain then is

Figure 35.1 TRADE CREATION AND TRADE DIVERSION IN A CUSTOMS UNION

Before the formation of the customs union, the United Kingdom imports refrigerators from Malaysia, where they cost £250 each to produce. There is a 30 percent (£75) tariff which takes the price to £325. Demand is 500,000 units, and local supply is 400,000, with 100,000's coming as imports from Malaysia. After the formation of the union, the United Kingdom imports refrigerators from Italy at a price of £300 each (there is no tariff), undercutting Malaysian competition. At the lower price, demand rises to 550,000 units, but production in the United Kingdom falls to 350,000 units. Imports rise to 200,000. There has been trade diversion of 100,000 units, and trade creation of 100,000 units. In the United Kingdom consumers have gained by paying a lower price. Their gain in consumer surplus is areas *a*, *b*, *c*, and *d*. But producers have lost because of lower prices. Their loss of producer surplus is area *a*. The government of the United Kingdom has lost tariff revenue of £75 on each of the initial 100,000 units of imports (areas *c* and *e*). The net gain to the United Kingdom is therefore areas *b* and *d* minus *e*, which may be either positive or negative.

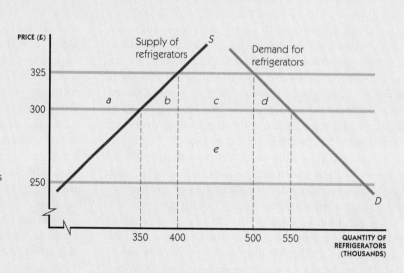

Before the formation of the customs union, the United Kingdom imports refrigerators from Malaysia, where they cost £250 each to produce. There is a 30 percent (£75) tariff which takes the price to £325. Demand is 500,000 units, and local supply is 400,000, with 100,000's coming as imports from Malaysia.

£325. People in Britain would then buy both British-made refrigerators (400,000 of them) and Malaysian refrigerators (100,000).

Now suppose that a customs union is formed between Italy and Britain. Refrigerators imported into Britain from Italy would now sell for £300, while Malaysian ones would remain at £325 (assuming that the common external tariff was at the old 30 percent). Consequently, Italian imports would replace Malaysian ones. But at the lower price, the British refrigerator industry might cut back supply to 350,000 per year. At the same time, consumers' demand might rise, say to 550,000 refrigerators per year. This leaves a gap of 200,000 refrigerators to be filled by imports. In this example, there has been trade creation of 100,000 units, the increase in the amount of imports into Britain, and trade diversion of 100,000,

the units whose source of supply has shifted from Malaysia to Italy.

Who gains and who loses from all this? Consumers gain because they now pay a lower price and buy more refrigerators. British producers lose, because they make fewer refrigerators and get a lower price for the ones they make. Consequently they make lower profits. The British government loses tariff revenue equal to £75 per refrigerator times 100,000 refrigerators. Overall, there might have been a gain or loss to the British economy, depending on the amounts of trade diversion and trade creation.

This analysis just looks at a single industry, in which the country joining the customs union is a net importer. There are likely to be other industries in which the country is an exporter, and in those industries the country might expect that its exports would increase when it joined the customs union.

This analysis also makes assumptions about the economy, which may not be completely valid in practice. It assumes that resources of labour and capital can be switched from one activity to another without unemployment. It assumes that the lower domestic production of refrigerators, in the example given, will permit greater production of something else, rather than causing unemployment. In practice, the changes involved in forming a customs union may cause unemployment at least temporarily, when it causes some industries to decline and others to expand. The argument also takes no account of the possibility that forming a customs union may, at least temporarily, lead some members into balance of trade surplus, while others go into deficit.

The argument also assumes, at least implicitly, that the economy is made up of competitive industries, each producing a different good, and that the economy is either an importer or an exporter of that good. In fact, trade among European countries does not follow that pattern. Most trade is in manufactured goods, which are produced in imperfectly competitive industries (the domestic appliances industry is such an industry, and so is the car industry, to give two examples), and most trade goes both ways. The United Kingdom is simultaneously both an importer and an exporter of cars and car components. The same is true in computers and electronics, pharmaceuticals, manufactured food products, and indeed in most industries. When industries are imperfectly competitive, and there is a lot of this kind of intraindustry trade, the creation of a customs union has additional effects, which may be more important than the ones considered so far.

Integration among Countries with Imperfectly Competitive Industries

When each manufacturer's products are different from all others, cutting tariff barriers among European countries increases the variety of products available to consumers, and an increased variety of products tends to make consumers better off. Consumers become able to choose not only among the products of British cheese producers, say, but also among those of French, Italian, Spanish, and Dutch producers, without the imports' having had a tariff paid on them and so being relatively expensive. At the same time, domestic manufacturers find that they can sell in a larger market, the whole of the customs union, without having to face tariff barriers. But on the other hand, they also have to compete, both in their home markets and in the markets of other member countries, with producers from the whole of the customs union: they have a bigger market but face more competition.

The size of the market is important when industries are not perfectly competitive and firms have increasing returns to scale. A larger market may allow firms to expand their rate of production, take better advantage of economies of scale, and produce at lower average costs. More competition may induce firms to reduce their prices relative to their production costs in an attempt to increase sales and profits.

In sum, therefore, it is argued that because industries are imperfectly competitive, firms enjoy increasing returns to scale, and products are not homogeneous, a customs union may benefit consumers via increased variety of products and lower prices due to both lower production costs and lower markups of prices over costs. These effects go beyond the effects analysed by Viner.

Another beneficial effect that, it is argued, may flow from a customs union is that the greater competition increases "X-efficiency." This argument is that firms are not producing as efficiently as possible and that exposing them to greater competition causes them to rethink how they produce and may lead to greater productivity. It has often been argued, for example, that the British car industry needs to be exposed to foreign competition in order to make itself competitive. According to the X-efficiency argument, increased competition may have much bigger beneficial effects by this route than it has by exploiting economies of scale more efficiently. However, the size of the potential X-efficiency gains are highly speculative.

Finally, it is claimed that the formation of a customs union may affect the rate of growth of the member countries in the long run and not just have a one-off effect on the level of national income or economic welfare via any of the effects just considered. It is claimed that lower prices and higher real incomes will encourage greater savings and investment in the customs union and that this will lead to faster accumulation of capital equipment, higher income, and more growth.

If it were true that economic integration would permanently raise the growth rate of the participating countries, the argument in favour of it would be much strengthened, because a small increase in the growth rate of real income has a much greater effect on wealth than a once-and-for-all step increase. (A simple example makes this clear. An annual income of £100, growing at 3 percent a year, at a discount rate of 4 percent a year, has a present value of £10,400. If the rate of growth of the income stream were to rise from 3 to 3.1 percent, that is, by one-tenth of a percentage point, the present value would rise to £11,555, which is 11.11 percent higher than the original present value. That increase could be achieved by a constant increase in income of £44.44 per year forever or by an initial increase of £11.11, growing at 3 percent per year.) However, estimated size of the effect of forming a customs union on growth is very imprecise.

THE SINGLE EUROPEAN MARKET

The "Single European Market" is an idea that goes beyond merely free trade in goods and services. The concept embodies free trade in all goods and services, and free mobility of labour and capital. Firms should not be able to charge different prices to consumers in different countries. This requires that all countries use common standards for the detailed specifications of manufactured goods. The plugs should be of the same dimensions; plumbing fixtures should be of the same standard sizes. National governments, when putting contracts out to tender for firms to supply goods (for example, when placing an order for new tanks for the army), should make the process open to firms in all countries in the EU.

Financial services—banking and insurance—should be available from firms situated in any EU country, not just the local companies. People wanting to work in EU countries should be able to use a qualification that is valid in any one country in all of them. A medical qualification that is acceptable for a doctor in Germany should be equally acceptable in Spain. A person wanting to buy a car should be free to buy it from a dealer anywhere in the EU.

These criteria imply radical policies to impose common standards across a wide range of goods and services, and educational qualifications. The Single European Market was intended to have come into effect on 1 January 1993. Of course, it did not. While there has been progressive change towards the Single European Market, all the required changes have not yet been made. There is still not complete deregulation in financial services or public procurement. In the motor industry, it is still not possible for people to shop around the whole of Europe looking for the best deal. If you want to register a car in Britain, it is effectively necessary to buy the car from a dealer in Britain. Educational qualifications are still not completely transferable between countries.

The Single European Market idea goes a long way beyond a customs union in the direction of increasing competition between firms in the EU, with the aim of reducing monopoly power and improving the allocation of resources. It would, for example, make it impossible for car dealers in different European countries to charge different prices for the same car, as happens now. The potential benefits are higher real incomes for people in the EU. The costs are the problems involved in establishing common standards for a large number of different goods and services. In many markets, this activity is controversial, and the European Commission is inevitably drawn into these controversies.

THE COMMON AGRICULTURAL POLICY

One of the most obvious and most heavily criticised features of the European Union is the Common Agricultural Policy (CAP). The vast amounts of surplus

CLOSE-UP: THE SINGLE MARKET—STILL SOME WAY OFF

Despite the intention to complete the single market by 1 January 1993, it remains some way off. The integration of markets in financial services like insurance and even banking has scarcely begun. Even quite a number of markets for manufactured goods are far from fully integrated. There are many examples of markets far from the single market ideal, of which the following are indicative

Agricultural equipment prices vary widely across the EU. Farmers in Britain pay 40 percent more for harvesters than those in Spain do. There are price differences of up to 196 percent in plant protection products and 37 percent in fertilisers, according to one survey. Partly the differences are due to different tax rates, but, these aside, large differences remain.

Computer prices differ greatly between EU countries, with Germany's (like the United States's) much cheaper than either Britain's or France's. The markets in these countries differ. In the United Kingdom there are few high-street shops selling computers, and Dixon's dominates the market. In Germany there are many local PC assembly firms selling cheap PCs. German consumers buy budget specifications, whereas the British buy more highly specified machines bundled with lots of extras which push up prices. Tax regimes differ. Nevertheless there remain price differences that are not explicable. They are not consistent with a single market.

Meanwhile the car market remains highly differentiated between countries; prices in the United Kingdom remain particularly high. This is partly due to the EU's concession to the motor trade, exempting it from normal EU competition laws and allowing exclusively franchised dealership networks to continue until 1999. The British competition authorities planned to investigate the market in 1998 (the Office of Fair Trading considered referring the motor trade to the Monopolies and Mergers Commission on grounds of anticompetitive behaviour and price fixing). The uncompetitiveness of the U.K. car market is sustained by the absence of international competition in car dealerships.

The market in electric power may approximate to a single market in twenty years, according to a recent study. There remains protection for local producers, much of it associated with protection for local coal mining. Some markets trading power between EU countries (Britain, Scandinavia, Spain, Switzerland, and the Netherlands) are developing but are far from universal. It is expected that pressure from consumers for lower prices, particularly when their visibility is increased by the Euro, will force the dismantling of individual countries' protective measures.

These examples show how far away the Single European Market remains despite strenuous efforts made in the years up to 1993.

Sources: "Single Power Market Likely in 20 Years," *Financial Times,* 3 December 1998; "Car Trade Faces Price Scrutiny," *Financial Times,* 28 October 1998; "A Byte of the Market," *Financial Times,* 22 November 1998; "Are These High Street Computer Prices PC?" *The Observer,* 22 November 1998; "EU Urged to Improve Single Market," *Financial Times,* 2 December 1998.

produce resulting from its subsidies and protected prices and bought up by the EU to maintain high prices have been lampooned in the press as wine lakes and frozen beef mountains. In other areas, such as milk, quotas have been used to limit production. These and related policies have absorbed the vast bulk of the EU's spending and have maintained high food prices for consumers in Europe.

The CAP has taken a large share of the total EC budget. In 1980 it was 73 percent of the total; in 1989 it was smaller but still 66 percent of the total. The total EC budget is around 1.3 percent of the total GDP of the EC, so agricultural spending via the CAP was around 0.85 percent of total EC GDP in 1989.

The purpose of the CAP was to maintain stable and adequate income levels for farmers in Europe. Many of the countries of Europe had large numbers of farmers after the Second World War, as Table 35.1 shows. The farm lobby has always carried considerable weight in France and Germany. Agricultural protection is not, however, a European peculiarity; many industrialised countries, not only those of Europe, have protected agriculture from foreign competition. The United States has protected its own agriculture to roughly the same extent as the EU has done; and Japan has a notoriously highly protected market for rice.

In addition to the protection of farm incomes, there has been a desire in France and Germany to prevent too much rural depopulation and to maintain traditional life in the countryside. This has been part of the motivation for agricultural support in the EC. Nevertheless, as Table 35.1 shows, agricultural employment has fallen substantially in most European countries. Indeed, the fall in agricultural employment and the rise in industrial employment has been one of the factors that has allowed rapid postwar economic growth in much of continental Europe. By contrast, Britain already had a very small agricultural sector in 1945 and was not able to grow on the basis of a growing industrial workforce released from a declining agricultural sector. The contrast between the size of the agricultural labour force in Britain and that in the other European countries is one of the reasons why the British have had a different attitude to agricultural support than have many of the continental countries of Europe.

Although European integration is closely associated

Table 35.1 SHARE OF AGRICULTURE IN TOTAL EMPLOYMENT (PERCENT)

Country	1950	1988
Denmark	23.0	6.3
France	28.3	6.8
Ireland	47.0	15.4
Italy	41.0	9.9
Netherlands	14.1	4.8
United Kingdom	67.0	2.2
West Germany	24.7	4.3

with the Common Agricultural Policy, the connection is an accidental one. A common policy towards agriculture is not an intrinsic part of the process of economic integration. There is, for example, no analogy to it for other industries. The CAP arose because of the EEC's desire to maintain a particular form of protection and support for agriculture, which has turned out to require detailed and complicated arrangements between EU members and to be very expensive for the EU's budget. There are alternative arrangements for agricultural support which would have been less inefficient and which would have permitted individual member states greater independence in formulating their policy towards agriculture.

The principles underlying the CAP were simple enough. The policy operated by setting prices for agricultural products (minimum import prices) below which prices in the EC were not allowed to fall while EC production was less than consumption. Imports from the rest of the world were allowed into the EC with the payment of a variable import levy which brought their price up to the EC's minimum import price for the good. If production in the EC exceeded consumption, then prices were allowed to fall to a lower level, the intervention price, at which the CAP would be willing to buy surplus produce from farmers.

Provided the CAP prices (the minimum import prices and the intervention prices) had been set at the right levels, the CAP would have been a policy that need have imposed no cost on the budget of the EC and indeed might have been a source of revenue. Provided the minimum import price for each agricultural product was set below the equilibrium market price that would exist in the EC in the absence of imports or exports but above the world price, EC production would have fallen short of demand, imports would have come into the EC to make up the difference, and the CAP would have collected levies equal in value to the quantity of imports times the difference between the EC minimum import price and the world price of the good in question.

This was probably a politically attractive system for supporting agricultural incomes, because it limited the fluctuations in the prices farmers received for their products that would have resulted from fluctuations in the world price (although it did not protect them from the effects of harvests of varying size) without imposing budgetary costs on the European Commission. The costs of protecting agriculture were concealed in the form of high food prices. This policy may have been politically more attractive than others that might have been used. For example, an alternative policy, and a policy that was used in the United Kingdom before 1973, was to allow food to be imported into the United Kingdom at world prices, so that consumers could buy food at world prices and farmers would have to sell their products at world prices. Farm incomes were supported by the government's paying farmers an amount equal to the difference between a support price and the world price for the goods they produced. This policy has the same direct effect on farmers as the CAP: farmers effectively receive a higher price than the world price for their produce, and the price they get is insulated from fluctuations in the world price. Consumers are able to buy food at world prices. The government, however, has to pay a subsidy to the farmers out of its tax and other revenues. These taxes impose costs elsewhere in the economy and are a visible reminder to the public of the costs of protecting agriculture.

Starting from the standpoint of this alternative system, the CAP can be thought of as this alternative system plus a tax (the same size as the production subsidy) on the consumption of agricultural goods and out of which the government is able to pay the farmers the subsidy (and have some money left over since the tax on consumption is applied to a larger tax base—consumption—than is the subsidy to production, providing that consumption in fact exceeds production and there are imports). It is possible to show that this alternative system is less harmful to the economy than the CAP, because while it would distort the production decisions of farmers just as much as the CAP would, it would not distort the decisions made by consumers of agricultural produce as the CAP would. The alternative system also has the merit that it would allow individual member states greater freedom in setting the level of subsidy for their farmers. Some European coordination would be needed, but nevertheless, the amount would be less than under the CAP.

While in principle, the CAP need not have become a budgetary black hole, the problem appears to have been that prices were set too high, perhaps because of the power of the farm lobbies or perhaps because the elasticity of supply in European agriculture was underestimated. If the CAP intervention price for a product is set above the price level that would equate EC supply with demand, then a surplus will be produced, which the CAP would have to buy and either store, to be sold in the future if at a later date supply were to fall short of demand, or sell at world prices outside the EC. In this case, the CAP becomes a cost item in the EC budget: the cost of buying up surplus production from farmers at the EC intervention price and selling it at the lower world price.

This appears to have happened on a large scale in the CAP over the last decades. It has caused the CAP to absorb the vast bulk of the EC's budget. The surplus produce, either sold directly by farmers with the aid of a subsidy in world markets, or sold by the CAP, has depressed prices in the rest of the world and has led to opposition from other countries, particularly the United States, to the EC's agricultural and trade policies. The negotiations over the Uruguay Round of GATT in 1993 and 1994 almost failed to reach agreement because of arguments between the United States and the EC over agricultural protection. Selling goods abroad at a lower price than they sell in the country where they are produced is called dumping. It is generally regarded as an unacceptable trade practice, and it violates GATT. Consequently it can give the countries on which goods are dumped legitimate grounds for retaliating, either by imposing tariffs or by using some other sanctions.

The growing cost of the CAP on the budget of the EC, as shown in Table 35.2, and pressure from other countries, particularly the United States, as a result of the EC's dumping of its surpluses on world markets, has strengthened the incentives to reform the system.

The obvious reform, from an economic point of view, is to cut the support and intervention prices of agricultural goods in the EC. Such attempts naturally encounter objections from the farm lobby, and they have been tempered by other measures aimed at cutting production without reducing farm incomes as much as simple price cuts would. The measures that have been used include setting quotas on production, as in the case of milk, for example; the recently introduced "set-aside" schemes; and moves away from paying farmers a guaranteed price for however much they choose to produce and towards a system of direct income support, which has the effect that beyond a certain output level, any additional output is sold at the (lower) world market price. Under the quota arrangements, farmers are allocated quotas of milk production. They are allowed to produce up to their quota, and if they overproduce, they are required to pay a penalty to the commission. They can sell or transfer their quotas to other farmers if they

do not want or are unable to use them, either completely or partly. Under the set-aside schemes, farmers are compensated for not planting at least 15 percent of their land with certain crops. Therefore, although they continue to receive a high price for those crops, the benefit they get relative to what they get if they do not grow them is diminished: they are paid a subsidy for growing crops, and they are paid a subsidy for not doing so.

At the same time as these measures were used, there have been continuing efforts to reduce EC prices relative to world prices and to reduce the number of crops for which CAP support is available. In recent years, world prices for agricultural products have risen, the stocks of surplus food have been sold off, and there is the prospect of bringing land that has been set aside back into production.

THE EUROPEAN MONETARY SYSTEM

European attempts to develop a customs union and single market have been paralleled by attempts to stabilise exchange rates within the EC. It is argued that movements in exchange rates, which affect the competitiveness of different member states, would disrupt the allocation of resources within the community. The countries with weak currencies would boom while the countries with strong currencies would slump. Without coordination on exchange rates, some governments might be tempted to use a deliberate devaluation of their currency to gain a competitive advantage over others in order to boost their own employment and output. After the experiences of competitive devaluations in the 1930s, the European countries after the Second World War wanted to avoid the possibility of a repetition. The devaluation of the pound in September 1992 when it left the Exchange Rate Mechanism (the system for regulating exchange rates which was the key element of the European Monetary System) is sometimes cited as an example of a country's using its freedom to manipulate the exchange rate in order to secure an unfair advantage. The desire to prevent

Table 35.2 EXPENDITURE ON THE COMMON AGRICULTURAL POLICY

	Million Ecus
1972	3,076
1975	4,598
1980	11,770
1985	19,971
1989	27,220
1992	35,829

Source: Commission of the European Communities, *Official Journal,* various issues.

exchange rate fluctuations for these reasons is one of the factors that drives the movement to Economic and Monetary Union (EMU).

For most of the period of the existence of the EC, its member countries have tried to limit the fluctuations of their exchange rates. After the collapse of the Bretton Woods system of pegged (but adjustable) exchange rates in 1973, the EC countries set up a system known as The Snake, which operated in various forms and with mixed success until 1979. It was intended to limit exchange rate fluctuations among them. In 1979 they set up the European Monetary System (EMS), which has survived with several modifications until the inception of EMU on 1 January 1999. The EMS was intended to allow exchange rates to adjust, in order to accommodate, at least partially, the differences in the inflation rates of member countries. But at the same time the EMS was intended to prevent the wild swings in exchange rates that might have resulted from speculative pressure on freely floating exchange rates.

In the EMS, each currency was assigned a central parity exchange rate in terms of each other currency. Provided the value of each currency stayed within a band of plus or minus 2.25 percent of its parity value, the monetary authorities in the member countries were free to pursue whatever monetary policies they thought fit. Once the value of two currencies reached the edges of the band, however, the monetary authorities were required to intervene in the foreign exchange markets to defend the weaker currency. If the lira had become very weak against the deutsche mark, for example, the Italian authorities would have been required to buy lire using other currencies. At the same time, the German monetary authorities would have been required to sell deutsche marks.

The intervention was intended to be symmetrical, so that all the burden of defending exchange rates did not fall only on the country whose currency was weak. The country with the weak currency, required to buy it up on the foreign exchange markets, might run out of foreign exchange reserves with which to buy it. By contrast, the country with the strong currency would always be able to supply more of its currency to the foreign exchange markets. The Bundesbank obviously cannot run out of deutsche marks, whereas it is possible for the Banca d'Italia to run out of deutsche marks, dollars, yen, or whatever reserve foreign currency it is

using to buy up surplus lire. The symmetry of the intervention was intended to make it more effective.

A device used by the EMS to ensure that symmetrical intervention could take place was a system of loans between central banks (the "very short term financing" facility), to ensure that the country with the weak currency could always obtain supplies of the strong currency. In the example of the weak lira and strong mark, the Bundesbank would have been required to lend marks to the Banca d'Italia, for a short period of time, with which the Banca d'Italia could buy lire on the foreign exchange markets.

Capital controls were also used to prop up the EMS. They were used to limit speculation, reduce exchange rate fluctuations, and enable foreign exchange intervention to work effectively. They took a number of forms. In many EC countries, until the late 1980s, residents were not free to buy and sell foreign currencies to whatever extent they wished; and they were not free to own real or financial assets in other countries to whatever extent they wished. They might be able to buy only a small amount of foreign currency each year to be able to travel on holidays or on business; only firms that could show that they needed foreign currency to pay for imported goods were allowed to buy it. Restrictions of this kind made it harder for speculators to buy or sell particular currencies and made it easier for the central banks to manage exchange rates. Foreign exchange controls were removed in Britain in 1979. They were gradually removed in other European countries, such as Belgium, France, and Italy, during the 1980s. Under the Single European Market programme, it was intended that they should have been completely removed by the end of 1992, and indeed they were all substantially removed.

In order to accommodate persistent differences in inflation rates between countries, the Exchange Rate Mechanism (ERM) also allowed for the parity exchange rates to be realigned from time to time. Except for very small ones, realignments had to be made with the agreement of all the countries in the ERM. In the early years of the operation of the EMS, the parities were realigned approximately once each year. Table 35.3 shows the dates on which currencies were realigned in the ERM and, for each realignment, the percentage by which the central parity exchange rate was depreciated against the German mark.

Table 35.3 REALIGNMENTS IN THE EUROPEAN MONETARY SYSTEM

Date			BFR[a]	DKR	FFR	NGL	IR£	LIT	PES	UK£
24	Sept	79	2	5	2	2	2	2		
30	Nov	79	0	5	0	0	0	0		
23	Mar	81	0	0	0	0	0	6.4		
5	Oct	81	5.5	5.5	8.8	0	5.5	8.8		
22	Feb	82	9.3	3.1	0	0	0	0		
14	June	82	4.3	4.3	10.6	0	4.3	7.2		
21	Mar	83	3.9	2.9	8.2	1.9	9.3	8.2		
22	July	85	0	0	0	0	0	8.5		
7	April	86	2	2	6.2	0	3	3		
4	Aug	86	0	0	0	0	8.7	0		
12	Jan	87	1	3	3	0	3	3		
8	Jan	90	0	0	0	0	0	3.7	0	
	Sept	92	0	0	0	0	0	[b]	5.0	[b]
	Aug	93	[c]							

[a] The currencies are: BFR, Belgian franc; DKR, Danish krone; FFR, French franc; NGL, Dutch guilder; IR£, Irish pound; LIT, Italian lira; PES, Spanish peseta; and UK£, pound sterling. The Spanish peseta entered the system in June 1989 and the British pound in October 1990. All figures given relative to DM, German marks.

[b] Pound and lira driven out of ERM.

[c] No realignments, but bands widened from 2.25 to 15 percent either side of central parity, except for DM/NGL which retained a 2.25 percent band.

Source: Official Journal of the European Communities, various issues.

Realignments became less and less frequent, and none (apart from a small technical adjustment of the lira in January 1990) occurred between 1987 and September 1992, when speculative pressure forced the pound and the lira out of the ERM. Another bout of speculation in August 1993 did not lead to a realignment, but it caused the ERM members to widen the acceptable bands of fluctuation around the central parities from 2.25 to 15 percent. The scale of speculation in the 1990s was much greater than it had been in previous years, partly because the removal of capital controls gave individuals and firms the ability to buy and sell currencies freely. The central banks were not able to defend exchange rates against it.

Nevertheless, there is an important question as to why the ERM failed to survive speculative attacks, as it had been devised so as to include strong defences against speculation. In theory, the central bank of the country with the strong currency, in practice Ger-

many, was required to give unlimited support to weak currencies when they hit the lower limit of their band of fluctuation. With sufficient intervention, it should have been possible to defend the bands for the pound and the lira in September 1992 and keep Britain and Italy in the ERM. If the Bundesbank had simply purchased pounds and lira in unlimited quantities at the intervention price, if necessary buying up the entire world supply of the British and Italian currencies, neither currency need have been devalued. Once it became clear to speculators that there was an unlimited commitment to the announced parities and bands, they would have unwound their speculative positions, allowing the Bundesbank to sell pounds and lira back to them and to buy back the deutsche marks it had sold them. The ability of the Bundesbank to supply deutsche marks is clearly unlimited, and consequently it can give unlimited support to weak currencies.

The ERM failed in the face of speculation because

the Bundesbank was unwilling to undertake unlimited intervention on behalf of the pound and lira. The Bundesbank hinted in 1992 that it thought that the pound should be realigned in the ERM: it believed the pound to be overvalued at its parity rate of DM2.95. The Bundesbank has also previously concluded an agreement with Italy that it would not undertake extensive intervention to support the lira. It had always been unwilling to allow its obligation to support other currencies to risk causing an increase in the German money supply. In addition, the domestic political support for the parity of the pound in 1992 did not appear to be very strong. Loud voices in Britain complained at the supposed iniquity of a situation in which monetary policy in Britain was dictated by a foreign power.

Despite the failure of the monetary authorities to fight off speculative attacks in 1992 and 1993, the formal structure of the EMS was maintained, and the movement towards monetary union proceeded without interruption.

THE MAASTRICHT TREATY AND MONETARY UNION

A committee chaired by Jacques Delors, the president of the European Commission until 1995, produced a highly influential report on monetary union in 1989, and most of the recommendations of this report were incorporated into the treaty that was eventually signed in Maastricht in 1993. It set out a gradual three-stage programme leading to monetary union in Europe.

The first stage of the Delors programme, which lasted until the end of 1993, was a continuation of the European Monetary System. Countries were intended gradually to reduce their inflation rates to a common low level, and to cut their government deficits to a low level also; they were required to liberalise financial markets and permit unrestricted movements of capital. As inflation rates converged, realignments within the ERM were expected to become less and less frequent. In the second stage of the Delors plan, which began at the start of 1994, countries were expected to move further towards fixing their exchange rates and the European Monetary Institute was set up, as a forerunner of a future European central bank.

At the start of the third stage, countries would irrevocably fix their exchange rates and begin to set up a **single currency;** a European central bank would begin to operate, regulating European monetary policy. The third stage was intended to begin between 1 January 1997 and 1 January 1999. In the event, the third stage began on 1 January 1999. The criteria were that countries had to have sufficiently low inflation rates and interest rates, their national debt and their government's deficit should be low enough (the debt has to be less than 60 percent of the gross domestic product, and the deficit less than 3 percent of the gross domestic product), and they should not have devalued their currencies for two years before joining. The criteria gave some room for maneouvre. Countries which did not quite satisfy the criteria but which were moving in the right direction with sufficient speed and conviction could be allowed to join.

Things did not go quite as planned. Instead of countries moving smoothly towards fixed exchange rates, with fewer realignments and smaller and smaller exchange fluctuations, the speculative attacks on the EMS in September 1992 and August 1993 caused realignments and a dramatic widening of the bands. Many people claimed that, effectively, the EMS no longer existed. Nevertheless, the European Monetary Institute was set up as planned in 1994, and European central banks studied how to carry out the practical steps needed to introduce a single currency, agreeing on a name for it—the Euro, devising new arrangements for clearing payments between banks in different countries, planning the design and printing of banknotes and minting of coins, changing slot machines, considering how to rewrite contracts in the new currency, and so on.

A serious obstacle to creating a monetary union like the Maastricht Treaty was that very few countries seemed likely to satisfy the Maastricht criteria. While inflation and interest rates in many European countries were converging towards a common low level, most countries had national debts much higher than the levels deemed acceptable by the treaty.

What is the significance of a country having a national debt no greater than 60 percent of the GDP and a government deficit no more than 3 percent of its GDP? How were these magic numbers derived? Why were they set at 60 and 3 percent, rather than, say, 100 and 5 percent, respectively? Why were limits of any size established?

The 15 members of the EU, whether in EMU or not, signed, in the Treaty of Amsterdam (the treaty which amends the treaty of Maastricht) in 1997, the Stability and Growth Pact (SGP) which takes further the limits on debts and deficits in the Maastricht Treaty. It states that countries whose deficits exceed 3 percent of their GDP will, except under specific conditions, be said to have an excessive deficit and that if they do not reduce it quickly, they will be made the subject of steadily increasing penalties imposed by the EU. In order to be able to use fiscal policy to moderate the business cycle, either by allowing automatic stabilisers to work or by using active fiscal measures, countries will need to keep their governments' budgets roughly in balance on average over the business cycle.

The purpose of the SGP is to prevent huge national debts from building up and to make sure there is no pressure on the European Central Bank to bail out countries that have problems paying the interest on them by buying up government bonds and thus printing money. It is one of the many defences intended to protect Euroland from inflation.

The SGP is controversial. Many have argued that it will in fact be a serious obstacle to stabilising policy, either because countries will be unable to achieve the on-average balanced budget needed to leave room for stabilization (more spending and less taxation during recession) or because even if they achieve balance, there will be inadequate scope for stabilising fiscal policy.

It has been argued that if governments spend on capital investment, then borrowing should be allowed against that, without counting against them in the SGP. This implies a golden rule in fiscal policy (borrow only to finance capital) akin to that introduced in 1997–98 in the United Kingdom. The counterargument is that it would require close monitoring, as the profligate would be tempted to dress up current spending as capital.

Besides the self-imposed limitations of the SGP, Europe has adopted additional limits on its ability to mitigate adverse shocks, by failing to introduce fiscal transfers between members to act as a collective insurance policy against asymmetric shocks. One proposal is that countries with above-average increases in unemployment should receive automatic budget contributions from the EU paid for by members experiencing below-average increases in unemployment. This proposal would, its proponents claim, offer additional stabilization without requiring a large increase in the budget of the European Commission, unlike many other schemes for providing European-level stabilization.

Such schemes would, of course, at best address only short-term stabilization. They would not affect the supply side of the continental economies, which is the source of persistently high European unemployment.

Sources: Samuel Brittan, "Shock Therapy," *Financial Times*, 3 December 1998, p. 20; Macro Buti, Daniele Franco, and Hedwig Ongena, "Fiscal Discipline and Flexibility in EMU: The Implementation of the Stability and Growth Pact," *Oxford Review of Economic Policy* 14, no. 3 (1998), pp. 81–97.

They were in fact designed to calm the fears of the low inflation countries of the EU about being involved in a monetary union with countries that had a poorer recent record on inflation, by disqualifying the high inflation countries from joining the union. European central bankers (who were strongly represented on the Delors committee) were keen to reduce the risk that they would have to print money to buy up the national debt of member countries. The limits on debts and deficits were motivated by a desire to ensure that countries in the union would not have strong incentives to create inflation as a way of reducing the burden of their national debts or get in a position where their national debts were so large that they were unable to pay the interest on them and were forced to default.

These arguments nevertheless do not lead to any precise bounds on national debts and deficits, and the magic numbers may appear somewhat arbitrary. Perhaps in recognition of this, and in recognition of the fact a country that had in 1994 an inherited national debt over 100 percent of its GDP would be unable to reduce it to 60 percent by 1999, the Maastricht Treaty allows for countries whose debts have been falling sufficiently to be judged eligible for entry into the EMU.

The negotiations leading to the decision on which countries to admit to the single currency in the first wave in January 1999 were intensely political. In the end, 11 countries were admitted: Austria, Belgium, Finland, France, Germany, Ireland, Italy, Luxemburg, the Netherlands, Portugal, and Spain. Britain, Denmark, Greece, and Sweden remained outside the Euro zone, or Euroland, as it has come to be known.

The figures in Table 35.4 show that not even Germany would have qualified under the strict Maastricht criteria on debts and deficits; other countries certainly would not. The Netherlands's national debt is above the 60 percent criterion; both the deficit and the debt in Belgium and Italy have far exceeded the Maastricht criteria; and, while the debt of the United Kingdom has been less than 60 per-

Table 35.4 NATIONAL DEBTS AND DEFICITS FOR SELECTED POTENTIAL MEMBERS OF A EUROPEAN MONETARY UNION[a]

	1990	1991	1992	1993	1994	1995	1996	1997	1998
Netherlands									
Debt	79.2	79.0	80.0	81.2	77.9	79.1	77.2	72.1	70.0
Deficit	5.1	2.9	3.9	3.2	3.8	4.0	2.3	1.4	1.6
Italy									
Debt	98.0	101.5	108.7	119.1	124.9	124.2	124.0	121.6	118.1
Deficit	11.1	10.1	9.6	9.5	9.2	7.7	6.7	2.7	2.5
Belgium									
Debt	125.7	127.5	129.8	135.2	133.5	131.3	126.9	122.2	118.1
Deficit	5.5	6.3	6.9	7.1	4.9	3.9	3.2	2.1	1.7
Germany									
Debt	43.8	41.5	44.1	48.0	50.2	58.0	60.4	61.3	61.2
Deficit	2.1	3.1	2.6	3.2	2.4	3.3	3.4	2.7	2.5
United Kingdom									
Debt	35.5	35.6	41.8	48.5	50.5	53.9	54.7	53.4	52.3
Deficit	0.9	2.3	6.2	7.9	6.8	5.5	4.8	1.9	0.6
France									
Debt	35.5	35.8	39.8	45.3	48.5	52.7	55.7	58.0	58.1
Deficit	1.6	2.1	3.9	5.8	5.8	4.9	4.1	3.0	2.9

[a] Debts and deficits are given as percentages of gross domestic product.

Sources: European Monetary Institute, Convergence Report (March 1998); European Commission Convergence Report 1998, European Economy No. 65 (1998).

cent of the GDP, the government deficit had exceeded 3 percent in several years prior to 1997. Even France has had too high a fiscal deficit. In the end it was judged that those countries which had not satisfied the strict criteria were making sufficiently strenuous moves towards them to be allowed entry. Table 35.4 makes clear the extent of last-minute fiscal belt-tightening that was undertaken to enable countries to squeeze in!

THE COSTS AND BENEFITS OF A SINGLE CURRENCY

The EMS and the limiting of exchange rate movements were regarded by many policymakers as merely a step on the way towards complete monetary union and a single currency in Europe. Despite the setbacks that occurred in 1992 and 1993 when speculation seemed to have blown the EMS apart, plans for the single currency were pushed forward, and it was introduced on schedule in January 1999.

The principal argument for a single currency in Europe is a microeconomic argument, based on a consideration of the fundamental role that money plays in the economy, as the medium of exchange. Money is the good that everyone is willing to accept in exchange for any other good, and so it eliminates the problem of barter economies, namely the double coincidence of wants. The choice of a particular good as a monetary unit is a **public good,** rather like a telephone system or a language. A telephone system is no use if hardly anyone has a telephone. There would be little reason for any one person to get a telephone in that case. The more people who have a telephone, the more useful the system is. Similarly, a language is more useful, the greater the number of the people who speak it. Likewise, in the case of a monetary standard, the more people who are willing to use it, the more useful it is. The U.S. dollar is a useful currency to carry around the world because many people in many countries are willing to accept dollars, regardless of whether it is legal tender in that country or not. Dollars are widely used for transactions in Latin America, and in eastern European

countries, where, for a variety of reasons, the domestic currency is of dubious value.

When people within an economy make many transactions with other people in that same economy and few transactions with people in other economies, the additional transactions costs caused by each economy's having a separate currency may be small. But when people travel a great deal between countries and there is a great deal of trade among countries, the advantage in having a single currency is likely to be much larger. It eliminates the transactions costs of changing money from one currency to another when traveling between countries or of buying and selling goods in different countries.

Another cost of having many different currencies is based on the risks and uncertainties faced by firms that trade internationally. Such firms face uncertainty about their costs and revenue if they buy and sell goods in various currencies, the values of which fluctuate relative to each other, as happens when exchange rates are not fixed. The value in deutsche marks of goods sold in Italy may be less than expected if the value of the lira falls unexpectedly relative to the mark. Costs of materials brought from Denmark may be unexpectedly high if the Danish crown appreciates unexpectedly relative to the mark. Of course, these unexpected currency movements may go in the other direction, leaving the firm in Germany better off rather than worse off. These risks increase the effective costs of trading between countries and may discourage trade.

Firms can to some extent reduce these risks even when currency values can fluctuate, by using forward exchange markets. For example, the forward exchange market would enable a German exporter to convert the revenue she expects to receive in a year's time in pounds sterling into marks at a price that is agreed today, although the actual exchange of pounds for marks does not take place until a year's time. The use of other financial instruments instead of the forward market, such as options and futures markets, can make these hedging operations fit more exactly the needs of firms. Nevertheless, the extent to which firms can reduce risk this way is limited. An investment in a new plant might typically enable a firm to produce goods for many years, and the investment decision depends on the projected value of the sales it will be able to make over many years.

When sales are for export, foreign exchange fluctuations many years ahead may affect the returns to the investment. The forward and futures markets in foreign exchange can reduce these risks up to about a year ahead but no further. Thus the firm will face inescapable risk from exchange rate fluctuations.

These microeconomic arguments in favour of a single currency are that it will reduce transactions costs and costs imposed by exchange rate risks, for individuals and firms doing business in several European countries. The savings of transactions costs represent real resource savings. They mean that banks will not need to employ people changing money from one currency to another. The removal of the risk of currency fluctuations will remove a discouragement to firms to invest in order to undertake business throughout the European Union. The size of the benefits of a single currency depend on the amount of trade and travel that takes place between European countries: the more there is, the greater the benefits. One estimate puts them at between 13 and 19 billion Ecus per annum in 1990, about 0.3 percent to 0.4 percent of the annual GDP of the European Community.

To set against these benefits, there are various costs. The main cost is a macroeconomic one. Countries that adopt a single currency lose the freedom to use the exchange rate as an instrument of policy. While they maintain separate currencies, France and Germany are in principle able to change the value of the exchange rate between the German mark and the French franc if they want to. If French goods had become uncompetitive relative to German goods and the French were not able to maintain a high level of employment without running a trade deficit, they might want to allow the French franc to depreciate relative to the German mark.

If the French and Germans were to adopt a single currency, the Euro, it would become impossible for them to change the exchange rate, just as it would be if they fixed the exchange rate between their two separate currencies. With a fixed exchange rate, if France had higher inflation than Germany or for some other reason had become uncompetitive relative to Germany, so that France was not able to maintain high employment and trade balance simultaneously, then to get back to equilibrium (a situation in which full employment and trade balance could be sustained in France), it would be necessary for France to have

lower inflation than Germany for a period of time. This might be brought about either by France's having low aggregate demand for goods for a time, associated with low inflation and relatively high unemployment, or by Germany's following an expansionary monetary policy and having relatively high inflation for a period of time. Unless wages and prices are very flexible, whichever of these policies is followed is likely to be costly. By contrast, changing the exchange rate has generally been viewed as a relatively costless way of changing the relative prices of the two countries.

This argument against a single currency relies heavily on two assumptions. One is that prices are sticky, so that changing the relative prices between two countries without using the exchange rate is costly. The other is that European countries are hit by a lot of idiosyncratic or asymmetric shocks.

If, instead of being sticky, wages and prices were very flexible; if wages adjusted very rapidly in response to, say, disequilibrium unemployment or excess demand for labour so as to restore equilibrium employment and if prices similarly responded rapidly to excess supplies of or demands for goods so as to restore balance very quickly, then there would be little incentive to use the exchange rate to change relative prices. Relative prices in the two countries would return to equilibrium levels very quickly without changing the exchange rate. The more flexible are wages and prices, the less useful a policy instrument is an adjustable exchange rate between two countries.

The second key assumption in this argument against a single currency is that countries in Europe are subject to many disturbances or shocks that affect their competitiveness relative to each other (so-called asymmetric or idiosyncratic shocks). Examples include Britain's unexpected resurgence of inflation in the late 1980s or the inflation in Germany caused by the process of unification of West and East in 1990. Another example is Italy which has had a long history of high inflation and has only recently, in the early 1990s, been able to reduce its inflation to a level near that of Germany. The recent history of inflation in Italy, Germany, and France is shown in Figure 35.2.

If shocks of this kind recur from time to time, they may cause unemployment or inflation in various members of the single currency block, as the countries that are affected try to restore their relative prices to an appropriate level. The more frequent

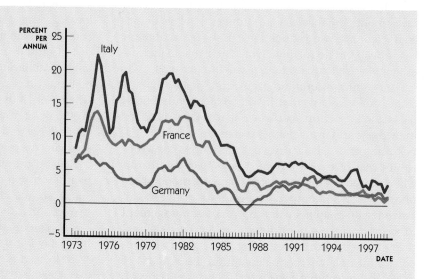

Figure 35.2 INFLATION IN FRANCE, ITALY, AND GERMANY

Over the last twenty years inflation rates in the three largest continental European countries have converged substantially. Although inflation in Italy has not quite fallen to the levels in France and Germany, it has come very close compared with its record in the 1970s and 1980s. The price of achieving convergence with German inflation rates has been high unemployment in both France and Italy. In both countries the currency has been substantially overvalued relative to the deutsche mark, as part of a deliberate policy of squeezing inflation out of the system. *Source: IMF, International Financial Statistics.*

and the larger such shocks are, the greater the problems for countries linked by a fixed exchange rate or using a single currency.

FISCAL POLICY WITH A SINGLE EUROPEAN CURRENCY

It is sometimes claimed that a single European currency would lead not only to the loss of an independent monetary policy but also to the loss of an independent fiscal policy. In fact there is nothing about a single currency itself that implies a single fiscal policy. However, growing economic integration implies that the ability of each European state to pursue an independent fiscal policy is becoming less and less useful.

It is important to distinguish here between two aspects of fiscal policy. One aspect concerns the allocation of resources in the economy—the microeconomic aspect of fiscal policy. The other concerns the level of economic activity, the rate of unemployment, and so on—the macroeconomic aspects of fiscal policy. Concerns about the loss of an independent fiscal policy have largely concerned the macroeconomic aspects rather than the microeconomic aspect.

There is of course no reason in principle why countries should not be able to set the level of provision of public services and the level of taxes according to their own preferences in a more integrated Europe. But growing integration is likely to limit this freedom. Some countries might want to have a more generously publicly funded health service, better public education, or a more generous national welfare and social security system than another. The desired pattern of taxes to pay for public expenditure may differ from country to country. One might want to have heavier taxes on spending while another might want to have heavier taxes on income. One country might want to have more redistribution from the rich to the poor than another. One country might want to have higher taxes on alcohol and tobacco than another. Desired taxes on fossil fuels may differ. And so the list goes on. The single currency makes little difference to countries' ability to sustain these differences.

CLOSE-UP: BOOM AND BUST ON THE EDGE OF EUROPE

For many, the main argument for Britain's staying out of EMU has been that Britain's economic cycle has been out of sync with the major continental economies, France and Germany. While Britain enjoyed falling unemployment and a boom in the years 1993 to 1998, France and Germany endured rising unemployment. In the first years of EMU, the continental economies would require much lower interest rates than would the United Kingdom. While the 11 EMU countries lowered their interest rates to 3 percent per annum in December 1998, Britain's interest rates were 6.5 to 7 percent, beginning to ease but still much higher. While France and Germany still had near record unemployment levels (11.6 and 10.6 percent respectively in October 1998), Britain's was at a cyclical low of 6.2 percent.

Lack of synchronization has, however, not kept either Ireland or Portugal out of EMU. Both experienced rapid growth during the 1990s and were enjoying boom conditions in 1998, with Ireland in particular close to a large explosion of property prices. Ireland's real GDP grew at roughly 8 percent per year between 1994 and 1998. In the case of Ireland, two factors may enable it to

make the transition to EMU monetary conditions smoothly. One is that its labour force is highly mobile. Irish workers have been moving back to Ireland as conditions have improved, meeting the growing demand for labour and keeping down wage inflation. Another is that Ireland is highly open: imports and exports together amount to about 160 percent of GDP. This will serve to dampen inflationary pressure also. Ireland's exports will have to remain competitive with those from alternative sources, and imports from Europe will have stable prices. Portugal also has considerable labour market flexibility and is highly open, but is closer to full employment than Ireland, with unemployment at 6.2 percent and falling. Ireland has little possibility of using fiscal policy to limit the growth of demand that results from falling interest rates.

The experiences of Ireland and Portugal in the early years of EMU will provide interesting examples of the consequences for countries that are out of sync from joining the single currency.

Source: Wolfgang Münchau, "EMU's First Boom and Bust," *Financial Times,* 8 October 1998, p. 21.

Differences in taxes and benefits may cause problems such as cross-border shopping to take advantage of lower prices in a neighbouring country, or people's living in one country while working in another to take advantage of lower income taxes. Poor people living on social security benefits might attempt to move to locations with relatively generous welfare benefits. The more integrated Europe becomes, the greater the mobility of labour between countries, the greater these problems will become, and the greater the pressure on countries to have similar tax rates. There has been concern in some European countries that their high levels of welfare provision will come under threat if their high taxes

cause people to move out of the country to avoid high income taxes or to shop out of the country to avoid high value-added taxes. Other countries might use low tax rates to attract industry, residents, and shoppers. There may potentially be competition between countries that will undermine the provision of public goods and the welfare state. Thus integration is likely to lead to growing pressures on countries to have similar tax rates and levels of public services. There is also good reason for countries to coordinate on what those levels should be. Nevertheless this coordination may be achieved by cooperation among several countries, each with its own tax-setting power.

The other aspects of fiscal policy are the macroeco-

It has long been argued that the introduction of a single European currency and a common monetary policy would bring along with it a need for a single fiscal authority and a common fiscal policy. The Eurosceptics' fears were whipped up late in 1998 when the German finance minister Oscar Lafontaine suggested that there was a need for much further harmonization of tax rates and that EU tax policy should be determined by qualified majority voting rather than unanimity. The British media gave the impression that all taxation in Britain might be determined in Brussels and that many tax rates would have to rise to bring them into line with higher rates in Germany, France, and other continental countries.

There is concern in some EU countries about harmful tax competition's being used by other countries to attract businesses to tax-favoured locations, and in some countries a number of very specific and highly distortionary tax incentives have been used. The EU is making efforts to remove these provisions. France and Germany are concerned about low levels of corporate taxation more generally and taxes on the interest on savings. Corporate taxes are relatively low in Britain at 31 percent as against roughly 40 percent on average on the Continent.

Lower corporate taxes may well attract business. The danger of harmonising taxes upwards is that firms can choose from among locations not only within the EU but also outside the EU. Coordination on higher corporate taxes may simply drive economic activity out of the European Union. There is a desire in Germany and France for the imposition of a common withholding tax on interest payments on the assets of nonresidents, at a rate of at least 20 percent. This proposal is directed primarily against Luxemburg,

which has no such tax and which attracts large amounts of savings from Belgium and Germany.

All these proposals for tax changes can be adopted only by unanimity, and the stated position of the U.K. government is to determinedly hold out against them. For the moment it is likely that there will be no further harmonization. But in the longer term, the growing mobility of capital and labour will as integration progresses increase the need for it.

The irony of the outrage of the British media and the Eurosceptics is that the European Community, as a customs union, was founded on tax harmonization: the harmonization of customs duties. All internal tariffs were abolished and a common external tariff introduced when the EC was set up. Beyond customs duties, other taxes have been harmonised little or not at all. Excise duties, such as the taxes on alcohol, petrol, and tobacco, have not been harmonised. (Differences in alcohol taxes between Britain and France lead the British to do huge amounts of cross-border shopping for wine, and so on, in northern France, to loud complaints from off-licences in southern England and at the loss of many millions a year in U.K. excise tax revenue. This brings pressure for tax harmonization from British businesses!) There is a minimum standard rate of value-added tax in the EU of 15 percent, but countries are allowed to charge a lower rate on certain things. Further harmonization is thought unlikely. On personal income taxes there has been no harmonization, and none is likely for some time.

The fundamental pressure for tax harmonization comes from the free movement of labour, capital, goods, and services throughout the EU. The

nomic aspects, which involve the balance between spending and taxation, the amount of government borrowing, and attempts by government to manage aggregate demand. Economic and Monetary Union has raised the spectre of the loss of the freedom to use fiscal policy in this way. States within the EU are increasingly open, and fiscal policy is less and less useful as a way of managing aggregate demand. The more integrated goods and labour markets in Europe become, the more open the economies of individual states and the less useful the ability to pursue independent fiscal policies will be. At the same time, the argument for a European fiscal policy becomes stronger. While individual states may become unable to affect demand effectively when they act independently of each other, they would be better able to influence aggregate demand by acting together and using a European Union–wide expansion or contraction of government expenditure. This is because, while individual EU states are relatively open economies, the EU as a whole is more closed.

Several arguments based on fiscal policy have been made against a single currency. One such argument is that a move to a single currency strengthens the power of a single European fiscal policy, while it weakens the effectiveness of the fiscal policy of an individual state. The more extreme form of the argument is that a single currency implies the *necessity* of a European fiscal policy. It is claimed that it implies a reduction in the sovereignty of the governments of individual states. A single currency may well reduce the ability of each national government to pursue whichever monetary and fiscal policies it wished, and so it is understandable that national politicians would feel that their position was weakened by it. But at the same time, more power to determine fiscal and monetary policies will reside at the level of the European Union, to be exercised by the European Central Bank and the Council of Ministers, or other EU institutions. These changes therefore involve a shift in the location where decisions are made and the way in which voters are represented. While national governments may lose sovereignty, EU institutions, in which voters in member states are represented, gain sovereignty. It is not clear therefore that individual voters in EU countries would lose sovereignty overall, still less that they would end up being economically worse off. If a single currency were to lead to resources' being better allocated and used more effectively, then European citizens may gain more *economic* welfare, without any loss of political freedom.

THE UNITED STATES OF EUROPE

A comparison is often made between the countries of the European Union and the states of the United States, as far as a single currency is concerned. In the United States, the dollar is used throughout the country, and it is taken for granted that this is the appropriate arrangement. The idea that individual states might have separate currencies is never seriously entertained as a practical possibility. In Europe, by contrast, a single currency has been a hotly debated issue. But many of the issues that arise in the United

States arise equally in Europe. While the scale of the problems may be different, the principles are the same. States on the East Coast and the West Coast and in the Midwest are geographically distant and have different industries. They are affected by different shocks at different times which might cause one state to boom while another has a recession. A rise in oil prices as in 1973 and 1979 leaves oil-producing states like Texas booming, while industrial states like New York and Pennsylvania go into recession; the growth of the computer industry in the Silicon Valley may leave California booming, while other states lag behind; and so on. Despite this, it is not suggested that they should have different currencies so that the Pennsylvania dollar could be devalued against the California dollar. The question that is asked is: how do the necessary adjustments take place in the United States? Why would they not take place in the same way in Europe? There appear to be several contributory factors.

Labour markets are more flexible in the United States than in Europe, and wages adjust more rapidly following shocks. Labour is also more mobile between states and regions of the United States than it is between European countries; consequently regions of the United States return to full employment more rapidly than European countries do.

The U.S. federal government's budget redistributes incomes among states. When a state has a high income, its residents pay more in income taxes and receive less in federal government benefits, and conversely when a state's income is low. Resources are transferred from the booming states to recessionary ones. The scale of these transfers is large: the marginal rate of federal income tax is 24 percent on most incomes and 28 percent on higher ones. It has been estimated that a $1 fall in income in a state induces a cut of $.40 in net transfers from that state to the federal government. These transfers via the federal government between states have the effect of cushioning the shocks that individual states suffer.

By contrast, there are no transfers on a comparable scale between EU member states via the European Commission. The structural and regional development funds of the EC, which are used to aid depressed regions, amount to only a small fraction of the budget of the EC, which is itself on the order of only 1 to 1.5 percent of the national income of the EU.

If there were to be transfers between states within the EU on the scale that occur in the United States, the budget of the EC would have to take up a much larger fraction of the national income of the EU than it does at present.

The states of the United States differ from those of the EU in that they have very little freedom to pursue independent fiscal policies. States in the United States can vary rates at which state taxes on incomes, sales, and property are levied, and they are responsible for a substantial fraction of total government spending in the United States. However, they are restricted by law in their ability to run surpluses and deficits and to borrow money to finance their spending. States are allowed to borrow to pay for spending on capital investment projects but have to repay loans over the life of the capital goods they create, and they have to pay for current spending out of tax revenue and grants from the federal government. This means that a state effectively cannot use its spending and taxation policies to try to counter unemployment in the state. An expansionary fiscal policy would have to consist of higher capital spending financed by borrowing (which would lead to higher repayments of debt in future years) or a balanced budget expansion of taxation and current expenditure.

The need for an independent fiscal policy is reduced in the United States by the cushioning effect of federal government taxes and spending. The incentive for the states to use independent fiscal policies is reduced further by the openness of individual states: in each state a large fraction of spending by consumers and firms falls on goods that come from outside the state and a large fraction of the demand for goods produced in a state comes from outside the state. Consequently, an expansionary fiscal policy in a state would have only a small effect on employment in the state, a large (negative) effect on the trade balance of the state, and a (positive) effect on the demand for goods in other states. In other words, an independent fiscal policy would be an ineffective policy for a U.S. state. These arguments apply in Europe to a smaller but growing degree.

In summary then, it appears that with a single currency Europe is, on the one hand, likely to have greater difficulties adjusting to fluctuations in employment and output in EU states than in the United State's states, because labour is less mobile between countries in Europe than between states in the United States, wages within EU countries are less flexible than in the United States, and the budget of the EU is not able to cushion fluctuations in income as much as the U.S. federal budget is. On the other hand, EU states have greater freedom to vary their own expenditure and taxation, and thus use fiscal policy to manage aggregate demand, than U.S. states have.

INDEPENDENT CENTRAL BANKERS

Another aspect of the Maastricht Treaty that emphasises its preoccupation with preventing inflation is the importance it gives to having a European central bank which is independent of elected officials and which has a constitutional responsibility for maintaining low inflation. Low inflation has become the dominant objective of monetary policy in recent years, in Britain, other European countries, the United States, Japan, Canada, and New Zealand. The idea that, as a means of achieving low inflation, the central bank should be independent of the influence of elected government officials has gathered widespread support.

Mistrust of the monetary control of elected governments arises from the belief that they are too prone to using expansionary monetary policy to improve their prospects of getting reelected, by bringing a short-term boom to the economy. The problem with short-term monetary expansions, aimed at generating a fall in unemployment and a rise in the GDP, is that the real economic benefits are temporary but the consequences for inflation are more costly and longer lasting.

Evidence for the desirability of having an **independent central bank** is drawn from the experiences of Germany and the United States, both of which have independent central banks, and other countries with similar institutional arrangements. Figure 35.3 shows that on average, countries with a more independent central bank have had lower inflation in the recent past. The Bundesbank was

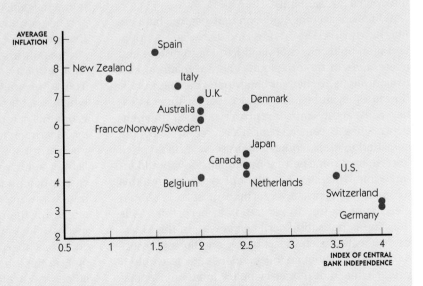

Figure 35.3 **CENTRAL BANK INDEPENDENCE AND INFLATION**

Alberto Alesina and Larry Summers examined indices of the independence of central banks and plotted them against inflation rates. The graph shows that there has been a clear negative association. Countries that have a more independent central bank have had lower average inflation. It is not clear whether independent central banks are a cause of low inflation or countries that prefer low inflation also prefer independent central banks. However, there are good reasons based on economic principles why the independence of monetary policy from elected officials leads to lower inflation. Source: Alberto Alesina and Larry Summers, "Central Bank Independence and Macroeconomic Performance," Journal of Money, Credit, and Banking 25, no. 2 (May 1993), pp. 157–162.

normally able to decide on monetary policy independently of the elected German government, although it has been overruled on one or two occasions. (One such was the occasion when it was forced by the German chancellor to accept the conversion of East German marks into West German deutsche marks at an exchange rate 1:1 in 1990.) Likewise the Board of Governors of the U.S. Federal Reserve System decide on the money supply and interest rates in the United States independently of the president or the Congress. Countries with an independent central bank have maintained lower inflation on average than countries whose central bank was under the control of elected politicians.

The Maastricht Treaty requires countries that are members of EMU and use the single currency to make their central bank independent of government. The policy response in Britain has been relatively modest. At first in the early 1990s the Bank of England was given very limited independence. It was allowed to produce an independent forecast of inflation in its three-monthly *Inflation Report* and to disagree publicly with the monetary policy that it is required to carry out by the chancellor of the exchequer. More recently, in May 1997, the Bank was finally given the freedom to conduct monetary policy independently. But the goals it is required to achieve are set out by the elected government.

While on average, independent central bankers may have printed less money and delivered less inflation than politically motivated finance ministers and chancellors of the exchequer, there remain at least two questions about their behaviour. One question is, how are they to be held accountable for their activities, while at the same time preserving their independence? If the central bank were required by the constitution of the country to preserve a stable price level, then at some point some public body should inquire into whether it had attempted to carry out this job in an appropriate way. The central bank should clearly not be free to run amok in perpetuity. This question is not satisfactorily dealt with in the Maastricht Treaty, which in fact barely mentions it. A second question about an independent bank is, would it use its control of monetary policy to attempt to stabilise the GDP of the country sufficiently? An independent central bank might produce lower inflation, but if it were to concentrate on inflation and pay no attention to the level of unemployment, there might be greater swings in output and employment than elected government officials would choose. In fact, it turns out that past evidence shows no signs of this.

FISCAL FEDERALISM AND SUBSIDIARITY

A major issue for many countries considering their participation in the single currency and EMU and in the further integration of Europe is the effect on their sovereignty. In Britain, a strong body of opinion has raised objection to the supposed loss of sovereignty of the British government to European institutions. The European Central Bank would take away Britain's ability to determine its own monetary policy, for example. Some go further and argue that it would also take away the British government's ability to determine its own fiscal policy. It is agreed that monetary union would place further limitations on a country's freedom to use fiscal policy. This is an issue that arises in all EU member countries. The loss of national sovereignty has been held as an argument against further integration.

The counterargument to such claims of the British "Eurosceptics" is based on the principle that sovereignty in a democratic state should be seen not as a property of its government but of its citizens. The government is merely an agent of the citizens which enables them to make collective decisions. From this perspective, the issue of sovereignty raised by integration looks much less problematic. Integration involves citizens of European countries establishing a different set of agencies through which to carry out joint decision making. It involves their taking away some powers from national governments and giving them to European institutions. It does not involve a loss of sovereignty for citizens of European countries, merely a different institutional expression of it, in the interests of greater economic and social efficiency. It may be natural that national governments resist the reduction in their own powers, but these arguments suggest that their claims should not be decisive.

The lack of accountability of European decision making to an elected legislature is a source of concern to many people. This is a problem that has arisen because the European Parliament has very weak powers to hold the European Commission or the European Council to account for its actions. This itself is a consequence of the national governments' being unwilling to allow the European Parliament to acquire powers, also a consequence of the smaller European countries' fears that they would have a smaller voice in the Parliament, where each country's number of seats is proportional to its population, than in the Council, where each country has one vote.

The concept of "**subsidiarity**" is intended to allay fears about excessive centralization and rule of Europe from Brussels. By *subsidiarity* is meant that decisions should only be taken centrally where there are clear benefits from doing so. Decisions should be taken in as local and decentralised a way as possible. Allocating tasks to different levels of government— local, regional, national, European—would lead to a federal fiscal structure. A clear example of fiscal federalism is provided by the United States, where the federal government is responsible for national defence, some health care and social programmes, and macroeconomic policy; states levy taxes on incomes and sales and are responsible for spending on a wide range of services—transport, some social programmes, police, justice, and higher education; and local communities are responsible for yet more local public services, such as schools, local police forces, and so on. Germany has a federal structure, in which spending decisions are made at the national level, the level of the states—the *Länder*, and the level of local communities. Britain has a relatively centralised structure, in which the national government in Westminster makes the bulk of taxation, spending, and other policy decisions, leaving only a little freedom of manoeuvre for local authorities. France also has a highly centralised public administration, with much control from Paris.

REVIEW AND PRACTICE

SUMMARY

1 A customs union is a number of countries with a common set of tariffs on imports into the union but no barriers to trade within the union. The formation of a customs union may but need not necessarily be a move towards free trade. It leads to both trade creation, which shifts production to lower cost producers, and trade diversion, which shifts production towards higher cost producers. The overall effects on the efficiency of the allocation of resources are ambiguous.

2 The formation of a customs union may allow firms with increasing returns to scale to expand production and consumers to experience greater variety of products. It may produce greater competition which may increase X-efficiency. It may conceivably affect the rate of economic growth, but the size of any such effect has been impossible to quantify.

3 The Common Agricultural Policy was an attempt to increase and stabilise farm incomes. It was intended to restrict imports of food and raise food prices by imposing a variable import levy. Raising prices in the EU discourages consumption and encourages production. It was intended not to require public expenditure. In practice it has led to production in excess of EC consumption and has been a source of waste and inefficiency.

4 Within a group of countries that trade extensively among themselves, a single currency brings benefits of lower transactions costs and greater efficiency in exchange. A cost is each country's loss of the exchange rate as an instrument of economic policy. The loss of this policy instrument is less important the more flexible wages and prices are, the more open the economy is, and the more common to the group as a whole the shocks that buffet individual countries are.

5 The formation of a single currency in Europe requires the establishment of a European central bank to manage the supply of the currency and, by doing so, to manage monetary policy for the Union. The EU has chosen to guarantee the central bank considerable independence to pursue its policies free of political interference. The European Central Bank has been given the responsibility for maintaining price stability; it is not required also to consider employment when setting policy.

6 While a group of countries may use a single currency, individual members of the group continue to be able to pursue independent fiscal policies. There is no necessary connection between a single cur-rency and a unified fiscal policy. Fiscal policy in any single country is limited by the degree of mobility of labour and capital between countries. Differences in tax rates cause economic activity to move between member states. Fiscal policy is also constrained by the need to prevent the debt-to-GDP ratio from growing too high.

7 The EMS was a system of target zones for exchange rates, aimed at limiting their volatility. Exchange rates were normally kept within narrow bands around agreed central parity exchange rates. The parities were changed or realigned from time to time. The system proved susceptible to speculative attack in 1992 and 1993 when members differed in their ability to maintain the same high interest rates as prevailed in Germany and central banks were unwilling to intervene sufficiently to maintain exchange rate bands.

KEY TERMS

customs union	trade creation	single currency	independent central bank
common external tariff	trade diversion		subsidiarity

REVIEW QUESTIONS

1 Why is trade creation a move towards free trade and trade diversion a move away from it?

2 What are the benefits of forming a customs union among economies many of whose industries contain a few large firms producing goods under conditions of increasing returns to scale?

3 How would a reduction in the minimum import prices and the intervention prices set by the Common Agricultural Policy affect production and consumption of food in the EU?

4 Why did the countries of the EU attempted to stabilise their exchange rates using the European Monetary System? How was the system intended to discourage speculation? How was it intended to survive a speculative attack if one occurred?

5 Why do some European countries wish to maintain their freedom to adjust their exchange rates to other European countries, rather than adopt a system of irrevocably fixed exchange rates?

6 How does the existence of either a system of irrevocably fixed exchange rates or a single currency, instead of the ERM, affect the ability of countries to follow independent fiscal policies?

7 Why did the EU placed such importance on the convergence of inflation and interest rates in the process of moving towards Economic and Monetary Union in Europe?

PROBLEMS

1 Suppose that a fall in world oil and gas prices depressed the North Sea oil industry, causing a recession in Britain, while Germany enjoyed a boom. And suppose that Britain had joined the single currency area.

How might the European Central Bank respond to this situation in setting monetary policy for Europe?

How does this compare with the way that monetary policy may have been determined under the same circumstances when the ERM was in operation (1979 to 1993)?

2 Should agricultural support be removed completely, leaving farmers to buy and sell at world market prices? Why is any agricultural support maintained in developed countries?

3 How might controls on international capital flows have enabled governments and central banks to have withstood the speculative attacks on the ERM in 1992 and 1993? Why were capital controls removed in the process of establishing EMU?

4 How might an individual country in a single currency area use a fiscal expansion to reduce unemployment? What would be the effect of such a fiscal expansion on the other member countries of the currency union?

5 A number of eastern European countries want to join the EU. What economic factors determine whether this would be beneficial:
(a) To the East European countries themselves?
(b) To the existing members of the EU?
(c) To the rest of the world?

6 Why have many Japanese car manufacturers set up plants in the EU rather than manufacturing in Japan and exporting completed vehicles to the EU?

7 "If the exchange rate is not freely adjustable, it is more important for a country to have a flexible labour market." Discuss.

8 How might a spiral of competitive devaluation arise among a group of countries with mutually floating exchange rates? What would be the consequences for (a) inflation and (b) unemployment?

9 It is sometimes claimed that freedom to devalue the currency may be of little use as a policy instrument for dealing with unemployment and a trade deficit if it leads to expectations of further devaluation and inflation. What is the basis of this claim?

CHAPTER 36

TRADE POLICY

In any clothing store, you will find clothes that have been manufactured all over the world: in European countries, the United States, Hong Kong, the Philippines, India, Malaysia, China, and many other countries. While people in Europe consume goods made all over the world, people in other parts of the world are at the same time consuming European goods. In Chapter 3 we saw that there are gains for all countries when they produce and trade according to comparative advantage.

In spite of gains from trade, countries have imposed a variety of barriers to trade. During the last fifty years there have been sustained international efforts to lower them. This chapter explores these barriers to trade and the major initiatives to remove them.

KEY QUESTIONS

1 Why and how do countries erect barriers to trade?

2 What is meant by fair trade laws? What is dumping, and why are economists often critical of antidumping laws?

3 Why are government subsidies to industries considered a barrier to trade?

4 Why is protection popular? Who are the winners and losers from free trade?

5 What are some of the institutions and agreements through which trade barriers have been reduced?

COMMERCIAL POLICY

Countries that have *no* barriers to trade are said to practice **free trade,** but most countries engage in some form of **protectionism;** that is, in one way or another they restrict the importation of goods. Policies directed at affecting either imports or exports are referred to as **commercial policies.** This and the next section take up the forms trade barriers take, their economic costs, and their economic and political rationale; the next section explores international attempts to reduce these trade barriers.

There are four major categories of trade barriers—tariffs, quotas, voluntary export restraints and other **nontariff barriers,** and a set of laws called "fair trade laws" that, by and large, actually serve to impede trade rather than promote fair trade.

TARIFFS

Tariffs are simply a tax on imports. Since a tariff is a tax that is imposed only on foreign goods, it puts the foreign goods at a disadvantage. It discourages imports.

Figure 36.1 shows the effect of a tariff. The figure shows a downward-sloping demand curve for the product, and an upward-sloping domestic supply curve. For simplicity, we consider the case of a country sufficiently small that the price it pays for a good on the international market does not depend on the quantity purchased. In the absence of a tariff, the domestic price is equal to this international price p^*. The country produces Q_s, consumes Q_c, and imports the difference, $Q_c - Q_s$. With a tariff, the price consumers have to pay is increased from p^* to $p^* + t$, where t is the tariff. Domestic production is increased (to Q_s')—producers are better off as a result. But consumers are worse off, as the price they pay is increased. Their consumption is reduced to Q_c'. Since production is increased and consumption reduced, imports are reduced: the domestic industry has been protected against foreign imports.

QUOTAS

Rather than setting tariffs, many countries impose **quotas**—limits on the amount of foreign goods that can be imported. Producers often prefer quotas. With limitations on the quantity imported, the domestic price increases above the international price. With quotas, domestic producers know precisely the magnitude of the foreign supply. If foreigners become more efficient or if exchange rates change in favour of foreigners, they still cannot sell any more. In that sense, quotas provide domestic producers with greater certainty than do tariffs, insulating them from the worst threats of competition.

Quotas and tariffs both succeed in raising the domestic price above the price at which the good could be obtained abroad. Both thus protect domestic producers. There is, however, one important difference: with quotas, those who are given permits to import get a profit by buying goods at the international price

Figure 36.1 EFFECT OF TARIFFS

In the absence of tariffs, the international price in a country will be p^*. The country will produce Q_s (the quantity along the supply curve corresponding to p^*), consume Q_c (the quantity along the demand curve corresponding to p^*), and import Q_c Q_s. A tariff at the rate t increases the price in the country to $p^* + t$, lowers aggregate consumption to Q_c' (the quantity along the demand curve corresponding to $p^* + t$), and increases domestic production to Q_s' (the quantity along the supply curve corresponding to $p^* + t$). Domestic producers are better off, but consumers are worse off.

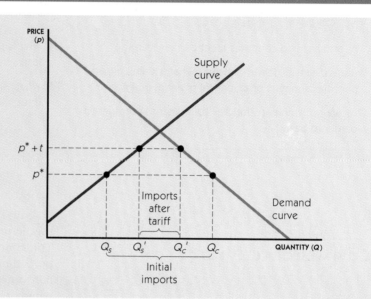

abroad and selling at the higher domestic price. The government is, in effect, giving away its tariff revenue. These profits are referred to as **quota rents.**

VOLUNTARY EXPORT RESTRAINTS

In recent years, international agreements have reduced the level of tariffs, and restricted the use of quotas. Accordingly, countries have sought to protect themselves from the onslaught of foreign competition by other means. One that became popular in the 1980s was **voluntary export restraints** (VERs). Japanese exports of cars to both Europe and the United States have been limited by voluntary export restraints.

There are two explanations for Japan's willingness to accept VERs. One is that it worries that its trading partners might take stronger actions, like imposing quotas. From Japan's perspective, VERs are clearly preferable to quotas, because with VERs the quota rents accrue to Japanese firms. The other

COMPARISON OF QUOTAS AND TARIFFS

Both can be used to restrict imports by the same amount, with the same effect on consumers and domestic producers.

With quotas, the difference between domestic price and international price accrues to the importer, who enjoys a quota rent.

With tariffs, the difference accrues to government as tariff revenue.

VERs (voluntary export restraints) are equivalent to quotas, except that the quota rents are given to foreign producers.

We can quantify the net loss to society from imposing tariffs. The difference between the amount consumers are willing to pay and what they have to pay is called consumer surplus. For the last unit consumed, the marginal benefit exactly equals the price paid, and so there is no consumer surplus. But for the first units consumed, individuals typically would be willing to pay far more—reflected in the fact that the demand curve is downward sloping in the following figure. In the initial situation, the consumer surplus is given by the triangle ABC, the area between the demand curve and the price line p*. After the price increase, it is given by the triangle ADE. The net loss is the trapezoid BCED.

But of this loss, the rectangle BDHF represents increased payments to producers (the increased price BD times the quantity that they produce), and HFGE is the tariff revenue of the government, (imports HE × the tariff). Of the increased payments to domestic producers, some is the cost of expanding production. The rest represents price and the marginal cost of production—increased profits. This is the area BIHD. Thus, the societal loss is represented by two triangles, EGC and HFI. The triangle EGC is similar to the loss to consumers arising from a monopolist's raising its price. The triangle HFI is the waste of resources resulting from the fact that as the economy expands production because of the tariff, the costs of domestic production exceed the costs of purchasing the good abroad.

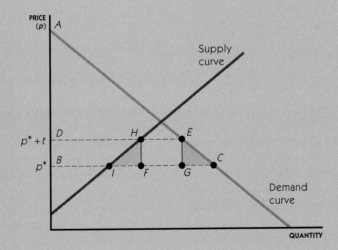

explanation is that VERs enable Japanese producers to act collusively. It may have been in their interest to collude to reduce production and raise prices in the absence of VERs, but such collusion would have been illegal under Japanese competition laws. The VERs imposed on Japanese car producers restrictions on output that they would have chosen for themselves had the law allowed it. The cost of the VERs are borne by European and U.S. consumers who pay higher prices for cars. As a means of protecting European and U.S. jobs, VERs are expensive and ineffective.

Quotas and VERs are very clear examples of nontariff barriers to trade. But there are many others. Among European countries, the many different product standards and regulations in different EU countries form an important barrier to trade, despite the efforts of the European Union to establish a single market. They are particularly important in markets for financial services and insurance. Health and safety regulations in various countries are sometimes used to create barriers to trade.

"FAIR TRADE" LAWS

Most people believe in competition. But most people believe that competition should be fair. When someone can undersell them, they suspect foul play. The government has imposed a variety of laws to ensure that there is effective and fair competition domestically. Laws have also been enacted by most countries to ensure "fair competition" in international trade. But most economists believe that in practice they are protectionist measures, reducing competition and restricting imports. To ensure fair competition, economists argue that the same laws that apply domestically should be extended internationally; that is, there should not be two standards of fairness, one applying domestically, one internationally. New Zealand and Australia, in their trade relations, have applied the same laws to trade between themselves that they do domestically. But elsewhere, progress has been limited.

ANTIDUMPIMNG LAWS

Dumping refers to the sale of products overseas at prices that are below cost and lower than those in the home country. Normally, consumers greet discounted sales with enthusiasm. If Russia is willing to sell aluminium to the European Union at low prices, why should Europe complain? One reason that might be of concern is predatory pricing. By selling below cost, the foreign companies hope to drive European firms out of business. Once they have established a monopoly position, they can raise prices. In such a case, European consumers gain only in the short run. In competitive markets, however, predation simply cannot occur, for in such markets, firms have no power to raise prices. In almost all of the cases where dumping has been found, markets are sufficiently competitive that predation is not of concern.

SUBSIDIES

The second trade practice widely viewed as unfair is for governments to subsidise domestic firms' production or exports. For example, the government may give certain domestic industries tax breaks or pay a portion of the firms' costs. These subsidies give companies receiving them an unfair advantage. Trade is determined on the basis not of comparative advantage but of relative subsidy levels.

The usual logic of economics seems to be reversed. If some foreign government wants to subsidise European consumers, why should they complain? Presumably, only if the subsidies are part of a policy of predation—if the subsidies are used to drive European firms out of business and establish a monopoly position, after which prices will be raised. Most foreign subsidies do not fall into this category.

Opposition to these subsidies arises from the companies who see their businesses hurt. While the gains to consumers outweigh the losses to businesses, the gain to each consumer is small, and consumers are not well organised. Producers, being far more organised, are able and willing to lobby government.

The European Union has been in dispute with the

United States over dumping agricultural produce. The Common Agricultural Policy has kept European prices for some food crops above world prices, by guaranteeing farmers a price for their produce. When Europe has had surpluses of some foods, it has tried to dispose of the surpluses by selling them on world markets, necessarily at the world market price. Farmers who sell produce this way are given a subsidy equal to the difference between the European price and the world price. As this entails giving producers a subsidy to export goods at less than the costs of production, it constitutes dumping.

This has been a very expensive and wasteful policy in Europe and has come about because of political pressure exerted by the farming lobby in continental Europe. Pressure on the EU budget has gradually brought down both the EU's spending on agriculture and its support prices, so that issue is gradually diminishing in importance.

POLITICAL AND ECONOMIC RATIONALE FOR PROTECTION

Chapter 3 showed how free trade, by allowing each country to concentrate production where it has a comparative advantage, can make all countries better off. Why, in spite of this, is protection so popular? The basic reason is simple: protection raises prices. While the losses to consumers from higher prices exceed the gains to producers in higher profits, producers have more political clout than consumers do.

There is an important check on the firms' ability to use the political process to advance their special interests: the interests of exporters, who realise that if the country closes off its markets to imports, other countries will reciprocate. Thus, exporting firms have often been at the forefront of advancing an international regime of freer and fairer trade through international agreements, of the kind that will be described in the next section.

But before turning to a review of these international agreements, we need to take a closer look at some of the other economic aspects of protection. While with free trade, the country as a whole may be better off, certain groups may be worse off. Those especially affected include displaced firms and workers, low-wage workers, and those in industries in which, without free trade, competition is limited.

DISPLACED FIRMS AND WORKERS

Where once Britain had a large textile industry based on cotton and wool, its comparative advantage in this industry has been lost to China and other Asian countries. Britain has a comparative advantage in pharmaceuticals and sophisticated engineering products. The same is true for Europe as a whole. The comparative advantage that Europe once had in textile manufactures and certain other manufacturing industries has been lost to developing countries in Asia and South America. Europe has a comparative advantage in relatively high-tech industries.

As firms in the textile industry have been driven out of business, their workers have had to find jobs in other industries. This applies also to steel, shipbuilding, and car manufacture, all of which have declined in Britain under the pressure of foreign competition. The losses in these industries are offset by gains in growing exporting industries. In principle, providing all the displaced labour and capital find uses in other industries and do not stand idle, the gainers would be able to more than compensate the losers; but compensation is rarely made, and so there is often resistance to the changes caused by trade.

There is often sympathy for workers displaced by the effects of trade. They are of course in a similar position to workers displaced by new technology. In an economy operating at a high level of employment, with a flexible labour market, it should be possible for these workers to find new jobs. Even then, they are likely to go through a transitional period of unemployment, they may be unable to get a job at as high a wage as the old one, and they may have to move to a new location to find work. Their worsened economic situation is offset by the improved position of workers in the exporting industries where wages tend to be higher than average.

When labour markets are not very flexible, as in most of Europe, displaced workers may become unemployed permanently or for a long time before finding new work. They may find that there are no jobs they can get reasonably close to their old work-place or that their skills are in surplus. Moving to a new area or developing new skills may be difficult or not worthwhile. When the wages that displaced workers could get are not much higher than the value of the social security and other benefits that they would lose on finding a new job, the incentive to search or move for one is low. In these circum-stances, which characterise much of Europe, shifts of comparative advantage and the growth of trade may be associated with the growth of structural un-employment which will be difficult for governments to eradicate. These conditions breed arguments for protection. Nevertheless, the appropriate response may be to increase labour market flexibility rather than to attempt to restrict trade.

BEGGAR-THY-NEIGHBOUR POLICIES

In Chapter 25 we saw that output may be limited by aggregate demand. Aggregate demand depends on consumption, investment, government expenditures, and net exports. Net exports equal exports minus im-ports. Increasing imports thus reduces net exports—reducing aggregate demand, national output, and employment. Policies that attempt to increase na-tional output by reducing imports are called **beggar-thy-neighbour policies,** because the jobs gained in one country are at the expense of jobs lost in another.

If one country imports less, other countries ex-port less. Restricting imports into Europe, say, by raising tariffs on imported goods may initially have a positive effect on European output. But the gains are likely to be temporary and limited. Europe's fewer imports will lead to lower exports, aggregate de-

mand, and imports in other countries; they lead to lower demand for European exports, even if there is no retaliation for higher tariffs.

The greater danger is that if one country imposes tariffs as a beggar-thy-neighbour policy, other coun-tries are likely to retaliate with high tariffs of their own, in order to protect their own employment. The worst instance of these beggar-thy-neighbour policies oc-curred at the onset of the Great Depression, when, in 1930, the United States passed the Hawley-Smoot Tariff Act, raising tariffs on many products to a level which effectively prohibited many imports. Other countries retaliated. As U.S. imports declined, incomes in Eu-rope and elsewhere in the world declined. As incomes declined and as these countries imposed retaliatory tariffs, they bought less from the United States. So U.S. exports plummeted, contributing further to the eco-nomic downturn in the United States. With incomes in the United States plummeting further, U.S. imports de-clined even more, contributing still further to the de-cline abroad, which then fed further into the decline in U.S. exports. The downturn in international trade that was set off by the Hawley-Smoot Tariff Act, charted in Figure 36.2, is often pointed to as a major contributing factor in making the Great Depression as deep and severe as it was.

WAGES OF SKILLED AND UNSKILLED WORKERS

There may be long-run effects of trade on the em-ployment and wages of skilled and unskilled work-ers, in addition to the problems caused by labour market inflexibility which slows down the process of adjustment. These are effects that would occur in a perfectly flexible labour market.

European countries, like North America, export so-

INTERNATIONAL TRADE AND JOBS

Opposition to imports is strongest when the economy is in a recession, but restricting imports as a way of creating jobs tends to be counterproductive.

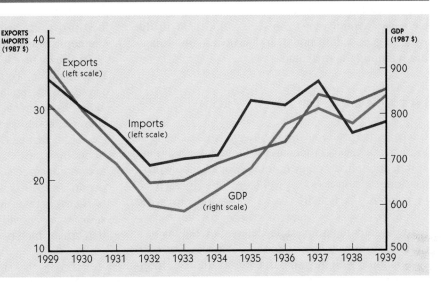

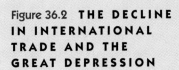

Figure 36.2 THE DECLINE IN INTERNATIONAL TRADE AND THE GREAT DEPRESSION

U.S. exports and imports fell dramatically during the Great Depression. One contributing factor to the decline in trade was the Hawley-Smoot Tariff Act introduced in 1930.

phisticated and high-tech products which use a high ratio of skilled to unskilled workers in their manufacture. By comparison, the industries that are losing out to foreign competition such as textiles use a higher ratio of unskilled to skilled workers. As trade has grown and European production has shifted away from industries like textiles towards high-tech industries, the demand for skilled workers has grown and the demand for unskilled workers has fallen.

This puts downward pressure on the wages of unskilled workers, relative to those of skilled workers. In Britain, there has been a widening gap in their pay, but at the same time unemployment of unskilled workers relative to skilled has remained high.

In continental Europe, where labour markets are less flexible, relative wages have not been free to change so much. Unemployment of unskilled workers has become a greater problem. In the United States, which is at the other end of the spectrum in terms of labour market flexibility, the skill differential in pay has widened considerably.

The fact that trade with the developing world is one of the causes of European unemployment problems might be taken as an argument against free trade. But this would ignore the alternative responses of increasing labour market flexibility to encourage wages to adjust and keep the economy at a higher level of employment and increasing educa-

EFFECTS OF TRADE ON WAGES AND EMPLOYMENT

International trade may lower the wages of unskilled labour and those working in industries where competition is limited.

International trade raises the wages of skilled workers.

If labour markets are not flexible, trade may cause higher unemployment among unskilled workers.

The appropriate response is not to restrict trade but to encourage labour market flexibility and enhance skills.

tion and training to shift the supply of labour away from unskilled and towards skilled labour. This latter policy would offset the forces that lead to the widening pay differential and growing unemployment among the unskilled.

INCREASED COMPETITION

International trade also has other adverse effects in industries where competition is limited. With limited competition, firms enjoy monopoly or oligopoly profits. Some of these extra profits are often passed on to workers. Particularly when those industries are unionised, workers may receive wages far higher than workers of comparable skill working elsewhere in the economy. International trade introduces more competition; with the increased competition, monopoly and oligopoly profits get competed away. Firms are forced to pay competitive wages—that is, the lowest wage that they can for workers with the given skill.

THE INFANT INDUSTRY ARGUMENT

While job loss and decreased wages and profits from international competition provide much of the political motivation behind protection, economists have asked, are there any *legitimate* arguments for protection? That is, are there circumstances where protection may be in the *national* interest and not just in the interests of those being protected? Two arguments have been put forward.

The first is the **infant industry argument.** Costs in new industries are often high, coming down as experience is gained. The infant industry argument is that, particularly in developing countries, firms will never be able to get the experience required to produce efficiently unless they are protected from foreign competition.

Economists have traditionally responded to this argument skeptically. If it pays to enter the industry, eventually there will be profits. Thus, the firm should be willing to charge today a price below cost to gain the experience, because today's losses will be more than offset by the future profits. But more recently, the infant industry argument has found more favour. Firms can only operate at a loss if they can

borrow funds. If capital markets do not work well, firms may not be able to borrow even if their eventual prospects are reasonable. This is a particular danger in developing countries.

This may be a legitimate argument. But it is not an argument for protection. It is an argument for assistance, which can take the form of loans or direct subsidies. Economists argue for direct assistance rather than protection because the assistance is transparent. Everyone can see that it is a subsidy to producers. Economists criticise protection because it is a hidden tax on consumers, with the proceeds transferred to producers. The lack of transparency encourages what is referred to as rent seeking: industries spend resources to persuade government to impose these hidden taxes which benefit themselves.[1]

STRATEGIC TRADE THEORY

Another argument for protection is that protection can give a country a strategic trade advantage over rivals by helping reduce domestic costs. There may be economies of scale: the larger the level of production, the lower the marginal cost. Protection ensures a large domestic sales base, and therefore a low marginal cost. The instances in which **strategic trade theory** might provide a rationale for protection appear relatively rare. Even then, they tend to be effective only when foreign governments do not retaliate by taking similar actions.

INTERNATIONAL COOPERATION

Recognising both the temptation of shortsighted trade policy and the gains from trade, nations large

---

[1] Rents refer to payments to a factor of production that are in excess of what is required to elicit the supply of that factor. In the absence of entry, protection would result in higher prices, yielding returns to the industry that are above their competitive levels; these higher returns are rents. The irony is that typically, the higher returns do attract entry, and the additional entry dissipates the rents—though prices remain high.

and small have since the Second World War engaged in a variety of efforts to reduce trade barriers. At the global level, the prominent effort is known as the **General Agreement on Tariffs and Trade.** On a slightly smaller scale, regional trading blocs have also been developed. The European Union, discussed extensively in the previous chapter, is such a trading bloc.

GATT AND THE WTO

After the Second World War, the countries of the world realised that there was much to be gained from establishing an international economic order in which barriers to trade were reduced. They established GATT. In 1995, this was succeeded by the **World Trade Organization.**

The GATT was founded on three guiding principles. The first was *reciprocity:* if one country lowered its tariffs, it could expect other countries in GATT to lower theirs. The second was *nondiscrimination:* no member of GATT could offer a special trade deal that favoured only one or a few other countries. The third was *transparency:* import quotas and other nontariff barriers to trade should be converted into tariffs, so their effective impact could be ascertained.

The GATT has proceeded in a number of stages, called **rounds** (the Kennedy Round, completed in 1967; the Tokyo Round, completed in 1979; and most recently, the Uruguay Round, completed in 1993). Collectively, the rounds have reduced tariffs on industrial goods markedly. The average tariff on manufactured goods was 40 percent in 1947. By 1992, they had been reduced to 5 percent, and the Uruguay Round reduced them still further.

The Uruguay Round was remarkable for two achievements. It began the process of extending the principles of free and fair trade to a number of much more difficult areas. There were, for instance, agreements to reduce agriculture subsidies, particularly export subsidies, and to ensure that intellectual property rights—patents and copyrights—were respected. Secondly, it created the WTO to help enforce the trade agreements. Previously, a country that believed that it was suffering from an unfair trade practice could bring a case to a GATT panel which would examine the evidence. Even if the panel was unanimous, however, in finding that an unfair trade practice had occurred, there was little in the way of effective enforcement. Under the WTO, a country injured by an unfair trade practice will be authorised to engage in retaliatory actions.

REGIONAL TRADING BLOCS

GATT and WTO have made some progress in reducing trade barriers among all countries. But the difficulties of reaching agreements involving so many parties have made progress slow. In the meantime, many countries have formed **trading blocs,** agreeing with their more immediate neighbours not only to eliminate trade barriers but also to facilitate the flow of capital and labour. Perhaps the most important of these is the **European Union,** the successor to the **Common Market,** which now embraces most of Europe, as we discussed in Chapter 35. The **North American Free Trade Agreement** will result eventually in a free trade zone within North America—that is, an area within which goods and services trade freely, without tariffs or other import restrictions. There are also many smaller free trade zones, such as those between New Zealand and Australia, and among groups of countries in Latin America and in Central America.

While the gains from internationally coordinated reductions in trade barriers are clear, the gains from regional trading blocs are more controversial. Reducing trade barriers within a region encourages trade by members of the trading bloc. Lowering barriers among the countries involved results, of course, in **trade creation.** But it also results in **trade diversion.** Trade is diverted away from countries that are not members of the bloc, who might, in fact, have a comparative advantage in the particular commodity. Under these conditions, the global net benefits will be positive if the trade creation exceeds the trade diversion. Typically, when trade blocs are formed, tariffs against outsiders are harmonised. If the external trade barriers are harmonised at the lowest common level (rather than at the average or highest levels) at the same time that internal trade barriers are lowered, it is more likely that the trade creation effects exceed the trade diversion effects.

The prospect of the free movement of both goods and financial capital in NAFTA caused a lot of con-

CLOSE-UP: MERCANTILISM—OLD AND NEW

Mercantilism is the name for the school of thought that was prevalent in Europe between about 1500 and 1800 and focused on building up the power and wealth of the state through the aggressive pursuit of exports. It also discouraged imports and thought that a country's strength was related to its store of gold and silver. Josiah Child, one of the better-known mercantilists, wrote in 1693: "Foreign trade produces riches, riches power; power preserves our trade and religion."

To have lots of products left over to export, the country had to produce more than it consumed, so citizens were exhorted to work hard for low wages.

Adam Smith, the father of modern economics, recognised the fallacies in mercantilism. A country's wealth, he argued, was measured not by its gold and silver but by the productivity of its resources. Smith pointed out that even from the standpoint of national power, a country's army does not run on gold and silver but on physical products like ships, food, clothing, and weapons.

The world has changed dramatically in the more than two centuries since Adam Smith formulated his attack on mercantilism. But the mercantilist spirit remains alive, and the criticisms of the new mercantilist arguments are direct descendants of Smith's analysis.

Modern mercantilists view exports as desirable today, not because they lead to the accumulation of gold but because they lead to job creation. By the same token, imports are viewed as undesirable, both because they lead to job loss and because they lead to dependency on foreigners.

Some countries, such as Japan and Korea, have successfully pursued strong export-oriented policies; and most economists believe that these policies have contributed to their economic success. But the reason is quite different from that of the older mercantilist theories that focused on the accumulation of riches. Japan and Korea did accumulate capital rapidly, but this was because of their extraordinarily high savings rates. Their export-oriented policies were important because to be successful in international markets, their industries had to be efficient and adopt high standards of production. Their export-oriented policies helped their industries become more competitive and adopt advanced technologies.

Today, in Europe, we recognise that trade is important, not because it creates jobs but because it leads to higher standards of living, because Europeans can specialise in producing those goods in which Europe has a comparative advantage, and because competition from abroad forces European firms to become more efficient. These are essentially the same reasons that Adam Smith put forward for why, though protection might benefit businesspeople, free trade would benefit the society as a whole.

cern in the United States. In the NAFTA debate, Ross Perot used the metaphor of a giant sucking sound: Mexico would suck up huge amounts of investment that otherwise would have occurred in the United States. The accusation was not just that goods produced today in Mexico would cost Americans jobs. It was also that U.S. firms would move down to Mexico, to take advantage of low-wage labour, and the capital that flowed down to Mexico would not be available for investment in the United States.

Such arguments are based on an important misconception. They fail to take account of the fact that capital markets are already global. The United States is not limited in its investment to savings in the United States. Capital will flow to good investment opportunities wherever they are. If there are good investment opportunities in the United States, capital will flow there, regardless of how much Americans invest in Mexico. Investment barriers impede this flow of capital to its highest productive use, thus lowering world economic efficiency.

The Perot argument is based on a zero sum view of the world—that what Mexico gains must come at the expense of the United States. Perot's argument is similar to the one that says when a country imports, it loses jobs: the gains to foreigners from their exports are at the expense of domestic firms, which otherwise would be creating these jobs. In Chapter 3, we saw what was wrong with this argument: the theory of comparative advantage says that when countries specialise in what they produce best, *both* countries are better off. Workers gain higher wages when they move into those sectors where their productivity is highest; and consumers gain from the lower prices. So too with investment. When investment flows to where its return is highest, world output is increased. Since the return to capital is increased when it is efficiently allocated, savings rates may also increase, so that the overall supply of funds will be higher. Higher savings rates and more efficient use of available savings will combine to give a higher world economic growth rate.

But just as not everyone necessarily gains from trade according to comparative advantage, so too not everyone will necessarily gain from the flow of capital to Mexico. There will be some investment diversion from other countries to Mexico, as Mexico becomes more attractive to investors throughout the world because of its improved access to the huge U.S. market. Most economists believe that the net effect on investment in the United States will be negligible and could even be positive. Industries within the United States that see their opportunities expand by selling more to Mexico will invest more, more than offsetting the reduced investment from firms that decline in the face of competition from Mexican imports.

In fact, investment flows augment the gains from trade that would occur in their absence because there are important trade-investment links. The U.S. companies producing abroad tend to use more parts from the United States, just as French companies producing abroad tend to use more parts from France. Thus, flows of investment often serve as a precursor to exports.

TRADE-OFFS BETWEEN REGIONAL AND INTERNATIONAL AGREEMENTS

The potential economic trade-off between increased trade within the region and the expense of reduced trade outside the region has led to concerns about the consequences of regional trading blocs. There is the prospect of a world dominated by these blocs—the EU, NAFTA, an Asian bloc, and so on—with free trade and capital flows within blocs, but with trade between them restricted by tariff and other barriers and with difficult trade relations between them. It raises the prospect that the economic separation of

AREAS OF INTERNATIONAL COOPERATION

Multilateral trade agreements—WTO
  Based on principles of reciprocity, nondiscrimination, and transparency.
  Uruguay Round extended trade liberalization to services and agricultural commodities and helped establish intellectual property rights.

Regional trade agreements—European Union, NAFTA
  Risk trade diversion rather than trade creation.
  But may be better able to address complicated issues, such as those involving investment or the Single European Market.

the blocs would be paralleled by political distance between them and uneasy, maybe dangerous international relations. The European part of the scenario has been called "fortress Europe."

Alternatively, and more optimistically, blocs may be seen as groups of countries that have achieved greater progress towards free trade among themselves than the world as a whole has, but nevertheless there continues to be global progress towards free trade. Regional blocs may be better able to reach agreements on liberalization of trade in a wider range of goods and services and of capital markets, than is possible globally. It is difficult to envisage a programme as ambitious as the Single European Market on a wider scale than the European Union.

REVIEW AND PRACTICE

SUMMARY

1 Countries protect themselves in a variety of ways besides imposing tariffs. These nontariff barriers include quotas, voluntary export restraints, and regulatory barriers. Quotas and voluntary export restraints are not banned by international agreement. While in recent decades there have been huge reductions in tariff barriers, there has been some increase in nontariff barriers.

2 While all countries benefit from free trade, some groups within a country may be adversely affected. In Europe and North America, unskilled workers and those in industries where, without trade, there is limited competition, may see their wages fall. Some workers, particularly the unskilled, may lose their jobs and may require assistance to find new ones. In the United States, the skill gap in pay has widened. In Europe, the unskilled suffer high unemployment but their relative pay has not fallen so much.

3 Laws nominally intended to ensure fair trade often are used as protectionist measures.

4 Concern about imports is particularly strong when unemployment is high. But beggar-thy-neighbour policies, which attempt to protect jobs by limiting imports, tend to be counterproductive.

5 The World Trade Organization, which replaced GATT, provides a framework within which trade barriers can be reduced. It is based on reciprocity, nondiscrimination, and transparency. The Uruguay Round of GATT extended trade liberalization to new areas, including agriculture and intellectual property and established the World Trade Organization.

6 Difficulties at arriving at trade agreements involving all of the countries of the world have resulted in broader regional agreements, including the European Union and NAFTA. Some of the risk from these regional agreements may arise from trade diversion rather than trade creation.

KEY TERMS

protectionism

nontariff barriers

quotas

voluntary export restraints

dumping

beggar-thy-neighbour policies

infant industry argument

strategic trade theory

General Agreement on Tariffs and Trade (GATT)

World Trade Organization (WTO)

North American Free Trade Agreement (NAFTA)

trade creation

trade diversion

REVIEW QUESTIONS

1 What are the various ways in which countries seek to protect their industries against foreign imports?

2 How do tariffs and quotas differ?

3 Why are consumers worse off as a result of the imposition of a tariff?

4 What are the laws designed to ensure fair international trade? How have they worked in practice?

5 What are nontariff barriers to international trade?

6 How is it that, while there are gains to free trade, some groups are adversely affected? Which groups in Europe are most adversely affected?

7 What are beggar-thy-neighbour policies? What are their consequences?

8 What do GATT and the WTO do? What are their basic underlying principles? What have been GATT's achievements? What further advances were accomplished under the Uruguay Round?

9 What is NAFTA? What are the advantages of regional free trade agreements?

10 What is meant by trade diversion versus trade creation?

PROBLEMS

1 Suppose that Japanese products go out of fashion in Europe. How would this affect Japan's exports? What would happen to the exchange rate? What would happen to national income in Japan, assuming the Japanese government did not take offsetting actions? What effect would this, in turn, have on European exports? On national income, again assuming that governments in Europe did not take offsetting actions? Use the diagrammatic techniques learned in earlier chapters to answer these questions.

2 Explain why the balance of trade between Japan and Europe would worsen as Europe went into a recession if at the same time, the United States were recovering from a recession.

3 Explain why, if the European Union succeeded in getting Japan to remove some of its trade barriers, the exchange rate between the yen and European currencies might change but the trade balance might not be affected much. Why would the removal of these trade barriers still be beneficial for Europe? What would happen to the exchange rate?

4 How might a government use regulatory policies to discourage imports?

5 If Portuguese workers receive 60 percent of the wages that German workers do, why don't all German firms move down to Portugal?

6 Should the European Union treat foreign-owned firms producing cars in the European Union (like GM) differently from European firms? Should VW, Fiat, and Renault be allowed to form a research consortium, excluding these producers? Should the European Union give money to a research consortium that excludes these firms? Should they be eligible for research funds themselves on an equal basis?

7 How should a government prioritise its efforts on opening foreign markets to its domestic firms, by the impact on domestic workers? By the impact on domestic companies? By the impact on domestic investors? How would you prioritise the following four examples?

(a) Opening the Japanese market to allow Toys-R-Us to open retail stores in Tokyo, selling toys made in China

(b) Opening the Japanese securities markets to ensure that Goldman Sachs and other similar non-Japanese investment firms can sell securities to Japanese pension funds

(c) Opening the Japanese car market to enhance the ability of VW and others to sell European cars in Japan

(d) Opening the Chinese car market to enhance the ability of Toyota and Mazda to sell U.S.-made cars to China

CHAPTER 37

ALTERNATIVE ECONOMIC SYSTEMS

The Soviet Union has dissolved, and formerly Communist countries all over eastern Europe and the Baltic areas are overhauling their economic systems, making them more market based. Even the most populous country in the world, China—though retaining communism as its *political* system—has committed itself to using markets in its economic life. Such an enormous change makes it difficult to remember the days of rivalry between the Soviet Union's communist economy and the mixed capitalist economies of western Europe and the United States. As recently as the 1970s, many Western observers, including reputable economists, considered it only a matter of time before the Soviet Union would draw even and eventually win the economic race.

Today the formerly Communist countries look to their western European neighbours and see much higher living standards. This chapter contrasts Soviet-style economies with those of western countries, highlighting the major differences that might account for their divergent growth paths and standards of living. Towards the end of the chapter, we consider the two major versions of socialism that differed from that of the former Soviet Union: the workers' cooperatives of the former Yugoslavia and the attempts by Hungary and China to incorporate elements of a market into socialism.

Studying these alternative economic systems is not only important in providing insights into the major economic and political conflict of the twentieth century. Understanding why socialism and communism have failed provides us insights into what makes markets work.

KEY QUESTIONS

1 What were the economic conditions that gave rise to the socialist idea?

2 What were the central characteristics of Soviet-style socialism? How did it differ from the market system in the way it allocated resources?

3 Why did it fail?

4 What are some of the principal reforms of Soviet-style socialism that have been tried, and how did they fare?

5 What problems do the former socialist economies face in making the transition to a market economy?

TERMINOLOGY

Several terms are useful in describing alternative economic systems. Under **socialism,** the government owns and operates the basic means of production—the factories that make cars and steel, the mines, the railways, the telephone system, and so on. Under **communism,** the government essentially owns all property—not only the factories but also the houses and the land. In practice, no government has abolished all private property. People still own the clothes they wear and durable consumption goods like cars and television sets.

The term *communism* is used to describe the economic system in countries that came under the domination of the Soviet Union and China in the years after the Second World War. These countries shared an economic system that involved not only state ownership of assets but also considerable central control of economic decisions. Because of the important role played by central planning, these economies are referred to as **planned economies.** These countries also had a political system that did not allow free elections, free speech, or a multitude of other rights found in democracies.

The economies of western Europe and the United States, in contrast, are commonly referred to as capitalist economies, because of the important role played by private capital. They are also called mixed economies, since government plays a large role, and market economies, because of their heavy reliance on firms and households interacting in markets.

Table 37.1 compares living standards in the Soviet-style economies just before the revolutionary events of 1989 to 1991 with those in the rest of the world.

THE ORIGINS OF SOCIALISM AND COMMUNISM

The eighteenth and nineteenth centuries produced the industrial revolution and, with it, a dramatic change in the structures of the economies and societies it touched. New technologies resulted in development of the factory system and increased movement of workers from rural to urban areas. In the fast-growing cities, workers often lived in squalid conditions. In order for families to eke out a living, children went alongside their parents to work in the factories, where they worked long hours in unhealthy conditions. Periodically economies faced a recession or depression. Workers were thrown out of their jobs and forced to beg, steal, or starve. Life for the unlanded peasants in the rural sectors was hardly more idyllic. In Ireland in the 1840s, for instance, a fifth of the population (half a million people) starved to death.

While the vast majority of people thus lived on the edge of survival, a few had considerable wealth, often inherited. Between the very wealthy and the poor was a small but growing middle class, mainly commercial and professional. (By contrast, today in Europe and the United States, it is the middle class, consisting of professionals, businesspeople, and high-wage workers, that is dominant.)

Were these conditions inevitable? Could they be

Table 37.1 COMPARISON OF LIVING STANDARDS BETWEEN PLANNED AND MARKET ECONOMIES

	GNP per Capita (1988 $)	Annual GNP Growth Rate (%) 1965–1988	Life Expectancy at Birth	Adult Illiteracy (%)
Soviet-style economies:				
USSR	2,660	4.0	70	< 5
China	330	5.4	70	31
Hungary	2,460	5.1	71	< 5
Market economies:				
U.S.	19,840	1.6	76	< 5
India	340	1.8	58	57
Italy	13,330	3.0	77	< 5
Egypt	660	3.6	63	56
Sweden	19,300	1.8	77	< 5

changed? If so, how? These questions preoccupied numerous social thinkers from the late eighteenth century on. Many saw the capitalist economic system as the culprit. The most influential critic of the capitalist system was a German man living in England named Karl Marx.

Marx believed that the force of history had led the economy inevitably to evolve from medieval feudalism to capitalism and that the economy, just as inevitably, would evolve from capitalism to socialism and eventually to communism. Not only would there be no private property, the state would make all allocation decisions. "From each according to his ability," wrote Marx, "and to each according to his needs."[1] Clearly Marx's vision of socialism provided different answers from those of the market economy to the basic economic questions of what to produce and in what quantities, how to produce it, for whom it should be produced, and who makes the decisions. The state, *not* the market, would decide what, how, and for whom.[2]

Among those who found Marx's ideas particularly attractive was a Russian revolutionary, Vladimir Ilyich Lenin. In October 1917, the Bolsheviks—the party of Lenin, with Marxism as its official ideology—seized the government. The first Communist government was established. Translating Marx's ideology into a programme for running a populous, poor, and largely undeveloped and rural country was no easy task. It was ironic that Russia, hardly touched by capitalism at the time of the revolution, became the first to try to implement Marx's ideas. Since Marx had predicted that countries would have to pass through the capitalist

[1] *Critique of the Gotha Program* (1875).

[2] In Marx's view, socialism and communism were transitional stages to an eventual time when the state would wither away. How production would be organised—how the basic decisions of what to produce, how to produce it, and for whom it should be produced would be made—in this eventual period was left unclear.

phase *on the way* to socialism, he had expected socialism to arise first in countries such as Britain or France.

Indeed, the economic system that we know today as communism is as much due to how Lenin and his successor, Joseph Stalin, adapted Marx's ideas to the situation they found in Russia as it is to Marx's original ideas. What Marx's reaction would be to what evolved there one can only guess, but a hint is provided by his comment on the ideas of the French Marxists: "As for me, I am not a Marxist."

DISILLUSIONMENT WITH MARKETS

In developed countries today, there is widespread confidence in markets and in the efficiency with which they allocate resources. To be sure, there are market failures, periods of unemployment, and pockets of poverty. But we have seen in this book how markets by and large allocate resources efficiently. We have seen as well how selective government interventions can remedy the market failures and, if there is the political will, at least partially address the problem of the inequality of income generated by the market.

But this confidence has not always been present; nor is it universal now. When the United States went into the Great Depression in 1929, followed by most of Europe, not to recover fully until the Second World War, millions were thrown out of jobs. The capitalist economic system did not seem to be functioning well. Today, to the billions of people still living in abject poverty in India, elsewhere in Asia, and in Africa and South America, markets have failed to meet their rising aspirations. And even within the industrialised countries, there are many who have not partaken of the general prosperity. For them the market system does not seem to have worked well.

It is not surprising, then, that many have sought an alternative economic system, which would generate faster sustained economic growth at the same time as it promoted greater equality. Throughout much of the twentieth century, many saw socialism as the answer. They believed that if the government controlled the economy, not only would recessions be eliminated, so too would what they saw as the chaos of the marketplace, for instance the excess expansion of capacity in one industry accompanied by shortages in another industry.

HOW SOVIET-STYLE SOCIALIST ECONOMIES WORK

Private property, prices, and the profit incentive play a central role in market economies. If these are abandoned in a Soviet-style socialist economy, what replaces them? Three major components are central planning, force, and political controls and rewards.

In Soviet-style economies, decision making, including coordination of economic activity, was to be done by government ministries, through central planning. Five-year plans were drawn up, with detailed targets—how much steel production was to be increased, how much food production, and so on. Individual plant managers were told not only what they were to produce but also how they were to produce it.

Market incentive schemes were also sometimes replaced by force. We saw in earlier chapters that some incentive schemes take the form of the carrot, some of the stick. The Soviet Union under Joseph Stalin preferred the stick. Those who did not meet their targets were rewarded with a sojourn in Siberia.

Political controls and rewards also helped replace the lack of economic incentives. Key positions in the economy went to faithful members of the Communist party. In the early days of the revolution, these included many who believed in socialism as an alternative, superior form of economic organization. Given their ideological commitment, economic incentives to work hard to meet the goals were relatively unimportant. And to the extent that incentives were important, they were provided by the potential for promotion. But as the years went by, membership in the party came to be seen as the vehicle for getting ahead, not as a matter of belief. Under Leonid Brezhnev, who was the first secretary (head) of the Communist party from 1964 to 1982, this cynical attitude spread. The party faithful not only received good jobs but enjoyed other benefits,

CLOSE-UP: MARXIST ECONOMICS

Of the many writers in the nineteenth century who advocated socialism, none was more influential than Karl Marx. His ideas not only influenced how socialism developed within the Soviet Union, they gave rise to the Marxist school of economics. Like any major school, ideas evolve, as do disagreements among its members. Following are a few of the major ideas.

One important idea concerns what determines or should determine prices. The answer given by the basic economic model is the law of supply and demand. Marx, by contrast, made use of what was called the labour theory of value, a set of ideas developed earlier by the British economist David Ricardo. The labour theory of value argued that the value of any good should be attributed to the workers who made it. A good that required more labour should be valued more highly, and vice versa. Marx considered the difference between what a good was sold for and the labour costs that went into making the good—the profits of the firm and the return to capital—as exploitation of workers. By contrast, in market economies profits are viewed as providing firms with incentives, and capital is seen as a scarce factor—like any other scarce factor, such as land or labour—that will be efficiently allocated only when it fetches a return.

Another important strand in Marxist thought is that the economic system affects human nature. This book has taken the preferences of individuals as given. The demand curves for chocolate bars and CDs, for example, have been based on the trade-offs that people are willing to make. And we have not asked why workers may shirk if they are not provided with incentives.

Many Marxists believe that under a different social system, people would be less materialistic, more concerned about helping one another, more committed to their jobs. During wartime, we often see changes in attitudes and behaviour. Whether human nature is sufficiently mutable that *some* social system might achieve these idealistic goals over long periods of time remains debatable. What is clear is that none of the Soviet-style economies succeeded.

A third strand of Marxist thought emphasises the link between politics and economics. Marxists claim that the answer to the question of "for whom" is provided by power—the economic power of monopolies and the political power of the wealthy. The wealthy use government to gain for themselves what they cannot achieve in the marketplace. Marxists cite instances of governments spending hundreds of billions of dollars to fight a war to preserve business interests, while claiming insufficient money to finance the rebuilding of urban ghettos or to provide free higher education for the poor. The debate on the validity of these claims, as always with moral issues and other value judgments, takes us beyond the boundaries of economics.

Marx may have been correct in his emphasis on the importance of economic factors in determining the evolution of society. In an ironic twist of history, though, economic forces appear to have injured socialism more than capitalism. It is the economic successes of the capitalist systems of the industrialised world, combined with the economic failures of the Soviet-style socialist economies, that led to the reaction against socialism in eastern Europe and the Soviet Union.

including access to special stores at which goods not generally available could be acquired.

A basic aspect of market economies, competition, was shunned. Just as the Communist party had a monopoly in the political sphere, no competition with government enterprises was allowed, and the government enterprises did not compete with one another. They did not, of course, eliminate all competition: there was still competition to be promoted to top positions and thus receive higher incomes and access to desirable goods. But success in this competition was not based on how efficiently you produced the goods that consumers wanted or how innovative you were in devising new products. Rather, success was measured by how well you complied with the bureaucratic targets and requirements and how well you performed in the politics of the bureaucracy and party.

The planned economy or central planning failed miserably in replacing markets. The central planners simply did not have the requisite information. Workers, for instance, were often mismatched with jobs. They were given job security, but this reduced their economic incentives. Pay, and even promotion, were generally not related to performance, and thus the incentives were undermined. Without economic incentives, workers often exerted the minimal level of effort that they could get away with.

Similarly, firms had no incentive to produce beyond the quotas assigned to them. Indeed, they had an incentive not to do so. If they showed that they could produce more with fewer inputs, in subsequent years their quotas would be increased. In the absence of a price system, shortages often developed, not only of consumer goods but also of inputs to production. Hence, firms squirreled away any extra raw materials they could get their hands on.

The absence of prices and profits had further debilitating effects. In market economies, returns to investment are the signals that determine how capital should be allocated. The quest for profits provides the incentive for entrepreneurs; equally important, losses are a signal for firms to close down. In socialist economies, with the state's owning all firms and therefore all profits, profits provide little incentive. And losses are seldom used as a basis for shutting down establishments. If a firm makes a loss, the government meets the deficit. János Kornai, a Hungar-

ian economist who teaches both in his native land and at Harvard, refers to this phenomenon as **soft budget constraints,** to contrast them with the harsh reality of budget constraints facing firms in a market economy. For the firm in a socialist system, there is no penalty for making losses, and no incentive to conserve on resources or to innovate.

In a way, it made sense for the Soviet government not to pay too much attention to profits, since the prices firms received for what they produced and the prices they paid for the inputs they used (including labour and capital) were not market-clearing prices. They did not represent the scarcity value of the resources used or of the goods produced. Thus, the profits were not a good measure of the benefits or costs of the firm's production. By the same token, since prices were not set at market-clearing levels, they did not reflect scarcity. Hence returns to investment—measured in rubles—were not a sound guide for allocating investments. Prices and wages provided little guidance for whether firms should try to economise more on labour or capital or other inputs.

It is perhaps no accident that the fields in which the Soviet Union achieved its greatest success—military research, space technology, and mathematics and physics—were all fields in which markets play a limited role even in capitalist economies. In the absence of prices and interest rates to guide investment, decisions were made on beliefs about the correct path of development. Stalin had two basic ideas. First, he recognised that resources that were not allocated to consumption could be given to investment. In terms of the production possibilities curve depicted in Figure 37.1, his first objective was to reduce consumption and move the economy from a point such as E_0 to E_1. One of the aims of the collectivization of agriculture was to do just that, to squeeze the farmers as much as possible. But urban workers' wages were also kept low. By keeping wages low and the supply of consumer goods limited, the Soviet planners in effect forced the economy to have high savings.

His second idea was to focus investment on heavy industry. Stalin considered huge factories, such as steel mills, the central symbol of modern economies, which distinguished them from less-developed, agrarian economies. He therefore invested primarily in heavy industry, providing little support for agri-

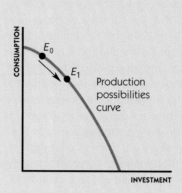

Figure 37.1 RAPID INDUSTRIALIZATION: MOVEMENTS ALONG THE PRODUCTION POSSIBILITIES CURVE

Soviet-style socialists believed that rapid growth of heavy industry was desirable, so they increased investment. But as the production possibilities curve shows, this can only be done at the expense of consumption. Central planners tried to move the economy towards a point such as E_1, with a high output of investment goods and a low output of consumption goods.

culture, consumer goods, or housing. The two ideas were in a sense intertwined. With low wages and low consumption, there was little need to invest in industries to provide consumption goods.

SOVIET-STYLE SOCIALISM AND INEQUALITY

The Soviet government, through its planning ministry, not only decided what was to be produced and how. It also provided the answer to the for whom question. In answering this question, three aspects of Soviet ideology played an important role. First, Soviet-style economies were committed to heavy industrialization and a deemphasis on agriculture. Not surprisingly, then, a large part of the burden of the costs was borne by agriculture. Forced collectivization in agriculture kept agriculture wages low. In effect, there were high taxes on agriculture.

Second, the programme of high savings and low consumption could be interpreted as putting an emphasis on the consumption of future generations at the expense of the consumption of the current generation.

Third, an attempt was made to reduce the inequality in society, at least according to the rhetoric of the leaders. The government determined every-

one's wages. It decided how much more a skilled worker got than an unskilled worker. Some goods it allocated directly, such as markets for housing and medical care.

Whether or to what extent Soviet-style socialist systems were successful in reducing inequality remains debated. On the one hand, after confiscating all land and other property, there were no longer any very rich people. Also, free medicine and highly subsidised food and apartments provided a safety net for the poor. Moreover, one of the major sources of poverty—unemployment—was eliminated. But on the other hand, differences in life-style between the worst-off members of society and high party officials remained enormous. Whole families of ordinary citizens lived crowded together in one room. And though no one starved, they spent long hours in lines to obtain the barest necessities of life. By contrast, high party officials enjoyed vacations along the beaches of the Black Sea, could buy goods unavailable elsewhere at stores reserved for party members, and had chauffeur-driven cars and other powers and perquisites enjoyed by relatively few within the capitalist world. Large wage differentials, commensurate with those observed in capitalist economies, also existed, though they may have translated into smaller differences in living standards, given the many things provided cheaply by the state.

THE BASIC ECONOMIC QUESTIONS UNDER SOVIET-STYLE SOCIALISM

1 What is produced?
  Heavy industrial goods
  Other goods as the state sees fit

2 How are goods produced?
  With technologies and inputs decided upon by the state (often capital-intensive technologies)

3 For whom are they produced?
  For future generations (high forced savings rates)
  For present generations according to the wages set by government (high "taxes" on agriculture)
  For government officials, who get high rewards

4 Who makes the decisions?
  Central planning authorities

Even the most vaunted achievement of socialism, prevention of the abject extremes of poverty, has in recent years been thrown into doubt. In the period 1960–61 in China, for example, demographers now estimate that as many as 20 million Chinese starved to death. In the democracies, a free press would have presumably ensured that a calamity like this could not have occurred. Something would have been done. In China, it went almost unnoticed.

FAILURE OF SOCIALISM

For several decades, Stalin's programme appeared successful. He was able to force net investment rates up to almost unprecedented levels, more than 23 percent of net national product in 1937, for example. Many factories were built. The official statistics suggested a path of rapid industrialization and growth. There is growing doubt about the reliability of the statistics, but there is little doubt that any gains were accompanied by political repression. The U.S.S.R.'s economic progress was interrupted by the Second World War, in which 20 million Russians are believed to have died, and the economy was greatly disrupted.

The period after the Second World War saw the spread of Soviet-style socialism to eastern Europe— Poland, Czechoslovakia, East Germany, Hungary, Ro-

mania, Bulgaria, Yugoslavia, and Albania—and, in 1949, to China.[3] In the case of the eastern European countries, at least, the spread was hardly voluntary. It was the price they paid for being liberated from the Germans by Soviet troops at the end of the war. Before the war, some eastern European countries had enjoyed reasonably high standards of living. Others, such as Albania, had been extremely poor and backwards.

The ensuing decades witnessed several changes in attitudes towards the Soviet-style socialist experiment. At first, the efficiency virtues of the system were lauded. The planning mechanism replaced the perceived chaos of the marketplace. Investment could be directed in a rational way. Resources could be quickly mobilised. Moreover, the government could force the high levels of savings required for a successful development programme. Textbooks as well as popular writings talked about a trade-off between growth and development on the one hand and freedom on the other. Strong central control was thought to be necessary for rapid growth. Moreover, it was thought that Soviet-style socialism could raise the quality of life to a level the market economy had not been able to attain. Basic human services like health and education could be brought to the masses.

[3] Mongolia had adopted Soviet-style socialism much earlier, in 1924. Cuba adopted a variant much later, under Castro in 1959. North Korea and North Vietnam both adopted Soviet-style socialism as soon as their governments were established.

CLOSE-UP: ENVIRONMENTAL DAMAGE IN THE SOVIET UNION

One of the alleged advantages of centrally controlled economies was that unlike ruthless capitalists, socialist firms would take into account the costs and benefits to all members of society. In the area of environmental protection, that promise was not kept. In fact, in the words of one recent study, "When historians finally conduct an autopsy on the Soviet Union and Soviet Communism, they may reach the verdict of death by ecocide."

Market economies often have difficulty dealing with pollution externalities. But in attempting to grow faster, Soviet central planners often made pollution problems worse. For example, oil and energy prices were held deliberately low, as a form of assistance to manufacturers who used oil as an input. But lower prices encouraged wasteful use of energy. When combined with a lack of antipollution measures, this produced literally sickening air pollution. Today in the industrial centre of what was called Magniogorsk, nine out of ten children become ill with pollution-related diseases like bronchitis, asthma, and cancer.

Highly intensive farming, in a situation where no one had a property right to the land and an incentive to protect it, led to massive pesticide use and soil erosion. Three-quarters of the surface water in what used to be the Soviet Union is now badly polluted, either from industrial or agricultural sources.

Perhaps the most publicised result of all was the explosion at the Chernobyl nuclear power station in 1986, which exposed perhaps 20 million Soviet citizens to excessive radiation. If that nuclear power plant had been forced to use safety equipment to avoid that externality, it might well have been shut down years earlier.

Rather than correcting the market failures that led to pollution, Soviet central planners had magnified them into ecological disasters.

Sources: "Rubbishing of a Superpower," *The Economist,* 25 April 1992, pp. 99-100; M. Feshbach and A. Friendly, *Ecocide in the USSR* (New York: Basic Books, 1992).

But as economies like Czechoslovakia and Hungary, which had been prosperous before the war, fell behind other European countries, concerns about the efficiency of the system were raised. Such systems could force their citizens to save more because they could repress consumption, but could they allocate resources efficiently? It became increasingly clear that the countries were not growing as fast as one would have thought. The higher savings rates did little more than offset the higher levels of inefficiency.

By the mid-1970s, inklings of an impending economic crisis became more and more apparent. While agricultural productivity in the United States and western Europe had boomed, in the Soviet-style socialist countries it had stagnated. Nikita Khrushchev, who led Russia from the death of Stalin until he was replaced

by Brezhnev in 1964, recognised the problems in agriculture and directed more of the country's investment there. But in 1973, the Soviet Union began buying massive amounts of wheat from the United States and other western countries to feed its people.

As Mikhail Gorbachev came to power in 1985 the magnitude of the problems the country faced became even clearer. It became evident that many of the statistics on industrial production had been more exaggerated than even many skeptics had thought. Indicators of well-being, such as infant mortality statistics, had similarly been distorted.

In most economists' judgment, the Soviet-style socialist experiment was a failure. Today, more than seventy years after the Soviet-style socialist experiment began in Russia, income per capita is an eighth of that

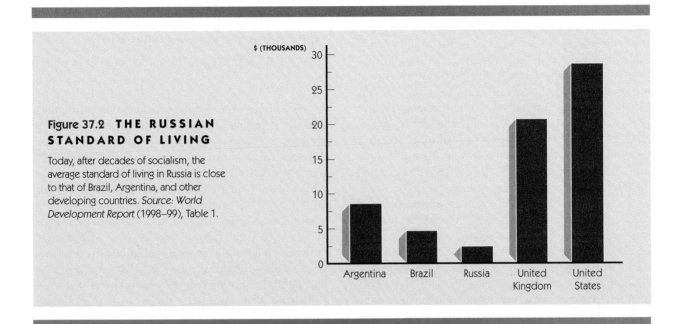

Figure 37.2 THE RUSSIAN STANDARD OF LIVING

Today, after decades of socialism, the average standard of living in Russia is close to that of Brazil, Argentina, and other developing countries. *Source: World Development Report* (1998–99), Table 1.

of the United Kingdom and a tenth of that of the United States. Russia finds its standard of living close to that of Brazil, Argentina, and other countries considered to be developing, as illustrated in Figure 37.2. The Soviet-style socialist experiment had remarkable achievements, like the Sputnik satellite, but a productive and growing economy was not among them.

REASONS FOR THE FAILURE

The continued success of the capitalist system and the failure of Soviet-style socialist economies can be attributed to incentives and markets, or the lack of them.

The socialists failed to recognise the importance of incentives. Workers, both in collective farms and in manufacturing firms, had no incentive to do more than was required. Managers similarly had no incentives. Firms could not keep any profits they made, and managerial pay in any case did not depend on the profitability of the enterprise. There was no competition, and the soft budget constraints—the fact that losses would be made up by the government—further attenuated managerial incentives.

Equally important, there was no incentive for in-

novation and growth. The increases in productivity of the labour force in capitalist economies over the past century, with the concomitant increases in wages, are in no small measure the result of the innovative efforts of entrepreneurs. These entrepreneurs almost surely did not succeed out of the desire to enhance the welfare of their workers; they were motivated by the lust for profits and the desire for returns to their savings. But as Adam Smith said, such motives provide a far surer guide to the enhancement of a nation's wealth than any other.

Socialists wanted to replace the market mechanism for allocating resources with central planning. But they encountered two further problems. First, the bureaucrats did not have the requisite information to know how to allocate resources efficiently. Managers of firms had no incentive to tell the central planners what the minimum inputs required to meet their production goals were. Rather, they had every incentive to claim they needed more than they really did. This made their job easier. And they had no incentive to exceed their goals, for if they did, the planners would raise their targets for the next year.

Second, planners could not perfectly monitor the various firms in the economy, to ensure that resources were used in the way intended. And firms had only limited incentives to comply with the planners' directives. They were not rewarded, and they knew they were only imperfectly monitored. Sometimes the managers could divert resources meant for the firm to their own private use. Their disdain for the planners was enhanced by the fact that the planners often put impossible demands on them, such as asking them to produce outputs without providing them the requisite inputs. To fulfill their quota, firms had to acquire the inputs from a "grey" market outside the planning system.

The socialists did not understand the importance of capital markets, interest rates, and profits. As this text has emphasised, capital is a scarce resource. It must be allocated efficiently. Prices provide the signals that make this possible. Because the Soviet-style socialist economies set prices by command rather than through markets, prices did not provide the necessary signals. Try as they might to use the planning mechanism to replace the market mechanism, socialist government planning boards simply did not have the requisite information to allocate investment efficiently.

Given the scarcity of capital, the Soviet strategy of heavy industrialization probably did not make much sense. It would have made more sense to focus attention on industries that required less capital.

The failure of worker incentives, the failure of planners to allocate resources efficiently, and the failure of firms to use resources efficiently largely accounted for the inefficiency of the system. But there were other factors as well. The drabness of life, the lack of opportunity afforded by the system, the long hours spent in lines trying to get rotten vegetables or a small portion of meat, all contributed to social malaise, evidenced by a high incidence of alcoholism, which impaired worker productivity. The worker under Soviet-style socialism seemed truly alienated from his work.

REFORMS IN THE SOVIET-STYLE SOCIALIST ECONOMIES

As the failures of Soviet-style socialism became more evident, a variety of reforms were discussed. Three courses of action were possible: try harder to make the socialist system work; give up on socialism and move to a market-based system; or find a third way, which would be neither capitalism nor socialism. For three decades, beginning with Khrushchev, the Soviet Union tried the first strategy. Workers were exhorted to work harder. Money poured into agriculture but left little traces of enhanced productivity. Campaigns—including one against vodka—were launched to increase worker productivity.

During 1990 and 1991, there was much debate over whether the first strategy should be abandoned. In October of 1990, Gorbachev announced that the Soviet Union would be converted to capitalism in 500 days. He soon dropped this programme, whereupon the economists who had been advising him on the market strategy resigned. It appeared as if there would be another attempt to make socialism work. But then, following the attempted coup in August 1991 and the dissolution of the Soviet Union, directions were changed again: most of the newly created republics seemed committed to adopting some form of market system.

People looking for a third solution sought ways of combining what they saw as the strengths of capitalism with those of socialism. Hungary made some attempt to do this. But perhaps the most successful experiment was in China, where the so-called responsibility system in agriculture essentially allowed farmers to sell most of what they produced in mar-

CAUSES OF THE FAILURE OF SOVIET-STYLE SOCIALISM

1 Failure to provide adequate incentives to workers and managers

Lack of competition, soft budget constraints, and lack of incentives to stimulate innovation and growth were major factors.

2 Failure of planning mechanism to replace markets

Planners lacked the requisite information to allocate resources efficiently.

Planners lacked the ability to monitor firms and make sure resources were used in the ways intended.

kets and to keep the proceeds. As a result, agricultural production skyrocketed during the late 1970s and early 1980s. The annual growth rate of grain production in the 6 years after the responsibility system was adopted (1978 to 1984) was 5 percent, compared with 3.5 percent in the 13 years before the new system (1965 to 1978).

MARKET SOCIALISM

An important idea behind several of the reform movements was market socialism, which argued that an economy could combine the advantages of market mechanisms with public ownership of the means of production. Oskar Lange—who was a professor of economics at the University of Chicago before returning to Poland after the Second World War, eventually to become a vice president of that country's Communist government—was a leading advocate.

Under market socialism, prices would serve the same allocative role that they do in capitalist economies. Prices would be set so that demand would equal supply. Firms would act like competitive price takers. They would maximise their profits at the prices they faced. They would produce up to the point where price equaled marginal cost. They would hire labour up to the point where the value of the marginal product of labour was equal to the wage. But since government owned all machines and buildings, it would take responsibility for all investment decisions. These decisions would be made according to a national plan, which defined the nation's priorities. The planning process would entail close interaction between the government planners and the firms, with the firms' informing the planners of what was required to meet various production goals.

In the 1930s, there was a great debate between the advocates of market socialism, including Oskar Lange, and a group of Austrian economists, including Ludwig von Mises and Nobel laureate Friedrich von Hayek. The Austrians did not believe that government could have the information required to efficiently allocate investment. They thought the task of allocating resources, or even setting market-clearing prices, was simply too complicated to be done by a government bureau. (As it turned out, they were largely correct.) And they did not believe govern-

ment-owned firms would act like private firms. In their view, market socialism was doomed to failure. The advocates of market socialism emphasised the fact that there were, in modern terms, pervasive market failures. Capital and risk markets were imperfect. There were externalities. Competition was imperfect. The market gave rise to great inequality. And capitalist economies seemed prone to periodic chronic illnesses—to recessions and depressions. Pointing out these failures, of course, does not prove that market socialism can do any better than, or even as well as, capitalism.

Market socialism faces two key problems: obtaining the requisite information to set prices and providing managers with incentives.

Information to Set Prices In order to set prices at market-clearing levels, planners have to know, in effect, both demand and supply curves. They have to know an enormous amount about what consumers want as well as firms' capabilities. But they seldom have this information, partly, as noted, because firms have no incentive to tell planners their capabilities. Even with good information, it is extraordinarily difficult for a government bureaucracy to set prices at market-clearing levels. In Lange's time it was still plausible to hope, as he did, that faster computers would solve the problem. But as better and better computers have been developed, it has become increasingly clear that the problems of setting simultaneously the prices of the millions of goods produced in a modern market economy cannot be solved by a computer, however advanced.

Indeed, it has become clear that while prices play a central role in how the market economy functions, they are only part of the market's incentive systems. Customers also care about the *quality* of the goods they purchase. For instance, for firms, having inputs delivered on time is essential. Consider producing nails in a socialist economy. Given a directive to produce so many nails, the nail factory produces short, stubby nails. When the directive is modified to include a specification for a longer nail, the factory responds by producing a nail with the cheapest steel it can get hold of; the result is that the nail splits when hit too hard. When told that the steel should not be too brittle, the firm finds a kind of steel that bends too easily to make it useful for many purposes.

In market economies, firms will not produce at

the market price unless they know they can sell the goods. In a socialist economy, the producer simply delivers the goods to another government enterprise, whose problem it is to sell the good. When China set too high a price for fans, for example, the factories produced more fans than could be sold. Meanwhile, there were huge shortages of most other consumer goods.

While setting prices wrong for consumer goods causes inconvenience, setting prices wrong for producer goods impairs the entire production process. If a firm producing an intermediate good cannot get some input it needs, it will not be able to provide its product to the firms that need it. A shortage at one critical point can have reverberations through other parts of the economy.

Incentives Under market socialism, managers often lack incentives. When the enterprise makes a profit, they cannot keep the profit. And when the enterprise makes a loss, the government makes up the deficit. Market socialism therefore does not resolve the problem of soft budget constraints. Furthermore, competition, which lies at the heart of the market's incentive system, is absent, and this lack of competition is reflected in all aspects of behaviour, including the incentive to produce goods that reflect what customers want.

Some aspects of the experiments with market socialism have been successful, at least as compared with Soviet-style socialism. As was noted, the responsibility system of agriculture in China has resulted in huge increases in agricultural productivity. But overall, the success of most of the experiments is more debatable. To some, market socialism lacks the best features of both capitalism and socialism: it lacks the market's incentive structure and traditional socialism's other mechanisms of economic control. Within Hungary, for example, which had gone the farthest along the road to market socialism before 1989, a consensus developed against market socialism.

In 1992, China embarked on further reforms, in which prices and investment were increasingly placed in the hands of individual enterprises. What distinguished this form of market socialism from capitalism was the ownership of enterprises. Most were state owned, owned by villages or townships, or cooperatives. The system, which had evolved

gradually since 1979, had produced remarkable results—growth rates which averaged in excess of 10 percent for almost two decades.

WORKERS' COOPERATIVES IN YUGOSLAVIA

Yet another type of socialist experiment occurred in Yugoslavia. Marshal Tito, a Communist who led the fight against the Nazis in Yugoslavia and became the country's leader after the Second World War, broke with Stalin in 1948. In the ensuing years, decentralization and decision making by firms became an important part of the Yugoslavian economy. Ownership of firms was turned over to the workers, who were responsible for choosing their own managers. (In practice, the Communist party exercised considerable influence both in the choice of managers and in the decisions made.)

The idea of worker-owned and -managed firms—cooperatives—has a long history throughout Europe and in the United States. Even today there are some enormously successful worker-owned firms—the John Lewis Partnership; Avis, the car rental company; and W. W. Norton, the publisher of this book. Ulgar, a successful household appliances firm, began as a worker cooperative in Mondragón, Spain. Today, with thousands of workers located in many separate plants, it is still run as a cooperative.

A major argument for cooperatives is that because the worker is also part owner, she has a greater commitment to the firm and more incentive to work hard. While this argument seems valid for cooperatives involving relatively few workers, it does not apply as well to large enterprises. And this proved to be a problem in Yugoslavia. Managers elected by a vote of the workers may be as remote as managers chosen by a board of directors. In cooperatives with thousands of workers, each worker gets back a negligible amount of any extra profits that result from anything he does. The most successful cooperatives thus are often the smaller ones.

In Yugoslavia, the cooperatives encountered another problem—lack of incentive to hire new workers. If new workers have the same rights as old workers, the profits of the enterprise must be divided more ways. Whether for this or other reasons, Yugoslavia was plagued with high unemployment rates.

Investment posed still a third problem. When Yugoslavian workers left their cooperative, they received nothing. There was therefore little interest in investing, at least in the long term, or otherwise increasing the market value of the enterprise. Workers did not have an incentive to make investments that yielded returns beyond the date of their retirement.[4]

Some of these problems are not *inherent* in cooperatives. For instance, in cooperatives in the United States and Europe, when a person retires or leaves the cooperative for any other reason, he takes his capital out. He is viewed as a part owner of the enterprise; the share he owns depends on the rules of the cooperative, typically how long he has been with the cooperative and in what positions he has served. By the same token, when a worker joins a cooperative, she has in effect to buy a share. (The company may loan her the money, so her take-home pay may be reduced until she has contributed her capital share.) The better the cooperative does, the more she will be able to receive when she leaves. This provides an obvious incentive for the cooperative to make good investment decisions.

TRANSITION TO MARKET ECONOMIES

Many former socialist countries, including Hungary, the Czech Republic, and Poland, are today committed to becoming market economies. Others, such as Bulgaria, Romania, and Albania, want *some* market reforms, but how many and how fast remains uncertain. The following discussion describes key problems facing countries as they move towards a market economy.

These problems of transition are exacerbated by the economic chaos in the former Soviet Union—the main trading partner of the eastern European countries. As these countries face the problems of transition, they face the additional burden of finding new markets to replace sales to the Soviet Union, which have plummeted. To make matters worse, the kinds of goods they produced for the Soviet Union are not the high-quality goods consumers in western Europe, Japan, and the United States want. Not only must they find new markets. They must also reorient their production.

MACROECONOMIC PROBLEMS

The first transition hurdle eastern European economies face is a period of disruption in which living standards, at least for some, fall below even the low level that they had been under socialism.

A central problem with socialism was that resources were inefficiently allocated. If the economy is to move from a point inside its production possibilities curve (such as *A* in Figure 37.3) to a point on the curve, resources will have to be reallocated. Factories will have to be shut down. Workers will have to be let go. These disruptions will be reflected in high transitional unemployment. Transitional unemployment is like frictional unemployment—the unemployment that occurs as workers move between jobs—magnified many times over. Poland, the first country to attempt the transition, experienced unemployment rates estimated at 25 to 35 percent. In Romania, miners, seeing their real wages cut by a third, rioted and succeeded in bringing down the market-oriented prime minister. The new prime minister, however, was an economist even more committed to market reforms.

Unemployment is particularly serious in eastern European countries, because they do not have the same kinds of safety nets that protect people forced out of jobs in western Europe and the United States. This is not surprising, since under the previous regime unemployment was not a problem. Firms retained workers even when they were no longer needed; they had no profit motive, no budget constraint. But now, in the transition, firms do face budget constraints. Moreover, since capital markets are not yet working well, new firms are not being cre-

---

[4] This list of problems that Yugoslavia faced is not meant to be exhaustive. There were others: lack of competition among people who purchased the farmers' produce, for instance, meant that farmers received lower prices for their goods, and this discouraged the farmers' production.

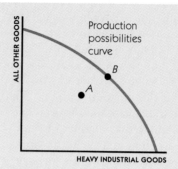

Figure 37.3 INEFFICIENCIES UNDER SOCIALISM

The Soviet-style socialist economies seemed to use their resources inefficiently, so that they operated substantially below the production possibilities curve, such as at point A. Moving the economy from A to a point like B on the production possibilities curve will entail substantial improvements in efficiency.

ated and old firms are not expanding production to absorb the workers who have been laid off.

Inflation receives considerable attention in eastern Europe these days, partly because it is felt by everyone, partly because typically wages do not keep pace with prices (so that living standards fall). But the fall in living standards is not caused by the inflation. It is caused by the economic disruption of the transition process, which simultaneously reduces output, leads to inflation, and lowers living standards. In Russia inflation was not brought under control until 1994, and even then it proceeded at the rate of 18 percent per year.

The reason inflation always seems to arise in the transition is easy to see. The Soviet-style economies were run with prices below market-clearing levels. In Russia, indeed, the price of bread was kept so low that farmers found it cheaper to buy bread to feed their pigs than grain. Shortages were endemic. Hence, once prices were freed, price increases were inevitable. A onetime price increase is not the fundamental worry, however. The danger is that it will lead to inflationary expectations which, once established, perpetuate inflation.

Huge government deficits contribute to inflationary pressures. As the government's control over the economy weakens, its revenue sources often diminish. Under socialism, it could simply seize corporate profits. If it wanted to increase profits and thus its revenue, government could just increase the prices charged or reduce the wages paid. As government

abandoned its role in wage and price setting, it lost its ability to raise revenue in this way. But cutting back on expenditures seems no easier in eastern Europe than elsewhere. Food subsidies are a major drain on the budget, but government threats to reduce them have met with stiff opposition. As profits shrank, and, for huge numbers of enterprises, turned into losses, the economies in transition faced a dilemma. They could subsidise those enterprises making losses or shut them down. With limited revenue, subsidies required deficit financing; and the debt contributed to inflationary pressures. If they were shut down, unemployment increased. Poland chose unemployment. Throughout much of the early 1990s, Russia seemed to choose inflation, with the unemployment rate remaining relatively low. Some countries got a large dose of both.

PRIVATIZATION AND COMPETITION

Prviate property and competition are at the centre of the market economy. *Allowing* competition is easy. The government can simply say that anyone who wants to set up a firm and has the necessary resources can do so. Generating and sustaining competition are more difficult.

One important way for eastern European countries to promote competition is through trade liberalization—opening up the economy to competition from abroad. But while most economists believe that trade liberalization will enhance economic efficiency in the long run, some are concerned about those who lose out in the competition, including people who lose their jobs. They give a variant of the infant industry argument, which goes like this. Enterprises in the former socialist economies have been insulated from competition for decades. It is unfair to suddenly subject them to competition and make their survival depend on this market test. They need time to learn how to compete.

Another way to promote competition is to sell off different parts of existing state enterprises to private entrepreneurs. There are few problems in selling off small businesses—hairdressers, retail stores, restaurants. The difficulties come in selling large enterprises like vehicle or cement factories. Selling them to foreigners raises a host of thorny problems. No country likes to see its factories owned by foreigners. And if a country sells the factories to buyers abroad at too low a price, it is as if the country is giving away its hard-earned savings to foreigners. In eastern Europe, there is a further problem. People with the most money include former party bosses. There is a bitter irony in seeing those who exploited the system under the Communist government for their own advantage retain their advantageous position, this time as capitalist bosses.

Different countries have approached the problem of privatization differently. The Czech Republic first privatised shops, restricted purchases of the shops to citizens (and prohibited their resale to foreigners for two years), and accepted the grim fact that many of the hated Communist bosses would now become capitalist bosses. Economic efficiency, in the minds of Czech reformers, was more important than revenge. The country distributed vouchers to all citizens, which the citizens used to bid for shares in the larger, privatising firms. Thus, in one stroke, the Czech Republic hoped both to privatise and to establish a viable stock market. With the widely distributed ownership of firms, they hoped to establish a people's capitalism. The next problem the Czechs face is that with no shareholders having a large stake in a firm, managers will run the firm with little outside check on their behaviour. There have been proposals to deal with this problem, such as the establishment of holding companies or investment banks, but no consensus has emerged.

Hungary, by contrast, has taken the view that the advantages of foreign ownership—in particular, the advantage of foreigners' expertise—outweigh the disadvantages. Government officials point out that almost 40 percent of Belgian firms are foreign owned with no adverse effects. They envisage a similar role for foreign ownership within their own economy.

Russia, like the Czech Republic, used vouchers, but a large fraction of the shares were distributed to the workers and managers of each enterprise. This raised questions about the extent to which managers will be subject to outside control.

SPEED OF TRANSITION

The pace of privatization has also varied greatly across countries and sectors. In Russia, by 1995, 55 percent of the large enterprises (outside of certain key sectors, such as energy) had been privatised. In the Czech Republic, 70 percent had been privatised. But in Romania and Bulgaria, privatization is proceeding at a very slow pace.

The former Soviet-style socialist economies face a difficult problem in deciding how fast to make the transition to capitalism. One approach is going "cold turkey," or shock therapy. Make the plunge, live through a short nightmarish period, and then enjoy a future prosperity. The other approach calls for a more gradual transition and considers political as well as economic issues. For instance, will the pain caused by going cold turkey be so great that support for the market will erode?

Poland tried the cold turkey approach, at least with respect to its macroeconomic adjustment. Inflation was brought under control, but at the expense of a drastic drop in output and employment, and the defeat of the government that undertook the plan. And even after the macroadjustments are made, the microeconomic problems—for instance, making factories more efficient, reallocating labour and capital—remain. Most of the other countries have moved more cautiously.

The problem is that the success of market economies depends on a host of long-established in-

The debate about the speed of transition has been heated—both inside the countries and from foreign commentators. Those advocating a quick transition have cited the famous aphorism, "You can't jump across a chasm in two steps." Advocates of a slower transition pointed out that "It takes nine months even to produce a baby," to which the advocates of fast transition replied, "But you can't be half pregnant."

What is at issue involves both economics and politics. If a fast transition results in high levels of unemployment, political disillusionment can set in, and political pressures may halt the reform process. When the reformers lost the Russian elections in December 1993, Strobe Talbott, who headed U.S. Russian policy (he subsequently became Deputy Secretary of State) criticised the "shock therapy" of rapid transition by saying there was too much shock and too little therapy.

He seemed to be suggesting that he thought that the transition had proceeded too rapidly, without sufficient attention to those hurt by it.

There was a quick response form market reformers, who argued that the problem was too slow, not too rapid transition. In a sense, both were correct. The slow transition was evidenced in low unemployment rates and low rates of privatization. But the rapid rates of inflation had left many older people (whose pensions did not increase with inflation) with a rapidly decreasing standard of living. In the rush to engage in economic reforms, too little attention may have been placed on the safety net.

Even those countries that managed to arrest and reverse the decline in GDP during transition faced a problem of increasing inequality.

---

stitutions, not just on the abstract concept of markets. And all these institutions have to be functioning reasonably well if the economy is to prosper. There must be credit institutions to sort out potential loan applicants, to monitor the loans, and to see that funds go where they are most productive and are used in the way promised. There must be a legal structure that ensures contracts will be enforced and determines what happens when one party cannot fulfill its contract (bankruptcy). There must be an antitrust policy that ensures firms compete against one another.

Beyond that, the more-developed countries have developed a set of safety nets to help certain segments of society, such as the unemployed. Since unemployment was not a problem in socialist economies, these societies do not have such safety nets. There may be a huge human toll if the transition, with its attendant unemployment, proceeds before

the safety nets are in place. Yet the budgetary problems facing all of these governments make it hard to institute such programmes quickly.

Those who advocate a more gradual transition to market economies believe that the long-run success of these economies will be enhanced by thinking through each of the components, trying to design the best possible institutions, adapting to the particular situations in which they find themselves, and borrowing where appropriate from western Europe, the United States, and Japan.

Today, almost all the countries of the former Soviet empire pay lip service to a commitment towards market reform. In some, the pace is so gradual as to be, to date, almost imperceptible. In Ukraine, market reforms were resisted as long as possible. But as inflation rates soared to over 100 percent per month and as the economy became unable to pay for its imports of energy—leading to factories threatened with closure, homes unheated, and farms unable even to get oil to run their tractors—a set of reforms was put into place in 1994. In other countries, such as the Czech Republic, the reforms have been rapid.

Even with rapid reforms, for most of the countries in transition it will take years, perhaps decades, to overcome the problems bequeathed by their Communist systems.

REVIEW AND PRACTICE

SUMMARY

1 Socialism grew out of the grave economic problems that characterised nineteenth-century industrial economies—severe recessions and depressions, unemployment, and bad working and living conditions.

2 Soviet-style socialism used central planning, under which government bureaucrats made all major decisions about what would be produced, how it would be produced, and for whom it would be produced. Competition was banned. Prices, set by the government, often did not reflect relative scarcities. Private property was restricted.

3 In socialist economies, firms and workers lacked incentives. Firms had little incentive to make profits since profits went to the state, and little incentive to avoid losses since the government would meet any deficits. Firms thus faced soft budget constraints. Similarly, socialism protected workers against layoffs. The trade-off was that this greater security created fewer incentives for efficiency and hard work.

4 In Soviet-style economies, the government used force to impose high savings rates (which meant low consumption) and decided where investment funds went, pushing heavy industrialization. Government often lacked the requisite information to make informed decisions concerning how to allocate re-

sources. Central planning was not able to replace markets.

5 The Soviet-style socialist experiment is today considered a failure by most economists. Russia's standard of living is no higher now than that of many developing countries.

6 Three possible reforms have been proposed for Soviet-style socialist economies: try harder to make socialism work, give up on socialism and move to a market-based system, and find a third alternative between socialism and markets. Today the focus is on the latter two strategies.

7 Among the problems faced by countries in their transition to a market economy are unemployment and inflation. These countries also do not have in place a safety net to protect those hurt in the transition process.

8 Privatising state-controlled firms has proved difficult in many countries, given the reluctance of governments to sell factories to foreigners or former party bosses, who are often the only ones with sufficient resources to buy the enterprises. Still, in many countries, there has been substantial progress in privatization, especially where voucher schemes have been employed.

KEY TERMS

socialism   communism   planned economies   soft budget constraints

REVIEW QUESTIONS

1 What were some of the problems that motivated Karl Marx's criticism of capitalism?

2 What are some of the central characteristics of Soviet-style socialism?

3 How is the rate of national savings determined in a socialist economy, as opposed to a capitalist economy? How is the allocation of capital determined in a socialist economy, as opposed to a capitalist economy? Who determines which goods are produced in a socialist economy?

4 Why are budget constraints soft in socialist countries and hard in market economies?

5 What is market socialism? What did its advocates claim? What are the main problems it faces?

6 What are workers' cooperatives? What did their advocates claim for them? What were the problems of workers' cooperatives in Yugoslavia?

7 What are the central problems facing countries trying to move from Soviet-style socialism to market economies? Why are inflationary pressures common in a socialist country that is moving towards a market economy? Why is rising unemployment common?

8 What benefits do socialist economies hope to gain from privatization? What are some of the problems facing privatization programmes?

9 What are the advantages and disadvantages of the cold turkey approach for a socialist economy in transition?

PROBLEMS

1 Explain how each of the following incentives is different in a socialist and a market economy:
   (a) The incentive of a manager to make wise decisions
   (b) The incentive of workers to exert their best efforts
   (c) The incentive of a bank manager to screen prospective borrowers carefully

2 Queues form when there is a shortage of goods. Use a supply and demand diagram to explain why socialist price controls tend to lead to queues.

3 Are the problems of soft budget constraints unique to socialist economies?

4 Why did the Soviet-style socialist economies have almost no safety nets of unemployment and welfare benefits?

5 In the Soviet-style socialist economies, housing was very scarce, and much of it was controlled by firms. What consequences might this have for labour mobility?

6 If you were a top official in a country that practiced Soviet-style socialism, would you rather have a very high income or access to a special store where all items are guaranteed to be in stock? Why?

7 Imagine that you are 60 years old and you work for a workers' cooperative in Yugoslavia. If you consider only your own self-interest, are you likely to support hiring more workers? Would you support long-term investments in capital?

DEVELOPMENT

Three-quarters of the world's population live in **developing countries.**
Life in the developing countries poses very serious problems. A large
percentage of the population has no housing; many people are starv-
ing to death; medical care is simply unavailable. The contrast between
life in some developing countries and life in the developed world is
significantly greater than the contrast between life in Britain today and two
centuries ago.

The developing countries pose some of the most poignant problems in economics. There are no simple answers, no easy formulas that, if followed, will ensure successful solutions. Still, as this chapter explains, economists have learned
a lot during recent decades about the process of economic development.

KEY QUESTIONS

1 In what ways, besides their grinding poverty, do the developing countries differ from the countries of western Europe, the United States, and Japan?

2 What are the impediments to growth in developing countries?

3 What policies can these countries pursue to improve their standards of living?

BACKGROUND

Statistics cannot convey the full measure of what it means to live in a developing country, but they can provide a start. In the United Kingdom, life expectancy at birth is about 77 years. In Peru, it is 65 years; in India, 61 years; in Nigeria, 52 years. In the United Kingdom, 6 infants die for every 1,000 live births; in Brazil, 57; in Pakistan, 95; in Ethiopia, 122. The average person in Britain completes 15 years of education, while the average African gets only 5 years. India, with a population 16 times larger than that of the United Kingdom, has a GDP roughly four-thirds that of the United Kingdom. This means that per capita income in India is about 8 percent of that in the United Kingdom.

The statistics connect to one another in a vicious cycle. Little or no education, malnutrition, and poor health care reduce productivity and thus incomes. With low incomes, people in the developing countries cannot afford better education, more food, or better health care. Life is hard in developing countries. In many African countries, whose standards of living were already low, population has been growing faster than national income, so that per capita income is falling. Life is getting worse, not better.

The United Nations and the World Bank (a bank established by the major industrialised countries after the Second World War that provides loans to developing countries) group countries into three categories: low-income countries, with GNP per capita of $785 or less in 1997; high-income countries, with GNP per capita above $9,655; and middle-income countries, with GNP per capita in between. The low-income countries are the developing countries. The high-income countries are referred to as **developed countries.** Because the basis of their higher level of income is their higher level of industrialization, they are also referred to as the **industrialised countries.** Figure 38.1 shows countries in the various income categories. In the Western Hemisphere, hardly 200 miles apart, lie one of the richest countries, the United States, with a per capita income of $28,740 in 1997, and one of the poorest, Haiti, with a per capita income of $330.

The income gap among the high-income countries, including the countries of western Europe, the United States, Canada, Japan, Australia, and New Zealand, has narrowed considerably over the past hundred years, but the gap between the high-income countries and the low-income countries has not. Figure 38.2 shows per capita income in several developing countries, ranging from $510 in Ethiopia to $2,940 in Egypt. Note that U.S. per capita income in 1997 was $28,740—56 and 10 times as large, respectively. However, there are signs that change is possible. Some countries have made notable progress in recent years.

First, several countries have moved from the circle of developing countries to the ranks of middle-income countries. These are referred to collectively as **newly industrialised countries,** or **NICs** for short. These success stories include the "gang of four": South Korea, Taiwan, Singapore, and Hong Kong. Just thirty years after the devastating Korean War, for instance, South Korea had moved from the category of developing country to that of major pro-

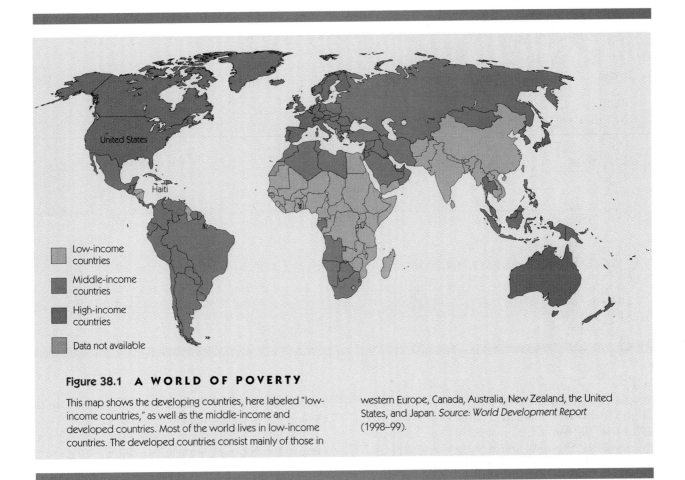

Figure 38.1 A WORLD OF POVERTY

This map shows the developing countries, here labeled "low-income countries," as well as the middle-income and developed countries. Most of the world lives in low-income countries. The developed countries consist mainly of those in western Europe, Canada, Australia, New Zealand, the United States, and Japan. *Source: World Development Report* (1998–99).

Legend:
- Low-income countries
- Middle-income countries
- High-income countries
- Data not available

ducer, not just of simple products such as textiles but of automobiles (the Hyundai) and computers (many of the IBM clones are made in South Korea), which require a reasonably high level of technological expertise. Even more impressive, Japan has moved from the ranks of middle-income countries to one of the most prosperous in the world.

Second, there have been pockets of remarkable progress *within* the developing countries. In the early 1960s, agricultural research centres around the world developed new kinds of seeds, which under correct conditions increase the yields per hectare enormously. The introduction and dissemination of these new seeds, accompanied by enormous improvements in agricultural practices—known as the **green revolution**—led to huge increases in output. India, for example, finally managed to produce enough food to feed its burgeoning population, and now sometimes exports wheat to other countries.

Third, even the grim statistics for life expectancy—57 in Bangladesh and 52 in sub-Saharan Africa (compared to 77 in the United Kingdom)—represent improvements for many countries. But these improvements have a darker side in some countries—a population explosion reminiscent of the Malthusian nightmare. Malthus envisioned a world in which population growth outpaced increases in the food

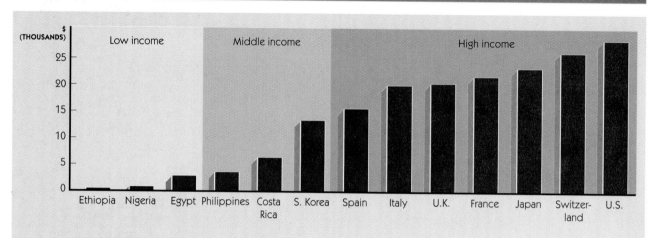

Figure 38.2 PER CAPITA INCOME LEVELS, 1997 (U.S.$)

Some middle-income countries like Egypt and Costa Rica have per capita incomes between five and ten times those of the world's poorest nations and yet have per capita incomes between five and ten times smaller than those of the world's richest nations. *Source: World Development Report* (1998–99), Table 1. Conversion to U.S.$ uses purchasing power parity.

supply. In Kenya during the early 1980s, for instance, improved health conditions enabled the population to grow at the remarkable rate of 4.1 percent a year; this doubled the population every 18 years, while output increased only at the rate of 1.9 percent a year.

Output increases do nothing to improve per capita income when the population grows even faster.

The 1980s was a particularly hard decade for some of the poorest countries, as Figure 38.3 shows. Sub-Saharan Africa had stagnated for the previous

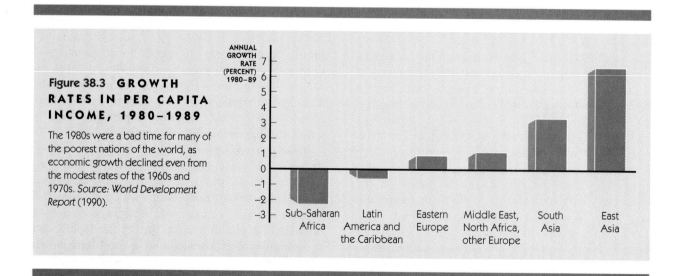

Figure 38.3 GROWTH RATES IN PER CAPITA INCOME, 1980–1989

The 1980s were a bad time for many of the poorest nations of the world, as economic growth declined even from the modest rates of the 1960s and 1970s. *Source: World Development Report* (1990).

Table 38.1 STANDARD OF LIVING MEASUREMENTS IN THE UNITED KINGDOM, UNITED STATES, MEXICO, AND INDIA

Category	U.K.	U.S.	Mexico	India
GNP per capita ($)	18,060	25,880	4,180	320
Life expectancy (years)	77	77	71	62
Agriculture as % of GDP	2	2	8	32
Energy consumption per capita (kilograms of oil equivalent)	3,718	7,662	1,525	235
Food as % of total household consumption	15	13	35	52
Medical care as % of total household consumption	6.1	14	5	3
Average annual inflation (GDP deflator): 1984–1994	5.6	3.3	40.0	9.7
Average annual growth of population (%): 1980–1994	0.2	1.0	2.0	2.0
Infant mortality rate (per 1,000 live births)	7	8	35	70
Population per physician	810	420	1,242	2,460
Population in cities of 1 million or more as % of total population	23	43	28	9

Source: World Development Report (1991–1996). Data are for the most recent year available, in most cases 1994.

quarter century.[1] But during the 1980s per capita income fell by 2.4 percent per year. Latin America had grown at a little more than 2 percent a year in per capita income for the previous quarter century. During the 1980s per capita income there fell by 0.7 percent a year.

LIFE IN A DEVELOPING COUNTRY

Just as there are large differences between the developing countries and the industrialised countries, so too are there large differences among the developing countries. The largest developing country of all, China, has a Communist government. The second largest, India, has an avowedly socialist government, but also functions as the world's largest democracy. Literacy standards in Costa Rica rank with those of the industrialised countries. But more than half of the adult population in sub-Saharan Africa is illiter-

[1] Sub-Saharan Africa is all of Africa south of the Sahara except South Africa.

ate. One must be careful in generalising about developing countries. Still, certain observations are true for *most* of them.

Table 38.1 summarises some of the most important dimensions of living standards—contrasting the United States and the United Kingdom, both high-income countries; Mexico, a middle-income country; and India, a low-income country. Incomes and life expectancies in most developing countries are low. A large fraction of the population lives in the rural sector and is engaged in agriculture. Lacking modern equipment like tractors, they work on small plots (often less than a hectare, compared with hundreds of hectares in many farms in the United Kingdom or the United States). In many cases, they even lack the resources to buy productivity-increasing inputs like fertiliser and pesticides, averaging less than half the fertiliser per acre used in more-developed countries. In many countries, most farmers are landless, tilling the landlord's land under **sharecropping** arrangements, in which the landlord gets half the output. In several countries, **land reform** has redistributed land to the peasants. Such land reforms were a precursor to the remarkable growth in

Figure 38.4 **RATES OF URBANIZATION**

The percentage of the population living in urban areas tends to be higher in developed countries than in developing countries. *Source: World Development Report* (1996), Table 9.

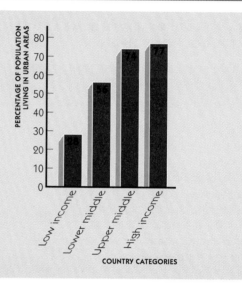

Taiwan and Japan. In other countries, such as the Philippines and Peru, the land reforms have been only partially successful.

Over the past fifty years, most developing countries have experienced gradual urbanization (see Figure 38.4). Those who live in the cities have a much higher standard of living, including access to better education and health facilities. The marked differences between the cities and rural areas have led some to refer to these economies as **dual economies.** While there are large income disparities between rural and urban sectors, there are equally large disparities within the urban sectors, with government workers and those few lucky enough to get jobs in manufacturing earning many times average wages. These high wages attract migrants from the rural sector, often resulting in high urban unemployment. Unemployment rates in some cities exceed 20 percent.

EXPLANATIONS OF LACK OF DEVELOPMENT

Part of developing country poverty arises from lack of resources. They have less physical capital per capita and less human capital, with high illiteracy rates and low average years of schooling. The lower levels of physical capital per capita are not the result of low savings rates; in fact savings rates of most are considerably higher than that of the United Kingdom (see Figure 38.5). Their high population growth rates mean that they have to save a lot just to stand still.

High population growth rates have another effect. They have increased enormously the proportion of the young, who are dependent on others for their income. And they have made the task of improving educational levels even harder.

There is a vicious circle here. Typically, more-educated women have smaller families. This is partly because they are more likely to be informed about family planning, but it is also partly because the opportunity cost of having children is higher for them; they must forgo more income.

Low education levels and lack of capital mean that these economies cannot avail themselves of much of the most-advanced technologies. With important exceptions, they specialise in low skill *labour-intensive* industries (products that require much labour relative to the amount of equipment they employ), like textiles.[2]

---

[2] There is, for an example of an exception, a large highly educated elite in India, which has become a centre for the development of computer software.

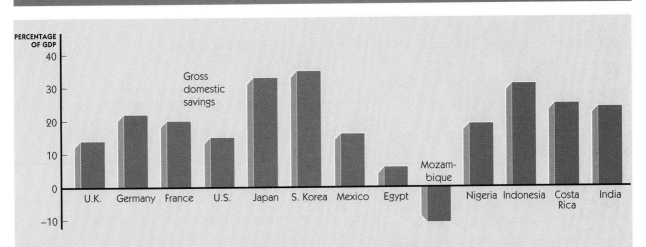

Figure 38.5 SAVINGS RATES, 1993 (PERCENT OF GDP)

Western Europe and the United States have moderate savings rates. Savings rates are generally very high among the fast-growing countries of Asia. Among poor countries there is a wide variety of savings rates, some very high, others very low or even negative. *Source: World Development Report* (1995).

IMPORTANCE OF CAPITAL

How much of the difference between developed and developing countries can be attributed to lack of capital as opposed to inefficient use of capital? If a shortage of capital in developing countries were the major difference between the developed and developing countries, the law of diminishing returns would predict that the return to capital in the industrialised countries would be much lower than the return in developing countries. The more capital a country has relative to its population, the lower the output per machine and the lower the marginal return to capital are. In other words, the shortage of capital in developing countries should make the return to capital greater. This difference in returns would naturally result in a movement of capital from

IMPORTANT DIFFERENCES BETWEEN DEVELOPED AND DEVELOPING COUNTRIES

	DEVELOPED COUNTRIES	DEVELOPING COUNTRIES
Per capita income	Over $9,655	Less than $785 per year
Production/Employment	Less than 10% of the workforce is in agriculture	More than 70% of the workforce is in agriculture
Urbanization	Less than 30% live in rural areas	More than 60% live in rural areas
Population growth rate	Less than 1.0%	Often more than 3.0%

the more-developed to the developing countries, as business firms searched out profitable investment opportunities.

The evidence shows some differences in the return to capital. But these differences are too small to demonstrate that a capital shortage is the major problem faced by the developing countries. Moreover, if a capital shortage were the major problem, the developing countries would use what capital they have very intensively. But this does not typically happen. For example, factories run extra daily shifts more often in developed countries than in developing countries.

A much more important impediment to growth in many developing countries is the lack of efficiency in the use of scarce funds. In Venezuela, which tried to invest its oil revenue as fast as it came in during the 1970s, output increased by 10 pence for every pound invested in capital equipment. In contrast, in the United Kingdom and other developed countries, each extra pound of investment results on average in an output increase of between 30 and 50 pence—three to five times higher. In many developing countries, greater investment simply does not lead to much increased output.

There are a number of reasons for this. Some

CLOSE-UP: TRANSNATIONAL CORPORATIONS AS A SOURCE OF CAPITAL

Developing countries lack capital, both to get the machines needed for greater production and to increase the human capital of their population. But where is that capital to come from?

Developing countries can, through savings, provide some capital themselves. Countries like Mexico, Brazil, and South Korea have shown a capacity to save more than 20 percent of GDP per year. By world standards, those countries are fairly well off. The poorest countries, like many in Africa or Asia, save only about 7 percent of GDP.

The other alternatives all involve investment capital coming in from abroad, whether through foreign aid, private bank loans, or direct foreign investment. The problem with depending on foreign aid is that there is not enough. For example, in one recent year the total foreign aid received by all developing countries was perhaps 1 percent of their combined GDP.

Another possibility is private financial capital, commonly in the form of bank loans. Banks in the United States tried this with a vengeance in the 1970s. But after the experience of countries like Brazil, Argentina, and Mexico not being able to repay their loans on time in the 1980s, banks in the developed world are not eager to plunge into a massive new round of lending. They put their toes in the water again in the early 1990s, only to be burned again with the Mexican peso crisis of 1995.

The final possibility is direct foreign investment, more commonly known as investment by multi-national or transnational corporations. This method has some obvious advantages. The transnational company has an interest in looking after its investment and managing it carefully; this means that the money is less likely to be spent inefficiently. The company, not the country, takes the risk. Moreover, the company doing the investment will often send new technology to the developing country and train workers there.

The main disadvantage of direct investment is political. The governments of developing countries often prefer loans or grants that they can spend as they wish over investment controlled by foreign business executives. In the past, developing countries often passed laws that discouraged foreign companies from investing. But as the options for obtaining capital from other sources dwindled, transnational corporations looked better as an alternative. The current level of direct foreign investment in developing countries is only about $10 billion (about £6 billion). However, according to a recent United Nations report:

> In an era of large international capital flows and rapid technological change, developing countries will increasingly look to transnational corporations for economic stimulation. For their part, transnational corporations will frequently be in a position to provide significant long-term benefits to many developing countries. An important component in the next generation of development policies is that this mutuality of interest continues to grow.

Source: United Nations Center on Transnational Corporations, *Transnational Corporations in World Development* (New York: United Nations, 1988), pp. 10–11.

economists, such as Walter Rostow of the University of Texas, have argued that at any moment a country has only a limited absorptive capacity for more capital. Developing countries lack the human capital, the experience, and technological know-how to pursue many projects simultaneously. The absorptive capacity is most limited in the poorest countries. When investments are pushed beyond absorptive capacity, they yield very low returns.

Many economists, however, believe that there are two more fundamental reasons for the low returns to capital: lack of developed capital markets to allocate capital efficiently, and well-intentioned government interventions which nonetheless support low-return projects. At least in the past, many countries thought that a symbol of development was having a steel mill or some other big factory, even if such a factory was unsuitable for the economic conditions of the country.

INEQUALITY

Many developing countries are also marked by high levels of inequality. Thousands of homeless people sleep in the streets along which the wealthy travel in expensive cars. Some of this inequality is simply due to the law of supply and demand. There is an abundance of unskilled labour and a scarcity of skilled labour and entrepreneurs, so that unskilled wages are low and those who have skills do well.

Indeed, earlier theories suggested that inequality contributed to economic growth. Sir Arthur Lewis, who received the Nobel Prize for his work on development economics, argued that what he called the **surplus of labour** kept wages low and profits high.

Workers earning subsistence wages could not save, but capitalists could, so that the higher profits contributed to a higher savings rate. In this view, there was a trade-off between growth and equality.

Today, many economists believe that growth and equality are really complementary, as evidenced by the East Asia miracle discussed later in the chapter.

FAILED GOVERNMENT POLICIES

Most of the countries of Asia and Africa were colonies of the European powers until the Second World War. As they got their independence in the aftermath of the war, the new governments took upon themselves the responsibility of promoting economic development. Almost all believed that strong government action would be required, with some, such as India, taking an avowedly socialist strategy. These ideas were partly in revulsion to what they saw as the exploitative capitalism of their colonial masters, partly a reflection of the seeming success of the Soviet Union's rapid industrialization.

PLANNING

In many developing countries, the government attempted to direct the overall course of the economy by planning. A Ministry of Planning would draw up a detailed plan, typically for five years, specifying how much each sector of the economy would grow, how

FACTORS CONTRIBUTING TO LACK OF DEVELOPMENT

Lack of physical capital

Lack of education

Lack of technology

Lack of developed capital markets

Government interventions that impair efficient resource allocation

Extreme income inequality

much investment would occur in each sector, where the output of each sector would go, and where each sector would receive its inputs. The Ministry of Planning had enormous powers, among them allocating investment funds and the foreign exchange required to import raw materials from abroad.

In many developing countries, the government undertook some of the investments itself, but it also gave powerful inducements to private firms to conform to the dictates of the government's plan, for example, by restricting access to needed foreign exchange only to approved investment projects or by making credit more readily available for approved investment projects.

In the last decade, there has been considerable disillusionment with planning—a disillusionment that set in even before the failures of the Soviet-style system became evident. Planned economies like India have done worse than unplanned economies like Hong Kong. There are good reasons for this. The 1960s' views on the need for planning ignored the extensive planning that goes on in all economies. For example, when the steel industry became established in South Yorkshire and South Wales, it made sure that there were sources of inputs and the transportation facilities to deliver these inputs—the coal and coke from the nearby coalfields, iron ore, and transport by water (sea or canal) and later by rail. It also made sure there was a source of demand. The issue is not whether planning is needed—it surely is—but whether the most effective place to do the planning is in a centralised government office or at the level of the firm. Today most economists are skeptical about the ability of a centralised office to do effective planning.

One of the main arguments for centralised planning was its presumed greater ability to coordinate. But the experience of the past quarter century has shown that centralised planning offices generally do not do a good job at coordination. One reason is that they often lack the requisite information. Another is that firms can more easily deal with the details of investment projects—deciding what kind of plant to construct, how to construct it, making sure that it is constructed in an efficient way, and so on—than can government officials. And these details, more than anything else, determine the success of the projects.

TILTING THE ECONOMY

The purpose of planning, of course, was to do more than just substitute for the markets' role in coordinating economic activity. It was also at least to tilt the economy in ways that would enhance growth.

Some ideas on how this might be done were borrowed from the Soviet Union, such as an emphasis on capital-intensive industries like steel. Many countries pursued a policy known as **import substitution,** stressing the substitution of domestically produced goods for goods previously imported. In this view, the hallmark of a developed country is modern industry. Rather than importing steel, automobiles, TV sets, computers, and other such products, a country should produce them itself in order to develop the skills necessary for modernization. It should produce, in other words, all the goods it had previously imported from the industrialised economies. This is the road to development that most of the larger developing countries, including India, China, and Brazil, undertook in the years after the Second World War. At times, each of these countries has taken import substitution to extremes, insisting, for example, on domestically produced computers even when they might not be able to perform the functions of imported computers.

India, like many other developing countries, has also placed a heavy emphasis on domestically owned businesses. At least 50 percent of each company must be owned by citizens of India. When Coca-Cola refused to disclose the secret of its closely guarded formula to its Indian-controlled subsidiary, the government shut down Coca-Cola.

But the import substitution approach has disadvantages of its own. Trade barriers set up to protect domestic firms can end up protecting inefficient producers. The absence of foreign competition means that there is an insufficient spur to innovation and efficiency. The profits to which trade barriers frequently give rise provide a source of government corruption. And the trade barriers remain years after they are introduced.

In some cases, the value added of the protected industry is actually negative. Consider a developing country car producer. Many of the car parts have to be imported. The value added of the car manufac-

CLOSE-UP: THE INTERNATIONAL DEBT CRISIS

Borrowing from abroad can make sound economic sense. For instance, much of the development of the railway networks of the United States, Argentina, and various developing countries in the nineteenth century were financed by bonds issued in Europe. Over the past two decades, many firms and governments of developing countries borrowed billions of dollars from banks in the developed countries, as the table here shows. But while the nineteenth-century railway companies were able to repay their debts, it became apparent in the 1980s that some of the countries that had borrowed heavily—particularly Brazil, Argentina, and Mexico—could not repay what they owed. The resulting crisis threatened the economic prospects of the developing countries and the financial viability of many banks in the rich countries.

The immediate cause of the problem was simple. In the 1970s, real interest rates were low, and banks were flush with "petro dollars"—dollars that oil producers, particularly in the Middle East, had earned from selling their oil at the high prices that prevailed beginning in 1973—and wanted to invest or deposit them abroad. Both borrowers and lenders were optimistic that the loans would create economic growth, and repayment would be easy.

Then three things happened. First, nominal and real interest rates soared in the late 1970s. The interest payments rose far beyond any level that the borrowers had imagined. Second, the world entered a recession in the early 1980s, and the worldwide slowdown in growth made it even

PUBLIC OR PUBLICLY GUARANTEED EXTERNAL DEBT

Country	1989	1994
Brazil	$84 billion	$151 billion
Mexico	76	128
India	54	99
Argentina	51	77
Indonesia	41	97
Egypt	40	33
China	37	101
Poland	35	42
Turkey	35	66
Nigeria	32	34
Venezuela	25	37
Algeria	24	30
Philippines	23	39
Morocco	19	23
Korea	17	55

Source: World Development Report (1996).

more difficult for the developing countries to pay back what they owed. Third, oil prices fell in the early 1980s. Some of the largest borrowers had been oil producers, like Mexico and Indonesia, and they had intended to repay their loans by selling oil.

But bad luck is not the only culprit. The banks are also to blame for failing to take into account the risks associated with the loans they were making. They should have realised, for instance, that prices for goods like oil are volatile. The banks also placed too much trust in the assurance of foreign governments that the loans would be invested productively. Much of the money was invested in projects that were probably not economically viable from the start. By contrast, some better-managed countries like the Republic of Korea borrowed heavily but invested the money wisely and have been able to repay it.

Massive defaults on loans were avoided only by debt rescheduling. As a payment came due, the banks lent the country more money, in effect postponing the date at which repayment was to occur. As a condition for this rescheduling, the lenders insisted that the borrowers "put their houses in order," cutting back, for instance, on their huge budget deficits. But this strategy of squeezing the developing countries to pay had its own problems. The only way the countries could repay was for them to grow more. But growth required additional capital, which foreign lenders were reluctant to provide. The only way out was to forgive some of the debt and then count on the rest's being repaid.

Debt forgiveness, which amounts to a gift to the debtor countries, also has its problems. For example, will forgiveness encourage countries to borrow more in the future than they have the capacity to repay? Is Brazil more deserving of such a huge gift than many poorer countries in Latin America or Africa, just because it borrowed more?

turer is not the total value of the car, but only the difference between the value of the car and the value of the imported components. Assume that because of sloppy manufacturing, a significant fraction of the imported parts are damaged. It might be cheaper for the country to import the entire car than import the components and assemble the car. Of course, with protection, the developing country car manufacturer may still be making profits. Consumers suffer, because they have to pay higher prices.

The problems are even worse when the protected industry is one like steel, whose product is used in other industries. Manufacturing cars in a developing country might be profitable if the company could only purchase steel at international prices. But if it is forced to pay inflated prices to buy domestically produced steel, it cannot compete with foreign producers. The government might try to offset this by subsidising the car manufacturers. A subsidy or trade protection in one sector thus grows into a complex of subsidies and trade protection in other sectors.

Although trade protection to stimulate import substitution generally leads to massive inefficiencies, it has proved successful for a time in some countries, such as Brazil, which enjoyed several decades of rapid growth before the debt crisis of the 1980s tainted that picture. Also, supporters of import substitution note that many of the most rapid bursts of growth of the current developed countries occurred in wartimes, when the economy was inwardly directed, not export oriented. These same supporters, looking at the experience of Japan, argue that at least for industrial goods, import substitution—the development of a domestic market—must precede exports. Before Japan was able successfully to sell cars abroad, it first had to develop a market for Japanese cars at home.

WHEN GOVERNMENT BECOMES THE PROBLEM

Sometimes government has impeded the development process. It has done this both by allocating inefficiently those resources over which it has direct control and by interfering in the function of markets so that *they* could not efficiently allocate resources. Countries following the Soviet model attempted to imitate not only its reliance on planning but also its pattern of development, with heavy emphasis on industries such as steel—whether such a pattern of industrialization was appropriate for those countries or not.

Mao Zedong, perhaps because he saw that wheat was the predominant grain consumed in the more developed countries, directed that vast areas be converted from rice to wheat. This land was not suited for wheat, and agricultural productivity suffered. The conversion to wheat fields depleted the land of its fertility, so that when it was eventually returned to growing rice, productivity was lower.

There are flops in the private sector as well, like the Ford Edsel or the nicotine-free cigarette in the United States—mistakes that cost the companies making them hundreds of millions of dollars. But the firm (its owners) bears the costs of these mistakes, and has a strong incentive to avoid making them. A company that makes a mistake cannot finance itself indefinitely. When the Ford Motor Company discovered that the Edsel was a mistake, it quickly discontinued production, cutting its losses. It knew and acted upon the basic lesson that such costs should be treated as bygones.

The government, by contrast, can support an unprofitable firm for many years. Also, the scale of mistakes governments make sets them apart from the mistakes of private firms. If a single farmer mistakenly decides to grow wheat rather than rice, the costs he faces are not comparable to the costs borne by China when Mao made his mistake.

Mao's mistake was an honest mistake of judgment, not a consequence of his pursuit of private interests. But some problems facing the developing countries arise from governmental corruption, and here private interests conflict with public ones. Corruption is often associated with the large role government plays in a developing country, particularly in restricting foreign trade. When the government imposes a high tariff or otherwise protects an industry, the protected firms can raise their prices and increase their profits. If there are only one or two such firms, they will be tempted to share some of the resulting profits with the government official responsible for the protection. And the government official, knowing this, has a strong incentive to ask the private firms to share some of the profits.

These problems arise in all countries. The building inspectors in New York have periodically been charged with accepting bribes to speed approvals, for instance. However, these problems are more likely to arise in countries where government salaries are low relative to the size of the bribes being offered, where institutions like a free press that might closely monitor this kind of corruption do not exist, and where government regulations are more pervasive.

Between honest mistakes and corruption lies a third category: rent-seeking activities. If government has the power to confer special benefits, people will seek those benefits for themselves. Firms will try to persuade government that they deserve protection from foreign competition, knowing that such protection will increase their profits. They may give outright bribes, or they may simply spend funds to help elect officials who are sympathetic to their views.

Critics of an activist role for government in development see these problems as casting serious doubt on the wisdom of government planning. We might *imagine* a government's improving on the market, they argue, but if we look more closely at how governments behave and take into account the natural incentives for counterproductive behaviour on the part of government officials (as opposed to the incentives for efficiency on the part of private firms), we see that government activity can and often does impede development.

THE EAST ASIA MIRACLE

As the development strategies based on planning, import substitution, and heavy industrialization were failing, the countries of East Asia had been pursuing a different set of strategies and achieving growth rates of 7 percent or more year after year. At these growth rates, GDP doubles every ten years.

Several ingredients were essential to their success. Governments in these countries also took an active role. But they pursued market-oriented policies which encouraged development of the private sector. They sought to augment and "govern" the market, not to replace it. A key policy was to ensure the macroeconomic stability of the economy, avoiding for the most part high inflation. As part of this strategy, governments maintained a high level of fiscal responsibility, eschewing the huge budget deficits that characterise many developing countries.

They sought to augment all the ingredients to growth, including fostering high savings rates—often in excess of 25 percent (see Figure 38.5). In Japan, more than a third of these savings went into accounts at the postal savings banks established by the government. These provided a secure and easy way, particularly for those in the rural sector, to save. In Singapore, the government established a provident fund, to which all workers were required to contribute 40 percent of their income. The money went not only to finance their retirement but also to purchase homes. More than 70 percent of all Singaporeans now own their own homes—in a country which, at independence in 1959, had an unemployment rate of more than 30 percent and negligible home ownership.

Many of the countries in East Asia began their growth spurt with a high level of literacy. But they pushed it even further, enhancing the opportunities particularly for women. These countries realised that if they were to become developed, they had to bridge the technological gap. Many countries, including Taiwan and Korea, sent thousands to the industralised countries to study science and engineering. And they devoted huge resources to establishing quality universities within their own countries.

These governments also influenced the allocation of capital in a myriad of ways. Banks were discouraged from making property loans and loans for durable consumption goods. This helped to increase private savings rates and discouraged property speculation, which often serves to destabilise the economy. As a result, more funds were available for investment in growth-oriented activities, like new equipment.

In addition, governments established development banks, to promote long-term investment in activities like shipbuilding, steel mills, and the chemical industry. These interventions have been more controversial and their success has been mixed. The steel firms in Taiwan and Korea are among the most efficient in the world. But soon after the chemical industry was established in Korea, the price of oil, an essential ingredient, soared, and the industry suffered losses for almost two decades. With the decline in oil prices, it is now doing better. Proponents of these initiatives argue that they have technological benefits for other sectors and are necessary as part of a long-term growth strategy.

The Japanese government took a variety of other initiatives to promote certain industries. Among its most noted successes was its entry into the computer chip market. By the early 1980s, Japan looked as if it would completely dominate that market, before Intel and other U.S. producers reasserted U.S. leadership. The dangers of government intervention are often symbolised by the Japanese government's failed attempt to discourage Honda (a manufacturer of motorcycles) from entering the auto market, arguing that there were already too many producers.

EXPORT-LED GROWTH

One factor that distinguished the countries of East Asia from less successful developing countries was their emphasis on exports. A growth strategy focusing on exports is called **export-led growth,** in contrast to the import substitution policy described earlier. Firms were encouraged to export in a variety of ways, including being given increased access to credit, often at subsidised rates.

In export-led growth, firms produce according to their long-term comparative advantage. This is not current comparative advantage, based on current resources and knowledge. It is dynamic comparative advantage, based on acquired skills and technology, and recognition of the importance of learning by doing—of the improvement in skills and productivity that comes from production experience. With exports, demand for the goods produced by a developing country is not limited by the low income of its citizens. The world is its market.

Advocates of export-led growth also believe that the competition provided by the export market is an important stimulus to efficiency and modernization. The only way a firm can succeed in the face of keen international competition is to produce what consumers want, at the quality they want, and at the lowest possible costs. This keen competition forces specialization in areas where low-wage developing countries have a comparative advantage, such as labour-intensive products. It also forces firms to look for the best ways of producing. International firms often take a role in helping to enhance efficiency. For instance, the clothing store chain Benetton has developed production techniques that combine large production runs with rapid adaptability in style and color. In this way, the firm has been able to take advantage of low-wage developing countries by producing most of what it sells in these countries.

Finally, export-led growth has facilitated the transfer of advanced technology. Producers exporting to developed countries not only come into contact with efficient producers within those countries, they also learn to adopt their standards and production techniques. They come to understand better, for instance, why timeliness and quality in production are important.

FOSTERING EQUALITY

Another distinctive aspect of East Asia's development strategy is its emphasis on equality. We have already noted several aspects of these egalitarian policies: Singapore's home ownership programme; the almost universal provision of elementary and secondary education, which includes women; and the land redistribution programmes that were the precursor of growth in several of the countries, including Taiwan and Japan. In many of these countries, government has also tried to curb excessive wage inequality and to discourage conspicuous consumption by the rich.

Their experience has shown that one can have high savings rates without either the oppressiveness of Soviet-style governments or vast inequalities. The equality measures have actually promoted economic growth. The land reforms have resulted in increased agricultural production; the sharecropping system previously in place had had the effect of a 50 percent tax on output. The high education levels have increased productivity directly and facilitated the transfer and adoption of more-advanced technology. And more education for women, as we have noted, is associated with declining rates of population growth.

But the greatest boon of equality for development may be through its political effects. Inequality frequently gives rise to political instability, and political instability has strong adverse effects on the economic climate. In such an atmosphere, both domestic and foreign firms will be reluctant to invest. The countries of East Asia not only managed to have remarkable political stability, but as their incomes grew, there was a strong trend towards democratization.

One of the policies these countries did *not* engage in was large-scale food subsidies. These are often justified as promoting equality, but in fact their effect is more problematic. This is because the food subsidies typically benefit mainly those in the urban sector and are often paid for out of taxes (or suppressed prices) in the agricultural sector. Since those in the urban sector are on average far better off than those in the rural sector, this type of redistribution takes from the very poor to give to the poor. Food subsidies also can be a major budgetary drain on the government, reducing funds for growth-oriented investments.

REDEFINING THE ROLE OF GOVERNMENT

The central question many developing countries are asking today is, what can we learn from the success of the East Asian countries and the failures elsewhere? What can governments do or refrain from doing to effectively facilitate economic growth? Today, there is widespread consensus on the main elements of a successful development strategy.

Macroeconomic Stability Governments need not only to maintain macroeconomic stability but also to constrain expenditures in line with their revenue.

Positive Investment Climate A favourable climate for investment, including foreign investment, enhances growth not only by increasing the stock of capital but also by facilitating the transfer of valuable technology.

Population Policy High rates of growth of population put a strain on almost any economy but especially on poor economies. Savings must be devoted to housing the growing population and providing capital to the new entrants to the labour force, leaving little for capital deepening, which would enhance productivity. Today, knowledge about contraception is widespread; but knowledge about the means to control population is not enough. People have to want to reduce family size. In the absence of a social insurance system, parents often rely on large families to ensure that there is someone to take care of them in their old age. The benefits of having children are of course more than economic. The evidence suggests that one of the most reliable ways of controlling population is to increase the cost—the opportunity cost—of having children; educating women does exactly that. That is why female education not only has a direct benefit, in increased productivity, but an indirect benefit, in reduced population growth.

Provide More and Better Education Education increases the productivity of the labour force and enables the economy to adopt more-advanced technologies.

Provide an Institutional Infrastructure Some examples of this type of infrastructure are an effective legal system, strong competition laws, and a regulatory system supporting a safe and sound financial system.

Provide a Physical Infrastructure In this area, the direct role of government versus the private sector has been evolving. Many countries have discovered that parts of the infrastructure—like toll roads—can be provided privately, relieving the government of both fiscal and managerial burdens.

Avoid Protectionism Avoid policies, such as protectionism, that reduce competition, leading to increased costs and prices.

While there is widespread consensus on these elements of a development strategy, some elements are more contentious. Most of the countries of East Asia actively promoted exports and the transfer and adaptation of modern technology. And most analysts of the East Asia experience give these policies considerable credit for their economic success. Yet critics worry that in other countries, these attempts by government to direct the development of the economy have been singularly unsuccessful; the programmes have been captured by special interests and used to enhance the profits of these special interests rather than to promote economic growth.

THE ROLE OF THE DEVELOPED COUNTRIES

What can the developed countries do to help? Direct foreign assistance has been declining in importance. Today, international capital markets are far better developed than they were fifty years ago, with funds investing in emerging markets becoming very prominent in the financial markets, like the City in London or Wall Street. Countries, like China and Thailand, that provide an investment-friendly atmosphere have little trouble attracting funds. Still, for the poorest countries, especially in Africa, there is a huge need for development assistance. And for all of the developing countries, there is a need for technical assistance and help in areas like education and health in which the private sector is not particularly interested.

There is an ongoing debate about how effective such assistance has been. There have been huge successes, some supported by private foundations as well as by government. The development of high-yielding crops with the support of the Rockefeller Foundation and the dissemination of the seeds and new technologies throughout the developing world have resulted in a "green revolution." Countries like India have become self-sufficient in food. But there have also been failures. Food aid sometimes depresses local prices, hurting farmers and discouraging domestic production. Some large projects have been criticised for damaging the environment and

In January 1994, the Mexican peso crashed, losing a quarter of its value (relative to the U.S. dollar) in a single day and, in the span of a couple weeks, more than 40 percent of its value. The U.S. government, other governments, and the International Monetary Fund were called to the rescue. While the IMF pledged $7.7 billion in credits, the United States lent more than $20 billion to Mexico.

To the media and much of the public, the crash of the peso seemed like a shock. But many economists, such as Rudiger Dornbush of M.I.T., had anticipated the crisis. The Mexican government had made extremely impressive economic reforms under President Salinas, the signing of NAFTA was a positive step for Mexico's economic future. But the Mexican government's macropolicies had been less sound. They had run moderate deficits over a number of years, which they had financed with short-term borrowing denominated in dollars. They had also worked hard to sustain the value of the peso—despite the much higher rate of inflation in Mexico than elsewhere. Thus, by late 1994, the peso was overvalued by at least 25 percent. Economists within the Mexican government realised this, but the government was unwilling to allow the peso to depreciate before the presidential election. The new Mexican government took only three weeks to recognise that it could not sustain the value of the peso. But it could not engineer a smooth reduction.

Many lost millions as a result of the decrease in the value of the peso. Still more millions were lost as the Mexican stock market crashed. Finally, those who had invested in Mexican bonds worried that the government would not be able to pay off bondholders when the debt became due. The U.S. government worried that the emerging turmoil would spread to other emerging markets, disrupting their growth plans. It also worried that an economic downturn in Mexico could lead to a flood of immigrants to the United States. These were among the reasons cited in favour of the Mexican bailout.

Critics of the bailout argued that the main beneficiaries were investors, who should have realised the risks they faced. The devalued peso would be good for the Mexican economy, as it promoted exports and discouraged imports. In fact, the Mexican trade deficit, which had swelled over the past few years, was reversed to a trade surplus in the first months of 1995.

The subsequent events did not fully resolve the question of whether the bailout should have taken place. Mexico went through a deep economic downturn, with unemployment and interest rates soaring. By the middle of 1996, the economy had shown signs of a slow recovery, though the banking system remained fragile; still, Mexico was able to repay half of its loans from the U.S. government.

Even with the bailout, other countries like Argentina were hit hard by the contagion effect, resulting from the loss of investor confidence. It is difficult to ascertain how much harder these countries would have been hit had there not been a bailout.

But both within the United States and abroad, a consensus emerged that the Mexico experience should not be repeated. In a meeting of the leaders of the industrialised countries held in

June 1995 in Halifax, Nova Scotia, they set in motion reforms which would increase the surveillance by the International Monetary Fund of the economies of the world, so that markets would be better informed concerning the risks that they face, and which would increase the funds available for lending in the event of a crisis. And discussions were begun on the development of "work-out arrangements" for countries, analogous to those available to firms in the event of bankruptcy. Whether these initiatives will suffice to avoid a similar crisis remains to be seen.

resulting in crop yields that were insufficient even to pay the interest on the loans.

Today, an increasing fraction of aid is distributed through multilateral development banks—the World Bank, the regional banks in Asia, Africa, and Latin America, and the European Bank for Reconstruction and Development (EBRD), which focuses on the economies of eastern Europe and the former Soviet Union.

Economists continue to emphasise the importance of trade for developing and developed countries alike. Giving developing economies access to the markets of developed countries is a win-win policy. Consumers in the developed countries win by having a greater variety of goods at lower prices. The developing country wins by having a huge market for its goods. Of course, as always with trade, some producers and their workers in the developed countries complain about the loss of jobs to these low-cost competitors. As argued in Chapter 3, the total benefits to trade generally outweigh the losses to certain groups.

THE PROSPECTS

The enhanced means of production that resulted from the industrial and scientific revolutions of the past two centuries have meant ever-rising living standards for most of those lucky enough to live in the developed countries of Europe and North America. And the past fifty years have extended the benefits of development to an increasing number of countries—in full measure to Japan and more mod-

AN AGENDA FOR DEVELOPMENT

How the developed countries can help
  Reduce trade barriers.
  Increase foreign aid.
  Facilitate foreign investment.

Growth-oriented policies for developing countries
  Reduce population growth.
  Increase quantity and quality of education.
  Provide a basic infrastructure (roads, ports, a legal system).
  Provide a favourable climate for investment, including foreign investment.

Facilitate development of capital markets (financial intermediaries).
Spend more government revenue on investment rather than consumption, such as food subsidies.
Develop a competitive export sector.

Policies that may inhibit growth
  Trade protection
  Regulations, licencing

erately to middle-income countries such as Singapore, South Korea, and Taiwan.

There are pockets of success elsewhere as well. The area around São Paulo in Brazil has the look and feel of prosperity. India, as noted above, has become self-sufficient with regard to food. Thailand has been flourishing. Success often seems precarious; for instance, for many of these countries, the debt crisis of the 1980s was a major setback, with growth's stalling, and in some cases, incomes' declining. The economic crisis in Southeast Asia in 1997 to 1999 was a significant setback. Still, the outstanding lesson of recent decades is that success is possible. There is the real prospect that more and more of these countries, if they pursue wise policies and enjoy political stability, will be able to pull themselves out of the cycle of poverty in which they have lived for centuries.

But for the most unfortunate countries, such as those in sub-Saharan Africa—which lack human and physical resources and have burgeoning populations that consume much of whatever gains they are able to obtain—the prospects are less optimistic. Lack of hope contributes to political instability, making economic progress all the more difficult.

REVIEW AND PRACTICE

SUMMARY

1 In developing countries, life expectancies are usually shorter, infant mortality is higher, and people are less educated than in developed countries. Also, a larger fraction of the population lives in the rural sector, and population growth rates are higher.

2 In recent years, newly industrialised countries (NICs) such as South Korea, Singapore, Hong Kong, and Taiwan have managed to improve their economic status dramatically. Other developing countries, like India, have expanded food production considerably. But the standard of living in some of the poorest developing countries, such as many African nations, has been declining, as population growth has outstripped economic growth.

3 Among the factors contributing to lack of development are lack of physical capital, lack of education, lack of technology, and lack of developed capital markets. The factors interact: low education levels impede the transfer of advanced technology; low incomes make it difficult to invest heavily in education.

4 Central planning has not been effective in developing countries. Governments lack the requisite information and often misdirect resources.

5 Import substitution policies have often been implemented through protectionist policies, which have raised domestic prices, often give rise to inefficiencies, and, when applied to intermediate goods like steel, have adverse effects on those industries that use the input.

6 The success of the countries of East Asia is based on activist government policies, which include helping develop and using markets rather than replacing them; promoting high levels of education, high savings, and strong support for education; improving capital markets, which facilitate an efficient allocation of scarce capital; promoting exports; and fostering equality.

7 Effective development policies include maintaining macroeconomic stability (including sound fiscal policies), creating a positive investment climate (including for foreign investors), controlling population, providing more and better education, providing an institutional infrastructure (including an effective legal system, competition laws, and a sound financial system), and ensuring that there is the necessary infrastructure (roads, electricity), which may be provided either publicly or privately.

8 Developed countries can help developing countries through the provision of aid (capital assistance), technical assistance, and opening markets to trade.

KEY TERMS

developing countries

developed or industrialised countries

newly industrialised countries (NICs)

green revolution

dual economies

import substitution

export-led growth

REVIEW QUESTIONS

1 List some important ways in which developing countries differ from more-developed countries.

2 What are the most important factors inhibiting growth in the developing countries? Why is capital shortage *alone* not the most important factor? What can be done to help overcome the problem of capital shortage? How do some of the factors interact with each other?

3 How does rapid population growth make it more difficult to increase a country's standard of living?

4 Why has centralised government planning failed? Does planning occur in market economies?

5 How and why have governments sometimes tried to tilt the economy, interfering with how markets by themselves would allocate resources? Compare import substitution and export promotion strategies. Why have export promotion strategies, by and large, been more successful than import substitution strategies?

6 What are some of the factors that contributed to the East Asia miracle?

7 Why might fostering equality promote economic growth?

8 What are some of the roles that government can play in promoting economic development and growth?

9 What are some of the roles that the developed countries can play in promoting economic development among the developing countries?

PROBLEMS

1 In the United Kingdom, the economy grew by 1.9 percent per year (in real terms) during the period 1990 to 1997. In India, the economy grew by 5.9 percent during the same period. However, population growth in the United Kingdom was 0.3 percent annually, while population growth in India was 1.8 percent annually. Which country increased its standard of living faster for the average citizen? By how much?

2 Nominal GNP in Kenya was 9 billion shillings in 1967 and 135 billion shillings in 1987. The price level in Kenya (using 1980 as a base year) rose from 40 in 1967 to 200 in 1987. And the population of Kenya increased from 10 million to 22 million in those twenty years. What was the total percentage change in real GNP per capita in Kenya from 1967 to 1987?

3 True or false: "Developing countries do not have much capital because their rates of saving are low. If they saved more or received more foreign aid, they could rapidly expand their economic growth." Discuss.

4 How might each of the following hinder entrepreneurs in developing countries?
(a) Lack of functioning capital markets
(b) Pervasive government control of the economy
(c) Lack of companies that offer business services
(d) A tradition of substantial foreign control of large enterprises

5 What is the economist's case for having the government be responsible for providing infrastructure? (Hint: You may wish to review the concept of a public good.)

6 If many developing countries simultaneously attempted to pursue export-led growth, what would be the effect in world markets on the quantities and prices of products mainly sold by developing countries, like minerals, agricultural goods, and textiles? What effect might these quantities and prices have on the success of such export-led growth policies?

7 Explain how the idea of import substitution conflicts in the short run with the idea of comparative advantage. Need the two ideas conflict in the long run? Why or why not?

8 Why might a family in a developing country feel economic pressure to have more children than a family in a developed country?

GLOSSARY

absolute advantage: the ability of a country to produce a good more efficiently (with fewer inputs) than another country. Absolute advantage is relative to, or over, that other country.

accelerated depreciation: a provision of the tax laws that allows for deductions from income for purposes of calculating tax liability for the depreciation of machines (that is, for their wearing out and obsolescence) that are in excess of the true decrease in value. This may entail, for instance, the use of a shorter life span than the actual life span of the machine or building.

accelerator: the effect on GDP of the increase in investment that results from an increase in output. For instance, the greater output leads a firm to believe the demand for its products will rise in the future; the resulting increase in investment leads to growth in output and still further increases in investment, accelerating the expansion of the economy.

accommodative monetary policies: monetary policies that accommodate changes in fiscal policy (or other changes in the economic environment) in ways that maintain the economy's macroeconomic performance

acquired endowments: resources a country builds for itself, like a network of roads or an educated population

adaptive expectations: expectations based on the extrapolation of events in the recent past into the future

adverse selection: the phenomenon that as an insurance company raises its price, the best risks (those least likely to make a claim) drop out, so the mix of applicants changes adversely for the company; now used more generally to refer to effects on the mix of workers, borrowers, products being sold, and so on, resulting from a change in wages, interest rates, prices, or other variables

aggregate consumption function: the relationship between aggregate consumption and aggregate income

aggregate demand curve: a curve relating the total demand for the economy's goods and services to each price level, given the level of wages

aggregate expenditures curve: a curve relating expenditures—the sum of consumption, investment, government expenditures, and net exports—and national income at a fixed price level

aggregate savings: the sum of the savings of all individuals in society

aggregate savings rate: the fraction of national income that is saved, calculated by dividing aggregate savings by national income

aggregate supply: the amount of goods that firms would be willing to supply, given their plant and equipment, assuming wages and prices are flexible and adjust so that the labour force is fully employed

aggregate supply curve: a curve relating the total supply of the economy's goods and services to each price level, given the level of wages

appreciation: the decrease in value of an asset; or a change in the exchange rate that enables a unit of currency to buy more units of foreign currencies

arbitrage: the process by which assets with comparable risk, liquidity, and tax treatment are priced to yield comparable expected returns

asset: any item that is long-lived, purchased for the service it renders over its life or for what one will receive when one sells it

asymmetric information: a situation in which the parties to a transaction have different information, as when the seller of a used car has more information about its quality than the buyer

automatic stabilisers: expenditures that automatically increase or taxes that automatically decrease when economic conditions worsen, and therefore tend to stabilise the economy automatically

autonomous consumption: that part of consumption which does not depend on income

average costs: total costs divided by total output

average productivity: the total quantity of output divided by the total quantity of input

average tax rate: the ratio of taxes to taxable income

average variable costs: the total variable costs divided by the total output

balanced budget policy: a policy that requires the government to have a balanced buget (that is, that prohibits a deficit)

balanced budget multiplier: the increase in GDP from an increase in government expenditures matched by an equal increase in taxes

balance sheet: the accounting framework that shows a firm's assets, liabilities, and net worth

bank run: a rush on a bank by its depositors to withdraw their funds, as they lose confidence in the bank's finances

barriers to entry: factors that prevent firms from entering a market, such as government rules or patents

barter: trade that occurs without the use of money

basic competitive model: the model of the economy that pulls together the assumptions of self-interested consumers, profit-maximising firms, and perfectly competitive markets

basic research: fundamental research; it often has a wide range of applications, but the output of basic research usually is not of direct commercial value; the output is knowledge, rather than a product. The output of basic research typically cannot be patented.

beggar-thy-neighbour policies: restrictions on imports designed to increase a country's national output that hurt the output of other countries at the same time

bequest savings motive: people's desire to save so that they can leave an inheritance to their children

Bertrand competition: an oligopoly in which each firm believes that its rivals are committed to keeping their prices fixed and that customers can be lured away by offering lower prices

bilateral trade: trade between two parties

black market: an illegal market in which proscribed trades occur. For instance, in war time, when coupons are required to buy certain basic commodities, it may be illegal to buy and sell coupons; black markets typically develop in which these coupons are traded.

boom: a period of time when resources are being fully used and GDP is growing steadily

breach: a violation of a contract by one of the parties to it

budget constraint: the limitation on the consumption of different goods because a household has only a limited amount of money to spend (its budget). The budget constraint *defines* the opportunity set of an individual when the only constraint the individual faces is money.

business cycle: the fluctuations in the level of economic activity in the economy. At one time, it was thought that these fluctuations were extremely regular; today, the term is used to refer to fluctuations even when they have no regular periodicity.

capital: funds used for investment; or the value of an individual's investment or a firm's capital stock

capital deepening: an increase in capital per worker

capital gain: the increase in the value of an asset between the time it is purchased and the time it is sold

capital goods: machines and buildings used to produce goods

capital goods investments: investments in machines and buildings [to be distinguished from investments in inventory, in research and development, or in training (human capital)]

capital goods markets: markets in which capital goods are traded

capital inflow: the inflow of capital (money) from abroad, to buy investments, to be deposited in banks, to buy government bonds, or to be lent within the domestic economy for any reason

capital loss: the loss that occurs when an asset is sold at a price below the price at which it was purchased. The difference is the magnitude of the capital loss.

capital market: the various institutions concerned with raising funds and sharing and insuring risks; it includes banks, insurance markets, bond markets, and the stock market.

capital outflows: flows of capital (money) out of the country

capital requirements: the capital that the government requires of banks (defined as a certain ratio of net worth to deposits) to ensure their financial viability

cartel: a group of producers with an agreement to collude in setting prices and output

causation: the relationship in which a change in one variable is not only correlated with but actually causes a change in another variable. The change in the second variable is a consequence of the change in the first variable, rather than both changes being consequences of a change in a third variable.

central bank: the bank that oversees and monitors the rest of the banking system and serves as the bankers' bank

centralization: the organizational structure in which decision making is concentrated at the top

centrally planned economy: an economy in which most decisions about resource allocation are made by the central government

central planning: the system in which central government officials (as opposed to private entrepreneurs or even local government officials) determine what will be produced and how it will be produced

certificate of deposit (CD): an account in which money is deposited for a preset length of time and which yields a slightly higher return to compensate for the reduced liquidity

chain-weighted real GDP: the method of calculating real GDP in which the percentage increase in output from each year to the next is calculated by comparing the value of output of both years in the earlier year's prices

circular flow: the way in which funds move through the capital, labour, and product markets among households, firms, the government, and the foreign sector

classical economists: economists before the 1930s who believed that the basic competitive model provided a good description of the economy and that if short periods of unemployment did occur, market forces would quickly restore the economy to full employment

classical unemployment: unemployment that occurs as a result of too-high real wages. It occurs in the supply-constrained equilibrium, so that rightward shifts in aggregate supply reduce the level of unemployment.

closed economy: an economy that neither exports nor imports

Coase theorem: the assertion that if property rights are properly defined, then people will be forced to pay for any negative externalities they impose on others, and market transactions will produce efficient outcomes

collude: act jointly to increase overall profits; for firms, more nearly as they would if they were a monopolist

command-and-control approach: the approach to controlling environmental externalities in which the government provides detailed regulations about what firms can and cannot do, including which technologies they can employ

commercial policies: policies directed at affecting either imports or exports

Common Market: the predecessor of the European Union

communism: an economic system in which the government owns all property and is responsible for most economic decision making

comparative advantage: a country's having greater *relative* efficiency in the production of one good compared to another good than another country. Comparative advantage is relative to, or over, that other country.

compensating wage differentials: differences in wages that can be traced to nonpecuniary attributes of a job, such as the degree of autonomy and risk

competition policies: policies designed to promote competition and to restrict anticompetitive practices

competitive equilibrium price: the price at which the quantity supplied and the quantity demanded are equal to each other

competitive model: the basic model of the economy, in which profit-maximising firms interact with rational, self-interested consumers in competitive markets, where all participants are price takers (that is, it is assumed that prices are unaffected by their actions)

complement: a good for which the demand (at a given price) decreases as the price of another good increases, and the price increases as the demand for the other good decreases. The goods are complements of each other.

compound interest: interest paid on interest; a savings account pays compound interest when, say, interest is credited to the account everyday, so that on subsequent days, interest is earned not only on the original principal but also on the credited interest.

constant returns: the quality of a production function such that increases in an input (keeping all other inputs fixed) increase output proportionately

constant returns to scale: the quality of a production function such that equiproportionate increases in all inputs increase output proportionately

consumer price index: a price index in which the basket of goods is defined by what a typical consumer purchases

consumer protection legislation: laws aimed at protecting consumers, for instance by assuring that consumers have more complete information about items they are considering buying

consumer surplus: what a person would be willing to pay minus what he actually has to pay for a certain amount of a good

consumption function: the relationship between disposable income and consumption

contestable markets: markets in which there is strong potential or actual competition; the theory of contestable markets predicts that even in a market with only one firm, that firm will make zero profits so long as there is strong potential competition (which will be the case if sunk costs are low).

contingency clauses: clauses within a contract that make the level of payment or the work to be performed conditional upon various factors

corporate finance: the branch of economics concerned with how firms raise capital and the consequences of alternative methods of raising capital

corporation tax: a tax based on the income, or profit, earned by a corporation

corporation: a firm with limited liability, owned by shareholders, who elect a board of directors that chooses the top executives

correlation: the relationship that results when a change in one variable is consistently associated with a change in another variable

cost-push inflation: inflation whose initial cause is a rise in production costs

countervailing duties: duties (tariffs) that are imposed by a country to counteract subsidies provided to a foreign producer

coupon rationing: a system of rationing (often used in wartime) in which, in order to buy some commodity, such as a pound of sugar, a coupon is required in addition to the price. Each individual or household is issued so many coupons for certain essential commodities each month.

Cournot competition: an oligopoly in which each firm believes that its rivals are committed to a certain level of production and that rivals will reduce their prices as needed to sell that amount

credit constraint effect: the result that when prices fall, firms' revenues also fall but the money they owe creditors remains unchanged so they have fewer funds of their own to invest. Because of credit rationing, they cannot make up the difference, so investment decreases.

credit rationing: the situation in which no lender is willing to make a loan to a borrower or the amount lenders are willing to lend to borrowers is limited, even if the borrower is willing to pay more than other borrowers of comparable risk who are getting loans

cross subsidization: the practice of charging higher prices to one group of consumers to subsidise lower prices for another group

crowding out: a decrease in private investment resulting from an increase in government expenditures

cyclical unemployment: the increase in unemployment that occurs as the economy goes into a slowdown or recession

deadweight loss: the difference between what producers gain and (the monetary value of) what consumers lose when output is restricted under imperfect competition; or the difference between what the government gains and what consumers lose when taxes are imposed

debt: capital, such as bonds and bank loans, supplied to a firm by lenders. The firm promises to repay the amount borrowed plus interest.

decentralization: the organizational structure in which many individuals or subunits can make decisions

decision tree: a device for structured decision making that spells out the choices and possible consequences of alternative actions

deficit: see **fiscal deficit**

deficit spending: spending more on expenditures than receiving in revenue, as by a government

deflation: a persistent decrease in the general level of prices

demand-constrained equilibrium: the equilibrium that occurs when prices are stuck at a level above that at which aggregate demand equals aggregate supply. Output is equal to aggregate demand.

demand curve: the curve showing the relationship between the quantity demanded of a good and its price, whether for an individual or for the market (all individuals) as a whole

demand deposits: deposits that can be drawn upon instantly, like current accounts

demand-pull inflation: inflation whose initial cause is aggregate demand's exceeding aggregate supply at the current price level

demand shocks: unexpected shifts in the aggregate demand curve

demographic effects: effects that arise from changes in characteristics of the population such as age, birthrates, and location

depreciation: the decrease in the value of an asset, in particular, the amount that capital goods decrease in value as they are used and become old; a change in the exchange rate that enables a unit of one currency to buy fewer units of foreign currencies

depreciation allowance: the provision of the tax laws that allows for deductions from income for purposes of calculating tax liability for the depreciation of machines (that is, for their wearing out and obsolescence)

deregulation: the lifting of government regulations to allow the market to function more freely

devaluation: a reduction in the rate of exchange between one currency and other currencies under a fixed exchange rate system

developed or **industrialised countries:** the wealthiest nations in the world, including western Europe, the United States, Canada, Japan, Australia, and New Zealand

developing countries: the poorest countries of the world, including much of Africa, Latin America, and Asia

diminishing marginal rate of substitution: the phenomenon that as the individual gets more and more of one good, less and less of another good is required to compensate her for a one-unit decrease in consumption of the first good. Since the marginal rate of substitution is the slope of the indifference curve, the principle of diminishing marginal rate of substitution is equivalent to the slope of the indifference curve's becoming flatter as the quantity on the horizontal axis increases.

diminishing marginal rate of technical substitution: the phenomenon that as the firm uses more and more of one input, less and less of another input is required to compensate it for a one-unit decrease in the first input. Since the marginal rate of technical substitution is the slope of the indifference curve, the principle of diminishing marginal rate of technical substitution is equivalent to the slope of the isoquant curve's becoming flatter as the quantity of input on the horizontal axis increases.

diminishing marginal utility: the phenomenon that as an individual consumes more and more of a good, each successive unit increases her utility, or enjoyment, less and less

diminishing returns: the phenomenon that as one input increases, with other inputs fixed, the resulting increase in output tends to be smaller and smaller

discount: the difference in price when assets sell at a price below the price that might be expected, given their expected returns or, more specifically, their observable attributes. Because the price of such assets is low, the return per pound invested is high; the higher return is said to reflect a *risk premium.*

discount rate: the interest rate charged to banks by the central bank

discouraged workers: workers who would be willing to work but have given up looking for jobs, and thus are not officially counted as unemployed

discretionary expenditures: government expenditures that are decided on an annual basis

disposable income: income after paying taxes

dissaving: negative saving. An individual is dissaving when consumption exceeds income.

diversification: spreading one's wealth among a large number of different assets

dividends: that portion of corporate profits paid out to shareholders

division of labour: the division of a production process into a series of jobs, with each worker's focusing on a limited set of tasks. The advantage of division of labour is that each worker can practice and perfect a particular set of skills.

double coincidence of wants: the situation in which each of two individuals has what the other wants; required in order for barter to work

downward rigidity of wages: the situation in which wages do not fall quickly in response to a shift in the demand or supply curve for labour, resulting in an excess supply of labour

dual economy: the separation in an economy between an impoverished rural sector and an urban sector that has higher wages and more-advanced technology, as in many developing countries

dual-use technologies: technologies that have both a civilian and a military use

due process: procedures designed to protect the public against the arbitrary use of government power

dumping: the practice of selling a good abroad at a lower price than at home, or below costs of production

duopoly: an industry with only two firms

durable goods: goods that produce a service over a number of years, such as cars, major appliances, and furniture

dynamically efficient: the property of an economy that appropriately balances short-run concerns (static efficiency) with long-run concerns (focusing on encouraging R & D)

dynamic consistency: the property of a government that actually carries out a proposed course of action

econometrics: the branch of statistics developed to analyse the particular kinds of problems that arise in economics

economic rents: payments made to a factor of production that are in excess of what is required to elicit the supply of that factor

economics: the social science that studies how individuals, firms, governments, and other organizations make choices and how those choices determine the way the resources of society are used

economies of scope: the situation in which it is less expensive to produce two products together than it would be to produce each one separately

efficiency wage: the wage at which total labour costs are minimised

efficiency wage theory: the theory that paying higher wages (up to a point) lowers total production costs, for instance by leading to a more productive labour force

efficient market theory: the theory that all available information is reflected in the current price of an asset

elastic: see **relatively elastic**

elasticity of labour supply: the percentage change in labour supplied resulting from a 1 percent change in wages

elasticity of supply: see **price elasticity of supply**

endogenous factors: properties of the economy itself, such as a tendency of the economy to become overconfident in expansions, which tends to generate or exacerbate economic fluctuations; more generally, in a model, any variable that is determined within the model itself

entrepreneurs: people who create new businesses, bring new products to market, or develop new processes of production

entry-deterring practices: practices of incumbent firms designed to deter the entry of rivals into the market

equation of exchange: the equation relating velocity, the value of output, and the money supply ($MV = PY$)

equilibrium: a condition in which there are no forces (reasons) for change

equilibrium price: the price at which demand equals supply

equilibrium quantity: the quantity demanded (which equals the quantity supplied) at the equilibrium price, where demand equals supply

equity, shares, or **stock:** terms that indicate part owner-

ship of a firm. The firm sells these in order to raise money, or capital.

equity capital: capital, such as shares (or stock), supplied to a firm by shareholders. The returns received by the shareholders are not guaranteed but depend upon how well the firm performs.

European Union: the agreement among most of the countries of western Europe not only to remove trade barriers but also to allow the free flow of labour and capital. It succeeded the Common Market.

excess capacity: capacity in excess of that currently needed. It is sometimes used by an incumbent firm to discourage new entrants.

excess demand: the situation in which the quantity demanded at a given price exceeds the quantity supplied

excess or **free reserves:** reserves that banks hold in excess of what are required

excess supply: the situation in which the quantity supplied at a given price exceeds the quantity demanded

exchange efficiency: the condition that whatever the economy produces is distributed among people in such a way that there are no gains to further trade

exchange rate: the rate at which one currency (such as pounds) can be exchanged for another (such as Euros, dollars, or yen)

excise tax: a tax on a particular good or service

exclusive dealing: a restrictive practice in which a producer insists that any firm selling its products not sell those of its rivals

exclusive territories: a vertical restriction in which a producer gives a wholesaler or retailer the exclusive right to sell a good within a certain region

exit the market: a consumer's leaving the market when he decides that at the going price, he would prefer to consume none of the market's good or service

exogenous shocks: disturbances to the economy originating outside the economy (such as wars or floods)

expectations-augmented Phillips curve: a Phillips curve relationship (that is, a relationship between inflation and unemployment) that takes into account the impact of inflationary expectations; as inflationary expectations increase, the inflation associated with any level of unemployment increases.

expected return: the average return—a single number that combines the various possible returns per pound invested with the chances that each of these returns will actually be paid

experimental economics: the branch of economics that analyses certain aspects of economic behaviour in a controlled, laboratory setting

export-led growth: the strategy that government should encourage exports in which the country has a comparative advantage to stimulate growth

exports: goods produced domestically but sold abroad

externality: a phenomenon that arises when an individual or firm takes an action but does not bear all the costs (negative externality) or receive all the benefits (positive externality) of the action

factor demand: the amount of an input demanded by a firm, given the price of the input and the quantity of output being produced. In a competitive market, an input will be demanded up to the point where the value of the marginal product of that input equals the price of the input.

factors of production: the inputs that are used in the production process

national debt: the cumulative amount that the national government owes

federal governmental structure: the organization of government such that activity takes place at several levels—national, state, county, city, and others

fiat money: money that has value only because the government says it has value and because people are willing to accept it in exchange for goods

final goods approach to measuring GDP: the approach to measuring GDP that adds up the total money value of goods and services produced, categorised by their ultimate users/purchasers (consumption by households, investment by firms, investment by government, and net exports)

financial intermediaries: institutions that link savers who have extra funds and borrowers who desire extra funds

financial investments: investments in stocks, bonds, or other financial instruments. These investments provide the funds that allow investments in *capital goods* (physical investments).

financial system: that part of the economy which includes all the institutions involved in moving savings from savers (households and firms) to borrowers and in transferring, sharing, and insuring risks; it includes banks, insurance markets, bond markets, and the stock market.

firm wealth effect: the result when lower prices or lower demand causes firms' profits and net worth to fall, and this makes them less willing to undertake the risks involved with investment.

fiscal deficit: the gap between government expendi-

tures and its revenue from sources other than additional borrowing

fiscal policies: policies that affect the level of government expenditures and taxes

fiscal stimulus: an attempt by the government to stimulate the economy (increase aggregate demand) through fiscal policy, that is, a reduction in taxes or an increase in expenditures

fixed costs: the costs resulting from fixed inputs, sometimes called **overhead costs**

fixed exchange rate system: an exchange rate system in which the value of each currency is fixed in relation to other currencies

fixed or **overhead inputs:** inputs that do not change depending upon the quantity of output. Fixed inputs may be fixed in the short run—may not depend upon *current* output—but may depend upon output in the long run.

flexible or **floating exchange rate system:** a system in which exchange rates are determined by market forces, the law of supply and demand, without government interference

flows: variables such as the output of the economy *per year*. Stocks are in contrast to flows; flows measure the changes in stocks over a given period of time.

flow statistics: measurements of a certain rate or quantity per period of time, such as GDP, which measures output per year

four-firm concentration ratio: the fraction of output produced by the top four firms in an industry

fractional reserve system: the system of banking in which banks hold a fraction of the amount on deposit in reserves

free-market economists: economists who believe that free markets are the best way the economy can achieve economic efficiency; typically, they believe that the basic competitive model provides a good description of most markets most of the time.

free reserves: see **excess reserves**

free rider: someone who enjoys the benefits of a (public) good without paying for it. Because it is difficult to preclude anyone from using a pure public good, those who benefit from the goods have an incentive to avoid paying for them, that is, to be free riders.

free trade: trade among countries that occurs freely, without barriers such as tariffs or quotas

frictional unemployment: unemployment arising from the "friction" associated with people moving from one job to another or moving into the labour force

full-employment deficit: the budget deficit that would

have prevailed if the economy were at full employment, thus with higher tax revenues and lower social security expenditures

full-employment level of output: the level of output that the economy can produce under normal circumstances with a given stock of plant and equipment and a given supply of labour

full-employment or **potential output:** the level of output that would prevail if labour were fully employed (Output may exceed that level if workers work more than the normal level of overtime.)

gains from trade: the benefits that each side enjoys from a trade

GDP deflator: a weighted average of the prices of different goods and services, where the weights represent the importance of each of the goods and services in GDP

GDP per capita: the value of all goods and services produced in the economy divided by the population

General Agreement on Tariffs and Trade (GATT): the agreement among the major trading countries of the world that created the framework for lowering barriers to trade and resolving trade disputes. Entered into after the Second World War, it has now been succeeded by the World Trade Organization (WTO).

general equilibrium: the full equilibrium of the economy, when all markets clear simultaneously

general equilibrium analysis: a simultaneous analysis of all capital, product, and labour markets throughout the economy; it shows, for instance, the impact on all prices and quantities of immigration or a change in taxes.

gift and inheritance taxes: taxes imposed on the transfers of wealth from one generation to another

Gini coefficient: a measure of inequality (equal to twice the area between the 45-degree line and the Lorenz curve)

green GDP: a measurement of national output that attempts to take into account effects on the environment and natural resources

green revolution: the invention and dissemination of new seeds and agricultural practices that led to vast increases in agricultural output in developing countries during the 1960s and 1970s

gross domestic product (GDP): the total money value of the goods and services produced by the residents of a country during a specified period

gross national product (GNP): a measure of the incomes of residents of a country, including income they receive from abroad but subtracting similar payments made to those abroad

horizontal equity: the principle that says those who are in identical or similar circumstances should pay identical or similar amounts in taxes

horizontal integration: the integration of a firm with other firms producing the same product (at the same level of production)

horizontal merger: a merger between two firms that produce the same goods

horizontal restrictions: restrictions (such as an agreement not to compete in price or to enter each others' markets) by competing firms at the same level of production (for instance, among producers, or among wholesalers, or among retailers)

hostile takeover: the takeover of control of a firm against its will by the management team of another firm

human capital: the stock of accumulated skills and experience that makes workers more productive

imperfect competition: any market structure in which there is some competition but firms face downward-sloping demand curves

imperfect information: the situation in which market participants lack information (such as information about prices or the characteristics of goods and services) important for their decision making

imperfect market economists: economists who see significant discrepancies between the basic competitive model and the conditions observed in market economies

imperfect markets: markets that do not satisfy the assumptions of the basic competitive model, such as where competition is less than perfect, information is less than complete, there are externalities, or markets are missing

imperfect substitutes: goods that can substitute for each other but imperfectly

implicit contract: an unwritten understanding between two parties involved in an exchange, such as an understanding between employer and employees that employees will receive a stable wage throughout fluctuating economic conditions

import function: the relationship between imports and national income

imports: goods produced abroad but bought domestically

import substitution: the strategy that focuses on the substitution of domestic goods for goods that were previously imported

incentive-equality trade-off: the exchange of desired things for equalities and vice versa. In general, the greater the incentives, the greater the resulting inequality.

income approach to measuring GDP: the approach to calculating GDP that involves measuring the income generated to all of the participants in the economy

income effect: the reduced consumption of a good whose price has increased that is due to the reduction in a person's buying power, or "real" income. When a person's real income is lower, normally she will consume less of all goods, including the higher-priced good.

income elasticity of demand: the percentage change in quantity demanded of a good as the result of a 1 percent change in income (percentage change in quantity demanded divided by percentage change in income)

income-expenditure analysis: the analysis that determines equilibrium output by relating aggregate expenditures to income

income-tested transfers: transfers to particular groups of individuals (such as the aged) based on their income

incomplete markets: markets in which no demand or supply exists for some good or for some risk or in which some individuals cannot borrow for some purposes

increasing returns: the quality of a production function such that increases in an input (all other inputs fixed) increase output more than proportionately

increasing, constant, or **diminishing returns to scale:** the situation in which when all inputs are increased by a certain proportion, output increases by a greater, equal, or smaller proportion, respectively. Increasing returns to scale are also called **economies of scale.**

indexing: the formal linking of any payment to a price index

indifference curves: curves that give the combinations of goods about which an individual feels equally (that is, which yield the individual the same level of utility)

income tax: a tax based on the income received by an individual or household

industrial policies: government policies designed to promote particular sectors of the economy

industry: a collection of firms making the same product

inelastic: see **relatively inelastic**

infant industry argument for protection: the argument that industries must be protected from foreign competition while they are young, until they have a chance to acquire the skills to enable them to compete on equal terms

inferior good: a good the consumption of which falls as income rises

infinite elasticity of demand: the situation in which any amount of a product will be demanded at a particular price but nothing will be demanded if the price increases even a small amount

infinite elasticity of supply: the situation in which any amount of a product will be supplied at a particular price but nothing will be supplied if the price declines even a small amount

inflation: the rate of increase of the general level of prices

inflationary spiral: a self-perpetuating system in which price increases lead to higher wages, which lead to further price increases

inflation inertia: the tendency of inflation to persist

inflation tax: the decrease in buying power (wealth) that inflation imposes on those who hold currency (and other assets, like bonds, the payments for which are fixed in terms of money)

information-based differential: a wage differential that results from imperfect information, for instance, the situation that a worker does not know the wage being offered by other employers and it would be costly for him to search to find out

informative advertising: advertising designed to provide consumers with information about the price of a good, where it may be acquired, or what its characteristics are

infrastructure: the roads, ports, bridges, and legal system that provide the necessary basis for a working economy

inputs: the various material, labour, and other factors used in production

insider-outsider theory: the theory that firms are reluctant to pay new workers (outsiders) a lower wage than current workers (insiders), because current workers would fear being replaced by the new, low-wage workers and would not participate in training and cooperating with them

inside traders: individuals who buy and sell shares of companies for which they work, making use of the inside information that they are able to glean from working there

intellectual property: proprietary knowledge, such as that protected by patents and copyrights

interest: the return a saver receives in addition to the original amount she deposited (loaned); or the amount a borrower must pay in addition to the original amount he borrowed

interest elasticity of savings: the percentage increase in savings resulting from a 1 percent change in the interest rate

interest rate effect: the situation in which lower interest rates (resulting from an increase in the money supply or a fall in the price level) induce firms to invest more

intertemporal trades: trades that occur *between* two periods of time

investment: from the national perspective, an increase in the stock of capital goods or any other expenditure designed to increase future output; from the perspective of the individual, any expenditure designed to increase an individual's future wealth, such as the purchase of a share in a company (Since some other individual is likely to be selling the share, that person is disinvesting, and the net investment for the economy is zero.)

investment function: the relationship between the level of real investment and the value of the real interest rate

investors: those who supply capital to the capital market (including individuals who buy shares of stock in a firm or lend money to a business)

involuntary unemployment: the situation in which the supply of those willing to work at the going market wage exceeds the demand for labour

isocosts: different combinations of inputs that cost the same

isoquants: different combinations of inputs that produce the same quantity of output

job discrimination: discrimination in which disadvantaged groups have less access to better-paying jobs

joint products: products that are naturally produced together, such as wool and mutton

junk bonds: bonds that are especially risky, that is, have a high probability of default

Keynesian monetary theory: see **traditional monetary theory**

Keynesian unemployment: unemployment that occurs as a result of insufficient aggregate demand. It arises in the demand-constrained equilibrium (where aggregate demand is less than aggregate supply), so that rightward shifts in aggregate demand reduce the level of unemployment.

kinked demand curve: the demand curve perceived by an oligopolist who believes that rivals will match any price cut but will not match price increases

labour force participation decision: the decision by an individual to actively seek work, that is, to participate in the labour market

labour force participation rate: the fraction of the working-age population that is employed or seeking employment

labour hoarding: the situation where (in an economic downturn) firms keep workers on the job, though they do not fully utilise them

labour market: the market in which labour services are bought and sold

labour turnover rate: the rate at which workers leave jobs

lag: the difference in time between two events, such as between the time the government recognises a problem and takes action and between the time the action occurs and its macroeconomic effects are fully realised

land reform: the redistribution of land by the government to those who actually work the land

law of supply and demand: the law in economics that holds that *in equilibrium* prices are determined so that demand equals supply. Changes in prices thus reflect shifts in the demand or supply curves.

leakage: income generated in one round of production that is not used to buy more goods produced within the country

learning by doing: the increase in productivity that occurs as a firm gains experience from producing and results in a decrease in the firm's production costs

learning curve: the curve describing how costs of production decline as cumulative output increases over time

liabilities: what a firm or a person owes to others

life-cycle savings: savings that are motivated by a desire to smooth consumption over an individual's lifetime and to meet special needs that arise in various times of life; saving for retirement is the most important aspect of life-cycle savings.

life-cycle theory of savings: the theory of savings that emphasises the importance of life-cycle savings and that savings will differ in different parts of an individual's life cycle

limited liability: the property that the amount an investor can lose is limited to the amount that he has invested. Corporations have limited liability.

limit pricing: the practice of charging a lower price than the level at which marginal revenue equals marginal cost, as a way of deterring entry by persuading potential competitors that their profits from entering are likely to be limited

linear demand curve: a demand curve that is a straight line, that is, in which demand is a linear function of price

liquidity: the ease with which an asset can be sold

local public goods: public goods that benefit only residents of a particular local area

long-run aggregate supply curve: the aggregate supply curve that applies in the long run, when wages and prices can adjust fully to ensure full employment

long-term bonds: bonds with a maturity of more than ten years

Lorenz curve: a curve that shows the cumulative proportion of income that goes to each cumulative proportion of the population, starting with the lowest-income group

lottery: a process, such as picking a name from a hat, through which goods are allocated randomly

Luddites: early nineteenth-century workers who destroyed labour-saving machinery rather than see it take over their jobs

luxury tax: an excise tax imposed on luxuries, goods typically consumed disproportionately by the wealthy

macroeconomics: the top-down view of the economy, focusing on aggregate characteristics

managerial slack: the lack of managerial efficiency (for instance, in cutting costs) that occurs when firms are insulated from competition

marginal benefit: the extra benefit resulting, for instance, from the increased consumption of a commodity

marginal cost: the additional cost corresponding to an additional unit of output produced

marginal costs and benefits: the extra costs and benefits that result from choosing a little bit more of one thing

marginal product: the amount output increases with the addition of one unit of an input

marginal propensity to consume: the amount by which consumption increases when disposable income increases by a unit

marginal propensity to import: the amount by which imports increase when disposable income increases by a unit

marginal propensity to save: the amount by which savings increase when disposable income increases by a unit

marginal rate of substitution: how much of one good an individual is willing to give up in return for one more unit of another; the slope of an indifference curve

marginal rate of technical substitution: how much of one input a firm can give up in return for one more unit of another and still leave output unchanged; the slope of an isoquant

marginal rate of transformation: the extra output of one commodity resulting from a decrease in output of another commodity in an economy in which all resources are fully and efficiently used; the slope of the production possibilities curve

marginal revenue: the extra revenue received by a firm for selling one additional unit of a good

marginal tax rate: the extra tax that will have to be paid as a result of an additional unit of income; the rate of tax at the margin

marginal utility: the extra utility, or enjoyment, a person receives from the consumption of one additional unit of a good

marketable pollution permits: permits issued by the government which allow a firm to emit a certain amount of pollution and which can be bought and sold

market clearing: the situation that exists when supply equals demand, so there is neither excess supply nor excess demand

market demand: the total amount of a particular good or service demanded in the economy

market demand curve: the curve that shows the total amount of a particular good or service demanded in the economy at each price. It is calculated by "adding horizontally" the values of the individual demand curves; that is, at any given price, the market demand is the sum of the individual demands.

market economy: an economy that allocates resources primarily through the interaction of individuals (households) and private firms

market failure: the situation in which a market economy fails to attain economic efficiency

market failures approach: the approach based on the belief that government may have an economic role to play when markets fail to produce efficient outcomes

market for risk: the market (the institutions and arrangements) in which risks are transferred (exchanged), transformed, and shared

market labour supply curve: the curve showing the relationship between the wage paid and the amount of labour willingly supplied, found by adding up the values in the labour supply curves of all the individuals in the economy

marketplace: the place where, in traditional societies, goods were bought and sold. In today's economy, only in the case of a few goods and services is there a well-defined marketplace.

market power: the ability of a firm to significantly affect price through its actions (such as sales)

market risks: risks that arise from variations in market conditions, such as changes in prices or demand for a firm's product

markets: places where goods or services (including labour) are bought, sold, and traded. The term is used today metaphorically; there is no single marketplace where any particular good is bought and sold; the collection of all the places where exchanges take place is thought of as "the market." See also **capital market.**

market structure: the organization of the market, such as whether there is a high degree of competition, a monopoly, an oligopoly, or monopolistic competition

market supply: the total amount of a particular good or service that all the firms in the economy supply

market supply curve: the curve showing the total amount of a particular good or service that all the firms in the economy together would like to supply at each price. It is calculated by "adding horizontally" the individual firm's supply curves; that is, it is the sum of the amounts each firm is willing to supply at any given price.

market surplus: the situation in which at the going price, the amount firms are willing to produce exceeds the amount households demand

maturity: the length of time before a loan or bond is due to be paid in full; a bond with a maturity of ten years will be paid off in full in ten years.

median voter: the voter such that half the population has preferences on one side of this voter (for instance, they want higher government expenditures and taxes), while the other half of the population has preferences on the other side of this voter (they want lower taxes and expenditures)

medium of exchange: an item that can be commonly exchanged for goods and services throughout the economy

menu costs: the costs to firms of changing their prices

merit goods and bads: goods that are determined by government to be good or bad for people, regardless of whether people desire them for themselves or not

microeconomics: the bottom-up view of the economy, focusing on individual households and firms

missing market: the situation in which there is a good or service which individuals would like to purchase (at a price at which that good could be profitably produced) but which is not available in the market; or more generally, the situation in which there is no market where a good or service can be bought or sold

mixed economy: an economy that allocates resources through a mixture of public (governmental) and private decision making

model: a set of assumptions and data used by economists to study an aspect of the economy and make predictions about the future or about the consequences of various policy changes

Modigliani-Miller theorem: the theorem that says that under a simplified set of conditions, the manner in which a firm finances itself does not matter

monetarists: economists who emphasise the importance of money in the economy; they tend to believe that an appropriate monetary policy is all the economy needs from government, and market forces will otherwise solve any macroeconomic problems.

monetary aggregates: statistics that describe the various measures of the money supply (M0, M2, and so on)

monetary policies: policies that affect the supply of money and credit and the terms on which credit is available to borrowers

money: any item that serves as a medium of exchange, a store of value, and a unit of account

money multiplier: the amount by which a new deposit into the banking system (from outside) is multiplied as it is loaned out, redeposited, reloaned, and so on, by banks

monopolist: the single firm in a monopoly, that is, in an industry in which there is only a single firm

monopolistic competition: the form of imperfect competition in which the market has sufficiently few firms that each one faces a downward-sloping demand curve, but enough that each firm can ignore the reactions of its rivals to what it does

monopoly: a market consisting of only one firm

monopoly and competition laws: laws that discourage monopoly and restrictive practices and encourage greater competition

monopoly rents: the profits that accrue to a monopolist as a result of its reducing its output from the competitive level to the monopoly level

monopsonist: the single buyer of a good or service

moral hazard: the danger for an insurance company that those who purchase insurance have a reduced incentive to avoid the risks that they are insured against

multilateral trade: trade among more than two parties

mutiplier: the factor by which a change in a component of aggregate demand like investment or government spending, is multiplied and so leads to a larger change in equilibrium national output

multiplier-accelerator model: the model that relates business cycles to the internal working of the economy, showing how changes in investment and output reinforce each other; the central ingredients of the model are the multiplier and the accelerator.

myopic expectations: "short-sighted expectations," for instance, simply assuming that today's prices will continue into the future

nationalization: the process whereby a private industry is taken over by the government, whether by buying it or simply by seizing it

natural endowments: a country's natural resources, such as a good climate, fertile land, and minerals

natural monopoly: a monopoly that exists because average costs of production are declining below the level of output demanded in the market, thus making entry unprofitable and making it efficient for there to be a single firm

natural rate of unemployment: the rate of unemployment at which the rate of inflation is zero

negative public savings: a fiscal deficit, where expenditures exceed revenue

negatively sloped curve: a curve in which as the variable measured along the horizontal axis increases, the variable measured along the vertical axis decreases

net capital inflows: total capital inflows minus total capital outflows

net domestic product (NDP): GDP minus the value of the depreciation of the country's capital goods

net export function: a relationship that gives the level of net exports at each level of income

net exports: total exports minus total imports

neutrality of money: a situation where an increase in the money supply simply increases prices proportionately and has no real effect on the economy

new classical economists: economists who, beginning in the 1970s, built on the tradition of classical economists and believed that by and large, market forces, if left to themselves, would solve the problems of unemployment and recessions

new Keynesian economists: economists who, beginning in the 1980s, built on the tradition of Keynesian economists and focused attention on unemployment; they sought explanations for the failure of wages and prices to adjust to make labour markets and possibly other markets clear.

newly industrialized countries (NICs): countries that have recently moved from being quite poor to being middle-income, including South Korea, Taiwan, Singapore, and Hong Kong

nominal GDP: the value of gross domestic product in a particular year measured in that year's prices

nominal interest rate: the percentage return on a deposit, loan, or bond. The nominal interest rate does not take into account the effects of inflation.

nonaccelerating inflation rate of unemployment (NAIRU): the level of unemployment at which actual (realised) inflation equals inflationary expectations. Below this rate of unemployment, the rate of inflation increases; above it, it decreases.

nondiscretionary expenditures: expenditures that are determined automatically, such as interest payments and expenditures on entitlements

nonexcludability: the property of pure public goods that it costs a great deal to exclude any individual from enjoy-

ing their benefits. In the extreme, it may be impossible to exclude.

nonpecuniary: not relating to money, for example, aspects of a job other than the wage it pays

nonrivalrous: the property of pure public goods that the consumption or enjoyment of the good by one individual does not subtract from that of other individuals

nontariff barriers: barriers to trade that take forms other than tariffs (such as regulations that disadvantage foreign firms)

normal good: a good the consumption of which rises as income rises

normative economics: economics in which judgments about the desirability of various policies are made; the conclusions rest on value judgments as well as facts and theories.

North American Free Trade Agreement (NAFTA): the agreement between Canada, the United States, and Mexico that lowered trade and other barriers among those countries

oligopoly: the form of imperfect competition in which the market has several firms, sufficiently few that each one must take into account the reactions of its rivals to what it does

open economy: an economy that is actively engaged in international trade

open market operations: central banks' purchase or sale of government bonds in the open market

opportunity cost: the cost of a resource, measured by the value of the next-best, alternative use of that resource

opportunity sets: a summary of the choices available to individuals, as defined by budget constraints and time constraints

output per capita: a country's output divided by the number of individuals in the country

outputs: the outcomes of a production process

overhead costs: the costs a firm must pay just to remain in operation. They do not depend on the scale of production.

Pareto efficient: the quality of a resource allocation such that no rearrangement can make anyone better off without making someone else worse off

partial equilibrium analysis: an analysis that focuses on only one or a few markets at a time

partnership: a business owned by two or more individuals, who share the profits and are jointly liable for any losses

patent: a government decree giving an inventor the exclusive right to produce, use, or sell an invention for a period of time

peak: the top of a boom

perfect competition: the situation in which each firm is a price taker—it cannot influence the market price. At the market price, the firm can sell as much as it wishes, but if it raises its price, it loses all sales.

perfect information: the situation in which market participants have full information about the goods and services being bought and sold (including the prices at which they are available at every location and all of their relevant characteristics)

perfectly elastic: infinite elasticity. A demand or supply curve is perfectly elastic if it is horizontal.

perfectly inelastic: zero elasticity. A demand or supply curve is perfectly inelastic if it is vertical, so the demand or supply is completely insensitive to price.

perfectly mobile capital: capital that responds quickly to changes in returns in different countries

permanent home hypothesis: the theorem that individuals base their current consumption levels on their permanent (long-run average) income

permanent-income savings motive: people's desire to even out their income so that they save in good years to tide them over in bad years

persuasive advertising: advertising designed to make consumers feel good about the products that are being sold and more inclined to purchase them; it does not inform them about price or any characteristic of the product.

Phillips curve: the curve showing the trade-off between unemployment and inflation such that a lower level of unemployment is associated with a higher level of inflation

physical capital: investments in plant and equipment, distinguished from investments in people, called human capital

piece-rate system: a compensation system in which workers are paid specifically for each item produced

planned economies: economies in which the government takes central responsibility for economic decision making, including developing plans for economic growth

planned and unplanned inventories: planned inventories are those firms choose to have on hand because they make business more efficient; unplanned inventories result when firms cannot sell what they produce.

policy ineffectiveness proposition: the proposition that some government policies are ineffective; for example, policies aimed at stimulating aggregate demand that at most change the price level

portfolio: an investor's entire collection of assets and liabilities

portfolio theories of monetary policy: theories that argue that monetary policy affects output through its effect on prices of various assets, in particular the prices of stocks

positive economics: economics that describes how the economy behaves and predicts how it might change, for instance, in response to some policy change

positively sloped curve: a curve in which as the variable measured along the horizontal axis is increased, the variable measured along the vertical axis increases

potential competition: competitive pressures that arise from the potential of firms to enter a market

potential GDP: a measure of what the value of GDP would be if the economy's resources were fully employed

precautionary savings motive: people's desires to save so that they will be able to meet the costs of an unexpected illness, accident, or other emergency

predatory pricing: the practice of cutting prices below the marginal cost of production to drive out a new firm (or to deter future entry), at which point prices can be raised again

premium: the price that assets sell at above that which might be expected, given their expected returns or observable attributes

present discounted value: how much an amount of money to be received in the future is worth right now

price: what must be given in exchange for a good or service

price ceiling: a maximum price above which market prices are not legally allowed to rise

price discrimination: the practice of a firm in which it charges different prices to different customers or in different markets

price dispersion: a situation that occurs when the same item is sold for different prices by different firms

price elasticity of demand: the percentage change in quantity demanded of a good as the result of a 1 percent change in price (percentage change in quantity demanded divided by percentage change in price)

price elasticity of supply: the percentage change in quantity supplied of a good as the result of a 1 percent change in price (percentage change in quantity supplied divided by percentage change in price)

price floor: a minimum price below which market prices are not legally allowed to fall

price index: a measure of the level of prices found by comparing the cost of a certain basket of goods in one year with its cost in a base year

price leader: in some oligopolies, a particular firm that sets the price, with other firms' quickly following suit

price level: some measure of the average prices in the economy. When analysing the product market as a whole, the equilibrium *price level* is given by the intersection of the aggregate demand curve and the aggregate supply curve.

price makers: firms that affect, or make, the price of a good or service as a result of their actions, especially as a consequence of their level of production

price system: the economic system in which prices are used to allocate scarce resources

price takers: firms that take the price of the good or service they sell as given; the price is unaffected by their level of production.

principal: the original amount a saver deposits in a bank (lends) or a borrower borrows

principal-agent problem: the problem of one party (the principal) who needs to delegate actions to another party (the agent) to provide the agent with incentives to work hard and make decisions about risk that reflect the interests of the principal

principle of consumer sovereignty: the principle that holds that each individual is the best judge of what makes him better off

principle of substitution: the principle that holds that in general there are many possibilities for substitution, both by consumers and by firms, so that an increase in the price of, say, an input will lead the firm to substitute other inputs in its place

Prisoner's Dilemma: a situation in which the non-cooperative pursuit of self-interest by two parties makes them both worse off

private marginal cost: the marginal cost of production borne by the producer of a good. When there is a negative externality, such as air pollution, private marginal cost is less than social marginal cost.

private property: ownership of property (land or other assets) by individuals or corporations. Under a system of private property, owners have certain property rights, but there may also be legal restrictions on the use of property.

privatization: the process whereby functions that were formerly undertaken by government are delegated to the private sector

producer price index: the price index that measures the average level of producers' prices

product differentiation: the fact that similar products (like breakfast cereals or soft drinks) are perceived to differ from one another and thus are imperfect substitutes

production efficiency: the condition in which firms cannot produce more of some goods without producing less of other goods. The economy is on its production possibilities curve.

production-facilitating function of inventories: the role of inventories in facilitating production, for instance, by avoiding costly stoppage of production as a result of an interruption of supplies

production function: the relationship between the inputs used in production and the level of output

production possibilities: the combination of outputs of different goods that an economy can produce with given resources

production possibilities curve: the curve that defines the opportunity set for a firm or an entire economy and gives the possible combinations of goods (outputs) that can be produced from a given level of inputs

production-smoothing function of inventories: the role of inventories in allowing production to continue at a steady level in the face of fluctuations in demand

productivity, or GDP per hour worked: how much an average worker produces per hour, calculated by dividing real GDP by hours worked in the economy

productivity wage differentials: wage differentials among individuals due to differences in productivity

product liability: the obligation of a producer to compensate victims of a defective product that has injured them

product market: the market in which goods and services are bought and sold

product-mix efficiency: the condition in which the mix of goods produced by the economy reflects the preferences of consumers

profits: total revenue minus total costs

progressive tax: a tax in which the rich pay a larger fraction of their income than the poor

property rights: the rights of an owner of private property; these typically include the right to use the property as she sees fit (subject to certain restrictions, such as zoning) and the right to sell it when and to whom she sees fit.

property tax: a tax based on the value of property

proprietorship: a business owned by a single person, usually a small business

protectionism: the policy of protecting domestic industries from the competition of foreign-made goods

public good: a good, such as national defence, which costs little or nothing for an extra individual to enjoy and which the costs of preventing any individual from enjoying are high

pure profit or **monopoly rents:** the profit earned by a monopolist that results from its reducing output and increasing the price from the level at which price equals marginal cost

pure public good: a good that possesses the properties of nonexcludability (in which it is *impossible* to exclude any individual from enjoying the benefits of the good) and nonrivalrousness (the consumption or enjoyment of the good by one individual does not subtract at all from that of other individuals)

quantity theory of money: the theory that the velocity of money is constant, so that changes in the money supply lead to proportional changes in nominal income (which also equals the value of output)

quota rents: profits that accrue to firms that are allocated the right to import a good subject to quotas as a result of the artificially created scarcity

quotas: limits on the amounts of foreign goods that can be imported

random walk: the way the prices of stocks move; the next movement cannot be predicted on the basis of previous movements.

rational choice: a choice process in which individuals weigh the costs and benefits of each possibility, and the choices made are those within the opportunity set which maximise net benefits

rational expectations: expectations for which people make full use of all relevant available past data

rationed goods: goods of which individuals get less than they would like at the terms being offered

rationing by queues: allocating scarce resources on the basis of who is most willing and able to wait the longest in a queue

rationing system: any system of allocating scarce resources, applied particularly to systems other than the price system; rationing systems include rationing by coupons and rationing by queues.

reaction function: in the analysis of oligopolies, the relationship between the level of output of one firm and the level of output of other firms (in Cournot competition), or the level of price of one firm and the prices of other firms (in Bertrand competition).

real balance effect: the result that as prices fall, the real value of people's money holdings increases and they consume more

real business-cycle theorists: economists who contend that the economy's fluctuations have nothing to do with monetary policy but are determined by real forces

real exchange rates: exchange rates adjusted for changes in relative price levels in different countries

real GDP: the real value of all final goods and services produced in the economy, measured in dollars adjusted for inflation

real income: income measured by what it can actually buy, rather than by the amount of money

real interest rate: the real return to saving; the nominal interest rate minus the rate of inflation

real product wage: the wage divided by the price of the good being produced

real wage: the nominal wage divided by the (consumer) price level

recession: two consecutive quarters of a year during which GDP falls

regressive tax: a tax in which the poor pay a larger fraction of their income than the rich

regulatory capture: a situation in which regulators serve the interests of the regulated rather than the interests of consumers

relatively elastic: the quality of a good such that the price elasticity of its demand is greater than unity

relatively inelastic: the quality of a good such that the price elasticity of its demand is less than unity

relative price: the ratio of any two prices; the relative price of apples and oranges is just the ratio of their prices.

rent: see **economic rent**

rent control: limitations on the level or rate of increase of rents that landlords can charge

rent seeking: behaviour that seeks to obtain benefits from favourable government decisions, such as protection from foreign competition

reputation: the "good will" of a firm resulting from its past performance. Maintaining one's reputation provides an incentive to maintain quality.

resale price maintenance: a restrictive practice in which a producer insists that any retailer selling his product sell it at the "list price"

reservation wage: the wage below which an individual chooses not to participate in the labour market

reserves: money kept on hand by a bank in the event that those who have made deposits wish to withdraw their money

reserve requirements: the minimum level of reserves that the central bank requires be kept on hand or deposited with the central bank

residual economic growth: that part of the growth of the economy that cannot be explained by increases in inputs

restrictive practices: practices of oligopolists designed to restrict competition, including vertical restrictions like exclusive territories

retained earnings: that part of the net earnings of a firm that are not paid out to shareholders but retained by the firm

revenue curve: the curve showing the relationship between a firm's total output and its revenue

revenue: the amount a firm receives for selling its products, equal to the price received multiplied by the quantity sold

right-to-work laws: laws that prevent union membership from being a condition of employment

rigid prices: prices that do not adjust when demand differs from supply

risk averse, risk loving, or **risk neutral:** given equal expected returns and different risks, risk-averse people will choose assets with lower risk, risk-loving people will choose assets with higher risk, and risk-neutral people will not care about differences in risk.

risk premium: the additional interest required by lenders as compensation for the risk that a borrower may default; more generally, the extra return required to compensate an investor for bearing risk

sacrifice ratio: the amount by which the unemployment rate must be kept above the NAIRU for one year to bring down inflation by 1 percentage point

sales tax: a tax imposed on the purchase of goods and services

scarcity: the limited availability of resources, so that if no price were charged for a good or service, the demand for it would exceed its supply

screening: differentiating among job candidates, when there is incomplete information, to determine which will be the most productive

search: the process by which consumers gather information about what is available in the market, including prices, or by which workers gather information about the jobs that are available, including wages

seasonal unemployment: unemployment that varies with the seasons

shadow price: the true social value of a resource

sharecropping: an arrangement, prevalent in many developing countries, in which a worker works land and gives the landowner a fixed share of the output

shortage: a situation in which demand exceeds supply at the current price

short-run aggregate supply curve: the curve showing the relationship between aggregate supply (what firms are willing to produce) and the price level that prevails in the short run. It is not assumed that wages adjust fully to ensure full employment (see long-run aggregate supply curve).

short-run production function: the relationship between output and employment in the short run, that is, with a given set of machines and buildings

short-term bonds: bonds that mature within a few years

signaling: conveying information, for example, a prospective worker's earning a degree to persuade an employer that he has desirable characteristics that will enhance his productivity

simple interest: interest that is paid only on the original principal (deposit), not on other interest earned by the principal

slope: the amount by which the value along the vertical axis increases as the result of a change of one unit along the horizontal axis; the slope is calculated by dividing the change in the vertical axis (the "rise") by the change in the horizontal axis (the "run").

Smith's "invisible hand": the idea that if people act in their own self-interest, they will often also be acting in a broader social interest, as if they had been directed by an "invisible hand"

smoothing consumption: consuming similar amounts in the present and future, rather than letting year-to-year income dictate consumption

social benefit: the benefit that accrues to society as a whole. The social benefit of an innovation includes not only the profits of the innovator but also the benefits that accrue to others, either as a result of the knowledge produced in the innovative process or because the new product is available at a price below that which the individual would be willing to pay.

social insurance: insurance provided by the government to individuals, for instance, against disabilities, unemployment, or poverty due to any cause

socialism: an economic system in which the means of production are controlled by the state

social marginal cost: the marginal cost of production, including the cost of any negative externality, such as air pollution, borne by individuals in the economy other than the producer

social science: the branch of science that studies human social behaviour; the social sciences include economics, political science, anthropology, sociology, and psychology.

soft budget constraints: budget constraints facing enterprises that can turn to government for assistance in the event of a loss

stagflation: high inflation combined with low growth and high unemployment

static efficiency: the efficiency of an economy with a given technology. Taxes used to finance basic research and monopoly power resulting from patents result in a loss in static efficiency.

static expectations: the belief of individuals that today's prices and wages are likely to continue into the future

statistical discrimination: differential treatment of individuals of different gender or race that is based on the use of observed correlations (statistics) between performance and some observable characteristics; it may even *result* from the use of variables like education that have a *causal* link to performance.

sticky prices: prices that do not adjust or adjust only slowly towards a new equilibrium

sticky wages: wages that do not adjust or are slow to adjust in response to a change in labour market conditions

stock option: an option to buy a share of a stock at a particular price (usually within a particular period of time). If the value of the share increases (above that price), the value of the option increases. Stock options are often used to reward corporate executives.

stocks: variables, like the capital stock or the money supply stock, that describe the state of the economy (such as its wealth) at a point in time. They are contrasted by flows.

stock statistics: measurements of the quantity of a certain item, such as capital stock or the total value of buildings and machines, at a certain point in time

store of value: something that can be accepted as payment in the present and exchanged for items of value in the future

strategic trade theory: the theory that holds that protection can give a country a strategic advantage over rivals, for instance by helping reduce domestic costs as a result of economies of scale

strike: the collective withdrawal of labour (usually organised by a union)

structural unemployment: long-term unemployment that results from structural factors in the economy, such as a mismatch between the skills required by newly created jobs and the skills possessed by those who have lost their jobs in declining industries

substitutes: two goods such that the demand for one increases when the price of the other increases

substitution effect: the reduced consumption of a good whose price has increased that is due to the changed trade-off, the fact that one has to give up more of other goods to get one more unit of the high-priced good. The substitution effect is associated with a change in the slope of the budget constraint.

sunk cost: a cost that has been incurred and cannot be recovered

supply-constrained equilibrium: the equilibrium that occurs when prices are stuck at a level below that at which aggregate demand equals aggregate supply. In a supply-constrained equilibrium, output is equal to aggregate supply but less than aggregate demand.

supply curve: the curve showing the relationship between the quantity supplied of a good and the price, whether for a single firm or the market (all firms) as a whole

supply shocks: unexpected shifts in the aggregate supply curve, such as an increase in the international price of oil or a major earthquake that destroys a substantial fraction of a country's capital stock

supply siders: economists who emphasise the importance of aggregate supply, in particular the responsiveness of supply to lower taxes and regulations; some argue that lowering tax rates leads to such large increases in inputs of capital and labour that total tax revenues may actually increase.

surges: unexpected large increases in imports

surplus: the magnitude of the gain from trade, the difference between what an individual would have been willing to pay for a good and what she has to pay; see also **market surplus.**

surplus labour: a great deal of unemployed or underemployed labour, readily available to potential employers

sustainable development: development that is based on sustainable principles, including particularly concern with avoiding environmental degradation and the exploitation of natural resources

tacit collusion: collusive behaviour among the firms of an oligopoly based on an implicit understanding that it is in each firm's best interest not to compete too vigorously; they tacitly understand that it is undesirable to undercut each others' prices, but there is no open discussion about price fixing.

takeover: the taking of control by one management team (one firm) of another firm

target savings motive: people's desires to save for a particular target, for example, to make a deposit on a house or to pay for school or college tuition fees

tax expenditures: the revenue lost from a tax subsidy

technological risks: risks facing a firm that are associated with technology, such as whether a new technology will work or be reliable

theorem: a logical proposition that follows from basic definitions and assumptions

theory: a set of assumptions and the conclusions derived from those assumptions put forward as an explanation for some phenomena

thin markets: markets with relatively few buyers and sellers

tie-in: a restrictive practice in which a customer who buys one product must buy another

time constraints: the limitations on the consumption of different goods imposed by the fact that households have only a limited amount of time to spend (24 hours a day). The time constraint defines the opportunity set of individuals if the only constraint they face is time.

time value of money: the fact that a pound today is worth more than a pound in the future

total costs: the sum of all fixed costs and variable costs

total factor productivity analysis: the analysis of the relationship between output and the aggregate of all inputs. Total factor productivity growth is calculated as the difference between the rate of growth of output and the weighted average rate of growth of inputs, where the weight associated with each input is its share in GDP.

trade creation: the generation of new trade as a result of lowered tariff barriers

trade deficit: the excess of imports over exports

trade diversion: the diversion of trade away from outside countries as a result of the lowering of tariffs between the members of a trading bloc

trade-off: the amount of one good (or one desirable objective) that must be given up to get more of another good (or to attain more of another desirable objective)

trade secret: an innovation or knowledge of a production process that a firm does not disclose to others

trading bloc: a group of countries that agree to lower trade and other economic barriers among themselves

traditional monetary theory: the theory (first developed by John Maynard Keynes, and therefore sometimes referred to as Keynesian monetary theory) that the nominal interest rate is the opportunity cost of holding money, that the demand for money decreases as the interest rate rises, and that the interest rate is determined to equate the demand for and supply of money

transactions costs: the extra costs (beyond the price of the purchase) of conducting a transaction, whether those costs are money, time, or inconvenience

transactions demand for money: the demand for money arising from its use in buying goods and services

Treasury bills: bills the government sells in return for a promise to pay a certain amount in a short period

trough: the bottom of a recession

two-tier wage systems: wage systems in which newly hired workers are paid lower wages than established workers

unemployment rate: the fraction of the labour force (those unemployed *plus* those seeking jobs) who are seeking jobs but are unable to find them

unitary price elasticity: the property of a commodity that the demand for it decreases by 1 percent when the price increases by 1 percent and the supply of it increases by 1 percent when the price increases by 1 percent. If the demand for it has unitary price elasticity, then expenditures on the good do not depend at all upon price.

unit of account: something that provides a way of measuring and comparing the relative values of different goods

utility: the level of enjoyment an individual attains from choosing a certain combination of goods

utility possibilities curve: a curve showing the maximum level of utility that one individual can attain, given the level of utility attained by others

value-added: the difference between the value of the output and the value of the inputs purchased from other firms in each stage of production

value-added approach to measuring national output: the approach in which the value-addeds of all the firms in the economy are added together

value of the marginal product of labour: the value of the extra output produced by an extra unit of labour, calculated by multiplying the marginal product of labour by the price of the good that is being produced

variable: anything which can be measured and which changes; examples of variables are prices, wages, interest rates, and quantities bought and sold

variable costs: the costs resulting from variable inputs

variable inputs: inputs that rise and fall with the quantity of output

velocity of money: the speed with which money circulates in the economy, defined as the ratio of income to the money supply

vertical equity: the principle that says that people who are better off should pay more taxes

vertical integration: the integration of a firm with its supplier or customer

vertical merger: a merger between two firms, one of which is a supplier or distributor for the other

vertical restrictions: restrictions imposed by a producer on wholesalers and retailers that distribute its products; more generally, restrictions imposed by a firm on those to whom it sells its products

voluntary export restraints (VERs): restraints on exports that are "voluntarily" imposed by an exporting country, though often in response to a threat that if such restraints are not imposed, the importing countries will impose import quotas

voluntary unemployment: the situation in which workers voluntarily drop out of the labour force when the wage level falls

voting paradox: the fact that under some circumstances there may be no determinate outcome with majority voting: choice A wins a majority over B, B wins over C, and C wins over A

wage discrimination: paying lower wages to women or minorities

wage-productivity curve: the curve that depicts the relationship between wages and productivity

wholesale price index: the price index that measures the average level of wholesale prices

work sharing: reducing all employees' hours by equal amounts rather than firing some workers

World Trade Organization (WTO): the organization established in 1995, as a result of the Uruguay Round of trade negotiations, replacing GATT, designed to remove trade barriers and settle trade disputes

zero elasticity: the property of a good that the quantity demanded or supplied does not change at all if price changes. The demand or supply curve is vertical.

INDEX